D1593511

Holy=Days and Holidays

Holy-Days and Holidays

A TREASURY OF HISTORICAL MATERIAL, SERMONS IN
FULL AND IN BRIEF, SUGGESTIVE THOUGHTS,
AND POETRY, RELATING TO

HOLY DAYS AND HOLIDAYS

Compiled by

EDWARD M. DEEMS, A.M., PH.D.

FUNK & WAGNALLS COMPANY
NEW YORK AND LONDON

Republished by Omnigraphics ● Penobscot Building ● Detroit ● 1992

Library of Congress Cataloging-in-Publication Data

Holy-days and holidays : a treasury of historical material, sermons in full
and in brief, suggestive thoughts, and poetry, relating to holy days and
holidays / compiled by Edward M. Deems.
      p.   cm.
    Reprint. Originally published: New York : Funk & Wagnalls, 1902.
    Includes bibliographical references.
    ISBN 1-55888-910-8 (lib. bdg. : alk. paper)
    1. Church year. 2. Holidays—United States. 3. Holidays—Canada.
4. Fasts and feasts—United States. 5. Holidays—Canada.
6. Homiletical illustrations. I. Deems, Edward Mark, 1852–1929.
BV30.H56   1990
394.2'6973--dc20   89-71091
                                                    CIP

∞

Printed in the United States of America

PREFACE

THE object of this book is to help busy people in our busy age to find and enjoy the very best that has been written on the vital events and great men whose memory society is trying to perpetuate.

The attempt has not been made to treat all the saints' days and special days of the ecclesiastical calendar. Only the most important days, such as are commemorative of the most significant facts and principles of the Christian faith, have been dealt with. On the other hand, days and anniversaries not in the Church calendars are included, such as Thanksgiving Day, New Year's Day and Old Year Day—occasions which are rich in suggestion to thoughtful minds. This work includes, besides the most important secular legal holidays, the anniversaries most widely observed in America, Great Britain, Ireland, and Canada.

As moral and educational influences, holy days and holidays are of inestimable value. For an example, the stimulus to Christian gratitude and patriotism that comes from the annual observance of Thanksgiving Day throughout the nation cannot easily be exaggerated.

The literature bearing upon holy days and holidays is vast, and greatly scattered, but some of the best thoughts of the brightest minds are now offered the readers of this volume, while it refers them to much more material, which has been excluded through lack of space.

The compiler takes this opportunity to thank all authors and publishers who have courteously contributed toward the completeness of this work. Every effort has been made to give full credit to all to whom credit is due, and any omission to do this has been unintentional.

The compiler also wishes to thank MONTROSE J. MOSES, B.S., for his invaluable assistance in matters relating to general literary form, and his help in the work of seeing the book through the press.

HOLY-DAYS AND HOLIDAYS is now given to the reading public both as a book of reference and as a book for recreation, with the sincere hope and conviction that it has a mission, and that it will be welcomed to its niche in the library of the reader and thinker of our times.

EDWARD M. DEEMS

THE MANSE,
HORNELLSVILLE, NEW YORK.

CONTENTS

KEY TO ABBREVIATIONS

[In order to give full credit to authors and publishers of the material used in this work, and in order to enable readers to follow up the quotations made in its pages, initials are placed at the end of articles, and this key explains their significance.]

A. G....Apples of Gold. New York: Am. Tract Society.

A. M....American Messenger. New York: Am. Tract Society.

A. P. L....Anglican and American Pulpit Library. New York: Edwin S. Gorham.

At. M....Atlantic Monthly. Boston: Houghton, Mifflin & Co.

B. A....Baptist Argus.

B. C. E....Brantford (Canada) Expositor. Brantford, Ontario.

B. E....Brooklyn Eagle. Brooklyn, N. Y.

B. J....Boston Journal. Boston.

B. M....Biblical Museum. New York: E. R. Herrick & Co.

B. O. K....By Order of the King.

B. W....British Weekly. London, England.

C....Congregationalist. Boston.

C. A....Christian Advocate. New York.

C. Ad....Central Advocate. St. Louis, Mo.

C. An....Current Anecdotes. Cleveland, Ohio: F. M. Barton.

Can. M....Canada Magazine. Toronto, Canada.

C. A. W....The Church at Work. New York.

C. B. F....Century Book of Facts. Springfield, Mass.: King-Richardson Co.

C. E. W....Christian Endeavor World. Boston.

C. G....Cut Gems. Cleveland, Ohio: F. M. Barton.

C. H....Christian Herald and Signs of Our Times. New York.

Ch. St....Chicago Standard. Chicago.

C. J....Chambers' Journal. London, England.

C. M....Century Magazine. New York: The Century Co.

C. O....Columbian Orations. (See Col. S.)

Col. S....Columbian Selections. Philadelphia: Porter and Coats.

Col. W....Collier's Weekly. New York.

C. P....Cumberland Presbyterian. Nashville, Tenn.

C. P....Church Press.

C. R....Contemporary Review. (See T. C. R.) London, England.

C. U....Christian Union. New York.

Cul....The Cultivator.

C. Up....Christian Uplook. Buffalo, N. Y.

C. W....Christian Work. New York.

C. Y. B....Canadian Year Book (1900). Toronto, Canada.

D. T. C. Y....Daily Thoughts for the Christian Year. New York: Brentano's.

E....Evangelist. New York.

E. G....Educational Gazette, Rochester, N. Y.

E. H....Epworth Herald. Chicago.

E. T....Every Thursday. New York.

E. Times....Expository Times. Edinburgh: T. & T. Clark. N. Y.: Scribner's Sons.

E. W....Everywhere. Brooklyn, N. Y.

F....Forward. Philadelphia, Pa. (Pres. Board of Publication.)

F. I....Foster's Cyclopedia of Prose Illustrations, Series I. New York: Funk & Wagnalls Co.

F. II....Foster's Cyclopedia of Prose Illustrations, Series II. New York: Funk & Wagnalls Co.

* F. I....Foster's Cyclopedia of Poetical Illustrations, Series I. New York: Funk & Wagnalls Co.

* F. II....Foster's Cyclopedia of Poetical Illustrations, Series II. New York: Funk & Wagnalls Co.

F. R....Fortnightly Review. London, England.

G. F....Gems for the Fireside. Washington: H. W. Bolton.

G. R....Golden Rule. Boston: Christian Endeavor World.

G. T....Great Thoughts. London, England.

H....Harper's Magazine. New York: Harper and Bro's.

H. A. C....Hymns for All Christians. New York.

H. A. C. Y....Homiletic Aids for Christian Year. New York: Thos. Whittaker.

H. L. S. E....Homiletic Library, Spence and Exell. New York: A. D. F. Randolph & Co.

H. P....Herald and Presbyter. Pittsburg, Pa.

H. R....Homiletic Review. New York: Funk & Wagnalls Co.

H. W....Harper's Weekly. New York: Harper and Bro's.

H. Y. P....Harper's Young People. New York: Harper and Bro's.

I....Independent. New York.
I. A....Illustrated American. New York.
In....Interior. Chicago.

J. E....Journal of Education. New York.

L. C....The Living Church. Milwaukee, Wis.
L. H. J....Ladies' Home Journal. Philadelphia, Pa.
L. Pu....London Punch. London, England.
L. W....Leslie's Weekly. New York.

M. R....Methodist Recorder. Pittsburg, Pa.
M. R. W....Missionary Review of the World. New York: Funk & Wagnalls Co.'

N. B. A. D. M. (1898)....Nebraska Bird and Arbor Day Manual (1898).
N. C....Nineteenth Century. London, England.
N. C. T. M....New Century Teachers' Monthly. D. C. Cook: Chicago.
N. T. A....National Temperance Advocate. New York.
N. Y. J....New York Journal. New York.
N. Y. O....New York Observer. New York.
N. Y. S....New York Sun. New York.
N. Y. T....New York Tribune. New York.
N. Y. Ti....New York Times. New York.
N. Y. W....New York World. New York.

O....Outlook. New York.
O. C. W....Our Church at Work. New York.

P....F. N. Peloubet's Select Notes on the International S. S. Lessons. Boston: W. A. Wilde & Co.
P. H....Pulpit Herald.
P. I....Pulpit Illustrator. Corning, N. Y.
P. J....Presbyterian Journal. Philadelphia.
P. M....Preacher's Magazine. New York: Wilbur B. Ketcham.
P. S. M....Popular Science Monthly. New York: McClure, Phillips & Co.
P. T....Pulpit Treasury. New York: E. B. Treat & Co.

P. Tid....Parish Tidings. Williamstown, Mass.

Q....The Quiver. New York.

R. H....Religious Herald. Richmond, Va.
R. R....Review of Reviews. New York.

S....Scribner's Magazine.
S. B....Sermon Bible. New York: Funk & Wagnalls Co.
S. C....Silver Cross. New York: King's Daughters.
S. J. M....St. James Messenger.
S. M....Scribner's Magazine. (See S.) New York: Scribner's Sons.
S. N....St. Nicholas. New York: The Century Co.
Sp....Spectator. London, England.
S. R....Sabbath Recorder. Plainfield, N. J.
S. S. D....Students' Standard Dictionary. New York: Funk & Wagnalls Co.
S. S. T....Sunday School Times. Philadelphia.
S. S. V....S. S. Visitor. New York: Am. Tract Society.
St....The Standard. Chicago.
St. D....Standard Dictionary. New York: Funk & Wagnalls Co.
S. Y. B. (1891)....Sermon Year Book. New York: Funk & Wagnalls Co.

T. C. R....The Contemporary Review.
T. T....Teacher's Treasury.

U. G. N....Union Gospel News. Cleveland, Ohio.
U. L....Universalist Leader. Boston.
U. S....Union Signal. Chicago.

W....Watchman, The. Boston.
W. A....World Almanac. New York: N. Y. World.
W. B. O....The World's Best Orations. St. Louis: Ferd. P. Kaiser.
W. C. M....Will Carleton's Magazine. Brooklyn, N. Y.
W. S....Washington Star. Washington, D. C.
W. T....Watchword and Truth. Boston.

Y. C....Youth's Companion. Boston.
Y. L. J....Young Ladies' Journal. New York.

Holy=Days

The holiest of all holidays are those
    Kept by ourselves in silence and apart,
    The secret anniversaries of the heart,
When the full river of feeling overflows.—
The happy days unclouded to their close,
    The sudden joys that out of darkness start
    As flames from ashes; swift desires, that dart
Like swallows singing down each wind that blows!

HENRY W. LONGFELLOW—*Holidays.*

NEW YEAR'S DAY

FROM very ancient times the first day of the year has been observed as a holy festival. Among the Jews we find directions for its proper observance in passages of the Old Testament Scriptures, like Numbers xxix: 1, 2. It was called the Feast of Trumpets, and is to this day carefully observed by pious Hebrews.

Among the old Romans the year began with the first of March, when the festival of *Ancylia* was celebrated with processions, and feasting and rejoicing. When the Roman calendar was changed so as to make January first the beginning of the year, the same sacredness was attached to the day. To show the contrast between heathenism and Christianity, Christians began to observe January first as a day of joy and of religious services.

Among the Hindus, the first day of the year is celebrated with sacrifices to the God of Wisdom, and festivities and rejoicing throughout India mark the day. In China and Japan the day is the most striking and joyous of all the religious observances. The Persians celebrate the New Year with customs similar to those which characterized the Hebrew Sabbatical Year.

The ancient Druids commenced their year on the tenth of March, the cutting of the mistletoe and banqueting, sacrificing, and feasting being customary. " On the first day of the year," Lyman D. Abbott tells us, " the Mexicans carefully adorned their houses and temples, and employed themselves in various religious ceremonies. One, which was at first, perhaps, peculiar to this season, tho it became subsequently of more frequent occurrence, was the offering to the gods of a human sacrifice."

It thus appears that among all nations and in all ages the first day of the new year has been and is regarded not only as a holiday but also and especially a holy day, a day of glad rejoicing and of reverent worship.

NEW YEAR'S EVE AND DAY

By Alice Morse Earle

THE sole record of the observance of the New Year by the Pilgrims in the New World, named New England, was most prosaic, most brief—" We went to **In New England** work betimes." Many of the good Puritan ministers thought the celebration or even notice of the day in any way savored of improper and unchristian reverence for the heathen god Janus. Yet these English settlers came from a land where New Year's Eve and New Year's Day were second in importance and in domestic observance only to Christmas. Throughout every English county New Year's Eve was always celebrated; in many it was called by the pretty name of Singing E'en, from the custom which obtained of singing the last of the Christmas Carols at that time.

In Scotland the last day of the year was called by the uglier name of Hogamanay, a name of unknown and inexplicable derivation; and in Scotland it was re-**In Scotland** garded as the most popular of all the Daft Days, as the Christmas holidays were termed. Scotch children of the poorer class in small towns still beg on that day from door to door at the houses of wealthier families for a dole of oat-bread, calling out " Hogamanay " or some of the local rhymes which are given in Chambers's POPULAR RHYMES OF SCOTLAND, such as:

> " Hogamanay,
> Trollolay,
> Give us of your white bread
> And none of your gray ! "

They also beg for cheese, which they call "nog-money," and Brand's POPULAR ANTIQUITIES gives this begging rhyme used by Scotch children:

"Get up, gude wife, and binno sweir,
 Deal cakes and cheese while ye are here;
For the time will come when ye'll be dead
 And neither need your cheese nor bread."

As the children on these forays are swathed in great sheets formed into a deep bag or pouch to carry the oatcake, they form quite a mumming and fantastic appearance on the by-streets and lanes.

In County Antrim, Ireland, among the Scotch-Irish, a similar custom obtains; and round oaten bannocks with a hole in the middle, like our doughnuts, are specially baked for gift cakes. In other Irish counties a cake is thrown outside the door on New Year's Eve "to keep out hunger" the ensuing year.

In Ireland and the Isle of Man

In the Isle of Man a curious belief and custom existed till the middle of this century. In each home the housewife smoothed the ashes over the kitchen floor just before stepping into bed. If there were found in the morning on the surface of the ashes anything resembling the print of a foot that pointed toward the door it indicated a death in the family within the year. But if the heel of the footprint were toward the door it was a sure proof that the family would be increased.

No English holiday was of much account that was not observed with flowing bowl. On New Year's Eve the wassail bowl was filled with spiced ale and drunk in families, and poorer folk tied a bowl with ribbons and begged for money for ale to fill and refill the bowl, singing:

"Wassail, wassail all over the town,
 Our toast it is white, our ale it is brown;
Our bowl it is made of a maplin tree,
 We be good fellows all, I drink to thee."

In some parts of England the old year is "swept out" by men and boys with blackened faces, dressed to represent sweeps; in others it is "burned out" with bonfires. Sometimes it is rung out with muffled bells that are unmuffled and rung clear after twelve o'clock.

Another curious local name for New Year's Eve a century and a half ago was "Scrutiny Night." In Merton College, Oxford, all the college servants then delivered up their keys to the warden and fellows, and the worthy servants received them again with a Latin address.

Scrutiny Night and Watch Night

The observance in the churches of what was named by the Methodists "Watch Night," and the ringing of the old year out and the New Year in, are our present American customs for New Year's Eve, and may they long continue. I think no one who has ever attended these beautiful midnight services or heard those bells—equally solemn and happy—has ever done so with indifference. Charles Lamb says:

"Of all sounds, of all bells most solemn and touching is the peal which rings out the old year. I never hear it without a gathering up of my mind to a concentration of all the images that have been diffused over the past twelvemonth. I begin to know the worth of that regretted time, as when a person dies."

In lack of other customs we might revive the pretty Derbyshire custom of a posset pot, into which is placed the wedding ring of the hostess, each unmarried drinker trying to catch the ring in his or her ladleful of posset, and thereby insure being married within a year. I am not sure that modern palates would relish, or modern stomachs digest posset which was thus concocted:

The Posset Pot

"Take eighteen Eggs, whites and all, taking out the treads, let them be beaten very well, take a pint of Sack, and a Quart of Ayle boyld, and scum it, then put in three quarters of a pound of sugar and a Little Nutmeg, let it boyl a walm or two, then take it off the fire, stirring the eggs still, put into them two or three ladles full of drink, then mingle all together and set it on the fire, and keepe stirring till you find it thick, then so serve it up."

Another popular compound was called "lamb's wool" and "powsowdy" was also much in vogue—boiled ale full of roasted apples and toasted bread and raisins and currants—but would prove doubtful fare nowadays. In Scotland was everywhere drunk a "hot-pint" made of beer, whisky, and eggs—a villainous compound.

When the clock struck twelve the house door was thrown open, as for an honored guest, and the New Year was ushered in with a shout of "Welcome!" and the first human incomer was watched for with much eagerness, a woman visitor being thought—rather ungallantly—to bring ill-luck; a light-haired man was also regarded with much disfavor. In Lancashire many swarthy, dark-haired men went from house to house on New Year's morn "to take the New Year in," receiving a gift of liquor or money from each host. In Scotland this "first-footing" was a ceremony of much importance; and so universal was the custom of visiting from house to house that a century ago, in Edinburgh, the streets were more thronged from twelve to one in the New Year's morning than at midday. As it was deemed unlucky to enter a house empty-handed, the visitors bore with them cakes, cheese, and bowls or kettles of "hot pint." As parties of friends met in the streets they exchanged cakes and buns and sipped each other's drink. It was also held everywhere to bring ill-luck if anything were carried out of the house before anything was brought in:

Various Customs

"Take out and take in,
Bad luck is sure to begin;
But take in and take out,
Good luck will come about."

In some portions of England the Bible was consulted, or "dipped," on New Year's morning as an oracle. This ceremony took place before breakfast. The **The Bible** book was opened at random, and **Used** the finger of the seeker was placed, without time even for hasty perusal, upon any chapter that chanced to be contained in the two open pages. The contents of this chapter were construed in some way into foretelling his fortune for the year. I should like to try the skill and ingenuity of these diviners with some of the chapters in Leviticus and Numbers.

A very pretty custom was that of tasting the "cream of the well," the first drink from spring or well on New Year's morn. The first pail of water drawn, "the flower of the well," insured positively the best husband in the parish to the water drawer.

"Twall struck—two neebour hizzies raise
An liltin gaed a sad gate;
The flower o' the well to our house gaes
An' I'll hae the bonniest lad yet."

The custom of exchanging gifts on New Year's is of long standing. It was a practice among the Romans and the Saxons, **New** and was for many years a time **Year's** of annual gift-offering to the **Gifts** royal family of England. In the reign of Queen Elizabeth these gifts assumed such proportions that it is thought the royal wardrobe and jewel case were principally supported by these New Year's presents which came from the highest in the land down to the dustman. The Queen made gifts also, but with a most thrifty eye to a tidy balance in her own favor. Agnes Strickland quotes this account of the method of the royal reception of New Year's gifts in a previous reign from a manuscript of the time of Henry VII.:

"On the day of the New Year, when the king came to his foot-sheet, his usher of his chamber door said to him, 'Sire, here is a New Year's gift coming from the queen.'

Then the king replied, 'Let it come in.' Then the king's usher let the queen's **Henry VII.** messenger come within the **and the** gate. Henry VII., sitting at the **New Year** foot of the bed in his dressing gown, the officers of his bed-chamber having turned the top sheet smoothly down to the foot of the bed when the royal personage rose. The queen in like manner sat at her foot-sheet and received the king's New Year's gift within the gate of her bed-railing. When this formal exchange had taken place between the king and his consort, they received, seated in the same manner, the New Year's gifts of their nobles."

This system of royal taxation lasted long and extended wide. Sturdy old Latimer dared to give King Henry VIII., instead of **Gifts to** a purse of gold, a Bible with **Royalty** the leaf boldly turned down at Heb. xiii: 4. The Commonwealth destroyed this burdensome observance of costly royal gifts on New Year's.

Gloves were a common gift among friends, and pins, when pins were rare and few in number. Oranges stuck with cloves, and apples, skewered on three sticks in the form of tripod legs, and gilded nutmegs were all given. Tho Christmas gifts were never exchanged in colonial days in New England, we learn from contemporary diaries that New Year's gifts of money, books, toys, etc., were given.

It is curious to find the Puritan Judge **Judge** Sewell, a hater of all holidays **Sewell's** and set-days, recording with **New Year,** much pleasure his being awak- **1700** ened on New Year's morning in sober Boston, in 1698, by a levet or blast of trumpets; and he celebrated January 1st, 1700 (which he seemed to deem the opening of a new century), by writing a very poor poem and causing it to be cried or recited through the town by the town crier.

The New Year's cakes of the Dutch set- **New** tlements were not an English **Year's** fashion; and the custom of New **Cakes** Year's calls as practiced to our **and Calls** own day on Manhattan Island was not of English origin. This latter custom lived to a good old age, died slowly, and is still deeply lamented.—I.

NEW YEAR'S DAY IN THE EAST

By Alcide de Andria

New Year's day in part of the Turkish Orient **is the gayest holiday of the year,** for it is also the day of St. Basil's festival. The **In the** celebration of the two feasts has become inseparable, so to speak, **Turkish** in the minds of the Greeks, and **Orient** the first of January is now known throughout the Levant as St. Basil's day.

But it is the Greek Church only which honors the saint on that date; the Latin Church observes simply his ordination day, some time in June, while the other Christian denominations have for him merely the same reverence as for the principal Greek Fathers, such as St. Chrysostom, St. Gregory Nazianzen, etc.

The Russians, tho following the same

ritual as the Greeks, hold no particular celebration on New Year's day in honor of St.

Russians and Greeks Basil: and the true Hellenes, those who live on Greek territory, seldom give importance to a saint's feast on January first.

So St. Basil's birthday is distinctly celebrated only by the Greeks who dwell on Turkish territory and are subjects of the Sultan.

They are known as Greek Rayahs. Of their fatherland they have preserved nothing, save the religion and an impure dialect, which varies more or less in every *vilayet,* or province and little resembles the harmonious and venerable mother tongue. This dialect in its varieties is by no means the modern Greek, which is a beautiful and very expressive language, rich in constructions, possessing a grammar, and also a vocabulary, almost as extensive as that of the ancient Greek. The Rayah dialects on the other hand are corrupt *patois* formed with words borrowed from Turkish, Hebrew, Armenian, Italian, and French.

Nor does the costume of the Rayahs resemble the true Hellenic dress, but rather that of the Mohammedans.

The ignorance, debasement, and sluggishness of the Rayahs are extreme, notwithstanding the efforts of the Greek government

The Status of the Greek Rayah cational institutions, in the hope that they may rise against their oppressors and succeed in shaking off their yoke. But it is likely to be long before these descendants of a noble race shall appreciate the philanthropic efforts of their freed brethren.

At present they have adopted nearly all the Turkish fashions, and lack ambition to improve their condition. They are fond of their ease, love drinking and smoking, and care for nothing beyond their material welfare.

Still they have remained faithful to their religion nevertheless; and follow all its rites with a respectful and blindly superstitious obedience. They observe all the holidays of the church, but prefer above all St. Basil's day.

Popular tradition represents St. Basil as a venerable man, clad in bishop's vestments, carrying incense, myrrh, and other Oriental

St. Basil perfumes. He is supposed to come on the eve of his birthday, reputed as January 1st old style, —January 12th according to the Gregorian calendar,—and distribute presents to children. He is the patron saint of the home and of the young. From Armenia to the Archipelago, and from the Black Sea to Syria, there is not a Rayah child who does not regard its New Year's presents as positive proof of his coming.

Among the young he ranks as high as St. Nicholas in Russia, Germany, and other countries; but among the old he is held in great veneration as one of the most eminent Greek Fathers, and also as the most elo-

quent promoter of monasticism throughout the East. Besides, he was a great philanthropist and an ardent apostle.

Cæsarea, the capital of the former province of Cappadocia, was St. Basil's native place. At the age of thirty-three he was made a presbyter, and a few years later bishop of the same city, a position which he held until his death, A. D. 379.

Elaborate preparations are made for his festival, which begins at an early hour on the evening of December 31st. The shop-

St. Basil's Eve, Dec. 31 keepers adorn their windows with an attractive medley of toys and holiday gifts. Oranges, dried and fresh fruit, imported and domestic table delicacies, candies, cakes, are either displayed in the show-cases or piled up in front of the stores, which are extravagantly lighted up for the occasion, and decorated with garlands of colored paper skilfully cut out in the shape of natural flowers. From the ceilings, from the chandeliers, from the pictures, from the top of the windows, they fall in grouped festoons.

The mild climate permits a large and variegated crowd to circulate through the streets and gather in the stores, and no sight is more picturesque than a street in the East on St. Basil's eve. There are to be seen people of communities and races having nothing in common but the land and the surrounding atmosphere; there are curious contrasts of complexion and wearing apparel; there the genuine attire of five races is on constant exhibition.

You see, for instance, the long, loose robes of the Jews, and the bright red or yellow silk garments worn by their wives. There are the short, wide breeches of the Turks, contrasting with the long ones of the Rayahs. The small red fez and the large vermillion one, designed to hang down on one side of the face like the Phrygian cap, are intermingled with the plain Derby and black silk hats of the European gentlemen, whose simple attire is made obtrusively plain by the bright-colored goods used by the natives.

Conceive, too, the variety of garments worn by the women. Imagine, for instance, the Parisian dress and bonnet of a European merchant's daughter, side by side with the loose yellow breeches, the lilac doublet, and the long green veil of a wealthy Armenian lady! Every day one sees embroidered bosoms, long garments sometimes trimmed with fur, robes, Cashmere shawls, and bright red silk slippers, on the women.

Among men it is not uncommon to behold bare legs and gorgeous holiday turbans; often a gallant Mohammedan, covered with rags and filth, carries in his belt an assortment of Damascus blades, yataghans, and jewel-encrusted firearms, worth a small fortune.

Two singular customs contribute to this holiday's particular character; one is the

" St. Basil's Cake " making of " St. Basil's cake," the other the singing of a song through the streets on the eve of the saint's alleged birthday.

Elaborate preparations for the kneading of the cake begin in every house two days, at least, before the festival, for much labor is involved in its confection. All the women of the family squat on a rug in the Turkish fashion, around a low circular pastry-table, and amidst gay stories and laughter the rolling-pin runs over the rich paste, while the housewives vie in decorating and forming the cakes. The commonest decorations are Oriental arabesques representing palms, flowers, shells, or grotesque figures with which to amuse the children, while the most skilful workers make dolls whose faces are red eggs firmly embedded in the paste.

These would seem simple to an American housekeeper; but in a country where cooking utensils and baking ovens are very rude, the undertaking requires much patience. The cake consists of butter, eggs, and sugar, and its flavoring is of certain spices. It is usually made very rich, so that it may keep soft for days after it is baked.

Housekeepers dread the task, for a large quantity of St. Basil's cake is made in each family. A large part of it is destined for the hospitals, the children's and orphan's asylums, the prisons, and the poor; another part is given away to callers, to servants, and to the boys who come around in the early evening to sing St. Basil's song.

New Year's eve is a great time for the Rayah boys. As soon as they ring the bell of a house the door is thrown **The Rayah** open and the voice of the mas- **Boys on** ter is heard, saying: **New** "Let the boys in at once! **Year's Eve** Give them money, fruit, and all that they can carry of St. Basil's cake. Come on, servants, fill their pockets while they give us their song!"

Then the poor children, delighted by the warm welcome of the host and the profusion of dainty things given them, sing with frenzy the romantic little tale of St. Basil, which ends with the calling down of numerous blessings on the generous family during the new year.

But the strangest thing of all is neither St. Basil's song nor St. Basil's **Confusion** cake; it is a curious mistake as **of a Date** to date which has prevailed among the Greek Rayahs for many generations. For history declares that the 1st day of January is not the anniversay of St. Basil's birth, but that of his death!— Y. C.

A GREETING TO THE NEW YEAR

By J. R. MILLER, D.D.

We are on the threshold of a new year. We do not know what the year holds for us, but we are not afraid of it. We have learned to look for kindness and goodness in all our paths, and so we go forward with glad hope and expectation.

It is always a serious thing to live. We can pass through any year but once. If we have lived negligently we cannot return to amend what we have slurred over. We cannot correct mistakes, fill up blank spaces, erase lines we may be ashamed of, cut out pages unworthily filled. The irrevocableness of life ought alone to be motive enough for incessant watchfulness and diligence. Not a word we write can be changed. Nothing we do can be canceled.

Another element of seriousness in living is the influence of our life on other lives. We do not pass through the year alone; we are tied up with others in our homes, our friendships, our companionships, our associations, our occupations. We are always touching others and leaving impressions on them. Human lives are like the photographer's sensitized plates, receiving upon them the image of whatever passes before them. Our careless words drop, and we think not where they fall, but the lightest of them lodges in some heart and leaves its blessing or its blight. All our acts, dispositions and moods do something in the shaping and coloring of other lives.

It is said that every word whispered into the air starts vibrations which will quiver on and on forever. The same is true also of influences which go out from our lives in the commonest days—they will go on forever. This should make us most careful what we do, what we say, and what quality of life we give to the world. It would be sad, indeed, if we should set going unholy or hurtful influences, if we should touch even one life unwholesomely, if we should speak even a word which starts a soul toward death.

Still another reason why life is so serious is because we must give account of it all. Jesus hinted at the large meaning of this truth when He said that for every idle word that men speak they must give account. If for the idle words—light, airy, trivial, empty words—how much more for the words which are filled with bitterness, or with malice, or with the poison of impurity, or with the evil of falsehood, of envy, of irreverence! We are not done with life as we live it; we shall meet it all again. This should make us exceedingly watchful over every word, act, and influence of our days. Nothing can be concealed. Every secret thing shall be brought to light. We should give the year nothing which we shall ever be ashamed to see again.

These things being true, how should we enter upon the new year? For one thing, we should begin it with Christ. Who is sufficient for the serious problem of living without the divine grace and help? One New Year's eve a trembling young Christian, who in the year just closing had been greatly helped by a strong friendship, said to the friend who had given the help, "May I put my hand in yours for another year?" The answer was, "Yes, but in Christ's first." There is no other hand that can guide us safely through the new and strange experiences.

Then we need great watchfulness if we would make the voyage of the year in safety. Tho we have Christ with us, this does not relieve us of our own share of the responsibility. God does not carry us on angel wings through this world. The devoutest pilot would not run his vessel over the sea by prayer alone, without giving heed to his compass and his chart. Pray as earnestly as he might for divine protection and guidance, he would watch every movement of his vessel and give it his utmost care. A life of prayer does not free us from duty. One of our Lord's words of counsel was "Watch!" We need to watch ourselves, for our hearts are deceitful. We need to watch against the evil there is in others about us. We need to watch that we are not swept upon fatal rocks by sudden storms.

Another suggestion for a prosperous new year is that we should fill its every hour with duty well done. Duty is a large word. It includes all that we owe to God—honor, love, obedience, faithfulness. It includes all that we owe to men. No year can be happy or beautiful with God left out. Some people strive to render all love's duties to their fellowmen, and then suppose they have done all that needs to be done. But all the while they have forgotten God, giving Him no honor, not seeking to do His will, never bowing in homage before Him. It is a poor life that has no heavenly outlook. A picture without sky is defective. A life without heaven in it. lacks the chief glory of life. Duty toward God must fill the year that is to be deeply happy. Prayer must bring down into all its days heaven's grace and strength. The flowers must have the sun and the rain and dew of the skies to fill their cups with fragrance. So do we need God's blessing in our life.

Then there are duties to man. If we love God we shall love our brother also. St. Paul said he was a debtor to every man, Greek or Barbarian. He meant that he owed to every one the duty of love. Every relation of life brings its obligations. We make gladness for ourselves only when we do our duty as well as we can, wherever we are. It never can be found in selfishness.

"He is dead whose hand is not opened wide
  To help the need of a human brother;
He doubles the length of his life-long ride
  Who gives his fortunate place to another;

And a thousand million lives are his
Who carries the world in his sympathies—
          To give is to live!"

Some people dream of happiness as something they will come to by and by, at the end of a course of toil and struggle. But the true way to find happiness is as we go on in our work. Every day has its own cup of sweetness. In every duty is a pot of hidden manna. In every sorrow is a blessing of comfort. In every burden is rolled up a gift of God. In all life Christ is with us if we are true to Him.

"The work which we count so hard to do,
  He makes it easy, for He works too;
The days that are long to live are His,
A bit of His bright eternities,
And close to our need His helping is."

If we have learned this secret, even the things that seem unpleasant and disagreeable yield joy in the doing. A traveler in South Africa saw some boys playing marbles, using pebbles. One of these rolled to the traveler's feet, and picking it up, it seemed to him only a rough stone, without beauty or worth. But as he turned it over a gleam of light flashed from one spot of it. It was a diamond. Duties seem dull and dreary to us, unattractive, hard, but they enfold secrets of happiness which we find when we accept them with love and do them cheerfully.

Another way to be sure of a good year is to make it a year of growth. We are in this world to grow. Each day should show its new line in every life and character. We should be better men and women at the end of the year than we were at the beginning. Yet we must remember that mere largeness is not always growth. One may be richer in estate and yet be poorer in mind and heart. Ruskin says, "He only is advancing in life whose heart is growing softer, whose blood warmer, whose brain quicker, whose spirit is entering into living peace."

      "The glory of our life
Comes not from what we do or what we
          know,
But dwells for evermore in what we are."

These are but a few suggestions of ways in which we may make the new year one of happiness and blessing. Let us give it nothing to keep which will not prove an honor to God's name and a blessing to the world; nothing which we shall not be willing to learn of again when we stand before the great white throne.—P. J.

A HAPPY NEW YEAR
By J. M. Buckley, D.D.

Few persons begin a new year without some sort of hope or determination that it shall be a happier year than the preceding. But most men and women come to the close of the year disappointed and discouraged. The year has been about the same as other years. The fond hopes of New Year's Day have been blasted. Is there any sure way by which the year to come may be a happier year than any of its predecessors? What is the secret of a happy year?

First, get rid of sin. Sin is not only the sting of death, but also the sting of life. "The way of the transgressor is hard." One who has never tried God's remedy for sin may dream that he is happy, but he is as one who dreams that he eats, but he waketh, and, behold, he is yet hungry. Sin is darkness, weakness, death. Some seek to cover their sins, but "he that covereth his sin shall not prosper." Some try to justify themselves in sin, but this is impossible, because each one is condemned by his own conscience. Some ignore the fact of sin and seek to silence conscience by multiplying iniquity, but this will only augment the dark account and heap higher the mountain under which the soul already groans. Some seek happiness in the good things of the world, in the pursuit of knowledge, or in the society of kindred spirits. While this joy is real, it is marred by the awful fact of unconfessed and unpardoned sin. Some study philosophy, some read amusing fiction, some reform their lives and mend their ways. All these expedients must fail. They have all failed. There is one way to get rid of sin. "Repent and be converted, that your sins may be blotted out." Then shall the soul take up the song of the psalmist, "As far as the east is from the west, so far hath he removed our transgressions from us."

Learn to serve. So long as we bend our energies and our wits to the task of securing the service of others we can never be happy. "It is more blessed to give than to receive." The mistake of this world is the belief that all blessedness is found in receiving. This fatal error is seen in the way most men use their friends. They cherish their friendship for what they can make out of them. Most men love their country for what they hope to get out of it. Many church members have no use for the Church except so far as they can make the Church serve them. Some ministers decline calls to Christian pulpits and refuse appointments or complain of them merely because the only interest they have in the Church is the salary or support it offers. The question should be, "How much can I put into that Church?" not, "How much can I get out of it?" Even in prayer men make this mistake. It is right to plead with God for help, because we are helpless, and He is an almighty helper. But when we never speak to God except to beg Him for help, we prove our ignorance of the great secret of life and happiness. If we love God, our hearts will be set on serving Him. We will not be content to have Him serve us. Jesus was servant of all. He came to minister. He taught us that the chief place is the place of a servant. The new year will be full of happiness in proportion to its fulness of service. Let one set about serving God, serving his kindred, serving the church, serving his country, serving his fellow-men, and fill each day full of service, and the year will be filled with joy.

Take no thought for the morrow. Much of the trouble of our past years has been borrowed trouble. We have suffered more from ills that never happened than from any other. We have the best of reasons for keeping the mind free from the troubles of to-morrow. One is, the trouble of to-day is sufficient. "Sufficient unto the day is the evil thereof." Moreover, we have the promise that the strength we need will come when it is needed: "As thy day, so shall thy strength be." Another reason is, God has hidden the future from us for this very purpose, that we might not worry over it. Overburdened souls are overburdened chiefly with borrowed burdens. They could bear present trouble, but they are carrying burdens for to-morrow in addition.

Learn the lesson of transformed sorrow. "Count it all joy when ye fall into divers temptations." All blessings abused become a curse, and all ills sanctified become a blessing. "All things work together for good to them that love God." Good men have been enriched more by their sorrows than by their joys. We have made more advancement in the darkness than in the light. If we count our burdens, our trials, our sufferings, all loss, we make a great mistake. "Count it all joy." "Your sorrow shall be turned into joy." Whatever the year shall bring will be a blessing to the righteous. We know not which will bring most good—gain or loss, pain or pleasure. Then leave to our heavenly Father the choice of the way. Let it be our concern to follow whithersoever He leadeth. Let the new year be a year of freedom from sin, a year of service, a year of trust in God, and it will be a happy year from first to last. It may be the hardest year we have known, but it will be the happiest.—C. A.

THE PLEA OF THE FUTURE

By Henry Armitt Brown

My Countrymen:—

The moments are quickly passing, and we stand like some traveler upon a lofty crag that separates two boundless seas. The century that is closing is complete. "The past," said your great statesman, "is secure." It is finished and beyond our reach. The hand of detraction cannot dim its glories, nor the tears of repentance wipe away its stains. Its good and evil, its joy and sorrow, its truth and falsehood, its honor and its shame we cannot touch. Sigh for them, blush for them, weep for them if we will, we cannot change them now. The old century is dying and they are to be buried with him; his history is finished and they will stand upon its roll forever.

The century that is opening is all our own. The years that are before us are a virgin page. We can inscribe them as we will. The future of our country rests upon us. The happiness of posterity depends upon us. The fate of humanity may be in our hands. That pleading voice, choked with the sobs of ages, which has so often spoken to deaf ears, is lifted up to us. It asks us to be brave, benevolent, consistent, true to the teachings of our history, proving "divine descent by worth divine." It asks us to be virtuous, building up public virtue upon private worth; seeking that righteousness that exalteth nations. It asks us to be patriotic, loving our country before all other things; making her happiness our happiness, her honors ours, her fame our own. It asks us in the name of charity, in the name of freedom, in the name of God!—W. B. O.

SERMONS AND OUTLINES

OUR GUIDE

By James Stalker, D.D.

Thou shalt guide me with thy counsel, and afterward receive me to glory.—Psa. lxxiii: 24

We are met this morning to wish one another a happy New Year, and let me wish you one and all a happy New Year. It is a good thing surely that we should begin the year with prayer, seeking to lay our life anew on God's altar; and it is good also, I think, to begin it in the Church, that our sympathies may not be confined within our own breasts, but be taught to circle round our friends and our fellow-members, and round the things and Kingdom of Christ. Now I like to give a New Year's day motto for the year, and it is often very delightful for me to find far on in the year that the New Year's motto is well remembered. I heard one of our elders, just a couple of months ago, quoting up at the mission last New Year's motto, and I am not sure but he quoted those of several years past. Now I am going to give you one to-day that I think will be very encouraging and helpful. You will find it in the Psalms—seventy-third Psalm, twenty-fourth verse: "Thou shalt guide me with thy counsel, and afterward receive me to glory."

The Word of God says a great deal about guiding. There are many prayers in it in which God's people ask for guidance, and there are many promises in it which God undertakes to guide His people. Now what does that imply? Who are they who need to be guided? Well, children do. When very young you know how a mother requires to take a child's hand, and even teach it to walk, and in many respects we are children. Some of us have just begun the Christian life, and even those of us who have been longer in it are in many respects children. You remember when Jeremiah was called to be a prophet, how he said at once, "Ah, God, I am a child;" and when Solomon was called to be a king, he said very much the same thing. Now when we think of our high vocation—for the Christian calling is both a prophetic, and a kingly and priestly vocation—we also say, "I am a child." We need to be guided. Then, again, strangers need to be guided. When we are in a foreign land we need to take a guide-book with us. When we are in a strange town we need to ask our way. Now every New Year as it comes is a foreign country. We have not passed this way heretofore. We do not know what the year contains. There are none who need guidance so much as the blind, and we may almost say that, as regards the future, we are blind. There is a dark curtain hanging before us, and we cannot penetrate the future, therefore we need some one to guide us.

Then, again, guidance is needed when any one's road is very adventurous or perilous. You know when travelers go away to Switzerland, and want to ascend the Alps, they have to take guides with them; and I believe that when the ascent is very perilous they are tied to the guide. Even that is not sometimes a perfect protection, because the guide may slip away; but if we are tied to our Guide, there is no fear that He will fail us. And our path is generally a perilous one. We are not going the broad highway of ordinary life; we are seeking the white heights of purity, the lofty heights of meditation and contemplation; and, therefore, we need a Guide to take us up the perilous and difficult way. And then, once more, the erring need a guide; and I think the most pathetic thought suggested by the words, "Thou shalt guide me," is how much we have gone astray in years past. There was a clear path, but how often we have turned to the right hand or to the left, and we know what the result of that has been, how disastrous both to us and to others; and when we remember our past errors, most pathetically and most earnestly of all do we say, "Thou shalt guide me."

"Thou shalt guide me *with thy counsel.*" There is, I am certain, an unconscious guidance in Providence. God sees us past many a peril that we do not see. There is a lovely phrase somewhere—I think it is in the Psalms—about guidance. It says, "I will guide thee with mine eye." What does that mean? It always makes me think of a mother, out in the open air, perhaps, sitting on a green, or in a room sitting with her charge; and her child is playing through the house, and she is sewing or knitting, but with the corner of her eye she is watching the little one all the time, and with her feet she pushes something out of the way to clear its path; or if she sees something sharp lying in the path she takes it quietly away. And I have no doubt unconsciously to us God thus guides us with His eye, taking many a perilous thing out of our path, shutting up many a by-way, controlling us often when we do not know it by His Providence, so that we are guided aright. But on the whole the guidance of Christians by God is a conscious guidance. "I will guide thee with my counsel." It is an intelligent guidance. We come to think God's thoughts about our life. It is a voluntary guidance. He does not lead us against our will, but He makes our will insensibly to harmonize with His, and, therefore, He guides us with His counsel. Where do we find that counsel? Well, we find it in His Word, and I am going to say to you now that we are gathered here to speak about guidance for the year—if we want really to be guided we must be searching the Word during the year more than ever we have done, more carefully than we have done. You that have any experience of this are aware how the Word throws light on every day's duties, and how the new difficulties and dangers of the way grow light by the Word of God. Another way in which He guides us by His counsel is by the preaching of the Word. And I would say to you who want to be guided, attend diligently upon the preaching of God's Word in His House. I think you can say that the sermons of the Sabbath day throw light upon the week, and your experience through the week often gives a wonderful meaning to the sermon. And then, last of all, God gives us His counsel through His Holy Spirit—by the Word, by preaching, and by the Spirit.

"Thou shalt guide me with thy counsel, and *afterward*. . . . " Do you know I think that is the best word in the whole verse. It is a perilous way, it is a difficult way we are going on, but there is a glorious afterward. There is an afterward even for this world, and there is a glorious afterward for the next world. Now, my dear people, I think there is nothing laid on my heart so much to say to you this morning as this— do not despair in yourselves. Do not think that your life has come to an end, that you have already seen the best of existence. No; the best is still in front. I think that is a glorious hope for the Christian. In regard to the merely natural life there comes a time when everything begins to give way. The body gets stiff, and begins to fail. Even the memory begins to be lost, and the mind is not so reliable as it once was. The tabernacle has to be taken down, but it is not so

with the inner life, the life of the spirit. Tho the outward man perish, the inner man is renewed day by day. Do not despair of yourself, but keep a bright hope for the future.

Some of us have been reading dear Dr. Bonar's life during the last few days. Well, it is a very beautiful book in many ways, but I think Dr. Bonar's life—to me, at all events—had its greatest charm and best lesson in this: that he never gave up. He never thought that his service to God was done, and he never thought that God's goodness to him was done. He was ripening and growing to the very end. And can we not say this—I felt it whenever I came to Glasgow—that that dear old man's very presence in Glasgow streets was a message and a sermon? We all felt here that merely to have him there was might, a tower of strength to religion, and an encouragement to us all. And I would say to you who are growing old, look for an influence of that kind. Even tho part of your activity has to cease, and some great scheme in which you have been engaged has to be laid aside, God has new forms of interest and activity for you. Do not look upon your life as done and over. I think, perhaps, we are far too apt to think our life is over. We soon begin to despair, and we do so in regard to the inner life. I dare say there is some one here who has been fighting hard with some sin or temptation, and you are beginning to despair. Don't despair! God will give you the victory yet. Perhaps some of you have been thinking, when you looked upon an advanced Christian, "I never could become like that. There is a beauty, a godliness that I never can attain." There is no beauty of holiness God cannot give to you and me. Keep looking to the future. There is always an afterward. We have not exhausted Christ yet. We have not exhausted God's grace yet. The well of salvation is still deep and flowing. Look ever to the afterward.

And then there is the afterward of the next world, to which the text, perhaps, specially refers. "Thou shalt guide me with thy counsel, and afterward receive me to glory." I was saying a short time ago—I forget whether in the pulpit or the prayer-meeting —that one of the peculiarities of our time is the growing faith in the religious importance of the present life, but along with that there goes too much the want of interest in the future life. Now, I think, while we lay hold of the one we should take care and not lose the other. There was a time in the history of Christianity, an age in Europe, when the next world, so to speak, engrossed this world; the light of the coming glory so dazzled men's eyes they could not see the importance of time; and so they fled from common life and hid themselves in monasteries and nunneries. Well, we have got over that, but perhaps we have got too much over that. I think we have recovered a great truth of Christianity, a great thought of Christ, in taking this world very seriously, in looking upon it as a matter of great importance.

There is a great work to do here in the present life; there is a vast deal we have to do for ourselves and others and God, and we cannot, perhaps, make too much of it. Yes; but while we grasp that truth which Christianity at one stage lost hold of, don't let us lose hold of the other truth—the glory that is to come. Of course, it is possible to cherish that as a very idle hope, and I suppose it is from that the reaction has come. Heaven has been spoken about in an unnatural way, and therefore by degrees people have come not to care about it at all. Ah, but it is capable of doing two things for you. You remember what St. John said: " Now are we the sons of God, and it doth not yet appear what we shall be; but we know that, when he shall appear, we shall be like him: for we shall see him as he is." Therefore he adds: "And every man that hath this hope in him purifieth himself, even as he is pure." If the thought of Heaven has that effect on us, if it makes us purify ourselves that we may be fit for that exaltation, if the sense that we are citizens of that glorious country lays on us an obligation that leads us to live up to the dignity of the sons of God, then that is no idle or useless hope. Then there is another practical issue, for the thought of Heaven and its glory makes us wish to take others there. Oh, when we see what men are living for, when we see how unhappy the most of them are, do you not feel the passion in your soul to try to take some of them to Heaven with you? I have often said, both in public and in private, one of my chief ambitions for this congregation is that it may consist of those who are not only going to Heaven themselves, but trying to take a great many others with them; and if the thought of Heaven has that effect on us, it will be by no means an idle or impracticable thought.

Let me go over these points again. " Thou shalt guide me." We need guidance for all the reasons I mentioned. " With thy counsel "; there is not only an unconscious guidance, but an intelligent, voluntary guidance; and " afterward "—there is a glorious afterward for Christian hearts; first, the afterward of this world, and, second, the afterward of the eternal world.—P. M.

DISCOUNTING THE FUTURE

By H. C. Potter, D.D.

Come ye, say they, I will fetch wine, and we will fill ourselves with strong drink; and to-morrow shall be as this day, and much more abundant.—Isaiah lvi: 12

In this picture, that exaggerated hopefulness which it describes seems to have been the result of intoxication. It is one who has filled himself with strong drink; who, from the midst of his revels, cries out, " To-morrow shall be as this day, nay, much more abundant."

In point of fact, however, such artificial stimulous is no wise necessary for the excitement of extravagant hopes. Such hopes are born out of circumstances the most discouraging and amid surroundings the most dismal and dreary. There is probably not a man in this church this morning who, having balanced his accounts and closed his books for the year yesterday, does not believe and expect that the year before us will be, as compared with the year that is behind us, better and more abundant. And this not at all because the year behind us has been so exceptionally bad and unprofitable, nor because the most lugubrious prophets admit that things in the business world must take a turn some time or other, but because, underneath the hopelessness of even the most chronic croaker, there is an indestructible substratum of expectation which is perpetually looking for and anticipating the dawn of a brighter day and a better era.

Let us bless God that it is so. I doubt whether life would be long endurable if it were otherwise. In fact, it is at the point when the spring of hopefulness fairly snaps that men and women break down. You who are a spectator of the struggle which your neighbor is making, whether it be for wealth or fame or, as in so many overtaxed lives and in so many sick chambers, for bare existence itself, you can see how hopeless that struggle often is. You can see the infirmities in your neighbor's plans or his powers or his partnerships that predict his failure as inevitably as dawn predicts the daylight. But he—let us thank God, I say, that it is so—he can neither read the stern prophecy of failure that is written across his present nor discern the dismal certainties of his future. And so, while you are thinking that you would almost go and hang yourself if you were in *his* place, he, perhaps, is quite clear that he would drown himself if he should be in yours. In other words we are all of us living largely upon hope—an ethereal diet, which is not to be purchased in the markets, but which has, nevertheless, a power of sustentation which no other food at all pretends to rival.

And yet, like some other forms of so-called nourishment, this is one which has a perilous power of enervation. Wretched as life would become if there were taken out of it that dim but deathless expectancy of better days and a more blessed lot, it is a singular illustration of the fact that every good is offset and qualified by its corresponding evil, that when we come to look at what has been the fruitage of many of the most ardent hopes of humanity, we find that the net result has been only too often indolence and inertness and apathy. Men talk about the future as tho the future were a sort of divinity who was coming down the gleaming slopes of time with both hands full of infinite riches and indiscriminate blessings. As in trade, people are fond of saying in bad times that things will "take a turn"—as if somewhere at hand there were a benevolent fairy who might at any moment, from a mere freak of good nature, empty her apronful of bounties into all the waiting and idle industries of the hour—so, *out* of trade, in art, in letters, above all, in religion, we are fond most of all of discounting the future, and of believing that, somehow, tomorrow shall be much more abundant, though we cannot for the life of us give the remotest reason why.

Now, it is worth while to remember that the future is simply and inevitably and inexorably the outgrowth and outcome of the present. It is the period in which one reaps what he has been sowing in the present. It is only that, and invariably that, and eternally that, and all the misery of life that does not come from man's *hereditary* sinfulness of nature comes from his more or less conscious and deliberate refusal to recognize this fact. We are all bemoaning the "hard times" and wondering why they do not get better, and when the golden future which is to make them better is to dawn. Well, the golden future will come when it has been honestly earned and its harvest faithfully sown, and not before. When men and women stop buying what they cannot pay for and spending what they have not earned, when we have had enough of calling houses our own which belong, in fact, to the mechanics who reared them or to the creditors with whose borrowed money we have adorned them—when, in one word, we are willing as a nation to live frugally, and spend moderately, and deal honestly with others and no less honestly with ourselves—then, when we have some fair dealing and plain living and chastened ambitions as our seed, shall we have permanent prosperity as our harvest. Yes, then, and not till then, tho we were to have a currency as hard and as precious as diamonds, with St. Paul for Chief Magistrate and the whole College of the Apostles as his Cabinet!

And so in every other department of life, however lofty or lowly its range, there are a great many estimable people who are expecting amid the kindlier atmosphere of the future to outgrow their infirmities. They are conscious of them; they bemoan them; they will do everything to be rid of them—but grapple with them. With them to-morrow will be as to-day, as good a time for such a task as to-day, only with this difference, that to-morrow will be much more abundant than to-day—more abundant in its opportunities, its inspirations, its freedom from hindrances. But, alas! that sort of tomorrow never comes.

The man or woman of ungoverned temper imagines that age will cool their blood and so diminish their provocations. But age weakens nothing save our powers of demonstration. I have seen a man of eighty in as towering a passion as a youth of eighteen; and that to-morrow to which he had been looking all his life to do for him that which he would not do for himself had achieved no more than the making his blind anger feeble and impotent in its expression. The ungoverned passion was all there, as ungoverned and undisciplined as in the beginning. And so of the rest of the infirmities of our nature. Does the lust of the flesh, or the lust of the eye, or the pride of life—do our covetousness and our selfishness and our untruthfulness go through a sort of transformation-scene process, and emerge at some given point in our future in the guise of the Christian graces or the cardinal virtues? Is the future a moral alchemist, under whose skilful manipulation the seven deadly sins become metamorphosed into the seven signs of saintly perfection? There is a perfectly easy method of answering that question. Ten years ago, the ten years which end to-day, were the future. Then as now, the New Year began in close conjunction with a Sunday. Then, as now, we were already discounting our future. Out of it was to come to us, somehow, a loftier plane of living. Somewhere in it we should meet the opportunity to make Christ a personal Friend and Master. Somewhere there would open to us the way out of a great many associations and intimacies that we were most anxious to be free from, if only it could be accomplished by some other means than by the ordinary means in such cases—namely, by rising up and abandoning them. Well, since then the future has become the past, and what have we to tell to-day of that future's magic potency?

In fact, is it not time, dear brethren, that we learned that the future does not create progress, but only reveals it? We are fond of looking back to the dark ages of the world's history and reminding ourselves how upon their darkness suddenly the light burst and the morning dawned, and the world became new and young again. Yes, the light did dawn, but it dawned because brave hearts and strong hands had hewn and cleft a way for it. We talk of the Reformation in Germany and in England, and recall how the light of a purer gospel flashed, as it were, simultaneously within the walls of monastic cells, whether those cells were at Oxford or at Erfurt. Ay, but who were within those cells? Dozing monks, who were making no struggle toward the light, and smiting no walls of lifelong prejudice to let it in? Ah! I think of Luther climbing painfully upon his knees that long and wearisome ascent of the Scala Sancta at Rome, where to-day you may see the disciples of the Roman obedience painfully and laboriously repeating the same penance. I think, I say, of Luther mounting one by one those same stairs and crying to himself in an agony of longing and aspiration: "Tell me, O! thou Holy One, *is* this the road to heaven?" And then, as there flashes into his expectant soul those words of the apostles, "The just shall live by faith," and he sees, as in a moment, the life of simple and loving trust opening before him, instead of a life of bitter and painful penance. I see in that experience a revelation given to one who had been wrestling, striving, praying, struggling to attain it; not to one who had sat down in drowsy idleness to dream until the future should bring near that revolution. And so, wherever light has broken on the world, we shall find that some earnest thinker and toiler, delving beneath the dull, dead surface of the times, has been digging the mine and laying the train that made some vast upheaval of the social or spiritual fabric of human society not merely a possible, but an actual thing. Such men, whoever they were, were not men who believed in the future half so much as they believed in and verified the present. They had learned what we need to learn, that the future is not an actor; that it is only a result, and that that which to-morrow does for us is simply to add up the transactions of to-day.

And thus we see the province and, if I may so speak, the function in the moral and spiritual world of Hope. That function is to inspire the present. When you are struggling up the steeps of duty, and when, amid the storm and darkness, you cannot see where you may safely plant your feet, then from beyond Hope flashes its rays of light and makes your pathway plain. When you are wrestling with the demon of evil in your own nature, and that struggle, as day after day you are called upon to renew it, seems so hard and so ineffectual, then Hope bids you see in such daily struggles the seed-time of your future triumph. You are sowing now—sowing in faith and hope. Be patient, then, and He who has never failed to bless the labors of the husbandman will not fail to bless your labors also. And so Hope whispers to you, "In due season ye shall reap if ye faint not," and thus gilds the often dry and cheerless horizon of your present with the distant dawning of a brighter future. But let us take care how we transform what God gave as an inspiration to effort, as a consolation in sorrow, into an excuse for apathy and neglect. If we sit still and fold our hands and intermit all effort, then we may be sure that our expectancy, in all the vastness of its irrational proportions, will be the precise measure of our disappointment. One cannot help feeling as if the world had found a new divinity, and that amid all its festering evils and unrighted wrongs it was content simply to worship the Goddess of the Future. Is the State corrupt? No matter! Let us wait for the redeeming influence of the "Future." Is the tone of morals lower than we would fain see it? Again, no matter. It will all come right "in the future." Above all, are our souls cold and lifeless and unaspiring? Are we still uninfluenced by the love of Christ and unenlightened by the indwelling power of the Spirit? Once more, "no matter," we

are saying. It will be different and better in the "future." But why? It is true that in the learned professions and in the case of almost all permanent success and prosperity in business, the prizes come to a man comparatively late in life, and that the chief encouragement through long years of obscurity and straitened means must needs be found in looking toward the tardy successes of the future. But in such cases what a record of quiet, steadfast, persistent toil and study has laid the foundations of that future; and when it comes, how plainly we see that the future has given the man nothing save the fruitage of those seeds of endeavor which he planted long ago in the waiting furrows of his past!

And, therefore, if I were asked to indite that legend or motto which should be the rule and law for every young life among us, I would write the one word "Now." If I were bidden to choose the watchword to be blazoned upon all the banners of our social reforms and philanthropic endeavors, I would choose the watchword "Now!" If it were given to me to trace upon the walls of our school-houses, and in the recitation-rooms of our colleges, and in every other place where minds and hearts are trained for manly science the single syllable that should best inspire and inform that service, that single syllable would be "Now!" Nay, if in this house of God, if in our separate houses, if in the chambers where we sleep and the closets where we kneel, one word might quicken and comfort us always, I would that it might be the one word, "Now!" "Now is the accepted time," and God has never anywhere told us that He will accept or honor that postponing trust that builds on any other. We have all read of that Persian prince who, having grown to man's estate and completed his education, divided his life into four decades. The first ten years of his life he would devote to travel, since travel, he rightly argued, was as much an educator as were books. The second decade he would employ in the affairs of government, since government is part of the duty of a prince. The third decade he would reserve for the pleasures and the benefits of friendship, since friendship is, after all, the melody and fragrance of life. And then the fourth decade he would give to God. It was a most taking and attractive plan of life. It seemed singularly equitable in its partition of time between rival and urgent claims. Nay, it seemed even generous in its recognition of the claims of religion. For the religion of the Brahmin, like the religion of the Hebrew and of the Christian, only asks for the devotion of one-seventh of one's time to God, and here there was pledged one-fourth. Yes, it seemed to be an admirable plan, but it was marred by one considerable defect. During the first ten years the prince died, and for that contingency he had made no provision whatever.

Dear brethren, let us take this simple story and sit down and read it between the lines. I will not speak of the men who have been discounting the future in the matter of their plans for others. We have had some examples of that of late, which are only weakened in their solemn and searching emphasis by any human endeavor to press them. I leave them, amid these last hours of a vanishing year, to your memories and your judgments. But how is it with our plans for ourselves? I cannot think that there is one of us here this morning who is determined always to leave God out of the account. I will not believe but that somewhere in your future you look for the coming of a moment which will make the love of God and of good in you the living and sovereign law. But when and how?

A gifted Englishman told us lately of his first night as a youth within the walls of his university: "Do any of us remember," he writes, "when leaving home and school and the boy's life behind us, we stood for the first time within college walls? The first night in the antique place, how wonderfully we were struck by it! As we looked out of our window on the still quadrangle, with the moonlight streaming down like some silvery flood upon the grave buildings and the grass, and heard the bells answering one another in the vocal air, it seemed as if the place were alive with all the dead. The thousand forms of famous men who came thither with unborn thoughts within them, which, when born, should move the world to passion and to power, appeared to thrill the air with their unseen presence. The silence was eloquent with those secrets which are told to hearts that listen in the hour of presentiment; secrets which, tho they seem our own thoughts, are, it may be, impressions from that silent world of souls of which our intellect knows nothing, but our heart so much. As we dreamed our dream, hope and fear, enthusiasm and depression interchanged

their glow and gloom within us. The past life—home and school and childhood—vanished for a time. We seemed to have been asleep and only now to have awakened. And with what a loosened rein we rode forward into the unknown fields of the future! Should it be failure or success, fame or a wasted life, enthusiasm deepening into work or grown craven in the chill of difficulty, pleasure decaying into pain or pain growing into the pleasure of conquest? And then we answered, 'Nay, it shall not be failure, but success—no wasted life, but one made famous and immortal by achievement.' Only, we would delay the struggle and postpone our fight until we had tasted something of the joys of college life and run, for once at least, its round of gaiety and dissipation. And so," he writes, who tells us thus much of so many human histories, "and so our vows of victory vanished like vapor in the midnight sky, and aspirations ended in an impotent and unborn hope!"

How many of us here are waiting for the opportunities of the coming year! With how many of us is it the unuttered hope that to-morrow, next week, next month, the next year may be as to-day in its privileges and opportunities only far more abundant? I pray God, my brother, that it may be so! I pray Him that He may have in store for you in that to-morrow such disclosures of Himself and of His truth as He has never before vouchsafed to you! But of one thing suffer me to assure you. If you would ever taste them you must begin to seek them now. We are told that the first day of the New Year is an appropriate time to form good resolutions. But the New Year is to-morrow, and therefore there is a better time for such a task, and that time is to-day. For "now is the accepted time; now is the day of salvation."—H. R.

THIS YEAR ALSO

By Rev. C. H. Spurgeon

This year also.—Luke xiii: 8

[The following short address was *written* by Mr. Spurgeon on his sick-bed. He sat up to write when he was able, but some of it was written with his head on his pillow.]

At the opening of another year, and at the commencement of another volume of sermons, we earnestly desire to utter the word of exhortation: but, alas! at this present the preacher is a prisoner, and must speak from his pillow instead of his pulpit. Let not the few words which we can put together come with diminished power from a sick man, for the musket fired by *a wounded soldier* sends forth the bullet with none the less force. Our desire is to speak with living words, or not at all. He who enables

us to sit up and compose these trembling sentences is entreated to clothe them with His Spirit, that they may be according to His own mind.

The interceding vine-dresser pleaded for the fruitless fig-tree, "let it alone *this year also*," dating as it were a year from the time wherein He spoke. Trees and fruit-bearing plants have a natural measurement for their lives; evidently a year came to its close when it was time to seek fruit on the fig-tree, and another year commenced when the vine-dresser began again his digging and pruning work. Men are such *barren* things that their fruitage marks *no certain periods,* and it becomes needful to make artificial divisions of time for them; there seems to be no set period for man's spiritual harvest or vintage, or if there be, the sheaves and the clusters come not in their season, and hence we have to say one to another, "This shall be the beginning of a new year." Be it so, then. Let us congratulate each other upon seeing the dawn of "this year also," and let us unitedly pray that we may enter upon it, continue in it, and come to its close under the unfailing blessing of the Lord to whom all years belong.

I. The beginning of a new year SUGGESTS A RETROSPECT. Let us take it, deliberately and honestly. *"This year also;"*—then there had been former years of grace. The dresser of the vineyard was not for the first time aware of the fig-tree's failure, neither had the owner come for the first time seeking figs in vain. God, who gives us "this year also," has given us others before it; His sparing mercy is no novelty, His patience has already been taxed by our provocations.

First came our *youthful* years, when even a little fruit unto God is peculiarly sweet to Him. How did we spend them? Did our strength run all into wild wood and wanton branch? If so we may well bewail that wasted vigor, that life misspent, that sin exceedingly multiplied. He who saw us misuse those golden months of youth nevertheless affords us "this year also," and we should enter upon it with a holy jealousy, lest what of strength and ardor may be left to us should be allowed to run away into the same wasteful courses as aforetime.

Upon the heels of our youthful years came those of *early manhood*, when we began to muster a household, and to become as a tree fixed in its place; then also fruit would have been precious. Did we bear any? Did we present unto the Lord a basket of summer fruit? Did we offer Him the firstling of our strength? If we did so, we may well adore the grace which so early saved us; but if not, the past chides us, and, lifting an admonitory finger, it warns us not to let "this year also" follow the way of the rest of our lives. He who has wasted youth and the morning of manhood has surely had enough of fooling: the time past may well suffice him to have wrought the will of the flesh: it will be a superfluity of naughtiness to suffer "this year also" to be trodden down in the service of sin.

Many of us are now in *the prime of life,* and our years already spent are not few. Have we still need to confess that our years are eaten up by the grasshopper and the canker-worm? Have we reached the half-way house, and still know not whither we are going? Are we fools at forty? Are we half a century old by the calendar, and yet far off from years of discretion? Alas! great God, that there should be men past this age who are still without knowledge! Unsaved at sixty, unregenerate at seventy, unawakened at eighty, unrenewed at ninety! These are each and all startling. Yet, peradventure, they will each one fall upon ears which they should make to tingle, but they will hear them as though they heard them not. *Continuance in evil breeds callousness of heart,* and when the soul has long been sleeping in indifference it is hard to arouse it from the deadly slumber.

The sound of the words "this year also" makes some of us remember *years of great mercy,* sparkling and flashing with delight. Were those years laid at the Lord's feet? They were comparable to the silver bells upon the horses—were they "holiness unto the Lord"? If not, how shall we answer for it if "this year also" should be musical with merry mercy and yet be spent in the ways of carelessness?

The same words recall to some of us our *years of sharp affliction* when we were, indeed, digged about and dunged. How went those years? God was doing great things for us, exercising careful and expensive husbandry, caring for us with exceeding great and wise care,—did we render according to the benefit received? Did we rise from the bed more patient and gentle, weaned from the world, and welded to Christ? Did we bring forth clusters to reward the dresser of the vineyard? Let us not refuse these questions of self-examination, for it may be this is to be another of these years of captivity, another season of the furnace and the fining-pot. The Lord grant that the coming tribulation may take more chaff out of us than any of its predecessors, and leave the wheat cleaner and better.

The new year also reminds us of *opportunities for usefulness,* which have come and gone, and of *unfulfilled resolutions* which have blossomed only to fade; shall "this year also" be as those which have gone before? May we not hope for grace to advance upon grace already gained, and should we not seek for power to turn our poor sickly promises into robust action?

Looking back on the past we *lament the follies* by which we would not willingly be held captive "this year also," and we adore the forgiving mercy, the preserving providence, the boundless liberality, the divine love, of which we hope to be partakers "this year also."

II. If the preacher could think freely he could wherry the text at his pleasure in many directions, *but he is feeble,* and so must let it drive with the current which bears it on to a second consideration: the text MENTIONS A MERCY. It was in great goodness that the tree which cumbered the soil was allowed to stand for another year, and prolonged life should always be regarded as a boon of mercy. We must view "this year also" as a grant from infinite grace. It is wrong to speak as if we cared nothing for life, and looked upon our being here as an evil or a punishment; we are here "this year also" as the result of love's pleadings, and in pursuance of love's designs.

The wicked man should count that the Lord's longsuffering points to his salvation, and he should permit the cords of love to draw him to it. O that the Holy Spirit would make the blasphemer, the Sabbath-breaker, and the openly vicious to feel what a wonder it is that their lives are prolonged "this year also"! Are they spared to curse, and riot, and defy their Maker? Shall this be the only fruit of patient mercy? The procrastinator who has put off the messenger of heaven with his delays and half promises, ought he not to wonder that he is allowed to see "this year also"? How is it that the Lord has borne with him and put up with his vacillations and hesitations? Is this year of grace to be spent in the same manner? Transient impressions, hasty resolves, and speedy apostasies—are these to be the weary story over and over again? The startled conscience, the tyrant passion, the smothered emotion!—are these to be the tokens of yet another year?

May God forbid that any one of us should hesitate and delay through "this year also"! Infinite pity *holds back the ax of justice;* shall it be insulted by the repetition of the sins which caused the uplifting of the instrument of wrath? What can be more tantalizing to the heart of goodness than indecision? Well might the Lord's prophet become impatient and cry, "How long halt ye between two opinions?" Well may God Himself push for a decision and demand an immediate reply. O undecided soul! wilt thou swing much longer between heaven and hell, and act as if it were hard to choose between the slavery of Satan and the liberty of the Great Father's home of love? "This year also" wilt thou sport in defiance of justice, and pervert the generosity of mercy into a license for still further rebellion? "This year also" must divine love be made an occasion for continued sin? Oh do not act so basely, so contrary to every noble instinct, so injuriously to thine own best interests.

The believer is kept out of heaven "this year also" in love, and not in anger. There are some for whose sake it is needful he should abide in the flesh, some to be helped by him on their heavenward way, and others to be led to the Redeemer's feet by his instruction. The heaven of many saints is not yet prepared for them, because their nearest companions have not yet arrived, and their spiritual children have not yet gathered in glory in sufficient number to give them a thoroughly heavenly welcome; they must wait "this year also" that their rest may be the more glorious, and that the sheaves which they will bring with them may afford them greater joy. Surely, for the sake of souls, for the delight of glorifying our Lord, and for the increase of the jewels of our crown, we may be glad to wait below "this year also." This is a wide field, but we

may not linger in it, for our space is little, and our strength is even less.

III. Our last feeble utterance shall remind you that the expression, "This year also," IMPLIES A LIMIT. The vine-dresser asked *no longer a reprieve* than one year. If his digging and manuring should not then prove successful he would plead no more, but the tree should fall. Even when Jesus is the pleader, the request of mercy has its bounds and times. It is not forever that we shall be let alone, and allowed to cumber the ground; if we do not repent we must perish, if we will not be benefited by the spade we must fall by the ax.

There will come a last year to each one of us; therefore let each one say to himself— *Is this my last?* If it should be the last with the preacher, he would gird up his loins to deliver the Lord's message with all his soul, and bid his fellow-men be reconciled to God. Dear friend, is "this year also" to be *your* last? Are you ready to see the curtain rise upon eternity? Are you now prepared to hear the midnight cry, and to enter into the marriage supper? The judgment and all that will follow upon it are most surely the heritage of every living man; blessed are they who by faith in Jesus are able to face the bar of God without a thought of terror.

If we live to be counted among *the oldest inhabitants* we must depart at last; there must be an end, and the voice must be heard —"Thus saith the Lord, this year thou shalt die." So many have gone before us, and are going every hour, that no man should need any other *memento mori,* and yet man is so eager to forget his own mortality, and thereby to forfeit his hopes of bliss, that we cannot too often bring it before the mind's eye. O mortal man, bethink thee! Prepare to meet thy God; for thou must meet Him. Seek the Savior, yea, seek Him ere another sun sinks to his rest.

Once more, "this year also," and it may be for this year only, the cross is uplifted as the *pharos* of the world, the one light to which no eye can look in vain. Oh that millions would look that way and live! *Soon the Lord Jesus will come a second time,* and then the blaze of His throne will supplant the mild radiance of His cross; the Judge will be seen rather than the Redeemer. Now He saves, but then He will destroy. Let us hear His voice at this moment. He hath limited a day; let us be eager to avail ourselves of the gracious season. Let us believe in Jesus this day, seeing it may be our last. These are the pleadings of one who now falls back on his pillow in very weakness. Hear them for your souls' sakes and live.— C. H.

OCCUPY TILL I COME

By Alexander Maclaren, D.D.

And he called his ten servants, and delivered them ten pounds, and said unto them, Occupy till I come.—Luke xix: 13

We have four things here, which, keeping to the metaphor of the text, I may designate as the Capital, the Business, the Profits, and the Audit.

I. THE CAPITAL.—A pound was a very little thing for a prince who was going to get a kingdom to leave with his servants to trade upon. The smallness of the gift is, I think, an essential part of the representation. May it not be intended to point out to us this lesson—how small after all, even the high gift that we all receive alike here is, in comparison with what we are destined to receive when the kingdom comes? Even the salvation that is in Jesus Christ, as it is at present experienced on earth, is but like the one poor pound that was given to the servants, as compared with the unspeakable wealth that shall be theirs—the ten cities, the five cities, and all the glories of supremacy and sovereignty, when He comes.

II. NOW A WORD ABOUT THE TRADING.—You Christian men and women ought to make your Christian life and your Christian service a matter of business. Put the same virtues into it that some of you put into your trade. Your best business in this world, as the *Shorter Catechism* has it, is to glorify God and to enjoy Him for ever. And the salvation that you have got, you have to trade upon, to make a business of, to work it out, in order that, by working it out, by living upon it, and living by it, applying its principles to daily life, and seeking to spread it among other people, it may increase and fructify in your hands.

III. THE PROFITS.—The immediate results are in direct correspondence and proportion to the immediate activity and diligence. The truths that you live by, you will believe more because you live by them. The faculties that you employ in Christ's service will grow and increase by reason of your employment of them.

IV. THE AUDIT.—"Till I come," or, "Whilst I am coming." As if all through the ages the king was coming, coming nearer. We have to work as remembering that everyone of us shall give an account of himself and his trading unto the Proprietor when He comes back.—S. B., vol. vii. p. 299.

LOT'S CHOICE*

TO SUNDAY-SCHOOL CHILDREN

By John Hall, D.D.

It is well for Lot's character that Peter put him down as a "righteous" man in his Second Epistle (ii: 7), for his life leaves it in doubt. He acted like a bad man several times, and he suffered for it. If ever you go to Europe, by Queenstown, you may see in the bay a wooden frame with a bell swinging and ringing with the waves. A fine steamer got on a rock there. It lies too low to be seen above water, but too high to let vessels over it safely. Like a beacon should be the report of this sore shipwreck long ago. There is a great rock, just out of sight, but in all men's way, and they should hear the warning-bell, tolling in Genesis, tolling in the Gospels, "Remember Lot's wife—remember Lot's choice!"

I. LOT FORGOT HIMSELF.—He had come out of Haran with his wiser uncle. He had lived and grown rich along with him. He had had the benefit of Abraham's good company and example, and doubtless worshiped at the altars which Abraham never failed to build. All this kept him right, and so long he was blameless; and very likely he thought

he would always get on just as well. If the strong angel who had to hurry him at last out of Sodom had met him and said, "Lot, beware; you will lose your religion in Sodom!" he would probably have replied: "Never fear; I know what I am doing; there is no danger!" He forgot how easily men are tempted; how much good company keeps us right; how great need we have of religious services to help us—in a word, he forgot himself.

Many people do just the same now. Living in a good family, with well-kept Sabbaths and pleasant church-helps, their way is hedged up. The rails are nicely laid for them, and they come to think they can go smoothly anywhere, and they rather like to go alone; so, when some chance is offered them, they set out, without any regret for what they lose, or any fear of what they meet. Sabbaths, friends, the church and all that, they say, "it is a pity to leave; but they will take care of themselves, and, in fact, they must" make money, or whatever else they have chosen. So Lot looked about

* From a New Year's Address. A. D. F. Randolph & Co.

and decided for the plain of Jordan. True, the people were awfully wicked, and the cities dens of sin. He thought of his cattle, and not of his children; of his substance, and not of his soul. He looked at it, as Fuller says, "with the eye of a mere grazier." What did he gain? He had reason, by and by, to move into Sodom, and, after a little, he and all belonging to him were made captives, and only rescued by the courage and quickness of Abraham. After a little longer, the whole place was burnt up, and he lost cattle and home, some of his children and his wife. He lived in daily vexation, without honor from the people, and he went out penniless and widowed and crushed under a load of sorrows. His choice proved bad every way.

When you shoot your arrows at a mark, let the arrowhead be a quarter of an inch to the right of the line to the mark, and it will be many yards to the right at the mark. When the riflemen take aim, let the muzzle of the gun point half-an-inch too low, and tne ball will fall many feet too low at the target. And so it is, boys, with the wrong choice. It is only turning a little bit wrong at the moment; but it is a great deal wrong in the long run. And as you cannot set the arrow right after you have pulled the string and let it go; as the very smartest rifle-shot cannot give the ball a friendly touch after he has fired, so, when the choice has been made, the natural consequences may be expected. Therefore choose cautiously and well. It is common enough to say, "Of two evils choose the less." This much-abused proverb needs explaining. If I must lose my thumb, or have the arm mortify, I choose to part with my thumb. But if I am between moral evil and physical, I will not choose either. The three Hebrew children might have avoided the furnace by idolatry. They would not worship an idol; and they did not *choose* the furnace. It was *forced* on them. If I am between two moral evils, I will not have either. "There is small choice in rotten apples." I am to reject both. A man is not to lie, to save from the necessity to steal; nor to break the Sabbath, lest he should not be able to pay his debts. Never choose to do wrong.

Now, my dear reader, you have to make decisions every day. What books will you read? What friends will you make? What studies will you follow? What pleasures will you enjoy? What will you do with your money? You can, if you please, do like Lot. You can make everything bend to self and present pleasure. You can turn your back on Sabbath-school, and teacher, and Bible, and church. You can choose to make the Sabbath an idle or a pleasure-seeking day. You can select a set of friends who care nothing about their own souls or yours. As you grow up, you can make up your mind that the one thing is to get on, make money and be somebody, no matter how it is to be done. And you may think in your heart that you will go no farther than is safe. But by and by you will come where

you must go farther and farther, and have to do more than you ever meant. Lot did not intend, possibly, to live in Sodom. But it could not be helped. Perhaps it was not safe to be away from a city. Perhaps his family wanted to have "some people to know." Perhaps his wife wished her children to be like the rest, and to get settled in life; and "better be out of the world than out of fashion," according to the devil's gospel. And so they went into Sodom, and his daughters were settled, and perished in the ruins of the place.

Have you a good friend, who loves you, who tells you the truth—whom you love? Cling to him. His friendship will bless you, and it glorifies God, who is pleased to see His creatures unselfishly bound together.

"Fall not out upon the way;
 Short it is, and soon will end;
Better far to fly the fray,
 Than to lose the friend.

"Christ hath sent you two and two,
 With an order to return:
Can ye meet the Master's view,
 If with wrath you burn?"

Lot made a bad decision when he parted company with his true friend, Abraham.

Children, if you saw a sea-beach covered with wrecks and bodies of sailors, would you not think it very dangerous; and if you were sailors, would you not keep away from it as far as possible? Well, children, the plan of *getting on at any cost* is such a shore; and it is covered with wrecks of body, of mind, of honor, of conscience, of means of life, and, one fears, too often, of the soul itself.

There is a castle, of which I want to tell you, with a splendid front. On that front is inscribed "God-fearing." Its right side is called Moderate Living; and the wall to the left—so strong and solid—is called Honest Principle. It has to the rear two fine towers, called Sabbath-keeping and Bible-reading, and a great crowd of people are safe and happy inside.

These people have a bitter enemy outside, who would fain destroy them, but he can do little harm in the castle. His name is the Devil, and he has an ally called the *world*. Could he only get them out! And so he goes to work, and around the gates he scatters those attractions "that nobody can object to." Here the world helps him. Shall they go out to them? "What harm can they do?" No; in themselves they are neither good nor bad. They go. Then, a little farther on, he has another set. "They have done one thing, and no harm came of it. Why not this as well? There is no evil in it" And so he proceeds, perhaps, through many years. You could not show the actual harm of any of these things by themselves. But they draw people away from their castle and from safety, and then their ruin is sure and easy. That was just Lot's case, and you know the result.

Keep within the castle, dear children, no matter what gay and charming scenes are spread to draw you out of it.

" The story of the past
   Comes up before our view;
How well it seems to suit us still—
   Old, and yet ever new!

" It is the oft-told tale
   Of sin and weariness—
Of grace and love yet flowing down,
   To pardon and to bless.

" No wider is the gate;
   No broader is the way;
No smoother is the ancient path
   That leads to life to-day.

" No slacker grows the fight;
   No feebler is the foe;
No less the need of armor tried—
   Of shield and spear and bow."

II. Lot treated Abraham badly.—So soon as trouble arose between his servants and those of the good man, to whom he owed so much, he forgot all, and was ready to leave him. Abraham likely saw how it was to be. Such men never want to quarrel, especially with their relations. So he made a noble offer to Lot. Now Lot should have left the choice to Abraham, if they must part. But he never thought of it. As a matter of course, he took what seemed best to him, and turned his back on his uncle.

It was ungrateful, mean, and selfish. Dear children, never do such wrong. When you are strong, stand by those who stood by you when you were weak. Never take advantage of a good man's softness. Never abuse good nature. Some are so gentle, they will bear a great deal; and some are so great in feeling, they will not resent injuries. Do not trade upon those fine qualities. Good men cannot respect or love you if you do. God is not likely to bless such a course. Rather learn to help the weak, than to lean on others, and you will grow stronger and happier in the attempt.

" For the heart grows rich in giving;
   All its wealth is living grain:
Seeds, which mildew in the garner,
   Scattered, fill with gold the plain.

" Is thy burden hard and heavy?
   Do thy steps drag wearily?
Help to bear thy brother's burden:
   God will bear both it and thee."

So Abraham found, when going out of his way and running such risks to save his kinsman.

Let us hope Lot was ashamed of himself when Abraham saved him from the kings and gave him back all again. Children sometimes forget their parents, and fling them off as if they were nothing to them. Many a careless daughter wounds a mother's heart. Young men will be bribed by the offer of a few dollars from the best friends and employers in the world, and quit those to whom they owe everything. This is all wrong. Next to God's love, the best thing in the world is the love of true human hearts. You cannot buy it with all the money in the mint. Don't sell it, boys and girls, for a handful of dollars. Be true, generous, grateful. There are many to whom you can make no return but that of the heart: they have a right to that from you. You are better for loving those who deserve it at your hand. You are worse for forgetting them as Lot did Abraham. You grow fickle, selfish, cold-hearted, and unhappy in yourself. You care for no one, and by and by no one will care for you.

III. Lot robbed God.—Why did Abraham leave Haran? Because God meant him and his to be separate from the worshipers of false gods. But Lot, who owed obedience to God's will in this, went among the idolaters. Abraham set up his altar wherever he went. Is it likely that Lot had an altar to God in Sodom? Abraham looked for a wife for Isaac among those who would not lead him to sin. Lot did not take any such trouble. His daughters married men of Sodom, " wicked before God exceedingly," but probably with nice houses and good positions. And little comfort he could have had in sons-in-law, who, when he warned them of ruin not a day off, thought him a fool. All through, he acts as if God was nothing. He is partner in the losses with the Sodomites, but the warning is nothing to him, and he goes back again as before. The next time God speaks, it is in the destruction of his married children and his unhappy wife. He escapes, indeed, with his two daughters, but even they show in their lives the ill effects of bad training and a life in Sodom.

Now my dear young friends, I wish you to be happy all this year, all your lives, all through eternity. But I know you cannot be happy if you rob God. He wishes you to be His, and to put His will first in everything. Nothing can make up to you for holding back God's due from Him. Robbing God, my dear boy, *does not pay* in any way. Don't believe that boy who wants you to deceive your mother or share his sins. You owe it to God to obey her. Don't you think God's eye and hand can follow you when you steal to the theater? Do not listen to that tempter who puts the glass to your lips and tells you, " Every fellow drinks." Do not believe the whisper in your heart that you can take forbidden joys and remain happy. The devil is a liar from the beginning. It is an old lie of his, that to make money and get rich in any way is a grand success. I wish you would learn by heart these lines:

" Gold filleth none!
   That which has life
Alone can fill the living;
   That which has love
Alone can fill the loving.
Gold is not life or love;
   It is not rest or joy;
It filleth coffers, hearts it cannot fill."

Riches in Sodom are little worth to Lot, and riches gained at the cost of disobeying God make the road to hell easy. The first thing, dear children, is to do God's will. Take heed to God, and He will take care of you. Despise Him, and you will be lightly esteemed.

There was a place at which Lot might have returned and escaped. He first settled toward Sodom (Gen. xiii: 12), not in it, but dangerously near it. Oh, how many things there are on which you might put "*Toward* Sodom!"

That boy at the corner in the dusk, making a man of himself, with three or four others, with a cigar, is "toward Sodom." The oath and the coarse word are the language of the place.

That girl to whom a gay dress is everything, and the display of it perfect bliss, no matter where it leads her, is "toward Sodom." That family whose carriage is at the door on a Sunday morning for a day's pleasure is "toward Sodom." That lad who goes into a godless business for immense profits is "toward Sodom." God help them, and pluck them back before the evil day comes, and the fire descends in judgment!

"What would have kept Lot right? So far as we can see, a right choice at this critical time. He should have said to Abraham, "Thy people shall be my people, and thy God my God." Better be with God's servants, and in God's service, than in Sodom and a prince. So, my dear children, be sure, it will be with you. Follow the Lord fully. Begin this year in His fear. He loves you; His Son died to redeem you from all iniquity, and to bring you to heaven. This is His will concerning you. Let that blessed will have its way. It will be best for you. Learn to say:—

"When obstacles and trials seem
  Like prison-walls to be,
I do the little that I can,
  And leave the rest to Thee.

"Ill that Thou blessest, is our good,
  And unblest good is ill;
And all is right that seems most wrong,
  If it be Thy sweet will."

Do not wrong yourselves. You can never be safe but in God's keeping. Do not turn away from the best friend you ever can have, who would have you near Him here and forever. Do not wrong the Lord God Almighty. Give your heart to Him, through and in Jesus Christ, His Son and your Savior. Choose the good part that shall not be taken away; and when palaces and cities have been burned up in the last fire, you, as the redeemed of the Lord, shall be safe in the city that hath no need of the sun.—H. R.

THE GOLDEN GATE OF OPPORTUNITY

By G. B. F. Hallock, D.D.

Ye have not passed this way heretofore.—Josh. iii: 4

The new year is a golden gate of opportunity. The children of Israel were just going to cross the Jordan and the message came to them, "Ye have not passed this way heretofore." We have not passed this new year's way heretofore. It was a prospect calculated to try the stoutest hearts among them; yet it was the opening up of many possibilities for noblest achievement. The ark, the symbol of God's presence, was carried before them. God was their leader. He must be ours. If we will accept Him as our guide in every path, if we will follow Him always, we will find that to us rivers will open and we shall be led into lands of glorious promise. The reason the ark was to be carried before the people was that they might know the way. It was a new path to them. "Ye have not passed this way heretofore." We, too, are constantly coming to experiences that are altogether new to us. Indeed, all life is in a sense new and strange. Every day's path is an untried one. Each year's path is also an untried one. The new century's path is an untried one. There are also many special times in life when it can be truly said to us, "Ye have not passed this way heretofore." It is so of youth, and to every happy-hearted child the counsel well may come: "Keep the ark always before you, and keep in sight of it, for you have not passed this way heretofore." It is true when a young man goes out from his home to try the world for himself. It is true of the young woman who steps forth from her father's door to go to the marriage altar. It is true when we are called to meet our first great sorrow. It is true when we take up our first serious responsibilities in life. It is true at the last when we are moving into the valley of the shadow of death.

But we wish to apply this truth especially to the opening of the year 1901.

I. The new year is a golden gate of opportunity, especially *in affording us new chance for coming into contact with Christ*. In it we may learn to know Him better than ever before. We may walk with Him, and talk with Him, and dwell "in the secret of His presence" as never before, if we will embrace the opportunities for fellowship the new year brings.

When Christ was on earth the words He so frequently used in speaking of the relations of His disciples to Himself were: "Follow me." But when He was about to leave for His heavenly home He gave them a new expression, conveying an idea much more intimate and spiritual: "Abide in me." It is to be feared that there are many earnest followers of Jesus from whom the meaning of this expression, with the experiences it promises, is very much hidden. While trusting in their Savior for pardon and help, and seeking in some extent to obey Him, they have hardly realized to what closeness of union, to what intimacy of fellowship, to what wondrous oneness of life and interest He invites as He says, "Abide in me."

II. The new year is a golden gate of opportunity *to appropriate Christ as never before.* We do not need so much to work for and pray to and commune with our Savior as we do to appropriate Him, to make Him "the soul of our soul, the life of our life." There is a mystical union between Christ and each believer transcending all the analogies of earthly relationships in the intimacy of its communion, in the transforming power of its influence and in the excellence of its consequences. It is a spiritual union.

It is a vital union. It is an indissoluble union. It is a union which gives us the power to assimilate His life, to reproduce His character, and to display in some degree all the graces He displayed.

III. The new year, therefore, is *a golden gate of opportunity for the cultivation of Christian character.* It gives us new chance for growth in grace. Each year should leave its mark upon Christians as it does upon trees, by an additional circle of growth. We should become larger, stronger, better with each passing year. Vegetable growth is unplanned for and unconscious, but growth in grace is largely the result of purpose and persistence.

IV. The new year is *a golden gate of opportunity for doing good.* We made a good many failures the past year. The new year is a chance to try again with the hope of doing better. Many a musician has desired, after a public pageant, to play his parts over again, believing that he could have done them accurately and well but for a small misunderstanding of some little note. During this year the concert will be repeated. The chances of life are open anew.—P. T., vol. xviii., p. 715.

THE NEW YEAR

Psalm xxxi: 15

To-day we wish each other "a happy new year." We seem to stand at a fresh starting-point. Naturally we wish each other well through it. Yet how many utter it with a sore heart. Text, a thought full of consolation to every believer. We stand on the threshold of the New Year. It is a solemn time. Consider thoughts suggested by text. It teaches us:

I. OUR DEPENDENCE ON GOD. The ungodly disown God's providential government. But believer rejoices that "the Lord reigneth." Reconciles him to present evils, and fortifies against future ones. He is convinced that nothing is casual or accidental. God has steered his bark from earliest infancy. Our time marked out by Him. Gives and takes away blessings, Amos viii: 11. No circumstance too trivial for Him. Look back on past and discern His hand. In His hand, too, are the Seasons of death as well as the occurrences of life. Death at last comes to all. Man lives on word of God's mouth. Our wisest course to cling to His love and faithfulness. Pillows dying heads of His people in Jesus' bosom. How many have thus passed away in past year. They appeal to us to "acquaint ourselves with God." Begin year by consecrating yourselves anew to Him.

II. OUR SECURITY IN GOD. This afforded David comfort and confidence. We are always exposed to perils. Let *text* assure us that in God's hand we are safe. We see this

constantly exemplified in Scripture. David hunted by Saul. Our Lord had His "hour," and could say to Pilate, John xix: 11. Paul furnishes a list of His perils. The Christian is immortal till His work is done. Like Elisha at Dothan he is in God's hand. None can hurt us without His permission. The promise is still sure. Is. liv: 17. Faith in this promise would banish care. Peter asks, Pet. iii: 13? While our times are in His hand we are safe tho in a den of lions. *Learn to seek God without delay.* Do not provoke Him to withdraw His support. Do not despise His patience and forbearance. Begin now to seek Him as you never sought Him before. Think to how little purpose you have hitherto lived. Ask Him for Grace to "number your days." True wisdom consists in knowing God in Christ. *Learn to serve Him without fear.* Servile fear is banished from a believer's service. Yet he often shrinks from boldly giving himself up for God's service. Fear of man brings a snare. Is. li: 12, 13. Let thought of His presence dispel fear. Every trial be pure will come duly weighed and meted. *Learn to trust Him without carefulness.* Where could our times be in better keeping? Shall proofs of His past love fail to banish anxiety? Shall we desire to wrest reins of government from His hands? He doeth all things well. To Him, then, let us commit ourselves and all belonging to us.—H. A. C. Y.

TO-DAY

By Charles F. Deems, D.D., LL.D.

Heb. iv: 7

Nothing unusual in to-day. We have made our routine of business, etc. Because " since the fathers fell asleep," etc.

Had there been signs you would listen to a voice, even the voice of man and certainly of God.

Let us study what is in " to-day."

I. THE VALUE OF A WHOLE LIFE.—The future as valuable as all Sibylline leaves. What would you take for your whole future life? What money? What pleasure? That whole future may be in this hour. Wholesale and retail. But why talk in market language? A day in saving a soul! "What shall it profit, etc." Price of Christ's blood. Past and future.

II. TO-DAY IS ALL THAT IS CERTAIN.—And that certain " to-day " is an instant. 3,600 certainties die in an hour; 86,400 in a day; 31,500,000 in a year. In this case each dead certainty makes a probability that the next will be the last. It is certain there is a last.

III. TO-DAY'S RELATION TO ETERNITY.—On a draft one-eighth of an inch may stand for miles. Life is the draft of eternity. Each moment represents ages.

IV. EACH DAY HAS ITS APPROPRIATE WORK.—(a) For our own soul's character building. Divide this whole work by the number of days of life. (b) For others: for the world. Divide this. Fail in *other* things, you may repair. But this is imperious. No insurance on time.

V. HOW MUCH MAY BE DONE IN A DAY!—Adam's fall. Israel's sin. Peter's sermon. Christ's death.

VI. ETERNITY GIVES VALUE TO TO-DAY.—What abides is more precious or painful than what is evanescent. Pain. Pleasure. Glory.

VII. TASK OF SOME DAYS MUCH GREATER.—Crisis. Disease. Law. Now is *your* " deciding " day. The whole case has been submitted.

VIII. TO-DAY IS PASSING.—It goes, goes, goes. You may hear His voice now. It may be awful silence hereafter. Strive to seize and hold to-day. There is NO TO-MORROW!—*Selected.*

THE DIMENSIONS OF LIFE

By Phillips Brooks, D.D.

And the city lieth four square, and the length is as large as the breadth: and he measured the city with the reed, twelve thousand furlongs. The length and the breadth and the height of it are equal.—Rev. xxi: 16

" The length and the breadth and the height of it are equal." There are then three directions or dimensions of human life to which we may fitly give these three names: length, and breadth, and height. The length of a life, in this meaning of it, is, of course, not its duration. It is rather the reaching on and out of a man in the line of activity, and thought, and self-development, which is indicated and prophesied by the character which is natural to him, by the special ambitions which spring up out of his special powers. It is the push of a life forward to its own personal ends and ambitions. The breadth of a life, on the other hand, is its outreach laterally, if we may say so. It is the constantly diffusive tendency which is always drawing a man outward into sympathy with other men. And the height of a life is its reach upward toward God; its sense of childhood; its consciousness of the Divine life over it, with which it tries to live in love, communion, and obedience. These are the three dimensions of a life,—its length, and breadth, and height,—without the due development of all of which no life becomes complete.

I. Consider the length of life in this understanding of the word. Here is a man who, as he comes to self-consciousness, recognizes in himself a certain nature. He cannot be mistaken. Other men have their special powers and dispositions. As this young man studies himself, he finds that he has his. That nature which he has discovered in himself decides for him his career. He says to himself, "Whatever I am to do in the world must be done in this direction." It is a fascinating discovery. It is an ever-memorable time for a man when he first makes it. It is almost as if a star woke to some subtle knowledge of itself, and felt within its shining frame the forces which decided what its orbit was to be. Because it is the star it is, that track through space must be its track. Out on that track it looks; along that line which sweeps through the great host of stars it sends out all its hopes; and all the rest of space is merely the field through which that track is flung: all the great host of stars is but the audience which waits to hear it as it goes singing on its way. So starts the young life which has come to self-discovery and found out what it has to do by finding out what it is. It starts to do that destined thing, to run out that appointed course. Nay, the man when he arrives at this self-discovery finds that his nature has not waited for him to recognize himself. What he is, even before he knows it, has decided what he does. It may be late in life before he learns to say of himself, "This is what I am." But then he looks back and discerns that, even without his knowing himself enough to have found it out, his life has run out in a line which had the promise and potency of its direction in the nature which his birth and education gave him. But if he does know it, the course is yet more definite and clear. Every act that he does is a new section of that line which runs between his nature and his appointed work. Just in proportion to the definiteness with which he has measured and understood himself in the sharpness of that line, which every thought, and act, and word is projecting a little further, through the host of human lives, toward the purpose of his living, toward the thing which he believes that he is sent into the world to do.

II. Look at the second dimension of life, which we call breadth. I have ventured to call this quality of breadth in a man's life its outreach laterally. When that tendency of which I have just been talking, the tendency of a man's career, the more loftily it is pursued, to bring him into sympathy and relationship with other men—when that tendency, I say, is consciously and deliberately acknowledged, and a man comes to value his own personal career because of the way in which it relates him to his brethren and the help which it permits him to offer them, then his life has distinctly begun to open in this new direction, and to its length it has added breadth. When a man has length and breadth together, we feel at once how the two help each other. Length without breadth is narrow and hard; breadth without length,

sympathy with others in a man who has no intense and clear direction for himself, is soft and weak. The man whom the world delights to find is the man who has evidently conceived some strong and distinct purpose for himself, from which he will allow nothing to turn his feet aside, who means to be something with all his soul, and yet who finds in his own earnest effort to fill out his own career the interpretation of the careers of other men, and also finds in sympathy with other men the transfiguration and sustainment of his own appointed struggle.

III. The height of life is its reach upward toward something distinctly greater than humanity. The height of life, its reach toward God, must be coextensive with, must be part of the one same symmetrical whole with the length of life, or its reach toward its personal ambition, and the breadth of life, or its reach toward the sympathy of brother-lives. It is when a man begins to know the ambition of his life not simply as the choice of his own will, but as the wise assignment of God's love, and to know his relations to his brethren not simply as the result of his own impulsive affections, but as the seeking of his soul for their souls because they all belong to the great Father-soul—it is then that life for that man begins to lift itself all over, and to grow toward completion upward, through all its length and breadth. That is a noble time, a bewildering and exalting time, in any of our lives, when into everything that we are doing enters the Spirit of God; and thenceforth moving ever up toward the God to whom it belongs, that Spirit, dwelling in our life, carries our life up with it, not separating our life from the earth, but making every part of it while it still keeps its hold on earth soar up and have to do with heaven, so completing life in its height by making it Divine.—S. B., vol. xii., p. 367.

NEW YEAR THEMES AND TEXTS

[From *The Homiletic Review*]

CHILDREN, New Year's Address to.—
Prov. viii: 17: Those that seek me early shall find me.
1. We have lost our way. We may not admit it, nor even know it. All the worse. We can find out whether this is so by comparing our life with the heavenly course in the Bible,—as a ship which has lost her compass may study her course from the stars.
2. Christ offers to be our guide. He has been near, tho not noticed, and is closest to those who feel that they are lost. His parables of the lost sheep, silver, son.
3. We can trust Him, for He knows every step of way. He has strength to hold us up, and He has never lost a life intrusted to His care.

4. Those that seek Him early shall find Him. We have to look for Him before He reveals Himself. Those who love their own way will not see Him.
5. Seek Him early.
(a) The wrong way leads to death.
(b) The wrong way fascinates and blinds us to better things.
(c) We may wait till too late.—From a Sermon by Rev. James Black.

DESTINY, Christ the Fit Ruler of.—
Rev. v: 9: They sung a new song, saying, Thou art worthy to take the book, and to open the seals thereof.
The "book" is the book of our destiny, which turns a new page with this new year. Christ alone is able happily to control that

turning. Our New Year will bring joy and progress rather than failure and sorrow, according as our destiny is put in the hands of Christ.

1. Christ has died for us and redeemed us from a guilty past.

2. Christ opens before us our true and high place as honored servants of God.

DISTRICTS, The Untraveled, of Life.— *Isa. xxvi: 3: Thou wilt keep him in perfect peace, whose mind is stayed on thee, because he trusteth in thee.*

The New Year opens out with uncertainty. The events of the year are known alone to the Omniscient God. The child of God realizes this. Hence we must cultivate: (1) The habit of trust. (2) The habit of faithfulness. (3) The habit of dependence.

The result of this will be: (1) A sense of duty. (2) A disciplined life. (3) A new view of things regarding the untraveled districts of life.

FUTURE, A Look into the.—1. *Jer. xxviii: 16: This year thou shalt die.*

The time of his death was declared to Hananiah because of his sin; but while not declared, the time of our death is equally fixed, and to some of us it is literally "this year."

2. *Luke xiii: 8:* Let it alone this year also.

A new year is a new opportunity.

3. *James iv: 13: Go to now, ye that say, To-day or to-morrow we will go into such a city, and continue there a year, and buy, and sell, and get gain.*

Do we include God in our plans for the year?

FUTURE, The Uncertainty of the.— *James iv: 14: Ye know not what shall be on the morrow.*

1. Our ignorance of the future is as obvious as any fact of our life; and we can see that it is essential to our reasonable life.

2. Because of our imperfection and sin it does not free us from trouble that the future is all under absolute law. Its events grow out of what precedes.

GOD, New Reason for Praising.—*Psalm xcvi: 1: Sing unto the Lord a new song.*

New praises for the New Year.

I. The old gifts of God have not been adequately praised.

1. His greatness and power.

2. His salvation.

3. Christ's fitness to arrange our destiny.

II. He has given new gifts that call for thanksgiving.

1. The mercies of the year.

2. The continued blessing of His presence. He "taketh pleasure in his people."

3. He extends His blessing into new fields.

HEED, The Unfolding Year Calls for Watchful and Devout.—*Mark xiii: 33: Take ye heed; watch and pray; for ye know not when the time is.*

JUDGMENT is What the Years and Seasons Are for, God's Rule of.—*Jer. viii:*

7: *The stork in the heaven knoweth her appointed time, and the turtle and the crane and the swallow observe the time of their coming; but my people know not the judgment of the Lord.*

KINGDOM, God's, in the New Year.— *Matt. vi: 33: Seek ye first the kingdom of God.*

1. The changes of time prepare the way for eternity

2. The spiritual New Year is the setting up of the kingdom of God.

3. Of all the interests of the new year none is so great as that progressive development of Christian character in us and around us which we call the kingdom of God.

4. Perhaps our practical wisdom would be to put God's kingdom first *in time*. Seek it in January, and on January 1.

LIFE, The True Limit of Our.—*Eccles. vii: 17: Why shouldst thou die before the time?*

Machinists speak of the "life of an engine," meaning the time it will run if used with care, not allowing for its destruction by collision or derailment. So a man's life is according to his natural endowment of strength, but may be cut short by sin.

The promise of the new year is conditional upon the highest wisdom of looking to God, and the true virtue which puts away sin and accepts grace.

MERCIES AND SONGS, A New Year's Meditation.—*Psalm ci: 1: I will sing of mercy and judgment.*

Song is the natural expression of a noble emotion of grief or joy.

I. God's mercies.

1. They are so full that sorrow seems an impertinence.

2. They put to shame our past fretting.

3. He, who alone could do it, extends His mercy over sin.

4. He puts forth mercy with fulness in proportion to sinful need.

5. Mercy is not unmindful of judgment, wakes deep sorrow for sin, but in penitence brings blessing.

II. Our songs.

1. We look away from our discontent toward God's grace.

2. We look at our advantage over those who know not God's mercy.

3. We recognize God's good purpose even in trials, and can give "songs in the night."

4. Those who triumph over great tribulation sing the sweetest song.—From a Sermon by Rev. James Black.

MORAL CHANGE, The Change of the Year Calls for a.—*Mark i: 15: The time is fulfilled. . . . Repent.*

NEW YEAR, God Opens the.—1. *Gen. viii: 22: While the earth remaineth, seedtime and harvest, and cold and heat, and summer and winter, and day and night shall not cease.*

Dr. Hawes said to his Sunday-school: "What season is this?" "Winter," they answered. "What will come next?" "Spring." "What after that?" "Summer." "How do you know?" Then Henry Camp, who grew up to be known as "the knightly soldier," stood up and answered: "Because the Lord has said, 'While the earth remaineth,' etc."

Because God reigns, the order of nature will not fail.

2. *Deut. xi: 12: A land which the Lord thy God careth for; the eyes of the Lord thy God are always upon it, from the beginning of the year even unto the end of the year.*

3. *Isa. xlviii: 6: I have showed thee new things from this time.*

4. *Isa. lxv: 17, 18: Behold, I create new heavens and a new earth: and the former shall not be remembered, nor come into mind; but be ye glad and rejoice forever in that which I create; for behold, I create Jerusalem a rejoicing, and her people a joy.*

NEW YEAR, Looking Forward to the. —*Psalm xci: 9-11: Because thou hast made the Lord, which is my refuge, even the Most High, thy habitation; there shall no evil befall thee, neither shall any plague come nigh thy dwelling. For he shall give his angels charge over thee, to keep thee in all thy ways.*

What the last Sabbath of the old year was, a period, has sprung up into an interrogation-point. What of the future?

1. It is a pathway ready for our feet. God carves a path for the river; much more for a man. We may break away from the path, but it is there.

2. Life is a failure apart from the divine path. God's intent touches all your purposes, and every thought not fitted into His is worthless. Even His forgiveness does not retrieve the loss of wilfulness.

3. How find the line of God's purpose?

(a) Life is so intricate that it needs a chart—the Bible.

(b) Each step well taken prepares us to see the next.

(c) If we *desire* to do His will, He will show us the way. "The secret of the Lord is with them that fear him."

4. To take God's will for ours is the consummation and acme of destiny; not the destruction of our will, but harmony with God's, so that both sound but one note.

5. The church labors to bring us to this. We enter the Kingdom of Heaven upon our knees. So shall we rightly enter the New Year.—From a Sermon by C. H. PARKHURST, D.D.

NEW YEAR, Our Year of Redemption, Christ Makes the.—1. *2 Cor. v: 17: If any man be in Christ he is a new creature: old things are passed away; behold, all things are become new.*

A new man in a new year.

2. *Heb. ix: 7: Into the second went the high priest alone once every year.*

So great an intercession it was fitting should not be made common by frequent and familiar repetition. The long year period makes us think of even greater intercession of Him who has entered in "once into the holy place." Do we entrust our case this year to Him?

3. *Matt. vi: 33: Seek ye first the kingdom of God and his righteousness.*

What to begin the year with.

NEW YEAR, The.—*Eph. v: 16: Redeeming the time, because the days are evil.*

I. "The days are evil." The outcome may be bad or good.

II. The value of time as relating to this life.

III. The value of time as relating to all the future.

PRAYER FOR CARE THROUGH THE YEAR.—*Luke i: 74, 75: That he would grant unto us that we, being delivered out of the hand of our enemies, might serve him without fear in holiness and righteousness before him all the days of our life.*

PROVISION FAR AHEAD.—*John iv: 14: Whosoever drinketh of the water that I shall give him shall never thirst; but the water that I shall give him shall be in him a well of water springing up into everlasting life.*

With the onward movement of time, natural desires, now only conscious, will become imperative. Wise provision for them is only common prudence.

REDEMPTION, The Year a Period in the Course of.—*Isa. lxiii: 4: The year of my redeemed is come.*

Accepting the idea of a race which grows slowly toward perfection, rather than of a community of faultless but unimproving beings, God has accepted the struggle of good and evil with all that is involved in it.

There is necessity for *time*, and each year makes a period of the struggle.

RESOLUTIONS, Shattered.—*Luke xv: 18: I will arise and go to my Father.*

I. It is well to make good resolutions at this time.

II. We should be very careful in making our resolutions.

III. We should hold tenaciously to our determination no matter what it costs.

IV. How to be able to keep our resolutions.

V. The best resolution for an unconverted person to make.

TEXTS, A Few.—*Luke xviii: 8: Let it alone this year also.*

We have been spared to see another year in order to bring forth fruit.

Gen. xlvii: 8: And Pharaoh said unto Jacob, how old art thou?

It has been said that a man is only as old as he feels. This is especially so with the spiritual man.

Job xxxii: 7: Days should speak, and multitude of years should teach wisdom.

We are not influenced nearly as much by either precept or example as we are by experience. What have the past years taught us in our experience of the things of God?

Psalm xc: 10: The days of our years are threescore years and ten; and if by reason of strength they be fourscore years.

This is a wise and merciful limit, for God only knows what fools or scoundrels many of us would become if allowed to live much longer.

TIME, and its Meaning.—*Eccles. viii: 5: A wise man's heart discerneth both time and judgment.*

Not material issues only, but moral. The year as the setting of a just and gracious providence.

TIME, The Old Forgotten in the New.— *Isa. lxv: 17: Behold I create new heavens and a new earth and the former shall not be remembered, nor come into mind.*

Sometimes in careless enjoyment of the present we neglect the wholesome and instructive lesson of past trials, and for this we are to blame. But sometimes a new time comes with so great uplift and enlargement that the past loses its importance or sinks out of thought. This latter is the thought of this scripture.

1. The new present may well eclipse the past when it includes the highest as well as the most practical interests suggested by the "new heavens and new earth."

2. The new present may claim our intensest interest when we see God's hand manifestly in it. "Behold I create new heavens and a new earth."

3. The new time claims us altogether when we see in it our redemption from former sorrows and sins.

Our present New Year may include all these elements of authoritative attraction.

UNCHANGING, God Alone.—1. *Psalm cii: 27: Thou art the same, and thy years shall have no end.*

2. *Psalm ciii: 17: The mercy of the Lord*

is from everlasting to everlasting upon them that fear him, and his righteousness unto children's children.

3. *1 Pet. i: 24, 25: All flesh is as grass, and all the glory of man as the flower of the grass. The grass withereth and the flower thereof falleth away; but the word of the Lord endureth for ever.*

YEAR, The Old and the New.—*Eccles. iii: 15: That which has been is now, and that which is to be hath been.*

1. The stability of nature is matter of experience. It must be so, because God governs by law and adheres to His chosen order. So we know that seedtime and harvest will be in the next year—just as in past years.

2. We also know that providence is to be as it has been; that the year to come will have light in it and dark in it for us and our fellows.

3. God has kept His promises in the past; He will keep them in the future. Last year He saved His Church from the assaults of infidels; He will do even the same in this year.

4. Look back, then, over the past year and recall the mercies of God in harvest, in domestic joy, in personal health, in spiritual gifts. Forecast from last year the Divine goodness to be revealed in the next.

5. Look back at the afflictions and chastisements of last year; look at their meaning, that you may avoid the sin, that you may get the good of the sorrow that will come again.

6. Our experience of last year should enable us to avoid its errors. We have been too worldly. Let the solemn hours of suffering and penitence, as they come back to memory, warn us to be more spiritually-minded. The danger to the Christian Church is the worldly spirit that has crept into it. Cultivate, above all things, personal piety.—R. M. HATFIELD, D.D.

SUGGESTIVE THOUGHTS AND ILLUSTRATIONS

ACTION, Pledge of.—A young Roman nobleman of the eleventh century, just married, during the nuptial feast joined in a game of ball, and to relieve himself of his wedding ring, took it off and placed it on the finger of a statue of Venus. The game ended, he went to reclaim the ring, but found it immovable, for the stone finger clenched upon it. Ever after he heard the whisper, " Embrace me ; I am Venus, whom you have wedded ; I will never restore your ring." Only by calling a priest to his aid was he able to recover his ring. A first act either wrong or right commits us, and is influential in shaping our character.—F. II.

AIM, A Christian.— The artist, when he paints, knows right well that he shall not be

able to excel Apelles; but that does not discourage him; he uses his brush with all the greater pains, that he may, at least in some humble measure, resemble the great master. So the sculptor, tho persuaded that he will not rival Praxiteles, will hew out the marble still, and each to be as near the model as possible. Thus the Christian man: forgetting all he has attained, he will press forward, crying, *Excelsior!* going upwards still, desiring to be conformed more and more to the image of Christ Jesus.—C. H. SPURGEON.

AIM, Effective.—A sharp-shooter from one of the Vermont regiments in the battle of —— fired ninety-six cartridges, three-fourths of which were effective. In the random shooting of common soldiers in battle it is estimated that no more than one bullet in four thousand does execution. The teacher or Christian worker who would save souls must make some particular heart his target and aim for it:—must select the best rifle and ammunition, and if he does not hit must try again, and again, till he has smitten the mark and secured the capitulation of the soul to Christ. So of every other object desired.—F. II.

AIM, Effort and.—At the battle of the Alma, when one of the regiments was being beaten back by the hordes of Russia, the ensign in front stood his ground as the troops retreated. The captain shouted to him to bring back the colors; but the reply of the ensign was, " Bring up the men to the colors."—F. I.

AIM, Execution and.—A gentleman calling on Thorwaldsen, found him, as he said, in a glow, almost in a trance, of creative energy. On his inquiring what had happened, " My friend, my dear friend," said the sculptor, " I have an idea, I have a work in my head, which will be worthy to live. A lad had been sitting to me some time as a model. Yesterday, when I bade him rest awhile, in so doing, he threw himself into an attitude which struck me very much. 'What a beautiful statue it would make!' I said to myself; 'But what would it do for? It would do—it would do—it would do exactly for Mercury drawing his sword, just after he has played Argus to sleep.' I immediately began modeling. I worked all the evening, till at my usual hour I went to bed. But my idea would not let me rest. I was forced to get up again. I struck a light, and worked at my model for three or four hours, after which I again went to bed. But again I could not rest; again I was forced to get up, and have been working ever since. O my friend, if I can but execute my idea, it will be a glorious statue." And a noble statue it is; altho Thorwalsden himself did not think that the execution came up to the idea. For I have heard of a remarkable speech of his, made some years after to another friend who found him one day in low spirits. Being asked whether anything had distressed him, he answered, " My genius is decaying." " What do you mean?" said the visitor. " Why! here is my statue of Christ: it is the first of my works that I have ever felt satisfied with. Till now, my idea has always been been far beyond what I could execute. But it is no longer so. I shall never have a great idea again." The same, I believe, must have been the case with all men of true genius. While they who have nothing but talents may often be astonished at the effects they produce by putting things together, which fit more aptly than they expected, a man of genius, who has had an idea of a whole in his mind, will feel that no outward mode of expressing that idea, whether by form or colors or words, is adequate to represent it.—F. II.

AIM, High.— Some time ago, half a dozen young men, dressed in green, were shooting at a target with bows and arrows, when the arrows of one of them invariably struck the earth, on account of his aiming too low. " *Aim higher,*" cried out one of his companions. " *Aim higher,* for your arrow-head is always pointed to the ground. He that aims at a barn-door will never hit the weathercock on the church-spire."

A father, giving advice to his son, said, " Let your objects be liigh and holy, and then the High and Holy One will give you strength and grace to attain them."

"What would you advise me to aim at?" asked a young man of a Christian friend. " At riches and honors," replied his friend, " if you mean to be satisfied with earth; but at Christian graces if you have any desire ever to enter heaven."—G. Mogridge.

AIM, Importance of Definite.—Lieut.-Col. M'Leroth, of the 95th British regiment, relates the following anecdotes of the skill of sharp-shooters, and the inefficacy of ordinary musketeers:—

In an action of some importance, a mounted officer of the enemy was on the point of being made prisoner. One only way presented itself, by which he had a chance of escaping: this was along the front of our line, within musket range. He embraced this alternative; and, altho the whole brigade fired at him, both man and horse escaped with impunity.

Another fact, from the same authority, is equally curious:

In order to cover themselves as much as possible from the enemy's aim, at the siege of Yorktown, our soldiers had each three bags of sand to lay on the parapet. Two of these were placed with their ends at a little distance from each other, and the third crossed over the interval, leaving a small loop-hole for the soldiers to fire through. The American riflemen, however, were so expert, that, on seeing a piece protruded through the hole, they levelled toward it, and, penetrating the opening, frequently shot the men through the head.—Percy.

AIM, Want of.— The French have recently published some statistics in regard to the recent war with Germany that are significant and instructive. They count now that during the war there came into France one million Germans, but there were only one hundred thousand Frenchmen killed; therefore, nine Germans in ten fired away for seven months and never hit any one, and the tenth fellow never fired but one effective shot. All this, too, in the age of needle-guns and most perfect military education.—W. F. Crafts.

ANXIETY, Prevention of.— We may consider the year before us a desk containing three hundred and sixty-five letters addressed to us—one for every day, announcing its trials, and prescribing its employments, with an order to open daily no letter but the letter for the day. Now, we may be strongly tempted to unseal beforehand some of the remainder. This, however, would only serve to embarrass us, while we should violate the rule which our Owner and Master has laid down for us: "Take, therefore, no thought for the morrow, for the morrow shall take thought for the things of itself."—WILLIAM JAY.

ASPIRATION, Heavenly.—What epic can equal those *unwritten* words which pour into the ear of God out of the heart's fulness! still more, those *unspoken* words which never find the lip, but go up to heaven in unutterable longing and aspirations! Words are but the bannerets of a great army, a few bits of waving color here and there: thoughts are the main body of the footmen that march unseen below.—H. W. BEECHER.

ASPIRATION, Universal.—Every man is born with aspiration. It does not develop in every man: neither do half the buds in trees blossom; but they are there. And there is aspiration in every man, whether you suspect it or not, and tho it may not blossom. Aspiration means tendril, twining, or any thing else by which one climbs upward, holding on by the way to whatever will support it. Some plants take hold by winding around, some by little roots, some by tendrils, some by hooks, and some by leaves that catch like anchors. But these things take hold, not for the sake of staying when they take hold, but only that they may climb higher. And so it is with men. We clasp things above by every part of our nature, one after another, not for the sake of remaining when we take hold, but that we may go higher. In other words, when, in the ordinary experience of life, we gain satisfaction, we do it almost only by feeding on each other. When we attain development, we do that in the same way. The soul feeds on soul whether for satisfaction or development.—H. W. BEECHER.

BEGINNING, Delayed.—It was said of Alfred De Vigny that he proposed making a great poem, and he had the capacity and genius to make it; but he spent his life in gathering materials for that poem. Sometimes his friends used to say to him, "Why don't you begin? You are getting on in life, and after awhile you will be too old to write the poem." And he would keep saying, "To-morrow I will begin." One morning the papers in Paris announced his death, his work all undone; he lay dead amid the magnificent materials he had with which to begin the poem.—TALMAGE.

BEGINNING, Evil. — That temptation that at first is but a little cloud as big as a man's hand, may quickly overspread the whole heaven. Our engaging in sin is as the motion of a stone down, *vires acquirit eundo,* "it strengthens itself by going," and the longer it runs the more violent. Beware of the smallest beginnings of temptation. No wise man will neglect or slight the smallest spark of fire, especially if he see it among barrels of gunpowder. You carry gunpowder about you. Oh, take heed of sparks.—JOHN FLAVEL.

BEGINNING, Faulty. — Some workmen were lately building a large brick tower, which was to be carried up very high. In laying a corner, one brick, either by accident or carelessness, was set a very little out of line. The work went on without its being noticed, but as each course of bricks was kept in line with those already laid, the tower was not put up exactly straight, and the higher they built the more insecure it became. One day, when the tower had been carried up about fifty feet, there was a tremendous crash. The building had fallen, burying the men in the ruins. All the previous work was lost, the materials wasted, and, worse still, valuable lives were sacrificed, and all from *one brick laid wrong* at the start. The workman at fault in this matter little thought how much mischief he was making for the future. Do you ever think what ruin may come of *one bad habit,* one brick laid wrong, while you are now building a character for life? Remember, in youth the foundation is laid. See to it that all is kept STRAIGHT.—T. T.

BEGINNING, Good.—When the ancients said that a work well begun was **half done,** they meant that we ought to take the utmost pains in every undertaking to make a good beginning.—POLYBIUS.

BEGINNING, Prayerful.—Victoria was aroused at midnight and informed that she was Queen of England. She asked her informer to pray, and they knelt down in prayer together. Thus began the prosperous reign of England's worthy queen.—F. II.

BROODING, A Remedy for.—"A reasonable amount of fleas is good for a dog; they keep him from broodin' on bein' a dog."—E. N. WESTCOTT in *David Harum.*

CAPACITIES, Special.—I am of the opinion that every mind that comes into the world has its own specialty—is different from every other mind; that each of you brings into the world a certain bias, disposition to attempt something of its own, something your own—an aim a little different from that of any of your companions; and that every young man and every young woman is a failure so long as each does not find what is his or her own bias; that just so long as you are influenced by those around you, so long as you are attempting to do those things which you see others do well instead of doing that thing which you can do well, you are so far wrong, so far failing of your own right mark. Everybody sees the difference in children. They very early discover their tastes. One has a taste for going abroad, another for staying at home; one for books, another for games; one wishes to hear stories, another wants to see things done; one is fond of drawing, the other cannot draw at all, but he can make a machine. This difference, as you advance, becomes more pronounced. You are more distinct in your conception of what you can do—more decided in avoiding things which you cannot and do not wish to do. Now, I conceive that success is in finding what it is that you yourself really want, and pursuing it; freeing yourself from all importunities of your friends to do something which they like, and insisting upon that thing which you like and can do.—EMERSON.

CHARACTER, Light of.— Have only one chief end. The head-light on an engine is a small lamp, back and set forth by a burnished reflector. Then it casts forth its brightness, pointing out and illumining the way for the speeding travelers. Your lamp may not be large, but if you will put behind and about it the burnished reflector of a consistent, concentrated life, it may shine forth into the darkness, guiding hurrying pilgrims safely through the night.—FOWLER.

CHILDREN, Treatment of.—If you make children happy now, you will make them happy twenty years hence by the memory of it.—KATE DOUGLAS WIGGIN.

CHRISTIANS, Aim of.—Even as a man that passeth through a strong flood or stream on foot, lest he stumble and fall down, setteth his eye steadily upon the firm land which he mindeth to attain unto, and marketh not the swift course of the water, and so goeth over safely, and is nothing dismayed; so, likewise, a sound and good Christian, passing the raging waves of present troubles, turneth away his sight, his thought, and all apprehension that he might otherwise have of the misery of them, and, lifting up his eyes to heaven, beholdeth there, with a spiritual regard, the inestimable treasures of the heavenly inheritance, which he striveth unto; and by this means easily surmounteth all horror and fear of torments and griefs, which commonly make alterations in men's heads, and casteth them headlong into desperation.—CAWDRAY.

CONCESSION, The First.—A woodman came into a forest to ask the trees to give him a handle for his ax. It seemed so modest a request that the principal trees at once agreed to it, and it was settled among them that the plain homely ash should furnish what was wanted. No sooner had the woodman fitted the staff to his purpose, than he began laying about him on all sides, felling the noblest trees in the wood. The oak now seeing the whole matter too late, whispered to the cedar. "The first concession has lost it; if we had not sacrificed our humble neighbor, we might have yet stood for ages ourselves."—ÆSOP.

COURTESY.—If you will be cherished when you are old, be courteous when you are young.—JOHN LYLY.

DAYS.—We are always complaining our days are few, and acting as if there were no end of them!—ADDISON.

DAYS.—Write it on your heart that every day is the best day in the year. No man has learned anything rightly, until he knows that every day is Doomsday.—EMERSON—*Society and Solitude. Work and Days.*

DAYS.—The days are made on a loom whereof the warp and woof are past and future time.—EMERSON—*Society and Solitude. Work and Days.*

DAYS, Common.— One of the chief dangers of life is trusting occasions. We think that conspicuous events, striking experiences, exalted moments have most to do with our character and capacity. We are wrong. Common days, monotonous hours, wearisome paths, plain old tools, and everyday clothes tell the real story. Good habits are not made on birthdays, nor Christian character at the New Year. The vision may dawn, the dream may waken, the heart may leap with a new inspiration on some mountain top, but the test, the triumph, is at the foot of the mountain, on the level plain.

The workshop of character is everyday life. The uneventful and commonplace hour is where the battle is won or lost. Thank God for a new truth, a beautiful idea, a glowing experience; but remember that unless we bring it down to the ground and teach it to walk with feet, work with hands, and stand the strain of daily life, we have worse than lost it —we have been hurt by it. A new light in our heart makes an occasion, but an occasion is an opportunity, not for building a tabernacle and feeling thankful and looking back to a blessed memory, but for shedding the new light on the old path, and doing old duties with new inspiration. The uncommon life is the child of the common day lived in an uncommon way.—MALTBIE D. BABCOCK, D.D.

DAYS, Divine.—The days are ever divine. They come and go like muffled and veiled figures sent from a distant friendly party; but they say nothing and if we do not use the gifts they bring, they carry them as silently away.—EMERSON.

DEFEAT.—To expect defeat is nine-tenths of a defeat itself.—F. MARION CRAWFORD.

DISAGREEABLE, Things.—Don't look too hard except for something agreeable. We can find all the disagreeable things we want between our own hats and boots.— HUNT.

DOUBT, When in.—When in doubt, tell the truth.—SAMUEL CLEMENS (MARK TWAIN).

DRUDGERY, What Men Call.—The every-day cares and duties, which men call drudgery, are the weights and counterpoises of the clock of time, giving its pendulum a true vibration, and its hands a regular motion; and when they cease to hang upon the wheels, the pendulum no longer swings, the hands no longer move, the clock stands still.— H. W. LONGFELLOW.—*Kavanagh.* Ch. XIII.

EMULATION, Necessity of.— Altho there may be some degree of pride in emulation, yet a laudable ambition should always be encouraged, especially in youth; for, without this, they will never rise to eminence in any thing. When we think of some of the greatest generals, historians, or poets, what was it but emulation that brought them to excel others? In short, without emulation, we sink into meanness or mediocrity; for nothing great or excellent can be done without it.—F. I.

EXAMPLE.—There is nothing so powerful as example. We put others straight by walking ourselves—MADAME ANNE SOPHIE SWETCHINE.

FAITH CORD, The.—In passing over the more perilous portions of the way (up the Alps) the tourist is roped to his guide. In that way you become one with him. That rope seems as a visible expression of your faith in him; and it is an interesting fact that the same word in Greek denotes "faith" and "rope." You are confident that your guide is not going to perish, and, bound to him by the palpable strands of a faith cord, because he lives you expect to live; because he stands, you expect to stand; he is not going to be lost in a crevasse, therefore you do not expect to be.

It is interesting, too, in what quiet, deft ways your guide will make that same rope a ministry of relief to you in the midst of the hard strains of the journey. In scrambling up a steep pitch, say the rugged slopes of the Matterhorn, with the breath almost out of you, the wind, it may be, threatening to topple you over, and the flying snow perhaps blinding you and almost suffocating you, just as you are beginning to wonder whether all this really pays, and whether, after all, you are not going to be obliged to give up before reaching the top, just then there comes a little tug at the rope that is bound around you, and just enough of the guide's surplus unweariness is made over to you to make you light and nimble and full of confidence again. That gentle pull at the rope is a kind of gospel lift, and means to you very much what it meant to St. Paul when in toiling up the hill of his difficulty he heard the voice of the Lord saying to him, "My strength is sufficient for you."—C. H. PARKHURST, D.D.

FORESIGHT.—Foresight is very wise, but fore-sorrow is very foolish; and castles are, at any rate, better than dungeons in the air.—SIR JOHN LUBBOCK.

FUTURE, Dodging the.—Dodging the future, in this world, is a success equal to that of the old woman who triumphantly announced that she had borrowed enough money to pay all her debts.—*Selected.*

GERMANY, New Year in.—There exists a very beautiful custom in Germany, which it would be well to imitate everywhere. On the first day of the New Year, whatever may have been the quarrels or estrangement between friends and relatives, mutual visits are interchanged, kindly greetings given and received—all is forgotten and forgiven. Let this custom begin with reconciliation to God, then friendship and fellowship may be found that shall be blessed and lasting.—F. II.

GOD, The Guidance of.—If God be our guide, He will be our guard.—MATTHEW HENRY.

GROANING AND GRUMBLING.—Groaning and grumbling under your burdens doesn't lighten them of one ounce of weight, but it does deprive you of that much breath, which might be useful in carrying the load.—*Selected.*

GUIDANCE.—There is no trouble about guidance, if only we want to be guided. The trouble lies here,—that we want to lead, not to be guided. Thus we fall into the ditch and possibly lead some one else there also. God has made abundant provision for our guidance in the smallest matters, if only we will avail ourselves of it.—A. F. SCHAUFFLER, D.D.

GUIDANCE.—The Lord went before them. . . . They saw Him by day in a pillar of cloud to guide them on the way, and by night in a pillar of fire to give them light. The glory of Israel was that manifested Presence, lacking which, Moses besought him to carry them up no farther.—G. A. CHADWICK, D.D.

GUIDANCE.—"He shall guide you into all the truth." That is not a promise of omniscience, but the assurance of gradual and growing acquaintance with the spiritual truth revealed in Jesus. Not to-day, nor to-morrow, will it all be known, but step by step we shall be led.—ALEXANDER McLAREN, D.D.

HOPE, Benefit of.—Hope is the most beneficial of all the affections, and doth much to the prolongation of life, if it be not too often frustrated, but entertaineth the fancy with the expectation of good; therefore they which fix and propound to themselves some end as the mark and scope of their life, and continually and by degrees go forward in the same, are, for the most part, long-lived; insomuch that when they are come to the top of their hope, and can go no higher therein, they commonly droop, and live not long after. —BACON.

HOPE, Refuge in.—"It was a dark, chill, misty morning, like to end in rain; one of those mornings when even happy people take refuge in their hopes."—GEORGE ELIOT.

HUMOR.—Honest good humor is the oil and wine of a merry meeting.—WASHINGTON IRVING.

INDIVIDUAL LIFE.—The higher and more consecrated the individual life, the clearer will probably be its recognition of its dependence upon and guidance by the God who is acknowledged in all its ways.—C. P.

INTENTIONS, Biblical.—The Lord discerns them. Heb. iv: 12. The chief value of good deeds, lies in their right intentions. Abraham offered Isaac not in deed but in intention; and the intention was accepted, Heb. xi: 17. *David* was commended because he desired to build the temple, 1 Kings viii: 18. *The widow's mite.* Mark xii: 43. *Mary*— What a noble eulogy. "She hath done what she could." Mark xiv: 8. The *Macedonian's* liberality, 2 Cor. viii: 3, 12. Wickedness lies not in acts only, but in intentions. *Looking* may be *lusting*, Matt. v: 28. *Hatred* is accounted murder, 1 John iii: 15. Jacob was a murderer when he wished to kill Esau, Gen. xxii: 41; Joseph's brethren, Gen. xxxvii: 20, 21; Saul wishing to kill David, 1 Sam. xviii: 25; Solomon wishing to kill Jeroboam, 1 Kings xi: 40. *Good intentions* cannot justify wrong actions. *Gideon,* Judges viii: 24-27. *Uzzah,* 2 Sam. vi: 6, 7. *James and John,* Luke ix: 54. *Peter,* John xviii: 10.—BOWES.

INTENTIONS, Transient.—No sooner does the warm aspect of good fortune shine, than all the plans of virtue, raised like a beautiful frost-work in the winter season of adversity, thaw and disappear.—WARBURTON.

JANUARY, The First of.—No one ever regarded the first of January with indifference. It is that from which all date their time, and count upon what is left. It is the nativity of our common Adam.

Of all sound of bells (bells the music highest bordering upon heaven), most solemn and touching is the peal which rings out the old year. I never heard it without a gathering-up of my mind to a concentration of all the images that have been diffused over the past twelve-month. All I have done or suffered, performed or neglected—in that regretted time. I begin to know its worth as when a person dies. It takes a personal color; nor was it a political flight of a contemporary, when he exclaimed: "I saw the skirts of the departing year." It is no more than what in sober sadness, every one of us seems to be conscious of in that awful leave-taking.—CHARLES LAMB.

JAPAN, New Year's Day in.—Somehow tho the sun may have shone just as brightly on the previous day, and indeed the whole year round, yet it all seems changed and different on this, the first day of the year (writes Onoto Watanna in *Leslie's Popular Monthly).* It is the spirit of the New Year! This is the time of universal peace and good will; when the inhabitants of the little empire start life anew with fine resolutions and promises for the future, and all ill-feeling done away with.

The first of January bears the significant title of Gansan (the Three Beginnings), meaning beginning of the year, beginning of the month, and beginning of the day. And to this might be added the beginning of a new and better life. What Christmas is to the Occidentals, New Year's is to the Japanese, altho greetings and congratulations are not confined to the first day of the year, but at any time between the first and the fifteenth.

The Japanese begin to prepare for the New Year nearly a month before, and in fact give their houses and possessions a thorough cleansing, just as the good American housewife does in the spring-time. Even the very poorest people do this, laying mats of rice straw, and cleaning every nook and corner with fresh bamboo dusters and brooms, which are said to symbolize prosperity and good fortune. And after the house has been aired and cleaned, it is decorated with pine and bamboo, for the Japanese venerate both of these, because they keep green through the entire winter and symbolize longevity. The Japanese read in the most insignificant natural objects some striking significance, and there is a meaning attached to almost every decoration or ornament in the house. The outside and gardens of the houses are also beautifully decorated, to say nothing of the streets, which present a most interesting and animated spectacle at this time.

On New Year's eve the streets and stores, which at this time display their most attractive goods, are thronged with people intent on buying the requisites for the coming year. At night the streets are beautifully illuminated with lines of big lanterns, family crests, flags, shop-signs, etc., hung from every store. On this eve many of the people remain up all night, and watch the old year out and the new year in, tho a few old-fashioned ones prefer the custom of rising very early in the morning to worship the first rising sun of the new year.—E.

JESUS, Illustration of Looking to.—The painter who undertakes to copy some masterpiece of art, sits down before it, sketches the outline upon his own canvas, reproduces the coloring of the model, adds item by item to his picture, constantly looking upon the original, noting its qualities and the deficiencies of his work, till, by scrupulous care and untiring endeavor, he has produced a *fac simile* of the original. The Christian's work is kindred. He has a better model, even Christ; but a harder task, for his canvas is treacherous and his work is lifelong.—F. I.

JESUS, Influence of Looking to.—It is related of Mr. Astor, that, when once fording the Susquehannah on horseback, he found himself becoming so dizzy as to be about to lose his seat. Suddenly he received a blow on his chin from a hunter, who was his companion, with the words, "Look up!" He did so, and recovered his balance. It was looking *on* the turbulent water that endangered his life; and looking *up* saved it.—F. I.

JEWISH NEW YEAR'S DAY, The.—The New Year is regarded by the Jews as a festival and the month in which it occurs (generally in our September) is looked upon as very sacred, for they believe that the destiny of every individual is now determined, and that the Creator, on the first day of Tishri, weighs the merits and demerits of all. Those who are meritorious are sealed to life and those who are guilty are sealed to death, whilst judgment upon those whose merits and demerits are equal is delayed until the Day of Atonement. Hence the intervening days between the New Year and the Day of Atonement are spent by the pious in praying, fasting, and imploring forgiveness. The day before the New Year is regarded as a fast, and after morning service in the synagog the Jews visit the graves of the dead, upon whom they call for intercessory prayers. In the evening they again repair to the synagog and on their return home for supper the table is laid with several kinds of sweet provisions, especially apples and honey. At an early hour the Jews go to their synagog and continue their devotions till about noon. Various prayers, blessings, and legends are strung together in addition to the ordinary morning service. The most important part of the service is the ceremony of blowing the *shophar* or ram's horn (compare Numb. xxix: 1 and Levit. xxiii: 24), which is done by a well-qualified person. This festival lasts for two days.

The first ten days of the month of Tishri are called the Ten Days of Repentance or Awful Days.—H. R.

LAUGH, A.—A laugh is worth a hundred groans in any market.—CHARLES LAMB.

LIFE.—It's good to live only a moment at a time; . . . it isn't for you and me to lay plans; we've nothing to do but obey and trust.—GEORGE ELIOT.

LIFE.—Some men pass through life wreathed with four-leaved clovers, and loaded down with horse shoes; while others are born on Friday, the thirteenth of May, and have opals given to them in the cradle.—BRANDER MATTHEWS.

LIFE.—Our lives are drugged with bric-a-brac. The disease of bric-a-brac, I think, is due to two influences,—the desire of uncreative minds to create beauty, and the mania for giving Christmas presents.—E. CHESTER.

LIFE, Business in.—Our grand business in life is not to see what lies dimly at a distance, but to do what lies clearly at hand.—CARLYLE.

LIFE, End of.—What is the end of life? The end of life is not to do good, tho many of us think so. It is not to win souls, tho I once thought so. It is *to do the will of God, whatever it may be*.—DRUMMOND.

LIFE, Object of.—Lady Huntingdon, one evening, was on her way to a brilliant assembly; when suddenly there darted into her soul these words, "Man's chief end is to glorify God and to enjoy Him forever," which she had committed to memory years before in learning the Westminster Shorter Catechism. From that hour, her whole life revolved round a new center. The guilty, trembling sinner, hitherto occupied with her poor self, gazed on the face of Him who died for her; and, as she gazed, her conscience found peace, and her heart a satisfying rest. Her whole life became one "living sacrifice."—J. BAILLIE.

LUCK.—Good luck will carry a man over a ditch if he jumps well, and will put a bit of bacon in the pot if he looks after his garden and keeps a pig. . . . Luck taps at least once in a lifetime at everybody's door, but if Industry does not open it, away it goes.—SPURGEON.

MAN, The Wise.—He is a wise man who wastes no energy on pursuits for which he is not fitted.—GLADSTONE.

MARK, To Hit the.—If you would hit the mark, aim a little above it. Every arrow that flies feels the attraction of earth.—H. W. LONGFELLOW.

MAZE, In the.—We remember once hearing a speaker tell how in his youth he and a young companion became lost in the maze at Hampton Court; they wandered about, tired, discouraged, but they felt sure they would find their way out presently, and they thought it would seem foolish to ask direction, tho they saw an old man working not far off. All their efforts, however, proved unavailing, and at last they came with red faces to ask the old man if he could possibly tell them how to get out of the maze.

"Why," he answered, "that's just what I am here for; why did you not say before that you wanted to get out?" And he put them at once on the right track.

Those young men learned that day not to rely so absolutely on their own wisdom and ability. There is One who stands ready to be our Counselor, our Guide, our Light in every labyrinth. Instead of yielding to worry, let us simply ask him to take us by the hand and lead us through.—Q.

MOTIVE, Want of.—What makes life dreary is want of motive.—GEORGE ELIOT.

NEW YEAR BREVITIES.—Lord Dundas, being wished a happy New Year, replied, "It had need be happier than the last; for I never knew one happy day in it." Wilberforce said, "The last year has been the happiest of my life." Romaine's new-year's wish for his people was, "God grant that this may be a year famous for believing!"—F. I.

NEW YEAR, Facing the.—A new year is upon us, with new duties, new conflicts, new trials, and new opportunities. Start on the journey with Jesus—to walk with Him, to work for Him, and to win souls to Him. The last year of the century, it may be the last of our lives! A happy year will it be to those who, through every path of trial, or up every hill of difficulty, or over every sunny height, march on in closest fellowship with Jesus, and who will determine that, come what may, they have Christ every day.—THEODORE L. CUYLER, D.D.

NEW YEAR NONSENSE.—A great many things are done in the name of New Year, which no doubt cause the fine old day to blush when it contemplates them.

Some people have a regular practice of making New Year resolutions—generally shattering them before January has hidden its cold head out of sight. Resolves, in order to be of any use, should be made every day in the year, and if necessary every hour in the day.

Some men go around calling upon their lady friends, drink every thing that is offered them on the way, from cider to sherry, and make their last call of the day upon their wives and families, carrying with them a pronounced case of inebriation. Thus is a good and courteous practice often turned into a shameful bit of traveling dissipation.

Some men do not take the pains to travel and collect the different drinks that are to make beasts of them, but go directly to the saloons, and carouse all day with equally wretched companions.

It is one of the characteristics of our dear old wicked whimsical now-and-then-idiotic human race, that it is perfectly competent to spoil anything in the world; that it can make almost anything into a curse, when it sets out.—W. C. M.

NEW YEAR THOUGHTS. — The thoughts of the New Year are not thoughts of the ease of attainment, secured or anticipated, but they are thoughts of the severity of the pilgrim path of life, and of the toilsomeness of the track; and these thoughts would prove disheartening to the bravest of us if we could not have faith in Him who has passed this way before, and who invites us to an unfailing trust in Him in hours of despondency or of cheer. He who has helped us hitherto will not desert us now.—S. S. T.

NOTHING IS EVER LOST.—*Eccles. iii: 15: God requireth that which is past:* The meaning of a sentence cannot be gathered into its last word; the last word takes significance from what has gone before. So with life. Dying utterances and even thoughts may not be taken into account. Every dying man *would be* a saint. A great Southern statesman said to those who asked if some one should pray for him, as his pulse was failing: " No; my life must be my prayer. This solemn moment is not so significant as the solemn years that are gone. Let them stand."— H. R.

PAST AND FUTURE.— The past is dead, and has no resurrection; but the future is endowed with such a life that it lives to us even in anticipation. The past is, in many things, the foe of mankind; the future is, in all things, our friend. For the past there is no hope; for the future there is both hope and fruition. The past is the text-book of tyrants; the future is the Bible of the free. Those who are solely governed by the past stand like Lot's wife, crystallized in the act of looking backward, and forever incapable of looking forward.—HENRY KIRK WHITE.

PATTERNS, Highest.—There is no manner of inconvenience in having a pattern propounded to us of so great perfection as is above our reach to attain to, and there may be great advantages in it. The way to excel in any kind is to propose the brightest and most perfect examples to our imitation. No man can write after too perfect and good a copy; and tho he can never reach the perfection of it, yet he is like to learn more than by one less perfect. He that aims at the heavens, which yet he is sure to come short of, is like to shoot higher than he that aims at a mark within his reach.—TILLOTSON.

PRESENT, The.—Look not mournfully into the Past. It comes not back again. Wisely improve the Present. It is thine. Go forth to meet the shadowy Future, without fear, and with a manly heart.—H. W. LONGFELLOW.

PROGRESS, Alternative of.—The more thorough a man's education is, the more he yearns for and is pushed forward to new achievement. The better a man is in this world, the better he is compelled to be. That bold youth who climbed up the Natural Bridge in Virginia, and carved his name higher than any other, found, when he had done so, that it was impossible to descend, and then his only alternative was to go on and scale the height, and find safety at the top. Thus it is with all climbing in this life. There is no going down. It is climbing or falling. Even an upward step makes another needful; and so we must go on until we reach heaven, the summit of the aspirations of time. —H. W. BEECHER.

PROGRESS, Conservative.—Spain once held both sides of the Mediterranean at the Straits of Gibraltar. So highly did she value her possessions, that she stamped on her coin the two Pillars of Hercules (as the promontories of rock were called) ; and on a scroll thrown over these were the words, *ne plus ultra*,—" no more beyond." But one day a bold spirit sailed far beyond these pillars, and found a new world of beauty. Then Spain, wisely convinced of ignorance, struck the word *ne* from the coin, and left *plus ultra*,— " more beyond." How many a man, whose conceit is great, thinks he has reached the limits of knowledge, when further investigation would open to him a continent of truth before unknown!—BISHOP SIMPSON.

PROGRESS, Laws of.— Gradual ascent is as necessary to the mind in order to its reaching a great idea, as it is to the body in order to its reaching a great height. We cannot ascend to the pinnacle of a cathedral which towers aloft in air, without either steps or an inclined plane. We cannot reach the summit of a mountain without first toiling up its base, then traversing its breast, and then successively crossing the limits where verdure passes into crag, and crag into a wilderness of snow. Even when we have gained the highest point, we are still, it is true, at an infinite distance from the blue vault of the firmament which stretches above our heads. Still we have a better and more exalted view of what that firmament is: we have at least risen above the fogs and mists which obscure its glory; and the air which encompasses us is transparent to the eye, and invigorating to the frame. Now, the law of man's bodily progress is also the law of his mental progress. Both must be gradual. No grand idea can be realized except by successive steps and stages which the mind must use as landing-places in its ascent.—GOULBURN.

PURPOSE, Dominant.—Peter the Hermit visited Palestine in the latter part of the eleventh century, and was so enraged at the Turks for their cruel treatment of Christians, that he resolved to rescue the holy soil. Returning he went through the towns of France and Italy, bareheaded and barefooted, bearing a heavy crucifix, and picturing with extreme eloquence and enthusiasm, the sufferings of the pilgrims to the holy places. He soon gathered an army of 60,000, which he led toward Jerusalem.—F. II.

PURPOSE, Emblem of.—A man's purpose of life should be like a river, which was born of a thousand little rills in the mountains; and when, at last, it has reached its manhood in the plain, tho, if you watch it, you shall see little eddies that seem as if they had changed their minds, and were going back again to the mountains, yet all its mighty current flows, changeless, to the sea. If you build a dam across it, in a few hours it will go over it with a voice of victory. If tides check it at its mouth, it is only, that, when they ebb, it can sweep on again to the ocean. So goes the Amazon or the Orinoco across a continent,—never losing its way, or changing its direction, for the thousand streams that fall into it on the right hand and on the left, but only using them to increase its force, and bearing them onward in its resistless channel.—H. W. BEECHER.

PURPOSE, Execution of.—Keep your eye fixed upon the mark, and don't flinch when you pull the trigger. The steady nerve is necessary to carry out the bold plan. Could the multitude of failures which are recorded every day be thoroughly examined into as to their cause, it would be found that a great proportion of them have resulted from a want of nerve at just the moment when an unwavering sight and steady pull would have accomplished the object. If one is to succeed, he must fix his eye on the mark, and never think otherwise than that he shall hit it. Many a huntsman whose marksmanship is none of the best has astonished himself by shots made under circumstances when he must up gun and blaze away, with scarcely time given him to know what he is firing at. This was because he had no opportunity to hesitate or waver when pressing the trigger. Let an enterprise be ever so boldly projected and energetically pushed, if the nerve fails at the last moment, good-by to success.—F. I.

PURPOSE IN LIFE.—Have a purpose in life, . . . and having it, throw such strength of mind and muscle into your work, as God has given you.—CARLYLE.

PURPOSE IN LIFE.—Do not dare to live without some clear intention toward which your living shall be bent. Mean to be something with all your might.—PHILLIPS BROOKS.

PURPOSE, Persevering.—On one bright summer day, the boy Warren Hastings, then just seven years old, lay on the bank of the rivulet which flows through the old domain of his house to join the Isis. There, as threescore and ten years later he told the tale, rose in his mind a scheme, which, through all the turns of his eventful career, was never abandoned. He would recover the estate which had belonged to his fathers. He would be Hastings of Daylesford. This purpose, formed in infancy and poverty, grew stronger as his intellect expanded, and as his fortune rose. He pursued his plan with that calm but indomitable force of will which was the most striking peculiarity of his character. When, under a tropical sun, he ruled fifty millions of Asiatics, his hopes, amidst all the cares of war, finance, and legislation, still pointed to Daylesford. And when his long public life, so singularly checkered with good and evil, with glory and obloquy, had at length closed forever, it was to Daylesford that he retired to die.—MACAULAY.

PURPOSE, Steadiness of.—Many who slumber in nameless graves, or wander through the tortures of a wasted life, have had memories as capacious, and faculties as fine, as Macaulay; but they lacked the steadiness of purpose, and patient thoughtful labor, which multiplied the "ten talents" into "ten other talents beside them." It is the old lesson, voiceful from every life that has a moral in it; from Bernard Palissy, selling his clothes, and tearing up his floor, to add fuel to the furnace, and wearying his wife, and amusing his neighbors with dreams of his white enamel, through the unremunerative years; from William Carey, panting after the moral conquest of India, whether he sat at the lapstone of his early craft, or wielded the ferule in the village-school, or lectured the village elders when the Sabbath dawned,—it is the old lesson, a worthy purpose, patient energy for its accomplishment, a resoluteness that is undaunted by difficulties, and, in ordinary circumstances, success.—W. M. PUNSHON.

RIGHT, The One Inalienable.—Thou hast but one inalienable right, and that is the sublime one of doing thy duty at all times, under all circumstances and in all places.—FREDERICK R. MARVIN.

SADNESS, Birds of.—"You cannot prevent the birds of sadness from flying over your head, but you may prevent them from stopping to build their nests there."—*Selected.*

SIN, Beginnings of.—Thieves, when they go to rob a house, if they cannot force the doors, or the wall is so strong that they cannot break through, then they bring little boys along with them, and these they put in at the windows; who are no sooner in but they unbolt the doors, and let in the whole company of thieves. And thus Satan, when by greater sins he cannot tell how to enter the soul, then he puts on and makes way by lesser, which insensibly having got entrance, set open the doors of the eyes and the doors of the ears; then comes in the whole rabble. There they take up their quarters; there, like unruly soldiers, they rule, domineer, and do what they list, to the ruin of the soul so possessed.—ALSOP.

SPIRIT OF MAN, The.—One can but admire that wise and beneficent ordination of Providence whereby the spirit of man asserts its power over circumstances.—SINGLETARY.

SUNSET IN LIFE, The.—If I can put one touch of a rosy sunset into the life of any man or woman I shall feel that I have worked with God.—GEORGE MACDONALD.

TIME.—That great mystery of TIME, were there no other; the illimitable, silent, never-resting thing called Time, rolling, rushing on, swift, silent, like an all-embracing ocean-tide, on which we and all the Universe swim like exhalations, like apparitions which *are*, and then *are not:* this is forever very literally a miracle; a thing to strike us dumb—for we have no word to speak about it.—CARLYLE.—*Heroes, and Hero Worship.* Lecture I.

TIME.—What is Time? The shadow on the dial, the striking of the clock,—the running of the sand,—day and night,—summer and winter,—months, years, centuries;—these are but arbitrary and outward signs, the measure of Time, not Time itself. Time is the Life of the Soul.—H. W. LONGFELLOW.—*Hyperion.* Bk. II. Ch. V.

TIME, The Calculation of.—We are indebted to the great Roman general and ruler, Julius Cæsar, for our year, for the length of our month, and for the extra day in leap-year; we are indebted to a studious pope, Gregory XIII., for a uniform chronology common to all civilized lands; to the far-away half-mythical Numa Pompilius for New Year's Day on the first of January, and the months as we know them. The Roman heathen gave us three of our week day names, and the heathenish and altogether ungodly Norsemen supplied us with the names of the other four, while the name of the Sabbath comes from the Jews. Heathen, Christian, and Jew, crowned pope, world-famous conqueror and obscure pirate of the seas, each and all have helped to make and shape our system of time for us. Surely the science of computing time may well be called cosmopolitan, since it is a result of the labor of the wise men of all lands, a labor that continued through three thousand years, and perhaps longer.—We are indebted to Christ for eternal life.—C. An.

TIME, Well Disposed.—When Drexelius was asked by his friend Faustinus how he could do so much as he had done, he answered, "The year has three hundred and sixty-five days, or eight thousand four hundred and sixty hours: in so many hours great things may be done; the slow tortoise made a long journey by losing no time."—BISHOP HORNE.

WILBERFORCE, BISHOP, Advice of.—A man said to Bishop Wilberforce, "Pray, sir, can you tell a plain man, in a single sentence, the way to go to Heaven?" "Certainly," was the instant reply, "turn to the right and go straight ahead."—*Selected.*

WISDOM.—Formerly we were guided by the wisdom of our ancestors; Now we are hurried along by the wisdom of our descendants.—L. T.

WISHING.—No amount of wishing will fill the Arno, or turn a plum into an orange.—GEORGE ELIOT.

WORLD, A Topsy-turvy.—The bat hangs upside down, and laughs at a topsy-turvy world.—ANON.

YEAR, The.—Beautiful is the year in its coming and in its going—most beautiful and blessed because it is always the "year of our Lord."—LUCY LARCOM.

POETRY

Annus Mirabilis.

This year the wondrous year shall surely be
To such as have the gift to hear, to see!
We greet, between prophetic smile and tear,
Annus Mirabilis—new year, strange year!
                    ÉDITH M. THOMAS.

Bless the Year.

O, tender Christ, bless Thou this year!
  Bless Thou its dawn, and bless
Its noontide and its evening Lord;
  And let each heart confess,
As days and weeks and months go by
  To help the year grow old,
That of Thy glory, King of Kings,
  The half not yet is told.
            MARY D. BRINE.—O. C. W.

Chance, The Main.

As the ancients say wisely,
Have a care o' the main chance,
And look before you leap;
For as you sow, ye are like to reap.
    SAMUEL BUTLER—*Hudibras, Pt. II.*
        Canto II., l. 490.

Day, The New.

Every day is a fresh beginning,
  Listen, my soul, to the glad refrain,
And spite of old sorrow, and older sinning,
  And troubles forecasted, and possible pain,
Take heart with the day, and begin again.
                    SUSAN COOLIDGE.

Death, Expect but Fear Not.

Expect, but fear not Death: Death cannot
    kill,
Till Time (that first must seal his patent)
    will.
Wouldst thou live long? keep Time in high
    esteem;
Whom gone, if thou canst not recall, re-
    deem.
    QUARLES—*Hieroglyphics of the Life
        of Man.* Epigram VI.

Deeds, The Power of.

  One deed may mar a life
  And one may make it.
                —*Selected.*

Destiny, In the Field of.

The tissue of the Life to be,
We weave with colors all our own,
And in the field of Destiny
We reap as we have sown.
RAPHAEL

Development, Man's.

I hold it truth with him who sings,
To one clear harp in divers tones,
That men may rise on stepping stones
Of their dead selves to higher things.
TENNYSON—*In Memoriam.*

Duty, Man's.

I did God's bidding and man's duty; so
breathe free.
BROWNING.

Eternity.

Out of eternity
This new day is born;
Into eternity
At night will return.

So here hath been dawning
Another blue day—
Think, wilt thou let it slip
Useless away?
CARLYLE.

Experience.

Others' follies teach us not,
Nor much their wisdom teaches;
And most, of sterling worth, is what
Our own experience preaches.
Selected.

Future, The.

" Yet in opinions look not always back;
Your wake is nothing; mind the coming
track.
Leave what you've done for what you have
to do,
Don't be ' consistent,' but be simply true."
O. W. HOLMES.

Height, Man's.

The heights by great men reached and kept,
Were not attained by sudden flight,
But they, while their companions slept,
Were toiling upward, in the night.
LONGFELLOW.—*The Ladder of St.
Augustine,* St. 10.

Hope.

The clouds may rest on the present,
And sorrow on days that are gone,
But no night is so utterly cheerless
That we may not look for the dawn;
And there is no human being
With so wholly dark a lot,
But the heart by turning the picture
May find some sunny spot.
Selected.

Hours, The Precious.

Waste not the precious hours in idle dreams,
Vain disputations, and perplexing themes;
This life's the seed-time of eternity,
And as thy sowing shall thy reaping be.
Be earnest, then, O man, while time is given,
To sow for righteousness, for God, and
Heaven.
G. MORISON

Life's Journey.

Does the road wind up hill all the way?
Yes, to the very end.
Will the day's journey take the whole long
day?
From morn to night, my friend.
CHRISTINA G. ROSETTI.—*Up Hill.*

Life's Way, On.

The world is wide,
In time and tide,
And—God is guide;
Then *do not hurry.*

That man is blest
Who does his best,
And—leaves the rest,
Then *do not worry.*
CHARLES F. DEEMS, D.D., LL.D.

Life, The Last of.

Grow old along with me, the best is yet to be,
The last of life for which the first was made;
Our times are in His hand, Who saith " A
whole is planned,
Youth shows but half; trust God,
See all, nor be afraid."
BROWNING.—*Rabbi Ben Ezra.*

Life, The Twofold.

He lives twice, who can at once employ
The present well, and e'en the past enjoy.
POPE.

Losses and Crosses.

Tho' losses and crosses
Be trials maist severe,
There's wit there ye'll get there,
Ye'll find nae otherwhere.
BURNS.

Move, All Things.

We sleep and wake and sleep, but all things
move.
The Sun flies forward to his brother Sun;
The dark earth follows, wheeled in her el-
lipse;
And human things returning on themselves
Move onward, leading up the golden year.
TENNYSON.—*The Golden Year.*

New, The.

Only a night from old to new;
Only a sleep from night to morn;
The new is but the old come true;
Each sunrise sees a new year born.
HELEN HUNT JACKSON.—Y. C.

New Year, The.

I see not a step before me
As I tread on another year,
But the past is still in God's keeping,
The future His mercy shall clear,
And what looks dark in the distance
May brighten as I draw near.
MARY G. BRAINARD.—Y. C.

New Year, The.

A Flower unblown: a Book unread:
A Tree with fruit unharvested:
A Path untrod: a House whose rooms
Lack yet the heart's divine perfumes:
A Landscape whose wide border lies
In silent shade 'neath silent skies:

A wondrous Fountain yet unsealed:
A Casket with its gifts concealed:—
This is the Year that for you waits
Beyond To-morrow's mystic gates.
          HORATIO NELSON POWERS.—Y. C.

New Year, The.

New Year, coming on apace,
What have you to give me?
Bring you scathe, or bring you grace,
Face me with an honest face;
You shall not deceive me.
          CHRISTINA ROSSETTI.

Plans, God's.

" God's plans, like lilies, pure and white unfold.
We must not tear the close-shut leaves
apart,
Time will reveal the calyxes of gold."
          From a Tract.

Power, Human.

I ask not wealth, but power to take
And use the things I have, aright;
Not years, but wisdom that shall make
My life a profit and delight.
          PHOEBE CARY.

Present, Past, and Future.

Threefold the stride of Time, from first to
last!
Loitering slow, the Future creepeth—
Arrow-swift, the Present sweepeth—
And motionless forever stands the Past.
SCHILLER.—*Sentence of Confucius. Time.*

Present, Past, and Future.

" To-morrow I will live," the fool does say;
To-day itself's too late;—the wise lived yesterday.
          MARTIAL.—*Epigrams*, Bk. V., Ep. lviii.

Problem, The Common.

The common problem, yours, mine, every
one's,
Is—not to fancy what were fair in life
Provided it could be,—but, finding first
What may be, then how to make it fair
Up to our means: a very different thing!
BROWNING.—*Bishop Blougram's Apology.*

Reward, Life's.

Be good, sweet maid, and let who will be
clever;
Do noble things; not dream them all day
long;
And so make life, death, and that vast forever,
One grand, sweet song.
          CHARLES KINGSLEY.—*A Farewell.*

Smile, The Test of a.

'Tis easy enough to be pleasant,
When life flows along like a song;
But the man worth while is the one who will
smile
When everything goes dead wrong.
For the test of the heart is trouble,
And it always comes with the years,
And the smile that is worth the praise of
earth
Is the smile that comes through tears.
          ELLA WHEELER WILCOX.

Strength and Weakness.

Strength alone knows conflict,
Weakness is below even defeat,
And is born vanquished.
          MADAME ANNE SOPHIE SWETCHINE.

Thought, New Year.

I would be quiet, Lord,
Nor tease nor fret;
Not one small need of mine
Wilt Thou forget.
          JULIA C. R. DORR.

Time.

Seize time by the forelock.
          PITTACUS, of Mytilene.

Time.

Time is the nurse and breeder of all good.
SHAKESPEARE.—*Two gentlemen of Verona,*
          Act III., Sc. 1.

Time.

O! Old Father Time grows tender and mel-
low,
As, roving the round earth, the sturdy old
fellow,
Year in and year out, keeps going and coming,
In winter's wild wrack, and in summer's
green blooming.
          LEWIS J. BATES.—*Time.*

Time and Tide.

For the next win he spurs amain,
In haste alights, and scuds away,—
But time and tide for no man stay.
WM. SOMERVILLE.—*The Sweet-Scented
          Miser.* Line 98.

Time's Glory.

Time's glory is to calm contending kings,
To unmask falsehood and bring truth to light,
To stamp the seal of time on aged things,
To wake the morn and sentinel the night,
To wrong the wronger till he render right,
     To ruinate proud buildings with thy hours,
     And smear with dust their glittering golden
     towers.
SHAKESPEARE.—*Rape of Lucrece.* Line 939.

Time, The Flight of.

The present is our own; but, while we speak,
We cease from its possession, and resign
The stage we tread on, to another race,
As vain, and gay, and mortal as ourselves.
          THOMAS LOVE PEACOCK.—*Time.*

Time, The Flight of.

The more we live, more brief appear
Our life's succeeding stages;
A day to childhood seems a year,
And years like passing ages.
CAMPBELL.—*A Thought Suggested by the
          New Year.* St. 1.

Time, The Flight of.

Time wears all his locks before,
Take thou hold upon his forehead;
When he flies, he turns no more,
And behind his scalp is naked.
Works adjourn'd have many stays;
Long demurs breed new delays.

Time, The Flood of.

The flood of time is rolling on,
We stand upon its brink, whilst they are gone
To glide in peace down death's mysterious
    stream.
Have ye done well?
    SHELLEY.—*Revolt of Islam.* Canto XII.
                   St. 27.

Time, The Greatness of.

Time is great, and greater no man's trust
Than his who keeps the fortress for his king.
Wearing great honors as some delicate robe
Brocaded o'er with names 'twere sin to tarnish.
    GEORGE ELIOT.—*The Spanish Gypsy.* Bk. I.

Time, The Hand of.

            Time has laid his hand
Upon my heart, gently, not smiting it,
But as a harper lays his open palm
Upon his harp, to deaden its vibrations.
    LONGFELLOW.—*The Golden Legend.*

Time, The Host.

          Time is like a fashionable host,
That slightly shakes his parting guest by the
    hand;
And with his arms outstretch'd as he would fly,
Grasps in the comer, welcome ever smiles.
    SHAKESPEARE. — *Troilus and Cressida.*
               Act III., Sc. 3.

Time, The Lack of.

He that lacks time to mourn, lacks time to
    mend:
Eternity mourns that. 'Tis an ill cure
For life's worst ills, to have no time to feel
    them.
    HENRY TAYLOR.—*Philip Van Artevelde.*
               Act I. Sc. 5.

Time, The River of.

A wonderful stream is the River Time,
    As it runs through the realms of Tears,
With a faultless rhythm, and a musical rhyme.
And a broader sweep, and a surge sublime
    As it blends with the ocean of Years.
    BENJAMIN F. TAYLOR.—*The Long Ago.*

Time, The Tread of.

Nought treads so silent as the foot of time;
Hence we mistake our Autumn for our prime.
    YOUNG.—*Love of Fame.* Satire V. Line
                      497.

Time, The Value of.

Know the true value of time; snatch, seize,
and enjoy every moment of it. No idleness,
no laziness, no procrastination; never put off
till to-morrow what you can do to-day.
    EARL OF CHESTERFIELD.—*Letters to his
             Son.* Dec. 26, 1749.

Time, The Waters of.

Unfathomable Sea! whose waves are years,
Ocean of Time, whose waters of deep wo
Are brackish with the salt of human tears!
Thou shoreless flood, which in thy ebb and flow
Claspest the limits of mortality!
And sick of prey, yet howling on for more,
Vomitest thy wrecks on its inhospitable shore,
Treacherous in calm, and terrible in storm,
    Who shall put forth on thee,
    Unfathomable sea?
              SHELLEY.—*Time.*

Time, The Wheel of.

No! no arresting the vast wheel of time,
That round and round still turns with onward
    might,
Stern, dragging thousands to the dreaded
    night
Of an unknown hereafter.
    CHARLES COWDEN CLARKE.—*Sonnet. The
             Course of Time.*

Time, The Work of.

    Ever eating, never cloying,
    All-devouring, all-destroying,
    Never finding full repast
    Till I eat the world at last.
             SWIFT.—*On Time.*

To-days and Yesterdays, Our.

    Our to-days and yesterdays,
    Are the blocks with which we build.
                LONGFELLOW.

Truth and Falsehood.

    Falsehoods which we spurn to-day,
    Were the truths of long ago;
    Let the dead thoughts fall away,
    Fresher shall the living grow.
                WHITTIER.

Work, God-appointed.

            I am glad to think
I am not bound to make the world go right,
But only to discover and to do
With cheerful heart, the work that God ap-
    points.
             JEAN INGELOW.

World, All's Right with the.

    The year's at the spring
    And day's at the morn;
    Morning's at seven;
    The hillside's dew-pearled;
    The lark's on the wing,
    The snail's on the thorn,
    God's in his heaven,—
    All's right with the world.
          BROWNING.—*Pippa Passes.*

World-Treasures.

The world is so full of a number of things,
I'm sure we should all be as happy as kings.
           R. L. STEVENSON.

Years, The Flight of.

Years follow'ng years, steal something ev'ry
    day;
At last they steal us from ourselves away.
    POPE.—*Imitations of Horace.* Bk. II.
             Ep. II. Line 72.

Years, The Trend of.

I hear the muffled tramp of years
    Come stealing up the slope of Time;
They bear a train of smiles and tears,
    Of burning hopes and dreams sublime.
    JAMES G. CLARKE.—*November.*

Year, The Next.

No backward glance shall hinder or appal me:
    A new life is begun;
And better hopes and better motives call me
    Than those the past has won.
          LILLIAN KNAPP.—Y. C.

The Cry of the New Century

God, give us men; a time like this demands
Strong minds, great hearts, true faith, and
 ready hands.
Men whom the lust of office does not kill;
Men whom the spoils of office cannot buy;
Men who possess opinions and a will;
Men who have honor; men who will not lie;
Men who can stand before a demagog
And scorn his treacherous flatteries without
 winking,
Tall men, sun-crowned, who live above the
 fog
In public duty and in private thinking.
For while the rabble with their thumb worn
 creeds,
Their proud profession, and their little deeds,
Mingle in selfish strife—lo!
Freedom weeps, wrong rules the land, and
 waiting Justice sleeps.—O. C. W.

The World for Christ—A New Year Rallying Song

By Fanny Crosby

[*Air, "From Greenland's Icy Mountains."*]

Arise, O Christian soldiers,
 And consecrate anew
Your all upon the altar,
 Of Him, who died for you!
Arise in faith united,
 And let this year record
Your undivided service,
 To Christ, our risen Lord!

O, rally 'round H's standard;
 Defend the cross you love;
And look to Him for wisdom
 And counsel from above.
Against the arch deceiver,
 Against the host of sin,
March on with steady purpose
 The world for Christ to win!

Be strong, O Christian soldiers,
 On Jesus cast your care!
And when the conflict rages
 Let every breath be prayer.
Fear not; the Lord is with you:
 'Tis He who speaks within;
March on with zeal and courage
 The world for Christ to win!

Go forth, go forth rejoicing,
 And in the Master's name,
To weary souls that perish
 Eternal life proclaim!
The crowning day is coming;
 The end of toil and sin;
March on through grace determined,
 The world for Christ to win!
 W. C. M.

Another Year is Dawning

By Frances Ridley Havergal

Another year is dawning!
 Dear Master, let it be,
In working or in waiting,
 Another year with Thee.

Another year in leaning
 Upon Thy loving breast,
Of ever-deepening trustfulness,
 Of quiet, happy rest.

Another year of mercies,
 Of faithfulness and grace;
Another year of gladness,
 In the shining of Thy face.
Another year of progress,
 Another year of praise;
Another year of proving
 Thy presence "all the days."

Another year of service,
 Of witness for Thy love;
Another year of training
 For holier works above.
Another year is dawning!
 Dear Master, let it be
On earth, or else in heaven,
 Another year for Thee!

Farther On

A New Year's Song

By Helen Boyden

Once again has old Time lifted
 All the curtains of the years,
Shows the good from evil sifted,
 Makes a rainbow of our tears.
While we gaze with tender yearning
 At the dear enchanted past,
Memory is slowly turning
 Pictures on life's canvas cast.

Some we long to keep for ever,
 Crying out to memory, "Hold!"
Others haunt us with a "Never!"
 Some are fancies, strange and old.
Ah, we're wiser now for grieving,
 Tho we cannot tell the "why;"
And the pain and joy we're leaving
 Thrill us with new mystery.

Up the steeps of time we falter,
 Hope and courage almost gone;
Nothing can our pathway alter,
 We must journey farther on!
Shadowy heights their crests uprearing
 Dare our mounting to the skies;
Treacherous depths in mist appearing
 Mock our weary, fearful eyes.

Courage, children! One beside us
 Holds our footsteps lest they stray:
Good or ill, whate'er betide us,
 Jesus keeps us "all the way:"
"It is well," for God has led us;
 Sing a requiem for the years
As we climb to heights above us,
 Past the clouds of doubt and fears.

Onward, upward—such is living;
 Gaining, losing, smiles and tears,
Partings, meetings, taking, giving—
 Thus we keep the march of years:
Trying, failing, trusting, praising,
 Yet a welcome strong and true
Let our lips and hearts be raising
 To this Year of "All things new."
 A. M.

Trust in the Future

By J. G. WHITTIER

I know not what the future hath
Of marvel or surprise,
Assured alone that life and death
His mercy underlies.

And so beside the Silent Sea
I wait the muffled oar;
No harm from Him can come to me
On ocean or on shore.

I know not where His islands lift
Their fronded palms in air;
I only know I cannot drift
Beyond His love and care.

The Future

By HENRY JEROME STOCKARD

As brave Columbus, drifting from that sea
Which mortal's keel had never dared before,
Came breathless on the banks of Salvador,
With veils of silver mist on slope and lea,
So borne by winds and streams of destiny,
But with no memory of our native shore,
Do we emerge, and life's vague land explore,
Here on the outpost of eternity.
He never dreamed those aisles that dimly rose
Upon his raptured vision skirted land
That spreads far as the zones of earth expand.
Sail on, O soul! brave life's outlying bars,
For heaven's blazing archipelagoes
Fringe continents wide as the range of stars.

Gradatim

By J. G. HOLLAND

Heaven is not reached at a single bound;
But we build the ladder by which we rise
From the lowly earth to the vaulted skies,
And we mount to the summit round by round.

I count this thing to be grandly true;
That a noble deed is a step toward God—
Lifting the soul from the common sod
To a purer air and a broader view.

We rise by things that are under our feet;
By what we have mastered of good and
gain;
By the pride deposed and the passion slain,
And the vanquished ills that we hourly meet.

We hope, we aspire, we resolve, we trust,
When the *morning* calls us to life and light;
But our hearts grow weary, and ere the
night
Our lives are trailing the sordid dust.

He Knows

MARY G. BRAINARD

I know not what will befall me!
God hangs a mist o'er my eyes;
And o'er each step of my onward path
He makes new scenes to rise,
And every joy He sends to me
Comes as a sweet and glad surprise.

I see not a step before me,
As I tread the days of the year,
But the past is still in God's keeping,
The future His mercy shall clear,
And what looks dark in the distance,
May brighten as I draw near.

For perhaps the dreaded future
Has less bitterness than I think;
The Lord may sweeten the water
Before I stoop to drink,
Or, if Marah must be Marah,
He will stand beside its brink.

It may be there is waiting
For the coming of my feet,
Some gift of such rare blessedness,
Some joy so strangely sweet,
That my lips can only tremble
With the thanks I cannot speak.

O, restful, blissful ignorance!
'Tis blessed not to know,
It keeps me quiet in those arms
Which will not let me go,
And hushes my soul to rest
On the bosom which loves me so.

So I go on not knowing!
I would not if I might;
I would rather walk in the dark with God,
Than go alone in the light,
I would rather walk with Him by faith,
Than walk alone by sight.

My heart shrinks back from trials
Which the future may disclose,
Yet I never had a sorrow
But what the dear Lord chose;
So I send the coming tears back,
With the whispered words "He knows."

New Year's Hymn

How beautiful it is to be alive!
To wake each morn as if the Maker's grace
Did us afresh from nothingness derive
That we might sing, "How happy is our
case!
How beautiful it is to be alive!"

To read in God's great book until we feel
Love for the love that gave it; then to kneel
Close unto Him whose truth our souls will
shrive,
While every moment's joy doth more reveal
How beautiful it is to be alive.

Rather to go without what might increase
Our worldly standing, than our souls de-
prive
Of frequent speech with God, or than to cease
To feel, through having wasted health or
peace,
How beautiful it is to be alive.

Not to forget, when pain and grief draw nigh,
Into the ocean of time past to dive
For memories of God's mercies, or to try
To bear all sweetly, hoping still to cry,
"How beautiful it is to be alive!"

Thus ever toward man's height of nobleness
  Strive still some new progression to con-
    trive;
Till, just as any other friend's, we press
Death's hand; and, having died, feel none
    the less
How beautiful it is to be alive.—W.

The White Flowers of January

"The aconites, and other white flowers of January,
the spirits of the dead blooms of summer."
                                    SIWAARMILL.

BY WILLIAM SHARP

The woodland ways were white; the boughs
    swung low
  With weight of snow;
There was a shimmer of dancing golden light,
  And through the glow
The goddess Flora moved in sudden flight.

But when she saw the dead blooms every-
    where
  Laid low i' the mold,
Her sunny wings she did unfold.
  Long did she brood amid that woodland
    bare
And the blooms withered there.

Then, with a smile, she called the snows to
    her;
  There was a stir,
A falling rustle, as when bird-wings whir
Alow i' the thickets in the twilight hour;
  And next, a glimmering shower.

Swift 'mid the green gloom flecked with
    white, she fled;
  But where each snowflake fell
There was a happy miracle;
Dead pansies, wind-flowers, violets, once more
    rose,
But now in white each petal did unclose.

Life

BY PHILIP JAMES BAILEY

Life's more than breath and the quick round
    of blood;
It is a great spirit and a busy heart.
The coward and the small in soul scarce do
    live. . . . .
We live in deeds, not years, in thoughts, not
    breaths,
In feeling, not in figures on a dial.
We should count time by heart throbs.
    He most lives
Who thinks most, feels the noblest, acts the
    best.
Life's but a means unto an end; that end
Beginning, mean, and end to all things,
  —God. . . . .
Upon the summit of each mountain—thought
Worship thou God. Keep thy spirit pure
From worldly taint by the repellent strength
Of virtue. Think on noble thoughts and
    deeds
Ever. Count o'er the rosary of truth;
And practice precepts which are proven wise.

It matters not then what thou fearest.
    Walk
Boldly and wisely in that light thou hast;
There is a hand above will help thee on.
                        From " Festus."

A New Year's Meditation

BY M. S.

The earth was brown and bare and cold;
Another year had swiftly rolled
Its twelve months round, and as its life went
    out, it seemed
To bring to mind all the fond hopes that man
    had dreamed,
Which in the waking never were fulfilled—
Every disappointment that had chilled
A single heart; every broken vow
Each day had known; and now
The year was going, with bowed and heavy
    head;
The whole earth sad,
And nature, too, seemed dead.

The heavens looked with pity on the earth
    below,
And, to hide its desolation, sent the snow.
All that long night the soft white flakes were
    whirled,
And when the morning came, their innocence
    and purity had clothed the world.
A bright New Year had dawned, which did
    not know
The sin and sadness that had come a year ago
The past was covered: God had sent this
    untried year to give
Another chance to man, that he might wake
    and hope and live.—O.

New Year's Morning

BY HELEN HUNT JACKSON

Only a night from old to new!
Only a night and so much wrought!
The Old Year's heart all weary grew,
But said: "The New Year rest has brought."
The Old Year's heart its hopes laid down,
As in a grave; but, trusting, said:
"The blossoms of the New Year's crown
Bloom from the ashes of the dead."
The Old Year's heart was full of greed;
With selfishness it longed and ached,
And cried: "I have not half I need.
My thirst is bitter and unslaked.
But to the New Year's generous hand
All gifts in plenty shall return;
True loving it shall understand;
By all my failures it shall learn.
I have been reckless; it shall be
Quiet and calm and pure of life,
I was a slave; it shall go free,
And find sweet peace where I leave strife."

The New Year

BY CELIA THAXTER

With the whirling and drifting of snows
  Comes breathless, the wild New Year,
While bitter the North wind blows
  O'er the fields that lie stark and drear.

Yet hope is alight in her eyes
  As she looks from the heart of the storm,
"Earth sleeps in her shroud," she cries,
  "But the life in her breast is warm.

"Death is but a dream of the night,
  And the hymn of joy is begun,
For slowly seeking the light
  The great globe turns to the sun.

"Behold, I will bring delight
  In place of the darkness and cold;
Safe under the meadows so white
  Is hiding the buttercup's gold.

"The blush of the sweet-briar rose
  Where is it treasured to-day?
I will call it from under the snows
  To bloom on its delicate spray.

"I will fling all the flowers abroad,
  And loose in the echoing sky
The beautiful birds of God,
  To carol their rapture on high.

"And the summer's splendor shall reign
  In place of the winter's dearth,
Her color and music again
  Shall gladden the patient earth.

"Look but with eyes that are pure
  On the gifts in my hand that lie,
And your portion of bliss is sure
  In the beauty no wealth can buy."

Hark to the New Year's voice
  Through the murk of the winter drear;
O children of men, rejoice
  At the tidings of home and cheer!
                                    Y. C.

The New Year

By Mrs. M. A. Kidde

New Year's Day in spotless robes
In the east is dawning,
As the old year glides away,
Giving us no warning.
Fold the record of the past—
Close the book forever—
  You can alter, you can mend,
What's within, no, never.

Let us take the Life Book new
With its leaves unspotted,
And with nobler purpose write,
Leaving it unblotted!
Let us trust and not despair;
Hope comes with the morning.
  "Peace on earth, good will to all"
With the New Year's dawning.
                                    O. C. W.

The New Year

By Rev. C. F. M'Kown

The New Year come! Its pathway lies
Hid by the mist of days unknown;
Faith sees bright stars illume its skies,
Hope bids each heart arise, press on.

The Old Year gone! The New Year come!
Thus speed the years till pathways blend,
Till old and new greet lustrous dawn
Of fadeless day, where time shall end.

New Year's, 1900

By E. S. Martin

One greeting more to one of noble fame,
  Our comrades since our birth; our fathers',
    too;
Into whose springtime hopes our grandsires
    came,
  Whose promises to them for us came true.

What struggles and what gains have filled his
    day!
What peerless triumphs of a mind set free!
What stubborn shrinking, oftentimes, to pay
  The woful birth-price of the is-to-be.

Hoary, sublime, deathless yet doomed to die,
  No other New Year's dawning his shall be.
Vouchsafe him, Time, such end that men shall
    cry—
  "Grand was thy passing, Nineteenth Cen-
    tury!"   S.

The New Year Dawns

By Louise Chandler Moulton

The New Year dawns—the sun shines strong
    and clear;
  And all the world rejoices and is gay:
The city-loving birds from spray to spray
Flit busily, and twitter in my ear
Their little frozen note of wintry cheer:
  From ruddy children with the snow at play
  Ring peals of laughter, gladder than in May,
While friend greets friend with "Happy be
    thy Year!"

So would I joy, if Thou wert by my side—
  So would I laugh, if Thou couldst laugh
    with me—
But left alone, in Darkness I abide,
  Mocked by a Day that shines no more on
    Thee:
From this too merry world my heart I hide—
My New Year dawns not till Thy face I see.
                                    Y. C.

New Year's Eve

By Mrs. Charles F. Thomas

Ye solemn bells! toll sadly,
  The old year's hours are few;
Sweet bells! ye'll soon ring gladly
  To welcome in the new.
But from old friends the parting
  Is sad and sore to me;
E'en now my heart is smarting,
  Old year! to part with thee.

New Year! thou coming stranger,
  From doubt, and fear and danger,
Thy hours may bring, I hasten
  To Jesus; tho He chasten,
He will from harm defend me;
  Still will His grace attend me
And so, whate'er betide,
  Safely, I shall abide.   P. J.

New Year's Eve

The night is starry, bright, and clear,
  With moonlight glimmering on the snow;
And midnight winds, with voices low,
Sing dirges for the dying year.

Old Year, I pray we part as friends!
  Sincerely we can say " Adieu! "
  And as we welcome in the New
We promise him to make amends—

We pledge ourselves to nobler deeds,
  To loftier thought and purer life,
  To be more faithful in the strife
For what our nobler nature pleads.

Remembering all the solemn past,
  Its lessons treasured in the heart,
  So we will live and act our part
As if this New Year were our last.

L. C.

New Year's Eve

By Alfred Tennyson

Ring out, wild bells, to the wild sky,
  The flying cloud, the frosty light;
  The year is dying in the night;
Ring out, wild bells, and let him die.

Ring out the old, ring in the new;
  Ring, happy bells, across the snow;
  The year is going, let him go;
Ring out the false, ring in the true.

Ring out the grief that saps the mind,
  For those that here we see no more;
  Ring out the feud of rich and poor,
Ring in redress to all mankind.

Ring out a slowly dying cause,
  And ancient forms of party strife;
  Ring in the nobler modes of life,
With sweeter manners, purer laws.

Ring out false pride in place and blood,
  The civic slander and the spite;
  Ring in the love of truth and right,
Ring in the common love of good.

Ring out old shapes of foul disease,
  Ring out the narrowing lust of gold;
  Ring out the thousand wars of old,
Ring in the thousand years of peace.

Ring in the valiant man and free,
  The larger heart, the kindlier hand;
  Ring out the darkness of the land;
Ring in the Christ that is to be.

The New-Year Mine

By Amos R. Wells

Every year's a hidden mine,
  Stoutly up, and work it!
What tho anxious toil is thine?
  Never think to shirk it.

Half the mine, as I am told,
  Harbors dust and ashes;
Half the mine is precious gold,—
  Ah, how bright it flashes!

Sink the shaft of Lazy Mind,
  (What a dreadful bore, sir!)
Dust and ashes you will find,
  That, and nothing more, sir!

Sink the shaft of Earnest Heart,—
  Lo, the treasure glances,
Gleaming gay in every part
  Where your pick advances!

See, my lad, the New-Year Mine
  Bright with promise-flashes!
Will you dig for treasure fine,
  Or only dust and ashes?

G. R.

A New Year's Reminder

By Mary F. Butts.

The season's joy you wish us—
  For that we thank you, dear;
Yet wishes are not quite enough
  To bring a glad New Year.

Watch day by day, my darling,
  For helpful work to do,
And through the new year you yourself
  Will make your wish come true.

C. U.

The Door of the New Year

By Lucy Larcom.

We pause beside this door:
Thy year, O God, how shall we enter in?

. . . .
The footsteps of a Child
Sound close beside us. Listen, He will speak!
His birthday bells have hardly rung a week,
Yet has He trod the world's press, undefiled.
" Enter through Me," He saith, " nor wander
    more;
For lo! I am the Door."

G. R.

Threshold of the New Year

We are standing on the threshold, we are in
  the opened door,
We are treading on a border land we have
  never trod before:
Another year is opening, and another year is
  gone,
We have passed the darkness of the night;
  we are in the early morn;
We have left the fields behind us o'er which
  we scattered seed;
We pass into the future which none of us can
  read.
The corn among the weeds, the stones, the
  surface mold,
May yield a partial harvest; we hope for
  sixty fold.
Then hasten to fresh labor, to thrash, and
  reap, and sow,
Then bid the new year welcome, and let the
  old year go—
Then gather all your vigor, press forward in
  the fight,
And let this be your motto, " For God, and
  for the Right."—Anon.

*F. I.

Uncertainty of the New Year

BY WILLIAM COWPER

Could I, from heaven inspired, as sure presage
To whom the rising year shall prove his
last,
As I can number in my punctual page
And item down the victims of the past;

How each would trembling wait the mournful sheet
On which the press might stamp him next
to die;
And, reading here his sentence, how replete
With anxious meaning, heavenward turn
his eye!

Then doubtless many a trifler, on the brink
Of this world's hazardous and headlong
shore.
Forced to a pause, would feel it good to think,
Told that his setting sun must rise no more.

Ah, self-deceived! could I prophetic say
Who next is fated, and who next to fall,
The rest might then seem privileged to play;
But, naming none, the Voice now speaks to
all.   *F. I.

Opportunity

BY EDWARD ROWLAND SILL

This I beheld, or dreamed it in a dream:
There spread a cloud of dust along a plain;
And underneath the cloud, or in it, raged
A furious battle, and men yelled, and swords
Shocked upon swords and shields. A prince's
banner
Wavered, then staggered backward, hemmed
by foes.
A craven hung along the battle's edge
And thought: "Had I a sword of keener
steel—
That blue blade that the king's son bears—
but this
Blunt thing!" He snapt and flung it from
His hand
And, lowering, crept away and left the field.
Then came the king's son, wounded, sore
bestead,
And weaponless, and saw the broken sword,
Hilt-buried in the dry and trodden sand,
And ran and snatched it, and with battle shout
Lifted afresh, he hewed his enemy down,
And saved a great cause that heroic day.
                                        C. E. W.

Opportunity

BY MABEL EARLE

One sought for rivers, thirsting, while a
spring
Watered, unseen, the grasses at his feet.
One roamed the world for wealth, while,
glittering,
Rich ores lay hid beneath his native street.

One lived apart with sorrow, desolate,
And yearned for love's sweet help, and
never smiled,
While, day by day, before his fast-barred
gate
Wandered with wistful eyes a homeless
child.

One longed in vain to fight for Christ his
Lord,
Out in the fierce, free strife with open ill,
While pride and self crept close, with unseen
cord,
And bound and led him captive at their
will.   C. E. W.

Opportunity

BY REV. BENJAMIN COPELAND

Before this truth be bared each brow—
The infinite is here and now!
As sacred as the stars, the sod—
As near to Heaven, as close to God.

Call nothing common or unclean,
Nor deem thou any service mean;
Forevermore this faith be thine—
All days, all duties, are divine.

E'en now, at thy reluctant feet,
The seed-time and the harvest meet;
"The morrow in the moment lies,"
Heed well the Voice; awake! arise!

He, only he, is free indeed,
Who in his heart holds fast this creed—
(A fadeless wreath for every brow),
The infinite is here and now!

New Year as Peacemaker

BY FRANK WALCOTT HUTT

I have made peace with my foes, peace with
the lost and the slain;
Hope and the Future are mine; over the living I reign.

For I have buried the old, buried and put
away,
And the whisper and curse of wrong I suffer
to fail to-day.

And the sorrow of dark regret, and the dread
of the vampire past,
Are dead on the white highways where the
Old Year breathed his last.

I am the glad New Year. Songs of the morn
I sing;
Songs of the triumph-soul, with the pardon
and peace I bring.
                                        I.

A New Year's Prayer

I want my heart made pure, dear Lord,
I want to know and love Thy Word;
To be all glorious within,
Freed from each spot and stain of sin.

I want the New Year's opening days
To fill with love, and prayer, and praise.
Some little things to do for Thee,
For Thou hast done great things for me.

I want some other soul to bring
To Thee, my Savior and my King.
Thou wilt not, Lord, my prayer deny,
For Thou canst all my wants supply.

In Jesus' name our prayer we raise,
Whose guiding hand has blessed our days.
And may we, Lord, in godly fear
Serve Thee through all this coming year.
Selected.

A New Year's Prayer

BY JOHN HALL, D.D.

O God, my good desires fulfil;
  The bad do Thou restrain;
Reveal to me Thy holy will,
  And make my duty plain.

Sustain me by Thy heavenly grace,
  And keep me in Thy fear:
Help me to run the heavenly race
  With Jesus ever near.

O Christ, my all-wise Prophet,
  I sit down at Thy feet;
Teach me to do the Father's will,
  For heaven make me meet.

O Christ, my great High Priest,
  Ascended now to heaven,
On Thine atoning work I rest,
  To Thee the praise be given.

O Christ, my glorious King,
  Thy law write on my heart;
And bring me to the heavenly home
  Where we shall never part.

There let me sing the song of songs;
  There let my praise be given,
To Father, Son, and Holy Ghost,
  The Trinity in heaven.
                            G. R.

Sonnet LXIV

BY WILLIAM SHAKESPEARE

When I have seen by Time's fell hand defaced
The rich-proud cost of outworn buried age;
When sometime lofty towers I see downrazed.
And brass eternal, slave to mortal rage;
When I have seen the hungry ocean gain
Advantage on the kingdom of the shore,
And the firm soil win of the watery main,
Increasing store with loss, and loss with store;
When I have seen such interchange of state,
Or state itself confounded to decay;
Ruin hath taught me thus to ruminate,—
That Time will come and take my love away.
This: thought is as a death, which cannot choose
But weep to have that which it fears to lose.

Teach Me Thy Way

BY MARIANNE FARNINGHAM

THE dark comes down ere it be late;
  I stand amid the shades and wait,
Not knowing whether left or right
  Will bring me to the open gate
Where I can pass to home and light.
  O God, with whom is endless day,
  Guide Thou my steps; teach me Thy way.

The distant lights like beacons shine;
  The city they illume is mine;
The friends I love are gathered there.
  Give me Thy help, O Guide divine,
For hope and faith are in my prayer;
  And morn will break and I shall stand
At daybreak in my fatherland.
                            C. E. W.

The Accepted Time

If you have a friend worth loving,
  Love him. Yes, and let him know
That you love him, ere life's evening
  Tinge his brow with sunset glow.
Why should praises ne'er be said
Of a friend—till he is dead?

If you hear a song that thrills you,
  Sung by any child of song,
Praise it. Do not let the singer
  Wait deserved praises long.
Why should one who thrills your heart
Lack the joy you can impart?

If you hear a prayer that moves you
  By its humble, pleading tone,
Join it. Do not let the seeker
  Bow before his God alone.
Why should not your brother share
Strength with "two or three" in prayer?
                            C. G.

The Three Voices

What saith the Past to thee?   *Weep!*
  Truth is departed,
Beauty hath died like the dream of a sleep,
  Love is faint-hearted;
Trifles of sense, the profoundly unreal,
Scare from our spirits God's holy ideal;
So, as a funeral bell, slow and deep,
So tolls the Past to thee. Weep!

How speaks the Present Hour?   *Act!*
  Walk, upward glancing;
So shall thy footsteps in glory be tracked,
  Slow, but advancing.
Scorn not the smallest of daily endeavor,
Let the great meaning ennoble it ever,
Droop not o'er efforts expended in vain,
Work as believing that labor is gain.

What doth the Future say?   *Hope!*
  Turn thy face sunward;
Look, where light fringes the far-rising slope
  Day cometh onward.
Watch, tho so long be the twilight delaying
Let the first sunbeam arise on thee praying;
Fear not, for greater is God by thy side
Than the armies of Satan against thee allied.
                            R. H.

The Eternal Years

BY FREDERICK FABER

How shalt thou bear the cross that now
  So dread a weight appears?
Keep quietly to God, and think
  Upon the Eternal Years.

Brave quiet is the thing for thee,
  Chiding thy scrupulous fears;
Learn to be real from the thought
  Of the Eternal Years.

One cross can sanctify a soul;
  Late saints and ancient seers
Were what they were because they mused
  Upon the Eternal Years.

Death will have rainbows round it seen
  Through calm contrition's tears,
If tranquil Hope but trims her lamp
  At the Eternal Years.

H. A. C.

The Old Year and Young Year

By NORA PERRY

I

Said the year that was old,
  "I am cold, I am cold.
And my breath hurries fast
  On the wild winter blast
Of this thankless December;
  Ah, who will remember
As I shivering, go,
  The warmth and the glow
That arose like a flame
  When I came, when I came?
For I brought in my hands
  From Utopian lands,
Golden gifts, and the schemes
  That were fairer than dreams.
Ah never a king
  Of a twelvemonth, will bring
Such splendor of treasure
  Without stint or measure,
As I brought on that day
  Triumphant and gay.
But alas, and alas,
  Who will think as I pass,
I was once gay and bold?"
  Said the year that was old.

II

Said the year that was young—
  And his light laughter rung—
" Come, bid me good cheer,
  For I bring with me here
Such gifts as the earth
  Never saw till my birth;
All the largess of life,
  Right royally rife
With the plans and the schemes
  Of the world's highest dreams.
Then—Hope's chalice filled up
  To the brim of the cup,
Let us drink to the past,
  The poor pitiful past,"
Sang the year that was young,
  While his light laughter rung.

Y. C.

The Building of the Year

By FRANK WALCOTT HUTT

Seek, if ye may, of them that read,
Whereto the year thy hopes shall lead;

Toward what proud heights, in lines of flame,
The world may look to read thy name;

But know that in the deepmost vales,
Where heroes strive and courage pales,

Amid the wilderness and fen,
Along the beaten paths of men,

Where, face to face with common things,
God's saints have known their stress and
  stings;

There, brave to share the lot of all,
Shalt thou endure thy part, or fall.

There only, shalt thou raze or rear
Thy building of Another Year.   G. R.

EPIPHANY

EPIPHANY (ἐπιφάνεια, ἐπι, upon, +φάινω show) in its general use means "any appearance or bodily manifestation, especially of a deity." * In the Greek, Latin, Anglican, and other branches of the Christian Church on January 6 the festival called Epiphany has been observed. The day gets its name from the fact that God in Jesus Christ manifested Himself to the world: at His advent, to the wise men from the East, on the occasion of His baptism.

The day has been called Twelfth Day as well as Epiphany, because it falls on the twelfth day after Christmas. So intimately is it associated with the festival of the nativity of Christ that some authorities claim that it was not kept as a separate holy day until A. D. 813. Speaking of the relation of Epiphany to Christmas, Bennett says: " The labored investigations given to this subject have quite firmly established the following conclusions: (1) Until near the close of the fourth century the Nativity was celebrated in the Oriental churches in connection with the Epiphany, or on January 6—this custom continuing in many parts of the East for a century or more later. (2) From a much earlier date the Nativity was celebrated in the Western Churches on December 25, and it occupies an important place in the most ancient liturgies. It is, however, impossible to fix the date when the change from January 6 to December 25 was made." †

Coleman says: " Christmas commemorates the birth of Christ; God Himself becoming man. This great event indeed is represented by two solemnities; the *birth* of Jesus on the twenty-fifth of December, when the Divine Being entered on His Earthly existence; and the day of His *baptism* on the sixth of January, when He first manifested Himself as Christ, the promised Messiah. On this occasion His Divine power and glory were publicly revealed; and for this reason the day is styled Epiphany, the manifestation."‡

So it would appear that Epiphany was first observed in the Eastern, or Greek, Church, where it celebrated Christ's manifestation of His Messiahship on the occasion of His Baptism; and after the fourth century it was observed in the Western, or Roman Catholic, Church, with especial reference to God's manifestation of Himself in Christ to the whole world, but especially to the gentile world. The Anglican Church, and all the churches observing Epiphany in America very appropriately use the day to magnify the cause of missions and hold up Jesus Christ as " The Light of the World."

OUTLOOK FOR THE WORLD'S EVANGELIZATION §

By Rev. J. A. Graham

I. *The results already attained,* more particularly during the last hundred years, give cause for gratitude. At the beginning of the modern missionary movement the churches were dead to the claims of the heathen world. Now every branch has its foreign mission board or society, whose work focuses the living interest of the best of its members. Before the famous meeting at Kittering, in 1792, only one or two agencies were at work

* Standard Dictionary.　† Christian Archæology, p. 456.　‡ Ancient Christianity Exemplified, p. 538.
§ A chapter (condensed) from *Missionary Expansion Since the Reformation*, 1895. (Revell.)

among the heathens; now there are about 150 separate organizations, with an annual income of over $12,500,000. Then there were but a few missionaries representing Christendom among non-Christians; now there is a great army with 10,000 missionary officers (one-third of them women), aided by 50,000 native workers, of whom 3,300 are ordained. Then the great mission fields were either unknown or closed to the free entrance of the Gospel; now the whole wide world, with inconsiderable exceptions, is open to its heralds. Then the converts of Protestant churches in heathendom were reckoned by the thousand, now there are said to be 3,000,000. Then the power of politics and the influence of the press were almost wholly, and often bitterly, opposed to foreign missionary enterprise; now the missionary is looked upon as the pioneer of civilization, and the valued ally of good government.

II. But notwithstanding past success, *only a beginning has been made* in the work of missions. The area actually occupied by Christian peoples is small compared with that of non-Christian nations, and large tracts of the earth's surface remain unevangelized. We rejoice over three million converts as the result of modern missions, but what are they to the thousand million unconverted? And the startling fact presents itself that during the period in which the three millions have been won, the natural increase of heathendom is reckoned at two hundred millions!

III. *Christians must be more earnest and self-sacrificing* if the whole world is to be speedily evangelized. The number of those who feel called to go to preach the Gospel to the heathen increases yearly, but their number is utterly inadequate to meet the urgent calls which open doors of opportunity are presenting to the churches. A great host of consecrated men and women—the very best

in Christendom—are at present needed in the world's harvest field. And *to help them go* there is required a larger proportion of the wealth of those who are unable to give personal service. What is being done by the poor Moravian Church shows what might be done by others. If even their standard were reached by the other reformed churches, these would be represented, says Mrs. Bird Bishop, by two hundred thousand missionaries, and would contribute $700,000,000 a year. "We spend," she adds (referring to the United Kingdom), "£160,000,000 ($800,000,000, or $20 a head) upon drink; we smoke £16,000,000, and we hoard £240,000,000 while our whole contributions toward the conversion of this miserable world are but one and a half million pounds, or ninepence (18 cents) a head."

IV. Yet, withal, *the present outlook is full of hope.* Of all the faiths in the world, Christianity alone presents the appearance of a world-wide religion. Mr. Gladstone has said that "the art, literature, the systematized industry, invention, and commerce—in a word, the power of the world—are almost wholly Christian." The Christian nations exercise political power over thirty-two out of the fifty-two million square miles of the earth's surface—Protestant Great Britain alone over one-fourth of the whole world—and the Christian peoples increase in a higher ratio than do the non-Christian. The hold of the non-Christian faiths is weakened as knowledge increases, while, as Dr. Barrows asserts, "It is vastly significant, and in accordance with the genius of Christianity, that the religion of Christ has in this century of intellectual progress, when superstitions have been dispelled by the light of truth, made more memorable and rapid conquests than in any previous period since the downfall of Roman paganism."—M. R. W.

THE FINGER OF GOD IN MODERN MISSIONS *
By Arthur T. Pierson, D.D.

Facts are the fingers of God. Altho indifference is not always born of ignorance, there will be little zeal without knowledge. To awaken a deep passion for the universal and immediate spread of Gospel tidings believers must be brought face to face with those grand facts which make the march of modern missions the miracle of these latter days.

Not to go back further, for four hundred years we can trace signal providences casting up this broad, level highway between the centers of Christendom and pagandom. Near the close of the sixteenth century a new route to the golden Indies by way of the Cape of Good Hope led to the chartering of the East India Company a few years later; and so, while the Pilgrims were sowing the seeds

of this Christian republic beneath the setting sun, Protestant England planted an empire toward the sunrise, and in the very heart of the pagan Orient. Unconsciously the leading nation of the Protestant Christian world was reaching out one hand eastward, and the other westward, to lay the foundations of a world-wide Church. Subsequent conflicts in America and India settled the question that in both hemispheres the Cross was to displace both the crescent and the crucifix.

By the middle of the eighteenth century, America and Asia are respectively held by the two foremost Protestant powers of the world. England has a firm foothold in the critical center of oriental missions, and in her hands holds the keys of the kingdoms of the East. This makes necessary, as a line of

* Brief portions of Dr. Pierson's paper on "God's Hand in Missions," written for an edition of David Brainerd's Memoirs—1884.

communication, an open highway for travel and traffic between the mother country and her eastern possessions. If Britain had any right in India, she had a right to a safe and peaceful road thither; and this political necessity was used of God ultimately to shape the attitude of every nation along that highway. Had England not held that highway to the Indies, the destinies of Europe and Asia might have been changed. Turkey would probably have been devoured by Russia, or divided between Russia and France; the Greek and Roman churches, crossing the mountains, might have swayed all Asia and kept out Protestant missions. Behold the hand of God, using English arms and diplomacy to hold popes, czars, and sultans in check; to shield converts from persecution by Turkish Armenians, Persian Nestorians, Syrian Moslems, or Indian Brahmins; and giving Britain a casting vote in the affairs of the Sublime Porte!

What means this providential establishment of British empire in India? It is an entering wedge driven into the heart of Asia; a wedge the direction of whose cleavage is still eastward, splitting in twain these gnarled and knotted trunks of moss-grown empires!

Meanwhile, from seed sown at Plymouth, develops another mighty, evangelizing power. The Protestant republic of America strides from Atlantic to Pacific, and, planting foot on the western shores, moves toward the eastern coasts of Asia, as tho there were no more sea. Here is God's counter-force moving from the opposite direction to meet England and oppose her entering wedge with the resistance of cooperation, as anvil opposes sledge-hammer. In other words, another irrepressible conflict has come. Commerce will have her highway round the world, and knocks imperatively at the sealed ports and barred gates of exclusive Oriental empires.

Our Republic leads the way. In 1853 Commodore Perry sails into the bay of Yeddo, spreads the Star Spangled Banner over the capstan, and the open Bible upon the flag, and, without firing a gun or shedding a drop of blood, peacefully opens the ports of Japan to the world. Five years later, four leading nations knock loudly at the gates of China, and the walled kingdom opens her doors, expressly stipulating by treaty that "any person, whether citizen of the country with which the treaty is made, or Chinese convert to the faith of the Protestant or Roman Catholic churches, who, according to these tenets, peaceably teaches and practices the principles of Christianity, shall in no case be *interfered with or molested.*" This one edict of toleration gave religious liberty to one-third of the population of the globe. At one titanic blow, God levels an obstacle as high as the Himalayas, and opens the way from Bosporus to the China sea, through the heart of Asia.

Passing by all other providential interpositions, let us emphasize the recent unveiling of Africa. In August, 1877, after 999 days from Zanzibar, Stanley, emerging at the mouth of the Congo, completes the transit of the Dark Continent. The dying cry of Jesus has rent the last veil in twain, and the missionary has only to follow the footsteps of the explorer. The same Providence that opens the door, prepares the forces of His Church for the crusade.

The missionary advance of this century is directly traceable to answered prayer. Since Luther nailed up his theses, there has been no historic hour so dark as the first half of the eighteenth century. Even England was, as Isaac Taylor said, in "virtual heathenism," with a lascivious literature, an infidel society, a worldly Church, and a deistic theology. Blackstone heard every clergyman of note in London, but not one discourse had more Christianity in it than the orations of Cicero, or showed whether the preacher was a disciple of Confucius, Mahomet, or Christ. In America, Samuel Blaine declared that "religion lay a-dying." In France, Voltaire, Rousseau, and Madame de Pompadour led society; and in Germany, Frederick the Great made his court the Olympus of infidels.

If Collins and Tyndal denounced Christianity as priestcraft, Whiston called Bible miracles grand impositions, and Woolston treated them as allegories; if Clark and Priestly openly taught the heresies of Arius and Socinus, and even morality was trampled under foot, what missionary activity could there be? To diffuse *such* "Christianity" would be disaster; but happily such a type of piety has no diffusive tendency or power. If it has any divine fire left, it has not a coal or even a spark to spare to light a blaze elsewhere.

The only hope of missions lay in a *revival* of religion, widespread and deep-reaching; and God gave that to His Church through a wonderful constellation of evangelists: Whitefield, the Wesleys, Grimshaw, Romaine, Rowlands, Berridge, Venn, Walker, Hervey, Toplady, Fletcher—these Bishop Ryle names as twelve of the apostles of that new Reformation which, between 1735 and 1785, woke not only England, but the Protestant world from the awful apostasy of irreligion and infidelity. At first even the Church resisted all efforts to revive her dying life. Whitefield found Scotch ministers opposing him by set days of fasting and prayer: and church doors shut against himself and Wesley, compelled that open-air preaching which was the great stride of the century toward the reaching of the masses.

But the Spirit of God was breathing on the dry bones. The fires, slowly kindled at first, burned brighter and hotter, caught here and there, spread far and wide, till even America, across the sea, was aflame. Within fifty years from Whitefield's first sermon at Gloucester, all Protestant Christendom thrilled with a renewed evangelical faith, and as evangelistic zeal is sure always to follow, out of these Pentecostal outpourings came the flaming tongues of witness. The Church, from her silver trumpets, pealed forth her summons to prayer for the effusion of the Spirit upon all disciples, and upon the whole habitable earth. Praying bands answered the trumpet peal in all parts of Britain, and from American shores came the echo, in 1747, of Jonathan Edwards's bugle "Call to Concerted Prayer." The tidal wave of revival rose higher and moved with greater momentum under the Haldanes, Andrew Fuller, Sutcliffe, Rowland Hill and others.

In 1792 the Warwick Association formally made the first Monday of, each month a "monthly concert of prayer" for the world's evangelization. No sooner did the revived Church, after this awful period of drought, begin to pray for a great rain, than a cloud like a man's hand appeared on the horizon; and in that same year (1792) the first Foreign Missionary Society was formed in England, and the next year sent to India its first missionary, William Carey, who, within the thirty years following, secured the translation of the Scriptures into forty tongues, and the circulation of two hundred thousand copies. Thus the revival of evangelical faith and of concerted prayer are the two pillars on which rests the arch of Modern Missions.

How fast that little cloud has grown, till the heaven is overspread, and there is a sound of the abundance of rain! During these eighty years the number of translations of the Word has increased *fivefold,* from fifty to two hundred and fifty, of Protestant mission societies *tenfold,* from seven to seventy; of male missionaries *fifteenfold,* from one hundred and seventy to twenty-four hundred; of moneys contributed *twenty-fivefold,* from two hundred and fifty thousand to six and a quarter million dollars; of con-

verts *thirty-fivefold,* from fifty thousand to one million six hundred and fifty thousand; and of mission schools *one hundred and seventyfold,* from seventy to twelve thousand!

The whole tide of thought has turned in the Church since William Carey first offered to go and meet the giant of heathenism. The wave, at its lowest ebb a century ago, now touches a flood-mark never before reached, and is still rising. Sydney Smith would no longer dare to sneer at the "pious shoemaker" of Paulersburg, or characterize his schemes as "the dreams of a dreamer who dreams that he has been dreaming." England is prouder of Carey than Athens was of Pericles, or Rome of Cicero, and lifts the statue of Livingstone to its lofty pedestal in the metropolis of the world, to inspire Christian colonies to push into the heart of the dark continent. American churches hurl their columns against the ranks of pagan and papal superstition, and erect missionary lectureships in the foremost institutions of learning to train youth to imitate the devotion of David Brainerd, Henry Martyn, and Alexander Duff.

In fact, the whole history of Modern Missions is a Burning Bush, whose every twig is aflame with the divine presence. We are standing on holy ground. Many and marked are the divine interpositions. We see the iron gates open of their own accord, obstacles suddenly sinking, continents unveiling their secrets, and missionary exploration going forward so rapidly that the maps of yesterday are out of date to-day!—H. R.

THE TRANSFORMING POWER OF THE GOSPEL *

By Arthur T. Pierson, D.D.

The Divine Hand has been conspicuous in the missionary work in the direct transformation of character, both individual and national. The fiercest, hardest, rudest of heathen have been subdued, softened, refined by the Gospel. Africaner, that monster of cruelty, who would kill an innocent man to make a drinking cup of his skull and a drum-head of his skin, was, at the touch of that Gospel, turned from a lion into a lamb. Guergis, the ferocious Koord, who would have killed his own daughter as she prayed for 'him, was struck by it into penitence, as bitter as Peter's, and as potent. He laid aside gun and dagger for Testament and hymn book, and made the mountains echo with the story of his great sins and great Savior, shouting with dying breath, "Free grace!" Even Fidelia Fiske could scarcely believe she saw the miracle of such a conversion. Sau Quala, the Karen, was by that same Gospel changed into an apostolic worker. He aided the missionaries in the translation of the Word, guided them for fifteen years through the jungles; then himself began to preach and plant churches—

within three years gathering nearly twenty-five hundred converts into more than thirty congregations—and refusing a tempting government position, rather than mix up God's work with secular labor, tho his poverty forced him to leave his lovely wife in loneliness.

So has the Gospel transformed whole communities. In 1878, the Ko Thah Byu Memorial Hall was consecrated, commemorating the fiftieth anniversary of the first Karen convent, whose name it bears, Karens built it at a cost of fifteen thousand dollars. It represented twenty thousand living disciples converted from demon worship, maintaining their own churches and schools, beside twenty thousand more who had died in the faith of Jesus. That hall confronts Shway Mote Tau Pagoda, with its shrines and fanes on an opposing hill—the double monument of what the Karens *were* and *are.*

The story of the Gospel in the South Seas should be written in starlight. John Williams, the blacksmith's boy, and the apostle of Polynesia, found idolatry of the most degraded type, and savages of the lowest grade

* See note to previous article; this is a continuation.

Yet his progress was one rapid career of conquest. Churches and schools grew, he knew not how. A lawless people adopt a code of laws and trial by jury. Printing presses scatter their leaves like the tree of life; and even a missionary society is formed with King Pomare as its president, and twenty-five hundred dollars as its first year's contribution. Within a year after he landed at Raratonga, the whole Hervey group, with a population of seven thousand, have thrown away their idols, and a church-building is going up, six hundred feet long. He turns to the Samoa group, and shortly has the whole people, sixty thousand, in Christian schools.

The tale of Fiji is not less wonderful. These cannibals built the very huts of their chiefs upon the bodies of living human beings, buried alive, and they launched their canoes upon living bodies as rollers; they slew infants and strangled widows. Human language has no terms to describe the abasement of this people, or their atrocious customs. Such deeds of darkness should be written in blood and recorded in hell. The Fijians are now a Christian people. In 1835 missionary labor began among them; seven years later the island of Ono had not one heathen left on it, and became the center of Gospel light to the whole group. To-day every village has its Christian homes and schools, and there are nine hundred churches on those islands.

So it was with new Hebrides. It was written as Dr. Geddie's Epitaph, that "when he came to Aneityum, there were no Christians; when he left, there were no heathens." These are but a few representative cases. Madagascar was so hopeless a field that the French governor of the island of Bourbon told the pioneer missionaries that they might as well try to convert cattle as the Malagasy. Yet the Gospel barely got a foothold there when it took such root that twenty-five years of fire and blood failed to burn out or blot out its impression. And now a Christian Church stands on the court grounds, and on the coronation table together lie the Laws of the Realm and the Bible, as the Higher Law of Madagascar, "that crown of the London Missionary Society."

The American Board of Commissioners for Foreign Missions, however, in 1879, declared at Syracuse, that the previous seven years in Japan furnish the most remarkable chapter in the history of the world, eclipsing not only Madagascar, but the early triumphs of Christianity. The "Lonestar" mission among the Teloogoos, almost abandoned as both helpless and fruitless in 1853, in 1878 blazed forth with a brilliancy like that of Sirius; within forty days nearly ten thousand converts were baptized. The experiences of Powell at Nanumaga, Duncan at Columbia, Judson in Burmah, Wheeler in Turkey, Johnson in Sierra Leone, Grant in Persia, Scudder in India, Wolfe in China, Mc'All in France, and David Brainerd in New Jersey, besides many more which we have not space to mention, furnish unanswerable proof that the Hand of God is in this work of modern missions.

While looking at the marvels of this missionary history, we must not forget how the subsidence of opposing systems has prepared the way for Gospel triumphs. When the first seventeen missionaries landed at Hawaii, God had gone before them, the old king was dead, the idols burned, the old pagan faith cast away as worthless, and the first death blow struck at the tabu system. The isles were waiting for His law. When McAll crossed the English Channel, the fields of France were already white for the sickle. Bouchard, Reveillaud, and others, had already forsaken Romanism, as the ally of ignorance and superstition; and a whole people were ready for a grand insurrection of thought, and resurrection of conscience. Tired of feeding on the ashes of Atheism and priestcraft, they hunger for the bread of life. God has let down the continent below the sea level. It is not so much a rising tide as a sinking land. But is His hand any the less conspicuous, when He thus floods the continents with the Gospel?—H. R.

PRESENT OBSTACLES AND OPPORTUNITIES, 1898

[Notes of remarks made in the discussion of this theme]

Rev. C. C. Baldwin, D.D., of China, said: We naturally like to look on the bright side, but it is well sometimes to look on the dark side also. It will be at least a good topic for faith. There are about a million temples in China, containing, say, from five to ten millions of idol gods. Besides these we have five hundred million manes or spirits of dead ancestors and others which are worshiped in or without the wooden tablets. The Chinese may give up the idols, but not so easily the ancestral worship. To do so is a grand test and climax of sincere faith in God, so far as a true heart surrender is concerned; for the whole practise seems to rest mainly on the beautiful doctrine of filial piety, which is dearer to them than aught else, unless we except the living family and worldly success.

Then there is the sad discouraging fact that the Chinese are gross materialists, none grosser, I am sure, in the whole world. It is an immense undertaking to them to look fairly at the moral and spiritual side, and to acknowledge fully moral distinctions, calling things by right names only. Ancestral worship and materialism are the prime difficulties in our work from the native side.

Rev. Gilbert Reid, said: There is one important obstacle in China, found not in the natives, but in ourselves, and that is the political character of Christianity, owing to the political complications with Christian nations. The Church is regarded as a political organization, backed up by foreign powers. The difficulty is in presenting Christianity in the right light. The Chinese do not see Christ as the loving, saving, helpful, uplifting friend. When they do see Christ as He is, He will be accepted.

J. C. Hepburn, D.D., Japan, said: The principal obstacles to missionary work in Japan are:

1. The intense nationalism of the Japanese and their superstitious loyalty to the Mikado.

2. The strong anti-foreign spirit of the people, and their regarding Christianity as a foreign religion, revolutionary and subversive to their inherited customs.

3. The influence of Buddhism, and the strenuous efforts made by the priests to antagonize Christianity, even adopting the methods used by Protestant missionaries in their work.

4. But the greatest of all obstacles is the natural repugnance of the human heart to the Gospel of Christ.

Mrs. J. T. Whitney, Micronesia: While in the Marshall Islands (with my husband, Rev. J. T. Whitney) I was trying to persuade a native young man to go as a teacher to another island. He said: " We Marshall Islanders are not like white people—we love our relatives and our homes." No wonder he said it, when he had seen so many white men who were mere driftwood. To counteract the influence of these low white men was one of the greatest obstacles in these islands.

Rev. J. L. Bruce, Brazil: The greatest obstacle in Brazil is the fact that we have a strongly organized Roman Catholic Church opposed to us. The Roman Catholics do not hold the simple truth nor the simple lie, but the truth mixed with the lie, or the truth perverted. Also, religion and morality have been thoroughly divorced, so that gross immorality and thorough devotion may exist in the same person. They think they have just what we wish to give them. On the other hand, our great difficulty is that we will undertake to combat a church by a church.

Rev. Wm. M. Nichol, Egypt: The obstacles in the line of work in Egypt are many, but let me mention these three: The learning of the Arabic language is difficult because of its many guttural sounds. The prevailing religion is Moslem, and it is hard to fight against, because it is a mixture of truth and error. Another difficulty is the position given to woman. She is liable to be divorced at any time, and divorce hangs over her head like the sword of Damocles.

Rev. T. W. Woodside, Africa: There are two classes of obstacles: first, from the natives themselves—the apathy—they are so content with what they have and are; second, obstacles from without, from immoral white men, rum, and slavery. The rum is the vilest kind of stuff, made of potatoes and doctored with sulphuric acid. Then there is slavery, not only among the natives, but

also among the white men; Portuguese, Dutch, and Englishmen buy slaves. This is not only domestic, but there is also slavery on the high seas. Slaves are shipped upon the high seas. There were one hundred slaves on the steamer on which we came home. They, of course, are not called slaves, but " contract laborers." They have contracts made out by a notary public, but they are fraudulently obtained.

Rev. C. D. Campbell, Mexico: Mexico has twelve and one-half million inhabitants. There are one hundred thousand Christians. The country is open from end to end. The two principal railroads are in the hands of Americans. The mines are going into their hands, but they are not Christians. The government is friendly to missions. Two states are without Christian workers. Medical missions will pay as well in Mexico as elsewhere, will speedily become self-supporting, and there is but one medical mission in Mexico.

Miss Emily C. Wheeler, Turkey: The opportunities in Turkey are: 1. The eighty thousand orphans to bring to Christ. Fifty-two recently converted. Generally Gregorians. 2. New villages opening, never before accessible. Self-supporting. 3. Mohammedans inquiring, " Who is this Jesus who makes these Armenians so brave?" One woman wishes to unite with the church. Have read the Bible. Opportunity for us to pray that the Holy Spirit may quicken the word and they may come to Christ. Ask the people in the United States to pray and give for this—give systematically, so we shall spend for missions as we ought, and not comparatively, as we do now, when shown in inches, seven feet for liquor and a quarter of an inch for foreign missions.

Rev. Gilbert Reid, China: One opportunity in China is found in a decree issued by the emperor to allow Western branches in all examinations. This is an educational opportunity. The second is the trend of thought and policy to open up China more fully to trade, and, of course, there will be more openings to missions. Thirdly, the customs under English direction are to collect the likin tax in five of the large provinces. Where the customs men go, missionaries can go. Fourthly, Americans have special opportunities, because they are free from the suspicion of territorial aggrandizement. We go as friends.

Dr. Chalmers Martin, Laos: The special opportunity of the Laos Mission at present lies in the fact that the French officials on the Upper Mekeng (Cambodia) River are now friendly to our missionaries, and that the Roman Catholics have not yet made an entrance to the field. If we can strike in this great region now, we have a free field; when once the Jesuits have appeared there, the history of the past and of other countries tells us that our opportunity as Protestants will be more limited, if it does not disappear altogether.

Rev. G. E. Stone, Arabia: Arabia is (1) A land of possibilities. (*a*) A country much more fertile and populous than generally supposed. (b) The people are largely town people, not ignorant Bedouin. (2) Arabia is a land of opportunity. (a) Politically, only partially under Turks. The interior is independent. The eastern and southern coasts under British influence. (b) People not as bigoted as in Turkey. Preaching in streets and bazaars at Bahrein. (c) Opportunity because everything is yet to be done. Only three missionaries at present on east coast, and one on the southern coast, with the reenforcements going out this year only nine or ten missionaries for ten million people. Arabia is promised for Christ, and He will give the victory.

Rev. H. Blodget, D.D., China: The West River has recently been opened in all its length to trade and trading vessels. The Yang-tse has been opened in like manner. These rivers flow through densely populated countries, and large numbers of missionaries are needed to reach the multitudes of people. A steamer has passed through the rapids of the Yang-tse, and the fifty millions **of Sze-chuen** are now accessible by steam communication. The number of missionaries there needs greatly to be increased. The province of Hunan has now two resident missionaries. This province has been intensely hostile to foreigners. No foreign missionaries, until very lately, have been allowed to locate within its borders. They have been hunted out with insult, abuse, and violence. Here have originated the vile placards and tracts against missionaries so widely circulated in China. The twenty million of this province call for a large number of laborers. China must be converted by Chinese. Christian workers must be trained in the field, yet a large number of missionaries from western lands will be needed to form the link to convey the blessing from the church in the West to the church in the East.

Mr. B. B. Blachly, Mexico: There are now about twenty colporteurs in Mexico. The great cry is, send us more colporteurs to work from house to house. Mr. H. P. Hamilton, Bible agent at Mexico City, said that thousands more copies of the Bible could be circulated if there were more workers. The great cry of the people is, give us the Word of God. The American Bible Society *must* have help, or their society will be a thing of history.

Dr. Cyrus Hamlin, Turkey: The portion of the field of the American Board which calls loudly for occupancy is that which borders the eastern part of the Bulgarian mission, comprising a portion of the Albanian— a very brave and heroic people, for whom Christianity has hitherto done little good. The Greek Church has converted about half of them; Islam has the other half. It is a common saying that they are bad Christians and bad Moslems, but splendid soldiers. They are now accessible to one missionary in Bulgaria. There are educated native agents ready to go to them with the Bible in their own language, and with Christian education they would be gladly received. Only a few thousand dollars are needed to inaugurate a most interesting mission without demanding a single new American missionary. The native force is ready for the work.

Rev. T. W. Woodside, Africa: I read a short time ago in one of the leading missionary magazines of the new mission station at Lake Moero, and there they remarked, " Now there is a chain of mission stations right across the Dark Continent." Let me explain just what that means: From Benguela inland for two hundred and fifty miles (twelve days' journey) there is not a station, not a missionary. There a station, with two families, then four days, and you come to another station; again three days, and you come to a third station. From there you make forty camps, or forty days' journey, to the little station Kavungu, of the English mission. From there another jump of fifteen days to the Garaganze mission, where you find two lone men, missionaries; another leap of fifteen or more days to Lake Moero, and this is the " chain of mission stations." These stations are mere points, lone links, and then to the north and south are large tracts where there is not a missionary.

Rev. J. W. Baird, Turkey: Sadder than the sway of the Turk over the holy places of Christianity is the reign of spiritual death over the Eastern Church of Salonica. Tho a thriving city, it is not now " the faithful city," nor, as a thousand years ago, do missionaries of the Gospel take the light of the Gospel to surrounding peoples. There is no preaching or other means of spiritual enlightenment. Education is coming in very rapidly. The Gospel can find an entrance. To the west of Macedonia are the Albanians, a most promising people, entirely without the Gospel. Servia and Bosnia, too, need missionary work at once.—M. R. W.

THE ECUMENICAL CONFERENCE ON FOREIGN MISSIONS, 1900

More comprehensive in its scope, wider in the range of themes discussed, undoubtedly to be further reaching in its effects and of greater potentiality in every way, was the Ecumenical Conference on Foreign Missions just ended as compared with those that preceded it. Notable as were the Ecumenical Conferences at Liverpool in 1866, and at London in 1878 and 1888, the New York Conference has exceeded them all not only in attendance and universal interest but in the magnitude of the issues which were presented for consideration. Since 1889 the preparations for this congress of missionaries were in progress, and the body of pains-taking men who brought the Conference into material being will undoubtedly have the gratification of knowing that their labors will induce a widespread and long continuing revival of interest in missionary work.

That result is inevitable. Each of the former conferences was attended with such revivals, with increasing intensity, and in view of all that has been accomplished at the Convention of 1900, as it will be known, it is certain that such a stimulus will be given to the cause of missions as to bring appreciably nearer that Christian millennium upon which the followers of the Church of Christ have set their hearts and minds—the evangelization of the world. Some of the more hopeful speakers, in fact, did not hesitate to declare that if the vast interest which the Conference aroused on two continents was properly taken advantage of, this end would be attained within the next two or three generations. They demonstrated, moreover, that there was method in their optimism. It was one of the features of the conference, this combining of intellectual vigor and earnestness of purpose with practical sagacity. It was again and again proved by the aid of statistics that the conversion of the world to Christianity was not so shadowy a vista or such a far off goal as most people are likely to believe. Eugene Stock, in one of his addresses, remarked that if any one had prophesied thirty years ago that the Church Missionary Society would have so many workers in the foreign fields as it has to-day he would have been laughed at. Yet the Church Missionary Society, which at the time it was formed was one only of a few, is now only one among over five hundred societies and auxiliaries which exist in this country and in Europe.

These organizations, it was shown, possess sufficient strength and experience to guide an enterprise indefinitely larger than the present missionary operations of the Church, if they were supported with more generosity. That the money power of the Church is capable of meeting the cost of a supreme and an immediate effort to evangelize the world, was proved by the assertion that if only one-fourth of the Protestants of America and Europe gave one cent a day to this object it would yield a fund of over $100,000,000 a year. Again it would take less than one-fiftieth of the Christian young men and women who will go out from Christian colleges in the United States and Canada within this generation to furnish, according to the estimate of conservative missionaries, a sufficient force of workers to achieve the evangelization of the world in this generation.

Attention was also drawn to the fact that in considering this possibility, not only the resources but the facilities at the disposal of the Church should be taken into account. Among these, mention was made of the work of the eighty-three geographical societies which have done so much to make the world known, of the greatly enlarged and improved means of communication, and of the development of the printing press, which has multiplied the power of the Church, to disseminate the Gospel. The Bible has already been printed in about four hundred out of two thousand languages, and due attention was called to the significance of these languages being spoken by about 1,200,000,000 people, while the remaining 1,600 languages are spoken by less than 300,000,000. These were some of the statistical arguments advanced by those who addressed the Conference in support of the contention that the early evangelization of the world is something more than a chimerical hope.

Apart from its practical purpose, there was a picturesque and romantic side to the Conference. There was something particularly impressive in that gathering of over two thousand missionaries from every part of the globe. Many of them were from remote and semi-civilized parts of the earth. There were men among them who have passed years of their lives in a constant uncertainty, sacrificing all home ties to the effort of lifting their fellows to a higher plane of belief and understanding. Few of them there were but could tell of some tragedy in their lives or of dangers through which they had passed. It was this knowledge which invested the Conference with an element of romance.

In some instances the bodies of the missionaries who stood last week upon the platform pleading the cause of the heathen were literally covered with the marks of their devotion and enthusiasm. Again, there were other missionaries, old in years and with patriarchal beards, who have for so long been preaching and conversing in native dialects as to have lost the faculty of fluent expression in their own language. It was little wonder, therefore, that for the most part these devout workers in the dark lands of the world should be somewhat somber of countenance and should manifest less exuberance of spirit than people whose habitations are laid amid the brighter surroundings of modern civilization.

The brief relaxation these missionaries had from their vigils and duties was deserved, and, altho their holiday was short, they will undoubtedly return cheered and encouraged by the belief that one of the results of the Conference will be to wipe away some of the indifference with which, generally speaking, many people have regarded them. These heroes of Christianity have awakened renewed interest upon both sides of the Atlantic. They have shown to those who sit in luxury at home that theirs is in every way a strenuous life; they have won battles without shedding blood; they have settled in regions where hatred of foreigners is a predominant characteristic, and have earned honor and affection from tribes whom travelers have reported as being devoid of all instincts of humanity and incapable of appreciating kindness.

There was probably no single subject appertaining to the welfare and spread of foreign missionary work that was not considered at the Conference. Meetings were held regularly, morning, afternoon, and evening, and often as many as half a dozen or more meetings were in progress at once. By the interchange of views, opinions, suggestions, and experiences, the best means not only of converting the heathen, but of raising him mentally, of educating him and generally fitting him to take better care of himself, were thoroughly ventilated. It was agreed that the most enduring and effective method of helping the ignorant native was to place him in a position whereby he could help himself. To this end the extension of schools and industrial training was advocated. The schools already in existence, it was shown, have done a wonderful amount of work, and have directly aided in furthering Christianity. Young men and women who have been trained in these schools in turn themselves become missionaries and do excellent work among their own races.

By every speaker who touched upon the qualifications necessary for the successful missionary of the future, it was maintained that only a thoroughly trained and equipped man or woman should be sent out to the foreign fields of work. The importance of medical missions was made particularly prominent. Medical missions, according to every voice that was heard upon the subject, are the pioneers and permanent agencies of evangelism. They can be planted where no other branch of evangelical work is possible. Heathens who fall sick are anxious for the ministrations of the white doctor, foreign tho he be, and consequently the medical worker has access to vast numbers who otherwise would have no intercourse with missionaries. Some of the speakers, indeed, went so far as to contend that no missionary should be sent out who had not some knowledge of medicine. The value of such a knowledge as a branch of evangelistic work in countries of intense prejudice, like China, was dilated upon. It has been almost solely due to women medical missionaries who have gone out to China that it has been possible to reach the Chinese women. It constantly happens that after the native doctors have failed to effect a cure with their incantations, burning of red paper, and other devices peculiar to them, the medical missionary has been appealed to. By that means alone has it been possible to obtain access to that most difficult of all places—the Chinese home.

Having secured that foothold, the medical missionary, after first giving physical relief to her patient, has then proceeded to expound the Gospel to her. By this means

only has it been possible to reach the thousands of native women who now profess Christianity. And it has been made clear during the last two weeks that the efficacy of a medical training as an adjunct to evangelistic work applies with as much force to other countries as it does to China.

One of the most significant of all the lessons that the Conference has served to teach has been the perfect comity which exists between all Protestant churches in mission work. From first to last representatives of all Protestant denominations sat and discussed great religious problems without a note of discord. It was an eloquent testimony to the harmony and unity of effort which prevails among them, so far as the Christianizing of the Pagan world is concerned. Undoubtedly not the least of the commendable results which will be the outcome of the Conference will be an even better mutual understanding among the various denominations than has hitherto existed. This will tend to prevent the overlapping and duplication of churches, as has sometimes happened in certain missionary districts. During the entire life of the Conference, denominationalism was totally forgotten and only the essentials of Christianity considered. In every paper that was read and in every address that was delivered there was a refreshing absence of anything approaching intolerance or dogmatism. Even when opinions or views differed there was uniform courtesy, and individualism gave way to catholicity.

Yet another notable feature of the Conference of which mention should not be omitted was the interest which it aroused in the laity. It is doubtful if there has ever been a convention open to both sexes where so many women have attended. Moreover, day after day there were present at the meetings men and women of all phases of life. Beginning with President McKinley and Governor Roosevelt, who welcomed the missionaries for the country and State respectively, the meetings have been attended by men who stand the highest in business, finance and the professions. They have given the most zealous attention to the work of the Conference, and it is reasonable to suppose that there has been inculcated in them a broader view of foreign missions than they held before.

" It is not opportunity men want; it is fire," Phillips Brooks once said, and that the New York Ecumenical Conference has succeeded in giving a warm and fervent stimulus to missions, time will unquestionably show.—N. Y. T.

EXTRACTS FROM ADDRESSES BEFORE THE ECUMENICAL CONFERENCE, 1900

The *Rev. Dr. James S. Dennis* read a report upon Centennial Statistics. The report contained the following figures:

Societies directly engaged in conducting foreign missions number 249, distributed as follows: United States, 49; England, 42;

Asia, 29; Africa, 28; Australasia and Oceania, 26; Germany, 15; Netherlands, 10; Canada, 8; Sweden, 7; West Indies, 11; Scotland, 7; Ireland and Norway, 4 each; Denmark, 3; France and Switzerland, 2 each; Wales and Finland, 1 each. The total income was $17,161,092, England leading off with $6,843,031; the United States, $5,403,-048; Germany, $1,430,151; Scotland, $1,280,-684. The total number of missionaries, including ordained physicians, lay missionaries, married women not physicians, unmarried women not physicians, is 13,607, divided as follows: England, 5,136; the United States, 4,110; Germany, 1,515; Scotland, 653. The different departments are in much the same proportion, tho there are some interesting points.

The *Rev. Dr. Arthur T. Pierson,* in speaking upon the " Superintending Providence of God in Foreign Missions," said:

He has opened the doors and made sea and land the highways for national intercourse and the avenues to national brotherhood. He has multiplied facilities for worldwide evangelization, practically annihilating time and space, and demolishing even the barriers of language. The printing and circulating of the Bible in four hundred tongues reverses the miracle of Babel and repeats the miracle of Pentecost. Within the last century the God of battles has been calling out His reserves. Three of the most conspicuous movements of the century have been the creation of a new regiment of medical missions, the Woman's Brigade and the Young People's Crusade. The organization of the Church army is now so complete that but one thing more is needful, namely, to recognize the invisible Captain of the Lord's hosts as on the field, to hear His clarion call summoning us to the front, to echo His word of command; and, in the firm faith of His leadership, pierce the very center of the foe, turn his staggering wings and move forward as one united host in one overwhelming charge.

The *Rev. J. Fairley Daly* asked two questions: " What has God been doing for foreign missions?" and " What have you been doing?" Then he answered them himself. In showing what God has been doing he said, among other things:

One hundred years ago the total sum subscribed by Protestant churches for foreign missionary work did not exceed $50,000. God has so opened His people's hearts that they now give $15,000,000. There were then only fifty missionaries, all men; now there are 10,500 of both sexes. There were then no native preachers, now there are 4,000. There were then about 100 native mission workers, now there are 7,000. There were then about 7,000 native communicants, now there are 1,500,000.

When Mr. Daly came to answer the second question he said he would not speak for America, but would only say that his own country spent in four days for strong drink an amount equal to that which it gave for foreign missions in one year, and

expended on tobacco in one month what it gave to foreign missions in twelve. Such puny efforts to spread the Gospel, he declared, were appalling.

Mr. Eugene Stock, editorial secretary of the Church Missionary Society, London, in a comprehensive address, reviewed the growth of missionary work during the last century. In part he said:

In rapidly surveying the missionary history of the nineteenth century let us take it in four periods of twenty-five years each. The early years of the century saw the establishment of two of the great missionary organizations, the British and Foreign Bible Society in 1800, and in 1810 the American Board of Commissioners. Two great struggles in the British Parliament marked the early years of the century, both of which had an important influence upon the missionary enterprise. In both cases it was William Wilberforce, the greatest Christian statesman England has produced, who led the Christian party to victory. In 1807 he carried the abolition of the British slave trade. In 1813 he compelled the East India Company to open the doors of India to missions. England from being the chief kidnapper of Africans became their deliverer. China missions began in 1807 with the going forth of Robert Morrison. New Zealand owes the Gospel to Samuel Marsden, who visited the cannibal islands in 1814.

The second quarter was a period of progress among the simpler races of the world. Missions spread rapidly among South Africans, in the Polynesian Islands, among the West Indies negroes and the simpler villagers of India. Alexander Duff, the mighty Scotchman, invented a new method to reach the higher classes and castes in India by the offer of a good English education. China's doors were at last ajar before the second quarter had run its course.

We are accustomed to think of Protestant missions being a century old or more, and we fail to realize how great a part of our progress has been achieved during the last fifty years. In 1850 there were in Africa no Niger Mission, no Congo Mission, no Zambesi Mission, no Nyassa Mission, no Tanganyika Mission, no Uganda Mission, no North African Mission. Moreover, there was no Japan Mission, no Corea Mission, no New Guinea Mission, no missions in the far north of Northwest Canada, no Melanesian Mission, no South American Mission. The China missions had only just begun. India was the most advanced field, but even in India there was no native church organization and none of the great missions. The long barred gates of Japan were gently pushed open by Commodore Perry in 1854.

The third quarter of the century was notable for martyr deaths in the mission field. Besides many missionaries and native Christians cruelly murdered in the Indian Mutiny, the southern hemisphere was especially stained with the blood of Christ's servants. The great Northwest mission of the Dominion of Canada, a vast field, was opened during this quarter.

The immense advance of the missionary spirit in England in the last twenty-five years —I cannot speak of America—is due in the main to the influence of evangelistic and spiritual movements in the Church at home. I refer to Mr. Moody's great campaigns of 1874-75 and 1882-84, the parochial mission movement, the Mildmay Conference, the Keswick Convention and the Children's Special Service Mission. In more recent years the most striking sign of the awakening has been the Student Volunteer Movement.

President Capen, of the American Board said, in part:

It is too late in the century to ask whether or not foreign missions pay, but it is always in order to ask the question how much they pay.

Perhaps we shall understand this a little better if we go back in imagination to the beginning of this century, when the American Board, the oldest of our foreign missionary societies, was born. The United States had just secured its independence. France was our ally, and everything that was French was popular, and the worst of it was French infidelity. We read that Yale University, which we are accustomed to think of now as the center of religious life, was a hotbed of infidelity and old Princeton only had one Christian student. Christianity, the religion of this country, one hundred years ago was at a very low ebb, and it was not much better in other nations. There were but seven foreign missionaries at the beginning of the century, employing only 170 male missionaries.

Now look about us and see the change! Let me call your attention to Hawaii. It is only eighty years ago last September since the first mission work was begun on that island. When the missionaries went there and saw the natives they almost doubted whether or not they were human beings. They found them eating raw fish with the dogs, and then, eating the dogs.

I want to call your attention to the heroism exhibited among the missionaries, which is equal to those of the martyrs of the first century. You have heard of Miss Shattuck. Everett P. Wheeler, of New York, said that Miss Shattuck stood for all the United States Government stood for—righteousness and law—and when a howling Mussulman mob tried to enter her schoolhouse she interposed the dignity of womanhood and the power of consecration. We speak of the early heroes, Carey and Judson, and we take no laurels from their brow when we speak of our missionary heroes and heroines of the present day. Our Nation had a Farragut, but we do not forget our Dewey, or our Sampson, or Captain Philip. This country had a Sedgwick and a Kearny, but we do not forget Lawton.

However we may feel about what is going on in the Philippine Islands, the blood of every American flowed a little quicker when he heard General Funston say, when an order was sent to him by a superior officer asking how long he could hold the place, replied, "Until we are mustered out." Our missionaries are doing that very same thing, and with no regiment back of them. Now, my point is this: That if a nation builds monuments to its heroes our Church should not forget its heroes and heroines.

An American bishop has told us that one educated Christian man will counteract the influence of a thousand illiterate and vicious men. If that is so, the million pupils in our schools now are a match for the billion of heathen, and in a very few years this million of pupils will pass out and another million will take their places. I pass by what missions have done for science with the single sentence that every missionary station is a scientific observatory. When the Gospel of the Son of God gets into a place it is a death blow to despotism. When a man becomes a child of God he wants everything that is Christian—Christian clothing, Christian furniture, Christian agricultural implements, and everything Christian. We have the motto that "Trade always follows the flag," but it is not true, as I could show you if I had the time; but this is true: "Trade always follows the missionary." That is proved true in the case of Hawaii. In 1843 the exports were $227,000 in Hawaii; last year they were $10,000,000. The total trade of those islands sixty years ago was less than $300,000. Last year it was $27,000,000.

Now, I am willing to admit that this is not the highest kind of an argument to appeal for missions, but I do say when we have men going around sneering and saying there isn't any good in foreign missions, it is well to have a few facts of this kind to throw at them to show how ignorant they are.

We all know the state of unrest throughout the world, just as it was apparently when Jesus came. Japan and China had their war, and China woke up. America had its war with Spain, and we are a world Power to-day as never before. Russia is pressing through Siberia into China, and the storm center is now in the China seas. There are three great nations in the world—the Teutonic, which embraces the Anglo-Saxon; the Latin and the Slav. I think the Latin are on the wane, and the battle is between the Slav and the Anglo-Saxon.

As to our duty: We have an open world, and we have, as President Angell has said, the men ready. The great need now is for money to help carry on this work. Besides money we need Christian statesmanship of the highest order. We want to confederate our work at home and abroad, so as to be able to strike the hardest blow possible. The greatest phenomenon of this century is the passion of men to save humanity, inspired by love of the Lord Jesus Christ. Let us press on. Let us give the money for this grand work, and God will consecrate it, and God will give us the victory.

The *Rev. Dr. George F. Pentecost* particularly emphasized the relations of the home Church to foreign missions. He said:

First, I would dwell upon the progress of the world during the nineteenth century. More has been accomplished in both material and spiritual lives during the last one hundred years than in all the centuries preceding since the birth of Christ.

This cannot be more distinctly shown than by statistics. One hundred years ago there were less than twenty foreign missionaries, only five mission stations and not even one thousand converts from paganism. Now there are 6,387 male missionaries, 6,287 female missionaries and 61,887 native helpers, all of whom are commissioned in the work by home churches. There are now 5,207 mission stations and 15,506 auxiliary posts. The annual expenditure of the home churches for foreign missions reaches the sum of $17,000,000. As a result there are now two million native communicants and ten million native adherents to the Church.

The greatest results of foreign missions are to be found in India. The religion of the Hindoos is a rock-ribbed and a rock-based belief, but the impact of Christianity has broken it into a dozen fragments. In Bengal, where more than seventy millions of people reside, there is one shattered remnant. In the Punjab there is another. Here one million have broken away from the old chains of caste. In Bombay is another religious faction, and so in different parts of the empire there are different schisms.

Thus it may be said that the missionaries in heathen lands have thus far been digging under ground, preparatory to a great over-turning. They are now doing a work similar to the undermining of Hell Gate. The great upheaval is soon to follow. To the eye not much appears to have been done, but deep down great influences are at work.

There are a million non-Protestants in this city. We ask for the reason. It is because of social distinctions. It is because of the crystallization of these people in their old habits of thought. But this is no reason why we should not go forth into foreign fields. It is by exporting that the imports of a nation are increased. That has been the experience of our own country. We should put into the virgin soil of pagan lands the plow of Christianity, where the harvest will be plentiful and the ultimate returns will be still more abundant.

The *Rev. Dr Maltbie D. Babcock* emphasized especially the demands of the new century. He said in part:

The true Christian cannot get away from foreign missions. The preachings of Jesus Christ were to all peoples. He exhorted His disciples to go unto the uttermost parts of the earth. Thus we must forget our prejudices against this race or that race, the Jew or the Italian. All are equal in the eyes of the Creator. Selfishness, the unwillingness to impart good to others, is the greatest curse which can rest upon humanity. And we must remember that we, too, are of pagan blood. Our ancestors were as savage and as needful of Christianity as these pagans among whom these missionaries are laboring in the dark East.—N. Y. T.

SERMONS AND OUTLINES

THE MISSIONARY FIELD

By R. S. Storrs, D.D.

The field is the world.—Matt. xiii: 38

It is always profitable, when one has gained the particulars of a subject that engages his attention, to secure one broad, general view of the whole, by which the particulars are themselves interpreted, co-ordinated and unified in a single impression.

After reading a book, paragraph by paragraph, page by page, I have found it advantageous at the end to read again the table of contents, and thus acquire one definite conception of all I have followed out in detail. You enter a European cathedral. The portal attracts you, the pillar, the capital, the arch, the chapel, the great and brilliant apse; but to obtain a satisfying and permanent impression, you select a point, within or without, where you can see the details in a grand unity; and this is the image you carry away. Or you may wander in the country at summer-tide, enjoy the meadow, the brook, the gentle hill, and the shadow of the forest; but it is from some elevation from which your eye sweeps the whole scene, that you detect the interrelation of each part with every other, and gain an impressive picture of the whole. So with the subject of Christian Missions before us. With its individual aspects we are familiar. We are acquainted with individual missionaries and their respective missions. Let us now look at the whole field. What is it? The Master says: "*The field is the world.*"

All parts and all peoples are included. No race is so savage and none so cultured as to be excepted. The Gospel is for the whole world; and that is a wider field to-day than when the New Testament was written. Beyond Roman cities and colonies little was then known of the world. It is not four hundred years since this hemisphere was known. Now, explorations are pushed in every quarter of the globe. No parts are unknown save those fenced in by ice, and even against these frozen barriers the energy

of modern enterprise is continually precipitated, to force a passage amid those Arctic
solitudes where no human foot has yet
walked.

Religion was once a divisive force, for the
very zeal with which early nations clung
to their own worship led them to look on
other religions with hostility. Buddhism, indeed, spread to contiguous nations; but
Christianity alone has overleaped all tribal
and racial bounds, and encircled the earth
in its beneficent sway, making itself welcome to communities who have seen in
it a character and culture they had never
known before. God has now wonderfully
prepared the earth for its progress, as
truly as He did in the early centuries by
the dispersion of believers, by the supremacy
of the Roman power and the Greek tongue.
By steam and by electricity the ends of the
earth are now nearer each other than were
Boston and Berlin a few years ago. Enormous changes, swift and dazzling—mighty
as well as swift—are as signal a preparative
for the conquests of grace as if God's own
hand had opened a passage amid the stars!

What is the purpose of all this? To make
the Gospel familiar to every man. Why?
To meet his immortal aspirations; to save
the soul. But some say that the heathen
will be saved without the Gospel, if they live
up to the inner light already imparted. The
testimony, not only of missionaries, but of
those who have lived among the heathen for
secular ends, is this: they are besotted, they
do not live up to this light, they do not seek
life through repentance, but grovel in lust
and in personal indulgence. The Gospel
comes as a new discovery. God is a Being
to be loved, as well as feared. New affections and purposes and aspirations are
awakened. The results are seen in character.
The command of God comes to each: " Thou
shalt love the Lord thy God." Thus society
is leavened. This renovation of the souls
of men is the first work aimed at. Then
there follows an intellectual impulse through
the truth, by argument and appeal, by proverb and by song, by library and school, by
philanthropic and political endeavor. All
things become new. As Correggio made the
manger bright by the illumination reflected
from the face of the infant Jesus, so the
Bible has illuminated society by its reflected
light, wherever it has been placed.

We owe all we have to this peerless, priceless boon: all that is sweetest and noblest
in social life, and all that is freest and most
prophetic in our political institutions. Our
ancestors were savages, feeding on roots and
acorns, worshiping gods of the storm and
pestilence, and sunk in moral debasement.
Our present civilization we owe to Christianity. Two centuries ago the site of many
a New England village of to-day was an
Indian hunting-ground. The personal and
social prosperity now witnessed there, the
beautiful family life, the sweetness, happiness, and hope enjoyed, are the fruitage of
the Gospel. Such results are more conclusive than mere abstract arguments. This

work of individual and social renewal we
are to undertake for all nations. He is mean
who does not desire to be useful to others.
As one draws near to the close of life, he
feels an intense enthusiasm; for as the days
are fewer they appear more precious. So
it will be if we recognize our privilege to
transmit the blessings we enjoy—the fruit
of sacrifice and service through centuries
past—to generations yet to come. Standing
on soil hallowed by noble lives, it will be
ignoble, ignominious, if we do not eagerly
engage in this godlike work. As we, by acts
of charity and love, make other lives brighter,
we shall deepen the sense of immortality
within ourselves and in others.

Then there is the most potential motive of
all—the love of Christ. He who has seen
Him and felt His presence and comfort in
darkness and trouble; who has heard when
standing under cloudy heavens the inspiring
voice of the Redeemer: " Fear not; I have
found a ransom for thee in my own blood
and life "—he has a motive for toilful and
continuous endeavor. Do you ask, How?
By what means? Your gifts, your voice,
your example may aid. He who illustrates
the Gospel in his life, unsoiled in the midst
of temptation, neither unduly elated by prosperity nor depressed by trial, he is an eloquent preacher of righteousness. The printing press is a means, and educational institutions as well; also efforts for the salvation of seamen, and many other methods
that reach out far beyond our own hand.
The finger of a child may move a lever to
set in motion the machinery of a mill. You
send written messages across the sea by a
steamer which you have not builded, along
railway lines you have not laid, through
mountains you did not tunnel; and so you
may, by the machinery of some society, set
in motion the water of life, or circulate the
messages of grace through wide and remote regions. They are unwise who speak
contemptuously of "machinery," for it
clothes and feeds us, it prints our books,
it carries us from city to city, it ornaments
and gives value to life. So the organized
work of such a society as the American
Board—carried on now for nearly five and
seventy years—is a blessed and beautiful
work, historic and honored. This board has
sent out as many consecrated men and
women as any, and instrumentally sent
thousands to heaven, and is an heir of their
prayer and blessing. It asks our gifts—not
small, but large gifts—because it needs them.
The cost of administration is a very small
percentage of the amount received.

And do you ask, " What is the prospect of
success? " Some scoff, and say that these
efforts are as futile as the attempt to stay
a stream by scattering on its bosom a handful of autumn leaves. Said one to me: " I
have lived in China. Your missionaries are
good men; but in one place, after much labor,
they made but two converts, and one of
them got into jail." It is easy to point to
failures, and we can also point out conspicuous successes. Chinese literature, its

ethics and classics, have been translated into modern tongues by the missionaries. They have there and everywhere enlarged the sphere of knowledge. It is one function of Christianity to reverse the curse of Babel. Pride scattered men, and the humble in Christ are united to all others by means of the Gospel in every land and language. The missionary is loved and honored by those who have been blessed by his work. That work will be successful. The Gospel that has lifted Germany, and England, and America, will not crack under the strain of the world. To it we may trace the blessings already enjoyed, and from it greater still may flow. Our Magna Charta, our Bill of Rights, our United States Constitution, we may trace to the leaves of the Bible brought to England by a pious monk from Rome; and this Gospel is to fill the earth. Our Lord has said that all power in heaven and earth is His, and that He will be with us alway to the end. What audacious blasphemy, if He be only man! Either this is a celestial voice, or that of one who is foolish and insane. There is no room to doubt. The same power that subdued Rome and evangelized barbarian Europe, and has ennobled our own civilization, will go on from victory to victory! You may believe it or not; it will make no

difference. The papers may sneer at the missionary cause, but it will make no difference. The Gospel is to conquer the earth! Now the question is, Will you take part? Not in this agency alone; but will you cooperate with God Himself? You do that when you turn coal to gas, and water to steam; when you make iron to swim and wire to talk; but in a grander sense you strike hands with God when you undertake work for Him in the field which is the world. This service makes life noble indeed. Nothing I saw or heard at our recent Long Meadow Centennial impressed me so much as the sight of an elderly lady and her sweet voice, as she bore loving testimony to the gladness of her service for Christ during many years in the Ottoman Empire. Before her friends, those who knew her in girlhood, she affirmed that there was no life so beautiful and precious as that of a missionary—a missionary woman amid Moslem or pagan civilization.

Animated by such an exalted, intrepid, heroic consecration, life will be illuminated with the brightness of immortality. Power will be glorified, and money itself will take on something of the beauty of heaven, shining, as it were, like bits of the golden pavement in the city of our God!—H. R.

THE MISSIONARY IDEA

By Charles H. Fowler, D.D.

As my Father hath sent me, even so send I you.—John xx: 21

The missionary idea came into the world with Christianity itself. Christ came needed, but hardly wanted. He was sent into the world, a missionary from heaven to earth. He came to emphasize and to illustrate God's infinite longing for the salvation of men. There is no thought so worthy our continued reflection as this supremest thought of God concerning our race. It is the one idea which God saw fit to utter. For this idea time continues its flight, and the earth continues to revolve; for its utterance God broke the silence of eternity, and came out and declared it, that, through the ages, we might know the center of His great purpose concerning men. We ourselves are not wont to put on it this emphasis, but, busied with the little piece of the divine garden under our eye, we only glance occasionally at the larger field, the world. Let us, therefore, return to and linger over this, the divine idea—the missionary idea. It is not the fruit of philosophy. Perhaps an argument might have been made on the grounds of human reason, but I assume your belief in the supernatural origin of the Gospel, in the Deity of Christ, the regeneration of man by the Holy Ghost, and the other verities of Christianity. " Go ye, *therefore*." Look back a little at the reach of this thought: Christ had lived and taught; had spent days in blessing the humble poor, and nights in prayer in moun-

tain solitudes; had looked into the hungry souls of the people, and felt their needs. He had been rejected by His own; had been betrayed by priest and disciple; had struggled in the garden, and confronted there the enemy of our souls; had borne the scourging, the hissing, hooting, and spitting; had staggered under the beam of the cross, died on Calvary, gone into our sepulcher, and risen more than conqueror, shouting, " Lift up, ye gates!" He had spoken the words of peace to His disciples, and breathed on them the breath of power, and now stands on Olivet, His little Church about Him, which He has taught and inspired. Angels beckon Him. With outstretched hands He says that all power is His, and bids them, therefore, to go out everywhere and teach all nations. Then do the heavens receive Him.

It seems that the conditions, under which this command was given, invest it with supreme binding authority over us. The Lord was organizing His forces, preparing the way for His kingdom. The Comforter was promised. Material obstacles were to be removed, and perils from men—even from viper or poison—were averted. All power was His; *therefore* they were to go—go into all the earth—tarrying not. But, in course of time, somehow, the spirit of the mission which they had undertaken seemed to be misunderstood. Paul is raised up and sent to the Gentiles. Thirty years after the ascension he expands the missionary idea, and says: " If any man have not the spirit of Christ, he is none of His." Christ came to minister, not to be ministered unto. Tho rich, He, for our sakes, became poor. Human birth, or position, or power, is nothing without the Spirit of the Master. This searching idea Christ, through Paul, impressed upon the Church. Then, through the generations it labored and suffered; its martyrs and confessors witnessed till the aged John, who had felt the throb of Jesus' breast—a son of thunder and of light and love—wrote the text, " As the Father hath sent me, even so send I you." God seemed to see the people dull, omitting the divinest truth of all, failing to grasp the missionary idea in its completeness. The heralds of the Lord are to go—go in the spirit of Jesus, and go, as Christ Himself was sent by the Father, embodying His divine, self-sacrificing love.

Calvary is a mystery to me; its vision is incomprehensible. I cannot understand how that the shoulders that bore the world should sink beneath the cross; how that the hand that held the globe should hang from a felon's spike. Yet I see the blind, the leper, the demoniac, healed and the dead raised; I hear the words, " He that hath seen me hath seen the Father," and my soul responds, " My Lord and my God ! " So I have assurance that the Son of man has power on earth to forgive sins. Behind Calvary, beneath the cross, older than the book, the sacrament, the sacrifice, the ceremonial—all the panorama of redemption—is the eternal love of God, who proposes to save man by the Redeemer, the Holy Spirit and the ministry of His Church. This love, which stoops to the guilt and need of man, is an infinite, shoreless ocean, beyond our thought or description. Here is the missionary idea. To apologize for it, is to apologize for Calvary, which is its expression.

We infer:—

I. That there exists, in the hearts of many, A LACK OF CONVICTION of the necessity which is put upon us to send the Gospel to the heathen. " God will take care of the heathen, and can save them without our assistance," it is said. But, if He has made any plan about their salvation, it will be as merciful as any we could make. It is folly to put our maudlin sympathy against His statements. Again, if He could save part of the race without a Redeemer, it might have been possible to save us, to save all, without the needless tragedy enacted on Calvary. No; it is a necessity for us, and for all, to accept the provisions which God has made. But you say that it is the blackest Calvinism to affirm that there are to be lost, because they failed in doing what they had no knowledge of. I answer that we are to be judged according to the light we have. Men everywhere vary in the delicacy of their moral sensibilities, as in other things; but each is judged according to what he has, and not according to what he has not, received. We

read in Romans, first chapter, that the invisible things of God " are clearly seen, being understood by the things that are made, so that they are *without excuse!* " This is spoken of the cultured Romans. The wrath of God was revealed upon them. You see their chances of heaven.

II. It is said, " WE HAVE HEATHEN AT HOME." We have not. There are, indeed, a few Chinese or Japanese here, of soft tread and unreplying tongue, but the objector does not refer to them. He refers to our English-speaking population. Now I affirm that the worst men have a great deal of knowledge of the truth. Go to the lowest ward of New York city, at the darkest hour of the night, and select a dozen cut-throats, and I am ready to say that these have more intellectual knowledge of God than any dozen heathen in any age or race, even if you include Plato, Socrates, and Confucius. These live among Sabbaths, sanctuaries, Christians, and some of them have been in our Sunday-schools. They are going to the bad because they will, yet they know better.

III. " IT COSTS." Yes, and the gift of God cost an infinite self-sacrifice. It is a part of the plan. We are to enter this co-partnership of sacrifice and service with this understanding. Mere faith in certain doctrines does not make stalwart Christians. Perfect love and trust do not make a young convert a ripe Christian in a minute. He may be clean, but yet in babyhood. He first has milk and then meat. An infant that could talk Greek or Hebrew would be a monstrosity; and so is he who, just converted, fancies himself a stalwart Christian, able to instruct aged saints in the knowledge of God. There are first the blade and the stalk, then full corn in the ear. Character is builded slowly, and by varied processes, among which are those of toil, trial, and self-sacrifice.

Again—

IV. Remember the FACILITIES WE NOW HAVE FOR THIS WORK. A few days' ride in a Pullman car to the Golden Gate, and a few days on the Pacific, and you are in the field at little wear or weariness. We are, by means of the telegraph, brought within speaking-distance of the laborers. Your gift to one of them beyond the Himalayas is thus received the day before you give it. It can be announced and acknowledged in forty seconds. More than this, the Gospel does succeed. Rome gave our white-haired Saxon sires the Gospel when they were savages. They sent a deputation, and, under the sky, heard the message, refusing to go within walls, or beneath a roof, lest they be bewitched. These barbarians were too low to be sold even as Roman slaves. The Feejee Islands have one hundred and two thousand attendants on public worship, out of one hundred and twenty thousand population. The Sandwich Islands were evangelized at a cost of a million and a quarter, and every year our business with them yields a profit of five millions. Yes, missions pay—they pay in every way—grandest of all, in the building of character. The patriot dies for his country, and the martyr for the cause he loves, and we revere their memory. Noblest of all are the triumphs of the grace of God in converted souls.

See yonder multitude in a Chinese city, gathered about a converted heathen who is preaching Christ! He stands on a box, and proclaims the word of life. A mob gather and drag him away, beat him with bamboo rods till blood flows from his face and back. He washes his stripes in a brook outside the town, adjusts his torn garments, prays for guidance, and returns. A second time he is pulled down from his position and beaten till he is left for dead. He recovers, returns, and is a third time seized, to be killed, but the police rescue him and place him in jail. From the barred window he speaks to the crowd once more, using the words of Paul, " None of these things move me, neither count I my life dear unto me." Is not his a grand character? Will you remain a forty-year-old baby, or aim to be a man, strong and stalwart, and made perfect through sac-

rifice and suffering if need be? Such a one, pounded by foes, scarred and cut from head to foot, yet with the vigor of an indwelling Christ, may stand before the King, who will say, " See what My grace has done! " God wants such heroic saints. Will you be one? Christ says: " Come unto me, and I will give you rest." You can't earn it or buy it. " I will *give* you rest." But hear! " Take my yoke upon you, and learn of me . . . ye shall find rest unto your souls." Habits of obedience, service, and sacrifice, crystallize into character. Here, in these heights of consecration, is supremest rest.

Go—go, then, in His name! " Freely ye have received, freely give." This world, staggering under sin, God puts upon the heart of the Church. He could, by His omnipotent grace, save it without us, but chooses to develop character by making us co-workers with Him. As Christ was sent, so are we. Will you go? Will you send? The Lord help you to do now as you will hereafter wish that you had done.—H. R.

THE PRINCIPLE OF CHRISTIAN MISSIONS *

By A. J. F. Behrends, D.D.

We then that are strong ought to bear the infirmities of the weak, and not to please ourselves. Let every one of us please his neighbor for his good to edification. For even Christ pleased not himself.—Rom. xv: 1, 3

These words outline the philosophy of Christian Missions.

There is an " ought " here, before whose imperative even Christ bowed, an obligation transcending all positive statutes, essentially divine. There is reasonableness here, for the obligation has regard to the neighbor's good. The energy thus exerted is, by implication, effective, inasmuch as Christ Himself leads the way in its exercise. Yet is it efficient without overriding personal responsibility, for the end is edification, upbuilding in personal character.

1. Here, then, is the obligation of the Church to evangelize the world; the specific commission, so often quoted and expounded, is only the application of a universal principle antedating and underlying it—the strong ought to bear the infirmities of the weak. The obligation meets us only when moral life appears; but there it is of primary and absolute authority. Great prominence is given, in some departments of modern science, to what is called the " struggle for existence," and the consequent " survival of the fittest." Nature is regarded as a great battle-field, where the warfare is fierce, merciless, and incessant; where strength is invested with the right and the certainty of sovereignty. And it has been claimed by not a few that this law of nature is no less supreme in human life and history. The strong are entitled to rule, and before their behests

the weak are to be dumb. We cannot, however, quite make up our minds that personal force is entitled to rule. It seems to us that the world needs wise men and good men, even more than strong men. We do not despise greatness, but we feel that it ought to be the handmaid of reason and of righteousness. Our native intuitions therefore teach us that, whatever may be true in the realm of nature, where moral law is not operative, in human life strength is secondary and subordinate. It has no title to sovereignty, except in so far as sovereignty is secured in obedience to what is reasonable and right—and that is simply reaffirming the apostle's thought that strength is under the obligation of service. Our pre-eminence makes us debtors to the race. Our superior advantages are a disgrace, and will prove a curse, bitter and blighting, unless we employ them to the utmost in the service of truth and of righteousness.

There is an apparent approach to this principle in the Spencerian doctrine of the sociological law and limitation of morality. There is an industrial and political fellowship before which every man is compelled to bow; and, as the nations are brought more closely together, the imperatives of this fellowship become more authoritative. The trades supplement each other. Disaster to one means suffering to all. Civil war may stimulate trade for a season, but the overproduction

* Preached April 25, 1884, at the ordination of Rev. Mr. Dwight as missionary to Western Turkey, in connection with the American Board of Commissioners for Foreign Missions.

thus encouraged is followed by the inevitable industrial retrenchment and financial embarrassment. Selfishness is thus confronted by inherent and necessary limitations, and even prudence suggests the law of universal benevolence. But this prudential benevolence, this "egotistic altruism," is altogether different from the principle of Christian missions. It is, after all, only a refined selfishness that bids you not trample on the weak, because in so doing you injure yourself. Benevolence, on such a basis, will always be cold, narrow, calculating: it never can be spontaneous, warm, and unstinted. Ours is no such mercenary service. We are summoned to a larger and a richer life. We are under the obligation of love, as interpreted by the eternal Son of God in His voluntary sacrifice for man's redemption. His glory was incapable of increase. His power could not be augmented. He came to give His life a ransom for many. The law that the strong *ought* to bear the infirmities of the weak is no mere temporary enactment, imposed for disciplinary ends; it has its origin in the essential life of God, and its most impressive illustration in the ministry and mediation of Jesus Christ. Worldly wisdom counts the obligation a sentimental dream. It had only sneers for the Christ, as both a fanatic and a fool. It regarded the martyr as a maniac. It cannot understand the spirit that supports the foreign missionary enterprises of the Church. The principle is one and the same with that under which our Lord endured the cross—the principle of love, the law that the strong *ought* to bear the infirmities of the weak.

2. But while we emphasize the indefeasible obligation of Christian missions, we insist equally on their supreme reasonableness. We are under the law of love, and our commission bears the seal of the divine authority. The pressure is both from without and from within; but it is a double pressure, commanding the approval of the calmest reason. For the divine authority is never arbitrary, finding its sanction merely or mainly in omnipotence; every command has its sufficient, reasonable ground, even where the same cannot be clearly discerned by man's thought. And love is never a blind, unreasoning, involuntary instinct of nature. It always contemplates the worth of its object, and how that worth may be maintained, guarded, and increased. You do not love a dew-drop as you love a flower; you do not love a flower as you love a nightingale; you do not love a bird as you love a child. As the object of your affection rises in the scale of being, your love changes in kind and in degree. Love is the first and the greatest of the fruits of the Holy Spirit; it is of divine origin, and of spiritual nature; and the Spirit of God always enlightens the reason and quickens the conscience by His presence. So that love must be both intelligent and righteous. It never works blindly. It has good reasons for what it does, and it never loses sight of definite ends. Sacrifice, for its own sake, it never demands or encourages. It does not bear the infirmities of the weak sim-

ply for the sake of bearing them. It summons us to please our neighbors only for their good to edification. It is not every whim that we are to humor. It is not every wish that we are to gratify. It is not every weakness that we are to condone. We are to seek our neighbor's upbuilding in all that is good. We are so to bear his infirmities that he may shortly be able to walk alone, and be helpful to others. In a word, the spirit of Christian missions is one of faith in man, as well as of love for man. He is recognized as outranking all other orders of existence, because created in the image of God, and redeemed by the God-man, Christ Jesus. The principle of love is justified to the reason by the high doctrine, appearing in the very first pages of the Bible, articulate in all its subsequent utterances, most impressively illustrated in the incarnation, and solemnly sealed in the resurrection from the dead and the ascension into glory: that man, tho framed in body of the dust of earth, is the heir of eternity, and the child of God. Sadly has he fallen, but he is not beyond rescue. He cannot be what he ought to be, and what he may be, until the grace of Christ has renewed and sanctified him; and therefore love impels to any sacrifice and endeavor that may place this grace within his reach.

The providence of God is a living endorsement of this doctrine. The history of Christian missions vindicates the adaptation and the adequacy of the Gospel of Christ to the moral wants of man. There is a gospel of progress by colonization and elimination. The ruder races are to be gradually weeded out and supplanted by a more vigorous stock. The Indian must go to the wall, the prey of civilized vices, for whose conquest he is wanting in moral energy. The tribes of Africa are doomed. The civilizations of India and of China are corrupt and effete; they are not worth saving, and their populations must disappear before the steady march of the Anglo-Saxon, to whom belongs the world's future. Over against this ambitious and heartless speculation is the fact that Christian missions have won their most signal triumphs among the tribes and races that a worldly wisdom had come to regard as hopelessly debased, and as doomed to extinction—among fetichists and cannibals—in Australia, New Zealand, New Guinea, the Sandwich Islands, Madagascar, and last, but not least, in the Micronesian Islands—that standing miracle of Christian evangelization, where the "Morning Star," representative of our American Sunday-schools, has for many years been making its annual visits with ever-widening beneficial results. The Bible declares that man is made in the image of God, and as such is capable of redemption; and the wondrous transformation is going on before our eyes; this is the twofold and unanswerable vindication of the reasonableness of our endeavor.

3. Here the question may be raised, Is there any necessity for interference with other religions and civilizations, for an active

and organized propagandism? Why not trust to the inherent forces of human nature, in the confident assurance that these will be sufficient, ultimately, to renew the face of the earth? The law of progress is elastic; why seek to reduce it to rigid uniformity in method and result? Why not leave China, India, and Africa to work out their own regeneration in their own way, as we have done? Because *we have not done it;* because our Anglo-American civilization owes its origin, its energy, its conquering superiority, to elements that were brought into it by the missionaries of Christianity. Until they came, our ancestors were ignorant, superstitious, cruel. That human nature is under a constitutional law of ethical progress is the purest of assumptions, contradicted by all ethnic testimony. All history shows that until the time of Christ the moral degeneracy of the world was rapid, continuous, and universal; and since then, the path has been an upward one only for those nations who have received the Gospel. Elsewhere the darkness still deepens, and no native prophets appear, clear of vision and strong of hand, to lift the millions from the grave of spiritual death. The Brahmo Somaj of India, under the leadership of Keshub Chunder Sen, has seemed to not a few prophetic of a near national self-regeneration. It repudiates alike Christianity and Hinduism, presenting as its creed a strange mixture of Oriental philosophy and Christian ideas. It reminds one of the ancient Gnosticism, in which both Christianity and the Greek philosophy were supposed to have found their higher interpretation and final reconciliation. The Indian Gnosticism finds its chief value in the confession that the East needs a new religion. National pride succumbs with difficulty; it would save at least a few fragments from the ruins of the Indian temples, incorporating them with the new Christianity to which Asia is to give birth; but the stone has smitten the colossal image of Indian heathenism, and there can be no cessation in the mighty moral and spiritual revolution until the Christianity of the New Testament is dominant throughout the great peninsula. And what India needs, Japan and China and Africa must have. They will not regenerate themselves. The forces requisite to produce such a result are not lodged in human nature. They must come from above. They must be carried abroad by those who have been made partakers of the heavenly light and life. The Gospel of Christ, in our hands, is the flaming torch that is to dissipate the world's darkness, and the mighty hammer under whose blows its chains are to be broken and its prisons demolished.

4. I have tried to set forth and vindicate the unconditional obligation, the inherent reasonableness, and the historical necessity of Christian missions. The strong ought to bear the infirmities of the weak. Such is the order of history, the law of reason, and the life of God. But the principle does not regard its beneficiaries as objects merely of pity, but as subjects of moral discipline. They are weak, not by misfortune, but by guilt. The actual preaching of the Gospel does not inaugurate for them the period of moral probation; the law is written on their hearts, conscience is active in the accusing and excusing thoughts, the truth is held down in unrighteousness, and they are without excuse. Heathenism discloses no organic law of ethical progress; it is not a stage in religious development; it is an equally fatal mistake to imagine that the unevangelized nations are innocent children of nature, or the irresponsible waifs of misfortune. They are men, and we must deal with them as men. Their slumbering and paralyzed manhood, drugged and weakened by deliberate wickedness, must be roused and quickened. Their spiritual personality, their original, constitutional, and indivisible moral accountability must be persistently recognized and addressed. They can enter the kingdom of heaven only through the strait gate, where the eternal law convinces them of sin and judgment. Remembering this, our task is immensely simplified, and the simplicity of method prepares the way for greater intensity and concentration in execution. It is not our business to inaugurate for any man the period of moral agency. With that, and with all conditioned upon it, we have absolutely nothing to do. Nor are we summoned to assume the moral, educational, and industrial activity of those to whom we carry the Gospel. They must, as men like unto ourselves, under the leadership of Christ, work out their own salvation. It is our sole business to make men the disciples of Christ. It is not our duty to educate them, or to emancipate them, or to civilize them, but to Christianize them. Culture, political liberty, industrial improvement, will follow; but none of the products of Christian civilization will come to stay until Christianity has taken root; and then they will come without foreign pressure. It was a timely utterance of President Angell, at Detroit, a few weeks since, made all the more impressive by the history of our American missions, when, speaking in behalf of China, he said: " The great empire will not receive and keep your locomotives and telegraphs until she has bowed the knee to your Christ. She will not yield her ancient civilization until she has surrendered her religion." We believe in schools, in literature, in deliverance from political tyranny, in social improvement; but all these must be the spontaneous outgrowth of something deeper and more radical—the life of the Holy Ghost in the souls of men. The tree must be planted before the fruits can be eaten.

5. And yet the simplicity and directness of our task also adds to its difficulty. For it is easier to carry a child than to teach it the use of its own feet. It is easier to do something for your neighbor than to spur him to help himself. It is easier to feed a beggar than to induce him to eat the bread of his own earning. It would be easy to cover the globe with a network of schools; to set up a printing press in every city and town; to

build a church for every thousand of the world's inhabitants. That would require only money. But the change would be nominal and apparent only. The hidden life must be stirred to mighty and continuous action, and that requires wisdom and patience even more than generosity. And so the question, than which none can be more momentous, recurs: "Is there sufficient energy behind the law whose authority binds us, whose reasonableness commands our hearty approval, whose necessity is apparent?" Is there any good hope of success? The task to which we are summoned is one of unparalleled boldness,

requiring the loftiest faith, the most unwearied patience, the most untiring and generous enthusiasm. Neither Alexander, nor Cæsar, nor Napoleon dreamed of such an empire as that to whose establishment Jesus Christ calls us. Is there energy adequate to the aim? Yes, verily. For He who commands us to this service is He who bore our infirmities, who died to save the race, and who rose again, fathoming our misery and guilt, leaping from the cross and the tomb to the throne of universal and eternal dominion. And by that sign we conquer!— H. R.

GIVING AND DOING FOR THE LORD

By F. N. Peloubet

Ex. xxxv: 20-27

I. THE OBJECT. The chapter in which the present lesson occurs contains an account of the call which Moses made upon the liberality of the people (vers. 4-20), at the divine command (Ex. xxv: 1-8), for materials for a sanctuary, and of the response of the people to that call (vers. 21-29). A small tax, amounting to half a shekel of silver, or about thirty cents of our money, was levied upon each man, according to the divine directions (Ex. xxx: 12-16), without regard to his wealth or poverty, in order to enforce the idea of the equal obligation of all to God. But beyond this the supply of the materials necessary for the building of the Tabernacle was left wholly to the voluntary offerings of the people, which were extremely liberal.

The Tabernacle and its furniture were to be as costly and as precious as possible, as an expression of honor to God, and a symbol of the preciousness of His presence and care. The whole expense must have been at least a million and a quarter of dollars.

The MISSIONARY WORK is one of the great instrumentalities for building up God's spiritual temple, the most costly and precious object in the world. Our Sunday-schools should know what this work is, the different societies which are working for it, and what they are doing, and especially those departments in which each one's own church is most engaged.

II. THE CONTRIBUTIONS FOR THIS OBJECT (vers. 20-29). The spoil of the Egyptians was brought as a free-will offering to Jehovah,—jewels and precious metals, skins and woven fabrics, spices, oils, and incense. They soon found the offerings of the people far above what was required; and they made the Tabernacle, with its furniture and vessels, the cloths of service, and the garments of the priests, after the pattern shown to Moses in the mount; and Moses blessed them.

Their *hearts* (ver. 21), their spiritual nature, feelings, intellect, and will, *stirred them up*, by the opportunity to express their gratitude to God, to aid in the cause of religion, and confirm and train the nation. The *blue,*

purple, and scarlet (vers. 23, 25) means the woolen yarn or cloth, dyed these colors, out of which to make curtains and coverings for the tabernacle, and vestments for the priest. *Onyx stones* (ver. 27) are most probably some variety of the stone known in modern times as the "onyx," a stone formed of strata of different colors. It is called the onyx, because, as the color of the flesh appears through the nail (Greek *onyx*) of the human body, so the reddish mass which is below shines delicately through the whitish surface of the onyx. The twelve stones were to be set in gold. The settings may have been separate, but it is much more likely they were connected in a square frame of gold, which was attached to the variegated cloth of the breastplate, as the settings of the onyx stones to the shoulder-straps of the ephod. *The ephod* consisted of two principal pieces of cloth, one for the back and the other for the front, joined together by shoulder-straps, below the arms; probably the two pieces were kept in place by a band attached to one of the pieces just above the hips. *The breastplate* was the most costly, beautiful, and glorious part of the high priest's dress. It was doubled, so as to form a kind of bag, a span in length and in breadth; it was worn on the heart of the high priest. It was enriched with twelve precious stones, all set in gold, each stone having written upon it the name of one of the tribes of Israel. It was made of linen, embroidered with colors and gold, and was fastened by golden chains to the onyx stones on the shoulders, and to the girdle of the ephod.

NOTE that these contributions were (1) free-will offerings, (2) rich and costly. They "gave till they felt it." (3) Very abundant, so that Moses had to tell them to give no more. (4) They worked, as well as gave. (5) Each one did his part, men and women, rulers and people. Calculate the amount of the gifts, if each member of the church and Sabbath-school should give, according to his ability, as freely and generously as these Israelites did.

WHO ONLY DOETH WONDROUS THINGS

By Sidney Dickinson

Ps. lxii: 18

Nothing is so wonderful, no, not the wildest dreams of poet's imagination, as what God has actually done for His people. The sending of His Son from heaven, His life and death expressing infinite love, and the transforming power of the Holy Spirit, are all transcendent wonders.

ILLUSTRATIONS. (1) The day of Pentecost. (2) The fruits of missions during the last fifty years. (3) In the *Boston Journal* of this morning, in which I am completing this lesson (May, 1891), is one of a series of letters from the Fiji Islands from a traveler, expressing his astonishment at the marvelous changes there, from a savage, ignorant, warlike race of cruel cannibals to a quiet and peaceful civilized people. An excellent illustration of these changes is at the missionary station in Mbau, where the present large and commodious Christian church is chiefly built of the walls of a former great heathen temple, in which the "devil priests" in fantastic and terrifying garb superintended the satanic cannibal feasts; and where the great stone of human sacrifice is now used as a baptismal font. Christianity has slowly overcome cannibalism and many other barbarous customs. Even as recently as twenty years ago missionary labor was hazardous. "When I was a school boy, Fiji was the synonym of all that was barbarous and cannibalistic; that I should ever travel to this land of the man-eaters in a steamer like a floating palace and lighted with electricity, never, I am sure, entered my head." "Among our ship's company from Melbourne was a missionary who thrice saw the fires kindled to roast him, and the executioner standing with his club awaiting the word to knock him on the head. Some providential influence prevented."—B. J.

THE WINNER OF SOULS

The fruit of the righteous is a tree of life; and he that winneth souls is wise.—Prov. xi: 30

The central thought of this whole passage from verse 17 to 30 is that a *true life terminates upon others*. The righteous becomes a sort of sacramental tree of life, imparting life, or, to use a very different figure, a fisher of men, a captor of souls. The emphasis is on the wisdom that wins men. A fisher does everything to get fish on his hook or in his net, to capture his prey. Piety must be winning not repulsive.

Consider the application.

1. To preachers. Every one who teaches truth is a lens through which truth reaches souls. How important that there be no false color in the medium lest a wrong and false hue be given to the truth. A young student preached in a theological seminary upon God's wrath, and so vindictive did he make God appear that a little boy who was present went home and told his mother that he heard a man preach "about a *wicked God*." The preacher needs a regenerate temper, otherwise he is liable to impart to his representations of God his own wilfulness, arbitrariness, impatience, censoriousness, etc.

2. To disciples. "Ye are our epistle"— it is to be feared many of these "living epistles" sadly need revision; they do great injustice to the original. Even Cretan servants and slaves "adorned the doctrine." The poor Indian in Mexico said he would "rather go to hell than to the same heaven with his Spanish tyrant and oppressor." How can we win men or be to them a tree of life while our own character and conduct repel? The exclusive sectarian bigot cannot teach charity; the bad tempered man is a poor instructor in gentleness, and the selfish man in self-sacrifice. Let us study Christ, as a winner of souls, with the woman at the well, etc. An infidel fled from the society of Fenelon lest he should be compelled to be himself a disciple. Hume acknowledged that his philosophy could not explain a true Christian life.—H. R.

THE HARVEST AND THE LABORERS

By F. N. Peloubet

Matt. ix: 35-38

I. THE EXAMPLE OF JESUS AS A MISSIONARY (vers. 35, 36). Jesus came from heaven as a missionary to this world, and He here gives us an insight into His method. (1) *He felt the needs of men.* He "so loved the world." He saw men perishing; He longed to save. (2) *He preached the simple Gospel.* The plain truths about the kingdom, and the way into it. (3) *He helps men's bodies as well as souls.* The Gospel that does not make men kinder, more helpful, more healthy, that does not seek to relieve want, and minister to the sick, and help every kind of need, is no true Gospel.

EXAMPLES. Every earnest Church is an example. Every mission station is an example. FACTS. Schools, colleges, hospitals, reformatories, houses for the aged, etc., spring up everywhere that the Gospel is preached and lived. Where there is the most Christianity, there are the largest efforts to relieve the temporal wants of men. PROOFS. These things are the proofs that we are sincere in offering the spiritual Gospel.

II. THE HARVEST (vers. 36, 37). The harvest is plenteous. (1) All without the Gospel in their hearts are included in this harvest to be gathered. (2) Investigate your own town or neighborhood and church district, and see how great this harvest is. (3) Look over the whole world and see how great is the harvest. (4) Consider what part of this harvest is given you to reap.

ILLUSTRATION. A chart has been constructed with the aim of awakening a new interest in the salvation of the world. It is divided into 1,434 one-inch squares, each representing a million people. 391 squares represent the 391 millions in Christian nations; seven squares, or seven millions, are Jews; 170 millions are Mohammedans; and 1,034 millions are in black for Pagans. The only mistake is in not dotting this mass of darkness with radiant stars for the places where mission stations are shining with Gospel light in the blackness of heathenism. But we thus see how plenteous is the harvest.

III. THE LABORERS (vers. 37, 38; 1-8). They are few, but we can make them more. (1) By prayer, (2) by becoming laborers ourselves, (3) by becoming better laborers. Have the scholars learn the names of the twelve Apostles, and something about them. NOTE in reference to them, and apply to present times: (1) Their call. God calls us (a) by the opportunity to do good, (b) by fitness to do it, (c) by His spirit. (2) With the call, Jesus gave them power and authority. (3) They were to preach the Gospel. (4) They were to do good. (5) The obligation was increased by the fact that they had freely received so much from Jesus.

THE GREAT COMMISSION

By F. N. PELOUBET

Matt. xxviii: 16-20

I. THE GREAT MEETING (vers. 16, 17). This, the great meeting, during the forty days, including the apostles and 500 disciples. Final instruction. Worship of Christ. Doubts of these men leading to our certainties.

II. THE GREAT COMMISSION. MISSIONARY (vers. 18, 19). Explain the passage. The grandeur of the idea. The nobleness of the work. Where our missionary work lies— home and abroad. What each of us can do. Objections to foreign missions. What has been already done. Necessity of obeying this command, to the growth and purity of the Church and of the individual Christian. The duty of baptism. The value to a young convert of a public profession of religion.

ILLUSTRATIONS. (1) Real light always shines, and the brighter the light, the farther it shines. (2) Flowing, moving water is pure. Stagnant water becomes impure. (3) The spinning top stands; stop its spinning, and it falls.

Archdeacon Farrar says that "he who talks of missions as a failure, uses the language of ignorant error as an excuse for unchristian sloth." We are apt to know the work of our own denomination only; but

read Dr. Christlieb on *Foreign Missions,* and the *World's Progress,* by Dr. Dorchester, and we shall begin to understand the marvelous extent of missionary work, and the conquering progress of the Gospel. In this country alone there were raised

		For Foreign Missions.
In the thirty years . .	1820 to 1850.	. . $8,666,600
In the next thirty years	1850 to 1880.	. . 43,007,090
		For Home Missions.
In the thirty years . .	1820 to 1850.	. . $5,382,000
In the next thirty years	1850 to 1880.	. . 45,331,700

At the end of the first 1,000 years from the birth of Christ there were 50,000,000 in Christian lands.
In the next 500 years the number was doubled, and there were 100,000,000 in 1500 A.D.
This number was doubled in the next 300 years, and there were 200,000,000 in 1800 A.D.
This number was again doubled in the next 80 years, and there are 415,000,000 in 1880 A.D.
And the progress is growing more and more rapid

III. THE GREAT COMMISSION. TEACHING (ver. 20). The duty and privilege of teaching and of being taught. What to teach. Where to learn it. The great encouragements from the presence of Jesus.

IV. THE ASCENSION and its lessons. What Jesus is now doing in heaven for us,—a living, guiding, loving, omnipotent Savior.

THE FOOD OF THE WORLD

By Alexander Maclaren. D.D.

Matt. xiv: 19, 20

I. Christ feeds the famishing world by means of His Church. "He gave the loaves to His disciples, and the *disciples* to the multitude."

1. The food, altho *supernaturally* provided, is carried to the hungry by the ordinary means; *the disciples gave it to the multitude.*

2. The disciples were prepared for their work. The first lesson they had to learn was the almost ludicrous disproportion between the means at their command and the necessities of the crowd. "How many loaves have ye? Go and see."

3. We must carry our poor and inadequate resources to Christ. "Bring them hither to me."

II. The bread is enough for all the world. "They did all eat, and were filled."

III. The bread which is given to the famishing is multiplied for the future of the distributors. "They took of the fragments that remained twelve baskets full."—H. R.

THE MISSIONARY DUTY OF THE CHURCH

By F. N. Peloubet

Matt. xxviii: 16-20

Observe that this command implies (1) that Christianity is a universal religion, not merely one of the religions of the world; (2) that it is adapted to all nations and all classes (Rom. i: 16), a claim which history has abundantly justified; (3) that not a natural development, but obedience to the principles inculcated by Jesus Christ, constitutes the secret of true civilization among all nations, and thus that Christian missions are the mother of civilization; (4) that from all nations the members of Christ's Church triumphant are to be gathered to God by obedience to this commission (Rom. x: 11-13)—Abbott. The very soul of our religion is missionary, progressive, world-embracing; it would cease to exist if it ceased to be missionary, if it disregarded the parting words of its Founder.—Max Müller.

1. This is the command of Christ. The Church cannot be obedient, and let one nation be without the Gospel. The duty is obligatory, not on ministers and missionaries alone, but upon the whole Church. The commission was given. not to the apostles only, but to the whole body of five hundred disciples.

2. This command includes home missions as well as foreign; our own neighborhood as well as more distant places. But missionary effort must not be confined to the home field. Every nation needs the Gospel as much as ours need it.

3. It is the nature of a living Christianity to be missionary. Max Müller says that of all religions, only the missionary religions are living. That Church is dead which is not anxious to preach the Gospel to every creature.

4. This is the only way the Church will keep pure. Nothing without this can keep the doctrine or life pure: organizations, creeds, persecutions—all have failed. But any Church which seeks to save souls will keep pure, because it cannot do its work without the great main doctrines of Christianity.

5. The true *Broad Church* cares for *the salvation of the world;* the *Narrow Church* is the one that cares chiefly for itself and for temporal things.

6. The Church at home is built up faster by working for the heathen.

7. The grandeur of this work exalts the individual Christians who give and labor.

8. It is blessed to have part in the final triumph of the Gospel.

THE DEMONIAC OF GERASA, TYPE OF HEATHENISM

Mark v: 20

1. Heathenism is a *place of Tombs.* Spiritual death and decay. Bodily disease, intellectual degradation and wreck of true faith.

2. Humanity is *possessed of unclean spirits.* Heathenism sacrifices to demons, not to God. The whole system of idolatry is Satanic.

3. Their name is *Legion.* Every conceivable form of inhumanity, cruelty, injustice, may be found linked with idolatry, caste, woman's thraldom, infanticide, torture, can-

nibalism, slavery, etc. Often paganism has been exceeding fierce, imperiling the lives even of travelers, not to say missionaries.

4. Heathenism feeds and has affinity for *the swine* of bestial and brutal lusts and passions. It panders to the animal nature and gives the body full sway. Witness polygamy, drunkenness, etc.

5. Heathenism is *materialistic,* valuing a herd more than a human being, and opposing a religion that makes man holy, if it imperils an unholy trade.

On the contrary—the Gospel casts out the evil spirit, brings those who are possessed to a right mind, shows its greatest proofs in its own transformed converts, and sends them out to be evangelists of its power. Its power is thus manifested in (1) Exorcism, (2) Transformation, (3) Evangelism. —H. R.

THE FESTIVAL OF EPIPHANY

By H. Melvill

John viii: 12

I. There is no figure more common in Scripture, and none more beautiful, than that by which Christ is likened unto light. Incomprehensible in its nature, itself the first visible, and that by which all things are seen, light represents to us Christ, Whose generation none can declare, but Who must shine upon us ere we can know aught aright, whether of things Divine or human. Itself pure and uncontaminated, tho visiting the lowest parts of the earth, and penetrating its most noisome recesses, what does light image, if not that undefiled Mediator who contracted no stain, tho born of a woman in the likeness of sinful flesh? Who can question that the rising of Jesus Christ was to the moral world what the sun is to the natural?

II. Without pleading that the state of the world, before Christ came, was a state of total darkness, we may yet affirm that Christ emphatically came as the light of the world. In no district of the earth—not even in Judæa, tho privileged with revelation—was there anything that could be called more than the dawning of the day. Types there were—significative ceremonies—mysterious emblems, but these do not constitute the day. At best, they were but a twilight, that gave promise of the morning; and if that be all we can affirm of Judæa, then certainly, until the light of which we have been speaking, there brooded over other lands a darkness that might be felt. Here and there were lingering traces of a patriarchical religion; but every year saw the gathering of thicker gloom, and streak after streak grew dim on the firmament.

III. Such was the state of the whole Gentile world when He appeared, whom the prophecy announced as "a light to them that sit in darkness and in the shadow of death." Was the testimony exaggerated, or has it been justified by events? Wheresoever the Gospel has been published and received as a communication from God, the darkness has fled as night flies before the sun. It hath hung the very grave with bright lamps, and rekindled the spirit of an almost quenched immortality. The pardon of sin, justification through the Mediator's righteousness, the gradual overcoming of the corruptions of nature, guidance in difficulty, guardianship in danger, comfort in affliction, triumph in death—all these are in the portion of him who follows Christ—followeth Him in faith as his surety, in obedience as his pattern. And are not these the light—yea, the light of life? —S. B., vol. iv., p. 57.

THE LIGHT OF THE WORLD

By F. D. Maurice

John viii: 12

I. Jesus had often spoken this word before. Every act of mercy He did, spoke to the men who were the subjects of it. St. John dwells specially upon His cure of blindness. He takes that as an instance, and the clearest and liveliest instance, of the effects which were produced by all His miracles. Each sufferer felt that a power of darkness had taken hold of him; that a portion of the beauty and joy of the universe was hidden from him. The appearance of a deliverer who could set him free from his plague, was the appearance of a Light. He was brought out of a cave; the air that breathed upon the rest of men, was breathing on him; the common sun was shining on him. Christ's word was light; the entrance of it into the soul gave light, and that light diffused itself through every part of the man. It brought health and vigor wherever it encountered sickness and decay.

II. Divines are wont to make distinctions between Christ the Teacher of the world at large, and Christ the Teacher of the heart and conscience of each man. They talk of an outward Christ and an inward Christ. The Evangelists indulge in no such refinements. The Christ who was born of the Virgin, who suffered under Pontius Pilate, reveals Himself—not to the eyes of those who actually see and handle Him, but to a spirit within them. And so there is no need of artificial rules and distinctions, such as doctors invent for their own confusion. The Light makes the distinction. It is not the distinction of Pharisee or Publican, of religious men or irreligious. It goes deeper than that. It is the distinction between that in every man which welcomes the light, and claims kindred with it, and that in every man which eschews the light and would fain extinguish it for ever. It expresses itself in these words, " He that followeth me shall not walk in darkness." The Light of the world is not put out. Now have death and the grave been converted into the great testimonies for life and immortality. Now may each man, who has the sentence of Adam upon him, know that he is a kinsman of the Son of God. Now may he follow Him; and so, when the darkness is thickest around him and within, not walk in it, but see the Light of Life.—S. B., vol. viii., p. 58.

SUGGESTIVE THOUGHTS AND ILLUSTRATIONS

ANGELS, Ministry of.—It is a great thought on this subject, that *the human race furnishes but a small part of the holy ministries of this world.* The ministry of angels probably swells what we call minorities to secret majorities. " Are they not *all* ministering spirits?" Invisible multitudes probably fill the air with their busy pinions in service to the right. One of England's great poets says of a noted champion of liberty :—

" Thou hast left behind
Powers that will work for thee; air, earth, and skies;
There's not a breathing of the common winds
That will forget thee. Thou hast great allies.
. . . Winds blow and waters roll
Strength to the brave."

But the friend of Christ has allies more imperial than skies and winds and waters.— PROFESSOR AUSTIN PHELPS.

CHURCH, The Light of the.—*Isa. lx: 1.* There is a little church on a lonely hillside where they have neither gas nor lamps, and yet on darkest nights they hold Divine service. Each worshiper, coming a great distance from village or moorland home, brings with him a taper and lights it from one supplied and carried by the minister of the little church. The building is thronged, and the scene is said to be " most brilliant." Let each one of our lives be but a little taper—lighted from the life of Christ, and carrying His flame—and we shall help to fill this great temple of human need and human sin with the light of the knowledge of the glory of God.—A. P. L.

EPIPHANY, The Festival of the.—The Festival of the Epiphany must be deemed of very high importance by a believing and thoughtful Christian. It does not merely commemorate one of the most beautiful incidents of our Lord's Infant Life, it asserts one of the most fundamental and vital features of Christianity: the great distinction, in fact, between Christianity and Judaism.

The Jewish religion was the religion of a race. . . . Was a merely national religion like this a full unveiling of the mind of the common Father of the human family? Was His eye ever to rest in love and favor only on the hills and valleys of Palestine? Was there to be no place in His Heart for more races, who lay east and west and north and south of the favored region? Or was the God of Israel like the patron deities of the heathen world, the God of Israel in such sense that Israel could lastingly monopolize His interest, His protection, His love; that heathendom, lying in darkness and in the shadow of death, would lie on in it for ever, without a hope of being really lightened by His Countenance or being admitted to share His embrace? It could not be. The Jewish revelation of God contained within itself the secret and the reason of its vanishing by absorption into the brighter light which should succeed it.—H. P. LIDDON.

GOD, One and.—One great principle of God's working in the affairs of His kingdom is that *He Works with minorities who are working for Him.* An old saying of the German reformers, which a modern reformer has untruthfully claimed as his own, was: " One, with God on his side, is a majority." " The battle is not yours, but God's."—P.

HEATHEN, The Light of the.—*Isa. lx: 1.* At a Church Missionary meeting the Bishop of Moosonee, furnishing proofs of the growing civilization of the Indians, said :— " I am here to speak of the conversion of men to God through the work of missionaries, and I can tell you of men who evidence by their lives that they have been born again of the Holy Spirit of God. While speaking some time ago to an Indian, I said to him, ' My friend, I should be glad if you would give me a picture of the Indians as they were before they received Christianity.' I took down the man's words in reply, from his own lips and they were these :—" Before we were Christians we were very, very wicked;

we knew nothing save the devil and the devil's works. We lied, we stole, we conjured; we thought we could prophesy. The Indians robbed men of other tribes; the Indians robbed each other; their lives were very, very wicked.' "—A. P. L.

JEWS, The King of the.—*Matt. ii:2.* Erasmus thought that the Magi did not adore Christ with Divine worship (as not knowing that He was God), but only with the homage which was due to Him whom they acknowledged as the " King of the Jews." But the Fathers generally teach otherwise.—A. P. L.

MAGI, The Gifts of the.—*Matt. ii: 11.* St. Leo says: " Frankincense they offer to God; myrrh to man; gold to the King: honoring with full intention the Divine and Human Nature in unity; because they believe with their hearts, they witness it by their gifts."—A. P. L.

MISSIONARY CONSECRATION.—A brilliant Oxford student was giving himself to the Wesleyan Missionary Society for African service. His tutor remonstrated. " You are going out to die in a year or two in that deadly climate. It is madness." The young man, who did die, after being on the field about a year, answered:

" I think it is with African missions as with the building of a great bridge. You know how many stones have to be buried in the earth, all unseen, to be a foundation. If Christ wants me to be one of the unseen stones, lying in an African grave, I am content, certain as I am that the final result will be a Christian Africa."—*Selected*

MISSIONARY INFLUENCE.—" The whole advance of Christianity has been a missionary movement. From the time that St. Paul went to Cyprus and Asia to the latest missions of any board of America, Christianity has been a missionary religion." —Secretary Judson Smith. One of the first privileges and duties of a strong church is to be a center of missionary influence. We are told to

" Measure our writings by Hesiod's staff, Which teaches that all has less value than half."

We should learn the same lesson in our churches. The large church that sends many of its best men and women to evangelize others, and supports them, will be stronger by the gift.—P.

MISSIONARY SERMONS, How Often to Preach.—Rev. John W. Etter, B.D., in a new work on Homiletics, entitled " The Preacher and his Sermon," says: " A *missionary* sermon must be preached as often as a congregation becomes lax in its zeal and contributions for missions. The pulpit must develop a missionary spirit in the Church, and through it ' Christians be kept in an habitual and alarming sense of the facts of the wretched, terrible state of the heathen, and of our ample ability and bounden and responsible duty to send them the Gospel." —H. R.

MISSIONARY SPIRIT, The.—When John Wesley was asked to go out to Georgia to preach the Gospel to the settlers and native Indians, his noble-minded mother not only gave her free consent, but said, " Had I a hundred sons, I should be glad to see them all engaged in such a blessed work, altho I might see them no more in this world."—H. R.

MISSIONARY WORK, MODERN, The Facilities for.—Gladstone's statement that the first fifty years of the present century eclipse all the centuries preceding in human progress is no exaggeration. Consider the triumphs of astronomical science in the perfection of the telescope and the invention of the spectroscope and in sidereal photography. Consider microscopic science and its present perfection and utility; the advance in medicine and surgery, and especially in the case of anesthetics; in the science and art of mining and the invention of giant explosives such as nitro-glycerine, dynamite, and giant powder; the perfection of photography and kindred methods of producing pictures by the aid of sunlight. Consider electricity as a motor, messenger, and illuminator, unknown one hundred years ago; anilin colors, the sewing machine, and the type-writer, the steam engine, the steam printing press, the sewing machine and the type-writer, the postal union and the wide world communication.—H. R.

MISSIONARY, Zeal of a.—Winfrid, or Boniface, having laid the ax at the roots of the trees, literally, in Germany, cutting down the oaks sacred to Thor, planting churches and making converts with remarkable success, longed for new fields and fresh conquests. When over seventy-five years of age, he set forth (so strong was his ruling passion) to win pagan Friesland to Christ. He appointed a bishop to succeed him at Mainz, and left everything, as if he did not expect to return. He took with him his shroud and St. Ambrose's treatise on the " Advantage of Death." With a company of eight, he entered upon his work, and met with good success. Many had been baptized. The pagans became alarmed, and went against him with an armed band. Boniface knew too well their bloody intent. He exhorted his followers not to resist, but to await the crown of martyrdom. He himself took a volume of the gospel for a pillow, and stretching his neck upon it for the blow, received his release in 755. Few are the names of missionary heroes more illustrious than his.—F. II.

MISSIONS AND SCIENCE.—Archdeacon Farrar sets forth forcibly the large debt of science to missions in these words: " Is it nothing that through their labor in the translation of the Bible the German philologist in his study may have before him the grammar and vocabulary of two hundred and fifty languages? Who created the science of anthropology? The missionaries. Who rendered possible the deeply important science of comparative religion? The missionaries. Who discovered the great chain of lakes in Central Africa, on which will turn its future destiny? The missionaries. Who have been the chief explorers of Oceanica, America, and Asia? The missionaries. Who discovered the famous Nestorian monument in Singar Fu? A missionary. Who discovered the still more famous Moabite stone? A missionary. Who discovered the Hittite inscriptions? A missionary."—*Selected.*

MISSIONS, Basis for.—The Baptist Missionary Society of England owes its existence and success to the unflagging zeal of the shoemaker, school-master, and preacher, William Carey, of Nottingham. He preached a powerful sermon from Is. liv: 23, of which the two leading divisions were, "Expect great things from God"—"Attempt great things for God." Under its influence a mission to the heathen was resolved upon. Mr. Carey became its first missionary, sailing for India in 1793. His expectations were not disappointed.—F. II.

MISSIONS, Era of.—It was not until Christians became inflamed with the zeal of Wesley, who said, "The world is my parish," and Whitefield, who saw in every man a brother, that missions assumed any importance among Protestants. To this epoch the great societies of England, date their origin. "The Society for the Propagation of the Gospel in Foreign Parts," the oldest of all, was organized in 1701; "Church Missionary Society," in 1799; "Scotch Missionary Society" in 1796; "London Missionary Society" in 1794; "Baptist Missionary Society" in 1792; "Wesleyan Missionary Society" in 1769. The foregoing are all in Great Britain. "The American Board of Foreign Missions" was organized in 1810; "The American Baptist Missionary Society" in 1814; "The Methodist Episcopal Missionary Society" in 1819; "The Episcopal Board of Missions" in 1820. Various minor societies exist, of later origin. The obstacles attending the beginning of new mission enterprises have been overcome. The great harvest of the heathen world is being rapidly gathered. Soon the inhabitants of heaven will shout, "The kingdoms of this world are become the kingdoms of our Lord and of his Christ." (Rev. xi: 17.)—F. II.

MISSIONS, Gold for.—John Sunday, the converted Indian chief of Upper Canada, addressing a missionary meeting in England, in his appeal to the benevolence of the people, previous to collection, said, "There is a gentleman, I suppose, now in this house; he is a very fine gentleman, but he is very modest. He does not like to show himself. I do not know how long it is since I saw him, he comes out so little. I am very much afraid he sleeps a great deal of his time, when he ought to be going about doing good. His name is Mr. Gold. Mr. Gold, are you here to-night? or are you sleeping in your iron chest? Come out, Mr. Gold; come out, and help us to do this great work, to send the gospel to every creature. Ah, Mr. Gold, you

ought to be ashamed of yourself, to sleep so much in your iron chest! Look at your white brother, Mr. Silver, he does a great deal of good in the world, while you are sleeping. Come out, Mr. Gold! Look, too, at your brown brother, Mr. Copper, he is everywhere! See him running about doing all the good he can. Why don't you come out, Mr. Gold? Well, if you won't come out and give us yourself, send us your shirt, that is a bank note, and we will excuse you this time."—F. II.

MISSIONS, Love for.—A late writer says, "Why was Christ's long journey from heaven? Why His long sojourn amidst poverty and scorn? Why His toilsome ministry in Galilee and Judea? Why the journey to Jerusalem, and the known betrayal, rejection, and cruel death there? Ah, "the Son of man came to seek and to save that which was lost." With the Spirit of the Master upon them, thousands have gone forth upon the same errand.—F. II.

MISSIONS, Martyrs of.—The missionaries' torch has been lighted in every land. Their bones scattered everywhere are the seed of a bountiful harvest, to be gathered when the earth shall be fully ripe. Some fell by the malaria of an inhospitable climate, like Melville B. Cox in Africa. Thousands of true martyrs have thus died for their faith. Rev. William Thielfall was martyred in Namaqualand, in 1825; Rev. J. S. Thomas in Kaffirland, in 1856; Rev. John Williams in Erromanga, in 1838; Rev. J. G. Gordon in the same place, in 1872; Rev. Thomas Baker in Fiji in 1867; Bishop Patterson and Rev. Mr. Atkin, in Malanesia in 1871. The only wonder is, considering the ignorance, superstition, and cruelty of the heathen, that so few have been called to shed their blood for Christ.—F. II.

MISSIONS, Mystery of.—Napoleon thought that he knew the world well. He had studied the history of great empires, but he said it was an inexplicable mystery to him that Christianity, beginning as it did with a few fishermen of the feeblest nation then on the globe, should in his time have risen to be so much more mighty than his own conquests, which had almost all the armies of Europe to back them.

"Oh, where are kings and emperors now,
   Of old that went and came?
But, Lord, thy church is praying yet
   A thousand years the same."

The same phenomenon was witnessed in the first attempt to establish American missions among the heathen. When one of the early meetings of the American Board was held at Bradford, Mass., less than twenty persons were in attendance, and they were hooted at by boys on the piazza of the hotel where they were in session.—P.

MISSIONS, Official Tribute to.—The English blue-book, published in 1875, after a summary of missions in India, about half of which are American enterprises, closes with the following tribute: "The government in India cannot but acknowledge the great obligation under which it is laid by these six hundred missionaries, whose blameless example and self-denying labors are infusing new vigor into the stereotyped life of the great population placed under English rule, and are preparing them to be in every way better citizens of the great empire in which they dwell."—F. II.

MISSIONS Pay Financially, Do?—The total cost of the work done in the Sandwich Islands was about one and one-quarter million dollars, the cost of six "ironclads," not one-half the expense of the tunnel proposed under the river at Detroit; at Harpoot fourteen congregations were formed, in as many years, at a total cost of $120,000, which is often spent on one church building at home. In India, Christian residents defray one-fourth the expense, seeing the value of the work with their own eyes. The Cincinnati bridge cost double all the work in Persia, which gave that land seventy schools, ninety congregations, and sixty native preachers.—M. R. W.

MISSIONS, Providence and.—Rev. John Thomas, founder of the Friendly Islands Mission, applied to the London Mission Society for permission to extend his work to the island of Haabai, whose chief desired his coming. He waited with some anxiety for a reply. About that time a box was washed ashore, and carried to one of the missionaries, containing a letter from the society authorizing the establishment of the mission. Neither the vessel to which the letter was entrusted, the crew, nor any of the freight, except the box containing the letter authorizing a new effort for the salvation of the heathen, which came to the right place at the right time, was ever heard from.—F. II.

MISSIONS, Result of Love for.—A poor Christian mechanic was much chagrined that he could give so little for missions when the subscription was passed among the workmen in the factory. He told his wife of it, and she was inspired to try to earn something for the cause of missions. She secured some silk-twist and a few button-moulds, and began the manufacture of silk buttons. She sent a sample to a New York merchant, saying that, if they would sell, the money was to be her husband's contribution for missions. She received answer, "Make as many as you choose; I can sell a hundred dozen." The wife made her venture unknown to her husband; but now he was let into the secret. Success crowned her efforts. Machinery supplanted hand labor. A large manufactory, extensive business, and ample fortune grew up from and rewarded their love and labor for missions.—F. II.

MISSIONS, The Spirit of.—The very soul of our religion is missionary, progressive, world-embracing: it would cease to exist if it ceased to be missionary, if it disregarded the parting words of its founder, "Go ye, therefore, and teach all nations," etc. The spirit of truth is the life-spring of all re-

ligion; and where it exists, it must manifest itself; it must plead, it must persuade, it must convince and convert. There may be times when silence is gold, and speech silver; but there are times, also, when silence is death, and speech is life,—the very life of Pentecost. Look at the religions in which the missionary spirit has been at work, and compare them with those in which any attempt to convince others by argument, to save souls, to bear witness to the truth, is treated with pity or scorn. *The former are alive; the latter are dying or dead.*—Max Müller.

MORAVIAN BROTHERHOOD, The.—*John vi: 1-14.* Most of us have only one talent, but he who has one talent sometimes makes ten of it. We have only five barley loaves, etc., which indeed in themselves are useless, but when given to Christ He can make them enough to feed five thousand. Take the one instance of kind words of sympathy and encouragement.

When Count Zinzendorf was a boy at school, he founded amongst his school-fellows a little guild which he called the "Order of the Grain of Mustard Seed," and thereafter that seedling grew into the great tree of the Moravian Brotherhood, whose boughs were a blessing to the world. The widow's mite! When they laughed at Saint Theresa, when she wanted to build a great orphanage and had but three shillings to begin with, she answered, "With three shillings Theresa can do nothing; but with God and her three shillings there is nothing which Theresa cannot do." Do not let us imagine, then, that we are too poor, or too stupid, or too ignorant, or too obscure to do any real good in the world wherein God has placed us.

If you bring no gift, how can God use it? The lad must bring his barley loaves to Christ before the five thousand can be fed. Have you ever attempted to do as he did? Have you, even in the smallest measure, or with the least earnest desire, tried to follow John Wesley's golden advice: "Do all the good you can, by all the means you can, in all the ways you can, to all the persons you can, in all the places you can, as long as ever you can?"—Farrar.

NATIONS, The Oneness of the.—When the Prophet of the Apocalypse looked upon the Holy City of the new creation, he saw that there was no longer any temple there—that was the symbol at once of religious fellowship and religious separation—*for the Lord God Almighty and the Lamb are the Temple of it;* he saw that it had no need of the sun—that was the symbol of the quickening energy of nature and the measure of time—*for the glory of God did lighten it, and the lamp thereof was the Lamb;* he saw *the nations* (not *the nations of them which are saved,* according to the gloss of the common texts) *walking in the light of it,* and so revealed in their true abiding power; he saw *the kings of the earth bring their glory into it,* offering, that is, each his peculiar treasures to complete the full measure of the manifested sovereignty of the Lord. This is the end; in this magnificent vision of faith the Church and the nations are at last revealed as one in the open presence of God. And meanwhile the promise is for our encouragement and for our guidance, as we strive to win for Christ the manifold homage of men.—BISHOP WESTCOTT.

SERMON, Outline for Missionary.—A most practical missionary sermon it would be which should candidly consider and answer these seven popular objections: (1) "The work of missions does not pay." (2) "Foreign peoples have their own civilizations and religions." (3) "There are plenty of heathen at home." (4) "Home Churches are even now loaded with debt." (5) "Foreign missionaries fare better than home pastors." (6) "Most of those who go abroad die soon, or return broken down." (7) "It costs five dollars to send ten abroad."—H. R.

STAR IN THE EAST, The.—We learn from astronomical calculations that a remarkable conjunction of the planets of our system took place a short time before the birth of our Lord. About 283 years ago, in December, 1604, the great astronomer Kepler saw a strange sight in the heavens,—a sight which occurs only once (or rather, is repeated two or three times at one period) in eight hundred years. It was the conjunction of the bright planets Jupiter and Saturn, close together at one point of the heavens. Five months later, in the following May, the wonder was repeated in a more wonderful way: Mars joined with Jupiter and Saturn, a fiery trygon in the constellation Pisces, in part of the heavens noted in astrological science as that in which the signs denoted the greatest and most noble events. The attention of the whole astronomical world was called to the sight; and this seemed to draw the notice to another sight,—the appearing of a new star in the constellation of the Serpent. First seen in October, 1604, it grew more and more brilliant, till it glowed like a planet; then its luster waned, its white light turned to yellow, then to red, grew duller and dimmer, and finally, at the end of two years, had vanished altogether. These unusual occurrences led Professor Kepler, who was as religious as he was scientific, to think that they might help to explain the strange star which the wise men saw in the east, and how it was that the star in the east led them to the King of the Jews; whether a conjunction of planets like this was the star in the east, or whether it led them to see and recognize the real star of the east, as this conjunction accompanied the new star which Kepler saw in the same part of the heavens, a blazing, burning world. The conjunction could occur but once in eight hundred years; take twice eight hundred years, and it brings us to within one or two years of the date of Christ's birth, the *exact* date of which is unknown. Several great astronomers, since Kepler's day, have made the same calculations,—Professor Pritchard, of the Royal Astronomical Society, and

Encke; and it rests on assured grounds that, about the time of Christ's birth, in the month of May, occurred this conjunction of Jupiter and Saturn, rising about three hours before sunrise, and therefore seen in the east. Suppose these wise men of Persia, the far East, seeing this wonderful sight in their clear skies, had started on their journey about the end of May: it would require at least seven months. The planets were observed to separate slowly till the end of July, when they slowly drew together again, and were in conjunction in September, when the wise men would have reached the nearer East, on the border of the desert. "At that time there can be no doubt that Jupiter would present to astronomers a very brilliant spectacle. It was then at its most brilliant apparition, for it was at its nearest approach both to the sun and the earth. The glorious spectacle continued almost unaltered for several days, when the planets again slowly separated, came to a halt, and then Jupiter again approached to a conjunction for the third time with Saturn, just at the time the Magi may be supposed to have entered the holy city, in December. And to complete the fascination of the tale, if they performed the journey from Jerusalem to Bethlehem in the evening, as is implied, then, about half an hour after sunset, the two planets might be seen from Jerusalem, hanging, as it were, in the meridian, and suspended over Bethlehem in the distance."—CONDENSED FROM UPHAM.

These circumstances would seem to form a remarkable coincidence with the history in our text. The true theory seems to be, that *the expectations of the Magi were aroused by the remarkable conjunction, and their watching was rewarded by the sight of the miraculous star.* This conjunction was a John the Baptist that heralded the true Star out of Jacob, miraculously shown in the heavens. "This theory recognizes the astronomical fact, and teaches, even more fully, the lesson that the *expectant* study of nature leads to the discovery of the supernatural. Equally with the last view, it shows us the Magi, because earnestly seeking the Messiah, led to Him by nature, by science, if astrology can be so termed." So Upham, Schaff, Abbott, and others.—PELOUBET on Matt. ii: 1-12.

TESTIMONY, More, Concerning Missions.—Only necessary to know the facts: "Any one who writes that Indian officials, as a class, have no faith in the work of missionaries as a civilizing and Christianizing agency in India must either be ignorant of the facts or under the influence of a very blind prejudice. . . . Missionary teaching and Christian literature are leavening native opinion, especially among the Hindus, in a way and to an extent quite startling to those who take a little personal trouble to investigate the facts."—SIR CHARLES U. AITCHISON.

"I do not think I can too prominently say that our gratitude to the American Marathi Mission has been piling up and piling up all the years of this century. . . . I take this public opportunity of conveying, on behalf of the Government of Bombay, our most grateful thanks for the assistance the people of the United States are rendering this government in pushing forward the cause of education in India."—LORD HARRIS, Governor of Bombay.

TRADITION, A Beautiful.—One tradition is beautiful. In the farthest East, it says, lived a people who had a book which bore the name of Seth, and in this was written the appearance of the star of the Messiah, and the offering of gifts to Him. This book was handed down from father to son, generation after generation. Twelve men were chosen who should watch for the star, and when one died, another was chosen in his place. These men, in the speech of the land, were called Magi. They went, each year, after the wheat-harvest, to the top of a mountain, which was called the "mountain of victory." At last the star appeared, and in the form of a little child, and over him the sign of the cross; and the star itself spoke to them, and told them to go to Judea. For two years, which was the time of their journey, the star moved before them, and they wanted neither food nor drink. Gregory of Tours adds that the star sank, at last, into a spring at Bethlehem, where he himself had seen it, and where it still may be seen, but only by pure maidens.—ELLICOTT.

WORLD, The Light of the.—Every tree, plant, and flower grows and flourishes by the grace and bounty of the sun. Leaving out of account the eruptions of volcanoes and the ebb and flow of the tides, every mechanical action on the earth's surface, every manifestation of power, organic and inorganic, vital and physical, is produced by the sun. Every fire that burns, and every flame that glows, dispenses light and heat which originally belonged to the sun. The sun digs the ore from our mines, he rolls the iron, he rivets the plates, he boils the water, he draws the train. Thunder and lightning are also his transmuted strength. And remember this is not poetry, but rigid, mechanical truth.—PROF. TYNDALL.

WORLD, The Light of the.—The Bartholdi Statue of Liberty enlightening the world. It is the gospel which enlightens the world, and, placed on the church for a pedestal, holds up Jesus to let all on the stormy sea of life see the light of the world and safely reach the desired haven.—P.

XAVIER, Francis.—When Francis Xavier was in Rome, preparing to go on his great mission to the heathen, he was heard by his friend Rodriguez uttering in his sleep the words, "Yet more, O my God, yet more!" In his dreams there had come to him a vision of his future career: of his sufferings, weariness, hunger, thirst, the storms to be battled, and the fiercer storms of heathen rage, the continents to be traveled, the rivers and seas to be crossed, dangers and death on every hand. But along with these he saw the nations that he would bring to Christ, islands, continents, empires, that would by his voice hear the Gospel of the kingdom; and he exclaimed, "*Yet more, O my God, yet more.*" More toil, more suffering, and more souls brought into eternal life.—P.

POETRY

Christ for the World

BY S. WOLCOTT

Christ for the world we sing;
The world to Christ we bring,
   With loving zeal:
The poor, and them that **mourn**,
The faint and overborne,
Sin-sick and sorrow-worn,
   Whom Christ doth heal.

Christ for the world we sing;
The world to Christ we bring,
   With fervent prayer;
The wayward and the lost,
By restless passions tossed,
Redeemed, at countless cost,
   From dark despair.

Christ for the world we sing;
The world to Christ we bring,
   With one accord;
With us the work to share,
With us reproach to dare,
With us the cross to bear,
   For Christ our Lord.

Christ for the world we sing;
The world to Christ we bring,
   With joyful song;
The new-born souls, whose days,
Reclaimed from error's ways,
Inspired with hope and praise,
   To Christ belong.

Attendants of the Epiphany

TR. FROM EPHRAIM SYRUS

A star shines forth in heaven suddenly,
A wondrous orb, less than the sun, yet greater—
Less in its outward light, but greater in
Its inward glory, pointing to a mystery.
That morning star sent forth its beams afar
Into the land of those who had no light;
Led them as blind men, by a way they knew not,
Until they came and saw the Light of men,
Offered their gifts, received eternal life,
Worshiped, and went their way.
Thus had the Son two heralds, one on high,
And one below. Above, the star rejoiced;
Below, the Baptist bore Him record:

Two heralds thus, one heavenly, one of earth.;
That witnessing the nature of the Son,
The majesty of God, and this His human
  nature.
O mighty wonder! thus were they the
  heralds,
Both of His Godhead and His manhood.
Who held Him only for a son of earth,
To such the star proclaimed His heavenly
  glory;
Who held Him only for a heavenly spirit,
To such the Baptist spoke of Him as man.
And in the holy temple Simeon held the
  Babe
Fast in his aged arms, and sang to Him:

  " To me, in Thy mercy,
    An old man, Thou art come;
  Thou layest my body
    In peace in the tomb.
  Thou soon wilt awake me,
    And bid me arise;
  Wilt lead me transfigured
    To Paradise."

Then Anna took the Babe upon her arms,
And pressed her mouth upon His infant lips;
Then came the Holy Spirit on her lips,
As erst upon Isaiah's, when the coal
Had touched his silent lips, and opened them:
With glowing heart she sang:

  " O Son of the King!
  Tho Thy birthplace was mean,
  All-hearing, yet silent,
  All-seeing, unseen,
  Unknown, yet all-knowing,
  God, and yet Son of man,
    Praise to Thy name!"

Christ's Dominion

By Isaac Watts

Jesus shall reign where'er the sun
Does his successive journeys run,
His kingdom spread from shore to shore,
Till moons shall wax and wane no more.

From north to south the princes meet,
To pay their homage at His feet,
While western empires own their Lord,
And savage tribes attend His word.

To Him shall endless prayer be made,
And endless praises crown His head;
His name like sweet perfume shall rise
With every morning sacrifice.

People and realms of every tongue
Dwell on His love with sweetest song,
And infant voices shall proclaim
Their early blessings on His name.

The Epiphany

By Frederick W. Kittermaster

Isaiah lx: 3

Beyond the barren mountain range
  Where Hor lifts up its sacred head,
And buried lies in mystery strange,
  As years work out their silent change,
The city of the dead.

Where proud Euphrates day by day
  Winds through the plain, or sleeping lies,
The watching Magi nightly pray,
And seek the future's hidden way
  From planet-lighted skies.

Through the unclouded midnight air,
  On vast infinity's dark page,
With deepest skill and constant care,
They read the golden letters there
  That wax not old with age.

Lo! as they gaze with deep intent,
  A star more brilliant than the rest,
The herald of some great event,
Moves through the gilded firmament
  Onward towards the west.

Then came the sound tradition brought
  From Peor's top in day of old,
What time the seer entranced caught
Prophetic power, and, spirit taught,
  The future did unfold.

A scepter shall from Israel rise,
  A star from Jacob doubly blest;
And now before their wondering eyes
The brilliant meteor walks the skies
  Still onward toward the west.

Where'er it leads, that fiery light
  Unhidden by the blaze of day,
And marking with intenser might
The darkness of the deeper night,
  They follow on the way.

With morning's blush, when sunsets fade,
  On over rock and steep and wild,
By palm and cedar-tree and shade,
Till in the homely manger laid
  They find the royal child.

Intruding doubts away they fling,
  Unheeding the unwonted stir,
They from their costly treasures bring
Free offerings for the infant King,
  Gold, frankincense, and myrrh.

Gold shadows forth His royalty
  While frankincense His priesthood shows,
And myrrh that He shall buried be;
And so the wondrous mystery
  With deeper meaning grows.

Epiphany Hymn

By Aurelius Clemens Prudentius

[Tr. by Edward Caswell. 1849.]

Bethlehem, of noblest cities
  None can once with Thee compare;
Thou alone the Lord from Heaven
  Didst for us Incarnate bear.

Fairer than the sun at morning
  Was the star that told His birth;
To the lands their God announcing,
  Hid beneath a form of earth.

By its lambent beauty guided,
  See, the Eastern kings appear;
See them bend, their gifts to offer,
  Gifts of incense, gold, and myrrh.

Offerings of mystic meaning:
    Incense doth the God disclose;
Gold a royal child proclaimeth;
    Myrrh a future tomb foreshows.

Holy Jesus, in Thy brightness
    To the Gentile world displayed!
With the Father, and the Spirit,
    Endless praise to Thee be paid.

The Three Kings

By F. W. Faber, D.D.

Who are these that ride so fast o'er the
    desert's sandy road,
That have tracked the Red Sea shore, and
    have swum the torrents broad;
Whose camel's bells are tinkling through the
    long and starry night—
For they ride like men pursued, like the van-
    quished of a fight

Who are these that ride so fast? They are
    Eastern monarchs three,
Who have laid aside their crowns, and re-
    nounced their high degree;
The eyes they love, the hearts they prize, the
    well-known voices kind,
Their people's tents, their native plains,
    they've left them all behind.

The very least of faith's dim rays beamed
    on them from afar,
And that same hour they rose from off their
    thrones to track the star;
They cared not for the cruel scorn of those
    who called them mad;
Messiah's Star was shining, and their royal
    hearts were glad.

But a speck was in the midnight sky, un-
    certain, dim, and far,
And their hearts were pure, and heard a
    voice proclaim Messiah's Star:
And in its golden twinkling they saw more
    than common light.
The Mother and the Child they saw in Beth-
    lehem by night!

And what were crowns, and what were
    thrones, to such a sight as that?
So straight away they left their tents, and
    had not space to wait;
They hardly stop to slake their thirst at the
    desert's limpid springs,
Nor note how fair the landscape is, how
    sweet the skylark sings!

Whole cities have turned out to meet their
    royal cavalcade,
Wise colleges and doctors all their wisdom
    have displayed;
And when the Star was dim, they knocked
    at Herod's palace gate,
And troubled with the news of faith his
    politic estate.

And they have knelt in Bethlehem! The
    Everlasting Child
They saw upon His mother's lap, earth's
    Monarch meek and mild;
His little feet, with Mary's leave, they pressed
    with loving kiss,—

Oh what were thrones, oh what were crowns,
    to such a joy as this?

One little sight of Jesus was enough for
    many years,
One look at Him their stay and staff in the
    dismal vale of tears:
Their people for that sight of Him they gal-
    lantly withstood,
They taught His faith, they preached His
    Word, and for Him shed their blood.

Ah me! What broad daylight of faith our
    thankless souls receive,
How much we know of Jesus, and how easy
    to believe:
'Tis the noonday of His sunshine, of His sun
    that setteth never:
Faith gives us crowns, and makes us kings,
    and our kingdom is for ever!

Oh glory be to God on high for these Ara-
    bian kings,
These miracles of royal faith, with Eastern
    offerings:
For Gaspar and for Melchior and Balthazar,
    who from far
Found Mary out and Jesus by the shining
    of a Star!   .   .

Let There Be Light

By John Marriott

Thou whose almighty Word
Chaos and darkness heard,
        And took their flight,
Hear us, we humbly pray;
And where the gospel's day
Sheds not its glorious ray,
        Let there be light.

Thou, who didst come to bring
On Thy redeeming wing
        Healing and sight—
Health to the sick in mind,
Sight to the inly blind—
Oh, now to all mankind
        Let there be light.

Spirit of truth and love,
Life-giving, holy Dove,
        Speed forth Thy flight:
Move o'er the water's face,
Bearing a lamp of grace,
And in earth's darkest place
        Let there be light.

Blessèd and holy Three,
Glorious Trinity,
        Wisdom, Love, Might;
Boundless as ocean's tide,
Rolling in fullest pride,
Through the earth, far and wide,
        Let there be light.

Song of the Wise Men

By David Vedder

Matt. ii: 10

Son of the Highest! we worship Thee,
Tho clothed in the robe of humanity;
Tho mean Thine attire, and low Thine abode,
We own Thy presence, incarnate God!

We have left the land of our sires afar,
'Neath the blessed beams of Thine own birth-
    star,
Our spicy groves, and balmy bowers,
Perfumed by the sweets of Amra flowers;
Our seas of pearl, and palmy isles,
And our crystal lake, which in beauty smiles,
Our silver streams, and our cloudless skies,
And the radiant forms, and the starry eyes
That lit up our earthly paradise!

We have turned us away from the fragrant East
For the desert sand and the arid waste,
We have forded the torrent, and passed the
    floods,
And the chilly mountain solitudes,
And the tiger's lair, and the lion's den,
And the wilder haunts of savage men,
Till Thine advent star its glories shed
On the humble roof, and the lowly bed,
That shelters, Lord, Thy blessed head!

Son of the Highest! we worship Thee,
Tho Thy glories are veiled in humanity!
Tho mean Thine attire, and low Thine abode,
We hail Thine advent, eternal God!

Missionary Convocation

By W. B. Collyer

Assembled at Thy great command,
Before Thy face, dread King, we stand;
The voice that marshaled every star,
Has called Thy people from afar.

We meet, through distant lands to spread
The truth for which the martyrs bled;
Along the line, to either pole,
The thunder of Thy praise to roll.

Our prayers assist, accept our praise,
Our hopes revive, our courage raise;
Our counsels aid, to each impart
The single eye, the faithful heart.

Forth with Thy chosen heralds come,
Recall the wandering spirits home;
From Zion's mound send forth the sound,
To spread the spacious earth around.

Sun of Righteousness

By W. Williams

O'er the gloomy hills of darkness,
    Cheered by no celestial ray,
Sun of righteousness! arising,
    Bring the bright, the glorious day;
        Send the gospel
To the earth's remotest bound.

Kingdoms wide that sit in darkness,—
    Grant them, Lord! the glorious light:
And, from eastern coast to western,
    May the morning chase the night;
        And redemption,
Freely purchased, win the day.

Fly abroad, thou mighty gospel!
    Win and conquer, never cease;
May thy lasting, wide dominions
    Multiply and still increase;
        Sway Thy scepter
Savior! all the world around.

Home Missions

By William C. Bryant

Look from Thy sphere of endless day,
    O God of mercy and of might!
In pity look on those who stray,
    Benighted in this land of light.

In peopled vale, in lonely glen,
    In crowded mart, by stream or sea,
How many of the sons of men
    Hear not the message sent from Thee!

Send forth Thy heralds, Lord, to call
    The thoughtless young, the hardened old,
A scattered, homeless flock, till all
    Be gathered to Thy peaceful fold.

Send them Thy mighty word to speak,
    Till faith shall dawn, and doubt depart,
To awe the bold, to stay the weak,
    And bind and heal the broken heart.

Then all these wastes, a dreary scene,
    That makes us sadden as we gaze,
Shall grow with living waters green,
    And lift to heaven the voice of praise.

Missionaries

By William Bingham Tappan

Onward, ye men of prayer!
Scatter in rich exuberance the seed,
Whose fruit is living bread, and all your need
    Will God supply; His harvest ye shall
        share.

To Him, child of the bow,
The wanderer of his native Oregon,
Tell of that Jesus, who in dying won
    The peace-branch of the skies, salvation,
        for His foe!

Unfurl the banneret
On other shores; Messiah's cross bid shine
O'er every lovely hill of Palestine;
    Fair stars of glory that shall never set.

Seek ye the far-off isle;
The sullied jewel of the deep,
O'er whose remembered beauty angels weep,
    Restore its luster and to God give spoil.

Go break the chain of caste;
Go quench the funeral pyre and bid no more
The Indian river roll its waves of gore,
    Look up, thou East, thy night is over
        past.

To heal the bruisèd reed:
Oh, pour on Africa the balm
Of Gilead, and, her agony to calm,
    Whisper of fetters broken and the spirit
        freed.

And thou, O Church, betake
Thyself to watching, labor, help these men:
God shall thee visit of a surety when
    Thou art faithful; Church that Jesus
        bought, awake, awake!

LENT

L ENT is a fast of forty days, not including Sundays. It begins with Ash Wednesday, and ends with the Saturday preceding Easter. The Roman Catholic, Anglican, and other Churches make it a season of special self-denial. It is sometimes called the quadrigesimal fast. Because of the mortifying of the flesh and special penance and prayer, Lent is preeminently the season of Spiritual revival in the Church. It is supposed to have had its origin in a desire to commemorate our Lord's forty days of fasting in the wilderness, and His temptation by Satan. At first it lasted only forty hours, the length of time our Lord lay in the grave, and was purely voluntary. In time, however, it developed into a regularly prescribed fast, and was observed by Christians generally. Its duration was extended to thirty-six days in the fifth or sixth century. Either Gregory the Great, in the sixth century, or Gregory II., in the eighth century, added the four days to make out the forty. Moses, Elias, and our Lord each fasted forty days, and many contend that this accounts for the forty days of Lent.

It is an interesting fact that nations and individuals in all ages and in all parts of the world have observed days and seasons of fasting and prayer. In Jonah iii: 7-8, we read of the fast observed by the Ninevites, when Jonah threatened them with Jehovah's judgment on their sins. The Jews from the beginning of their existence as a distinct nation observed days of fasting.* While our Lord and the Apostles did not command fasting, their language anticipates such an exercise of the soul on fitting occasions.† The Mohammedans, annually kept their ninth month, Ramadan, as a fast, abstaining from food and drink, from the rising to the setting of the sun, and otherwise curbing their natural appetites. That fasting was a practice of the New Testament Church is shown by such passages as Acts xiv: 23. And the history of the Christian Church shows that believers of all nations and denominations, as organized bodies and as individuals, have believed in the efficacy of lenten thought, self-examination, fasting, and prayer.

LENTEN THOUGHTS

One of the most impressive features of the great experience which the Lenten season commemorates was its solitariness. Withdrawn from all companionship in the silence and loneliness of the desert those tremendous temptations came and were resisted which afforded the first test of the divine strength of Christ. In this experience, as in all the experiences which made up the story of his life, all men and women have a share. The great temptations, the great trials, those things which shake and shape us, come to us in solitude. Sometimes, under the spell of the contagion of feeling which a great crowd breathes out, men and women perform decisive acts; but for the most part those things which determine character come about in silence and solitude.

All the deepest experiences are allied with solitariness. There is a beautiful significance in this, since it is only as we withdraw ourselves from men that we find ourselves face to face with God. He who does not find the Creator in the creation and the Father in the brother as he goes about the world from day to day will never find him in any desert places; but he who does thus find the divine in the human, and who renders his service to God in His helpfulness to men, finds no place so filled with a great companionship as those

* Lev. xvi: 29; Judges xx: 26; 2 Chron. xx: 3; Jer. xii: 3. † Matt. vi: 16-18; ix: 15.

solitary places which men call deserts. To be alone by ourselves, if we are right with our fellows, is to be with God.

It is only in the silence of the world's work and the world's activities that the still, small voice speaks the deepest truths. The years in the desert were years of mighty discovery and growth to Moses, the days in the wilderness were days of a final revelation to Christ; it has happened again and again in the history of the world that men have been withdrawn from their fellows in order that they might be prepared for some great disclosure of truth. He who believes in God and serves Him is never alone. It is only the atheist or the man of unfaithful life who is really solitary; that which seems to be a desert, and which may be a place of supreme trial, is also a place of angelic visitation and of divine consolation.—C. U.

CHRIST'S LAST WORDS: "IT IS FINISHED"

Finished means not merely ended; it means completed, perfected, accomplished.

The long agony is finished. The throbbing brow and aching limbs, the feverish veins and pain-racked nerves, the taunting priests and gaping onlookers and heartbroken disciples, begin to fade. The end has come. At such a time memory crowds into a moment the events of a lifetime. His life passes in review before the Sufferer. All the scenes of the Passion—the march from Jerusalem, the wailing women, the cruel scourging, the shameful buffeting, the cowardly Pilate, the malignant Caiaphas, the denying Peter, the forsaking twelve, the betraying Judas—move before him like shadows and are gone. The poverty, the loneliness, the hostility of enemies, the desertion of disciples, the misunderstanding of friends, the recreancy and apostasy of the nation, the short-lived popularity with the feeble multitude in Galilee, the rancorous hate of the hierarchy in Jerusalem, the temptation of the Evil One—all is now over. The earthly is finished. Sorrow has done its worst. Its brief reign is over for the Divine Sufferer. The Passion is fulfilled.

Human malignancy is finished. It has accomplished its desire, realized its cherished plan, fulfilled its purpose, reached its end. The Son of God has not resisted evil, and evil has done to Him what it would. The malignant powers have had full freedom, and have wreaked their worst upon the Savior of mankind. "This is your hour," said Christ, "and the power of darkness." What sin unrestrained would do in its hour is attested. It can go no further than to whelm in contumely and to kill the Son of God and Savior of the world. The tares are fully grown, and this is their poisonous fruitage—such recompense for such love. The crucifixion of the world's Redeemer is the culminating sin of the world. "Sin, when it is finished," says James, "bringeth forth death." The tragedy of this hour is not the apparent death of the Son of God; it is the real death of priest and soldier—the insensibility to patient love in the horrible triumph of the one and the scarcely less horrible indifference of the other. Nothing that human misery has ever looked upon through tearful eyes, or human shame through downcast eyes can quite equal this scene of perfect love luminous in a scene of darkness which it cannot illumine, warm in this atmosphere of deathly coldness which it cannot recover to life. Sin is fulfilled.

The revelation of divine love is finished. It began in the day when the morning stars sang together, and man was given this palace beautiful for his home. It continued in the day when the prophet interpreted the mystic voice of conscience in a law so clear, so definite, so responsive to man's own nature, that no man could fail to see that "it was holy, pure, and good." It was carried on through all the wayward steps of a nation which refused to feed in green pastures, or lie down beside still waters, or be led in the paths of righteousness for Jehovah's sake. It was emphasized in the voices of prophets bearing witness, in an almost unbroken line, to One who pitieth them that fear Him, as a father pitieth his children, who forgiveth all their iniquities, healeth all their diseases, redeemeth their lives from destruction, and crowneth them with loving-kindness and tender mercies. But it was completed in the Incarnation, the Passion, and the death of the Son of God. Not even divine love can go further than this. "God commendeth his love toward us, in that, while we were yet sinners, Christ died for us." Beyond this, is and can be nothing. The cross of Christ is the final fruit of God's love. In that cross His love is fulfilled.

Redemption is finished. Sin has done its worst; it has brought up its last reserve, and is conquered. In its hour—the hour of darkness—it is vanquished. The taunt of the priests is the triumph-song of the Christian: "He saved others, himself he cannot save." This is why He saved others—because Himself He could not save. If He had come down from the cross, the cross would not have delivered. Had He not been more than conqueror, He would not have conquered. As nothing remains to manifest the blackness of human sin, and nothing to reveal the warmth and light of God's love, so nothing to complete the victory over sin. "It is finished," was cried with a loud cry; it is not the voice of resignation, nor a battle-cry; it is the shout of triumph.

As on a great battle-field there is one pivotal point on which the whole issue turns, one critical hour to which all before has led, from which all that follows issues, in which the victory is really won, so that it remains only to push retreat into flight, and flight into rout, and rout into irretrievable defeat, so the long campaign between good and evil culminates in Calvary and the hour of the crucifixion. That was the critical hour in the world's history. Could Christ have faltered or flinched or drawn back then, all would have been lost. He did not; and all was gained. The battle was really finished then, and has never been for a moment doubtful since. All that remains for His followers

is, armed with His courage, inspired by His spirit, employing His methods, to complete the victory which He has won. When from the other world we look down upon this, we shall see that the long battle does not wait to be finished for the day of judgment; that the victory was really achieved on the day of crucifixion; and that the judgment does but record the results of what was truly finished in that great hour.—C. U.

SERMONS AND OUTLINES

THE TRIAL OF CHRIST'S PERSONAL VIRTUE

By S. E. Herrick, D.D.

Then was Jesus led up of the Spirit into the wilderness to be tempted of the devil.—Matt. iv:1

Led of the Spirit to be tempted of the devil. Simultaneously played upon by two forces directly opposite in kind, and the perfected character of the man, Jesus Christ, was the resultant of these two forces so contrasted in His experience. Without either of these He would not have been the perfect man that He was. He did not begin life a perfect man. He became perfect, we are told, through suffering. "He grew in wisdom," says the Evangelist. "He learned obedience," says the apostle, "by the things that he suffered." He rose, through temptations resisted, from grace to grace, ever graduating, as it were, through the strife, into some new mastership of spiritual acquisition. This was His life's epitome—led of the Spirit and tempted of the devil—His whole biography in eight words. This is also the universal genesis of virtue. There is no virtue on earth, and there never was any, that was not begotten in precisely this way. This is the burden of life, and of life's attainment, which is set before every man. No doubt we have often wished that it might have been otherwise. We do not like this perpetual antagonism of life; this warfare of the flesh and the spirit on the soul's arena; the wings of life taking upward against the gravity of the body of death. If we could always and only be led by the Spirit without feeling at all that terrible devil pressure—but no! they go together.

Led of the Spirit, tempted of the devil, and it is that devil pressure that makes Gethsemane, and gives its burden and its bitterness to the cross. Led of the Spirit to be tempted of the devil. Some people think to escape the antagonism by simply throwing themselves wholly upon the leadings of the Spirit; giving themselves to the fierceness of the temptation; willing simply to be tempted of the devil, without any of the Spirit's leading:—simply letting temptation sweep them away wherever it will. There is no antagonism about such a life—it is easy. If a man wishes to throw himself at the mercy of the waves, they will carry

him whither they please. Such people become like wandering stars—nothing in them but the centrifugal force of life; and when borne out into the darkness—it is too painful to follow their course, even in imagination.

Wo will, sooner or later, be to the man who expects to be led of the Spirit without being also tempted of the devil, or who determines that he will be tempted of the devil without, at the same time, being led of the Spirit.

Is it a good thing, then, to be tempted of the devil? Nay, I did not say that, but I said: "What God hath joined together let no man put asunder." It is a good thing to be led of the Spirit *and* to be tempted of the devil. Did not Christ, very shortly after this experience of His, teach His disciples to pray, "Lead us not into temptation"? No; He did not teach them to pray any such thing. It reads quite differently if you read the whole of it: "Lead us not into temptation, *but* deliver us from evil." It is balanced by a divine delivering force; that is the thing he deprecates. A tempest is not a bad thing for an oak, save when the oak has no roothold—then it is a bad thing—but a tempest is a good thing for an oak if it have a roothold. The whole trend of Bible teaching is that temptations under the Spirit's leadership are themes for thanksgiving rather than for repining. "Blessed is the man that endureth temptation." "Count it all joy, my brethren, when ye fall into manifold temptations."

There is no grander spectacle to be beheld on this round earth than the man who is beset on every side by various buffetings, oppressed by evil suggestions, persecuted by solicitations to self-indulgence, pursued by the lusts of the flesh and of the eye and of the pride of life, and yet enabled to encounter them all—feeling the full force of their impact, and yet able to resist them all in the might of a divine energy that has been put within him by the Spirit of God. Great possibilities of evil are in any temptation, to be sure, but only in temptation by itself; only in temptation as divorced from that resisting force which God has abundantly supplied for its modification and transformation. When the twain are grappling, there are in that conflict great possibilities, and of that grappling comes all human virtue. Character is born of it. What is character? What do you mean by it? Character is something far greater than untempted innocence. Untempted innocence is not character. Adam before he sinned had innocence, but he had no character. Character begins with the first resistance to temptation, or with the first yielding to it. That is the point at which character begins. It does not begin before that. No man has character until he has met temptation, and either resisted it or yielded to it.

Think about that word "character" for a moment. It carries an abiding significance in itself. It means something that has been scored or engraved. It comes down to us from the olden time when all writing was done with some hard substance, with bone or ivory, with an iron pen, so that every letter was scored or cut into the substance written upon, and the letter so scored was called a character, because it was "carassed" into the substance written upon, cut in. We mean now by the word certain abiding results which have been scored into the soul of a man by the experiences of life, by some searching trial. Temptations leave a mark, and that mark is always significant whether we have overcome the temptation or it has overcome us. The temptation leaves a mark, and that is character.

Holiness, what is it? Simply innocence, no more than innocence. It is innocence that has endured the test, and that bears the mark —of endurance. What is unholiness? Why, that is innocence too, but it is innocence that has succumbed under the stress, and bears the mark; that has broken down under pressure. That is sin, that is unholiness. Holiness and unholiness, both are character. Now I know of no words in the biography of our blessed Lord that bring Him down so closely and tenderly into the fellowship of our human sympathies as these words of the text, "Then was Jesus led up of the Spirit into the wilderness to be tempted of the devil." They are words which seem, on the surface, to be preliminary or prefatory to an epistle of His life, but as we stop to ponder them we feel how fully He was with us. I think there are no words for which we ought to be so devoutly grateful, not even those that tell us of His crucifixion or of His resurrection. Because here we see Him, the Son of God, putting Himself down into our conditions, taking life at just our level—if I may so express it—and going through with its great struggle which we all have to undertake. Of course I do not mean now the struggle for bread and butter. I am not speaking of that, tho He had to endure that also, but I mean now that higher conflict which every one knows who has ever had one noble thought start within him; who has ever had one higher ambition awakened within

him, and who has felt a something trying to drag him down from those higher things.

That is what I mean by the struggle with life which every one has to feel. An everlasting fight it is, and a universal one, this struggle between the endeavor to be sons of God and the temptation to be only children of the flesh and of earthliness. Jesus, I say, entered Himself into this same conflict, and precisely at the same level with us. We see Him, made like unto us, taking upon Himself the same susceptibilities to evil, having just such possibilities as you and I—and I say this in its fullest meaning—with just such possibilities as you and I have, for if it was not possible for Him to sin, then He was not tempted as we are to sin. Having just the same possibilities that you and I have, "We have not a High Priest that cannot be touched with the feeling of our infirmities." If it was not possible for Him to sin, He could not have been touched with our infirmities—He did not have infirmities. He knew, in His own personal experience, just what we feel when appetite suggests that we should become, just for the sake of gratifying it, less like the man and more like the brute. He knew in His own experience just what we know when the ambition for popular influence suggests that in order to gain that influence we plunge into some vulgar and vainglorious and sensational display. He knew just what we experience when, feeling that our path is rugged and the way upward is slow, we are tempted to take some short cut to wealth, and so to ease and comfort, which, if we proceeded in strict uprightness and the fear of God, we might not so readily reach. Nowhere else does Jesus come closer to us than just here on this path of our daily experience, when "tempted of the devil."

This story of Jesus is worth nothing to us if it is not true. The Gospels are no better than almanacs to us if this is not true. In order to make His experience available and in the highest degree healthful to us, we must take note of the way in which He has received in His own life these two contrasted truths. We must take notice of the order in which He allowed Himself to be subjected to their play. Notice how carefully the statement is made, "Then was Jesus led up of the Spirit to be tempted of the devil." It will not do for us to reverse this order, as some of us do at times, and come to be tempted of the devil with the expectation that we shall be led of the Spirit. I see men doing that occasionally; I have done it myself. If we are really led of the Spirit, then let Him lead whithersoever He will, and we shall be likely to receive not detriment but blessing. But if we are going merely of our motion, the temptation into which we enter will shortly prove defeat and disaster. Keep in the order; be led of the Spirit, and let Him lead you wheresoever He pleases, and you can be tempted of the devil with safety; but do not be tempted of the devil with the expectation that you are going to be led of the Spirit.

Let us look a little more particularly at this

experience of our Elder Brother, and see what was the nature of this spiritual leading; what is meant by this word of the Evangelist as he tells the story of Jesus' life; what is meant by this "leading of the Spirit," this reinforcement and cooperation which were vouchsafed to him as some special preparation against attack. It is one of the unnecessary hindrances to our understanding of the record, arising from the dividing of the Bible into chapters and verses, that we almost always think of the beginning of a new chapter as the beginning of a separate narrative. Nowhere is this artificial division more of an impertinence, almost amounting to a profanity, than at this point. "Then was Jesus led up of the Spirit into the wilderness to be tempted of the devil." That is no place for the story to begin, and the man was impertinent and profane when he cut up the Bible in that way. I do not want my conversation cut up in that way and given to men in disconnected bits. You would not like to have your conversation cut up in that way, but ministers have to submit to it a good deal.

Read the preceding words, "Jesus when he was baptised went up straightway from the water, and lo, the heavens were opened to him, and he saw the Spirit of God descending as a dove, and coming upon him. And lo, a voice out of heaven saying: This is my beloved Son, in whom I am well pleased. Then was Jesus led up of the Spirit into the wilderness to be tempted of the devil"—led by that same Spirit that had just descended upon Him, with the full, clear, unmistakable disclosure of His Sonship; with the words of the Father ringing in His ear, the same Spirit that comes to us, His disciples, as the apostle says, by the spirit of adoption or of sonship by which we cry, Abba, Father. That heavenly preparation under which Christ went forth into the wilderness to meet His trial was not some mystic, undefinable influence. The leading of the Spirit is set forth just as clearly as the story of the devil is told. They are both told together, and should never be cut apart.

Many people are inclined to think that the action of the Spirit of God is something that exists only in the imagination of weak enthusiasts. It is no such thing. Here we have it given us with the utmost clearness—the way in which, and the end to which, the Spirit came to Jesus Christ. It came bringing down into the mind of Christ this clear strong assurance, that He was God's beloved Son, that God was His Father. Not that He had not known it before; He had known it before, even from His childhood, as He had had the Spirit before from His childhood. But there came to Him at this point such an impressive and powerful assurance and conviction of Sonship that, under the burden and glory of the thought, He was constrained to go away, away alone by Himself into the wilderness, to contemplate in solitude far from the influence of men, the relations in which He stood—the Son of God! the Son of God, well beloved. How, henceforth, should He bear Himself? That was the thought. What does sonship mean? what does it demand of me? He was asking. What towards God, if I am His beloved Son? What towards man, my brother, if I am God's Son? What if I bear myself a true Son in my Father's house, may I expect from my Father? What may I expect from my brethren, who neither know my Sonship nor their own?

These were the questions that were burning like fire through His bones, as He went out under that impression of the Spirit into the wilderness. These were the questions which He answered there, and kept on answering through all His life and with His death. This explains all the thoughts, and nothing else does explain them. This explains all that follows; the character of the temptation; the Sermon on the Mount—that was no extemporaneous affair. It was made in the wilderness during these forty days. It was forged under heat. He did not just open His lips and pour out that Sermon on the Mount. Under this grand, this unquestionable assurance of His relations to the Father were wrought out all these matchless expositions of the essentials of human wellbeing that are in the Beatitudes. This dowry of the Spirit upon Him fits into the whole Sermon on the Mount, and explains it as nicely and as accurately as in some fine piece of mechanism one cog-wheel explains and interprets another. The story of the temptation explains and interprets the Sermon on the Mount in the same way.

Now this was the end of the Spirit's power and leading upon Him by which He became equipped and fortified against the attack which was so sure to fall. You can see if this is not so. Look at these contrasted forces which are let loose upon Him. We have already looked at the leading of the Spirit, what the nature of it was. In what shape did the temptation come? See if the one does not exactly correspond to the other. "If thou be the Son of God." What had the divine Spirit just said to Him? "This is my beloved Son, in whom I am well pleased." The first words of the tempting devil are, "If thou be the Son of God, command these stones to be made bread." "If thou art the Son of God cast thyself down, and he will send his angels to hold thee up." All these temptations were addressed to this one point in His affections. This was the bull's-eye of the target to which every fiery dart was directed. "If thou be the Son of God." The whole endeavor was to shake Him and loosen Him at this point of His conviction of His divine Sonship; to make the poor hungry man disbelieve that He is the Son of God, and that God is treating Him like a Son; to make Him act as if He was not a Son; to make Him plunge into some unfilial course, to break into some temper of dissatisfaction. See how the contrasting forces play back and forth. The Spirit divine and the spirit devilish. Like deep calling unto deep. If you are the Son of God there is no need that you should go hungry. Turn the stones to bread if you are hungry. Nay, says the Sonly spirit, my Father made the stones to be stones and not something else. A son lives not alone by the bread which he can find or can make in his father's house; he maintains his sonship by obedience, not by making bread. Let him obey, if he is a son, every word that proceedeth from his father's mouth, then he will maintain sonship, not by making bread.

If you be the Son of God, the devil says, you can win the following you ought to have among your brethren by giving some grand proof before their eyes. Your Father will sustain you, and your brethren will flock around you. No, replied Jesus, a son will not tempt his father to break what he knows to be one of that father's laws, and the force of gravity is just as much one of My Father's laws as a law of the Decalog graven on stone, and every law of nature is just as much so as a law of Moses. If there was any necessity for so doing, no doubt My Father would be willing that I should suspend or modify that law, but there is no necessity, and I will not be unfilial.

So He was led of the Spirit and tempted of the devil. To and fro the forces played on Him, and they are working on the character of every man in precisely the same way. This is the method and the *rationale* of their operation. That temptation of the wilderness stands typical of all temptations. There is no human trial that does not still range under it. Look at the last temptation that came to you, perhaps this morning or last night, or take the very next one that meets you and study it, and you will find that this is at the heart and center of it—that you are God's child, and it is your greatest obligation and your clearest privilege to bear yourself as God's child in this world, which is simply a part of your Father's house, and the temptation is always to do something that will break down your character at the point of sonship. I care not what may be the external form which the temptation takes; it may spring out of the fires of youthful appetite, or the suggestions of ambition or of covetous desire, or the narrowness or restrictions of your poverty, or your pains or weakness, and the meagerness of your life itself, with its dry and barren monotony, or out of your wealth and ease and comfort, but whencesoever it comes, the evil essence, the subtle, evil spirit of temptation will be, in every case, that you shall be, or do, or say, what is unfilial, what will tend to break down God's Fatherhood and your own sonship, in your heart and life; what will put estrangement between you and Him, of whom your spirit has been begotten. It comes to me as the great conviction of my life that we need to be born again each day into the sense of a divine sonship; to have descend upon us in ever-increasing measures that same spirit of adoption by which we cry, "Abba, Father." Then, led up into every day and its experiences by that Spirit, as temptations earthly, sensual, and devilish rise upon us, they will simply work for us, as they did for our Elder Brother, "a far more exceeding and eternal weight of glory."—H. R.

SELF-RENUNCIATION THE LAW OF SELF-PRESERVATION

By Joseph Roberts, D.D.

Verily, verily, I say unto you, except a grain of wheat fall into the earth and die, it abideth by itself alone; but if it die, it beareth much fruit. He that loveth his life (or soul) loseth it; and he that hateth his life (soul) in this world shall keep it unto life eternal.—John xii: 24, 25

How can it be affirmed that gain is loss and that loss is gain? To formal logic this statement is absurd. You might as well say that something is nothing, or that down is up, or that the south is the north. The statement violates the principle of contradiction—that which Sir William Hamilton declares to be the highest of all logical laws, the supreme law of thought. Yet the statement is not a mere rhetorical paradox, but an exact statement of the deepest law of life, the fundamental law of self-sacrifice and glorification of the Son of Man. . . .

"Loveth his life, ..." "hateth his life . . ." "eternal life." Do you like paradoxes? Nature is full of paradoxes. Some men are accustomed to apply "paradox" as if it were a term of reproach, and implied absurdity. But all that the term properly implies is that the burden of the proof lies with him who maintains the paradox, since men are not expected to abandon the prevailing belief until some reason is shown. . . . As we said, nature is full of paradoxes. The water which drowns us as a fluent stream can be walked upon as ice. The bullet which, when fired from a musket, carries death, will be harmless if ground to dust before being fired. The crystallized part of the oil of roses, so grateful in its fragrance—a solid at ordinary temperatures, tho readily volatile—is a compound substance, containing exactly the same elements, and in exactly the same proportions, as the gas with which we light our streets. The tea, which we daily drink with benefit and pleasure, produces palpitations, nervous tremblings, and even paralysis if taken in excess; yet the peculiar organic agent called "thein," to which tea owes its quality, may be taken by itself (as thein, not as tea) without any appreciable effect. . . .

Thus you see that nature is full of paradoxes, and not nature only, but also the teaching of the Teacher from heaven. According to His teaching, the only true gain is through loss; the only true enrichment is through giving; the only true victory is through suffering and humiliation; and the only true life is through death. "He that loveth his life loseth it; and he that hateth his life in this world shall keep it unto life eternal." His own life was subjected to this law.

More than once did the Lord express—in the words which He here emphatically repeats—the course of life which those must lead who would follow Him. On several great occasions He impressed this law of spirit of life upon the minds of His disciples. After calling the Twelve, in His commission to them, to place His own claim on their affections as greater than that of the father, mother, friend, and calling for self-denial and self-sacrifice, He said: "He that findeth his life shall lose it; he that loseth his life for my sake shall find it." (Comp. Matt. x: 39; xvi: 25; Luke ix: 24; xvii: 33.)

This is the watchword of Christ and it should be our watchword also. In the text He is applying to His own case this universal law of the divine life, of which He was on the point of giving the crowning, climacteric expression by His suffering and death. . . . Brethren, do you grasp this great thought? Do you understand this great law of the moral and spiritual world? What is it? It is the fundamental law of self-sacrifice. What does it mean? It means this: That self-renunciation is the law of self-preservation; and conversely, that the law of self-preservation is the law of self-destruction.

Let us try to realize this law, and pass on now to the consideration of it under the following divisions:

I. First, then, let us look at the vicarious death of Christ in the light of this law. "Verily, verily I say unto you, except a grain of wheat fall into the earth and die, it abideth by itself alone; but if it die, it beareth much fruit."

This is true, not only of wheat, but of every other seed; every seed must die in order to bear fruit, There is no harvest without death. All nature, conceived of as animated by the breath of God, and sustained by His Almighty Word, contains in her phenomena the most pregnant symbols of all the truths in the spiritual world. And in these words, which were first spoken to the Greeks, Christ does not appeal to the testimony of the prophets, but to the secretly prophesying similitude of nature. "Therefore, nature herself, as well as the divine prophecy in Israel, speaks of a redeeming death."

Since the fall of mankind was foreseen, and the plan of their redemption laid in the deep counsels of eternity, the Creator implanted types in nature of this great principle—life through death, gain through loss. From this divine ordinance of fruit springing from the seed, of the new growth from the death of the old, we have the most primitive prophecy of the mystery of the atonement which pure creation contains. Indeed, we may look upon the whole world as one great parable to which the Gospel supplies the clew. How patent

and beautiful is this analogy to illustrate that change from weakness to power, from springing forth afresh of life out of death! From death in its general sense, and from death in its special sense, namely, as the wages of sin, new life has sprung forth. Such a wonderful idea is this; death is the source of the natural and the spiritual harvest. Christ could not be a source of eternal life without dying, but through His death He became a source of life, increase, fruitfulness, and glorification.

1. His death is the reviving power in the moral world to all united to Him through faith.

The grain of wheat must fall to the ground and die, in order to become a reviving energy. It must undergo death-like change, and death-like transformation before it springs up and bears fruit. So the eternal Son voluntarily sinks down into the earth of death and curse, "into the domain and destiny of sinful men, not to remain there, but to rise out of it as the Glorified Glorifier, the risen Raiser of Men."

In the history of nations, in the life of men, in the plan of redemption, as well as in nature, it is a law of universal operation that out of self-renouncing, self-sacrificing resignation of all, the benediction of richer fruitfulness, of glorified, multiplied existence, springs forth. If Christ had not died He would "abide alone,"—alone in the presence of His Father, alone in the bosom of eternal silence, but without any of the sons of men. Through His death He became the source of a reviving power and fruitfulness. The incarnation and the death of the Son of Man form the spiritual power that is to create the world anew. If we would become one with God—and what higher glory or felicity is conceivable?—let us ever remember that Christ in His obedience and atoning death is the medium. "For as the Father hath life in himself, even so gave he to the Son also to have life in himself." "For as the Father raiseth the dead and quickeneth them, even so the Son also quickeneth whom he will."

"The Son of Man came to give his life a ransom for many." This is what the Holy Ghost said of His death by the pen of inspiration—"Who gave himself a ransom for all, to be testified in due time." "A ransom" —do you know what a ransom means? It means an equivalent or satisfaction for things forfeited or lost. "He gave himself a ransom for all." Let us take note of the word "for." The vicariousness of the sacrifice is implied in the word "for." A vicarious act is an act for another. The Son of Man "poured out his soul unto death" for us, and "bare the sin of many." And when the great tragedy of Calvary had taken place, it was said that "His own self bare our sins in his body on the tree." In all these statements the death of our Lord is set forth as the pivot, as the soul and center of the mysterious transaction of redemption "for" others. . . .

How original and divine is this scheme— life through death, fruitfulness through destruction! A grain of wheat is small and insignificant, yet what a mystery is contained in it! A little child may hold scores of them on the palm of its hand, yet all the wisdom, all the science, and all the philosophy of the world could not produce one grain. To produce one grain of wheat there is necessary the cooperation of all the laws, forces, and influences of nature. If evolution is simply the history of the steps by which the world has come to be what it is, then, according to the investigation of science within the last ten years into the origin and growth of wheat, wheat apparently does not come under the law of evolution. It does not come under the law of the "survival of the fittest." I do not intend now to indicate the course and scope of these searches more than to say that the record of history and the deposits of geology testify that wheat has no development, no descent. It has never been found in a fossil state; it has no existence whatever in the deposits of geology. And, further, it has never been found in a wild state in any country, nor in any age; and never existed where man did not cultivate it. Wheat is an exception in the vegetable kingdom, for the reason that it has no power whatever to perpetuate its own existence, like some other growing and living things. A crop of wheat left to itself, in any latitude or country, in the third or the fourth year from its first planting, would entirely disappear. In regard to the "staff of life," man is the High Priest who was ordained to administrate between God and Nature. It has no power to master its surrounding difficulties so as to become self-perpetuating, and never exists where men do not cultivate it. Thus, it does not come under the law of the "survival of the fittest."

This is also as true of our Redeemer as of a grain of wheat. He descended from heaven. The plan of our salvation originated in the Divine Mind. Christ is the "Bread of Life," "For the bread of God is he which cometh down from heaven, and giveth life unto the world." He is the dispenser of this heavenly vital energy. He communicates His spiritual life and essence itself to His own, and therefore makes them like Himself, first spiritually, then corporeally. This is the universal law of life: "a deathlike metamorphosis," as a condition whereon depends the renewal of life, is type of the fundamental law in the Kingdom of God; which law provides that we, by priestly surrender of our own wills to the will of God, do obtain new kingly life from God.

And besides this, let us carry this thought further. It was not the life but the death of Christ that multiplied Him a thousandfold. "But if it die it bringeth forth much fruit." Had this first seed-corn died and fallen into the earth, it would be alone in its peculiar preeminence, just as Jesus stood in His power of the Spirit, His divine human life and energy, incommunicable, independent of, and above the rest of the human race, before He died. But now what a thousandfold fruit does He bear! From the time He gave up His soul as an offering for sin, "He sees his seed and prolongs his days." We may imag-

ine that we see in an acorn all that may arise from it—an oak, a ship, a navy—for an acorn has a life-germ that is capable of increase and multiplication; but we cannot imagine the results of the suffering and the death of Christ to humanity. The Son of God, and He alone, through His omniscience could clearly foresee and foretell the spiritual results of His obedience unto death. This earth is the only wheat country in the great universe of God; and the Grain of Wheat is bringing forth much fruit. And in the time of the harvest God will say to the reapers, "Gather the wheat into my barn." Yes, and this barn is the eternal Kingdom of our Lord Jesus Christ.

2. This principle involves, further, that the Son of Man is glorified in His death.

When He explained His system, in brief, to the Greeks, He said, "The hour is come that the Son of Man should be glorified." As the Son of Man, the normal and the central Man, by His dying, the divine energy of His person will be set free and exerted for all mankind. Nature arrives at the true and the beautiful by passing through death into new life. The higher form of existence is obtained only through extinction of the lower form that preceded it. The food perishes in the process of digestion to reappear in vivified flesh and blood. So in a symbolical analogy the grain of wheat dies in order to prolong and glorify itself.

When Christ uttered the words "The hour is come: glorify thy Son," He realized all the grief and pain which were to come. But the dark cloud of suffering and death could not hide from Him the results in His glorification. He saw both the star and cloud, and knew well which of the two was transient, and which would endure. The hour was at hand, and the sacrifice and the struggle were real when His calm soul was troubled. Oh! what a tremendous self-sacrifice that death of the cross involved. Yet, in the face of His sufferings, Christ said, with a burst of triumph: "Now the Son of Man is glorified." And what is very remarkable, in five brief clauses He repeats the word "glorify" five times, as if to His view a coruscation of glories played at that moment above the cross. He was glorified, He is to be glorified in the results of His death—"bring forth much fruit."

II. Once more. Self-renunciation is the law of self-preservation; and conversely, self-preservation is the law of self-destruction in the life of men. "He that loveth his life (his own soul), shall lose it; and he that hateth his life in this world shall keep it unto life eternal."

The way to eternal life is to hate oneself. Death of self, the death of egoism that clings to the outward life of appearance, is the condition of the transition from the old life to the new. Thus, the Master and the servant are under the same law. There is no other way to preserve or redeem against ourselves than by self-hating and self-renouncing surrender of ourselves to death. That which held good for the Master in its own peculiar, unapproachable sense—as of the seed which He alone could sow, the sacrifice which He alone could offer—is not less on that account a type for us and fulfilled in us. The disciple, then, must be like his Master, the servant like his Lord. There are many things in which we cannot resemble Him—in freedom from sin, in knowledge, in wisdom, and power. But in this highest quality of all, in the divinest faculty and grace, we can be like Him. We can sacrifice ourselves; this is merely a necessary means to a higher end. Sacrifice is the indispensable condition of success. We must renounce in order to prevail.

Now, how many of us are willing to follow Christ in the regeneration of society until we get sight of Calvary? We are willing to make what we call "reasonable sacrifice." What do you mean by reasonable sacrifice? There is nothing reasonable in this universe but the entire sovereignty of the law of self-sacrifice in the personal life. There is nothing more reasonable in the moral order than sacrifice. There is but one reasonable sacrifice for you and me, and that is to have our wills to be nailed upon the cross of an entire self-renunciation in the service of Christ. "I beseech you, brethren, by the mercies of God, that ye present your bodies a living sacrifice, holy, acceptable unto God, which is your reasonable service."—H. R.

LENT

By Rev. E. P. Cachemaille

I will be sorry for my sin.—Ps. xxxviii: 18

At this season we are reminded of our Lord's fasting, temptation, sufferings and death. This should make us think why He suffered so much. He suffered and died for our sins. Then at this season especially we ought to think upon our sin, and the text tells us how we ought to think about it.

I. "I will be SORRY."

Not only "afraid," tho sin is something to be afraid about. (*Illust.*—Adam, Judas Iscariot.) Nor, "I will try to hide it, or forget it;" but, like Peter, who wept bitterly, "be sorry." Sorry for whom? Not only the person against whom you have done wrong—*e. g.*, if you have told your mother a lie, you will be sorry before her—but also "against thee, thee only, have I sinned."

II. "Sorry FOR MY SIN."

Not only for the disgrace it has brought upon me, or the suffering it has caused me; but for my having broken God's holy commandments and grieved the Holy Spirit.

III. "Sorry for MY sin."

Whose? Sad to see others sin; should never rejoice over it, but pray God to forgive them, and be sorry for them. But here I have to be sorry, not only for my brother's or schoolfellow's sin, but for my own.

"I will be sorry." Father, mother, teacher, minister, friends, all who know how wicked my sin is, will be sorry. But these are not enough. I, too, must be sorry.

Ask God, for Christ's sake, to make you truly sorry for your sin, by the teaching of the Holy Spirit. Ask Him to forgive you for Christ's sake, and to wash you in the precious blood that cleanseth from all sin. Ask Him to help you to show that you are really sorry by forsaking the sin.—P. T.

ASH WEDNESDAY

By E. M. A.

Matt. iv: 1

Why this season is called Lent? Why this day Ash Wednesday? Let us use the season; hope to profit by it.

(Forty days Moses was on the Mount. Forty days Jonah was crying out to the Ninevites.)

Think to-day of Jesus tempted. Why? For our sakes. (1) To teach us to expect temptation. (2) To show us how to meet it.

Let us look at the Catechism, and see how it warns us against three kinds of temptation. What did your Godfathers and Godmothers promise for you? (Let answer be repeated.)

I. The devil and all his works. Subject mysterious, yet we know: (1) He puts bad thoughts into our minds. (2) Urges us to use wrong words. (3) Tempts us to evil deeds. All his works are wrong, evil, against God.

II. The pomps and vanity of this wicked world. Its sinful pleasures. May have many pure pleasures; but there are such as lead us *from*, not *to* God. Its outward show and pomp help to turn our thoughts, and so our desires, from Him. (Contrast Lot's choice with Daniel's.)

III. The sinful lusts (or desires of the flesh). (1) Such as laziness (perhaps too lazy to say prayers, or help another). (2) Greediness; letting our appetite master us. (3) Selfishness; as shown in thinking more of self than others; eagerly seizing best place or piece, etc.

Let us fight as Jesus did, with the sword of the Spirit. "It is written."—P. T.

THE PURPOSE OF FASTING

By W. C. Smith

Matt. vi: 16-18

Properly speaking, fasting is not so much a duty enjoined by revelation as it is the natural expression of certain religious feelings and desires. There is but one special fast ordained in the Old Testament, and there is none at all ordained in the New. Yet one cannot fail to see that the exercise is nevertheless quite in accordance with the whole tenor of a true religious life of all ages; and that, if it is not expressly commanded, it is only because nature itself teaches us in certain circumstances thus to afflict the soul. These circumstances which would obviously suggest this exercise are twofold.

I. Fasting is the natural expression of grief, and therefore the natural accompaniment of godly sorrow. It is a mistaken kindness to press dainties on the heart when it has no appetite for aught but its sorrow. Better let it have its fill of grief—better every way for body and mind. Spiritual sorrow in the same way suggests, and is the better for, this exercise of fasting.

II. Fasting is also a wise method of keeping down the law of the flesh which is in our members. Rich and poor will be the better for a fast now and then, to mortify the flesh, to weaken the incentives to evil, to subdue in some measure the carnal nature, and give freer play and power to the spiritual man within.

III. Our Lord counsels His people, (1) that their fasting must be real, sincere, genuine—a thing to be seen, not of men, but of God; (2) that fasting in the Christian Church should be altogether private, and even secret, not only not in order to be seen of men, but absolutely hidden from them. Religion does not consist in a sour visage or morose habit —nay, more, religion is not properly a sorrowful thing. The Gospel was not sad tidings, but glad tidings for all mankind, and we are not acting fairly by it unless we strive so to present it, in all its winning and attractive beauty, that men shall be led to seek after Jesus. Christianity has its godly sorrow, has its heartgrief for sin, has its fasting and mortifying of the flesh; yet we do it utter injustice unless we also make it appear that it is, taken as a whole, the only true blessedness and peace and joy, the only walk with God which is gladness everlasting.—S. B., vol. v., p. 144.

FAST DAY

By Phillips Brooks, D.D.

Moreover when ye fast, be not, as the hypocrites, of a sad countenance; . . . that thou appear not unto men to fast, but unto thy Father which is in secret.—Matt. vi: 16-18

Let us ask what is the use of fasting, for so we shall best come to understand the true methods and degrees of fasting. All bodily discipline, all voluntary abstinence from pleasure of whatever sort, must be of value either as a symbol of something or a means of something. These two functions belong to it as being connected with the body, which is at once the utterer and the educator of the soul within. No man can be a better man save as his pride is crushed into repentance, and as the sweltering, enwrapping mass of passions and indulgences that is around him is broken through, so that God can find his soul and pour Himself into it. This, then, is the philosophy of fasting. It expresses repentance, and it uncovers the life to God. It is the voluntary disuse of anything innocent in itself, with a view to spiritual culture.

I. Consider first the value of fasting as a symbol. It expresses the abandonment of pride. But it is the characteristic of a symbolic action that it not merely expresses but increases and nourishes the feeling to which it corresponds. And if abstinence is the sign of humility it is natural enough that as the life abstains from its ordinary indulgences the humiliation which is so expressed should be deepened by the expression. Thus the symbol becomes also a means.

II. Note the second value of fasting—its value directly as a means. The more we watch the lives of men, the more we see that one of the reasons why men are not occupied with great thoughts and interests is the way in which their lives are overfilled with little things. The real Lent is the putting forth of a man's hand to quiet his own passions and to push them aside, that the higher voices may speak to him and the higher touches fall upon him. It is the making of an emptiness about the soul, that the higher fullness may fill it. Perhaps some day the lower needs may themselves become, and dignify themselves by becoming, the meek interpreters and ministers of those very powers which they once shut out from the soul. There will be no fasting days, no Lent, in heaven. Not because we shall have no bodies there, but because our bodies there will be open to God, the helps and not the hindrances of spiritual communication to our souls.—S. B., vol. v., p. 143

MEDITATION ESSENTIAL TO THE DEVELOPMENT OF SPIRITUAL LIFE

By A. E. KITTREDGE, D.D.

And He said unto them, Come ye yourselves apart into a desert place, and rest awhile; for there were many coming and going, and they had no leisure so much as to eat.—Mark vi: 31

You will see by the context the occasion for these words. It was an hour of triumph and of trial. The disciples had just returned from the mission upon which Christ had sent them two by two. During their absence a terrible event had taken place in the prison-house of Herod. Word was just now brought to Christ and His disciples announcing the death of John, the forerunner of Christ. Then, crowds of people, sick in body, sick in soul, friends, enemies, had been thronging them until the disciples had forgotten to provide even for their hunger. Then Christ said to them, " Come ye yourselves into a desert place, and rest awhile," etc.

Now, I take this to teach the need of withdrawal from the noise and bustle of the world, that man's own good may be subserved; that quiet, earnest, continuous meditation is essential to the development of spiritual life. Such a theme as this seems out of place in the universal hurry that surrounds life to-day. This tidal wave of feverish excitement has invaded even the church, the pulpit. Not a few pulpits have surrendered to sensationalism. Said a man to me, " You must keep things buzzing in the church as in the world, if you would interest people." Of course, activity in church affairs is important. But our danger is the neglect of the inner spiritual life.

The essentials of strong spiritual character are, not church membership, nothing outward; but are, hatred of sin, love to God as revealed in the Bible, loyalty to the divine will, an ever deepening passion for the souls of men, etc. Now, these essentials are developed by meditation.

I remark—

1. That this spiritual meditation must be *quiet*. When a boy, I thought it strange that the Savior should say, " When thou prayest, enter into thy closet, and when thou hast shut the door," etc. I thought the shutting of the door trivial. It is not trivial. You shut the world out, and yourself in with Christ. Elements of Christian growth are (a) knowl-edge of yourself, (b) knowledge of Christ. Quiet meditation secures this knowledge. The spirit uses but two channels (a) The Word, (b) Prayer. The spirit uses these in the still hours. The accountant and the scholar demand quietness in solving their problems. Yet the Christian, who has infinitely more important problems to solve, etc. Believer, what a travesty are often our prayers; we devote a few moments in the morning to a hurried prayer, in the evening to a sleepy prayer, and devote all the rest of the day to the world. O believer, enter thy closet and shut that door, etc.

2. This spiritual meditation must be *fervent*. Jacob wrestling with God, etc.

3. This spiritual meditation must be *resolute*. England's greatest engineer was said to be a man of no great natural talent, yet he performed wonders, bridged torrents, pierced mountains for his viaduct, etc. When he came to a difficulty that seemed insurmountable, he would shut himself in his room and neither eat nor drink, that he might concentrate all his mind on that difficulty. At the end of two or three days he came out of the room with the look and step of a conqueror, and gave orders which seemed to his men like inspirations. Let this unyielding resolution mark our prayers to God. A man takes a check to a bank. It is not enough to hand in the check. He *waits* for an answer. We must *wait* on God.

The highest conception of prayer is not that of a pump-handle, to bring up the water of life. The highest conception of prayer is seen at the Last Supper, in the beloved disciple leaning on the breast of Christ, *not uttering a word*, just lying there. As an old divine once said, we should fall on our knees and *grow* there.

The cry was heard 3,000 years ago, " O Israel, to your tents!" In this age, when our spiritual life is so feverish, runs to assemblies, to talk, and is so shallow, the cry comes, " To your closets, O Israel! "—H. R.

APOSTOLIC SERVICE AND TEMPTATION

By JOSEPH PARKER, D.D.

And at Lystra there sat a certain man, impotent in his feet, a cripple from his mother's womb, who never had walked.—Acts xiv. 8-18

This is the kind of man who is always looking out for religious excitement or entertainment. Christianity always *begins with the cripple*, with the poor, with the outcast, with the friendless. The one cry of Christianity is, " Give me a man," and the answer is always a cripple. This the Church's proper defense: it has a seat for the cripple who cannot stand. Paul perceived that the man had "faith to be healed." This man also is everywhere. That you are in church has a whole heartful of meaning. You *do* believe. *Perceiving* that he had faith. What eyes those men had! They knew faith when it was only a gleam in the eye. The wise preacher must have the critical eye which pierces the core of the case. Why did Paul speak "*with a loud voice*"? Some people object to loud voices; they say they could hear quite as well if the preacher did not exert himself so. It is not enough to hear. An utterance must not deliver its own syllables only, but take with it heart, blood, fire, music, life. *The gods are come down.* Every life has its hand-to-hand fight with hell. This was the devil's hour: if they get over that bridge, the Apostles will be safe. Their self-knowledge was their salvation. "Sirs *we are men of like passions with you.*"

The narrative sheds light on Christianity itself; it makes men do *what they never did before.* This man had never walked. It does not make us do things a little better—it makes us do things we had never done. The *attention paid* to Paul and Barnabas was natural; its root is right. But the preacher must never become the priest. Paul must not separate himself from human sympathy. When the priest of Jupiter saw what was done, he said: "We have never seen anything like this." He would have put the knife to Jupiter's throat. So Christianity indicates itself *by the men it makes:* a noble manhood convinces the priest of Jupiter. The man *leaped and walked.* A man leaping is always beside himself. We cannot live leaping; but we must do so at first. It would be pleasant to see some of us leaping a little; it would do the preacher's heart good to see some people trying to fly a little! Without enthusiasm, what is the Church? It is Vesuvius without fire; Niagara without water; a firmament without a sun!—H. R.

THE TRUE METHOD OF SECURING A REVIVAL

By Frederick Wagstaff

Be watchful, and strengthen the things that remain, that are ready to die.—Rev. iii: 2

In an age when so much is said and thought about revivals, the passage before us is peculiarly appropriate. The early part of this chapter gives a description of a church which needs a revival, and the text contains a divine command as to the proper methods to be taken in order to secure that revival. The great secret, after all, consists in rightly cherishing those things that are already possessed.

I. WHAT ARE THE THINGS WHICH REMAIN IN SUCH A CHURCH?

1. There is, in the first place, some degree of *church organization.* There was, in the case of Sardis, a "name to live"; they had "received" the oracles of God. It was a Church, altho a weak one. The fire of godliness was there, albeit the flame was well-nigh extinguished. There were the germs of life, tho they were very feeble, and could scarcely be seen. Yet this imperfect existence God did not despise, since the apostle was directed to address an epistle to the Church. Christ will not break the bruised reed, nor quench the smoking flax.

2. They had some of the *Church ordinances.* They had the Word of God. The ministry of the Gospel was still an actual fact; "remember how thou hast *heard,* and hold fast," etc. The preaching of the Gospel, if not accompanied by the saving power of former days, was still a privilege in their possession. There may have been a lack of what is sometimes called "unction" in the preaching; but there was no false doctrine taught. They were not warned against what they heard, but, on the contrary, were charged to remember it and hold it fast.

3. They appear to have carried out to a certain extent some of the *undertakings to which a Christian Church may address itself.* "I know thy works." The works of this Church are twice alluded to, and in the second instance there is an intimation that God had not found them perfect. It is literally: "I have not found thy works full to the brim." They are not the works of a truly healthy Church. It is as if God had said:" Go back to thy first love and repentance; get filled with grace, and the works of a Christian life will flow abundantly."

4. There was also *the presence of a few godly men.* In Sardis there were a "few names which had not defiled their garments." To them a promise is given that hereafter they shall walk with Christ in white. They are spoken of as fighting for the truth, and to such as should overcome there is a promise of the triumphal robes and honors of the victorious.

Here, then, are the things that remain. Perhaps it may be said the catalog is not a very promising one. It might be worse; there might have been *no* organization—no ordinances—no Christian work—no true believers. But what shall be done with a Church like that at Sardis? There must be improvement or destruction; for the things that remain are "ready to die."

II. WHAT IS THE DIVINE METHOD OF SECURING A REVIVAL?

Human ingenuity would probably resort to one or other of these two methods: (1) Some would suggest entire *reconstruction.* They would remove the weak and sickly plants, and till the ground afresh. They would throw down the tottering walls of the old structure, and build anew from the foundation. (2) Others would seek to accomplish the end desired by *introducing some powerful revival element,* such as they have heard of as successful elsewhere—revival preaching, revival services, revival hymns.

God's plan differs from both these. He neither destroys nor calls in the aid of foreign excitement. He simply says: " Strengthen the things that remain." Literally, " Make fast the surviving things that are about to perish." Here then we have—

1. *Church organization consolidated.*
2. *Church ordinances more diligently observed.*
3. *Church work more actively performed.*

Some one has well said: " I believe earnest Christian work to be the divinest remedy for almost every Church disease. An almost in-

fallible preventive it must be; for men building Zion's walls with a sword in one hand and a trowel in the other are sure to return this answer to the troublers of Israel, who tempt them into the valley: ' We are doing a great work, so that we cannot come down. Why should the work cease while we leave it and come down to you?' The workers in our Churches are seldom, if ever, found among the disturbers of their peace and the hinderers of their progress."

4. *Godly men multiplied.* Thus bestirring itself about "the things that *remain*," the Church will be reminded of things once possessed and lost; and so, one by one, the full privileges of its life will be regained, and a complete and blessed revival ensured.—H. R.

SUGGESTIVE THOUGHTS AND ILLUSTRATIONS

CHRIST'S FAST and Mortification.— On one of these forties Tertullian dwells with peculiar emphasis; often bringing out the relation between the forty days of our Lord's Temptation and the forty years of Israel's trial in the wilderness. His fast as the true Israel, as fulfiller of all which Israel after the flesh had left unfulfilled, as the victor in all where it had been the vanquished, was as much a witness against their carnal appetites (for it was in the indulgence of these that they sinned continually. Exod. xv: 23, 24; xvi: 2, 3) as a witness against Adam's. It was by this abstinence of His declared that man was ordained to be, and that the true man would be, lord over his lower nature. In this way Christ's forty days' fast is the great counter-fact in the work of redemption, at once to Adam's and to Israel's compliances with the suggestions of the fleshly appetite; exactly in the same manner as the unity of tongues at Pentecost is the counter-fact to the confusion of tongues at Babel (Gen. xi: 7-8; Acts ii: 6-11), to which the Church would draw our attention in the selection of the latter as one of our Whitsuntide lessons.—ARCHBISHOP TRENCH.

CHRIST'S FAST Our Example.—Our Savior's fast, like every act of His life, bears the character of an example, and instructs us that this particular exercise of religion, while it exposes to temptations of its own, is yet in itself a great preliminary safeguard against sin—a source of facility for vanquishing all temptation. That there are demoniacal possessions which no means without this can reach effectually, is the express assertion of our Savior on another occasion; and His example here, no less than His precept to His chosen followers there, instructs us forcibly that, while Christianity is the most mild and liberal of institutions, its founder, no preacher in the desert like Elias, or His forerunner the Baptist, but one who came " eating and drinking," as His censors remarked, neither fearfully flying nor morosely disdaining the

ordinary converse and habits of mankind,— it yet requires the highest prudence and assistances of grace proportional, to maintain this intercourse with the world either with safety to ourselves or benefit to others; and these assistances are to be found where our Lord and Savior Himself sought them—in occasional retirements, in meditation, prayer, and fasting.—W. H. MILL.

CONFLICT.—Frequent conflicts render the Christian strong. They fit preachers for their work,—*oratio, meditatio, tentatio, facunt theologum.*—A. P. L.

DAYS, Forty.—For forty days this fast of the Lord endured. But wherefore for exactly this number, for forty, and neither more nor less? . . . On a close examination we note it to be everywhere the number or signature of penalty, of affliction, of the confession, or the punishment of sin. Thus it is the signature of the punishment of sin in the forty days and forty nights during which God announces that He will cause the waters by the deluge to prevail (Gen. vii: 4, 12 ; in the forty years of the Israelites' wanderings in the desert (Num. xiv: 33) ; in the forty stripes with which the offender should be beaten (Deut. xxv: 3) ; in the desolation of Egypt which should endure forty years (Ezek. xxix: 11). So also is it the signature of the confession of sin. Moses intercedes forty days for his people; the Ninevites proclaim a fast of forty days; Ezekiel must bear for forty days the transgression of Judah. . . . And in agreement with all this, resting on the forty days' fast of her Lord, is the Quadragesimal Lent fast of the Church; and so, too, not less the selection of this Scripture of the Temptation to supply the Gospel for the first Sunday in that season, as being the Scripture which duly laid to heart, will more than any other help us rightly to observe that time.—ARCHBISHOP TRENCH.

DEVIL, Craftiness of the.—*Matt. iv.* When Satan first comes to tempt, he is modest, and asks but a little. He digs about and loosens the roots of faith, and then the tree falls the easier on the next gust of temptation.—A. P. L.

DEVIL, Persistency of the.—*Matt. iv.* The enemy of man's salvation deems it no small torment to abandon his suffering victim, and the longer he has had possession, the more reluctant is he to quit (Mark ix: 21).—A. P. L.

EARTH, Inheriting the.—*2 Cor. vi: 10.* Bishop Burnet treated with most distinguished regard such clergy in his diocese as were eminent for their piety and most attentive to the souls of their people. One of these had frequently expressed the importance of well understanding our Lord's meaning in the Beatitudes and of this in particular, " Blessed are the meek, for they shall inherit the earth." Many anxious inquiries yet left this clergyman unsatisfied in his mind of the just and true explanation. In this state of mind, he happened in a morning's walk to observe a very wretched-looking hovel, and walking toward it, he heard, to his surprise, a voice of joyous praise. He looked in at the window, and saw a poor woman with a piece of black bread and a cup of water before her. With her eyes lifted up to heaven, she was repeating the words, " All this, and Jesus Christ too! All this, and Jesus too!" The clergyman here learned that they who inherit this earth are they who possess Jesus Christ.—A. P. L.

EMBER AND ROGATION DAYS.— Ember and Rogation Days are certain periods of the year devoted to prayer and fasting. Ember Days (twelve annually) are the Wednesday, Friday, and Saturday after the first Sunday in Lent, after the feast of Pentecost (Whit Sunday), after the festival of the Holy Cross (September 14), and after the festival of St. Lucia (December 13). Ember Weeks are the weeks in which the Ember Days appear. Rogation Days are the three days immediately preceding Holy Thursday or Ascension Day.—W. A.

FASTING.—Don't flatter yourself that you have been very good, if your fasting has been a matter of necessity.—*Selected.*

FASTING AND SELF-CONTROL.—*But I keep under my body, and bring it into subjection, etc.—1 Cor. ix: 27.* In Christianity we have this principle which men had approached from various sides engrafted into the religion which is to meet man's inmost needs—man is a complex being, body, soul, and spirit; he must not neglect his body; it is useful, it is blessed, it is holy; but the body, if a good servant, is a terrible master—within every man the will must reign supreme, and therefore the will must show its supremacy. Where Satan is leading hundreds upon hundreds of his victims captive in gluttony and drunkenness all round us, the will of the Christian must be able to show his body temperate, curbed, restrained. He must be able to say, so far from being allured into excess, I can voluntarily cut off those things which

men think pleasant or necessary, and forego their very use. When the world is following pleasure and ease, and neglecting the eternal interest of the soul, the Christian ought to be able to say, instead of being entrapped by pleasure, I can of my own free will lay it aside if need be. Where the world shrinks from unpleasant duties, the Christian ought to be able to say, I welcome pain, I welcome suffering as something which God sends me. The flesh is a spoilt child, it cries out for everything which it sees or wants. The will is the disciplinarian who thwarts it, curbs it, controls it, and does not mind in what way, if in any way, it can make it obedient. What is an army without discipline? What are the great forces of nature, unless we can regulate them? What is man without self-control?— W. C. E. NEWBOLT.

FASTING AS AN ACT OF OBEDIENCE.—*Obey them that have the rule over you.—Heb. xiii: 17.* If this be any one's first Lent, I would give some simple rules which may smooth some difficulties. Let it be an act of obedience. A sacred poet of our own says, " the Scripture bids us fast, the Church says now." Thus shall we do it more simply, not as any great thing; not as of our own will, but as an act of obedience; so will the remarks of others (if such there be) less disturb us, as knowing that we are doing but little, and that, not of our own mind. But little in itself, it is connected with high things, with the very height of Heaven and the depths of hell; our Blessed Savior and our sins. We fast *with* our Lord, and *for* our sins. The Church brings us nigh to our Lord, Whose fast and the merits of Whose fasting and Passion we partake of. We have to " humble our own souls with fasting" for our own sins. Remember we both. Review we our past lives; recall we to our remembrance what chief sins we can; confess them habitually in sorrow, with the use of Penitential Psalms and especially that daily medicine of the penitent soul, the fifty-first. Fast we, in token that we are unworthy of God's creatures which we have misused. Take we thankfully weariness or discomfort, as we before sinned through ease and lightness of heart. And thus, owning ourselves unworthy of all, think we on Him, Who for us bore all; so shall those precious sufferings sanctify thy discomfort, the irksomeness shall be gladsome to thee which brings thee nearer to thy Lord.—E. B. PUSEY.

FASTING, Benefits of.—*As they ministered to the Lord, and fasted, the Holy Ghost said.—Acts xiii: 2.* It is, we believe, because this duty is so little practised as a regular habit that its benefits are so undervalued. It is often eagerly commenced in a fit of transient zeal, but the natural inclinations raise their remonstrance—it is found wearisome and painful—and after one or two attempts entirely laid aside. But is it not true, that this is scarcely giving it a trial? To be appreciated, and its benefits felt, it must be a habit—be practised often—and become, as it were, a portion of our regular religious service. Thus, that which at first was performed with difficulty is rendered easy; and we learn at last, that the ancient Saints in primitive days knew human nature better than we do, and when they urged those who should come after them to "crucify the flesh" as a source of spiritual benefits, were only giving the result of their own experience. This, then, is that discipline, by whose severity we are to weaken the force of passion, and of those appetites which else assert the mastery over the soul and bind it down to earth. "I keep under my body," says St. Paul, "and bring it into subjection; lest that by any means when I have preached to others, I myself should be a castaway." And St. Chrysostom declares "Fasting restrains the body and checks and bridles its inordinate sallies, but makes the soul much lighter, and gives it wings to mount up and soar on high." —BISHOP KIP.

FASTING, True.—*Matt. iv.* Our fasting should be accompanied with abstinence from evil; we must fast from our passions and vices: without this, bodily fasting is unprofitable. Take heed that you make not your fasting to consist only in abstinence from meats. True fasting is to refrain from vice. Tear in pieces all your unjust obligations. Pardon your neighbor. Forgive him his trespasses. Fast not to stir up strife and contention. You eat no flesh, but you devour your brother (Matt. xxiii: 14). You drink no wine, but you cannot refrain from doing injury to others. You wait till night to take your repast, but you spend all the day at the tribunal of the judges. Wo be to you, who drink without wine. Anger is a kind of inebriation, which does no less trouble the mind than real drunkenness (Isa. lviii: 4-11; Jer. xiv: 12; Mark ii: 18).—A. P. L.

FASTS, Church.—The Roman Catholic Days of fasting are the forty days of Lent, the Ember Days, the Wednesdays and Thursdays of the four weeks in Advent, and certain vigils or evenings prior to the greater feasts. In the American Episcopal Church the days of fasting or abstinence to be observed, according to the Book of Common Prayer, are the forty days of Lent, the Ember Days, the three Rogation Days, and all the Fridays of the year except Christmas Day. In the Greek Church the four principal fasts are those in Lent, the week succeeding Whitsuntide, the fortnight before the Assumption, and forty days before Christmas.—W. A.

LIFE, The Austerity of.—*By His wounds the Lord calls His Church to austerity of life.*—There is no master so gentle or so severe as Jesus, for He gives the most generous invitation and the kindliest welcome when we come to Him; He lays on us the hardest service and demands of us the hardest sacrifices after we have come.

"Peace be unto you," He said that night to the disciples, and He breathed upon them that they might receive His Spirit; but before James lay a speedy martyrdom, and before John a lonely exile, before them all bonds and sufferings. For Christ hath two words of power: one is "Come," which

draws us to His side, where there is peace for evermore; and the other is "Follow," which draws us after Him, where He carries His cross in the paths of life. The wounds of Christ are first of all the hope and hiding-place of the soul; afterwards they turn into the soul's standard and obligation.

As there is a false Christianity which banishes the cross from thought, there is another which banishes the cross from life; and, as the one makes no distinction between Jesus and other teachers, save His deeper wisdom and His higher goodness, so the other does not separate the Christian life from the world life, except in a finer degree of purity and of charity; but the true Christianity, which has made the sacrifice of Christ its distinctive principle of thought, makes the same sacrifice its rule of life. It does not pretend that it is easy to follow Christ, or that the cross is light to carry, but rather teaches that the Christian must be prepared upon occasion to pluck out the right eye and cut off the right hand, to hate father and mother, to sell all that he has, to part from all whom he loves, to do work which he dislikes, to associate with unattractive people, to deny himself in heart and life, in his reason also and in his affections, even as Christ Himself did, and for the same cause,—the love of God and the love of man. So the Church comes to carry the print of the nails upon her hands and her feet, and the world knows that she is the body of Christ.— IAN MCLAREN.

SELF-MORTIFICATION, Necessity of. —*Mortify therefore your members which are upon the earth.*—*Col. iii: 5.* Believe me, the way of mortification is the only way of spiritual emancipation. Holy desires without discipline will never make us free. Emotional confessions not issuing in discipline will never strike off our chains. Constant attendance on the means of grace in the sanctuary or in the closet not issuing in discipline will never set our feet at liberty. Helpful indeed are these to those who seek to live the mortified life, but without the practice of mortification they cannot secure our spiritual freedom. This is ours only when our lower nature is mortified in imitation of and in dependence on Jesus, and Him crucified. On this matter I pray you do not allow yourself to be deceived. For no law of spiritual life is more certain or more imperative than this law of mortification. There cannot be such a thing as the perseverance in Christian life of an unmortified Christian who has come to years of discretion. Obedience, we repeat, is religion; and mortification is the essential condition of obedience, for it is the condition of its actual expression and of the recovery of that spiritual freedom without which that expression is impossible for sinful men.—GEORGE BODY.

SIN IS AGAINST GOD.—This fact—that a sin is against God—is that in which consists the greatness of its guilt; for, even among men, we measure the guilt of crimes, not by the actual injury resulting from them, but by their injurious tendencies. The traitor who has attempted the life of his sovereign, the rebel who has tried to overthrow his authority, are rightly held as guilty when they fail as if they had succeeded. They are punished, not for the harm that their rebellion or their treason has done, but for the harm which rebellion and treason must do if not repressed. Now, what is a sinner but a rebel? He who sins has defied the sovereign authority of his God; he has set the will of the creature against the Creator. It is true that such rebellion can harm only the rebel himself—the wickedness of man no more extendeth to God than his goodness does. The potsherd of the earth seeks in vain to strive with his Maker; nevertheless, his sin has in it all the malignity of treason. The revolt of his will, if it were only successful, would end in the dethronement of God. . . . Is it not plain, then, that disobedient opposition to God is the very deadliest crime possible in a system, the well-being of which depends upon the perfect submission of all things to His will, and that a sinner is a miserable anomaly in the midst of an obedient universe—a wretched rebel against almighty power and eternal law, who for the sake of the peace and safety of creation, must be subdued, or destroyed utterly and forever?—ARCHBISHOP MAGEE.

SIN MAN'S GREAT ENEMY.—No doubt we shall all of us, one day, come to see (whatever we may think about it now), that Sin is our only real enemy, the one thing to be really afraid of. Even the sting of Death is only Sin. And it is always the part of a wise, as well as of a brave man, to look his worst enemies in the face, to study their nature and character, and the secret of their power of mischief, that he may the better know how to be on his guard against them, how to meet them, how to disarm and overcome them. *Sin* is not the same thing as *Crime.* When we speak of *Crime,* we are thinking of something which is an offense against human law, punishable in this life by sentence of a human tribunal. When we speak of *Sin,* we are thinking of something which is an offense against a far higher power, and which may have farther reaching and more enduring consequences. Not all sins are crimes such as human law either does or could, or perhaps ought to, punish. And not all crimes or offenses against human laws are sins. For human law—tho one of the most sacred things on earth, and challenging, as a rule, our reverent respect and obedience as a matter of conscience—is not infallible. It may prescribe things which an enlightened conscience cannot conform to, whatever the consequences may be. . . . Sin and Crime are not, then, absolutely identical and coextensive. A sin may be no crime; a crime may be not only no sin, but an act of the highest goodness.—P. G. MEDD.

SUFFERING.—Out of suffering have emerged the strongest souls; the most massive characters are seamed with scars; martyrs have put on their coronation robes, glittering with fire, and through their tears have the sorrowful first seen the gates of heaven. —*Selected.*

TEMPTATION.—*Matt. iv.* Satan will seldom come to a Christian with a gross temptation; a green log and a candle may be safely left together; but bring a few shavings, then some small sticks, and then larger, and you may soon bring the green log to ashes.— A. P. L.

TEMPTATION AND AFFLICTION.— *Matt. iv.* Remember that a time of affliction is a time of temptation. Satan will not be wanting in any opportunity or advantage of setting upon the soul. When Pharaoh heard that the people were entangled in the wilderness, he pursued them. And when Satan sees a soul entangled with its distresses and troubles, he thinks it is his time and hour to assault it. He seeks to winnow, and comes when the corn is under the flail. Reckon, therefore, that when trouble cometh, the prince of this world cometh also, that you may be provided for him. Then is the time to take the shield of faith, that we may be able to quench his fiery darts. If they be neglected, they will inflame the soul. Watch, therefore, and pray, that you enter not into temptation, that Satan does not represent God falsely unto you. He that durst represent Job falsely to the all-seeing God, will. with much more boldness, represent God falsely unto us, who see and know so little. Be not ignorant of his devices, but in every way set yourself against his interposing between God and your souls, in a matter which he hath nothing to do with. Let not this makebate by any means inflame the difference.—A. P. L.

TEMPTATION AND HOLINESS.—*Matt. iv.* He forced him not; he touched him not; only said, " Cast thyself down ": that we may know, whosoever obeyeth the devil, casteth himself down; for the devil may suggest; compel he cannot.—A. P. L.

TEMPTATION AND PRAYER.—*Matt. iv.* Very strikingly do the gospels illustrate for us our danger, and the daily value of this petition. At about the same time strong temptation came to our Lord, to Peter, and to Judas Iscariot. It came to our Lord; but the tempter found nothing in Him, no point of vantage. It came to Peter, secure as he thought himself from its attacks; heedless, therefore, and unwatchful, he entered into temptation and fell; the tempter found something in him, and used his opportunity. Temptation came also to the unhappy traitor. and carried all before it, the tempter entered into him, and made him his prey.—A. P. L.

TEMPTATION Follows Graces.—*Matt. iv: 1.* Christ is no sooner out of the water of baptism, than He is in the fire of temptation; whence we learn that great manifestations of the love of God are usually followed with great temptations from Satan.—A. P. L.

TEMPTATION the Road to Glory.— *Matt. iv.* None can be crowned unless he conquer, nor conquer unless he fight, nor fight unless he have enemies and temptations. (2 Tim. ii: 3-5; Jas. i: 2.)—A. P. L.

TEMPTATION, The Safe Course in.—The sentinel picketed to watch the enemy does his duty by giving the alarm if the enemy approaches—not by advancing single-handed to the conflict. So the duty of a Christian, watchfully discerning the approach of temptation, is to convey the case to God; it is foolhardiness to adventure into the combat unsent and unprovided for.—Budington.

TEMPTATIONS, To Live Without.—I find it most true, that the greatest temptation out of hell is to live without temptations; if my waters would stand, they would rot. Faith is the better for the free air and the sharp winter storm in its face; grace withereth without adversity. The devil is but God's master-fencer, teaching us to handle our weapons.—A. P. L.

TEMPTER, The.—*Matt. iv.* Behind temptation and evil there is here recognized the baneful agency of a personal tempter, an evil one. Our great writers of fiction invariably have a demon in human character plotting the ruin of a hero or heroine; but whose malevolent designs are, as a rule, thwarted by a counteracting good agency. And this, to those who see below the surface of things, is true of life. The Holy Scriptures tell the children of God that they have, in a fallen spirit, an unscrupulous foe, who is the father of lies: " Your adversary the devil, who goeth about as a roaring lion, seeking whom he may devour "; the calumniator of God, and of all that is good; the accuser of the brethren whose assaults they must encounter, with whom they will have to wrestle, against whom they must watch and pray; and, in order to withstand and resist him successfully, they must arm themselves with the panoply of God. And this prayer, to be delivered from evil, is a cry to " the stronger than the strong," for help in an unequal contest; to the " Advocate with the Father," for His interposition on our behalf; to the " Good Shepherd," to deliver His sheep from the teeth of the destroyer and " to save them to the uttermost," both of peril and of need.—A. P. L.

ULYSSES and the Enchanted Isle.—We are told that when Ulysses was passing by the coast of the Enchanted Isle, where the Sirens lived and sang, he had to have his ears stopped with wax, and himself bound to the mast of the ship, lest he should wish to listen to their song, and so become intoxicated with pleasure, and never get beyond that shore, as had been the case with all others.—A. P. L.

POETRY

Ash Wednesday

By John Keble

When thou fastest, anoint thine head, and wash thy face; that thou appear not unto men to fast, but unto thy Father which is in secret. Matthew vi: 17, 18.

Yes—deep within, and deeper yet
  The rankling shaft of conscience hide.
Quick let the swelling eye forget
  The tears that in the heart abide.
Calm be the voice, the aspect bold,
  No shuddering pass o'er lip or brow,
For why should Innocence be told
  The pangs that guilty spirits bow?

The loving eye that watches thine
  Close as the air that wraps thee round—
Why in thy sorrow should it pine,
  Since never of thy sin it found?
And wherefore should the heathen see *
  What chains of darkness thee enslave,
And mocking say, Lo, this is He
  Who owned a God that could not save?

Thus oft the mourner's wayward heart
  Tempts him to hide his grief and die,
Too feeble for Confession's smart,
  Too proud to bear a pitying eye;
How sweet, in that dark hour, to fall
  On bosoms waiting to receive
Our sighs, and gently whisper all!
  They love us—will not God forgive?

Else let us keep our fast within,
  Till Heaven and we are quite alone,
Then let the grief, the shame, the sin,
  Before the mercy-seat be thrown.
Between the porch and altar weep,
  Unworthy of the holiest place,
Yet hoping near the shrine to keep
  One lowly cell in sight of grace.

Nor fear lest sympathy should fail;
  Hast thou not seen, in night-hours drear
When racking thoughts the heart assail,
  The glimmering stars by turns appear,
And from the eternal home above
  With silent news of mercy steal?
So Angels pause on tasks of love,
  To look where sorrowing sinners kneel.

Or if no Angel pass that way,
  He who in secret sees, perchance
May bid His own heart-warming ray
  Toward thee stream with kindlier glance,
As when upon His drooping head
  His Father's light was poured from Heaven
What time, unsheltered and unfed,†
  Far in the wild His steps were driven.

High thoughts were with Him in that hour,
  Untold, unspeakable on earth—
And who can stay the soaring power
  Of spirits weaned from worldly mirth,
While far beyond the sound of praise
  With upward eye they float serene,
And learn to bear their Savior's blaze
  When Judgment shall undraw the screen?

* Wherefore should they say among the people, Where is their God? Joel ii: 17.   † Matthew iv: 1.

The Stricken Deer

By William Cowper

I was a stricken deer that left the herd
Long since: with many an arrow deep infix'd
My panting side was charged, when I with-
drew,
To seek a tranquil death in distant shades.
There was I found by one who had Himself
Been hurt by the archers. In His side He
bore,
And in His hands and feet, the cruel scars.
With gentle force soliciting the darts,
He drew them forth, and heal'd, and bade me
live.
Since then, with few associates, in remote
And silent woods I wander, far from those
My former partners of the peopled scene;
With few associates, and not wishing more.
The Task, Bk. iii. l. 108.

Lenten Fasting

By George Herbert

Welcome, dear feast of Lent; who loves not
thee,
He loves not temperance, or authority,
But is composed of passion.
The Scriptures bid us fast; the church says,
Give to thy mother what thou wouldst allow
To every corporation.

The humble soul, composed of love and fear,
Begins at home, and lays the burden there,
When doctrines disagree:
He says, in things which use hath justly got,
" I am a scandal to the church, and not
The church is so to me."

True Christians should be glad of an occasion
To use their temperance, seeking no evasion,
When good is seasonable;
Unless authority, which should increase
The obligation in us, make it less,
And power itself disable.

Then those same pendent profits, which the
spring
And Easter intimate, enlarge the thing,
And goodness of the deed.
Neither ought other men's abuse of Lent
Spoil the good use; lest by that argument
We forfeit all our creed.

'Tis true, we cannot reach Christ's fortieth
day;
Yet to go part of that religious way
Is better than the rest:
We cannot reach our Savior's purity;
Yet we are bid, " Be holy e'en as He."
In both let's do our best.

Who goeth in the way which Christ hath
gone,
Is much more sure to meet with Him, than
one
That traveleth byways.
Perhaps my God, tho He be far before,
May turn, and take me by the hand, and more,
May strengthen my decays.

Yet, Lord, instruct us to improve our fast
By starving sin, and taking such repast
As may our faults control;
That every man may revel at his door,
Not in his parlor, banqueting the poor,
And among those his soul.

Acceptable Fasting

By Francis Quarles

Is fasting then the thing that God requires?
Can fasting expiate, or slake those fires
That sin hath blown to such a mighty flame?
Can sackcloth clothe a fault, or hide a shame?
Can ashes cleanse thy blot, or purge thy of-
fense?
Or do thy hands make heaven a recompense?
By strewing dust upon thy briny face?
Are these the tricks to purchase heavenly
grace?—
No! tho thou pine thyself with willing want,
Or face look thin, or carcass ne'er so gaunt;
Altho thou worser weeds than sackcloth wear,
Or naked go, or sleep in shirts of hair;
Or tho thou choose an ash-tub for thy bed,
Or make a daily dunghill on thy head,—
Thy labor is not poised with equal gains,
For thou hast naught but labor for thy pains.
Such holy madness God rejects and loathes,
That sinks no deeper than the skin or clothes.
'Tis not thine eyes, which, taught to weep by
art,
Look red with tears (not guilty of thy heart) ;
'Tis not the holding of thy hands so high,
Nor yet the purer squinting of thine eye;
'Tis not your mimic mouths, your antic faces,
Your Scripture phrases, or affected graces,
Nor prodigal upbending of thine eyes,
Whose gashful balls do seem to pelt the skies;
'Tis not the strict reforming of your hair,
So close that all the neighbor skull be bare;
'Tis not the drooping of thy head so low,
Nor yet the lowering of thy sullen brow;
Nor wolfish howling that disturbs the air.
Nor repetitions, or your tedious prayer:
No, no! 'tis none of this that God regards—
Such sort of fools their own applause re-
wards;
Such puppet-plays to heaven are strange and
quaint;
Their service is unsweet, and foully taint:
Their words fall fruitless from their idle brain—
But true repentance runs in other strain;
Where sad contrition harbors, there the heart
Is truly acquainted with the secret smart
Of past offenses—hates the bosom sin
The most which the soul took pleasure in.
No crime unsifted, no sin unpresented,
Can lurk unseen; and seen, none unlamented.
The troubled soul's amazed with dire aspects
Of lesser sins committed, and detects
The wounded conscience; it cries amain
For mercy, mercy—cries, and cries again;
It sadly grieves, and soberly laments;
It yearns for grace, reforms, returns, repents.
Aye, this is incense whose accepted savor
Mounts up the heavenly Throne, and findeth
favor;
Ay, this is it whose valor never fails—
With God it stoutly wrestles, and prevails;

Ay, this is it that pierces heaven above,
Never returning home, like Noah's dove,
But brings an olive leaf, or some incense
That works salvation, and eternal peace.

A True Fast

By Robert Herrick

Is this a Faste—to keep
　　The Larder leane,
　　　And cleane,
From fat of veales and sheepe?

Is it to quit the dish
　　Of flesh, yet still
　　　To fill
The platter high with fish?

Is it to faste an houre,
　　Or rag'd to go,
　　　Or show
A downcast look and sowre?

No; 'tis a Faste to dole
　　Thy sheaf of wheat,
　　　And meat,
Unto the hungry soule..

It is to faste from strife,
　　From old debate,
　　　And hate;
To circumcise thy life.

To show a heart grief-rent,
　　To starve thy sin,
　　　Not bin:
And that's to keep thy Lent.

Lent

By F. W. Faber, D.D.

Now are the days of humblest prayer,
When consciences to God lie bare,
And mercy most delights to spare.
　Oh hearken when we cry,
　　Chastise us with Thy fear;
　Yet, Father! in the multitude
　　Of Thy compassions, hear!

Now is the season, wisely long,
Of sadder thought and graver song,
When ailing souls grow well and strong.
　Oh hearken when we cry,
　　Chastise us with Thy fear;
　Yet, Father! in the multitude
　　Of Thy compassions, hear!

The feast of penance! Oh so bright,
With true conversion's heavenly light,
Like sunrise after stormy night!
　Oh hearken when we cry,
　　Chastise us with Thy fear;
　Yet, Father! in the multitude
　　Of Thy compassions, hear!

Oh happy time of blessed tears,
Of surer hopes, of chast'ning fears,
Undoing all our evil years.
　Oh hearken when we cry,
　　Chastise us with Thy fear;
　Yet, Father! in the multitude
　　Of Thy compassions, hear!

We, who have loved the world, must learn,
Upon that world our backs to turn,
And with the love of God to burn.
　Oh hearken when we cry,
　　Chastise us with Thy fear;
　Yet, Father! in the multitude
　　Of Thy compassions, hear!

Vile creatures of such little worth!—
Than we, there can be none on earth
More fallen from their Christian birth.
　Oh hearken when we cry,
　　Chastise us with Thy fear;
　Yet, Father! in the multitude
　　Of Thy compassions, hear!

Full long in sin's dark ways we went,
Yet now our steps are heavenward bent,
And grace is plentiful in Lent.
　Oh hearken when we cry,
　　Chastise us with Thy fear;
　Yet, Father! in the multitude
　　Of Thy compassions, hear!

All glory to redeeming grace,
Disdaining not our evil case,
But showing us our Savior's face!
　Oh hearken when we cry,
　　Chastise us with Thy fear;
　Yet, Father! in the multitude
　　Of Thy compassions, hear!

The Second Sunday in Lent

By John Keble

*And when Esau heard the words of his
father, he cried with a great and exceeding
bitter cry, and said unto his father, Bless me,
even me also, O my father. Genesis xxvii:
37. (Cf. Hebrews xii:17. He found no place
of repentance, though he sought it carefully
with tears.)*

" And is there in God's world so drear a place
　Where the loud bitter cry is raised in
　　vain?
Where tears of penance come too late for
　　grace,
　As on the uprooted flower the genial
　　rain? "

'Tis even so; the sovereign Lord of souls
　Stores in the dungeon of His boundless
　　realm
Each bolt, that o'er the sinner vainly rolls,
　With gathered wrath the reprobate to
　　whelm.

Will the storm hear the sailor's piteous cry,
　Taught to mistrust, too late, the tempting
　　wave,
When all around he sees but sea and sky,
　A God in anger, a self-chosen grave?

Or will the thorns, that strew intemperance's
　　bed,
　Turn with a wish to down? will late re-
　　morse
Recall the shaft the murderer's hand has sped,
　Or from the guiltless bosom turn its course?

Then may the unbodied soul in safety fleet
  Through the dark curtains of the world
    above,
Fresh from the stain of crime; nor fear to
    meet
  The God, whom here she would not learn
    to love:

Then is there hope for such as die unblest,
  That angel wings may waft them to the
    shore,
Nor need the unready virgin strike her breast,
  Nor wait desponding round the bride-
    groom's door.

But where is then the stay of contrite hearts?
  Of old they leaned on Thy eternal Word,
But with the sinner's fear their hope departs,
  Fast linked as Thy great Name to Thee,
    O Lord:

That Name, by which Thy faithful oath is
    past,
  That we should endless be, for joy or wo:
And if the treasures of Thy wrath could
    waste,
  Thy lovers must their promised Heaven
    forego.

But ask of elder days, earth's vernal hour,
  When in familiar talk God's voice was
    heard,
When at the Patriarch's call the fiery shower
  Propitious o'er the turf-built shrine ap-
    peared.

Watch by our father Isaac's pastoral door—
  The birthright sold, the blessing lost and
    won,
Tell, Heaven has wrath that can relent no
    more,
  The Grave, dark deeds that cannot be un-
    done.

We barter life for pottage; sell true bliss
  For wealth or power, for pleasure or re-
    nown;
Thus, Esau-like, our Father's blessing miss,
  Then wash with fruitless tears our faded
    crown.

The True Lent

By W. M. Punshon

There's winter on the hills to-day,
  The sad wind soughs o'er churchyard knolls,
And weary nature seems to say,
  "'Tis Lenten-tide for sinful souls."

The barb is in our heart to-day;
  Sore crushed with sense of ail and sin,
We feebly strive and faintly pray,
  'Gainst danger near, for grace within.

We mourn our pride and passion's stain,
  The earthly in our hearts enshrined;
The rebel flesh, too oft in vain
  Commanded by the nobler mind;

And all of human curse or care
  Which lurks life's dangerous paths among,
To quench the altar-flame of prayer,
  Or hush the heavenward strain of song.

From Pain to Pain

By F. W. Faber, D.D.

From pain to pain, from wo to wo,
With loving hearts and footsteps slow
To calvary with Christ we go.
  See how His Precious Blood
    At every Station pours!
  Was ever grief like His?
  Was ever sin like ours?

Repentance

By Charles Mackay

By the red lightning rent and riven,
  And stretch'd along the plain,
Can the tall oak extend to heaven
  Its gay, green boughs again?
Or when a star hath lost its track,
  And faded from on high;
Can aught restore the lost one back
  To glory and the sky?

No; the tall oak no more can spread
  Its green leaves to the blast,
Nor can the meteor which hath fled
  Recall its splendors past.
Can man, deep sunk in guilty care,
  And press'd by human ill,
Gain triumph o'er his dark despair,
  And find a solace still?

Yes! He who for our ransom bled
  Holds back the avenging rod,
When meek contrition bows her head,
  Repenting, to her God:
Tho dark the sin—tho deep the heart
  Be sunk in guilt and pain,
Yet Mercy can a balm impart,
  And raise it up again.

Repentance and Faith

By Rev. W. Alexander

There was a ship, one eve autumnal, onward
    Steered o'er an ocean lake;
Steered by some strong hand ever as if sun-
    ward:
    Behind, an angry wake;
Before, there stretched a sea that grew in-
    tenser,
    With silver-fire far spread,
Up to a hill mist-gloried, like a censer,
    With smoke encompassèd;
It seemed as if two seas met brink to brink,
A silver flood beyond a lake of ink.

There was a soul that eve autumnal sailing
    Beyond the earth's dark bars,
Toward the land of sunsets never paling,
    Toward Heaven's sea of stars:
Behind, there was a wake of billows tossing;
    Before, a glory lay.
O happy soul! with all sail set, just crossing
    Into the Far-away;
  The gloom and gleam, the calmness and the
    strife,
  Were death before thee, and behind thee
    life.

And as that ship went up the waters stately,
Upon her topmasts tall
I saw two sails, whereof the one was greatly
Dark, as a funeral pall.
But oh! the next's pure whiteness who shall
utter?
Like a shell-snowy strand,
Or when a sunbeam falleth through the
shutter
On a dead baby's hand;
But both alike across the surging sea
Helped to the haven where the bark would
be.

And as that soul went onward, sweetly speed-
ing
Unto its home and light,
Repentance made it sorrowful exceeding,
Faith made it wondrous bright;
Repentance, dark with shadowy recollections
And longings unsufficed,
Faith, white and pure with sunniest affections
Full from the face of Christ:
But both across the sun-besilvered tide
Helped to the haven where the heart would
ride.

A Few Selections

Fasting, Private.

When thou a fast would'st keep,
Make not thy homage cheap
By publishing its signs to every eye;
But let it be between
Thyself and the Unseen,
So shall it gain acceptance from on high.
                          BERNARD BARTON

Fasting, Senseless.

Who can believe with common sense
A bacon slice gives God offense;
Or, how a herring has a charm
Almighty vengeance to disarm?
Wrapp'd up in majesty divine,
Does He regard on what we dine?
                          JONATHAN SWIFT

Life's Foe.

Conquer but self, the mightiest foe in life,
And of no other need'st thou stand in fear;
For none will care to prove himself the peer
Of Him who vanquishes in such a strife.
                          W. H. BIRCKHEAD

Through Trials

FROM THE GERMAN OF KOSEGARTEN

Through night to light. And tho to mortal
eyes
Creation's face a pall of horror wear,
Good cheer, good cheer! The gloom of mid-
night flies;
Then shall a sunrise follow, mild and fair.

Through storm to calm. And tho his thun-
der car
The rumbling tempest drive through earth
and sky,
Good cheer, good cheer! The elemental war
Tells that a blessèd healing hour is nigh.

Through frost to spring. And tho the biting
blast
Of Eurus stiffen nature's juicy veins,
Good cheer, good cheer! When winter's
wrath is past,
Soft murmuring spring breathes sweetly
o'er the plains.

Through strife to peace. And tho with bristling front
A thousand frightful depths encompass
thee,
Good cheer, good cheer! Brave thou the battle's brunt,
For the peace march and song of victory.

Through sweat to sleep. And tho the sultry
noon,
With heavy, drooping wing, oppress thee
now,
Good cheer, good cheer! The cool of evening soon
Shall lull to sweet repose thy weary brow.

Through cross to crown. And tho thy spirit's
life
Trials untold assail, with giant strength,
Good cheer, good cheer! Soon ends the
bitter strife,
And thou shalt reign in peace with Christ
at length.

Through wo to joy. And tho at morn thou
weep,
And tho the midnight find thee weeping
still,
Good cheer, good cheer! The Shepherd loves
His sheep;
Resign thee to the watchful Father's will.

Through death to life. And through this vale
of tears,
And through this thistle-field of life, ascend
To the great supper in that world whose years
Of bliss unfading, cloudless, know no end.

Temptation of Adam by Eve

BY JOHN MILTON

This tree is not, as we are told, a tree
Of danger tasted, nor to evil unknown
Opening the way, but of divine effect
To open eyes, and make them gods who taste;
And hath been tasted such: the serpent wise,
Or not restrain'd as we, or not obeying,
Hath eaten of the fruit, and is become,
Not dead, as we are threaten'd, but thence-
forth
Indued with human voice and human sense,
Reasoning to admiration: and with me
Persuasively hath so prevail'd, that I
Have also tasted, and have also found
Th' effects to correspond; opener of mine eyes,
Dim erst, dilated, ampler heart,
And growing up to Godhead; which for thee
Chiefly I sought, without thee can despise.
For bliss, as thou hast part, to me is bliss;
Tedious, unshared with thee, and odious soon.
Thou therefore also taste, that equal lot
May join us, equal joy, as equal love.

Renouncing the World

By Jane Taylor

Come, my fond, fluttering heart,
  Come, struggle to be free;
Thou and the world must part,
  However hard it be;
My trembling spirit owns it just,
But cleaves yet closer to the dust.

Ye tempting sweets, forbear;
  Ye dearest idols, fall;
My love ye must not share,
  Jesus shall have it all:
'Tis bitter pain, 'tis cruel smart,
But ah! thou must consent, my heart.

Ye fair enchanting throng!
  Ye golden dreams, farewell!
Earth has prevail'd too long,
  And now I break the spell:
Ye cherish'd joys of earthly years;
Jesus, forgive these parting tears.

But must I part with all?
  My heart still fondly pleads;
Yes; Dagon's self must fall,
  It beats, it throbs, it bleeds:
Is there no balm in Gilead found
To soothe and heal the smarting wound?

Oh, yes, there is a balm,
  A kind Physician there,
My fever'd mind to calm,
  To bid me not despair.
Aid me, dear Savior; set me free
And I will all resign to Thee.

Oh, may I feel Thy worth,
  And let no idol dare,
No vanity of earth,
  With Thee, my Lord, compare.
Now bid all worldly joys depart,
And reign supremely in my heart.

PALM SUNDAY

PALM SUNDAY (Dominica in Palmis) is the last Sunday in Lent, the first day of Holy Week and the Sunday immediately preceding Easter. It commemorates Our Lord's triumphal Entry into Jerusalem, accompanied by the multitude who greeted Him with hosannas, waving palm branches and scattering them before Him in the way. *(Matt. xxi: 1-11; Mk. xi: 1-11; John xii: 12-16.)* There is evidence that as early as the fifth century the feast of palms (βαίων ἑορτή) was observed in the East. But as observed in the Greek and Roman Catholic churches of to-day, its celebration dates from the tenth century.

At St. Peter's Church, in Rome, Palm Sunday is celebrated elaborately every year. Splendidly arrayed for the occasion, the Pope is brought into the Church, borne aloft on the shoulders of eight men. His court is in attendance, and the priests bring him palm branches on which he pronounces a blessing and sprinkles holy water. The great procession then starts, the day's ceremonies and services closing with high mass. All who attend the ceremony are granted thirty years' indulgence. Each one who has been present on the occasion takes away his palm branch, which is supposed now to be a charm against diseases, and which is kept in some cases to be burned to ashes on the next Ash-Wednesday. The supreme thought of Palm Sunday is: " Christ is King."

HOLY WEEK

There is a true piety in the observance of anniversaries. That home has lost something of the sacredness, something of the beauty to which it has a right, in which the children's birthdays are not high days; and where to these happy anniversaries the birthdays of father and mother, and their wedding day, are also home holidays, the cord of love and of parental and filial piety becomes all the stronger. So it is with religious anniversaries. From Thanksgiving Day we have come to recognize the value of celebrating Christmas and Easter. We have risen above that natural reaction against holy days with which their perversion inspired our Puritan ancestors, and have come to see that the most precious days in the year ought to be those which commemorate the most important events of our Lord's life on earth. In a more general observance of the same holy days, we find a bond of union which seems to give us a foretaste, or at least a vision, of that time when Christ's last prayer will be answered, and all Christians shall be one.

The round world over, this week is observed as the most sacred of all the year. There is hardly a country on the globe which does not now hold some to whom its observances are among the most precious of their experiences. And tho in America, the majority belong to denominations which have not, until recently, been wont to think much of holy days, yet in the whole field of Christendom the majority is very heavily on the other side. So, in the observances which we are learning to find so spiritually helpful and quickening, we have the further stimulus of this sense of oneness, knowing that we join with an innumerable company of worshipers. The coming Sabbath is Easter, and on that day, at least, the whole Christian world is one in commemorating and rejoicing in the Risen Lord.

And now we are beginning to feel the solemnity of these days which precede that glorious event. It was on this very Thursday, so many hundred years ago, that our Lord first broke the bread and blessed the wine for His disciples. Can any hour be more sacred, any remembrance more precious than this? Can we whose life is in Him spend the evening of this day better than by doing this in remembrance of Him? It was to-night that He prayed in the Garden. It was to-morrow morning very early that He stood before Pilate, and all the slow minutes of the day mark a new step in His Passion, a new pang, a new anguish, endured for us. How shall we sleep to-night and to-morrow go eagerly about our business, our money-making, or our pleasures, as if these things had never been?—E.

SERMONS AND OUTLINES

THE DAY OF PALMS

By Rev. George Hodges, D.D., LL. D.

On the next day much people that were come to the feast, when they heard that Jesus was coming to Jerusalem, took branches of palm-trees and went forth to meet him.—John xii: 12, 13

Yesterday He was at Bethany. Last night they made Him a supper there, and Mary anointed His head and feet with the precious ointment—for "the day of my burying," He said, looking on into the darkness of this week's tragedy. The little village was full of Passover pilgrims, and there was much going and coming, over the hill road which led to Jerusalem. The news that the Prophet of Nazareth was on His way to the feast would speedily be carried into the city.

People were full of expectation. They had been debating one with another as to the likelihood of His coming. Some feared He might be kept away by fear of priests and sentries. It was the topic of the hour.

Jesus had now been going up and down the country for three years. He had preached in city after city. Many had seen His miracles. It was known through all the length and breadth of Judea, and Samaria, and Galilee, that this new Prophet had arrived, claiming to be the Messiah. Everybody was interested in Him. It was known also that His claims were utterly disowned by all the prominent churchmen, and that at last the religious authorities had publicly proclaimed Him to be a deceiver and a dangerous person, and had given orders that He should be arrested.

Most people, especially in Jerusalem, sided, as the world's way is, with those who were in authority. Many others were quite different, but were interested in the day's happenings, as people are, and ready to join a crowd at any time to go in any direction. Others there were in whose hearts sounded still some word which Jesus had spoken in the streets of their town, in whose eyes was still the sight of Him as He went along one day, which they well remembered—blessing little children, healing the sick, comforting the sad.

A strange and terrible thing it seemed to them that He should now be hunted after like a thief by Scribes and Pharisees. If He came to the Passover, He came in peril of His life. They knew that, and they dreaded what might come to pass. And there were His enemies, also, wondering what He would do. And, when men came running over the side of the hill into the city, bearing the news that Jesus was at Bethany, and would upon the morrow enter into Jerusalem, there was a stir among the people.

Thus, as Jesus nears Jerusalem, presently **this great crowd, shouting and singing,** comes in sight. And every one's heart is stirred. The multitude from Jerusalem turns back escorting Him; the multitude from Bethany follows on behind Him. He is in the midst of them. And some pull off their long cloaks and cast them in the road, and others break off branches from the trees, green with the first leaves of spring, and spread them in the way. They carry palm-branches in their hands, and sing. And as they go they describe one to another the good deeds they have seen Him do, and they rejoice and praise God with a loud voice for all His mighty works, crying: "Hosanna, blessed be the Lord; peace in heaven and glory in the highest."

Some of the Pharisees, who have come out with the crowd, are suddenly alarmed, hearing this name of "king," and seeing this great enthusiastic multitude sweeping on down into the crowded city. "Master," they cry, "rebuke thy disciples." To which Jesus answers: "I tell you that, if these should hold their peace, the very stones would immediately cry out."

You see with what intensity He speaks. He has been silent, hitherto, listening to the voices of the shouting crowd, and looking into their eager faces, thinking His own sad thoughts. This to Him is no holiday procession. He is indeed a king, and in the Lord's name does He come; but He is to be rejected; He knows that. The cross is at the end of the road.

Now the way descends into a valley, with a hill upon the right and a wall of rocks upon the left; then it rises again, and suddenly the Holy City lies outspread across a deep ravine, terrace upon terrace, crowned with the Temple tower, all white with marble walls and set about with shining roofs, like gems. Here it was, no doubt, that "He beheld the city, and wept over it;" wept, not with silent tears, but with long lamentation. For Jesus loved that city. Every stone of it was precious in His eyes. He had come to it again and again, as the prophets came in the old time; preaching in the streets and in the synagogs and in the courts of the Temple, bearing the messages of God. And few had heeded.

Outside, in the country, ignorant people, unprivileged people, had listened and believed. And even in the town of Galilee, where men thought more about their business than they did about the services of the church, there had been many disciples, and some had been willing to give up everything and follow Him. But here, in Jerusalem, the religious city, where dwelt the priests and doctors of the law, where the tower of the holy temple dominated all the buildings of the town and where the church was the supreme interest of all the citizens—here had Jesus preached and done His deeds of mercy and blessing. And they had despised and hated Him.

And the day of divine visitation had come, the last of all the manifold opportunities which the town had had, the final call of God, and the city lay there, beautiful beyond expression, but deaf and dumb and blind. For this did Jesus weep, saying: "If thou hadst known, even thou, at least in this thy day, the things which belong unto thy peace! But now they are hid from thine eyes."

After all the elaborate preparations to receive Christ, He came and was rejected. He came so simply, so naturally, speaking so directly to the hearts and lives of men, caring so little for all their costly ceremonies and their fine ritual, that they did not know Him. They had deceived themselves by their emphasis upon the dress and posture of religion, by their interest in the forms and ceremonies of the church. They had dwelt so long upon the mere externals of devotion that they had ceased to be devoted. And Jesus looked upon the religious city, with its stately Temple crowning the summit of the hill, with its streets full of men and women preparing for the great church festival of the divine redemption of their fathers, and wept over it; looked upon these throngs of people on their way to church to keep their Easter feast, and wept to see them.

Such a difference there is between churchgoing and religion, between righteousness and ritual, between our way of looking at things and Christ's way. We are busy, we are interested in many matters which have something to do with the Christian religion, in the service, in the singing, in the adornment of the house of God. How much does it all mean? Jesus Christ looks upon our stately churches; does He rejoice in them as the comely shrines of a pure devotion, or does He behold them as He beheld Jerusalem, looking into our hearts and seeing cause for lamentation?

On moves the rude procession, with waving palms and singing, Jesus riding in the midst. Thus comes the King. In Rome there have been scenes of triumph when some conqueror enters with his soldiers to the sound of music, all the people throwing flowers before him and shouting in the streets, and behind him are led his captives, the princes of some unfortunate province, bound in chains; and all along the way the spears glitter and there is clash of armor. But here comes another King, the King of peace, the King of love, in very different fashion.

The road leads down the mountain, past the Garden of Gethsemane, over the Kedron bridge, into the city. And here is noise and tumult, people running together and heads thrust out of windows, the whole city moved, and everybody saying, "Who is this?" And the bearers of the palm-branches answer, not with the same confidence which they had shown as they sang along the road, but retreating a little from their high enthusiasm in the presence of their unsympathetic questioners: "This is Jesus, the Prophet of Nazareth of Galilee"—a perfectly safe saying.

"Hosanna to the Son of David," they had been singing. "Blessed be the King that cometh in the name of the Lord." They do not sing that in the streets.

By and by there will be another crowd in these same streets, and some of these same people in it crying: "Crucify him!" That is the way with crowds. Jesus rides on, silent and sad, knowing how little it all means. In every company, in every congregation, some are present because their hearts are filled with sincere interest and genuine devotion, and they cannot stay away.

Others are there because they have seen people going in that direction and have gone with them, or because it is the conventional thing to do, and they join their voices in the general acclaim because it is the way of human nature, doing what their neighbors do. This Palm-Sunday crowd vanishes away and is heard no more. There is a little company of true disciples standing afar off, watching the end, when the darkness falls upon the cross. But when the crowd utters no voice, is not visible, sits trembling at home, or is on the other side, when the tragedy comes. When Jesus needs men to stand up in the midst of his enemies and speak for Him, these loud singers of Palm Sunday are not there.

There are two kinds of religion: The religion of the crowd, and the religion of the consecrated heart. Many people who account themselves good Christians are good Christians only in the crowd. It is so easy to go with the multitude! Opposition tests religion, so that we may see of what sort our religion is. Some unsympathetic and incredulous questioner comes, like the people who looked down from the windows, crying, "Who is this?" and then—what do we say?

Along the streets the simple procession moves, up to the Temple, into which Jesus enters and looks about, making no comment. He sees the priests and the people, He sees the money-changers and the traders. But He stands there silent. Presently, but not to-day, He will come again and drive away these intruders who are turning the house of prayer into "a house of merchandise" and a "den of thieves."

Then the sun goes down, and in the dusk, only the twelve disciples with Him, He leaves the city and seeks the peace of Bethany. The Day of Palm is over.—H. R.

THE GLORY OF THE KING

By Alexander Maclaren, D.D.

Now unto the king eternal, immortal, invisible, the only wise God, be honor and glory forever and ever. Amen.—1 Tim. i: 17

With this burst of irrepressible praise the apostle ends his reference to his own conversion as a transcendent, standing instance of the infinite love and transforming power of God. Similar doxologies accompany almost all his references to the same fact. This one comes from the lips of "Paul the aged," looking back from almost the clôse of a life which owed many sorrows and troubles to that day on the road to Damascus. His heart fills with thankfulness that overflows into the great words of my text. He had little to be thankful for, judged according to the rules of sense; but, tho weighed down with care, having made but a poor thing of the world because of that vision which he saw that day, and now near martyrdom, he turns with a full heart to God, and breaks into this song of thanksgiving. There are lives which bear to be looked back upon. Are ours of that kind?

But my object this morning is mainly to draw your attention to what seems to me a remarkable feature in this burst of thanksgiving. And perhaps I shall best impress the thought which it has given to me if I ask you to look, first, at the character of the God who is glorified by Paul's salvation; second, at the facts which glorify such a God, and, last, at the praise which should fill the lives of those who know the facts.

I. First, then, notice the God who is glorified by Paul's salvation.

Now what strikes me as singular about this great doxology is the characteristics, or, to use a technical word, the attributes of the Divine nature which the apostle selects. They are all those which separate God from man; all those which present Him as arrayed in majesty, apart from human weaknesses unapproachable by human sense, and filling a solitary throne. These are the characteristics which the apostle thinks receive added luster, and are lifted to a loftier height of "honor and glory," by the small fact that he, Paul, was saved from sins as he journeyed to Damascus.

It would be easy to roll out oratorical platitudes about these specific characteristics of the Divine nature, but that would be as unprofitable as it would be easy. All that I want to do now is just to note the force of the epithets; and, if I can, to deepen the impression of the remarkableness of their selection.

With regard, then, to the first of them, we at once feel that the designation of "the King" is unfamiliar to the New Testament. It brings with it lofty ideas, no doubt; but it is not a name which the writers of the New Testament, who had been taught in the school of love, and led by a Son to the knowledge of God, are most fond of using. "The King" has melted into "the Father." But here Paul selects that more remote and less tender name for a specific purpose. He is ', the King"—not "*eternal,*" as our Bible renders it, but more correctly "the King of the Ages." The idea intended is not so much that of unending existence as that He molds the epochs of the world's history, and directs the evolution of its progress. It is the thought of an overruling Providence, with the additional thought that all the moments are a linked chain, through which He flashes the electric force of His will. He is "King of the Ages."

The other epithets are more appropriately to be connected with the word "God" which follows than with the word "King" which precedes. The apostle's meaning is this: "The King of the ages, even the God who is," etc. And the epithets thus selected all tend in the same direction. "Incorruptible." That at once parts that mystic and majestic Being from all of which the law is *decay.* There may be in it some hint of moral purity, but more probably it is simply what I may call a physical attribute, that that immortal nature not only *does* not, but *cannot,* pass into any less noble forms. Corruption has no share in His immortal being.

As to the "invisible," no word need be said to illustrate that. It too points solely to the separation of God from all approach by human sense.

And then the last of the epithets, which, according to the more accurate reading of the text, should be not as our Bible has it, "the only *wise* God, but "the only God," lifts Him still further above all comparison and contact with other beings.

So the whole sets forth the remote attributes which make a man feel, "The gulf between Him and me is so great that thought cannot pass across it, and I doubt whether love can live half-way across that flight, or will not rather, like some poor land bird with tiny wings, drop exhausted, and be drowned in the abyss before it reaches the other side." We expect to find a hymn to the infinite love. Instead of that we get praise, which might be upon the lips of many a thinker of Paul's day and ours, who would laugh the idea of revelation, and especially of a revelation such as Paul believed in, to absolute scorn. And yet he knew that he was saying when he did not lift up his praise to the God of tenderness, of pity, of forgiveness, of pardoning love, but to "the King of the ages; the incorruptible, invisible, only God;" the God whose honor and glory were magnified by the revelation of Himself in Jesus Christ.

II. And so that brings me, in the second

place, to ask you to look at the facts which glorify even such a God.

Paul was primarily thinking of his own individual experience; of what passed when the voice spoke to him, "Why persecutest thou me?" and of the transforming power which had changed him, the wolf with teeth red with the blood of the saints, into a lamb. But, as he is careful to point out, the personal allusion is lost in his contemplation of his own history, as being a specimen and test-case for the blessing and encouragement of all who "should hereafter believe upon Him unto life everlasting." So what we come to is this—that the work of Jesus Christ is that which paints the lily and gilds the refined gold of the Divine loftinesses and magnificence, and which brings honor and glory even to that remote and inaccessible majesty. For, in that revelation of God in Jesus Christ, there is added to all these magnificent and all but inconceivable attributes and excellences, something that is far Diviner and nobler than themselves.

There be two great conceptions smelted together in the revelation of God in Jesus Christ, of which neither attains its supremest beauty except by the juxtaposition of the other. Power is harsh, and scarcely worthy to be called Divine, unless it be linked with love. Love is not glorious unless it be braced and energized by power. And, says Paul, these two are brought together in Jesus; and therefore each is heightened by the other. It is the love of God that lifts His power to its highest height; it is the revelation of Him as stooping that teaches us His loftiness. It is because He has come within the grasp of our humanity in Jesus Christ that we can hymn our highest and noblest praises to "the King eternal, the invisible God."

The sunshine falls upon the snow-clad peaks of the great mountains and flushes them with a tender pink that makes them nobler and fairer by far than when they were veiled in clouds. And so all the Divine majesty towers higher when we believe in the Divine condescension, and there is no god that men have ever dreamed of so great as the God that stoops to sinners and is manifest in the flesh and Cross of the Man of Sorrows.

Take these characteristics of the Divine nature as set forth in the text one by one, and consider how the Revelation in Jesus Christ, and its power on sinful men, raises our conceptions of them. "The King of the ages"—and do we ever penetrate so deeply into the purpose which has guided His hand, as it molded and moved the ages, as when we can say with Paul that His " good pleasure" is that, " in the dispensation of the fulness of times, he might gather together in one all things in Christ." The intention of the epochs as they emerge, the purpose of all their linked intricacies and apparently diverse movements, is this one thing, that God in Christ may be manifest to men, and that humanity may be gathered, like sheep round the Shepherd, into the one fold of the one Lord. For that the world stands; for that the ages roll, and He who is the King of the epochs hath put into the hands of the Lamb that was slain the Book that contains all their events; and only His hand, pierced upon Calvary, is able to open the seals, to read the Book. The King of the ages is the Father of Christ.

And in like manner, that incorruptible God, far away from us because He is so, and to whom we look up here doubtingly and despairingly and often complainingly and ask, "Why hast Thou made us thus, to be weighed upon with the decay of all things and of ourselves?" comes near to us all in the Christ who knows the mystery of death, and thereby makes us partakers of an inheritance incorruptible. Brethren, we shall never adore, or even dimly understand, the blessedness of believing in a God that cannot decay nor change, unless from the midst of graves and griefs we lift our hearts to Him as revealed in the face of the dying Christ. He, tho He died, did not see corruption, and we through Him shall pass into the same blessed immunity.

"The King . . . the God invisible." "No man hath seen God at any time," nor can see Him. Who will honor and glorify that attribute which parts Him wholly from our sense, and so largely from our apprehension, as will he who can go on to say, " the only begotten Son which is in the bosom of the Father, he hath declared him." We look up into a waste heaven; thought and fear, and sometimes desire, travel into its tenantless spaces. We say the blue is an illusion; there is nothing there but blackness. But "he that hath seen me hath seen the Father." And we can lift thankful praise to Him, the King invisible, when we hear Jesus saying, "Thou hast both seen him, and it is he that talketh with thee."

"The only God." How that repels men from His throne! And yet, if we apprehend the meaning of Christ's Cross and work, we understand that the solitary God welcomes my solitary soul into such mysteries and sacred sweetnesses of fellowship with Himself that, the humanity remaining undisturbed, and the Divinity remaining unintruded upon, we yet are one in Him, and partakers of a Divine nature. Unless we come to God through Jesus Christ, the awful attributes in the text spurn a man from His throne, and make all true fellowship impossible.

So let me remind you that the religion which does not blend together in indissoluble union these two, the majesty and the lowliness, the power and the love, the God inaccesible and the God who has tabernacled with us in Jesus Christ, is sure to be almost an impotent religion. Deism in all its forms, the religion which admits a God and denies a revelation; the religion which, in some vague sense, admits a revelation and denies an incarnation; the religion which admits an incarnation and denies a sacrifice; all these have little to say to man as a sinner; little to say to man as a mourner; little power to move his heart, little power to infuse strength into his weakness. If once you strike out the thought of a redeeming Christ from your religion, the temperature will go down alarmingly, and all will soon be frost-bound.

Brethren, there is no real adoration of the loftiness of the King of the ages, no true apprehension of the majesty of the God incorruptible, invisible, eternal, until we see Him in the face and in the Cross of Jesus Christ. The truths of this Gospel of our salvation do not in the smallest degree impinge upon or weaken, but rather heighten the glory of God. The brightest glory streams from the Cross. It was when He was standing within a few hours of it, and had it full in view, that Jesus Christ broke out into that strange strain of triumph, "Now is God glorified." "The King of the ages, incorruptible, invisible, the only God," is more honored and glorified in the forgiveness that comes through Jesus Christ, and in the transforming power which He puts forth in the Gospel, than in all besides.

III. Lastly, let me draw your attention to the praise which should fill the lives of those who know these facts.

I said that this apostle seems always, when he refers to his own individual conversion, to have been melted into fresh outpourings of thankfulness and of praise. And that is what ought to be the life of all of you who call yourselves Christians; a continual warmth of thankfulness welling up in the heart, and not seldom finding utterance in the words, but always filling the life.

Not seldom, I say, finding utterance in the words. It is a delicate thing for a man to speak about himself and his own religious experience. Our English reticence, our social habits, and many other even less worthy hindrances rise in the way; and I should be the last man to urge Christian people to cast their pearls before swine, or too fully to "Open wide the bridal chamber of the heart," to let in the day. There is a wholesome fear of men who are always talking about their own religious experiences. But there are times and people to whom it is treason to the Master for us not to be frank in the confession of what we have found in Him. And

I think there would be less complaining of the want of power in the public preaching of the Word if more professing Christians more frequently and more simply said to those to whom their words are weighty, "Come and hear, and I will tell you what God hath done for my soul." "Ye are my witnesses," saith the Lord. It is a strange way that Christian people in this generation have of discharging their obligations that they should go, as so many of them do, from the cradle of their Christian lives to their graves, never having opened their lips for the Master who has done all for them.

Only remember, if you venture to speak you will have to live your preaching. "There is no speech nor language, their voice is not heard, their sound is gone out through all the earth." "The silent witness of life" must always accompany the audible proclamation, and in many cases is far more eloquent than it. Your consistent thankfulness manifested in your daily obedience, and in the transformation of your character, will do far more than all my preaching, or the preaching of thousands like me, to commend the Gospel of Jesus Christ.

One last word, brethren. This revelation is made to us all. What is God to you, friend? Is He a remote, majestic, unsympathizing, terrible Deity? Is He dim, shadowy, unwelcome; or is He God whose love softens His power, whose power magnifies His love? Oh, I beseech you, open your eyes and your hearts to see that that remote Deity is of no use to you, will do nothing for you; cannot help you, may probably judge you, but will never heal you. And open your hearts to see that "the only God" whom men can love is God in Christ. If here we lift up grateful praise "unto him that loveth us and hath loosed us from our sins in his blood," we, too, shall one day join in that great chorus which at last will be heard saying, "Blessing and honor and glory and power be unto him that sitteth upon the throne, and unto the Lamb forever and ever."
—H. R.

WHO IS THIS THAT COMETH FROM EDOM?

By Phillips Brooks, D.D.

Who is this that cometh from Edom, with dyed garments from Bozrah?—Isaiah lxiii: 1

The victory of Christ; the destruction of evil by good; the conquest over the devil by the Son of God, at cost, with pain, so that as He comes forth His robes are red with blood; the redemption of mankind from sin by the Divine and human Savior,—this is the largest and completest meaning of the ancient vision. Wherever there is good at work in the world, we Christians may see the progress of the struggle, and rejoice already in the victory of Christ. It does us good. It enlarges and simplifies our thought of Christ's religion. We shall conquer. But when we say that, we are driven home to Him and Him

alone, as our religion. Look at the method of His salvation, first, for the world at large, and then for the single soul.

I. "WHO IS THIS THAT COMETH FROM EDOM?" Sin hangs on the borders of goodness everywhere, as just across the narrow Jordan valley Edom always lay threatening upon the skirts of Palestine. So right on the border of man's higher life lies the hostile Edom, watchful, indefatigable, inexorable, as the old foe of the Jews. Every morning we lift up our eyes, and there are the low black hill-tops across the narrow valley, with the black tents upon their sides, where Edom lies in wait. Who shall deliver us from the bad world and our bad selves? The Savior comes out of the enemy's direction. His whole work had relation to and issues from the fact of sin. If there had been no sin, there would have been no Savior.

II. Look next what He says to His anxious questioner. (1) We ask Him, " Who is this?" and He replies, " I that come in righteousness, mighty to save." The Savior comes in the strength of righteousness. He will be the negotiator of no low compromise. He wants to set up the standard of absolute holiness in the midst of a nature all conquered and totally possessed by Him. (2) It is no holiday monarch coming with a bloodless triumph. The power of God has struggled with the enemy, and subdued him only in the agony of strife. Only in self-sacrifice and suffering could even God conquer sin. (3) He has conquered *alone*. He had fellow-workers, but they only handed round the broken bread and fishes in the miracle, or ordered the guest-chamber on the Passover night. They never came into the deepest work of His life. With the mysterious suffering that saved the world they had nothing to do. (4) What was the fruit of this victory over Edom which the seer of Israel discovered from his mountain-top? It set Israel free from continual harassing and fear, and gave her a chance to develop along the way that God had marked out for her. Christ's salvation sets men free; it takes off the load of sin; it gives us a new chance; and says to the poor soul that has been thinking there was no use of trying to stagger on with such a load, Go on; your burden is removed. Go on; go up to the home that you were made for, and the life in God.—S. B., vol. iv., p. 195.

THREE CONTRASTS

By Dr. A. F. Schauffler, D.D.

Matt. xxi: 12

I. The Actual.—This event was the nearest to a triumphant progress that Jesus ever made on this earth. Yet, in reality, it was a very simple affair. With a few plain disciples, and a number of very simple people who sang His praises, He entered the city as unlike a conqueror as possible.

II. The Possible.—He could have summoned a vast throng of those whom He had restored to bodily health. Lazarus and Bartimeus, the ten lepers, the widow of Nain's son, the ruler's daughter, Peter's mother-in-law, a host of those from whom He had cast out evil spirits, and a whole army of others who in one way and another had been healed by Him, could easily have been summoned to take part in that procession. Such an army as the world never saw might have marched up the hill with Him. This would have been a triumphal procession worth seeing, indeed! Moses and Elijah, who appeared on the Mount of Transfiguration, might have joined the procession, and the twelve legions of angels He once said were ready at His call. Heaven would swiftly have emptied itself a second time, and each created angel would joyfully have come down to do Him honor. Not all of earth's monarchs together could have summoned such a train of followers as Christ could have had, if He had only spoken the word. The imagination would fail to picture the scene of His triumphal procession, had He chosen to exert all His powers to make it a regal occasion.

III. The Triumphal Procession to come. —There is to be a great triumphal procession in which Jesus will one day be the leader; for in that day He will call forth all His resources, and will march in real triumph! The great procession of the universe is yet to come; for the day is coming when the Son of man will return to this earth " in his glory, and all the angels with him." The apostle John tells us, " I saw heaven opened; and behold, a white horse, and he that sat thereon was called Faithful and True. And the armies which are in heaven followed him upon white horses, clothed in fine linen, white and pure; and he hath on his garment and on his thigh a name written, King of kings and Lord of lords." At that time heaven shall be drained of all its resources to make that procession worthy of the Son of God. Prophecy had foretold His coming in humility, and it came to pass. But prophecy has also told of His coming again in glory, and that, too, shall come to pass.—S. S. T.

THE COMMENCEMENT OF CHRIST'S CORONATION PROCESSION

Mark x: 46-52

Discrepancies in three accounts. Some assert two miracles, but plainly one recorded by independent witnesses.—Silence of one witness ought not to invalidate testimony of another. Mark, in specifying Bartimeus, does not contradict Matthew. No stumbling block here to faith, proofs of independent character of Evangelist's testimony.—Christ on way from Ephraim to Jerusalem.—His journey took form of festal procession.—Full of interesting incidents.—Commencement inaugurated by this miracle.—Regard procession in three aspects, and consider :—

I. WHAT IT SIGNIFIES.—It was Christ's ratification of His people's Messianic hopes. Previously shunned publicity; hour not come. —Now case altered; Prophet begins journey to Holy City.—Appeal of Bartimeus.—Pleasant news for sinner, " Jesus passeth by."— Times when Jesus places Himself within reach.—Yet we slight such opportunities, say with Jacob, Gen. xxviii : 16. But if we felt guilt, cry like Bartimeus.—Then wrestle, " I will not let thee go."—Then cry find sympathetic echo in God's ear.—But Bartimeus also manifested signal faith.—Uses Messianic title, not " Jesus of Nazareth."—" No man say Jesus is Lord but by Holy Ghost."— Matt. xxi : 22. O that we had this faith.— Beggar's cry proclaims the character of procession.—Jesus does not check it, but stops to answer it.—Hint lost on followers—see entry to Jerusalem.

II. HOW THE CROWD REGARDED IT.—Various motives actuated followers.—Disciples alone knew real object of journey.—Others by curiosity, malignity, ambition, while many mere Passover pilgrims.—All acknowledged Jesus as leader; enthusiasm excited. Coronation procession of kings.—Elated at having recognized Messiah; enforce His claims on polished citizens of Capital.—Beggar's cry jarred : " hold thy peace."—This view of Christ's progress repeats itself.—The Church follows in Master's train.—But mistake character of progress, points of royal progress.— Forget king calls for " broken hearts and

contrite spirits."—Illustrate. False ecclesiasticism and ritualism act on consciences as crowd on Bartimeus.—Awakened sinner referred to miserable substitute for living Christ.—But these not the only hindrances.— Our own hearts ; worldly friends.—Temptations without combine with solicitations within to stifle the cry :—

" What various hindrances we meet,
  In coming to the mercy seat ;
  Yet, who that knows the worth of prayer,
  But wishes to be often there."

For there find " Son of David "

III. HOW CHRIST HIMSELF TREATED IT.—As a journey of redemption for awakened sinners. Thankful for difference between Christ's estimate of human misery and His servants. —Tho journey important, and " straitened," yet stops.—Touch of nature in fickleness of crowd.—Wants no friendly hand, for voice brings.—As beggar clutched garment, now as sinner throws it away.—Thanks, Bartimeus, for this lesson.—Hear Christ's voice in word. —Fling aside garments of self-righteousness.

" Just as I am, poor, wretched, blind ;
  Sight, riches, healing of the mind ;
  Yea, all I need in Thee to find,
  O Lamb of God I come."

V. 51. Why put question.—How many suppliants would be confused by such a question ; no clear idea of want.—But not so here ; come then and you will receive answer. V. 52. Now procession sweeps onward.—Now see true significance, since outset thus signalized.—Spiritual sight needed for intelligent following of Jesus.—H. A. C. Y.

CHRIST'S ENTRANCE INTO JERUSALEM

By J. C. HARE, D.D.

Much people that were come to the feast, when they heard that Jesus was coming to Jerusalem, took branches of palm trees and went forth to meet him, etc.—John xii : 12, 13

I. We, too, like the people in the text, should go forth to meet our Savior, whenever He comes to us. So we would go forth to meet Him, some may perhaps be thinking, if He would indeed come to us, as He came to Jerusalem, in the body, that our eyes might see Him, and that our ears might hear His words so full of grace and truth. But we should remember, that if Jesus Christ were abiding at this day upon earth, He could only be in one place at one time. If He were dwelling here with you, all the rest of the world would be without Him. But now that He is in Heaven, He can be in all places at all times, just as the sun is not only with you in your garden, but quite as much with your neighbor in his corn-field, and with the sheep on the hills, and with the sailors on the broad sea.

II. But how are we to know when Christ is coming to us? If He does not come to us in the body, how and in what does He

come? In everything, if you will but believe it, sin alone excepted. If we did but behold the hand that brings all our blessings to us, if we saw how they are brought to us by Him who cometh in the name of the Lord, they would become doubly, nay tenfold more lovely and precious, from the light of His love shining upon them. You know what a difference it makes in the brightness and beauty of everything in the world, when the sun is shining upon it—how cold and cheerless earth, sea, and sky would be without the sun—what freshness and gladness beam from them as soon as they are bathed in its light; such, so great, yea, still greater is the difference which it makes in the whole color and aspect of our lives, if we look at the events which befall us, as ordained and sent to us by the love of our heavenly Lord and Savior. In every dispensation and visitation of life, Christ comes to us, sin alone excepted. He came, not to conquer our great enemy once for all, but in order that He might be continually with us, with every one who believes in Him, standing by our side whenever we are attacked, strengthening our arms, nerving our hearts, bidding us to be of good courage, for that the enemy has already been conquered; bidding us lift up our souls to heaven, for that He has gained us sure inheritance, if we will but strive to make it sure in the kingdom of His Eternal Father—S. B., vol. viii., p. 119

CHRIST'S ENTRY INTO JERUSALEM

Outlines of a sermon by GEORGE H. SMYTH to the children in the House of Refuge, New York.

Much people that were come to the feast . . . took branches of the palm-trees, and went forth to meet him, and cried Hosanna, etc.—John xii: 12, 13

Christ was now approaching the end of His ministry. His fame had, for three years, spread far and wide; great crowds went out of the city to meet Him. Some threw their garments in the way—as a young nobleman once threw down his cloak, when the road was muddy, for Queen Elizabeth to walk over. Others cut down branches and cast them in His way, just as the children of our own country used to strew flowers in the way where Washington was to pass. Palm was an emblem of joy, peace, and victory, and was, therefore, appropriately used on this occasion.

This scene in the life of the Lord Jesus teaches:

(1) That all that God has said in His Word will come true. Five hundred years before, this entry of Christ into Jerusalem was predicted and minutely described by the prophet Zechariah. (See ix: 9.) (2) The fulfilment of prophecies that are past is a sure guaranty of the fulfilment of those that are future. "I, the Lord, have spoken it, and will do it." Read in your Bibles what has been said about the coming, rejection, and crucifixion of Christ; about the destruction of Jerusalem, of Nineveh, Babylon, Tyre, and Sidon; the dispersion of the Jews, and see how surely it has all come to pass, and learn from it all: (3) A lesson of trust in God—in all that He says in His Word, concerning you. Believe God when He says that you are a sinner, "For all have sinned"—"None righteous, no, not one." And when, believing this, and

feeling it, and in deep sorrow for sin, you ask, "What shall I do to be saved?" "Believe on the Lord Jesus Christ and thou shalt be saved," there and then saved when you believe. (4) A lesson of human weakness. The crowd that now shouted, "Hosanna to the Son of David," four days after cried, "Crucify him," "Away with this fellow and give us instead the murderer Barabbas." Oh! how we need to offer the prayer we so often sing, carelessly, I fear:

> "Savior, more than life to me,
> I am clinging, clinging close to Thee;
> Let Thy precious blood applied,
> Keep me ever, ever near Thy side."

(5) We should best celebrate this day by receiving Christ gladly into our hearts. That day when He entered the city He went into the temple and cleansed it. Let Him come in and cleanse our hearts. He is just outside now, waiting to come in. Listen! "Behold, I stand at the door, and knock; if any man hear my voice, and open the door, I will come in to him and will sup with him and he with me."

Christ wept over Jerusalem—He is yearning over you just now.

(The speaker closed with Mr. Moody's story of Mr. Dorset, the missionary of London, about the dying young prodigal, who had been expelled from his father's house. See Moody's sermon in *Glad Tidings*, page 72.)—H. R.

CHRIST IS KING

BY CHARLES F. DEEMS, D.D., LL.D.

John xviii: 37

CIRCUMSTANCES OF HIS ARRAIGNMENT.—Charged with plotting against Cæsar. Yet it was just because He would *not* do so that they hated Him. But He did constantly claim to be King. It was not a figurative expression but literal. They understood Him to speak literally: and when He entered Jerusalem in triumph, He should have corrected if not so. He was executed on the ground of that assumption.

I. CHRIST IS A KING. He claims it—if not fool or knave, He *is* a King. Over that "Kingdom of God"—that Society "called"—that *nation* in the nations.

II. IN THAT "KINGDOM OF GOD" HE DOES ALL THAT THE OLD JEWISH KINGS DID. But His Kingdom was not in the Jewish nation—nor in the Roman Empire. The thought that it was, was their mistake.

1. He refused to forbid the payment of

Cæsar's tax—not concerned about Jewish independence—nor Roman rule—but He *created a people*—and *maintained the supremacy of that Kingdom* and *takes tribute from the world.*

2. He is Supreme Judge—like old Jewish Kings.

3. *He is leader of forces*—Generalissimo—like the old Hebrew Kings.—All the seekers after truth rally to Jesus.

III. BUT HIS KINGDOM IS UNSECULAR.

1. Did not reach His throne like other Kings.

2. Does not support His throne like them.

3. Its objects, nature and tendency not worldly. (a) His disciples did not fight for Him. (b) He forbade it.

IV. ITS NATURE SHOWN IN THE TEXT. He came to bear witness to the Truth. He revealed the Truth. His royal power lay in His having the whole Truth. His martyrdom for truth.

He thus plants Himself: (1) In the intellect. (2) In the heart of man.

And so His Kingdom is not of this world. It is everlasting. Each man a king as he holds to the truth.

JESUS, THE KING

By J. VAUGHAN, D.D.

Pilate therefore said unto him, Art thou a king, then? Jesus answered, Thou sayest that I am a king, etc.—John xviii: 37

It was not as the Son of God that Jesus said this, but as the Son of man. It would have been nothing that the second Person in the Blessed Trinity should have been a King; of course He was, and much more than a King. But that poor, weak, despised man, that was standing there before Pontius Pilate, that was a King; and all Scripture confirms it. It was the manhood of Christ that was there. This is the marvel, and here is the comfort.

I. The subjugation of the universe to the King Christ is now going on, and it is very gradual; we see not yet all things put under Him. Little by little it is extending itself: "One of a city, ten of a family." The increase will grow rapid and immense. When He comes again, at once to Him every knee shall bow and every tongue shall swear: "For he must reign, till he hath put all enemies under his feet. The last enemy that shall be destroyed is death." Grand and awful! rather to be felt, than understood; where our little thoughts drift and drift for ever, on an ocean without a shore.

II. We pray: "Thy kingdom come." How much of that rich prayer is yet answered? how much are we waiting for? Three things it means: Thy kingdom in my heart; Thy kingdom over all the nations; Thy kingdom in the Second Advent. (1) The throne of God is set up in me. Sin is there, but now sin is only a rebel. It does not reign as it once did. (2) The second; it is being accomplished, and God bless the missions. (3) The third; we long and look for it with outstretched neck, and hail each gleam on the horizon.

III. When you go to this King in prayer, do not stint yourselves before His throne. Seek regal bounties. Ask for largesses worthy of a king. Not after your own little measure, but after His, according to that great name, which is above every name that is named in earth or heaven; and prove Him, on His heavenly throne, whether He will not open now the windows of heaven, and pour a blessing that there shall not be room enough to receive it.—S. B., vol. viii., p. 269.

CHRIST OUR KING

For this Melchizedek, king of Salem, priest of the most high God, etc.—Heb. vii: 1-4

All sorts of grotesque theories have been advanced about Melchizedek. He was not at all a supernatural person, but merely a Canaanitish king who united in himself the kingly and priestly offices. Tho not one of the chosen people, he was a worshiper of the true God.

His appearance was sudden and momentary. As Abraham was returning from his battle with the five kings, he was met by Melchizedek, before whom he made obeisance, receiving a blessing and "paying tithes of all." In this shadowy figure, so dimly and briefly outlined, the writer of the Epistle

to the Hebrews finds a suitable illustration of the royal priesthood of Jesus. He describes him as "without father, without mother, without descent, having neither beginning of days nor end of life." This is rhetorically correct, since the narrative gives none of these particulars. The point which the Apostle makes is this: "Christ is not a priest of the Aaronic order, but rather after the order of Melchizedek—that singular priest-king who appears for a moment and is gone, without lineage or posterity, unborn and undying, so far as the vision goes."

It is impossible to consider the Kingship of

Jesus without reference to His priestly office also. His miter is His diadem. His crown of glory is His crown of thorns. Like Melchizedek, He combines both offices in Himself. Observe His superiority to the Aaronic priests.

I. HE STANDS LIKE MELCHIZEDEK, SOLITARY AND ALONE. Since the entrance of Christ on the pontifical office, there can be no other priest. No man must presume to usurp or supplement His function as Mediator between the sinner and God. "What can I do for you?" asked a passer-by of Diogenes in his tub. "Nothing," was the reply; "only stand out of my light."

II. HIS PRIESTLY WORK IS EFFECTIVE. He offered Himself on Calvary, a sacrifice "once for all." There can be thenceforth no more sacrifice for sin. All the lambs and bullocks and turtle-doves of the ceremonial economy find their fulfilment in Christ. These were but foregleams of Him. To say that our sacrament is a "sacrifice" is to contravene the whole philosophy of the Gospel. The "elevation of the Mass" is nineteen centuries out of date.

III. CHRIST IS A PRIEST FOREVER. Other priests have come and gone; one has followed another; but Christ abideth always. He ever liveth to make intercession for us. Heb. vii: 25.

IV. HE IS A ROYAL PRIEST. Here is the chief aptness of the similitude. Melchizedek was called "King of Righteousness and King of Peace." Christ is King over all and blessed forever. (1) His priesthood is made effective by His Kingship. Darius would have delivered Daniel from the den of lions had it been possible; our King makes our deliverance possible by His sacrifice for us. (2) He is worthy of loyal service and complete surrender; as Melchizedek received of Abraham "tithes of all." Nothing that we have is too good for Christ. All our gold and myrrh and frankincense must be laid before His feet. (3) In His blessing is fulness of life. Abraham did not disdain to receive the benediction of Melchizedek. Our Lord stands ready always to say to all who will submit themselves to His sovereignty, "Peace be unto you."—H. R.

THE THRONE AND THE RAINBOW

BY C. S. ROBINSON, D.D.

And he that sat was to look upon like a jasper and a sardine stone: and there was a rainbow round about the throne, in sight like unto an emerald.—Rev. iv: 3

Look—

I. AT THIS WONDERFUL THRONE.—Of course we understand such a thing to be the symbol of government, of the Divine government in the universe, for that Being on the seat of royalty is God. But what do the other emblems mean? The whole chapter seems to glitter with a blaze of precious jewels, some of them with strange names. (1) The exalted monarch is said to be like a jasper and a sardine stone. I find the soberest commentators agreed in declaring that what is here called jasper must be the diamond, and the sardine is only what we call a carnelian, that is, a flesh-colored gem in hue, as the name signifies. And hence these expositors would have us believe that this personage, with a Divine brightness and a human expression, is none other than the Lamb in the midst of the throne. (2) The attendants. The very nobles are crowned, and wear royal raiment; their ordinary seats are thrones. (3) This vision teaches that

earth can always and everywhere be seen from heaven. (4) Observe once more, this is an unimpeachable government. These living creatures are worshiping while watching.

II. THE RAINBOW.—This represents a covenant, as the other represented a rule. (1) The ancient covenant has in it the promise of the covenant of grace. (2) Its appearance just here in John's vision is welcomed more for its graciousness than for its antiquity. (3) Observe how well this vision teaches us that God's covenant is completed This rainbow is a circlet; it goes around the throne. (4) The covenant is abiding; it will stand for ever. (5) This covenant is to each of us individual and personal.

III. NOTE THE COLLOCATION OF THE TWO SYMBOLS.—(1) God's promise surrounds God's majesty; (2) God's grace surrounds God's justice; (3) God's love surrounds God's power; (4) God's glory surrounds God's children.—S. B., vol. xii., p. 291.

SUGGESTIVE THOUGHTS AND ILLUSTRATIONS

CHRIST, The Coming of.—I. THE EARTH IS MORE INTERESTING SINCE CHRIST CAME.— He comes " meek." He had but one triumph. And there He was sitting on the colt of an ass. Jesus knew that poor forlorn thing. Meekness consistent with power—the meek *Dawn*—the meek *Spring.* II. HE COMES A KINSMAN.—" Son of David " a royal—but also a human title. In John xiv: 18 He says, " I will not leave you *orphans;* I will come again." III. HE COMES IN THE NAME OF JEHOVAH. —In the *spirit* and *power* of Jehovah. His benignity and miracles show us what our God is. IV. HE COMES A KING.—He comes to His poor. Not to every poor man, not man who is poor by drink or crime. Especially those who are poor because of their *sacrifices for others.*—CHARLES F. DEEMS.

CHRIST, The Enthroned.—In the beautiful cathedral of Orvieto, among its brilliantly decorated ornaments of sculptures and paintings, is one of Fra Angelico's greatest works, " Christ Enthroned." By his left hand he steadies the globe. His right hand is raised in divine supremacy. But in that hand is the print of the nail. Ah, it is the wounded hand that is so raised; it is by that hand He controls the world! Ah, it was by His sufferings that He became the enthroned Christ. His earthly crown was the crown of thorns. And our beloved who have gained their crowns—kings and priests and conquerors they—owe their victory to His cross alone. The disciple is not above his Master; but every one when he is perfected shall be as his Master. Sharing with Him labor and sacrifice, they are enthroned with Him. " Ye are they that have continued with me in my trials; and I appoint unto you a kingdom, even as my Father appointed unto me, that ye may eat and drink at my table in my kingdom; and ye shall sit on thrones." With the glorious company of the apostles, the goodly fellowship of the prophets, the noble army of martyrs, they lift their praise to Him who loved them and washed them from their sins by His blood. If now they could speak to us from their illuminated homes, they would admonish us to be faithful unto death, and would assure us of the crown of life, of which they well know, but concerning which we vaguely wonder.—BURDETT HART.

CHRIST, The Enthusiasm for.—We are accustomed to say that this same multitude, who on Sunday shouted Hosanna, cried " Crucify him! " on the following Friday; that " the whole enthusiasm of the multitude at the end is nothing more than the last upstreaming brilliancy of an evening sun, before it vanishes beneath the horizon." But Richard Glover is doubtless nearer the truth when he says, " The whole of that enthusiasm was not excitement. If most of the gladsome voices were silenced by the cross, very few, if any of them, took up the other cry, ' Crucify him! ' Doubtless many of those who sang Hosanna that day, asked at Pentecost, ' What must I do to be saved? ' and were among the first believers. In times of great religious excitement all emotion is not spiritual, but much of it is good and will endure.". " This story," says Dr. Robinson, " proves Christ's *fitness to evoke religious enthusiasm.* It is a frightful mistake to suppose, and a wilful perversion to assert, that Christianity as a scheme of faith is tame, insipid, and lifeless." There never has been anything on God's earth so adapted to kindle all the enthusiasm of the soul, and to make it an enduring flame. Blessed are they who have felt and continue to feel a deep, abiding, glowing enthusiasm for Christ and His Gospel. As Christ said to the Pharisees at this time (Luke xix: 40) " If these should hold their peace, the very stones would immediately cry out." Only stony or dead hearts never feel enthusiasm for Christ.— P.

END, The Beginning of the.—We have now reached the most picturesque event of our Savior's life. The Passover rapidly approached. The roads from all quarters were crowded with the assembling worshipers. Not only the great mass of the inhabitants of Palestine, but many foreign Jews thronged from every quarter,—from Babylon, Arabia, Egypt, from Asia Minor, Greece, and Italy, probably even from Gaul and Spain.—MILMAN. The question uppermost in the minds of them all was, " Can this Nazarene be *the* MESSIAH ? " Our lesson opens with the first day of Christ's last week of earthly life, and " shows to what a pitch of expectation and enthusiasm the people were aroused."—P.

ENTRY, A Triumphal.—When (at the close of the Franco-Prussian war) the German army entered Paris, they had a regular triumphal procession, and the world admired the splendor of their achievements. The papers were full of pictures of that event, and German artists have represented it again and again on canvas. But there were many things about that triumphal entry that were not dwelt upon by writers or painters. Behind that army what a sea of wo surged! How many dead strewed the way, and how many burned villages and towns marked their progress! How many widows and orphans were the consequence of that march, and, to this day, how much of poverty and distress bears witness to the dreadful progress of the German armies! Yes, the grandeur of the scene, as the German emperor marched past the triumphal arch on the Champs Elysées, was more than counterbalanced by the bloodshed and havoc that lay behind him. This was a triumphal entry of an earthly monarch, and it is the kind of march to which the world has been accustomed ever since the days of the Roman emperors. What a different kind of a triumphal entry is that of which we read to-day. —Rev. A. F. Schauffler, D.D.

GARMENTS IN THE WAY.—At that time (1834), when some of the inhabitants of Bethlehem, who had participated in a rebellion (against the Turkish government) were already imprisoned, and all were in deep distress, Mr. Farrar, then English consul at Damascus, was on a visit to Jerusalem, and rode out with Mr. Nicolayson to Solomon's Pools. On their return, as they made the ascent to enter Bethlehem, hundreds of people, male and female, met them, imploring the consul to interfere in their behalf, and afford them his protection, and all at once, by a sort of simultaneous movement, they spread their garments in the way before the horses.—Dr. Edward Robinson.

JESUS, The King.—" Thus (by the use of the three languages of the title on the cross of Jesus) to power (Latin), to culture (Greek), and to piety (Hebrew), was the sovereignty of Jesus declared, and it is still declared by means of such language. Power, culture, and piety, in their noblest forms, pay homage at the feet of Jesus."—J. R. Vincent. Thus in the chief tongues of men who proclaimed in jest what became a living truth,—that Jesus is king: the king to whom all nations and peoples should yield allegiance. " He is a king with many crowns; He is a king in the religious sphere, the king of salvation, holiness, love; He is king in the realm of culture; the treasures of art, of song, of literature, of philosophy belong to Him; He is to be king in the political sphere, in trade, commerce, and all the activities of men." And it is through the crucifixion that Jesus becomes king, and founds His kingdom, and draws the hearts of men to be His loyal subjects.—P.

JESUS, The Prince of Peace.—The triumph on this day was the triumph of the Prince of Peace. In its methods: The kingdom of Christ is one of moral influences. " Truth is His scepter; love, His force. He not only dispenses with, but disowns, all force. Christ's kingdom has been extended to every land, and has only been hindered by the force sometimes used to extend or to secure it. Meet error with truth, injustice with honor, selfishness with love, and you will understand, by attaining, something of that meek majesty of Christ which has proved so omnipotent."—R. Glover. In its results: Jesus has come to bring peace into all the world by righteousness. His reign will bring peace into the soul, now a troubled seat of war, into the community so often arrayed in contending factions; between nations, and everywhere; peace, which passes understanding, and which flows like a river.—P.

JESUS, The Prince of Peace.—He mounted, that He might enter the holy city

with all the significance of a triumph. He would not enter it, indeed, like a haughty warrior on His steed. He was the Prince of Peace. Neither would He enter it in a bedazzlement of purple and pomp and pageantry. He was the meek and lowly One. And yet He was a Conqueror and a King. All the ideas that were incarnated in His career, and emblazoned in His final sufferings and death and resurrection, are destined to be triumphant.—Morison. His riding in this triumphal procession was an object lesson, a living parable, setting forth the fact that He was a king; that His kingdom was at hand; and also " the spiritual peculiarities and dignities and glory of the reign of Christ. It is a reign of peace, humility, and meekness, because of love."—P. Palm Sunday also prefigured the entire history of the church here below. The history of the church is the march of the glorified Lord Jesus across continents and centuries. He advances on the earth as on the road to Jerusalem, with the calm majesty of a sovereign; He takes possession of things and of men; He makes them His instruments and His servants, just as on Palm Sunday He used the ass which did not belong to Him, and drew forth a glorious homage from all those mouths which on that day had no voice for Him. Saluted by the songs of all the churches in all the countries where His name is known, advancing from nation to nation, He marches toward the final domination of the whole world.—Prof. Frederic Godet.

MESSIAH, Jesus Presents Himself as the.—The purpose of this riding into Jerusalem was to set forth, as in a living parable, that He was the Messiah, the expected king, and to present Himself to the Jews for their acceptance. It was the final offer to those who had rejected Him as a teacher, that they might accept Him as the Messiah, and save themselves and their nation from destruction. (1) He came as a king, as God's ambassador, kingly as God is kingly, in spirit, in moral exaltation, seeking willing subjects, desiring to do only good, and to destroy only incorrigible evil. (2) He came in accordance with prophecy uttered centuries before (Isa. lxii: 11; Zech. ix: 9). (3) He came as the Prince of Peace, the riding on an ass being a symbol of peace, as riding on a horse was the symbol of war. His kingdom will be one of peace through righteousness,—peace with God, peace with the laws of the universe, peace with one another, peace of conscience, peace among all the faculties of the soul,—peace that passeth understanding, unspeakable and full of glory.—P.

PALM-TREE, Use of the.—The palm-tree, from its erect and noble growth and its heavenward direction, is used in Psalm xcii: 12, as an illustration of the righteous. Its branches are also used as emblems of victory or triumph. In the heavenly Jerusalem, the great multitude who stood before the thone and before the Lamb, are represented as " clothed with white robes, and palms in their hands."—F. II.

PEACE, The Prince of.—I. THE PRINCE OF PEACE TRIUMPHS OVER EVIL MEN.—Note the power of Jesus; the power of one doing right; the weakness of those in the wrong. Apply to the evils that need to be cleansed from the heart and from the church. ILLUSTRATION. Remember the state of the great cathedral of London, as painted in the literature of Elizabeth and James, when mules and horses laden with market produce were led through St. Paul's as a matter of every-day occurrence, and bargains were struck there, and burglaries planned, and servants hired, and profligate assignations made and kept.—ELLICOTT. II. THE PRINCE OF PEACE TRIUMPHS OVER SORROW AND DISEASE (ver. 14). These the works that belong to the house of prayer. God is ever working them in and through cleansed hearts and cleansed churches. III. THE PRINCE OF PEACE AND CHILDREN'S PRAISE (vers. 15, 16).

POMPEY'S TRIUMPH.—In September, B. C. 61, about ninety years before Christ's triumphal entry, the most magnificent triumph ever seen in Rome was given to Pompey. For two days the grand procession of trophies from every land, and a long retinue of captives, moved into the city along the Via Sacra. Brazen tablets were carried, on which were engraved the names of the conquered nations, including 1,000 castles and 900 cities. The remarkable circumstance of the celebration was, that it declared him conqueror of the whole world.—P.

PROCESSION, The Invisible.—If Christ had opened the eyes of those looking upon this scene as the eyes of Elisha's servant were opened, so that they might see the invisible, and hear the inaudible, no pen could picture the real triumphal procession. They would have seen the vast multitude of those whom He had healed and comforted and saved from sin, Lazarus and Bartimeus, the ten lepers, the widow of Nain's son, the ruler's daughter, Peter's mother-in-law, a host of those whom He had raised from the dead, those from whom He had cast out devils, the blind He had made to see, and the lame that now walked, the lepers He had cleansed, those who had been delivered from the bondage of their sins and brought into the light of the gospel. There would join them the angels who sang at His birth, Moses and Elijah, who appeared on the Mount of Transfiguration, and the twelve legions of angels He once said were ready at His call. Heaven would swiftly have emptied itself, and all its choirs would joyfully have come to do Him honor, and sing their songs of joy over many sinners brought to repentance.—PELOUBET.

PROCESSION, The Triumphal.—*Matt. xxi: 8, 9.* "And a very great multitude, R. V., *most of the multitude,* because only a few could find branches. The crowds came from two directions, from the city (John xii: 12), and crowds of pilgrims from all parts thronging into the city by the Jericho road. By a census taken in the time of Nero,

it was ascertained that there were 2,700,000 Jews present at the Passover. Being visitors, they would have abundant leisure for any procession or excitement. "Spread their garments." The loose blankets or cloaks worn over the tunic or shirt. "In the way." "Thus manifesting, extemporizingly, their high idea of our Lord. It was customary, in royal processions, to spread decorative cloth, or carpet, upon the ground, that the feet of royalty might not be defiled, or that dust might not arise."—JAMES MORISON.

QUEEN, Only One.—A beekeeper, expert in knowledge of bees and their habits, says there can be but one queen to a colony, and as soon as the first queen is born she will go around to the other queen cells, rip them open and kill the about-to-be-born queens just as fast as she can. It is thus that she disposes of all possible rivals. Her course meets with the entire approval of the other bees; in fact, if two queens happen to be born at the same time, the bees bring them together at once and make them fight until one or the other is dead. Two queens would be worse than none at all. If the queens are disposed to tolerate one another and will not fight when brought together, the other bees will force them to it, and they are obliged to combat for supremacy. Surely a man ought to be as wise as a bee, and whenever he is, he knows that Christ's word is true, that "no man can serve two masters."—*Selected.*

RALEIGH AND THE QUEEN.—This was somewhat on the principle that actuated the heart of young Sir Walter Raleigh when, on Queen Elizabeth coming to a miry part of the road, and hesitating for an instant how to step across, he "took off his new plush mantle, and spread it on the ground. Her Majesty trod gently over the fair foot-cloth."—JAMES MORISON.

SORROW OVER THOSE WHO REFUSED TO JOIN IN THE TRIUMPH.—*Luke xix:41-44.* One touching incident is related by Luke only. As the procession began to descend from the summit of the Mount of Olives, the glories of Jerusalem in all its splendor burst upon Jesus' view. "It rose terrace upon terrace, a city of palaces." "If," says Canon Tristram, "the prospect be impressive now, what must it have been when the grand colonnade of Herod, gleaming with white marble, ran along the southern face of that platform for a thousand yards, and reaching a height of two hundred feet? Then, too, the golden gate showed its gorgeous façade; but the dazzling marble and gilding of Herod's temple dominated over all else, so that the city seemed built for the temple, not the temple for the city." Here, while others shouted, Jesus wept over the city, for the sins of its people, who, in rejecting Him, sealed the ruin of the city and the nation. "He was crossing the ground on which, a generation later, the tenth Roman legion would be encamped, as part of the besieging force destined to lay all the splendors before Him in ashes."

"The contrast was indeed terrible between the Jerusalem that rose before Him in all its beauty, glory, and security, and the Jerusalem which he saw in vision dimly rising on the sky, with the camp of the enemy round about it on every side, hugging it closer and closer in deadly embrace; then another scene in the shifting panorama, and the city laid even with the ground, and the gory bodies of her children among her ruins; and yet another scene, the silence and desolateness of death, not one stone left upon another."—EDERSHEIM. Even in the midst of our rejoicing over the triumphs of Christianity, we should weep over those who will not come and be saved.—P.

TRIUMPH OF JESUS, The.—Commerce, railroads, printing presses, inventions, wealth, civilization are aiding His triumph, paving His way, and advancing His glory. All are cast down before Him in His onward march. And all the redeemed, ten thousand times ten thousand and thousands of thousands, are singing His hosannas, and joining in the song, "Worthy is the Lamb that was slain to receive power, and riches, and wisdom, and strength, and honor, and glory, and blessing." Jesus still weeps over those who refuse to come to Him to be saved. But His triumph is increasing, and soon

"The gospel banner, wide unfurled,
Shall wave in triumph o'er the world;
And every creature, bond and free,
Shall hail the glorious jubilee."
                                        P.

VISION, The Present.—The triumphal procession of Christ is still going on. Already it numbers countless millions, who, as these people cast their garments before Jesus as He rode in triumph, have cast their talents, their money, their time, all that they possess, before Him, to aid His cause, and hasten His success.

"Ride on triumphantly; behold, we lay
Our lusts and proud wills in Thy way."

"They know that to Him they owe all that is dearest in life. From Him they have received pardon and grace, and a title to eternal life. I see among them the redeemed drunkard, who was miserable, and blind, and naked, and half demented, but who now is clothed, and in his right mind. I see there the harlot, who now is refined, and trying to live a Christ-like life. Old men and young boys, feeble women and robust maidens, all saved by the power of the Lord, unite in that throng. Multitudes of Sunday-school children are there too, and join their voices with those of the others in singing His praise.'—A. F. SCHAUFFLER.

POETRY

Alleluia

BY ROBERT ROBINSON

Lord of every land and nation,
"Ancient of eternal days,"
Sounded through the wide creation,
Be Thy just and lawful praise.
Alleluia! Amen.

For the grandeur of Thy nature,
Grand beyond a seraph's thought,
For created works of power,
Works with skill and kindness wrought.
Alleluia! Amen.

For Thy rich, Thy free redemption,
Dark through brightness all along;
Thought is poor, and poor expression;
Who can sing that awful song?
Alleluia! Amen.

"Brightness of the Father's glory,"
Shall Thy praise unuttered lie?
Shun, my tongue, the guilty silence;
Sing the Lord who came to die.
Alleluia! Amen.

From the highest throne in glory,
To the Cross of deepest wo,
All to ransom guilty captives—
Flow my praise, forever flow.
Alleluia! Amen.

Go, return, immortal Savior;
Leave Thy footstool, take Thy throne;
Thence return, and reign forever;
Be the kingdom all Thine own.
Alleluia! Amen. Amen.

The Name of Jesus

BY CAROLINE M. NOEL

At the name of Jesus
Ev'ry knee shall bow,
Ev'ry tongue confess Him
King of glory now.
'Tis the Father's pleasure,
We should call Him Lord,
Who from the beginning
Was the mighty Word.

At His voice creation
Sprang at once to sight,
All the angel faces,
All the hosts of light,
Thrones and dominations,
Stars upon their way,
All the heavenly orders
In their great array.

Humbled for a season,
To receive a name
From the lips of sinners
Unto whom He came,

Faithfully He bore it
Spotless to the last,
Brought it back victorious,
When from death He past.

In your hearts enthrone Him;
There let Him subdue
All that is not holy,
All that is not true:
Crown Him as your Captain
In temptation's hour:
Let His will enfold you
In its light and power.

Brothers, this Lord Jesus
Shall return again,
With His Father's glory,
With His angel train;
For all wreaths of empire
Meet upon His brow,
And our hearts confess Him
King of glory now. Amen.

A New Hymn

By S. F. Smith, D.D.

Haste to Thy conquest of the world,
O King, with glory crowned;
Gather Thy trophies far and wide
Wherever man is found.

Ride in swift triumph o'er the earth,
Lift up Thy sceptered hand;
Thine is the kingdom, Thine the right,
Ride forth o'er sea and land.

Then round the conquered world Thy praise
In waves on waves shall ring;
And shore to shore, and sea to sea,
In answering chorus sing.

Adoring thousands at Thy feet
In faith and love shall fall;
And countless souls, redeemed from sin,
Shall crown Thee Lord of all.

Then he that sowed in patient hope,
Through all the weary years,
Shall find at last abundant sheaves,
And joy for toil and tears.
                                        E. T.

Jesus Reigns

By T. Kelly

Hark! ten thousand harps and voices
Sound the note of praise above;
Jesus reigns, and heaven rejoices;
Jesus reigns, the God of love:
See, He sits on yonder throne;
Jesus rules the world alone.

King of glory! reign for ever—
Thine an everlasting crown;
Nothing, from Thy love, shall sever
Those whom Thou hast made Thine own;
Happy objects of Thy grace,
Destined to behold Thy face.

Savior! hasten Thine appearing;
Bring, oh, bring the glorious day,
When, the awful summons hearing,
Heaven and earth shall pass away;—
Then, with golden harps, we'll sing,—
"Glory, glory to our King!"

Thy Kingdom Come

There's a light from the cross! There's a
light from the Word!
It is flooding the earth with the joy of the
Lord!
And hearts that were aching
In darkness, and breaking,
Are chanting His praises in blissful accord.

Bow down, Eastern mountains! The Savior
has come!
And sing, O ye fountains, in every wide
zone!
To every dark nation
The glad proclamation
Is offering welcome and pardon and home.

Ay! crumble to dust in your temples of
gold,
Ye idols so ancient and stony and cold!
The people are yearning
For comfort, and learning
The best, sweetest story that ever was told.

There's a light from the cross. There's a
light from the Word!
And the kingdoms of earth are the realms
of our Lord!
O Savior victorious,
So tender, so glorious!
We praise Thee, we bless Thee, in reverent
accord!—S. C.

The King

By Mary F. Butts

How plain soe'er the house or poor the
guests
The royalest of all sits at thy board,
Shares thy small space, waits longingly to
give
Full measure of the comfort of His love.
How great thy dignity! How little need
That men should power or place or goods
bestow!

O give Him access to thy pent-up heart;
No longer poor the place where God takes
part.—G. R.

The Lord Is King

By Charles Wesley

Rejoice, the Lord is King,
Your Lord and King adore;
Mortals, give thanks and sing,
And triumph evermore:
Lift up your heart, lift up your voice,
Rejoice, again I say, rejoice.

Jesus the Savior reigns,
  The God of truth and love;
When He had purged our stains,
  He took His seat above:
Lift up your heart, lift up your voice,
Rejoice, again I say, rejoice.

His kingdom cannot fail,
  He rules o'er earth and heaven;
The keys of death and hell
  Are to our Jesus given;
Lift up your heart, lift up your voice,
Rejoice, again I say, rejoice.

He all His foes shall quell,
  Shall all our sins destroy,
And every bosom swell
  With pure seraphic joy:
Lift up your heart, lift up your voice,
Rejoice, again I say, rejoice.

Rejoice in glorious hope;
  Jesus, the Judge, shall come,
And take His servants up
  To their eternal home:
We soon shall hear the archangel's voice,
The trump of God shall sound, Rejoice.

Palm Branches

Tr. by Theodore T. Barker

O'er all the way green palms and flowers gay
  Are strewn this day in festal preparation,
Where Jesus comes to wipe our tears away;
  E'en now the throng to welcome Him
  prepare.

Refrain.

Join all and sing, His name declare,
  Let every voice resound with acclamation,
Hosanna! Glory to God!
  Praise Him who cometh to bring us salva-
  tion!

His word goes forth, and peoples by its might
  Once more regain freedom from degradation;

Humanity doth give to each his right,
  While those in darkness find restored the
  light.   Refrain.

Sing and rejoice, O blest Jerusalem,
  Of all thy sons sing the emancipation,
Through boundless love; the Christ of Beth-
  lehem
  Bring faith and hope to thee forevermore.
  Refrain.

The Song of the Seraphs

By Matthew Bridges

Crown Him with many crowns,
  The Lamb upon His throne:
Hark, how the heav'nly anthem drowns
  All music but its own!
With His most most precious blood
  From sin He set us free:
We hail Him as our matchless King
  Through all eternity.

Crown Him the Lord of love:
  Behold His hands and side,
Rich wounds, yet visible above
  In beauty glorified:
No angel in the sky
  Can fully bear that sight,
But downward bends his burning eye
  At mysteries so bright.

Crown Him the Lord of peace,
  Whose power a scepter sways,
From pole to pole, that wars may cease,
  And all be prayer and praise:
His reign shall know no end,
  And round His piercéd feet
Fair flowers of Paradise extend
  Their fragrance ever sweet.

Crown Him the Lord of Heaven,
  One with the Father known,
One with the Spirit through Him given
  From yonder radiant throne!
To Thee be endless praise,
  For Thou for us hast died:
Be Thou, O Lord, through endless days
  Adored and magnified.

COMMUNION SUNDAY

ALTHO the holy sacrament of the Lord's Supper was instituted on Thursday evening of Passover Week, yet it is almost universally celebrated in the churches on Sunday. This ordinance is also called the Lord's Supper, because instituted by Him; and the Eucharist, or giving thanks, with reference to Christ's giving thanks at its institution and His ministers giving thanks at the time of the distribution of the bread and wine. At the Communion Christians partake of the sacrament as a memorial of Jesus Christ, especially of His vicarious sufferings and death on the cross. The Communion is as old as Christianity itself. *(Matt. xxvi: 26-29; Mark xiv: 22-25; Luke xxii: 17-20; 1 Cor. xi: 23-25.)*

In Exodus xii: 1-36 we have an account of the institution of the greatest of the three annual feasts of the Jews, the Passover. In the year 30, A. D., on Thursday night of Passover Week, *i. e.*, on the 14th of Nisan, corresponding with our April 6, Jesus Christ and His twelve apostles were assembled in the upper room of a house in Jerusalem. There they ate the Passover Supper, in the course of which, probably after Judas had gone out, our Lord took a portion of the unleavened bread, offered a prayer over it, broke it and distributed it among the apostles, saying: " Take, eat; this is my body, which is broken for you. This do in remembrance of me." In like manner, after they had supped, He took the cup of wine, which it was the custom to drink at the Passover, and blessed it and gave it to the apostles, saying: " Drink ye all of it. For this is my blood of the new testament, (or covenant) which is shed for many for the remission of sins."

With these words and actions Christ founded the Sacrament of the Lord's Supper. There is nothing in the account to indicate clearly where and how often the .Lord's Supper is to be observed, and by whom it ought to be administered. Various individual Christians and denominations of Christians have drawn various inferences as to the true answers to these questions. So the history of the church tells of the many ways in which the Lord's Supper has been observed, and of the discussions, sometimes amounting to controversies, as to certain features of this sacrament. Especially have opinions differed as to the meaning of our Lord's words, " This is my body." Very early in the history of the church the question arose as to whether this language is to be taken literally or figuratively. The Greek and Roman Catholic churches have insisted on the literal interpretation of the words, and hold that at the communion, the bread and wine are changed into the actual body and blood of Christ. This doctrine is called transubstantiation. The Lutheran doctrine is called consubstantiation, and teaches that while the bread and wine are not turned into the actual body and blood of Christ, yet the language of the Lord is not figurative, but literal, and there is, when the Lord's Supper is properly administered, a real tho mysterious, union of Christ, *unio sacramentalis,* and the elements used, so that both are partaken of at one and the same time. The Reformed view is that the language is not literal, but Christ meant, " This broken bread represents my broken body, and the wine in the cup represents my blood which was poured out for you." The Reformed view insists, however, that Christ is in some mysterious but real way present in a peculiar manner, and is partaken of spiritually by all who partake of the Lord's Supper intelligently and with faith. The Westminster Shorter Catechism (A. D. 1647) thus answers the question "What is the Lord's Supper?" (Q. 96.) It is "a sacrament, wherein, by giving and receiving bread and wine, according to Christ's appointment, His death is showed forth; and the worthy receivers are, not after a corporal and carnal manner, but by faith, made partakers of His body and blood, with all His benefits, to their spiritual nourishment and growth in grace."

For a detailed account of the theories and practices relating to the Lord's Supper, see the articles on The Lord's Supper in the various encyclopedias and dictionaries of Biblical and religious knowledge, especially the SCHAFF-HERZOG ENCYCLOPEDIA OF RELIGIOUS KNOWLEDGE (Funk and Wagnalls), and THE INTERNATIONAL CYCLOPEDIA (Dodd, Mead and Co.)

THE LORD'S SUPPER

BY PROF. E. J. WOLF, D.D.

The importance of its history in four books of the New Testament emphasizes the importance of this ordinance. It was solemnly instituted by our Lord on the night before His passion. It was celebrated by His disciples, at first daily and in connection with a simple social meal, called the *agape,* or Feast of Love, and then it was for a long period observed every Lord's Day, but only within the circle of the Church.

The Agape

Immediately after the conclusion of the homiletic or missionary services, in which the public participated, the promiscuous assembly was dismissed (the word *missa,* thus used, giving its name afterward to the entire sacramental service; German, *missa;* English, *Mass*), and the elements, common bread and wine mingled with water, were consecrated by the presiding official and then distributed by the deacons to the congregation, and also to the sick and the prisoners who were prevented from being present. An elaborate sacramental liturgy, comprising suitable prayers, doxologies, and responses, which became the basis of all subsequent formularies of this kind, developed at an early day around the solemn rite, and it has been commonly regarded throughout the Christian Church, as the highest and holiest part of divine worship.

Missa or Mass

Historians are unanimous in their testimony that from the beginning this sacrament was viewed as a great mystery, to which was attached profound doctrinal significance and the highest spiritual efficacy. With the visible elements, it was believed, were mystically the body and blood of the Lord. Those who in faith partook of this Supper enjoyed essential communion with Christ. They partook of a

The Mystery of the Sacrament

"spiritual food, indispensable to eternal life." The first Christian theologians were not given to sharp distinctions between the outward sign and the invisible substance which it represents. "The real and the symbolical were so blended," says Hagenbach, "that the symbol did not supplant the fact, nor did the fact dislodge the symbol." Yet they distinguished the two things constituting the Supper as *terrena et cælesti.* In some places they speak distinctly of signs, and the Alexandrians are classed with those holding spiritualistic views; then again they "speak openly of a real participation in the body and blood of Christ," while not a single passage in the Fathers asserts the elements to be merely signs or symbols.

Of the doctrine of a total change of the elements into the body and blood of Christ not a trace is found in the Ante-Nicene Church. Later, many of the Fathers used phraseology which seems to involve the doctrine of a real change, and a disposition toward that theory is apparent, yet according to Baur these "are only an obscure and exaggerated identification of figure and fact." The same teachers use also representations which exclude a change. The idea of a sacrifice came now likewise to be connected with the Sacrament, at first only in the sense of a celebration of the one Sacrifice of Christ, but gradually in the sense of an unbloody but actual repetition of that sacrifice. The ascription of a priestly character to the clerical office contributed largely to the development of this notion. As late as the ninth century, a treatise maintaining in earnest a complete change of the elements, called forth an extensive and violent controversy, altho it doubtless only set forth in definite statements what was then the popular belief. Two

Change of the Elements

centuries later the denial of the Change of Substance led to the condemnation of Berengar by several synods, and in A. D. 1215, at the Fourth Lateran Council, the doctrine of Transubstantiation was pronounced an article of faith by Pope Innocent III.

The Reformers with one voice repudiated both the doctrine of Transubstantiation and that of the Sacrifice of the Mass, as Wycliffe **The** had done before. When, however, they came to formulate **Reformers** the positive elements of the doctrine for the Evangelical Church, so wide a difference emerged that the unity of Protestantism was shattered upon this rock. Luther was at first predisposed to a symbolical and purely subjective interpretation; but he felt bound by the clear word of Scripture to accept the doctrine that, along with the elements there are present, and received, sacramentally and supernaturally, the glorified body and blood of the Lord Jesus Christ, which believers partake of to their spiritual strength, unbelievers to their judgment. Exception to this view, he argued, could only be taken on grounds of reason; and if reason may rule supremely on this doctrine, "you open the way for it to sweep away every doctrine."

Zwingli maintained the purely symbolical, commemorative, and subjective character of the Supper, and on this account Luther declined Church-fellowship with **Other** him. Calvin's position was me- **Views** diating between the theories of Luther and Zwingli. He also taught clearly, a Real Presence, but one not mediated through the bread and wine, as this would conflict with the doctrine of particular election, which limits the actual offer of grace to believers. "The believer, by means of faith, partakes in the Sacrament, only spiritually but yet really, of the Lody and blood of the Lord, through a power issuing from the glorified body of Christ, whereas the unbeliever receives only bread and wine." This view superseded the Zwinglian in the Confessions of Switzerland, and passed into all the Reformed Creeds of the Continent, and of Great Britain, including the xxxix articles.

The dogma developed by Luther has ever remained the distinguishing feature of the Lutheran system. It has also been held by many in the Church of England, **Luther** and by Episcopalians in this country. The Sacerdotal view of the ministry prevalent in the latter communion has favored both the doctrine of a change of substance and that of a sacrifice— the two go together, apparently—errors from which the Lutherans have escaped by their New Testament conception of the ministerial office.

While all the Reformed Confessions of the XVIth century contained the Calvinistic view of the Lord's Supper, the current teaching and popular belief in all but Lu- **Zwing-** theran and Episcopal Churches **lianism** has long been that of Zwinglianism. The Supper is wont to be celebrated as a solemn spiritual exercise, recalling the atoning death of our Lord, and indicating the union of His followers. A reaction in favor of higher views has of late appeared, especially among Presbyterian and Reformed theologians.—H. R.

SERMONS AND OUTLINES

THE LORD'S SUPPER

By Rev. Charles A. Savage

The proper attitude to assume with relation to the Lord's Supper is a golden mean between idolatry and indifference.

Indifference to the Sacrament casts contempt on an ordinance instituted by our Savior Himself, and one that is full of holy meaning. An idolatrous reverence for it not only violates the Second Commandment, but dishonors Christ.

This indifference may be overcome, and this superstitious reverence may be modified, by a proper emphasis on the following considerations:

I. The Lord's Supper should be regarded as a Festival, and not as a Fast. Our chief thought should be one of exultant gratitude. The cross is not so much for us a symbol of sacrifice as of victory. It does not stand so much for shame as for glory. Our eyes **have** been opened to see not so much guilt **there,** or punishment there, as Atonement and reconciliation with God. A proper emphasis of this side of the Atonement exalts Christ— kindles anew in us the flame of love—stimulates devotion.

II. We should come to the Lord's Table with the confident expectation of meeting Christ there, and of receiving there a blessing.

Unbelief of a positive promise blocks a blessing. Our doubt as to His willingness to do what He has said He will do, while it does not destroy His willingness to give, weakens our ability to receive. Expecting large blessings from God insures large blessings, not as a reward of the expectancy, but because the capacity of the aqueduct which taps the infinite reservoir is measured by the faith that builds it.

III. This expectation of meeting Christ at His Table, and of receiving His blessing, will demand and insure a thoughtful, prayerful preparation for it. We need not try to work

ourselves up to any prescribed state of religious feeling. Real communion with God
does not imply excited emotions. Christ is
not transfigured on the mountain top of
ecstasy. The preparation we need is calm,
candid contemplation. We need for a while
"to sit alone with our conscience, in some
siiently solemn place." We need to look inward as a preparation for looking outward,—
examine our hearts that so we may see the
value of the provision made to make them
clean; question our deepest longings, to enable us to understand the royal provision to
satisfy them; give attention to the cry of
our heart loneliness; that we may understand what communion with Christ may
mean.

IV. We should look to the Sacrament for a
special revelation of Christ and His truth.
The purpose of the communion service is to
afford us an opportunity to take into our
spiritual natures something from the outside.

Some spirit, foreign to itself, is to be taken
into our souls and assimilated for spiritual
strength and growth. That spirit is the living
Christ. Since the knowledge of Him is
eternal life, every increase of that knowledge
is an increase of the life power within us.

The vitality of the Sacrament is the Christ
in it.—both as the truth and the life. The
Parable, as it fell from the lips of Jesus,
and the Sacrament as instituted by Him, are
akin. Both are disclosures, through some
door opening into some common material
thing, of the spiritual reality within and behind them. The Parable opens a door into
the mystery of the Kingdom of Heaven,—
the Sacrament into the hearts of the King
of Heaven. It is more than a vision that
we see. It is an eternal reality. The plea
then is for a true spiritual " Elevation of the
Host," a revival of the consciousness of the
Real Presence of Our Lord in His Sacrament. Not the Lateran transubstantiation,
or the consubstantiation of Luther, but an
acceptance of Christ's Real Presence is a
protest against the conception of His fictitious presence. The Sacrament is something more than a scenic display. Its purpose is deeper than that of a mere memorial.
Paul speaks of its observance, wherein there
is no discernment of the Lord's Body, as a
profanation. Christ's Body to-day is a
spiritual body. His real presence is a spiritual presence. The bread and the wine are
material symbols, but the spiritual reality
is present in them, for these symbols were
ordained by Christ Himself for this very purpose, to represent Him.

V. The Lord's Supper may be made more
profitable for us if we emphasize it as a
bond of brotherhood. A communion with
Christ, it is also a communion with each
other, and not only among the few gathered
within the walls of a single sanctuary; it is
the fellowship of the ages. In the name of
our common Christ, "encompassed by so
great a cloud of witnesses," we sit with
them in heavenly places whenever we come
to the Communion Table of our Lord.

There is inspiration in this thought of
brotherhood. As the vision comes to us of
"the multitudes whom no man can number
out of every kindred and nation and tribe
and tongue, gathered at the marriage supper of the Lamb," as we recall His words,
"I will no more drink of the fruit of the
vine, until that day when I drink it new
with you in my Father's Kingdom," we feel
strong in the wide reaching brotherhood
begun here, to be consummated in the many
mansions.

Then, too, the Lord's Table offers special
opportunity for intercession and prayer.
If we have got there a clearer conception
of how our Father " spared not his only-begotten Son," we see clearer, too, how that
"with him he is ready, also, freely to give
us all things." So the vision of God's love
stimulates our love, and as the great Augustine has said: " By loving, not by traveling
we come near to Him who is everywhere."
Loving God is knowing God, and knowing
God is eternal life; with all that eternal life
means. A better acquaintance with our
Heavenly Father thus means larger measures
of His beneficence. The light of His smile,
the look of His eye, is an answer to every
prayer.

So while the Lord's Table presents a
favorable opportunity for special supplications on our own behalf and for a renewal of our consecration, the solemnity
of the occasion, the peculiar significance of
it, the atmosphere of prayer pervading it,
all combine to open our hearts in intercession for others. Prayer for the extension
of Christ's Kingdom is most effective when
we are in the audience chamber of the
King.

A proper emphasis of this opportunity, and
the suitably availing ourselves of it, cannot
fail to increase the profit of the communion
to our own souls. Not the blessing that we
get, but the one that we share, is most truly
blessed.

VI. The observance of the Supper is not a
matter of moods, but of duty and of privilege.
Our emotions are not always under our control. Our feelings are not altogether trustworthy indications either as to our spiritual
condition or our spiritual needs. Efferves-
cence in the spiritual world is no more substantial than in the natural world. We need
spiritual strength, nourishment, uplift. We
stand in special need along these lines when
our love is cold, when our faith is weak,
when our Christian purpose is wavering.
Such a condition of heart as this, so far from
being a reason for staying away from the
Lord's Supper, is the strongest reason for
attending it.

" We go to be filled with Christ and emptied of self, to warm our hearts at the flame
of His love, to stimulate our faith by the
touch of His life.

"If our covenant with Him has been
broken, we have double need to avail ourselves of the New Covenant in His blood,
which He has shed for many, for the remission of sins."—I.

THE LORD'S SUPPER: A EUCHARIST

By Rev. David Gregg, D.D.

Jesus took bread, and blessed, and brake it. . . . And he took the cup, and when he had given thanks, he gave it to them.—Mark xiv: 22, 23

The blessing of the bread and the giving of thanks over the cup, in the Lord's Supper, are similar acts. This is evident from the words of Paul. In 1 Corinthians x: 16, he calls the cup over which thanksgiving is offered, "the cup of blessing": "The cup of blessing which we bless, is it not the communion of the blood of Christ?" If this be true, then Jesus offered two thanksgivings at the institution of the Lord's Supper—one over the bread and one over the cup. In using the Passover wine, which stood as the index of the productiveness of the land, the Hebrews were vehement and prolonged in their expressions of gratitude and thanksgiving to God. Jesus, in building up the Lord's Supper out of the Passover, carried the thanksgiving of the old ordinance into the new. Because of His emphatic twofold thanksgiving, the Lord's Supper was known to the early Church by the name of the Eucharist—*i. e.,* "the Thanksgiving." The term Eucharist, which means "thanksgiving," is the Greek word Anglicized. As the Lord's Supper was a vast advance upon the Passover, the thanksgiving of Christ was a great remove beyond the thanksgiving of the Hebrews. He saw higher things; He saw grander purposes of God. They saw Canaan, He saw heaven. They saw the past, He saw the future. Let us not forget that Christ gives character to the ordinances which He institutes, and through which He communicates to His people His thoughts, His grace, His hopes, His feelings, His spirit—Himself. Was the Lord's Supper a thanksgiving to Him? Then it must be a thanksgiving to His people who sit down with Him in this ordinance and receive of His fullness.

We want to look at the Lord's Supper as an ordinance of thanksgiving, that we may have greater desire and pleasure and profit in its celebration. God unfolds to us the different attributes of this beautiful ordinance, that we may be attracted to it. He means every attribute to be a persuasive argument enforcing obedience to the command: "This do in remembrance of me."

I. It must be a thanksgiving ordinance in order to represent aright the feast which it supersedes.

It supersedes the Passover. Why? Not because it is in contrast with the Passover: not for the reason that one man is made to supersede another in office, because his predecessor was wrong and an opposite policy must be followed. The Lord's Supper supersedes the Passover because it is in the same line and is an advance in the same direction. It comes in under the necessity of growth, just as the fruit follows the blossom. It is not without design that the Passover cup

and bread are made the cup and bread of the Lord's Supper. There is a unity in the two ordinances. They are both social in character, and emblematical, in a large measure, of the same doctrines. They are both commemorative. The advance in the execution of God's great purposes, and the entrance of man upon the grander realities of an accomplished redemption, require an enlargement of the ordinance, and demand that the typo-symbolical Passover give place to the purely symbolical Lord's Supper. It is evident that the spirit of the old ordinance must be carried into the new, developed and intensified.

What was the reigning spirit of the Passover? Joy and thanksgiving. We are accustomed to look upon the old Jewish religion as a yoke, and we have Scripture for this. But let us not lose sight of this fact: It was a yoke that drew after it a great load of blessings and of prospects. It was a religion of feasts, and carried with it only one divinely-appointed fast-day—the day of atonement. The sacred times were joy times; and these returned and left, came and went, until the Year of Jubilee was reached. Then there was a fresh start to the jubilees beyond. The services demanded by this religion were many; but the spirit which God meant to reign in all was the spirit of the feast-day. Look at the Sabbath of the Jews, which is so discounted by modern public opinion: it is regarded as severe, and grinding, and enslaving. If one judged the Jewish Sabbath by popular estimation, he must conclude that God meant to afflict the Hebrews when He put them under the Sabbath ordinance. Bad as the Sabbath was for the Jew, we must conclude that it was awful for the stranger within the gates, who was compelled to honor the Sabbath law. But what saith the Word? It gives the true reason for the Sabbath: "Six days shalt thou work, and on the seventh thou shalt rest, that thine ox and thine ass may rest, and *the stranger may be refreshed.*"

In God's sight, the Sabbath meant refreshment; and hence He told His people to call it "a delight." The Passover was not an exception among the religious appointments of the Jews. It was full of thanksgiving memories. It recalled the safety of the Hebrews from the death-angel, who turned Egypt into a house of mourning; it spoke of the omnipotent arm made bare; it lifted to view the origin of the nation and the source of national blessings; and it spoke of the Abrahamic covenant. For fifteen centuries it made the Israelites feel that God's goodness to their fathers was God's goodness to them. To them it made the difference between slavery and freedom, ignorance and knowledge,

Egypt and Canaan. When I read the history of the Passover I do not wonder that it was the one occasion of the sacred year in which the people of God sung the grand Hallel of the Scripture psalter. It was a praise season, and it was fitting that the praise psalms should be used.

II. THE LORD'S SUPPER MUST BE A THANKS-GIVING ORDINANCE BECAUSE OF ITS GROUPING OF GREAT FACTS.

Men often take the facts which it exalts, and look at them, and place them out of the relations in which the Lord's Supper has placed them. The result is, the whole nature of the institution is changed, and this changed their feelings and moods and expectations. They substitute for joy and thanksgiving the spirit of fear, superstition, legalism. They claim to be Scriptural, because the facts with which they deal are the very facts exalted by the Lord's Supper. We grant that the facts with which they deal are the very facts ex-alted by this ordinance; but we make this emphatic: they have been wrung from their proper relations as grouped and arranged by the Lord's Supper. A fact taken out of its Scripture grouping and wrongly placed, is like the safety beacon taken from the harbor pier and run up over the rock that wrecks the ship. Truth, out of God's appointed place, is deceptive. The human face, as God has made it, possesses a wonderful charm. It is a thing of beauty, and a joy. It courts study and scrutiny. No one tires of looking into a beautiful face. The reason for this is, God has given to every feature and organ its proper place, and the setting of all is mutually helpful. Separate the face into parts, and look at it in a dissected state. Take the human eye, severed from the countenance, and look at it. Dissection is its disthronement. Its fascinating power has gone: it is a dull, dead, repulsive thing. To appreciate the human eye you must see it reigning in the midst of the beauty of the human face. Like the features of the human face, the facts exalted by the Lord's Supper must be viewed in their di-vinely-appointed associations.

Let us remember that the Lord's Supper is an ordinance given to the friends of Jesus Christ who have entered upon the saved life, and intended to help them realize their privileges. The Lord's Supper takes the most terrible facts of history and experience, and groups them with the grandest of realities in such a way that our souls break forth into hallelujahs.

There are no more terrible facts than these: —the existence of sin; its hold upon the human heart; man's deadness by nature in trespasses and in sins; the awful wrath of God against sin. These facts, looked at alone standing by themselves, fill with fear and gloom and despair. They separate us from God as far as hell is separated from heaven. Now all these facts are exalted by the Lord's Supper, but they are not exalted alone. This is what a great many people overlook. These facts are linked to the grandest and most glorious realities in the spiritual realm. The terrible fact of the existence of sin is linked with the fact of a Savior and a completed re-demption. Have we not in this ordinance bread and wine? And are not these bloodless emblems? The bloody emblems of the former economy spake of a sacrificial death to the accomplished; but these bloodless emblems of the present dispensation speak to us of that death as accomplished. They repeat the victorious shout of the dying Christ, "It is finished."

The terrible fact of our sentence of death under the law is linked with Christ's sub-stitution and His suffering in our low place— "This is my body which is broken for you." The terrible fact of our deadness by nature is linked with the fact that we "take and eat," and thus allow Christ to enter into us and live in us. This is the grouping of facts as we have them in the Lord's Supper. The ter-rible things are linked to glorious things, and the glorious things are first. It is first Jesus, then the sinner. This is the order in which we are to read the facts: *The Savior,* who has delivered us from our sins; *the Savior,* who has suffered for us; *the Savior,* who has completed forever our redemption; *the Savior* sustaining us in the saved life and living in us. It is your privilege to lift the voice of thanksgiving and shout, "There is therefore now no condemnation to them who are in Christ Jesus."

Turn to the grouping of other facts in the Lord's Supper, and learn the same lesson, viz.: that the facts, as presented by the Lord's Supper, make it a thanksgiving ordinance. It presents the fact of Christ crucified, but it does not leave this sad fact to stand alone: it joins it with the fact of Christ risen. We do not only see the cross, but we see the empty tomb, and the empty tomb means that the crucifixion has accomplished its purpose. The Lord's Supper brings before us the per-sonal absence of Jesus from the world. It recalls the separation at Olivet. As we walk with Jesus and His disciples, we see in the distance a brightness like a burning star. It draws nearer, and the splendor enlarges until it fills the whole dome with a glory beyond the noon-day sun. What is this wonder? It is the majesty of the holy angels whom the Father has sent to take Christ to His reward. Encircling Jesus, they bear Him up through the clear atmosphere and away from His dis-ciples. This personal absence of Jesus, whom we keep in remembrance by the Lord's Sup-per, is exalted before us by this ordinance; but it is exalted in connection with His per-sonal coming again. "Ye do show the Lord's death till he come." There is no weightier fact than His coming again. It carries in it the prepared mansions, the fulfilment of prophecy, the kingdom of glory, the meeting of departed friends, and the glorious reign as kings and priests unto God. The grouping of these facts can mean nothing else but joy and thanksgiving to those who are in Christ Jesus.

III. THE LORD'S SUPPER MUST BE A THANKSGIVING ORDINANCE BECAUSE OF ITS RE-LATION TO THE COVENANT OF GRACE.

It is a seal of the covenant of grace.

Christ's words are, "This cup is the new testament (or covenant) in my blood." These words are a parallel with those He utters when He puts the bread into our hands, "This is my body broken for you;" *i. e.,* this bread is a symbol speaking to you and assuring you that My body was broken for you. This cup is the seal, the evidence, the assurance of the covenant ratified and made effectual by My blood.

What are we to understand by the New Covenant? Christ represents His people and undertakes for them. He does this because, having violated the covenant of works, they are covenant-breakers and debtors to God, and can no longer enter into covenant upon their own responsibility. Christ, in putting the cup into our hands, tells us that He is our covenant, and that true covenanting at His table is the taking of Him and the hiding of our life with Christ in God. Hence the only acts which He prescribes in the Lord's Supper for us, in our relations to Him, are these: "Take and eat;" "Take and drink." These actions indicate that at the Lord's table we are to be receptive. The covenant-making and the covenant-fulfilling, these Jesus does Himself. He asks us only to accept of Him and His work. This view brings before us and keeps before us the teaching of the Gospel—that God can do nothing but give, and we can do nothing but take; that salvation is altogether of grace. This view strikes a killing blow at that spirit of legalism and self-sufficiency which would make this feast of grace a place of bargaining with God and a medium of offering Him good works at a premium.

Let us awaken to the truth that the Lord's Supper *is* a seal of the covenant of grace.

The use of a seal is to confirm, to attest the truth and value and reliability of that to which it is affixed. That canceled mortgage which the Father keeps and shows to His children is a seal, a witness of His past sacrifice and labor by which He purchased the home for His loved ones. It assures them of His forethought for them. It is an assurance that all the debt is paid. Like it, the Lord's Supper speaks to us of the sacrifice of Jesus Christ, by which He paid the price of our redemption. With the Eucharistic character of the Lord's Supper before us.

1. *Let us celebrate it in the exercise of faith.* It is "by faith that we are made partakers of the body and blood of Christ." Faith corresponds to the bodily acts of eating and drinking. Through eating and drinking, food, which is foreign to us, becomes part of us. It beams in the eye, quivers in the lip, throbs in the heart, enters into the mysterious chambers of the brain, and becomes thought and life. Through our faith, Christ, with His thoughts and purposes and spirit, passes into our souls and lives by and in us. Our cause for thanksgiving is, Christ in us the hope of glory.

2. *Let us celebrate it in the exercise of joy.* The apostle teaches us that there is "joy and peace in believing." We have joy when we dwell under the arch of the rainbow, and feel our safety as we look out upon the retreating storm and hear the mutterings of the distant thunders. We recognize the bow as the token of God's protecting covenant, and without fear and hesitancy we go out to enjoy it. Like freedom from fear should characterize our dealings with the Lord's Supper. It is the bow of the New Covenant.—H. R.

THE LORD'S SUPPER A DECLARATORY RITE

By Alexander Maclaren, D.D.

Ye do show the Lord's death till he come.—1 Cor. xi: 26

These words occur in the course of the oldest narrative of the institution of the Lord's Supper. The Apostle declares that he received his information directly from Jesus Christ. So that we have here an independent witness to the facts. The testimony carries us back beyond the date of the earliest of our existing gospels, and brings us within five-and-twenty years of the Crucifixion. By that early period, then, the Lord's Supper was universally observed; and not only so, but it had been in existence long enough to have been corrupted. The corruptions are instructive, as is also the apostolic method of dealing with them.

The abuses to which the Apostle refers, and which are his sole reason for mentioning the Lord's Supper at all, are mainly two, both of which cast great light on the earliest form of the ordinance. Some Corinthians were accustomed to make it an occasion for gluttony and intoxication, and some were accustomed to eat, as the Apostle says, "their own supper," so breaking the unity which the rite was in part intended to express.

How would it have been possible for abuses of that sort to arise unless the first form of the observance of the Lord's Supper had been associated with a common meal, and the domestic aspect been prominent in it? And how would individual hurry in partaking each one of his own supper have been possible if there had been present an officiating priest to do his magic ere the rite could be observed? It is a strange picture, to our eyes, which necessarily arises from the consideration of these two abuses. And it is a long road from the upper room where the Corinthian Church met to the "tremendous sacrifice of the Mass."

The Apostle's way of dealing with the abuses is quite as remarkable as the abuses themselves, and quite as illuminative of the true significance and sacredness of this ordinance. I simply take the words before us as they lie, noting the three points which he emphasizes in order to enforce his doctrine of the sanctity. of the Lord's Supper. It is a proclamation. It is a proclamation of the death of Christ. It is a proclamation perpetually "till he come." That is all, and He thinks it is enough.

Now, then, let us deal with these three things.

1. First, this great thought that the essential characteristic of this ordinance is that it is a declaration.

What it declares we shall have to speak about presently. It is its nature, not its theme, that I first note. The word rendered "show forth" means fully to proclaim aloud by word of mouth, and it is generally employed in reference to the preaching of the Gospel, or of the Word of God. Plainly, then, the Apostle wishes to parallel the two things, the oral declaration of the Gospel, and the symbolical declaration of the same verities, as standing on precisely the same ground, and differing only in regard of the method which is adopted for their proclamation, and the senses to which they are directed. A parable is a spoken symbol; a symbol is an acted parable. The one and the other lay hold upon the material, and bend it, flexible as it is, to become the illustration and partial embodiment of the spiritual. Such is, as the Apostle says, the nature of this rite. It stands on the same level as any other method of declaring the truths which it declares, and its only distinction lies in the peculiarities of the method adopted, which is a symbolical presentation to the eye of the facts which are given to the ear in what we ordinarily call the preaching of the Gospel.

Now, it is clear that I am not forcing too much meaning into a single expression, because, throughout this whole context, there is not a single word that goes beyond such a conception of the Lord's Supper. It is a memorial, and, as the Apostle says in my text, the reason why it is a memorial is because it is a proclamation. Or, to put it into other words, by the rite we declare to ourselves and to others the Christian facts, and the declaration helps us to bring them to mind, and to feed upon Him whom they reveal to us.

Nothing beyond that lies in this context. And the omission of any reference to anything unique, mystical—still more, supernatural—in the rite, is all the more remarkable if you remember the purpose that induced the Apostle to speak about it at all, viz., to rebuke irreverence, and to elevate the notions of the Corinthian Christians as to the sanctity of the ordinance. If he had shared the ideas of the people who call themselves his "successors," how could he have refrained from using that conclusive argument, when his purpose was to enforce the sacredness of the rite? The only reason why he did not use it was because he never dreamed of it, nor had it ever entered into the horizon of the Christian consciousness of his day.

The sacredness lies in the proclamation which it makes, and that is sacredness enough.

But then, brethren, as every king's crown and every wedding ring bear witness, all symbols are apt to run to seed, and there gathers round them, by swift accretion, almost necessarily, at all events generally, something that is far more than symbolical, even a superstitious use of them. Therefore our Lord, recognizing the needs of sense, has made concession to sense in the two ordinances of His Church; and recognizing the dangers of symbol, has rightly limited the symbols to the two appointed by Himself. But men have not lived at that lofty elevation. And paganism, when it came into the Church, grasped at the symbols, and translated them as it had translated those belonging to the system of idolatrous worship which in name was rejected and in spirit too often retained. All that is vulgar, and all that is sensuous, and all that is weak in humanity, clings to the outward rite, and transforms it into a power. And so we find that the baleful shadow of priestcraft is creeping over England again to-day, and that the center of gravity of Christianity is being shifted from personal union by faith with Jesus Christ to participation in an outward form which brings the benefits of union with Him.

And I for my part believe—tho it may sound, in these days of esthetic worship and growing regard for ceremonial, extremely and archaically Puritan and narrow—I believe that there is no logical standing-ground between these two conceptions of the Lord's Supper, "Ye do show the Lord's death," and on the other hand the extreme Roman Catholic view, to which so many people to-day seem to be so rapidly drifting. You nonconformists used to understand the limits of ritual and the place of ordinance. Some of us, I am afraid, are beginning to falter in our repetition of the ancient witness which our fathers have borne.

II. Notice here the theme of the proclamation.

"Ye do show the Lord's death." Now I need not remind you, I suppose, that there is perhaps no better evidence of an historical fact than the almost contemporaneous origin, and continuous duration, of some commemorative symbolical act, as the history of all nations may tell us. And it should be taken fairly into account, in estimating the historical evidence for the veracity of the Gospel narratives, that almost simultaneously with the events which they profess to record there sprang up, and there has continued to exist ever since, this rite. The book of the Acts of the Apostles shows us that immediately after Pentecost the disciples "continued steadfastly in the breaking of bread"; and that at a later period they were in the habit of assembling on the first day of the week for the same purpose. So I claim this long-practised rite, which can be traced up almost to the open grave of the Master, as a very strong attestation of the historical veracity of the Gospel narratives. Thus, in the lowest sense, we do proclaim the Lord's death.

But the force of the words goes far beyond that. Note, then, and give to it due importance in your conception of what the Gospel truth and Christ's teachings are, the fact that He Himself chose out from all His history His death as the thing which day by day loving hearts were to remember, and hungry souls were to feed on. Why was that? Why was it that He passed by all the rest and fixed on that? It seems to me that the ordinance of the Lord's Supper ought to exercise the influence of a barrier against all attempts to minimize or to diminish the significance and the importance of Christ's death. What do Churches which have ceased to proclaim the full doctrine that the death of Christ is the life of the world do with that rite? Neglect it. Let it drop into desuetude. Explain it away by all sorts of obviously insufficient explanations. But there it stands. Not His words of gentleness; not His deeds of power; not His teachings of wisdom and of truth; not His revelation of God by the beauty of a perfected humanity and the patience of inexhaustible tenderness, are what He desires to be remembered by; but that death upon the cross. Surely, surely, that indicates a unique influence and power as residing there.

And that same conviction is enforced if we remember that the showing of the Lord's death, which is accomplished in this rite, shows it under very distinct conditions, explanatory of its meaning and power. For the duplication of the memorials into the bread and the wine taken apart indicates a death by violence; and the language of the institution points us to deep mysteries—the body " broken " or given " for you," and the " blood shed for the remission of sins." The same death is conveyed by the associations which our Lord was careful to establish between this feast of the Christian Church and the Passover feast of the Jewish. He swept aside the sacrifice that was made for the redemption of Israel from the captivity of Egypt, and He said, " Forget the shadow and remember the substance; forget the sacrifice that was made of the Lamb, unbroken in bone, and remember the other of Him whose body was given for you, the Lamb of God, the Passover for the sins of the world."

The same declaration of redeeming power, as lying in the death of Christ, is enforced by the other reference, which our Lord Himself has bid us see, to the new covenant in His blood, the covenant of which the articles are remission of sins, the mutual possession of God by the redeemed soul, and of that soul by God, the direct knowledge of Him, and the continual inscribing of His law upon the heart.

And so, brethren, we have not to look back to that death as simply the touching martyrdom of the purest soul that ever lived. We have not to look back to Christ's work as having been done as they who reject His propitiatory death are forced to regard it— chiefly in His life of gentleness, in His words of teaching, in His deeds of power and of piety; but we have to recognize this unique

fact that His death is the center of His work, and in a peculiar sense the fountain of salvation for us all. " Ye do show the Lord's death."

And " ye do show," too, the conditions of our partaking of it, viz., that we should feed upon Him; the heart on His love, the will on His commandments, the understanding on His word, and the whole sinful man upon His atoning death. " He that eateth my flesh and drinketh my blood hath eternal life."

III. Lastly, note the perpetual duration and prophetic aspect of the proclamation.

" Ye do show the Lord's death till he come." Now, I suppose I do not need to dwell upon the thought that that distinctly implies that all through the ages of the Church the Apostle contemplated the continuance of this rite of witnessing, but I rather desire to suggest to you how, in the very rite itself, there can be distinguished, not only a commemorative aspect or a backward look, but a prophetic aspect, and a symbol of that which is to come.

" Till he come." All symbolical worship carries in itself the witness of its own cessation, and points onward to the time when it shall not be needed. It is, as I said, a concession to sense; it is a confession of weakness. It is, if not inconsistent with, at least in some measure incongruous with, the highest genius of the Christian dispensation. That is no reason for precipitate dispensing with external form. No man can judge another in regard of that matter. There is need for a great deal more charity, both on the side of those who incline to the Quaker freedom from all ritual, and of those who incline, by natural disposition, to the other side, than is usually practised. It is no proof of spiritual maturity to try to do without the help of external rites. It is no proof of spiritual immaturity to cleave to them, if only it be distinctly understood that the whole value of them lies, not in what they are, but in what they signify. But still the existence of symbolical worship is a prophecy of its own cessation. It digs its own grave, as it were; and just because here we need the bread and the wine to help us to remember the death, the taking of these in compliance with the temporary necessity itself carries our thoughts, or ought to carry them, onward to the time when, Christ Himself being present with His Church, and they sitting at His table in His Kingdom, the symbols shall be no more needed. " I saw no temple therein." " Ye do show . . . till he come."

Again, the memory of His death is fitted, and intended, to quicken the hopes of His return. For the two belong to one another, and are bolted together, if I might so say, like the two stars revolving round a common center. He being what He is, the cross and the open sepulcher cannot be the last that the world is to see of Him. The death demands the throne, and the throne certifies the return. So the memory of the past brightens into hopes for the future; and the radiance behind us flings its reflection forward on to the darkness before, and illuminates that with a sister luster. He has come and died, therefore He will come and reign.

And then, still further, hope is inextricably intertwined with memory; because, in this domestic rite, we see the symbol that the Master Himself has given us of the calm felicities of that life beyond. He Himself said, on that last night when He sat at the table, "I appoint unto you a Kingdom, that ye may sit at my table in my Kingdom,"; feeding on Christ then in reality, as we now do in symbol and imperfectly by faith; companioned by Christ according to His gracious promise, "I will sup with him and he with me," as in the depths of spiritual communion we now partially do; reknit to those whose empty places at this board below make some of us always solitary and often sad; and having the Master Himself to bless the feast and to part the viands.

"They shall go no more out." From the Supper-Room Christ went to His cross; the traitor to his gibbet; the beloved Apostle to his denial; the rest to forsake and to fly. But from that feast there will be no going forth, and the the the loftier service of heaven shall not interrupt participation in Jesus, for His servants shall serve Him and see His face.

Brethren, the one question for us all is, "Do I feed upon Jesus Christ? Do I discern that body as broken for and given to me? Do I know that my sins are remitted by the shedding of His blood?" No participation in outward rites will bring or sustain the spiritual life. Partaking of Jesus Christ alone can do that, and rites help to partake of Him in the measure in which they bring His death to heart and mind, and so help faith to grasp it as the means of our salvation. His solemn words. "Whoso eateth my flesh and drinketh my blood hath eternal life," are degraded when they are understood as referring to the external ordinance. In the same conversation He Himself interpreted them when He said, "He that believeth on me hath everlasting life."

"Believe, and thou hast eaten," said Augustine. "Eat, and ye shall live forever," says Jesus Christ.—H. R.

AT THE COMMUNION TABLE

By H. Lyman

And he took the cup and gave thanks.—Matt. xxvi: 27

The symbolism of the text—its power.

First "The Cup." The cup presents two aspects: (1) As viewed by Jesus—the Savior. (2) As viewed by man—the sinner.

1. Man sees in the cup *(a)* forgiveness *(b)* reconciliation, *(c)* freedom from sin, *(d)* eternal life. No wrath foams upon the surface, no bitter dregs beneath.

2. What did Christ see in the cup? *(a)* His death as a felon. *(b)* The hiding of the Father's countenance. *(c)* Himself as bearing the guilt of sin.

Second: "Gave thanks." Jesus shrank from that cup, yet took it and gave thanks. "Father, I thank Thee for this opportunity to magnify Thy great law. I thank Thee for the millions whom by this act I shall redeem, and that I am thus permitted to give testimony of My great love to man. I thank Thee that in this very triumph of Satan his downfall is sealed." Then, with the serenity of unspeakable grace, He drank the cup, draining it to its dregs, and in that act He tasted death for every man, and finished the sacrifice impending from the foundation of the world.

Infinite benevolence and infinite foresight were necessary to inspire this thankfulness in Jesus.

Remark: If Jesus the Savior could take the cup that symbolized His death and give thanks, how thankfully should man take the cup that symbolizes his salvation.—H. R.

CHRIST AND THE COMMUNION

By J. Culross

And as they did eat, Jesus took bread, and blessed, and brake it, and gave to them, and said, Take, eat: this is my body, etc.—Mark xiv: 22-25

I. This service carries us back over dim tracks of time to the beginning of the Gospel. We think of scattered bands of our ancient brethren, in the midst of surrounding heathenism, gathering as we do now around the Table of our Lord. They regarded the crucified Jesus as the Son of God, and the Savior of the world. It is not altogether difficult to place ourselves in the position of those ancient saints, and to enter into their state of heart as they gathered round the Lord's Table. There was an unconscious recognition—all the more profound and joyful that it was unconscious—of their being one through the love that embraced them all. It was not, however, that their minds were occupied about one another. It was the Lord Himself whom they thought upon; His holy form it was that rose up before the eye of faith; the festival was one of love, and memory, and hope, bringing up to faith the sacred Person of the Lord, and kindling all blissful emotions. In such experiences believing men may share to-day, to the same extent as believing men of the first century.

II. What is this communion to our Savior? What was in His heart when He established this ordinance? The answer rises to our lips at once. (1) There was undying love to His own. That love is the abiding mystery of the Gospel. Never before did it get such utterance; never before did it appear so tender and intense, so full and overflowing. (2) There is another thing beyond even this. It tells out His desire for fellowship with His own—just as when He took Peter and James and John with Him into the garden, and said,

"My soul is exceeding sorrowful even unto death; tarry ye here and watch with me." There is unfathomable mystery here—that He, so to speak, should lean on us, but it is a part of the blessed mystery of His brotherhood. Brotherhood is no mere name with Him; but a blissful verity. In all, save sin, His heart was like our own; and just as we have pleasure in the love that our friends bear toward us, and in knowing that we live in their memory, so does He delight in the love with which saved men love Him. It is part of the reward of His sorrows, part of the joy that was set before Him, for which He endured the Cross, despising the shame.— S. B., vol. vi., p. 357.

PREPARATION FOR THE LAST SUPPER

Outlines of a sermon by STEPHEN H. TYNG, SR., D.D.

Then came the day of unleavened bread, when the passover must be killed, etc.—Luke xxii: 7-20

Jesus was in Bethany, near Jerusalem, preparing for His great trial. It was Thursday morning. The passover is just at hand. It is a day of preparation, the Lamb to be offered is Himself. Go, said He to His disciples, and prepare—get ready—for Me; let it be heart preparation.

1. This *preparation was general.* Its outward nature we do not know; where it was to be was the first question of the disciples. A vast preparation had been going on from the foundation of the world, and the work was now to be finished. All the Old Testament teachings, histories, prophecies, and events were a preparation for the death on the cross. "Go, prepare to meet Me around that table." It was as much my table as it was Peter's, and I have just as much right to lay my head on Jesus' bosom, then, as had the beloved John.

2. *When, or at what time,* concerned the disciples. Your time to prepare is *now.* The time has come; childhood is all gone, and the heart is unchanged, now prepare to meet Him. If youth has passed, *now* is your time, before manhood is gone.

3. *The character of this command.* It is imperative—" Go " now. Grotius, who lived to be fifty before he made this preparation, said, " I have passed the whole of my life laboriously doing nothing." Cast away your sins,

your prayerlessness. " I have lost ten years; I give the rest to Jesus," should be the resolution of youth. It was three miles to Jerusalem. It required a *start* at once, and then He would *show* them how to *prepare.* Are there clouds or doubts as to duty? Christ will make all right. No hour for this preparation is too early. No matter how young, *prepare.* Go into the city, and you will meet a man bearing a pitcher of water. Go where he goes, and there I will eat the passover. By the *water* and the *blood* of the impending sacrifice you will be saved. The pitcher is the sign of the water in baptism—the preparation. Last Sabbath I sat where seventy years before my mother offered me in baptism.

Oh, if you have not accepted, you have refused this feast.

Lastly. You will need to carry nothing in there. The feast is prepared.

" Just as I am, without one plea."

This perfect obedience supplies everything. All that we want is the free gift already furnished. This was the last of Christ's pilgrimage, the journey from Bethany to Jerusalem. The Sunday following He rose from the dead, prepared for His kingdom of glory. The preparation I urge upon you is, that you may be ready to enter that Kingdom.— H. R.

DESIRE FOR COMMUNION

By T. D. WITHERSPOON, D.D.

With desire have I desired to eat this passover with you before I suffer.—Luke xxii: 37

The passage from Judaism to Christianity was as noiseless and unostentatious as the unfolding of the bud into the full flower, or the development of the gray dawn into the per-

fect day. There was no flourish of trumpets; no great convocation of ecclesiastical leaders; no blazonry of public proclamation to the world; but in the little upper chamber, where the Master and His twelve disciples were seated about the board, the passover was merged into the Lord's Supper; the prefigurative gave way to the commemorative; the old dispensation joined hands with the new; and as, shortly before, circumcision had yielded its place to baptism, the Church of God, with its changed seals of an unchanging covenant, came forth to enter upon its new and worldwide career.

It is this relation of the Passover to the Lord's Supper which gives to the words of the text a peculiar significance for us, and should cause a lively response in every heart to the intense desire with which He desired to partake of the feast with His disciples. This desire arose, no doubt, out of various considerations connected with the feast which He was about to observe.

I. It was to Him what the Lord's Supper is to us, an ordinance, the observance of which was enjoined with peculiar solemnity, and He desired to keep it as the expression of His filial obedience. He would give one more evidence that His meat and His drink was to do the will of Him that sent Him.

II. The relation of this Passover to His great mediatorial work now just about to be accomplished inspired His desire that it should be celebrated. He was the true "Paschal lamb." The blood sprinkled upon the door-posts and lintels was symbolic of His blood; the flesh eaten with bitter herbs, of His flesh, which He would give for the life of the world. And as the Lord's supper has the same significance, we should desire it that the same great spiritual realities may be exhibited and sealed to our faith.

III. In the companionship of the disciples at the table He could see even in advance the first fruits of the salvation He had come to secure. And in the faces of Peter, James, and John He could see the earnest pledge of that great multitude whom no man could number, who would sit down at the ten thousand times ten thousand communion tables of all ages and climes. Therefore He said to them, and through them to us, "I have desired to eat this passover with you."

Finally, the words, "before I suffer," indicate His expectation to receive in this communion with His disciples and with His Father at the table strength for the baptism of suffering that was to follow. He was man, with all human sensibilities and all sinless infirmities. He needed strength and support and sought it here, as He did afterward in the garden, when He said: "What, could ye not watch with me one hour?" If the Sinless One felt this need of strength through God's appointed feast, let us come with the assurance that we also may be strengthened for whatever conflicts, temptations, and trials may lie along our path.—P. T.

THE IMPORTANCE OF THE SACRAMENT

By Charles F. Deems, D.D., LL.D.

1 Cor. xi: 24

The Sacrament a *monument* requested by Jesus; twenty-five years after Paul reminded the Church in Corinth of its institution.

In remembrance of Christ:

I. All who believe that there *is* such a beautiful, good, holy, loving being as Christ in the universe.

II. That *He has done* so much *for us.*

1. Loved $\{$ (a) When *we did not love Him.* us. $\{$ (b) When *we were unlovely.*

2. Gave Himself for us. $\{$ Voluntary love. $\{$ Self-sacrificing.

III. Then He is *still doing* something for us.

1. Managing our providences.
2. Preparing our homes.
3. Interceding for us.

IV. That He was *an innocent sufferer.*—If an *impostor* He would not have instituted this supper.—All who believe Him innocent *ought to* observe this Sacrament.

V. *That He has risen.*—He knew His disciples could not keep one without the other.—Keep the monument over His grave adorned with fresh flowers and wet with fresh tears:

(a) It will *make you better and happier.*
(b) It will *impress the world.*

THE SACRAMENTAL CUP

Outlines of a sermon by Rev. T. A. Nelson, D.D.

This cup is the new testament in my blood: this do ye, as oft as ye drink it, in remembrance of me.—1 Cor. xi: 25

In individual, family, and national life, etc., we have our seasons of commemoration, to keep alive the memory of notable days or deeds. These seasons are observed with festive joy or a fast of the Spirit. So, too, Christianity has its memorial-day—not ushered in by the noise of cannon or blare of trumpets; not to be observed with gorgeous pageantry or imposing ritual, but rather as a holy resting time—a feast to be kept with solemn gladness of heart.

The institution of this feast was the instinct of love. We delight in being remembered by those who share our affection; so Christ desires to be remembered by those who love Him, and the thought of Him is to pervade the whole life.

But this remembrance has a wise purpose in relation to ourselves.

I. REMEMBRANCE BEGETS HUMILIATION, by revealing the measure of our guilt. The cup brings before us the *Cross*, and the Cross recalls our sin. We judge of the curse of slavery by what it cost us to blot it out—enormous expenditure of treasure; a million of graves furrowing the land; tens of thousands of hearts and homes desolated forever. We are prone to look upon sin lightly; but when we touch the cup to our lips it brings the vision of the Cross; we see the blood; we hear the groans of the broken heart of Jesus. The sun darkens; the earth quivers in sympathy with the dissolution of its Lord; and in the awful horror of that scene we read our sin, fathom its turpitude; then, bowing our heads, cry: "God be merciful to us sinners!"

II. IT QUICKENS HOPE. The day not only recalls our sin, but also our sacrifice. Through it we see "help laid on One mighty to save." It is at once the expression of God's wrath toward sin and His love toward the sinner. It not only speaks of our disobedience, but reminds us of One who for us fulfilled the law and became obedient unto the death. So we touch the cup to our lips and hope springs afresh.

III. IT INSPIRES TO NEW ACTIVITY THROUGH GRATITUDE.—Having been forgiven much, we love much, and love prompts to sacrifice and service. We feel with Paul the constraining power of this love.

It is this vision of the Holy Grail which sustained the martyr at the stake, and which to-day leads men over the seas and into the heart of unexplored lands, that they may carry thither the sweet message of the Gospel. We touch the cup to our lips at once as the inspiration and pledge of grateful service.

IV. IT LIFTS OUR LONGINGS HEAVENWARD. Every heart and every household has its treasured souvenirs of those who once were with us but are not, for God has taken them. How sacred such relics! To view them is to

" Sigh for the touch of a vanished hand,
And the sound of a voice that is still."

So, when reverently we press the cup to our lips, memory is busy with the past and imagination with the future, we do desire " to depart and be with Christ." Thought springs upward from the cross to the crown, and we long to be with Him—" to see the King in his beauty and to behold the land that is very far off."—H. R.

SUGGESTIVE THOUGHTS AND ILLUSTRATIONS

ATONEMENT, The Infinite.—*Is. i: 18.* You see the Thames as it goes sluggishly down to the arches, carrying with it endless impurity and corruption. You watch the inky stream as it pours along day and night, and you think it will pollute the world. But you have just been down to the seashore, and you have looked on the great deep, and it has not left a stain on the Atlantic. No, it has been running down a good many years, and carried a world of impurity with it, but when you go to the Atlantic there is not a speck on it. As to the ocean, it knows nothing about it. It is full of majestic music. So the smoke of London goes up; and has been going up for a thousand years. One would have thought that it would have spoiled the scenery by now; but you get a look at it sometimes. There is the great blue sky which has swallowed up the smoke and gloom of a thousand years, and its azure splendor is unspoiled. It is wonderful how the ocean has kept its purity, and how the sky has taken the breath of the millions and the smoke of the furnaces, and yet it is as pure as the day God made it. It is beautiful to think that these are only images of God's great pity for the race.—C. UP.

BREAD, The Living.—*John vi: 51.* Jesus had said that He was " the bread of life," and now He says: " I am the living bread." There is a difference. " Bread of life " puts emphasis on the effect, " living bread " on the cause. " As ' living water ' is running from a fountain in perpetual stream, and not a measured quantity in a tank, so ' living bread ' is bread which renews itself in proportion to all needs like the bread of the miracle."—BRUCE. Whoever eats this living bread feels the quickening power of an endless life.—C. G.

CHRIST, On the body of.—When Thou wert in the world, dear Master, Thou didst dwell in a body, like men. Now Thou hast gone from the world Thou hast no other body than those of Thy children on the earth. But Thou hast bidden me to be Thy body, me and all the host of those that love and serve Thee. When Thou wert on the earth, what wonderful things Thy body did! Thy lips that kissed the little ones and stilled the tempest. Thine eyes, that looked upon Peter, and saw Nathanael under the fig-tree. Thy hand, that touched the blind to sight and lifted the dead into life again. Thy feet, that bore Thee up and down among the homes of the poor, and sick, and sinful. Thine ears, that never were closed to a cry of need. Thy tongue, that uttered the wisest words of all the earth. Thy heart, that broke upon the cross. And whatsoever things Thy body did for Thee upon the earth nineteen hundred years ago, the church, Thy body,—I, and the other men and women that love Thee and serve Thee,—must do now. We must walk upon Thine errands, and speak Thy words, and look Thy glances, and stretch out Thy hands of loving sympathy, and rebuke for Thee, and heal for Thee, and daily die for Thee upon our smaller crosses. What can I say, *what can I say*, before this great duty, this awful responsibility? I will remember that I am not *all* Thy body. Thou didst not ask Thy hand to do the work of Thy mouth, or Thy feet to do the work of Thine eyes. Neither wilt Thou ask me to do the work of any other part of Thy body, but just my own work, and I am only a very small part of Thy great body, the Church. And I will remember, too,—above all, I will remember,—that Thou art in Thy body. The hand does not move by its own might, nor the tongue speak with its own wisdom; and if Thou wilt move me, I can easily be hand for Thee; and if Thou wilt inspire me, I can easily be voice for Thee. O may this thought be with me continually, "*I* must not speak, *I* dare not act; I am Christ's body, and it is His to use me as He will." And thus, dear Lord, wilt Thou come and abide in me.—G. R.

COMMUNION, Conditions of Acceptable. —"This psalm (xv.) is no mirror for the self-righteous to see themselves in." When we come to the Lord's table we ought to search our hearts and see what earth-stains still cleave to us. For holiness becometh God's house. The pure in heart shall see God. The guest-friends of the Lord Jesus ought to be eminent for practical holiness. Psalm xv. may well become the communicant's companion. Perowne says of it: "Such is the figure of stainless honor drawn by the pen of a Jewish poet. Christian chivalry has not dreamed of a brighter. We have need often and seriously to ponder it. For it shows us that faith in God and spotless integrity may not be sundered; that religion does not veil or excuse petty dishonesties; that love to God is only then worthy the name when it is the life and bond of every social virtue. Each line is, as it were, a touchstone to which we should bring ourselves. To speak truth in the heart—to take up no reproach against a neighbor—would not the Christian man be perfect (τέλειος) of whom this could be said? And that other trait in this divine character,—" who honoreth them that fear the Lord."—is there a surer test of our spiritual condition than this, that we love and honor men *because they love Christ?* "—C. G.

COMMUNION, Divine.—How many beautiful expressions suggest sweet thoughts as to the believer's near communion with God: *Abiding* before God. Ps. lxi: 7; under the shadow of the Almighty, Ps. xci: 1; in the light, 1 John ii: 10; in the love of Jesus, John xv: 4, 10; as the branch in the vine, John xv: 4, 5; the beautiful emblems of constant nourishment, calm security, and upholding trust. *Dwelling* in the secret place of the Most High, Ps. xci: 1; in God, 1 John iv: 16; implying the ideas of refuge and rest, *delighting in the Lord*, Ps. xxxvii: 4 Isa. lviii: 14—"If desire be love in motion like a bird on the wing; delight may be compared to love at rest, rejoicing in its own happiness." *Drawing near*, Ps. lxxiii: 28; as with Abraham's reverence and confidence, Gen. xviii: 23. *Entering into the holiest*, Heb. x: 19. *Fellowship*, 1 Cor. i: 9; 1 John i: 3; symbolized by eating and drinking together, as in the ancient sacrifices, and now in the Lord's Supper. *Sitting in heavenly places* in Christ Jesus, Eph. ii: 6. our heart and hope being there already.—BOWES.

COMMUNION, Sacramental.—Especially in acts of sacramental communion with his Lord does the Christian gather up and consecrate the powers of his life-long communion with heaven. Then it is that he has most vivid impressions of the nearness of God to his soul, a most comfortable assurance of strength for his need.—MACKARNESS.

COMMUNION, Spirit and Substance of. —*Matt. xxvi: 26.* I heard a Christian Jew say, detailing the present Jewish method of keeping the passover, that always, through the centuries back and now, on every paschal table there have been, and are, set a plate and a cup for the coming One. And that Jesus broke the bread into this plate, and took the cup waiting for the coming One, and so declared Himself the coming One, as He gave bread from the plate for the coming One, and wine from the cup for the coming One, to His disciples. I think this wonderfully beautiful and significant. Christ is the long promised coming One. He has come. Also, this Christian Jew said the bread and the wine were simply symbolic and memorial. Yonder hangs a photograph of your friend. "There is my friend," you say. You say it truly, but you mean that picture simply represents your friend. So the broken bread and the poured wine are symbols of, *represent*, the atoning Christ. Do not wait upon and hang your thought about the symbols. Press beyond them to the Christ they represent. Yield yourself in faith and love to Him, not to them, when in obedience to His command, you eat the bread and drink the wine in remembrance of Him.—S. S. T.

LORD'S SUPPER, Above.—*Matt. xxvi: 29.* Supposing for one moment that the divine Son of God was limited by the flesh more than the church formerly thought; suppose Jesus did expect to return at an early day, as per Mark xiv: 25 (Dr. McGiffert); and grant even that which I do not grant, that the Savior did not institute the Supper in the sense in which the apostle Paul and the Church Militant have ever observed it,—what then? If you take away every foundation for the use of this Sacrament, out into the future we go, we shall prophesy that whereas

" Years have past; in every clime,
Changing with the changing time,
Torn by factions, rock'd by storms,
Still the sacred table spread
Flowing cup and broken bread
With that parting word agree,
' Drink and eat. Remember me;' "

and whereas for hundreds of years back, and we know not how many hundreds and thousands of years in the future, the disciples of the Lord have kept up and will keep up this precious service in memory of Him, and as a symbol of feeding upon Him, be it resolved that it is the sense of every Christian that He will unquestionably celebrate the eating of the bread and the drinking of the wine with the Church triumphant.—C. J. TUTHILL, D.D.

LORD'S SUPPER, Import of the.—A Malay youth, who was being educated in Scotland, as he came out of church one Sunday, was asked, " What have you seen in church to-day? " He answered, " I see people take bread and wine." " And what does that mean? " " The body and blood of Jesus Christ." " Is it really the body and blood of Jesus Christ? " " O, no," said he, " not all same; it keep in mind—keep in mind His body and blood—He die for sinners."—F. II.

LORD'S SUPPER, Memorial.—The Lord's Supper comes to us like a ring plucked off from Christ's finger, or a bracelet from His arm; or rather like His picture from His breast, delivered to us with such words as these, " As oft as you look on this, remember me,"—JOHN FLAVEL.

LORD'S SUPPER, Real Presence in the.—Rev. Dr. Cumming, of London, says that in the Highlands of Scotland he once met a lady of noble birth, who asked him if he believed in the " real presence." " Certainly I do," he said; " I am very glad," she replied, " but you are the first Protestant clergyman I ever met with who did." " We attach different meanings to the same words," said Dr. Cumming. " I believe in the real presence of our Lord wherever two or three are gathered together in His name. I cannot believe as you do about the real presence, when I consider the words ' In remembrance of me.' Memory has to do with the past, with an absent friend. To eat and drink in remembrance of one who is actually present before one's eyes is an absurdity."—F. II.

LORD'S SUPPER, Title in the.—The Lord's Supper being an evident proof that the New Testament is in full force, (it being the cup of the New Testament in His blood, Matt. xxvi: 28), it tends much to our satisfaction, as the legal execution of the deed by which we hold and enjoy our estate. So that when He saith, " Take, eat," it is as much as if God should stand before you at the table with Christ, with all the promises in His hand;

and say, " I deliver this to thee as My deed."—JOHN FLAVEL.

LORD'S SUPPER, Typical.—When the miner in the American prairie sinks a shaft to strike the coal formation, he finds, far below, the images of beautiful plants, lying like lacework spread out upon tables of ebony; images of ferns, and leaves, and flowers, which, millions of years ago, perhaps ceased, from some change of climate, to open in the cold spring-time, and hence to fall into autumn. There these pictures lie, telling us where was the summer-time, where the drifting snows fell. Yet as these dimly shadow forth more perfect adaptations in nature and nature's growth, so do these humble memorials, the bread and wine, shadow forth dimly—the bread of which if a man eat he will never hunger, and the wine which we shall drink new in the kingdom.—*Selected.*

REMEMBRANCE of Me, In,—*I Cor. xi: 34.* The Lord's Supper is more than a memorial. But its memorial significance should not be ignored. The Paschal supper commemorated an event; the Lord's Supper commemorates a person. Salvation is due not simply to what Jesus did, but to what He was and is and evermore shall be. Believers are to remember *Him* as crucified, risen, exalted, glorified, and ruling over all for their salvation.—C. G.

SACRAMENT, Reconciliation Before the.—George IV. desired the sacrament and sent for the Bishop of Winchester to administer it. He became angry with the messenger he sent, because of what he considered unnecessary delay. He reprimanded the servant, discharged him, and immediately requested the bishop to proceed. This the bishop refused while any anger remained in the king's mind toward any fellow-creature. The king, recollecting himself said, " My lord, you are right." He then sent for the offending servant, became reconciled to him and restored him to his place, after which the sacrament was duly administered.—F. II.

SALVATION, The Cup of.—*Psalm cxvi: 12-14.* The Psalmist recalls the time when Jehovah mercifully delivered him from death. How shall he repay the kindness? There is but one way. He will take the cup of salvation and publicly acknowledge Jehovah as his helper. The " cup of salvation " formed part of the sacrificial meal connected with the thank-offering. The Lord's Supper is a feast of joy. It brings sweet reminder of the Friend that sticketh closer than a brother; a love that is stronger than death; of a salvation unspeakably glorious, for which the only return believers can make is to accept it with humble gratitude, and acknowledge before the world that Jesus has sole right to their love and fealty.—C. G.

POETRY

Bread of Heaven

BY JOSIAH CONDER

Bread of Heaven, on Thee I feed,
For Thy flesh is meat indeed;
Ever may my soul be fed
With this true and living bread;
Day by day with strength supplied,
Through the life of Him who died.

Vine of Heaven, Thy blood supplies
This blest cup of sacrifice;
'Tis Thy wounds my healing give;
To Thy cross I look and live.
Thou my Life, O let me be
Rooted, grafted, built on Thee.

Bread of the World

BY REGINALD HEBER

Bread of the world, in mercy broken,
Wine of the soul, in mercy shed,
By whom the words of life were spoken,
And in whose death our sins are dead:

Look on the heart by sorrow broken,
Look on the tears by sinners shed;
And be Thy feast to us the token
That by Thy grace our souls are fed.

Closer than a Brother

BY J. NEWTON

One there is, above all others,
Well deserves the name of Friend;
His is love beyond a brother's,
Costly, free, and knows no end.

Which of all our friends, to save us,
Could or would have shed his blood?
But our Jesus died to have us
Reconciled in Him to God.

When He lived on earth abaséd,
Friend of sinners was His name;
Now above all glory raiséd,
He rejoices in the same.

Oh, for grace our hearts to soften!
Teach us, Lord, at length, to love;
We, alas! forget too often
What a Friend we have above.

Till He Come

BY E. H. BICKERSTETH

"Till He come:" oh, let the words
Linger on the trembling chords:
Let the little while between
In their golden light be seen;
Let us think how heaven and home
Lie beyond that—" Till He come."

When the weary ones we love
Enter on their rest above,
Seems the earth so poor and vast,
All our life joy overcast?
Hush, be every murmur dumb;
It is only—" Till He come."

See, the feast of love is spread,
Drink the wine, and break the bread;
Sweet memorials,—till the Lord
Call us round His heavenly board;
Some from earth, from glory some,
Severed only—" Till He come."

Communion Hymn

BY JOHANN FRANK (1650)

TR. BY CATHERINE WINKWORTH

Deck thyself, my soul, with gladness;
Leave the gloomy haunts of sadness.
Come into the daylight's splendor;
There with joy thy praises render
Unto Him, whose boundless grace
Grants thee at His feast a place,
He whom all the heavens obey
Deigns to dwell in thee to-day.

Hasten as a bride to meet Him,
And with loving reverence greet Him,
Who with words of life immortal
Now is knocking on the portal;
Haste to make for Him a way,
Cast thee at His feet, and say:
"Since, O Lord! Thou com'st to me,
Never will I turn from Thee."

"Ah, how hungers all my spirit,
For the love I do not merit!
Ah, how oft with sighs fast thronging
For this food have I been longing!
How have thirsted in the strife
For this draught, O Prince of Life!
Wished, O Friend of man! to be
Ever one with God through Thee!

"Here I sink before Thee, lowly,
Filled with joy most deep and holy,
As with trembling awe and wonder
On Thy mighty works I ponder;
On this banquet's mystery,
On the depths we cannot see;
Far beyond all mortal sight
Lie the secrets of Thy might.

"Sun, who all my life does brighten,
Light, who dost my soul enlighten,
Joy, the sweetest man e'er knoweth,
Fount, whence all my being floweth!
Here I fall before Thy feet:
Grant me worthily to eat
Of this blesséd heavenly food,
To Thy praise and to my good.

"Jesus, Bread of life from heaven,
Never be Thou vainly given,
Nor I to my hurt invited
Be Thy love with love requited;

Let me learn its depths indeed,
While on Thee my soul doth feed;
Let me here, so richly blest,
Be hereafter, too, Thy guest."

Before the Cross

By J. Allen

Sweet the moments, rich in blessing,
Which before the cross we spend;
Life, and health, and peace possessing,
From the sinner's dying Friend.

Truly blesséd is this station,
Low before His Cross to lie,
While we see divine compassion,
Beaming in His gracious eye.

Love and grief our hearts dividing,
With our tears His feet we bathe;
Constant still, in faith abiding,
Life deriving from His death.

For Thy sorrows we adore Thee,
For the pains that wrought our peace,
Gracious Savior! we implore Thee
In our souls Thy love increase.

Here we feel our sins forgiven,
While upon the Lamb we gaze;
And our thoughts are all of heaven,
And our lips o'erflow with praise.

Still in ceaseless contemplation,
Fix our hearts and eyes on Thee,
Till we taste Thy full salvation,
And, unvailed, Thy glories see.

Take My Heart

Anonymous

Take my heart, O Father! take it;
Make and keep it all Thine own;
Let Thy Spirit melt and break it—
This proud heart of sin and stone.

Father, make me pure and lowly,
Fond of peace and far from strife;
Turning from the paths unholy
Of this vain and sinful life.

Ever let Thy grace surround me,
Strengthen me with power divine,
Till Thy cords of love have bound me:
Make me to be wholly Thine.

May the blood of Jesus heal me,
And my sins be all forgiven;
Holy Spirit, take and seal me,
Guide me in the path to heaven.

Jesus All in All

By Ray Palmer

Jesus, Thou Joy of loving hearts,
Thou Fount of life! Thou light of men!
From the best bliss that earth imparts,
We turn unfilled to Thee again.

Thy truth unchanged hath ever stood;
Thou savest those that on Thee call;
To them that seek Thee Thou art good,
To them that find Thee, All in All.

We taste Thee, O thou Living Bread,
And long to feast upon Thee still;
We drink of Thee, the Fountain Head,
And thirst our souls from Thee to fill!

Our restless spirits yearn for Thee,
Where'er our changeful lot is cast;
Glad, when Thy gracious smile we see,
Blest, when our faith can hold Thee fast.

O Jesus, ever with us stay;
Make all our moments calm and bright;
Chase the dark night of sin away,
Shed o'er the world Thy holy light!

The Lamb's High Feast

By Robert Campbell

At the Lamb's high feast we sing
Praise to our victorious King,
Who hath washed us in the tide,
Flowing From His piercéd side.

Praise we Him, whose love divine
Gives His sacred blood for wine,
Gives His body for the feast:
Christ the victim, Christ the priest.

Where the paschal blood is poured,
Death's dark angel sheathes his sword;
Israel's hosts triumphant go
Through the wave that drowns the foe.

Praise we Christ, whose blood was shed,
Paschal victim, paschal bread;
With sincerity and love,
Eat we manna from above.

Mighty victim from the sky,
Hell's fierce powers beneath Thee lie;
Thou hast conquered in the fight,
Thou hast brought us life and light."

Hymns of glory and of praise,
Risen Lord, to Thee we raise;
Holy Father, praise to Thee,
With the Spirit, ever be!

Grateful and Tender Remembrance

By Rev. Gerard Thomas Noel

If human kindness meets return,
And owns the grateful tie;
If tender thoughts within us burn,
To feel a friend is nigh;

O shall not warmer accents tell
The gratitude we owe
To Him, who died, our fears to quell,
Our more than orphan's wo?

While yet His anguished soul surveyed
Those pangs He would not flee,
What love His latest words displayed,
"Meet, and remember Me."

Remember Thee, Thy death, Thy shame,
Our sinful hearts to share!
O memory, leave no other name
But His recorded there.

The Sacrament

By Arthur Cleveland Coxe

Body of Jesus, O sweet food!
Blood of my Savior, precious blood!
On these Thy gifts, Eternal Priest,
Grant Thou my soul in faith to feast.

Weary and faint, I thirst and pine,
For Thee my bread, for Thee my wine,
Till strengthened, as Elijah trod,
I journey to the mount of God.

There clad in white, with crown and palm,
At the great supper of the Lamb,
Be mine with all Thy saints to rest,
Like him that leaned upon Thy breast.

Savior, till then I fain would know
That feast above by this below,
This bread of life, this wondrous food,
Thy body and Thy precious blood.

Hymn of the Last Supper

By John Pierpont

The winds are hushed; the peaceful moon
Looks down on Zion's hill;
The city sleeps; 'tis night's calm noon,
And all the streets are still;

Save when, along the shaded walks,
We hear the watchman's call,
Or the guard's footsteps, as he stalks
In moonlight on the wall.

How soft, how holy is this light!
And hark! a mournful song,
As gentle as the dews of night,
Floats on the air along.

Affection's wish, devotion's prayer,
Are in that holy strain;
'Tis resignation, not despair,
'Tis triumph, tho 'tis pain.

'Tis Jesus and His faithful few
That pour that hymn of love;
O God! may we the song renew
Around Thy board above!

The Last Supper

By Robert Hall Baynes,

Calm lay the city in its double sleep,
Beneath the paschal moon's cold silvery
light
That flung broad shadows o'er the rugged
steep
Of Olivet that night.

But soon the calm was broken, and the sound
Of strains all sweet and plaintive filled the
air;
And deep-toned voices echoing all around
Made music everywhere.

The holy rite is o'er; the blessed sign
Is given to cheer us in this earthly strife;
The bread is broken and out poured the wine,
Symbols of better life.

The bitter cup of wrath before Him lies
And yet as up the steep they pass along,
The mighty victim to the sacrifice,
They cheer the way with song.

We ne'er can know such sorrow as that night
Pierced to the heart the suffering Son of
God;
And every earthly sadness is but light
To that dark path He trod.

And yet, how faint and feeble rise our songs;
How oft we linger 'mid the shadows dim;
Nor give the glory that to Him belongs
In eucharistic hymn.

Oh for an echo of that chant of praise;
Oh for a voice to sing His mighty love;
Oh for a refrain of the hymns they raise
In the bright home above.

Touch Thou our wayward hearts and let
them be
In stronger faith to Thy glad service given,
Till o'er the margin of time's surging sea
We sing the song of heaven.

The Supper Instituted

By Isaac Watts

'Twas on that dark, that doleful night,
When pow'rs of earth and hell arose
Against the Son of God's delight,
And friends betrayed Him to His foes.

Before the mournful scene began,
He took the bread, and blessed, and brake:
What love through all His actions ran,
What wondrous words of grace He spake!

" This is My body, broke for sin;"
Receive and eat the living food:"
Then took the cup, and blessed the wine,
" Tis the new covenant in My blood."

" Do this," He cried, " till time shall end,
In memory of your dying Friend;
Meet at My table, and record
The love of your departed Lord."

Jesus, Thy feast we celebrate;
We show Thy death, we sing Thy Name,
Till Thou return, and we shall eat
The marriage supper of the Lamb.

At the Table

By Isaac Watts

How sweet and awful is the place,
With Christ within the doors,
While everlasting love displays
The choicest of her stores.

While our hearts, and all our songs,
   Join to admire the feast,
Each of us cry, with thankful tongues,
   " Lord, why was I a guest? "

" Why was I made to hear Thy voice,
   And enter while there's room,
When thousands make a wretched choice,
   And rather starve than come? "

'Twas the same love that spread the feast,
   That sweetly forced us in;
Else we had still refused to taste,
   And perished in our sin.

Pity the nations, O our God;
   Constrain the earth to come;
Send Thy victorious word abroad,
   And bring the strangers home.

The Supper of Thanksgiving

BY HORATIUS BONAR

For the bread and for the wine,
For the pledge that seals Him mine,
For the words of love divine,
   We give Thee thanks, O Lord.

For the body and the blood,
For the more than angel's food,
For the boundless grace of God,
   We give Thee thanks, O Lord.

For the chalice whence we sip
Moisture for the parchéd lip,
For the board of fellowship,
   We give Thee thanks, O Lord.

For the feast of love and peace,
Bidding all our sorrows cease,
Earnest of the kingdom's bliss,
   We give Thee thanks, O Lord.

For the heavenly presence-bread,
On the golden table laid,,
Blesséd banquet for us made,
   We give Thee thanks, O Lord.

For the paschal lamb here given,
For the loaf without the leaven,
For the manna dropped from heaven,
   We give Thee thanks, O Lord.

Only bread and only wine,
Yet to faith the solemn sign
Of the heavenly and divine!
   We give Thee thanks, O Lord.

For the words that turn our eye
To the cross of Calvary,
Bidding us in faith draw nigh,
   We give Thee thanks, O Lord.

For the words that fragrance breathe,
These poor symbols underneath,
Words that His own peace bequeath,
   We give Thee thanks, O Lord.

For the words that tell of home,
Pointing us beyond the tomb,
" Do ye this until I come ",
   We give Thee thanks, O Lord.

Till He come to take the bread,
Type of Him on whom we feed,
Him who liveth and was dead!
   We give Thee thanks, O Lord.

Till He come we take the cup,
As we at His table sup,
Eye and heart are lifted up!
   We give Thee thanks, O Lord.

For that coming, here foreshown,
For that day to man unknown,
For the glory and the throne,
   We give Thee thanks, O Lord.

GOOD FRIDAY

GOOD FRIDAY is the sixth day of Holy Week, and the culmination of that week as well as of the lenten season. It is the anniversary of the death of our Lord, and is meant to emphasize the truths connected with His crucifixion. Because He by His death obtained for humanity the highest good, it is called Good Friday.

The events of that first Good Friday, which the Church celebrates annually, were as follows: Early in the morning Jesus was brought before the High Priest and the Sanhedrin, where He declared Himself to be the Messiah, and was condemned and mocked. *(Matt. xxvi: 59-68; Mark xiv: 55-65; Luke xxii: 63-71; John xviii: 19-24.)* Next the chief priests and rulers took Him before Pilate, to obtain His crucifixion. *(Matt. xxvii: 1, 2 and 11-14; Mark xv: 1-6; Luke xxiii: 1-5; John xviii: 28-38.)* Pilate declared His innocence, but sent Him to Herod, who sent Him back to Pilate. *(Luke xxiii: 6-12.)* Jesus was scourged, mocked, and bore His cross to Calvary, where He was crucified. *(Matt. xxvii: 15-34; Mark xv: 6-32; Luke xxiii: 13-43; John xviii: 39, to xix: 1-27.)* Jesus died on the cross, supernatural signs accompanying His death, and the centurion gave his testimony. *(Matt. xxvii: 45-56; Mark xv: 33-41; Luke xxvii: 44-49; John xix: 28-30.)* Finally the body of Jesus was taken down from the cross, embalmed and buried. *(Matt. xvii: 57-61; Mark xv: 42-47; Luke xxiii: 55, 56; John xix: 31-42.)*

In the very early life of the ancient church, the day began to be observed as a strict fast, in preparation for Easter, and was called the " Festival of the Crucifixion " (πάσχα σταυρώσιμον), the " Day of Salvation," etc.

Constantine forbade the holding of courts, markets, etc., on Good Friday. (Eusebius, Vita. 1-4.) In the early centuries, on Good Friday "the customary acclamations and doxologies were omitted, and no music was allowed but of the most plaintive description. No bell was rung for divine worship on that day. None bowed the knee in prayer, because by this ceremony the Jews reviled Jesus. Neither was the kiss of charity used on this day, because with a kiss Judas betrayed his Lord. The sacramental elements were not consecrated on Good Friday, but a portion for the use of the priest was reserved from the day before; the altars were divested of their ornaments, and black veils and draperies were used to cover them; and the gospel of John was read, because he was a witness of our Lord's passion." *

To this day the Greek and Latin churches observe Good Friday with severe solemnity. The altar lights are extinguished, the altar furniture is covered, the usual communion is omitted and the bells in the church towers remain silent.

Good Friday is observed with increasing interest by the Church of England, and the Protestant Episcopal Church. And in Great Britain and the United States a marked increase in the observance of Holy Week, especially Good Friday, is observable in the non-ritualistic churches.

* DICTIONARY OF RELIGIOUS KNOWLEDGE, Abbott and Conant, p. 398. (New York, Harper & Bros.)

Of course, the supreme thought of the day is the atonement which was accomplished by the vicarious sufferings and death of Jesus Christ on the cross, where " He suffered for our sins, the just for the unjust, that he might bring us to God, being put to death in the flesh, but quickened in the Spirit." *(1 Peter iii.: 18.)*

THE CRUCIFIED ONE

The Christian Church does not abate a whit of its early passion of loyalty for Him who died on the cross. To the cross they had followed Him, too far off, in their first disappointment and fear; but never again did they make that cross anything less than their glory and boast. His resurrection and ascension lifted their allegiance to a sublimity in fervor in which they suffered martyrdom with joy. Nothing was too much which they could do for Him. That they might only know Him, they prayed for the privilege of filling up what was behind of His sufferings, and were willing to be made conformable to His death. They sang His name; they took His name; they carried His name throughout the world.

No less loyal to the Crucified Christ is the Church of this youngest century. Human investigation has reached no results in religion or morals higher than were taught by the Peasant of Galilee. After our furthest excursions into the realms of loftiest scholarship, we come back to the same cross before which Peter and John bowed, and there we too bow, and there we too ask and receive the pardon of our sins and gain the impulse which carries us to a better life; and with the two Apostles we proclaim and boast the name once despised but now honored: " Be it known unto you all, and to all the people of Israel, that in the name of Jesus Christ of Nazareth, whom God raised from the dead, even in him doth this man stand before you whole."

Within the last year (1893) the religions of the world have put themselves on exhibition in Chicago, and asked us to compare them with the religion of Christ. What wonder if some looked to see whether, in the far East, Buddhas and sages might not have discovered, and taught under another inspiration, an ethics and a religion as pure as those of Jesus? But the search has been made, and we find that there is none other name under heaven, given among men, equal to His. We find that it is the religion of Jesus, with its definiteness, its purity, its authority, which is replacing the teachings of Confucius and Gautama. Egypt, Assyria, Persia, India, China, Arabia, have opened their sacred books to this generation, and they have shown to us platitudes and beauties, puerilities and truths, coarse polytheisms and fine phrasings of storms and seasons; but nowhere do we find the firm, sure, simple, lofty, satisfying truth of God, as in the Gospels which tell the teachings of Jesus Christ.

In Him was life, and the life was the light of men. In His light, and His only, would we walk. Still the Church sings the old and faithful saying of its earliest liturgy:
" If we died with Him, we shall also live with Him:
If we endure, we shall also reign with Him:
If we shall deny Him, He also will deny us:
If we are faithless, He abideth faithful:
For He cannot deny Himself."—I.

THE DEATH OF THE CROSS

The Cross is to us an emblem of glory; to the Romans and Jews of our Lord's time it was an emblem of guilt. We venerate it; they thought of it as a curse. We bow to it; they turned from it as the accursed tree which bore felons as its awful fruit. We wear beautiful ivory and gold crosses and adorn our churches with them as precious symbols; they shuddered with a feeling of dread revulsion as they passed the great wooden instruments of death.

The Cross is precious to us, not for what it is in itself; not for its beauty, or its history, not even because our Lord died upon it; but because it illustrates, as no other object could, the love of Christ. It was not that He suffered as an innocent man, many in the history of the world have been unrighteously condemned; it was not that He

died praying for His executioners, tho few, or none, have had this grace; it was not that He died for friends, some have even dared to do as much; but Christ the God-man commended His love in that He died for a world of sinners. Men have been found brave enough and good enough to sacrifice themselves for a righteous person, or a righteous cause, and thus have made themselves immortal. Christ died for a race in rebellion against His Father's laws and His Father's rule, and for all the race, as much for those who reviled, persecuted and executed the Son of God, as for His own disciples, His mother and His brethren.

In what, then, do we rejoice? In His death? Nay, that was cruel and ignominious. Peter denounced it fiercely as the work of wicked hands. It is revolting to us because it was an outrage on justice to take the life of one in whom the judge declared he found no fault. It was the love of Christ for us, as shown in His willingness to suffer the death of the cross, that reaches our hearts and warms our nature into a life of love and devotion. It was necessary to God's plan of salvation that Christ should die, and so He who thought it not robbery to be equal with God, humbled Himself and became obedient unto death, even the death of the cross.

The cross had terrors for our Lord. We know this by His night of agony in the Garden of Gethsemane, when He prayed earnestly that if it were *possible* the cup that was even then being pressed to His lips might be taken away. But it was not possible. The loving Father would have saved Him from that hour and the terrible hours which were to follow; but we must believe that He could not save the Only Begotten without sacrificing the world, nor save the world without sacrificing the Christ. And so in humble obedience the Savior submitted Himself to the ordeal. And He was glorified in the obedience of His sufferings. His glorification lay in the way of the cross, and He was led as a lamb to the slaughter, offering no resistance, and expiating no sin of His own.

His example has been the inspiration of many who have suffered for principle. While John Brown was in the Charleston (Va.) jail, awaiting the day of execution, he wrote in this triumphant strain to his sister:

"Oh, my friend, can you deem it possible that that scaffold has no terrors for your poor, old, unworthy brother? I thank God, through Jesus Christ my Lord, it is even so. I am now shedding tears, but they are not tears of grief of sorrow; I trust I am nearly done with those. I am weeping with joy and gratitude I can in no other way express. . . . I am waiting cheerfully the days of my appointed time, fully believing that for me now to die will be to me of infinite gain and of untold benefit to the cause we love."

The scaffold had no terrors for him. He was but to suffer what the guiltless Jesus had suffered before him and for him. Death is not to us what it would have been if there had been no Christ to triumph over it. He went down to death, but He also came up out of it, that He "might destroy him that had the power of death," and "deliver them who through fear of death were all their lifetime subject to bondage."

If, then, we sing with great gladness,

"In the cross of Christ I glory,"

we do not rejoice in the instrument of torture, nor in the cruel death thereon, nor in the terrors which our Lord suffered; but because in these extreme sufferings, from which His sensitive and innocent soul revolted, He showed us the quality of His love for sinful creatures, and how to obey and to make sacrifice, and even to die. For we know by His example that through Him we die that we may enter upon eternal life.—I.

EXALT THE CROSS OF JESUS CHRIST

BY THEODORE L. CUYLER, D.D.

A certain creed has recently been promulgated by an eminent and genial minister who is more distinguished for his brilliant and fascinating Scotch stories than for the depth and clearness of his theology. This amorphous production is presented as an ethical creed for the promotion of Christian living; it is very good as far as it goes; but its author should bear in mind that true Christian living comes from a Christian heart that has been renewed by the Holy Spirit. While his new creed affirms the Fatherhood of God, it utterly ignores the divinity of the Lord Jesus Christ, and does not even mention the Holy Spirit; worst of all, it maintains a deadly silence in regard to the glorious central truth of revelation, the *cross of Calvary!* Brief as is the so-called "Apostles' Creed," it is dear to all Christendom, because it contains the core-truths which this new formula strangely ignores.

The New Testament does present a beautiful and sublime system of ethics, it also presents a beautiful and heaven-born fabric of theology; and they are interdependent. The Christ is a perfect model for pure and holy living; He is the divine Teacher who reveals the thoughts of God to us. But He is more than our model, He is more than our Master. He is our *Savior.* "Thou shalt call his name JESUS, for he shall save his people from their sins." He came to earth to seek and to save the lost, and this only could be accomplished by the Cross of Calvary. No example that He has set for us, however faultless, no teachings that fall from His lips, however sublime, could save the meanest soul that lies under the condemnation of sin. As I am a sinner, I must suffer as a sinner the punishment due to my guilt. But my compassionate Savior—all glory to His name! took my place, and suffered for me. He was bruised for my iniquities. He satisfied the claims of God's broken law. He made it possible that God might be just, and yet justify us when we lay our hands in faith on the head of our atoning Redeemer, and there confess our sins. He made it certain that we can be saved when our guilt is hidden in His wounds, and our souls are cleansed by His blood. The creed of all true Christians, of whatever name, was condensed by our own Dr. Ray Palmer into just three lines:

"My faith looks up to Thee,
Thou Lamb of Calvary
Savior divine!"

Good Christianity means cross-bearing for our Master; good preaching means cross-lifting before the eyes of all men. "And I," said the loving Redeemer, "if I be lifted up will draw all men unto me." This does not refer to His final exaltation in Heaven, but to His sacrificial death on Calvary. When He told Nicodemus that the Son of Man must be lifted up, He predicted His own crucifixion, and defined the great single purpose of it to be this: "Whosoever believeth on him shall not perish, but have everlasting life." How unwarranted is the assertion that Jesus preached chiefly a divine system of ethics, but did not make prominent the Atonement, or the salvation of sinners by His Cross! From the manger of Bethlehem, every footstep of Jesus moves straight toward that Cross; His whole earthly mission converges there. After the descent of the Holy Spirit on the day of Pentecost, the only gospel that was preached was the gospel of atoning blood. It was the keynote of the mightiest human preacher that ever trod our globe. Whatever else Paul omitted, he never omitted the "faithful saying that Christ Jesus came into the world to save sinners." When recalling his ministry among the Corinthians he reminded them that he was determined not to know anything among them save Jesus Christ, and Him crucified. In an ecstasy of self-forgetful adoration he cries out: "God forbid that I should glory save in the cross of our Lord Jesus Christ, by whom the world is crucified into me, and I unto the world!" Toward that Cross his finger constantly pointed; beside it he loved to linger. And the central theme of the great Apostle has been the central theme of the greatest preachers the world has ever known. No story has such power to move and melt and change the hearts of men as the story of the Cross. "No mother ever sang it over the pillow of her babe without tenderness; no child ever read it without a throbbing heart; no living man can peruse it with utter indifference; and no dying man ever listened to it without emotion. The Cross will be remembered when everything else in the history of this earth is forgotten." My dear reader, in that solemn hour when you and I stand between two worlds, and when we reach that unseen and eternal world, no object in the universe will be of such infinite importance to us as the Cross of our Lord and Savior Jesus Christ.

Good old Gilbert Tennent—a preacher once famous in New Jersey—was missed on a certain Sabbath morning after the close of the Church service. His family went in search of him. They found him in a woods near the Church, lying on the ground, and weeping like a child. They inquired the cause of his emotion. He told them that after preaching on the love of his crucified Savior, he had gone out into the woods to meditate. He had got such views of the wondrous love of God in sending His Son into the world to die for sinners that he was completely overwhelmed. The glory of the Cross seemed to smite him down, and to break his very heart as it had melted the heart of Paul. He saw no one save Jesus only. A clear, distinct look at Jesus is what every sinner also needs to convict him of guilt, and to break him down. The preaching which melts hard hearts is Christ preaching—Cross preaching—it wounds and it heals; it kills sin, and brings to the penitent soul new life. No other preaching so surely commands the blessing of the Holy Spirit. We ministers should find our highest duty and our holiest delight in simply lifting up the atoning Lamb of God before the eyes of our congregations. And nothing else can touch and fire the true believer like the vision of his crucified Savior.

This was the favorite theme of my beloved old friend Spurgeon, who was the most successful preacher of our times. In his racy and pungent way he once said to his divinity students: "When you see a preacher making the gospel of the Cross small by degrees, and miserably less until there is not enough of it left to make soup for a sick grasshopper —get you gone! As for me I believe in the *colossal*—a need as deep as Hell, and a grace as high as Heaven. I believe in an infinite God, and an infinite atonement—in an infinite love and mercy—and in an everlasting covenant ordered in all things and sure, of which the substance and reality is an infinite Christ."

I am also fully persuaded that the most effectual antidote to the current skepticism, is to present the incarnate Son of God, and with the omnipotence of the Holy Spirit to press His claims. The crucified Savior is the only cure for infidelity. Brethren in the ministry! cut that truth as with the pen of a diamond on your heart, and on your sermons. No skeptic can out-general you on that ground. If you can get him there, and hold him there, the Cross of Christ may conquer him. *Exalt the Cross!* God has hung the destiny of the race upon it. Other things we may do in the realm of ethics, and on the lines of philanthropic reforms; but our main duty converges into setting that one glorious beacon of salvation, *Calvary's Cross,* before the gaze of every immortal soul.—I.

THE CROSS

By Charles F. Deems, D.D., LL.D.

How must the cross have seemed to the disciples of Jesus who hovered about the outskirts of the crowd, or cowered, brokenhearted, in lonely chambers in the city? O what a dire disappointment it was to their hearts! O what a tight puzzle it was to their brains! O what a sore trial it was to their faith! Was not this the Prophet of God?

Had He not made displays of power that were credentials of His Divine mission? And would God send out so spotless a man to die ignominiously?

For we must strive to recollect what the cross was. We have wrought it in gold and wreathed it with flowers, and worn it as an ornament, and placed it at the head of all human symbolisms, until we have transfigured it. It had none of these associations originally. It was the meanest of all the engines of torture. The guillotine has something respectable in it, as it was for the decapitation of princes as well as robbers. The gallows is not so mean as the cross; for, when there was slavery among us, and a master and his slave were convicted of a capital crime, they perished on the same scaffold. But the cross was reserved for the lowest and vilest malefactors. It added deepest ignominy to death. Tacitus called crucifixion the torture of slaves.

Now, when they saw their Master hanging there, it was indescribably puzzling as well as painful. He had been so good, so sweet, so pure, so what all men's ideal of the perfect man has ever been! He had shown such power, stilling the winds, multiplying bread, opening deaf ears and blind eyes, cleansing lepers and raising the dead, doing all those things that they had been taught to believe belonged only unto God to do. How could He let Himself be crucified? How could the great eternal God allow this model of goodness and beauty to be crushed out of the world? The cross gave them a disappointment sadder than ever had fallen on men before, sadder than any since. It was the bitterest blighting of hopes recorded in the history of humanity.

But Jesus—how did it all seem to Him? He knew what was in Pilate's mind, and what in the minds of the chief-priests and the Jewish rabble, and the Roman centurion and the brutal soldiery, and His fainting mother, and His disheartened, disappointed friends. He knew that they felt that they were parting from Him forever. He heard the gibes and jeers of the mocking crowd, the roar of the unfeeling mob, the groans and cries of the blessed Virgin, and the frightful noise wherewith the earthquake burst open the tombs and ripped the Temple's veil from top to bottom. He saw the darkness coming on Temple and Tower and Calvary, and on His own soul, like the shadow of hell. But through it all He beheld a vision of glory. But above it all He heard a shout of triumph! And He died satisfied!—C. W.

SERMONS AND OUTLINES

THE VOICE OF THE CROSS

By Amory H. Bradford, D.D.

There they crucified him.—Luke xxiii: 33

These words describe an event by no means uncommon in that cruel age. In themselves they are not unique enough to attract attention; as a part of the ministry of Jesus Christ they have relations to all ages and climes. The death of Christ was not so painful as that of the two thieves who hung by His side. Considered simply as a historic fact, it was the death of one who by legal process had been adjudged to be a criminal. It has been called a sacrifice, but there was no altar, no fire, no priest. There has always been a tendency to surround the cross with artificial scenery. In it the dramatic instinct has found a fruitful subject. Artists have followed the example of theologians, so far as their art would allow them. I have always considered Gérôme's painting of " The Crucifixion " peculiarly noble because it shows only the three crosses, and stretching from their feet the shadows of those hanging upon them. The attempt to put infinite agony into a human face always fails. Ethical and spiritual sensibility defy the painter's brush even more than the logician's formula or the theologian's system. If the crucifixion in itself was not more tragic than thousands of other events, in what do we find the great and vital mystery of Calvary? Because of its relations to humanity, because it has been a fountain of moral regeneration, because it has been a source of salvation and new life, we are led to ask concerning the personality of Him who died that death. The cross alone proves nothing concerning Christ or His mission, but what followed shows that no ordinary mortal there poured out His soul in death, and that the life which then culminated was not like that of other men. You cannot begin with the cross as a fact in history and reach any adequate conclusion concerning the Man; but beginning with the work of Christ you are led by a process swift and irresistible to something like the faith of Peter—" Thou art the Christ, the Son of the living God."

Concerning the relation of the death of Christ to the Deity and the moral order, speculation has been common and useless. Salvation is as mysterious as the action of the elemental forces. How gravitation operates no one knows; how the energy in a sunbeam is communicated to a flower no one understands; how electricity can be manipulated so that a man may hold a pen in Chicago and write his signature in New York, baffles imagination; and until such facts are explained, no one need be dazed at the mystery of spiritual life. The cross in its relation to man is what claims our attention. If that cross were still standing, endowed with life and power of speech, what do you think would be its message to us in these latter years of the nineteenth century? We speak of the "Voice of the Cross." By that we mean the motive which is brought to bear upon every man to cooperate with those divine forces which found expression on the cross. And by the cross we do not mean simply Calvary and the wood that was there raised, but that suffering and sacrifice which were the symbol of the eternal love of God. If Christ was only a man, then the appeal is no greater than that which comes from any heroic death. But the cross reveals at the same time the love of God and the ideal life of man. Its call runs throughout the earth, as that of the sunshine and the rain. Every sunbeam seems to have a voice for the farmer, telling him that winter is past, and the time for the sowing of seed has come. The raindrops and the sunbeams call those who till the soil to cooperate with unseen forces for the realization of the harvest. No farmer understands how the ground is made ready for the seed, and as little how the seed grows after it is sown. And yet he may take advantage of the forces in nature, and compel the earth to bring forth harvests. Even the dullest savage may cooperate with the universe, they two working together for the support of the life of man. As rain-drops and sunbeams appeal to the farmer, so the cross on which the divine love broke into expression appeals to all, telling them that no man is left to himself; that, so to speak, redemption is in the nature of things; that God works with all who will work with Him; that the divine invitation, "Whosoever will, let him come," has in it a deep and sublime philosophy; that it is literally true that there is not a human being so humble or oppressed that he may not link his puny self to the great love of God, and by it be led into the fulness of the divine life. I have sometimes imagined the cross to be a living being, with a voice which, ringing down the centuries and throughout all lands, carries ever this message: The true life of man is that which culminated when our Master died.

To what does the Cross call men?

It calls to personal holiness. The teaching and mission of our Lord point toward the impartation to man of the very life of God. All have that life in the sense that they have existence, but all have not the nature of God, which is holiness. What is meant by holiness? Perfect goodness. Goodness is a word which every one understands. There have at different times been different moral ideals. In one age, the bravest have been considered the best; in another, the shrewdest; but holiness, in the sense of unalloyed goodness, has always been recognized as the finest flower of human character. In its Biblical usage, holiness comes from the sacrificial system, in which only animals perfectly sound were offered to God. That perfection was in our Master. Holiness is a state of moral purity. Some words need no definition. Pure as the air! Pure as the light! Pure as Christ! To think of an unholy imagination or an unworthy desire in the whiteness of His nature is blasphemous. But holiness is not only perfect health and purity; it is also something set apart for the service of God. A man with not one thrill of passion, not one desire for personal aggrandizement, but with ambition to be great for the sake of at last giving all to God, suggests what holy character is. It is not weakness; it has no kinship with merely sentimental piety. It is a positive quality—the sum of all virtues. A holy man cultivates every faculty to the utmost, acquires every possible art, disciplines his mind, trains his thought, acquires grace of action and expression, completes his manhood, in order that at last he may offer a finished and beautiful sacrifice to Him whom he delights to honor. Patience, temperance, love, have been called weak; and yet patience requires more strength than passion; temperance, more resolution than audacity; and love, both bravery and endurance. In the old time Cæsar was the hero; in the new time, Jesus upon the cross, dying that He may heal the woes of humanity, is the hero. To what does the cross call? To Christlike holiness; to the realization that every gift and grace, every faculty and energy, every motive and thought, belong to God. Pure as the water without a taint! as a diamond without a flaw! as the light that bathes the world in splendor! What were men intended to be? What Christ was. What word condenses His character better than any other? Holiness. No thought of self! no plan for self! everything for humanity! So pure in heart that He could see God! To that all are called—to the very character of Him who hung upon the cross. Is the ideal high? It cannot be too high. Is it an impossible ideal? When Robert Morrison started for China, an incredulous American said to him: "Mr. Morrison, do you think you can make any impression on the Chinese?" "No," was the reply; "but I think the Lord can." That ideal of perfect, flawless, stainless purity, can it ever be realized by such things as ourselves, stained by unholy memories and polluted by foul thoughts? Is not that a height beyond our reach? I fancy that I hear some incredulous man say, as he looks out over the fields loaded with snow: "The idea that a harvest will ever grow in these cold and icy fields is absurd? It is absurd to you and me, but not to Him who can send His sun to melt the snow and His rain to nurse the seeds that were sown before the snow had fallen. To the very life of God we are called. It is impossible to us, but not impossible to Him.

The Cross appeals to all to fill their lives with service and sacrifice. On the cross was the noblest example of self-sacrifice for the sake of those who have nothing to return that this earth has seen. "Let this mind be in you which was also in Christ Jesus." He "came not to be ministered unto, but to minister." Service and sacrifice are the natural language of love. Other men may have ambition for themselves, but a Christian must do as his Master did—make the most of himself for the sake of humanity. The life that ended on the cross, how little it is understood! We bear the sacred name; rear buildings for His worship; wear the symbol of sacrifice in jewels on our persons; talk about the cross; but how many know that there is but one material of which a cross can be made? There was never yet one cross of gold or silver or precious stones; the only material that can get into that shape is love; and love must manifest itself in service which will not shrink from sacrifice. Love without service is like a sunbeam without light. The mother must minister to her child. A friend must seek to be helpful to his friend. The first recorded word of Christ was: "Wist ye not that I must be about my Father's business?" and His last: "It is finished." What lies between these words? Constant ministry. When He said, "Let him that is chiefest among you be servant of all," He outlined the form that the Christ-life must take. The voice of the cross calls to what the cross symbolized. "Ah, but," you say, "that was all very well for Him who came for the accomplishment of a special work, but it has no meaning to us." No meaning for us? Are there not as great evils to-day as when He came? Do not millions bend beneath indescribable sorrow? Have all men even yet the truth? Do all know that they are children of God? Have the doors between this and the spirit life been thrown open? The very work which faced the Master still remains. He began that which His followers must complete. Take two or three illustrations.

The poverty of the world is not so great as when the Christ was here, but it is still appalling beyond description. Think of 95,000 families in one city with only one room to a family! Think of 210,000 human beings in New York this year on the verge of starvation! Think of little children in factories when they ought to be in school! Think of women with children to support making shirts at ten cents apiece; finding their thread, paying their rent, fuel, light, clothing, everything, out of that wage! Think of the wretchedness and poverty that surge even to the curbs of the palaces of the rich! Lazarus and Dives touch elbows. Why do thousands of men cheer the name of Jesus and hiss the mention of the Church? Because deep in their hearts they recognize that the cross stands for brotherhood, for helpfulness, for a real gospel to the poor, while they believe that those who bear the name of Jesus have forgotten the message that He spoke. A young student from Oxford, a resident of Mansfield House in East London, with thrilling and pathetic earnestness said not long ago: "Some of us have sworn that we will take no rest until these terrible conditions are done away." Such utterances have been heard before. That splendid enthusiasm will wear itself out, and that young man, if he persists, will sink into an untimely grave. He may live to the age of his Master, but he will hang upon his cross long before the work is completed. The cry of humanity is bitter and terrible. "The cry of the children," rings in the ears of those who heap up gold. Into this confusion rises the clear, sweet voice of Him who hung upon the cross: "Inasmuch as ye did it unto one of the least of these my brethren, ye did it unto me."

Poverty is not nearly so common as sorrow. Many suffer hunger; all sooner or later feel sorrow. Who can speak wisely of the disappointments that embitter? of the losses that make us wonder if there is love anywhere? of the disease that consumes those who are dearer to us than our lives? Who can tell what death—that strangest of mysteries in a world of life—means? Death obtrudes his hideous face into all happy associations, until sometimes it seems as if the sunlight were only a mockery and the very air poison. The work of Christ complete! He who came to bind up the broken-hearted—His work complete! Why, it seems as if it had hardly begun. The Apostle said: "Bear ye one another's burdens, and so fulfil the law of Christ." Enter into each other's life. Be helpful. Let those who have joy minister to those who are without it. From that cross I seem to hear a voice which comes straight to us, saying: "Thou shalt love one another as I have loved you." That means, you should enter into one another's life and bear one another's burdens, as I have entered into your life and borne your burdens. Over against sorrow and suffering the Master has put Fatherhood and immortality. "Our light affliction, which is but for a moment, worketh for us a far more exceeding and eternal weight of glory." "Blessed are they that mourn, for they shall be comforted." Ring out the message wherever hearts are breaking and eyes are filled with tears! All things are in the Father's hands; not one is utterly alone; no life is without purpose, and all things are moving upward.

The desolation of poverty and sorrow are as nothing when compared with the desolation of sin. The same selfishness that nailed Jesus to the cross still stalks through the earth. The same forces of evil are at work now as of old. In the morning multitudes go out pure as the light—in the evening they return beaten down, defeated, despairing. There is poverty because men choose evil rather than good. There is sorrow because men forget to love one another. Our Master had one mission above all others—by service and sacrifice to bring men from the sway of sin and sorrow into the life and love of God. His life was given to humanity. Study His career, and see if you can get anything out of it except ceaseless effort to destroy poverty, to break the clouds of sorrow, to find the secret places in which lurk the powers which work evil among men. All for man, and nothing for Himself. To that His followers are called. Wherever His story goes, there also goes the mute appeal that men should be as He was. Oh, what a world this would be if competition could go out, cooperation come in and prevail! How much of sorrow would go if all would help one another, and never in any way hinder; if all would work together to overcome sin and destroy evil! I seem to hear a voice calling to you and to me, saying: "You believe in me? then follow me. You believe in the cross? then live the life of the cross. You believe in the love of God? the love of God can manifest itself only in the love of man." Let us dare to be singular! dare to go against traditions and theories! dare to do anything that is not wrong, if thereby we may help a little to do away with poverty, and cause rifts in the clouds through which the light of God's love may shine into the broken hearts of brother men. Into the midst of the controversies concerning the mysteries of time and eternity; into the midst of competitions among the Churches; into the midst of those who use wealth as if there were no judgment; close beside those who are ungenerous and unkind, that living cross moves, with the streaming hands and the pierced side, and everywhere sound with thrilling pathos the words—"As thou hast sent me into the world, even so send I them into the world." The voice of the cross reaches to all men. It entreats us to fight against every usage or custom which is at variance with love. It summons us to war against every theory which confuses a man with a thing. It insists that all shall have the opportunity of growing into the divine likeness. It would have us go into business houses with a scourge of small cords, and drive out those who pay wages which necessitate starvation or sin. It summons the faithful to enter Churches which make discriminations based on wealth, and lift high the Gospel which cannot be bought with a price. It calls us to be brothers; to put our hearts at the disposal of those whose hearts are broken, and, in some way and at any cost, to find all who are without God and without hope, and then to be willing even to die that they may be brought to the Father's house and the Father's love.

Many other messages come from that cross. It asks, "Can you question the final outcome of the conflict between evil and good? Can you doubt that what has been begun at so great cost will be surely completed?" You have sometimes been at sea in the midst of the wild, black night. Not a star is visible. The rush and roar of the waters is in your ears. The desolate, awful ocean is around, and blackness of darkness above and beneath. Thus do we sometimes picture the world in which we live—evil around, evil within, evil behind, and an abyss before us! But that is not a true picture. Nature is not heartless. The elemental forces are beneficent. All things work for good. When despondency concerning the final victory comes, the cross seems to move nearer, the very wounds in the hands and feet, and the spear-print in the side, to find voices which ask, Can you believe that the work which the Savior began can be defeated? The call of the cross is to holiness, to service and sacrifice, to faith in the final triumph of good; it calls all who bear the Christian name to realize that they are in fellowship with the Son of God in saving the world. The cross utters its voice in our ears. It seems to say: "You are blest with all that you need; you have friends and love; I bring to you the greatest of all possible privileges. Power will cease, wealth will go, friendships must end; I offer to you fellowship with me in the work of bringing all men into actual brotherhood, and into the realization, not only of Fatherhood, but of immortality." Two voices sound from that living cross which has moved down the ages and stands by our sides to-day. One speaks to those who have taken the Christian name, saying: "Rise to your privilege! the servant is to be as his Lord! My work is your work! where I went you are to go! what I did you are to do! those who were dear to Me should be dear to you! the more you have the more you should give! the more nearly perfect you make your life the richer will be its achievement for God and humanity!" Are we heeding that voice?

Yet once more that cross moves closer, and yet more intensely and eagerly He who hangs upon it seems to speak to us, and the burden of His words is: "I bring to you that which is highest and best for time and eternity; I bring to you the assurance that there is no grief and no sorrow that is not always in the Father's sight and may not be turned into blessing. I bring to you a power by which evil thoughts and tendencies may be destroyed. I bring to you whose memories are full of sad and bad recollections the assurance that no life can have been so wicked, no past so foul, no strength so far gone, as to cut off from the love of God and His willingness to save." Are you willing to hear that voice and to respond to its invitation?—O.

THE CRUCIFIXION

By F. W. Farrar, D.D., D.C.L.

There they crucified him, and the malefactors, one on the right hand, and the other on the left.—Luke xxiii: 33

On these great solemn days of the church sermons are the least needful. The day itself preaches to us. Its lessons, its services, its memories are so many sermons; and every Sunday of the year helps to explain and to emphasize the lessons of those great facts of which Christmas Day, Good Friday, and Easter Day are special memorials. Eighteen and a half centuries have flowed back into the dark abyss of time since that first Good Friday, yet how fully does the fourfold narrative of the Gospels enable us to call up the most memorable event in the world's history! A turbulent afternoon in spring, an execution, a surging crowd, the eve of a great annual festival which has brought thousands to Jerusalem, the dim, unconscious sense of some great crisis and tragedy, rocks tremulous with earthquake, a sky darkening with preternatural eclipse! Stand amid that vile, promiscuous crowd; what is the spectacle which has summoned them together? There are three crosses on Golgotha; on the right hand and on the left are two robbers, crucified for murder and rebellion; on the central cross, with its mocking title of scorn over His head in three languages, "This is the King of the Jews," with women weeping at His feet as tho their hearts would break, hangs a sinless Sufferer, One who had lived as never man lived, One who spake as never man spake, One who had loved His brethren as never man had loved before! Guilt and innocence are alike nailed upon those crosses; redeeming Godhead and ruined humanity hang tortured there; and that Sufferer was the Savior of mankind.

Now, those three crosses symbolize two opposite, two eternal, conflicting facts—they are the signs of an awful defeat, and of an unutterable victory; they are the proof of an appalling misery and of an irresistible, triumphant hope.

I. THE AWFUL DEFEAT.

Gaze at which cross you will, you will see in it the fall, the degradation, the utter corruption of humanity, the acme, the zenith, the triumph—and at this moment it might have seemed the final triumph—of the enemy of souls. Death itself, death at the best, is full of awe; death even when the mute, beseeching appeal of every glance is anticipated by love, when every pang is soothed, when every tear is wiped away with the touch of consummate tenderness; death even when prayers and hymns are uttered softly by the dying bed, and children's faces look upon it, and every eye is wet with tears!

But death like this! Death in the cruelest and vilest form which has ever been invented, even by the base and cruel East; a death of ghastly and lingering torture, which even cruel nations, brutalized by despotism, and inured to blood, regarded as the supreme form of all that was miserable and execrable! And this death, inflicted in slow, horrible agonies, and the devilish inventiveness of torture by man upon his brother man when he is in the full flush and prime of his life! Death when the living man, who was made to be "but little lower than the angels," in the supreme moment of his destiny is loaded with nameless insult, and hounded out of the world with fiendish execration! Does not the mind shudder at it? Does it not look like the enthronement of the most hideous and malignant of the principalities of evil as lord over the life of man? From what other source could spring these frightful insults against

the majesty of manhood, against the awfulness of death? Said not our Lord Himself, "This is your hour and the power of darkness"?

And does not the voiceless horror become yet more horrible when we think that on those three crosses hang those who represent alike the loftiest and the lowest humanity—represent manhood taken up into Godhead, and manhood degraded into demonhood—represent guilt, innocence, repentance, ending their lives in the same dire anguish, under that darkening sky, in the common horror of the tragedy of apparent failure too awful for any human imagination to conceive?

1. For guilt was there, and guilt is the darkest problem which this world knows.

That impenitent robber, perhaps a follower of Barabbas, familiar with who knows what scenes of blood and plunder, with who can tell what scenes riding like a nightmare on his breast, does he not represent the horror of the doom of finished crime? Yes, he was a criminal; but no criminal was always a criminal; no man is made in a moment a votary of vice. The child is innocent. The first step toward the ruined man is nothing worse than inconstancy of mind and lack of faith in God. "First cometh to the mind a bare thought of the evil, then the strong imagination of it, then delight and evil motion and full consent; and so, little by little, our wicked enemy getteth complete entrance for that he is not resisted in the beginning."

That wretch, that impenitent murderer, in his agony, was once a prattling and innocent child, and some proud young Hebrew mother had bent over his cradle, and parted his dark hair, and guided his pattering footsteps, and folded his little hands to pray. Little by little, through slow, invisible gradations of degeneracy, inch by inch, step by step, from carelessness to vice, from vice to sin, from sin to crime, he had sunk to this. Sin had triumphed in his mortal body and over his immortal. The powers which war against man's soul had gained over that man so dread a mastery that even here and now, on the cross, he can blaspheme and perish in his evil courses, and go to his own place. The death of an impenitent criminal by the hands of his brother man on the cross, or on the scaffold, is the grimmest and ghastliest of grim and ghastly tragedy. Let us drop the curtain over it. No ray of light can pierce that midnight, save such as shines unseen by us behind the veil.

And that other robber, the penitent, what good there must have been once in him if his faith could leap like a dying flame out of these white embers of his life! We know not whether the legend of him be true, that in youth, when he was a robber, he had spared the Virgin Mother and her Child in the flight to Egypt; but in him, even more than in the other, we see the shipwreck of fair hopes, the ruin of faculties created for heavenly ends, the growth of sins unresisted, the rushing avalanche of final ruin which overwhelms those sins! The remission of sins is not the remission of their consequences; the penalty of violated law must be paid even by the penitent, and paid to the uttermost farthing.

2. And between those two hangs on the cross the Perfect Man, the Sinless Sufferer. On the white robes of His divine humanity there had never been a stain; over the blue heaven of His holiness there had never floated even the shadow of a cloud. He had been all love, all wisdom, all innocence. He had been the Word become flesh, He who clothed Himself " with light as with a garment, and spreadeth out the heavens like a curtain" had been content to dwell in a tent like ourselves, and of the same material—had come down from the starry heights of heaven, amid angels' songs, to live through a sweet infancy, a gracious boyhood, and a winning youth of humble obscurity—to us a divine example to show us the Father, the All-purity, All-tenderness, All-compassion, to heal the leper, to open the eyes of the blind, to go about doing good, to release the tortured soul of the demoniac, to preach the Gospel to the poor, to undo the heavy burden, and let the oppressed go free.

And thus He had lived, and thus the world rewarded Him! For lies and baseness, for selfish greed and destructive ambition, for guilty wealth and mean compliance, the world has a diadem; for perfect holiness it has the cross! The darkness quenched the Light, His own disowned Him. They had repaid by hatred that life of love; envy, malice slander, calumny, false witness, had done its work. Jesus had been excommunicated, hunted as a fugitive, with a price upon His head, buffeted, insulted, spit upon, mocked, scourged, crowned with thorns—thus had the world shown its gratitude to its Redeemer; and the end was here! After thirty hours of sleepless agony Jesus was hanging upon the cross. Infinite malignity! Could there be any greater proof of man's ruin than the fact that this was the sole reward which was requited to immeasurable love?

3. And the mass of mankind. too, the mass of ordinary, average humanity at its lowest, was represented in that scene—the common herd and scum, and low, coarse, average of humanity in all ranks. The stream of humanity in its muddiest vileness was flowing under those kingly and closing eyes. I think an ignorant, obscene mob of godless men, mere fevers of lust, and leprosies of uncleanliness, and ferocities of brutal rage, is of all sights the one which makes one shudder most. It is a multitudinous infamy of baseness, stupidity, and savagery. This crowd was a sink of the dregs of many nations. The Roman soldier was there, coarse and cruel and ignorant and corrupt; drinking, gambling, swearing at the foot of the cross; the Jew of many nations was there, narrow, fanatical, a chaos of relentless hatreds; the supple, unclean Greek was there, from all the corrupted shores and cities of Asia and Africa ; and the hoarse murmur of their jeers and blasphemies, in which even the crucified wretches beside Him joined, mingled themselves with the sobs of those poor Galilean peasant women in His dying ears! The King of men: and this is

what manhood had become! And yet the divine love can still love on unashamed in the face of the enormities which wronged it.

4. And, saddest of all, there was religion there—what called itself religion, believed itself to be religion, was taken for religion by the world; and the corruption and perversion of religion is almost viler and more perilous than godlessness when religion has sunk into mere callous conventionalism and mere irreligious hypocrisy. A city which they called the Holy City lay before Him, white, beautiful, vocal with religious songs, busy with festive preparation, but its heart defiled with blood, and a band of invincible darkness lying across its radiant sunlight. The elders, who should have taught the people, had been the deadliest in their yells of " Not this man, but Barabbas!" The Pharisees, who made the greatest pretense of being the sole representatives of the Orthodox Church, passed by Him, a band of self-deceivers, wagging their heads, and taunting with jeers His awful agony. The priests, who slew the victims, who burnt the incense, who trod the golden Temple courts, they had been the worst of His enemies, the most active of His murderers! What shall be done in the world when its very religion has become irreligious, when its very baptisms need baptizing, when it has sunk into a mass of usurping ambition, human ordinances, deceiving illusions, and historic lies? Guilt itself is a less hopeless spectacle than religion which has no love and no truth in it. What shall we think of priest and Pharisees who crucified the Lord of Glory? Yet the most dreadful fact of all history is that the church, or what calls itself the church, what taunteth itself as the only church, and anathematized and excommunicated all other religious bodies, has ever been at deadlier enmity with God's prophets even than the world, and has chanted its loudest hallelujahs over St. Bartholomew massacres and the ashes of slaughtered saints.

And now the Holy City was using the secular arm of heathen Rome, and religion was firmer even than irreligion in murdering the Son of God. Well might earth groan and tremble and fiends rejoice! " It was their hour and the power of darkness."

Thou palsied earth, with noon-day night all
    spread;
Thou sickening sun, so dim, so dark, so red;
Ye hovering ghosts that throng the starless
    air,
Why shakes the earth, why fades the light?
    Declare
Are those His limbs, with ruthless scourges
    torn?
His brows all bleeding with the twisted
    thorn?
His the pale form, the meek, forgiving eye,
Raised from the cross in patient agony?
Be dark, thou sun; thou noon-day night,
    arise
And hide: oh, hide! that dreadful sacrifice!

II. THE UNUTTERABLE VICTORY.

And so came the end. Seven times only in brief sentences He had broken His kingly silence—once to pray for His murderers; once to promise Paradise to true repentance; once in human tenderness to His mother; one brief cry of spiritual desolation; one single word, the only word recorded in the four Gospels, the one word of physical anguish, Διψῶ, "I thirst;" one loving, trustful prayer; then the one victorious, triumphant, divinely-exultant word, Τετελέσται "It is finished." Finished was His holy life; with His life, His struggle; with His struggle, His work; with His work, the redemption; with the redemption, the foundations of the new world. Over the world, rulers of this darkness, here intensified, here concentrated, Christ had triumphed for ever and ever more.

For, thank God, there is the other side of this great and terrible day of the Lord.

1. If it was the hour and power of darkness, it was also the hour and power of infinite deliverance. If it was the proof of an appalling ruin, it was also the pledge of an illimitable hope, for we know that the cross, which looked like the uttermost victory of Satan, bruised the head of Satan, and that the seeming victory of death was the rending from death of its shameful sting.

Nothing is further from the way in which Christ's apostles and Christ Himself teach us to regard the cross than the morbid, effeminate, gloating luxury of self-stimulated emotion. The unnatural self-torture of the flagellant, the hysterics of the convulsionary, the iron courage of the mistaken penitents, are manifestly out of place in contemplating that cross, which is the symbol of sin defeated, of sorrow transmuted, of effort victorious, which is the pledge of God's peace with man, and man's peace with God, which is the comfort of the penitent, which is the inspiration of the philanthropist, which is the symbol of divine charity on fields of slaughter, which was the banner in the van of every battle which good has waged with ill! The cross does not mean whipping, anguish, morbid wailing, morose despair; it means joy, it means peace, it means exultation, it means the atonement, it means the redemption, it means the liberty of humanity, it means the advance of holiness, it means the remission of sins!

Nothing is more futile than to merge ourselves in a sort of luxury of imaginative and artificial wo over the physical sufferings of Christ. There is not one word in the whole New Testament to encourage such worship. Christ is not suffering now; He is not now upon the cross; He is among heaven's eternal glories and infinite beatitudes. He is not now the crucified; He is not now the dead, not now the absent, not now the humiliated; but, as has been truly said, He is the Incarnate, the Present, the Living, the Prince of Peace on earth, the everlasting King in Heaven! What His life is, what His commandments are, what His judgments will be, these He impresses on us—not only what He once did, or what He once suffered. And what He now requires of us is what He is now doing; that is, the pure, joyful, beautiful practise of primitive and unperverted Christianity. And the fall from that faith,

and all the corruptions of its abortive practise, may be summed up briefly as habitual and too exclusive contemplation of Christ's death instead of His life, and the substitution of His past sufferings for our present duty.

2. It was a tremendous sacrifice; never let us forget that! Let it bring home to our hearts, with infinite sense of shame, the exceeding sinfulness of sin. It is for that, and not for Christ, that we are called upon to mourn. Better even the crude fanaticism of the Jogi or the Dervish, better the self-immolating rapture of the wretches who flung themselves under the car of Juggernaut, than the insolent self-satisfaction of liars and adulterers and slanderers who yet dare to be terribly at ease in Zion! Let us never forget how much it cost to redeem our souls, how exceeding must have been the sinfulness of that sin which needed such a sacrifice; yet let us, at the same time, bless God beside the cross that if no plummet can sound the abyss of human degradation, neither is there any instrument which can measure the altitude of God's love! "I saw," said George Fox, "that there was an ocean of death and darkness, but an infinite ocean of light and love flowed over the ocean of darkness, and in that I saw the infinite love of God."

For he must be blind, indeed, who does not recognize what the cross has done. You may judge of its effects by this, that when Christ died He left but a timid and miserable handful of disappointed Galilean followers, terrified, helpless, infinitely discouraged—and that now, nearly nineteen centuries after His death, we see the two immense proofs of His divinity, historically in all that we mean by Christianity and in all that we mean by Christendom, and individually in the blessed belief that there is forgiveness in God; so that "if any man sinneth we have an advocate with the Father, Jesus Christ the righteous, and he is the propitiation for our sins; and not for ours only, but also for the sins of the whole world."

3. Nor, lastly, is this all. If one arm of the cross points, as it were, to infinite forgiveness, the other points to illimitable hope. Truly, we need it still! Life is still a dark and stormy sea, strewn with innumerable shipwrecks, and its restless water still casts up mire and dirt. . . . As far as the world is concerned God's saints may still have cause to cry in age after age, "How long, O Lord, how long?" but as far as each human soul is concerned, it may, in Christ, escape from evil and doubt and misery and death, "as a bird out of the snare of the fowler," and find by experience the fruition of the eternal promise, "Thou shalt keep him in perfect peace whose mind is stayed on thee." For because Christ died, and liveth forevermore, access is ever open to the foot of the Throne of Grace, mercy is unfailing to the cry of penitence, grace is inexhaustible to the servant who offers himself wholly for the Master's use.

Darkness and earthquake, the shame and anguish of Good Friday, are but the prelude to the bursting dawn and glorious spring of

Easter! By the cross we, too, are crucified with Christ; but alive in Christ. We are no more rebels, but servants; no more servants, but sons! "Let it be counted folly," says Hooker, "or fury, or frenzy, or whatever else; it is our wisdom and our comfort. We care for no knowledge in the world but this, that man hath sinned, and that God hath suffered; that God has made Himself the Son of Man, and that men are made the righteousness of God!"—H. R.

THE FIRST GOOD FRIDAY

By Phillips Brooks, D.D.

Who his own self bare our sins in his own body on the tree, that we, being dead to sins, should live unto righteousness; by whose stripes ye were healed.—1 Peter ii: 24

St. Peter is speaking of the crucifixion of our Lord. The first Good Friday had passed away years before; and already there had come into the disciples' hearts a deep understanding of that which took place on that first Good Friday. The comprehension of Christ's death, the variety and richness of its meaning, the way in which it should be looked at —all this had become clear to the disciples before these epistles were written to describe for the Christian world, through all the Christian centuries, the meaning of the great sacrifice. And yet it had all really been there on the afternoon of the first Good Friday. When the last breath was breathed by the suffering Savior there was taken into the disciples' souls, in its potentness, all the meaning of the work which His death wrought, as that meaning came afterward to them more consciously when they used it in their teaching.

Let us think, on this Good Friday afternoon, of what His death accomplished in the world. We may not attempt to tell the whole of the rich story. Many men in many ways have told it. And sometimes they have taken views which seem contradictory, but which simply indicate the richness of that event, whose multiplied meaning no man can completely comprehend. Let us not think that we can tell it all; but let us try to see what a change had entered into human life when Christ died, when His death was complete on that first Good Friday afternoon.

I. It was the change which comes when any soul, even a soul that has seemed to lay least hold upon humanity, passes away. Think for a moment. Suppose such a death were the only death that had ever taken place. We should know that this soul had gone to be nearer to God, to have more clear manifestations of His presence and His love. We should know that he had carried this humanity of ours into some strange experiences, which yet must be forever the same experiences that have been passed through in this world. The multitudes of human creatures for whom there has been no death have stood upon the beach and watched this one soul pass out into the sea.

Think what a change must have happened in the death of this one dying soul, the only soul that had ever passed from life into death. There must have been a certain change in the balance of all life, when the double life, with its two hemispheres, had been transported from one side to another of its existence. Indeed, we should feel that the whole great balance of God's universe had changed; that there was a difference which must be felt to the farthest bounds of God's universe. There must have been a sense as if something had happened to the universe; something whose influence we could not begin to understand, but which we must feel, as this first life passed out from our sight into the other world, and we knew it had gone to God. It would seem as if that soul had gathered everything up that had happened to it here, and deposited it, and left it as its contribution to the world out of which it had passed. Other men would be continually adding to their lives. There would be for them no solemn summing up of life, no leaving of a man's career as a bequest behind him. But this man would seem to have left behind him the distinct meaning of his existence, different from the meaning of any other existence that had ever taken place, as a finished and final contribution to all the life the world was to live henceforth.

Then comes the thought of that man's own experience; of how it must have opened and enlarged; how those things which lay as unconscious germs in his nature must have opened and unveiled themselves. As we watched him going, we could almost see in his face the anticipation of the change; the development in his own soul of that toward which he was looking forward in the world where he was soon to live. Now all these things belong, it seems to me, to any death. There is a change in the soul itself, a change in the world it leaves behind, a change in the world to which it goes. Heaven and earth and a human soul, all of them, are made different by the transfer from this side of death to the other side of death. This applies to any soul that dies—to that soul which died this morning in some unknown chamber in our city.

II. But let us think how much greater the change must have been to Him who passed from life to death on that first Good Friday. The fulfilment of the Savior's life, the accomplishment of the purposes which had been forever in the soul of God; and those new inspirations and impulses and joys and hopes and judgments which have been in this world of ours from the time that Jesus died—all of these came and took their place among the facts of the universe when Jesus passed out of this world with the cry, " It is finished! "

Yet it is possible to state it much more simply. We may say that on the first Good Friday afternoon was completed that great act by which light conquered darkness and goodness conquered sin. That is the wonder of our Savior's crucifixion. There have been victories all over the world, but **wherever** we look for the victor we expect to find him with his heel upon the neck of the vanquished. The wonder of Good Friday is that the victor lies vanquished by the vanquished one. We have to look deeper into the very heart and essence of things before we can see how real the victory is that thus hides itself under the guise of defeat.

Think how it was with the friends of the victor and the friends of the vanquished on the evening of that Good Friday. The friends of the victor, who were they? A few women with broken hearts, cowering under the great horror through which they had just passed, and a few souls besides who had been won so that they could not help giving themselves to Jesus as their Lord and Master, and who now had seen Jesus, their Master and Lord, perish. Yet, as we read the story to-day, there is something so subtle which comes forth from it to us! We find still remaining underneath all their sorrow a deep suspicion that their Master had conquered, after all. What does it mean, this unbroken faith in Jesus, in so much that they still rejoiced to call themselves by His name; that they clung to one another, wanting to be in the company of those who loved Him; that they had nothing to talk about a day or two afterward as they journeyed, but their hopes of Him; so that they could say, " It is all over and has failed," while still in their hearts lay the inextinguishable hope which told them that this defeat was a victory, after all?

On the other hand, who were the friends of the vanquished that day? They were the Pharisees, shouting their triumph, going to one another and congratulating one another upon the work they have done, saying, " We have killed Him at last. Did you hear His expiring groan? Did you see Him hanging on the cross? " And yet, in the souls of those same Pharisees there was a fear and a doubt; so that they went to Pilate, saying, " Let us have a guard, that there may not be any possibility of His escaping from the tomb." It is the power of evil all through the ages, triumphant in what it thinks its victory, yet with a suspicion at heart that it has been beaten, and is being beaten all the time by righteousness. Is not this the meaning of Good Friday? That which seems to have conquered has been conquered, and that which seems to have been conquered has conquered. Evil has been trampled under foot, tho it boasts itself to be master of the world. Good has smitten evil, altho good seems to have been trodden under foot by sin. Victory has come by defeat. Overcoming has been attained by undergoing.

It is that which is going on everywhere to-day. Evil seems to be everywhere conquering good, and yet good is everywhere conquering evil. Oh, let us believe it! Before the cross of Jesus, let us believe it; so that we shall be able to rejoice in the good which seems to be broken down and defeated, knowing all the time in our souls that it really is the conqueror, and must be declared the conqueror some day. So shall we join the disciples of our Lord, keeping faith in Him in spite of the crucifixion, and making ready, by our loyalty to Him in the days of His darkness for the time when we shall enter into His triumph in the days of His light. And the beauty of it is that the same method runs throughout the disciples' work which ran through His work. Christ's method is repeating itself in the work of His disciples forever and ever. As He who first gained the great victory overcame by undergoing the power of evil, shall we be surprised if that is the sort of victory that God calls upon us to gain? It is the victory which it is always the best to gain, which makes the richest victory for any soul.

III. Think how it is everywhere. Everywhere, men who are ready to undergo, in humiliation and patience and faith, by and by find out that they have overcome, just as Jesus did.

You are poor and distressed, and in want of things that belong to this daily life. Every day the sun rises upon you and finds you in poverty. Every day the sun sets upon you and leaves you in poverty still. Oh! in patiently bearing that poverty, learn continually to trust the riches of the great God; and in the course of years you will know that you have overcome by undergoing, that your soul has grown rich, and that you have echoed the greater victory of Christ.

You are shut out from knowledge that you would like to gain. You would like to give your days to study, to drink deep of the fountains out of which flows the wisdom that men find everywhere hidden in the midst of this wondrous world. But you cannot, for you are driven to do some drudging work. You go and take that work and do it, full of trust and loving obedience. What is the result? There grows in you a wisdom such as books cannot give. Submitting to ignorance you conquer ignorance.

You want to help your fellow men. You have to set yourself against the prejudices and dispositions of your fellow men, and so you win their disesteem. You wish that they would praise you. You long for their approbation and do not get it. You sacrifice it. But out of your surrender there comes an opportunity of saving and helping your fellow men such as come to no popular idol; and you, the despised man, have within your soul the rich knowledge that God has given you that privilege. Once more, have you not overcome by undergoing?

And so of our life in general. Life seems too much for you, too great a burden and too great a task; yet, if you are patient, brave, and cheerful, by and by you will find that you have conquered life and are its lord. It seems to beat you down with every blow; but at last, there you stand, with your feet upon it, and are victor over it, and have gained out of it that which God gives to souls that do conquer life—character and strength and faith and love; and the wish to help and the power to help your brethren; to teach the souls that are being beaten and bruised and conquered by life the way to conquer it and compel it to give them the tokens of victory.

These are the ways in which each day is to be to us Good Friday. We are to be sacrificed to evil, and by sacrificing ourselves to evil become victors over evil.

It is easy to distort the truth. But we have only to turn to the helpfulness of Jesus in order to see that there is no truth in such doctrines as men have run after in their fantastic efforts to overcome the world. The essence of that by which Jesus overcame the world was not suffering but obedience. Yes, men may puzzle themselves and their hearers over the question where the power of the life of Jesus and the death of Jesus lay; but the soul of the Christian always knows that it lay in the obedience of Christ. He was determined at every sacrifice to do His Father's will. Let us remember that, and the power of Christ's sacrifice may enter into us, and some little share of the redemption of the world may come through us as the great work came through Him.

Let us stop there. Good Friday brings to us these inspirations. And Good Friday and the days to come bring duties into which these aspirations may be borne. God grant us so to have entered into the spirit of this day, as that we shall go forth to the days that yet remain to us in this world impelled by one consuming wish, the wish that we may be fit instruments, in true consecration and entire obedience, for doing some little fragment of the will of God upon earth. So we shall have entered into that victory over life which, tho it came by death, did surely come to Jesus and shall surely come to those who are sacrificed with Him.—H. R.

THE ATONEMENT

By Dwight L. Moody

Be ready always to give an answer to every man that asketh you a reason of the hope that is in you, with meekness and fear.—1 Peter iii: 15

I was a partaker of the Gospel many years before I was able to *give a reason* for the hope that was within me, but now I think I am prepared not only to give a reason, but to give it in meekness and temerity. Especially ought we to be able to speak about the Atonement.

The *first glimpse* that we get of the Atonement is there in the third chapter of Genesis, where it says that the seed of the woman shall crush the serpent's head. Well, you know there couldn't be any bruising without blood. But the first actual shedding of blood was there in the twenty-first verse, where we read that Adam and Eve were provided with coats of skins. Of course, animals had to be killed, and that was the beginning of the shedding of the blood of the innocent for the guilty. Even as Adam and Eve went out of Paradise they must have said to themselves that God loved them very dearly, altho He was punishing them for their sin.

Then we find that Abel's sacrifice was more esteemed by God than the sacrifice of his brother Cain. Away back there in the morning of creation God had marked out a way of atonement for sin, and because Abel followed that way God loved him. Cain probably said to himself, that he did not like the shedding of blood. The offering of golden grain and luscious fruits seemed to him a more reasonable sacrifice. These two boys were the same, with this difference. Every man that has a religion of his own to-day is a follower of Cain and, like him, discards the atonement by blood. But Abel reached Heaven by Cain's murderous act; and as he was the *first mortal that ever entered heaven,* there must have been a *solo* sung there once. He was the first to sing the song of redemption, which has since swelled into such a tremendous chorus.

Just as we find the first dispensation commenced with blood, so we find the second dispensation commenced in like manner. The first thing Noah did after he came out of the ark was to offer up sacrifices of clean animals and put *blood* between him and God. Abraham, the friend of God, walked in the self-same way, and on Mount Moriah was willing to offer up his only son, Isaac, in whom was all his expectation. God interposed for him, but not for His own Son, who died for you and me on Calvary in sight of that self-same Mount Moriah.

Perhaps as Abraham stood there the veil was lifted, and looking down the vista of time he *saw Christ* carrying His cross up the side of Calvary. Then comes the time of Moses and the sacrifices of the paschal lamb. Altho there were a quarter of a million lambs offered up by the Jews, yet we always find them referred to as "the lamb." Some say we ought to preach up Christ's life and not His death. Well, these Jews did not tie the live lambs in their *front yards.* If they had, none of them would have escaped when death came to every first-born that night. They killed the lamb, and put the blood as a token upon each door-post. Mind you, they did not put it on the step, where it would be trodden under foot, but on the posts.

A good many of us, I fear, are trampling the blood of Christ under foot. Moses was not safer that night than a child six years old. A good many of you are saying you wish you were as good as Dr. Backus, or some other holy man of God; but if you are behind the Blood you are *as safe as Dr. Backus* or anybody else. Of course, there is such a thing as growth in grace, and we will talk about that by and by; but what we want to think about now is the first principle of Christianity.

The Israelites were not only to have the token of the blood, but they were to *eat* the lamb as well. Why? Because they had a perilous journey before them, and it was necessary that they should be strong. So you must feed on Christ as well as accept His atoning blood if you want to succeed in walking faithfully the Christian's pilgrimage on earth. You have a good many large families down here, and Christ is enough for every family. By and by, however, the Israelites, when they insisted upon having a king, literally, if I may be allowed the expression, voted God out, and then they began to feel God's judgment. There are *two classes* of persons I find—those who believe in all judgment and no mercy, and those who believe in all mercy and no judgment. These must go hand-in-hand—mercy and justice must kiss each other.

Then came Christ, the very Lamb of God Himself, to take away the sins of the world. If Christ had committed one sin Himself He would have had to die for that Himself, but as He was sinless, He became a substitute for each of us. The story is told of a man who was *conscripted under Napoleon,* who furnished a substitute, who was killed. It happened that the man was conscripted again, but he took the ground that he was technically dead, as the substitute had died in his place. When an appeal was taken to Napoleon the Emperor decided that in the law the man was exempt.

This may be true or it may not, but of one thing I am certain, and that is, Jesus Christ died in your stead and mine for our sins, and we are now exempt from the law if we have faith to accept the substitution that has been made. If God has accepted it we ought to be able to. Now, if He has died for us, oughtn't we to live for Him. Who now will lift their voice against Jesus Christ, the Redeemer of their souls? Oh, how ungrateful we are! It isn't manly, it isn't noble, for us to doubt or to be raising our voices in resistance to the Son of God.—C. H.

THE LONELINESS IN DEATH

By C. J. Vaughan

Isaiah lxiii: 3

There is a loneliness in death for all men. There is a mysterious something which makes the bystanders feel that before the last breath the embarkation has begun. There is a silence of the soul to earth and earth's thoughts which seems to enter its protest alike against sobs and words—seems to bespeak the forbearance of the surviving towards the solemn, the mysterious act of stepping across the threshold of sense, into the very presence of the invisible God. There was this loneliness then, as of course, in the death of our Lord. In Him it was deepened and aggravated by the foregoing loneliness of His life. But we have not reached *the* loneliness yet. The context will give us one clue.

I. " I have trodden the winepress alone; and of the people there was none with me." There could not be. " I looked, and there was none to help." If there had been, this particular death had not been died. Christ was doing something in which He could have no assistance. His was a death not with sinners, but for sin; a death, therefore, which none else could die, in that which made it what it was in its truth and in its essence.

II. The divinity, the deity of Christ was another cause of the loneliness. Deity is loneliness, not in heaven, but on earth. If Christ was very God, He must live alone and He must die alone upon earth. It accounts for everything. His Divine Spirit, His soul indwelt of the Holy Ghost, must have been a solitude.

III. Loneliness often is isolation. Lonely men and women—lonely by circumstance or by disposition or by choice—are commonly selfish. Neither atonement nor deity made a solitary, in this sense, of Jesus Christ. He died that we might never be lonely—no, not in death. Tho He trod the winepress alone, yet He was not alone in this sense. He trod it for us. The loneliness was His; the sympathy is ours. The cross was His desolation; it is our comfort; it is our ornament; it is our " joy and hope and crown of rejoicing."—S. B., vol. iv., p. 197.

GROUPS AT THE CROSS AND WHY THEY WERE THERE

By Rev. William N. Pile

And they crucified him, and parted his garments, casting lots; that it might be fulfilled, etc.
—Matt. xxvii: 35-43

The assembling of the groups at the cross of Christ was but the work of an hour, but the causes reached back to centuries. There are many kinds of heredity—family, class, communal, national, racial. We inherit the tendencies of our ancestors in all these relations, and they are fostered by tradition, until we fill up the logical sequence of their feelings and doings, and thus ally ourselves with them in spirit; unless we discover that they were wrong, and by a new impulse repudiate them, and bend our energies to counteracting them. It was these inherited tendencies that brought these groups to the cross.

The soldiers represented Rome, the mistress of the world, who had inherited the spirit of conquest and worldliness from Babylon, Medo-Persia, and Greece. She embodied the heathenism of centuries, and stood up against the Prince of princes because there was in his claims implied opposition to her power.

Another group was composed of rulers, elders, and scribes—representatives of the Jewish nation. They embodied the formalism and hypocrisy of centuries of apostasy from God, and hence clamored for the blood of their own Messiah. As the prophet has declared, they joined hands with the Romans against the Lord's anointed.

The third group contained Mary, the mother of Jesus, John, the beloved disciple, and other believers—representatives of the true Church, imbued with the spirit of prophecy, devout, faithful among the faithless, neither afraid nor ashamed of the cross.

Lastly, there was the outer group of indifferent or curious ones, of all nations—representative of the world, of the unsaved, to which the gospel of the cross was to go.

We may draw two lessons from these groups at the cross.

The first lesson is that we should be very careful to know what tendencies we have inherited, and to judge of them by the word of God. We cannot throw the blame of our misdeeds upon our ancestors, for God has not made them, but His word, the standard of judgment.

The second lesson is that our characters and destinies will be determined at last by our attitude toward the cross.—H. R.

MAN'S UNBELIEF

By H. Bonar, D.D.

They cried, saying, Crucify him, crucify him!—Luke xxiii: 21

The Cross the expression of man's unbelief. Crucifixion was the death of the outcast only,—the *Gentile* outcast. "Crucify him," then, meant. "Let Him die the worst of deaths, the Gentile death, the death that is so specially connected with the curse; the death that proclaims Him to be not merely an outcast from Israel, an outcast from Jerusalem, but an outcast from the Gentiles, an outcast from the race."

I. It was thus that man rejected Christ—civilized man, educated man, religious man! It was thus that the natural heart spoke out, and showed the depths of its enmity and atheism—the extent of its desperate *unbelief*. All unbelief is rejection of the Son of God. Whatever be its evasions and subterfuges, and excuses, and fair pretences, this is its essence—rejection of the Christ of God.

II. And why this desperate rejection; this feeling of man toward the Christ? For many reasons; but chiefly for this, that God's religion, of which Christ is the beginning and the ending is so thoroughly opposed to man's religion, or man's ideas of religion, that to accept Jesus of Nazareth would be a total surrender of self, a confession of the utter absence of all goodness, an overturning of every religious idea or principle which the flesh had cherished and rested on. Man's alternative is—the denial of self, or the denial of Christ; the rejection of his own claims to be his own Savior, or the rejection of the claims of Christ; the crucifixion of the flesh, or the crucifixion of Christ. Allow unbelief to take its own way and, run its course, and it will end in the crucifixion of the Lord of glory. It will prefer self, the flesh, the devil, worst of criminals to Christ. "Not this man, but Barabbas!"—S. B., vol. vii., p. 326.

THE LIFTING UP OF JESUS

John xii: 32

Introduce subject by sketch of previous incidents from v. 20.

I. WHAT IS THE MEANING OF THIS "LIFTING UP?"—v. 33 explains it—of His death.—In this sense, understood by the people, v. 34.—But it may be Scripturally understood in other senses, for instance, to preach the gospel is to lift up Jesus.—His exaltation into heaven is a "lifting up" Acts v: 31.—So the double meaning of the word in Genesis xl: 13 and 19.—So Jesus lifted up both to shame and glory.—Confine our attention now to former sense.—Evident allusion to type of brazen serpent. John iii: 14.—It was "lifted up" that no perishing Israelite might fail to see it.—So Jesus was "lifted up."—Believer not removed from midst of temptations, but "kept from the evil."—He has a refuge continually open to him. 1 John ii: 1.—This type proves the Divine predetermination.—In events connected with death of Christ, an entire absence of accident. So Acts ii: 23.—The salvation of man occupied mind of God beginning.—Law and prophets testified that a plan had been devised.—Jesus must die but die a peculiar kind of death.—John xviii. 31, a fulfilment of the text.—The so-called blasphemer not "stoned" but "lifted up" on cross.—This testifies to extent of His humiliation.—A punishment reserved only for slaves, and vilest criminals.—But in Christ's case, tenfold more degrading.—His claims to be the Messiah denied.—A murderer's release demanded instead of His.—His kingly claim derided by the Roman soldiers.—Crucified between two thieves.—Mocked in his dying agony by the spectators.—Well might He say, Lament. i: 12.—Well might the sun be darkened.—"Lifted up" with His crown of thorns, the fruit of an accursed earth.—Well may we now bow our heads with shame.—But was He not then "lifted up" to glory also?—Yes, then made the first successful charge on Satan's host.—As "second Adam condemned sin in the flesh."—His blood

blotted out handwriting. Col. ii: 14, 15.—When He was crucified, sin and death were also crucified.—The enemy was slain—the gulf bridged over.—Once more His "lifting up" proves that the shame of His Cross was not intended to be concealed.—"This thing was not done in a corner." Acts xxvi: 26.—Crowds of Jews then in Jerusalem.—Everything combined to attract attention to His crucifixion. Luke xxiv: 18.—Apostles claimed that their Master died a malefactor's death.—"Christ crucified" preached by every faithful minister.—In doing so, there is still the same strange mingling of humiliation and triumph.—As Ezra iii: 12, 13, so now in raising Christ's spiritual temple.—Our duty, to speed forth the message.

II. WHAT IS THE EFFECT PRODUCED BY IT?—But all men are not so drawn to Him.—But only a general statement setting forth its natural tendency.—We must understand it is in some sense as we understand. Gal. iii: 24.—Appeal to history of Church.—This doctrine powerful to human sympathies.—It forced its way against Jewish prejudices, etc.—It has established its influence over every European nation.—In vain do infidels adduce Mohammedanism as a parallel.—Mohammedanism was propagated by very different means—Growth of Christianity an illustration of Zech. iv: 6.—"I will draw all men unto me," but how? John xviii: 36; 1 Cor. i: 17; Gal. v: 24.—Not by force of arms, etc.—Its attraction consists in power of God's love manifested by it.—It produces "Godly sorrow for sin."—It animates our faith.—It assures us of the Divine liberality, Rom. viii: 32.—It kindles a flame of love in our hearts.—On that accursed tree is fulfilled. Cant. i: 3.—He was "lifted up" as a standard around which soldiers rally. Is. xi: 10.—The cross sparkles with glory to the eye of faith.—What attraction does the Cross present to you?—H. A. C. Y.

THE TITLE ON THE CROSS

John xix: 10

Every detail of the crucifixion ordained and foretold. Acts iv: 27-28.—In the hour of His deepest humiliation proclaimed King.—Finger of God guided Pilate's hand.—Tells out His royalty to Greeks, Romans, and Jews.—Vindicates justice of His sentence by publishing the crime of the sufferer.—Also expresses His contempt for the Jews.—But compelled by a higher power to be a witness for the truth.—Draw near to the cross and consider.

I. A REPROACHFUL TITLE.—A pretender to power who fails, is exposed to contempt.—

The murderer by wholesale is applauded as a conqueror.—On this basis the Roman Empire was founded.—Pilate's idea of "a King" was that of a rebel seized with arms in his hands.—Hordes of robbers at this time defying the Imperial government.—The leader of such a band would have inspired Pilate with respect.—But to Jesus he says: "Art thou the King of the Jews?"—Surely, Cæsar has nothing to fear from such a pitiful rival.—Such the king who must be enthroned in our hearts.—Are you willing to confess this rejected malefactor?—If you doubt He is your King read the prophecy. Ps. xxii: 16, 17; Is. liii: 3, 5.—With light from such passages, again read title, *text*.

II. A VINDICATING TITLE.—His enemies brought many charges against Him.—Pilate by this title vindicates His innocence.—By the Roman governor's confession, Jesus is a King. —The cross His throne.—For His redeemed ones He hangs there.—Where now the fear of Pilate when threatened? v. 12.—As Christ's innocence vindicated so His people's. Ps. xxvii: 56.—How often have names of saints been covered with reproach, yet brought out triumphantly.

" Detraction's a bold monster, and fears not
To wound the fame of princes, if it find
But any blemish in their lives to work on."

But none in His. yet defamed.—Heed not reproaches, but look at dying Lord. 1 Peter iv: 14.—God changed His cross into a throne, on which read text.

III. A PROPHETICAL TITLE.—Declares His right to enter all Kingdoms by His Gospel.—

Written in three languages as if to predict universality of His sway.—Signifies that the powerful, the wise, and the worshipers of God are His subjects.—So Caiaphas. John xi: 51, 52.—" Not for that nation only "—a wider design. Ps. xcvi: 10.—God bringing to pass His promise. Ps. ii. 8.—He lays foundation of His kingdom on the cross.—Not when preaching on the Mount of Beatitudes.—Not when lighting up the meaning of ancient oracles.—Not when stilling the tempest, etc.— Not when greeted with rapturous hosannahs. —If this were all, He would have been without a Kingdom.—No Jerusalem would have l een built; no banner of liberty waved; no longings for a better land excited.—The city had to be founded in the blood of the covenant.—John xii: 32. and we may ask Is: 8—Yes, that title remains the same till prophecy fulfilled. Habak. ii: 14.—On this solemn anniversary be humbled.—Seek for faith to behold our King.—May He govern our spirits and hearts.—Let us swear allegiance to His sacred standard.—H. A. C. Y.

PRE-EMINENT GLORY OF THE CROSS OF CHRIST

Gal. vi: 14

Tho the cross is a stumbling-block and foolishness to the unsaved, it is the power and wisdom of God to the saved. This plan of redemption came forth from the glory of the eternal world, becomes the chief glory of all revelation, is lifted into the highest glory of the eternal world of the redeemed. Paul knew this glory of the cross by the Spirit in his experience and preaching in a two-fold way:

I. THE POWER OF THE CROSS TO CRUCIFY THE WORLD UNTO THE BELIEVER.—(1) By revealing the surpassing glory of the eternal and spiritual above the temporal and material. 2 Cor. iv: 18. (2) By revealing the dignity and destiny of man as a son of God and an heir of glory. Rom. viii: 15-39. (3) By re-

vealing the only power that can create the new heavens and new earth in which dwelleth righteousness. Heb. i: 8; Heb. ii: 7-10; 2 Pet. iii: 13.

II. THE POWER OF THE CROSS TO CRUCIFY THE BELIEVER TO THE WORLD.—(1) By revealing the perfection and glory of the divine character and law in condemning sin. Self-righteousness and self-will can no more live in the Spirit's blaze of the holiness of God than paper can retain its whiteness in the glowing flames. (2) By revealing the marvelous suffering love of God in atoning for sin and forgiving the penitent sinner. (3) By proving an inspired safeguard against the lusts of the flesh, the lust of the eye and the pride of life.—C. G.

THE LAMB OF GOD

By JOHN HALL

Rev. v: 6

I. Notice the descripition that is given of Christ: a Lamb. " Behold the Lamb of God, which taketh away the sin of the world." That was Jesus of Nazareth. You cannot read the Old Testament without understanding the same thing clearly; " He is led as a lamb to the slaughter." That also is Jesus of Nazareth. There is a fitness in His being presented as a Lamb in His own personal character. Morning sacrifices, passover lambs —these and kindred institutions of the Old Testament all point in the same direction.

II. This Lamb slain even yonder in heaven to the vision of the Apostle bears traces of having been slain. God deals with angels one by one. The angels are not a race. Like the trees of the forest, each one stands upon his own root. I feel thankful that we belong to a race. Christ took not on Him the nature of angels. We are a race, and are dealt with as a community. We stood in the first Adam, and he sinned; Christ is the second Adam, and we can stand in Him, and be saved; and there is the philosophy of the Lamb slain.

He came that He might undo what the first representative did. He came that He might stand for His people, that He might be in their room. He is slain, for the wages of sin is death; He is slain, for the law was broken, and He magnifies it; He is slain, because there was a penalty, and before angels, and principalities, and powers God is to be seen as forgiving for a cause, and that cause is the atoning death of the Lamb of God; "God so loved the world that he gave his only-begotten Son, that whosoever believeth in him might not perish, but have eternal life." That is a familiar text. Look into the meaning of it, and below the surface. The world is like a great house, with vessels to honor and vessels to dishonor; He loves it as His great house, but let it be our care that we be not the vessels to dishonor.

III. The Lamb slain is on the throne. In one breath the preacher tells us about Christ as a Victim, Christ as a Priest; in the next breath he tells us about this same Crucified One as on the throne. Yes, it is a strange combination. Man never could have made it; human intellect never could have originated it.

IV. The Lamb slain is standing in the midst of the throne. Fourteen or fifteen times in the Scriptures Christ is connected in this way with the throne; but this picture, standing, is peculiar. It is here and in one other place, here very fitly standing is the attitude of activity. The man on duty, the man who has to do things, the man who has to put his strength into things, stands up. Christ is Mediator, He is High-priest still: He ever liveth to make intercession; He is Prophet still; He is teaching all His people; He is King; He is standing, and nothing escapes His vision.—S. B., vol. xii., p. 296.

SUGGESTIVE THOUGHTS AND ILLUSTRATIONS

ATONEMENT, Accepting the.—When a sacrifice under the law was brought to be slain, he that brought it was to put his hand upon the head of the sacrifice, and so it was accepted for him, to make an atonement (Lev. i: 4), not only to signify that now it was no more his but God's, the property being transferred by a kind of manumission, nor yet merely that he voluntarily gave it to the Lord as his own free act; but principally it signified the putting off his sins, and the penalty due for them, upon the head of the sacrifice, and so it implied in it an execration as if he had said, "Upon thy head be the evil." So the learned observe, the ancient Egyptians were wont expressly to imprecate when they sacrificed, "If any evil be coming upon us or upon Egypt, let it turn and rest upon his head," laying their hand, at these words, on the sacrifice's head. And upon that ground, says Herodotus, the historian, none of them would eat of the head of any living creature. You must also lay the hand of faith upon Christ your sacrifice, not to imprecate, but to apply and appropriate Him to your own souls, He having been made a curse for you.—JOHN FLAVEL.

ATONEMENT, Appropriating the.—Now we may say, "Lord, the condemnation was Thine, that the justification might be mine; the agony Thine, that the victory might be mine; the pain was Thine, and the ease is mine; the stripes Thine, and the healing balm issuing from them mine; the vinegar and the gall were Thine, that the honey and sweet might be mine; the curse was Thine, that the blessing might be mine; the crown of thorns was Thine, that the crown of glory might be mine; Thou paidst the price, that I might enjoy the inheritance."—JOHN FLAVEL.

ATONEMENT BY THE CROSS.—Let us no more admire the enormous moats and bridges of Caligula across to Baiæ, or Trajan's bridge over the Danube (stupendous work of stone and marble) to the adverse shores, whilst our timber and our trees, making us bridges to the furthest Indies and antipodes, lead us into new worlds. In a word (and to speak a bold and noble truth), trees and woods have twice saved the whole world; first by the ark, then by the cross; making full amends for the evil fruit of the tree in paradise, by that which was borne on the tree in Golgotha.—EVELYN.

ATONEMENT, Effects of the.—It is said of Zeleucus, a king of the ancient Locri, that he enacted a law, the penalty of which was that the offender should lose both his eyes. One of his sons became a transgressor of that law. The father had his attachment to his son, and the law he himself had promulgated as righteous in its requirements and in its penalty. The lawgiver, it is said, ordered his son into his presence, and required that one of his eyes should be taken out; and then, in order to show mercy to his son, and at the same time maintain the penalty of the law, he sacrificed one of his own eyes as a ransom for the remaining eye of his child. The king was the lawgiver; he therefore had the power to pardon his son, without inflicting the penalty upon him, and without enduring any sacrifice himself. Every mind, therefore, would feel that it was a voluntary act on the part of the king; and such an exhibition of justice and mercy, maintaining the law and saving his son by his own sacrifice, would impress all minds with the deepest reverence for the character of the lawgiver, and for the sacredness of the law. But another effect, deep and lasting in its character, would be produced upon the son who had transgressed the law. Every time that he looked upon his father, or remembered what he had suffered for his transgression, it would increase his love for him, increase his reverence for the law, and cause an abhorrence of his crime to rise in his soul. His feelings would be more kind towards his sire, more submissive to the law, and more averse to transgression. Now, this is precisely the effect necessary to be produced, in order that pardon may be extended to transgressors, and yet just and righteous government be maintained.—WALKER.

ATONEMENT, Idea of.—The experience of poor Jack, a deaf-mute, is thus given by Charlotte Elizabeth :—

His sublime idea of the RED HAND was ever present. He had told me, some years before, that, when he had laid a good while in the grave, God would call aloud, " Jack! " and he would start and say, " Yes, me Jack." Then he would rise and see multitudes standing together, and God sitting on a cloud, with a very large book in His hand (he called it " Bible-book "), and would beckon him to stand before Him, while He opened the book and looked at the top of the pages, till he came to the name of John B. In that page, he told me God had written all his " bads," every sin he had ever done ; and the page was full. So God would look, and strive to read it, and hold it to the sun for light; but it was all "*no, no nothing, none.*" I asked him, in some alarm, if he had done no bad. He said yes, much bads ; but, when he first prayed to Jesus Christ, He had taken the book out of God's hand, found that page, and, pulling from His palm something which he described as filling up the hole made by the nail, had allowed the wound to bleed a little, *passing His hand* down the page, so that, as he beautifully said, " God could see none of Jack's bads, only Jesus Christ's blood." Nothing being thus found against him, God would shut the book, and there he would remain standing before Him, till the Lord Jesus came, and saying to God, " My Jack," would put His arm around him, draw him aside, and bid him stand with the angels until the rest were judged.—F. I.

ATONEMENT, Illustrating the.—A deaf and dumb boy was taught by a kind friend. This kind lady could speak to him only by signs and pictures. She drew upon a paper a picture of a great crowd of people, old and young, standing near a wide, deep pit, out of which smoke and flames were issuing. She then drew the figure of One who came down from heaven, and this was to represent Jesus Christ the Son of God. She explained to the boy that when this person came, He asked God not to throw the people into the pit, if He Himself agreed to be nailed to a cross for them, and how, as soon as He bowed His head on the cross and died, the pit was shut up and the people saved. The deaf and dumb boy wondered much, but he made signs that the person who died on the cross was but one, and the crowd very many. How could God be contented to take one for so many? The lady took off her gold ring and put it beside a great heap of withered leaves of flowers, and asked the boy which was the best, the one gold ring, or the many, many dry leaves. The boy clapped his hands with delight, and spelled the " One! one! " And then to show that he knew what this meant, and that Jesus was the one who was worth all the rest, he ran and got his letters, and looking up, spelled the words, " Good, good One! " He had learned that day that Jesus alone had saved the crowd of people, or sinners, and he stood wondering at His love.—A. A. BONAR.

ATONEMENT, Jewish Custom of.—The following is a report made by a committee of the Church of Scotland of their observations among the Jews: " We spread our mats on the clay floor at Jassy, and attempted to sleep, but in vain. We cared less for this, however, because it was the night preceding the day of atonement, and we had thus an opportunity of seeing the curious ceremony which then takes place. On the eve of that solemn day it is the custom of the Jews to kill a cock for every man, and a hen for every woman. During the repetition of a certain form of prayer, Jews or Jewesses move the living fowl round their heads three times, then they lay their hands on it, as the hands used to be laid on the sacrifices, and immediately after give it to be slaughtered. We rose before one in the morning, and saw the Jewish Shochet or ' slayer ' going round to the Jewish houses, waking each family, and giving them a light from his lantern, in order that they might rise and bring out their ' Chipporah ' or ' atonement,' namely, the appointed cock and hen. We walked about the streets; everywhere the sound of the imprisoned fowls was to be heard, and light seen in all the dwellings of Israel. In two houses the fowls were already dead and plucked. In another we came to the window, and saw distinctly what was going on within. A little boy was reading the prayers and his widowed mother standing over him, with a white hen in her hands. When he came to a certain place in the prayer, the mother lifted up the struggling fowl, and waved it round her head, repeating these words, ' This be my substitute, this be my exchange; this fowl shall go to death, and I to a blessed life.' This was done three times over, and then the door of the house opened, and out ran the boy carrying the fowl to the Shochet, to be killed by him in the proper manner."—F. II.

ATONEMENT, Need of.—A man on the Malabar coast had long been uneasy about his spiritual state, and had inquired of several devotees and priests how he might make atonement for his sins ; and he was directed to drive iron spikes, sufficiently blunted, through his sandals, and on these spikes to walk a distance of about four hundred and eighty miles. He undertook the journey, and traveled a long way, but could obtain no peace. One day, he halted under a large, shady tree, where the gospel was sometimes preached; and, while he was there, one of the missionaries came, and preached from the words, "The blood of Jesus Christ his Son cleanseth us from all sin." While he was preaching, the poor man's attention was excited, and his heart was drawn; and, rising up, he threw off his torturing sandals, and cried out aloud, "This is what I want!" and became henceforward a witness of the healing efficacy of the Savior's blood.—F. II.

ATONEMENT, Objection to the.—"He tasted death for every man." "He gave himself a ransom for all." "He is a propitiation for the sins of the whole world." That all are not saved is no objection. It is suggested by a popular expositor, that, in material nature, much goodness seems wasted. Rain and dew descends upon flinty rocks and sterile sands; floods of genial light come tiding down every morning from the sun on scenes where no human foot has trod; flowers bloom in beauty, and emit their fragrance, trees rise in majesty, and throw away their clustering fruit, on spots where as yet there has never been a man; wealth sufficient to enrich whole nations is buried beneath the mountains and the seas, while millions are in want; medicine for half the ills of life is shut up in minerals and plants, while generations die without knowing of the remedy which Nature has provided; it is no objection, therefore, to the universality of the atonement, that all are not benefited by it. Its benefits one day will be universally enjoyed. There are men coming after us who shall live in those solitary wastes, enjoy the beauty and the light which now seem wasted, appropriate the fruits, the wealth, and the medicine which for ages have been of no avail. It will be even so with the death of Christ. There are men coming after us that shall participate of the blessings of that atonement, which generations have either ignorantly rejected or wickedly despised.— Dr. Thomas.

ATONEMENT, Pagan.—There is a record of an ancient Hindoo custom, in which the offender brought a horse to a priest, and confessed his sins over the head of the animal, with certain religious rites. The horse was then turned into the wilderness and supposed to bear away the sins of the offender. This custom was similar to the scapegoat of the Israelites.—F. II.

ATONEMENT, Voluntary.—A sacrifice that struggled, and came not without force to the altar, was reckoned ominous and unlucky by the heathen; our sacrifice dedicated Himself, He died out of choice, and was a free-will offering.—John Flavel.

BLOOD, Accusing.—Abel's blood, and so Christ's, cry unto God, as the hire of the laborers unjustly detained, James v: 4; or as the whole creation, which is in bondage through our sins, is said to cry and groan in the ears of the Lord, Rom. viii: 22, not vocally but efficaciously. How sad is the case of those that have no interest in Christ's blood; but instead of pleading for them, it cries to

God against them, as its despisers and abusers! Every unbeliever despises it; the apostate treads it under foot. To be guilty of a man's blood is sad; but to have the blood of Jesus accusing and crying to God against a soul, is unspeakably terrible.—John Flavel.

BLOOD, Cleansing.—A poor tempted Scotchman in great distress of mind proceeded to put himself in order for church, and while washing his hands, no one by, he heard a voice say, "Cannot I in my blood as easily wash your soul as that water does your hands?" "Now, Minister," he said, in telling me this, "I do not say there was a real voice, yet I heard it distinctly, word for word, as you now hear me. I felt a load off my mind, and went to the table and sat under Christ's shadow with great delight."—Dr. Guthrie.

BLOOD, Custom of Purifying by.—A custom of purifying by blood, practised in ancient Phrygia, is thus explained: "When a person desired to be purified, he was placed by the priests in a pit prepared for the purpose, which was covered by a platform. This platform was perforated with many small holes; then a beast for sacrifice was brought and slain on this platform, so that its blood might flow through these perforations upon the person beneath. As the blood came down upon the head, the hands, the feet, the limbs, and the whole person, he was considered purified."—F. II.

BLOOD OF CHRIST, a Mystery.—A reader of the Bible was assailed by an infidel with such expressions as these: "That the blood of Christ can wash away sin is foolishness; I don't understand or believe it." The Bible student remarked, "You and Paul agree exactly." "How?" "Turn to the first chapter of Corinthians and read the eighteenth verse: 'For the preaching of the Cross is to them that perish foolishness; but unto us which are saved, it is the power of God.'"—F. II.

BLOOD OF CHRIST, Comfort from the.—The commentator Bengel, during an illness, sent for a theological student and requested him to give him a word of consolation. The youth replied, "Sir, I am but a pupil, a mere learner; I don't know what to say to a teacher like you." "What!" said Bengel, "a divinity student, and not able to communicate a word of scriptural comfort!" The student, abashed, contrived to utter the text, "The blood of Jesus Christ, the Son of God, cleanseth us from all sin." "That is the very word I want," said Bengel, "It is quite enough," and taking him affectionately by the hand, dismissed him.—F. II.

BLOOD OF CHRIST, Equality of the.— Just before the civil war came on, during the days of slavery, I was in Boston. They were very exciting times there then, and Dr. Kirk was preaching on the subject of the cross. It was during the great strife, when there was a great deal of hatred and suspicion against foreigners then in our country. It was in the time of the Know-Nothing party, and there was a great deal of feeling against the blacks, and a great deal of feeling against the Irish. Dr. Kirk said when he came up to the cross to get salvation, he found a poor black man on the right and an Irishman on the left, and the blood came trickling down from the wounded side of the Son of God and made them all brothers, and all alike, and equal. That is what the blood does. It makes us all one kindred, and brings us all into the family of God.—Moody.

BLOOD OF CHRIST, Experience of the.—During the civil war a New York minister went among the soldiers in the hospital, and preached to them the way to Christ. He found one man whose eyes were closed and who was muttering something about " blood, blood," and the old doctor thought he was thinking of the carnage of the battle-field and the blood he had seen there, and going to him, he tried to divert his mind; but the young man looked up and said, " Oh, Doctor, it was not that that I was thinking of; I was thinking how precious the blood of Christ is to me now that I am dying. It covers all my sins."—F. II.

BLOOD OF CHRIST, Hope in the.—Rev. J. Brown, of Haddington, on his death-bed said: " The Gospel is the only source of my comfort, and every sinner is as welcome as I. How pleasant that neither great sins nor great troubles can alter these consolations. Ever since God dealt savingly with my heart I have never had any comfort in the thought that my sins were small, but in the belief that the blood of Christ cleanseth from all sin."—F. II.

BLOOD OF CHRIST, Meditating upon the.—Five persons were studying what were best means to mortify sin. One said, to meditate on death; the second, to meditate on judgment; the third, to meditate on the joys of heaven; the fourth, to meditate on the torment of hell; the fifth, to meditate on the blood and sufferings of Jesus Christ; and certainly the last is the choicest and strongest motive of all. If ever we would cast off our despairing thoughts, we must dwell and muse much upon, and apply this precious blood to our own souls; so shall sorrow and mourning flee away.—Brooks.

BLOOD OF CHRIST, Preached.—I was in a city in Europe, and a young minister came to me and said, " Moody, what makes the difference between your success in preaching and mine? Either you are right and I am wrong, or I am right and you are wrong." Said I, " I don't know what the difference is, for you have heard me and I have never heard you preach. What is the difference? " Said he, " You make a good deal out of the death of Christ, and I don't make anything out of it. I don't think it has anything to do with it. I preach the life." Said I, " What do you do with this: ' He hath borne our sins in his own body on the tree '? " Said he, " I never preached that." Said I, " What do you do with this: ' He was wounded for our transgressions; he was

bruised for our iniquities, and with his stripes we are healed '? " Said he, " I never preached that." " Well," said I again, " what do you do with this—' without the shedding of blood there is no remission '? " Said he, " I never preached that." I asked him, " What do you preach? " " Well," he says, " I preach a moral essay." Said I, " My friend, if you take the blood out of the Bible, it is all a myth to me." Said he, " I think the whole thing is a sham." " Then," said I, " I advise you to get out of the ministry very quick, I would not preach a sham. If the Bible is untrue, let us stop preaching, and come out at once like men, and fight against it if it is a sham and untrue; but if these things are true and Jesus Christ left heaven and came into this world to shed His blood and save sinners, then let us lay hold of it and preach it, in season and out of season." In the college at Princeton this last year, when the students were ready to go forth into the world, the old man, their instructor, would stand up there and say, " Young men, make much of the blood. Young men, make much of the blood! " I have learned this, that a minister who makes much of the blood, and makes much of substitution, and holds Christ up as the sinner's only hope, God blesses his preaching. And if the Apostles didn't preach that, what did they preach? You take the great doctrine of substitution out of the preaching of Paul, Peter, John, James, and Philip and of all those holy men, and you take out all that they preached. And so, my friends, there don't seem to be one ray of hope for the man that ignores the blessed, blessed subject of the blood. " Without the shedding of blood there is no remission."—Moody.

BLOOD OF CHRIST, Relying on the.—An old herdsman in Dartmoor, England, was taken to a London hospital to die. There his grandchild used to visit and read to him. One day, she was reading to him the first chapter of the first epistle of John, when she reached the seventh verse, " And the blood of Jesus Christ, his Son, cleanseth us from all sin," the old man raised himself and stopped the little girl, saying with great earnestness: " Is that there, my dear? " " Yes, grandpa." " Then read it to me again; I never heard the like before." The little girl read again: " And the blood of Jesus Christ, his Son, cleanseth us from all sin." " You are quite sure that is there? " " Yes, quite sure." " Then take my hand and lay my finger on the passage, for I should like to feel it." So she took the old blind man's hand and placed his bony finger on the verse, when he said, " Now read it to me again." The little girl read, with her soft, sweet voice: " And the blood of Jesus Christ, his Son, cleanseth us from all sin." " You are quite sure that is there? " " Yes, quite sure." " Then if any one should ask how I died, tell them I died in the faith of these words: ' And the blood of Jesus Christ, his Son, cleanseth us from all sin.' " And with that, the old man withdrew his hand, his head fell softly back on the pillow, and he silently passed into the presence of Him whose "blood cleanseth us from all sin."—F. II.

CHRIST, Death of.—The death of Socrates, peacefully philosophizing with his friends, appears the most agreeable that could be wished for; that of Jesus, expiring in the midst of agonizing pains, abused, insulted, and accused by a whole nation, is the most horrible that could be feared. Socrates, in receiving the cup of poison, blessed the weeping executioner who administered it; but Jesus, in the midst of His tortures, prayed for His merciless tormentors. Yes! if the life and death of Socrates were those of a sage, the life and death of Jesus were those of a God.—ROUSSEAU.

CROSS, Apparition of the. Constantine saw in mid-heaven, above the brightness of the sun at noon-day, a cross of wondrous shape, and on it read the legend, "In this sign conquer!" The army also saw it. Before the battle of the Milvian bridge, he put the cross, with the name of Christ upon it, in place of the Roman eagle on his standards. His soldiers hailed it as a symbol of divine protection and pledge of victory. This occurred in 312. When Julian the Apostate came to the throne, he caused the removal of the cross from the standards, and substituted for it the images of his heathen gods. Christian soldiers in his army often refused to bear them, and on this account suffered martyrdom. Such were Bonosus and Maximilian, who refused to carry images of Jove and Hercules on their standards, and after excruciating torture with loaded thongs, and then upon the rack, steadfastly affirmed, "We will have nothing to do with your standards loaded with idols!" Rather than handle the idols, they went to their death A. D. 363.—F. II.

CROSS, Christ on the.—*1 Cor. ii: 2.* There is no more efficacious method of conquering all temptations, there is no more compendious way of gaining all the virtues, than perpetually to contemplate, affectionately to consider, diligently to wait upon, Christ hanging on the cross. I suppose that the especial cross from which we are at this moment suffering always seems the very one from which we should most have shrunk. If, therefore, it needs the more courage and patience, then we may be sure it is the truer and better friend to us.

The traitor was gone (John xiii: 31). His presence had been a restraint, and now that that spot in their feast of charity had disappeared, the Master felt at ease; and like some stream out of the bed of which a black rock has been taken, His words flowed more freely: "*Therefore,* when he was gone out, Jesus said."

Like the pellucid waters of the Rhine and the turbid stream of the Moselle, that flow side by side over a long space, neither of them blending discernibly with the other, so the shrinking from the cross and the desire were contemporaneous in Christ's mind.

The New Testament generally represents the cross as the very lowest point of Christ's degradation; St. John's Gospel always represents it as the very highest point of His glory. And the two things are both true; just as the zenith of our sky is the nadir of the sky for those on the other side of the world.

As the sun behind a cloud, which hides it from us, is still pouring out its rays on far-off lands, so Christ, veiled in dark sunset clouds of Calvary, sent the energy of His passion and cross into the unseen world, and made it possible that we should enter there.

As one who precedes a mighty host, provides and prepares rest for their weariness, and food for their hunger, in some city on their line of march, and having made all things ready, is at the gates to welcome their travel-stained ranks when they arrive, and guide them to their repose; so Christ has gone before, our Forerunner, to order all things for us *there.*

All His life long Christ had been revealing His heart, through the narrow rifts of deeds, like some slender lancet windows; but in His death all the barriers are thrown down and the brightness blazes out upon men.

All through His life He had been trying to communicate the box of ointment exceeding precious, but when the box was broken, the house was filled with the odor.

There blends, in that last act of our Lord's —for His death was His act—in strange fashion, the two contradictory ideas of glory and shame, like some sky, all full of dark thunder-clouds, and yet between them the brightest blue and the blazing sunshine.

All His life long Christ was the light of the world, but the very noontide hour of His glory was that hour when the shadow of eclipse lay over all the land, and He hung on the Cross dying in the dark. At His eventide " it was light," and " He endured the Cross, despising the shame "; and, lo! the shame flashed up into the very brightness of glory, and the very ignominy and the suffering were the jewels of His crown.—A. P. L.

CROSS, Clinging to the.—A great crucifix stood up at the outskirts of Noyon, France, and there at midnight the moonlight showed a woman kneeling, with her arms thrown around the tree, and her head bent to the ground; and I could not but hope that she was a true penitent, in error, but still clinging with her heart to Christ as she clung with her arms to the cross; anyway, at that midnight hour, in that lonely spot, a woman bowed by some secret grief to the earth, and seeking relief in prayer under the shadow of that lofty cross and its divine burden, was a solemn and touching sight.—GUTHRIE.

CROSS, Glory of the.—Its glory produces powerful effects wherever it shines. They who behold this glory are transformed into the same image, 2 Cor. iii: 18. An Ethiopian may look long enough to the visible sun before it changes his black color; but this does it. It melts cold and frozen hearts; it breaks stony hearts; it pierces adamants; it penetrates through thick darkness. How justly it is called marvelous light! 1 Pet. ii: 9. It gives eyes to the blind to look to itself; and not only to the blind but to the dead! It is the light of life; a powerful light. Its energy is beyond the force of thunder; and it is more mild than the dew on the tender grass. It communicates a glory to all other objects, according as they have any relation to it. It adorns the universe; it gives a luster to nature, and to Providence; it is the greatest glory of the lower world that its Creator was for a while its inhabitant. A poor landlord thinks it a lasting honor to his cottage that he has once lodged a prince or emperor; with how much more reason may our poor cottage, this earth, be proud of it, that the Lord of glory was its tenant from His birth to His death? Yea, that He rejoiced in the habitable parts of it, before it had a beginning, even from everlasting! Prov. viii: 31.—M'LAURIN.

CROSS, Glory of the.—*Gal. vi: 14.* Today men mount the ensign of the cross on their banners, blazon it on the baldric of knighthood, and lift it high on their spires above the smokestacks of their workshops, as if they would elevate it above the smoke of toil, the mist and malaria of earth, into the realm of perpetual calm and ceaseless sunshine and starshine, a silent, golden finger ever pointing to the heaven of their hopes. Notaries impress it on the seals of courts, art glorifies it upon the canvas, music sings its praises, beauty weaves it as an amulet on its alabaster bosom, and grief carves it as an epitaph of wounded love and resurrection hope upon the marble door of the tomb.

" In the cross of Christ I glory,
    Towering o'er the wrecks of time,
All the light of sacred story
    Gathers round its head sublime."
    —P. H.

CROSS, Index of the.—It is related of the celebrated scholar, Humboldt, that when he was traveling in tropical America, going chiefly by night to avoid the heat of the day, that his superstitious guides greatly reverenced the constellation of the Southern Cross, and directed their course by it. At that time this constellation reached the mid-heavens just before the break of day, so that its passage over the meridian was an indication that morning was approaching. He says frequently, when he was following after his train, and wearied by a night-long tramp, he could hear the guides shout, " Courage, comrades, the Cross begins to bend." So may the Christian soldier hear and regard this voice in the hour of his trials. In the darkness, and the weariness of life-long labor, it is enough to know that the cross bends at the earnest pleading of faith and uplifted prayer to God. You know where your strength lies, where you may burnish your weapons, where you may, indeed, stand forth renewed perpetually in the strength of grace. The cross of Christ is with us, and the power of that cross is efficacious to save to the uttermost.—DR CURRY.

CROSS, Legend of the.—A procession of Christians, singing hymns, having a cross carried at their head, come to a place called Tetramphodos, where stood a statue of Venus and a marble altar. As the cross was borne along the idol fell down of itself, and was broken in pieces.—F. II.

CROSS, Might of the.—The cross was two pieces of dead wood; and a helpless, unresisting Man was nailed to it; yet it was mightier than the world, and triumphed, and will ever triumph over it.—HARE.

CROSS, Our Only Hope in the.—On a rude cross by the side of an Italian highway is the motto *Spes unica*. The cross is the altar upon which the atonement for our sins was made.—F. II.

CROSS, Our Sins on the.—We must nail our sins to the cross of Christ, force them before the tree on which He suffered; it is such a sight as sin cannot abide. It will begin to die within a man upon the sight of Christ on the cross, for the cross of Christ accuseth sin, shames sin, and by a secret virtue feeds upon the very heart of sin. We must use sin as Christ was used when He was made sin for us; we must lift it up, and make it naked by confession of it to God; we must pierce the hands and feet, the heart of it by godly sorrow, and application of threatenings against it, and by spiritual revenge upon it.—BYFIELD.

CROSS, Power of the.—There is an Irish fable to the effect that Forannan, abbot of Waulsor, felt called to leave his native isle. He went to the sea shore with twelve companions, and not being able to procure a boat, they made a huge wooden cross, and casting it into the sea, and standing on it were wafted to the Flemish shore. Probably a raft of timbers laid crosswise had grown into a cross.—F. II.

CROSS, Power of the.—*1 Cor. i: 24.* The most imperial preacher of this century was Thomas Chalmers. During the earliest years of his ministry his preaching was mainly ethical; his Gospel was a Gospel of morality. He aimed to reform his hearers from such vices as dishonesty, profanity, falsehood, licentiousness, and cruelty. After a few years new light burst upon him, and his ministry became intensely evangelical. His testimony is very remarkable. He declared that while he was simply trying to reform men of their vices, he " never heard of any such reformation having been effected! If there were such cases, they never came to my knowledge. It was not until the free offer of forgiveness of sin through the atoning blood of Christ was urged upon men that I ever heard of any of these subordinate reformations."—*Selected.*

CROSS, Predominance of the.—Describing the artistic glories of the Church of St. Mark at Venice, Mr. Ruskin says: " Here are all the successions of crowded imagery showing the passions and the pleasures of human life symbolized together, and the mystery of its redemption; for the maze of interwoven lines and changeful pictures lead always at last to the Cross, lifted and carved in every place and upon every stone; sometimes with the serpent of eternity wrapped round it, sometimes with doves beneath its arms and sweet herbage growing forth from its feet; but conspicuous most of all on the great rood that crosses the Church before the altar, raised in bright blazonry against the shadow of the apse. It is the Cross that is first seen and always burning in the center of the temple; and every dome and hollow of its roof has the figure of Christ in the utmost height of it, raised in power, or returning in judgment.—A. P. L.

CROSS, Refuge of the.—A popular allegorical picture represents a huge cross hewn out of the rock standing upon the rugged shore of a stormy sea. A half-drowned female clings to it as her only hope, while another clutches her garments in that desperate struggle for safety. That sea is life and that cross is Christ.—F. II.

CROSS, Resting upon the.—Often does the wanderer, 'mid American forests, lay his head upon a rude log, while above it is the abyss of stars; so the weary, heavy-laden, dying Christian leans upon the rugged and narrow cross, but looks up the while to the beaming canopy of immortal life—to "those things which are above."—G. GILFILLAN.

CROSS, Soldiers of the.—A brave warrior of old time being delayed, prayed to the gods that the battle might not be ended before his arrival. The true soldier loves the warfare, despises its perils, and glories in its hardships. The Christian's Leader bore His own cross, and perished upon it. To follow His steps must be our pleasure.—F. II.

CROSS, Taking up the.—The old crusaders used to wear a cross upon their shoulders. This was their badge of service. Peter the hermit tore up his gown and distributed the pieces among the enthusiastic volunteers. It was then the fashionable and honorable thing. So to-day a profession of religion and pew in some church is the passport to respectability. The cross is the ornament of pride or adornment of beauty, with no thought of its sacred import and responsibility, "a cheap substitute for a struggle never made, and a crown never striven for."—F. II.

CROSS, The.—The most consummate wisdom made choice of the cross, of poverty, and meanness.—*Selected.*

CROSS, The Key of Paradise.—We do not sail to glory in the salt sea of our own tears but in the red sea of a Redeemer's blood. We owe the life of our souls to the death of our Savior. It was His going into the furnace which keeps us from the flames. Man lives by death; his natural life is preserved by the death of the Creature, and his spiritual life by the death of the Redeemer.—SECKE.

CROSS, The Pathos of the.—If Jesus had been an infinite hater, who had incarnated himself for a mission of mischief, and we could have caught Him and nailed Him to the cross, of course it would have been an impotent thing. We should not have extinguished hate in the infinite heart. We should, however, have made the feeble protest of our race against hatred.

But when He loves us and comes to us with a yearning heart and a wooing way, and seeks to win our love by all the sweetest advances of holy and loftiest affection, and when we, with wicked, unloving hands, do murder Him, we cannot quench His love. He sends down from the cross such indescribably sweet looks of love, as if He were saying in His heart, "Oh, I would rather have these tearing nails and piercing thorns from your dear hands than take the softest and brightest crown from the hands of any other beings."

This is the supreme glory of love. There never was anything like it in all the universe before. The angels that had worshiped Him had never seen such love. He had never so revealed Himself to them. They knew He was good. They knew that He delighted in the happiness of His children and of His creatures, but they had never seen divine love put to such trial before and rise to such radiance. Then they saw the glory of God, the glory of His power, the glory of His wisdom, the glory of His truth, and the glory of His love, shining in the face of Jesus. It streamed down all time and through all the universe. No world He ever made, no throne He ever erected, no rank of angels He ever created, so reflects His glory as the Cross.—CHARLES F. DEEMS.

CROSS, Traces of the.—Thor the thunderer, Scandinavian hero god, was always represented with a hammer in his hand. With this hammer he crushed the head of the great Midgard serpent, destroyed the giants, and restored to life the dead goats which drew his car, and consecrated the pyre of Baldur. Thor's hammer was a cross. As such it appears on old Scandinavian coins. So says Baring-Gould in his "Legend of the Cross." The sign of the cross was made by the Scandinavians, and may have been copied by the Christians from them. On the destruction of the temple of Serapium in Egypt, A. D. 389, a sign resembling the cross was found engraved upon the stones. It was interpreted to mean, "The life to come." The heathen claimed it as a symbol of their god Serapis. Sozomen, Socrates, and Rufinus relate this. Rufinus says, "The Egyptians are said to have the sign of the Lord's cross among those letters which are called sacerdotal, of which letter or figure this they say is the interpretation, 'The life to come.'" Baring-Gould says that the cross was a religious symbol to the lake-dwellers, that beneath it they laid their dead to rest, and trusted in it to guard and revive the loved ones whom they committed to the dust. Mortilett, who investigated the tombs of the lake-dwellers in Italy, concludes that the cross was a religious emblem, of frequent use, a thousand years before Christ.—F. II.

CROSS, Use of the.—God's scholars have learned to think of the cross that it is the frame-house in the which God frameth His children like to His Son Christ; the furnace that fineth God's gold; the highway to heaven; the suit and livery that God's servants are served withal; and the earnest and beginning of all consolation and glory.—BRADFORD.

CROSS, Victory of the.—This is the weapon that has won victories over hearts of every kind, in every quarter of the globe. Greenlanders, Africans, South-Sea Islanders, Hindus, Chinese, all have alike felt its power. Just as that huge iron tube, which crosses the Menai Straits, is more affected and bent by half an hour's sunshine than by all the dead weight that can be placed in it, so in like manner the hearts of savages have melted before the cross when every other argument seemed to move them no more than stones. "Brethren," said a North American Indian after his conversion, "I have been a heathen; I know how heathens think. Once a preacher came and began to explain to us that there was a God; but we told him to return to the place from whence he came. Another preacher came and told us not to lie, nor steal, nor drink; but we did not heed him. At last, another came into my hut one day, and said, 'I am come to you, in the name of the Lord of heaven and earth. He sends to let you know that He will make you happy, and deliver you from misery. For this end He became man, gave His life a ransom, shed His blood for sinners.' I could not forget his words. I told them to the other Indians, and an awakening begun among us. I say, therefore, preach the sufferings and death of Christ our Savior if you wish your words to gain entrance among the heathens." Never did the devil triumph so thoroughly as when he persuaded the Jesuit missionaries in China to keep back the story of the cross.—RYLE.

CRUCIFIXION, Application of the.—An irreligious German minister sat opposite a picture of Christ on the cross, under which was the inscription, "I did this for thee; what hast thou done for Me?" It was fastened by the Holy Spirit upon his conscience. In his thoughts by day and dreams by night the one question was, "What hast thou done for Me?" He felt the burden removed and rejoiced. He died not long after triumphing in redeeming love.—F. II.

CRUCIFIXION, Cruelty of.—Of all the devices of a cruel imagination, crucifixion is the masterpiece. Other pains are sharper for a time, but none are at once so agonizing and so long. One aggravation, however, was wanting, which, owing to the want of knowledge in painters, is still, we believe, commonly supposed to have belonged to the punishment. The weight of the body was borne by a ledge which projected from the middle of the upright beam, and not by the hands and feet, which were probably found unequal to the strain. The frailty of man's frame comes at last to be its own defence; but enough remained to preserve the pre-eminence of torture to the cross. The process of nailing was exquisite torment, and yet worse in what ensued than in the actual infliction. The spikes rankled, the wounds inflamed, the local injury produced a general fever, the fever a most intolerable thirst; but the misery of miseries to the sufferer was, while racked with agony, to be fastened in a position which did not permit him even to writhe. Every attempt to relieve the muscles, every instinctive movement of anguish, only served to drag the lacerated flesh, and wake up new and acuter pangs, and this torture, which must have been continually aggravated until advancing death began to lay it to sleep, lasted on an average two or three days.—FONTENELLE.

CRUCIFIXION, Impressing the.—A little girl asked her mother, who had a withered hand, how it became so deformed. Her mother told her that her crib took fire and in rescuing her she had burned herself. "It was for you my child, that this poor hand suffered." But for this loving interposition the child would have been burned up. Then the mother told her of the exposure of her soul to sin and death and that Christ came to her rescue. She added that when we get to heaven and behold the wounds of Christ, and ask, what are these wounds? He will reply "I was wounded for your transgressions; I was bruised for your iniquities."—F. II.

CRUCIFIXION, Pre-eminence of the.—If you have not yet found out that Christ crucified is the foundation of the whole volume, you have read your Bible hitherto to very little profit. Your religion is a heaven without a sun, an arch without a keystone, a compass without a needle, a clock without spring or weights, a lamp without oil. It will not comfort you. It will not deliver your soul from hell.—RYLE.

DEATH PROPHESIED, The.—*Jno. xii: 32-33*. I. The important event the text anticipates. Our Lord here refers to the crucifixion. The exaltation of Christ in the ministry of the Gospel comprehends: (1) The recital of the manner of the Redeemer's death. (2) The declaration of the great design of His death. (3) The proclamation of His power to save, with the terms on which He saves.

II. The grand purpose the text reveals: (1) The point to which He attracts.—"unto me." (2) The manner in which He attracts —the view of the Divine character presented by the lifting up of Christ on the Cross is eminently attractive. (3) The scale on which He attracts—"all men."—J. RAWLINSON.

FLOWERS, Never Withering.—*Heb. x: 23*. In the reign of Queen Mary of England, a man named Palmer was condemned to die. Before his death he was earnestly persuaded to recant, and among other things, a friend said to him, "Take pity on thy golden years and pleasant flowers of youth before it is too late." His beautiful reply was, "Sir, I long for those springing flowers which shall never fade away." When in the midst of the flame, he exhorted his companions to constancy, saying, "We shall not end our lives in the fire, but make a change for a better life; yea, for coals we shall receive pearls."—A. P. L.

GETHSEMANE IS AS PARADISE.— When God's children pass under the shadow of the cross of Calvary, they know that through that shadow lies their passage to the great white throne. For them Gethsemane is as paradise. God fills it with sacred presences; its solemn silence is broken by the music of tender promises, its awful darkness softened and brightened by the sunlight of Heavenly faces and the music of angel wings.—DEAN FARRAR.

GUILT, Transfer of.— For a long time before the conversion of the Rev. C. Simeon, he had been in the deepest distress, envying even the dogs that passed under his window. In Passion week he met with the expression in BISHOP WILSON ON THE LORD'S SUPPER "that the Jews knew what they did when they transferred their sins to the head of their offering." "The thought rushed into my mind," says he, "What! may I transfer all my guilt to another? Has God provided an offering for me, that I may lay my sins on His head? Then, God willing, I will not bear them one moment longer. Accordingly I sought to lay my sins upon the sacred head of Jesus, and on the Wednesday began to have a hope of mercy; on the Thursday that hope increased, and on Friday and Saturday it became more strong; and on the Sunday morning (Easter Day) I awoke early, with these words upon my heart and lips:

"'Jesus Christ is risen to-day! Hallelujah! Hallelujah!'"

From that hour he had peace.—F. II.

JESUS, Blood of.— Poets have loved the music of the mountain stream, as it tinkled down the hills amidst the stones, or murmured under leafy shades. Scripture speaks of the voice of God as the voice of many waters. So it is with the precious blood of Jesus; It has a voice which hears, speaking better things than the blood of Abel, more than restoring to Him again the lost music of His primeval creation.—FABER.

REDEMPTION, Light of.— Suppose you are standing over against some palace, and it is near midnight. Forth from that palace gate there comes a procession: the prince has come forth, attended by many of his train. He has not gone far, however, before you hear that he has dropped a beautiful gem. He is anxious about that gem, not simply for its intrinsic value, but it was the gift of one he loved. He calls for lights. You never saw the prince in your life, and in that dim darkness you have not been able to see much,

except a very imperfect outline of him. But now a lamp has come, and the prince, in his anxiety to find his gem, takes the lamp in his own hand, and there he is looking for the lost gem. Now the light which falls on the road where that gem is lying goes up into the face of the prince; and while he finds the gem, you see him as you never would have seen him but for that loss. Now it is like that with the revelation of God. When He came forth from the retirement of eternity for the salvation of souls, there was light which, while it was thrown on the poor lost sinner, that he might be found, was thrown upon the face of God, who came to seek him and to save him.—COLEY.

REDEMPTION, Ownership by.— A benevolent gentleman went South many years ago and purchased a slave. When he returned to the North, he said to the man, "You are now free, you can go where you please." "But," said the slave, "I will stay with you." Supposing he was not understood, he again said, "You are free to go wherever you please." The man replied, "I will stay with you; you bought me, and paid the price with your money, and I shall stay and serve you: I do not wish to go anywhere else." So it is with me; I have been bought at a great price, and I do not wish to serve any one but Jesus.—WM. McALLISTER.

REDEMPTION, Prefigured.— Nature is full of indications of divine attributes. Natural law, through all time, and round the world, conveys hints and germs of heaven, of hell, of vicarious suffering, and of remedial mercy. It teaches those four things. Disobey and suffer, obey and enjoy; these are its first and fundamental lessons, which are the rude seed-forms of those higher truths, purity and heaven, impurity and hell. Then throughout the world we see illustrations of the fact that one man can suffer for another. In the mother's suffering, and in the father's watch and care, the child grows out of impurity and rudeness into purity and gentleness. Vicarious suffering is a law of the household and of society. Remedial mercy is also a truth which nature hints. It is one of the eternal truths of God's nature. In the natural world, within certain bounds, a man's wrong-doing may be repaired, if he turn from his transgression and repent. There is provision for every bone to knit together again when fractured, for every muscle to heal when lacerated, and for every nerve when shattered and diseased to return again to health. Thus in nature we see prefigured the great scheme of redemption. Purity gives heaven; impurity eternal wail and wo. But there is vicarious suffering to bring men from the one to the other. If through Christ there be repentance and turning from evil, there is also health and restoration. And these things are indicated in nature—when we know how to see them there—but are authoritatively taught only in the New Testament. In nature they are as twilight, while in the gospel they glow with noonday brightness.—BEECHER.

POETRY

Atonement and Death

By Archibald Lampman

Col. i: 21, 22

Along the hills and by the sleeping stream
A warning falls, and all the glorious trees—
Vestures of gold and grand embroideries—
Stand mute as in a sad and beautiful dream,
Brooding on death and nature's vast undoing;
And spring that came an age ago and fled,
On summer's glory, long since drawn to red,
And now the fall and all the slow soft ruin,
And soon, some day, sweeps by the pillaging
    wind,
The winter's wild outrider, with harsh roar,
And leaves the meadows sacked and waste
    and thinned,
And strips the forest of its golden store,
Till the grim tyrant comes, and then they sow
The silent wreckage, not with salt, but snow.
                                        —S.

Calvary

By F. P. P.

Under the Eastern sky,
Amid a rabble's cry,
A Man went forth to die
    For me.

Thorn-crowned His blessèd head,
Blood-stained His every tread,
Cross-laden, on He sped,
    For me.

Pierced glow His hands and feet,
Three hours o'er Him beat
Fierce rays of noontide heat
    For me.

Thus wert Thou made all mine;
Lord, make me wholly Thine;
Grant grace and strength divine
    To me.

In thought and word and deed
Thy will to do. Oh, lead
My soul, e'en tho it bleed,
    To Thee!—E. T.

Calvary

By Mrs. C. F. Alexander

There is a green hill far away,
    Without a city wall,
Where the dear Lord was crucified,
    Who died to save us all.
We may not know, we cannot tell
    What pains He had to bear;
But we believe it was for us
    He hung and suffered there.

He died that we might be forgiven,
    He died to make us good,
That we might go at last to heaven,
    Saved by His precious blood.

There was no other good enough
    To pay the price of sin;
He only could unlock the gate
    Of heaven, and let us in.

Oh, dearly, dearly has He loved,
    And we must love Him too,
And trust in His redeeming blood,
    And try His works to do.
For there's a green hill far away,
    Without a city wall,
Where the dear Lord was crucified,
    Who died to save us all.

Cross and Crown

Anonymous

The cross for only a day,
    The crown forever and aye;
The one for a night that will soon be gone,
And one for eternity's glorious morn.

The cross then I'll cheerfully bear,
    Nor sorrow for loss or care;
For a moment only the pain and the strife,
But through endless ages the crown of life.

The cross till the conflict's done,
    The crown when the victory's won;
My cross never more remembered above, .
While wearing the crown of His matchless
    love.

His cross I'll never forget,
    For marks on His brow are set;
On His precious hands, His feet and side,
To tell what He bore for the church, His
    bride.

My cross I'll think of no more,
    But strive for the crown set before;
That ever through ages my song may be
Of His cross that purchased my crown for
    me.

The work of redemption done,
    His cross and His crown are one;
The crimson and gold will forever blend,
In the crown of Jesus, the sinner's friend.
                                        —C. P.

Under the Cross

By Horatius Bonar

Oppressed with noonday's scorching heat,
    To yonder cross I flee;
Beneath its shelter take my seat;
    No shade like this for me!

Beneath that cross clear waters burst,
    A fountain sparkling free;
And there I quench my desert thirst;
    No spring like this for me!

A stranger here, I pitch my tent
    Beneath this spreading tree;
Here shall my pilgrim life be spent;
    No home like this for me!

For burdened ones a resting-place
  Beside that cross I see;
Here I cast off my weariness;
  No rest like this for me!—

Agony of the Crucifixion

By C. P. Layard

Suspended on the cross! On His pale brow
Hang the cold drops of death; through ev'ry
    limb
The piercing torture rages; ev'ry nerve, ,
Stretched with excess of pain, trembles con-
    vulsed.
Now look beneath, and view the senseless
    crowd;
How they deride His sufferings, how they
    shake
Their heads contemptuous, while the bitter
    taunt,
More bitter than the gall they gave, insults
The agony of Him on whom they gaze
But hark! He speaks, and the still hovering
    breath
Wafts His last prayer to all-approving
    Heaven:
" Forgive them, for they know not what they
    do!"

Cause of the Crucifixion

By James Montgomery

I asked the heavens, " What foe to God hath
    done
  This unexampled deed?" The heavens
    exclaim;
" 'Twas man; and we in horror snatched the
    sun
  From such a spectacle of guilt and shame."
I asked the sea—the sea in fury boil'd,
  And answered with his voice of storms,
    " 'Twas man—
My waves in panic at his crime recoil'd,
  Disclosed the abyss, and from the center
    ran."
I asked the earth—the earth replied aghast,
  " 'Twas man—and such strange pangs my
    bosom rent,
That still I groan and shudder at the past."
  To man, gay, smiling, thoughtless man I
    went,
And asked him next; He turned a scornful
    eye,
  Shook his proud head, and deigned me no
    reply.

Miracles at the Crucifixion

By Reginald Heber

Thou palsied earth, with noonday night o'er-
    spread!
Thou sickening sun, so dark, so deep, so red!
Ye hovering ghosts, that throng the starless
    air,
Why shakes the earth? Why fades the light?
    Declare!

Are those His limbs, with ruthless scourges
    torn?
His brow, all bleeding with the twisted
    thorn?
His pale form, the meek, forgiving eye,
Raised from the cross in patient agony?

Mystery of the Crucifixion

By Ray Palmer

Wonder of wonders! On the cross He dies!
Man of the ages, David's mighty Son,
The Eternal Word, who spake and it was
    done,
What time, of old, He formed the earth
    and skies.

Abashed be all the wisdom of the wise!
Let the wide earth through all her king-
    doms know
The promised Lamb of God, whose blood
    should flow,—
For human guilt the grand, sole sacrifice.

No more need altar smoke, nor victim bleed:
'Tis finished!—the great mystery of love.
Ye sin-condemned, by this blood, 'tis de-
    creed.

Ye stand absolved; behold the curse removed!
O Christ! Thy deadly wounds, Thy mortal
    strife
Crush death and hell, and give immortal
    life!

The Crucifixion

By John G. Whittier

Sunlight upon Judea's hills!
  And on the waves of Galilee,
On Jordan's stream, and on the rills
  That feed the dead and sleeping sea.
Most freshly from the greenwood springs
  The light breeze on its scented wings;
And gaily quiver in the sun
The cedar tops of Lebanon!

A few more hours, a change hath come!
  The sky is dark, without a cloud!
The shouts of wrath and joy are dumb,
  And proud knees unto earth are bowed.
A change is on the hill of Death,
The helméd watchers pant for breath,
And turn with wild and maniac eyes,
From the dark scene of sacrifice!

That Sacrifice!—the death of Him,
  The High and ever Holy One!
Well may the conscious Heaven grow dim
  And blacken the beholding sun.
The wonted light hath fled away,
Night settles on the middle day,
And earthquake from his caverned bed
Is walking with a thrill of dread!

The dead are waking underneath!
  Their prison door is rent away!
And, ghastly with the seal of death,
  They wander in the eye of day;

The temple of the cherubim,
The house of God is cold and dim;
A curse is on its trembling walls,
Its mighty veil asunder falls!

Well may the cavern-depths of earth
Be shaken and her mountains nod;
Well may the sheeted dead come forth
To gaze upon a suffering God!
Well may the temple-shrine grow dim,
And shadows veil the cherubim,
When He, the chosen one of Heaven,
A sacrifice for guilt is given!

And shall the sinful heart alone
Behold unmoved the atoning hour,
When Nature trembles on her throne,
And Death resigns his iron power?
Oh, shall the heart, whose sinfulness
Gave keenness to His sore distress,
And added to His tears of blood,
Refuse its trembling gratitude!

Gethsemane

By Ella Wheeler Wilcox

In golden youth when seems the earth
A summer-land of singing mirth,
When souls are glad and hearts are light,
And not a shadow lurks in sight,
We do not know it, but there lies
Somewhere veiled under evening skies
A garden which we all must see—
The garden of Gethsemane.

With joyous steps we go our ways,
Love lends a halo to our days;
Light sorrows sail like clouds afar,
We laugh, and say how strong we are,
We hurry on; and hurrying, go
Close to the borderland of wo,
That waits for you, and waits for me—
Forever waits Gethsemane.

Down shadowy lanes, across strange streams,
Bridged over by our broken dreams;
Behind the misty capes of years,
Beyond the great salt fount of tears,
The garden lies. Strive as you may,
You cannot miss it in your way.
All paths that have been, or shall be,
Pass somewhere through Gethsemane.

All those who journey, soon or late,
Must pass within the garden's gate;
Must kneel alone in darkness there,
And battle with some fierce despair.
God pity those who cannot say,
" Not mine, but Thine; " who only pray
" Let this cup pass," and cannot see
The purpose in Gethsemane.—*F. I.

Gethsemane

By John B. Douglas

Where Olivet casts its grateful shade,
O'er Kedron's limpid stream,
Down where the olive's drooping leaves
Repel the sun's fierce beams.

The spot where my poor, trembling soul,
In love and faith draw near,
And on its consecrated soil
Oft drops the silent tear.

And when the evening star hangs low,
O'er Olivet's wooded crest,
In faith I wander through its groves,
And feel my soul is blest.

O, holy spot, in my poor heart,
Thou art alone supreme—
The mecca of my soul's desires,
The acme of my dreams!—P. J.

A Hymn for Good Friday

Anonymous

When the Christ, my Lord hung dying,
Dying on the shameful tree,
Men in all their madness mocked Him;
Yet no word at all said He.
But when at His side a sinner,
Hanging there in shame to die,
Pleading, sought His loving favor,
Swiftly came love's glad reply.

" When thou comest to Thy kingdom,
Lord," he cried, " remember me."
" Aye, to-day, with Me in glory,"
Jesus answered, " thou shalt be."
Was not this most wondrous pity,
So to bless a dying thief;
E'en amid His own deep anguish,
Thus to give a soul relief?

Still He hears the needy pleading,
Still He hears when sinners pray,
Answers every plea in mercy,
Sends no soul unblessed away.
Guilty, weary, sin-stained, laden,
Fear not now on Him to call;
Tho your sins be without number,
Freely He'll forgive them all.

Tell it in the highest heaven,
Tell it in the depths below,
Tell it to the lost and outcast,
Tell it in the haunts of wo;
To the very chief of sinners
Let the blessèd tidings go:
He who asks to be forgiven,
Shall the Savior's mercy know.—B. W.

Who is He

By Henry Hart Millman

Bound upon th' accursèd tree,
Dread and awful, who is He?
By the prayer for them that slew—
" Lord, they know not what they do! "
By the spoiled and empty grave;
By the souls He died to save;
By the conquest He hath won;
By the saints before His throne;
By the rainbow round His brow;
Son of God, 'tis Thou! 'tis Thou!

EASTER

EASTER is the festival of our Lord's resurrection, and is one of the most joyous days observed by the church. It corresponds with the Passover of the Jews, and in the early church *pascha* designated the festival of Christ's crucifixion; later, it meant both the festival of the crucifixion and the resurrection, and after the fourth century it was limited to the latter feast. The term Easter was first used when Christianity was introduced among the Saxons, and Bede traces it to *Eostre,* a Saxon goddess, whose festival was celebrated annually in the spring.

Great ecclesiastical controversies raged around the question of the actual day to be celebrated, and were finally settled only by the decree of the Council of Nicæa, 325 A. D. By that decree it was fixed on the Sunday immediately following the fourteenth day of the Paschal moon, which happens at, or on the first Sunday after, the vernal equinox. In the Roman Catholic Church elaborate rites are still observed, and only to a less extent in the Lutheran and Episcopal bodies, while throughout all Protestant churches the festival is being celebrated more and more.

The key to the observance of Easter is set in the joyous assurance of the statements and predictions of the gospels and the epistles, in the exultant strain of St. Paul, *1 Thess. iv: 13-18,* and in the glorious hymn of the Resurrection, *1 Cor. xv: 20-58.*

EASTER IN THE EARLY CHURCH

When the morning of the Festival of the Resurrection dawned, the early Christians gave signs of universal joy. The Risen One was present to the eye of faith; the resurrection of Christ served to believers as a sure pledge of their own resurrection to eternal life. This transition from death unto life was placed before their eyes, by the great number of the baptized, who, on Easter Eve, were admitted by thousands, and who, on Easter Morn, clad in their white garments, as signs of purity, united for the first time with the assemblage of believers at the Holy Supper. In order to call forth universal joy they sang Psalm cxxviii: 24: " This is the day which the Lord hath made; we will be glad and rejoice in it." It is in allusion to this circumstance that Chrysostom (A. D. 345-407), golden mouthed preacher of Constantinople, in an Easter sermon, remarked: " Death is now only a sleep. Death which before Christ's resurrection had a fearful aspect is now an object to be despised. On this day Christ freed human nature from the do-minion of human nature and brought it back to its original dignity. Let no one be dejected to-day on account of his poverty, for this is a spiritual Feast; let no man pride himself on his riches, for he cannot contribute to this feast with his wealth. Here all distinctions are taken away. There is one table for the rich and poor. For the bond and free Divine Grace knows no respect of persons."

Augustine, the great Bishop of Hippo (A. D. 395-430), says: " Since our existence is divided into two sections, the one under the temptations and sufferings of this present life, and the other that which is attained in the security and joy of eternity through Christ, so the circle of the Easter Festival is divided into two sections, the time before and after Easter. The time before Easter points us to the conflict of this present life, the time after Easter to the blessedness which we can obtain through Christ. The Lord's Passion shows us the present life of suffering. The Resurrection and glorification of the Lord shows the life which we shall receive."—C. A. W.

EASTER IN THE EARLY CHURCH

Very great indeed was the honor paid to this " Feast of the Resurrection " by the early Christians. We read that it was regarded by them as " the crown and head of all festivals," altho as a religious observance, Easter Day was not distinguished from other Sundays except by " the vastness of its congregation, and the dignity of its services."

Gregory, who was Bishop of Nyssa, of Cappadocia, in A. D. 380, draws a very vivid picture of the joyous crowds, who, by their dress and their devout attendance at Church, sought to do honor to the festival. He says, " all labor ceased, all trades were suspended; the husbandman threw down his spade and plow and put on his holiday attire, and the very tavern keepers left their gain in order to be present at the Easter service. The roads were empty of travelers, and the sea of sailors, for all tried to be home on this great day.

All Christians assembled everywhere as members of one family. The poor man dressed like the rich, and the rich wore his gayest and brightest attire whilst those who had no good clothes of their own borrowed of their neighbors. Even the little children put on their new clothes and were bright and happy." We would therefore remark that it is evident that the present custom of wearing new and bright clothes on Easter is at least fifteen centuries old!—*Selected.*

AN EASTER IN JERUSALEM

By J. L. Leeper, D.D.

Of all times to be in Jerusalem Easter is accounted the most desirable. Men anticipate an inspiration in standing by the tomb of our Lord at that ·season when His resurrection is thought to have taken place. They have a curiosity also to witness those august ceremonies, those pious frauds and orgies which, strange to say, have gathered around the tomb of the Savior during Passion week. So tho expecting to find the old town, " ram-jam full " they push onward in haste to Jerusalem for the Greek Easter. Thus did we. My friend and I had traveled extensively in eastern Europe and had " done " Egypt, but all the time we were " going up to Jerusalem at the season of the Passover." The nearer we drew the more it seemed as if the world was headed in the same direction. Those who understand the meager accommodations for such a multitude are likely to engage quarters beforehand. We had done so. Through the kindness of my friend, the Rev. Edwin S. Wallace, then United States consul at Jerusalem accommodations had been secured at Pension Hughes. Ordinarily Jerusalem is " insufferably dull." But once a year it shakes off its lethargy and bestirs itself into a new life that attracts from the four quarters of the earth. As every one knows, its atmosphere is proverbially religious. It is, in fact, as I shall know later, the habitation of cranks and fanatics. Hither queer people religiously flock. It is more even than of old the religious metropolis of the world. There are other religious centers for races, nations, and sects; but Jerusalem is the " religious hub " of the universe. All sects and creeds say, " If I forget thee, O Jerusalem—." All this is best illustrated at the Easter season, the most important ecclesiastical week in the year. Then the pilgrims are coming, coming from the North, South, East, and West. The Jews, to observe the Passover, to weep over the desolations of Zion, are coming from Persia, Arabia, Africa, and from every part of Europe.

Toward Jerusalem

The " Religious Hub " of the Universe

Christians, of every sect, Greeks, Latins, Armenians, Syrians, Copts; of every color, black, brown, and white, are coming to commemorate the events of Passion Week. Moslems from India, Arabia, Persia, Afghanistan and every part of the Turkish Empire are coming at this season, for to them the Temple Area is second in sacredness only to the Kaaba at Mecca. The peasants and swarthy Bedouins flock from the desert and hill country to filch their share of the shekels coming from afar. We would deem it a great privilege to be translated to the days of the Apostles and witness the Passover Week at Jerusalem; but here we have an assemblage in some respects on a vaster scale, for not only are the hills and valleys dotted with tents as in olden time and the narrow streets full of all manner of men in every variety of costume, but now Gentiles join the throng that were then never heard of.

The great event opens with Palm Sunday. In those to whom seeing only is believing, let us hope that the inventions and fakes of Holy Week may awaken the true spirit of devotion. It is doubtful whether any more profane orgies were ever enacted in a heathen temple than the monkish shows performed around the reputed sepulcher of our Lord. On Palm Sunday His triumphal entry is commemorated. In the days of the Crusaders it was represented in detail; a priest riding upon an ass over the traditional route impersonated Jesus, and a crowd went before and after bearing palm-branches and crying, " Hosanna." Now, however, the spirit of devotion finds vent in protracted processions around the sepulcher, in which pictures and candles, vestments and jewels, figure largely. The burning incense, the flashing lights, the gorgeous robes and bejeweled crown (of really great value) of the Greek patriarch awaken a superstitious awe in the peasant pilgrim from the steppes of Russia, the mountains of Syria, and the deserts of Arabia and Abyssinia, who has never before witnessed such a display of princely magnificence. On Thursday there is another dress

Religious Representations

parade, another unholy exhibition of feet
washing on an elevated platform in the Court
of the Holy Sepulcher, designed to illustrate
the solemn occasion in the " upper room "
when Jesus to teach the lesson of humility
deigned to wash the disciples' feet. This is
followed by another profanation representing
the agony in the Garden. Each succeeding
day has its round of ceremonies culminating
in the miracle of Holy Fire scheduled to take
place on Saturday afternoon, in the Church
of the Holy Sepulcher.

Before entering upon a detailed account of
this shameful superstition let me take the
reader hurriedly through this " holiest shrine
of the Christian world," the
The Church of the Holy Sepulcher Church of the Holy Sepulcher.
It consists of a tattered and
incongruous mass of buildings,
embracing convents, chapels,
shrines, caves, and natural elevations, now far within the walls
of the present city. Its location
was determined by St. Helena, the mother of
the first Christian emperor and the mother of
church traditions and superstitions, with the
aid of a miracle which enabled her to discover
the true cross as well as locate the Holy
Sepulcher. As to the merits of the discovery
and the correctness of the site I shall say
nothing now except that I have no faith in
either. At another time I shall be pleased to
discuss the question and give illustrations of
what I believe and what many **Protestants** believe is the real Calvary and the veritable
sepulcher of our Lord. St. Helena erected a
church upon the site of her find. Of this
basilica, which was more than once demolished
by war and devastated by fire only a few
fragments remain. At the beginning of the
twelfth century the Crusaders erected a large
church which embraced not only the site of
the sepulcher, but of all the events connected
with the last days of our Lord upon earth,
and all the Biblical events that could with any
probability be located in Jerusalem. Of this
the sites remain identified, and many traces
of the structure, but it has been several times
restored. Architecturally it has no beauty.
Two domes rise from the mass, one covering
the site of the sepulcher and the other the
Greek possessions. Its original portals, one
of which has been walled up, are approached
through an open court perhaps a hundred feet
square, in which venders are squatted ex-
posing for sale their relics, rosaries, curios,
and trinkets of all kinds in discordant and
multitudinous tongues. This court is entered through two small doorways from
streets on either side which are constantly
guarded by Moslem soldiers and through
which no Jew is permitted to enter upon the
pain of death. The Christian hates the Jew
because he crucified the Savior, the Moslem
because he killed a great prophet. As we
enter the one open portal we have a suggestion
of the mass of superstition to which we are
to be treated within. Three marble columns
flank the sides, in one of which there is a
flaw. Through this crack we are informed
the fire is to leap forth at the last judgment

which is to destroy the world. Passing
within we find a sacred medieval museum.
Here every church of pre-reformation days
has possessions and an altar. Their ceremonies and forms of worship are still punc-
tiliously observed. Greeks, Romanists, Syrians, Copts, and Armenians all have a corner
and are contending for more space, the chief
conflict being between the descendants of the
Crusaders supported by France and Spain and
the descendants of the original Greek occu-
pants supported by Russia. It is a perpetuation of the old conflict between the church
East and West. This contest for prestige in
the Holy Sepulcher and for other sacred sites
was one of the chief causes of the Crimean
war which cost one hundred and twenty-five
thousand lives and many millions of money.

The first shrine we approach after passing
the portal is the " Stone of the Anointing,"
whereon the body of Jesus was laid to be
prepared for burial. It is per-
The Stone of Anointing haps six feet by two, and elevated two feet. It is flanked by
a step convenient to kneel upon.
As tourists threatened to carry
off the original in small bits it was found
necessary to protect it by another so that the
stone exposed is not the real one. This
stone, like every similar one in the cathedral
is worn smooth as glass by the kisses of
myriads of pilgrim devotees through the
centuries. It was necessary for my friend
and dragoman and Moslem guard to ward
them off while I took a picture in which
half a dozen persons were grouped awaiting the conclusion of my nefarious deed.
Near to this and in the center of the rotunda
is the sepulcher, a marble building twenty-
six feet long and eighteen feet wide. I approached it with a feeling of awe seldom
experienced, and what wonder? For fifteen
hundred years it has been accepted by the
Christian world as the site of the burial of
our Lord. A desire for its possession gave
birth to one of the greatest movements in
history—the Crusades. For its acquisition
the blood of thousands and tens of thousands
was shed. On July 15, 1099, the victorious
Crusaders approached it with unsandaled feet
singing songs of praise. When I desired to
enter it I took my place in a line of pilgrims
which also quickly formed behind me. By
several severe thumps I received upon my
head I am reminded of the low, narrow passage way into the Sepulcher. At the other
end I found myself in a very small compart-
ment with barely room for the guardian priest
and myself to turn around in. To the right
was a marble slab, worn smooth by the kisses
of millions, which covers the rock couch on
which the body of our Lord is said to have
been laid. The place was ablaze with forty-
three lamps, the property of the contending
sects. As the air was heavy and impure and
others impatiently followed I tarried but a
moment and returned to the rotunda with a
mingled feeling of sorrow and disgust, with
not less reverence for my adorable Lord but
with a stronger antipathy for the miserable
avarice which has fastened lie upon lie on the

credulous to answer its own mercenary ends. Space will not permit me to even enumerate the shrines included within this sacred exposition building. There is the altar of Melchisedec and that on which Abraham offered Isaac. There are the spots where our Lord was mocked and scourged, with the fragment of the column to which He was bound; there is the hole in the rock in which the true cross stood and the stone which the angel rolled away from the sepulcher and on which He sat. There are a score of other sites none of which perhaps are so correct as that of the navel of earth for any point on a sphere is

Within the Temple a center. It will require further demonstration, however, to prove that from this spot the clay was taken with which to create Father Adam. Each and all of these sites are attired as a characteristic holy place, the receipt for making which would seem to be first to locate at the most convenient place, then to shut out the light, then to vitiate the air with smoking tallow lamps, then to accumulate lace and tinsel and tawdry finery and then open the show at a bishleck a head. Before these shrines dirty priests in semifemale attire are marching and countermarching, kneeling and kissing, and making the gloomy caverns and arches resound with their vain repetitions, as if they thought they would be heard for their much speaking, while at every corner a Moslem custodian stands with drawn saber to prevent the diverse sects from flying at each others' throats. With these so-called Christians as witnesses, how long will it take to convince the Moslems that Jesus was not only a great prophet but the Prince of Peace?

The last scene in this drama of idolatrous performances was an effort to reproduce the descent of the Holy Ghost in tongues of fire

The Descent of the Holy Ghost upon the great day of Pentecost. So gross is this imposture that the Latins long ago gave it up. The priests of other sects which participate, tho they may disclaim its miraculous character, cannot wash their hands of the fact that the people before whom they pose as leaders and teachers do believe that it comes from heaven, and they refrain from removing the delusion.

It was Saturday noon when we with others assembled at the United States consulate to be conducted in safety through the rabble to

The Cavas this greatest of all spectacular performances in the Holy City. Among the number was Mr. Fleming H. Revell, the wellknown publisher of Chicago, and his family. His Honor, the consul, had secured us standing room in a small alcove in an upper gallery, for eight francs, or two dollars apiece; but not even he assumed the responsibility of conducting us thither through the motley crowd. His cavas performed that duty. This is the attendant of an officer who, like the ancient Roman lictor, goes before and clears the way. He is a sort of body-guard and in appearance much more imposing than his mas-

ter. He is fitted out in splendid costume with baggy pants, and waistcoat covered with gold braid, rosettes, and shining buckles, and carries in his hand a loaded truncheon which answers the double purpose of staff and club. As he advances, he strikes it upon the ground and the clanging sound it gives forth is a warning that somebody is approaching for whom "nobodies" must clear the way. In this instance either for increased safety or out of regard for the dignity of his company, or because these fellows needed a job, His Honor provided two such majestic creatures to precede us. On and on they led us, striking their gong and raising their voice of warning, through the crowded bazaars, through the wicket gate into the outer court. Now the living mass of every nation under heaven with a Babel chatter rolled aside like billows before the giant vessel. Then into the cathedral we went, up stairways, through corridors, into "fat men's miseries" to our appointed station.

The scene that now ensued has been often described but never adequately portrayed. Nor can it be adequately depicted by my pen.

A Motley Audience In front and beneath us stretched a sea of humanity, filling the rotunda, galleries, chapels, and winding passages of the great cathedral. From the living mass yells, wild howls, and shrieks arose as from demons in the bottomless abyss. Some were cries of religious exultation as "This is the tomb of Jesus Christ," frantically repeated, but in an unknown tongue; others were execrations of a hated sect, as, "We are happy, the Jews are miserable." While giving expression to religious joy, their mouth was full of cursing and bitterness. Amid the tumult the Moslem guard was heard, "God save the Sultan." Now and then there was a *mêlée* in which whips and the butts of muskets and sabers were freely used. Sometimes the slightest provocation, as an Armenian mistakingly blowing out the lamp of a Greek, has prolonged the strife and arrested the descent of the Holy Fire. Often heads are bruised, blood is shed, and in one instance as many as three hundred were slain. In the swaying mass men and women are crushed or trampled under foot.

At length lines of soldiers form around the sepulcher between which processions, first of the Greeks, then of the Armenians and Copts, careful not to impinge, are conducted. They bear embroidered banners, in absence of images, which they dare not display in the Moslems' presence. The idea is that the fire will

The Holy Flame not descend until a certain number of rounds have been completed. The processions having concluded, that there may be no possibility of imposture, yet that the imposture may be more complete, the hundreds of lights within and without the sepulcher are extinguished. The heavenly flame is now soon expected to flash forth from the port-hole like openings on either side of the sepulcher, one for the Greeks and the other for the Armenians, to rekindle the holy candles. The strain now becomes intense, the cries unearthly, and the struggle frantic. Men in their eagerness to get nearer the apertures leap upon the shoulders of the swaying multitude and walking over their heads wedge themselves into the compact mass at a nearer point. And what wonder? They have come thousands of miles, they have anticipated it with a life-long expectancy, they have stood the night through and the day through without food and drink that they might touch their lips with a live coal off Heaven's altar. Two stand close to the opening with extended hands clenching it within. This privilege to first catch the heavenly flame they have purchased beforehand at auction at a great price. Would they pay three hundred dollars, relatively to them much more, for a spark from a lucifer match? They would plunge a dagger into the heart of a man who would be guilty of so base an insinuation. At length on schedule time the fire invisible descends; it flashes forth. Ten thousand arms are outstretched to catch the flame as it leaps from taper to taper beneath the lofty dome, up stairways, through galleries, into innermost passages and recesses, and all so quickly as to appear almost instantaneous. Runners are waiting without with hooded torches to bear the fire from Heaven to the sacred shrines at Bethlehem, Nazareth and every altar throughout the land. The officiating priest, overcome with the heavenly glory within is snatched from the sepulcher and borne away in his princely robes to repent of what he knows and what Dean Stanley says is "probably the most offensive imposture to be found in the world."

I turned away from the church of Basil and Chrysostom, thankful that my religion did not consist in an unseemly contest about an empty tomb, less precious even were its identification correct, than the tomb of St. Stephen and St. Paul, or any grave containing the ashes of the holy dead, but in the adoration of the Lord of Life, who, having risen triumphant from His sepulchral tenement, sits, the great Intercessor, on the right hand of His Majesty on high.—In.

EASTER AND THE GREEK CHURCH IN ST. PETERSBURG *

By Gideon Draper, D.D.

A wide contrast with the metropolis of the British Empire is presented by the capital of the Russian Kingdom. Four days and nights of travel sweep one over the intervening distance of 1,500 miles, across the Channel, through Holland and Germany, *via* Berlin and Königsburg, famous for the residence and life-long teachings of Kant. The home he occupied has disappeared, a monument has been erected to his memory, and the University, to which he attracted so many students, to-day numbers 900, in a city of 16,000 † inhabitants.

The approach of St. Petersburg is monotonously uninteresting, but the entrance into the city is reassuring. Many novelties await the stranger, and there is much to impress his attention favorably. St. Peters-English correspondents affect burg not to see the latter; the old-time rivalry of the two nations forbidding just appreciation. The wide streets, spacious squares, and colossal buildings evince great enterprise and vast expenditure of money in this modern capital of 860,000 ‡ population. The noble Neva, most majestic of rivers, courses through the middle of the town, with its pure and rapidly-flowing waters, source of wealth, health, and ever-new delight. On its quays are many of the finest public and private buildings of the metropolis, and drives and promenades that scarcely any other city can equal. But the centers of attraction to the new-comer are the Greek churches, foremost of which, in all the empire, is St. Isaac's, in close proximity to the temporary home of your London (?) correspondent. Its immense proportions, massive columns, golden dome surmounted by a gigantic silver cross, make it an object of beauty far and near, while the incalculable riches of its interior invite protracted study.

In Russia the Greek Church is seen in its glory. Since the year 1589 it has had its Patriarch independent of Constantinople, and in the next century the nominal tribute was abrogated and the necessity of applying, on the part of Moscow, to Constantinople for the confirmation and consecration of its ecclesiastical head. Peter the Great, who introduced Western civilization into a hitherto semi-barbaric empire, did not assail the Greek religion, but made especial effort for its enlightenment through reason and the Holy Scriptures, and to dispel ignorance and superstition from its priests and people. To this end he became patron of all the arts and sciences, invited learned men from various lands into the country, established schools and abolished persecution. He granted to all Christian

The Greek Church

---

* Written in 1886.
† The latest reports give the population of Königsburg as 161,666.
‡ The population of St. Petersburg at present is about 1,500,000. In 1897, the official report was: for the city, 1,132,677; for the suburbs, 134,346—total 1,297,023.

sects, dissenting from the Greek religion, full liberty. The Emperor suppressed the high office of Primate, lest it should be prejudicial to his own authority, and made himself in a limited sense, Sovereign Pontiff and head of the Russian Church. The Holy Synod was established, at whose head, however, is a layman, representative of the Czar, who has a negative on all its resolutions until they are presented to the Emperor. This nobleman is minister of the crown for the department of religion. The office is now filled by one who was tutor to the present ruler, Nicholas II., a son of a priest, and not distinguished for the toleration that characterized his predecessors.

The Greek Church vigilantly preserves its orthodoxy. The motto of the university in St. Petersburg is characteristically Russian: "Orthodoxy, autocracy, nationality." Orthodoxy is everywhere and always supreme. The slightest approach to heresy is resented, and proselytism continues to be prohibited. The Holy Synod exercises a sharp censorship over books and journals. The publication and circulation of tracts, formerly permissible, is now under ban.

The Greek churches and chapels in the northern capital, numbering nearly two hundred, are well attended. Multitudes of men, women, and children, of every walk in life, are continually coming and going, and with the external appearance of great devoutness and sincerity. That the many crossings and genuflections touch the real character in most cases may be questioned. Many are the instances of crime committed, either immediately after or before the most punctilious religious rites.

The Greek Church, while rejecting statues, retains pictures, mosaics, bas-reliefs, all that can be represented on a flat surface, holding that this is not a violation of the command, "Thou shalt not make unto thee any graven image."

Among the four great fasts, that of Lent comes first, and is most rigidly observed for the seven weeks between Carnival and Easter.
The Fasts As the latter approaches, the Church services multiply. Upon the preceding Thursday is the elaborate ceremony of the "Washing of feet."

Through especial favor your correspondent passed through the priest's, or private door in the great Cathedral, and even obtained a chair, amid the standing, crowding thousands. No seats are provided for the worshipers. The exercises continued three hours. St. Isaac's Cathedral ranks first in all the Kingdom. It is an immense and imposing structure, with four large porches ornamented and supported by colossal granite pillars; the great dome, covered with resplendent gold, and surmounted by a solid silver cross, seventeen feet in height. The interior is inconceivably rich in pillars, mosaics, pictures, precious stones, and gold. Lighted with myriads of tapers, it presented a weird appearance.

The music was quite incomparable. The soprano voices of thoroughly trained boys mingle with the profoundest bass to which one ever listened, and produce a magic effect. The enforced absence of instruments is unnoticed. The human voice is made to imitate the sweetest notes of softest sounds. Chanting, singing, reading prayers, with continual bodily contortions, constituted the service.
The Service There was no instruction from the Word, and no part for the gazing multitudes. They were simply idle spectators, but with many crossings and kneelings. The Church service is rapidly read by the priests in the ancient Slavonic, so that the people cannot understand. They are each provided with a taper, symbol of the Holy Spirit, and the revenue from the enormous sale of which, wellnigh defrays the ordinary expenses of the church. But upon this memorable occasion, the processions of the magnificently-robed priests and bishops, the prolonged ceremonies culminating in the "Washing of the feet" on a raised platform in the middle of the Cathedral, was of intense interest and held rapt attention to the end. As a spectacle, it was one of the finest ever witnessed by the writer. One easily sees the hold of the Church and Church Service on the ignorant, untaught masses. They are indeed sheep, with many priests, but no shepherd.

On Good Friday Christ's image lies in state and throughout Saturday, thousands kiss His hands and feet, and drop coins in the church treasury. On Easter
Easter Eve eve the climax is reached. The people are exhausted with prolonged fasting. At midnight the priests make the circuit of the church in elaborate procession, searching for the dead Christ; re-entering the church, after a two hours' service, the golden doors of the Holy of Holies are thrown open, and the metropolitan advances, holding the cross in his hands, and announces, "Christ is risen." "He is risen" is caught up by the people, and resounds amid universal kisses and embraces, the bells sending out a merry peal, the cannon firing, and all the city aflame with lights and holy joy. Then follows the blessing of the food brought for the purpose; oddly-shaped loaves of bread, towers of white cheese, red-colored eggs, sugar, honey, fruit, etc., at three o'clock A. M., and the hungry, fainting multitudes disperse for feasting, riding, and in many cases, drunkenness. And for the ensuing three or four days, the festivities and debauchery continue.

In contrast, how striking, increasingly appreciated and loved, the simple religious service in the "British and American Church," with the varied nationalities, including Russians, hungering for the Word, and at the close of the day, four penitent ones arising and declaring "Jesus, my new Master, Thee I call."

The orthodoxy of the great Eastern Church, as of some Western churches, has sore need of being set on fire from Heaven.—P. T.

THE RESURRECTION OF CHRIST A FUNDAMENTAL DOCTRINE

By Benjamin B. Warfield, D.D., LL.D.

It has been customary in the past to look upon the resurrection of Jesus as the very citadel of the Christian position. Friend and foe have been at one in so regarding it. Upon it as his Gibraltar, the Christian man has entrenched himself. It has seemed to him to be the rock on which he could securely build the house of his faith, and upon which the rain may descend and the floods come and the winds may blow without effect. Similarly it has seemed to the assailants of Christianity, that so long as this rock stood unconquered all their enginery was in vain.

It appears now that all this is a mistake. The importance of the resurrection of Christ, we are told, has been greatly exaggerated. It is not denied that from the beginning Christians have looked to it as their support and stay. It is not denied that it has been their enthusiastic conviction of its reality that has from the first enheartened them in their Christian living, and given force to their proclamation of the Gospel. Professor Harnack, for example, allows that " the firm confidence of the disciples in Jesus was rooted in the belief that He did not abide in death, but was raised by God," and that their conviction of His resurrection, because it was " the pledge of the resurrection of all believers," became " the mightiest power through which the Gospel has won humanity." But he thinks it a matter of profound indifference to us whether this conviction was sound or a delusion. " The conviction of having seen the Lord," he tells us, " was no doubt of the greatest importance for the disciples and made them evangelists; but what they saw cannot immediately help us." " To believe on the ground of appearances that others have had is a frivolity which will always revenge itself through rising doubts." It can, indeed, never be necessary " to have faith in a fact: " religious belief must not hang on history and must be independent of all facts, " which would hold good apart from that belief." Whether Christ rose from the dead cannot, therefore, be of moment to the Christian; all that is of any significance is the religious conviction that He was " not swallowed up in death, but passed through suffering and death to glory, that is, to life, power, and honor." " Faith has nothing to do with the knowledge and the form in which Jesus lives, but only with the conviction that He is the living Lord." And in the case of the resurrection of Christ this detachment from history is especially well for Christianity. For there is really no sound reason for believing that Jesus rose from the dead in the literal sense which has been attached to those words. " The mere fact that friends and adherents

of Jesus were convinced that they had seen Him . . . gives to those who are in earnest about fixing historical facts not the least ground for the assumption that Jesus did not continue in the grave." The candid historian will indeed feel bound to surrender the fact of the bodily resurrection of Christ to the assaults of recent criticism.[*]

The effect of this new attitude toward the resurrection of Christ, if it could be justified, would obviously be to turn the flank of the Christian position. Christianity has concentrated her defense at this impregnable point, and feels herself safe until it be captured. The new foeman bows politely and declares that he prefers to enter the Christian domain by some other road; the so-called Gibraltar, if it be rock at all, and not a mere stage construction of laths and brown cloth, holds no key-position and may best be simply neglected. Christianity is not built on the rock of fact in any case, he tells us; it is a castle in the air, adjusting itself readily, as it floats over the rough surface and solid earth, to all sorts of inequalities and changes of ground, and is best entered by disengaging ourselves from the soil and soaring lightly into its higher precincts. No doubt the professed purpose of this new determination of the relation of Christianity to fact is to render Christianity forever unassailable from the point of view of historical science; if it is independent of all details of history it cannot be wounded through the critical reconstruction of the historical events which accompanied its origin. But the obvious actual effect of it is to destroy altogether all that has hitherto been known as Christianity; the entire detachment of Christianity from the realm of fact simply dismisses it into the realm of unreality. Men may still call by the name of " Christianity " the possible " iridescent " dream which still remains to them, but a " Christianity " which stands out of relation to historical facts is plainly a very different thing from the old Christianity, all of whose doctrines are facts, and which was, above all things, rooted in historical occurrences. And this is particularly apparent with regard to the facts of the resurrection of Jesus. If Christianity is entirely indifferent to the reality of this fact, then " Christianity " is something wholly different from what it was conceived to be by its founders, and from what it is still believed to be by its adherents.

It is to be borne in mind that neither Professor Harnack, nor the more radical members of the school he so brilliantly represents, ventures to deny that the conviction of the reality of Christ's bodily resurrection formed

[*] A. Harnack, " History and Dogma," E-T., vol. i., pp. 85, 86; compare the later tract, " Christianity and History," p. 54.

the center of the faith of the founders of Christianity. It would certainly be difficult for any candid mind to doubt a fact so broadly spread upon the surface of the New Testament record. Our Lord Himself deliberately staked His whole claim upon His resurrection. When asked for a sign, He repeatedly pointed to this sign as His single and sufficient credential (John ii: 19; Matt. xii: 40). The earliest proclaimers of the Gospel conceived witnessing to the resurrection of their Master as their primary function (Acts i: 22; ii: 32; iv: 33; x: 41; xvii: 18). The lively hope and steadfast faith that sprang up within them they ascribed to its power (1 Peter i: 3; i: 21; iii: 21). Paul's whole gospel was the gospel of the risen Savior; to His call he ascribes his own apostleship, and to His working all the elements of the Christian faith and life. There are in particular two passages in his epistles which in an almost startling way reveal the supreme place which was then ascribed to the resurrection of Christ. In a context of very special power he declares roundly that "if Christ hath not been raised" the Apostolic preaching and the Christian faith are alike vanity, and those who have believed in Christ lie yet unrelieved of their sins (1 Cor. xv: 14-17).* His meaning is that the resurrection of Christ occupied the center of the Gospel that was preached by him and all the Apostles and that had been received by all Christians; so that if this resurrection should prove to be not a real occurrence, the preachers are convicted of being false witnesses of God, the faith founded on their preaching is proved an empty thing, and the hopes conceived on its basis are rendered void. Here Paul implicates with himself the whole Christian community, teachers and taught alike, as suspending Christianity on the resurrection of Christ as its fundamental fact. And so confident is he of universal accord on the indispensableness of this fact to the very existence of Christianity, that he uses it as his sole fulcrum for prying back the doctrine of the resurrection of believers into its proper place in the faith and hearts of his skeptical readers. "If dead men are not raised, neither hath Christ been raised," is his one argument, and he plies it as one who knows full well that none will deny the one if it be seen to involve the denial of the other. In some respects even more striking are the implications of such phraseology as one meets in a passage like Phil. iii: 10. Here the apostle is contrasting all the "gains" of the flesh with the one "gain" of the Spirit, Christ Jesus the Lord. As over against "the excellency of the knowledge of Christ Jesus his Lord," he declares that he esteems "all things," as but refuse, the heap of leavings from the feast that is swept from the table for the dogs, if only he may "gain Christ and be found in him;" "if only," he repeats, he "may know him and the power of his resurrection and the fellowship of his sufferings, becoming conformed to his death; if by any means he may attain unto the resur-

rection from the dead." The structure of the passage represents the very essence of the saving knowledge of Christ to reside in knowing "the power of his resurrection." That is to say, Paul finds the center of gravity of the Christian life no less than of the Christian faith in the fact of the resurrection of Christ.

It would seem, then, as if it would not be easy for Christians of to-day to ascribe to the resurrection of Christ a place more fundamental to Christianity than was given it by the first preachers and authoritative founders of Christianity. We are possibly more apt to fail to apprehend the variety of the aspects in which it presented itself to them as lying at the very roots of their Christian faith. It will, therefore, doubtless repay us to remind ourselves cursorily of some of the various ways in which the resurrection of our Lord evinces itself as fundamental to the Christian religion.

It is natural to think, first of all, of the place of this great fact in Christian apologetics. It is quite obvious that it is the fundamental fact of Christianity from this point of view. Opinions may conceivably differ as to whether, as a mere abstract proposition, it would have been possible to believe in Christianity as a supernaturally given religion, had Christ remained holden of the grave. But it is scarcely disputable that, in the actual circumstances, His failure to rise again would have thrown the gravest doubt on the validity of His claims. And it admits of no doubt whatever that the fact that He did rise again, being once established, supplies an irrefragable demonstration of the supernatural origin of Christianity, of the validity of Christ's claim to be the Son of God, and of the trustworthiness of His teaching as a Messenger from God to man. In the light of this stupendous miracle, all hesitation as to the supernatural accompaniments of the life that preceded it, or of the succeeding establishment of the religion to which its seal had been set,—nay, of the whole preparation for the coming of the Messenger of God who was to live and die and rise again, becomes unreasonable and absurd. The religion of Christ is stamped at once from heaven as divine, and all marks of divinity in its preparation, accompaniments, and sequence become at once congruous and natural. And as the resurrection of Christ is (despite Professor Harnack's scoffs) "the most certain fact in the history of the world," —attested as it is by evangelists and apostles, by Paul himself, and the five hundred brethren whom he summons as co-witnesses with him; by the course of events itself which otherwise would remain inexplicable, by the monument of the Christian Sabbath, persisting as its witness through all ages, by the visible power of God sealing the testimony of His servants through His efficient working in the hearts and before the eyes of many, and by the divine success and progress of the gospel and the resurrection in the first age and through all

* Compare R. M. Edgar, "The Gospel of a Risen Savior," p. 27, and the passages there adduced.

subsequent ages—so no fact can be conceived of more power to break down opposition to the strange doctrines of Christianity and to vanquish the world before its divine Lord. From the empty grave of Jesus the enemies of the cross turn away in unconcealable dismay. Those whom the force of no logic can convince, and whose hearts are steeled against the appeal of almighty love from the cross itself, quail before the irresistible power of this simple fact. Christ has risen from the dead! After two thousand years of the most determined assault upon the evidence which demonstrates it, that fact stands. And so long as it stands Christianity, too, must stand as the one supernatural religion.

But the fact of Christ's resurrection holds no more fundamental place in Christian apologetics than it does in the revelation of life and immortality which Christianity brings to a dying world. By it the veil of sense was lifted and men were permitted to experience the reality of that other world to which we are all journeying. We cannot begin to estimate the value to those first disciples who were to live in the world as part of it while they held their real citizenship in heaven—to become fellows with Christ in His sufferings and be made conformable to His death—of the visible and tangible proof which was given them by the presence of the resurrected Lord with them for forty days, of the reality of the life beyond the grave. This association with one who had died and yet lived—lived not through a return to earthly life like Lazarus, but in the power of His endless life—could not but revolutionize their consciousness, and enable them to endure as those who had actually seen the invisible. No wonder that thereafter it seemed as if death had no terrors for these men. If they had not all, like Paul, been caught up to the seventh heaven, heaven had been brought down to them and had been made to enter into their most intimate experiences. They knew that there was life on the other side of death, that the grave was but a sojourning place, that, tho their earthly dust-dwelling were dissolved, they had a building of God, a house not made with hands, eternal in the heavens. And those of us, who come later may see with their eyes, and handle with their hands, the Word of life. We can no longer speak of a bourne from which no traveler e'er returns. The middle wall of partition has been broken down and the boundary become but an invisible line by the resurrection of Christ. That He who died has been raised again and ever lives in the form of a complete humanity, is the fundamental fact in the revelation of the Christian doctrine of immortality.

Equally fundamental is the place which Christ's resurrection occupies relatively to our confidence in His claims, His teachings, and His promises. By it the seal was set to all the instructions which He gave and to all the hopes which He awakened. He Himself staked, as we have seen,—His credit on His rising again. He declared that no sign should be given that adulterous generation but the sign of Jonah, and that He would restore in three days the destroyed temple of His body. Had the sign failed all His claims would have fallen with it. And as the sign did not fail, but after three days He returned from the bowels of the earth according to His word, He has evinced His ability to perform all His words. It is He that had power to lay down His life and take it up again; who has said, "Come unto me, all ye that labor and are heavy laden, and I will give you rest;" who has promised to be with those that serve Him "alway even unto the end of the world;" who has announced to them the forgiveness of their sins. It is another instance of the challenge, "Whether is it easier to say, Thy sins be forgiven thee, or to say, Arise and walk?" That He could not be holden of death, but arose in the power of His deathless life, gives us to know that "the Son of Man hath power on earth to forgive sins." And the fulfilment of these explicit predictions do but point us to a deeper fact. The Lord of life could not succumb to death. Had Christ not risen we could not believe Him to be what He declared Himself when He "made himself equal with God." But He has risen in the confirmation of all His claims. By it alone, but by it thoroughly, is He manifested as the very Son of God who has come into the world to reconcile the world to Himself. It is the fundamental fact in the Christian's unwavering confidence in "all the words of this life."

There is even a deeper truth than this. The resurrection of Christ is fundamental to the Christian's assurance that Christ's work is complete and redemption is accomplished. Our stripes were laid upon Him and He bowed His head and died. And is that all? Is it enough to say that He "was delivered up for our trespasses?" Or must we not be able to add that "He was raised for our justification?" Else what would assure us that He was able to pay the penalty and deliver those who were bound? That He died manifests His love, and His willingness to save. That He rose again manifests His power, and His ability to save. We are not saved by a dead Christ who undertook but could not perform, and who lies there still, under the Syrian sky, another martyr of impotent love. If we are to be saved at all, it must be by one who did not merely pass to death in our behalf, but who passed through death. If the penalty was fully paid by Him, it cannot have broken Him, it must needs have broken upon Him. Had He not emerged from the tomb, all our hopes, all our salvation would be lying dead with Him unto this day. But as we see Him issue from the grave we see ourselves issue with Him in newness of life. Now we know that His shoulders were strong enough to bear the burden that was laid upon them, and that He is able to save to the uttermost all that come unto God through Him. The resurrection of Christ is thus the indispensable evidence of His completed work, His accomplished redemption. It is just because He rose again that we know that the full penalty was paid, the ransom was sufficient, the work was done, the sacrifice was accepted, and we have been bought with a price and are His purchased possession forever. Because Christ has risen, we no more judge that "if one died for all, then all died," that "the body of sin might be done away," that we know that having died with Him, "we shall also live with Him"—with Him who "being raised from the dead, dieth no more." In one word, the resurrection of Christ is fundamental to the Christian hope and to the Christian confidence. All our assurance of salvation is suspended on this fact.

It is but to concentrate our views upon one element of this hope when we note specifically that the resurrection of Christ is fundamental to our expectation of ourselves rising from the dead. That He rose from the dead manifests the salvation which He brings to man as one which works through supernatural power and produces supernatural effects. And we have not exhausted the scriptural view of the power of His resurrection until we perceive that His resurrection drags ours in its train. When He arose, men saw the great spectacle of the conquest of death, the reversal of the curse pronounced on man's sin, the presentation to God of the first fruits from the grave. When He arose, it was not merely as an individual who had burst the bonds of death; as Paul's language suggests, "the resurrection of the dead" had come (Rom. i: 4)—it was the beginnings of a great harvest. In Christ's resurrection, therefore, the Christian man sees the earnest and pledge of his own resurrection; and by it he is enheartened as he lays away the bodies of those dear to him, not sorrowing "as the rest that have no hope," but with hearts swelling with glad anticipations of the day when they shall rise to meet their Lord. "For if we believe that Jesus died and rose again, even so them also that are fallen asleep in Jesus will he bring with him." Had Christ not risen from the dead, could we nourish so great a hope—that what is sown in corruption shall be raised in incorruption, what is sown in dishonor shall be raised in glory, what is sown in weakness shall be raised in power, what is sown a body under the dominance of a

sinful self shall be raised a body wholly the servant of the Spirit of God? Is it not evident that the resurrection of Christ is fundamental to the Christian's hope that the dead in Christ "shall be raised incorruptible?"

We have touched only on some of the outstanding aspects of the bearing of the resurrection of Christ on our Christian faith and life. But enough has been said to show that we have in it a decisive proof of the divine origin of Christianity; a revolutionary revelation of the reality of immortality, a demonstration of the truth of all Christ's claims and the trustworthiness of all His promises, an assurance of the perfection of His saving work, and a pledge of our own resurrection. Are these things not fundamental to Christianity? If we can be content with a Christianity without them, we may satisfy ourselves with a "Christianity" to which it is indifferent whether Christ actually rose from the dead. A "Christianity" which can dispense with the immediately supernatural, to which the preexistence and the proper Deity of Christ are unknown, which discards the expiatory work of Christ, and which looks for no resurrection of the body—may readily enough do without the fact of the resurrection of Christ. But when it comes to that, may we not also do very well without such a "Christianity?" What has it to offer to the sin-stricken human soul? What is it to him to be assured that One lived two thousand years ago, the aroma of whose holy life shines through all the rust of the ages and impresses the observer of it with the conviction that He must have found a God of love with whom He could walk in the midst of this world of thorns? Here and now, in his own heart he finds a God of justice, where wrath is inextinguishably revealed against all unrighteousness. Enough for us that for a Christianity which will meet the needs of sinful man, a Christianity which does not offer to him merely the impression of a holy life, but provides him with salvation by a divine Redeemer, a resurrected Lord is indispensable. The fact of the resurrection of Christ is, in a word, certainly fundamental to a Christianity that saves.— H. R.

SERMONS AND OUTLINES

EASTER

By S. S. Mitchell, D.D.

This much, at least, will the mind possessing the minimum of religious faith be willing to admit, that on the subject of the resurrection and the future life, no book promises more to the student than the one which we call the Bible. Let us then, this morning, turn to it, and in it, to the fifteenth chapter of the First Epistle to the Corinthians, for a brief study of its teachings, endeavoring, so

far as may be, to read and to ponder its words as if we had never read or heard them before.

But first, two or three general thoughts. Our world has a measureless interest in the great doctrine set within the Easter Day, unto which God, in His good providence, again has brought us. When I was making one of the celebrated passes of the Alps, with a few steps out of the throng and excitement of the living tourist, I was in a little chapel, the walls of which were lined with human bones and the skeletons of the human frame. O! what a change was that. From the excitement and joy of the Alpine tourists, unto the quiet of the little room, where other human forms, their earth journeyings forever over, were moldering silently into dust. And as I sat there, the thought came into my mind, "What, and if all the skeletons of those who have wearied with their earth travel were so exposed, so massed!" Then whole houses, then whole blocks, then whole cities, then city after city, would be full of these unmoving forms. Then through alleys, then through avenues, then through great cities, then through mighty kingdoms, one might walk through one continuous museum packed with the rigid and unbreathing forms of those once quick with life and human power. And this is earth's interest in the doctrine accentuated by this Easter morning. Its crust is rich with the ashes of that which was once a human form, instinct with life, and thrilling with the hopes and fears and passions of a sentient soul. Thirty millions of human bodies, with every great revolution of the heavens, are thus added to the dust of Earth.

"All that tread
The globe are but a handful to the tribes
That slumber in its bosom. The hills
Rock-ribbed and ancient as the Sun, the vales
Stretching in pensive quietness between—
The venerable woods—rivers that move
In majesty, and the complaining brooks
That make the meadow's green; and, poured
Round all old Ocean's gray and melancholy
          waste,
Are but the solemn decorations all
Of the great tomb of man."

Ah! in his case, reason must have suicided, or fled to brutish beasts, if a man cannot think seriously and feel deeply upon the problem of this Easter morning.

And then our personal interest in this truth, how great and solemn is this. Forms have fallen from our very side into the darkness and stillness of the grave. Out of our arms which held them in the embrace of passionate love, death has torn human lives. To some of us the sun will never again shine so brightly; this life never be so full of joy and hope; our hearts never cease their ache and pain until they lose all feeling, in the numbness and torpor of their own decay. That which was most and sweetest to us—which was life's crown and every day's delight—that has grown pale, rigid, repulsive before our very eyes, and we have buried it in the cold and unfeeling earth. The form which was all beauty in our sight, which we embraced—kissed—caressed—which was the light of our life—that along a loathsome path, is finding its dark way back unto formlessness and nothingness and void. And this is the measure of our personal interest in the truth which this morning's sun illumines—

this question, "Shall I see and know the loved form again?" To the thoughtful mind, to the sore heart, language cannot frame a question, in deep, pathetic interest, comparable to this one of future recognition and future repossession. And even this is not the full measure of our interest in this great matter. The shadows darken over our own pathway. We also move toward weakness, toward decay—unto sickness, the last shivering moan, the last awful gasp—into the dark grave and corruption and nothingness. O! cover it from my sight, for I see every living form before me, laid out in the pallid mockery of death! Shut away the vision, for I behold a long row of black and hollow graves yawning for the warm and loving human hearts before me! O! hide it from my eyes, for I see foul and loathsome corruption crawling over, eating into the life and beauty of a thousand human faces.

Such, my hearers, is your interest in the doctrine framed by this Easter morning. If there is a book in this world which has anything of credible value upon the subject, then ought you thankfully and gladly to open that book this morning. If from earth or heaven, there is any voice of light or truth, any whisper of hope or consolation, then ought you, in this hour to strain your ears to catch its every syllable. And to help you here I open the Bible to the chapter which I have named, as to the most definite and authentic message which our world has ever received upon the measureless theme—the words of which as plentiful as the tears of human sorrow, and through all the ages of Earth's sin and of Earth's death, have fallen upon the closed casket and into the hollow grave.

The inspired teacher begins upon his great subject by the assertion of the resurrection of Jesus of Nazareth. "For I delivered unto you, that which I also received, how that Christ died for our sins according to the Scriptures, and that he was buried, and that he rose again the third day."

Endeavor, I pray you, my hearers, to bring before you, as clearly as possible the condition of the world unto which the Apostle spake. For forty centuries, it had been digging the human grave, and burying its human dead. For forty centuries, in one unbroken column, the race of man had been marching into the shadows. And of all the millions who had descended into the shadowed valley, not one had ever returned. No dead human form through all the centuries had risen up into a post-mortem life. There was in all Earth's area not one empty grave. No human heart believed, no human voice declared that there was such a grave—a grave robbed by the power of a victor stronger than man's great enemy, death. It was therefore a new and wonderful message which the Apostle communicated, when unto the dying race of man he lifted up his voice in the words: "One human form has risen from the dead; one grave of earth is empty; the man Christ Jesus who was dead, is alive again." Ah! these were new and strange words for earth to hear—that earth which was so full of human graves. They were the bringing in of a new hope. They formed a creed which was revolutionary—they were a revelation. Of course such a new and startling declaration demanded proof, and the Apostle proceeds to give it: " He was seen of Peter, then of the twelve; after that he was seen of above five hundred at once, of whom the greater part are yet alive. After that he was seen of James; then of all the Apostles; and last of all he was seen of me also."

Here are six separate appearances of the risen Jesus. Peter saw Him; the twelve saw Him; five hundred at one time saw Him; James saw Him, and Paul, the writer, saw Him. My hearers, if this testimony is insufficient to prove the resurrection of Jesus, then it could not be proved by any evidence addressed to the human senses. Take a parallel case in our day. Suppose that one of his late Cabinet affirmed that he had seen him, that our late martyr President * had been raised from the dead; add now to this the testimony of all the members of the Cabinet; strengthen this evidence by the affirmation of all the heads of department at Washington; add to this the eye-witness of half a thousand men; and then upon all this place the testimony of a cautious, educated and most eminent man outside altogether the circles of the preceding witnesses, and you have evidence of weight corresponding to that which the Apostle adduces. And in view of it, may I not say this, that such an accumulation of personal testimony would be sufficient to prove any event, to convince any mind.

But further consider. The disciples did not expect the resurrection of Jesus. Listen to the mournful and hopeless strain as it breaks forth from the conversation of the two disciples on their way to Emmaus. " We trusted that it had been he who should have redeemed Israel." We trusted, but our faith was a delusion. We fondly hoped, but our hopes have been blasted. All is lost: all is lost. So all the disciples thought. They all forsook Jesus, all abandoned His cause—turned from the life and mission unto which He had called them. One by one, and by the personal appearance of Jesus, had they to be convinced of Jesus' resurrection, in the face of, and against their firm conviction that He was dead. Recall how long Thomas held out.

Then again. The disciples, thus incredulous, were all convinced. Not one of them held out against the proof furnished them. From the over-sanguine Cephas to the doubting Thomas, all at length gave in, all believed. And more than this even. They staked their lives upon the truth so proven to them. One by one, each of the eleven, save it may be John, went to a martyr's death, believing, affirming, proclaiming, the fact of Jesus' resurrection. Now, men do not stake their earthly all upon a baseless fancy; they do not die for a dream.

But more than this even. Paul was outside the circle of the twelve, an educated dialectician, an adroit and able man, a prominent unbeliever in, and persecutor of, Christianity—and he, too, was convinced, and through a life of great toil and suffering went unto a violent death, joyfully, triumphantly preaching a risen Jesus. Such, my hearers, is the first word of this wonderful chapter upon the subject of the resurrection. Its declaration is, Jesus of Nazareth has arisen from the dead. And now from this fact so stated and proven its writer takes a step forward, asking this question: " How say some among you that there is no resurrection of the dead? " That is, how can you say so. How can you continue to say so, when Jesus has risen from the dead? Many had so said. The Sadducees denied the resurrection altogether. Athenian philosophy laughed at it. All the Gnostic sects of the East had regarded it as wholly undesirable. Rationalism through all the centuries has proclaimed it as incredible.

But how can you call it incredible, says the Apostle? What has taken place certainly may again occur. If a dead human form has once risen from the grave, walking before men in the body which died, then other human forms may rise from the slumber of the tomb. The resurrection which has once taken place, whatever else it may be, however wonderful, however mysterious and incomprehensible, is not incredible. It may be believed. And this, too, was a wonderful word to a world full then, as now, of " farewells to the dying and of mourning for the dead." Over all Earth's scarred and grave-ridged surface it kindled the light of this great hope: These moldering ashes may live again in human form. By the testimony of the senses Jesus is alive from the dead, and by the emptiness of Joseph's sepulcher, by Mary's risen Son, the resurrection is not incredible. Bereaved hearts may wrap themselves around with its sweet hope; human graves may be made vocal with its promise! the dying race of man come unto victory through faith.

But to advance with our study. Beyond the credibility of the resurrection, our teacher now goes, and boldly declares its certainty. In this shape, Jesus Christ as the new man, the Lord from heaven, has come into the world to destroy all man's enemies, and to lead the human race forward into a new order of being, in which death shall be swallowed up of life. This is the teaching in the Apostle's own words: " For since by man came death, by man shall also come the resurrection of the dead. For as in Adam all die, so also in Christ shall all be made alive. For he must reign, till he has put all his enemies under his feet. The last enemy that shall be abolished is death. And when all things have been subjected unto him, then shall the Son also himself be subjected unto him that did put all things under him, that God may be all in all." That is, the present age of human history is a redemptive and temporary one. Sin having disarranged the fair

* President James A. Garfield.

order of the first creation, the Son of God has undertaken the restoration, or restitution of all things. This includes the utter destruction of these enemies of the human race which through the long and weary years of Earth's sin have preyed upon the hopes and the happiness of men. Primary and foremost among these enemies—their chief indeed—is Death. And is he not an enemy? Behold the fair form of the human body; how it writhes in pain—how it burns with the fateful fever fire—how tissue once velvety in its softness turns into crisp and a foulness which runs with a thousand sores. See the human eye—love and intelligence are dying out of it! Look upon the human form—in a helplessness worse than that of infancy it cannot lift its hand. Behold the human form divine, once all strength and beauty, a joy to look upon, now helpless, now marble-cold, and now, in its corruption turning away the dearest gaze of human affection. An enemy to the human heart also, is Death. Behold father and mother clasping their dear one but all too weak to resist the violence of the dark angel. Behold the mourners as they go about the streets—their hearts are under the coffin lid. See the tears as they chase each other down the cheek of human sorrow—it is Rachel weeping for her children with eyes which this world will never see dried. O! death! death! How men hate thee! How the living fear thee! Thou art the Damoclean sword suspended over the head of human joy; thou art the worm gnawing at the root of human peace; thou art the dread enemy who upon the pale horse dost drive through happy homes and over loving hearts, evermore tearing a path of ruin and of anguish through the world of human life. Sin's ravage—sin's victory art thou—the archenemy of God the living, and of man the dying one.

And this enemy, says the Apostle, Jesus Christ shall destroy. Not at once, not quickly, as men count time. The great enemy shall die hard—shall be the last to contest the onward sweep of the great Redeemer's power. Slavery shall cease from earth, but death shall remain. Despotism shall perish from the way of the advancing King, but death shall continue. Ignorance and superstition shall flee as shadows before the rising sun, but death shall still hold his ground and swallow down his prey. Still, but not always. Forward and still forward sweeps the conquering Redeemer—God's mighty Son. Backward and still backward are pushed the ranks of the great enemy. Farther and still farther into earth's darkness reaches the light of redeeming mercy. Now the world seems to grow fair, as if in near approach to her promised deliverance. Creation's groans begin now and then to sweep upward into a strain of hope and joy—when suddenly the everlasting doors fly open wide, and with the re-appearance of the Lord from Heaven —Humanity's second head and man's Almighty Deliverer—rolling over all Earth's scarred surface, echoing in her every hollow grave and lifting itself up to highest heaven,

rises the shout "Death is swallowed up in victory—its sting plucked out by the hand which bears the prints of the nails—its victory turned into everlasting defeat and shame by Him, who, in dying, did abolish death." So does the Apostle teach that the divine Son, who has undertaken for earth and man, shall exercise His redeeming power until the last enemy shall be destroyed, and, as proof of this, He points to Jesus' risen body as the earnest of the coming victory. "Christ the first fruits, afterward them that are Christ's at his coming." The Redeemer's resurrection, the single sheaf —pattern and pledge of the glorious harvest which shall yet wave over all "God's acre."

But to proceed with our study. Beyond the assertion of the credibility of the resurrection, beyond the declaration of its certainty even, the Apostle now passes to a brief exposition of the nature of the resurrection body. He hears the voice of an objector saying, "With what body do they come? You speak of a resurrection, but where is the body to be raised? Death is the end of the human organism—its atoms dispersed, rejoin the unorganized material universe—the earth, the air, the water claiming each its share— so the human body is dissolved, is annihilated. Resurrection! What shall be raised? Where is there any body to raise? With what body do they come?" Thus the objector. And to him the Apostle thus replies: "Thou foolish one! Before your eyes continually is the spectacle of life springing up out of death. '*That which thou sowest is not quickened except it die.*'" The very condition of its new and risen life is the death of which you speak. Take any one of the seeds which with every spring, fall into the soil of earth. Its dissolution takes place. The earth acting upon the substance of the seed deorganizes it—dispersing its atoms— utterly annihilating its form. And yet notwithstanding this death, yea! in virtue of this very process of dissolution there comes forth the new and beautiful life of the waving stalk. The seed of wheat dies, but the blade of living green starts up from its ashes, waves above its tomb. The corn-kernel falls into dissolution and nothingness, but the stalk of corn lifts up the shout of victory from this grave of defeat. So of every seed. "*Except a corn of wheat fall into the ground and die, it abideth alone.*" Death is the condition of its new and higher life. So also is the resurrection of the dead. It is sown in corruption—it is raised in incorruption. Out of its death comes forth, at the word of Creator's power, the body of a new and glorious life. It is quickened because it dies.

And further the Apostle. The new life which thus springs up out of the ashes of death shall be very different from the old life. There is a natural body and there is a spiritual body, and these two are widely unlike. "That which thou sowest, thou sowest not that body which shall be, but a bare grain, it may chance of wheat, or of some other grain."

And how true this is, how common is its illustration. The farmer does not sow the living grass blade, but the tiny grass seed. He sows not the waving stalk of corn, but the bare grain—the corn-kernel. So also in the flower garden. The hyacinths of spring, the roses and the carnations of summer were not sown as such. Nay, but a tiny seed was dropped in the earth—or a bulb was planted. And what a difference between these two, the flower seed and the flower. Exquisite form, matchless coloring, sweetest odor, all the qualities of high and beautiful life array the latter. A bare seed is the former. Look into the wheat bin. There lie the bare seeds—the natural bodies—but no artist would think of sitting down before them. Now turn your eyes upon the field of living grain as the winds of summer billow its surface. What beauty—what a glory! The bare grains have risen from death in a body of living green, matchless in the splendor of a new and a higher material body. So is the resurrection of the human form. It is sown corruptible—it is raised incorruptible; it is sown in weakness—it is raised in power; a low, inferior, imperfect body is sown—one of glorious perfection rises up from this, as from a seed. There is a natural body and there is a spiritual body, and the former comes first—is the seed of the latter? As we have borne the image of the earthly, so also shall we bare the image of the heavenly. Flesh and blood, the present material organism of the human body, cannot inherit the kingdom of God. No! but we shall all be changed. This corruptible shall put on incorruption, and this mortal shall put on immortality; and so a new, a perfect, a gloriously beautiful human form shall step forth upon the plane of the endless life. And this new human body, still further says the inspired teacher, which is to spring up out of what we call death, and which is to be so superior and glorious, shall nevertheless continue the individuality and identity of the present body. "Thou sowest a bare grain, but God giveth it a body, even as it pleased Him and to every seed its own body." Thus to the dying kernel of corn is given its own body; so to the dying grain of wheat; so to all the countless seeds which with every revolving year die within the bosom of Mother Earth. Each of these comes forth with its own body. The wheat never springs up into the corn; from the ashes of the corn-kernel there never grows up the stalk of wheat. There is no power beneath the throne of the Creator which can change the calla lily into the rose. To all eternity these two have each their "own body." So of every flower seed. It comes forth evermore with its own body, that is with its own peculiar form, and odor, and color—with its own inalienable individuality of life and beauty. So untransmutable is the God-given individuality of the particular life. Upon a subject about which we know little, this much we can say surely. The identity of the human body consists not in the sameness of material particles. These are alike in all

bodies. Besides, too, they are in a constant flux. The particles which form your body to-day, have in time past been parts of many other human bodies. Yet when they come unto you, when they were laid hold of by the principle of your life, they formed you, the same body which you always have and always shall possess. So through all the changes and inter-changes of material particles in this world the one and the self-same body is continued, and so out of all the wounds, and the weakness, and deformity, and imperfection of the present body, shall be lifted up the spiritual body—gloriously unlike to that out of which it came, and yet the continuation of its individuality, the undisputed successor to its identity. Thus in this world and before our eyes, out of sickness and weakness and decay, which left but a mere skeleton of the human form, the man rises up into new health and strength, walking before human sight in the grace and beauty of a new life, and yet with the same body which lay upon the bed, wasted, deformed, repulsive. So out of the greater malformation of death, out of the emaciation, out of the disfigurement, out of the corruption which we lay in the earth, shall arise, I know not when, perhaps in the very death hour, the same form, the identical body, revivified, incorruptible, surprisingly glorious.

"Immortal form shall still divide
The unmortal soul from all beside
And I shall know Him when we meet."

Such, in brief, my Christian hearers, is the teaching of the Apostle upon the subject of the resurrection.

First: The body of Jesus rose from the dead, rendering credible the resurrection.

Secondly: The resurrection of Jesus as the Redeemer of the human race, is prophetic of, and leads surely and gloriously unto the general resurrection.

Thirdly: The future and permanent body shall be from and out of the death of the present one, and tho greatly different from it, shall yet continue and perpetuate its identity.

And now, says any one of you, "This is a hard saying—who can hear it?" Not harder I say in reply, than any other of the fundamental truths of the Christian religion; not harder than soul existence or soul immortality; not harder than the incarnation; not harder than self-existent being. In truth all these doctrines of our religion are the utterance of a revelation, and are in no wise discoverable by or demonstrable by reason. Now, if you say, speaking out of the atmosphere of rationalism which in our day pours itself through home, and school, and Church, that you cannot receive that which you are not able to understand, my reply is, then you can have no creed—for life is an insoluble mystery; and so is death, and so is the universe, and so is sin, and so is the Christ, and so is God. And to these the resurrection only adds another mystery. To reject it on rationalistic grounds is therefore as inconsistent as it is unchristian—it is in the words of

Jesus, greatly to err, since the doctrine itself is written in the Scriptures, and underwritten by the power of the Almighty God.

But I bring not to you, this morning, the resurrection as a dogma to be forced upon your mind, but as a sweet hope to be ministered unto your heart. If you say, " I cannot receive it," I have for you no word of reproach, but only a sentiment of deep regret, that you, in your little, troubled, sorrowing, dying life, cannot this morning reach unto the comfort and inspiration of the resurrection. It is my heart which at this hour more than my head speaks unto you. I feel the sorrow drops as yet undried upon my cheek, and the pain yet sharp in my heart, with every waking hour. That which was to me Earth's fairest life-blossom—that in which I saw most of the beauty of life and of the superior beauty and glory of God the life-giver—this have I seen sicken and wither and fall into the human grave. And now, this morning, standing almost within sight of the fading flower and the dissolving beauty, I listen and no voice comforts, save the voice of the risen Savior, and no hope is counted worthy of admittance by my heart and myself save the hope of the resurrection. To His voice, who has brought life and immortality to light, my bewildered mind listens gladly, tho it understands but poorly; and with the hope which He brought in through His mighty victory, with this my sore and weary heart eagerly assays to wrap itself around, if so be that it may benumb its pain, and bring a sense of warmth into its cold and cheerless habitation. And so upheld, so inspired, all the days of my appointed time shall I wait in hope, and at the last, along the returnless path, shall go in most willing quest of that which was Earth's whitest light and sweetest joy, and which, for the perfecting of the heavenly home, I believe is forever mine through Jesus Christ my Lord. And so I hope and pray it may be with all of you. For every earth hour of weakness and sorrow may the faith of Jesus bring you strength and inspiration; and at the last, through the faith of Jesus, and the resurrection, may you be able calmly and hopefully to die.—P. I.

HAS CHRIST RISEN?

By the Rev. Canon Liddon, D.D.

It is the Spirit that beareth witness — 1 John v: 6

On Easter Day we were considering St. Paul's argument that without faith in the resurrection of Jesus Christ serious Christianity is impossible; that, when the resurrection is denied apostolic doctrine, and Christian faith are alike empty of their vital force, or, as the apostle says, " are vain; " a Christ who died and never rose from death is not the Christ of the New Testament. He is not the Christ of Christendom; a Christ such as this would never have converted the world, and the Christianity, so to call it, which centers in such a Christ as this will not long even interest it. A Christ who dies, but who never has conquered death, is plainly an intellectual makeshift. He is a creation and the toy of souls who are passing, whether consciously or not, from the faith of their fathers to infidelity. If it can be shown that Christ did not really rise from His grave, Christianity sinks at once to the level of a purely human theory of life and conduct whose author altogether failed to make good His language to Himself. Certainly His religion has played too great a part in human affairs to be forgotten by history. But it would, in the event contemplated, have forfeited all right to obtrude itself any longer on the attention of mankind as God's last and greatest revelation of Himself to His rational creatures. It is natural to ask What is the evidence that Christ really did rise from the dead? And here, as St. John says in this epistle, " It is the Spirit that beareth witness." St. John, indeed, is speaking immediately of that faith in our Lord's eternal Sonship which overcomes the world; but then since the resurrection is the main proof of our Lord's divinity, since He was declared to be "the Son of God with power " as regards His higher, holy nature by the resurrection from the dead, it follows that the Spirit must also bear witness, in some sense of the word, to the resurrection.

And He does this in two ways. It is His work that the historic proofs of the resurrection which have come down to us, and which have addressed themselves directly to our natural reasoning faculties have been marshaled, recognized, preserved, transmitted in the Church of Christ. The Spirit, as we Christians believe, bears witness in the sacred pages of the New Testament to the resurrection of Jesus; but He also bears another witness, as we shall presently see in His action, not so much on the intelligence as on the will of a Christian believer.

Let us ask ourselves, first of all, what is the evidence with which we are supplied on the subject of the resurrection—what is there to be said on the subject to a person who believes—I will not say in the supernatural inspiration, but in the general trustworthiness of the writings of the first Christians. In order to know that our Lord did really rise from the dead we have to satisfy ourselves that three distinct questions may be answered. Of these the first is this: Did Jesus Christ really die upon the cross? For, if He merely fainted or swooned away, then there was no resurrection from death; then He merely recovered consciousness after an interval. The

Evangelists, each one of them, say expressly that He did die; and the wonder is, not that He died when He did after the three hours' agony on the cross, but with all His sufferings at the hands of the soldiers and of the populace before His crucifixion—with all these sufferings He should have lived so long. But suppose that what looked like death on the cross was merely a fainting fit, would He have survived the wounds in His side inflicted by the soldier's lance, through which the blood yet remaining in His heart escaped? We are expressly told that the soldiers did not break His limbs and that He was already dead, and before Pilate would allow His body to be taken down from the cross he ascertained from the centurions in the land that He was already dead.

But, suppose again, against all this evidence, that when He was taken down from the cross He was living, then He must have been suffocated by Joseph of Arimathea, and Nicodemus when they embalmed Him. They rubbed a hundred pounds weight of myrrh and aloes over the surface of His body, and then they bound bandages tightly around each of His limbs, and His head, and His body before they laid Him in the grave. The Jews carefully inspected and sealed the tomb; they had sentinels placed there; they were satisfied that the work was thoroughly done. To do them justice, the Jews have never denied the reality of our Lord's death; it is impossible to do so without a paradox. The second question is this: did the disciples take our Lord's dead body out of the sepulcher? They would not have wished to do it; why should they? What could have been their motive? Imagine yourselves, my brethren, in the position of the disciples when convinced of the reality of our Savior's death. They either believed in His approaching resurrection, or they did not. If they did believe it, they would have shrunk from disturbing His grave as an act not less unnecessary than profane; if they did not believe in it, and, instead of abandoning themselves to unreflecting grief, allowed themselves to think steadily, what must have been their estimate of their dead Master? They must now have thought of Him as of one who had deceived them, or was Himself deceived. If He was not a clever impostor who had failed, he was a sincere but feeble character, who had Himself been the victim of a religious delusion.

On either supposition, why should they arouse the anger of the Jews and incur the danger of swift and heavy punishment? What would have been gained for good and simple-minded men by persuading the Jews under those circumstances that He had risen, or that He was the Messiah, or that His anticipations had come to pass, if all the while they themselves knew that He was dead and that His body had only been shifted by themselves from one resting-place to another? If they were religious adventurers, they could not have hoped to succeed. The attempt would have been no less fruitless than absurd. The world, after all, is not converted to a new religion by sleight of hand; and in order to believe that the apostles would not have wished to remove our Lord's body from the sepulcher, it is only necessary to credit them with ordinary common sense. But had they wished they surely could not have dared it. Until Pentecost they were, by their own account, timid men. When Jesus was arrested all the disciples "forsook him and fled." St. Peter denied Him; only St. John ventured to follow Christ to Calvary, to stand near the cross. For some days after the great catastrophe the disciples did not presume to show themselves in public for fear of the Jews. When our Lord stood in the midst of the council chamber they took Him for a phantom; they were seized with terror. Were these the men to risk a desperate struggle with the guard of soldiers and to take a dead body out of its tomb at the dead of night? Even if one or two of the disciples would have ventured on such an enterprise, could they have counted on the cooperation of the others? Would not they have dreaded betrayal by some one of their companions, who might have denounced them, whether from motives of rivalry or motives of honesty to the Jewish authorities?

And, once more, had they desired and dared to remove our Lord's body from its grave, such a feat was obviously beyond their power? The tomb was guarded by soldiers; every precaution had been taken by the Jews to make it secure. The great stone at the entrance could not have been rolled away without much disturbance, even if the body could have been removed without attracting attention. The character of the guards themselves was at stake. Had they countenanced or permitted any such crime their almost inevitable detection would have been followed by severe punishment. In after years, you will remember, St. Peter was released from prison by an angel, and the sentinels were punished by death. Certainly, the guard at the sepulcher was largely bribed by the leading Jews to say that the body of Jesus had been taken away by the disciples while they slept. Whatever the eagerness of the soldiers might have been to touch the money, they would have been cautious in circulating such a report as this, and the Jews could not have ventured to treat it as practically true. When they imprisoned and scourged St. Peter and the other apostles, when they persecuted to death first St. Stephen and the other servants of Christ, they did not accuse their victims in any one instance of having stolen Christ's body from His grave and then circulating a false report of His resurrection. The charge was merely that they had preached the resurrection after having been ordered to be silent.

And a third question is the following: What is the positive testimony that goes to show that Jesus Christ did rise from the dead? There is, first of all, the witness of all the apostles. They affirmed publicly that during forty days they saw Jesus Christ alive; that they had conversed with Him; that they ate and drank with Him; that they touched

Him. They gave their lives in attestation of this fact. Their conduct after the day of Pentecost is that of men whose trustworthiness and sincerity of purpose are beyond dispute. You and I, my brethren, unless we were strengthened by Divine grace, might, too, probably, hesitate to give our lives for what we knew to be undoubted religious truth; but, at least, we should not—I will not say die—we should not, you and I, make any considerable sacrifice for the sake of impressing the world with the truth of an occurrence which we believed in our hearts to be very doubtful.

Next, there is the testimony of a large number of persons besides the apostles. Take the case of the three thousand converts of St. Peter's first sermon on the day of Pentecost. Here were three thousand people professing belief in the resurrection fifty days after the date of the occurrence. They had every means of verifying its truth or falsehood. They were on the spot; they could decide the time; they could collect and investigate the current stories; they could take them from the Jews; they could cross-question the guards; they could compare; they could analyze the conflicting opinions flitting around them; they had unrivaled opportunities of satisfying themselves as to its truth or falsehood, and at the risk of comfort, nay, of life, they publicly professed their belief in its truth. They could not be Christians without making this profession; they had no hesitation about making it.

Or, consider the case of the two hundred and fifty or more persons still living when St. Paul wrote his first Epistle to the Corinthians—persons who had seen the risen Jesus. On one single occasion during the forty days after that He was seen of about "five hundred brethren at once, of whom the greater part remain until this present, but some are fallen asleep." There is no doubt about the document containing this assertion. The most destructive of the negative schools of modern criticism ranks this first Epistle to the Corinthians among the four books of the New Testament whose genuineness and authenticity it still holds to be beyond dispute. There is no reason for questioning the accuracy of the apostle's information; and the significance of the statement in history could not be exaggerated. Five hundred persons could not be simultaneously deceived. Their testimony would be considered decisive as to any ordinary occurrence, when men wished only to ascertain this simple truth.

And the force of this flood of testimony is not really weakened by objections which did not, you will observe, directly challenge it; but which turn on accessory or subordinate points. For instance, it is said that the evangelical accounts of the resurrection itself, and of our Lord's subsequent appearance, are difficult to reconcile with each other. At first sight they are, but only on first sight. In order to reconcile them, two things are necessary; first, patience; and, secondly, determination to exclude everything from the narrative which does not lie in the texts of the

Gospels. Two-thirds of the supposed difficulties are created by the riotous imagination of the negative commentators. Left to themselves, the evangelists do not, indeed, tell us a great deal that we should really like to know, but, at least, they do not contradict each other. If they had forged the whole story, and had written with any degree of concert, they would have been at once more explicit and less careless about appearances than they are; they would have described Jesus bursting forth visibly from the grave in a blaze of splendor, terrifying His guards, welcoming His faithful followers, who would have been collected on the spot. They would have written just as the painters have painted, without any admission of ignorance, without any reserve, without permitting any suspicion of difficulties. As it is, these are just what might be expected in four narratives of the same event, written at different periods, by different authors, who had distinct sources of information at command. Each says what he has to say with blunt and simple directness, without an eye to the statement of the others, or to the possible comments of the hostile critics.

To show their agreement in detail would, of course, carry me far beyond our limit; suffice it now to say, that in describing the resurrection, as elsewhere, so here, Scripture takes no precautions against hostile judges. Scripture speaks as might a perfectly truthful child in a court of justice, conscious only of its integrity, and leaving the test, whether criticism or apology, of what it says, entirely to others. It proceeds on the strong conviction that in the end, in this, as in other matters, wisdom is justified of her true children.

It is further objected, that the resurrection was not sufficiently public. Jesus, it appears, ought to have left His grave in the sight of a crowd of lookers-on, and when risen, He ought to have hastened to show Himself to the persons least likely to believe in His resurrection—to the Jews at large, to the high priests, to Pilate, to His executioners; even, it is of late hinted, to a scientific commission of some kind, which might have first investigated, and then drawn up a report upon the subject.

Here, it is obvious, first of all, that the guards may very well have seen our Lord leave His tomb. Scripture, at least, says nothing on the point; but the guards were terrified to the verge of death from horror at the sight merely of an angel at the sepulcher; and any number of witnesses who would have been present would, in all probability, have been as frightened as the guards. Our Lord's object was not to strike terror, but to convince, to reassure, to console. It was not easy to do this when the disciples first saw Him after He had risen. But nothing would have been gained by their seeing Him leave His tomb. They knew that He had been laid in it dead; they saw Him alive before their eyes, and they put the two facts together. Nor is the old objection of Celsus, that Jesus Christ ought to have shown Himself to the

Jews and to His judges in order to rebuke their unbelief, one whit more reasonable. Had He appeared to the Jews, would they, think you, have believed Him? Would they not have denied His identity, or else argued that a devil had taken His form before their eyes, just as before they had dared to ascribe His miracles to Beelzebub?

There was no greater reason for our Lord showing Himself to the unbelievers of that day than for His showing Himself to the unbelievers of each succeeding century from then until now. He gives evidence to all of us to make faith easy and reasonable; but He does not give, except in very rare instances, such as that of St. Thomas, that particular kind of evidence which captious belief may, from time to time, demand, possibly for no other reason than because it says that such evidence will not be given. They who cried on the day of Calvary, "Let him come down from the cross and we will believe him," would not really have believed Him if He had taken them at their word. Unbelief is the product of a particular state of heart and mind; much more than that, it is the product of an absence of a particular sort of evidence. The Jews had ample opportunity of ascertaining that the resurrection was a fact if they had desired to do so; but, as it was, they were not in a mood to be convinced even by the evidence of their senses. It was with them as with the brethren of the rich man in the parable—" If they hear not Moses and the prophets, neither will they be persuaded though one rose from the dead." If the testimony of the apostles and of so many other persons was insufficient, the appearance of the risen Lord Himself would not have done more than add to the list of their rejected opportunities, and so add to their condemnation.

Far deeper than these objections is that which lies against all miracles whatever as being at variance with that conception of a rigid uniformity in the processes of nature which is one of the intellectual fashions of our time; suffice it to say that any idea of natural law which is held to make a miracle impossible is also inconsistent with intelligent belief in the existence of God. When a believer in God talks of a law of nature he can never mean more than God's uniform mode of working in a particular instance. He cannot mean anything that is independent of God, any force or impact, which, if originally coming from God, has now acquired a right to maintain itself in spite of Him, or is, at any rate, somehow out of His reach. To hold this idea of the law of nature is to hold that God is not Master of the universe—in other words, that He is not Himself. That He does work uniformly is matter of observation, and He is only what we should anticipate from that law of order which is an attribute of His eternal being. Without such general uniformity in the background of the miracle there will be nothing striking in the miracle; but if God is omnipotent, so that His eternal moral attributes alone can limit His powers of action, then it cannot be de-

nied that miracle is always possible, and if God be a moral Being who, as such, desires the interest of His moral creatures, and deems it higher than that of the inanimate and irrational beings around Him, then miracle, at least in great crises in human moral history, is to be expected.

The only real question for the serious believer in God is whether the producible evidence for an alleged miracle is sufficient. From the nature of the case it is impossible, my brethren, to give more than a scanty and imperfect outline of a great subject like the evidence of the resurrection within the compass of a sermon; but it is to be wished, in these days especially, that Christians would make themselves better acquainted with the grounds of their faith than too many of us are. Some old-fashioned but useful books as Sherlock's " TRIAL OF THE WITNESSES," in which the evidence of the resurrection is discussed conformably with the rules of the English bar, would do a great deal of good if they were better known. Undoubtedly new points have been raised since Sherlock's time, and, to a certain extent, the controversy has shifted its ground; but, in the main, his method of presenting the case is of lasting value, and it is better suited to our national [English] tastes and temper than the works of some more recent and more ambitious apologists.

Here, then, we are coming round to the point from which we started; for it is natural to ask, " Well, why, if the resurrection can be proved by evidence so generally sufficient, was it at the time, and is it still, rejected by a great many intelligent men? " The answer to this natural and legitimate question will be of practical importance to all of us. There can, I apprehend, my dear brethren, be no sort of doubt that, if an ordinary historical occurrence, such as the death of Julius Cæsar, is attested as clearly as the resurrection of our Lord—not, we will suppose, more clearly nor less—as having taken place nineteen centuries ago, all the world would believe it as a matter of course. Nay, more: if an extraordinary occurrence traversing the usual operations of God in nature were similarly tested, it would be easily believed if only it stood alone as an isolated wonder connected with no religious claims, implying no religious duties, appealing only to the bare understanding, and having no bearing, however remote, upon the will. The reason why the resurrection was not always believed upon the evidence of those who were witness to it was because to believe means for a consistent and thoughtful man to believe in and accept practically a great deal else. To believe the resurrection is to believe implicitly in the Christian faith. The divine Person of our Lord, the atoning work of our Lord, the teaching authority of our Lord, the efficacy of His perpetual intercession in heaven, and of the great means of grace He has given us on earth, depend on and are bound up with His resurrection. It is no more a speculative question whether Jesus Christ did or did not rise from the dead; it is an eminently practical question. The intellect is not more interested in it than the will; perhaps it is even less interested. If the intellect alone could have the decision of the question in its keeping, the number of unbelievers would be comparatively small. The real difficulties of belief lie, generally speaking, with the will; and nothing is more certain—I may add nothing is more alarming—than the power of the will to shape, to check, to promote, to control conviction. For the will, too, has reasoning power, so to call it, of its own; the will is, in a sense, a second reason within us. It looks ahead, does the will; it watches the proceedings of the understanding with jealous scrutiny; it watches, and, if need be, it interferes. It sees the understanding on the point of embracing a conviction; which means it knows very much more than speculative assent; which means action or suffering, that is to say, something entirely within its own province—the province of the will. It sees the conviction all but accepted; it sees the understanding stretching out its arms, as it were, to welcome the advancing truth, and it mutters to itself, "This must not be, or I shall be compromised; I shall have to do or to endure what I do not like." And such is the power of the will, the sovereign faculty in the human soul, that it can give effect to this decision. It can baulk and thwart the straightforward action of the intellect; it can give it a perverse twist; it can even set it thinking actively how best to discredit and refute the truth which but now it was on the point of accepting.

And this is what happened to the Jews of the Pentecost period. Those Jews had no prejudices against miracles; on the contrary, they expected miracles to occur from time to time. They entirely believed in the astonishing miracles in their own past history, altho many of these miracles rest upon evidence far less cogent than that which could be produced for the resurrection of Jesus Christ. Had it been for them only a speculative question, they would have believed in the resurrection, too; but, so far from being a speculative question only, it was charged with practical consequences. The will of the Jew instinctively suggested to him, "If Jesus of Nazareth rose from His grave, then a great deal will follow for which I am not prepared. Then He is the Messiah, then the present order of things will be seriously changed; new duties, new sacrifices, will be expected of me and mine. I must see if His resurrection is so very certain, if there is not some natural explanation of it to be found, if it is not due to a trick or to a hallucination; anyhow, it must not and it cannot be accepted as true. It may triumph at the bar of probable evidence. Granted; but common-sense, as I understand common-sense, it against it." This is something like what the Jew would have thought to himself, and his will would have carried the day against his understanding. And thus we may understand what it is that the Spirit does to produce faith. He does not set aside or extinguish the operations of the natural reason.

Reason, too, is a guide to truth which our God has given us; but He does change by His merciful and wonder-working touch the temper, the direction of the will; and thus He sets the reason free to do some sort of justice to the evidence before it. It is thus within us that the "Spirit beareth witness." The evidence of the resurrection is of such a character that an unspiritual man with no more than average powers to understand the value of a probable, as distinct from a mathematical argument, can at once see its strength and force. But this perception is useless unless the will be ready to do its part, or, at least, not to interfere with the verdict of the intellect. And it is the Spirit which secures this.

The evidence for the resurrection was not stronger on the day of Pentecost itself than it was on the day before; but the descent of the Spirit made all the difference—made it possible for the three thousand converts to do the evidence some sort of justice. And we can see, too, why it is that St. Paul makes so much of faith, especially faith in a living Christ, in all his great epistles. Faith is for him not merely the assent of the understanding; it is also the assent of the will. It is even less an intellectual than a moral act, and thus it is a test and criterion, not only or chiefly of the worth of a man's headpiece, but pre-eminently of the rectitude of his dispositions, of the goodness of his heart. This is one reason why it justifies. In a true act of faith the whole moral nature of man concurs in the justifying assent that is given to the revealed truth. If the understanding were alone concerned, there would be no more reason for our being justified by faith in a crucified and living Christ than for our being justified by faith in the conclusions of a problem in Euclid. It is because the will must endorse the verdict of the understanding, and so must mean obedience as well as mental assent, that "by grace ye are saved, and that not of yourselves, it is the gift of God."

At the close of Easter-week let us remember this. Pray, dear brethren, for the divine and eternal Spirit, who witnesses to the resurrection, as in the sacred books of scripture, so by His action upon hearts and wills of men. Remember there is no man can say that Jesus is the Lord but by the Holy Ghost; so no man can profess, to any purpose, faith in Christ's resurrection but by the Holy Ghost. "It is the Spirit that beareth witness" now, as nineteen centuries ago, by that influence on the will of man which leaves the intellect at liberty to do justice to the evidence before it. Pray that most blessed Spirit so to teach your hearts and wills that you may, at least, have no reason for wishing the resurrection to be untrue. Pray Him for His gracious assistance that you may recover or may strengthen the great grace of faith and have your part in the blessed promise of the apostle: "If thou shalt confess with thy mouth the Lord Jesus, and shalt believe in thy heart that God hath raised him from the dead, thou shalt be saved."—H. R.

AN UNRISEN CHRIST

By Richard S. Storrs, D.D.

And if Christ be not risen.—1 Cor. xv: 14

It is an appalling supposition: we almost stand aghast before it as presented to us by an inspired apostle. There are some suppositions which we are angry to have made when they concern even the things of present worth. If any one say to us, Suppose it turns out that all of your coins and bars of gold are nothing but brass and gilded lead; that all of your title-deeds to property are worthless; that your nearest friend, most intimate in your life, is merely a crafty impostor; that with all the appearances of health which you have there is in you a disease before which death is imminent—we do not wish such suppositions made to us, and we are offended and angry when they are; and yet they concern only the earth and our earthly experience. But this supposition of Paul goes farther and reaches higher. If Christ be not risen, what He affirms as the consequence is palpably true; then is our preaching unmeaning; then is your faith empty of power and purifying knowledge. But there are other consequences than these which he did not mention, and perhaps could not bear to particularize, on which it is meet for us to dwell.

If Christ be not risen, then death has absolute power in the world. If the cross of mankind kills, so that there can ,be no future making alive, then Christ Himself becomes the greatest witness to this fact; the wisest and most powerful and purest of men having no defense against death and no power afterward of returning into life. That is true if Christ be not risen; and every grave is sealed forever, and death is the signal of eternal sleep. Then all the prophecies which went before concerning the Messiah are superfluous, extravagant, and false. When Simon spoke to Him as the Son of God on earth, the Lord of Glory, before whom the beautiful gates were opened; when Hosea and Daniel and all the others pointed to this mighty King of Israel and King of the world —it was not an utterance inspired from on high, and full of truth and authority, it was simply the fancy of their own mistaken minds. It cannot be that all this line of prophecy was intended to terminate upon the life of a young man dying at thirty-three, hardly known at all outside of a small section of country, and whose remembrance and influence naturally closed with His death. We might as well suppose one of the ancient aqueducts, built with its mighty arches spanning the Campagna, league after league, and reaching back into the five hills, was constructed by imperial enterprise and ambition in order to bring to the city a few trickling drops of water that should close their flow after the first hour had passed.

And then there goes back a dismal doubt to us, to say the least, over all the miracles which are recorded as having been wrought by the Master—back to the divine. It is not credible that the swell of harps in the heavens, of angelic instruments, should have celebrated the coming to earth of a human being; yes, and after a little to have His life crushed out in bloody destruction by the rage of the Jews and by the Roman nails and spears. We doubt everything in the miracle if this last miracle is not maintained, "if Christ be not risen," as says the apostle. And then He is not the unique and holy Son of God. There is no other authority, no other significance, in His declaration of truth and duty, than belongs to a wise and instructed man. He is not declaring to us the thought of the Almighty, He is not giving us the revelation as He sees it, and the discovery in the way of life as it lies before His divine mind; but He is giving us theories such as other men give, out of the Christian world as well as within it; there is no authority in what He says. If He be merely the man Jesus, crushed on the cross and not rising after it, then there was not a voluntary element in His death. He was killed because He could not help it. He was killed because the spearhead of the Roman pierced the flesh and divided the heart. He was killed because those around Him determined that He should be, and He had no power of resistance, no power of rising again. And so there is in His death no voluntary element and there is no remission of sin, for that comes with the voluntary sacrifice of the Master on behalf of those who are sinners— as He said Himself, "My blood shed for many, for the remission of sins;" "My life, which I give for the life of the world." Then there is no present Lord in whom we may trust, to whom we may consecrate ourselves, on whom we may depend, praying to Him for life and succor and all that we need; and there is no living Lord in His kingdom or. the earth, and there is nothing to come except confusion and disaster, such as was before His disciples; nothing at the end of it but destruction, as there was nothing for His life on the earth, lofty and lovely as it was, except final death, from which there was no return.

There is no Gospel—it is literally true— there is no Gospel "if Christ be not risen;" no glad tidings of great joy to be proclaimed to the world; no mighty announcement of life beyond the grave; His words concerning that are merely human words and uncertain. He had no power to open to us the horizons of life out beyond the grave, closing on earth. We cannot know that anything which He said of the future is certainly true, if He did not illustrate and exemplify what He said in His own actual resurrection; otherwise His words are mere day-dreams in the air. Then the Bible is rent in every part; the prophecies, songs, gospels, acts, epistles, and revelations too, torn into strips. There is no authority for the Scripture and no truth in it; no Son of God dying by His own consent, and rising again for the glory of God and the welfare of man.

Now, these are not suppositions which are drawn out extravagantly in order to show the value of that superstition, "if Christ be not risen." These are the things which men affirm who deny the resurrection. They say frankly, "Christ was a human person, like any one else, only better in character and perhaps with a subtler intuition of truth, but He died and was buried, and that was the end; and the ancient prophecies have no authority for it; and the testimony of gospels and of the apostles in their epistles has no authority; and we deny the divine nature and supremacy of the Master on earth."

These are the results: "if Christ be not risen," then is our preaching unmeaning; then your faith is empty and vain. But also these consequences follow in this epistle before us: that death is the triumphant conqueror of the world, and there is no escape or hope of anything afterward; and that the prophecies are vain and fictitious, and miracles are legendary and fanciful and poetic. There is no unique Son of God in the world, and His death was not voluntary, and therefore not for the remission of sin any more than the death of any martyr; and what He told us of the life beyond the grave was altogether a human suggestion. He did not illustrate it in His own experience, and He is not the living Lord whom we can trust; not a living Lord to carry His kingdom in the world, and the Bible is wrong and there is no Gospel. Death is more terrible, and the world is gloomier, and the grave is more appalling, and the future more awful than if there had not shot over the earth a gleam of apparent illumination from the coming of the Christ and the rising of the Lord.

You have seen the landscape on a dull and murky day, how, with a sudden shock of light shot upon it, it seemed all illumined, and the clouds closed again, and the landscape was darker and gloomier than before by reason of the contrast with that solitary and fleeting gleam of splendor. So it is with the world. "If Christ be not risen," as the apostle presents the supposition, then is the world lonelier and darker than ever before He came.

It seems as if Paul's hand must have trembled as he wrote the word; that his voice must have trembled as he dictated it to another; and so he seems to hurry on to the sublime affirmation which stands only a few verses after, in the 20th verse, "But now is Christ risen from the dead and become the first fruits of them that slept." That dismal and dreary supposition which I made a moment ago, "if Christ be not risen," was only

a rumor against it that it might illuminate this majestic fact, "but now is Christ risen from the dead and become the first fruits of them that sleep."

Think of the consequences reversing the others which followed from the admission of that transcendent act; to him so marvelous; to him so full of glory and promise, and to us, I trust, as well. Christ is risen from the dead; then all this prophecy in the earlier time is true and has been fulfilled, and all the miracles related of Him take versimilitude, become probable beforehand, as we look back from the resurrection, sublimest of them all, in which they all come to their climax and consummation, which irradiates all that went before, walking on the sea, and breaking bread for the multitude, and turning water into wine, and opening the eyes of the blind and the ears of the deaf, and lifting the dead into life again. He could do it all; in Him was power to lift Himself into life after death and break the gates of the sepulcher. All this: and then we have this Son of God in the world, and we can listen to His words, tender as those of human friends and authoritative as those of God Himself, speaking within, and hear every gracious invitation and promise, and know that underneath it and behind it is divine wisdom and life and eternal being.

Then His death was voluntary. He arose from the dead after death; then all the world combined could not have taken His life, even to dim it in its luster, unless He consented. It was a voluntary death. He walked toward it, knowing what was coming. He took it upon Himself. It was for a sufficient purpose, that. He might make redemption for man, atonement for the sin of the world, blotting out our transgression from the book of God's remembrance. Then He is with us, and we may trust Him, and He is with His kingdom, carrying it forward, and the gates of hell shall never prevail against it. Then what He said of the other life is true. He showed it in His example and life; and we ought to obey His word, to be His disciples when the time comes, and should glory in the expectation. Then we have the old Bible back; that which has been the foundation of civilization in every land which has possessed it; that which God makes the Book for the world. We do not strike out one part or another part of the prophecy on record; we have the whole compacted together by this mighty keystone in the arch, the resurrection of the Son of God and the glorious manifestation given by Him as the divine representative and Son in the world. Then the world is beautiful; it is not a place of graves; it is a place of graves that are to be opened. It is not the city of the dead. They who are dead to human view are living unto God. It is a portal of paradise instead of a place of graves, and there is light upon it every Easter morning such as never was before on sea or shore until the Master had risen from the grave.

These are the consequences of that great affirmation of the apostle, "But now is Christ risen from the dead and become the first fruits of them that sleep." It is almost as if he said, Pardon me for the supposition, dismal and dreary, involving the world in gloom and overshadowing your hearts with fear, anxiety, and dread, "if Christ be not risen." Oh, let the thought go, for "now is Christ risen from the dead," and through Him the horizons of life are widened and the heavens are opened and the glory comes into view.

There are two thoughts which I will suggest briefly, which we may well consider in view of this; and the first, of course, is, what reason we have for gratitude to God, profound and constant, that He has given us proof of the resurrection of Christ, so ample, so full of meaning, so absolute in its power to produce conviction on any reasonable man. He might have left a mere verbal statement of it, and then the aspiring and believing spirit might have accepted it. But He has given us such testimony to it as cannot be brought to the establishment of any other historical fact in the world. It is certain that the death of the Master was complete. It was not His friends merely who saw that death, tho they saw it and were overwhelmed with sadness and grief in view of it. They heard His last words; they could almost see the spirit passing out from the closing lips. They knew He was dead. The soldiers knew it—they who had, with determined and stolid rage, carried Him to His death—and they were proficient in the signs of death. Many things they did not know. They knew the phenomena of death as well as any surgeon in the world to-day knows it, and they pronounced Him dead. And the Jews, raging against Him, knew that He was dead. They had seen it and they heard the testimony of the soldiers and the testimony of those who loved Him. They were triumphant in their knowledge that at last they had killed Him and He was out of their way forevermore, this falsely-pretending Messiah, as they held Him to be. And modern surgical science has even demonstrated the physical occasion of His death in the legend of the heart. It was death, public, not private; then there might have been a simulation. It was a death the result of a judicial process, a death inflicted by anger and by brutal power. It was not a death the result of disease; it was a death the result of determined violence, which was to be satisfied with nothing but the accomplished purpose.

Certainly He was dead; if testimony can prove anything, that was proved. And it is as certain that He was seen again in life, and seen by many. Testimony to that is as absolute. It is the testimony of His friends, who knew Him personally and could not be deceived as to His identity—friends who were not expecting the event, by which their minds, as it were, were almost overwhelmed, as if they had seen a spirit. It was the testimony of those who could not understand what they saw, but it was before their eyes. And they were incredulous to the last, like Thomas, "Except I see the hand and the

side, I will not believe." They could not believe and would not; and yet they testified that they saw Him again, and they could not be deceived in regard to it. It was not the testimony of those who saw Him for a moment in a passing glimpse, but of those who saw Him repeatedly at intervals, here, there, and elsewhere, during a period of forty days. It was the testimony given by those who were ready to seal their witness by their blood, and who did it against the rod of the Jew, against the proud malice and hate of the Roman. They testified to this fact that they had seen Him—500 of them at once; many of whom, Paul says, were living at the time when he was writing to the Corinthians, twenty-two or twenty-five years afterward. If any testimony can prove any fact, this fact of the reappearance of Christ after His completed death is established. Unless all judicial processes of inquiry into alleged facts are mere confusion and bewilderment, this fact is established certainly, upon constant evidence, by a sufficient number of unimpeachable witnesses.

You have heard the vision of heaven which came unto Stephen in the agony of his death, and that given to Paul on the way to Damascus; and the evidence of that testimony of St. Paul cannot be overstated. In blinding glory he saw the Lord and heard His voice. The persecutor became the apostle, and he who hunted Christians to the death preached the Lord to all whom he could reach.

It is an event, this of the resurrection, which is demonstrated by the effect of it on the spirit of the apostles. Take Peter, for example. Here he is before the Master has come to the cross in the early hours of that Friday morning. Frightened by circumstances, he denies three times that he knows the Man at all. His whole spirit has gone into a collapse of utter fear. The Master is taken and carried to the cross; it seems to make this appear more complete, if possible, and a permanent impression in Peter's life. On the other hand, he met the Jews and declares to them this risen Christ, preaches to them with power and earnestness which they cannot withstand. "This Jesus, whom you, with wicked hands, have crucified and slain, has God raised from the dead, whereof ye are witnesses; therefore repent, every one of you." This was the man who was frightened almost to death by the question of the servant in the house. There is some element there which you must concede, in order to account for the collapse on the one hand and the consummation on the other—the utter timidity and the absolute courage; and the only way to explain it is this fact of the resurrection of Christ: that explains everything.

Think of that early Church, with mechanics and slaves, tinkers and weavers, as a philosopher of the time said, thinking to withstand the Roman power. You might as well set an eggshell to withstand the stroke of a ball from a mighty gun. Something held them together; gave them continual inspiration; something told them that the Church was to live and be triumphant; and in the entire development of Christians afterward the same spirit went on in them. Christendom never came from an unbroken grave. It would have been buried in that grave, as Judas thought it was going to be, and as the Jews thought it was going to be, except there had been a resurrection from the dead. Then you can explain Christendom, Churches, and literatures, if Christ rose again; but otherwise they cannot be explained at all. Our whole civilization rests on the broken Cross of the Master, and it is incredible that a civilization like this, in a world advancing steadily for eighteen centuries, has been founded on a lie. You impeach the sanity of the race in that statement. No, it is founded upon a rock, the faith of the Christian. It is founded upon his own present experiences. We see Christ clear to us in our hour of extreme need, when we come to Him in prayer and rise to Him in praise; and we see Him in His kingdom, turning difficulties into instruments of advance, overcoming obstacles by means unperceived beforehand, and converting disaster itself into victory.

Yes, these are the consequences of the fact affirmed by the apostle, and blessed be God that He has not left it to a written statement; that He has built the truth of the resurrection of Christ into the history of mankind. He has made it as certain as if it were written on the arch of heaven. That is the reason for gratitude. With what joy should we welcome the coming of the day which reminds us of this stupendous fact in the history of the world—the Cross of Christ and the resurrection that followed; redemption and heaven side by side! Every Lord's day should bring its note of triumph into our life. It is not for meditation only on philosophical or theological themes; it is not for grief only tho that is appropriate as we meditate on our sin: but every Lord's day should give noble impulse to our spiritual life, lift us to higher elevations of thought and aspiration and expectation, and send us forth equipped better than before for life's struggle, conquerors of the world. That is the usefulness, privilege, and glory of the Lord's day, and every service ought to have that note of triumph in it. The grave is broken; that is the meaning and suggestion of every service of the Lord's house. Most of all, when the very anniversary comes and we are carried back to the cross and to the sepulcher from which the Master came, should this note of triumph be in our hearts or on our lips: songs of triumphant praise should sound from organ and voice. When we go home, it should be with a feeling that the world is consecrated, the sepulcher has been broken, and that life is lovelier than ever, and duty more beautiful, and death not terrible. So we should walk with an elastic step, with a light shining over our faces and in our eyes, and with music on our lips as we go to our homes; and if any one ask, Whence came this new expression? Whence came this sweeter and more victorious tone? we should be able to say to them, It is natural, for to-day I have walked with the risen Christ; to-day I have walked as conqueror of the Cross with Him who conquered it; to-day I have walked near the gates which He entered who broke the bars of the sepulcher and ascended in glory to heaven.— H. R.

CONSIDER THE LILIES OF THE FIELD

By Charles Kingsley

Matt. vi: 26, 28, 29

I. What has this text to do with Easter Day? Let us think a while. Life and death; the battle between life and death; life conquered by death; and death conquered again by life. Those were the mysteries over which the men of old time thought, often till their hearts were sad. And because our forefathers were a sad and earnest folk; because they lived in a sad and dreary climate, where winter was far longer and more bitter than it is, thank God, now: therefore all their thoughts about winter and spring were sad; and they grew to despair, at last, of life ever conquering death, or light conquering darkness. All living things would die. The very gods would die, fighting to the last against the powers of evil, till the sun should sink for ever, and the world be a heap of ashes. And then—so strangely does God's gift of hope linger in the hearts of men—they saw, beyond all that, a dim dream of a new heaven and a new earth, in which should dwell righteousness; and of a new sun, more beautiful than ours; of a woman called "Life," hid safe, while all the world around her was destroyed, fed on the morning dew, preserved to be the mother of a new and happier race of men. And so to them, heathens as they were, God whispered that Christ should some day bring life and immortality to light.

II. "So it pleased the Father," says St. Paul, "to gather together in Christ all things, whether in heaven or in earth." In Him were fulfilled, and more than fulfilled, the dim longings, the childlike dreams, of heathen poets and sages, and of our own ancestors from whom we spring. He is the Desire of all nations, for whom all were longing, tho they knew it not. And now we may see, it seems to me, what the text has to do with Easter Day. Be not anxious, says our Lord, for your life. Is not the life more than meat? There is an eternal life which depends not on earthly food, but on the will and word of God your Father; and that life in you will conquer death. Consider the lilies of the field. All the winter they are dead, unsightly roots, hidden in the earth. What can come of them? But no sooner does the sun of spring shine on their graves than they rise into sudden life and beauty as it pleases God, and every seed takes its own peculiar body. Even so is the resurrection of the dead.—DISCIPLINE AND OTHER SERMONS.

CHRIST'S RESURRECTION THE TYPE OF OURS

By Rev. F. B. Meyer

Like as Christ was raised up from the dead by the glory of the Father, even so we also should walk in newness of life.—Rom. vi: 4

The sons of Zarephath, Shunem, and Nain were brought back from the dead, as were Lazarus and Eutychus, but these did not share in the resurrection. Their bodies were not changed from corruptible to incorruptible, from mortal to immortal; they were still death's prisoners on parole. But over the risen body of Christ or His disciple, death has no power. Enoch and Elijah were "translated," "changed," like those who are alive at Christ's coming again; mortality was swallowed up of life.

Christ is the first-born of the dead; and His resurrection shows the law and method of ours. The points of resemblance we may indicate.

I. HE ROSE, AS WE SHALL, BY THE POWER OF THE HOLY SPIRIT.—In each period of His life He was dependent upon the Spirit; and the same Spirit who had nestled to His heart in His baptism hovered over the grave in Joseph's garden; and on the third day loosed the pains of death, because it was not possible He should be holden of it. The Holy Spirit forgets no body which has been made His temple. He shall "quicken our mortal bodies."

II. HIS RESURRECTION WAS UNOBTRUSIVE, like all divine work; like the unfolding of flowers. The doors of our tombs will open on noiseless hinges; the fetters will drop lightly from our hands; our bodies will rise into immortal beauty like a dream.

III. HIS RESURRECTION WAS LEISURELY.—The burial-clothes were folded and laid aside, as Christ without haste rose in majesty. God's children shall not go out by flight, for the Lord has gone before them, and His glory shall be their rereward.

IV. HIS RESURRECTION WAS IRRESISTIBLE.—When Joseph and Nicodemus left Him in the tomb, the guards tried to hold Him fast. But God said, and will say for us: "Let my people go."

V. HIS RISEN BODY WAS LIKE HIS MORTAL BODY.—As in the buried seed, the principle of vitality was unchanged. His glorious body was different from the body of His humiliation, yet it was the same. He could vanish and pass through doors, yet they knew Him the same. So those that sleep in Jesus become fairer, stronger, swifter, more apt for service, yet wake with the endeared features, familiar tones, and happy companionship.

VI. WHAT CHRIST DOES IN RENEWING OUR SOULS HE WILL YET DO IN RENEWING OUR BODIES.—This will be the top-stone in the edifice of redemption.—H. R.

CHRIST'S RESURRECTION THE PROMISE AND PROPHECY OF OUR OWN

By T. DeWitt Talmage, D.D.

But now is Christ risen from the dead, and become the first fruits of them that slept.—1 Cor. xv: 20

On this glorious morn, amid these flowers, I give you an Easter greeting. This morning Russians meeting Russians greet each other with, "Christ is risen!" and the reply, "Christ is risen, indeed!" In Ireland, and parts of England, the superstitious belief is still held that the sun dances on Easter morn. We forgive the superstition in the thought that the material world is in sympathy with grace.

I find in the text a prophecy of our own resurrection. Before I finish I hope to pass through every cemetery and drop a flower of hope on the tombs of all who have died in Christ. Rejoicing in Christ's resurrection we rejoice in the resurrection of all the good.

The greatest of all conquerors is not Alexander, or Cæsar, or Napoleon, but death. His throne is in the sepulcher. But his scepter shall be broken, for the dead in Christ shall arise.

There are mysteries around this resurrection of the body which I can't explain. Who can unravel the mysteries of nature? Who can explain how this vast variety of flowers have come from seeds which look so nearly alike? Tell me how God can turn the chariot of His omnipotence on a rose leaf? Mystery meets us at every turn.

Objects one: The body may be scattered— an arm in Africa, a leg in Europe, the rest of the body here. How will it be gathered on the resurrection morn?

Another objects: The body changes every seven years. It is perishing continually. The blood-vessels are canals along which the breadstuff is conveyed to the wasted and hungry parts of our bodies. Says another: A man dies; plants take up parts of the body; animals eat the plants, and other men eat the animals. Now, to which body will belong these particles of matter?

Are these all the questions you can ask? If not, ask on. I do not pretend to answer them. I fall back on these words, " All that are in their graves shall come forth."

There are some things, however, we do know about the resurrected body.

1. It will be a glorious body. The body, as we now see it, is but a skeleton to what it would have been were it not marred by sin.

2. It will be an immortal body.

3. A powerful body—unconquerable for evermore—never tired.

May God fill you to-day with glorious anticipations! Oh, blessed hope!—H. R.

RESURRECTION THOUGHTS AND OUTLINES

Personal Questions.—1. *How is our resurrection possible? 1 Cor. xv: 35.* " With what body do they come? "

One of Faraday's workmen by accident dropped a valuable silver cup into a strong acid bath, in which it was presently dissolved. Faraday cast in another acid which precipitated the silver, tho in a shapeless mass, but in a few days a silversmith had refashioned it and made it more beautiful than before. God's chemistry is as perfect as Faraday's.— REV. GEORGE F. PENTECOST.

2. *How can we make the resurrection our own? Rom. vi: 4.* " Like as Christ was raised from the dead by the glory of the Father, even so we also should walk in newness of life."

(*a*) *In heaven.* Many of our dear ones are there; some starred names in every family record. Toward them we look. " One family we dwell in him."

(*b*) *In our children.* Froebel's motto, carved on his tomb, is: " Let us live for our children." Make your investment in them, and five years will show you the return of manhood and womanhood for childhood.

(*c*) *By personal reformation.* The Christian's privilege is to forget the things that are behind and reach toward those that are before.

Naaman's flesh came again " as the flesh of a little child." You may have renewal by grace.

The Uplifting Power of the Resurrection.—" *If ye then be risen with Christ, seek those things which are above." Col. iii: 1.*

(*a*) Christ is ascended to heaven, and draws our thoughts and hopes heavenward.

(*b*) In Christ's death for sin we died to sin.

(*c*) Our true life now is unseen and religious.

(*d*) The future will reveal Christ and true Christians.

Conclusion. Give then to death (*mortify*) the things that should be dead, and rise with the risen Lord into the higher life.

New Life for the Twentieth Century.— *Rom. vi: 4.* " Newness of life." In these early days of the new twentieth century, we ask how we can enter into the new life.

I. The new time offers great opportunities.

(*a*) It offers cooperation with great movements now in progress.

(*b*) In Christ it offers a strong drawing heavenward.

II. We need to seize the opportunities.

(*a*) The heathen Greek said: " Know the opportunity."

(*b*) Christ said: " If thou hadst known, even in this thy day! "

(*c*) The Holy Spirit says: " To-day, if ye will hear his voice! "

Conclusion. Believe in the great movements of the time, and in the part God has given you in them.

The Resurrection of a Church.—*Like as Christ was raised up from the dead by the glory of the Father, even so we also should walk in newness of life.—Rom. vi: 4.*

The collective words of the Apostle show that he thought of the resurrection of the church.

I. *This is a fact accomplished:*

(*a*) In heaven. This has been attained by many members of this Church. Count up the starred names on your roll, and look up at the stars. Among them God has set some whom you have not recorded.

In Chinese ancestor-worship there is an element of beauty and truth.

" One family we dwell in Him:
One Church, above, beneath."

(*b*) In our children. The Church might adopt Froebel's motto: " Let us live for our children." " Children's Day " will soon show the Easter promise fulfilled. The startling prominence of children shows our knowledge of their quick succession to us. In work for them " He that soweth and he that reapeth may rejoice together."

II. *It is our duty to discern and Christianize these facts.*

(*a*) Discern Christ in them all.

(b) Have Christian faith in good movements.

(c) Take them to heart with patience and Christian resolution.

Christ's Resurrection Proves the Reality of the Supernatural.—*If Christ be not raised your faith is vain.—1 Cor. xv: 17.*

Whether the supernatural be a reality, was a vital question to Paul, and is to us. It is fundamental to all religion, and to all right and joyful thought.

I. *What proof of the supernatural may we expect?*

(a) Not proof that compels belief. Such demonstration belongs to mathematical, but not to vital, truths, which move our hearts.

(b) Not proof equally convincing to all. Men will believe more or less readily according to their ideas of (1) God, or (2) sin.

(c) We may expect reasonable evidence, adequate to satisfy (1) keen reason, or (2) plain candor.

II. *What evidence of the resurrection do we find?*

(a) Concurrent writings by six independent witnesses.

(b) Writings which were first given out challenging living witnesses and a skeptical age.

(c) Accordant behavior in the church:

(1) The courage of their convictions.

(2) The practise of corroborative ordinances.

These proofs are definite and reasonable beyond any comparison with Indian myths, Islam, Mormonism, etc. The supernatural is proved.

III. *The resurrection of Christ accords with the feelings of good and wise men:*

(a) As to death.

(b) As to the new spiritual life.

Conclusion.—(1) Religion rests on a basis of fact, not on our moods. (2) Religion contains an element of success and triumph. On Easter it was thought meet always to pray standing erect. (3) Religion centers in Christ.

Death Swallowed Up in Victory.—*Death is swallowed up in victory.—1 Cor. xv: 54.*

There are two evils in death: the personal fear of it, and unconsoled bereavement. Experience of both these is world-wide, and we need deliverance from both. He who is free from heartbreak at the death of others is apt to blench when he himself looks death in the face; and the brave soul who is not afraid to die trembles and agonizes at the death of those he loves.

God, therefore, early began to speak to men about this, and we find the accumulated wisdom of such in Job's friends, and Balaam, and sometimes the higher strains of Isaiah's poetry and Paul's lofty prose.

Paul makes the following points:

I. *Death makes no break in normal Christian progress.*

See 1 Cor. xv: 46-50.

" There is no Death! What seems so is
    transition.
This life of mortal breath
Is but a suburb of the life elysian,
    Whose portals we call Death."
                                        LONGFELLOW.

II. *The change is necessary to progress.*

Home is not destroyed by sending children away to school. The painfulness is in our faulty condition. See 1 Cor. xv: 50-54.

III. *The meaning of the change appears when we see Christ.*

What we need is a renewal of character. This comes in the new birth, and the new birth is the apprehension of Christ.

Conclusion.—Are you in the true line of progress? Is this your hope for your children? Is it your own hope?—H. R.

SCIENCE AND THE RESURRECTION

By a Physician

*But some man will say, How are the dead raised up? and with what body do they come?
Thou fool, that which thou sowest is not quickened, except it die.—1 Cor. xv: 35, 36*

The chapter from which these words are taken is full of sound reasoning, based upon scientific facts. St. Paul seems to comprehend clearly the doubts and fears possessed by his hearers respecting the possibility of the resurrection of the dead. Therefore, in order to set their minds at rest and give them faith, he reasons with them, plainly, clearly, and simply, taking as an illustration the well-known process of germination, that is, the process by which the embryo seed leaves its state of torpidity and becomes developed into a living plant. The seed is, to all intents and purposes, dead; but it is not so, for if placed in the ground, and warmth and air being supplied in due proportion, the seed which before appeared to be dead is gradually changed into a living plant. It is well known that the seeds of plants retain their vitality for many years if carefully stored away and kept from those influences essential to their growth. Dudley, a noted specialist on the subject, mentions a case in which young plants were raised from seeds found in an ancient urn with some coins of the Emperor Hadrian. Another writer gives an instance of seeds capable of germination which were discovered in a Roman tomb supposed to be fifteen or sixteen centuries old.

Now, we know that when all things answerable for germination are supplied, the seed, by absorption of moisture, is softened and swollen. It then undergoes certain chemical changes. The changes consist partly in the converting of the starch into sugar, and are accompanied by the evolution and production of heat as the fluid matters are absorbed by the embryo plant. The seed continues to increase in size until it bursts through the softened outer covering and arises an independent living plant; and yet this independent plant is not composed of a single atom that can be recognized as the substance of the seed. There has been a gradual but marvelous change; nothing has been destroyed, but all has been changed.

Priestly, by his discovery of the gas called oxygen, has taught us that there can be no destruction, and likewise no creation, that disappearance really means change, and not annihilation. We cannot create, neither can we destroy anything; therefore the total sum of energy in the world to-day is the same as it was in the beginning—no more, no less, only changed, but still here in essential, tho not in the same form. St. Paul when he uttered these words about the seed, using them as an argument and testimony in favor of the resurrection, must have known something about the indestructibility of matter, altho his knowledge may not have been so definite and perfect as ours is at the present time.

St. Paul, in choosing the subject of the seed, does so in order to enlarge the boundaries of our faith in the resurrection of the dead; and science, if we understand it aright, does much to assist us in confirming that faith. Therefore the more carefully and minutely we examine the facts which science has taught us and compare those facts with the Bible truths, the more shall we have cause to believe in the immortality of the soul. Science and religion work hand in hand. The more complete the one the more firmly shall we believe in the other, and shall exclaim in adoration and wonder, as the Psalmist of old, " O Lord, how manifold are thy works, in wisdom hast thou made them all, the earth is full of thy riches." The faith St. Paul wishes to instill into the minds of his hearers is the heavenly faith, a faith which rests neither on the Church councils nor authority of any kind here, but on the words of God himself, who distinctly states in these words that He is the resurrection and the life: " he that believeth on me, tho he were dead, yet shall he live."—*Selected*. P. M.

IMMORTALITY

By Phillips Brooks, D.D.

1 Cor. xv: 41

This is part of St. Paul's great argument for immortality. The reasoning is quite clear. He speaks of the splendor of heavenly things. He has been claiming man's resurrection on the strength of Christ's resurrection. Christ has risen and entered into His glory; man because he too has a human nature like Christ's, must rise.

I. St. Paul bases the argument for immortality on the richness and splendor of this mortal life. Because this world is so great and beautiful, therefore there must be another greater and still more beautiful. St. Paul makes heaven not a compensation, but a development. His doctrine seems to teach that immortality is not a truth to be distinctly striven for as an end, but a truth which will hold itself around the man who deeply realizes the meaning of life, the man who realizes living, how identity and variety blend and unite to make the richness and solemnity of living. To quicken identity with variety, to steady variety with identity, is to make a man always keep himself and yet always feel the power of new conditions around him.

II. Consider the consequences of this truth of identity and variety. (1) It will produce self-respect. If you can only know two things—first, that you are a different creature from any that the world has ever seen since Adam, and, secondly, that you are a branch of the tree of life from which sprang Isaiah and St. John—there must come self-respect from both these truths when they are really wrought and kneaded into the substance of the human nature. "There is one glory of the sun, and another glory of the moon, and another glory of the stars." There is the ground of self-respect. (2) Then see how inevitably respect for others is bound up in such self-respect as this. The absorbing character of great enthusiasm is a matter of the commonest observation. He who cares very earnestly for anything is apt to care very little for other things, and to be indignant that other people do not care as much as he does for the thing he cares for. But surely it must be possible for men to be profoundly devoted to their own work and yet profoundly thankful for the work which other men are doing, work which they cannot do, and whose details and methods it is not in their nature to understand! " All things are yours, and ye are Christ's, and Christ is God's." That every thing should reach its best, that every man should do his best in his own place, in his own line, that every star should shine brightly in its own sphere, comes to be the wish and prayer and purpose of my life. (3) To Paul this truth was a proof of immortality. We want the life of earth now, the life of heaven by and by, and all clear with its own glory, and our humanity capable of them both, capable of sharp timely duty here and now, capable also of the supernal, transcendental splendor of the invisible world when the time shall come; the glory of the star first, the glory of the sun at last.—S. B., vol. ix., p. 378.

A RESURRECTION STUDY

He that descended is the same also that ascended up far above all heavens, that he might fill all things.—Eph. iv: 10

I read sculptured on the grave of Shakespeare the quaint inscription:

"Good friend, for Jesus' sake forbear
To dig the dust encloséd here.
Blest be the man that spares these stones,
And curst be he that moves my bones."

The dust and the bones the grave there holds are all the world now has of what was Shakespeare. That which he has done remains indeed a truest treasure, a mighty, pervasive, victorious force and influence. But to that which he has done, nothing he is now doing can be added. Shakespeare's self went yonder, long ago, into the eternities. Of Shakespeare's self the world is bereaved.

When the great Napoleon was resplendent in Berlin, a conqueror, he went to the Church in Potsdam, a little distant from Berlin, where Frederick the Great is buried. At the solemn hour of midnight, if I remember rightly, he descended to the vault beneath the Church, bade that the coffin of the mighty Prussian king and warrior be opened; amid the flickering light of torches, he gazed long and earnestly upon the shriveled dust the coffin held, and bore away as trophy the mighty warrior's sword. But it was not the great Frederick whom Napoleon saw; it was but the dust of him. No glimpse of Frederick's self could any mortal man get vision of.

But in how marked contrast to the stern truth about all others, stands out the truth concerning Jesus Christ our Lord.

He is dead. The grimmest death captured Him on the cross. He is buried. The tomb is sealed. Will it be with Him as with all others? The disciples fear so. The Scribes and Pharisees hope so, believe so. But then follows—glorious Resurrection and Ascension.

He is *different* from all others. Notice the *difference*.

All others pass into Death and *disappear*. Christ *reappears*.

All others pass into Death and *leave the world*. Christ *comes back to the world*.

All others leaving the world in Death, as far as we know, *have nothing more to do with it*.

Christ out of death comes back to the world to tell it that tho He ascends to the Father, He *will be still in the world a power and a presence*.

First. Who thus arose from the dead and ascended? Our Scripture replies the Same. He descends into birth in my human nature, into temptation, weariness, suffering, death. And now the nadir-point is reached. The descent begins to change into ascent—resurrection, ascension. And He is the *Same* still. He does not slough off my nature. He does not cease brotherhood with me. He who rises and ascends is—the Same.

Second. To what purpose did this Christ who is the Same ascend? Heb. vi: 24; 1 John ii: 1. For Intercession and Advocacy.

Third. For what further purpose did this Christ who is the Same arise from the dead and ascend? That He might dispense the Holy Spirit, who is the omnipresent Christ, for presence with me and help for me.

"No fable old, nor mystic lore,
  Nor dream of bards and seers,
No dead fact stranded on the shore
  Of the oblivious years;—

"But warm, sweet, tender, even yet
  A present help is He;
And faith has still its Olivet
  And love its Galilee.

"The healing of His seamless dress
  Is by our beds of pain;
We touch Him in life's throng and press,
  And we are whole again."—H. R.

THE RISEN LIFE

By the Rt. Rev. F. D. Huntington, D.D.

If ye then be risen with Christ, seek those things which are above, where Christ sitteth on the right hand of God.—Col. iii: 1

I. There are two kinds of death: the failure of the vital force, which we dread of all things; and the cessation of that disordered, diseased condition of the soul which makes our life all wrong, and sometimes ruins it. This may be called the death of death; and from it we rise into a new and worthy life.

II. This risen life we may have here and now, as multitudes do, making their course true, pure, noble, more glorious; keeping their senses chaste and clean, their affections sweet, their conscience healthy. The breath of this new life is prayer. It is a present heaven which all who are Christ's may have.

III. Its practical attainment is in seeking "those things which are above." We seek things "above" what is low, mean, impure, false, cruel, profane.

IV. To attain this, establishes the Kingdom of God, the better social state, as a present fact.—H. R.

SUGGESTIVE THOUGHTS AND ILLUSTRATIONS

ANESTHETIC, Death an.—*1 Cor. xv: 55.* I have sometimes thought that, as far as a divine act can be illustrated by one that is human, the wondrous transformation of death into a ministry of life is foreshadowed by the surgeon's inventive skill, in superinducing the semblance of death by an anesthetic when a critical operation is to be performed. The flesh is laid open by an incision of the knife, but not a nerve quivers, and the patient revives, unconscious of pain. The drugs used for this purpose are of such a deadly character that in some instances a breath too much would prove fatal, and they are handled with the utmost caution and dread under ordinary circumstances; but, under the surgeon's skill, they are made to perform this helpful ministry.

So God takes this dreaded thing we call death, and makes of it an anesthetic (for does not Paul speak of the death of the believer as a sleep?), and, under its soothing ministry, the change is wrought in the child of God which fits him for immortality. I have heard patients, after the severest operations, assert, with all the assurance of conscious satisfaction: "I felt no pain!" And so the Christian cries triumphantly: "O death, where is thy sting?"—C. G.

CHRIST, Resurrection of. — *Biblical types and Illustrations. Isaac* received back from the dead. Gen. xxi: 10-14; Heb. xi: 19, "he received him in a figure" (or for a type). *Joseph* raised from the prison to the throne, Gen. xxxix: 20; xli: 39-45. *Jonah* restored, after three days and three nights in the whale's belly, Matt. xii: 40. *Eliakim* signifies the resurrection of the Lord, Isa. xxii: 20; see ver. 21-24. *The ark* resting after the flood on Mount Ararat, on the seventeenth day of the seventh month; the very day Christ rose, as some think, Gen. viii: 4.—JUKES ON OFFERINGS. *Aaron's rod that budded,*—life springing out of death. "Just as Aaron was declared to be the man of God's choice in the matter of the priesthood, by the signs of resurrection life in his rod, which budded while all the other rods remained dead; so is Jesus declared to be the chosen one of God—His great high priest, the antitype of Aaron, by the resurrection from the dead; or, as it might have been rendered, "from among the dead ones."— A. L. NEWTON. The *first-fruits* offered as a pledge of the harvest, the morrow after the passover Sabbath, Lev. xxiii: 9-14. See 1 Cor. xv: 20, "Christ the first-fruits." *The first-born,* having the pre-eminence—the beginning of strength and highest in rank; see Col. i: 18, Christ "the first-born from the dead;" Rev. i: 6, "The first-begotten of the dead." *The living bird* let loose at the cleansing of the leper, Lev. xiv: 53. *The scapegoat* probably, Lev. xvi. *The corn of* wheat—first dying, then rising into life, John xii: 24. *The temple destroyed* and raised, John ii: 19. The TIME of Christ's resurrection is variously counted. *The first day,* the early morning, Luke xxiv: 1. As we now count the days, the resurrection of Christ was, as it were, a new starting-point of time. *The third day* from his death, according to the Hebrew mode of reckoning. "It is *ten times* expressly said that our Lord rose, or was to rise again, on the third day."—BOWES.

CHRIST, Risen with.—Seek the things above. That is the first thing. It is your privilege, your possibility and your duty to reach the highest, holiest, and happiest life that divine grace can impart to you. Just what happened to the disciples when they sought and obtained the "power from on high," may in no small measure be your experience if you will seek a fresh baptism of the Holy Spirit and make a fresh and full surrender of yourself to Christ. That will be a re-conversion. What a different man Peter is in the Book of the Acts of the Apostles from the crude, inconstant Peter in the Book of John! No more vain boastings and cowardly lies now! Peter on the Day of Pentecost is as superior to Peter in Pilate's courtyard, as a stalwart man is to a puny, stumbling child. He had risen with Christ and into Christ. He had been baptized into a clearer illumination, and lifted into a close, vital, and victorious union with his Lord. It was a prodigious push that carried the sleeper in Gethsemane and the coward in Pilate's yard up to the heroic thunderer whose sermon converted three thousand souls.

Something similar to this in kind—tho not in degree—has happened to thousands of God's people. They have awakened to their low condition. Instead of quenching the Holy Spirit they have come to Jesus on their knees in honest confession, and have sought a new baptism. They have begun to clear out the sins that have monopolized most of the house room in their hearts. They have sought a re-conversion, a fresh quickening from on high. New light has burst in, new strength has been imparted, new joy has been kindled. They have flung off the grave-clothes and "put on Christ." Now they can sing with Charles Wesley:

Thou, O Christ, art all I want—
More than all in Thee I find.
—T. L. CUYLER.

EAR-MONTH, The.—The Jewish year began with Abib, the ear-month, when the early corn was in the ear, in point of time and meaning nearly equal to our April, the opening month, and in the order of nature the first month of the year. Life starts anew with Abib, with April. The sun ascending from the east, the Easter sun, has then conquered the frozen soil and gently compelled its countless germs to reveal themselves. *Surrexit* is then everywhere the word. Thus, from Joseph's new tomb He has come forth whose mission it is to give life to the world. The Church, that is, life in its highest and most enduring form, is coeval with the first Easter. *Resurrexit!*—C. G.

EASTER.—The word itself reveals its origin and meaning. It is an Eastern word and means something from the East. The sun has returned from his northern resort and shines again from the east, bringing warmth and revival in his rays, "The winter is past, the rain is over and gone, the flowers appear on earth, and the time of the singing birds is come." Who has done this? Easter has done it. But who is Easter? Why, Easter is the beautiful goddess who has wiled Sol or Jupiter from his northern home to come away with her. Easter is the fair goddess of spring, whom our pagan Saxon forefathers were wont to worship before they ever heard of Jesus. And this is whence she came.—C. G.

EASTER.—We see in Easter not merely a memorial of a long-gone past, but a witness to the truth that the grave is always empty; that the living are never to be sought among the dead, and that a divine presence ever walks the earth, the companion now as then of those whose eager questioning needs answer, and whose earnest but perhaps almost despairing hope needs inspiration which only He can give. . . . Death is the separation of spirit and body. Science can define neither life nor death. We only know that this spirit withdraws and leaves the dwelling untenanted; the musician stops playing, locks his instrument and goes away; the king abdicates his sovereignty over his earthly domain and departs and presently the kingdom with no king on the throne, dissolves; the organ, with no organist to play upon it, falls in pieces; the tent, abandoned by its tenants, drops in hopeless ruin on the ground. But this affords no slightest reason for thinking that the king is dead, the organist is extinguished, the tenant has ceased to be.—LYMAN ABBOTT.

EASTER, Glorious.—One real, thoroughly authenticated resurrection lightens all the darkness of the world. Men had been going down into death by the million and no one coming back. The mighty chasm of the grave had devoured the nations and races for thousands of years, but no one had given a look or waved a hand to tell the effects on the soul. The most horrible fancies and fears filled the mind as it was being forced step by step and hastening breath by breath toward the bottomless grave. But there was no hope or light, or reprieve and men went shuddering or shrieking into the dread unknown.

But when the ideal man went into the grave and came back at will unchanged, a crushing burden was lifted off every heart. Moses, Martha, and their people believed in a resurrection, but it had no definiteness. Jesus came out of the bonds of death because it was not possible that He should be held of it.

In Him we study the effects of death. *(a)* He was the same in purposes, loves, and devotion to ends previously dear to Him. He went right on with the same work, rallying and reviving His disciples and showing how His previous work was to be carried on by them. Hence we should say that death had no effect whatever on mind and affection more than a night's sleep. *(b)* Death had no effect on the body. It was the same on the resurrection morning as at life's evening. It had no power to prevent its possible and speedy glorification. Resurrection power must be vastly greater than the power of death. This last cannot even destroy. It only takes away the sustaining power of the spirit and leaves natural processes to work in their own way. Death is the highest power of nature, but it is nothing to the power of life. Transfiguration was only a natural flourishing of the forces of life. Ascension and glorification were only the natural fruit of such blossoming.

It is not surprising that some of the best poetry that has sprung out of jubilant human hearts has had the Easter for its theme.—BISHOP WARREN.

EASTER, The Coming.—Easter always falls on the Sunday after the full moon, next after March 21st. The idea in fixing it by this standard, was that Easter might always occur at the Spring full moon, at which time the first Easter, or our Lord's Resurrection, took place. Easter is the great festival of the Church, and well it may be since the triumphant words: "HE IS RISEN," were the seal and climax, and crown, of Christ's whole incarnation and work as Redeemer.—S. J. M.

EGGS, The Origin of Easter.—There fell from heaven one day, long, long ago, an egg of immense size; it rested on the Euphrates, where doves descended and hatched it, when out from it arose in splendid beauty Easter, or Venus; and that explains why eggs are a favorite food during the festival of this lovely deity. When the early Christians came to our Saxon lands, conquering for Christ, they preserved this feast, but changed its application. "We will maintain your celebration," they said, "but it shall henceforth mean the resurrection of Christ." And that explains why it is that this joyous Christian festival bears an old heathen name. Similarly with the egg; it was retained, and since from its shelly sepulcher there issued a new and winged thing of life and beauty; it was easily made to fit in finely with the Christian faith in the resurrection of the dead.—C. G.

GRAVE, The Three Days in the.—In the Jewish reckoning of days every part of a day is counted. The body of Jesus was laid in Joseph's rock-hewn tomb in the suburban garden near Golgotha on Friday night, and remained in it all Saturday and Saturday night—three days therefore. On the morning of the third day He rose from the grave. This was the first glad Easter, and it teaches us that as Jesus rose from the grave with His body, so shall we rise with our body. There are in Rome some very old burying places called the catacombs, and on the walls there are many epitaphs to Christians buried there, some very beautiful. One of these epitaphs is this: *Tentianus vivit*—that is, "Tentianus lives." That seems a strange thing to put on a grave, yet it is perfectly true. The love of that Christian is alive, and his body will rise again. But sometimes we see a long epitaph on a tomb, all about death. The people who write these gloomy epitaphs have forgotten the resurrection. There was a great painter once called Albert Durer. He lies buried in his native city of Nuremberg, in Germany, and on his tombstone they have put the word *Emigravit*—he has gone to another country.

Where was the soul of Jesus during the three days between the crucifixion and the resurrection? In the place of departed spirits. When the third day came, the soul came back into the body again. So it will be with us; our bodies will be laid in a grave in the cemetery (which means a *sleeping-place*), and our souls will be in the place of departed spirits, and when the great day of our resurrection comes, we shall have bodies into which our souls will come again. God, who made the first man out of the dust, can make our bodies again out of the dust. One of the old saints, St. Chrysostom, explains this very well. He says that when we pull down a house in order to rebuild it, or repair its ruins, we take the inhabitants out of it lest they should be injured by the rubbish, and we find them some other dwelling till the house is rebuilt and beautified. So when God perceives our worn-out body, all falling to pieces from sickness and old age, He calls out our soul for a time, and takes it to some part of His great kingdom; and when the time comes, He will place our soul back again in a restored and beautified body. We all know something of death, for it comes to all houses sooner or later. But I want you to feel that altho death comes to all our bodies, we are just as much alive five minutes *after* death as we were five minutes before. The soul has just gone from one kind of life to another. "I am the Life," that was a name Jesus called Himself. He is the Giver of life to our souls when they are dead in sins, and makes it possible for them to live forever.—P. M.

HOPE, Prisoners of.—*Zech. ix: 11, 12.* When I stand by the grave side, and see four men lower the casket into its resting place, the scene is not unlike that of another, where four men from the roof of a house in Capernaum let down their friend out of sight, but into the immediate presence of Christ. They cover up the roof, which is only part of their faith's work, assured that their friend is all right and will walk out another way liberated and with new life. So cover up the grave. Your dear ones are in the presence of the Risen Christ. Fear not! By His mighty power they will walk out another way liberated and glorified in the heavenly life.—J. E. Holden, D.D.

IRIDESCENCE OF DECAY.—*1 Cor. xv: 43, 44.* It is said that the beautiful iridescence found on ancient vases, buried for long centuries, was not put upon them by the master hands that made them, but is the result of decay. By some chemical change in the darkness they held secret commerce with sunlight and rainbows.

If this apparent destruction of man's handiwork can bring beauty above his skill, what shall not we say of the utter impotency of death to hurt or destroy any human beauty of person or character, in which each is co-worker with God. How blessed to read even of our dying bodies. "It is sown in dishonor; it is raised in glory: it is sown in weakness; it is raised in power: it is sown a natural body; it is raised a spiritual body." "We shall bear the image of the heavenly"—"fashioned like unto his glorious body." (Phil. iii: 21.)—Pallete. C. G.

JESUS CHRIST, Resurrection Life of.—It is said that a century ago an infidel German princess, on her death-bed, ordered that her grave be covered with a great granite slab, and that around it should be placed solid blocks of stone, and the whole be fastened together with clamps of iron: and that on the stone should be cut these words: —"This burial place, purchased to all eternity, must never be opened." Thus she meant publicly to proclaim that her grave would never be opened—never. It happened that a little seed was buried with the princess, a single acorn. It sprouted under the covering. Its tiny shoot, soft and pliable at first, found its way through the crevice between two of the slabs. And there it grew slowly but surely, and there it gathered strength until it burst the iron clamps asunder, and lifted the immense blocks and turned the whole structure into an irregular mass of upheaved rocks. Up and up through this mass of disordered stones grew the giant oak, which had thus broken the bars of the sepulcher. That oak grows there to-day a veritable tree of life.

In every grave on earth's green sward is a tiny seed of the resurrection life of Jesus Christ, and that seed cannot perish. It will germinate when the warm south-wind of Christ's return brings back the spring-tide to this cold sin-cursed earth of ours; and then they that are in their graves, and we who shall lie down in ours, will feel in our mortal bodies the power of His resurrection and will come forth to life immortal.—Dr. David Gregg.

JESUS, The Resurrection of.—A German journal quotes in favor of this resurrection two thinkers who are not usually appealed to in favor of the miraculous elements of Christianity, namely, Lessing and Schleiermacher. Lessing said: "The witnesses of the resurrection, through the testimony of the resurrection, established Christianity, and by means of its individual and its historic effects, this religion has authenticated itself as a miraculous religion. The witnesses, however, were the only ones who had before them the foundation on which they could venture with perfect assurance to rear a great superstructure. We see this superstructure before us. What fool will dig with curiosity at the foundation of this house merely for the purpose of convincing himself of the excellence of the foundation? I now know better that the foundation is good because it has stood so long that those could know it who saw that foundation laid." Schleiermacher's testimony is: "Whoever, for the sake of rejecting the miraculous, refuses to believe in the literal resurrection of Christ, and prefers to suppose that the disciples were deceived, and took inner vision for outward fact, attributes such great mental weakness to the disciples that he not only destroys all their testimony respecting Christ, but also implies that when Jesus chose such disciples He did not know what was in them."—H. R.

RESURRECTION, Figures of the.—
Awakening out of sleep (Isa. xxvi: 19). Morning after night (Ps. xlix: 14). A tree cut down and sprouting again (Job xiv: 7). A corn of wheat rising through death (John xii: 24). Israel's deliverance (Ex. xii: 37). Moses at the bush (Luke xx: 37). The seed sown (1 Cor. xv: 37).

"Paul saw our grave in the furrow of the plow, our burial in the corn dropped into the soil, our decay in the change undergone by the seed, our resurrection when, bursting its sheath, it rises green and beautiful above the ground that was once its grave."—GUTHRIE.

RESURRECTION-FLOWER,   The.—
There is a plant found in sandy deserts and arid wastes called *Anastatica*, or the Resurrection-Flower, from a remarkable power of recovery which it has. When it has flowered, its leaves drop off, its branches become hard and dry, and the plant, in a little while is seemingly dead. But so soon as it touches water again, it gradually expands, its leaves unfold, and life returns. It is a parable. If in its death-like state it is a figure of the backslider, its resurrection figures the above source of revival; the backslider must get back to the Fountain of Living Water again. —A. P. L.

RESURRECTION OF CHRIST.—Rom. iv: 25. Without His Resurrection, the death of Christ would be of no avail, and His grave would be the grave of all our hopes (1 Cor. xv: 17). A Gospel of a dead Savior would be a miserable failure and delusion. The Resurrection is the victory of righteousness and life over sin and death.—A. P. L.

RESURRECTION, The.—The understanding has its joys no less than the heart and a keen sense of intellectual joy is experienced when we perceive the truth, or any part of it, resting on a secure basis. A man is happy when he has attained to know the causes of things. The chemist, the historian, the mathematician, the anatomist, are examples. Christ's resurrection is such a fact to the Christian. It is the foundation on which the Christian creed rests. This was the reason it had such a prominent place in apostolic preaching.—CANON LIDDON.

RESURRECTION, The—A curious superstition leads the custodians of one of the temples in Japan to renew the whole of the structure every ten years. The work of renewal is always going on, a little at a time. Every new part is an exact *fac-simile* of the part it is made to replace; and in this way the identity of the first structure is maintained. And this has never ceased for a thousand years. The temple of the body is always being renewed after the same fashion. In the resurrection it will be renewed at once rather than part by part.—SELBY.

RESURRECTION, The.—It was for the glory that was set before Him that Christ endured the humiliation and suffering of the cross. Let us keep our eyes fixed steadily on the crown immortal, and then our sacrifices and services, and sufferings for Christ's cause, will seem light and trivial in comparison. . . . The seal of the Sanhedrim, a regiment of soldiers from the town, a floor of rock, a roof of rock, a wall of rock, a niche of rock, cannot keep Christ in the crypt. Tho you pile upon us all the boulders of the mountains, you cannot keep us down. The door of the tomb will be lifted from its hinges and flung flat in the dust.—TALMAGE.

RESURRECTION, The.—Epitaph on the late Charles Reade, written by himself.

Here lie,
By the Side of his Beloved Friend,
the Mortal Remains of
Charles Reade,
Dramatist, Novelist, and Journalist,
His last Words to Mankind are on this
Stone.

I hope for a resurrection, not from any power in nature, but from the will of the Lord God Omnipotent, who made nature and me. He created man out of nothing which nature could not. He can restore man from the dust; which nature cannot. And I hope for holiness and happiness in a future life, not for anything I have said or done in this body, but from the merits and mediation of Jesus Christ. He has promised His intercession to all who seek it, and He will not break His word; that intercession, once granted, cannot be rejected; for He is God, and His merits infinite: a man's sins are but human and finite. "Him that cometh to me, I will in no wise cast out." "If any man sin, we have an advocate with the Father, Jesus Christ the Righteous, and he is the propitiation for our sins."—A. P. L.

RESURRECTION, The Christian Risen with Christ—And now, how am I conformable to Thee if when Thou art risen, I lie still in the grave of my corruptions? How am I a limb of Thy body; if, while Thou hast that perfect dominion over death, death hath dominion over me; if, while Thou art alive and glorious; I lie rotting in the dust of death? I know the locomotive faculty is in the head; by the power of the Resurrection of Thee our Head, all we Thy members cannot but be raised. As the earth cannot hold my body from Thee in the day of the second Resurrection, so cannot sin withhold my soul from Thee in the first. How am I Thine, if I be not risen? and if I be risen with Thee, why do I not seek the things above, where Thou sittest at the right hand of God?—A. P. L.

SELECTIONS, Various.

DEATH.—Death is not a thing to be dreaded by the believer: it is "a sleep." Tired, we lay our heads on Jesus' bosom, and awake in heaven!—*Selected.*

FUTURE, THE.—There is, I know not how, in the minds of men, a certain presage, as it were, of a future existence; and this takes the deepest root, and is most discoverable, in the greatest geniuses and most exalted souls.—CICERO.

GRAVE, THE.—Paul saw our grave in the furrow of the plow; our burial in the corn dropped in the soil; and our resurrection in the grain bursting its sheath to wave its head in the summer sunshine.—*Selected.*

GRAVE, THE.—The grave is the apparent doorway through which we pass to heaven; but the true doorway is not so large—it is closely fitting to each man.—*Selected.*

IMMORTALITY.—In vain do individuals hope for immortality, or any patent from oblivion, in preservations below the moon; men have been deceived even in their flatteries, above the sun, and studied conceits to perpetuate their names in heaven.
Sir THOMAS BROWNE—*Hydriotaphia.*
Ch. V.

IMMORTALITY.—There is nothing strictly immortal, but immortality. Whatever hath no beginning may be confident of no end.
Sir THOMAS BROWNE—*Hydriotaphia.*
Ch. V.

IMMORTALITY.—Immortality is the glorious discovery of Christianity.
CHANNING—*Immortality.*

PAST, PRESENT, FUTURE.—I came from God, and I'm going back to God, and I won't have any gaps of death in the middle of my life.
GEORGE MACDONALD—*Mary Marston.*
Ch. LVII.

SEPULCHER, Woman at the.—Was it not most meet that a woman should first see the risen Savior? She was first in the transgression; let her be first in the justification. In yon garden she was first to work our wo; let her in that other garden be the first to see Him who works our weal. She takes first the apple of that bitter tree which brings us all our sorrow; let her be the first to see the Mighty Gardener, who has planted a tree which brings forth fruit unto everlasting life.—SPURGEON.

POETRY

Bird, Like a

Let us be like a bird for a moment perched
On a frail branch where he sings;
Tho he feels it bend he continues his song,
For he knows that he has wings.
VICTOR HUGO.

Easter Answer, The

Said Death to Life,
"The world is mine;"
Said Life to Death,
"*And thou art thine!*"
W. F. WARREN.

Easter Lilies, Like

Like Easter lilies, pure and white,
Make Thou our hearts, O Lord of Light!
Like Easter lilies, let them be
Sweet chalices of love to Thee!
EMMA C. DOWD.

Easter Morn

O chime of sweet Saint Charity,
Peal soon that Easter morn
When Christ for all shall risen be,
And in all hearts new born!
That Pentecost when utterance clear
To all men shall be given,
When all can say My Brother here,
And hear My Son in heaven!
J. R. LOWELL.

Immortality

No, no! The energy of life may be
Kept in after the grave, but not begun;
And he who flagg'd not in the earthly strife,
From strength to strength advancing—only he;
His soul well-knit, and all his battles won,
Mounts, and that hardly, to eternal life.
MATTHEW ARNOLD—*Immortality.* St. 4.

Immortality

Nothing lovely ever dies,
But passes into other loveliness,
Star dust or sea foam, flower or winged air:
If this befall our poor unworthy flesh—
Think thee! what destiny awaits the soul!
Anon.

Immortality

Immortality
Alone could teach this mortal how to die.
D. M. MULOCK—*Looking Death in the Face.*

Last, At

But all lost things are in the angels' keeping,
Love;
No past is dead for us, but only sleeping,
Love;

The years of heaven will all earth's little
pain
  Make good,
Together there we can begin again
  In babyhood.
  HELEN HUNT—*At Last.* St. 6.

Man, The Good

When the good man yields his breath
(For the good man never dies.)
  MONTGOMERY—*The Wanderer of
        Switzerland.* Pt. V.

Resurrection

One short sleep past, we wake eternally;
And death shall be no more; death, thou
  shalt die.
  DONNE.—*Sonnet.*

Resurrection, Man's

Shall man alone, for whom all else revives,
No resurrection know? Shall man alone,
Imperial man! be sown in barren ground
Less privileged than grain, on which he
  feeds?
  YOUNG—*Night Thoughts.* Night IV.
  Line 704.

The Power of an Endless Life

Thou wilt not leave us in the dust:
  Thou madest man, he knows not why;
  He thinks he was not made to die;
And Thou hast made him; Thou art just.
  TENNYSON—*In Memoriam.*

Risen with Christ

BY EMILY HUNTINGTON MILLER

O soul of mine, to life's new rapture born,
Canst thou forget the splendor of that morn,
When, through the chill and silence of thy
  night,
Stole the warm radiance of the Easter light?

Did not thy Lord, before the dawn of day,
Unseal thy tomb and bid thee come away?
And in that sacred garden, cool and dim,
Amid the lilies didst thou not walk with
  Him?

Then why shouldst thou, all trembling and
  afraid,
Still bring thy spices where thy Lord was
  laid?
Unto the heavens lift up thy downcast eyes;
Thy Lord is risen, and thou with Him didst
  rise.

Not for the trump of doom and judgment
  hour
Waits, through slow years, the resurrection
  power.
To-day He lives; to-day His life may be
Eternal life begun, O Soul, in thee.—I.

Easter

BY GEORGE T. PACKARD

The flowers by the garden tomb
  Each lent to each its sweet,
And made a fragrant pathway
  For the coming of His feet.

Glad Easter unto Easter
  Its own blest radiance gives,
And shining ranks of festivals
  Repeat the cry, He lives!—Y. C.

Easter

BY MARY CLARKE HUNTINGTON

That Easter when the stone was rolled away.
  The world was dewy fresh and morning
    fair;
The birds sang matins to the dawning day;
  Shy flowers shed perfume on the windless
    air;
And those who came with spices where He
    lay
Found angel vision—and the stone away!

That Easter when the stone was rolled away!
  How many centuries have passed between
Our first glad Easter and this later day!
  How much of sin and grief the world has
    seen!
Yet those of us who come with hearts to
    pray
Find angel vision—and the stone away.
  C. E. W.

Easter

BY MRS. E. C. WHITNEY

What rapturous joy thrills the pulse of the
    morning?
  What meaneth this swelling of timbrel and
    choir?
This incense of lilies, before the red dawn-
    ing
  Has quenched in the meadow its crystals
    of fire?

Oh, say! dost thou hear it? Of ill recks it
    warning?
  This deep, surging echo of past holy
    strains?
They break on my faint heart as on that dim
    morning
  When Judah's bright star rose o'er Beth-
    lehem's plains.

In the night's desolation, the cliffs and the
    vales
  Voiced with wild acclamation the earth's
    dreadful throes;
While from her bosom, quaking, ascended
    the wails
  Of the weepers in Israel, for Olivet's woes.

Not the chaotic clashing of supernal forces,
  Not the sobs of Golgotha that now greet
    mine ear,—
" Deo Jubilate, Gloria in Excelsis! "
  'Tis the song of the angels! My soul,
    dost thou hear?

From the hills of Moriah to Pisgah's lone
    crest
  Throbs the psalm of Redemption. O Is-
    rael, hear!
Awake, thou that sleepest, go, speed thee in
    quest
  Of these strains so prophetic that ravish
    the ear.

Go, hush thee in Zion the dirge of the
weeper;
  Bestrew not His grave with thy cypress
  and rue,
Nor with aloes and myrrh enfold Calvary's
lone sleeper,
  For the day-star has risen! Strike the
anthem anew!

In the hush of the dawn, in the morn's
saffron glow,
  The day's golden splendor, He comes,
Savior, King!
The holy Shechinah illumines His brow,
  His footsteps are led by cherubim's wing.

His tender feet press the brown mold of the
vale,
  And it blooms with the fragrance of
Sharon's sweet rose;
The withered heath sings, and the thicket
and dale
  In life's resurrection with fresh verdure
glows.

He speaks,—and the morning stars gather to
listen;
  He smiles,—and the flocks upon Carmel
rejoice;
"Rabboni!" oh, well may human eyes glis-
ten
  At sound of that tender, compassionate
Voice!

Bring hither the ivy, the myrtle and palm,
  And fill thy white censers with rarest perfume;
Bring chalice of spikenard and sweet Mecca's
balm,
  For the dear feet of Him Who brings life
from the tomb.

Fling wide your great portals, ye hills of the
blessed,
  That He Who without your proud walls
trod for men
The wine-press, may enter. Shout, oh, ye
oppressed!
  "In the highest be glory!" "Amen and
Amen."—Y. C.

An Easter Awakening

By J. L. S.

Time was when all my senses shrank
  At sight of death.
The face, expressionless and blank,
  And truant breath,—
The narrow tufted bed and scent
  Of drooping rose,
Were all a grim admonishment
  Of future woes.
I thought of horrors to be passed
  Upon the way.
My soul with trembling stood aghast,—
  Too late to pray.

. . . . . .

But when I saw her lying there
  So calm and sweet;
With roses in her wavy hair,
  And at her feet;

With lilies of the valley spread
  Upon her breast,—
I quite forgot that she were dead,—
  Such peaceful rest.
Then came this hallowed thought: If she
  Could start so glad
Upon a journey, that for me
  All terrors had,—
Could I not seek that self-same way
  O'er down and fell,
And travel on without dismay,
  And smile farewell?

. . . . . .

I trusted in I knew not what,
  Perhaps in pelf;
She trusted God in all, and not
  In pain-racked self.
And when I found that Christ had died,—
  Lay cold and still;
And rose, a body glorified,
  By His own will,—
This thought, like brightest sunshine, fell
  On me astray,
That Christ had come on earth to dwell,
  To show the way
Thro' vale and shadow—where He led
  She followed on,
And felt secure as in her bed,
  To rise at dawn.
And I—well, I have grasped the truth
  Their lives have taught.
And whether called in fading youth
  Or age is naught;
For with a smile I'll kindly greet
  The coming dawn;
And where He leads, with eager feet
  I'll follow on.

P. J.

A White Easter

By Jessie F. O'Donnell

Oh, the wondrous, glistening Easter,
  Shining in the morning light!
Silently the world had blossomed
  Like a white rose in the night;
Softly smiled the winter landscape
  To the sunbeams' glances bright.

Then I knew the wild ice Spirit
  Swift this marvel great had wrought;
Crystal robes for trees and bushes
  In the darkness he had brought,
With the rainbow's gorgeous colors
  In their diamonded fringes caught.

Every tree wore jeweled flowers,
  Flashing like a monarch's crown,
All the tiny twigs and branches
  With a weight of gems bent down;
Every stump and post unshapely
  Had a crystal column grown.

"He is risen!" cried the maples
  To our listening hearts beneath,
Pointing fingers white to Heaven,
  "He has conquered even Death."
"He is risen!" soft the crystals
  Echoed in their frosty breath.

And if ever speech were silver
　　Then it was as clear and sweet,
"He is risen!" all the ice-sprays
　　Seemed to tenderly repeat,
While they swayed in Easter sunlight,
　　And dropped jewels at our feet.

"He is risen!" cried our own hearts,
　　"Death's mysterious veil unrolls,
And forever Death's dark kingdom
　　He has conquered and controls;"
And were ever silence golden,
　　'Twas the stillness in our souls.
　　　　　　　　　　　　W. C. M.

Beautiful Easter

By Harriet McEwen Kimball

Day of the Crucified Lord's Resurrection;
　　Day that the Lord by His triumph hath
　　made;
Day of Redemption's seal of perfection;
　　Day of the Crown of His power displayed;
Beautiful Easter, dazzlingly bright;
Sun-Day that filleth all Sundays with light!

Queen of all festivals; glad culmination
　　Of the bright feasts that encircle the year;
Glimpsing the Life, in a transfiguration,
　　That shall at length in its glory appear.
Beautiful Easter; day in its height;
Sun-Day that filleth all Sundays with light!

Banish the gloom in the house of the
　　mourner
　　Keeping the vigil that sorrow compels;
Melt the cold walls of that prison forlorner
　　Where unbelief in its solitude dwells;
Beautiful Easter, dazzlingly bright;
Sun-Day that filleth all Sundays with light!

Pierce with thy rays those saddest of places
　　Hearts that are darkened by sin or despair;
Stream o'er the earth's most desert-like
　　spaces
　　Making them blossom than Eden more
　　fair;
Beautiful Easter, dazzlingly bright;
Sun-Day that filleth all Sundays with light!

Day of the hope that is almost fruition;
　　Day of Christ's message of "Peace" to
　　His own;
Day of the pledge that His creatures' con-
　　dition
　　He will transform to a glory unknown;
Beautiful Easter, dazzlingly bright;
Sun-Day that filleth all Sundays with light!

He who redeemeth, consoleth, forgiveth;
　　Who His own body raised up from the
　　dead,
Holdeth all evil in bondage and liveth,
　　Source of all blessing, our Life and our
　　Head.
It is His Glory that maketh thee bright,
Sun-Day that filleth all Sundays with light!
　　　　　　　　　　　　Y. C.

Easter Day

By John Keble

Oh! day of days! shall hearts set free
No "minstrel rapture" find for thee?
Thou art the Sun of other days,
They shine by giving back thy rays.

Enthronéd in thy sovereign sphere
Thou shedd'st the light on all the year:
Sundays by thee more glorious break,
An Easter Day in every week:

And week-days, following in their train,
The fulness of thy blessing gain,
Till all, both resting and employ,
Be one Lord's day of holy joy.

Then wake my soul to high desires,
And earlier light thine altar fires;
The world some hours is on her way,
Nor thinks on thee, thou blessed day:

Or, if she thinks, it is in scorn:
The vernal light of Easter morn
To her dark gaze no brighter seems
Than Reason's or the Law's pale beams.

"Where is your Lord?" she scornful asks:
"Where is His hire? we know His tasks;
Sons of a King ye boast to be;
Let us your crowns and treasures see."

We in the words of Truth reply,
(An angel brought them from the sky),
"Our crown, our treasure is not here,
'Tis stored above the highest sphere:

"Methinks your wisdom guides amiss,
To seek on earth a Christian's bliss;
We watch not now the lifeless stone;
Our only Lord is risen and gone."

Yet even the lifeless stone is dear
For thoughts of Him who late lay here;
And the base world, now Christ hath died,
Ennobled is and glorified.

No more a charnel-house, to fence
The relics of lost innocence,
A vault of ruin and decay;—
The imprisoning stone is rolled away.

'Tis now a cell, where angels use
To come and go with heavenly news,
And in the ears of mourners say,
"Come, see the place where Jesus lay."

'Tis now a fane, where love can find
Christ everywhere embalmed and shrined;
Ay gathering up memorials sweet,
Where'er she sets her duteous feet.

Easter Flowers

With gentle home-work doing all for love,
　　Making some life the better for our own;
Smoothing some path for other feet to tread,
　　Cheering some heart that has to work
　　alone.

So shall we live the nearer to our Lord,
So shall we labor through these holy hours;
Till Easter suns shall hail the Golden Day,
And joyful hands shall wreath the Easter
flowers.—O. C. W.

Easter Hymn of Athens

By Hezekiah Butterworth

They stood in the shadows, the Court and
the people,
And waited the midnight, the priests chant-
ing low.
Each hand clasped a torch, in the darkness,
unlighted,
In the palpitate air but one Light rose aglow.
The thin moon sank golden o'er Salamis
waters,
The lambent stars burned o'er Hymettus,
and white
The Acropolis lifted its blossoming marbles
Theseus's ghost 'mid pale columns of night.
"He will rise! He will rise!" breathed the
Patriarch lowly;
"He will rise! He will rise!" said the
people, and still
The priests chanted on, the one Christ-light
above them,
And faded the moon from the Capitol Hill!

A sound rends the sky, the deep voice of the
cannon,
And *Christos anesti!* ascends from each
tongue,
From the Christ-flame in air has the King
his torch kindled,
And the flame is fast speeding the people
among.
Each jubilant torch swiftly kindles another,
The One Flame is filling the city with light;
The noble the shepherd boy hails as a
brother,
And the shout of "Anesti!" leads onward
the night.
They are shouting, the temples of Pan and
Apollo,
They are singing, the shrines of the Muses
again,
From Pelion's pines to the groves of Ilissos,
From the gardens of Plato, to Marathon's
plain!
The old shrines are shouting "Anesti!
Anesti!"
Minerva is vanished, and Delphi is dumb,
And Theseus's columns are empty and
broken,
But the Zeus long unknown to his altar has
come!

Haste! haste to Mars' Hill, where once stood
the Apostle,
'Mid the close-crowding temples of Victor
and seer;
The priests in the night the sweet canon are
singing.
Haste, haste ye the glorious anthem to hear!
The hymn of St. John of Damascus is thrilling
The heart of the watchers with rapture divine!

The moon has gone down but over Hymettus,
The stars of the morning like vestal lamps
shine.

"Hail, morn of Resurrection!
To earth proclaim the word!
Now comes to hope immortal
The passover of God;
Lord, shrive our hearts from evil
And give our spirits sight,
That we may hail with gladness
The Resurrection light!

"All hail! said Jesus risen,
All hail! our lips shall say.
Ye heavens, be bright and joyful
This Resurrection day!
Lord, shrive our hearts from evil,
And give our spirits sight,
That we may hail with gladness
The Resurrection light!

"Let people unto people
Proclaim the joy abroad,
Our Christ has died and risen
The Passover of God,
Lord, shrive our hearts from evil,
And give our spirits sight,
That we may hail with gladness
The Resurrection light!"

'Tis morning in Athens, the broad sun is
shining
On lone Caryatids, through Propylons dumb,
But the cross gleams above the dead shrines
of the city,
The Zeus long unknown to his altars has
come,
The white palace sleeps in the shade of the
mountain,
The west wind breathes balm, and the silver
chimes cease,
And Peace leads the hours for the Lord has
arisen,
And blesses the earth with the gladness of
peace!   Y. C.

Easter Lilies

By Mary A. Denison

O lilies, pure and splendid!
O lilies, holy and white!
I greet with a Christian's greeting
Your lessons of love and light.

You bring to my mind a picture
Of One who was spotless too,
Who took for His world-read lesson
A sermon of faith from you.

O lilies, joyous and stately!
With never a thought of pride,
What treasures of trust and sweetness,
Come with you at Easter Tide!

What zest for a holy living!
What hope in a Christian's death!
What gentleness, charity, beauty,
You teach with each fragrant breath!

Do you know that the dear Lord Jesus,
Rose in His kingly might?
That the world is His royal capture,
And Heaven His throne of Light?

Glad may ye be, and singing,
Like me, to the Christ above,
For blessings on those who give you,
As tokens of Easter love!

Y. C.

Easter Lilies

BY MABEL EARLE

More holy than stole or mitre
They stood in the holy place.
The altar candles were brighter
Burning above their grace—
Spirits of love, grown whiter
From looking into His face.

One of the three was swaying
To music we could not hear
And one of them leaned down, saying
His name in the silence clear,
And one smiled upward, praying
As if He were very near.

Y. C.

Easter Morning

BY PHILLIPS BROOKS

Tomb, thou shalt not hold Him longer;
Death is strong, but life is stronger;
Stronger than the dark, the light;
Stronger than the wrong, the right;
Faith and hope triumphant say,
" Christ will rise on Easter day!"

While the patient earth lies waking
Till the morning shall be breaking,
Shuddering 'neath the burden dread
Of her Master, cold and dead,
Hark! she hears the angels say,
" Christ will rise on Easter day!"

And when sunrise smites the mountains,
Pouring light from heavenly fountains,
Then the earth blooms out to greet
Once again the blesséd feet;
And her countless voices say:
" Christ has risen on Easter day!"

C. G.

For Easter Morning

BY LOUISE CHANDLER MOULTON

The glad dawn sets his fires upon the hills,
Then floods the valleys with his golden
light,
And triumphing o'er all the hosts of night
The waiting world with new-born rapture
fills:
And, hark! I seem to hear a song which
thrills
The trembling air of Earth with Heaven's
delight,
And straight uplifts with its Celestial might
Souls faint with longing, compassed round
with ills.

" Christ, Christ is risen!" The unseen singers sing—
" Christ, Christ is risen!" The echoing
hosts reply—
The whist wind knows a passing seraph's
wing,
And holds its breath while shining ones go
by:
" Christ, Christ is risen!" loud let the anthem ring—
" He lives—He loves—He saves—we need
not die."—Y. C.

Easter Thanksgiving

BY MARGARET E. SANGSTER

Thank God for the dear ones safe to-day,
Safe at home on the happy shore,
Where the smile of the Father beams for ay,
And the shadow of pain shall fall no more.
Thank God for the hearts that have done with
sin,
For the eyes that shall never be blind with
tears,
Thank God for the beautiful, entered in
To the perfect rest of the deathless years.

Thank God to-day for the pilgrim feet
Which have trodden the last of the toilsome
way,
For the strong, for the frail, for the babes so
sweet,
Who have left forever this crumbling clay;
Who have changed earth's trial and loss and
moan
For the victor's palm and the voice of
praise,
Who dwell in the light of the great white
Throne,
And join in the songs which the ransomed
raise.

Thank God to-day for the hope sublime
Which fills our souls in the darkest hours;
Thank God that the transient cares of time
Are wreathed in the glory of fadeless
flowers;
Thank God for the rift in the desolate grave;
'Tis the soldier's couch, not the captive's
prison;
He hallowed its portal, who died to save,
And we write o'er its arch, " The Lord is
risen!"

C. G.

Cato's Soliloquy on Immortality

BY JOSEPH ADDISON

It must be so—Plato, thou reasonest well!
Else, whence this pléasing hope, this fond de-
sire,
This longing after immortality?
Or, whence this secret dread and inward
horror
Of falling into nought? Why shrinks the
soul
Back on herself, and startles at destruction?
'Tis the divinity that stirs within us:
'Tis heaven itself that points out an hereafter,
And intimates eternity to man.

Eternity! thou pleasing, dreadful thought!
Through what variety of untried being,
Through what new scenes and changes must
    we pass?
The wide, unbounded prospect lies before me;
But shadows, clouds, and darkness rest upon
    it.
Here will I hold. If there's a Power above
    us—
And that there is, all Nature cries aloud
Through all her works—*He* must delight in
    virtue,
And that which *He* delights in must be happy.
But when? or where? This world was made
    for Cæsar.

I'm weary of conjectures—this must end
    them.
Thus am I doubly armed. My death and life,
My bane and antidote, are both before me.
This, in a moment, brings me to an end;
But this informs me I shall never die.
The soul, secured in her existence, smiles
At the drawn dagger and defies its point.
The stars shall fade away, the sun himself
Grow dim with age, and Nature sink in years;
But thou shalt flourish in immortal youth,
Unhurt amidst the war of elements,
The wrecks of matter, and the crush of
    worlds.—From *Cato.*

Joy Cometh in the Morning

By Annie L. Muzzey

'Tis in your heart, beloved, that the Easter
    morning breaks,
  Your slumbering consciousness of Love
    with thrilling joy awakes;
Your thought goes out a minister of good to
    heal and bless
  The suffering and desolate who need your
    tenderness.

'Tis in your heart, beloved, that the Easter
    lilies bloom,
  The sweet flowers of affection whose in-
    cense cheers the gloom;
Go forth and spill their fragrance, whatever
    wind may blow,
  The lilies of Ascension thro' all the years
    must grow.

'Tis from your heart, beloved, that the stone
    is rolled away,
  The Life for all men given pulses in your
    life To-day;
The banners of Love's marching hosts are to
    the breeze unfurled,
  And the dawn-light of the Kingdom is
    streaming down the world.

Ring out the bells, beloved, the joyous Easter
    bells,
  Celestial harmony along their cadence rolls
    and swells,
The blesséd Christ is risen in the hearts that
    throb and thrill
  Responsive to Love's law wherein we may
    all laws fulfil.—Y. C.

Joy Cometh in the Morning

By Ada Melville Shaw

I buried my bulbs in the garden,
  'Twas night of the year;
The sky was o'ershadowed with weeping,
  The garden was drear;
I gave the brown bulbs to earth's keeping,
And left them there somberly sleeping
  Till day should appear.

The cold rain beat down on my garden;
  Ah, pitiless rain!
My bulbs—would they perish ere waking,
  My planting in vain?
The tempest swept on without breaking;
My faith for fair flowers was shaking;
  I wept in my pain.

Gray dawn slowly crept o'er my garden;
  I sought it with sighs.
Lo! there through the soft mold appearing,
  Glad sight for sad eyes,
Green life to the daylight uprearing,
O foolish heart, what of thy fearing,
  Thy faithless surmise?

When springtime was warm in my garden,
  What splendor was there!
White chalices heavenward turning,
  O, royal cups fair!
Tall lilies, in golden hearts burning,
Beneath the glad sunbeams' fond yearning,
  Their sweet incense rare.

Weep not o'er the tomb in thy garden,
  O soul sore bereft!
Tho sorrow thy spirit is shaking,
  Strong comfort is left;
The seals of the dread tomb are breaking,
Behind their grim guard life is waking,
  The darkness is cleft.

Eternity lighteth thy garden;
  Look up, tear-dimmed eyes!
Forget the lone night of thy weeping
  In morn's sweet surprise;
Thy dear ones thou hast from their sleeping;
Death held them delayed in his keeping;
  Lo, none but Death dies!—C. E. W.

The Holy Morn

By Edwin Forrest Hallenbeck

'Tis the Lord's day, day of resurrection!
Gloom of night and mist of early dawn have
Fled. With glory-light the sun looks out
    upon
A reverent world. Nature's mighty chorus
Shouts its halleluiahs unto God. The hills
With humble mien approach Jehovah's throne.
The trees with dew-be-diamonded robes of
    green
Draw near. Meadow and hillside bring from
    out
Their blossom'd wealth garlands for the altar
Of their king. Streamlets lisp a dreamy note
Of praise. Golden grain-fields bend into the

Attitude of prayer; orchards humbly bow
While morning winds put worship's voice
  into
Their lips. And as the day goes on apace,
Adoration at the shrine of nature's
God becomes intense; choirs of singing birds
Bring melodies of joy to Him who gave
Them breath, until the voice of forest sings
Refrain to field, and peak responds to peak,
And every note in glad creation's scale
Has fervent part in holy gratitude,
And admonition to the sons of men;
" Pay homage to the God who reigns above;
With humble spirit worship at His throne,
'Tis the Lord's day, day of resurrection! "
       —E.

Resurrection

By M. A. De Wolf Howe, Jr.

Through the length of the year the grave
  must take,
'Tis the Easter earth that can only give;
Then bury the meaner self, and wake
To the life that the nobler self may live.

Before the dawn of the Easter sun
  Hide deep in the mold the dearest sin,
The unnoted lie or the wrong begun;
  Let the shadeless right once more begin.

Bury the pride that has sprung from naught,
  The envy and hate of a blackened hour;
Arise to the Christ-life purely fraught
  With love as white as the Easter flower.
       —Y. C.

The Resurrection

By H. L. L.

Breezes of spring, all earth to life awaking;
  Birds swiftly soaring through the sunny
    sky;
The butterfly its lonely prison breaking:
  The seed upspringing which had seemed to
    die.

Types such as these a word of hope have
    spoken,
  Have shed a gleam of light around the
    tomb;
But weary hearts longed for a surer token,
  A clearer ray, to dissipate its gloom.

And this was granted! See the Lord as-
    cending,
  On crimson clouds of evening calmly borne,
With hands outstretched, and looks of love
    still bending
  On His bereaved ones, who no longer
    mourn.

" I am the Resurrection," hear Him saying,
  " I am the Life: he who believes in Me
Shall never die; the souls My call obeying,
  Soon where I am for evermore shall be."

Sing Hallelujah! light from heaven appearing
  The mystery of life and death is plain;
Now to the grave we can descend unfearing,
  In sure and certain hope to rise again!—E.
     From the German.

Outside and In

In Memoriam, S. M. B.

By Charles F. Deems, D.D.

I stood beside a swinging gate
  The two great worlds dividing,
Outside poor sinners weep and wait,
  Inside are saints abiding.

How grim and dark and dread is seen
  The outside of that portal
Whose inside's glorious golden sheen
  Streams on the eyes immortal!

Outside, the winds of winter shriek
  With howl and lamentation;
Inside, melodious accents speak
  Of spring's regeneration.

Outside I saw the snow-clad grave
  Of a babe who had just been dying;
Inside, his feet, wingéd and fleet,
  O'er fields of light were flying.

Outside I heard a father's plaint,
  And a mother's cry outbreaking;
Inside there shouted many a saint
  At the babe's new saintly waking.

Outside, bereavéd children wept,
  O'er little steps retreating;
Inside, the cherubs harp-**strings** swept,
  The new-born cherub greeting.

Outside were war, and want, and wo,
  Graves and homes melancholy;
Inside, the landscape stood aglow
  In soft light, still and holy.

Outside, upon a cross of blood,
  Hung God's great Victim dying;
Inside on throne He radiant shone
  And angels heard Him crying—

" Outside, O men, are Death and Sin;
  Inside, the Life Immortal;
Fear not to let your loved ones in
  To Life thro Death's dark portal! "

The Riddle

From the French of Louise Bertin

By Louise Imogen Guiney

If death be all, why on our hopeless travel,
  Laughs the young green of beauty's April
    tree?
And when the frost the woven leaves unravel,
  What need for us to sadden as we see?

Or why, if life be all, shards in the grasses,
  And ever in the wayside rose a spite?
Why must we pay, yea, soul by soul that
    passes,
  Blood for man's zeal, and tears for man's
    delight?—I.

Tired

BY NEWELL LOVEJOY

We are so tired, my heart and I,
Sweet is the swell of the poet's sigh;
Sweet is the ring of the minor chords;
Sweet is the chime of the measured words.
But, oh! when life is so hard and dull,
We miss the joy of the beautiful,
And echo it back like a bitter cry—
" We are so tired, my heart and I."

Tired of sowing the barren grains,
Tired of taking the useless pains
Of the futile faith, the unheeded word,
And the weary sickness of hope deferred;
While the counted sands drop fast away,
Through the feverish night and the restless
    day,
And the reeds we lean on break, one by one,
And the sad, ungranted prayers go on.

The winds sweep over the cowering plain,
Through the creeping mist sobs the ceaseless
    rain;
The chill and heaviness all around,
Like a chain the aching temples bound;
Dream, fancy, sacrifice—what is it all?
Climbing, struggling, slip and fall,
Over the sea hangs the dull gray sky:—
We are so tired, my heart and I.

Break through the clouds, O Easter light!
Wake up, brave sense of truth and right;
Lay on the shrine of our risen Lord
The useless talent, the broken sword;
Lay there doubts, griefs, and wants and cares,
And the erring darlings of many prayers;
From the cross on earth to the crown on high,
Let us look together, my heart and I.—Y. C.

SUNDAY

SUNDAY. (AS. *sunnan daeg; sunnan,* gen. of *sunne,* sun; *daeg,* day.) " The first day of the week, observed by Christians in honor of the resurrection of Christ, as a day of rest from secular occupations and devoted to the worship of God; the Lord's day; the Christian Sabbath." *

The old Testament Sabbath and the New Testament Sunday, or Lord's Day, being essentially the same, the history of the day dates from the creation of man. In Gen. ii: 1-3, we read: " Thus the heavens and the earth were finished and all the host of them. And on the seventh day God ended his work which he had made; and he rested on the seventh day from all his work which he had made. And God blessed the seventh day, and sanctified it: because that in it he had rested from all his work which God created and made." Many scholars find a reference to Sabbath observance in Gen. iv: 3, " And in process of time (literally, *at the end of days*) it came to pass that Cain brought of the fruit of the ground an offering unto the Lord." Many also find a reference to the Sabbath in the account of the flood, wherein we are told that Noah twice sent out the dove to seek dry land on the seventh day. *(Gen. viii: 6-12.)* The sixteenth chapter of Exodus *(Ex. xvi: 5, 22, 23)* distinctly shows Sabbath observance in connection with the gathering of the manna, before the moral law was given at Mt. Sinai. The fourth commandment, in the Decalogue, is devoted to reminding men that after six days of work the next, the seventh day, must be devoted to rest and to God. In subsequent Old Testament history and prophecy the Sabbath is not referred to very frequently, but often enough to show its continuity of obligation and observance. *(1 Chron. ix: 23; Neh. xiii: 15-21; Ezek. xl: 1; Is. lvi: 2; Amos viii: 5.)*

When Christ came, He found the Sabbath covered with the barnacles of tradition and man-made regulations, many of which were as absurd as they were burdensome. These He removed with unsparing hand. He claimed that " The Son of man is Lord also of the Sabbath." *(Mark ii: 28.)* He observed it carefully as He did all the moral and ceremonial law of the Old Testament Church. Faithfully He attended the services of the temple and of the synagog. The apostles also honored the Sabbath.

Since our Lord's resurrection, the day of the week on which the Sabbath (Heb. *Shabath,* rest from labor) has been observed has been changed by almost all Christians from Saturday to Sunday. In the apostolic age of the Church, both Saturday and Sunday were observed by Christians, out of consideration of the conscience of the Jewish converts; but gradually the observance of Saturday became almost obsolete. A small fraction of Christians, however, seem all along conscientiously to have believed that God means that Saturday only is the true Sabbath. In our day, the Seventh Day Baptists are the principal, if not the only denomination of Christians adhering to the Jewish Sabbath, or Saturday.

The author of EIGHT STUDIES OF THE LORD'S DAY thus summarizes the facts and events which led to the transition of the observance of Sabbath from Saturday to Sunday, from the seventh day of the week to the first day:

* Standard Dictionary.

"In the various books of the New Testament, a number of passages refer to the meetings of Christians, but only a portion of them connect these meetings explicitly with the Lord's Day. It would seem as if the Divine Inspirer of the Scriptures had permitted only these glimpses to appear in this part of the Sacred Canon, in order that at the proper time men might see that while the day might in them be traced to a distinct source, the true conception of its character was to be drawn from a larger view. These glimpses are sufficient, but no more than sufficient. They present before us the first week of the new era, showing how our Lord emphasized the first day of the week, not only by His resurrection and His visits to His disciples, but also by His abstention from them until the next first day. Then the seventh return of the first day is presented, showing by visible manifestation the entry of the Divine Being upon a new discipline of mankind through the Church. Then, after about twenty years, a view is presented of a European Church holding its regular assemblies on the first day of the week, and, by apostolic directions, regularly gathering the alms of its members on that day. After perhaps another year, there is a view of a Church in Asia Minor likewise assembling regularly on the first day of the week for preaching and the Eucharistic Supper; while an apostle, whose tardy vessel brought him into their harbor just too late for one of these meetings, tarried a week, tho pressed for time, in order to attend the next. *(Acts xx: 16.)*

"Five and twenty years, perhaps, later, a scene appears in whose foreground is an aged apostle, the last survivor of the original college, refreshing his solitude at Patmos by lofty communings with Heaven on the Lord's Day. In the distance is a circle of churches to whom the divine messages and the Apocalypse are being transmitted, who also have learned the expressiveness of this short title for the first day of the week, and understand the appropriateness to the Lord's Day of peculiar religious privileges and enjoyments in the special and spiritual worship of the Lord.

"Within the next half century, Pliny and Justin—heathen and Christian, persecutor and martyr—wrote, with many others, their testimony to the observance of the Lord's Day by Christians in general,—and the secular history of the day begins."

Of all holy days none is more worthy of the epithet than the Sabbath. Its antiquity, its rest for body, mind, and spirit, its worship of God and study of His word and works, the great events of which it reminds us, God's resting after creating the universe and man, and Christ's resurrection from the dead, with all the significance of that august event, combine to make it the sweetest and holiest of all the holy days.

Longfellow says " Sunday is the golden clasp that binds together the volume of the week."

THE DEFENSE OF THE SABBATH

By John Hall, D.D., LL.D.

We stand up for this day of rest because it takes us back to the origin of the race and comes from the hand of our Creator. "Oh, yes," says somebody, "now he is going to the Old Testament; have we not had enough of that? We are in the nineteenth century, and under the New Testament." I do not want you to think meanly, dear friends, of the Old Testament. It is not obsolete. Take all the great institutions that you have, and you will find that the elements of them are in that Old Testament and presented in such a way as to prepare us for receiving and intelligently accepting them. The family, the state, the nation, marriage, the rights of property, the Church, the officers of the Church, these and very many other institutions of the like kind that we have among us have their germs in the Old Testament, and that man mistakes his Bible gravely who supposes he can understand the New if he ignores the Old.

"God rested the seventh day." "Why?" says somebody, "was He weary, was He tired?" The strongest human minds do not rest only because they are tired. What is contemplation? What is reflection? What makes the strongest men reflective? What is reflection? Bending the mind back upon the past. So He rested for an example to you and me and for the framing of an institution that would be good for His creatures, not the intelligent only, but the unintelligent creation that He had called into being. He rested on that day from all His work, and there are a good many things in the history of the human race outside of the Mosaic narrative that go to corroborate the impression we have touching that matter.

What a curious thing it is that the number seven, for example, should be so generally a significant number as it has become. I could understand the number five becoming a typical number; we have five fingers, ten fingers, five toes, ten toes, but as to the number seven there is nothing of that suggestive nature about it. We have the Seven Ages and the Seven Heavens and the Seven Wise Men and the Seven Wonders of the world. We have a great number of these sevens spread by tradition all over the race wherever it has gone, just as we have the week. Tradition gives unconscious but mighty corroborative arguments in favor of that simple narrative that we have in the opening book of Genesis. Nor are we left to those strong probabilities. Somebody may say, "Ah that resting and that suggestion of a day of rest for me—that is due altogether to Moses, and is not to be found anywhere until you come to Sinai, and the ages after Sinai." History does not bear that out. Scholars will tell you about the Nineveh Calendar, and if you take such men as Sayce and Le Normande and the greatest and most accurate antiquarians, they will tell you, on the authority of that Nineveh Calendar, that six hundred years before the days of Moses the week was a well understood institution, and the very name that the Syrians had for the day of rest was "Sabbatu," the very word that we get in and from our Hebrew Scriptures.

We stand for this day, then, because it is coeval with the history of the race, and it comes to us with the stamp and appointment of our Creator. Then we come down a little further and we get to what men know as the Decalog, and all that are here recollect the words which we learned, many of us,

from the lips of our mothers or our fathers, "Remember the Sabbath day to keep it holy. Six days shalt thou labor and do all thy work, but the seventh is the Sabbath of the Lord, thy God." Now, of course, you know very well that efforts have been made to break the force of that remembrance. No wonder that men made these efforts. Tell me to remember a thing and that implies that it has been present to me before. "Remember the Sabbath," implies, it has been argued truly, that it has been before the mind already. Attempts have been made to break the force of that, but they have been made, I venture to say, absolutely in vain, and that they are in vain is made the clearer when you take into account the concluding part of that one of the Commandments, "For in six days the Lord made heaven and earth," and so on. What would be the meaning, what the sense, what the fitness, and what the propriety, of giving this reason annexed if it were not a thing already understood and in relation to which it was proper to say strictly, "Remember" this old institution; "Remember this day to keep it holy?"

One may say, "Ah, but the Decalog was a comparatively new thing, and it made a set of moral rules for a dispensation that was to pass away." All Christendom rejects that theory. All Christendom stands for the Decalog. All Christendom accepts the Decalog as something permanent in its nature, and no man believes that it for the first time made sin. It did not need the Sixth Commandment to make Cain a murderer, it did not need the Fifth Commandment to make him a dishonorer of his father. These commandments did not create virtues and vices. They defined them, they stated them, they put them in such a way that the human judgment might be able to distinguish clearly between the right and wrong, between what God demands and what God will condemn.

Then we come to the third consideration, namely, the resurrection of our blessed Savior. A threefold cord is not easily broken; here we have creation, divine legislation, our Lord's resurrection, giving a new turn altogether to the attitude in which men are to stand toward God and bringing the face into a fulness of light that was not enjoyed before. Now here it is that I want you especially to give me attention and to exercise your judgments upon the statements I want to make to you. "But," says some one in speaking of this matter, "our Lord Jesus Christ, the founder of our Christian system, does not tell people anywhere that they are to give over keeping the day that they have been keeping and that they are to take another." Now I want you to keep in mind that that is but a secondary consideration in the matter. Where the day shall come, whether at the beginning of the week or at the end of the week, is a secondary matter. The great thing is that there should be a seventh portion of the time given to rest. That is the great thing. Where it comes is a matter of detail, as we shall show by and by.

Now touching that statement—" the Lord Himself here on earth did not make the change of the day." Think for a moment, most of those to whom I speak are in the habit of going to Church and joining in the services and hearing the precious Word. You can comprehend then what is put before you. Our blessed Lord did not in person found any of the institutions that we have now. He for good and sufficient reasons left that to be done by those who came after Him. He trained His Apostles, He invested them with authority, He promised them touching the Holy Spirit, He departed, and that Spirit came when He had departed, and they, carrying out His will and under the influence of His Divine Spirit, framed the institutions that we have now. Christ Jesus never built a church edifice, Christ Jesus never gathered a Christian congregation, Christ Jesus never presided in a Christian meeting, Christ Jesus never established the institutions; He sowed the seed, and He gave the promise of the Spirit to His Apostles, and He endued them with the power, so that men in His name and by His authority gave the world the institutions in which we rejoice as Christian institutions, and all that was done according to a fixed and definite plan which theologians can explain to you if you take the trouble to look into their arguments upon that subject.

Then the question is, What did these men, endued with the Spirit and doing the things that would glorify Him that He might glorify the Father, do? Now I recall to your knowledge what you already have seen in your Bibles. On the first day of the week these men were in the habit of meeting together, meeting together to remember and rejoice in the resurrection, meeting together to worship God and receive instruction, meeting together as the followers of the risen Savior. It was not what they were used to. Those of them that were Hebrews did indeed for long continue to keep the Hebrew Sabbath and to keep it concurrently with the observance of

the first day of the week, and as long as that remained simply a matter of venerable usage, the Apostles had nothing to say against it; but when an attempt was made to perpetuate these features of Judaism as against Christianity, then, as you can see in your Bibles, they spoke out against those things. They, on the other hand, did not keep as a day holy the day of their Lord's entombment, the day when He was lying in the grave, the day when they were in the deepest sadness and sorrow. They did not keep that, but they kept the day when He rose, when their sadness disappeared, when their burden was lifted from their shoulders, and when they met again to rejoice, as they got understanding of His character, in a risen Redeemer who had conquered death and the grave.

It is a rather curious thing, a coincidence probably, that we have in the narrative to which I allude five times the meeting on the first day of the week mentioned in the New Testament story. Five times exactly in the narrative of Genesis we have an allusion to the week. A curious coincidence, it will be said, between the two things, and yet not so strange probably, after all. The finished work of the Creator was marked by the day of rest, and the finished work of the new Creator, who came to redeem and make all things new, was worthily commemorated in the same fashion, and the usage started with absolute uniformity on the part of the early Church, on the part of the Apostles as a whole, on the part of Paul himself in relation to " the collection," and other things; all these indicated that the clear, definite, and established usage by men who had the gift of the Spirit, and who were to put in shape what Christ taught them, as the germs of truth—their uniform usage was to keep that day, the first day of the week, which is now to us the Christian Sabbath. If, therefore, an argument is needed upon that matter, it is possible for us to set up an argument to which there is no adequate and conclusive rejoinder.—P. T. VII.

HOW SHALL WE SPEND THE SABBATH ?

By Dwight L. Moody

This is a serious question for young and old. When I was a boy, the Sabbath lasted from sundown on Saturday to sundown on Sunday, and I remember how we boys used to shout when the Sabbath was over. It was the worst day in the week to us. I believe it can be made the brightest day in the week. Every child ought to be reared so that he shall be able to say, with a friend, that he would rather have the other six days weeded out of his memory than the Sabbath of his childhood.

" Sabbath " means " rest," and the meaning of the word gives a hint as to the true way to observe the day. God rested after creation, and ordained the Sabbath as a rest for man.

" Remember the rest-day to keep it holy." It is the day when the body may be refreshed and strengthened after six days of labor, and the soul drawn into closer fellowship with its Maker.

Suppose some gentleman gave fifty thousand dollars for the purpose of building a new Church; what would be said if the gift was applied to build stores or some other building? Yet we are distinctly told that the Sabbath was made for man, and hence it was intended that man should use it as a Sabbath; but how often it is used for other purposes!

Suppose, again, that one man was met on a road by another man to whom he gave six dollars, and kept only one dollar for himself, to pay his expenses to the end of the journey. Suppose the other turned on him, knocked him down, and took away the one dollar, would not his ingratitude arouse our indignation? Yet God ordained the Sabbath that men might have time to worship Him; but how often do we rob God of the day!

True observance of the Sabbath may be considered under two general heads: cessation from work, and religious exercises.

A man ought to turn aside from his ordinary employment one day in seven. There are many whose occupation will not permit them to observe Sunday, but they should observe some other day as a Sabbath.

Ministers and missionaries often tell me that they take no rest-day; they do not need it because they are in the Lord's work. That is a mistake. When God was giving Moses instructions about the building of the tabernacle, He referred especially to the Sabbath, and gave injunctions for its strict observance; and later, when Moses was conveying the words of the Lord to the children of Israel, he interpreted them by saying that not even were sticks to be gathered on the Sabbath to kindle fires for smelting or other purpose. In spite of their zeal and haste to erect the tabernacle, the workmen were to have their day of rest. The command applies to ministers and others engaged in Christian work to-day as much as to these Israelite workmen of old.

All merely secular work ought to be avoided. An infidel was introduced by a gentleman to a minister with the remark, "He never attends public worship."

"I hope you are mistaken," said the minister.

"By no means," said the stranger. "I always spend Sunday in settling my accounts."

"Then, sir," was the solemn reply, "you will find that the judgment-day will be spent in the same way."

A woman forgot to send home some washing on Saturday. The next morning she told a little girl that lived with her to take the bundle under her shawl to the lady. "Nobody will see it," she said.

"But isn't it Sunday under my shawl, auntie?" asked the child.

In judging whether any work may or may not be lawfully done on the Sabbath, find out the reason and object for doing it. Exceptions are to be made for works of necessity and works of emergency. By "works of necessity" I mean those acts that Christ justified when He approved of leading one's ox or ass to water. Watchmen, police, stokers on board steamers, and many others, have engagements that necessitate their working on Sunday. By "works of emergency" I mean those referred to by Christ when He approved of pulling an ox or an ass out of a pit on the Sabbath day. In case of fire or sickness a man is often called to do things that would not otherwise be justifiable.

A Christian man was once urged by his employer to work on Sunday. "Does not your Bible say that if your ass falls into a pit on the Sabbath, you may pull him out?"

"Yes," replied the other; "but, if the ass had a habit of falling into the same pit every Sabbath, I would either fill up the pit or sell the ass."

The good effect on a nation's health and happiness produced by the return of the Sabbath, with its cessation from work, cannot be overestimated. Lord Beaconsfield said: "Of all divine institutions, the most divine is that which secures a day of rest for man. I hold it to be the most valuable blessing conceded to man. It is the cornerstone of civilization, and its removal might affect even the health of the people." Mr. Gladstone told a friend that the secret of his long life is that amid all the pressure of public cares he never forgot the Sabbath, with its rest for the body and the soul. The constitution of the United States protects the president in his weekly day of rest. He has ten days, "Sundays excepted," in which to consider a bill that has been sent to him for signature. Every working man in the republic ought to be as thoroughly protected as the president. If working men got up a strike for no work on Sunday, they would have the sympathy of a good many.

But "rest" does not mean idleness. No man enjoys idleness for any length of time. When one goes on a vacation, one does not lie around doing nothing all the time. Hard work at tennis, fishing, and other pursuits fill the hours. A healthy mind must find something to do.

Hence the Sabbath rest does not mean inactivity. "Satan finds some mischief still for idle hands to do." The best way to keep off bad thoughts and to avoid temptation is to engage in active religious exercises.

As regards these, we should avoid extremes. On the one hand we find a rigor in Sabbath observance that is nowhere commanded in Scripture, and that reminds one more of the formalism of the Pharisees than of the spirit of the gospel. In former times in Connecticut they had laws like this: "No one shall run on the Sabbath, or walk in his garden or elsewhere, except reverently to and from Church." Such strictness does more harm than good. It repels people and makes the Sabbath a burden.

On the other hand, we should jealously guard against a loose way of keeping the Sabbath. Already in many cities the day is profaned openly. Sunday newspapers are issued wholesale, not only turning the minds of readers away from godly things, and thus acting as a positive barrier in the way of religion, but also keeping newsboys away from Sunday school to sell papers, and keeping trains running in order that they may be distributed.

Make the Sabbath a day of religious activity. First of all, of course, is attendance at public worship. "There is a discrepancy," says John McNeill, "between our creed about the Sabbath day and our actual conduct. In many families at ten o'clock on Sunday attendance at Church is still an open question.

There is no open question on Monday morning—'John, shall you go to work to-day?'" A minister rebuked a farmer for not attending Church, and said, "You know, John, you are never absent from market." "O," was the reply, "we *must* go to market."

Some one has said that without the Sabbath the Church of Christ could not, as a visible organization, exist on earth.

But we must not mistake the means for the end. We must not think that the Sabbath is just for the sake of being able to attend meetings. There are some people that think they must spend the whole day at meetings or in private devotions. The result is that at nightfall they are tired out, and the day has brought them no rest. The number of Church services attended ought to be measured by the person's ability to enjoy them and get good from them, without being wearied. Attending meetings is not the only way to observe the Sabbath. In Lev. xxiii: 3, the Israelites were commanded to keep it in their dwellings as well as in holy convocation. The home, that center of so great influence over the life and character of people, ought to be made the scene of true Sabbath observance.

Many mothers have written to me at one time or another to know what to do to entertain their children on Sunday. The boys say, "I do wish 't was night," or, "I do hate Sunday," or, "I do wish Sunday was over." It ought to be the happiest day in the week to them, one to be looked forward to with pleasure. In order to this end, many suggestions might be followed. Make family prayers especially attractive by having the children repeat some verse or story from the Bible. Give more time to your children than you can give on week-days, reading to them and perhaps taking them to walk in the afternoon or evening. Show by your conduct that the Sabbath is a delight, and they will soon catch your spirit. Set aside some time for religious instruction, without making this a task. You can make it interesting for the children by telling Bible stories and asking them to guess the names of the characters. Have Sunday games for the younger children. Picture-books, puzzle-maps of Palestine, etc., can be easily obtained. Sunday albums and Sunday clocks are other devices. Set aside attractive books for Sunday, not letting the children have these during the week. By doing this, and by having extra delicacies at meals, perhaps, the children can be brought to look forward to the day with eagerness and pleasure.

Apart from public and family observance of the Sabbath, the individual ought to devote a portion of the time to his own edification. Prayer, meditation, reading, ought not to be forgotten. Think of men devoting six days a week to their body, which will soon pass away, and begrudging one day to the soul, which will live on and on forever!

If your circumstances permit, engage in some definite Christian work,—such as teaching in Sunday school, or visiting the sick. Do all the good you can. Sin keeps no Sabbath, and no more should good deeds. There is plenty of opportunity in this fallen world to perform works of mercy and of religion. Make your Sabbath down here a foretaste of the eternal Sabbath that is in store for believers.

"If thou turn away thy foot from the Sabbath, from doing thy pleasure on my holy day; and call the Sabbath a delight, the holy of the Lord, honorable, and shalt honor him, not doing thine own ways, nor finding thine own pleasure, nor speaking thine own words ['thine own' as contrasted with what God enjoins], then shalt thou delight thyself in the Lord; and I will cause thee to ride upon the high places of the earth, and feed thee with the heritage of Jacob thy father, for the mouth of the Lord hath spoken it."—G. R.

THE CHRISTIAN SABBATH

When De Tocqueville, the celebrated publicist of France, first came to this country, he was the guest of the Hon. John C. Spencer, then living in Canandaigua, N. Y. The village is delightfully located in the heart of a rich farming country, and was then mainly on one broad, beautiful street, on, or near which, were all the Churches of the village. The inhabitants were mostly of New England origin, and were a remarkably Church going people. De Tocqueville arrived there toward the end of the week; and on Saturday, as the country people came in, in crowds, to make their purchases and close up the business of the week, he spoke with surprise of their numbers and of their comfortable and thrifty appearance.

On the morning of Sunday, a bright, cool, delightful day, as he looked out after breakfast, he was still more surprised to see no one in the streets, and that all was as quiet and still as if the place had been deserted. And he asked Mr. Spencer, "What does this mean?" "Why," said Mr. Spencer, "it is Sunday." But this was no satisfactory explanation to the Frenchman; and when asked still further as to its meaning, Mr. Spencer replied, "Wait until the bells ring, and then you will see."

At half-past ten o'clock the bells from all the churches rang out their call to divine worship, and soon the broad walks of the street were crowded with people neatly and comfortably, and many of them expensively dressed, and all quietly thronging their way to the churches. And again De Tocqueville asked Mr. Spencer the meaning of all this; he was told in reply that this was the American way of keeping the holy Sabbath; and that every Sunday the great masses of the people laid aside their labor and all secular occupations and went up to the house of God, there to be instructed in truth, and directed in duty, both for this world and the next. And as De Tocqueville pondered the spectacle, and heard the explanation, he raised his hands, and with deep earnestness said, " Mr. Spencer, France must have your American Sabbath, or she is ruined! "

And when a gentleman asked the late Professor Agassiz, " What was the thing above all which most struck you in coming to this country? " the great naturalist gave as his answer, " Your American observance of the Lord's day."

In the Prussian Parliament petitions were not long since presented asking the government " to secure to the working classes their rest day; " for the Sabbath, which they took for pleasure, has been seized by Mammon for work—as, sooner or later, it always will be when its sacredness is broken down—and now the working men, when they find they are compelled by their employers to work on the Sabbath, want to get back again the rest and quiet of the Sabbath day. And in answer to their petitions, the government instructed its agents in England and the United States, to inquire into the Sabbath laws and customs of these two countries, with a view to adopting them in Prussia.

And when the Japanese are giving up their six resting days in each month and fixing on four—the first days of the weeks, corresponding to our Sabbaths—as their rest days, it surely is not for us to break down the rest and sacredness of our holy day.

" In giving us the Sabbath," said Coleridge, " I feel as if God had given us fifty-two springs in every year." And Count Montalembert, in his report to the French Parliament, soon after the overthrow of the French Republic, pleading earnestly for the full restoration and retention of the Sabbath, says: " In all our towns, and throughout too large a portion of our country districts, the Sabbath rest is violated, and the worship which was the consequence and condition of this rest is abandoned. At the same time the soul is deprived of its nourishment and the body of its repose. The poor man and the workingman are delivered up, unprotected, to the every-day increasing influence of error and evil. Thus the profanation of the day has become the ruin of the moral and physical health of the people, at the same time that it is the ruin of the family and of religious liberty."

True, perfectly true, every word of it. The Sabbath is, emphatically, the poor man's and the workingman's day. And there is no surer way to break down the health, as well as the morals and religion of the people, than to break down the Sabbath. To say nothing of the Divine law, on mere worldly grounds it is plain that nothing is more conducive to the health, intelligence, comfort, and independence of the working classes, and to our prosperity as a people, than our Christian American Sabbath.—A. M.

THE SUNDAY NEWSPAPER

By Herrick Johnson, D.D.

Let us be honest. The Sunday newspaper is not the Sunday religious or semi-religious paper; it is not the Sunday moral reform or semi-moral reform paper; it is the Sunday newspaper. Just that and that only; only that and nothing more. It is not the newspaper in partnership with Sunday to promote mutual interests and to share the profits. The only mutual interests that are promoted are those represented by that maxim of the boy in tossing up the penny: " Heads I win; tails you lose." The profits all go to the newspaper, and Sunday stands all the losses. The Sunday paper is simply the daily newspaper thrust into Sunday; published seven days in the week instead of six; unchanged as to its essential character. It is enlarged, indeed, greatly enlarged, but neither revised nor reformed, and certainly not sanctified or glorified.

When the newspaper first appeared on Sunday it changed its clothes a little. It was padded with pious homily as they pad the sacred concerts with " Sweet By and By " and the " Doxology in long meter; " but the wolf soon got tired of trying to look like a sheep, and now the wolf enters Sunday, a stark wolf, pure and simple, with scarcely a bit of the woolly fleece he put on when he was keeping up appearances. And you can see no difference between the Sunday and the Saturday paper save as to magnitude. It is a great mosaic; a huge conglomerate of all sorts of material pertaining to the world, the flesh, and the devil. It is a vast blanket of information, some of it—a great deal of it—not inherently unwholesome; but all of it secular, worldly, of the earth earthy; and some of it—very often a great deal of it—vicious, pernicious and unclean. It is just such a dish as we have served to us every other day of the week, except as to size, and it is seasoned and garnished and tricked out with every possible device to tempt the appetite and to gorge the social, literary and sensational stomach. It is a sheet like unto the sheet of the apostolic vision; like it in this, that it is a " great sheet " and " full of all manner of four-footed beasts and creeping things," but unlike it in this, that it was never " dropped down from heaven," and of its contents it never could be said, " What God has cleansed." This is the Sunday newspaper.

To be literally exact in this matter, let me cite the figures published not long since by the New York *Mail and Express*. These figures are made from an actual measurement, inch by inch, of the columns of the leading New York Sunday papers, which are certainly on a par with any Sunday publishing dailies in the country. On a certain Sunday, of political, special, sensational, criminal, and gossipy matter, the *Tribune* published eighty-three columns, the *Herald* eighty-one columns, the *World* one hundred and twelve columns, the *Sun* eighty-six columns, and the *Times* eighty-eight columns. What a mass of stuff that is to begin and go through God's day with! We have too much of it on other days. Does not the better nature of every one of us cry out: "Give us a rest at least one day in seven from this unwholesome dumpage!" But is there no religious reading in these Sunday papers? O yes; here are the bits of lamb-like fleece, by exact mathematical measurement, furnished on a subsequent Sunday. The *Tribune* published eighty-one columns of political, special, sensational, criminal and gossipy matter, *and three-quarters of a column devoted to religion!* The *Herald* eighty-four columns, with three-quarters of a column devoted to religion! The *World* ninety columns, with one-half a column devoted to religion! The *Sun* ninety-seven columns with one and three-eighths columns devoted to religion! The *Times* sixty-eight columns, with one-eighth of a column devoted to religion! It would be difficult to imagine what possible effect that little homeopathic pill of "sweetness and light" could possibly produce alongside that vast dose of crime, worldliness and sensationalism.

And this suggests another count in the indictment against the Sunday newspaper. It is tempting hundreds and thousands to stay away from the sanctuary, and making it manifold harder for the truth to reach those who go. Ruskin says, in view of the thronging activities of our times, the rush and roar of our busy life, the push and press and ambitions of trade, a minister on Sunday morning has "just thirty minutes to raise the dead in." The Sunday newspaper is another huge stone laid on that sepulcher making it just so much harder to raise the dead. Think how the appetite must be whetted for the word of God by reading column after column of such a paper, seasoned by the most adroit reportorial caterers for the special delectation of literary and sensational stomachs.

Another count I bring is, that not content with a single city, the Sunday newspaper, by "thunder-ball railroad extras" and "lightning flyers," is invading the peaceful Sabbath observance of cities and towns of the country for miles and miles away, and going with "banners flying" to disturb by "crowds" and "cheers" and "mobs of newsboys" the Sabbath of other populations.

This is the fearful indictment against it— that it is keeping an army of workmen from the day of rest they ought to have; it is educating an army of newsboys to trample on the Sabbath, and so counteracting the best influences that Christian people are trying to throw around them; it is thrusting itself into the face of a Sabbath-loving people as no other business is allowed to thrust itself; it is assaulting the Sabbath in quarters that are not reached by any other Sabbath-assaulting agency; and in this respect it is a most insidious and subtle evil, reaching a class of our community that the Sunday saloon and Sunday theater and the Sunday concert never touch, sweeping through the very best ranks of workingmen and even into the homes of religion; it is honey-combing society with false notions about the Sabbath, and it is deadening the spiritual sensibilities even of many of the people of God. The indictment is made, the evidence presented, the case submitted; and confident appeal is made, not only to Christian conscience, but to the considerate judgment of manly and self-respecting labor, and to that broad catholic intelligence which believes that the best interests of society and the State are wrapped up in the preservation of the American Sabbath.

Meanwhile, what are the friends of the Sabbath going to do about it! Well, first of all, *we must get and keep a conscience, into the warp and woof of which shall be woven the Divine authority of the Sabbath law,* "Remember the Sabbath to keep it holy." If we base the Sabbath on mere human expediency we base it on sand, just as we would found honesty if we adopted it simply as a "policy." This is no basis for the Sabbath, to put it on the ground of mere expediency. I do not question the propriety of using this argument as a means of influencing a certain class of men. Many will join in this Sunday movement and work heartily in the defense of Sunday as a rest-day in the interests of health and morals and good citizenship, who will not come to the higher ground. But we can never permanently keep our Sabbath on a basis of expediency. The gospel of the body is clear and unmistakable, but the greed of capital will overtask labor provided always a further supply is ready to take its place. No, the anchorage for the Sabbath is in the fact that it is a divine institution.

God commands its observance. There it is, in the bosom of His law as given in the Decalog. That is enough for anyone who believes in God. As God appointed it, He has told us how to keep it. We must not divide it up by giving Him a part only. "Remember the Sabbath *day*." Not the Sabbath morning, leaving the afternoon for recreation and desecration. "Remember the Sabbath day to keep it holy," not simply to rest. The Jews had loaded the day with traditions. Christ simply unloaded it of these justifying works of necessity and mercy. We hear a good deal of the need of a public conscience. But there is no possible public conscience apart from individual consciences. What we want is a good deal more of the individual conscience and I venture to say, *ministerial* conscience; a conscience *in the ministry* that will guard sacredly all the interests of this day, and that will see to it that even the hem of the garments of the ministry is not touched with the taint of any questionable Sabbath indulgence, so that month in and month out, year in and year out, the ministry will be consistently and unchallengeably free to declare God's words concerning this matter.

Let us be rid of the taint I say, of all questionable indulgence, and then take appeal from God's word to every Christian conscience, to merchants and lawyers and legislators, who acknowledge the obligations of loyalty to Christ. Let us righteously rebuke the profanation of the day, and wakefully see to it that, while legislation establishing any form of religion is scrupulously guarded against, legislation *hostile to God's Sabbath law is unalterably kept off the statute books*. With a sweet reasonableness and with a firm conviction of the rightfulness of our cause, I am sure that, with anything like a Christian sentiment and a united Christian effort we can carry this cause and preserve our Sabbath. O for a breath of the old Puritan! Doubtless he was sometimes too austere. Doubtless he sometimes looked as if all hope had been washed out of his face. I believe his Sabbath was a little too grim. But what men it made! Men of the martyr spirit. Men of heroic mold. Men of the stuff that is food for the rack and the stake. Men that had an almost infinite scorn for the reign of the turtle dove. You could trust them, lean on them, depend on them. They were great fearers of God, but they feared neither man nor devil. With Christ's gentleness wrapped around this unyieldingness may we make the Sabbath fight, and win!—In.

SERMONS AND OUTLINES

WHY THE LORD'S DAY IS KEPT BY CHRISTIANS

By Reese F. Alsop, D.D.

This is the day the Lord hath made; let us rejoice and be glad in it.—Ps. cxviii: 24

I propose to apply these words this morning to the Christian Sunday, or Lord's Day, and try to show why we keep it as our sacred day.

First, let me call your attention to a contrast. If you turn to the fourth chapter of the Gospel according to St. Luke at the 16th verse, you may read: " Jesus entered, as his custom was, into the synagog on the Sabbath day." And if then you turn to the 20th chapter of the Acts, at the 7th verse, you may read: "And upon the first day of the week, when they were gathered together to break bread (that is, in the Holy Communion), Paul discoursed with them, intending to depart on the morrow." Here Jesus keeps the Jewish Sabbath—that is, the seventh day. His apostles, after His ascension, seem to be keeping another day.

. . . .

Now the two passages to which I have just asked your attention show us that away back in the days of the Apostles this contrast began. Judaism held fast to her own old day. Christianity began at once to set apart another day. Why was this? What is our reason, what is our authority, for keeping the first day instead of the seventh?

There seem to be very strong reasons for the seventh. It was sanctified by the long usage of the old Jewish Church. The Fourth Commandment says: " Remember that thou keep holy the Sabbath day. Six days shalt thou labor, . . . but the seventh is the Sabbath of the Lord thy God." Times without number was it declared to Israel that Jehovah would bless or forsake them precisely as they kept or profaned His Sabbath. And to all this add, that Jesus Himself revered the seventh day. His custom was, we are told, to enter into the synagog on the seventh day and take part in the worship; nor did He say one word or do anything to empty the seventh day of its sacredness. Its abuses and hard restrictions He set aside, but the Sabbath, as made for man, for mercy, for healing and blessing, He honored.

How came we, then, to have made the change? A Jew might say to us: " You profess to honor the Old Testament. You recite the Fourth Commandment every Sunday in your Church worship. You own, as your founder and guide, Jesus Christ, who went into the synagog for worship on the seventh day. You admit that He kept that day. You can show no command in all your Scripture for making the change. And yet you keep, not the seventh day, but the first. What have you to say for yourselves? Are you not inconsistent, recreant to your own sacred writings, disobedient to the word and example of your Lord?" The arraignment, you see, is a strong one. The accuser is not easily answered. Now, in answer to his charge, I propose to show you this morning that in the Old Testament there was a remarkable foreshadowing of the coming change; and then I propose to point out to you by what steps and under whose authority that change, thus foreshadowed, was brought to pass. I shall have to ask your very close attention.

A careful reading of the passages bearing upon the subject will show that Moses instituted not only a Sabbath day, but a Sabbath system. This system has in it five members, which fall into two groups—one group of three and another group of two. The first three clearly affix sanctity to the last in a series of seven. There was the Sabbath day, which was the last in seven days. There was the seventh month, which was peculiarly sacred as having in it the great day of atonement, and three or four extra days of rest thrown in. Finally, there was the seventh year, which was the sabbatic year, when all farm land was to lie fallow, and Hebrew slaves go free. Now notice that in each of these three, making the first group, it was the seventh—the seventh day, the seventh month, the seventh year—to which the sanctity was attached. But this was not all of the system. There was, as I have said, the other group, with its two members. There were the feast of Pentecost—of Weeks, as it used to be called by the Jews—and the Year of Jubilee. That these were a part of the sabbatic system becomes evident upon the slightest examination. Their place was fixed by the count of weeks multiplied by weeks; that is, by multiplying seven by seven. From the Sabbath (the Jewish Sabbath) after the Passover feast, seven times seven were counted to bring Pentecost. The same was done, of years instead of days, to bring the year of Jubilee—a week of years; that is, seven years multiplied by seven made forty-nine.

But now there comes in something very remarkable. Were the analogy of the seventh day, the seventh month, the seventh year, carried out, Pentecost would fall on the forty-ninth day after the Sabbath following the Passover, and the Year of Jubilee would fall on the forty-ninth year. It does, in either case, nothing of the kind. Pentecost falls on the first day of the week following the forty-ninth day. And so in the count to the Jubilee year, that wonderful year which was to give liberty to the captive, the opening of the prison to them that were bound, land to the landless, freedom to the debtor, lifting up to them that were down. That year fell, not on the last day of a series of seven times seven years, but, again, on the first day of the next series. The fiftieth day was Pentecost; the fiftieth year was Jubilee. That is, in each case, the series of days or years were allowed to come to a full end, and then the first day, the first year, of the next series, was taken. This is a very interesting fact, and one which until recently was never brought especially to my own notice; and yet it bears most strongly upon the subject we have before us this morning.

And in this connection note this: that among all the feasts of the Jews, Pentecost was the only one that had no backward look, but only a forward look. The Passover commemorated the deliverance from Egypt. The feast of Tabernacles recalled the wilderness life. Pentecost had nothing to do with the past, but rejoiced only in the present and in the future. And, again, among all the institutions of Moses, there was not one which to all seemed so much an earnest and foretaste of better things to come, as the year of Jubilee. It was felt to be an anticipation of a veritable kingdom of God. It came, at

last, to be identified with the coming Messiah—as if Messiah, when He came, could do no better thing than bring to earth the blessedness of the Jubilee year. And so it came to pass, that when Jesus preached in the synagog of Jerusalem, and read a passage which all who heard it understood to apply to the year of Jubilee, and then said, "This day is the Scripture fulfilled in your ears," He was understood by all to be claiming to be the Messiah.

Here, then, was a subtle intimation of a change to come. The one feast· among the Jews which looked not backward but forward, began on the first day of the week. The great year which foreshadowed the blessings of Messiah's reign—that, too, fell not on a seventh year, or a forty-ninth, but the fiftieth—that is, the first of a new series. If, then, the spirit of the Jubilee was realized, as Jesus declared it was, in His coming, and if the highest meaning of Pentecost was realized in the outpouring of the Holy Ghost, then need we wonder to find the new dispensation adopting, not the rule of the seventh day, the seventh month, the seventh year, but the higher rule of the first day after the series of sevens has been completed. That, as a matter of fact, such rule was adopted; that it was done, if not with the direct command, yet most evidently with the sanction of our Lord and of His Spirit, a study of the facts shows. Without detaining you, I can only run hastily through the argument.

The first Sunday after the crucifixion was the day of Christ's resurrection. By that resurrection, the apostle tells us, Jesus was declared with power to be the Son of God—that is, His Lordship was affirmed by the direct act of the Almighty. More or less of what happened on that Sunday, you remember. We glanced at the facts last Sunday evening. Notice one thing. We read the account in the Gospel for the morning. The disciples were gathered together, and Jesus, now risen, appeared to them, talked with them, blessed them. Then He disappeared. We can imagine, in spite of the joy which must have throbbed through all the week in their souls, how they wanted to see Him again. The fact was so stupendous, so hard to realize, that it dazed and must have half crazed them at first. To quiet their apprehension, to fix even more strongly their faith, to make them sure that, after all, they had not been deceived by a now-vanished form—yea, to convince Thomas, who had been absent, they felt, every one of them, we may be sure, that they needed to see Him again. They doubtless looked, longed, and prayed for it with an intensity of desire. But day after day passed, and He came not. In spite of their gladness, the strain upon their souls and their minds must have been almost painful. Wednesday, Thursday, Friday, and still no further signs of their risen Lord. Saturday came, and with it, perhaps, kindling anticipation. On this day, so sacred among the Jews—this day on which He was wont to worship with them so regularly in the synagog, this day made, as He has told them, for man—on this day surely He would come; He would distinguish it again by showing Himself to His disciples. No, the day passed, and He left them still unvisited.

Then came the first day of the week. Gathered together for worship, they waited, and lo, He came again, and blessed and lightened them. This second appearance on the eighth day of the new era must have started their thought. They would now feel that His absence in a certain way implied His return; that, as He then returned on the octave of the resurrection, they might perhaps expect Him on the next. They felt that thus He had emphasized the week, and already, perhaps, they realized that He had begun to honor its first day. Whether their expectations that He would appear again on the next first day were realized, we cannot positively say. There were four more Sundays before the ascension, and at least four times more He did appear—once to the apostles (seven of them) on the shores of the Lake of Tiberius; once to five hundred brethren on the mountain in Galilee, once to James, and once again to all the apostles. Those appearances may have been on successive Sundays. There is nothing in Scripture inconsistent with the supposition. If they did so recur, we can easily understand that before the fourth had come those disciples would have come to look forward with intense anticipation to the first day of the week, and even naturally begun to call it the Lord's Day. After the ascension, following, as it did, after the sixth Sunday, they would look no more for a bodily appearance. There was, however, something else to look for—the promise of the Father; power from on high was to come; and Jesus had told them to tarry in Jerusalem until it did come.

We pass now over one Sunday, and come to the eighth (counting the first). This eighth Sunday, then, is the fiftieth day after the Jewish Sabbath when Jesus lay in the tomb. It is the Jewish Pentecost. Quite early in the morning, the disciples gather together. It is not to keep the Jewish feast, for those services are held later, in the temple. It is for communion and worship. Gathered in that upper room, they pray, and as they pray the gift comes—the rushing, mighty wind; the cloven tongues, as of fire; the power which makes that day an epoch in the Church's history, almost as great as the resurrection day. And remember that that comes on the seventh Sunday after the first Easter day—another honor put upon this day, another mark to set it apart for Christian thought, from all other days.

That the day thus honored by our Lord and by the Holy Spirit found a hold and place in the reverence of the Church, is plain. Some twenty years after this, Paul was writing to the Church at Corinth, which he himself had established two or three years before. He wished to give them some direction as to the gathering of benevolent offerings, and he tells them that the best thing to do is to take their collections on the first day of the week, for that is what his words mean.

His direction, you see, takes it for granted that a regular assembly of the Christian people of Corinth was held for worship on the first day of the week.

Now take another intimation. About a year after that letter to Corinth, we catch another glimpse of this observance. Paul, at the end of his third missionary tour, had turned his face back toward Jerusalem. He left Philippi in one of the sailing vessels which coasted along the shore, and he was detained some six days coasting across the north of what we call the Archipelago, and so much was he delayed that he did not reach Troas until Monday. At Troas, as the result of former labors, there was a church. Now there are indications that Paul felt under great pressure to get to Jerusalem as soon as he could. Nevertheless, he abides in Troas seven days. Why? we wonder. What keeps him in that little place for seven days, when he is in a hurry to get to Jerusalem? Simply this: he wanted to attend the full meeting of the Church on the next Sunday. His slow passage had made him miss one Sunday, and he waits for the next, and we are told that on the first day of the week, when the disciples came together to break their sacramental bread, Paul preached unto them, ready to depart in the morning—feeling, apparently, that he had strained a point even to stay so long. Here we find that the Lord's day is the set occasion for the Church's assembling for worship.

If now we turn to the Book of Revelation, we find that the first day of the week had then (and this book was probably written some time between the years 60 and 70) its name, which was generally well known. John, an exile for the gospel of Christ on the Island of Patmos, tells in rapt vision what the Lord showed unto him; and we are not surprised to find that it was on the Lord's Day that the Lord saw fit to draw aside the veil and give him those rare glimpses of the world to come. John says, " I was in the spirit on the Lord's Day."

Put, now, all these intimations together: the strange foreshadowing in the Old Testament of a change to come, from the seventh day of the week to the first; the honor given to the first day by the resurrection, and then by the appearance of our Lord to the disciples on the next first day, and His probable appearance on four more. Add to this the outpouring of the Holy Ghost on the first day, and the evident custom of the Church's assembling on the first day of the week for the purposes of worship; then John's vision at Patmos on the Lord's day; and are you not ready, with all these intimations, to take the words of the text, and say, " This is the day the Lord hath made; we will rejoice and be glad in it."

That it so impressed the early Church is plain from the two extra-Scriptural witnesses. We have, in the year of our Lord 104, Pliny's letter, in which he described to the Emperor what the Christians were wont to do. He says this: " On a stated day the Christians meet to sing a hymn to Christ as God, to take an oath to commit no theft, adultery, or fraud, and to partake together of food."

It is easy for us to see here a heathen description of a Christian Sunday and its worship. What the set day was, spoken of by Pliny, is shown clearly·by a letter of Justin Martyr, written some thirty-five years later, who declared that " on the day called Sunday the Christians held their assemblies for reading the Scriptures, prayer to Christ, alms-giving, and the Lord's Supper."

And so my chain of proof is as strong as I can make it. That a day thus honored by Christ and the Spirit, thus sanctioned and instituted by the apostles, thus taken for its sacred day of worship by the whole Church of the first century—that such a day should have taken the place of the Jewish Sabbath, and held that place through all the Christian centuries, is not surprising. That it has so done is a simple matter of fact, About other things Christians have differed. Other usages have changed; modes of worship have varied from age to age. But by a consent that is practically universal, Christians always and everywhere have consented together to honor and keep the first day of the week. They have now, as perhaps they have always had, differing views as to its obligation, differing opinions as to the way in which it ought to be kept, differing views as to the source of its sanctity. None the less, they have united in the feeling that it ought to be kept, and kept it has been, from the resurrection-day down through all the ages of time, through changes moral, political, social—through war and peace, through adversity and prosperity, through persecution and trial—Christian men and women have ever held the first day of the week as holy to their Lord, who on that day broke the bars of the grave and the gates of death. Nor is the unanimity strange when we remember the heart thought of the day.

The Sabbath was to the Jew the token of the covenant between Jehovah and His people, and it was a badge of loyalty toward Jehovah. That thought the Christian Sunday has inherited. It is the Lord's day, the token of the new covenant betwixt our Lord and those who rejoice to call him Lord. Yea, it is not too much to say that it is the badge of loyalty of Christians toward their Lord. That is its meaning, that is its purpose, that is the wrought-out effect, in soul and life, of its right keeping. "True loyalty to Christ will keep it, will honor it, will call it sacred, and, as it keeps it, that loyalty will grow warmer and deeper and fuller, till its highest joy is to serve, and at last to see, the King in His beauty."—H. R.

THE SABBATH

By Howard Crosby, D.D.

If thou turn away thy foot from the Sabbath, from doing thy pleasure on my holy day, and call the Sabbath a delight, the holy of the Lord, honorable; and shalt honor him, not doing thine own ways, nor finding thine own pleasure, nor speaking thine own words; then shalt thou delight thyself in the Lord, and I will cause thee to ride upon the high places of the earth and feed thee with the heritage of Jacob thy father; for the mouth of the Lord hath spoken it.—Isaiah lviii: 13, 14

The only correction to be made in this passage from the Authorized Version is " and shalt honor it (the Sabbath) by not doing thine own ways." The 53d chapter of Isaiah shows us the Messiah suffering and dying for sinners. The 54th and 55th chapters show the enlargement of God's Church that follows, and give the invitation to all to enter, and then come four chapters (lvi., lvii., lviii., and lix.), showing the evils which the church in its growth would have to contend with. In this portion, which stands between the invitation and the description of the glorious Church, embracing the Gentiles (chapter lx, etc.), note the peculiar position of the Sabbath commandment. We first find the Sabbath observance as a distinctive mark of the faithful ones who form the germ of the future developed Church in its glory. In chapter lvi: 2, the Sabbath keeper is the blessed one, and in verses 4 and 6 the eunuchs and strangers (classes excluded from the Old Testament ritual) are invited into the new Church, and in each case the keeping of the Sabbath is made a seal of their taking hold of God's covenant of grace—" thus saith the Lord unto the eunuchs that keep my Sabbaths and choose the things that please me and take hold of my covenant," etc.; "also the sons of the stranger . . . every one that keepeth the Sabbath from polluting it and taketh hold of my covenant." Then afterward comes the declaration " for mine house shall be called a house of prayer for *all people.*"

So evidently is all this prophecy a view of the Messianic church, and is utterly inapplicable to the Jewish Church. Now in the very heart of this passage (including the four chapters above indicated) occurs the remarkable emphasis of the Sabbath with which we have headed this article. The theme is still the same. It is the renewed Church coming out from the old church, which had become corrupt. The light was to break forth as the morning, the Church was to become like a watered garden, the waste places were to be built, the foundations raised up, the breach repaired and the paths restored. It is right after all this, and shortly before the clear picture of the universal Church in the 60th chapter, that we have this exaltation of the Sabbath as a distinguishing mark of God's people. The conclusion is irresistible. The Sabbath is no circumscribed Jewish institution. It belongs to God's Church of all ages. It is a holy sacrament, an outward and visible sign of the inward and invisible grace of the Church. It stands here imbedded in the picture of the Messianic Church, just as it stands imbedded in the Decalog, which also was given, not to the Jewish Church, but to the universal Church of God. The details of the passage we have given show that it is God's day ("my holy day") in which man is to withdraw from his accustomed works, pleasures, and ways to find his delight in holy thoughts, words, and actions, a day ordained in the mercy and love of God to prevent man from being carnalized by his earthly occupations.

We see, then, how unsound and pernicious is the flippant relegation of the Sabbath to the old Jewish Church, and understand that the only Sabbath observance which the apostle condemned was the false, hypocritical, formal, and absurd observance practiced by the corrupt Jews of his day, to avoid which abuse of the holy time, the Lord's day, the first day of the week, the day of our Lord's resurrection was substituted for the Jewish Sabbath, and became the Christian Sabbath.

The Sabbath is ever a vital element in true piety. As the Sabbath is neglected, religion loses its purity and power. Disregard of the Sabbath is a sure sign of a low state of religious life.—H. R.

SABBATH DUTIES*

By G. D. Boardman

Ex. xx: 8-11

I. The duty of work.—This is man's normal condition. (1) For the soil's sake. Nature's capacities are latent as well as vast, and need the quickening, unfolding, marshaling powers of a tireless, and skilful labor. (2) For man's own sake. He who does not use his faculties is as tho he had none. Indolence and barbarism go hand in hand. (3) For God's sake. Stewardship.

II. The duty of rest.—The seventh day is to be a day of rest for the body, jaded with the toils of the week: a day of rest for the mind, jaded with the cares of the week: a day of rest for the heart, jaded with the griefs of the week.

III. The duty of worship.—"Keep it holy." The Sabbath, if I may so say, is God's weekly toll on mankind, the periodical tribute which He demands in token of human fealty.

THE SABBATH

By Charles F. Deems, D.D., LL.D.

Isaiah lviii: 13, 14

I. How the Sabbath is to be sanctified.—Avoiding everything which would indicate want of high respect for the Sabbath. "Turn away thy foot," etc.

II. Our language must show our respect for it.—Call the Sabbath "a delight" call the holy day of Jehovah "honorable." Our language must show that we do not consider it a useless restraint. We must honor those that honor it. Call it so, (a) to God in praising Him for it. (b) Call it so to others, endeavoring to induce them to enjoy its blessings. (c) Call it so to our own hearts, not desiring to have the blessed hours pass.

III. We must feel that in honoring the Sabbath we are honoring Him, Jehovah. (1) Not to do our own ways. (2) Not to find our own pleasure. (3) Not speaking our own words.

Heaven is called "a Sabbatism." Hence we may learn how to keep the Sabbath on earth.

IV. The fruits of this: (1) We shall *delight* ourselves in it. The more cheerfully we engage in religious duties the more pleasure we shall find. (2) *Honor.* Ride upon high places. Washington and the elder John Adams. (3) *Profit.* Feed with the heritage of our Father. Six days devotion to toil will develop the resources of this country.

This passage seems to take for granted that whoso keepeth the fourth commandment, will keep all the other commandments of God. Show that this general principle is correct.

He who violates the Sabbath will be led to other sins. Show this also. The abnormal state of body and mind induces a desire for stimulating pleasures.

A Sabbath breaker is a God-robber. His moral principles become relaxed. He fails to receive the religious impressions of the Sabbath. Show this in the annals of crime. A gentleman for twenty years visited convicts; nearly all traced their ruin to neglect of the

* Biblical Museum (J. C. Gray), p, 213.

Sabbath. Three hundred and fifty executed, nine-tenths neglected the Sabbath. Auburn State Prison. Of one thousand two hundred and thirty-two convicts, only twenty-six had been observers of the Sabbath. We never can succeed in putting down the Sabbath breaking until a right public opinion in the Church is generated. Is it any worse to steal, to commit adultery than to violate the Sabbath? Picture a world without a Sabbath. Picture a world where the Sabbath is universally observed.

THE SABBATH QUESTION

Christianity has given us the Sabbath, the jubilee of the whole world, whose light dawns welcome alike into the closet of the philosopher, into the garret of toil, and into prison cells, and everywhere suggests even to the vile, the dignity of spiritual being.—Ralph Waldo Emerson.

The Sabbath was made for man.—Mark ii: 27

It is manifest to the careful observer that the Sabbath Question is to be, in the near future, one of the decisive battlefields between the friends and enemies of Evangelical Christianity. It is to-day even a graver question than any which excites the theological world; for its relations are world-wide; and it also interests and moves the *masses*, especially the working class and pleasure seekers, as no other question does. Already the conflict has begun. Agencies, forces, influences, of all kinds are combining and drilling their forces for a grand assault, all along the line, on the Puritan Sabbath; and tho as yet there has been only a little skirmishing here and there, there is reason for serious alarm on the part of the friends of the Sabbath.

I. Let us glance at what is doing for the overthrow of the Sabbath: (1) The greatest danger of all is *the laxity which prevails in the Family.* The change which fifty years have wrought, even in New England households, is a sad and startling one. The swing from over-rigid discipline has been way over to extreme laxity or liberalism, in its observance. You see it in the custom of going to Church but *once* on Sunday, in calling, visiting, and traveling on Sunday, and in many other ways, even on the part of members of the Church. *Here the work of reform must begin.* (2) The inroad of foreigners in such great numbers is a standing menace to us. They bring the old world Sunday with them (a day of pleasure), and everywhere, in city, and country, they cast their influence against the American Sunday. (3) Adverse legislation, and the pernicious example of those in authority in truckling to a false public sentiment. Every year legislation is sought tending to destroy the sanctity of the Sabbath and make it a day of mere pleasure and vicious indulgence, and the clamor of politicians, and the foreign element, and the rum interest, and infidel intolerance, waxes louder and louder. Hence the desperate efforts to *get rid of our laws restraining the Sunday traffic,* especially liquor selling. Hence also the opening of museums and libraries, and converting our public parks into places of Sunday entertainment. (4) And, back of all this and many other active hostile agencies, the *Great Liquor Power* of the country, with its money and its organized forces, is the deadly enemy of the Sabbath. It would fain blot out the day. It interferes with its accursed trade and profits. It would have all restrictions removed, and free and full scope given to beastly indulgence. And the fact is notorious that its money is freely given, its efforts put forth, to defeat all legislation and all other attempts to improve the observance of Sunday on the part of its friends. Rum and the enemies of the Sabbath are leagued together for its overthrow.

II. In view of such a condition of things it is imperative that all who reverence the Sabbath and desire to preserve it, must sound the alarm and rally to the support of all wise measures to defeat the designs of its enemies and create a right public sentiment. The true law of the Sabbath must be restored in the family. The Sunday-school power must be enlisted in the cause. The pulpit of the land must be stirred up to give forth a mighty blast. The religious press must give out no uncertain sound. As far as possible the better class of our secular newspapers must be persuaded to lend a helping hand, when our dearest interests as a nation are imperiled. Our legislatures must be jealously watched, to prevent assault from such a source, and wherever practicable, its action sought in defence of this great bulwark of Christianity. Citizens' Leagues should be formed in every city and town to see to it that our Sabbath laws respecting the sale of liquor, confectionery, gambling, and the like, are rigidly enforced. And all possible aid should be given to those who are seeking to enlighten the public mind and keep the sacred day from profanation. A book published in New York (1885), called "The Sabbath for Man," contains a vast amount of information and facts, statistics, correspondence, appeals, arguments, etc., on the Sabbath Question, as it stands to-day throughout Christendom, that sheds much light on the matter, and we wish it might obtain universal circulation.—H. R.

THE EARLY SABBATH: A TYPE OF THE HEAVENLY

By John Cairns, D.D.

Heb. iv: 9

Heaven is a perpetual Sabbath. The word translated "rest" means "the keeping of a Sabbath." This is proved to remain to the people of God in this way. In the 95th Psalm God exhorts Israel to hear His voice lest they should be excluded from His rest. This could not be God's creation rest, which was long over; nor the rest of Israel in Canaan, for Joshua gave them this rest long before the Psalm was written. There was therefore a future rest which would be fully entered on when there was no longer any cause for God to swear, "They shall not enter into My rest." Tho there may be anticipation of this by faith, the majority of interpreters agree that the apostle refers more to the rest of glory than of grace. And this future rest is a *Sabbath* rest. We may then consider the ideas associated with the Sabbath below, and transfer them to the heavenly Sabbath.

1. REST is the fundamental idea of the Sabbath; not mere physical rest, but rest *in* God, and *from* all that would hinder rest in Him. It is partially attained by the believer even here, but the true Sabbatism will only be attained in Heaven, both in its negative and positive aspects. The negative aspects include rest from *sin,* from *sorrow and pain,* from *labor and fatigue,* and these hindrances are only removed that the soul may find its positive and satisfying rest in God. This is its true end, and every faculty here finds its center. The mind rests in the knowledge of God, the heart in reconciliation with Him, the will in choice and possession of Him. There is nothing better to long for, but more of God, to all eternity, and as the object infinitely exceeds the faculty, there is room for an everlasting Sabbath of complete repose, and yet of constant progress in which God is all, and in all.

2. COMMEMORATION.—The Sabbath has had from the beginning a memorial character. The Paradisaic Sabbath was a memorial of creation, the Jewish Sabbath a memorial of deliverance out of Egypt, the Christian Sabbath a memorial of Christ's rising from the dead. The heavenly Sabbath will be a memorial of all the history, the deliverance, and the final exodus out of this world of the people of God. The rest of Canaan commemorated the gracious Providence of the old covenant, the rest of the heavenly Canaan will consummate and commemorate the Providence of the New.

3. WORSHIP.—From the first the Sabbath has been associated with worship. In the heavenly Sabbath, worship will be consummated. We cannot tell whether we should take literally the descriptions of the worship in the New Jerusalem, but we may be sure it will contain three elements: (1) Gratitude, (2) Sympathy, (3) Consecration.

But this rest is only for the people of God. They that believe enter into rest. Even God cannot bring them in by any other way. It was unfit that unbelieving Israel should enter Canaan; with regard to heaven it is unfit and impossible. There is no rest out of God, out of Christ, and the unbeliever is out of Both. —*E. Times,* vol. xii., p. 273.

SUGGESTIVE THOUGHTS AND ILLUSTRATIONS

BEER, The Great Sabbath Breaker.— Every other enemy to Sabbath observance succumbs before the strong influence of public opinion. Even the directors of the World's Fair (1893), backed by all the plausible opinions of some good men, and by the long, and loud, and sordid cry for "liberty" by Anarchists who have little regard for the laws of either God or man, and by others who fail to see what concerns their own best interests both for this world and the next, have been obliged to yield to the sanctified common sense and influence of the overwhelming majority of the American people. But beer— this modern Goliath of Gath, continues to defy the armies of the living God, and contemptuously asks questions, as the big Philistian bully of old did, of all who oppose its progress, and curses them by its gods. But the doors of the beer saloons will yet be closed when the American people rise in their strength, and demand that God's holy day shall be observed by all men who have voluntarily put themselves under the government of American laws, and who claim the protection of the American flag. The victory which has just been won in shutting the gates of the great Columbian Exhibition on the Lord's Day should encourage all Christian people to gird on their armor anew, and to demand from the beer desecrators of God's Day an observance that will not be offensive to American Christian people. This sin against God, this crime against man, this disgrace to a

Christian nation, this curse to the world should be immediately wiped out by an outraged Christian public.—*Selected*.

DESECRATION, Process of Sabbath.— Official investigations made in recent years by the German government, in reply to the bitter cry of Sunday toilers, showed that in Prussia fifty-seven per cent. of the factories—more than half—and seventy-seven per cent. of the establishments devoted to trade and transportation—more than three-fourths—were in operation on the so-called holiday Sunday. The downward steps of the continental Sunday are: Holy day, holiday, workday, devil's day, despot's day.—U. L.

LABOR IN AUSTRIA.—REV. C. M. SHELDON: I have just found what seems to me the best Sabbath news from Europe for a long time; so I forward it straight to you, as there is not time to reach you *via* Washington.

The Swiss *Sonntagsfreund* of Zurich says: "In Austria Sunday rest for shop assistants and others has at last received some measure of consideration after long delay. Shops other than those for the sale of provisions, and inclusive of pawn-brokers, traveling pedlers, and others are to have complete rest Sunday from June 16th to September 30th. From October 1st to June 15th there is to be a permitted sale of goods till 11 A. M., and the sale of food stuffs is to be allowed from 6 to 10 A. M. and from 4 to 8 P. M. The rest of the year articles of food can be sold from 5 to 10 A. M. All other labor is to be prohibited. The employe working in the evening is to be free from attendance on the next Sunday, or to be allowed half a day off the following week. Men and women employed in factories are to be permitted Sunday abstinence during the whole year."—J. B. DAVISON.

LABOR, Sunday Railroad.—(By a railroad employe.) There are over one million slaves in the United States. They may be found on the railroads, street cars and with other corporations. I charge a Christian people to be indirectly the primary cause of the beginning and the continuation of such a state of affairs. We are slaves of what? Sabbath desecration. It has come to be, Violate the fourth commandment or starve. How is the Christian responsible? By using and countenancing such a practice.

But a short time ago, a minister gave over the evening service into the hands of the Young People's Society, that he might start on Sunday evening for Chicago.

In order for that train to arrive at the place where this servant of God resides, on Sunday evening, it must necessarily leave its terminus on Sunday morning. Several entire train crews are ordered into service; telegraph operators must be at their key to keep track clear, and trains apart; ticket agents must be on duty to sell tickets; and throughout the entire system of that road hundreds of men worked on Sunday as on any other day to carry that Christian to his destination.

I hear it said, the train would have been run just the same. This is the lie Satan puts into the Christian's mouth.

You and I know trains, street cars, etc., are run to put money into the stockholders' pockets. Did not professing Christians patronize Sunday trains they would never be run.

What is the cure? Practical Christianity. God's people may pray continuously until the breath leaves the body, but still the shriek of the steam car whistle, and the clanging of the street car bell will mingle with their prayers on Sunday.

There is too much of that kind of religion now. All for self! "Oh, Lord! Save me, and my wife, and my children, and I shall be grateful and serve Thee!" Don't try to dodge it. It's true, only too true. Think of others.

Well, what is the cure? Organized Christian work. First, public sentiment aroused from the pulpit, awakening the people out of their slumber to a realization that God will hold them responsible. Second, the forming of non-sectarian organized bodies, pledging themselves to refrain from all kinds of enjoyment or convenience that deprives a fellow man of his Sabbath, and the withdrawal of all from any Sunday breaking corporation, and the bestowing of this patronage upon that corporation first giving positive proof of a strict Sabbath observance.

It will work, for God will make it a success, and a million men will be freed from the soul blighting curse of Sunday labor. The secular press with its railway advertising patronage, and passes, does not dare to lift its voice against this flagrant wrong; and unless the Christian press does so soon, God will blight their fair prospects, and justly too.

This may seem a very serious charge to bring against a Christian people, but it is true.

Again I reiterate, the Church of to-day is **partly** responsible for myself and a million of my brothers laboring on Sunday at the risk of our souls' salvation.—*Selected*.

NEWSPAPERS, The Bane of Sunday.— Keep your Sundays free for earnest reading. Burn up the Sunday newspaper. It is an indefensible, intolerable curse. It exists simply and solely to swell the income of wealthy and greedy newspaper proprietors. A Christian ought to be ashamed to have it in his house. Is not a man sufficiently secularized by six days' contact with the world without dipping his mind on Sunday morning once more into the muddy stream in which he has dipped himself on the preceding six days? What can be expected of a Christian in public worship who comes to Church with a newspaper stuffed into his mind? He is cold as a clod to the touch of the preacher and lowers the spiritual temperature of the entire congregation.—C. E. JEFFERSON. (C.)

SABBATH AND FREEDOM, The.—An eminent United States jurist has declared that "where there is no Christian Sabbath there is no Christian morality; and without

this, free government cannot be maintained."
—*Selected.*

SABBATH-BREAKER, Fate of the.—A worldly man, living on the shores of a beautiful lake built a yacht for pleasure excursions. The minister called upon him, and expressed his fears that it would demoralize the young people, and prove a Sabbath-breaker. The man said, defiantly, "That is just what I'll name my boat. She shall be called the Sabbath-Breaker." She was launched upon a Sunday, and her trial trip was made also on a Sunday. Many were invited to the excursion. Her ill-omened name floated on the flag, and caused many to refuse to go on board. A large company went, and mirth and music made them forget their fears. Suddenly, a squall of wind struck the boat. She capsized, and fifty of her passengers were drowned. Just above the water floated her name, "The Sabbath-Breaker."—F. II.

SABBATH-BREAKER, Heaven of the. —There is a place in Paris, called the Champs-Elysées, or the plain of heaven, a beautiful public walk, with trees and gardens. It is the chief scene of the Parisian's Sabbath desecration, and an awful scene it is! Oh, thought I, if this be the heaven the Parisian loves, he will never enjoy the pure heaven that is above.—M'CHEYNE.

SABBATH BREAKING, Effects of.—In New Hampshire there were two neighborhoods—the one of six families, the other of five families. The six families disregarded the Sabbath. In time, five of these families were broken up by the separation of husbands and wives; the other by the father becoming a thief. Eight or nine of the parents became drunkards, one committed suicide, and all came to penury. Of some forty or fifty descendants, about twenty are known to be drunkards and gamblers and dissolute. Four or five have been in State prison. One fell in a duel. Some are in the almshouse. Only one became a Christian, and he after first having been outrageously dissipated. The other five families that regarded the Sabbath were all prospered. Eight or ten of the children are consistent members of the Church. Some of them became officers in the Church; one is a minister of the gospel, one is a missionary to China. No poverty among any of them. The homestead is now in the hands of the third generation. Those who have died, have died in the peace of the gospel. Oh! is there nothing in remembering God's holy day? —TALMAGE.

SABBATH-BREAKING, Legend of.—A German legend says that ages ago an old man went into the forest one Sunday morning to cut wood. Having gathered a bundle of sticks he threw it over his shoulder and took his way homeward. He met a man in Sunday clothes, going towards the Church, who asked him, "Do you know that this is Sunday on earth, when all must rest from their labors?" "Sunday on earth or Monday in heaven, it is all the same to me," laughed the Sabbath-breaker. "Then bear your bundle for ever,"

answered the stranger; "and as you value not Sunday on earth, yours shall be a perpetual Monday in heaven; and you shall stand for eternity in the moon, a warning to all Sabbath-breakers." Thereupon the man was caught up into the moon, where he has stood with the bundle on his back ever since. —F. II.

SABBATH-DAY SLOTH AND TRIFLING.—God's rest-day is for man's benefit physically and spiritually. If kept in such a way as to insure benefit in both ways, there must be no neglecting of the proper modes of caring for the body. It needs rest and should have it, in right proportion and with proper care. But slothfulness will not secure its refreshment, nor will irregular and immoderate eating or drinking, nor will slovenly indulgence in dress assist towards it. When proper time has been given to sleep, and suitable ablutions observed, then dress should not be neglected, but attended to with a carefulness suited to the day, and sacred reading and devotions observed, and the sanctuary visited with reverence for holy worship, and when the remainder of the day is spent in quiet restfulness, if not in active religious work, the evening will come with a holy calm, with a spirit of satisfaction, and with a refreshment gained to both body and soul, that the slothful and trifling have not secured by all their dawdling, and stupid idling, and over eating and drinking, and excursioning. In the proper keeping of this fourth command of God there is a great reward both for the body and soul.—P. T.

SABBATH DESECRATION.—The desecration of the Christian Sunday is a social danger against which it behooves us to set our face, and take timely precautions before it assumes proportions too formidable to be easily eradicated. A close observer cannot fail to note the dangerous inroads that have been made on the Lord's Day in our country within the last quarter of a century. If these encroachments are not checked in time the day may come when the religious quiet now happily reigning in our well-ordered cities will be changed into noise and turbulence; when the sound of the Church bell will be drowned by the echo of the hammer and the dray; when the Bible and the Prayer-Book will be supplanted by the newspaper and the magazine; when the votaries of the theater will outnumber the religious worshipers, and salutary thoughts of God, of eternity, and of the soul will be checked by the cares of business and by the pleasures and dissipations of the world.—CARDINAL GIBBONS. (I.)

SABBATH, Desecration of the.—The importance of the religious observance of the Sabbath is seldom sufficiently estimated. The violation of this duty by the young is one of the most decided marks of incipient moral degeneracy. Religious restraint is fast losing its hold upon that young man, who, having been educated in the fear of God, begins to spend the Sabbath in idleness, or in amusement. And so also of communities. The desecration of the Sabbath is one of those

evident indications of that criminal reckless-
ness, that insane love of pleasure, and that
subjection to the government of appetite and
passion, which forebodes that the "beginning
of the end" of social happiness, and of true
national prosperity, has arrived.—WAYLAND.

SABBATH, Emblem of the.—The green
oasis, the little grassy meadow in the wilderness, where, after the week-days' journey,
the pilgrim halts for refreshment and repose;
where he rests beneath the shade of the lofty
palm-trees, and dips his vessel in the waters
of the calm, clear stream, and recovers his
strength to go forth again upon his pilgrimage in the desert with renewed vigor and
cheerfulness.—READE.

**SABBATH IS CHALLENGED TO
PROVE ITS VALUE, The American.**—It
it well for those engaged in the Rescue of the
Sabbath to understand the sources from
which the attacks upon the sacred day are
made. Most of these attacks come from
money considerations.

The railroads that are desecrating the day
do it for money; the Sunday newspaper proprietors issue papers not for philanthropy,
but to make money—and so all along the line.
We have, especially among the foreigners
who have recently come among us, a class
of citizens who are ignorant of the value
of the day. They know but little of the
American Sabbath, and what little they hear
of it through prejudiced channels has a
tendency to make them dislike it.

These foreigners are to be met with kindness and with reason. If they challenge you
to prove to them the value of the American
Sabbath, be prepared to give them reasons
why this institution, which has done us so
much good for the last hundred years, should
be continued. Let us be assured that unless
the reasons are forthcoming; unless God's
people become aroused to a higher reverence
and affection for the day; and unless they
pray for it, speak for it, and work for it,
the legal American Sabbath will be an institution of the past. It is on trial. Its observance as a legal rest day depends upon the
votes of the people.—*Selected.*

SABBATH IS, Where No.—Where no
Sabbath is, there is no religion. But for this
day, earthly things would have engrossed all
our thoughts. Honor, wealth, and pleasure
are the real sirens which charm mankind to
shipwreck and death. To their songs the
ear of man is by nature attuned, and the heart
beats in regular response. But for the Sabbath, the world as a canker would rust, corrupt, and consume all disposition to piety, and
all hope of Heaven. The soul would be be-
numbed; religion would die; God would be
forgotten; the death of Christ would be vain;
mankind would cease to be saved; and
Heaven would fail of her destined inhabitants.—DWIGHT.

SABBATH-KEEPING NATIONS.—Wil-
bur F. Crafts, Ph.D., superintendent of The
Reform Bureau, Washington, D. C., has said:
"The supreme fact of living history is that

the Sabbath-keeping nations are literally riding on the high places of the earth. I have
not read in a year a news item so significant
as the statement of that very reliable paper,
the *Baltimore Sun,* that two-thirds of the
world's mail is in the English language. That
means that one-fourteenth of the world's
population sends two-thirds of the mail, and
that means a corresponding pre-eminence in
intelligence and wealth. On the other hand,
the Sabbathless and Sabbath-breaking nations
are poor—poor physically—Italy once, and
France twice in ten years have cut down their
standard for soldiers; poor mentally—they
have the greatest illiteracy; poor morally—
they have the most vice; poor financially—
their workmen, despite longer hours per day
and one more work day in the week, get the
lowest wages; and they are also the worst
off politically, vibrating between the extremes
of despotism and anarchy, while Sabbath-
keeping people enjoy the golden mean of liberty under law."—U. G. N.

SABBATH KEEPING PAYS.—Many
persons are sceptical as to the advantages of
the Sabbath in a secular aspect. Here is a
fact from Belfast, Ireland. The Omnibus Company resolved to discontinue running their
vehicles on the Sunday. They did this, and
the result was that they saved their sharehold-
ers 12 1-2 per cent. in the outlay of money
for horses during the first twelve months.
The Divine law has reference to horses as
well as men, and experience shows that the
need of one day's rest in seven is necessary
for the beast of burden. How much greater
therefore is the need for man, whose physical and mental energies render the day of
rest doubly necessary; yea, imperative.—*Selected.*

SABBATH NEWS.—Pennsylvania leads
her sister states in Sabbath laws and in their
observance. The Sabbath laws of Illinois are
very weak. There is no law for the closing
of theaters or other places of amusement or
ball games on Sunday. Illinois friends of the
Sabbath are obliged to fall back on the general line of not allowing any disturbance or
nuisance.—*Selected.*

SABBATH REST, Saving.—*Josh. i:8.*
In a retired valley of Joshu in India, there is
a little hamlet of charcoal burners. A few
years ago their manner of life was the rudest
possible. There seemed no glimmer of hope
for better things.

A missionary, in passing through the valley, spoke to the people. Two men became
interested and purchased copies of the New
Testament. Their employers soon noticed a
change in the grade of charcoal from these
two men—it was more carefully burned, better
packed, and free from stones and grass. This
charcoal was looked upon as a special brand,
and brought a special price. On Sunday
work was suspended, and these men, with
their families, gathered for religious worship
and the study of the Bible.

Shortly after, they began to reclaim the
mountain land about them, to plant wheat and

garden stuff, and recently one has become forehanded enough to build a neat frame house in place of his old hut. His employers say he is the most efficient and trustworthy man in the mountain. He himself says he owes his new vigor to his weekly day of rest, and that without it and his Testament he could not do his work.—C. G.

SABBATH SUNSHINE.—But on the Sabbath I watch the earliest sunshine and fancy that a holier brightness marks the day when there shall be no buzz of voices on the exchange, nor traffic in the shops, nor crowd nor business anywhere but at church. Many have fancied so. For my own part, whether I see it scattered down among tangled woods, or beaming broad across the fields, or hemmed in between brick buildings, or tracing out the figure of the casement on my chamber floor, still I recognize the Sabbath sunshine, and ever let me recognize it. Some illusions—and this among them—are the shadows of great truths. Doubts may flit around me, or seem to close their evil wings and settle down, but so long as I imagine that the earth is hallowed and the light of Heaven retains its sanctity on the Sabbath—while that blessed sunshine lives within me—never can my soul have lost the instinct of its faith. If it has gone astray, it will return again.—NATHANIEL HAWTHORNE.

SABBATH, The.—The apathy of many of the so-called friends of the Lord's day is a danger of no small consideration. There are those who really are in sympathy with the institution of the Sabbath. They love it and enjoy its sacredness and blessings, but are careless and indifferent in regard to the dangers that beset it. They sing to themselves a requiem of security and peace when there is no peace or safety.

They need to be aroused from their slumber and shown the real situation. If eternal vigilance is the price of liberty, it is also at this moment the price of the perpetuity of this God-given institution—the Christian Sabbath.—REV. G. W. M. RIGOR.

SABBATH, The Last.—When that last Sabbath comes—the Sabbath of all creation—the heart, wearied with its tumultuous beatings, shall have rest; the soul, fevered with its anxieties, shall enjoy peace. The Sun of that Sabbath will never set, or hide his splendors in a cloud. The flowers that grow in its light will never fade. Our earthly Sabbaths are but dim reflections of the heavenly Sabbath, cast down upon the earth, dimmed by the transit of their rays from so great a height and so distant a world. The fairest landscapes, or combinations of scenery upon earth, are but the outskirts of the paradise of God, fore-earnests and intimations of that which lies beyond them; and the happiest Sabbath-heart, whose very pulse is a Sabbath-bell, hears but a very inadequate echo of the chimes and harmonies of that Sabbath, that rest, where we " rest not day and night," in which the song is ever new, and yet ever sung.—CUMMING.

SILENCE.—Where the song's gone out of your life, you can't start another while it's a-ringing in your ears; it's best to have a bit o' silence, and out o' that, maybe, a psalm will come by and by.—EDWARD GARRETT.

SUNDAY, Carrying.—I had a friend in Syracuse, who lived to be one hundred years of age. He said to me, in his ninety-ninth year, " I went across the mountains in the early history of this country. Sabbath morning came. We were beyond the reach of civilization. My comrades were all going out for an excursion. I said, ' No, I won't go, it is Sunday.' Why, they laughed. 'We haven't any Sunday here.' ' Oh! yes,' I said, ' you have. I brought it with me over the mountains.' "—TALMADGE.

SUNDAY, The Puritan.—The Puritan Sunday was too caste in its rules; but, in my opinion, better for the interest of man and beast than the license of the modern Sunday in our great cities. England, Scotland and the Canadian provinces are in advance of us in the observance of the Sabbath Day. We are gradually, but certainly, opening the doors of traffic and amusement, our railroads being the leaders in these regards. Laws recognizing the Lord's Day as one dedicated to worship, to works of charity, and to rest from labor should be enforced.—SENATOR FRYE. (I.)

SUNDAY, Typology of.—The eighth day is always typical of resurrection. The eighth day, the day after the seventh or Sabbath, answers to the first day of the week on which Christ rose; it is, however, the first day in reference to seven having gone before. Seven days include the periods proper to the first creation. The eighth day, as it takes us beyond and out of these—that is, beyond the limits of the old creation—brings us in type into a new order of things and times—into the new creation or resurrection.—A. JUKES.

SUNDAY, Using.—Make the Lord's day the market for thy soul; let the whole day be spent in prayer, repetitions, or meditations. Lay aside the affairs of the other parts of the week; let the sermon thou hast heard be converted into prayer. Shall God allow thee six days, and wilt thou not afford Him one?—BUNYAN.

WAR AND SUNDAY.—Captain Philip (U. S. N.) always spoke about the war with Spain, and reminded us that the side that opened fire first on the Sabbath would lose every time; so I was very glad last Sabbath when I saw the Maria Teresa fire the first shot.

On another occasion he was called on board the flagship, together with the commanding officer of the fleet, for a council of war, and went on board at half past nine that Sunday morning. The decision was reached to bombard the forts at two o'clock that afternoon, when Captain Philip spoke up and said:

" Admiral, this is Sunday, I do not think we should fight to-day. We may be sorry if we do." Whereupon the admiral apologized for even calling them together at all that day, but admitted he had been so pressed he had entirely lost track of the days, so the battle was deferred until the next morning, with the result of no damage to us."—C. G.

WARNING, A.—Why do many Christians, including pastors, concentrate all their ten commandment law-breaking on the commandment requiring the keeping of the Sabbath day holy? Why not change off and break some of the other commandments? "Thou shalt not steal," "Thou shalt not kill," etc. Is there any more binding force in these commandments? Let us be careful not to look at this from a nineteenth century standard of loose American ways, but from a Scriptural standard.—*Selected.*

WEEK, The Best Day of The.—A writer in Harper's *Bazar* says on this subject—and we would emphasize the remark on the church service—"That is profound philosophy which counsels parents to make Sunday the happiest day of the week. And the chief requisite to this is that they give themselves to their children—at church as well as at home. The Sunday school must not be allowed to usurp the place of the church service. The child nestled in the family pew at his mother's side, holding his father's hand, enters naturally from the shelter of warm human love into the mystery of divine love, and the house of God very early becomes to him the gate of heaven.

"For very little children it is a pretty plan to set aside for Sabbath use the most attractive toys, the favorite pictures and stories, the sweetest child songs and hymns, and to join with them more than ever in their plays and their quiet moods, until, when they wake Sunday morning, they shall exclaim, with a four-year-old of our acquaintance, 'Oh, I'm so glad it's Sunday!'"—E.

POETRY

Sunday Morning Bells

By Dinah Maria Mulock Craik

From the near city comes the clang of bells:
Their hundred jarring diverse tones combine
In one faint misty harmony, as fine
As the soft note yon winter robin swells.
What if to Thee in thine infinity
These multiform and many-colored creeds
Seem but the robe man wraps as masquer's weeds
Round the one living truth thou givest him—
Thee?
What if these varied forms that worship prove,
Being heart-worship, reach Thy perfect ear
But as a monotone, complete and clear,
Of which the music is, through Christ's name, love?
Forever rising in sublime increase
To "Glory in the highest,—on earth peace?"

A Nation's Contrition

By Margaret J. Preston

[These lines were written in 1893, before the decision to close the World's Fair on Sunday.]

O God! beneath whose folded hand
   So long was hidden away
The secret of the wondrous land
   We glory in to-day.

We thank Thee that with faith profound
   Our sires their sails unfurled,
And claimed as henceforth hallowed ground
   This unsuspected world.

That here they suffered, toiled and bled,
   For leave to keep Thy laws;
That here pure martyr-blood was shed
   For freedom's holiest cause;

That through what Christian men have done,
   By stress of conscience driven,
No other land beneath the sun
   Owes half so much to Heaven!

Now in the zenith of our fame
   The nations come at call,
To learn the secret that we claim
   Must hold the world in thrall.

What is it? Not our armaments
   On ocean or on shore;
Not vaunted freedom's proud pretense,
   Not gold's uncounted store.

Our faith hath made us what we are;
   Beneath these skies so broad,
From Southern cross to Northern star,
   Our people worship God!

Our statescraft rests on His commands,
   Divinely given to men—
The creed of all illumined lands,
   Sinai's engraven Ten!

This *was* our boast: Alas, too late!
   To-day we dare defy
Heaven's ordered law; we hesitate,
   We abrogate, deny.

O Christian people! pour your prayers
   From hearts subdued and riven;
Contrite, that thus our Nation dares
   The Majesty of Heaven!

Rest

By Johann Wolfgang von Goethe

Rest is not quitting
The busy career;
Rest is the fitting
Of self to one's sphere.

'Tis the brook's motion,
Clear without strife,
Fleeing to ocean
After this life.
'Tis loving and serving
The highest and best;
'Tis onward, unswerving,
And this is true rest.

The Day of Rest

By George Klingle

O sweet, fair day of silence,
When echoes come and go,
Of voices praising Him, the King,
Who died so long ago;

As tho in benediction
It brought us nearer heaven,
His face to see, His own to be,—
Day sweetest of the seven.

The Sabbath Bells

By Charles Lamb

The cheerful Sabbath bells, wherever heard,
Strike pleasant on the sense, most like the voice
Of one who from the far-off hills proclaims
Tidings of good to Zion: chiefly when
Their piercing tones strike sudden on the ear
Of the contemplant, solitary man,
Whom thoughts abstruse or high have chanced to lure
Forth from the walks of men, revolving oft,
And oft again, hard matter, which eludes
And baffles his pursuit—thought-sick, and tired
Of controversy, where no end appears
No clue to his research, the lonely man
Half wishes for society again.
Him, thus engaged, the Sabbath bells salute
Sudden! His heart awakes, his ear drinks in
The cheering music; his relenting soul
Yearns after all the joys of social life,
And softens with the love of human kind.

Sabbath Evening

By George Denison Prentice

How calmly sinks the parting sun!
Yet twilight lingers still;
And beautiful as dream of heaven
It slumbers on the hill;
Earth sleeps, with all her glorious things,
Beneath the Holy Spirit's wings,
And, rendering back the hues above,
Seems resting in a trance of love.

Round yonder rocks the forest trees
In shadowy groups recline,
Like saints at evening bowed in prayer
Around their holy shrine;
And through their leaves the night-winds blow,
So calm and still, their music low
Seems the mysterious voice of prayer,
Soft echoed on the evening air.

And yonder western throng of clouds,
Retiring from the sky,
So calmly move, so softly glow,
They seem to fancy's eye
Bright creatures of a better sphere,
Come down at noon to worship here,
And, from their sacrifice of love,
Returning to their home above.

The blue isles of the golden sea,
The night-arch floating high,
The flowers that gaze upon the heavens,
The bright streams leaping by,
Are living with religion; deep
On earth and sea its glories sleep,
And mingle with the starlight rays,
Like the soft light of parted days.

The spirit of the holy eve
Comes through the silent air
To feeling's hidden spring, and wakes
A gush of music there!
And the far depths of ether beam
So passing fair, we almost dream
That we can rise and wander through
Their open paths of trackless blue.

Each soul is filled with glorious dreams,
Each pulse is beating wild;
And thought is soaring to the shrine
Of glory undefiled!
And holy aspirations start,
Like blessed angels, from the heart,
And bind—for earth's dark ties are riven—
Our spirits to the gate of heaven.

A Sabbath Hymn

By O. E. Roberts

Rise hallowed morn, whose earliest ray
Tells of a tomb no longer sealed.
Bright angels roll the stone away
And sin and death their empire yield.

O'er all the earth the morning chime
Calls on the sons of men to pray.
People and tribes of every clime
Rejoicing hail the sacred day.

Released from toil and earthly care,
Our spirits feel a sweet repose.
A holy calm fills all the air
The peace which God alone bestows.

Thy Spirit's work in souls sincere
Continue Lord, nor take Thy rest
Till every heart that worships here,
Renewed on earth, in heaven is blest.—E.

Sabbath Morn

N. F. S. Grundtvig

From death, Christ, on the Sabbath morn
A conqueror arose;
And when each Sabbath dawn is born
For death a healing grows.
This day proclaims an ended strife,
And Christ's benign and holy life.

By countless lips the wondrous tale
  Is told throughout the earth;
Ye that have ears to hear, oh, hail
  That tale with sacred mirth!
Awake, my soul, rise from the dead,
See life's grand light around thee shed.

Death trembles each sweet Sabbath hour,
  Death's brother, Darkness, quakes;
Christ's word speaks with divinest power,
  Christ's truth its silence breaks;
They vanquish with their valiant breath
The reign of darkness and of death.

The Sabbath

BY REV. HENRY OSTRAM

O Sabbath! 'tis of thee,
Sweet day of liberty
  And worshiping;
Type of the soul's repose,
Day when my Lord arose,
Blessed at creation's close,
  Of thee I sing.

Thou treasure-house of prayer,
Thou balm for pain and care,
  Thou fount of praise;
Thy mornings breathe release,
Thine evenings whisper peace,
Thy anthems never cease,
  Thou psalm of days.

Forth on thy wings of white,
Plumed in celestial light,
  Sweet Sabbath day:
Fly all the earth abroad,
Till all thy beauty laud,
Till all adore thy God,
  All hope, all pray.

Merge heaven into home,
And where sad strangers roam,
  A friendship give;
Soothe ev'ry toiler's pain,
Wash every sinner's stain,
Hallow on land and main
  All men that live.

Our father's God to thee,
Author of sanctity,
  To Thee we sing;
May all the world revere
This day so old, so dear,
O bring Thy presence near,
  Great God, our king.

The Sabbath.

BY EDWARD BULWER, LORD LYTTON

Fresh glides the brook and blows the gale,
  Yet yonder halts the quiet mill;
The whirring wheel, the rushing sail,
  How motionless and still!

Six days' stern labor shuts the poor
  From nature's careless banquet-hall
The seventh an angel opes the door,
  And, smiling, welcomes all!

A Father's tender mercy gave
  This holy respite to the breast,
To breathe the gale, to watch the wave,
  And know—the wheel may rest!

Six days of toil, poor child of Cain,
  Thy strength thy Master's slave must be;
The seventh the limbs escape the chain,—
  A God hath made thee free!

The fields that yester-morning knew
  Thy footsteps as their serf, survey;
On thee, as them, descends the dew,
  The baptism of the day.

Fresh glides the brook and blows the gale,
  But yonder halts the quiet mill;
The whirring wheel, the rushing sail,
  How motionless and still!

So, O weary heart!—but, lo,
  The church-spire, glistening up to heaven
To warn thee where thy thoughts should go
  The day thy God hath given!

Lone through the landscape's solemn rest,
  The spire its moral points on high.
O soul, at peace within the breast,
  Rise, mingling with the sky!

They tell thee, in their dreaming school,
  Of power from old dominion hurled,
When rich and poor, with juster rule,
  Shall share the altered world.

Alas! since time itself began,
  That fable hath but fooled the hour;
Each age that ripens power in man
  But subjects man to power.

Yet every day in seven, at least,
  One bright republic shall be known;
Man's world awhile hath surely ceased,
  When God proclaims His own!

Six days may rank divide the poor,
  O Dives, from thy banquet-hall;
The seventh the Father opes the door,
  All holds His feast for all.

Various Selections

DAYS, COMMON.—
God gives us through the common days,
The level stretches, white with dust,
When thought is tired, and hands upraise
Their burdens feebly, since they must;
Through days of slowly fretting care,
When most we need, the strength of prayer.
  M. E. SANGSTER.

EASTER SUNDAY.—
'Twas Easter-Sunday. The full-blossomed
  trees
Filled all the air with fragrance and with
  joy.
  LONGFELLOW—*Spanish Student.* Act I.
  Sc. 3.

LITANY, MORAVIAN.—
    From untimely projects,
    From needless perplexity,
      And from all sin—
    Good Lord deliver us.

LORD'S DAY, THE.—

O day of rest! How beautiful, how fair,
How welcome to the weary and the old!
Day of the Lord! and true to earthly care!
Day of the Lord, as all our days should be!
　　　LONGFELLOW—*Christus.* Pt. III.
　　　　　　　John Endicott. Act I. Sc. 2.

MEDITATION.—

By all means use some time to be alone,
Salute thyself; see what thy soul dost wear,
Dare to look in thy chest, for it is thine own;
And tumble up and down what thou findest
　there.
　　　　　　　　　G. HERBERT.

SABBATH, THE.—

How still the morning of the hallow'd day!
Mute is the voice of rural labor, hush'd
The plowboy's whistle, and the milkmaid's
　song.
　　　GRAHAME—*The Sabbath. Song.*

The Sabbaths of Eternity,
One Sabbath deep and wide.
　　　TENNYSON—*St. Agnes Eve. l.* 33.

So sang they, and the Empyrean rung
With Halleluiahs. There was Sabbath kept.
　　　MILTON—*Paradise Lost.* Bk. VII.
　　　　　　　　　Line 632.

See Christians, Jews, one Sabbath keep.
And all the western world believe and sleep.
　　　POPE—*The Dunciad.* Line 99.

SUNDAIES.—

Sundaies observe; think when the bells do
　chime,
'Tis angel's musick; therefore come not late.
　　　HERBERT—*The Temple. The Church
　　　　　　　　　Porch.*

SUNDAY.—

Of all the days that's in the week,
　I dearly love but one day,
And that's the day that comes betwixt
　A Saturday and Monday.
　　　HENRY CAREY—*Sally in Our Alley.*

SUNDAY.—

The Sundaies of man's life,
Thredded together on Time's string,
Make bracelets to adorn the wife
Of the eternal, glorious King.
On Sunday heaven's gates stand ope;
Blessings are plentiful and rife,
More plentiful than hope.
　　　HERBERT—*The Temple. Sunday.*

SUNDAY ETHICS.—

For, bless the gude mon, gin he had his own
　way,
He'd na let a cat on the Sabbath say
　" mew; "
Nae birdie maun whistle, nae lambie maun
　play,
An' Phœbus himsel could nay travel that
　day,
As he'd find a new Joshua in Andie Agnew.
　　　MOORE—*Sunday Ethics.*

SUNDAYS, ON.—

On Sundays, at the matin-chime,
The Alpine peasants, two and three,
　Climb up here to pray;
Burghers and dames, at Summer's prime,
Ride out to church from Chamberry,
　Dight with mantles gay,
But else it is a lonely time
Round the Church of Brou.
　　　MATTHEW ARNOLD—*The Church of
　　　　　　　　　Brou.* II. St. 3.

WISH, A.—

" I sometimes wish the good Book had said,
' Remember Saturday night to keep it holy.'
Sunday would be smoother if it had."
　　　　　　　　　ANNA BREATH.

The Sepulcher on Sabbath Morning

BY THOMAS HASTINGS

How calm and beautiful the morn
　That gilds the sacred tomb,
Where Christ the crucified was borne,
　And veiled in midnight gloom!
Oh! weep no more the Savior slain,
The Lord is risen, He lives again!

Ye mourning saints, dry every tear
　For your departed Lord;
" Behold the place, He is not here,"
　The tomb is all unbarred:
The gates of death were closed in vain,
The Lord is risen, He lives again!

Now cheerful to the house of prayer
　Your early footsteps bend;
The Savior will Himself be there,
　Your Advocate and friend:
Once by the law your hopes were slain,
But now in Christ ye live again!

How tranquil now the rising day!
　'Tis Jesus still appears,
A risen Lord, to chase away
　Your unbelieving fears:
Oh, weep no more your comforts slains,
The Lord is risen, He lives again!

And when the shades of evening fall,
　When life's last hour draws nigh,
If Jesus shines upon the soul,
　How blissful then to die!
Since He has risen that once was slain,
Ye die in Christ to live again!

Sundays

BY HENRY VAUGHAN

Bright shadows of true rest! some shoots of
　bliss;
Heaven once a week;
The next world's gladness prepossest in
　this;
A day to seek;
Eternity in time; the steps by which
We climb above all ages; lamps that light
Man through his heap of dark days; and the
　rich
And full redemption of the whole week's
　flight!

The pulleys unto headlong man; time's
  bower;
  The narrow way;
Transplanted paradise; God's walking hour;
  The cool o' the day!
The creature's jubilee! God's parle with dust;
Heaven here; man on those hills of myrrh
  and flowers;
Angels descending; the returns of trust;
A gleam of glory after six-days-showers!

The Church's love feasts; time's prerogative,
  and interest
Deducted from the whole; the combs and
  hive,
  And home of rest.
The milky way chalked out with suns; a clue,
That guides through erring hours; and in full
  story
A taste of heaven on earth; the ledge and cue
Of a full feast; and the out-courts of glory.

First-day Thoughts

By John G. Whittier

In calm and cool and silence, once again
  I find my old accustomed place among
  My brethren, where, perchance, no human
    tongue
  Shall utter words; where never hymn is
    sung,
  Nor deep-toned organ blown, nor censer
    swung,
Nor dim light falling through the pictured
  pane!
There, syllabled by silence, let me hear
The still small voice which reached the
  prophet's ear;

Read in my heart a still diviner law,
Than Israel's leader on his tables saw!
There let me strive with each besetting sin
  Recall my wandering fancies, and restrain
  The sore disquiet of a restless brain;
  And, as the path of duty is made plain,
May grace be given that I may wake therein,
Not like the hireling, for his selfish gain,
With backward glances and reluctant tread,
Making a merit of his coward dread.—
  But cheerful, in the light around me
    thrown,
  Walking as one to pleasant service led,
  Doing God's will as if it were my own,
Yet trusting not in mine, but in His strength
  alone!

Sunday

By James Edmeston

When the worn spirit wants repose,
  And sighs her God to seek,
How sweet to hail the evening's close,
  That ends the weary week!

How sweet to hail the early dawn,
  That opens on the sight,
When first that soul-reviving morn
  Sheds forth new rays of light!

Sweet day, thine hours too soon will cease;
  Yet, while they gently roll,
Breathe, Heavenly Spirit, source of peace,
  A Sabbath o'er my soul!

When will my pilgrimage be done,
  The world's long week be o'er,
That Sabbath dawn which needs no sun,
  That day which fades no more?

ASCENSION DAY

A SCENSION DAY, or Holy Thursday, is an important festival in the Greek, Roman, and English churches. It is held on the fortieth day after Easter, ten days before Whitsunday, and commemorates the ascension of our Lord into Heaven. It is one of the six days for which the English church appoints special psalms. The Church of England also especially recommends it as a fitting day for the receiving of the Holy Communion. It is certain that its observance dates from the earliest times; the first mention of it being found in the Apostolic Constitutions; but St. Augustine believed it to have been instituted by the apostles themselves, or by the primitive bishops immediately succeeding them. Of this, however, there is no satisfactory proof.

In the Middle Ages, the rites and ceremonies of Ascension Day went in some cases beyond the bounds of reason, and became superstitious and ridiculous. Such was the custom of drawing an image of Christ up to the roof, to represent His ascension, and the casting down an image of Satan into flames, to represent his falling as lightning from Heaven.

In the Roman Catholic Church of our times, on Ascension Day, after the Gospel has been read, the Paschal candle is extinguished, denoting our Savior's leaving the earth; the altar is decorated with images, relics, and flowers; and the priests and their attendants are attired in white vestments.

Bishop Pearson, in a sermon on Ascensiontide, makes the following clear and important statements concerning the event, and truth of Ascension Day:

" The ascent of *Christ* into Heaven was not metaphorical or figurative, as if there were no more to be understood by it, but only that He obtained a more heavenly and glorious state or condition after His resurrection. For whatsoever alteration was made in the body of *Christ* when He rose, whatsoever glorious qualities it was invested with thereby, that was not His ascension, as appeareth by those words which He spake to Mary, *Touch Me not, for I am not yet ascended to My Father.* . . . Now this kind of ascension, by which *Christ* had not yet ascended when He spoke to Mary after His resurrection, was not long after to be performed; for at the same time He said to Mary, *Go to My brethren, and say unto them, I ascend unto My Father and your Father.* And when this ascension was performed, it appeared manifestly to be a true local translation of the Son of Man, as Man, from these parts of the world below into the heavens above; by which that body, which was before locally present here on earth, and was not so then present in heaven, became substantially present in heaven, and no longer locally present on earth. For when He had spoken unto the disciples, *and blessed them,* laying His hands upon them, and so was corporally present with them, even *while He blessed them He was parted from them.* . . . This was a visible departure, as it is described, a real removing of that body of Christ, which was before present with the apostles; and that body living after the resurrection, by virtue of that soul which was united to it."

The Scriptural authority for the event which this day celebrates is to be found in the brief statements contained in Mark xvi: 19; Luke xxiv: 51, and in the more detailed account, Acts i: 4-12.

CHRIST'S CORONATION DAY

By Rev. Talmadge Root

Holy Thursday holds no such place in the thought and life of the Church as Easter or Good Friday. This is not strange, for in the New Testament the Ascension receives no such emphasis as the Resurrection. It is not mentioned by Matthew, John or Mark, for in the best manuscripts the second Gospel ends abruptly at xvi: 8. Luke, in his Gospel and Acts, is our sole authority for the event. Even the allusions to it (Jn. vi: 62; xx: 27; Acts i: 22), are few and unemphatic in comparison with those to the Resurrection.

These facts raise the question, not indeed as to the occurrence of the event, but as to its real significance. The Resurrection was an event significant in itself. Life beyond the grave could have been demonstrated only as it has been, by one well-attested case of rising from the dead. Its significance lies in the fact itself. Hence it is that the Gospels dwell with such fulness upon the details which convinced the disciples that the very body which died upon the cross lived again in tangible reality.

Not such the significance of the Ascension! Then, it would signify Christ's final departure from earth. In that case how can we explain the "great joy" with which the disciples returned to Jerusalem? Or reconcile Luke with Matthew, who not only mentions no departure as Jesus' last words: "Lo, I am with you all the days even unto the end of the world?"

The phenomena themselves cannot have such literal value. The disciples did not, and could not, see Jesus ascend into heaven and take His seat at the right of God. What they did see was that He was "taken up" until "a cloud received him out of their sight." "Up" is the direction of heaven only symbolically, not literally. An upward pointing finger every minute sweeps through an arc of 15', and in 12 hours indicates the opposite direction in absolute space. "Up" gains its significance from its close association with moral ideas. The Ascension was a *symbolic* event.

It is none the less important and historical. Many historical events possess importance not from what they were in themselves, but from what they symbolized. Such was the significance of the signing of the Declaration of Independence. Such is the coronation of a king. To ascend the steps of a throne and to be crowned with a circlet of gold do not in themselves confer authority! They have value only because custom and sentiment have made them symbolize royal power. We remark, "In 1625, Charles I. ascended the throne of England," without a thought of the actual scene, meaning that he assumed royal authority. In the same sense Christ "ascended," not to depart from earth, but to take the throne of His Kingdom on earth. "He sat down at the right hand of God." God's reign does not consist in sitting upon a distant throne! It consists in omnipresent power and authority. To sit at His right hand means to share His Authority and Omnipresence. This is Matthew's interpretation: "Jesus came . . . saying, All authority is given unto me in heaven and on earth."

It is impossible to perceive by the senses even the authority of a king. Therefore men seek to make it visible and tangible by the ceremonies of coronation. Still less can we perceive the spiritual authority of Christ. The more necessary was it that it should be impressed upon the imagination of believers by the visible event of the Ascension. This was Luke's understanding of the event. It was, indeed, the termination of knowledge of Christ "after the flesh;" and left a vivid hope of beholding Him again "in like manner." But the very fact that Luke places his fuller account not at the close of the Gospel, but at the commencement of Acts, referring to the "former treatise" in which he had narrated "all that Jesus *began* both to do and to preach," shows that he regarded the Ascension not as the termination but the real beginning of Jesus' personal leadership.

Sense of the present reign of the Living Christ is the great need of the Church. So soon as it is ignored, heresy begins. Admit that Christ is absent, and the claims of the Pope to be His vice-regent are logical, if not conclusive. Regard His reign as postponed, and our only hope for the victory of His cause is His return. But it is not so! He would not thus desert to the devil the world that He died to redeem! He has not abandoned His followers to suffer and toil alone! He walks in the midst of the seven golden candlesticks—not part of the furniture of heaven, but the churches that live on earth "to make disciples of all nations." His was the ascension of a throne! We celebrate His Coronation Day!

THE ASCENSION OF OUR LORD

Sometimes we need a sharp reminder of the world unseen. God meets us out of the shadow. The mystery is simply the obscuring cloud, like that which hid the solar eclipse from this part of its path across the continent. The cloud did not change the event, nor arrest the swing of the planet or shadow through interstellar spaces. To those whom Christian experience has ripened, personal religion is a vision of the Christ. He is all and in all. The old difficulties of thought have passed like the cloud; the personality of Jesus stands out radiantly clear and full of present comfort and promise.

His Ascension marked a stage in His revelation, but it only brought Him nearer to us. To have lingered among the early disciples would have limited His mission and sequestered Him from the later Church. As the Resurrection opened the grave, the Ascension opened heaven. Every word of His now is a voice from the unseen addressed to each one of us. We hear the Gospel as if He spake from glory; we lift our eyes from the smiling face of the world on a day of early summer, and lo! the Lord our God looks down upon our brightened vision and our kindling faith and love. Ah, Thou art with us still! We are not in a world apart; this is a world where Christ is, and the other world is here also. If we believe in this world, we believe in that world. If we believe in the world that God has made for us here, we believe in the world that Jesus has made for us there. The two are separate, yet they are also one.

Perhaps our greatest difficulty is also our heaviest sorrow if we begin to yield to it. The separation of the unseen, which is its largest claim on our confidence, begets sometimes a doubt and, sometimes, forgetfulness. Doubt is sorrow and forgetfulness is danger. Behold the world where Christ has taken our beloved to a perfect life, and if we believe, our grief is the birth of joy. Be conscious of the world to come, and you are saved from the snares of this present world. This is the old, old truth and the world-old struggle. We still keep up the fight with the sun which would blot from our thoughts the greater Unseen. And the vision of our Lord going hence to be nearer, closer in all that concerns us here and hereafter, is a reminder of our relation to heaven, a promise to him that overcometh.—E.

SERMONS AND OUTLINES

THE LESSONS OF OUR LORD'S ASCENSION

By H. Kern, D.D.

Afterward he appeared unto the eleven as they sat at meat, and upbraided them with their unbelief and hardness of heart, because they believed not them which had seen him after he was risen, etc.—Mark xvi: 14-20

Beloved in the Lord! It is the coronation festival of our King and Lord Jesus Christ, the glorious Son of God, that we with joyful heart celebrate this day. For with the ascent of the Savior into heaven, from which this anniversary day receives its name, He has entered upon the real and undisputed possession of His royal reign, in which from this time on He rules over all things that are in heaven and on earth. He was saluted as a triumphant victor over the broken power of death and darkness by the heavenly hosts, filling all the heavens with joyous hallelujahs; the entire kingdom of everlasting life celebrates this glorious festival of joy, because the Son, the only begotten Son of the Eternal Father, who had left heaven and come upon the earth for the purpose of saving lost mankind, now, after the contest is over and the victory achieved, returns as the exalted world-Redeemer and again resumes His place in the middle of the eternal Holy of Holies in heaven. How can it be otherwise than that this day shall also be celebrated with gladness and thanksgiving by Christians here on earth? Is it not deserving of the greatest joy to know that from this time on our Savior is in heaven as the Lord over all, that we have in the seat of almighty power above a Ruler who had at one time been a man as we are and who is not ashamed to own us, poor mortal beings, as His brethren; who does not dwell in unapproachable majesty above us and our needs, but is like unto us and regards us as like unto Him. Indeed, this is a day of joy; but it is at the same time a day for earnest reflection, and that for the very reason that our divine Lord and King looks upon us as like unto Him and wishes to draw us to Him. As great as is the joy of this truth, so great is also the responsibility attached to it. Our Lord and Savior Jesus Christ has on this day been exalted to the throne of heaven's sacred shrine. This is the lesson found in the gospel words for to-day. "Follow me!" He cries out unto us, He who has preceded us to the world above; "follow Me from the darkness and dust of the earth up to holier, higher aims and goals." Especially do we find in these words the exhortation which the Lord at the close addresses to His disciples, not to live in quiet ease and for the enjoyment of earth's goods, but for earnest work, for steady faithfulness and fidelity, in faith, in service, in contest and progress on the road to heaven; and as a reward for this fidelity is held out the joy which is promised to us in His ascension. The lessons of admonition found in this ascension for us are these:

I. Deep Humility;
II. Diligent Service;
III. Joyful Hope.

I. Beloved, the Lord loved His disciples from the beginning to the end; He, however, praised them but rarely, but often upbraided and rebuked them. Why was this? It is easy to say that this was because they were weak, sinful human creatures, men who not through their own powers but only through the grace of God's spirit could learn to think, speak and do that which is good. Therefore we cannot be surprised to read in to-day's gospel lesson that even at the end, just as He was about to depart and ascend to the throne of His majesty, He upbraided them on account of their unbelief, which they had displayed over against the announcement of His resurrection. We cannot be surprised, still less does this mislead us, that we find ourselves approving the words of the Lord, as tho *we* had the right to find fault with what the Apostles did and said. No; this we should for the best of reasons leave to God and the Savior alone, for all the faults which we find in them are also our faults, and are only for this reason so clearly portrayed in the Scriptures in order that we thereby may all the more clearly learn to see our own failings and in the light of such knowledge bend the heart and soul in deep humility. What right have we to upbraid them for displaying unbelief over against the message of Christ's resurrection, we who in our actions and words daily display a similar unbelief? For to believe in the resurrection of the Lord means to rejoice in the risen Lord, and with hearts full of gratitude, comfort and consolation in the light of the great victory of the Conqueror of Death to glory in our faith and calling.

Instead of this it occurs only too often that this whole matter of the resurrection of the Lord practically is regarded as something like a beautiful old story, which once a year, on Easter Day, forms the topic of edifying discourse, but otherwise belongs to the regions of myth and story. As a consequence of this, the modern world has to a great extent lost the Christian joyfulness resulting from the Lord's resurrection, as also the blessed assurances that this faith brings. As a further result, the cares and concerns of love constantly press down upon us without the counteracting power of a joyful hope and certainty in the Lord. The spiritual loss of the lack of full faith in the risen Lord is felt in all the walks and stations of life. The joyful message that Christ has arisen, that Christ has conquered all the powers of darkness, that His resurrection is for us the guarantee that we too shall rise unto everlasting happiness, is in the saddest and most sorrowful hour of our lives to prove to dispel our ills and sufferings. Indeed, this is the light in which we should daily look upon this great work of the Lord; and since we do not in our heart of hearts think of the resurrection thus, we not only lose the spiritual joys arising from this conviction, but belong also to that class of people whom the Lord should upbraid for their unbelief every day.

Therefore when we this day speak of the great truth that as His adherents we should follow Him on His path to glory above, on the road that leads to heaven, we should on this day too be the first ones keenly to feel conscious of the fact that our faith and trust in His resurrection is not that power, factor, and force in our lives which it was intended to be. In view of this our hearts should feel deeply humiliated that we are such unfaithful followers of Him who has gone before, conquering and to conquer for our salvation. He who is ascending a high ladder should never, for fear of falling, look downward, but constantly upward. Only thus, too, can we attain our heavenly goal, when we keep the high ideals and aims of Christian life before us. But in order to learn to trust the grace that draws us upward, we must first have learned to know the depths out of which we are ascending. To appreciate fully the glorious blessings of the kingdom of God's grace, we must first have walked through the valley of humiliation and come to the conviction of our sure need of God's boundless mercy.

II. And through His grace the heart that by humble self-knowledge has been properly prepared to receive the seed of the Spirit is filled with a holy confidence and with an eager desire to seize the gracious helping hand of the Lord. Then, however, it is also necessary that we serve with the measure of grace that has been given us. No matter how weak the disciples were at this time, and however much the Lord was compelled to upbraid them, He did not on that account say that He could not use them in the service and work of His kingdom. But rather He commands them to go out and spread the glorious gospel news of forgiveness of sins and reconciliation with God, of the destruction of Satan's kingdom. And the disciples did what had been commanded them. They did not regard their own weakness, but began to preach in the name of the Lord and of Jesus Christ; and, behold, they succeeded better and better every day. They did not themselves know how this all happened, but the better they succeeded the more confirmed they became in their faith, the more joyful in the performance of their high and holy calling, for nothing tends so much to the increase of faith as to see the kingdom of our Savior spreading and becoming a power in the hearts of the people. For this reason it is a blessed privilege to labor in the kingdom of the Lord as a gospel messenger and worker, and to contribute one's strength to the upbuilding of the walls of Zion.

By these means the little flame of faith in the heart becomes a consuming fire. This we must learn to know, we who have the work of the Apostles to-day, and are their weak followers and imitators, to the purpose that the kingdom of God may come. In preaching the gospel the ministers themselves may be the greatest gainers; the privilege of laboring thus increases our faith and confidence in Him whose ambassadors we are. And to a still greater degree this is the case with those who labor without among the heathen nations and are in Gentile lands, the fishers of men, drawing into the net of the gospel of Christ the souls of the many. They, seeing the progress of their works, rejoice in a strengthened trust and faith, the more they labor, the more they toil. The same is true of all Christians whose hearts and hands are in the work of the Lord. It is the high mission of a new redeemed soul to labor for the upbuilding of the kingdom of the Lord, to win souls for the Savior, notwithstanding all weakness of faith, and doing such labor our own souls are to gain and be strengthened, and we are to advance on the way to heavenly glory. For none is too weak or too small to help the one common work of the Church of God on earth. Children can often win their parents for the Lord by their childlike, pious life; the poor widow, who may be in need of bread, may, by her example of trust and faith, be an object lesson for many that are without, and teach them to learn to love the Lord and His word. A poor peasant, by the firmness of his faith, may become the source of strength for the doubting faith of the learned. In every station and walk and condition of life, we can, by our conversation, word, and deed, declare to others the glories and blessings of a heart centered in a risen and ascended Lord.

III. But with all this we should never lose courage or be filled with forebodings of failure. If we enter upon the work of the Lord in such a spirit, nothing substantial and successful is accomplished. If in Christ's name we undertake Christ's work, there will be no time for lamentations or complaints. There are no reasons for such a thing. The spirit of God has been promised from above to be strong in those who are weak. Your Savior is your strength; He abides with you to the end of days. In a few plain words, the Evangelist says, "He was received up into heaven and sat down at the right hand of God." Blessed are we that we know this, blessed are we that we have such a kind Lord. He is seated on the throne of power and rules all things wisely and well. He guides and directs all things from His exalted seat of power, with His all-overlooking eye of majesty, with the all-conquering glance of His eye, with His all-embracing love. He directs the destinies of nations and individuals, notwithstanding the opposition of all evil powers and forces. All, great and small, are in the hollow of His hands; and especially are the members of His Kingdom of grace the objects of His never-ceasing and loving solicitude and care. Our faith in our Heavenly King as such a ruler must cast the brightest of sunshine in our lives and labors. It must draw us to Him. It must fill our hearts with cheer and joy, gladly and willingly to serve Him and work in His cause. The heart that is sealed by His Spirit in His kingdom has the blessed hope in the Lord who has ascended on the throne of majesty to rule and reign forever. Let us therefore on this day, while humbly remembering our lack of faith in Him and His gospel, yet glorify our King in His majesty, and with hearts full of confidence and implicit trust, pray and petition to Him constantly to send us from His throne of grace the Spirit that makes us fit for heaven and that will eventually make us partakers of the glories of the eternal heaven beyond the grave. Amen!— H. R.

THE ASCENDED CHRIST

By Charles F. Deems, D.D., LL.D.

When he ascended up on high, he led captivity captive, and gave gifts unto men.—Eph. iv: 8

Into the history of our race came the history of the career of Jesus. That changed all the relations of humanity to the universe and to itself. That furnished a reason for the existence of humanity. That now maintains the support of humanity. That predicts the future of humanity.

The life of Jesus is the foundation of the Christian religion. Now, in regard to that religion it is well to remind ourselves that it is not merely a philosophy or a science, but the inspiration of a new spiritual life. We must not forget that to live the life of a Christian does not demand any particular culture, or mere intellectual assent to any propositions, or the belief in any series of doctrines. It does not depend on a philosophy or a theology, but it does hang on a man's belief in a fact. One single historical fact, thoroughly believed and lived upon, followed out to all its logical consequences in practical living, will make any man a Christian.

The history of eighteen centuries shows this. Men have held to manifold forms of philosophy, and believed, and taught many and diverse theories of theology, and have lived and worked under all kinds of ecclesiasticism, and yet have manifestly been Christians; but no man has failed to believe in the fact of the Ascension of the Risen Body of Jesus and been a Christian, no matter what else he believed. He could not be. The denial of the Resurrection of Jesus is as distinct and complete an abandonment of the Christian religion as the denial of the existence of the Jehovah of Sinai would be of Jewish religion, or a denial of the existence of God would be of all religion. The resurrection and the ascension of Jesus make a hinge, the resurrection part of which takes hold upon earth, and the ascension part on heaven.

It is indispensable to believe that Jesus the Christ rose from the dead. No matter what we think of Him, no matter which other part of His history we accept or reject, no matter what opinion we have of His form and character, if He did not raise Himself from the dead, if the Galilean Prophet's dust is still reposing in some unknown Syrian grave, His claims are all worthless; He is not the highest spiritual authority in the universe, as He claimed; He is not the Creator of the world, as He claimed; He cannot be the Savior of the world, as He claimed. If He did not rise from the dead, all He said and all He did can be treated by mankind as the words and the deeds of one who must have been either a fool or a knave. All Christianity goes down with the denial of the resurrection of Jesus.

This was perceived and announced in the very first years of Christianity by its teachers, and especially by its very greatest thinker, the Apostle Paul, who asserted that if Christ had not risen from the dead, all the preaching of Christian teachers and all the belief of Christian disciples was in vain. That point is settled. To believe that Christ did not rise from the dead as thoroughly abrogates Christianity as to believe that there is no God.

Now this is a very interesting feature of the case, that our religion rests not on a theory, but on a fact. A theory may or may not be a mistake, but a fact is always susceptible of proof. And it is very important to remember that nothing which ever occurred in the history of the world has any more evidence to support it than the fact that Jesus of Nazareth, who was crucified and who was buried, rose from the dead. Nothing alleged to have occurred in the days of William the Conqueror, nothing in the wars of Frederick the Great, can bring to the thinking man of the eighteenth century more evidence than the resurrection of Jesus from the dead. That is the Easter Day part of the hinge.

To-day we have assembled to consider the other, the Ascension Day portion of the divine fact on which swings our redemption. To get the full force of it we must remember something of the forty days preceding this crowning event of our Lord's earthly history. I call your attention briefly to the facts that He was seen first by one woman, then by several women, and then by one disciple, and then by two, and then by ten of the disciples, and then by the whole eleven, and then by five hundred of the disciples at once. He also appeared to James, His younger brother. At these appearances our Lord ate, and drank, and showed His hands and His feet. It is to be remembered that these were acts repeated

through nearly six weeks, in which His apostles were being taught more deeply as to His natural existence as a man and as to the divine side of His nature. It is important to recall the fact that, having appeared in the body which He brought out of the tomb, He always came among them without announcement, and always departed without adieu.

That resurrection and those appearances were absolutely essential to the consummation of their faith. If He had not risen all their hopes would have failed, and their three years of remarkable relations with Jesus would have been to them sometimes as an enigma, but generally as the remembrances of a dream. It could have been of no spiritual benefit to them, and they could never use it for the spiritual benefit of others.

It is also to be remembered that our faith in the fact of the resurrection of Jesus does not depend wholly upon the testimony of the immediate eye-witnesses, but that there are thousands of historical facts, the existence of which in our present knowledge of the laws of human thinking cannot be accounted for without the assumption of another fact—namely, the resurrection of Jesus. They are such as these: The head of a body of religionists, in whom they believed as having power to resist all force, is murdered on a certain Friday in A. D. 30. That Friday night there was not a single one of them who believed he would ever see Him again. There was no plan and no purpose for the future, and there was no purpose because there was no object. On the following Sunday evening they were reassembled, their hopes were rekindled, they were again a body with a head. They asserted the resurrection of their leader, they asserted it to His murderers, who. if they still had possession of His body, if they had not lost it, could have produced it. The production of that body was absolutely essential to the maintenance of their own ground and to the destruction of the new religion; but they failed to produce that body. The disciples had seen it. It was dead or it was alive. If dead it was no more to them out of the grave than in the grave. But alive it supplied them with every intellectual consideration and furnished them with every spiritual stimulus to carry this Gospel to the ends of the earth.

In half a century it had overrun the Roman Empire; it was in the remote provinces, it was in Italy, it was in distant and humble hamlets, it was in the city of Rome. Far to the front there was the resurrection. "Jesus and the resurrection," this was the theme of the teaching of the apostles; this was the inspiration of their eloquence; this was the captivating power of their zeal. To account for the history of eighteen centuries since A. D. 31 is absolutely impossible without the assumption of the resurrection of Jesus Christ from the dead as a fact. Look at an existing fact here before our eyes, the presence in this Church of this great body of Knights-Templar,* part of a great institution this moment in the United States

* This sermon was delivered on Ascension day, May 7, 1891 before Columbian, Palestine, Manhattan, Ivanhoe, Constantine, and York Commanderies of Knights-Templar.

of America, a land far off and unknown when Christ was crucified, but in which every day two or more temples are erected to His worship. I look down upon this body of uniformed and armed men, the Knights-Templar of the city of New York, and I ask any thinker to account for the phenomenon on the assumption that the resurrection of Jesus Christ from the dead is a myth and not a fact.

We have come together to celebrate the ascension of Jesus, the other part of what I have ventured to call the great hinge on which Christianity swings. The sacred Scripture of the New Testament gives the following account of that last appearance of Jesus to mortal eyes. St. Mark tells us that after the Lord had spoken unto His disciples, " He was received up into heaven, and sat on the right hand of God." St. Luke tells us, in his Gospel, that after Jesus had given the promise to His apostles that they should be endued with power from on high, He led them out to Bethany, on the Mount of Olives; that He lifted up His hands and blessed them, and that while blessing them He was parted from them and was carried up to heaven. This same writer, who was the only educated man in the company, in writing the Acts of the Apostles enlarged the account, telling us that after Jesus had promised His apostles that they should receive power from on high after the Holy Ghost had come upon them, and that they should become His witnesses to the utmost parts of the earth, He was taken up from the circle of men among whom He stood, and a cloud received Him out of their sight; and that while they stood gazing into heaven two men stood by them in white apparel, saying, " Ye men of Galilee, why stand ye gazing up into heaven? This same Jesus who is taken from you shall so come in like manner as ye have seen him go into heaven." There are two other facts mentioned in this account: one is that Jesus received divine worship from His disciples before the two men spoke to them, and that immediately afterward they returned to Jerusalem and began to organize for work.

The importance of the record in regard to the Ascension can scarcely be overrated, and yet Christendom has seemed to content itself with observance of the Resurrection. But reflect a moment upon what would be the state of the case if the departure of Jesus had not taken place just as recorded in the Gospel. The Lord either might have made His farewells to the apostles and left them, going away naturally as He had been accustomed to do before His death, or He might have made a valedictory and have disappeared as He had been accustomed to do during the forty days immediately after the resurrection. In either case there would have been an incompleteness in His career, and, however majestic and beautiful the outlines of His life, it would always appear to succeeding generations something like a pyramid whose apex was lost in a mist.

No; the earthly career of our Lord was open, rounded, and complete. The extremes of human society saw Him as a human babe, over whose public stable-cradle Jewish peasants and Oriental sages bent. Out in the open air, on mountain or by sea-side, or in public synagog or crowded temple, He taught through all His ministry, doing nothing in secret, keeping no esoteric doctrine for cultivated Nicodemuses while teaching something else to the fishermen of Galilee and the common dwellers by the Jordan. He died in the sight of people from every part of the earth, at a point in full view of Jerusalem when it was crowded with visitors assembled at a solemn feast. After His resurrection He had appeared to apostles and disciples, men and women, in several places, by the space of about six weeks.

What now was to be done with that body? Should it evanesce? What, then, was to become of that religion which is to surpass all the religions of the world in spiritual power, because it does not consist in theological doctrines, however true, or ethical precepts, however sound, or in ritualistic ceremonials, however esthetic or imposing, but in personal devotion to a Person who is divinely human and humanly divine? Would not it also have evanished from among men?

No! No! The grand personality of Jesus grew grander and more personal to the end. On the slope of the Mount of Olives, surrounded by a number of persons who should afterward be able always to correct and confirm each other's recollections, He talked with His apostles, told them that some special baptism of the Holy Ghost was about to come upon them, that when it came they should receive spiritual " power " and should then become witnesses to Him unto the utmost parts of the earth. His glowing description of their coming career of power and glory fixed every eye on Him. Each saw Him and all saw Him. While they were gazing He began to rise. The circle widened with a sense of awe. No man knew what was to be next; the Master seemed to grow taller and more majestic, fuller of a divine beauty than had ever shone on mortal face before. And He no longer touched the ground, but rose, rose slowly, shooting into the eye of each disciple in turn a look of love and confidence, a look brighter than the sun and wider than the sky, a look that oversplendored each man's intellect and made each man's heart swell like an ocean-tide. " He went up," up, up, through that clear Syrian air under that pure Syrian sky, " while they looked steadfastly toward heaven, as He went up."

As the ages have passed, the more the Scripture has been studied, more and more Christians have come to find the power and comfort which reside in the fact of the Lord's Ascension. It illuminates all the previous life of the Christ. It shows how His birth was an incarnation, and that He must have had a pre-existence in a divine glory in which He was so much at home when His earthly career closed. To Nathanael, one of His earliest disciples and the most guileless, He said, " Hereafter ye shall see heaven open, and the angels of God ascending and descending upon the Son of Man" (John i: 51), and to the cultivated Nicodemus He had said, "No man hath ascended up to heaven but the Son of Man, who hath descended from heaven" (John iii: 13). When one of His most profound discourses had set His disciples to doubting, He said to them, "What and if ye shall see the Son of Man ascend up where he was before?" (John vi: 62). In view of His approaching death He said to His circle of chosen apostles, "I came forth from the Father, and am come into the world: again, I leave the world, and go to the Father" (John xvi: 28).

The effect of the Ascension upon the first apostles was instantaneous, powerful, and transforming. Naturally, while this stupendous event was taking place they would be in an absorbing rapture, but such states of exaltation are neither wholesome nor helpful. The men in white had put to them the question why they stood there gazing up to heaven. The gaze was natural, but not normal. Men must not let any visions of heaven turn them from any duties of earth. Whatever revelation God makes to the spirit is plainly to give the spirit strength to do its earthly work.

So the disciples returned unto Jerusalem, banded together, united with them godly women, and so stood ready for the next marching orders. When those orders came they found that the Lord was working with them, and as they traveled to the ends of the earth, their ascended Lord, now sitting at the right hand of God, which to them must have meant the possession of omnipotence, wrought with them. If He had still been upon earth, no matter to what majestic heights He may have risen, He could not have been so stimulating to their faith as when sitting at "the right hand of God." A star in the heavens may be equally near to two persons on the planet, altho they be in antipodes, while it would be impossible to erect in Jerusalem, or in Rome, or in Paris, or in New York, or in San Francisco, a tower so lofty as to be simultaneously beheld by the people in all these cities. So Jesus never seemed nearer to His apostles than He did when He returned to the Father and took His seat at the right hand of God. It is the crowning fact in His career.

The Apostle Paul groups in culminating order the three facts which, based upon the incarnation, are the foundation of the hope of our redemption—Christ's death, Christ's resurrection, and Christ's ascension. "Who is he that condemneth?" the apostle asked; and his answer is, "It is Christ that died, yea rather, that is risen again, who is even at the right hand of God, who also maketh intercession for us" (Rom. viii: 34). He might have died, and yet the work of our salvation be left incomplete. He might have risen, and yet the work of our salvation be left incomplete. The completing fact is that He is ever at the right hand of God. On the cross His sufferings made a powerful plea for our sins. His emergence from the tomb made a powerful plea for our immortality. But both would

have failed but for His ascension, in which He took a glorified human body up through the ranks of cherubim and seraphim, of angels and archangels, who parted to let Him pass in superb majesty up to the throne to eternity, where He placed His glorified human body at the right hand of God, to be forever in the sight of God the Father and in the sight of all principalities of the invisible world; where He ever liveth, making intercession for us, which intercession would be powerless without that presence.

It is never to be forgotten that those two men in white, perhaps angels from the upper glory, who turned the apostles away from gazing into the trackless ether through which their Lord had ascended to the gates of glory, turned them away to the hard work and rugged hardships attendant upon carrying the Gospel to the nations, gave them for comfort the wonderful promise, "This same Jesus, which is taken from you into heaven, shall so come in like manner as ye have seen him go into heaven."

First notice the preservation of the identity of Jesus, Mary's Babe, the Boy of Nazareth, the Master of the Apostles, the crucified, buried, risen, ascended Jesus is "this same Jesus." No change, no transfiguration breaks in upon the identity of our Lord. When Stephen, soon after the Ascension, was gazing into the heavens, and saw Jesus at the right hand of God, he beheld the very same person who broke the bread and delivered the wine at the Last Supper, the same person who had expired on the cross, had risen from the grave, and had been seen by the apostles ascending into heaven. Let us never lose sight of that wonderful fact.

Another great truth is, He is to come again upon earth, "this very same Jesus." We must remind ourselves that in the Old Testament Scripture which they held in their hands, the Jews, at the time of the birth of our Lord, had just as clear a promise of the First Advent as we have now of the Second, and yet they had conned those Scriptures and repeated them, losing sight of their grand meaning, so that He came and went, and many of them saw Him many and many a time and never knew Him. Now He is to come again. It is an utter waste of time for any man to strive to determine *when* that shall be, but there is nothing in the future more certain than that He will come, and that He will come out of the heavens; that as His body was not dissipated into the ether, but carried in perfect organism, glorified into the heavens, so "in like manner," in that glorified organism, the Son of God shall come down among men again.

My Brethren, *He may be coming now.* When He first appeared incarnate among men, the birth of the Bethlehem Babe was as noiseless as this morning's dawn. But sectarian Jerusalem, so very near His cradle, was so absorbed in theological disputes and civil insubordination, and imperial Rome was in such a turmoil of politics and corruption, that neither of these centers of civilization knew when he arrived. Centuries had elapsed since the promise had been made of the coming Seed of David, the Messiah, the Deliverer, the Person who should unite in Himself the offices of prophet, priest and king. Great national and political changes had occurred; the heroic Maccabean period had passed, the Roman Conquest had been completed, and still the Deliverer had not come.

My brethren, let us be on our guard! He may choose an Ascension Day on which to revisit the earth. While we worship here He may be already arriving, or it may be next Sunday; but soon or late, He will come. Let us be found ready. Let no sword be laid away. Let no vigilance be relaxed. Let every man of us every day be prepared to salute the coming Captain of our salvation when He shall enter our asylum, or our home, or our city. How should men live who, on such a day as this, come uniformed and armed into a venerable edifice erected for His worship! O knights! should any of us allow these lips, which have taken the solemn vows of the Red Cross, to be polluted with words of falsehood or of filth? O knights! should any of us, whose vows so bind us to deliver the oppressed, be found as oppressors when the Lord shall come again? Shall any of us, in the campaign against infidelity and vice, be found wavering in our loyalty, or sunk in sensual wassail, when our majestic Lord shall turn His holy eyes upon us?

Shall our feet, which are drilled to keep step to the march of the Christ's legions, ever walk into a saloon, the headquarters of the devil, our Captain's chief foe, or cross the threshold of the house of her whose "feet go down to death, and whose steps take hold on hell?" When your steps are directed to your place of business, or to your home, or to your Church, or to your asylum, oh! my brethren, go expecting the Son of God, expecting to find the Commander-in-Chief. At every turn, in all your walks of life, expect to confront "this same Jesus" come back to earth once more.

And so, brethren, let us His followers, His sworn followers, Knights of the Cross, of the Red Cross, let us never forget the vows we have made to follow Him as our Divine Leader. Whither did He go when He walked as the Son of Man among the children of men? He went down to the sorrowful and to the sinful. So to the sorrowful and the sinful let us go like the Captain of our salvation, carrying helpfulness in our hands and love in our hearts. What was the battle our Captain fought? It was a battle for the weak against the strong, and for the right against the wrong. He never antagonized a human hope or a human heart. He smote evil, only evil, and stood for the right, only for the right. Now, my fraters, dear brothers, Sir Knights, let our swords be like His sword, bathed in heaven. In our homes, in our business, in politics, in science, in our social life, in every way, let our sword be the sword of the Spirit, never drawn without cause, never wielded without right, never sheathed without honor.

It may be a long and weary battle, but we shall be brought off more than conquerors, and over every pilgrimage-path and upon every battle-field let us remember that when He ascended up on high "He led captivity captive, and gave gifts unto men," and that He will give us the gifts of faith, of hope, and of charity; that He will minister unto us the grace of wisdom, of courage, of strength, and of fortitude, and while we are living, and when we are dying, may we ever utter thus our prayer to the Father, "Grant, we beseech Thee, Almighty God, that as we believe Thine only begotten Son to have ascended into the heavens, so we may also in heart and mind continually ascend, and with Him continually dwell."—H. R.

ASCENSION DAY AND PENTECOST

(Selections from the German)

BY PROF. GEORGE H. SCHODDE, PH.D.

Ascension Day a Festival of Faith

Luke xxiv: 50-53

Glorious facts are revealed in these verses. They can be compared with the starry heavens; each fact more glorious than the preceding; the longer we look and contemplate, the greater is the abundance of rich truths here opened to our view. The ascension Gospel is one of comforting importance, of powerful effect, and deep and earnest significance. It is—

I. THE REAL FESTIVAL OF FAITH; which fact is recognized. (1) In its significance *for* us, namely, that we learn how *heaven has been opened for us*, as it is our Savior who has entered heaven; and (2) in its effects *in us*, namely, that *it opens our hearts for heaven*, for heaven is the place to which our Savior has been exalted. The Savior, first, led His disciples to Bethany, but only after He had passed through Gethsemane and Calvary. This is emblematic of His way of leading man's soul, first through the valley of humiliation and recognition of sin. But, then, He blessed them, which is emblematic of His grace given by faith to those who have learned to look for help to Him alone. Faith looks only to the outstretched hand of the Savior. Then, further, He departs to heaven; indicating what shall be the reward of those whose faith has made them His,

His own ascension, the certain assurance that where He is, there those too shall be, who are His own.

II. THE SUBJECTIVE EFFECTS OF THE ASCENSION GOSPEL, namely, that it unlocks and prepares our hearts for heaven. (1) The apostles *worshiped* Him, indicative of how their hearts had been opened to a recognition of His true character and work. (2) They returned to Jerusalem, *with great joy;* their hearts and lives were filled with the full joy of confident faith. (3) They were *continually in the temple blessing God;* their lives thus became one of constant *devotion, consecration and service to Him.*—THEODOSIUS HARNACK.

Sermon Sketches on the Gospel Lesson for Ascension Day

Mark xvi: 14-19

14 Afterward he appeared unto the eleven as they sat at meat, and upbraided them with their unbelief and hardness of heart, because they believed not them which had seen him after he was risen.

15 And he said unto them, Go ye into all the world, and preach the gospel to every creature.

16 He that believeth, and is baptized, shall be saved; but he that believeth not, shall be damned.

17 And these signs shall follow them that believe: In my name shall they cast out devils; they shall speak with new tongues.

18 They shall take up serpents, and if they drink any deadly thing, it shall not hurt them; they shall lay hands on the sick, and they shall recover.

19 So then after the Lord had spoken unto them, he was received up into heaven, and sat on the right hand of God.

What does the Ascension of the Lord signify?
1. The only worthy conclusion of His life on earth.
2. The all-supporting corner-stone of His life in heaven.

The Ascension of the Lord, the glorification of the Lord.
1. As a Prophet.
2. As a High Priest.
3. As a King.
The glory of the Lord on His Ascension Day.
1. He is raised up to heaven.
2. He sits at the right hand of the Father. All things are fulfilled in the Lord's glorification.
1. His disciples go out to the ends of the earth.
2. He himself takes possession of the heaven of heavens.
How does the Lord depart from His disciples?
1. He upbraids them for their unbelief.
2. He gives them His last commands.
3. He comforts them with great promises.
4. He remains with them by His word and wonders.
How the Lord's departure can comfort us.
1. That He has left us faith, through which we can overcome the world.
2. That He is sitting at the right hand of the Father, and that through Him we too can come to the Father.
The way through Christ to Eternal Bliss. It leads:
1. Through Repentance.
2. Through Faith.
3. Through work in Love.
The earth in the Light of Christ's Ascension is—
1. A school for faith.
2. A place full of promises.
3. A temple for God's honor.
Heaven in the Light of Christ's Ascension is—
1. Highly exalted above this earth.
2. Opened for this world.
3. Has come down to this earth.
The Testament of the Lord in ascending to heaven.
1. It consists of the saving Gospel to all men.
2. It consists of wondrous powers in the believers.—NEBE.

THE ASCENSION

So then after the Lord had spoken unto them, he was received up into heaven, and sat on the right hand of God.—Mark xvi: 19

The ascension, the crowning incident in Christ's career.—All these incidents are historical facts.—Each has been assailed by skeptics, especially His ascension.—Their arguments as to its impossibility are not worth answering.—But we must answer argument, from silence of two evangelists.—Notice fragmentary character of the gospels, John xxi: 25.—To make complete record they must be grouped together.—Independent witnesses who describe facts as impressed upon their observation.—Each evangelist, too, has a prominent design which regulates his selection of incidents for description.—Still this does not satisfactorily account for silence of Matthew and John.—Yet unreasonable to argue from this their ignorance of it.—Such a theory tenable only from total absence of any reference to it.—As acquaintances of the risen Jesus, must have believed in His ascension.—The ascension the necessary adjunct of the resurrection.—References in St. Matthew xxviii: 18, xxvi: 64.—References in St. John xx: 17, vi: 62.—Indirect confirmation of

Luke's detailed account and this brief record of St. Mark.

CONSIDER CHRIST'S ASCENSION.

I. AS A RETURN HOME. History of Christ on earth full of mystery and difficulty.—As God He must be omnipresent. John iii :13.— Yet as God's servant He left heaven for a time.—Earth the place of His exile till Father's purposes accomplished.—Into these He threw Himself as " His meat and drink," so finding pleasure.—Yet must have felt privation—hence His hours of retirement.—By these exercises the tedium of His exile was relieved.—True He was always conscious of His Father's presence, but with restrictions. —Therefore Luke xii : 50 may mean simply a desire for painful ordeal to be quickly over.— But also language of one who knows that this fiery baptism is the only means by which His soaring spirit can be released.—Till then " straitened "—longs for return home.— " Home," the magnet which attracts the true children.—If Absalom in Geshur longs for it, if prodigal longs for it, à fortiori the Son. —He knows no cold reception against Him. Ps. xxiv : 9.

II. AS AN EXALTATION. Again revert to difficulty presented by Christ's deity, connected with His exaltation.—As God He could receive no addition to His prerogatives, etc.—As Mediator it is that He is exalted.— His sojourn on earth was a state of degradation.—No language could adequately describe extent of it.—Love drew Him down to undergird our frail humanity.—Then He showed what mere " dust and ashes " is capable of.—He had been exalted in His baptism—in the wilderness—before His enemies —by His miracles—even on His cross—above all in His resurrection.—But a higher honor reserved, as resurrection made Him a King de jure, so ascension, a King de facto.—" All power given to me," etc., as the Son of Man. —This indeed worthy of admiration, " the worm " of Ps. xxii : 6 elevated to loftiest throne.—Phil. ii : 9-11, " Names at which the world grew pale."—But this " name " a source of blessing.—Evidence of grandeur of His exaltation is Rev. v : 11-13.

III. AS A NEVER-ENDING MARCH OF TRIUMPH. The ascension, the link connecting Christ's work on earth with His reign in Heaven.—Not seated there in idle state; carries on government.—As on earth unwearied in labors, so in heaven—John xii : 32. Magnetic attraction of ascended Jesus at work.— The ascension the signal for commencement of the Church's successful warfare.—Refer again to Matt. xxvii : 18, and connect v : 19.— In carrying out this commission, power of ascended Redeemer seen.—Preaching may be " foolishness," but wisdom justified in using its means.—Causes ever fresh peals of joy in heaven.—Thus the war is being waged with varying success, but Acts ii : 47.—Prophecy points to glorious future, Eph. i : 22, 23 ; Rev. xxi : 2.—Pleasant to meditate on Redeemer's exaltation.—The King will subdue every foe. —Under His scepter you are sure of safety.— See in the dispenser of God's mercy, the administrator of God's favor, and the very embodiment of God's love.—H. A. C. Y.

LESSONS FROM THE ASCENSION

And it came to pass while he blessed them, he was parted from them, and carried up into heaven.—Luke xxiv: 51

The Ascension was the appropriate bloom and culmination of the Resurrection. Had Christ, after the Resurrection, died a natural death, or had He simply disappeared from view into unknown obscurity, the Resurrection, as a proof of His divine power, and pledge of His undimmed and undiminished existence would have gone for nothing. And the Ascension of our Lord has some most precious lessons for us.

1. Since our Lord has ascended we are *never to think of Him as dead.* A French writer suggested *the* parallel to me. Out from the southwest extremity of Africa a cape is thrust, which, in the earlier times, was held to be a fatal barrier to navigation. Many had been drawn by wind and current into the swirling waters round it, but, it was said, none had ever reappeared. They called it the Cape of Storms. But at last, a bold navigator determined, if possible, to vanquish the dreaded cape. He sailed resolutely round it. He opened for Europe the route to the East Indies. He changed the Cape of Storms into the Cape of Good Hope.

So was there thrust out into human life the black, stormy, inscrutable Cape of Death. What became of those who at last had rounded it ? Whither had they disappeared ? On its thither side was there any land of activity and life, or were they submerged in the dark waters ?

That had been the ceaseless, wondering question of humanity for ages. For that question man, of himself, had never been able to gain perfectly clear and satisfactory reply. There is no sadder page in literature than that in which John Stuart Mill represents himself as hanging about the tomb of his dead wife at Avignon, with the hope of his life gone out, and with no vision for the future that was not shut off and ended by that grim tombstone.

But, right in this very region of death Christianity is full of speech and certainty. Christianity points with unhesitating finger to her risen Lord. *He* has rounded the black and inscrutable Cape of Storms, and changed it for us henceforth into the Cape of Good Hope. He has brought life and immortality to light. He is death's victor. And the Ascension is assurance that death hath *no more* dominion over Him. Therefore, since Christ has *risen* and *ascended* we are never to think of Him as dead.

Since our Christ is thus alive we are to be sure that *all the great offices* pertaining to His exaltation are in *active exercise*.

(*a*) He stands in heaven to-day the *living head of His redeemed Church*. We are members of His body. Not till the head dies can the body die.

" Since Christ and we are one,
    Why should we doubt or fear?
If He in heaven has fixed His throne,
    He'll fix His members there."

(*b*) He stands in heaven to-day our *priestly advocate*. It is the purpose of our lives that we sin not; and yet if we do sin, we need not despair; we have an advocate with the Father, even Jesus Christ the righteous—His advocacy evermore avails in our behalf.

(*c*) He stands in heaven to-day *as the controller of all things in God's providential government*. " *All* power is given unto me in heaven and in earth." It is His pierced hand which is on the helm of things. What a foundation for faith!

2. Since our Lord has ascended we are *never to think of Him as distant*—believe it, those apostles who saw and conversed with Jesus, who walked by His side, who rested in His bosom, who sat at His feet, were immeasurably more distant from Him than we may be to-day, if we will have it so. Contact of spirit with spirit—nothing can be nearer, more intimate. To those He stood by in actual, bodily shape, He could be but *external* form, *external* voice, *external* shape. John and Peter could not get nearer to Him than we can now get to one another, through eye-glance, ear, touch, bodily companionship. But now, having ascended, our Lord has sent *His Spirit* whose office it is to unite in subtle and deathless companionship our spirit with His own omnipresent Holy Spirit. His *inner* presence by the Holy Ghost is the special boon and issue of His ascension. " He hath poured forth this." We are never to think of our ascended Lord as distant, since the adorable Paraclete is with us.

" Closer is He than breathing,
    And nearer than hands and feet."

3. Since our Lord has ascended we are never to think of Him as *different*. " He that descended is the *same* also that ascended." Our Lord has not laid aside His brotherhood with us. He wears yet our human nature. Tho glorified man, He is *man* still. So to our Brother's heart *prayer must* find its way; from him to us a *perfect sympathy* must ever flow.—H. R.

THE ASCENSION

By Rev. C. O. Eldridge

He was taken up and a cloud received him out of their sight.—Acts i: 9

The Son of Man was in Heaven while yet on earth, tho not in the same sense. He is now on earth tho in Heaven, but not in the same sense. By His ascension we understand that divine act by which His manifest corporeal presence was lifted from earth to Heaven.

I. CHRIST WAS NOT OF THE WORLD WHILE IN THE WORLD. He was indeed born in Bethlehem, yet never spoke of that as His origin. He ever claimed a higher origin. He said: " I came forth from the Father and am come into the world: again, I leave the world and go unto the Father." To the Jews He said, " Ye are from beneath; I am from above: ye are of this world: I am not of this world." " If God were your Father ye would love me, for I proceeded forth and came from God; neither came I of myself, but he sent me." And when His earthly ministry drew near its close He asked the Father to restore Him " to the glory which I had with thee before the world was," and added, "Thou lovedst me before the foundation of the world."

Such claims would have been scouted as the dreams of a madman, but that His life agreed with them. His teachings were those of a master, not of a scribe. He taught them as one having authority. His miracles showed a divine power over Nature—water blushed into wine; bread increased in His hands; the winds were quiet at His bidding and the waves became solid under His feet; sickness fled at His command and spirits diabolic and human were subject to Him.

His death was an essential part of His great work. Speaking of this, He said, " Therefore doth my Father love me, because I lay down my life, that I might take it again. No man taketh it from me, but I lay it down of myself. I have power to lay it down, and I have power to take it again. This commandment have I received of my Father."

Thus He taught that His resurrection was also in the program, and after this He seemed less of the world than before; for tho His body bore the nail and spear-prints, it appeared and disappeared as it had not done before. It seems to have been visible only to His friends, and already to have indicated tokens of its higher destiny.

II. HIS ASCENSION WAS A FITTING CLOSE TO HIS EARTHLY MINISTRY. The earthly portion of His work being completed nothing could be gained by a longer sojourn. That He might carry into effect His mediatorial work it was necessary He should take His place above. He could not die again: death had no more dominion over Him. If He had secretly departed and been simply missing, His friends would have been left in most painful perplexity and uncertainty. It was quite in harmony with His whole life, death, and resurrection, that He should ascend bodily from among them in the clear daylight. They saw Him go, they traced His ascent till the heavens received Him: they knew He was gone, and they never sent to search for Him as the sons of the prophets had searched for Elijah on the mountains.

Here was a magnificent triumph over the law of gravitation. Here was the royal ascent by which our Solomon went up to the house of the Lord. The everlasting gates lifted up their heads and the King of Glory entered in. It was all of a piece—His life, His death, His resurrection, His ascension, all were triumphs.

III. THE ASCENSION OF CHRIST WAS ESSENTIAL TO THE WELFARE OF HIS CHURCH.

1. That He might take His true position as head over all things to His Church. As Mediator, all power had been given Him in Heaven and on earth; it was meet therefore as He had the authority that He should take the throne.

2. That, as our High Priest, He might appear in the presence of God for us.

3. That, as a returning Conqueror, He might receive and distribute royal gifts, and

especially that He might bestow the Spirit upon His Church.

IV. THE ASCENDED SAVIOR IS MORE FULLY OURS THAN EVER BEFORE. We have not lost Him: we know Him better than while He lived here, and He is ours still.

1. He is the *object* of our *faith*. Ours is not merely a Christmas Day religion, nor one which rests upon His life and teaching only; neither is it merely a Good Friday religion, lingering at the cross, or an Easter Sunday religion, rejoicing at an empty sepulcher; it embraces all these, but goes beyond them all, and triumphs in an ascended, enthroned Redeemer who bestows upon us the Holy Ghost: yet is divinely present with us always, even to the end.

2. He is the confirmation and *pledge* of our *hopes*. It might have been thought incredible that God should raise the dead, but Christ has risen, the first fruits of the resurrection of His people. He has shown us the way out of the grave. Our exaltation might seem unlikely, but it is already accomplished in Him.

" He hath raised our human nature,
In the clouds to God's right hand."

Thus our glorified humanity is already with God upon the throne. He is there as our Forerunner to prepare for us, as our Head, a pledge that His members shall follow.

3. He is the *center* of our *affections*. Doubly true now that He is lifted up to the throne, that He shall draw all eyes and hearts unto Him. It would have been difficult for us, as for the disciples, to lift our hearts to things above if He were here still. Our treasure is in Heaven. Our Head is there. "If ye then be risen with Christ, seek those things which are above, where Christ sitteth at the right hand of God."—P. M.

ASCENSION DAY

BY J. OSWALD DYKES

Acts i: 1-11 (with Luke xiv: 15-53)

I. It is quite necessary to seize firmly and hold fast by this thought, that the acts of Apostles and all subsequent acts of their true successors are, as Bengel says, a continuation of Christ's own history, if we would understand St. Luke's opening section of Church history, or any after section of it from St. Luke's day till now. The one event in which St. Luke finds the meeting place of these two eras is the Ascension. It finds a place at the end of his Gospel, and at the beginning of his Church history, because it is really common to both.

II. Unlike the feebleness of good wishes on men's dying lips, the strong benediction of the Prince of Life commands and confers a blessing, while from His radiant face and form, and down from His uplifted hands, there rains into the souls of the eleven a rain

of gracious influences, of hope and courage and content and gladness. Then, like a thing of rarer quality, which by its own upward virtue ascends through the grosser atmosphere below, His blessed body rose with a still and slow and stately movement into the pure bright upper air. Nor stayed; but followed by the fixed gaze of the amazed men, rose on, until, still raining blessings down, He reached the region where white clouds rest. Then suddenly there swept beneath His feet a cloud that shut him from their envious eyes. This was no time for idle, melancholy despondencies, that root themselves in the past—for profitless longings after that which is not. Gazing into heaven will not fetch Christ back, nor any other departed. Let us return to Jerusalem. Earth has its calls to duty, and heaven will chide us if we do not heed them. Let this be the spur which quickens labor and the hope which cheers exhaustion, that " This same Jesus who is taken from us into heaven, shall so come in like manner as they saw him go into heaven."—S. B., vol. viii., p. 339.

OUR ASCENDED LORD

1 Pet. iii: 22

" Who is gone? " Consider how *differently* He has gone.

Take any one of the world's greatest leaders—Napoleon. It stands there just at the turn of the stairs in the palace at Versailles. You come upon it suddenly. It is a sculpture of the great Napoleon smitten with death. The majestic forehead; the thin, set lips; the eye which seems to pierce you with its eagle glance even in its marble similitude. But death is on him. You can mark it in the relaxed posture, in the weakening hands; you can almost see the irregular convulsive movement of the chest. "*Sic transit gloria mundi*"—this is the legend sculptured on the pedestal. So, at last, death claimed the man before whom the world trembled. So he is gone.

Take the greatest of civic leaders—Abraham Lincoln. Said Secretary Stanton of him: " Here lies the most perfect ruler of men that ever lived." So he is gone.

Take Socrates—greatest of uninspired religious teachers. But death baffles him and captures him. Here is Socrates on trial for his life, saying to the Athenians: " Or perhaps do I differ from most other men in this; and if I am wiser at all than any one, am I wiser in this? That while not possessing any exact knowledge of the state of matters in Hades, I do not imagine I possess such knowledge." Here is Socrates again, under sentence of death, talking to his friends just before he drank the hemlock: " Well, friends, we have been discoursing for this last hour on the immortality of the soul, and there are many points about that matter on which he were a bad man who should readily dogmatize." Then he drank the hemlock. So he is gone.

Have you enough thought about and grasped the meaning of the abysmal difference of the going of our Lord and Savior Jesus Christ? He died, indeed, as all His brother men had died, or shall. It was real death He met upon the cross. But He was not, in any wise, holden by death as death has held and shall hold—save only those who shall be alive at the Lord's second coming—all the rest. He rose out of death, and from the Resurrection He bloomed into the Ascension.

So He is gone; but oh, how differently! Consider next how *similarly* He is gone. He was born into our nature and remains in our nature, for in our nature He ascended. So neither by the experiences of death nor resurrection nor ascension is He divided from us. Ah, how one with us He was—in weariness, temptation, toil. Not less one with us is He now, for He is gone *in our nature still.*

Consider *whither* He is gone. He is " gone into Heaven and is on the right hand of God."

What is Heaven?

(*a*) The place of the special Divine manifestation (Ps. cxxxix: 7-12).

(*b*) A *place*. Our Lord is there in veritable *bodily* presence.

(*c*) And in this Heaven our Lord is on the right hand of God—the place of utmost honor, the place of the utmost felicity.

(*d*) And remember our Lord is in Heaven at the right hand of God as our *Representative.* Think of how the Scripture labors to tell the truth of the believer's oneness with the Lord—foundation and building; husband and wife; vine and branches; members and head.

(*e*) As our *Forerunner*—" whither the Forerunner hath for us entered "—*i. e.,* harbinger; the first number of a series. His presence there is pledge of our entrance there; the first flower of the spring is pledge of all the succeeding flowers.

Consider to *what* He has gone—to supreme and eternal rule. Angel and authorities and powers being made *subject* unto Him. Angels fly for Him. Providences do His bidding. History is only the evolution of His purpose.

Learn, first, since our Lord is thus gone, we may be sure of the *final triumph of His cause.*

" Well roars the storm to Him who hears
A deeper voice across the storm."

Learn, second, since our Lord is thus gone, what *resource* for us.

Learn, third, since our Lord is thus gone and I trust Him, *I cannot know defeat.*

Learn, fourth, since my Lord is thus gone, let my love go *upward* to Him.

Learn, fifth, since my Lord is thus gone, let me be sure *He will master for me death's strangeness.*

Learn, sixth, the utmost folly of refusing submission to a Lord thus gone.—H. R.

THE LAST BEATITUDE OF THE ASCENDED CHRIST

By A. Maclaren

Rev. xxii: 14

I. If we are clean, it is because we have been made so. The first beatitude that Jesus Christ spoke from the mountain was, " Blessed are the poor in spirit;" the last beatitude that He speaks from heaven is, " Blessed are they that wash their robes." And the act commended in the last is but the outcome of the spirit extolled in the first. For they who are poor in spirit are such as know themselves to be sinful men; and those who know themselves to be sinful men are they who will cleanse their robes in the blood of ·Jesus Christ. (1) This mysterious robe, which answers nearly to what we mean by character, is made by the wearer. (2) All the robes are foul. (3) The foul robes can be cleansed; character may be sanctified and elevated.

II. The second thought that I would suggest is that these cleansed ones, and by implication these only, have unrestrained access to the source of light; " Blessed are they that wash their robes, that they may have the right to the tree of life." That of course carries us back to the old mysterious narrative at the beginning of the book of Genesis. The tree of life stands as the symbol here of an ex-ternal source of life. I take " life " to be used here in what I believe to be its predominant New Testament meaning, not bare continuance in existence, but a full, blessed perfection and activity of all the faculties and possibilities of the man, which this very apostle himself identifies with the knowledge of God and of Jesus Christ. And that life, says John, has an external source in heaven, as on earth.

III. Those who are cleansed, and they only, have entrance into the society of the city. The city is the emblem of security and of permanence. No more shall life be as a desert march, with changes which only bring sorrow, and yet a dreary monotony amidst them all. We shall dwell with abiding realities, ourselves fixed in unchanging, but ever-growing, completeness and peace. The tents shall be done with; we shall inhabit the solid mansions of the city which hath foundations, and shall wonderingly exclaim, as our unaccustomed eyes gaze on their indestructible strength, " What manner of stones and what buildings are here?" And not one stone of these shall be thrown down.—S. B., vol. xii., p. 379.

SUGGESTIVE THOUGHTS AND ILLUSTRATIONS

ASCENSION, Christ's.—Christ's offering Himself on earth, answered to the killing of the sacrifice without the veil; and His entering into heaven, there to intercede, answered to the priest's going with blood and his hands full of incense within the veil. So that this is a part, yea, a special part, of Christ's priesthood; and so necessary to it, that if He had not done this, all His work on earth had been ineffectual; nor had He been a priest, that is, a complete and perfect priest, if He had remained on earth, Heb. viii: 4; because the very design and end of shedding His blood on earth had been frustrated, which was to present it before the Lord, in heaven. So that this is the perfective part of the priesthood; He acted the first part on earth in a state of deep abasement, in the form of a servant; but He acts the second part in glory, whereto He is taken up, that He may fulfil His design in dying, and give the work of our salvation its last completing act.—John Flavel.

ASCENSION DAY.—We celebrate this day the Ascension of our great Judge into heaven, where He sits upon His throne and has all the world before Him; every human soul; with its desires and aims, its thoughts, words, and works, whether they be good or bad. Every man who is running now his mortal race is from first to last before the eye of Him who as on this day ascended with human nature into heaven. But we also celebrate the entrance of Christ into heaven to sit there in another character, viz., as our Mediator, Intercessor, and Advocate. He sits there as High Priest, to present to the Father His own atonement and sacrifice for the sins of the whole world. It is our Lord's supreme place in the universe *now*, and His reign over all the worlds, visible and invisible, which we commemorate in His Ascension. We are especially told in Scripture never to think of our Lord as having gone away and left His Church; but always to think of Him as now reigning, now occupying His throne in heaven, and from thence ruling over all. He rules in His invisible dominions, among the spirits of just men made perfect; He rules in the Church here below, still in the flesh. There He receives a perfect obedience, here an imperfect one;

but He still rules over all; and tho we may, many of us, resist His will here, He overrules even that resistance to the good of the Church, and conducts all things and events by His spiritual providence to their great final issue. Let us worship our Lord Jesus Christ, then, both with fear and love; but also remembering that in those in whose heart He dwells, perfect love casteth out fear. —J. B. MOZLEY.

ASCENSION, Difficulties of the.—We may confess, there are some special difficulties presented by this event when we contemplate it, ask what it means, consider what it involves. It is not only that, whereas Christmas brings the Eternal into our very midst, the Ascension "parts Him from our sight," hides Him behind the veil of the unseen world; it is also impossible to answer the questions that may be raised as to the actual removal of Christ's human body into "the heavenly places," or, as St. Paul once phrases it, "far above all the heavens." But can we expect to answer them? It has been well said that "physical difficulties in such a case are practically trifling," because we do not understand the conditions of existence attaching to that which, as belonging to the Incarnate, is in truth the "body of God;" nor, in fact, do we know, in any full sense, what is meant by "the highest heaven," considered as the scene of our Lord's glorified life. Nor must we look for the heaven of "God's right hand" among the skies which astronomy has examined, and which, as St. Peter says, "are in the way to be dissolved." At the same time we are well assured that the Resurrection of Christ carried with it His Ascension; given the one, the other follows; He could not tarry on earth—He could not but go up on high, that is, transfer His bodily existence into some inmost sanctuary of Divine glory, some central home of eternal power and life.—W. BRIGHT.

ASCENSION, Effect of the.—Note the effect wrought on the disciples by the Ascension of Christ—an effect, you observe, not of sorrow, but of joy. In place of being disheartened by the separation, they were mightily encouraged, and "returned to Jerusalem with great joy: And were continually in the temple, praising and blessing God." Shall we grieve that the Visible Presence is withdrawn, and that there is no longer on earth the mighty and mysterious Personage who put away sin by the sacrifice of Himself and discomfited through dying the enemies of God and man? Not so! There is no reason for sorrow that He quits the earth on the wings of the wind. We could not detain Him below, we would have Him as our Mediator within the veil. This and this only, can secure to us those spiritual assistances through which we ourselves may climb the firmament.—H. MELVILL.

ASCENSION, Fable of.—The body of Romulus disappeared suddenly, and no remnant of it or of his clothing could be discovered by the most diligent search. One report is that he disappeared from the temple of Vulcan; another that he was holding an assembly outside the city when there was great darkness, fearful thunderings, and a resistless tempest, which terrified and scattered the people. When this had subsided, the people came together again, but Romulus could not be found. It was thence reported by the patricians, that Romulus had been caught up to heaven, and would be to the Romans a propitious god. Thus Romulus became one of the gods of Rome. This was confirmed by the oath of his devoted and famous friend, Julius Proclus, who swore that he met Romulus while traveling on the road, clad in the most dazzling armor. Astonished at the sight, he cried out, "For what misbehavior of ours, or by what accident, O King, hast thou so untimely left us?" He answered, "It pleased the gods, my good Proclus, that we should dwell with men for a time, and having founded a city which shall be the most powerful and glorious in the world, return to heaven, from whence we came. Farewell, then! Go, tell the Romans that by the exercise of temperance and fortitude they shall attain the highest pitch of human greatness, and I, the god Quirinus, will ever be propitious to you."—F. II.

ASCENSION, Lessons of the.—By the Ascension all the parts of life are brought together in the oneness of their common destination. By the Ascension Christ in His Humanity is brought close to every one of us, and the words "in Christ," the very charter of our faith, gain a present power. By the Ascension we are encouraged to work beneath the surface of things to that which makes all things capable of consecration. We ponder these lessons of the Presence of Christ Ascended about us and in us all the days to the end of the world, and the sense of our own weakness becomes perhaps more oppressive than before. Then it is that the last element in our confession as to Christ's work speaks to our hearts. He is not only present with us as Ascended: He is active for us. We believe that He sitteth on the right hand of God the Father Almighty.—BISHOP WESTCOTT.

ASCENSION, Need of Christ's.—The Apostle makes a priest's exaltation so necessary a part of his priesthood, that without it he could not have been a priest. "If He were on earth he should not be a priest," Heb. viii: 4; that is, if He had continued here, and had not been raised again from the dead, and taken up into glory, He could not have been a complete and perfect priest. For just as it was not enough for the sacrifice to be slain without, and His blood left there; but it must be carried within the veil, into the most holy place before the Lord, Heb. ix: 7; so it was not sufficient that Christ shed His own blood on earth, except He carry it before the Lord into heaven, and there perform His intercession work for us.—JOHN FLAVEL.

ASCENSION, The.—*Luke xxiv: 50-53.* May 18, forty days after the crucifixion.

50. *And he led them out* of the city, where He had been giving His last instructions. *As far as,* until they were over against *Bethany. Blessed them.* No mere form, but a real, enduring blessing.

51. *He was parted from them.* By beginning to ascend upward. *And carried up into heaven.* The tense of the original is picturesque, and indicates a continued action, a gradual going up out of their sight. Compare the more detailed account, Acts i: 9-11.

It was at this time, that the great change came over His body described in 1 Corinthians xv: 51-53. When a cloud had received Him out of their sight two angels bade them be comforted, for the time was coming when He should return. Of the present appearance of Jesus we have a hint in the transfiguration, when "His face did shine as the sun and his raiment was white as the light" (Matt. xvii: 2); and in the Revelation (i: 12-16), where He is seen with "eyes as a flame of fire, and his feet like unto fine brass as if they burned in a furnace: and his voice as the sound of many waters, and his countenance was as the sun shineth in his strength."

52. *And they worshipped him.* They gave Him the religious worship due only to God. *And returned to Jerusalem with great joy.* Every sorrow had been turned into joy. ILLUSTRATION. The seven fears turned into seven joys, in Arnold's LIGHT OF ASIA.

53. *And were continually in the temple,* at the hours of worship. They were regular in attendance.

The temple was the visible symbol of worship.

The courts of the temple were open to all Jews. As yet no prejudice had arisen against Christians, and they were not powerful enough to excite active opposition. Jesus had called the temple His Father's house, and it was natural that His disciples should love to worship there, *praising and blessing* God, because He had done such great things for them and for the world. The new religion was full of hope and joy, light and gladness, in contrast with the religion of the Jewish traditions, and with the gloom occasioned by the death' of their Master.—P.

BETHANY, The Place of Christ's Ascension.—He led them out as far as Bethany. We can imagine the feelings of the disciples as they trod the familiar road, for they had often been to Bethany together. The inner signification of Bethany is the House of Sorrow; and it is a beautiful illustration, both of the tenderness and of the completeness of His triumph, that, on His way to His highest exaltation, He should pass the place of His deepest sorrow, and that thence He should ascend straight to the house not made with hands, eternal in the heavens.—W. M. PUNSHON.

CHRIST ASCENDED, As a Sun of Righteousness.—Christ is to the moral world what the sun is to the natural world. (1) He is the source of light. (2) He is the source of power. Nearly all the power in the world comes directly or indirectly from the sun. (3) He is the source of life. (4) He is the source of comfort and cheer. (5) He is the source of the beauty of holiness; all the glories of color come from the sun.—P.

CHRIST ASCENDED, Why.—To ascend on high must have meant for Christ a large increase of His quickening influence, more power to act beneficially on human minds and hearts, to purify and energize, to inspire and elevate, as hitherto He had not been able. That was His supreme ambition, the height for which He sighed; and was it not even thus that He went up gloriously at last from the cross and the grave, mounting from thence to be a greater saving and subliming force than He had ever been before, to beget repentance and remission of sins beyond what He had ever done?—S. A. TIPPLE.

CHRIST ASCENDED, Why.—"*I go to prepare a place for you.*" There is prepared a place not merely for all, but for *you,* a personal preparation in glory *for* each child as by grace *in* each child; a room, a house, for each nature adapted to its needs.—ABBOTT. Heaven is a prepared place for a prepared people.—VAN DOREN.

PREPARING US FOR THE PLACE. Jesus went away not only to prepare a place for us, so that it will be ready for us as one by one we go home, but to prepare us for the place, to fit us for heavenly enjoyments and heavenly service. It is quite as essential that we should be prepared for heaven as that heaven should be prepared for us. The same double process is going on with reference to that part of our Father's home in which we may dwell in this life. He is opening doors of opportunity, and preparing a sphere, a place for us on earth, and also preparing us for the sphere He would have us fill, and the work He would have us do.—P.

CHRIST ASCENDED, Why.—Consider the Ascension in the light of its declared purpose: "That he might fill all things." (1) When we see the only-begotten Son, clothed in a body like our own, exalted above all the heavens, in that sight we have before us the all-glorious and controlling center of all the spheres, the key which interprets the testimony of prophecy, the gathered first fruits of a new and redeemed world. The Gospel contains a gospel for nature as well as for man, the prediction of the day when the strife of elements shall cease, and when the powers of darkness shall be swallowed up of light. (2) By Christ's ascension our nature is endowed with an exalted fulness and clothed with a glory becoming the Son of God. "A parcel of clay," to use the words of Archbishop Leighton, "is made so bright and set so high as to outshine all the flaming spirits of eternity and the stars of the morning." And with such a miracle of grace who can regret his connection with a sinful history which conditions so great a salvation?—W. PULSFORD.

CHRIST ASCENDED, Why.—A number of years ago a delegation of Sioux Indians was present at a public meeting in the Philadelphia Academy of Music. Red Cloud, whose burly form and natural eloquence had attracted much attention, was called upon to speak. Turning to Mr. G. H. Stuart, he said: "Red Cloud wants to ask you one question,— Who made us? Did you ever see the Great Spirit or His Son? You have told Red Cloud that the Great Spirit came down from heaven, and dwelt among the white men, and that He went up again. (Pondering for a few minutes.) What did He go up again for? Red Cloud has come and he wants to find out." Many others want an answer. Jesus Himself answered the question (John xvi: 7).

1. Only by His going away could the Holy Spirit come and take His place. With Him in bodily presence in any one place, the attention of His people would be called away from the spiritual and universal nature of His Church, to that which was outward, and temporal, and earthly. The work of the Holy Spirit would be hindered and hampered. Statecraft, politics, government by force, would naturally arise, turning the thoughts away from new hearts and spiritual lives.

2. His bodily presence could be only in some one place, toward which all men would tend. "A present bodily Jesus involves a geographical Church." Now abiding on the right hand of God, He is enabled to be the omnipresent Savior of all men, as would not be possible if He were in the body, tho as King in Jerusalem. His Holy Spirit is everything to all men everywhere that He Himself would be if present with each one to aid, to comfort, and to guide. "The Holy Spirit," says Boardman, "gives us one and the same Church, even the Holy Catholic Church throughout all lands and times and names." Professor Stokes compares the centralization of the Roman Catholic Church at Rome, which, "instead of securing the universality of the Church, strikes a deadly blow at it," and the centralization of the British Empire at London. Now in the unseen heavens is "the common destiny, the true Fatherland of all the sons of God."

3. The ascension was a noble and fitting close of the earthly career of Jesus; far better than to die again, as Lazarus did, or than to remain always on earth in His body,—the only alternatives. Jesus' life thus became also a type of our lives, an inspiration toward such living as would bring the most glorious and perfect ending of our earthly careers that is conceivable through our resurrection existence in glorified spiritual bodies.

4. It completed the proof of His divine nature and mission. It was the crowning of His life with success.

5. It showed the continued reality of Christ's existence, linking this world with the other, and showing how He could be the ever-living Savior in heaven, whom Stephen saw at the right hand of God, who came to Paul on the way to Damascus, who is ever with His people, even to the end of the world. The last view of Christ is not upon the cross, but ascending from Olivet into glory; not in agony of atonement, but in the act of blessing; not in seeming defeat, but in manifest triumph. We worship, not a dead, but a living Savior, to whom we shall go, with whom we shall be in glory, and whom we shall love and serve through endless ages.

6. Thus His children are taught to live by faith and not by sight, and are trained in character and manhood by the responsibility of carrying on His work. The present system trains "governors and governed, kings and subjects, parents and children, teachers and pupils, all alike."

7. The doctrine of the ascension, with its hope of future glory, with its transfigured Son of Man (not son of Jew or Greek, but of man) on the throne, "adds new dignity to life," for the lowliest shall be changed into the likeness of His glorified body. "It is an ever-flowing fountain of dignity, of purity, of mercy."—P.

CHRIST, Ascension of.—The *high priest* entering the Holy of Holies once every year, on the day of Atonement. Lev. xvi; Heb. ix: 24-26. The Holy of Holies, where the symbol of Divine glory rested, typified heaven; and within that mysterious shrine the high priest, after he had made atonement for himself, for the sanctuary, and for the people, was to enter; and, dressed in the white linen robes common to the priesthood (not in the gorgeous robe of his high priesthood), was to sprinkle with blood before the mercy-seat seven times, taking with him also a censer full of burning coals, and sweet incense, beaten small. The *ark* carried up, with pomp and rejoicing, to Mount Zion. Ps. xxiv; lxviii: 18. *Moses* going up into the mount to receive the law, Deut. x, and *Elijah's translation to heaven,* followed by the double portion of his spirit being given to his successor, have generally been acknowledged by the Church as figures of Christ's ascension. Some add *Samson's* victoriously carrying up the gates of Gaza to the top of the hill. Judges xvi: 3.—BOWES.

CHRIST, Ascension of.—He wished to leave them in such a way that they should not think He had simply vanished from them, and wait for His present re-appearance.—GEIKIE. His ascension is not His separation from His people, but the ascension of His throne and the beginning of His reign as the head of the Church which "is his body, the fulness of him that filleth all in all" (Eph. i: 23).—REV. COM. There has been a stupid objection raised, that, as the world is turning around all the time, going up would not necessarily lead to any point in the sky called heaven. But if there is such a central point, any being going up from this world a short distance could change his course to that direction, no matter in which direction he started.—P.

CHRIST, Ascension of.—In public, in the daylight, on holy Olivet, the Lord finished with glory the career which He began in obscurity. He finished His earthly career, but not His human life. His ascension perpetuated His incarnation. He did not evacuate His human body, but carried it with Him to the right hand of God—with its nail prints and its thorn scars. Touched with a feeling of our infirmities, our great High-priest has passed into the heavens. There He ever liveth to make intercession for us. With His pierced hands He is able to save to the uttermost them that come unto God by Him. He is able to lift them up to the place where He reigns. This gives place and locality to heaven. Heaven is somewhere. It is where the holy feet of Jesus stand, and, therefore, where the weary feet of His pilgrims may rest. It is where His lips, which left the earth pronouncing blessing, still speak, and, therefore, where the happy ears of His saints may hear His blessed words of love and wisdom; where loving eyes behold Him, the chief glory of that glorious place, and the fairest object.—R. S. BARRETT.

CHRIST, Ascension of.—By our Lord's Ascension into Heaven, we mean His disappearance into the spiritual realm which pervades the material. And that realm, as He has Himself assured us, consists of various spheres of being. The common notion about heaven, I suppose, is that it is one vast place in which the whole human race together with the angels, shall be assembled after the general judgment, and there live for ever in ceaseless adoration. Very different is the view which our Lord gives us of heaven. He describes it as a world of many abodes. "In my Father's house are many dwelling-places; if it were not so I would have told you." In other words, it is natural to expect that there should be different dwelling-places, different spheres of being, different plans of existence in the spiritual world; so natural indeed is it that, were it otherwise, our Lord would have made a special revelation on the subject; . . . our own instincts confirm our Lord's declaration.—MALCOLM MCCALL.

CHRIST, Ascension of.—I suppose that our first impressions are to consider the Ascension of our Lord as the very greatest event connected with His appearance on earth. To our own mind, undoubtedly, nothing could be so solemn, so exalting, as the changing this life for another; the putting off mortality and putting on immortality; and all this we connect with the thought of the removal from earth to heaven. And had Christ been as we are, His Ascension would have been spoken of very differently from what it is now; and the account of His Resurrection would have been justly deemed incomplete without it. But to Christ, if I may so speak, His Resurrection was natural, it was His death that was the miracle of His love. Surely, as we need not to be told that Lazarus died again after *his* resurrection, as we know that it follows, of course, because he was a man and no more; so we need not be told that Christ, after *His* Resurrection, ascended into heaven. We know that it follows, of course, for the dwelling of the Most High God is not in earth, but in heaven.—THOMAS ARNOLD.

CHRIST, Ascension of Elijah and of.—The ascension of Elijah may be compared to the flight of a bird, which none can follow; the ascension of Christ is, as it were, a bridge between earth and heaven, laid down for all who are drawn to Him by His earthly existence.—BAUMGARTEN.

CHRIST, Body, The, of the Ascended.—Consider first the question of a body possibly existing in heaven. If Adam had kept His state of innocence, he would not have died, nor would he, we imagine, have continued for ever in Paradise, among the trees and the beasts of the earth. We believe that he would have been translated in his body, glorified, to heaven. Enoch was thus removed, and afterwards Elijah. Again, Moses, tho his body had been hidden in the earth, appeared after a thousand years, above a hill of Palestine, and was heard to talk. Whence did his body, and that of Elijah come? None can say. It is enough for our purpose to admit that their presence at the Transfiguration is a proof that bodies can exist somewhere above the range of the lower earth.—C. W. FURSE.

CHRIST, Exaltation of.—When the Jewish rulers, who had sworn the life of Jesus away before the tribunal of the Roman governor, heard first of His Resurrection, they remonstrated with the witnesses: "Ye intend to bring this man's blood upon us." The Resurrection of Jesus had no other meaning to them than vengeance. They reasoned: "If He whom we slew is exalted, wo unto us!" But to these very men the apostles preached pardon. They proclaimed that Jesus is exalted for the purpose of showing mercy to His murderers. He is exalted to give, and He gives even to them. He gives to all, and upbraideth not. Now that He is exalted, and His enemies are in His power, instead of taking vengeance, He gives remission of sins. The water is exalted into the heavens in order that it may give rain upon the earth—it is exalted to give. It is drawn up, as by a resurrection; and arises pure into the heavens, that it may be in a capacity to send refreshing to the thirsty ground. In the same way He who comes as rain on the mown grass was exalted that He might give—that He might give Himself, as the living water, to His own.—ARNOT.

CHRIST, Exalted Giver.—As in the Roman triumphs, the victor ascending up to the Capitol in a chariot of state used to cast certain pieces of coin among the people for them to pick up, which he used not to do at other times, so our Lord Jesus Christ, in the day of His triumph and solemn inauguration into His heavenly kingdom, scatters some heavenly jewels that the thief might pick up, which He doth not, and will not, do every day; or as in these days, it is usual with princes to save some notorious malefactors at their coronation, when they enter upon their kingdom in triumph, which they seldom do afterward, so did Jesus Christ act toward this thief.—T. BROOKS.

CHRIST, Gift of the Ascended.—"Wherefore, he saith, when he ascended up on high, he led captivity captive, and gave gifts unto men. And he gave some, apostles; and some, prophets; and some, evangelists; and some, pastors and teachers; for the perfecting of the saints, for the work of the ministry, for the edifying of the body of Christ." As when Roman heroes returned from blood-red fields, and the senate awarded them a triumph, they rode in their chariot drawn by milk-white steeds through the thronging streets of the capital, so did Jesus Christ when He led captivity captive receive a triumph at His Father's hands. The triumphal chariot bore Him through the streets of glory, while all the inhabitants thereof with loud acclaim saluted Him as Conqueror.

"Crown Him! crown Him!
Crowns become the victor's brow!"

It was the wont of the Roman conqueror as he rode along to distribute large quantities of money which were scattered among the admiring crowd. So our glorified Lord scattered gifts among men, yea to the rebellious also He gave those gifts that the Lord God might dwell among them; in this manner, then, to grace the triumph of Jesus, the Spirit of God was liberally poured out upon the Church below.—SPURGEON.

CHRIST IN HEAVEN, The Ascended. —Christ is already in that place of peace, which is all in all. He is on the right hand of God. He is hidden in the brightness of the radiance which issues from the everlasting throne. He is in the very abyss of peace, where there is no voice of tumult or distress, but a deep stillness—stillness, that greatest and most awful of all goods which we can fancy; that most perfect of joys, the utter, profound, ineffable tranquillity of the Divine Essence. He has entered into His rest. That is our *home*; here we are on a pilgrimage, and Christ calls us to His many mansions which He has prepared.—J. H. NEWMAN.

CHRIST IN THE CLOUD.—A suffering believer once remarked to a friend: "When I am very low and dark I go to the window, and if I see a heavy cloud I think of those precious words, '*A cloud received him out of their sight*,' and I look up and see the cloud sure enough, and then I think—well, that may be the cloud that hides Him. And so you see there is comfort in a cloud."—H. R.

CHRIST IS DOING, What the Ascended.—In the Cologne Cathedral hangs the original pencil drawing of the cathedral by Meister Gerard, about 1250, "whose great genius conceived and put into existence these plans, whose fulfilment would require centuries of labor." The work was begun, but war and political changes left it unfinished. For several centuries the plans disappeared. Then, in new circumstances, these drawings were "hunted from garrets in which they had slumbered," and in 1830, almost six hundred years after the plans were made, work was again begun, and carried to completion.

Jesus was going on now to carry out the plans formed "from the foundation of the world," and begun by Him during His bodily life. The new kingdom is wondrously beautiful, but it is not yet completed. —P.

CHRIST OUR ADVOCATE, The Ascended.—"We have an advocate with the Father, Jesus Christ the righteous." 1 John ii: 1. The word here translated *Advocate* was translated *Comforter* in John xiv: 16, 26; xv: 26; xvi: 7. It sometimes means one who takes up his client's cause to carry it through by pleadings and acts,—an *advocate;* sometimes one who goes forth to make peace between two parties, beseeching for an offender,—an *intercessor;* sometimes one who stands by the sinking sufferer, uttering words of consolation and strength,—a *comforter.* All these offices concur in Jesus Christ, who is our Advocate to urge our cause, an Intercessor to make our peace, our Comforter to fill us with joy.—J. W. ALEXANDER.

CHRIST OUR INTERCESSOR, The Ascended.—*Jno. xvii: 9.* Once, I suddenly opened the door of my mother's room, and saw her on her knees beside her chair, and heard her speak my name in prayer. I quickly and quietly withdrew, with a feeling of awe and reverence in my heart. Soon I went away from home to school, then to college, then into life's sterner duties. But I never forgot that one glimpse of my mother at prayer, nor the one word—my name— which I heard her utter. Well did I know that what I had seen that day was but a glimpse of what was going on every day in that sacred closet of prayer, and the consciousness strengthened me a thousand times in duty, in danger, and in struggle. When death came, at length, and sealed those lips, the sorest sense of loss that I felt was the knowledge that no more would my mother be praying for me. In John xvii. we hear Christ praying for us—just once, a few sentences; but we know that this is only a sample of the intercession for us that goes on forever. Nothing shall interrupt this pleading, for He ever liveth to intercede.—J. R. MILLER.

CHRIST OUR INTERCESSOR, The Ascended.—*Heb. vii: 25.* There arises from all parts of the world, at the morning and evening, and through the labors of the day, a perpetual incense of adoration and petition; it contains the sum of the deepest wants of the human race, in its fears and hopes, its anguish and thankfulness; it is laden with sighs, with tears, with penitence, with faith, with submission; the broken heart, the bruised spirit, the stifled murmur, the ardent hope, the haunting fear, the mother's darling wish, the child's simple prayer; all the burdens of the soul, all the wants and desires nowhere else uttered, meet together in that sound of many voices which ascends into the ears of the Lord God of Hosts. And mingled with all these cravings and utterances is one other voice, one other prayer, their symphony, their melody, their accord, deeper than all these, tenderer than all these, mightier than all these—the tones of One who knows us better than we know ourselves, and who loves us better than we love ourselves, and who brings all these myriad fragile petitions into one prevalent intercession, purified by His own holiness and the hallowing power of His work.—HENRY B. SMITH.

CHRIST, Presence of the Ascended.— Should a visitor go his way and say, " I came to see how Christ looked in a Christian country, and I found many spurious Christs and many miscalled gospels, but, the Christ of St. Luke and St. John I did not find," why he speaks but idle words; for wherever there is at work the Spirit of righteousness there is the Son of man, the ascended, the ever-living Christ, not in the sects, not in our little systems, which are born and perish in a day, not in the petty cobwebs men may spin, but in a million inarticulate prayers, in the numberless acts, and words, and thoughts of righteousness and love that every day go up to heaven from obscure saints, men and women struggling to be true and good against temptations to be bad of which we can form no idea. " Behold, I am alive for evermore."—A. AINGER.

CHRIST, Seeing the Ascended.—His own voice, speaking a welcome, will be sweeter music than the seraphs' song. What a thrill it brings to the soul when one first beholds Niagara, or Mont Blanc, or Westminster's towers, or St. Peter's dome! How the heart quickens when the eye first sees some world-famed man—Gladstone, or Bismarck, or Tennyson! But to think, oh, to think, we shall see Jesus! . . . Even the thought throws us upon our knees; but the reality!—The ascended Lord! The Divine Man! The Everlasting Son! The King in His beauty! God help us all to be faithful. —R. S. BARRETT.

CHRIST WORKS FOR MAN, How the Ascended.—There are two closely connected ways by which Christ after His glorification began a new work for mankind, the one inward, towards God; the other outward, towards the world. The first is the exercise of an immeasurably increased power of intercession. In the Epistle to the Hebrews we appear to be given to understand that so far from having accomplished and laid aside His priestly function with His death, our Lord was first truly consecrated to His priesthood on the morning of the Resurrection (Heb. v: 5, 6). The sacrificial task was not at an end when His life was laid down on Calvary, which answered to the slaughter of the typical victims. The whole point of the sacrifice lies in the presentation of that life, enriched and consecrated to the utmost by having undergone death, and still and for ever living, in the inmost presence of God. Christ then has passed within the veil to complete His merciful work for men, by pleading for them, . . . appearing for them " in the presence of God,"—and by pleading for them in the irresistible power which His perfect discharge of His mission has given Him.

CONDUCT, Relation of the Ascended Lord to Daily.—Paul never thought of the precepts which belong to the ordinary business of earth as standing aloof from the revelations of the Divine world or as merely added to them. He supposed that the Ephesians ought to know that they were sitting with Christ in heavenly places, in order that they might not lie or allow filthy communications to proceed out of their mouths. He did not suppose that it was necessary to tell those for whom he asked that they might know the unsearchable riches of Christ that they should not deceive, nor slander their neighbor, nor be thieves nor adulterers. If the saints in Ephesus considered it an insult to hear these plain broad exhortations they must go to some other teacher than St. Paul. —F. D. MAURICE.

POETRY

The Ascension Day

BY JOHN KEBLE

Why stand ye gazing up into heaven? This same Jesus, which is taken up from you into heaven, shall so come in like manner as ye have seen him go into heaven. Acts i: 11.

Soft cloud, that while the breeze of May
　Chants her glad matins in the leafy arch,
Draw'st thy bright veil across the heavenly way,
　Meet pavement for an Angel's glorious march:

My soul is envious of mine eye,
　That it should soar and glide with thee so fast,

The while my groveling thoughts half buried lie,
　Or lawless roam around this earthly waste.

Chains of my heart, avaunt I say—
　I will arise, and in the strength of love
Pursue the bright track ere it fade away,
　My Savior's pathway to His home above.

Sure, when I reach the point where earth
　Melts into nothing from the uncumbered sight,
Heaven will o'ercome the attraction of my birth,
　And I shall sink in yonder sea of light:

Till resting by the incarnate Lord,
　Once bleeding, now triumphant for my sake,

I mark Him, how by seraph hosts adored
He to earth's lowest cares is still awake.

The sun and every vassal star,
All space, beyond the soar of angel wings,
Wait on His word: and yet He stays His
car
For every sigh a contrite suppliant brings.

He listens to the silent tear
For all the anthems of the boundless sky—
And shall our dreams of music bar our ear
To his soul-piercing voice for ever nigh?

Nay, gracious Savior—but as now
Our thoughts have traced Thee to Thy
glory-throne,
So help us evermore with Thee to bow
Where human sorrow breathes her lowly
moan.

We must not stand to gaze too long,
Tho on unfolding Heaven our gaze we
bend,
Where lost behind the bright angelic throng
We see Christ's entering triumph slow
ascend.

No fear but we shall soon behold,
Faster than now it fades, that gleam revive,
When isuing from His cloud of fiery gold
Our wasted frames feel the true sun, and
live.

Then shall we see Thee as Thou art,
For ever fixed in no unfruitful gaze,
But such as lifts the new-created heart,
Age after age, in worthier love and praise.

The Ascension

By Charles Wesley

Our Lord is risen from the dead,
Our Jesus is gone up on high;
The powers of hell are captive led,
Dragged to the portals of the sky.

There His triumphal chariot waits,
And angels chant the solemn lay:—
" Lift up your heads, ye heavenly gates,
Ye everlasting doors, give way.

" Loose all your bars of massy light,
And wide unfold the ethereal scene;
He claims these mansions as His right;
Receive the King of glory in."

" Who is this King of glory, who? "
" The Lord that all His foes o'ercame;
The world, sin, death, and hell o'erthrew;
And Jesus is the conqueror's name."

Lo, His triumphal chariot waits,
And angels chant the solemn lay:—
" Lift up your heads, ye heavenly gates,
Ye everlasting doors give way."

" Who is this King of glory, who? "
" The Lord of glorious power possessed,
The King of saints and angels, too:
God over all, forever blessed."

The Ascension

By Christopher Wordsworth

See, the Conqueror mounts in triumph
See the King in royal state,
Riding on the clouds His chariot
To His heavenly palace-gate;
Hark, the choirs of angel voices
Joyful halleluiahs sing,
And the portals high are lifted,
To receive their heavenly King.

Who is this that comes in glory,
With the trump of jubilee?
Lord of battles, God of armies,
He has gained the victory;
He who on the cross did suffer,
He who from the grave arose,
He has vanquished sin and Satan,
He by death has spoiled His foes.

Thou hast raised our human nature
On the clouds to God's right hand,
There we sit in heavenly places,
There with Thee in glory stand;
Jesus reigns adored by angels,
Man with God is on the throne,
Mighty Lord, in Thine ascension
We by faith behold our own.

Lift us up from earth to heaven,
Give us wings of faith and love,
Gales of holy aspiration
Wafting us to realms above;
That, with hearts and minds uplifted,
We with Christ our Lord may dwell
Where He sits enthroned in glory
In the heavenly citadel.

So at last when He appeareth,
We from out our graves may spring
With our youth renewed like eagles',
Flocking round our heavenly King,
Caught up on the clouds of heaven,
And may meet Him in the air,
Rise to realms where He is reigning
And may reign forever there.

The Ascended Lord

By Thomas Kelly

The Head that once was crowned with thorns
Is crowned with glory now;
A royal diadem adorns
The mighty Victor's brow.

The highest place that heaven affords
Is His, by sovereign right,
The King of kings, and Lord of lords,
And heaven's eternal light.

The joy of all who dwell above,
The joy of all below
To whom He manifests His love,
And grants His name to know.

To them the cross, with all its shame,
With all its grace, is given;
Their name an everlasting name,
Their joy, the joy of heaven.

They suffer with their Lord below,
They reign with Him above;
Their profit and their joy to know
The mystery of His love.

The cross He bore is life and health,
Tho shame and death to Him;
His people's hope, His people's wealth,
Their everlasting theme.

Hail the Day

By Charles Wesley

Hail the day that sees Him rise,
Ravished from our wishful eyes!
Christ, awhile to mortals given,
Re-ascends His native heaven.

There the glorious triumph waits,
Lift your heads, eternal gates!
Wide unfold the radiant scene,
Take the King of glory in!

Him tho highest heaven receives,
Still He loves the earth He leaves:
Tho returning to His throne,
Still He calls mankind His own.

Lord, tho parted from our sight,
High above yon azure height,
Grant our hearts may thither rise,
Following Thee beyond the skies.

He Is Gone

By Arthur Penrhyn Stanley

He is gone; a cloud of light
Has received Him from our sight;
High in heaven, where eye of men
Follows not, nor angels' ken;
Through the veils of time and space,
Passed in to the holiest place;
All the toil, the sorrow done,
All the battle fought and won.

He is gone; towards their goal
World and Church must onward roll:
Far behind we leave the past;
Forward are our glances cast:
Still His words before us range
Through the ages, as they change:
Wheresoe'er the truth shall lead,
He will give whate'er we need.

He is gone; but we once more
Shall behold Him as before;
In the heaven of heavens the same,
As on earth He went and came.
In the many mansions there,
Place for us He will prepare:
In that world unseen, unknown,
He and we shall yet be one.

Glory's King

By Charles Wesley

God is gone up on high,
With a triumphant noise;
The anthems of the sky
Proclaim the angelic joys:

Join all on earth, rejoice and sing,
Glory ascribe to glory's King!

God in the flesh below,
For us He reigns above;
Let all the nations know
The Savior's conquering love:
Join all on earth, rejoice and sing,
Glory ascribe to glory's King!

All power to our great Lord
Is by the Father given;
By angel hosts adored
He reigns supreme in heaven:
Join all on earth, rejoice and sing,
Glory ascribe to glory's King!

Till all the earth renewed
In righteousness divine,
With all the hosts of God,
In one great chorus join:
Join all on earth, rejoice and sing,
Glory ascribe to glory's King!

The Ascended Savior

By Charles Coffin, Tr. by John Chandler

O Savior, who for man hast trod
The winepress of the wrath of God
Ascend, and claim again on high
Thy glory, left for us to die.

A radiant cloud is now Thy seat,
And earth lies stretched beneath Thy feet;
Ten thousand thousands round Thee sing,
And share the triumph of their King.

The angel-host enraptured waits:
" Lift up your heads, eternal gates! "
O God and Man! the Father's throne
Is now, for evermore, Thine own.

Our great High-Priest and Shepherd, Thou
Within the veil art entered now,
To offer there Thy precious blood,
Once poured on earth a cleansing flood.

And thence the Church, Thy chosen bride,
With countless gifts of grace supplied,
Through all her members draws from Thee
Her hidden life of sanctity.

O Christ, our Lord, of Thy dear care
Thy lowly members heavenward bear;
Be ours with Thee to suffer pain,
With Thee for evermore to reign.

The Soul Ascending with Christ

By Caroline May

Thou art gone up on high
Beyond that starry sky,
So far, so fair!
And while our searching eyes
Traverse the wondrous skies,
Jesus, our souls would rise
To see Thee there!

Let us Thy power receive;
That as we do believe

Thou hast arisen,
We, too, may rise with Thee,
And dwell continually
Happy and pure and free
From earth's dark prison.

Once Thou on earth didst dwell;
Once the abodes of hell
Thou didst behold;
Once Thou didst lie so low,
All a world's waves of wo
Over Thy head did flow,
Anguish untold.

Jesus, belovéd Lord,
Thou wast for sin abhorred,
For man beloved;
Thus Thou didst show to God
Thou hadst the wine-press trod,
Thou His just wrath and rod
For man removed.

Now we look up to Thee,
Ascended Christ, and see
Thee on Thy throne;
Thou our strong Advocate,
For us dost mediate,
There, with Thy power and state
Fully made known.

Now Faith and Hope appear,
Like those two angels dear,
On that grand day,
Who stood by, clad in white,
When clouds of dazzling light,
Up through the heavens so bright,
Caught Thee away.

Soon at Thy own right hand,
In that far upper land,
We shall declare
All Thou for us hast done;
Triumphs Thy power has won,
Grace, long ago begun,.
Perfected there.

Then what a joy 'twill be,
Praising, adoring Thee,
Our hearts in tune,
Joining with heaven's glad host
Thy wondrous love to boast,
Father, Son, Holy Ghost,
Godhead Triune!

Reigning in Light

By Matthew Bridges

Rise, glorious Conquer'r, rise
Into Thy native skies;
Assume Thy right;
And where, in many a fold,
The clouds are backward roll'd,
Pass through those gates of gold,
And reign in light.

Victor o'er death and hell,
Cherubic legions swell
The radiant train:
Praises all Heaven inspire;
Each angel sweeps his lyre,
And claps his wings of fire,
Thou Lamb once slain.

Enter, incarnate God!
No feet but Thine have trod
The serpent down:
Blow the full trumpets, blow,
Wider yon portals throw,
Savior, triumphant, go,
And take Thy crown.

Lion of Judah, Hail!
And let Thy name prevail
From age to age:
Lord of the rolling years,
Claim for Thine own the spheres,
For Thou hast bought with tears
Thy heritage.

Worthy the Lamb

By James Allen

Glory to God on high,
Let praises fill the sky!
Praise ye His Name.
Angels His Name adore,
Who all our sorrows bore,
And saints cry evermore,
"Worthy the Lamb!"

All they around the throne
Cheerfully join in one,
Praising His name.
We who have felt His blood
Sealing our peace with God,
Spread His dear fame abroad:
"Worthy the Lamb!"

Join all the human race,
Our Lord and God to bless;
Praise ye His Name!
In Him we will rejoice,
Making a cheerful noise,
And say with heart and voice,
Worthy the Lamb!"

Tho we must change our place,
Our souls shall never cease
Praising His name;
To Him we'll tribute bring,
Laud Him our gracious King,
And without ceasing sing
"Worthy the Lamb!"

He is Gone, and We Remain

By Arthur Penrhyn Stanley

He is gone and we remain
In this world of sin and pain:
In the void which He has left,
On this earth of Him bereft,
We have still His work to do,
We can still His path pursue;
Seek Him both in friend and foe,
In ourselves His image show.

He has gone! unto their goal
World and church must onward roll;
For behind we leave the past;
Forward all our glances cast:
Still His words before us range
Through the ages as they change;

Whereso'er the truth shall lead,
He will give whate'er we need.

He is gone! but we once more
Shall behold Him as before,
In the Heaven of heavens the same
As on earth He went and came:
In the many mansions there,
Place for us He will prepare:
In that world, unseen, unknown,
He and we shall yet be one.

Gazing Up

BY CHARLES WESLEY

Master, Lord, to Thee we cry,
On Thy throne exalted high;
See Thy faithful servants, see,
Ever gazing up to Thee.
Grant, tho parted from our sight,
High above yon azure height,
Grant our hearts may thither rise,
Following Thee beyond the skies.

Ever may we upward move,
Wafted on the wings of love;
Looking when our Lord shall come,
Looking for our heavenly home:
Then may we with Thee remain,
Partners of Thine endless reign;
There Thy face unclouded see,
Find our Heaven of heavens in Thee.

Ascension Hymn

BY THE VENERABLE BEDE

A hymn of glory let us sing;
New hymns throughout the world shall ring;
By a new way none ever trod
Christ mounteth to the throne of God.

The apostles on the mountain stand,
The mystic mount in Holy Land;
They with the Virgin Mother see
Jesus ascend in majesty.

The angels say to the eleven,
"Why stand ye gazing into heaven?"
This is the Savior, this is He;
Jesus hath triumphed gloriously!

They said the Lord should come again,
As these beheld Him rising then,
Calm, soaring through the radiant sky,
Mounting its dazzling summits high.

May our affections thither tend,
And thither constantly ascend,
Where, seated on the Father's throne,
Thee, reigning in the heavens, we own!

Be Thou our present joy, O Lord,
Who wilt be ever our reward!
And as the countless ages flee,
May all our glory be in Thee!

WHITSUNDAY

IN the Church year there are two cycles of festivals: The *Semestre Domini* and the *Semestre Ecclesiae*. The holy days of the former refer to our Lord's life, and Whitsunday is the last of them. It is meant to commemorate the descent of the Holy Spirit on the infant Christian Church in Jerusalem on the Day of Pentecost, which fell on the fiftieth day after our Lord's resurrection.*

Whitsunday is very intimately associated with its Jewish predecessor, Pentecost, not only chronologically and historically, through the events recorded in Acts ii, but also in its inner significance, as being a feast of thanksgiving for the first fruits of the Spirit.† St. Augustine emphasizes this thought in his *Ep. 54, Ad Januar.*

The day seems to have been observed from the very beginning, having been engrafted on the Day of Pentecost. At first the whole period of fifty days was observed, but gradually the last day came to monopolize the attention of the Church. It is mentioned as a separate feast by such early writers as Irenæus (130-200 A. D.), and Tertullian (160-240 A. D.). The latter several times mentions the fact that this was one of the principal times for baptism in the early Church.

Whitsunday is in contrast with Lent, in that no fasting was enjoined, and prayer was offered standing rather than kneeling. All the Whitsunday customs of the early Church were of a joyful nature. The exhibitions of the theater and the circus were suspended, and the ceremonials and liturgy of the Church increased.

The English name is thought by not a few authorities to be Whitsun Day, not Whitsunday, and to be the same as the name Pentecost, coming through the German Pfingsten. Most of the older writers on the English Church festivals, however, have claimed that originally the name was either White Sunday or Wit Sunday. In the former case they derived the word from the chrisoms of the newly baptized, and in the latter from the outpouring of wit, the Old English for wisdom, upon the apostolic church on the Day of Pentecost.

In commenting on Whitsunday's sublime event, and its significance, W. H. Hutchings, writes:

" There they continued where they were gathered together, the small band of disciples, the mustard-seed which was to grow into the great tree of the Catholic Church; there they awaited the Advent of the Comforter; musing on the past, * * * and, intent on the future, with holy anxiety picturing to themselves what this Other Comforter should be,—not knowing whether He would appear in human guise, or as an angel of light, or whether He would be all Divine; wondering how He should be to them what Jesus had been in His personal ministry, and how He would even have a closer fellowship with them, and that, not for a time, but ' for ever.' They continued in supplication, listening to every sound, expecting His arrival every moment, when suddenly—the building trembled with the sound of a rushing, mighty wind, and to their amazement, there

* Luke xxiv : 49; John xiv : 16-26; Acts ii.   † Rom. viii : 23.

spread out upon them and around them from one center a seraphic shower,—tongues of fire like one vast halo of glory, and ' sat upon each of them,'—and the Apostles were filled with the same Spirit which had dwelt from the days of Nazareth in the Manhood of Jesus. It was the enlargement of the Spirit's Home in Human Nature,—as He had been able to ' rest ' on Christ, so now the fiery tongue ' sat ' upon each of them, so calm and abiding is that Presence. O dearly bought Mystery! All the Mysteries of our Lord led the way for this; His Birth, Life, Death, Resurrection, Ascension, Glorification, were so many stages in procuring it. ' I am come,' saith Christ, ' to send Fire on the earth.' "

PENTECOSTAL TIMES

By Rev. William M. Davis

Three facts stand out as we read the story of the Day of Pentecost:

First, the right and normal condition of the Church; second, that this should be its permanent condition, and third, that this is not its condition to-day.

The question is at once forced upon us, " Why do we not have Pentecostal times in the Church now? " Should we not seek the reasons and ought we not try to remove the obstacles, if any there be, that stand in the way of such a bright consummation?

Are the days when the multitudes pressed about Jesus to be no more? Is the Spirit of the Lord straitened that He does not answer prayer? Have the days forever gone when the " Word of the Lord shall prosper " and men shall cry out " What must I do to be saved? "

If God will help us look at facts and conditions, let us try to see if we cannot get some ray of light and some glimmers of truth in answer to this question, " Why do we not have Pentecostal times in the Church to-day? "

I. Perhaps it is because the Church does not pray for this as it did in days of old. You will find that Pentecost never comes without prayer. Jacob " saw God face to face," but it was only after he had wrestled all night in prayer. Jonah sent God's message ringing through Nineveh till king and peasant sat in sackcloth and ashes, but only after he had prayed. Daniel faced lions and dangerous human foes, but you remember three times each day that window was opened toward Jerusalem. No time of blessing was ever enjoyed in the Church of God that was not preceded by prayer.

Does the Church now pray for Pentecostal days? Do those who visit churches here and there hear ministers praying and people praying for Pentecostal outpourings? When God looks down from heaven and sees the father at the family altar and the mother at the bed-side with her children at her knee, does He hear one great universal anthem of prayer from the whole Church, united with one accord in faith and triumphant for Pentecostal

days? Of one thing we can be sure. Until God does see such scenes and hear such prayers, Pentecostal times will never come.

II. It may be that another reason why we do not have Pentecostal times is that the Church don't expect them—ay, worse—mayhap don't want them! There are churches, I am sure, where attendants would be very much put out indeed if the pews were to be filled with strangers and outcasts and publicans and harlots and sinners. If these people for whom Christ died were to crowd into some of our churches, as no doubt they would if Pentecost were fully come, the people already there would feel so uncomfortable that they would soon look for another corner lot on which they could build a church that they could call theirs!

The Church don't expect Pentecost. We have heard it said many times, " Oh, these were special occasions and God does not do now as He did in those days." Does He not? Explain then how it was that the monk of Erfurt, single handed, shook the mightiest organization that this world has ever seen to its foundation! Tell me why it was that when Wesley and Whitefield preached in England, they had audiences of ten and fifteen thousands which hung breathless on their burning words! Explain how Spurgeon filled Surrey gardens and Exeter Hall for years and years with weeping thousands, if God does not work now as He did in Pentecostal times!

It is the enemy of souls that tries to persuade the Church that God does not work now as He used to. And so the Church does not expect it. The Church is even almost surprised when there is a moving in the tops of the trees, and when the waters of the silent pools are simply stirred.

III. It may be that we do not have Pentecostal times because we do not have Pentecostal preachers.

Preachers are human and we shall not arraign them overmuch. The day was when it could be said, " Like priest, like people," but the day now is when it might better be said, " Like people, like priest." Preachers are too often what the people make them, and if you have any fault to find with the priest look to his people. The demand of the people is for a preacher that will " draw," that will " take," that will " fill the church," not with sinners but with sitters, not with prayers but with pay-ers! And so the preacher is forced to make frantic efforts to do what the people want. In spite of himself, he thus gets his message from the people instead of from his God. He preaches what he thinks they will like instead of what God tells him they need. He takes up topics that will draw men to church, instead of Scripture that will draw them to Christ. This ought not so to be. It is not so, of course, in all cases, but it is lamentably so, perhaps unconsciously, in many. Preachers thus become man-made instead of God-made. They choose their profession instead of God choosing them. Pentecostal times will not come until we have in our churches Pentecostal preachers and Pentecostal sermons.

Can you imagine how that crowd would have looked that day, as they surged about the Spirit-filled disciples, if Peter had arisen and preached to them a sermon on " Friendship " or on " Candor " or on " Love of Praise " or on " The African War "? Prepared and anxious for the word of the Eternal, as that multitude was, it would have risen in righteous wrath and driven Peter from its midst if he had made such a hideous mistake. I don't believe that multitude wanted even magnificent music, or a beautiful ritual, or a splendid ceremony of any kind. What it wanted was the Word of God and it wanted it quickly.

When prayer and faith have prepared a people for a message, wo! wo! be to the ambassador of God who fails to give it straight from the throne itself! That was what Peter gave that multitude; or rather the Spirit gave it through Peter. He gave Scripture, not an emasculated Scripture, but the words of David, Joel, and the prophets of old, and he linked that Scripture to existing needs and circumstances. He gave his hearers Christ. Every word was made to palpitate and throb with Christ not as an ethical teacher, a great reformer, a matchless character or an ideal man but Christ crucified, Christ risen, Christ enthroned and regnant, Christ the forgiver of sin and Christ the Savior of men. And he gave it with such Holy Ghost power that men did not applaud him, but censured themselves. They did not say " What a great preacher Peter is," but " What a vile sinner I am." " Other preachers reach my ear but Latimer reaches my heart," said a courtier of the long ago. Ah, when we have Pentecostal preachers and sermons we will have Pentecostal times in the Church.

IV. It may be that another reason why the Church and world do not have Pentecostal times to-day lies in the fact that the Church and world do not have Pentecostal ideas of religion.

Is there enough of conscience in to-day's conception of religion? When Peter pointed his finger at that multitude and thundered out his accusation, " Him ye have taken and by wicked hands have crucified and slain," conscience like a feathered arrow pierced them to the heart. We talk a great deal to-day about morality and ethics and enlightenment and culture and " sweetness and light." Sin, rebellion against God, guilt and doom are regarded as old fashioned terms and as out of date. We have not fully learned what Chalmers learned after twelve years of work in the ministry, " that the system of ' Do this and live ' gives no peace and is not worthy of obedience."

In the Church and world to-day we still have people who are trying to earn God's favor by a right life, utterly misconceiving the teaching of Scripture.

Till we get the Pentecostal idea of religion, that the best man is a sinner, that he is lost utterly and forever, no matter what he may do to save himself, and that until he has repented and believed in Jesus Chirst, we cannot expect, or have, Pentecostal times in Church.

V. Perhaps the most potent reason why we do not have Pentecostal times to-day is that we do not have a Pentecostal baptism of the Holy Spirit. It was after the Spirit had descended that Peter preached and three thousand were added to the Church. Here, after all, is the *sine qua non,* the baptism of the Holy Spirit. Once we have secured that, all the rest will follow. Take cold iron and try to weld it; how fruitless is the effort. Hammer it, twist it, turn it, use utmost skill and it is of no avail. Put that iron in the fire, let it be softened and made malleable, then lay it on the anvil and each stroke tells, and it can be fashioned to our will.

The Holy Spirit must soften and melt men's hearts and then we may look for Pentecostal blessings in the Church.

How can we get that baptism of the Holy Spirit? That is the important question.

The Chinese tell a fable of a great potter of the long ago who was ordered to make a set of dishes for the Imperial table. He tried and tried; he used all his skill in order to bring out the beauty and the gloss that he desired, but all his efforts seemed to fail. At last, in utter despair of ever accomplishing his task, he threw himself into the furnace with his wares, and they say that such heavenly beauty never gleamed and glistened from mortal handiwork before nor since!

Would we know how to get the Holy Spirit for Pentecostal blessings and power? We must learn the secret of China's imperial potter and cast ourselves into the furnace of prayer, into the furnace of surrender, into the furnace of fire, and as God honored such devotion at Pentecost, He will assuredly honor it to-day!—P. J.

THE LITERATURE OF THE OFFICE AND WORK OF THE HOLY SPIRIT *

By Rev. D. N. Beach

In preparing this paper I have consulted nothing not accessible in English. Neither have I consulted periodical literature, nor literature of an occasional nature, like collections of sermons or encyclopedia or dictionary articles, except in the case of three sermons of the seventeenth century, hereafter to be mentioned, and the article in SMITH'S DICTIONARY OF THE BIBLE. Two works of importance which I have wanted very much to see, and have searched diligently for, I have been unable to find, viz.: Bishop Heber on the PERSONALITY AND OFFICE OF THE COMFORTER (the Bampton Lectures for 1816), and Burton's TESTIMONIES OF THE ANTE-NICENE FATHERS TO THE DOCTRINE OF THE TRINITY AND THE DIVINITY OF THE HOLY GHOST (1831).

The last named work, together with Swete's HISTORY OF THE DOCTRINE OF THE PROCESSION OF THE HOLY SPIRIT, FROM THE APOSTOLIC AGE TO THE DEATH OF CHARLEMAGNE (1876), and the closing division of Smeaton's CUNNINGHAM LECTURES for 1882, headed HISTORICAL SURVEY OF THE DOCTRINE OF THE HOLY SPIRIT, are to be commended as authorities on the history of the doctrine. Swete and this division of Smeaton I have been able hardly more than to look into.

From what has been said, it will appear how small a portion of the entire literature of this subject I am to survey at present.

Of the earlier writers I have consulted Archbishop Tillotson's SERMON ON THE UNPARDONABLE SIN AGAINST THE HOLY GHOST; Barrow's sermons ON THE GIFT OF THE HOLY GHOST, and on THE DIVINITY OF THE HOLY GHOST; and Owen's DECLARATION AND VINDICATION OF THE DOCTRINE OF THE TRINITY (1676), and DISCOURSE CONCERNING THE HOLY SPIRIT (1674). Barrow's two sermons amount to a tolerably complete treatise, in his comprehensive, weighty and admirable manner. Owen on the TRINITY is brief, and much in the method of modern systematic theologians. On the HOLY SPIRIT, on the contrary, he is elaborate and exhaustive. The work is faulty in treating at length many topics to which his theme stands related merely—as, for instance, the person of Christ, in connection with the relation of the Holy Spirit to the incarnation. I have seen, nevertheless, nothing which approaches this work in grasp of the subject, in depth, and in essential suggestiveness.

Coming now to works of the present century, I have examined the treatment given the subject by Dwight, Hodge, Van Oosterzee, and Henry B. Smith, among the systematic theologians—in the case of Hodge, both in his THEOLOGY and (more homiletically) in his CONFERENCE PAPERS (1879). Of these writers the least formal and the richest in treatment is Dwight.

I have also examined Oehler (Old Testament), and Van Oosterzee and Weiss (New Testament), among biblical theologians. Oehler recognizes amply the place of the Spirit of God in the Old Testament, but does not find as yet its personality. Van Oosterzee finds the latter in the New Testament, but Weiss seems not to, except in the Paraclete of John, which, he says, " is represented as a person in the speeches of Christ in the Gospel, without this idea being assimilated with the Johannean system of doctrine" (vol. ii., p. 405). Even in John, Weiss finds the Holy Spirit principally "the Spirit of truth " (p. 407) ; and, viewing the Spirit in this aspect, he agrees with our previous essayist—if I understood him—in affirming that the Paraclete " can testify to the world only by the instrumentality of believers, and in that way lead it from the sin of its unbelief " (p. 405.)

I now proceed to speak of fifteen works, to be found (with the possible exception of Robert Hall's) in volumes by themselves. Seven of these may fairly be pronounced treatises on the subject, and I speak of them first.

I mention, then, Cardinal Manning's TEMPORAL MISSION OF THE HOLY GHOST; OR, REASON AND REVELATION (1865) ; and his INTERNAL MISSION OF THE HOLY GHOST (1875). These books have intrinsic value. They have value also as a recent exposition of Roman Catholic views on this subject. The former volume—as the secondary title, " Reason and Revelation," suggests—develops the Spirit's outer, or " temporal " function, as that of establishing truth. Offset, to reason are, here, the Church, the letter, and, after that, the interpretation of Scripture, together with tradition—all under the oversight of the Spirit. Thus, competent authority is afforded for the mind to rest upon. In the latter volume the more spiritual or " internal " work of the Spirit is treated.

I mention next Moberly's ADMINISTRATION OF THE HOLY SPIRIT IN THE BODY OF CHRIST (the Bampton Lectures for 1868). And I mention this work next, because the Romish positions as regards authority are not more faithfully defended in the first mentioned of Cardinal Manning's treatises than the Anglican views as regards " apostolical and ecclesiastical teaching and authority," and as regards " the two sacraments of the Gospel and the two great sacramentals, ordination and absolution " (p. 33), are in this book. On the Spirit's work in these channels the book is an elevated discourse, and its appendix, in

---

* No literature of a later date than 1884 has been examined for this review.

the form of "Notes," is heavy with citations on churchly matters.

More satisfactory, because more catholic, are the four remaining members of this group.

The least valuable of them, I had almost said, is Bickersteth's SPIRIT OF LIFE; OR, SCRIPTURE TESTIMONY TO THE DIVINE PERSON AND WORK OF THE HOLY GHOST (1869), written in a flowing, easy style; exhaustive in its Scripture citations; warmly Christian in spirit; beautifully reverent toward Him who was to be sent when Jesus should depart; but painfully uncritical, particularly in its treatment of the Old Testament testimony.

Of a nobler tone, because, while not less devout, more truly intelligent, are the others: Simeon's OFFICES OF THE HOLY SPIRIT, FOUR SERMONS PREACHED BEFORE THE UNIVERSITY OF CAMBRIDGE IN THE MONTH OF NOVEMBER, 1831; Julius Hare's MISSION OF THE COMFORTER (five sermons before the same University, March, 1840), WITH NOTES, and Smeaton's DOCTRINE OF THE HOLY SPIRIT (the Cunningham Lectures for 1882).

Simeon's book confines itself to the offices of the Spirit, as does Hare's, but covers more ground and is written more tersely.

Hare's work, on the other hand, which—whether wittingly or not, I cannot say—follows Simeon in a measure, while more diffuse than Simeon's, carries more warmth and conviction. Confined tho it is to an exposition of the expediency of Christ's departure, and of the Spirit's mission as regards sin, righteousness, and judgment, it is suggestive of much more.

Better than either—except as regards the warming power of Hare—is Smeaton's volume. Professor in New College, Edinburgh, its author is, to say the least, orthodox *enough;* but from a conservative point of view, he has produced a candid and critical book. His first division presents the biblical testimony, disposed according to the method of Biblical Theology, under successive epochs for the Old Testament, and under successive types of doctrine for the New Testament. The second division consists of the "Lectures" proper; the first on the personality and procession of the Spirit; the remaining five on His offices. Division III.—already alluded to—is an admirable survey of the history of the doctrine from the age of the apostles.

The remaining eight books fall naturally into pairs.

The first two are: THE PARACLETE: AN ESSAY ON THE PERSONALITY AND MINISTRY OF THE HOLY SPIRIT, WITH SOME REFERENCE TO CURRENT DISCUSSIONS (1875); and J. B. Walker's DOCTRINE OF THE HOLY SPIRIT; OR, PHILOSOPHY OF THE DIVINE OPERATION OF THE REDEMPTION OF MAN (1869). Of these books, THE PARACLETE is incomparably the abler, and Walker incomparably the clearer. Both set out to be somewhat complete treatises. I have thrown them out, however, from the class of treatises strictly speaking, because each undertakes to set forth a philosophy on the subject—a purpose incompatible, I think,

with a proper treatment of the theme. THE PARACLETE—one of the most suggestive of books, tho rather unhealthfully so—thus, by its reasonings, prepares the way for a polemic against Mill, Huxley and others.

Next are to be mentioned: Faber's PRACTICAL TREATISE ON THE ORDINARY OPERATIONS OF THE HOLY SPIRIT (1813); and Professor Phelps' NEW BIRTH; OR, THE WORK OF THE HOLY SPIRIT (1866). Both of these books, it need not be said, are admirable; but the objective point in them is hardly so much the Holy Spirit, as man needing renovation and holiness. Faber's work is very direct and simple; Professor Phelps' has more of a homiletical coloring, deliberately pausing, for example, to discuss methods of preaching in their relation to its theme.

There come next: Robert Hall's WORK OF THE HOLY SPIRIT (1809); and Scribner's PRAY FOR THE HOLY SPIRIT (1875),—the former, but for its brevity, fit to be classed with the treatises; but both practically hortatives toward more reverence for, and a more earnest seeking after the Spirit. As such they are much to be praised, particularly Robert Hall's few and earnest pages.

Lastly, there are two books on this subject which I may call devotional: Cutler's WORK OF THE SPIRIT; OR, DOCTRINAL AND PRACTICAL MEDITATIONS ON THE NATURE AND WORK OF THE HOLY GHOST (1873)—strictly devotional, with Scripture, meditation, and poetry for each day of the year, treating the topic in an orderly and somewhat complete manner; and Robert Philip's LOVE OF THE SPIRIT TRACED IN HIS WORK (3d ed., 1836). This latter is a dissertation on the Holy Spirit from the point of view of His yearning love. The attempt is made to show that not Christ Himself is animated by a more tender and personal love toward men than is the Holy Spirit. The book becomes, under this plan of treatment, one of the sweetest and most moving of writings—a real devotion.

I make, in conclusion, the following remarks:

I. As the matter of the Holy Spirit is, in the nature of the case, one to be experimentally known, if known at all to advantage, and as, also, even experimental knowledge requires correctives and guides, I venture to suggest the helpfulness of a considerable amount of reading on this subject, and, if I were to be so bold, I should suggest, by way of saving time, the consecutive reading, say, of four books; First, Hare, for its soundness and its warming quality; then, Smeaton, for a comprehensive and thorough presentation of the whole subject (his is the best single book on it of which I know); then—if one has patience—Owen, to correct whom Smeaton will have served, and than whom, corrected, there is not a profounder work on the subject in English, if in any language; and lastly, Philip, whose wonderful book as a devotion, I last mentioned. Then, if a daily devotion were wished, Cutler; or if something with man as the objective point, Faber. But these last two I make supplementary. The first four are enough.

II. Do we realize enough the peril that attends such a theme? Upon it Irving went to wreck. Plymouth Brethrenism, with its meetings under the presidency of the Holy Spirit, and its holding to be wrong to pray for the Spirit because the Spirit is present, is a more substantial, but hardly less pernicious error than that of the Irvingites. When we contemplate what happened to so able and good a man as Irving through error here, we may all well beware. But how? By somewhat wide reading on the subject, as I have suggested; by study, especially of the Scriptures; and as the most spiritual of the apostles advised, by proving the spirits (1 John iv: 1), "for God is not a God of confusion, but of peace" (1 Cor. xiv: 33).

III. I should not be candid did I not say that the methods of Biblical Theology are raising—and I cannot see but properly—certain questions about the doctrine of the Holy Spirit. I have alluded to the guarded position of Oehler—necessarily guarded, while treating of the Old Testament. Also, to the attitude of Weiss. I should not feel justified, from insufficient study of him, in affirming the details of Weiss' view. But as I understand him he finds exegetical grounds for a somewhat less personal conception of the Holy Spirit than I have been in the habit of accepting. Yet no man can doubt the reverence of his view; or that it has, to his mind, exegetical foundation. I suspect that this statement will be laid heavily against Weiss by some, but I hardly think by any who have read him carefully. For one, I want to see this side of the subject fairly discussed, as well as the other. If it is erroneous, may it not be that it gets its rise in the defects—intrinsically, or as expounded—of a truer contrary view? Here let us know, by following on to know (Hos. vi: 3).

IV. Finally, these tendencies are to be noted in the literature of the subject:

1. The *devotional* tendency—impossible to be, within proper limits, enough commended —Philip, Cutler, even Cardinal Manning, on the *Internal Mission*.

2. The *hortative* tendency—Robert Hall, Scribner, as well as so many of our current papers and addresses (equally deserving, many of them, to be printed); this tendency, also, within proper limits, commendable.

3. The *conglomerate* tendency, if I may so say—shown alike by treatises on conversion and kindred subjects, under the name of the Holy Spirit, and by treatises (like *The Paraclete*) seeking to construct a philosophy of the Spirit. I shrink from this class of books, admirable intrinsically tho some of them are.

4. Then, *treatises* on the Holy Spirit that may be properly so styled—some on the offices, and some on person and offices, and some on person, offices, and history of the doctrine as well. These are the really helpful books—helpful to the **understanding** and to the heart—tho from the uncritical works of this class I feel that we should also shrink.

But what I mourn in books on the Holy Spirit is a too formal treatment of the whole subject, as if it were all sure, and could all be mapped and marked out. This is particularly the method of the systematic theologians in their published works. What study and meditation I have been able to give to the subject (and it is a theme which has been much in my thought for years) have left on me the impression that we have here the unsounded depths of mystery in Deity. And when I say that, I draw a distinction between vagueness and mystery. Undoubtedly much may be known, and accurately known, about the Holy Spirit; and it is our duty to proceed to know it; but how little of all that is to be known! I seem—if I may say it reverently—to know the Father; I seem to know the Lord Jesus; but the Holy Spirit, to whom I continually pray, I seem not to know. And the more I know Him, the less I seem to know Him. And, when I see Jesus wishing to withdraw Himself, in order that the Spirit may (the more completely) come—saying "it is expedient" (John xvi: 7); when I hear Him declare that the one sin unpardonable is against that blessed Spirit—I seem to get glimpses of more than any of the ordinary expositions reach unto, viz., of that in God, which all else in God right chivalrously pays homage to, and would lift into loftiest regard. In this range may we not look for what is latest to be found, and greatest, in God; and for what to know (when we shall know it), will be to know God indeed? *—H. R.

* During the discussion which followed the paper, which was prepared at the request of and read before the Boston (Congregational) Ministers' Meeting, two works, not mentioned by the essayist, were especially commended: John Howe's (1630–1705) OFFICE AND WORKS OF THE HOLY SPIRIT, and Dr. J. P. Thompson's THE HOLY COMFORTER (1866).

SERMONS AND OUTLINES

PENTECOSTAL BLESSINGS

By Rev. Dekan W. Pressel

John xiv: 23-31

It is Pentecost! In one of our grand old Pentecostal hymns we sing:

" O Holy Ghost, descend, we pray,
　Abide with us from day to day,
　Thy temple deign to make us!
Let Thy bright beams, Thou heav'nly Light,
Dispel the darkness of our night,
　To joy and gladness wake us."

The echo of this hymn should arouse a Christian congregation to celebrate this festival day
(1) As a day of joyous remembrance; (2) as a day of earnest humiliation; (3) as a day of grateful encouragement.
I. " O Holy Ghost, descend, we pray, abide with us from day to day." That which Christ in our text before His departure promises to His disciples became a reality and a fact on Pentecost. The Acts of the Apostles tells us that when the days were fulfilled the faithful were found together, united by the bond of the one love for the ascended Lord, in the one obedience to His Word, in the one confidence in the certainty that He would fulfil His promises, waiting for the bestowal of His power from on high. There, then, just as our first parents once noticed the approach of their God by the rustling of the evening air, they too felt the living and life-giving breath of Jesus as tho seized by a terrible wind. They were fired with enthusiasm; they broke forth in laudation of the mighty deeds of the eternal God; they spake as tho they were filled with sweet wine, and in many tongues gave utterance to the wonders of His grace; and in joyful contemplation listened to a discourse concerning the crucified and risen Christ; their enthusiasm was enkindled in three thousand converts, who came to repentance, and were baptized in the name of Jesus. They continued in the breaking of the bread and in prayer, in teaching and instruction, and came together daily in the temple, having all things in common, divided among themselves their goods and possessions, and together and with one heart they praised the Most High, and won the goodwill of all the people. The Lord, however, added daily to their number those who were to be saved. Behold, this was the entrance of the Holy Spirit on that Pentecost day in accordance with the promises of the Lord. See, then, the Church of Christ was born and came into existence and into the world, like dew from heaven. Behold, in this way God's dwelling-place was established among men; His grace from heaven was implanted into

the hearts of men, which came out of the heart of the Father in heaven and of His exalted Son to bless this miserable earth. Pentecost indeed! Truly it is a day of glorious remembrance; and, like none others, it urges us to pray, " O Holy Ghost, descend, we pray, abide with us from day to day."
II. " Thy temple deign to make us." *Us*—not only that assembly of people who two thousand years ago peacefully and contentedly, in faith and joy, celebrated the first Pentecost. It is *we;* it is *we* who ask for this boon now; the Christianity of to-day; our congregations, our families, our present generation with all its classes and conditions of men, with its entire society and in all its individuals. Oh, Christian friends, if we apply to ourselves the measure of that Pentecost, then this is indeed also a day of earnest humiliation. Then with groans beyond utterance we must pray on this festival day, " Thy temple deign to make us! " For if we compare ourselves with the Christians of that great day, how can we do otherwise than in contrition of heart declare that we have been far from reaching the ideal and the fact of those days. There we see the presence of a new power on every tongue, because in every soul and in every heart the fire of the Holy Ghost had been enkindled; and therefrom came their intense love for Him who had been sent by the Father, in whom we can and should love each other, He who is love itself. Feel the pulse of this present generation, and, alas, how sluggishly the blood of Christian life flows!
In large sections and parts of the modern world this life seems to be altogether gone, not a spark seemingly remains; but in the room thereof there glows with all the greater power the flames of selfishness, sin, and wickedness. Whenever we think earnestly of this, we feel and know it to be the case; and every honest heart confesses that the zeal is weak for the Lord and His cause, for Him who has redeemed and saved lost mankind through His sufferings and death, and not through gold or silver. He has bought us; we are His; and it is His will that we should live in joy and eternal righteousness in His kingdom, in innocence and blessedness. Certainly, in view of this contrast, the spirit of Pentecost is also a solemn institution for reflection and humiliation. If the spirit of Pentecost has no deeper lessons to teach us than that we accept the words of Jesus as the Word of the Father who has sent Him; as the lamp and light of the truth, as the fountain of eternal life and bliss, as the rule for Christian faith

and life, as the firm foundations and pillars of Christian prosperity and growth—if we learn this, embrace it, love it, cling to it, then how we must deplore the fact that so many have departed from the Lord and His Word in the carelessness, pride, and evil propensities of their hearts.

When, on the other hand, over against this, we see in the first Christian Pentecost the joy and happiness of the Holy Ghost, the faith and love of the primitive Christians, in whom the spirit of Jesus Christ has been implanted by the Holy Ghost, in whom the peace of which the world knows nothing has become a joyful reality, and love to God and love to their fellow-men is the controlling factor in their hearts, so that they live in peace, without contention and quarrel, without envy and strife, without anger and hatred, then, then indeed we see a condition of affairs with which our own day and generation presents a lamentable contrast. In the thousands of contests and struggles that agitate the hearts of men and society everywhere there is one cry heard over all, and that is for peace. The Pentecost peace is found so rarely in our day; and for that reason this festival is an admonition to earnest humiliation and prayer that the spirit of our times may be transformed and transfused by the Spirit of Pentecost from on high. In the spiritual bitterness and darkness of to-day this is the only fountain of hope and reformation.

III. " Let Thy bright beams, Thou heav'nly Light, dispel the darkness of the night, to joy and gladness wake us." Pentecost day also offers the Christian an abundance of material and occasions for most grateful encouragement. Did the great and glorious sun of the first Pentecostal day succeed in banishing all the darkness of that day, to scatter all the clouds? The Gospel has preserved for us enough of evidences to the contrary, and shows us that even then the world and its evil were arrayed against the Pentecost spirit with bitterness and determination. The multitude of those who opposed the Spirit was vastly greater than the number of those who submitted to His influence. Grace was then as little as it is now irresistible. Some mocked and scoffed, and the outpouring of the Holy Ghost was only an occasion for an expression of their adherence to the world. Peter exhorted them to accept deliverance from an evil generation. Then already it appeared that faith is not of every man. Therefore it is not surprising that in our day, too, there should be many who fall away from grace, as there are many who do not accept the proffered boon of salvation at all.

The prince of this world is active now as ever against the influence of Divine grace in our hearts and in the world. Yet notwithstanding this opposition, we have all reasons for reassurance that faith in the Lord and trust in His Word and promises will eventually gain the victory. Of this fact Pentecost gives us the testimony and evidences always. The Spirit, who as the Comforter was to take the place of the Lord in the hearts of the faithful came in reality, without again departing; and He has shown Himself more powerful than the world ever since. Otherwise Christ vainly would have been wiped out of existence long ago. The Sun of the first Pentecost that came forth as a bridegroom out of his chamber, rejoicing as a strong man to run a race, was no passing meteor. He has been a hero in the Church; a warrior whose armor has been impenetrable. The rays of this Sun which warmed and vivified the souls of the first disciples, and out of humble, frightened fishermen made heroes with hearts of iron, that Spirit has been alive in the Church ever since, as countless martyrdoms by fire and sword have testified in all generations. The rays of this Sun have always been powerful. Think only of the Reformation, the second Pentecost of the Christian Church, a new seal of the promises of Christ to His Church; and has the Church ever since not experienced the presence and power of this benign Spirit? Is not this grace, this present and living reality, in the Church of our God?

Therefore let not your hearts be afraid. He who has promised to be with His Church and His children always, even to the end of days, He is present with us yet in and through His Spirit, no matter what the dangers that vex and perplex us may be. We have ground for the certain hope of final victory in the Pentecostal promises and spirit. Let us therefore prayerfully, hopefully, and joyfully join in the petition:

" Oh, Holy Ghost, descend, we pray,
Abide with us from day to day,
   Thy temple deign to make us!
Let Thy bright beams, Thou heav'nly Light,
Dispel the darkness of the night,
   To joy and gladness wake us,
That we, to Thee
Truly living, to Thee giving
Pray'r unceasing,
Still may be in love increasing."—H. R.

THE BAPTISM WITH THE HOLY GHOST

By J. W. A. Stewart, D.D.

Ye shall be baptized with the Holy Ghost.—Acts i: 5

I. The Holy Spirit is the Spirit of absolute moral perfection. and stands for purity. The baptism with the Spirit begets a life that is holy. The presence of the Holy Ghost whom Jesus gives acts like fire against sin. " Our God is a consuming fire," means the condemnation and punishment of the wicked and impenitent; but also the purifying of all whom Christ baptizes with the Holy Ghost.

II. The Holy Ghost stands for power. In the baptism with the Holy Ghost that power is applied in working in the believer the complete salvation promised by Christ, the complete deliverance from the power of sin.

III. The Holy Ghost stands for the spiritual enlargement of the believer. Through baptism with the Spirit the Christian is led into all the heights and depths of spiritual knowledge and experience. The apostle prays, "that ye may be strengthened with might through his Spirit in the inward man."

IV. The Holy Ghost stands for power for service, and His baptism gives this power. "He that believeth in me," said Jesus, "out of his belly shall flow rivers of living water. This spake he of the Spirit which they that believed on him were to receive." A Spirit-filled man is, under Christ, a source of eternal life to those about him. You recall the words of Christ to His disciples: "But ye shall receive power when the Holy Ghost is come upon you." We all know of the mighty working of that power through Peter, and John, and Paul, and the early Church.—H. R.

THE PENTECOSTAL FEAST

By Rev. Henry Smith

Deut. xvi: 9-12

In the Law of Moses we find references made to three great feasts, viz., Passover, Tabernacles, Pentecost. Each feast had a very prominent place in the heart and mind of the nation. All were intended to promote some great moral and spiritual purpose. That purpose was to foster and evoke joy. Judaism was not a joyless religion; much less should Christianity be.

The Pentecost was a corn festival originally. The Feast of Tabernacles being a fruit festival. Modern Jews have lost sight of the Pentecost as a corn harvest, and so have modern Christians, but at our thanksgiving service we may find it profitable

I. To REMIND OURSELVES OF THE SACRED CHARACTER OF THE HARVEST.

The harvest field should be a holy place. Alas! it is not always such. But in the harvest field, if anywhere, we may see the hand and the glory of God.

II. GOD TOOK CARE TO TEACH THE PEOPLE THE SACREDNESS OF COMMON THINGS.

To those who have eyes to see a *grain* of

corn is suggestive of some of the deepest mysteries of the kingdom. The small grain suggests a reign of law. The working of wisdom, love, and patience. There is a close relation between the intellectual and the spiritual, and the physical underlies them both. The Jews were in a true sense what the nation's cornfields enabled them to be. England's town and city life is largely what England's cornfields and the cornfields of other lands give. Christ sought to teach the people of His day the sacredness of the common corn.

III. THIS FEAST WAS INTENDED TO BE A RENEWED BOND OF BROTHERHOOD.

Plenty sometimes hardens the emotional life (*cf.* the rich fool. Some modern millionaires). God intends it should be otherwise. See how Levite, stranger, fatherless and friendless, was thought of in the Jewish Pentecost.

IV. IT WAS A SEASON OF SETTING WRONG THINGS RIGHT IN THE FAMILY AND NATIONAL LIFE.—C. G.

ST. PETER'S PENTECOSTAL SERMON

By Bishop Harvey Goodwin

Then they that gadly received his word were baptized, etc.—Acts ii: 41, 42

Consider the several points noted in the text, as showing the result of St. Peter's sermon.

I. In the first place, the persons who had been baptized, and so added to the Church, remained in the apostles' doctrine and fellowship; that is, they joined themselves to their company, listened to their teaching, and acted accordingly; they were not ashamed to confess that they belonged to the new society who owned a crucified Master, and they did not wish merely to adopt a new name, and not withal to show by their conduct that

their Christian name was a reality. As a general rule, it is clear that the effect of the conversion which was produced by St. Peter's sermon was true and vital; tho there were some who disgraced their profession, yet as a general rule, the profession which was made under the influence of St. Peter's words was fully borne out by the lives of the converts.

II. Another point mentioned concerning the converts is, that they remained steadfast in the breaking of bread; this phrase has in the New Testament a peculiar signification, and generally means that which undoubtedly it does mean in this case, namely, the celebration of the sacrament of the Lord's Supper. And the converts remained steadfast in the partaking of the Holy Communion. In our own days, it is nothing remarkable for a Christian to listen to a sermon, and yet hold back from the breaking of bread; people think that listening to a sermon commits them to nothing; that the breaking of bread does; that the one is amusing, and the other certainly awful. What does this prove but that the heart is wrapped up in impenetrable folds of worldliness, or self-satisfaction, or carnal security.

III. Lastly, those who were converted by St. Peter's address remained steadfast in prayer. This was the proper fruit of a sermon. The sermon is rightly appreciated, it is manifestly blessed by the Holy Ghost, when it leads persons to value and join heartily in the Church's prayers. The prayers are not the mere introduction to preaching, but preaching is intended to make people pray.—S. B., vol. viii., p. 359.

THE FAITH OF PENTECOST

By C. J. Vaughan, D.D.

Behold, are not all these which speak Galileans? And how hear we every man in our own tongue, wherein we were born?—Acts ii: 7, 8

I. There are but two postulates necessary to the faith of Pentecost, or Whitsuntide: the first, God is Almighty; and the second, Christianity is of God. Given these two principles, all is intelligible. The new Gospel was a word, was a message, was a testimony, was a proclamation; these were its names for itself. Therefore it must find a voice and it must get a hearing. It was a failure if it did not. There must be a miracle. Men's eyes and ears must be made cognizant of God's intervention, must be appealed to, as St. Peter appeals to them on this occasion, " He hath shed forth this which ye now see and hear." I know not how else the Gospel could ever have got out of little Palestine; how else the Gospel could ever have gained, in the first instance, the attention of mankind.

II. These Galileans speak still. Each one of them, being dead, yet speaketh. No philosopher, no poet, no orator, ever spake as they speak. To have written a page in the Bible is to have an immortality of speech. There is no book like it, its enemies themselves being judges. Men feel that the Bible is something to them which none other book is. It has words of eternal life, which must be heard in their integrity, and heard in the birth-tongue. How is this and why? The Spirit of God touched their lips and therefore it is life or death to listen.

III. The Spirit of God is not dead but living. The miracle of Pentecost was a token, was a symbol, was a proclamation—of what? Of the advent of the Holy Ghost, in all His fulness, to abide with us for ever. We want still God's Holy Spirit; and still, as in times of old, He lives and works in Christ's Church. Not in the Church as an establishment, as an institution, as an aggregate of humanity or a center of worship. It is by making the separate stones temples that the Spirit builds into one the great temple. It is by opening to the praying soul the secrets of Scripture, that the Spirit causes these long dead Galileans to speak and preach to us. By bringing a spiritual ear to the spiritual utterance, so that spiritual things may be interpreted to the spiritual in that which is the common, the unchangeable language of hearts and souls.—S. B., vol. viii., p. 349.

THE HOLY GHOST

By Joseph Parker, D.D.

Have ye received the Holy Ghost?—Acts xix: 2

I. Why should not each of us put this question to his own heart as a personal inquiry, as a question that ought to be answered as before God, without equivocation, without self-deception, and without any attempt to deal triflingly with the piercing and all-important interrogative? If we treat the question in this way, it will become to us a judgment-seat; and why should we not ever and anon arrest ourselves in the hurry and rush and delirium of life, to ask a question or two that shall pierce the heart and bring us to a right knowledge and a proper estimation of ourselves? The Divine mediation is a progress. From the beginning to the end, from the outline, the shadow, the type, to this great spiritual personality, this sovereignty of the Holy Ghost, there has been progress, advancement, culmination; and in all these I see a grandeur most impressive and instructive. Now, are we in the line of that progress, are we as far on as our opportunities have enabled us to be? or are some of us still lingering far behind? Have some of us turned back to the beggarly elements? Is it not matter of debate with the heart whether it has passed through the process called regeneration—whether it has passed from death unto life?

II. What is the one decisive sign by which we may know whether we have received the Holy Ghost? Is it to be a mere sentiment, an impression upon the mind, a religious hope? or is it to be something more decisive, emphatic, and incontrovertible? What is the one decisive sign that a man has received the Holy Ghost? Let me approach that question through two others. Have you received the poetic spirit? How do you prove it? Not by prose, but by poetry. Have you received the heroic spirit? How do you prove it? Not by cowardice, not by craven-heartedness, but by adventure and by freely encountering peril in all its thousand forms and possibilities of visitation. Have you received the Holy Spirit? The decisive sign is love of holiness; not power of theological debate; not only contending for the faith once delivered to the saints, not only outwardly irreproachable character, but love of holiness;

not reputation, but reality; a heart that pants after the holiness of God; life concentrated into one burning prayer to be sanctified, body, soul, and spirit; life a sacrifice on God's altar,—that is what I mean by saying that holiness is the one decisive test of our having received the Holy Ghost. Alas! are not some professing Christians afraid to say the word "holy"? I find this in the course of my study of human nature and my intercourse with men, that I should be almost startled if I heard some men say the word "holy." They hope; they assent; they would fain believe; they are not without some idea that so-and-so may be the case; but a rich, ripe, unctuous, emphatic expression of Christian experience would be from their lips almost an anti-climax, if not a profanity. We are not called upon to do with as little Christianity as possible; it is not "Just get over the line, and that will do;" it is this: "Be ye perfect, as your Father in heaven is perfect; be ye holy, as God is holy." This is the vocation to which we are called, and if, when men ask us if we have received the Holy Ghost, we only answer them by some theological mystery which neither they nor we can understand, then we lie not unto men, but unto the Holy Ghost.—S. B., vol. ix., p. 54.

SUGGESTIVE THOUGHTS AND ILLUSTRATIONS

BAPTISM, Pentecostal and Seclusion. —*Acts i: 14-21.* The pentecostal *baptism* and the pentecostal *seclusion* were related to each other not as power and accident, but as power and *condition*. Walls of prayer *excluding all entrance of the world* must enclose the room which is to be filled with the Holy Ghost. This is a causal necessity. An *engine* open on one side of its cylinder to the steam from the boiler, and on the other side to the air without, would either only blow off without turning a wheel, or else blow up itself and the machinery. How then can men seeking worldly intercourse presume to pray for the might of the Holy Spirit? A worldly-minded man filled with the power of the Holy Ghost would be an anomaly in the dynamics of heaven and earth.—REV. DUBOIS H. LOUX, Ph.D. (C. G.)

CHRISTIANITY.—Whatever the age, or the intellect of the passing age, may be, even if ever arise again such a galaxy of great minds as dawned upon this country three hundred years ago, tho all those great minds start upon their glorious career, comprising and intensifying all the light engendered by, before, and since the time of Shakespeare, Bacon, Newton, then, tho they enhance that light tenfold by their own bright genius, till a thousand waking nations gleam, like hilltops touched with sunrise, to guide men on

the human road, to lead them heavenward, all shall be no more than a benighted river wandering away from the stars of God. Do what we will and think as we may, enlarging the mind in each generation, growing contemptuous of contempt, casting caste to the winds of Heaven, and antiquating prejudice, nevertheless we shall never outrun or even overtake Christianity. Science, learning, philosophy may regard it through a telescope; they touch no more than astronomy sets foot upon a star. To a thoughtful man, who is scandalized at all the littleness felt and done under the holy name, until he almost begin to doubt if the good outweigh the evil, it is reassurance to remember that we are not Christians yet, and comfort to confess that on earth we never can be. For nothing shows more clearly that our faith is of Heaven than the truth that we cannot rise to it until it raise us thither. And this reflection is akin to the stately writer's sentiment, that our minds conceive so much more than our bodies can perform to give us token, aye, and earnest, of a future state.

Of all the creeds which have issued as yet from God, or man, or the devil, there is but one which is far in advance of all human civilization. True Christianity, like hope, cheers us to continual efforts, exalts us to unbounded prospects, flies in front of our best success. Let us call it a worn-out garb when we have begun to wear it; as yet the mantle is in the skies, and we have only the skirt with the name on it.—R. D. BLACK-MORE, Author of " LORNA DOONE." (P. M.)

CHURCH, Contributing for a. — A worthy Quaker who lived in a country town in England was rich and benevolent, and his means were put in frequent requisition for purposes of local charity and usefulness. The townspeople wanted to rebuild their parish Church, and a committee was appointed to raise funds. It was agreed that the Quaker could not be asked to subscribe towards an object so contrary to his principles; but then, on the other hand, so true a friend to the town might take it amiss if he was not at least consulted in a matter of such general interest. So one of their number went and explained to him their project; the old Church was to be removed, and such and such steps taken towards the construction of a new one. " Thee was right," said the Quaker, " in supposing that my principles would not allow me to assist in building a Church. But didst thee not say something about pulling down a Church? Thee may'st put my name down for a hundred pounds."—F. II.

HOLY SPIRIT, Agency of the.—Unconverted men often say, " If these things are so, if they are so clear and great, why cannot we see them? " And there is no answer to be given but this, " Ye are blind." " But we want to see them. If they are real, they are our concern as well as yours. Oh, that some preacher would come who had power to make us see them! " Poor souls, there is no such preacher, and you need not wait for him. Let him gather God's light as he will, he can but pour it on blind eyes. A burning glass will condense sunbeams into a focus of brightness; and if a blind eye be put there, not a whit will it see, tho it be consumed. Light is the remedy for darkness, not blindness. Neither will strong powers of understanding on your part serve. The great Earl of Chatham once went with a pious friend to hear Mr. Cecil. The sermon was on the Spirit's agency in the hearts of believers. As they were coming from the Church, the mighty statesman confessed that he could not understand it all, and asked his friend if he supposed that any one in the house could. " Why yes," said he, " there were many plain, unlettered women, and some children there, who understood every word of it, and heard it with joy."—DR. HOGE.

HOLY SPIRIT, Biblical.—The Gift of the Spirit is frequently described by words expressive of abundance and continuance. Thus the Holy Ghost is spoken of as—*Coming*, as a mighty and powerful impulse, as in the case of Othniel, Jephthah, Samson, etc., personally, and upon the Church collectively. *Poured out*, Ps. li: 23; Isa. xliv: 3; Joel ii: 28, 29; Zech. xii: 10; Acts ii: 17, 18. *Shed* abundantly, Titus iii: 6. *Clothing*, Judges vi: 34; 1 Chron. xii: 18, margins; so Luke xxiv: 49—" endued," or invested with the Spirit. *Dwelling*, Ps. lxviii: 18; John xiv: 17; Rom.

vi: 9; 1 Cor. iii: 16, and also vi: 19. *Abiding*, John xiv: 16. *Supplying* the wants of the Church Phil. i: 19. The Greek word here (Phil. i: 19), is taken from the office of the Choregus, whose place it was to supply the chorus, at his own expense, with ornaments and all other necessaries. So the Holy Spirit supplies the wants of the Church. St. Luke's Gospel contains the most frequent references to the Holy Ghost of all the gospels. In the first four chapters, we read of Zacharias and Elizabeth, John the Baptist, Mary, Simeon, and our Lord Himself, being filled with, or moved by, the Holy Ghost. A STRIKING CONTRAST. Thomas, tho one of our Lord's chosen apostles, who had been with Him during His ministry, and heard Him so often foretell His own resurrection, yet refused to believe the resurrection, until compelled by sight to say, " My Lord," John xx: 18. Elizabeth—less favored—when Mary came to see her before He was born, at once acknowledged her as " the mother of my Lord," Luke i: 43. " Elizabeth," we read, " was filled with the Holy Ghost," ver. 44. FILLED WITH THE SPIRIT—FULL OF THE HOLY GHOST. How often these pregnant expressions occur; denoting the energizing, ennobling power of the Spirit in the heart of God's saints. They are generally marked by some special result following. Take, *e. g.*, the following cases: *Bezaleel*—Exod. xxxi: 3; xxxv: 30, 31—" filled with the spirit of God; " to prepare the materials for the tabernacle. *Zacharias and Elizabeth*—Luke i: 41, 67—inspired with the spirit of prophecy. *John Baptist*, Luke i: 15, 16. (See the beautiful connection.) The *disciples* at Pentecost, and afterwards—Acts ii: 4; xiii: 52—endued with the ordinary and extraordinary gifts of the Spirit. *The seven deacons*—Acts vi—qualified for their important offices; filled with wisdom, ver. 3; faith, ver. 5; and power, ver. 8. *Peter*—Acts iv: 8; xiii: 19, 20—emboldened to confess Jesus Christ without fear. *Stephen*—Acts vi: 5— witnessing a good confession; rejoicing in the midst of danger, vi: 15; calm in the hour of death, vii: 55. *St. Paul*—Acts ix: 17; xiii: 9 —even from the commencement of his ministerial course, was filled with the Holy Ghost. —BOWES.

HOLY SPIRIT OF GOD, The.—The Holy Spirit of God is our Guide. Who will displease his Guide, a sweet comfortable Guide, that leads us through the wilderness of this world? As the cloud before the Israelites by day, and the pillar of fire by night, so He conducts us to the Heavenly Canaan. If we grieve our Guide, we cause Him to leave us to ourselves. The Israelites would not go a step further than God by His angel went before them. It is in vain for us to make toward Heaven without our blessed Guide.— SIBBES, 1577-1635.

HOLY SPIRIT'S WORK, Conviction of Sin the.—*John xvi: 8.* The revisers have improved this verse by changing " reprove " to " convince " (cf. A. V. margin.) The Greek word ἐλέγχειν in some passages in the New Testament means simply " rebuke," as in Luke iii: 19; in others "convince," as here: in others again "convict," as in James ii: 9. Conviction of sin is pre-eminently the work of the Holy Spirit. Says Julius Charles Hare (in THE MISSION OF THE COMFORTER): *To convince the world of sin,*—to produce a living and lively conviction of it,—to teach mankind what sin is,—to lay it bare under all its masks,—to trace it through all the mazes of its web,—and to light on it sitting in the midst thereof,—to show it to man, not merely as it flashes forth ever and anon in the overt actions of his neighbors, but as it lies smoldering inextinguishably within his own bosom,—to give him a torch wherewith he may explore the dark chambers of his own heart,—to lead him into them, and to open his eyes so that he shall behold some of Sin's countless brood crouching or gamboling in every corner,—to convince a man of sin in this way, by proving to him that it lies at the bottom of all feelings, and blends with all his thoughts;—to convince the world of sin, by showing it how sin has tainted its heart, and flows through all its veins, and is mixed up with its lifeblood;—this is a work which no earthly power can accomplish. No human teacher can do it. Conscience cannot do it. Law, in none of its forms, human or divine, can do it. Nay, the Gospel itself cannot do it. Altho the word of God is the sword of the Spirit, yet unless the Spirit of God draws forth that sword, it lies powerless in its sheath."—C. G.

HOLY SPIRIT, The.—As the sails of a ship carry it into the harbor, so prayer carries us to the throne and bosom of God. But as the sails cannot of themselves speed the progress of the vessel, unless filled with a favorable breeze, so the Holy Spirit must breathe upon our hearts, or our prayers will be motionless and lifeless.—TOPLADY, 1740-1778.

HOLY SPIRIT, The.—One of the three great articles of the Christian faith is a belief in God the Holy Spirit, who, in answer to prayer, bestows upon us His supernatural guidance and assistance. Assuming this to be true, there remains no room for comparison between this and the influence of purely natural culture. It seems desirable to mention this, lest, in arguing upon other grounds, this momentous power in Christian faith should appear to be overlooked.—A. P. L.

PENTECOST, The Christian.—Next to the day of Christ's death, the day of Pentecost was the greatest day that ever dawned on our world. It was the first day of the last and best dispensation of revealed religion. It was, as it has been well called, "the birthday" of the Christian Church. It was the first day of the new creation, in which the elements which had previously existed in a state of chaotic confusion began to be fashioned and arranged by the plastic power of the Spirit of glory and of God.—MORRIS. (F. II.)

PENTECOST, The Day of.—*Acts ii: 1-47.* The day of Pentecost was characterized by a great miracle, a great sermon, and a great revival.

The miracle was not only the inauguration of the dispensation of the Holy Spirit and the solemn investiture of the Church with its functions as a witness-bearing and world-reaching Church, but also a specific equipment of the Apostles for their work. The mighty wind and the tongues of fire were symbols of God's mysterious, vitalizing power and His illuminating and warming presence. The gift of tongue symbolized the bloodless character of the Christian warfare, and the power of the preached word.

The sermon of Peter was preached from the strange text: "These men are full of new wine," a text which disclosed the old tendency of the Sadducees to deny the miraculous. Even as to-day, men love to explain away the supernatural. Upon it Peter preached a plain, honest, earnest, doctrinal sermon which produced a wonderful revival. There was nothing of rhapsody in the sermon, and nothing of uncertainty in its results. On the contrary we are expressly told that the converts continued steadfast— a statement especially encouraging to us in these days when revivals are disparaged and their results are considered transitory.— FRANCIS L. PATTON, D.D., LL.D.

SPIRIT OF GOD.—Ordinances are but as the sails of a ship, and ministers as the seamen that manage those sails. The anchor may be weighed, the sails spread, but when all this is done there is no sailing till a gale come. We preach, pray and listen, but there is no motion Christward until the Spirit of God blows upon us.—FLAVEL, 1627-1691.

SPIRIT, Witness of the.—*Rom. viii: 16.* That the world deny any such testimony in the hearts of believers, and that they look on it with scorn and treat it with derision, proves only that they are unacquainted with it; not that it is an illusion. It is a sensible and true remark of the French philosopher Hemsterhuis, in regard to certain sensations which he was discussing: "Those who are so unhappy as never to have had such sensations, either through weakness of the natural organ, or because they have never cultivated them, will not comprehend me."—A. P. L.

SPIRIT, Witness of the.—*1 Cor. ii: 4.* The witness of the Spirit is taken in a sense quite too limited, when it is taken as merely a practical testimony in the conscience, the feelings, the heart, and not at the same time as a testimony borne by the Spirit of God, as the Spirit of Truth, through the medium of the thoughts of men. We know that the chief witness, on which all else depends, is that which is borne in "demonstration of power."—A. P. L.

TRUTH, The Spirit of.—*John xiv: 17.* The Holy Ghost is the living, personal, divine unity of complete revelation; and, as such, the Spirit of Truth (John xv: 26; xvi: 13). He is the Spirit of Truth, inasmuch as He makes objective truth subjective in believers, in order to the knowledge of truth. Objectively He is the Spirit of God (Rom. viii: 14), and God Himself (Acts v); the Spirit of the Father (Matt. x: 20); the Spirit of Christ (Rom. viii: 9); the Spirit of the Lord (2 Cor. iii: 17), the Holy Spirit (Acts ii). Subjectively He is the Spirit of Truth, the Spirit of wisdom and revelation (Eph. i: 17); the Spirit of power, of love, and of a sound mind (2 Tim. i: 27); the Spirit of Adoption, of prayer (Rom. viii: 15); the Spirit of Sanctification (Rom. i: 4, of life (Rom. viii: 10), of meekness (1 Cor. iv: 21), of comfort (Acts ix: 31), of glory (1 Pet. iv: 14), of sealing, of the earnest of eternal life (Eph. i: 13, 14), of all Christian charismata (1 Cor. xii: 4). As the Spirit of Truth, the Holy Ghost applies to believers the full truth of the perfect revelation of God in Christ.—A. P. L.

POETRY

The Church

By Samuel John Stone

The Church's one foundation
Is Jesus Christ her Lord;
She is His new creation
By water and the word:
From heaven He came and sought her
To be His holy bride;
With His own blood He bought her,
And for her life He died.

Elect from every nation,
Yet one o'er all the earth,
Her charter of salvation,
One Lord, one faith, one birth;
One holy name she blesses,
Partakes one holy food,
And to one hope she presses,
With every grace endued.

'Mid toil and tribulation,
And tumult of her war,
She waits the consummation
Of peace for evermore;
Till, with the vision glorious,
Her longing eyes are blest,
And the great Church victorious
Shall be the Church at rest.

Yet she on earth hath union
With God the Three in One,
And mystic sweet communion
With those whose rest is won:
O happy ones and holy!
Lord, give us grace that we
Like them, the meek and lowly,
On high may dwell with Thee.

Various Selections

Wherever God erects a house of prayer,
The devil always build a chapel there.
Defoe—*The Trueborn Englishman.*
Line 1.

God never had a church but there men say,
The devil a chapel hath raised by some wyles,
I doubted of this saw, till on a day
I westward spied great Edinburgh's Saint
Gyles.
Drummond—*Posthumous Poems.*

No sooner is a temple built to God, but the
devil builds a chapel hard by.
Herbert—*Jacula Prudentum.*

And storied windows richly dight,
Casting a dim religious light.
Milton—*Il Penseroso.* Line 159.

No silver saints, by dying misers giv'n,
Here brib'd the rage of ill-requited heav'n:
But such plain roofs as Piety could raise,
And only vocal with the Maker's praise.
Pope—*Eloisa to Abélard.* Line 137.

Who builds a Church to God, and not to
Fame
Will never mark the marble with his Name.
Pope—*Moral Essays.* Ep. III.
Line 285.

The People of God

By James Montgomery

People of the living God,
I have sought the world around,
Paths of sin and sorrow trod,
Peace and comfort nowhere found.

Now to you my spirit turns,
Turns, a fugitive unblessed;
Brethren, where your altar burns,
O receive me into rest.

Lonely I no longer roam,
Like the cloud, the wind, the wave;
Where you dwell shall be my home,
Where you die shall be my grave.

Mine the God whom you adore,
Your Redeemer shall be mine;
Earth can fill my heart no more,
Every idol I resign.

Descent of the Holy Spirit

By John Keble

Swiftly and straight each tongue of flame
Through cloud and breeze unwavering came,
And darted to its place of rest
On some meek brow of Jesus blest.
Nor fades it yet, that living gleam,
And still those lambent lightnings stream;
Where'er the Lord is, there are they;
In every heart that gives Him room,
They light His altar every day,
Zeal to inflame, and vice consume.

Gift of the Holy Spirit

THOMAS H. GILL

Day divine, when in the temple,
    To the first disciples came
Glory new and treasure ample,
    Mighty gifts and tongues of flame!
Day to happy souls commended,
    When the Holy Ghost was given,
When the Comforter descended,
    Bringing down the joy of heaven.

Hath the Holy Ghost been holden
    By those ancient saints alone?
Only may the ages golden
    Call the Comforter their own?
No; their portion we inherit;
    Ours the sorrow, ours the sin:
We beseech the Holy Spirit;
    We the Comforter would win.

Grieving the Holy Spirit

BY GEORGE HERBERT

And art Thou grieved, sweet and sacred Dove,
        When I am sour
        And cross Thy love?
Grieved for me? the God of strength and
        power
Grieved for a worm, which, when I tread,
I pass away and leave it dead.

Then weep, mine eyes, the God of love doth
        grieve:
        Weep, foolish heart,
        And weeping live;
For death is dry as dust. Yet if we part,
End as the night, whose sable hue
Your sins express: melt into dew.

When saucy mirth shall knock or call at door,
        Cry out, get hence,
        Or cry no more.
Almighty God doth grieve, He puts on sense:
I sin not to my grief alone,
But to my God's, too; He doth groan.

O take thy lute, and tune it to a strain,
        Which may with thee
        All day complain.
There can no discord but in ceasing be.
Marbles can weep; and surely strings
More bowels have, than such hard things.

Lord, I adjudge myself to tears and grief,
        E'en endless tears
        Without relief.
If a clear spring for me no time forbear,
But runs, although I be not dry;
I am no crystal, what shall I?

Yet if I wail not still, since still to wail
        Nature denies;
        And flesh would fail,
If my deserts were masters of mine eyes:
Lord, pardon, for Thy Son makes good
My want of tears with store of blood.

Guidance of the Holy Spirit

BY JOHN MILTON

He to His own a Comforter will send,
The promise of the Father, who shall dwell
His Spirit within them, and the law of faith
Working through love, upon their hearts shall
        write,
To guide them in all truth.

Influence of the Holy Spirit

BY JOHN MASON

There is a Stream, which issues forth
    From God's eternal Throne,
And from the Lamb, a living stream
    Clear as the crystal stone.

The stream doth water Paradise;
    It makes the angels sing;
One cordial drop revives my heart;
    Hence all my joys do spring.

Such joys as are unspeakable,
    And full of glory too;
Such hidden manna, hidden pearls,
    As worldlings do not know.

Eye hath not seen, nor ear hath heard,
    From fancy 'tis concealed,
What Thou, Lord, hast laid up for Thine,
    And hast to me revealed.

I see Thy face, I hear Thy voice,
    I taste Thy sweetest love:
My soul doth leap: but O for wings,
    The wings of Noah's dove!

Then should I flee far hence away,
    Leaving this world of sin!
Then should my Lord put forth His hand,
    And kindly take me in!

Then should my soul with angels feast
    On joys that always last!
Blest be my God, the God of joy,
    Who gives me here a taste.

Litany to the Holy Spirit

BY R. HERRICK

In the hours of my distress,
When temptations me oppress,
And when I my sins confess,
        Sweet Spirit, comfort me.

When I lie within my bed,
Sick in heart, and sick in head,
And with doubts disquieted,
        Sweet Spirit, comfort me.

When the house doth sigh, and weep,
And the world is drowned in sleep,
Yet mine eyes the watch do keep,
        Sweet Spirit, comfort me.

When God knows I'm tossed about
Either with despair or doubt,
Yet before the glass be out,
        Sweet Spirit, comfort me.

When the tempter me pursueth
With the sins of all my youth,
And reproves me for untruth,
Sweet Spirit, comfort me.

When the judgment is revealed
And that opened which was sealed,
When to Thee I have appealed,
Sweet Spirit, comfort me.

Offices of the Holy Spirit

By John Hey

The Spirit of God
From heaven descending, dwells in domes of
clay;
In mode far passing human thought, He
guides,
Impels, instructs: intense pursuit of good,
And cautious flight of evil He suggests,
But in such gentle murmurs, that to know
His heavenly voice, we must have done His
will.

Power of the Holy Spirit

By Harriet Auber

Our blest Redeemer, ere He breathed
His last farewell,
A guide—a Comforter, bequeathed,
With us to dwell.

He came in tongues of living flame
To teach, subdue;
All-powerful as the wind He came,
As viewless too.

He comes, His graces to impart;
A willing guest,
While He can find one humble heart
Wherein to rest.

He breathes that gentle voice we hear
As breeze of even;
That checks each fault, that calms each fear,
And speaks of heaven.

And all the good that we possess,
His gift we own;
Yea, every thought of holiness,
And vict'ry won.

Spirit of purity and grace,
Our weakness see;
O make our hearts Thy dwelling-place,
And worthier Thee.

Prayer to the Holy Spirit

Veni Creator Spiritus

Come, Holy Ghost, our souls inspire,
And lighten with celestial fire:
Thou the Anointing Spirit art,
Who dost Thy sevenfold gifts impart.
Thy blessèd unction from above
Is comfort, life, and fire of love:
Enable with perpetual light
The dullness of our blinded sight:

Anoint and cheer our soilèd face
With the abundance of Thy Grace;
Keep far out foes; give peace at home;
Where Thou art Guide, no ill can come.
Teach us to know the Father, Son,
And Thee of Both, to be but One;
That, through the ages all along,
Thy praise may be our endless song.
A. D. 1662

River of the Holy Spirit

By William Hurn

There is a River, deep and broad,
Its course no mortal knows;
It fills with joy the Church of God,
And widens as it flows.

Clearer than crystal is the stream,
And bright with endless day;
The waves with every blessing teem,
And life and health convey.

Where'er they flow, contentions cease,
And love and meekness reign;
The Lord Himself commands the peace,
And foes conspire in vain.

Along the shores, angelic bands
Watch every moving wave;
With holy joy their breast expands,
When men the waters crave.

To them distressèd souls repair,
The Lord invites them nigh;
They leave their cares and sorrows there,
They drink, and never die.

Flow on, sweet Stream, more largely flow,
The earth with glory fill;
Flow on, till all the Savior know,
And all obey His will.

Temples of the Holy Spirit

By Charles Jenner

If yet the Holy Spirit deigns to dwell
In earthly domes, 'tis not those defiled
With pride, with fraud, with rapine, or with
lust;
'Midst the rough foliage of the thorny brake,
The clustering grape not blushes, and the fig
Decks not the prickly thistle's barren stalk;
Even thus shall all be measured by their
fruits.

Lead, Kindly Light

By John H. Newman

Lead, kindly Light, amid th' encircling
gloom,
Lead Thou me on;
The night is dark, and I am far from home,
Lead Thou me on;
Keep Thou my feet; I do not ask to see
The distant scene; one step enough for me.

I was not ever thus, nor prayed that Thou
Shouldst lead me on;
I loved to choose and see my path; but now
Lead Thou me on.

I loved the garish day; and spite of fears,
Pride ruled my will; remember not past
  years.

So long Thy pow'r hath blest me, sure it still
  Will lead me on
O'er moor and fen, o'er crag and torrent, till
  The night is gone.
And with the morn those angel faces smile,
Which I have loved long since, and lost
  awhile.

The Spirit's Hour

By John Ward Stimson

My mocking bird, full oft, in vesper twilight
  still,
  Croons in a low refrain to south winds
    soughing by,
And tunes his glowing throat to echo back
    each trill
  Of far-off fading notes from warblers in
    the sky.
When every murmuring chord has sunk be-
    yond my reach,
He sits, alert there, still, himself the sound to
    teach.

So too that " still small voice " which broods
    o'er poet soul,
  So sacred, sweet and low, mysteriously shy!
Ye cannot catch Its call, nor hear Its char-
    iot's roll
  When fanning seraph wings and thun-
    dering hosts go by,
Except in holy tryst ye wait, nor deaf nor
    blind,
Like pure Eolian harp kissed by the autumn
    wind.—E.

Veni Sancte Spiritus

By F. W. Faber, D.D.

Come Holy Spirit! from the height
Of heaven send down Thy blessèd light!
  Come, Father of the friendless poor!
Giver of gifts, and Light of hearts,
Come with that unction which imparts
  Such consolations as endure.

The Soul's Refreshment and her Guest,
Shelter in heat, in labor Rest,
  The sweetest Solace in our wo!
Come, blissful Light! oh come and fill,
In all Thy faithful, heart and will,
  And make our inward fervor glow.

Where Thou art, Lord! there is no ill,
For evil's self Thy light can kill:
  Oh! let that light upon us rise!
Lord! heal our wounds, and cleanse our
    stains,
Fountain of grace! and with Thy rains
  Our barren spirits fertilize.

Bend with Thy fires our stubborn wills,
And quicken what the world would chill,
  And homeward call the feet that stray:
Virtue's reward, and final grace,
The Eternal Vision face to face,
  Spirit of Love! for these we pray.

Come Holy Spirit! bid us live;
To those who trust Thy mercy give
  Joys that through endless ages flow:
Thy various gifts, foretastes of Heaven,
Those that are named Thy sacred Seven,
  On us, O God of love, bestow.

Whitsunday

By John Keble

*And suddenly there came a sound from
heaven as of a rushing mighty wind, and it
filled all the house where they were sitting.
And there appeared unto them cloven tongues
like as of fire, and it sat upon each of
them. And they were all filled with the Holy
Ghost.—Acts ii: 2, 3, 4.*

When God of old came down from Heaven,
  In power and wrath He came;
Before His feet the clouds were riven,
  Half darkness and half flame:

Around the trembling mountain's base
  The prostrate people lay,
Convinced of sin, but not of grace;
  It was a dreadful day.

But when He came the second time,
  He came in power and love,
Softer than gale at morning prime
  Hovered His holy Dove.

The fires that rushed on Sinai down
  In sudden torrents dread,
Now gently light, a glorious crown,
  On every sainted head.

Like arrows went those lightnings forth
  Winged with the sinner's doom,
But these, like tongues, o'er all the earth
  Proclaiming life to come:

And as on Israel's awe-struck ear
  The voice exceeding loud,
The trump, that angels quake to hear,
  Thrilled from the deep, dark cloud.

So, when the Spirit of our God
  Came down His flock to find,
A voice from Heaven was heard abroad,
  A rushing, mighty wind.

Nor doth the outward ear alone
  At that high warning start;
Conscience gives back the appalling tone;
  'Tis echoed in the heart.

It fills the Church of God; it fills
  The sinful world around;
Only in stubborn hearts and wills
  No place for it is found.

To other strains our souls are set:
  A giddy whirl of sin
Fills ear and brain, and will not let
  Heaven's harmonies come in.

Come, Lord, come Wisdom, Love, and Power,
  Open our ears to hear;
Let us not miss the accepted hour;
  Save, Lord, by Love or Fear.

CHILDREN'S DAY

ORIGIN AND DEVELOPMENT OF CHILDREN'S DAY

By James A. Worden, D.D.

[From a leaflet published by the Presbyterian Board of Publication.]

FROM early times, pastors have devoted certain Sabbaths or parts of Sabbaths to special services for children. Many years ago certain pastors were accustomed to devote one Sabbath every three months to certain forms of service in behalf of the Sabbath-school.

Then grew up an almost universal custom of holding Sabbath-school anniversaries, either upon a Sabbath or upon some week-day evening. Here we have the several elements of the evolution of Children's Day. An effort was unavoidably made to systematize and correlate those several customs of recognizing the children's place in the public worship of the Lord's Day. As a result of this widespread endeavor there gradually obtained a consensus of thought and practice.

Who it was that first suggested an annual Children's Day that should combine the idea of an anniversary, a special children's service, in the beautiful season of the year, on which all parts of the country and all Sabbath-school workers could unite, it is impossible to discover. Perhaps it sprang up naturally in many child-like hearts at once. It would be as easy to fix the exact hour at which spring re-visits the earth after the storms of winter, as to fix the date of the exact origin of Children's Day. And to write a history of its development would be no easier than to undertake to record the annals of the blossoming of spring flowers and the budding of the trees. We only know that whereas it was winter, now it is spring, and so Children's Day is come, on which the Church rises and shines and sings and puts on its beautiful garments. If any claim that the Methodist Episcopal Church in its General Conference, was the first ecclesiastically to recognize Children's Day they are probably correct; but long before this, hundreds of Presbyterian schools were observing the day of joy and gladness without reference to the authority of Church courts.

But when, in 1883, many years after Presbyterian Sabbath-school workers had been accustomed to do this, the General Assembly said, " It hereby designates the second Sabbath in June as the Children's Day on which special services for the children shall be held, and the vital topics of the Christian nurture and the conversion of the young shall be pressed upon the thought of the entire congregation," the whole vast forces of the Sabbath-school gladly and loyally wheeled into line. So that two years later it is recorded: " The General Assembly notices with approval the observance by our Churches and Sabbath-schools of the second Sabbath of June, designated by a former General Assembly as Children's Day, and emphasizes the importance of seeking the presence and power of the Holy Spirit in these services, that they may not be simply attractive, but profitable, contributing to the conversion and Christian nurture of the young." Superintendents, officers, teachers, and scholars supported this effort with joyous faith and earnest cooperation.

What more powerful object-lesson, setting forth the love of Christ and of Christ's Church to the young, than the services of Children's Day? What clearer demonstration of the identity of Church and Sabbath-school could be given? I venture to say that the children and youth of the Presbyterian Church never have doubted, since the establishment of Children's Day, the Church's supreme interest in, and love for them; and they have reciprocated this interest and love with all the enthusiasm of their youthful spirits.

One of the most beautiful incidents in the life of our Lord occurred when He was on the direct road to Jerusalem and Calvary, and was surrounded by an excited and wondering multitude; when, in this very crisis of His work, He stopped to give an opportunity to mothers and fathers to bring their young children to Him that He might put His hands upon them and bless them. And when the disciples rebuked this parental solicitude as an interference with the greater and more important work of healing and teaching the crowds, Jesus rebuked them and said, " Suffer the little children to come unto me, and forbid them not, for of such is the kingdom of God." And He took them up in His arms, put His hands upon them and blessed them. Is not this Children's Day the outgrowth of the " same mind that was also in Christ Jesus "?

The Christian appreciation of childhood is one of the significant marks of this new and brighter era; and it brings with it a baptism of new and simpler love, the hearts of the fathers being turned to the children, and the hearts of the children to their fathers. Longfellow expresses our heart's sentiment when he sings:

> " Ah! what would the world be to us,
>   If the children were no more?
> We should dread the desert behind us
>   Worse than the dark before.
>
> .   .   .   .   .   .
>
> " Come to me, oh ye children,
>   And whisper in my ear,
> What the birds and the winds are singing
>   In your sunny atmosphere.
>
> .   .   .   .   .   .
>
> " Ye are better than all the ballads
>   That ever were sung or said,
> For ye are living poems,
>   And all the rest are dead."

CHILDREN'S DAY SUGGESTIONS

Few special days in the average Sunday-school are looked forward to with such eager expectancy on the part of the scholars as Children's Day. Even fathers **A Day of** and mothers, big brothers and **Oppor-** sisters, who perhaps seldom en-**tunity** ter church doors, go then if at no other time. With many schools it is practically the end of a year's work and an anniversary corresponding to Commencement Day in our public schools. But in every school it may be a day of unusual opportunity for presenting the joy of the Christ-life and the friendship of the All-loving One to many who perhaps are not reached at other times during the year. Besides this, the memory of a happy Children's Day, with its birds and flowers, its music and fluttering banners and all kindred associations of loving helpfulness, has often been in after years the breath which stirred to flame a loyalty for the church that had become an uncertain flicker. This being the case, pastor, superintendent, and teachers should spare no pains in planning to make the day a golden one in the circlet of the year.

Children's Day not only affords opportunity for providing an especially happy time for the school as a whole, but the different departments, as well as individual teachers, may take advantage of the occasion to devise many helpful plans for their own special classes.

With some the celebration of Children's Day lasts all day, taking the place of Church and Sunday-school, or giving color to these.

Hours for the Exercises Often it takes the place of the morning or the evening church service. Again it is confined to the Sunday-school hour. In some instances a special afternoon service is held. The morning church hour is sometimes given over to a program by the smaller children, and the evening service to the older boys and girls. Where the morning church service is confined to the regular order, the hymns and anthems may be selected with the idea of being especially helpful to children and easily understood by them, and the sermon is prepared with reference to the children. The Sunday-school attends in a body, seats in the front or in the gallery being reserved for the members. In this case the exercises by the scholars themselves follow later in the day.

Children's Day Programs Published exercises and cantatas may be had in abundance, and a selection to fit the needs of any school may easily be made. Some are quite simple, while there are others more elaborate.

Home-made Programs It is not difficult to prepare a home-made program by selecting suitable songs from various books, and using such recitations and desirable exercises as are readily copied from books or clipped from Sunday-school papers, magazines, and similar sources. Such a program may be prepared without expense, and is often more satisfactory than one secured ready prepared. When a program is to be made in this way, the choosing of material should be given into the hands of one or more persons who will use taste and judgment in making selections.

It is necessary to use care in assigning pieces. Give each one only what is within the range of his capability to understand and render well. Often little folks are asked to memorize recitations too difficult for their years, while other children are sometimes given selections too young for them.

Both music and recitations should be of real worth and dignity. When such pieces as "Like as a Father," "The Palms," and Gounod's "Praise Ye the Father," and such classics as Lowell's "Vision of Sir Launfal," can be as readily learned as something of less worth, there is little excuse for spending time in storing the mind with mere jingles. Music and poetry memorized for Children's Day may as well be something that will also enrich the mind for a lifetime.

It is usually wisest to let one committee of three or four do all the planning both of the program and the decorations. But when the work is thoroughly outlined, it **Committees** can be subdivided so as to give as many as possible something to do, thus lightening the load for the main committee. Different classes may be requested to attend to parts of the decorations, while teachers may take charge of drilling those in their classes who are to take part in the exercises.

Often a sub-committee takes charge of the decorations, under the direction of the general committee, so that wherever it is necessary the decorations can be made to accommodate the needs of the program committee, if for instance special designs of arches, shields, or crosses are needed to illustrate some recitation or exercise. If one committee keeps the general result clearly in view, the different parts of the work can be given profitably to as many as are willing to help carry it on, and "many hands make light work."

Rehearsals Rehearsals should not be allowed to interfere with the Sunday-school hour. The songs may be practised at the time usually given to singing other music, but most of the rehearsing should be done outside the regular Sunday-school session. An evening in the week or a Sunday afternoon may be chosen. The smaller children can usually have their rehearsals on a week-day afternoon. Whatever the time selected, the drilling should be frequent and thorough, so that no halting, half-prepared parts shall mar the exercises when the important time comes. If various teachers rehearse their own classes at least a week before the final day, the general committee should personally hear all numbers on the program in order to strengthen the weak places and correct mistakes before it is too late. It is seldom wise to leave much rehearsing to busy mothers at home.

Children's Day as Promotion Day Children's Day is coming to be recognized as one of the most suitable times for transferring scholars from one department to another. Such transfer occurs in nearly all schools, at least from the Primary Department into the Juvenile, and from the Juvenile into the Main School. A public recognition of this promotion is proper whether scholars pass into a higher class by regular examination or simply because of becoming old enough for transfer.

Promotion Exercises A prominent place on the program is usually given to the promotion or graduating exercises. In one school graduating classes occupy front seats, the girls dressed in white, the dark suits of the boys brightened by buttonhole bouquets. When their turn comes they take their places on the platform and the examination questions are asked by the Primary Superintendent. The class answer, some in turn and some in concert.

When the first and twenty-third Psalms, the Commandments, and the Beatitudes have been repeated and the catechism questions answered, the diplomas are awarded by the pastor. Then comes a short address of welcome from the superintendent of the main school. Following this a tiny tot from the primary department comes upon the platform with a basket of bouquets for the graduates, as a little good-by gift from the infant class. It is sometimes hard to tell which the graduates receive most proudly—the diplomas or the bouquets.

When there is more than one graduating class they may take turns in their order—primary, juvenile, and so on, depending upon how elaborate a system of grading is followed.

The annual graduating exercises prove a means of wonderful helpfulness, not only to the school but to many homes. Parents who have shown little interest in the Sunday-school are almost sure to be present to witness the promotion of their children.

Small diplomas and certificates of promotion of varying prices and degrees of elegance may be bought from the different Sunday-school supply houses. The prices **Graduat-** of these range from one to five or **ing** ten cents each. The diplomas are **Diplomas** printed on linen paper to imitate **and** parchment. When rolled and tied **Certifi-** with a bit of ribbon they are **cates** greatly prized by the children. Diplomas for the girls may be tied with blue ribbon and those for the boys with pink, or a different shade may be selected for each child.

Sometimes promotion cards are used instead of diplomas. A promotion certificate which is much liked by the children is made of cardboard about 12x14 inches. In the center is space for the child's name, the name of the school, the superintendent, etc. Around the four sides in the form of a border are places for seals to be attached—a green seal for the first examination, a red seal for the second, and so on, the number of seals depending upon the length of the course of study. These seals are usually in the form of large gold paper stars gummed on the back and with a bit of colored ribbon hanging from them.

Another plan is to have the list of names of those who graduate placed on a large card, handsomely framed and hung near the superintendent's desk where all may inspect it from time to time.

A teacher can prepare home-made diplomas or have some friend who is a fine penman help her in doing so. Such a diploma, being the work of the teacher's own **Home-** hands, would be more prized per- **made** haps than any that could be pur- **Diplomas** chased. If certificates of promotion are used instead of diplomas, they can be cut from bristol board and ornamented with one of the penny prints of Hofmann's "Boy Jesus" or some other appriate picture.

Something like the following can be made by using two colors of ink, ruling the lines and the borders red.

First Congregational Sunday School

*This certifies that....................
has passed a satisfactory examination in
the Primary Department and is promoted
to the.............................*

Chicago,...................1900.

....
Teacher.

....
Primary Supt.

....
Supt. of Main Room.

Some Sunday-schools give certificates on Children's Day to all who pass satisfactory examinations on the lessons of the year. **Promotion** These examinations are conduct- **Certifi-** ed previous to Children's Day, **cates** and the awards made as a part **for All** of the exercises on that day. Thus a pupil may earn a new certificate each year. Another plan, which however involves more expense, is to give at the first examination a handsome certificate in a frame, with places for seals around the edge of the certificate. Each Children's Day those who have passed the examination bring back their certificates to have a new seal attached. New scholars receive their certificates at this time.

In Churches that practise infant baptism, the baptism of young children is one feature **Baptism** of the Children's Day program. **of** In some cases those of the Sun- **Children** day-school graduating classes who wish to do so, are received into Church membership on this day.

Much inspiration and enthusiasm is added to the exercises by a processional of the whole school. If the exercises are to be held in the auditorium of the Church, **The** as they usually are, the school **Proces-** gathers in the Sunday-school **sional** room and the procession is formed by classes,—primary children first in the line and the others following in their order. Another plan is to have the Boys' Brigade, if there is one in the school, lead the procession. It is always necessary to have as leaders two who will not be timid and who will take short, even steps. When this is attempted, be sure that the Bible classes join in the procession. This will do much to prevent the older boys from hanging back through fear of doing something not quite consistent with their dignity. A cornet at the head makes it much easier for the children to sing well while marching. A large number of songs are well adapted to be used as marching songs, tho "Onward, Christian Soldiers," seems to be the favorite. An organ prelude preceding the entrance in procession gives visitors an opportunity to be seated.

Where schools have for the various classes banners which can be carried in the procession, doing this increases the interest.

Banners and Flags in the Processional Teachers may plan to add to the interest, as well as to the class spirit, by preparing banners for their classes. They can be fashioned from delicate colors of cambric or cheesecloth, and bordered with flowers or ferns. The mottoes can be cut from gold or silver paper and put on with a little paste. Flags large and small may be carried in addition to the banners. A school thus equipped with banners and flags flying, and marching to some majestic Church hymn, is a sight to stir the heart of the least enthusiastic and fire with new zeal the sometimes discouraged workers.

Flowers have always had so large a part in the celebration of Children's Day that many call it Flower Sunday. It should be Flower **Flowers** Sunday, not only because of the use of flowers in the decoration of the Church and Sunday-school rooms, but because of the distribution of the flowers afterwards among the sick and aged and others who might not otherwise have the opportunity of enjoying them. Some schools at Easter distribute to each child plants and bulbs to be cultivated and brought to Church on Children's Day as a part of the decoration, then given away afterward to brighten some home.

Children should be encouraged to bring flowers from the woods and fields and from their home gardens to help in the decorations. Let them have as large a part as possible in making the Church beautiful. One Sunday-school gives each class one of the fourteen large windows to decorate, while a number of classes help to decorate the platform.

Plenty of green branches add greatly to the beauty of the decorations. Oak branches are easily procured and the leaves do not wither quickly. Potted plants, palms, and ferns can also be borrowed from various homes by sending a competent person to carry them to the Church and afterward ·return them safely. Some of the larger boys may be enlisted to attend to this part of the work.

Some schools on Children's Day present each child with a small plant or bulb to be kept and cared for. Sometimes these are given with the thought of cultivating them for some future celebration. One school gave out one Children's Day several hundred young chrysanthemum plants, with the understanding that they were to be prepared for a Chrysanthemum Show early in November. To this exhibition a small admission was charged and the proceeds used to assist the poor during the winter. Some of the plants were sold and others were distributed among the sick. The same plan might be adopted with bulbs or some other plants, and they could be cultivated to use in decorating for Harvest Home or Rally Sunday. There is much helpfulness in thus keeping before the children a definite purpose from month to month. In any case the thought should be not only to make the rooms fragrant and beautiful for the special services, but to share with others these most beautiful of summer's treasures.

Different ways of distributing the flowers may be adopted. They can be packed in **Distribution of Flowers** baskets and sent to hospitals or Flower Missions, or turned over to the Flower Committee of the Church young people's society for distribution. If, however, the children themselves have a part in the distribution, it will mean more to them, and perhaps to the recipients. One of the souvenir programs tied to the stems of the flowers will interest the sick ones to whom bouquets are sent, and give them the sense of being really in touch with the joyous celebration.

In these days when artificial flowers are so inexpensive and easily made, as well as really beautiful, it is often desirable to use them in **Artificial Flowers** addition to the real flowers. When an emblematic figure—a cross, a star, or a shield—is to be fashioned, artificial flowers are more suitable than real ones. Artificial flowers may also be formed into letters for mottoes, made into arches, crosses, and garlands, twined with ropes of evergreen, or hung in bunches from the chandeliers.

A pretty exercise for some of the tiniest tots of the Primary Department is the forming of a white shield bearing a blood-red cross. The shield is first made of thin board covered with sprays of evergreen or with dark green crépe paper. Holes are bored for the stems of the flowers, and a number of children, each bearing a large white blossom, recite appropriate verses about faith, as they place the flowers in the shield. Then come children with red blossoms, each one reciting a verse about the cross, and inserting their flowers, thus making the form of a cross on the white background.

Canaries in their gilded cages make a beautiful addition to the decorations. A cage with a bunch of flowers and greenery may be hung **Birds** from each chandelier. The twittering of the birds during the service and their rippling songs, joining with the children's voices, are a fitting accompaniment on this day of rejoicing and pleasure-giving.

June 14, the anniversary of the adoption of the Stars and Stripes by Congress, is now set apart as Flag Day. Some have found it helpful to celebrate this in connec-**Children's Day as Flag Day** tion with Children's Day. Flags and bunting are used with the flowers in decorating, flags carried in the procession and tiny flags worn with bunches of flowers by the children, while the exercises are planned to place an emphasis on patriotism. One teacher suggests that a girl wave the Stars and Stripes while the audience join in singing

"America" and in the Salute to the Flag: "We give our hearts and our heads to God and our Country—one country, one language, one flag, and one God"—the sentiment of all Christian patriots.

A beautiful service that the children will never forget, and which will make glad the **Children's Day as Grandparents' Day** heart of many an aged one, is a Children's Day service to which the grandfathers and grandmothers are especially invited. Let it be understood by the children, in planning the exercises, that the preparations are to be made with this in view. Then when Children's Day morning arrives, seats can be reserved for the guests of honor, to whom written invitations have been previously sent. Wherever possible, let conveyances be sent to bring to the Church those too feeble to walk. Have the children feel that these guests are their special company, and plan in every way to make the service a delightful one for them. At the close of the exercises a company of boys may act as escorts to the carriages and busses, while the girls may present the old people with bouquets or other souvenirs.

Babies who are enrolled as members of the Cradle Roll class may be invited to visit the Primary Department at the regular Sunday-**Cradle-roll Babies at Sunday-school** school session on Children's Day. Some special exercises can be planned to interest the mothers, and a motion song or exercise will please the baby visitors. The delight of the small lads and lassies at seeing "our baby" in Sunday-school is unbounded. Thus the ties between the home and Sunday-school are made the firmer by a visit from "mamma and baby."

Girls dressed in white and carrying baskets **Collections** trimmed with small flags and flowers may act as collectors.

Girls may act as ushers, tho some of the young men who do not care to take part in any other way may be enlisted to do this and give valuable aid.

Beautiful souvenir programs can be prepared at little expense. If Children's Day is also celebrated as Flag Sunday, the program may be printed or copied with mimeograph on the reverse side of a paper or pasteboard flag. Handsome cards, with flower designs on one side, may be used as souvenirs, printing the order of exercises on their backs. Programs with a half-tone print of a child's

head or a copy of some appropriate picture need not be expensive.

A beautiful custom observed yearly by some schools is that of decorating the graves of Sunday-school members each Children's Day. **Decorating Graves on Children's Day** In the afternoon the school assembles and goes in a body to the cemetery, bearing wreaths and bouquets. After the graves of all who have been members of the school have been decorated, the scholars gather under the trees and join in song and prayer. Thus are the children strengthened in the thought that "Death is but the covered way that leads at last to light," and that those gone before have but stepped into another room of the Father's house, while we on this side are as truly in His presence.

A choir of the older boys and girls carefully chosen and drilled for Children's Day, will add greatly to the exercises. If the regu-**Choir** lar order of Church service is followed they may take the place of the regular choir on this day. Quartets, duets, and anthems can be rendered by them with beautiful effect. Not only will this add to the enjoyment of the day, but as the members of our choirs for the future must come from the ranks of the boys and girls of to-day, it is most fitting that they should thus in childhood begin their musical service to the Church.

One number always included in the Children's Day program by a certain New Jersey Sunday-school is a resumé of the past year's lessons, prepared for the occasion by one of the teachers, and recited by a boy or girl. Another plan is to have a recitation of the Golden Texts for the past year given by a class composed of as many of the scholars as are able to do so. A floral button, bearing a Scripture text awarded at this time is a souvenir the children will greatly prize.

An interesting program is sometimes planned to help in cultivating the missionary spirit, and the collection devoted to mission-**A Missionary Program** ary causes. Recitations and readings telling of the condition of children in other lands can be found in abundance. The songs should be of the same order, and the central theme of the whole program emphasize the blessedness of children in a land where Jesus is known and loved, and the joy of spreading the news to other children less favored.—N. C. T. M.

IMPROVED METHODS OF SUNDAY-SCHOOL TEACHING

By Ellen Kenyon Warner

An interesting address on the above subject was given at one of the Sunday sessions of the Martha's Vineyard Summer Institute by its President, Dr. William A. Mowry. Dr. Mowry's recommendations were substantially as follows:

The Sunday-school has for its object to teach a high morality and a true religion. Its text-book is the Bible. The Bible is a history of the best development of the race. Its concrete moral teachings are always of interest to the young. About twenty-five years ago a uniform plan for Bible study in the Sunday-schools originated in this country and spread to Canada and England. The advantages that have been realized in the use of this plan can hardly be overestimated. But the scheme should be broadened, so as to take in practical subjects; and the methods of teaching in the Sunday-school should follow true pedagogic principles. The laws of psychology, too, should be observed in the government of the Sunday-school.

The kindergarten system, where once introduced under competent teachers, is never abandoned. It should have a place in every Sunday-school where there are five or six children of the right age. This lowest class should have the best teacher in the school. A large class with a superior teacher is better than smaller classes with poor teachers. This primary class should follow the International Lessons. They should have placed before them in a graphic manner the stories of the Bible, especially those of the New Testament. The Golden Rule should be so paraphrased for them as to bring it within their easy comprehension, and then should be learned. Suitable memory gems should be studied and learned.

Children of the ages between five or six and nine or ten should constitute a junior department. These classes should take up the International Lessons. The classes should be small, and the question of discipline should receive careful attention. The most tactful teachers available should be secured, and the classes should have separate rooms. This is provided for in some Sunday-schools by having the class-rooms ranged around the assembly-room and cut off from it by rolling doors, which can be slid back, throwing all the rooms into one for general purposes.

A senior department, corresponding with the high school, and composed of the pupils from fourteen to eighteen years of age, should also pursue the International course, but upon a higher plane of study. The personality of the pupils should be studied. Above this grade a great change is needed. A variety of subjects adapting the Sunday-school in-

struction to adults of all ages, tastes, and interests should be compassed. A critical study of the life of Christ by all authors should be made. Particular books and chapters of the Bible may receive the same critical study. The literature of the Bible; recent Oriental explorations; a comparative study of sacred and profane history—these and other subjects are suitable for adult attendants upon the Sunday-school, and would interest and draw in great numbers of those who now leave its classes because the instruction falls below their level of study. This department for general higher study might be called the collegiate department. There should also be a theological department. Each of these departments should be found in every Sunday-school that has five or six persons for each.

The Sunday-school should give a course in the Christian doctrine, teaching the technical and fundamental principles of the Christian religion. It should take up a study of ethics, dwelling upon those virtues that especially belong to the teachings of Christ. The development of religion from a world standpoint; the history of the Jewish Church; the founding and subsequent history of the Christian Church—some one at least of these or kindred subjects might be taken up in almost any Sunday-school. In larger towns more than one of these subjects might be followed. There is no lack of literature. Teachers may be found among the townsmen and women who have read in these several lines until they have developed enthusiasm for special subjects or characters within the proper scope of Sunday-school work. Here a lawyer may be found who has made a special study of the Book of Job; there a doctor who believes that no other such man ever lived as Paul. Enlist these people in the work of the Sunday-school. The present system drives them out.

Every Sunday-school should have courses of lectures on how to control and interest children. All the Sunday-schools in one place should have classes in pedagogy, under the teaching of a paid expert. These classes should make a special study of discipline.—I.

THE CHILDREN'S SERVICE

To the Editor of the Homiletic Review: I have just seen in one of my foreign exchanges a plan for a children's service, which has in it, to me, some novel and suggestive features. The plan has been pursued for a number of years with very satisfactory results. says the article before me, by the Rev. John Richardson, in his parish in England. Every month the clergyman sends to each family in the parish a letter, such as the one given below, together with a printed outline of the coming children's address. The children and young people thus know what texts they will be asked to repeat in the church and the subject on which they will be catechized. I take the liberty of sending you two of these outlined discourses as

samples of what is thus printed and distributed. They are full of suggestions not only for the young, but for all ordinary hearers. The series embraces four subjects—The Lord Jesus Christ: 1, His Wonderful Life; 2, His Dreadful Death; 3, His Resurrection and Glory; 4, His Expected Return.

Respectfully,

J. A. A.

" My Dear Friend: I am very anxious to see the young of our parish grow up in the knowledge and love of the Lord Jesus Christ. and I propose a plan to you in which I shall be very glad to have your help.

" A list of subjects like the present will be sent early in every month to the house of every person who will accept it, and the request made is that you will carefully instruct your children and young servants in them during the month. On the afternoon of the last Sunday in each month the young people will be catechized on the things contained in the monthly paper; and if you will allow your children to be present, and attend yourself, I shall be greatly obliged.

My sole object is to help in the religious education of the young of our families, and I ask your prayers and assistance.

" Believe me,
" Yours very sincerely,
" (Signed)   JOHN RICHARDSON, *Vicar.*

" P.S.—Additional copies of this paper may be had at my house."—H. R.

SUNDAY-SCHOOL STATISTICS OF ALL COUNTRIES, 1900

COUNTRIES	SUNDAY-SCHOOLS	TEACHERS	SCHOLARS
EUROPE			
England and Wales......................	37,201	585,457	5,976,537
Scotland.............................	6,275	62,994	694,860
Ireland	3,584	27,740	308,516
Belgium	89	310	4,112
Austria	212	513	7,195
Denmark	506	3,043	55,316
Finland	6,853	11,534	147,134
France........	1,450	3,800	60,000
Germany..	5,900	34,983	749,786
Greece.	4	7	180
Italy	403	654	10,969
Netherlands	1,560	4,600	163,000
Norway	550	4,390	63,980
Portugal..........................	11	56	1,066
Russia.....	83	777	15,524
Spain.	88	180	3,230
Sweden...........................	5,750	17,200	242,150
Switzerland..........................	1,637	6,916	113,382
European Turkey.................	35	175	1,564
ASIA			
India included Ceylon.	5,548	10,715	197,754
Persia...........................	107	440	4,876
Siam.....................	16	64	809
China.....	105	1,053	5,264
Japan ....;	150	390	7,019
Central Turkey....	516	2,450	25,833
AFRICA................................	4,246	8,455	161,394
NORTH AMERICA			
United States........	123,173	1,305,939	9,737,432
Canada	8,386	69,521	576,064
Newfoundland and Labrador	359	2,275	22,976
West Indies	2,185	9,673	110,233
Central America and Mexico.	550	1,300	15,000
SOUTH AMERICA........................	350	3,000	150,000
OCEANICA			
Australasia.	4,766	54,211	586,029
Fiji Islands......	1,474	2,700	42,909
Hawaiian Islands........................----	230	1,413	15,840
Other Islands....	210	800	10,000
THE WORLD	224,562	2,239,728	20,287,933

[The total number of teachers and scholars in the world, according to this report, was 22,508,661. The table does not include the schools of the Roman Catholic and Non-Evangelical Protestant churches. The number of scholars in Roman Catholic Sunday-Schools in the United States is estimated by clerics at 800,000.—C. B. F.]

SERMONS AND OUTLINES

FINDING WISDOM

By Joseph Parker, D.D.

(A Sermon for Children)

A certain man went forth to find a Queen of whom he had heard many things that touched his hope and made him glad. He was told how kind she was to every one; how rich; how ready to give all she had; and how she made those who found her, richer than merchants and loftier than princes. And it came to pass that this man took his staff in his hand and went forth to put to the test all that he had heard of this Queen, so great and kind; and as he said farewell to those at home, he added that he would soon return and tell the stirring tale to his children and his friends. He took but little with him, for he said he would soon be home again; a week at the most, and he would come back rich and strong, if all that he had heard should prove to be true. So saying, he passed the little wicket, waved his hand and went on his way without fear or shame.

On the third day he came within sight of the great Queen's house, and when he saw that it stood on a high hill and knew that behind it must be the great and wide sea, he felt a little afraid. But he was sure there must be some way up to the house, else how could the Queen herself get into it? So he took heart again and went on like a brave man. Now began the slope. Then came a wicket not larger than the one he had passed three days ago at his own house, and there he was told to leave his staff. He left it and went on. Presently he was spoken to by some one hidden in a large shrub, and the word he heard was, "Go home again; what thou hast heard is untrue; go back and dream no more." But the man saw the great Queen's house in front, and therefore he thought that what he had heard from the bush was a lie, so on he went. Then he saw a sweet child plucking flowers, and he said, "Is this the right road?" And the child said, "Yes." He asked again, "Is the great Queen at home?" And the dear child said, "She is always at home," and having said this, she gave him a sweet white flower she had just plucked. "They grow nowhere else," said she, "and my mother is always glad for those who come to see her to take one; it will not die, it is not like any other flower you ever saw." The man was pleased; he said, "Thank you much; my little girl shall have it when I go home." On he went, and as he went the house seemed to go back and to be farther from him. Then the road took a sudden turn, and for a time he lost sight of the great Queen's house altogether. A voice then said to him, "Go home; seek her not; they are fools who come this way." The man was afraid, and wished he had not

given up his staff, but still he went on until the road turned again and divided into two parts, one going to the left and the other going to the right.

What to do he could not tell. Should he go and ask the little girl? She might be gone, and then his time would be lost. He would try the left road, but he soon found that it turned downward and not upward, by which he knew it must be wrong, for the great Queen's house was on a lofty hill. Then he turned to the right hand, and that brought him round by a high rock which overhung the narrow path and threw a very deep shadow on the road. The rock was between him and the sun, so the wind was cold, and the outlook was bleak and chilling. And there came a voice out of a cave, saying, "Turn back; go home; think of those you have left behind." Then the man trembled and thought he would return, and he would have done so had he not seen a boy higher up whose hand he thought was beckoning him forward. On he went again, and soon the road began to go upward. This pleased the man, for he knew that the great Queen's house stood on a high hill. But just here the road was very rough; it was like the channel of a mountain torrent; stones great and small choked up the way; still, on he went, and as he went the light came again, and the wind was warmer, and flowers were blooming at his feet. Then the great Queen's house came in sight, and the man's heart was full of joy. What a house it was! So high, so wide, without a stain or a flaw of any kind, the sun gilding the windows with rich light, and rare plants climbing high up the sunny walls. But there was no one to speak to. Where was the boy? Was it a boy or was it a man who looked like a boy through the distance? All was silent. A feeling of strangeness came upon the man and turned his gladness into fear. The road had been long and not always smooth—here and there, indeed, it had been quite dangerous, and now that he had walked it every inch he knew not what to do. What he thought was a door was not a door at all. The door would be on the other side, but he saw no way round, so he wandered and strained his eyes, and almost wished he had never come.

But his trouble was over in a moment, for a friendly voice said to him:
"Hast thou come to the feast to-day?" And the man answered, "What feast?" "Hast thou not heard that the great Queen hath killed her beasts, she hath mingled her wine, she hath also furnished her table; she hath sent forth her maidens, who cry upon

the highest places in the city. Whoso is simple let him turn in hither as for him that wanteth understanding, she saith to him, Come eat of my bread and drink of the wine which I have mingled! All things are ready."

"But," said the man, "I did not know there was a feast. I heard that the great Queen would make me rich; is not that true which I have heard?"

"Certainly; length of days is in her right hand, and in her left hand riches and honor. She is more precious than rubies, and all the things thou canst desire are not to be compared unto her. Wouldst thou see the great Queen of Light?"

"For that purpose have I come all this weary way," said the man.

"Sawest thou not her Son upon the hill where the road is roughest?"

"I saw a young figure, but knew not who or what it was."

"It was the great Queen's Son; if the Son shall make thee free, thou shalt be free indeed; He alone can take thee in; He will find an open door for thee in that solid wall, yea, the seven pillars shall bow before Him rather than entrance shall not be found."

Then the man turned round and behold the Son was at hand, and with many a welcome did the Son bring back the man's shrinking confidence and fading hope.

"Yea," said He, "forsake her not, and she shall preserve thee; love her, and she shall keep thee; exalt her, and she shall promote thee; she shall give to thine head an ornament of grace, a crown of glory she shall deliver to thee;" and, so saying, the unseen door fell open, and sounds of music were heard from those who were gathered at the great Queen's holy feast, and the man went in and beheld the Queen; her eyes were as the sun shining in a deep lake, and her voice was solemn, sweet and peaceful, as a voice heard in a glad dream.

"And hast thou come alone?" said she.

"I have left my friends at home," the man replied, "and now I would they were all here, and that we might never go elsewhere."

"And thou hast seen the sweet child?" said the Queen.

The man remembered. It was the little girl. He looked at the white flower, touched it lovingly, and smiled as one smiles who is well content.

"And didst thou find enemies on the road?"

"Yea, surely, and they urged me home again."

"Blessed are all they that overcome," said the great Queen. And as she said so a new window seemed to open in the western wall, and the man felt as if he passed into a trance as the Son gently led him forward. When afterward asked about it, the man said: "He showed me a pure river of water of life, clear as crystal; in the midst of the street of it, and on either side of the river, was there the tree of life, which bore twelve manner of fruits, and yielded her fruit every month, and the leaves of the tree were for the healing of the nations. And when I would have passed over, the Son said to me, ' Strait is the gate and narrow is the way, but strive to enter in.' So I awoke, and I was glad with a new joy."

Then the man knew that the great Queen's name was Wisdom; that her shining house stands upon a high hill; that the road is rough; that enemies are here and there upon it; but he also knew that one sight of the great Queen's face was worth ten thousand times the trouble he had gone through in climbing to her sunny and holy dwelling place.

"My only fear," said the man, "is going home again, the road is so long and some parts so rough."

"Ah, no!" said the Son, "thou returnest by another road. for her ways are ways of pleasantness, and all her paths are peace." So the man followed down flowery slopes, where no lion was, nor any ravenous beast had ever come, and swiftly did they come to the wicket, and away went the man, staff in hand, to bring his dear ones to the great Queen's house. His children saw him, and shouted welcome, and ran to greet him, and when they saw him there were tears in his eyes, but they were tears of joy. Then the good wife came and plied him with many questions, and said:

"Oh, such dreams have I had! I thought I should never see you more; dreams about enemies lurking in bushes, and about wolves, and little children, and steep places, and I am so glad it is not true!"

"It is every word true," said the good man; "I have gone through it all; and now we must make haste, for the great Queen waits."

"And are you rich?" said the eager wife.

"Forever!" was the brief reply.

And the explanation came little by little. At first it was disappointing, but by and by it was better, and then better still, and at last they all started together, and, thank God, they all found the way to the great Queen's house, and every one was blessed, and enriched, and crowned. They lived forever in the great Queen's house, and never went out but to do the great Queen's errands. And such errands they were—to ask the poor, and the sick, and the mean to come; to bring in the hungry, the thirsty and the heavy laden; to tell the wanderers that whosoever would might come in, and to assure the very worst that none would be turned away.— H. R.

THE LITTLE MAID

2 Kings v: 2-4

Notice three things about her: Her bad fortune; her good fortune; her good use of her good fortune.

I. HER BAD FORTUNE.—She lived, we may suppose, in a quiet country home. Had parents to care for her, brothers and sisters to play with; her young life was bright and happy. One day rough soldiers rush into house and wrench her away, amid tears of all. This was her bad fortune.

No wars in America for many years past. Old men even have not seen a foreign army plundering and slaying in this country and carrying captive. True, our soldiers and sailors have had to carry on wars away, and at home. You will very likely never see a great battle in this land. Do you remember petition, "From our enemies," etc.? In Litany, "From plague, . . . battle," etc." National anthem of English Church, "Confound their politics," etc. So that there is little likelihood you will ever be taken captive to a strange land. But you will have to endure many troubles. Tears often roll down your cheeks even now. Greater trials are before you. Bear the little ones now, that you may be able to bear great ones when they come. Thank God He has placed you in a land of peace, and has yet dealt gently with you.

II. HER GOOD FORTUNE.—Soldiers have taken her a long way—to Damascus, perhaps. She is glad journey is over. She trembles to think what may happen to her. They hear that their captain's wife wants a waiting-maid. They bring her and sell her. Thus she is at last out of their rough hands, and finds herself in fine house with nice work. This was her *good fortune*.

Why was she chosen by this grand lady? Must have been many other little captive maids there. There was something, I think, neat in her dress and pleasing in her manner that attracted. All boys and girls not like this. She was most likely, modest, gentle, and quiet. If you wish to be liked and successful, you must be humble, have respect for those set over you—parents, teachers, etc. Avoid a rough manner, etc. We do not expect in children soberness of old age; but we expect them to be serious sometimes. Each young person should be, what little girl was once called, a bit of blue sky. Blue sky is bright and clear, so you should be cheerful and contented. But blue sky very calm, never moving, like face of person thinking upon solemn subject. There is a time to laugh and a time to be serious.

III. HER GOOD USE OF HER GOOD FORTUNE.— Naaman, fine, soldierly man, esteemed by Benhadad; loved by people whose lives and property he had saved by his bravery in battle. What a hearty reception they would give him on his return from some victory.

But when he takes off armor, and lays aside robes, lo! he is covered with scales of leprosy. Little maid would pity him. Pity is good; we should pity those in pain; pity not enough. In her compassion she was like Jesus weeping at the grave of Lazarus, but as He proceeded to dry the sisters' tears by restoring their brother, so she will do what she can. So you must help others to get rid of their troubles. Must do this even for your enemies; for Naaman was her enemy, and had killed many of her people. Yet she returns good for evil. How like Jesus, again! "Father, forgive them," etc.

What remedy does she propose? She has not forgotten Elisha; knew he could heal diseases. She speaks to mistress about him, saying, "Would God," etc. (verse 3). What surprise these words must have caused! How slow every one would be to believe her, and call her a silly little thing. And yet, strange to say, her mistress and master, and even the great king, believe her. Astonishing! I cannot account for it, except by supposing that, having never known her to tell a lie on any previous occasion, could not doubt her now. Beware of telling first lie. Afterwards people will not trust you. [*Illust.*—Dr. Livingstone was very proud of one of his forefathers, who, calling children round deathbed, said, "I have examined family, find all honest. Should any of you become dishonest, you do not belong to us. Dishonesty runs not in our blood; therefore be honest."] So I have examined character of little maid, and find in it no traces of untruth. If any of you give way to lying, you are no relation to her. Untruth runs not in blood of her real descendants. Therefore be ye truthful.

Relate rest of story about Naaman. His cure. His conversion.

Here press two points: (*a*) Remembering God when from home; (*b*) missionary spirit.

(*a*) Sore trial to ministers and teachers to find elder ones who leave our schools leave us entirely. Mingling with the careless, etc., they gradually forget what they have been taught, forget their God, their soul, eternity. Not so the little maid. Far from home, from pious parents—for must she not have had pious parents?—she still thinks upon God of her fathers. Oft tempted to go with mistress to temple of Rimmon. But no; she continues faithful amongst strangers and idolaters. Here give charge to continue with us tho absent from us.

(*b*) Note, she was a "little" maid; and yet means of mighty good. She wished to see heathen family with whom she lived converted. Illness of her master gave opportunity to do this, which she did not let slip. Result—Naaman was led to serve true God. Thus she was a little Jewish missionary to the Gentiles. You are little, but may do much good in same way. You have heard of God, been taught about Christ. Thousands ignorant of this; would you not like to share with them your knowledge? Would not like to be thought selfish. Then give your little pennies and dimes to send out missionaries to teach multitudes lying in darkness, etc., to come into light. Pray God to bless your little gifts to the heathen for whom they are intended. —*Selected.*

CHILDREN'S SERVICE

The Lord is my shepherd.—Ps. xxiii: 1

This is what David said at a time when he was in great trouble, brought on him by a bad son—Absalom. David was driven into a wilderness by this rebellious son; but he remembers that it is not all darkness—there is a bright side to the picture. He turns away his thoughts from the dark side and looks at the brightness, and his feelings find expression in this beautiful psalm. His painful position here in the wilderness reminds him of the tender and beautiful relation sustained by a shepherd to the sheep which he tends, feeds and guards. This relation God sustains to us:

I. He TENDS US.—God did not make us, and then leave us to ourselves. He has not done so with anything which He created. A blade of grass, a sparrow, a lily, are all mentioned in the Bible as receiving God's care; and they are mentioned to show us that God, who cares for such things, will much more care for us. He never leaves us. He abides forever with His sheep—a constant and never-tiring Shepherd.

II. He FEEDS US.—It was the duty of the Eastern shepherd—to whom David refers—to find ample pasture for his flock—to lead them hither and thither, that plenty might be found. God gives us our daily bread. The Lord provides. He feeds the young ravens. He furnishes food for all living things; and, above all and before all, He provides for His children, opens His bountiful hands, and satisfies the wants of every living thing.

III. He GUARDS US.—Like a good shepherd, He protects us from harm. Fierce beasts prowled about ready to devour the sheep, and the shepherd had, therefore, to be on constant watch against them. Shepherds often exposed themselves to danger while guarding the sheep. Our Shepherd laid down His life for His sheep. We have enemies who seek to devour us. Our enemies are very numerous, very cunning and very strong. David said if the Lord had not been on his side he would have been devoured. God is represented as our "Shepherd," "Shield," "*Wall of Fire,*" etc., etc. He never wearies, ever watches. Like a gentle nurse, He guards us night and day. No father, no mother is so loving, true and constant as God. To be the subjects of God's shepherdly care we must be His sheep. Only such have any claim on, or right to expect, the protection, sustenance and guardianship of God.

God the child's ally.—" Workers together with him."—2 Cor. vi: 1.

God calls upon every hand to help in His work, however small and feeble. It is not our skill or strength which will secure the results sought, but God's presence with us. God is our ally; we work *with* Him. Many a child has spoken a word, or done a deed, which, by God's blessing, has been the means of great good. One child against the world, with Christ to help him, is always in a majority. He cannot fail. There is no such word as fail to one who has God on his side. God waters the seed sown by tiny hands as readily as that scattered by His full-grown servants.—H. R.

WHAT THE LILIES TEACH US

BY REV. W. H. BOOTH, D.D.

Consider the lilies.—Matt. vi: 28

Who spoke these words? What scholar can name the mount? Uncertain—called the Mount of Beatitudes. Why? The sermon on the Mount. Probably the month of May. Christ drew lessons from a great variety of objects. Who can mention some? The mind —the bird—the storm, etc. We should learn from everything. "Consider." We must not simply look or listen, but examine, think about, and remember. The scene: Jesus in the midst probably sitting on some slight elevation. The disciples around Him. Who can name these disciples? The sun shining brightly. Everything spring-like, and not far off a field of lilies. Not like our lilies of the valley: about three feet high, all colors— white, purple, and blue. Pointing to them as they stand in their delicate beauty, He adds, "Consider the lilies," etc. See if they do not teach the very truths I am inculcating. We learn from them something concerning

I. OUR FATHER'S POWER.—Our earthly father is weak. There are many things he would do for us, but cannot. Our heavenly Father is almighty. We do not form our ideas of His power from big things only.

A butterfly's wing, or a daisy, tells us as much about Omnipotence as mountain or sea. The mightiest forces in universe not noisiest or most striking. Earthquakes, volcanoes, thunderstorms, hurricanes, tell us of God's power. But the light of sun, or moon, or law of gravitation tell us more. What would be the consequence if these were to fail. Illustrate by steam hammer used in foundries, which will crush with fearful force, or break a nutshell without injuring the kernel. The latter impresses more than the former with wonder. Variety in color, size and form of lilies another indication of God's power. Men repeat; God never. Our resources are so limited that we patent a good invention. God's resources so boundless He never needs to make two alike. A minister once told some children whom he was addressing that no two blades of grass, daisies, etc., were alike. They could not believe it; went to search, found it true, came back and confessed that he was right. *Learn.*—This power will *punish* or *save* us. We must all come into contact with it, either in the hands of *our Father* or our *Judge*. The lilies teach us also something concerning

II. Our Father's care.—The beauty and delicacy of all the parts. Compare the real and artificial flowers. Man's best imitation poor when placed by the side of God's creation. Nothing imperfect or slovenly in God's smallest works.

Note concerning lilies—

1. *They are comparatively insignificant, yet cared for.* Nothing too small for God's observation or providence. He knows the sparrows that die. He tells the swallows when to fly. He "paints the wayside flower." He "feeds the young ravens when they cry." He who hurts one of God's weakest and smallest creatures does it under His eye. *Learn.*—If God cares for birds and flowers, He must care for children more. Mungo Park learned this in the African desert, when stripped by savages and left to die. He had given himself up for lost, when he saw a small piece of moss, not an inch in size, clinging to a small stone, and perfect in its miniature beauty of flower. He thought, if God can take care of this little bit of moss in the desert, He can take care of me. This inspired him with energy; he rose to his feet, and after traveling some distance found friends and shelter.

2. *They are perishing, yet cared for.*—In a few weeks at most their beauty fades, and they disappear. Their life is short, yet no less care is bestowed upon them than upon the oak or the baobab, which often live a thousand years. How much more likely that God should care for us, who are to live for ever.

3. *They often grow amongst thorns, yet are cared for.*—This is very common in Palestine. But thorns do not destroy them. They make it difficult for man to reach or gather them. Many children are like "the lily among thorns." Drunken father or mother, or both, prayerless homes, cruel masters, pestilential neighborhood, evil examples—all tend to choke everything good. Yet as Jesus came out of Nazareth, so such lives may be shielded by God's providence and transformed by His grace. The lilies teach us also something concerning

III. Our frailty.—That is, our weakness and liability to sickness and death. When the south wind blows, which comes from the burning sands of Arabia, they wither and die in twenty-four hours. Not more frail than our lives. More than half the population of the world die before they are seventeen years old. Sickness wastes rapidly. Children especially are soon deprived of strength and sink into the grave. How many such cases we remember. Visit the graveyard and notice how many short graves.

" Nipped by the wind's untimely blast,
Parched by the sun's directer ray,
The momentary glories waste,
The short-lived beauties die away."

They also teach us something concerning

IV. Our future life.—When stem and flower wither, root does not die; it remains buried in the earth, to produce new life another year. When you wrap yourselves in wool and fur to keep out cold, God wraps up these bulbs to keep them from perishing. He covers them with mantle of snow. Altho invisible, they are not destroyed. When spring comes they re-appear, often more beautiful than before. Sometimes one root would bear fifty blossoms. Death is our winter. The body is laid in the ground. When the springtime of the resurrection comes, it will rise again more beautiful than ever. There are differences between the bodies of earth and those of heaven. No more hunger, or pain, or crying, or sin. Illustrate: Child admiring drops of rain on leaf after storm. Sun shining makes them look like crystals. Presently absorbed by heat. Child began to weep. Father pointed up to sky, where rainbow was arching the heavens. "There," he said, "the drops are far more beautiful up there than down here." The most happy and lovely lives here will be far more so in heaven. "They shine, as the stars, for ever and ever." The lilies also teach us something concerning

V. Jesus Christ.—He is called the "Lily of the Valley." "The fairest amongst ten thousand and altogether lovely." There are spots and flaws in the character of all others; none in His. Abraham, Lot, Noah, Job, David, Peter, Paul, were all imperfect. Christ alone is stainless and pure. Going into hot-house one day, was immediately struck with the appearance of a tall, slender, perfectly white flower of the lily species. There were others of various sizes and colors, but this one excelled all the rest in purity and stateliness. An emblem of Him who was "holy, harmless, undefiled," etc., "the fairest among ten thousand," etc.

1. *We may learn from everything around us.*

2. *We should study Nature and the Bible side by side.*—H. R.

THE STRONG MAN'S PALACE

By Rev. S. Winchester Adriance

Matt. xii: 29; Luke xi: 21, 22.

Jesus was very fond of painting pictures for those around Him. I do not mean that He sat down with a real brush and paint and canvas and painted in that way. His pictures were word-pictures. All His parables were like beautiful stories, and when any one tells a story so plainly that it seems as if you could see all that he is talking about—that is word-painting. Your mind does see them. Now this picture of the Strong Man's Palace is a word-picture. They had brought to Jesus a poor, miserable man. A great many things were the matter with him. He was blind, and that was bad enough. No beautiful sky, no green fields or daisies or lilies or birds, could he see in summer, no pure white snow in winter, and not even the kind face of Jesus could he see. But that was not all. He was dumb, too. He could not speak with any one, but just mumbled away his queer sounds. Nor could he sing, and all the way he could make people understand was by making signs with his fingers.

Still, for all that, he might have been happy. But he was miserable. There was an evil spirit in him that caused all this distress, and made his life wretched to himself and to all that loved him. So they brought him to Jesus, and as quickly as Jesus spoke, the evil spirit came out, and then he could speak and see. But some wicked people were angry at Jesus, and said that He was a bad man, and that the evil-spirit came out from the man because it was a friend of Jesus. Jesus said: "No, if I were bad I would love to have the bad stay in the man. But because I am good and want to do him good I cure him." And then He told this story of the Strong Man's House. In another place (Luke) Jesus calls it a wonderful palace. But a bad strong man had somehow or other gotten through the door, had moved all his goods in, had armed himself from head to foot with spears and knives, and there he was, saying to himself, "I am going to use this palace just as I like, and invite all my friends here." But, alas! this strong man was unclean and all his goods and friends were unclean. He left stains all over the palace, on the walls, on the floor, and whatever his hands or his feet touched was made filthy. Bad pictures were there, bad words and stories were said, and the longer he stayed the worse it was, until it did not seem at all like the sweet, beautiful palace it once was. Now a palace is meant for everything nice. It ought to have beautiful pictures on the walls, and clean floors, often of stones inlaid with wonderfully-colored marble. It has carved pillars, broad halls and sunny windows.

By and by, another still stronger Man, a great and good King, who really owned the palace, came by. With a quiet but clear voice He said to the porter at the door, "Let me in; this house is mine." And the bad man inside heard the voice. Now, altho the bad king hated the good King, yet he was afraid of Him. But the knock at the door made him very angry, and he made a horrible struggle. First he ordered the porter not to open the door, and then, trembling with rage, he tore around the palace, breaking everything he could find, and saying: "I will not leave." Then the Good Man broke through the door, rushed upon the bad man, took all his weapons away, and bound him hand and foot. The heart of the Good Man was sad to see the dirt and ruin all around. But He knew what to do. "Can this be the once beautiful palace?" He wondered. But He knew what to do; He went into every room, had everything washed, threw out and burned all the old pictures, spread on the table good food, and called the porter at the door to sit down with Him to eat, saying to him, "I will be your friend." Now and then the old man who had been staying around, came and listened, and whispered under the door to the porter, "Let me in." But the Good Man heard his voice and said "Begone."

Can you tell me who the bad man is?

Can any tell me what his goods are?

Can any tell me what this palace is?

Can any tell me who the porter is at the door?

Can any tell me who is the Good Strong Man?—H. R.

A FEW ANECDOTES

She Took Out the "If"

A little girl was awakened to anxiety about her soul at a meeting where the story of the leper was told.

One day, a poor leper came to Jesus and worshiped Him, saying, "Lord, if thou wilt, thou canst make me clean." And Jesus put forth His hand and touched him, saying, "I will; be thou clean;" and immediately his leprosy was cleansed.

Well, this dear little girl, who was anxious, said, "I noticed there was an 'if' in what the man said, but there was no 'if' in what Jesus said; so I went home and took out the 'if' by my granny's fireside; and I knelt down, and I said, 'Lord Jesus, Thou canst,

Thou wilt make me clean; I give myself to Thee.' "

My beloved little reader, have you thus come to Jesus? Oh! do come to Him! He can, He will make you clean—yes, whiter than snow. You are a sinner, and sin is a far worse disease than leprosy. Nothing can take it away but the blood of Jesus. Come to Him this very minute. For "behold, now is the accepted time; behold, now is the day of salvation!"—*Selected.*

"All About Our 'Straggles'"

Our Juniors take great delight in singing the song by Johnson Oatman, entitled, "There's not a Friend like the Lowly Jesus, No, Not One." Where the chorus reads, "Jesus knows all about our struggles," one of our sweetest little voices was heard singing above the rest, "Jesus knows all about our straggles."

Was she so far out of the way?—Rev. W. K. Crosby.

Whose Superscription?

Victor Hugo, describing the work of the comprachicos, those devilish instruments of the tyranny of a devilish age,—buying children to disfigure them into dwarfs, or other monstrosities—says: "These are the audacities of monarchical terrorism. The disfigured one was marked with the fleur-de-lys; they took from him the mark of God, they put on him the mark of the king."—B. O. K.

God on the Other Side

We had been teaching our little three-year-old boy the Sunday-School lesson. It was about Nehemiah's prayer. While undressing him for bed, his mother began to question him about what he had learned. In reply to one question he said: "It was Nehemiah, an—an—and God around on the other side."

In our haste we often forget that God is behind every good cause; and act as if all depended on ourselves; or as tho God took no notice of how we cast a ballot or neglect our duties.—S. I.

Two Stories

One little girl came forward in the meeting here. Her mother was a Church member. When she went home and said, "I have been converted; I have given my heart to Jesus to-day," her mother said, "You are too young; you don't know what it means."

Then the little girl went off crying with a broken heart.

When Church members degenerate and backslide that way, what wonder that we accomplish nothing? What wonder it is charged upon us that we are but dead forms, that we are but sounding brass and a tinkling cymbal? It is even so, and I cannot deny it when I talk with a skeptic many a time.

I knew a little child who went home out of one of our meetings. Her father was a great big, swearing man, a wicked man. She approached him timidly, almost afraid to tell him about it. He noticed it, and said, "What is it, daughter? What do you want to tell me? Speak it out."

So she said, "Papa, I don't know what you will think, but I went forward in the meeting to-day, and have been converted. I have given my heart to God, and I am going to pray for you."

The great big, swearing man looked at his little girl, who was only nine or ten years old and said, "Do you mean it?"

"Yes, papa, I mean it," said the little one.

Putting his arms around her he drew her head down on his breast, and the tears began to fill his eyes as he said, "You were afraid of wicked old papa, weren't you? But papa's glad if you mean it; he wouldn't do a thing to keep you back."

The infidelity of the Church breeds more skepticism and agnosticism than all the Ingersolls and Putnams in America.—M. B. Williams. B. A.

Bad Home Examples

There is too much home religion like that which led the Scotch boy to ask about heaven: "Will feyther be there? Then I'll nae gang!" and the little girl sent up-stairs to ask God to give her a better temper, to add, "and please, Lord, make mamma's temper better, too."

Going Alone

"Me want to go my lone," said a little tot, refusing her father's proffered hand, as she made her way painfully along over the slippery sidewalk. In a moment she had fallen, but she picked herself up repeating the words, "Me want to go my lone." Again she fell. This time her lips quivered as she rose, but to her father's words, "Daughter, take hold of papa's hand," she only replied as before, "Me want to go my lone."

This was repeated several times, the faltering steps becoming more and more bewildered and halting. Finally, after an unusually severe fall, she came back to her father, and, without a word, put her little hand in his big, strong one, looking up into his face with tearful yet trusting eyes. At last she was safe, The way was easy. With that sustaining arm she knew that all danger was past.

We think, perhaps, in the blind confidence and ignorance of youth, that our own strength is sufficient. We strive to forge ahead, but falter and fall by the way. At last it is borne in upon our saddened, weary souls that we need a higher strength, a larger and finer intelligence. Then it is that, like the little child, we come back to our Father, and with trusting faith place our hand in His. Then it is that we know for the first time what security and true guidance is.—S. S. T.

Outdone by a Boy

A lad in Boston, rather small for his age, works in an office as errand boy for four gentlemen who do business there. One day the gentlemen were chaffing him a little about being so small, and said to him:

" You will never amount to much; you never can do much business; you are too small."

The little fellow looked at them.

" Well," said he, " as small as I am, I can do something that neither of you four men can do."

" Ah, what is that? " said they.

" I don't know as I ought to tell you," he replied. But they were anxious to know and urged him to tell what he could do that neither of them were able to do.

" I can keep from swearing," said the little fellow.

There were some blushes on four manly faces and there seemed to be very little anxiety for further information on the point. —C. A.

SUGGESTIVE THOUGHTS AND ILLUSTRATIONS

BOY, A Converted.—I knew a boy some years ago, whose father was a miserable drunken wretch and infidel, and he would not allow a praying man under his roof, for he said a man that prayed was nothing but a black-hearted hypocrite. Somebody got hold of his little boy and got him into the Sabbath-school, and he was converted. One day afterward the old man caught him praying, and he took him by the collar and jerked him to his feet, commanding him with oaths never to be caught doing that again or he would have to leave home forever. Twice after that he caught him in the act of praying, and the last time told him to leave his house forever. The little fellow packed up his things in a handkerchief, went down into the kitchen where his mother was and bade her good-by, then went and bade his little brother and sisters good-by, and as he passed his father on his way to the door, he reached up his arms to put them around his father's neck, and said: " Good-by, father. As long as I live I will pray for you," and he went down the street, but he had not gone a great while before his father came after him and said, " If that is Christianity, I want it." And the boy went back and prayed with his father and led him to Christ.—MOODY.

BOY, Heroic.—A boy who had been trained by the missionaries in the Loyalty Islands. set sail in a fishing boat with three other persons. A little way out they were capsized, but clung to the keel for support. After being sixteen hours in the water, they drifted ashore, upon Woody Island, where neither water nor provisions of any kind could be procured. Their long exposure and exhaustion made it necessary that something should be done at once. The boy called Billy proposed to swim to another island. three and a-half miles away. In his exhaustion it was a most hazardous enterprise. On starting he said : " Suppose me catch the land, me see you again; suppose me die, good-by." He reached the island, obtained aid and rescued his companions. All were full of gratitude and praise for him. He said, " Don't think of me. Thank God; it is God who has done it."—F. I.

BOYS AND MOTHERS.—Some one has written beautifully of the boy in the following manner. Here is a whole sermon in a few sentences:

Of all the love-affairs in the world, none can surpass the true love of a big boy for his mother. It is a love pure and noble—honorable in the highest degree to both. I do not mean merely a dutiful affection. I mean a love which makes a boy gallant and courteous to his mother, saying to everybody plainly that he is fairly in love with her. Next to the love of the husband, nothing so crowns a woman's life with honor as this second love, this devotion of her son to her. And I never yet knew a boy turn out bad who began by falling in love with his mother. Any man may fall in love with a fresh-faced girl, and the man who is gallant enough with the girl may neglect the worn and weary wife; but the boy who is a lover to his mother in her middle age is a true knight, who will love his wife as much in the sear-leafed autumn as he did in the daisied springtime.—*Selected*.

BOYS, Danger to.—We once saw the sentence " Perishable, don't switch off," chalked on a car belonging to a freight train. Careless conductors sometimes leave freight cars on side tracks for a day. Here was one that could not be left even one day off the main track. It had fruit, or something else, on board, which must be gotten to market at once. A day lost might bring the fruit in a day late. Those boys in your class are " perishable property." Don't lose your hold of them an hour. Don't " switch " them off the track by any carelessness or irregularity, or dullness or severity of yours. Hold them firmly and steadily.—J. H. VINCENT.

CHILDHOOD.—Childhood, in being the period when the currents of life take their rise and assume their direction, is well paralleled by the watershed. The Mississippi and the Red River of the North have their sources but a few miles apart, on opposite sides of the same watershed. But what a difference those few miles make in the character and usefulness of the two streams ! The one starts northward, and, flowing 750 miles, empties itself into Lake Winnipeg, the other flows southward, and sweeps majestically along for 2,800 miles, bearing on its bosom the commerce of a mighty country, enriching millions of busy toilers, and never stopping till its waters are mingled with those of the measureless sea.—H. R.

CHILDREN, Putting Stumbling Blocks in the Way of.—(1) By teaching that children cannot become Christians while young; (2) by neglect of their religious training; (3) by the example of parents who are more interested in worldly things than in religion, who neglect family prayer, and the Church, and Sabbath-school; (4) by "all conduct on the part of the Church, the teacher, or the parent which tends to repress, chill, or check the enthusiasm of childhood for Christ, and darken its simple faith in Him;" (5) by faultfinding with the Church and good people in their presence, thus lessening their respect and reverence for them. (6) Children are hindered from coming to Christ by building the audience rooms, conducting the worship, forming the choir almost solely for the benefit of the adults, and doing very little for the convenience and instruction of the children.

Compare the disciples hindering little children from going to Jesus (Mark x: 13, 14).—P.

CHILDREN'S AGE, The.—Nearly all the Christian denominations have come to adopt the second Sunday in June as "Children's Day!" In some of the Churches it is called by other names, as "Rose Sunday," for example. Not only do we have a Day for the special benefit of the children, but it may almost be said that this is the Children's Age. Naturally the religion of Him who said, "Suffer the little children and forbid them not to come unto me," has ever put emphasis upon the necessity of caring for the children. The Churches all have their children's societies of various kinds, while the community pays especial attention to, and taxes itself heavily in the interest of the proper training and culture of the children. The law books of all the states of our own land are covered with statutes in the interest of those who are the hope of the future.

Beyond the school laws there are many enactments for the prevention of cruelty to children. In Massachusetts children under fourteen years of age are forbidden employment in manufacturing, mechanical and mercantile establishments, while the public schools are in session unless they can read and write. In New Hampshire, an act has been passed prohibiting the employment of children under ten years of age. In Michigan, the employment of children under ten years of age by showmen, the giving of obscene books, pamphlets, etc., to minors, and the exhibition of the same in view of passing children, are prohibited. In New York, by a bill passed in 1885, children under twelve years of age, unable to write, are prohibited employment. Children's Aid Societies, and Societies for the Prevention of Cruelty to Children, exist in all the large cities of the land.—P. I.

CHILDREN, Save the.—Were we more anxious about the children we would do more work of a Christian kind. The old man seems to be beyond our reach, but the little child seems to be made for Christ. It would seem—do not let us shrink from the term—*natural* for every little child to put out his arms to cling to the Child of Bethlehem. Save the children and you will purify society; expend your solicitude upon the young, opening, tender life, and you shall see the result of your concern after many days. Services should be constituted for children; the old people have had the sanctuary too long; their ears are sated with eloquence; their minds are stored with names that never turn into inspirations; Churches might be built for children, and preachers trained to speak to them alone. We have reversed all things and thus have gone astray. . . .

A poet says he was nearer heaven in his childhood than he ever was in after days, and he sweetly prayed that he might return through his yesterdays and through his childhood back to God. That is chronologically impossible—locally and physically not to be done, and yet that is the very miracle which is to be performed in the soul—in the spirit; we must be "born again."—REV. JOSEPH PARKER.

CHILDREN'S QUESTIONS, How to Answer.—When children ask you questions about gray hairs, and wrinkles in the face, and sighs that have no words, and smiles too bright to be carved upon the radiant face by the hands of hypocrisy,—when they ask you about kneeling at the altar, speaking into the vacant air, and uttering words to an unseen and in an invisible Presence,—when they interrogate you about your great psalms, and hymns, and anthem-bursts of thankfulness, what is your reply to these? Do not be ashamed of the history. Keep steadily along the line of fact. Say what happened to *you*, and magnify God in the hearing of the inquirer.—REV. JOSEPH PARKER.

CHILDREN, Taking Care of the.—One chapter in George William Curtis' volume, PRUE AND I, is called "*Mr. Titbottom's Spectacles.*" The magical quality of these spectacles was, that when their owner looked through them at people he ceased to see them as they ordinarily appeared on the street; he saw their real essential character personified. Wonderful were the revelations that were made. He looked at one man and saw nothing but a ledger. Another was simply a billiard cue, another a bank bill, another a great hog, or a wolf, or a vulgar fraction. On the other hand, he saw the good that others failed to see. One of his school teachers was a deep well of living water in which he saw the stars. Another was a tropical garden full of fruits and flowers. In one woman's heart lay concealed in the depth of character great excellencies like pearls at the bottom of the sea, little suspected by most, but perhaps love is nothing else than the sight of them by one person. Another, called an old maid, was a white lily, fresh, luminous and fragrant still. Another's nature was a tropic in which the sun shone, and birds sang, and flowers bloomed forever. His wrinkled grandmother appeared as a Madonna, "and I have yet heard of no queen, no belle, no imperial beauty whom in grace, and brilliancy, and persuasive courtesy she might not have surpassed."

It is with some such vision that the angels often see in the child and the lowly possible saints and martyrs, men and women who shall change this world for the better, angels excelling in strength, with victors' crowns and harps of heavenly praise.

So, too, should the Church see these possibilities in her children and never for one moment despise them. That Church will be most successful which does the most for her children, trains them, educates them, welcomes them, arranges services for them, favors the Sunday-school, furnishes them with the best rooms, and plenty of books and everything that contributes to their nurture.

The town, too, is wise that does not despise her children, but cares more for school-houses than for roads, and selects her teachers more carefully than any other officers of the town.

Good old Dr. Tyng said, at one time, "In my Church I haven't hesitated for years, when the choice came between one child and two old men, to take the child." And the life and prosperity of that Church, under Dr. Tyng as its pastor, showed the wisdom of this Christ-like way of estimating childhood.—P.

CHILDREN, The Faith of.—A Christian mother once came to me to ask my counsel concerning her son. He had admired and loved his Sunday-school teacher; but he had learned that that teacher was accustomed to attend the theater, and at once he lost confidence in his teacher's Christian character. "Nothing that that teacher can say will now have any influence with my son," said the mother. "What can I do? Shall I take my boy out of that class? It seems useless for him to remain there any longer." The question is not in such a case whether the teacher had a moral right to pursue the course which he did concerning theater-going; but whether it was wise for him thus to endanger his influence with his scholars.—Rev. H. Clay Trumbull.

CHILDREN TO LOOK UP, Teach the.—Among the old Romans there prevailed the touching custom of holding the face of every new born babe toward the heavens, signifying by their presenting its forehead to the stars that it was to look above the world into celestial glories. That was only a vain superstition; but Christ has taught us how to realize the old Pagan yearning.—Dr. L. A. Banks.

CHILD'S ANALYSIS OF MOTIVE, A.—A child will not, as a rule, go far astray in analysis of his own motives. In this matter it were well if some grown-up children would be as honest in owning the real motives governing neglect of God's word, and of prayer. Little Raymond is generally a thoughtful

boy, if not always a model in conduct. I sometimes think he is better than most boys. His nature has been refined by much suffering of body. One day he had done something he knew to be wrong. When going to his bed his mother said:

"Ray, are you not going to pray to-night?"

"No," said he.

"Why not?" questioned his mother.

The answer came after a moment of thought, his face hidden in the bed-clothes: "Because, Mamma, I am ashamed to pray."—Rev. W. K. Crosby.

CONVERT, A Young.—A woman whose testimony we are prepared unhesitatingly to endorse, told us that in one of Mr. Hammond's meetings, held in Glasgow last spring, a young lady came up to her and said:—

"Do you not remember me?"

"No, I do not," was the reply.

"Do you not remember a little child four years old, whom you found in one of Mr. Hammond's meetings, seventeen years ago, weeping very bitterly, and whose nurse was afraid to take her home, to whom you spoke kind words about Jesus?"

"Yes, I do, perfectly," was the reply.

"I was that little girl, and I then became a Christian, and have continued so ever since," was the unexpected answer.

The truth is, we have not sufficient confidence in the Spirit and Word of God when we speak to children with the one distinct aim of leading them at once to the Savior. It is not enough to sow in their young minds seeds of truth which may ripen by and by. Our duty is to tell them plainly they are lost sinners, whom Jesus came to save. When they learn their condition as the Scripture states it, and when they hear of the gracious Savior,

Who left His throne on high,
And came into the world to die,

their young hearts are touched, and an impression often is made which no lapse of time can efface. We have been far too faithless about the conversion of children. We have learned somehow or other to regard childhood as an unpromising field, which it is a loss of labor to cultivate; while in truth it is the most hopeful field into which any servant of Christ can enter.—Selected.

EXAMPLES, A Few.—Dr. Arnold, a great teacher, and the father of Matthew Arnold, said: "All who have meditated upon the art of governing mankind, have felt that the fate of empires depended on the education of the young."

It was the remark of John Bright, that great and good statesman, "I think that the influence of a good man and a good woman teaching ten or twelve children in a class, is an influence in this world and the world to come, which no man can measure, and the responsibility of which no man can calculate. It may raise and bless the individual. It may give comfort in the family circle. For the blessing which the child receives in the school it may take home to the family. It may check the barbarism even of the nation."

The following is the testimony of our great orator Webster: "If we work upon marble, it will perish; if we work upon bronze, time will efface it; if we rear temples they will crumble to the dust; but if we work upon immortal souls, if we embue them with right principles of action, with just fear of wrong and love of right, we engrave on those tablets something which no time can obliterate, but which will grow brighter and brighter to all eternity."

The following, is from the brilliant French writer, Edmond About: "Our children," he says, "are side altars in the temples of our lives; manhood's power of reasoning and calculation are sorry substitutes for their distinct consciences. He who plants a tree does well; he who fells and saws it into planks does well; he who makes a bench of the planks does well; he who sitting on a bench teaches a child, does better than the rest. The first three have added to the common capital of humanity; the last has added something to humanity itself."—*Selected.*

GIRL'S GIFT, A Little.—A child, dying, wished to give something to the missionary cause. All she had left was a canary bird she dearly prized. That she gave. It was brought to the missionary meeting. The story was told, and one in the audience arose and bid $300 for the bird; $400 was bid; another, $500, and it was sold. That little girl's gift was not despised by God, or man.—*Selected.*

RAJAH, A Thoughtful.—Ali Schind, one of the Rajahs of India, was noted for the uprightness of his dealings, and for his nice sense of honor, even towards the lowest of his subjects. One day while out hunting with his courtiers, he became hungry, and ordered some of the game they had taken to be dressed for an immediate repast. This requirement had been anticipated by his attendants, and they had brought with them bread, sauces, plates, and all they needed—all except *salt,* which had been forgotten. There was, however, a village near by, and a boy was hastily despatched to procure some. The Rajah, hearing the order given, called after the lad to inquire whether he had taken money to pay for the salt. At this his attendants expressed some surprise, wondering that so great a man should trouble himself about such trifles, and adding that those who had the happiness of living under his dominion had no right to murmur, if he should claim at their hands gifts of much greater value than a handful of salt.

"Justice," replied the Rajah, "is of as much importance in *little* as in great matters; and the fact of my conferring benefits on my subjects at one time gives me no right to oppress them in the smallest particular at another. All the wrongs and oppressions under which mankind groan began in *little* things, and if we would prevent great sins or great calamities, we must strive against the *beginnings* of evil."

Let our young readers mark this, and if they desire to become good and great men, let them in *childhood* form habits of integrity, virtue, and piety.—C. W.

STRAWBERRIES, The First.—A little girl once had a bed of strawberries. Very anxious was she that they should ripen and be fit to eat. The time came.

"Now for a feast," said her brother to her one morning, as he picked some beautiful ones for her to eat.

"I cannot eat these," said she, "for they are the first ripe fruit."

"Well," said her brother, "all the more reason for our making a feast, for they are the greater treat."

"Yes; but they are the first ripe fruit."

"Well, what of that?"

"Dear father told us that he used to give God the first out of all the money he made, and that then he always felt happier in spending the rest; and I wished to give God the first of my strawberries too."

"Ah! but," said her brother, "how can you give strawberries to God? And even if you could, He would not care for them."

"Oh! I have found out a way," said she. "Jesus said, 'Inasmuch as ye have done it unto one of the least of these my brethren, ye have done it unto me,' and I mean to go with them to Mrs. Perkins' dying child, who never sees a strawberry; they are so poor."

Away went the children to give them to the dying child, and when they saw her put out her thin arms and take the ripe, round fruit in her little shriveled fingers, and when they saw her eyes glisten, and her little faded lips smile, they felt as if they had a richer treat than if they had kept the ripe fruit for themselves; and something within them told them that God had accepted their little offering.—*Selected.*

SUNDAY-SCHOOL, Faithful to the.—James Kershaw, of England, once a poor boy, but afterward a member of Parliament, revisited the Sabbath-school of his early days, and looked over the old class-books. He was gratified to see that for seven years while a scholar, and fourteen years while a teacher, he had not once been absent. He then expressed his conviction that his attachment to the Sabbath-school and his deep regard for the Sabbath, were the foundation of all his blessings, temporal and spiritual.

SUNDAY-SCHOOL, Recommendation of the.—A wholesale liquor dealer one day accosted Moses F. Odell, the well-known superintendent of Sand Street M. E. S. S., Brooklyn: "I want you to send me a first-rate clerk—one that you can recommend. He must be prompt, smart, and reliable. In short, he must be a first-class Sunday-school boy." "Why do you want a clerk out of my Sunday-school? You're not a Christian; you don't attend Church; your children are not in the Sunday-school." "Oh, that's all very well," replied the German free-thinker, "I can take care of myself; but I won't have anybody in my store that I can't trust. I know these Sunday-school boys, and they'll do to tie to. They won't drink my liquor, nor rob my till." It must be said that Sunday-school boys do not do the foul work of liquor dealers, but the indorsement is good.—F. II.

SUNDAY-SCHOOLS, Advantage of.—A little boy said to his irreligious mother, as she smoothed his dying pillow, " Oh, mother, you have never taught me anything about Jesus; and had it not been for the Sabbath-school teachers, I should now be dying without a hope in Him, and must have been lost forever."—F. II.

SUNDAY-SCHOOLS, A Tribute to.— " What gives you the greatest satisfaction as you take a retrospective view of your long and eventful life, doctor?"

This was the question put by a visitor to one whose name stands for all that is good and noble, and one who has earned an enviable reputation as scholar and linguist; but the answer came promptly:

" My connection with various Sunday-schools, both as scholar and teacher."

The young man who told of the interview, granted for his father's sake, said: " This answer seemed to me so suggestive of weakening power that I thought those who say that ' his mind has brightened as his hair was whitened,' were mistaken. I think he must have read my thoughts, or judged me by the average youth, for after a moment's silence the venerable doctor said emphatically:

" ' Yes, my young friend, as I review my threescore years and ten, all the honors heaped upon me because of my research along the lines in which you are so greatly interested, dwindle to nothingness in comparison to the satisfaction I feel in knowing that until the Lord shut me in I never absented myself from Sunday-school, where new treasures were unfolded as teacher and scholar studied the Book of books.'

" I wanted to talk of the books of which he was the author," said my informant, " but there was no opportunity, for when the aged scholar was once started on his love of Bible study, all else was crowded out. But I am free to confess that after listening to one who is surely a type of ' Thine age shall be clearer than the noonday,' I was ready to give heed to the parting injunction: ' Make it your first aim to study the Bible, for its precepts alone make life worth the living.' "—HELENA H. THOMAS.—U. G. N.

SUNDAY-SCHOOLS, Mission of.—A new and beautiful flower has recently been discovered in the State of Texas. It is called the compass flower, because all its petals point to the north. In sunshine and in storm, by day and by night, the little flower points northward, and tho the traveler may perchance be lost in the Texan wilds, yet, if he can only find one of these little compass flowers, he may, by looking at it, find his bearings and ascertain the true and right way. Now, the mission of the Sabbath-school is to sow the seeds of truth in the heart of the little ones; those seeds will spring up as the seeds of flowers, and the blossoms will appear, beautiful and lovely in the sight of heaven, and as this compass flower points toward the north, they will point toward Christ. And gazing upon these compass flowers of truth, planted by the instrumentality of some humble Sunday-school teacher, many a poor wanderer may be brought back to the way of peace and righteousness.—*Anon.*

TONGUES, Velvet.—When I was a boy, I and a number of my playmates had rambled through the woods and fields till, quite forgetful of the fading night, we found ourselves far from home; we had lost our way. It happened that we were nearer our home than we thought, but how to get to it was the question.

By the edge of the field we saw a man coming along, and we ran to ask him to tell us. Whether he was in trouble or not I do not know, but he gave us some very surly answer. Just then there came along another man who, with a smile on his face, said, " Jim, a man's tongue is like a cat's; it is either a piece of velvet or a piece of sandpaper, just as he likes to use it and to make it; you always seem to use your tongue for sand-paper." And then he pleasantly told us the way home. Try the velvet, children.—S. S. V.

POETRY

The Children's Hour

BY HENRY WADSWORTH LONGFELLOW

Between the dark and the daylight,
  When night is beginning to lower,
Comes a pause in the day's occupations,
  That is known as the children's hour.

I hear in the chamber above me
  The patter of little feet,
The sound of a door that is opened,
  And voices soft and sweet.

From my study I see in the lamplight,
  Descending the broad hall stair,
Grave Alice and laughing Allegra,
  And Edith with golden hair.

A whisper and then a silence;
  Yet I know by their merry eyes
They are plotting and planning together
  To take me by surprise.

A sudden rush from the stairway,
  A sudden raid from the hall,
By three doors left unguarded,
  They enter my castle wall.

They climb up into my turret,
O'er the arms and back of my chair;
If I try to escape, they surround me;
They seem to be everywhere.

They almost devour me with kisses,
Their arms about me entwine,
Till I think of the Bishop of Bingen
In his Mouse-Tower on the Rhine.

Do you think, O blue-eyed banditti,
Because you have scaled the wall,
Such an old mustache as I am
Is not a match for you all!

I have you fast in my fortress,
And will not let you depart,
But put you into the dungeon
In the round tower of my heart.

And there will I keep you forever,
Yes, forever and a day,
Till, the walls shall crumble to ruin,
And molder in dust away.

Beauty of Childhood

By Nathaniel Parker Willis

Beautiful, beautiful childhood! with a joy
That like a robe is palpable, and flung
Out by your ev'ry motion! delicate bud
Of the immortal flower that will unfold
And come to its maturity in heaven!
I weep your earthly glory. 'Tis a light
Lent to the new-born spirit, that goes out
With the first idle wind. It is the leaf
Fresh flung upon the river, that will dance
Upon the wave that stealeth out its life,
Then sink of its own heaviness. The face
Of the delightful earth will to your eye
Grow dim; the fragrance of the many flowers
Be noticed not, and the beguiling voice
Of nature in her gentleness will be
To manhood's senseless ear inaudible.

Crown of Childhood

The cows are lowing along the lane,
The sheep to the fold have come
And the mother looks from the cottage door,
To see how the night comes over the moor,
And calls the children home.

Their feet are bare in the dusty road,
Their cheeks are tawny and red;
They have waded the shallows below the mill,
They have gathered wild roses up the hill,
A crown for each tangled head.

The days will come, and the days will go,
And life hath many a crown,
But none that will press upon manhood's
brow
As light as the roses resting now
On the children's foreheads brown.
F. *I.

A Farewell

By Charles Kingsley

My fairest child, I have no song to give you;
No lark could pipe to skies so dull and gray;
Yet, ere we part, one lesson I can leave you,
For every day:

Be good, sweet maid, and let who will be
clever;
Do noble things, not dream them, all day
long:
And so make life, death, and that vast forever
One grand, sweet song!

Blessing upon Children

By James Grahame

" Suffer that little children come to Me,
Forbid them not." Emboldened by His words,
The mothers onward press; but, finding vain
The attempt to reach the Lord, they trust
their babes
To strangers' hands; the innocents, alarmed
Amid the throng of faces all unknown,
Shrink, trembling, till their wandering eyes
discern
The countenance of Jesus, beaming love
And pity; eager then they stretch their arms,
And, cowering, lay their heads upon His
breast.

Example for Children

By Charles Wesley

Lamb of God, I look to Thee,
Thou shalt my example be;
Thou art gentle, meek, and mild:
Thou wast once a little child.

Fain I would be as Thou art,
Give me Thy obedient heart;
Thou art pitiful and kind:
Let me have Thy loving mind.

Let me above all fulfil
God my heavenly Father's will;
Never His good Spirit grieve,
Only to His Glory live.

Loving Jesus, gentle Lamb,
In Thy gracious hands I am:
Make me, Savior, what Thou art;
Live Thyself within my heart.

I shall then show forth Thy praise;
Serve Thee all my happy days;
Then the world shall always see
Christ, the Holy Child, in me.

Weariness

By Henry Wadsworth Longfellow

O little feet! that such long years
Must wander on through hope and fears,
Must ache and bleed beneath your load;
I, nearer to the wayside inn
Where toil shall cease and rest begin,
I am weary, thinking of your road!

O little hands! that, weak or strong,
Have still to serve or rule so long,
Have still so long to give or ask;
I, who so much with book and pen
Have toiled among my fellow-men,
Am weary, thinking of your task.

O little hearts! that throb and beat
With such impatient, feverish heat,
  Such limitless and strong desires;
Mine, that so long has glowed and burned,
With passions into ashes turned,
  Now covers and conceals its fires.

O little souls! as pure and white
And crystalline as rays of light
  Direct from Heaven, their source divine;
Refracted through the mist of years,
How red my setting sun appears,
  How lurid looks this soul of mine!

Children

By Henry Wadsworth Longfellow

Ah! what would the world be to us
  If the children were no more?
We should dread the desert behind us
  Worse than the dark before.

What the leaves are to the forest,
  With light and air for food,
Ere their sweet and tender juices
  Have been hardened into wood,—

That to the world are children;
  Through them it feels the glow
Of a brighter and sunnier climate
  Than reaches the trunks below.

Come to me, O ye children!
  And whisper in my ear
What the birds and the winds are singing
  In your sunny atmosphere.

For what are all our contrivings,
  And the wisdom of our books,
When compared with your caresses,
  And the gladness of your looks?

Ye are better than all the ballads
  That ever were sung or said;
For ye are living poems,
  And all the rest are dead.

Hymn for Children's Sunday

Anonymous

Ten thousand thanks, O Lord, be Thine,
  For flowers to crown this summer land,
For dews to fall and sun to shine,
  For birds to sing and airs so bland!

But more we thank Thee for the flowers
  That bud and blossom in the home,
Like song-birds, making glad the hours,
  Wherever straying feet may roam.

Fairer than all these flowers of June,
  The children at their work or play;
Sweeter their song, with hearts in tune,
  Than wild bees' hum or skylarks' lay!

Lord, bless them with June's wealth of life,
  Grown golden for the life above!
Make strong to win in hours of strife,
  And crown them with Thy saving love!

Hark to the Children's Voices

By George Edward Martin

Hark to the children's voices!
  Hark to their cry so clear!
"Jesus, the Christ, is coming,
  Jesus is drawing near:
Near to the city portals,
  Near to the church's door,
Near to the homes of the rich of earth
  And the lowly, whose lot He bore."

Refrain

Lift up your heads, ye portals,
  Swing open, wide and high!
Jesus, the King, is coming,
  Jesus is drawing nigh!
Singing, because He bids us,
  Loudly the challenge rings—
Swing open wide ev'ry heart-door now,
  At the call of the King of kings!

Hark to the children's voices!
  Hark to their cry so clear!
"Jesus, the Christ, is coming,
  Jesus is drawing near—
Faith, with her heav'nly vision,
  Hope, with her sunny cheer,
Love in whose light Faith knows no night
  And Hope hath no blame or fear."
                Refrain.

Hark to the children's voices!
  Hark to their glad refrain!
Out from the temple holy
  Calling to men again:
"Open your hearts, oh sinners,
  Welcome the Savior King,
Live in the light that can know no night,
  In the joy of the ransomed sing."
                Refrain.

Greeting Song

By Laura E. Newell

We would greet you now, this joyous Children's day,
With a garland of sunshine and song.
We would bid you welcome; heaven cheer your way!
May your hearts all be happy and strong!

Duet.

  Onward, onward march!
    Marching all together;
  Life shall still be bright,
    Till the day is done;
  Onward ever as we roam!

Refrain

We are marching onward in the narrow way,
  And we greet you with anthems of praise.
In the golden sunshine of this Children's day,
  We our hearts unto heaven would raise.

How the Father's love to us this day is shown,
  As His goodness and mercy we see:
We would follow Jesus, who doth love His own;
  Oh salvation is boundless and free!

DUET.

Christian soldiers, on!
Onward, valiant ever;
Fearless, strong and true,
We'll our way pursue,
Till His glory we shall view.
REFRAIN.

Ancient Hymn

BY ST. AMBROSE

Shepherd of tender youth,
Guiding in love and truth,
Through devious ways;
Christ, our triumphant King,
We come Thy name to sing,
And here our children bring,
To shout Thy praise.

Thou art our holy Lord;
The all-subduing Word,
Healer of strife;
Thou didst Thyself abase,
That from sin's deep disgrace
Thou mightest save our race,
And give us life.

Ever be Thou our Guide,
Our Shepherd and our pride,
Our staff and song:
Jesus, Thou Christ of God,
By Thy perennial word,
Lead us where Thou hast trod,
Our faith make strong.

So now, and till we die,
Sound we Thy praises high,
And joyful sing:
Let all the holy throng,
Who to Thy Church belong,
Unite and swell the song
To Christ our King!

Jerusalem

BY GEORGE EDWARD MARTIN

Last night as I lay sleeping, there came a
dream most fair:
I stood in old Jerusalem, beside the temple
there:
I heard the children singing, and ever as they
sang,
Methought the voice of angels from heaven
in answer rang.

REFRAIN

Jerusalem! Jerusalem!
Lift up your gates and sing
Hosanna in the highest!
Hosanna to your King!
Hosanna in the highest!
Hosanna to your King!

And then methought my dream was changed,
the streets no longer rang:
Hush'd were the glad Hosannas the little
children sang:
The sun grew dark with mystery, the moon
was cold and chill,
As the shadow of a cross arose upon a lonely
hill.

REFRAIN

Jerusalem! Jerusalem!
Hark how the angels sing
Hosanna in the highest!
Hosanna to your King!
Hosanna in the highest!
Hosanna to your King!

Well May the Church Keep Children's Day

BY GEORGE EDWARD MARTIN

Well may the Church keep Children's Day,
And thus draw near the Son,
Who gained His richest human realm,
When children's hearts were won.
Well may the Church keep Children's Day,
And thus draw near the skies,
For in the children's sunny hearts,
The light of heaven lies.

Well may the Church keep Children's Day,
She keeps her greatness then,
E'en now the Christ uplifts a child,
Above all sinful men.
Oh, happy day! Oh, heavenly hour!
When thus the Church shall stand,
Like Christ with smile and touch of grace,
Amid the children's band. Amen.

Sunbeam Band

BY LAURA E. NEWELL

FIRST CHILD

We're a little band of sunbeams,
Happy, happy all day long,
And our lives are full of sunshine,
As our hearts are full of song.

SECOND CHILD

Hither, thither, playing, straying,
Do we wander to and fro,
Gathering the sweetest blossoms,
Singing gaily as we go.

THIRD CHILD

Smiling as the skies above us,
On this lovely Children's Day,
Thankful for the friends who love us,
Joyful in our work or play.

FOURTH CHILD

You may think a band of sunbeams
Have not any work to do;
But we have, and help each other
Trying to be good and true.

FIFTH CHILD

Jesus loves us. Do you wonder
That our hearts are glad and light?
When on earth He blessed the children,
And He made dark places bright.

SIXTH CHILD

So would we, a band of sunbeams,
Strive to scatter light and joy,
And to help to make earth better,
While God's praise our tongues employ.

ALL

And, whatever may befall us,
   We God's sunbeams still would be,
Trusting Him who loves the children,
   And who cares for you and me.

In the Way He Should Go

BY REGINALD HEBER

By cool Siloam's shady rill
   How fair the lily grows;
How sweet the breath beneath the hill
   Of Sharon's dewy rose.
Lo, such the child whose early feet
   The paths of peace have trod,
Whose secret heart, with influence sweet,
   Is upward drawn to God.

By cool Siloam's shady rill
   The lily must decay;
The rose that blooms beneath the hill
   Must shortly fade away.
And soon, too soon, the wintry hour
   Of man's maturer age
May shake the soul with sorrow's power,
   And stormy passion's rage.

O Thou, whose infant feet were found
   Within Thy Father's shrine,
Whose years, with changeless virtue crowned,
   Were all alike divine!

Dependent on Thy bounteous breath,
   We seek Thy grace alone,
In childhood, manhood, age, and death,
   To keep us still Thine own.

The Sweet Story

BY MRS. J. LUKE

I think, when I read that sweet story of old,
   When Jesus was here among men,
How He called little children as lambs to His
      fold,
   I should like to have been with them then.

I wish that His hands had been placed on
      my head,
   That His arm had been thrown around me,
And that I might have seen His kind look
      when He said,
   " Let the little ones come unto me."

Yet still to His footstool in prayer I may go,
   And ask for a share in His love;
And if I now earnestly seek Him below,
   I shall see Him and hear Him above :—

In that beautiful place He is gone to prepare
   For all who are washed and forgiven :
And many dear children are gathering there,
   " For of such is the kingdom of heaven."

TRINITY SUNDAY

(June)

TRINITY SUNDAY immediately follows Whitsunday, and is set apart for the honor of the Holy Trinity. Much obscurity surrounds the date of the origin of this holy day. It seems not to have been known to the fathers of the early centuries, and no corresponding festival has been discovered at any time in the separated Greek Church. Benedict XI. introduced it into the calendar in 1305, but the general establishment of Trinity Sunday as a common festival of the Western Church dates from the decree of John XXII., who died in 1334.

" The late appearance of Trinity Sunday among the settled Holy Days of the Church is to be readily understood in the light of the unique character of that celebration. It is not, as other feasts, the commemoration of an event—not the memorial of a phase of divine, or angelic, or saintly activity or passion. It is rather the commemoration of a systematized result of many separate and several facts of revelation—of the nexus and relation of several simple propositions, each of which, involving the Infinite and the Self-Existent, involves also the unthinkable and the incomprehensible. In its ontological doctrine, there is nothing necessarily of human interest. Reason is dazzled and transcended; the festival is a festival of faith, of orthodoxy, of a creed." *

Trinity Sunday concludes the festival part of the Church Year in the West, and in the Anglican Church the Sundays from Whitsuntide to Advent are counted as the first, second, etc., till the twenty-sixth Sunday after Trinity.

In the course of a sermon on Jude 3, Bishop W. R. Huntington thus writes of the importance of the doctrine of the Trinity: "The doctrine of the Divine Trinity in Unity has proved itself the conservator and upholder of other beliefs which appeal more evidently to the affections than it does itself, but which, experience has proved, will in the long run stand or fall with it. This is the reason why Trinity Sunday is made the crown and climax of that part of the Christian year which commemorates the life of Christ. All the momentous truths that lie scattered along our path from the first Sunday in Advent to Whitsunday, are gathered up into a single sheaf to-day, and this strong formula serves as a three-fold cord to bind them into unity. Take, for example, the belief of which Christmas Day is the commemoration, namely, the union of the Divine and the human in the person of Jesus Christ. It is the doctrine of the Eternal Fatherhood and the Eternal Sonship which alone can keep, as experience would seem to teach, that precious faith of the Savior's Divinity bright and clear. But the doctrine of the Eternal Fatherhood and the Eternal Sonship is part of the mystery of the Holy Trinity. Disown the threeness of the Godhead, and presently your teaching about Christ's Divinity will become thin, shadowy, vague. Again take the doctrine of the Atonement, the belief in the sacrificial character of the death of Christ; certainly all must acknowledge the tremendous hold which that has had upon the affections of men. . . . Deny the essential Deity of Christ, declare Him to be a creature, and a creature only, and what doctrine could be more monstrous than such a one as the Atonement?"

* CHURCH SEASONS; By Alexander H. Grant, M. A., p. 221. (Thomas Whittaker, New York.)

SERMONS AND OUTLINES

OUR TRINITARIAN PRAYERS

By Robert Balgarnie, D.D.

I

" As he " (the Trinitarian worshiper) " directs his prayers, now to one " (person of the Trinity), " now to another, they sit apart within his faith; and his awe, his aspiration, his affection, flow into no living unity."—Dr. James Martineau.*

Thus justly and incisively Dr. Martineau puts his finger upon a weak point of our devotions. He acquits us of Tritheism, and fairly enough explains to his co-religionists our standpoint as Trinitarians, yet his charge against us of thought-confusion in our worship is unquestionably true. In our anxiety to be orthodox we have come to acquire a habit of thought and expression in public prayer that can hardly be described as either rational or scriptural. If we closely analyze our mental vision in addressing the Deity, we seem to have three divine beings before our spiritual eye instead of one. We conjure up a misty conception of three celestial thrones, one occupied by the Father, another by the Son, and the third by the Holy Ghost. We address the first in the name of the second, imploring, as we do so, the aid and influence of the third. In the venerable Litany of the English Church an appeal is made for mercy to " God the Father of heaven; " this is followed in similar terms by prayer to the Son as Redeemer of the world; then succeeds a like petition to the Holy Spirit; after which comes the adoration of the Trinity; the prayer concludes with earnest supplication to the Son as Lord.†

Who is the central object of worship in this prayer for mercy? If we scrutinize our inner consciousness while offering it we must frankly acknowledge that there is " no living unity." Our thought seems to wander in the presence chamber from Father to Son, and from Son to the Blessed Spirit; we localize their thrones by habit, we appeal to each consecutively, but with no unified conception in our minds of one divine image and likeness—one conceivable and approachable form, in whom the fulness of the Godhead is embodied; one whom we can worship with all reverence and affection in spirit face to face.

It does not help us out of our difficulty here to return to the dreary controversies of the early Church. Origen, Clement, Irenæus, Tertullian, and others were confronted in their times by theories of the Godhead and tendencies of religious thought utterly unlike those that beset us; and the conclusions they arrived at were only satisfactory when viewed in relation to the Gnostic and other heresies of their age. Like ancient ships of the Le-

vant, they were built and shaped for other seas than ours.

Neither does the Unitarian sword cut the Gordian knot. As Dr. Martineau has shown in his second volume of " Addresses," his own co-worshipers are not altogether unbeset with difficulties. Putting names aside and concentrating our thoughts on realities, he frankly admits:

" The Father, in the sense which I have endeavored to explain, *is really absent from the Unitarian creed*. . . . Did Trinitarians perceive this, they would be less disposed to charge us with believing in only a cold, distant, and awful God. . . . Tell them that the object of our belief is their *second person,* not their first, and they will feel how false is the accusation; for it is precisely around Him, as the very center and solar glory of their faith, that all their trust and reverence move, and in Him that their affections burn and glow. If it is in Him that we also put our faith, tho under another name, then we are at one with all Christendom in the very focus and fervor of its religious life." ‡

There are some misconceptions that have to be cleared away before the chief point of this thesis can be dealt with.

1. We have been taught—taught wrongly—to regard Jehovah of Old Testament scripture as " the Father," the first person of the glorious Trinity. In spite of New Testament teaching to the contrary, this vital error, I fancy, is almost universally prevalent. Altho we are expressly informed that " all things," without exception, " were made " by the co-eternal Son, we still attribute the creation of the world and the introduction of man to the act of the Father, and constantly distinguish in our prayers between God the Creator and Christ the Redeemer of the world. Moses heard God's voice at the bush, and saw Him at the mountain face to face, and we are told that no man hath ever seen or heard the Father, we continue to think of the Father—not the Son—as the " covenant God of Israel." Altho Jehovah Sabaoth, seen and worshiped by Isaiah in the temple, in the vision that effected his conversion and gave him the call to the prophetic office,§ is described in the Fourth Gospel as Christ the Son—then

---

* *The Christian Reformer*, February, 1886.
† In striking contrast with the English Litany stand the Public Prayers of the Church of Scotland, which are addressed exclusively to the Father (*v. Directory*). This is unity indeed, but the unity desiderated by the Unitarian.
‡ " A Way out of the Trinitarian Controversy."   § Isaiah vi.

anticipating His incarnation*—we still think of and address the Father as the occupant of the mercy-seat when we kneel, as Isaiah did, in confession and prayer for forgiveness. And altho we know that "the Father" judgeth no man, but hath committed all judgment unto the Son, that all should honor him even as they honor the Father," we cannot apparently divest our minds of the thought that it is the Father who "will bring every work into judgment." The Old Testament "Jehovah" has thus become to us "the Father of Heaven" in our prayers. This is the *genesis* of our error. It is in following this false light that we have been led into confusion of thought in prayer.

2. Even New Testament Scripture is often popularly misread on this subject. We are distinctly told in the Gospels, *e. g.*, to attribute the birth of Christ to the power of the Holy Ghost, and that He should "therefore be called the Son of God;" yet the voices from heaven that acknowledged Him as the "Only Begotten and Well Beloved" at His baptism, on Hermon at His transfiguration, and at His passion are supposed to be the utterances of the first person of the Trinity and not of the third.

We also, being regenerated, are, in another sense, "born of the Spirit;" we are the children of the Holy Ghost; in strictest theological doctrine it is the third person of the Trinity, not the first, who has begotten us by the incorruptible seed and made us "sons and daughters of the Lord Almighty." Is it not, therefore, of Him our Lord speaks when He says, "I ascend unto my Father and your Father; to my God and your God?" "Our Father in heaven" is God, the Holy Ghost.

3. Our space here will not permit examination of those passages in St. John's Gospel where our Lord, in His conscious humanity, speaks of His relationship to His Father; yet most, if not all, are capable of being understood of God the Spirit. "I am in the Father, and the Father in me"—the indwelling God is the Holy Spirit. "We will come and take up our abode with him." "No man can come unto me except my Father, who hath sent me, draw him." Conversion is the work of the Holy Ghost. But we are already prepossessed of the idea that the reference is to the first person of the Trinity, and thereby miss possibly the point, power, and beauty of the allusion.

4. The imagery of the Epistle to the Hebrews, in which our Lord is represented as our Great High Priest seated at His Father's right hand in the heavens, there making continual intercession for us, altho a divinely inspired truth and of priceless value to our faith, is nevertheless answerable for not a few of these human misconceptions. We cannot isolate and separate our Lord's humanity as if it stood apart from his Deity.

It was the Deity *within Him* that was propitiated and reconciled to us by the priestly sacrifices of His humanity. It was on the altar of His Deity which was "greater than, and sanctified the gift," that He offered the sacrifice of His human nature, and so made peace between God and man.

They tell in Greek legend of a wounded warrior who held aloft his maimed arm before the judges of his country in silent yet eloquent appeal for the life of his son, a prisoner at their tribunal. The plea was allowed, and the youth was spared. So the "wound prints" of our Lord's humanity make silent but effectual intercession for us. But the nail-pierced hands are now outstretched *to us,* and through them "God in Christ" appeals to us to become reconciled to Him.

5. It may be thought to militate against the ascription of Fatherhood to the Holy Spirit that He was "sent" as the "Comforter" at Pentecost, and "proceedeth from *the Father* and the Son."† "I will pray the Father, and he will give you *another Comforter,* that he may abide with you forever, even the Spirit of truth. . . . I will not leave you comfortless (ὀρφανούς) I will come to you."‡

Were these promises exhausted in the outpouring of the Spirit? Was He the *other* Advocate? Was He waiting for His advent till the Savior's departure? Was it impossible for Him to come while Jesus remained on earth? Had He not been in the world from the beginning?§ What mean the words "I will not leave you orphans, I will come to you?" Is there not something here that we, with our many prepossessions, have overlooked? Was there not something in the divine constitution of our Lord's personality that only required a spiritualized and glorified body to reveal its omnipresent attributes and its omnipotent love? Did not the Holy Ghost descend on Jesus at His baptism and *remain* on Him, thus enshrining itself in His human spirit, and becoming embodied in His humanity? Was it not *This* that "baptized" the disciples and the first converts at Pentecost, enabling them thenceforth to manifest and exemplify the Spirit of Christ? God hath sent forth *the Spirit of His Son* into your hearts, crying, "Abba, Father." ‖

(*a*) Peter has explained the phenomena of Pentecost as the fulfilment of Joel's prediction: "I will pour out my Spirit upon all flesh, and your sons and daughters shall prophesy." But Joel's prediction was the promise of *Jehovah,* the second person of the glorious Trinity. It was *His* spirit, therefore, that "fell" upon the Church at Jerusalem, making all men confess that "the Lord was among them of a truth." The Father-Spirit had been in the world from the beginning.

(*b*) "I will not leave you comfortless; I will come to you." That Christ fulfilled His

---

* John xii: 41.
† *Filioque,* Not in Greek text of Easter Creed.—Bishop Westcott, "THE HISTORIC FAITH," p. 199.
‡ John xiv: 16-22.
§ *The Expositor,* November, p. 368.
‖ "That imparted spirit acts upon us as the agent of one who is still truly human. He is 'the spirit of Jesus'" (Acts xvi: 7).—Canon Mason, "THE FAITH OF THE GOSPEL."

piedge, and "after a little while" returned in spirit to His own is the unequivocal testimony of the early Church. Wherever two or three met together in His name there He was in their midst. When they preached "the power of the Lord was present to heal." No one might say, "Who shall ascend into heaven to bring Christ down from above?" Saul of Tarsus saw and heard Him on the way to Damascus; John in Patmos; Peter at Cæsarea; Stephen at his martyrdom: "*the Spirit of the Lord* caught away Philip" at Gaza; "*Domine quo vadis?*" And Chrysostom's renown as a preacher commenced with the day when his half empty Church was filled by Christ and His angels. "Lo, I am with you alway, even to the end of the world."

And is not this the hope and joy of the Church of all ages—that Christ is with us? that our living Lord is in the midst of us? that He still walks in the midst of the lamp-

stands? and that "whosoever shall call upon him shall be saved?"

What constitutes revival times but a sense of His presence? Why is He the subject of revival hymns and the object of revival prayers but because it pleases God at such seasons "to reveal his Son in us" and "the light of the knowledge of his glory in the face of Jesus Christ?"

(*c*) The third person of the blessed Trinity is not "sent," does not "proceed;" He fills immensity with His presence. Like the light and air of heaven, He pervades the universe. Like the ocean waters that cover the basins of the seas, the gulfs, the bays, the creeks, the inlets—nay, every little crevice and shell along the shore, "He filleth all in all." "In him we live, and move, and have our being."

The argument against the Fatherhood of the Spirit, therefore, is not quite conclusive.— H. R.

OUR TRINITARIAN PRAYERS

By ROBERT BALGARNIE, D.D.

II

"Given self, to find God."* As we have been created in the " image and likeness " of the Trinity, the world's earliest Bible, the first and clearest revelation of the mystery of the Godhead will be found in man himself. If man resembles his Maker not only in his moral attributes, and in these but dimly, but in the nature and constitution of his being; if soul, body, and spirit be three conceivable hypostases in one visible personality, we have been divinely furnished, from the beginning of our history, with an intelligible clew to the doctrine of the Three-One God. No better analogy, at all events, has ever presented itself.

Taking this, then, for the purposes of our argument meanwhile, as the divine *epitome* of the Book of God, let us see to what it leads as regards the three persons of the adorable Trinity, reserving the right to compare its conclusions ultimately with the direct teaching of Scripture. The soul or life within us represents the Father; the Spirit, with all that is comprehended under that term—the mind, the will, the affections —will represent the Holy Spirit; while the outward visible form, that embodies and expresses both, will be the representative of the co-Eternal Son. In both cases these are one.*

Should any one object to this detailed analogy, I would say that we cannot otherwise conceive or think of the Trinity at all. It is only by such analogy that the subject is comprehensible. "The invisible things of him from the creation of the world, are clearly seen, being understood by the things that are made, even his eternal power and Godhead" (Θειότης) divinity.†

I. THE FATHER.—According to this analogy, then, the Father is the life or soul of the universe. He is essentially and emphatically the Living One. To impart life is His prerogative. In this self-existent, all-pervading, and changeless Life the Son and Holy Spirit are equal and co-eternal with the Father; for that life or soul is one. In this respect the persons of the Trinity are undistinguishable; each is infinite, ever-living, and immutable. This is what we mean when we speak of each as God.

But as that which animates the mind and body of the human frame is silent, formless in itself to us, undefinable and incomprehensible, so the Supreme Life "passeth knowledge." "No man hath seen God at any time." No one has ever heard His voice or seen His shape. "He dwells in the light inaccessible." "We go forward, but he is not there; and backward, but we perceive him not." He is beyond the comprehension of any created intelligence. "Canst thou by searching find out God?" One thing we do know of this Infinite Life, and that by revelation—His infinite, unchanging, everlasting love.

We call Him "Father" to indicate His relationship to the Eternal Son, and there is no other name by which He has revealed Himself. The ancient Egyptians thought of Him as *the Nameless Supreme*, to whom all their deities and gods were subordinate. He had no temple among them, altar, or form of worship; but in their thoughts He was "God over all, blessed forever." The Greek philosophers followed their example, speaking of Him as the 'Ον. Our Scandinavian ancestors called Him the "Al-Fadur," placing

* *Imago Dei, Homiletic Review* for April, 1892.　　　　† Rom. i : 20.

Him above Odin and Thor and all in Valhalla. He would appear at Raquarök.

> " Yet there shall come
> Another Mightier;
> Altho Him
> I dare not name.
> Farther onward
> Few can see
> Then when Odin
> Meets the Wolf."
>
> *Ancient Saga.*

It was this probably that led the Hebrews, in imitation of the Egyptians, to suppress the name Jahve in their worship, styling it " incommunicable," refusing to write or pronounce it, and foolishly confounding " Jehovah, the Son," with the Eternal Father. Sad to think, our translators, like the LXX, have condoned their folly.

But if we address our prayers, as we are directed to do by the Church but not scriptural authority, to the All-Father, to Him whose name is ineffable, whose being is incomprehensible, only naming the Son as the plea for acceptance and the Spirit as a help to our infirmities in the act of devotion, we can have no possible or conceivable Object of adoration before our mental eye, no holy locality in earth or heaven toward which to direct our thoughts; no throne, visible by men or angels, to which we can make spiritual approach; we only look blindfold into space, and address a centerless infinitude. Even the Unitarian, as Dr. Martineau confesses, adoring *"Jehovah"* of Old Testament Scripture as " the Father," is in reality worshiping the Son.

II. THE HOLY SPIRIT.—Man made in the image and likeness of the Trinity is conscious of a spirit within. Besides the life, or soul, we are sensible of a power to reason, decide, love, hate—a power that differentiates us from the brutes and elevates us above the mechanical laws of nature. Something infinitely superior, yet analogous to this, we are divinely taught, and our experience confirms the revelation, exists in the Godhead we worship, a spirit of holiness, of ineffable wisdom and love. Where we might have turned a deaf ear and obdurate heart to mechanical force we are influenced by divine persuasion, argument, and affection. Thus our spirits bear witness to the existence, character, and attributes of the heavenly Spirit, and our will submits to His authority. The mind of that Spirit is in the Bible, and we make it the night-lamp of our path.

But how shall we conceive of that Spirit as an external object of worship? How shall we pray to that which inspires and prompts our prayers, without which we cannot pray? Our worship in this case can only take the form of silent submission, consenting to be filled and influenced by the fulness, opening our eyes to the light, our ears to the truth, and surrendering our wills to His ruling. The will of the Spirit is that we should accept Christ; and in His worship and service He (the Spirit) is honored, obeyed, and glorified.

III. THE CO-ETERNAL SON.—Enshrined in the light that centers the infinitude of the invisible God, sat One from eternity, in the Divine nature and essence, who was " the express image of his person" ($\chi\alpha\rho\alpha\kappa\tau\dot{\eta}\rho$ $\tau\tilde{\eta}\varsigma$ $\dot{\upsilon}\pi o\sigma\tau\dot{\alpha}\sigma\epsilon\omega\varsigma$) " He was God," and " in the form of God." Whatever that form was, it was that, and that alone, that made angelic and other worship possible. To that form, as the empty space began to fill with worlds and their inhabitants, all faces turned, all worship ascended, all prayer arose.

From that " form " went forth the words that called everything into being, that gave it shape and purpose, that gave it law and order. " All things were made by him, and without him was not anything made that was made."

We have been taught to call that " form of God " " the Son," and to speak of Him as " begotten of the Father " from the poverty of human language and the feebleness of human intellect to express or grasp " the deep things of God." It was language that might have risen spontaneously to an archangel's lips if brought suddenly and for the first time since his creation into the presence of the Visible in the bosom of the Invisible, of the Comprehensible on the throne of the Infinite, of the Approachable where he had expected the Inaccessible. " He is the Son in the bosom of the Eternal Father." But there was no priority of existence or inequality of power to give birth to the term of relationship. " In the beginning was the Word, and the Word was with God, *and the Word was God.*"

In the Old Testament ages the Son revealed Himself in human form to man, whom He had created in His own " image and likeness." His name was " Jehovah," and under that name He was and still is the only Divine object of worship to the Hebrew tribes. The Jews to this hour worship the Son as we do, altho under another title, and denying His incarnation.

" The Word became flesh and dwelt among us," and the New Testament era began. " In him dwelt all the fulness of the Godhead bodily." In His sinless humanity, as in a temple, the Father and blessed Spirit stood enshrined; and the manifestations of the Divine Unity—the Three-One God in Christ—became the central truth of Christianity. " Let all the angels of God worship him " was the decree attendant on His birth. " Let every knee bow to him," was the decree that accompanied His ascension.

The introduction of the word " Lord " in place of Jehovah to New Testament Scripture, as well as to the English and other versions of the Old Testament, altho to be deprecated in the interests of evidence and as a liberty taken with the inspired text, has nevertheless been so far useful that it facilitates the construction of the Christian Litany.* It is the " new name " that unites

---

* It is to the honor of the American Company of Revisionists that they have restored the name Jehovah to the English Bible.

the past with the present, that breaks down "the wall of partition" between the Hebrew worshiper of Jehovah and the Christian worshiper of Christ, that makes both one in adoration of the Incarnate Son. "We have one Lord, one faith, one baptism, one God and Father of all," in Him "who was, and is, and is to come." "He is the Everlasting Father and Prince of Peace." In Him is realized for us the unity of the Godhead, the embodiment of all we seek to worship, "the Alpha and Omega, the beginning and the end—ὁ παντοκράτωρ—the Almighty."

Is it necessary to add, in concluding this article on trinitarian prayer, that it is *to God,* our reconciling Father in Christ, that we pray? We have only to recall, in our approaches to the throne of heaven, the midnight scene on Hermon, when the indwelling Deity of our blessed Lord's nature was seen by His disciples shining through His humanity, as the shechinah of the temple shimmered through the veil "when his face did shine as the sun, and his raiment was white as the light," in order to realize that the Object of our worship is divine.* It is God we appeal to, looking at us through human eyes; listening to us through human ears; speaking to us in human language and by human lips; and wiping from our cheeks the

tears of sorrow with gentle human hands—to "God in Christ, reconciling the world unto himself, not imputing unto men their trespasses." Nearer than this we may not go; higher than this we cannot soar; in that presence is fulness of joy; at that right hand are pleasures forevermore.

This, then, appears to be the solution of our trinitarian difficulty: to concentrate our thoughts and our affections on God the Son as He is revealed to us in Christ; to adore Him as the Creator, Preserver, all-wise Ruler and Redeemer of the world; to worship Him as the ever-present King and Head of His Church; and to look forward to the eternal enjoyment of His presence in heaven, as the consummation of our happiness, as "all our salvation and all our desire."

"Almighty God, who hast given us grace at this time with one accord to make our common supplications unto Thee, and dost promise that when two or three are gathered together in Thy name, Thou wilt grant their requests, fulfil now, O Lord, the desires and petitions of Thy servants, as may be most expedient for them; granting us in this world knowledge of Thy truth, and in the world to come life everlasting. Amen." (*A Prayer of St. Chrysostom*).—H. R.

THE TRINITIES

By Frederick D. Power, D.D.

Moreover, brethren, I declare unto you the gospel which I preached unto you, which also ye have received, and wherein ye stand; by which also ye are saved, if ye keep in memory what I preached unto you, unless ye have believed in vain. For I delivered unto you first of all that which I also received, how that Christ died for our sins according to the Scriptures; and that he was buried; and that he rose again the third day according to the Scriptures.—1 Cor. xv: 1-4

It is by no means a fanciful thought that the main facts and teachings of Scripture are presented to us under the form of trinities—groups consisting of three important constituents. We do not wonder at this interesting fact when our experience with everything outside of the Bible brings us constantly into contact with triune divisions of things. In the world of nature we have the three kingdoms: animal, vegetable, and mineral. In the realm of matter we have existence under three forms, solid, liquid, and gaseous. In our own being we have body, soul, and spirit. In the heavens we have sun, moon, and stars; and in the earth; air, land, and sea.

In approaching the revelation of God in His Word we are prepared to notice the same exhibition of three in one, and even the most sublime and essential elements of Christianity developed and exhibited in a succession of trinities.

1. Whether the word "trinity" be Scriptural or not, and we discard the expression "The Trinity" because of its unscriptural-

ness, it still expresses the thought of this peculiar division as seen in the three distinct persons in the unity of the Godhead. Of this one fact we are sure, the sacred Oracles teach that the one living and true God is in some inexplicable manner triune, for He is spoken of as one in some respects and as three in others. Addressing Himself in the creation, God said: "Let us make man in our image, after our likeness." Our Lord declared: "If any man love me he will keep my commandments, and my Father will love him, and we will come unto him and make our abode with him." Sending forth His disciples, He commanded: "Go ye therefore and teach all nations, baptizing them into the name of the Father, and of the Son, and of the Holy Spirit." Of Christ, John declares: "In the beginning was the Word, and the Word was with God, and the Word was God." Of the Holy Spirit, Peter affirms in his rebuke of Ananias: "Why hath Satan filled thine heart to lie to the Holy Ghost? Thou hast not lied unto men,

* Here as elsewhere, the Lord, as the Son of Man gives the measure of the capacity of humanity (Bishop Westcott, "THE HISTORIC FAITH," p. 264).

but unto God." The Apostolic benediction proclaimed: "The grace of our Lord Jesus Christ, the love of God, and the communion of the Holy Spirit be with you all." "There are three that bear record in heaven, the Father, the Word, and the Holy Spirit, and these three are one."

Here is a mystery, the stupendous mystery of the Christian religion, the ineffable mystery of three persons in one God. We cannot define it. Every human attempt at definition involves it in deeper mystery. The arithmetic of heaven is beyond us. Yet this is no more mysterious and inexplicable than the trinity of our own nature; body, soul, and spirit; and no man has ever shown that it involved a contradiction or in any way conflicted with the testimony of our senses or with demonstrated truth; and we must accept it by the power of a simple faith, or rush into tritheism on the one hand or unitarianism on the other.

2. Going still further into the examination of this arrangement of trinities, we take the Divine Person mentioned in our text, Christ, the Second Person of the Godhead. At once there comes before us the trinity of offices filled by our Lord,—prophet, priest, and king. Man could not be saved unless in one divine person all three of these should be combined. Christ could not be the Christ if God were not all three of these dignities and glories united in His single person.

Prophet He was, typified by all the illustrious personages of the Hebrew race, the Oracle, the Teacher, the Spokesman for God who should make known the fulness of revelation, and that to all mankind. "God, who at sundry times and in divers manners spake in times past unto the fathers by the prophets, hath in these last days spoken unto us by his Son." Priest He was, the only and all-sufficient Priest of the Christian Church. None other can stand between man and his God. None other can exercise sacerdotal functions except in the sense that all Christians are kings and priests unto God. A priest is He, foreshadowed faintly by the servants of the Jewish sanctuary; yet more beautifully adorned than the family of Aaron in all the splendid robes of the temple, more glorious in communications than the mysteriously glowing Urim and Thummim on the high-priest's ephod before the mercy-seat, more potent in intercession than all the priesthood under the law, seeing that He offered Himself on the altar, and opened up a new and living way into the very holy of holies by His own blood of atonement. "This one, because he continueth forever, hath an unchangeable priesthood, wherefore he is able to save unto the uttermost them that come unto the Father by him." "Such an high priest became us, holy, harmless, undefiled, separate from sinners, and made higher than the heavens, who needeth not daily, as those high priests, to offer up sacrifice first for his own sins and then for the people's, for this he did once when he offered up himself."

King He was, 'Ο Χριστος the Christ, the Anointed of God. "I have set my King upon my holy hill of Zion." "Blessed and only Potentate, the King of kings and Lord of lords." All-glorious, all-powerful, all-governing, He reigns over His people and over all the earth. "God hath highly exalted him and given him a ₁name that is above every name, that at the name of Jesus every knee should bow, of things in heaven and things on earth and things under the earth, and every tongue should confess that Jesus is the Christ, unto the glory of God the Father."

Thus the Christ is invested with a triune power. In one Being these three offices meet in their perfection, and we accept Him in all His glory, personal and official.

3. Then the doctrine of Christ, the facts which constitute the Gospel, are unfolded to us in a trinity. Three distinct facts are here: First, that "Christ died for our sins according to the Scriptures;" second, that "he was buried;" and third, that He "arose again the third day according to the Scriptures." It is not possible to measure the infinite import of these three facts. There would be no gospel without them, no salvation, no proof of the divinity of Jesus, no ground of faith. The gospel is the power of God unto salvation; not faith, not repentance, not baptism, not hope, not love. We are saved by Jesus Christ, and the action which saved us is set forth in these facts—the death, burial, and resurrection of Jesus.

Too often men make the mistake in supposing their salvation is secured, not by what they believe, but by the fact that they do believe; not by the facts of the gospel, but by the feelings of ecstasies of their own natures; not by the Son of God and His personal service, but by their apprehension of the truth of the gospel and tacit acceptance of its teaching. In other words, they substitute a saving faith for a saving gospel, and find the proof of pardon in the revulsion of feeling in their own hearts rather than in the express declaration of God's Word. Was it so with these Corinthians? The gospel which Paul preached unto them, which they also received, wherein they stood, and by which they were saved, consisted of the facts of the death, burial, and resurrection of the Messiah. Without the death of Christ the gospel could not be begun. The shedding of blood was necessary to remission of sins. Expiation, atonement must be made that the sinner may be saved from punishment. Some one must be wounded for our transgressions, bruised for our iniquities. God's justice must be satisfied, God's honor vindicated. Man's conscience must be pacified, man's sins pardoned. So the Son died. The cross was an element of the gospel. Without the burial of Christ the gospel would not be complete. The prophecy must be fulfilled; "He made his grave with the wicked and with the rich in his death." By our Lord the tomb has been forever sanctified. The valley of the shadow of death becomes the valley of the opening of life. Death, instead of being the jailer of hell and the grave, becomes the porter of heaven. All that he can now do is to cause the Christian to sleep in Jesus, to release the immortal spirit from the fetters which bind it to earth, and deposit the weary body in the tomb. The grave is an element of the gospel. Without the resurrection the gospel would not be perfected. Before this great consummation the gospel is not proclaimed save in promise. The fulness of the glad tidings is not realized. The kingdom of heaven is preached as at hand. Not until the long-tied bands of the grave are broken, the stone rolled from the mouth of the sepulcher, and the newly-risen One walks forth into the garden, is the divinity of Jesus proven and the sublimest revelation of God complete; not until then does the glorious King of kings appear with all authority in heaven and in earth, and say to His representatives: "Go ye into all the world and preach the gospel to every creature; he that believeth and is baptized shall be saved, and he that believeth not shall be condemned."

Hence the resurrection is the demonstration of the gospel. "If Christ be not risen, then is our preaching vain, and your faith is also vain; ye are yet in your sins." Hence the apostles, in going forth to convert the world, were to lay this down as the foundation of their preaching, that Jesus Christ was raised from the dead that all men might believe on and obey Him. Hence the resurrection is essential to the confirmation of the faith of Christians in His person, seeing He is declared to be the Son of God, with power according to the spirit of holiness by the resurrection from the dead," demonstrating the truth of the Word, "Thou art my Son, this day have I begotten thee," and of the promise, "I will give thee the sure mercies of David." Hence the resurrection is a most pregnant proof of the all-sufficiency of His satisfaction: "He was delivered for our offenses and raised for our justification." Hence on the fact of the resurrection is built our faith in His promise to give life and glory; for how could we believe Him to be the Author of life who remained under the power of death? Would not all hope have been buried in His grave? And is not His resurrection the cause, pattern, and argument of ours? And rising Himself to glory, honor, and immortality, does He not raise His people also with Him?

What a glorious truth is here! The heathen sorrowed without hope. The Jews had only vague assurance of a resurrection. The myth of the Phenix was but a myth. A shattered pillar; a ship gone to pieces; a race lost; a harp lying on the ground, with snapped strings, its music gone; a flower-bud crushed with all its fragrance in it—these were the sad utterances of their hopeless grief. The thought that death was the gateway of life came not to cheer the parting or brighten the sepulcher. But look at the grassy mounds in the light of this truth. *Resurgent!* The eye of faith sees

them change into a field sown thick with the seeds of immortality. Blessed field! what flowers shall spring there! What a wild shout shall be the harvest-home of the resurrection day! In neighboring fields, "Whatsoever a man soweth that shall he also reap;" but here what a difference between that which is sown amid mourners' tears and that which shall be reaped amid angel joys!—between the poor body we return to the earth, and the noble form that shall spring from its ashes! Lazarus' putrid corpse with health glowing on its cheek is nothing to the change that then shall be wrought in a moment, in the twinkling of an eye, at the last trump. From east and west, from north and south the armies gather. Yesterday, bones, carcasses, rottenness, worms, corruption, dust—to-day, multitudes in glorified and immortal bodies; thronging the many mansions of the Father's house.

The death, the burial, the resurrection of Jesus—these are the three facts of the gospel. The mere existence of these facts, however, does not save men. The mere admission that they are true does not secure the end that God designed. In order that this may be done they must be received; every man must actually and truly appropriate them to himself. Practically it is as important to understand how the gospel may be received as it is to understand the nature and component parts of the gospel, for what is the gospel to a man if it be not received by him? What are the Bible, the Church, the pardon of sin, the death of Christ, all the sublime facts and teachings of the Christian religion, if personally and receptively a man knows them not?

4. This brings us to another trinity—the reception of the gospel involves obedience to three distinct precepts. We must truly and heartily believe the gospel; honestly and sincerely repent of our sins; and actually and formally accept it by a reverent and obedient baptism. Thus the understanding recognizes and accepts the gospel as true, the affections delight in and embrace it as good, the will obeys it and approves it as right. The records of the Acts of the Apostles and the Epistles to the Churches make clear the essentiality of this triune obedience. After conforming to these three precepts, and not before, we are regarded as having come into fellowship with Christ and His Church. Paul, writing afterward in allusion to the doctrine of the gospel, as he had delivered it, declares: "I thank God that ye have obeyed from the heart the form of doctrine which was delivered unto you; being then made free from sin, ye became the servants of righteousness."

What was the doctrine? The death, burial and resurrection of Christ. And what was the form or type of this doctrine? Death to sin, burial with Christ by baptism, a resurrection in the likeness of His rising to walk in newness of life. To the people on Pentecost Peter preached this trinity of facts, —how Christ died for our sins according to the Scriptures, was buried, and rose again; and the three thousand rendered this trinity of obedience; they believed, and were commanded to "repent and be baptized in the name of Jesus Christ for the remission of sins." "And as many as gladly received the Word were baptized. and the same day there were added unto them about three thousand souls." As Christ's death, Christ's burial, and Christ's resurrection must be all assured facts, so of human obedience there must be no uncertainty. no contingency, no doubt whatever that all the elements in the trinity of our acceptance are complete. The apostles recognized no man as fully obedient to the gospel and worthy to be enrolled in the Church until obedience to all three of these precepts had been rendered. Is not the gospel the same in our day? Are not the terms of acceptance unchanged?

5. Receiving now the trinity of facts in a trinity of obedience, we have a triune blessing. We are "saved," or receive the "remission of sins," the "gift of the Holy Spirit," and the hope of eternal life. This is the trinity of blessings which heaven bestows on the Christian. First Christ comes, takes away his sins, purifies his heart, pacifies his conscience, assures him of the wiping out of his past record. Then the Spirit is given, enlightens, comforts, sanctifies, gladdens, directs, strengthens, and takes up His abode within him.

Then in view of the brevity of human life, of the pain which the thought of losing this new-born joy must bring, He fills the Christian with the assured hope of an everlasting life, of higher joys. of richer glories, of more abundant delights, of sweeter friendships, of more lasting rewards which shall be developed out of these present gifts of the gospel. Oh, what happiness! Who can refuse it? Who does not long for it? Where is there a heart in all the world that does not in serious reality hunger and thirst for this blessing which the gospel alone pretends to give?

6. But there is more. Out of this trinity of blessings grows another trinity—a trinity of responsibilities. In the gospel which we have received we are to stand, and three principles are necessary to standing—faith, hope, and love. All Christian living is marked and covered by this trinity of conduct. Faith here is the growth, development, continuance of the seed-faith which embraces the gospel. It is the daily looking to Jesus, the seeing of Him that is invisible. Hope here is the carrying forward and upward of the original hope, the strengthened and matured form of that assurance received when the conditions of salvation were accepted. That was a joy, a gladness; this is a stimulus, a safeguard. That was an evidence that we had been saved from our past sins; this is a power that keeps us forever from being lost. Love is the climax of this trinity. Love is the end of the commandment. Love is the active principle of our standing which embraces all practise of Christianity toward God and man. Faith

looks up, hope reaches up, love climbs up. So looking steadfastly, hoping constantly, loving fully, we can only stand and wait all the days of His appointed time till our change come.

7. One more trinity, and the saved soul shall stand in the presence of the ever-adorable Trinity of the Godhead: Glory, honor, immortality! By degrees the Christian has come higher and higher. Body, soul, and spirit, touched and overshadowed by the great facts of the gospel—the death, burial, and resurrection of Jesus—brought into entire harmony with these by obedience to three great precepts—faith, repentance, and baptism,—and kept in preparation and expectancy by three great conditions—faith, hope, and love,—are ready for transfiguration, translation into the presence of the Most High. Glory is the supernal brightness the Father bestows, honor the renown of victory won by the Christian soldier on hard-fought fields, immortality the deathless bliss of a deathless being in the presence of the throne!

Now see in all these trinities a climacteric effect. All three are essential in every case to the perfectness of the unity which they form, and the last is absolutely necessary to crown the series. God is goodness, wisdom, power. His goodness might influence Him to create, His wisdom devise the universe, but must not His power be exercised to perfect His work? The Father of our spirits is all that is expressed in the address, "Our Father which art in heaven;" the Son is all that is set forth in the name "Immanuel;" but must not the Spirit come to reveal to us the Father and the Son? In Christ as prophet He is the teacher sent from God. in Christ as Mediator He is the High Priest of our profession, but are these anything without His kingly dignity and power by which He rules and reigns in the midst of His enemies? In the gospel His death and burial are glorious, stupendous, facts, but without the resurrection what are they? He is not the Son of God, His sacrifice is vain, our faith also is vain.

In our acceptance of the gospel, "without faith it is impossible to please God," and except men repent they must perish, but without obedience can we have the full assurance of pardon? "Faith without works is dead." We are "baptized into Christ," "baptized into his death." So the command to believers was, "Repent and be baptized every one of you in the name of Jesus Christ for the remission of sins," and to the believing penitent, "Arise and be baptized and wash away your sins, calling upon the name of the Lord." In the unit called salvation the remission of past sins is a blessing, the gift of the Holy Spirit is a greater blessing, but what would either or both of these be without the third, the hope of eternal life? In the trinity of Christian living, faith is nothing, hope is nothing without love. This is the climax. "Tho I have the tongues of men and of angels, and have not love, I am as sounding brass and a tinkling cymbal."

" And now abideth faith, hope, love; and the greatest of these is love." Heaven, glory, what is that? Honor—what joy can it bring without immortality? It is for an eternity we want these joys and splendors—not for a century, a lifetime, a decade, a year, or a day!

So passing through the whole series in every case, accepting all and doing all, we shall receive all. Is the measure full with you, my friend? In the trinity of obedience is there one thing left undone? Fulfil your duty. The completion of the joy, the certainty of the assurance depends upon the perfectness of your obedience, the perfectness of your service.—H. R.

THE TRINITY

BY JOHN A. BROADUS, D.D.

For through him we both have access by one Spirit unto the Father.—Ephesians ii: 18

The apostle Paul had been engaged in what we call "Judaizing." It was understood that all Gentiles who became Christians must also become Jews. He says: " Wherefore remember, that ye being in time past Gentiles in the flesh, who are called uncircumcision by that which is called the circumcision, in the flesh, made by hands; at that time ye were without Christ, being alienated from the commonwealth of Israel, and strangers from the covenant of promise. having no hope and without God in the world. But now in Christ Jesus, ye who sometimes were far off are made nigh by the blood of Christ. For he is our peace, who hath made both one." The Jews were accustomed to speak of themselves as near by and the Gentiles as far off. " And hath broken down the middle wall of partition between us," meaning the gates of the temple from the outer court—in which alone the Gentiles were permitted to come. " Having abolished in his flesh the enmity, even the law of commandments contained in ordinances; for to make in himself of twain one new man, so making peace." Paul is speaking to the Gentiles, and by his personal influence and by the help of zealous brethren at Jerusalem, it was considered right that this barrier should be broken down between the Gentiles and the Jews, and that they should be united in one faith. So Paul presents the plea contained in our text: " For through him we both have access by one Spirit unto the Father." One God and Father, one faith, one baptism—all one spiritual body—tho so widely separated, yet one in Jesus Christ. The Jews, tho so widely separated from the Gentiles, would, through Jesus Christ, both have access by one Spirit unto the Father.

But do you observe that in making that plea he brings out " God the Father," " God the Son," and " God the Holy Spirit?" For through Him—that is, Christ, we both have access by one Spirit unto the Father.

Is the preacher going to dare to preach a sermon on the " Trinity"? Have not we been told many times that ours is so practical an age that people don't want to hear about the great doctrines of Christianity? Now, friends, I don't believe that—I believe that intelligent people are very willing and sometimes very glad to hear about the highest truths of

the Christian system, provided their attention is called to the devotional aspect of the truths. The text presents to us: " God the Father," to whom we have our access; " God the Son," through whom we have access; and " God the Holy Spirit," by whom we have our access.

My friends, it is a very wonderful thing to think of, that God who made the universe—the Eternal, the Omnipotent, the Almighty, the All Knowing—became man and lived among us, and died for us, that we might have salvation and eternal life, who " in the beginning was the Word, and the Word was with God, and the Word was God. The same was in the beginning with God "—Son of God—somehow distinct, yet God, but that Word became flesh and dwelt among us, as the apostle says, " full of grace and truth." " And we beheld his glory, the glory as of the only begotten of the Father." We looked upon Him and our hands handled Him. He was in the beginning, He was with God, He was God, He became flesh, He dwelt among men. O friends, we are used to it, we have heard it over and over, we have heard it all our lives; but it is the most wonderful thing that ever happened since the Creation. We read of the doubt of the Apostle Thomas; but he was convinced at last that his Lord had risen from the grave. Said Thomas, " Except I shall see in his hands the print of the nails, and put my finger into the print of the nails, and thrust my hand into his side, I will not believe. Then came Jesus, the doors being shut, and stood in the midst, and said, Peace be unto you. Then saith he to Thomas, Reach hither thy finger, and behold my hands; and reach hither thy hand, and thrust it into my side: and be not faithless, but believing. And Thomas answered and said, My Lord and my God." It did seem to Thomas too good to believe, he could not believe it. But when Jesus asked him to put his finger into His side—into the print of the nails—he broke out, " My Lord and my God." But Jesus did not rebuke him because he doubted. " Jesus saith unto Thomas, Because thou hast seen me, thou hast believed: blessed are they that have not seen and yet have believed."

Sometimes I am tempted to say to some of my congregations, You don't believe that God became a man, lived on earth among men, died on the cross, was buried and the third day rose again, and as the God-man ever lives to intercede for us, but we will stir ourselves to take hold of that stupendous fact; the Scriptures teach it. Why, a little child who reads the New Testament will see that Jesus Christ is God, and when you search for the truth, you will find in the ninth chapter of Paul's Epistle to the Romans and the fifth verse: "Whose are the Father's, and of whom as concerning the flesh Christ came, who is over all, God blessed for ever." And in the first chapter of Hebrews we read concerning the Son: "But unto the Son he saith, Thy throne, O God, is for ever and ever." Everywhere in the Scriptures it is plainly declared that Jesus of Nazareth is the eternal Son of God, and it is strikingly and manifestly declared that the Holy Spirit is also God. Men blaspheme the Holy Spirit, they try to deceive themselves regarding the Holy Spirit. "The grace of the Lord Jesus Christ, and the love of God, and the communion of the Holy Spirit"—so the Scripture teaches—that is what we call "the doctrine of the Trinity." Children, I don't suppose you know the meaning of the "Trinity." It means three in one; it is the idea that God the Father, God the Son, God the Holy Spirit is one God. These three are somehow different from one another and yet One in God—three in oneness—tri-unity or "Trinity." But you say, "How can three be one? we believe anything that we cannot understand?"

My dear friends, please tell me what you do understand. Do you know what life is? Why, all the physiologists and metaphysicians cannot tell us what life is; nobody can define "life"; nobody can account for life, yet you believe in life; you believe that you have a soul somewhere in your body, you know it, but you cannot understand it; and if we do not understand the nature of the "Trinity," does it make any difference? But you say, "What have I to do with anything that I do not understand the nature of?" Look at the wires running all along the streets in every direction; now, when these wires are connected with the electrodes of the battery, electricity flows along the wires. Now, you cannot see that electricity, you cannot weigh it, it does not seem to have any weight; it is a mighty power, but you do not know the nature of it; nobody knows the nature of it. But, if we put ourselves in the right relation with that unknown quantity—for it is coming into our lives in a dozen different ways, it is coming into our homes—therefore, if we put ourselves in a right relation with it, it will be of advantage to us. And if we put ourselves in a wrong relation with it, it will kill us, for it is a dangerous and powerful element. And just so it is in regard to the "Trinity." If we put ourselves in right relations with the Trinity, according to the Scripture teachings,

in right relations with God the Father, God the Son, God the Holy Spirit, we shall be infinitely blessed in time and in eternity, living, dying, forever. But if we put ourselves in wrong relations with God the Father, God the Son, and God the Holy Spirit, we shall be ruined, as we deserve to be. We cannot understand the nature of the "Trinity," we cannot explain it. But, friends, we do live in a practical age and therefore we ought to see the practical importance of these great truths and their practical nature; we ought to take hold of them in a practical way and to let alone the practical varying nature of that which we do not know. Children, do you believe that Jesus Christ is the eternal Son of God? This is a very wonderful thing, is it not? that the Son of God became man and dwelt among us, that the Son of God suffered and died on the cross. This is a very shameful death, a very disgraceful death, more disgraceful than the scaffold or the electrocuting chair, but the Son of God died this shameful and disgraceful death, then was buried in the sepulcher and rose the third day, and carried that body up to the mediatorial throne on high; and we are invited to put our trust in Him as our Savior, to follow in His footsteps, to imitate His blessed example, to live as His disciples, and then we shall be saved.

It is indeed a wonderful thing that the God-man died on the cross. You say, "Could God die?" I answer "No." You say, "Could God suffer?" I answer, "I suppose not." But then the God-man suffered in His human nature. Yet it was not simply a good man that suffered and died, it was the God-man, and what a wonderful significance that gave to His atoning death; He lived for us, suffered for us, died for us; His being God gave an importance to that fact; as our Redeemer He died that we might live. But you say, "How could it be right that one person should die for another?" Why, the noblest thing that any person ever did was to suffer for another, and some have died for others, yes, voluntarily suffered and died that another might live; see the loving sacrificial devotion of a parent for his children; he would suffer, yes, die for his children; see the many examples of friend suffering for friend. So you see that it would not do but that the Savior should suffer in order to redeem the world. But you say, "How could His suffering and dying for me do me any good?" God says plainly in His Word that through atoning blood, through human sacrifice of life alone He could forgive men their sins, and it is on that ground that He is willing to forgive the sins of the world. And if God says that it was necessary, that it was all right for Christ to suffer and die for me, all I have to do is to accept it and come through Christ to the Father, who died for me that I might receive salvation. If God is satisfied, why should not I be satisfied? If God has made this marvelous provision, and He says that it is all right to obtain salvation on that ground, I shall have to whether I understand it or not, and I ought to be glad, whether I understand it or not, that He has provided that way.

But the only way to understand it is to take hold of it in a practical way; you cannot understand it if you stand off from it. It is like swimming, you cannot understand it unless you take hold of it in a practical way and resolve to learn to swim, then plunge in the water and strike out; that is the only way to learn to swim, and the only way we can ever do anything practical; in the doing of it we will understand better the nature of it. And we must come near to our Savior, confess our sins to Him and trust Him; then we will understand more clearly this life and the eternal life; and we shall understand how our sins, which are many, may be forgiven because of what our Savior has done in our behalf. And it is not merely what He has done in the past, but what He is doing now. The apostle Paul says in the Epistle to the Hebrews, "Wherefore he is able to save them to the uttermost that come unto God by him, seeing he ever liveth to make intercession for them." The Savior is now busy carrying out the designs of the creation and preparing a place for us; and we are to think not merely how He once died for us, but how He ever lives for us.

And our prayers, which are ever unworthy, if offered in His worthy name will be acceptable to God; all His infinite love goes to give value to my poor prayers and yours, when we offer them in His name. So we are taught also that this Savior who came to this earth, and lived, and suffered, and died that we might live—this Savior will come again to earth and receive His own unto Himself. Now, I know nothing about the discussions regarding the millennium; I do not know as much about it as I did thirty years ago; but there is this great and wonderful fact that He will come again; we are to be ushered into His eternal presence, and we that have loved and served Him will be received by Him into eternal glory; all men will have to appear before the judgment seat of God. Then let us look at the work of God, the Holy Spirit, and our relations with Him—it is He alone that can work a change in our moral nature. We are sinful, we are prone to do wrong, it is hard for us to do what is right; the little boy who has acquired a wrong habit knows how hard it is to stop doing that wrong and to try to do right. But God, the Holy Spirit, will come into our hearts and work such a change in us that we will hate the sin and love the holiness; and this is called being born over again—made into a completely new creature—and it is God's Holy Spirit that works that great change. So when we set out to love and work and serve Christ with all our powers, the Holy Spirit will help us in all our ways; He will help us to know our duty and to do it, and somehow, as more and more we need it, the Holy Spirit will go on renewing and sanctifying us. The Holy Spirit will come to us by asking for it. You

believe that human fathers and mothers are able to give good things unto their children; and some of you parents know what a joy and comfort it is for you to give any good thing that seemeth good for the children to them, and how hard it is for you to refuse them when you think it is not good for them to have anything; and if the human parents are able to give good things unto their children, how much more able is God to give the Holy Spirit to them that ask for it and that earnestly seek for it. But the Holy Spirit enables us to pray for what you or I do not understand how to pray for. And so, my dear friends, we must seek the Holy Spirit to guide us and help us; and we must trust ourselves unto the Savior and ask, through the Holy Spirit, Christ's blessing to sustain, strengthen and sanctify us.

This, friends, is what I call the doctrine of the Trinity, that through the Divine Savior we have our access in one Holy Spirit unto the Father. And so we may come boldly unto the throne of grace if we set out earnestly to live a life of piety. Look at that little girl who is going out into the darkness of the night—thick darkness has settled down; she says, "It is so dark outside, I hear a strange noise, I am afraid to go out into the dark;" but the child's father comes and takes the little one's hand in his strong hand; she feels it clutching her little hand and now she starts out into the darkness without fear. And that is the attitude of the human soul to God; it should trust itself to the loving Savior and to the gracious Holy Spirit, setting out to walk through the darkness guided by His sustaining hand, and thus it will reach safety at last.

My friend, are you a Christian? won't you try to be a more earnest one, rejoicing in God your Father in Jesus Christ your Divine Redeemer, in the Holy Spirit that can sanctify and strengthen you? Whether your days be many or few, devote them to the service of the Blessed Savior. My friend, are you a Christian? won't you take hold of this blessed truth more strongly? You say there are questions that you cannot answer, that you cannot understand—let the questions alone. You know of many who have taken hold of this blessed truth and have found joy, love, strength in its service, and have died in its comfort. Oh, that every heart among us might be moved at this hour to take hold of this blessed truth. Jesus Christ, the Divine Savior, who once lived on this earth and suffered and died for you, now bends from the mediatorial throne ready to receive your petition—He who gave Himself for us and ever lives to make intercession for us. Life is a very strange thing in many ways, but the strangest and saddest thing of all is that people should let themselves be told of the redeeming love and renewing grace of Our Lord and Savior Jesus Christ, and then go out and walk about in the world as tho He had never trod the earth before. God help us to live as those ought to live who know the story of salvation. Amen.—P. T.

THE IMPORTANCE OF BELIEVING ON THE SON

He that believeth on the Son, etc.—John iii: 36

The Spirit utilized John's peculiar love to Jesus as a vehicle for conveying the great truth, which permeates all John's writings, *that God now regards men only as they regard His Son* (John v: 22, 23).

To reject the Son and yet worship the Father is to be a " liar," an uncandid self-deceiver, preferring his " darkness " to the clear " light " of the " true God," now fully revealed by Jesus Christ (1 John ii: 22; v: 20).

So here we see that

I. *There is no eternal life apart from " the Son."*

This is the leading thought, carried on from the verse preceding—a fitting close to this cardinal chapter.

It is reasonable, too; for

1. A perishing world has been redeemed by the blood of God's Son; to save men otherwise would be self-contradiction (Gal. ii: 20, 21).

2. " Thou shalt not surely die " (which is still the devil's master-key for the human heart-door) would otherwise triumph over truth and justice. Salvation save through Christ would degrade God and exalt the devil and the sinner (Rom. iii: 19, 20).

3. A sinner must therefore either be saved through Christ or perish (Acts iv: 12; 1 John v: 11, 12).

II. *Every man must assume some attitude towards the Son; and is held responsible by God for it.*

No evasion possible; His yoke must be either accepted or declined—and *practically* too; belief must fructify into " obedience," and *vice versa*. The heathen will be tested otherwise, since they cannot " believe on him of whom they have not heard " (Rom. x: 14).

III. *" Belief " or " unbelief " is the crucial test of man's attitude toward God's Son.*

God sent His Son to die for me, because I could not save myself.

1. Have I gratefully placed " on the Son " my reliance for salvation? (Gal. ii: 15, 16).

2. Or have I haughtily turned away? (Rom. x: 3).

3. Or, have I listlessly passed Him by, more deeply concerned about other things? (Matt. xxii: 5; Heb. ii: 1, etc).

4. Or, am I a self-contradicting hypocrite —*both* " believing on the Son and having eternal life," *and* " obeying not the Son and never to see life? "

5. *Practical belief is God's test of character*—God's separating " fan."

(*a*) All *docile* and *candid* lovers of " light " believe (Matt. xi: 25-27).

(*b*) All unbelief is due to " love of darkness," " an evil heart of unbelief."

(*c*) Even intellectual unbelief is by Christ traced to the " will " (John vii: 17). There is no mystery in Christ greater than the mystery of God and the universe.

IV. *The reward of belief is " eternal life ":*

1. *Now*, through the Spirit. " Hath " (1 John v: 7-12; Eph. i: 14).

2. " Forever with the Lord " (Rom. viii: 16, 17; 1 Thess. iv: 17).

V. *The punishment of unbelief is abandonment to eternal blindness and eternal wo.*

1. *Abandonment by God:* " Abideth on him; " refusing salvation, he is left under wrath.

2. *Eternal blindness:* " Shall not see life; " never see God as " *Love* " (John xvii: 3; Psa. lxiii: 3). No " final restoration " is hinted at.

3. *Eternal wo:* " The wrath of God; " not " annihilation," else why creation? but the everlasting displeasure of God purposely manifested against a rejecter of His " beloved Son."—BETA. H. R.

THE TRINITY, THE SOURCE OF GRACE AND PEACE

Rev. i: 4, 5

Authorship of this Book clearly declared.— St. Paul in his epistles, mentions office and authority.—But St. John had no need to do so.—None likely to confound him with some other John.—Strange that any should have disputed its authorship.—Begins with salutations of grace and peace.—Desires that they might be enriched with fulness of blessing.— Grace had already brought them out of darkness.—But desires they might enjoy more.— It, bestowal assured, when consider source.— *Text.*

I. FIRST PERSON OF THE TRINITY, STYLED, TEXT. Difficulty in finding language to set

forth God.—Scripture employs various methods.—Usual way to proclaim His attributes. Comp. Exod. xxxiv: 6.—Here uniqueness of God's nature.—" Is, and was. and is to come," *i. e.,* the self-existent One.— So at burning bush, " I Am."—His presence pervades all space, covers all time.—Time has a relation to material things, none to God.—Mind bewildered in contemplating Him.

II. THE THIRD PERSON IN THE TRINITY, STYLED, TEXT.—Evidently refers to Holy Spirit, for introduced between Father and Son.—Contradicted notion of created intelligence, as ch. viii: 2.—Seven the number of the Holy Spirit.—Spirit works in the Church, sealing elect, etc.—Began His work at Creation.—So ever since, striving with waywardness, inspiring men of God, overruling Kings, etc.—In redemption, especially, Holy Spirit, active.—Overshadowed Virgin Mary, anointed Christ,

"Thou the anointing Spirit art,
Who dost Thy sevenfold gifts impart."

These sevenfold gifts in Is. xi: 2.—Christ received these for men, to fulfil Is. xv: 9.—Evidences every day of its being fulfilled.—The Spirit's energy set forth in ch. v: 6.—Horns, eyes, spirits, and in a sevenfold degree. III. THE SECOND PERSON.—Introduced last, for more to say of Him.—Dwells upon name, Jesus Christ, threefold office. (1) PROPHET, "faithful witness."—Came as teacher confirming words by works.—No teacher so persuasive, "spake of what seen." —His tidings unpalatable, yet preserved.— His faithfulness evidenced before Pilate, John xviii: 37.—"A good confession," convincing to Pilate.—A king of the truth attracting sympathetic souls.—Exposes worth-

lessness of Satan's testimony.—Seeks to reinstate men in the truth of their humanity. (2) PRIEST.—"First-begotten from the dead."—In person of Christ, death assumed new character.—Became a womb from which new life to spring, "first-begotten."—From it a glorious progeny.—Claim kindred with exalted Head.—Hung on cross and lay in grave, as people's representative.—As a priest offered Himself, would it be accepted.—That question answered on resurrection morn.— Then problem solved, veil withdrawn, death the gate to life. (3) KING.—"Prince of the Kings of earth."—Kingly office asserted, ": many crowns."—Christ's offices culminate in, and derive value from His death.—His witness perfected in death, and its truth demonstrated by resurrection.—So priestly office.—And now kingly office springing out of obedience to death.—A name above every name, conferring eternal life.—Supreme in heaven, "let angels worship," in hell, "holds keys," on earth, till "all kings fall before him."— Fitting title at opening of this book, which describes fortunes of the Church.—In vain do earthly powers rebel against Him.—From this triune Jehovah issue grace and peace for every humble believer.—H. A. C. Y.

TRINITY SUNDAY

BY BISHOP BROOKE F. WESTCOTT, D.D.

Rev. iv: 8, with 1 John v: 20

To-day we are called upon to keep the festival of revelation. Every other great festival of our Church commemorates a fact through which God has been pleased to teach men something of His purpose of love; Trinity Sunday encourages us to reflect for a brief space on that final truth, most absolute, most elementary, most practical, which gives unity and stability to all knowledge. The view of the Divine nature which it offers for our devout contemplation is the charter of human faith. I. The conception of the Triune God is not given to us first in an abstract form. The abstract statement is an interpretation of facts, a human interpretation of vital facts, an interpretation wrought out gradually in the first years of the Church, and still mastered gradually in our individual growth. We are required each, in some sense, to win for ourselves the inheritance which is given to us, if the inheritance is to be a blessing. We learn through the experience of history and life how God acts, the Father, the Son, and the Holy Spirit, and by the very necessity of thought we are constrained to gather up these lessons into the simplest possible formula. So we come to recognize a Divine Trinity, which is not sterile, monotonous simplicity. We come to recognize One in whom is the fulness of all conceivable existence in the richest energy.

One absolutely self-sufficient and perfect, One in whom love finds absolute consummation, One who is in Himself a living God, the fountain and end of all life. II. The conception of the Triune God illuminates the idea of creation. It enables us to gain firm hold of the truth that the learning which we observe under the condition of time answers to a Being beyond time; that history is the writing out at length of that which we may speak of as a Divine thought. The same conception illuminates the idea of the Incarnation. It enables us to see that the Incarnation in its essence is the crown of the Creation, and that man, being made capable of fellowship with God, has in his very constitution a promise of the fulfilment of his highest destiny. III. This truth is not speculative, but practical. The Christian conception of God is the translation into the language of thought of the first Christmas, Easter, and Whitsuntide. By our faith in these facts we confess that the Divine life has been united with human life. We confess, even if we do not distinctly realize the force of the confession, that the Divine life is the foundation and the end of human life. And we live, so far as life deserves the name, by this faith by which consciously or unconsciously we are stirred to toil and sustained in sacrifice.—*Oxford Review and Journal*, May 24th, 1883.

SUGGESTIVE THOUGHTS AND ILLUSTRATIONS

DIVINITY, Proofs Which Our Lord Gave of His.—When Ulysses returned with fond anticipations to his home in Ithaca, his family did not recognize him. Even the wife of his bosom denied her husband—so changed was he by an absence of twenty years, and the hardships of a long-protracted war. It was thus true of the vexed and astonished Greek as of a nobler King, that he came unto his own, and his own received him not. In this painful position of affairs he called for a bow which he had left at home, when, embarking for the siege of Troy, he bade farewell to the orange-groves and vine-clad hills of Ithaca. With characteristic sagacity, he saw how a bow, so stout and tough that none but himself could draw it, might be made to bear witness on his behalf. He seized it. To their surprise and joy, like a green wand lopped from a willow tree, it yields to his arms; it bends till the bow-string touches his ear. His wife, now sure that he is her long lost and long lamented husband, throws herself into his fond embraces, and his household confess him the true Ulysses.—THOMAS GUTHRIE.

FATHER, God Our Heavenly.—God bears not in vain the name of a Father; he fills it up to the full. It is a name of indulgence, of hope, of provision—a name of protection. It argues the mitigation of punishment; a little is enough for a father. In all temptations, oh, let us by prayer fly to the arms of our heavenly Father! and expect from Him all that a father should do for his child. But yet we must remember the name of a father is a word of relation; duty is expected from us; we must reverence Him as a father with fear and love. He is a great God, we ought to fear Him; He is merciful, yea, hath bowels of mercy, we ought to love Him; if we tremble before Him, we forget that He is loving; and if over-bold, we also forget that He is a great and holy God. Therefore we should always go to the throne of grace with reverence, holy love, and confidence in the name of Jesus.—SIBBES.

FATHER, God the.—The full meaning of God's fatherhood was not brought out in Old Testament times as we understand it now, tho it was known and recognized by pious saints. See 1 Chron. xxix: 10; Ps. ciii: 13; Isa. lxiii: 16—rather nationally than personally. THE GOSPEL OF ST. JOHN is the Gospel which speaks most of God as the "Father." It contains about one hundred references, with many varieties of expressions. Eph. iii: 15—"Of whom the whole family in heaven and earth is named." Some refer this to Christ, but more generally it is referred to the Father. God's ownership over the Church is involved in its being named from Him. To give a name to a person or a place denotes lordship over it, or interest in it; as a father gives his own name to a child; a husband to a wife; a conqueror to a conquered city.—BOWES.

GOD IS LIGHT.—*John i: 5.*—As the sentence, "God is a Spirit" (John iv: 24) is immediately followed by "and those who worship him must worship him in spirit and in truth," so this sentence must be taken as a principle, the application of which is in the sequel. The sentence is through and through ethical and practical. St. John wants no science without practice. He does not allow an enlightenment of the mind without a corresponding bias and purifying of the will.—A. P. L.

GOD, Son of.—In order to understand Jesus Christ our Savior, and the meaning of His coming, we need to know who He was before He came. We learn from John i: 1-3, and Heb. i: 2, 3, that He was existent from eternity, that He "was with God, and was God," that he was "the effulgence of his glory, and the very image of his substance."

The divine nature of Christ is not a mere theory, far away from human life, but is a fact essential to one who would reveal God to men, and be the Savior of men. He speaks to us from personal knowledge of God, of His love, His care, His readiness to forgive, His nearness to men, His fatherhood. He tells us about heaven and immortal life from His own experience. Only the Son of God could possibly make atonement for sin. Only He could have power to save us at all times and in all places, to be our ever-present friend, our perfect example, our infallible guide.

Dr. Gladden, in his PUZZLING QUESTIONS, (pp. 184-6) compares the soul to a very intricate and curious piece of mechanism, which nobody has been able successfully to operate, "on which mechanical experts of all countries have tried their hands, with very unsatisfactory results." "But here is one who knows you through and through, who knows what you are, and what you are not, but ought to be, and what you may be, and how you may live the only life that is worth living. He is one to trust and obey."

When sovereigns wish to ascertain for themselves how their subjects live, they leave their robes of state behind, and move incognito among their people, mingling with the crowd, as belonging to them. Thus their subjects speak out their feelings freely, and they become acquainted with them.—From MARCUS DODS.

LIBRARY. EXPOSITOR'S BIBLE ON JOHN, vol. ii. p. 344, for above illustration in full; OUR ELDER BROTHER (by E. P. Tenney, King-Richardson Company), p. 413, for illustration from Lessius; SUGGESTIVE ILLUSTRATIONS ON JOHN, for further illustrations; BURNING QUESTIONS, by Dr. Gladden, " Who is Jesus Christ?" for a wealth of testimonies.—P.

GOD, The Fatherhood of.—In the New Testament, God is made known to us as a Father; and a brighter feature of that book cannot be named. Our worship is to be directed to Him as our Father. Our whole religion is to take its character from this view of the Divinity. In this He is to rise always to our minds. And what is it to be a father? It is to communicate one's own nature, to give life to kindred beings; and the highest function of a father is to educate the mind of the child, and to impart to it what is noblest and happiest in his own mind. God is our Father, not merely because He created us, or because He gives us enjoyment, for He created the flower and the insect, yet we call Him not their father. This bond is a spiritual one. This name belongs to God because He frames spirits like Himself, and delights to give them what is most glorious and blessed in His own nature.—A. P. L.

GOD, The Infinite.—Unity added to infinity increases it not, any more than a foot added to infinite space. What is finite vanishes before that which is infinite, and becomes absolutely nothing. For instance, our understanding, in respect of 'God's; our righteousness compared with the Divine.—A. P. L.

GOD, The Name.—This word is spelled in four letters in almost every language, viz.: Latin, *Deus;* French, *Dieu;* Greek, *Θεός;* German. *Gott;* Scandinavian, *Odin;* Swedish, *Codd;* Hebrew, *Hdou;* Syrian, *Adad;* Persian, *Syra;* Tartarian, *Idgu;* Spanish, *Dios;* East Indian, *Esgi,* or *Zeui;* Turkish, *Addi;* Egyptian, *Anum,* or *Zeut;* Japanese, *Zain;* Peruvian, *Sian;* Wallachian, *Zene;* Etrurian, *Chur;* Irish, *Dieh;* Arabian, *Alfa.* The name appropriated by the Saxon nations (" the Good ") is unequaled, except by the most venerable Hebrew name, Jehovah.—A. P. L.

GOD, The Nature of.—" God is spirit " (John iv: 24) ; " God is light " (1 John i: 5) ; " God is love " (1 John iv: 5). All from the pen of St. John are the briefest and profoundest definitions, or Divine oracles rather, concerning the nature of God, which can be found anywhere. The first refers mainly to His metaphysical, the second to His intellectual, the third to His moral essence; but of course the line cannot be distinctly drawn.—A. P. L.

JESUS CHRIST LORD OF ALL, Revealed Truth Proclaims.—As, with the genius that aspires to immortality and anticipates the admiration of future ages, the painter leaves his name on a corner of the canvas, so Inspiration, dipping her pen in indelible truth, has inscribed the name of Jesus upon all we see—on sun and stars, flower and tree, rock and mountain, the unstable waters and the firm land; and also on what we do not see, nor shall till death has removed the veil, angels and spirits, the city and heavens of the eternal world. This is no matter of fancy. It is a fact. It is a blessed fact. No voice ever sounded more distinctly to my ear, than that of revealed truth, proclaiming Jesus, Lord of all.—THOS. GUTHRIE.

TRINITY, Derivation of.—The word " Trinity," in its Latin form *Trinitas,* is derived from the adjective *trinus,* " threefold," or " three in one." It is nowhere employed in Holy Scripture, but was a term invented and used as early as the second century, to express the doctrine by a single word, for the sake of brevity and convenience.—BISHOP HALL.

TRINITY, Glory to the.—That holy man, St. Francis, of Assisi, found appropriate expression of the ardent devotions of his soul in the constant repetition of the doxology " Glory be to the Father, and to the Son, and to the Holy Ghost; as it was in the beginning, is now, and ever shall be, world without end. Amen." He recommended the same exercise to others, who found it very helpful to spirituality.—F. II.

TRINITY, Incomprehensibility of the. —An infidel was scoffing at the doctrine of the Trinity. He turned to a gentleman, and said, " Do you believe such nonsense?" " Tell me how that candle burns," said the other. " Why the tallow, the cotton, and the atmospheric air produce light," said the infidel. " Then they make one light, do they not?" " Yes." " Will you tell me how they are three, and yet but one light?" " No, I cannot." " But you believe it?" The scoffer was put to shame.—F. II.

TRINITY IN UNITY, the.—The light of the sun, the light of the moon, and the light of the air, in nature and substance are one and the same light, and yet they are three distinct lights: the light of the sun being of itself, and from none; the light of the moon from the sun; and the light of the air from them both. So the Divine Nature is one, and the persons three; subsisting, after a diverse manner, in one and the same Nature.—R. NEWTON.

TRINITY, Names of.—The two principal names which are applied to deity in the Old Testament are Jehovah and God (in Hebrew, *Elohim*). The former is God's proper name, and clearly applics to the divine essence. This name is always singular, and may be rendered, " He who exists." The other name, *Aleim* or *Elohim,* is plural. And the question occurs, Why is the name Jehovah, which refers to His essence, always singular? Plainly, to express the unity of the divine essence. Why is the other, *Elohim,* plural? As clearly to denote a plurality of persons in the Godhead.—FIELD.

TRINITY, Symbol of the.—This symbol, light, is composed of three parts, one visible and two invisible; first, illuminative rays, which affect our vision, and by their Fraunhofer lines bring to us a knowledge of the substance of the suns from which they spring; second, chemical rays, which cause growth, and give the results of photography; and, third, the principle called heat, separate from either. So is God revealed—three persons in one God. No man hath seen the Father, or the Holy Ghost: but the Son has been seen of men. Each of these component parts is capable of separate and independent action. Each can be sundered from the other, and still retain its full efficiency. The illuminative rays still stream with their incredible swiftness, still bloom with incomprehensible color, and still bear their records of other worlds, after the other two component parts have been turned to other work. There could be no other so happy illustration of the incomprehensible triune nature of God.—Dr. H. W. Warren.

TRINITY, Understanding the.—He who goes about to speak of the mystery of the Trinity, and does it by words, and names of man's invention, talking of essence and existence, hypostases and personalities, priority in co-equality, and unity in pluralities, may amuse himself and build a tabernacle in his head, and talk something—he knows not what; but the renewed man, that feels the power of the Father, to whom the Son is become wisdom, sanctification, and redemption, in whose heart the love of the Spirit of God is shed abroad—this man, tho he understand nothing of what is unintelligible, yet he alone truly understands the Christian doctrine of the Trinity.—Jeremy Taylor.

TRINITY, Unity of the.—A converted Indian gave the following reason for his belief in the Trinity: "We go down to the river in winter, and we see it covered with snow; we dig through the snow, and we come to the ice; we chop through the ice, and we come to the water; snow is water, ice is water, water is water; therefore the three are one."—F. II.

TRIUNE GOD, The.—Is a conception for which we can never find a complete illustration; but it is a suggestive fact that every ray of sunlight is composed of three kinds of rays, which perform three distinct kinds of work: the heat-rays, the light-rays, and the actinic, or chemical rays.—H. R.

POETRY

To a Clover Leaf

By Eliza Atkins Stone

O tiny trinity of green,
Thou perfect three-in-one!
Lowly I kneel before thy shrine
Wilt hear mine orison?

To-day I feel a kinship near,
With all things secret, shy;
Too close about my spirit draws
The myriad mystery.

The sun is over glorious,
Awful the arch of sky,
And the high altars of the earth
Seem not for such as I;

But, hushed and hidden here with thee,
The wondrous All I read,
In gentle symbol charactered,
Accordant to my need.—I.

Ode to God

By Derzhavin

O Thou eternal One: whose presence bright
All space doth occupy, all motion guide;
Unchanged through time's all-devastating flight;
Thou only God! There is no God beside!
Being above all beings! Mighty One!
Whom none can comprehend and none explore;
Who fill'st existence with Thyself alone:
Embracing all—supporting—ruling o'er—
Being whom we call God—and know no more!

In its sublime research philosophy
May measure out the ocean-deep—may count
The sands or the sun's rays—but, God for Thee
There is no weight nor measure: none can mount
Up to thy mysteries. Reason's brightest spark,
Tho kindled by Thy light, in vain would try
To trace Thy counsels, infinite and dark:
And thought is lost ere thought can soar so high,
Even like past moments in eternity.

Thou from primeval nothingness didst call
First chaos, then existence: Lord! on Thee
Eternity had its foundation; all
Sprung forth from Thee—of light, joy, harmony,
Sole origin: all life, all beauty Thine.
Thy word created all, and doth create;
Thy splendor fills all space with rays divine.
Thou art, and wert, and shalt be! Glorious! Great!
Light-giving, life-sustaining Potentate!

Thy chains the unmeasured universe surround,
Upheld by Thee, by Thee inspired with breath!
Thou the beginning with the end hast bound,
And beautifully mingled life and death!
As sparks mount upward from the fiery blaze,
So suns are born, so worlds spring forth from Thee:
And as the spangles in the sunny rays
Shine round the silver snow, the pageantry
Of heaven's bright army glitters in Thy praise.

A million torches lighted by Thy hand
Wander unwearied through the blue abyss:
They own Thy power, accomplish Thy command,
All gay with life, all eloquent with bliss.
What shall we call them? Piles of crystal light—
A glorious company of golden streams—
Lamps of celestial ether burning bright—
Suns lighting systems with their joyous beams?
But Thou to these art as the noon to night.

Yes! as a drop of water in the sea,
All this magnificence in Thee is lost:
What are ten thousand worlds compared to Thee?
And what am *I* then? Heaven's unnumbered host,
Tho multiplied by myriads, and arrayed
In all the glory of sublimest thought,
Is but an atom in the balance, weighed
Against Thy greatness, is a cipher brought
Against infinity! O, what am I then? Naught!

Naught! yet the effluence of Thy light divine,
Pervading worlds, hath reached my bosom too;
Yes! in my spirit doth Thy spirit shine,
As shines the sunbeam in a drop of dew.
Naught! yet I live and on hope's pinions fly
Eager towards Thy presence; for in Thee
I live, and breathe, and dwell; aspiring high,
Even to the throne of Thy divinity.
I am, O God! and surely *Thou* must be!

Thou art! directing, guiding all, Thou art!
Direct my understanding, then, to Thee;
Control my spirit, guide my wandering heart;
Tho but an atom 'midst immensity,
Still I am something, fashioned by Thy hand!
I hold a middle rank 'twixt heaven and earth,
On the last verge of mortal being stand,
Close to the realms where angels have their birth,
Just on the boundaries of the spirit-land!

The chain of being is complete in me;
In me is matter's last gradation lost,
And the next step is spirit—Deity!
I can command the lightning, and am dust!
A monarch, and a slave; a worm, a god!
Whence came I here?. and how so marvelously
Constructed and conceived? unknown, this clod
Lives surely through some higher energy;
For from itself alone it could not be!

Creator, yes! Thy wisdom and Thy word
Created *me!* Thou source of life and good!
Thou spirit of my spirit, and my Lord!
Thy light, Thy love, in their bright plenitude
Filled me with an immortal soul, to spring
Over the abyss of death, and bade it wear
The garments of eternal day, and wing
Its heavenly flight beyond this little sphere,
Even to its source—to Thee—its Author there.

O thoughts ineffable! O visions blest!
Tho worthless our conceptions all of Thee,
Yet shall Thy shadowed image fill our breast,
And waft its homage to Thy Deity.
God! thus alone my lonely thoughts can soar;
Thus seek Thy presence, Being wise and good!
'Midst Thy vast works admire, obey, adore;
And when the tongue is eloquent no more,
The soul shall speak in tears of gratitude.

God's Glory

By Oliver Wendell Holmes

Lord of all being, throned afar,
Thy glory flames from sun and star;
Center and soul of every sphere,
Yet to each loving heart how near.

Sun of our life, Thy quickening ray
Sheds on our path the glow of day;
Star of our hope, Thy softened light
Cheers the long watches of the night.

Our midnight is Thy smile withdrawn;
Our noontide is Thy gracious dawn;
Our rainbow arch Thy mercy's sign;
All, save the clouds of sin, are Thine.

Lord of all life, below, above,
Whose light is truth, whose warmth is love,
Before Thy ever-blazing throne
We ask no luster of our own.

Grant us Thy truth to make us free,
And kindling hearts that burn for Thee,
Till all Thy living altars claim
One holy light, one heavenly flame.

Herein is Love

By Frederick W. Faber

My God, how wonderful Thou art,
 Thy majesty how bright!
How glorious is Thy mercy-seat,
 In depths of burning light!

How dread are Thine eternal years,
 O everlasting Lord!
By prostrate spirits day and night
 Incessantly adored.

Oh, how I fear Thee, living God,
 With deepest, tenderest fears,
And worship Thee with trembling hope,
 And penitential tears.

Yet I may love Thee too, O Lord,
 Almighty as Thou art,
For Thou hast stooped to ask of me
 The love of my poor heart.

No earthly father loves like Thee,
 No mother half so mild
Bears and forbears, as Thou hast done
 With me, Thy sinful shild.

My God, how wonderful Thou art,
 Thou everlasting Friend!
On Thee I stay my trusting heart,
 Till faith in vision end.

Eternal Spirit!

By Rev. William H. Bathurst

Eternal Spirit! by whose power
Are burst the bands of death,
On our cold hearts Thy blessing shower,
Revive them with Thy breath.

'Tis Thine to point the heavenly way,
Each rising fear control,
And with a warm, enlivening ray
To melt the icy soul.

'Tis Thine to cheer us when distressed,
To raise us when we fall;
To calm the doubting, troubled breast,
And aid when sinners call.

'Tis Thine to bring God's sacred Word,
And write it on our heart;
There its reviving truths record,
And there its peace impart.

Almighty Spirit! visit thus
Our hearts, and guide our ways;
Pour down Thy quickening grace on us,
And tune our lips to praise.

Te Deum Laudamus

By Clarence Augustus Walworth

Hark! the loud celestial hymn,
Angel choirs above are raising:
Cherubim and seraphim
In unceasing chorus praising,
Fill the heav'ns with sweet accord:
Holy! holy! holy Lord!

Lo! the apostolic train
Join Thy sacred Name to hallow!
Prophets swell the loud refrain,
And the white-robed martyrs follow;
And from morn till set of sun,
Through the Church the song goes on.

Holy Father, Holy Son,
Holy Spirit, Three we name Thee,
While in essence only One,
Undivided God we claim Thee;
And, adoring, bend the knee,
While we own the mystery.

Spare Thy people, Lord, we pray,
By a thousand snares surrounded;
Keep us without sin to-day,
Never let us be confounded.
Lo! I put my trust in Thee,
Never, Lord, abandon me.

Three in One

By Gilbert Rorison

Three in One, and One in Three,
Ruler of the earth and sea,
Hear us, while we lift to Thee
Holy chant and psalm.

Light of lights, with morning, shine:
Lift on us Thy light divine;
And let charity benign
Breathe on us her balm.

Light of lights, when falls the even,
Let it close on sin forgiven;
Fold us in the peace of heaven,
Shed a holy calm.

Three in One, and One in Three,
Dimly here we worship Thee:
With the saints hereafter we
Hope to bear the palm.

Thrice Holy

By Christopher Wordsworth

Holy, holy, holy Lord,
God of Hosts, eternal King,
By the heavens and earth adored;
Angels and Archangels sing,
Chanting everlastingly,
To the Blessèd Trinity.

Since by Thee were all things made,
And in Thee do all things live,
Be to Thee all honor paid;
Praise to Thee let all things give,
Singing everlastingly
To the Blessèd Trinity.

Thousands, tens of thousands, stand,
Spirits blest, before the throne,
Speeding thence at Thy command,
And, when Thy commands are done,
Singing everlastingly
To the Blessèd Trinity.

Cherubim and Seraphim
Veil their faces with their wings;
Eyes of angels are too dim
To behold the King of kings,
While they sing eternally
To the Blessèd Trinity.

Thee apostles, prophets Thee,
Thee the noble martyr band,
Praise with solemn jubilee,
Thee, the Church in every land,
Singing everlastingly
To the Blessèd Trinity.

Halleluiah! Lord, to Thee,
Father, Son, and Holy Ghost;
Godhead One, and Persons Three;
Join with us the heavenly host,
Singing everlastingly
To the Blessèd Trinity.

The Trinity Adored

By Rev. James Wallis Eastburn

O Holy, holy, holy Lord,
Bright in Thy deeds and in Thy Name,
For ever be Thy Name adored,
Thy glories let the world proclaim.

O Jesus, Lamb once crucified
To take our load of sins away,
Thine be the hymn that rolls its tide
Along the realms of upper day.

O Holy Spirit from above,
In streams of light and glory given,
Thou source of ecstasy and love,
Thy praises ring through earth and Heaven.

O God Triune, to Thee we owe
Our every thought, our every song;
And ever may Thy praises flow
From saint and seraph's burning tongue.

Trinity Hymn

BY EDWARD COOPER

Father of heaven, whose love profound
A ransom for our souls hath found,
Before Thy throne we sinners bend:
To us Thy pardoning love extend.

Almighty Son, incarnate Word,
Our Prophet, Priest, Redeemer, Lord,
Before Thy throne we sinners bend:
To us Thy saving grace extend.

Eternal Spirit, by whose breath
The soul is raised from sin and death,
Before Thy throne we sinners bend:
To us Thy quickening power extend.

Jehovah,—Father, Spirit, Son,—
Mysterious Godhead, Three in One,
Before Thy throne we sinners bend:
Grace, pardon, life, to us extend.

Analogies of the Trinity

BY MARTIN F. TUPPER

There be three grand principles—life, generation. and obedience—
Shadowing, in every creature, the Spirit, and
the Father, and the Son.
There be three grand unities, variously
mixed in trinities,
The rose, and the ruby, and the pearl; each
one is made of three;
And the three be the like ingredients, mingled in diverse measures.
Thyself hast within thyself body, and life,
and mind;
Matter, and breath, and instinct, unite in all
beasts of the field;
Substance, coherence, and weight, fashion
the fabrics of the earth;
The will, the doing, and the deed, combine
to frame a fact:
The stem, the leaf, and the flower; beginning,
middle, and end;
Cause, circumstance, consequent; and every
three is one.
Yea, the very breath of man's life consisteth
of a trinity of vapors,
And the noonday light is a compound, the
triune shadow of Jehovah.

Hymn to the Trinity

BY WILLIAM CROSWELL DOANE

O Holy Father, who hast led Thy children
In all the ages, with the fire and cloud,
Through seas dry-shod; through weary
wastes bewildering;
To Thee, in reverent love, our hearts are
bowed.

O Holy Jesus, Prince of Peace, and Savior,
To Thee we owe the peace that still prevails,

Stilling the rude wills of men's wild behavior,
And calming passion's fierce and stormy
gales.

O Holy Ghost, the Lord and the Life Giver,
Thine is the quickening power that gives
increase.
From Thee have flowed, as from a pleasant
river,
Our plenty, wealth, prosperity and peace.

O Triune God, with heart and voice adoring,
Praise we the goodness that has crowned
our day;
Pray we, that Thou wilt hear us, still im-
ploring
Thy love and favor, kept for us alway.

Blest Trinity

BY HERVEY DODDRIDGE GANSE

Eternal Father, when to Thee,
Beyond all worlds, by faith I soar,
Before Thy boundless majesty
I stand in silence, and adore.

But, Savior, Thou art by my side:
Thy voice I hear, Thy face I see,
Thou art my friend, my daily guide;
God over all, yet God with me.

And Thou, Great Spirit, in my heart
Dost make Thy temple day by day:
The Holy Ghost of God Thou art,
Yet dwellest in this house of clay.

Blest Trinity, in whom alone
All things created move or rest,
High in the heavens Thou hast Thy throne,
Thou hast Thy throne within my breast.

Trinity Sunday

BY JOHN KEBLE

*If I have told you earthly things, and ye
believe not, how shall ye believe, if I tell you
of heavenly things?—St. John iii: 12.*

Creator, Savior, strengthening Guide,
Now on Thy mercy's ocean wide
Far out of sight we seem to glide.

Help us, each hour, with steadier eye
To search the deepening mystery,
The wonders of Thy sea and sky.

The blessèd angels look and long
To praise Thee with a worthier song,
And yet our silence does Thee wrong.

Along the Church's central space
The sacred weeks with unfelt pace
Have borne us on from grace to grace.

As travelers on some woodland height,
When wintry suns are gleaming bright,
Lose in arched glades their tangled sight;

By glimpses such as dreamers love
Through her gray veil the leafless grove
Shows where the distant shadows rove;

Such trembling joy the soul o'erawes
As nearer to Thy shrine she draws;
And now before the choir we pause.

The door is closed—but soft and deep
Around the awful arches sweep
Such airs as soothe a hermit's sleep.

From each carved nook and fretted bend
Cornice and gallery seem to send
Tones that with seraph hymns might blend.

Three solemn parts together twine
In harmony's mysterious line;
Three solemn aisles approach the shrine:

Yet all are One—together all,
In thoughts that awe but not appal
Teach the adoring heart to fall.

Within these walls each fluttering guest
Is gently lured to one safe nest—
Without, 'tis moaning and unrest.

The busy world a thousand ways
Is hurrying by, nor ever stays
To catch a note of Thy dear praise.

Why tarries not her chariot wheel,
That o'er her with no vain appeal
One gust of heavenly song might steal?

Alas! for her Thy opening flowers
Unheeded breathe to summer showers,
Unheard the music of Thy bowers.

What echoes from the sacred dome
The selfish spirit may o'ercome
That will not hear of love or home?

The heart that scorned a father's care,
How can it rise in filial prayer?
How an all-seeing Guardian bear?

Or how shall envious brethren own
A Brother on the eternal throne,
Their Father's joy, their hope alone?

How shall Thy Spirit's gracious wile
The sullen brow of gloom beguile,
That frowns on sweet affection's smile?

Eternal One, Almighty Trine!
(Since Thou art ours, and we are Thine)
By all Thy love did once resign,

By all the grace Thy heavens still hide,
We pray Thee, keep us at Thy side,
Creator, Savior, strengthening Guide!

The Blessed Trinity

BY REGINALD HEBER

Holy, holy, holy! Lord God Almighty;
Early in the morning our song shall rise to
    Thee,
Holy, holy, holy, merciful and mighty;
God in three persons, blessed Trinity.

Holy, holy, holy! all the saints adore Thee,
Casting down their golden crowns around the
    glassy sea,
Cherubim and seraphim falling down before
    Thee,
Which wert, and art, and evermore shalt be.

Holy, holy, holy! tho the darkness hide Thee,
Tho the eye of sinful man Thy glory may
    not see,
Only Thou art holy; there is none beside
    Thee
Perfect in power, in love, and purity.

Holy, holy, holy! Lord God Almighty;
All Thy works shall praise Thy name, in
    earth and sky and sea:
Holy, holy, holy, merciful and mighty;
God in three persons, blessed Trinity. Amen.

Trisagion

BY JAMES MONTGOMERY

Holy, holy, holy Lord
    God of hosts! When heaven and earth
Out of darkness, at Thy word,
    Issued into glorious birth,
All Thy works before Thee stood,
And Thine eye beheld them good,
While they sang with sweet accord,
Holy, holy, holy Lord!

Holy, holy, holy! Thee,
    One Jehovah evermore,
Father, Son, and Spirit, we,
    Dust and ashes, would adore;
Lightly by the world esteemed,
From that world by Thee redeemed,
Sing we here, with glad accord,
Holy, holy, holy Lord!

Holy, holy, holy! All
    Heaven's triumphant choir shall sing,
When the ransomed nations fall
    At the footstool of their King:
Then shall saints and seraphim,
Hearts and voices, swell one hymn,
Round the throne with full accord,
Holy, holy, holy Lord!

The Triune God

BY HORATIUS BONAR

Glory be to God the Father,
    Glory be to God the Son,
Glory be to God the Spirit,
    Great Jehovah, Three in One:
    Glory, glory,
    While eternal ages run!

Glory be to Him who loved us,
    Washed us from each spot and stain;
Glory be to Him who bought us,
    Made us kings with Him to reign:
    Glory, glory,
    To the Lamb that once was slain!

Glory to the King of angels,
    Glory to the Church's King,
Glory to the King of nations,
    Heaven and earth, your praises bring:
    Glory, glory,
    To the King of glory bring!

Glory, blessing, praise eternal!
    Thus the choir of angels sings;
Honor, riches, power, dominion!
    Thus its praise creation brings.
    Glory, glory,
    Glory to the King of kings!

ALL SAINTS' DAY

(November)

A LL SAINTS' DAY is a holy day of the Greek, Romish, Anglican, and Episcopal churches. Chrysostom tells us that as early as the fourth century, a festival was celebrated by the Eastern Church in honor of all the saints on the Sunday after Whitsuntide, and called All Saints' Sunday. It is, however, as late as the seventh century before such a day was observed in the Western Church.

Pope Boniface IV. having obtained possession of the pantheon at Rome, fitted it for Christian worship, dedicated it to the Virgin and all the saints, and its day of dedication, May 13, was annually celebrated for all the saints. Later Pope Gregory III. dedicated a church to the honor of all the saints, on November 1, and, in the ninth century, the Anglican and Frankish Churches having been induced to introduce an all-saints' festival on November 1, this date became generally accepted. The day was popularly called All Hallow's Day, whence it became the custom to call the evening before All-hallow e'en, and in Scotland and Ireland certain sports and festivities, said to be relics of Druidism, were indulged in.

In the Anglican Church All Saints' Day is still observed; in most other Reformed churches it has fallen into disuse.

On the supreme idea of this day, the life of the blessed in Paradise, Bishop Webb says: "We may think of those who have gone before us, as having consciousness about themselves and about each other, and as being able to recognize each other, and as having a condition of identity, which some sort of blessed bright form will give them. Search the Scriptures yourselves. Take every passage which discloses the individuality of those who have gone into the invisible world; you will scarcely be able, it seems to me, to come to any other conclusion. There will also be, amongst other marks of life and consciousness, Memory. You know what Abraham said to one, 'Son, remember!' Look back upon thy life. Think of what you did with the means God gave you. Think of those who were so close to you, at your very gate. . . . There will be, then, this great bond and link between one part of our life and another, which seems almost indispensable to our individuality and to our consciousness, the wonderful prerogative of Memory. Together with this there will be a *progress,* a growth, in knowledge, in holiness. St. Paul learned in Paradise what he did not know before, here on earth; and shall not we learn the power and meaning of truths to which we have not yet attained? Shall not God reveal to us, in Paradise, the truths which some holy men clearly see already, but whereunto we ourselves cannot honestly say that we have attained? 'God shall reveal even this unto you.'"

THE GLORIES OF IMMORTALITY

By Alexander Carson

With respect to the nature of the glory of the Heaven of heavens, the Scriptures do not appear to afford much precise and specific information. It would appear in general, from the Book of Revelation, that the chief employments and happiness of the saints consist in the praises of their ever-blessed Redeemer. On earth, tho they have not seen

Him, they love Him above all things. But in Heaven their happiness is perfect in the perfect love of Him.

The representation of the new Jerusalem is evidently figurative, and therefore we are not warranted to say that any of the specific objects mentioned in this description actually exist. We ought not to conceive Heaven as being really a city, with such walls, gates, pavements, etc. This representation has no doubt an important meaning, but this importance would be infinitely diminished by supposing that it is a literal description. A city thus built would be the most glorious that the imagination could conceive, to be made of earthly materials, but it is a faint figure of the glory of the true Heaven.

Some have thought that the risen body will not possess any powers of sensation. With respect to sight and hearing this is manifestly false. How much of the pleasure of the heavenly inhabitants consists in the sweet and loved songs of praise to God and the Lamb! And for what is all the glory of heaven, if not to gratify the eye? Light is the most glorious object on earth, and the enjoyment of the light of Heaven appears to be among the most eminent felicities.

The angels of Heaven are called angels of light—as distinguished from the angels that kept not their first love, who are reserved in chains of everlasting darkness to the judgment of the great day. Now, it appears to me that the former are so called from the light in which they dwell, rather than from their knowledge, or from the nature of their works, as Macknight understands the passage. It would be difficult to point out a distinguishing ignorance in the fallen spirits, and angels of light would be a very indefinite and distant expression to denote that they are continually employed in promoting truth and virtue. Believers may be distinguished from the children of this world, as the children of light, because they are enlightened in that great truth of which the others are ignorant.

God is also said to dwell in light—" who only hath immortality, dwelling in the light which no man can approach unto; whom no man hath seen, nor can see." This light is so exceedingly glorious that no man in his present state can approach it. But the time will come when even the eyes of the saints will be able to bear that light, for "they shall see God." "Flesh and blood shall not inherit the kingdom of God," but the glorious spiritual bodies of the saints will enjoy it. What must be the brilliancy of the light of Heaven when a glance of it now overpowers any of the human race? "At midday, O king, I saw in the way a light from Heaven above the brightness of the sun, shining round about me and them which journeyed with me. And when we were all fallen to the earth," etc. "And when I could not see for the glory of that light, being led by the hand of them that were with me," etc.

Some have supposed that God will never be visible and that the promise that we shall see God means only that we shall see the light in which He dwells. It is dangerous to advance too far on such a subject. But I am not willing even here to limit Scripture language by views of possibility. That one spirit may have a perception of another corresponding to what we call visible is surely not only possible but certain. If so, why may not our spirits have such a perception of God? And that it is impossible for the glorified eye of the saint to have a perception of God is more than I will say. Let it suffice us that "we shall see God." Let us leave the manner of this to Himself. "Take heed," says Christ, "that ye despise not one of these little ones; for I say unto you that in heaven their angels do always behold the face of my Father which is in heaven." And if angels behold the face of God, it will not be impossible for us. To behold His face must imply to view Him in His glory; we need not, therefore, confound ourselves by any subtle inquiries about the way of seeing a spirit. God is everywhere: it is possible to make us sensible of His presence, whatever part of space we may at any time occupy. This is an unfathomable subject, but tho it represses arrogant inquiries beyond what is written, it opens up a boundless field of expectation of our future state. Having such a God as a Father, what may we not expect?

The reward of the saints is frequently exhibited with very animating effect, under the figure of the crowns of the victors in the Grecian games, and of the conquerors who obtain a triumph on their return to their country. In these games the greatest men of the times entered as competitors for the glory of victory, and even kings thought themselves honored by obtaining the prize. The victor was rewarded with a crown of leaves, and was received with unbounded honor by the vast multitudes assembled from all parts of Greece. Now, after all the self-denial of their former lives and unwearied diligence in preparatory exercises; after all the toils, dangers, and sufferings in the arduous struggle, they thought this crown of leaves a high recompense. It raised them upon a pinnacle of glory, to be viewed with admiration by all countries. Yet, as the apostle says, they had in prospect only a corruptible crown; we have in our view an incorruptible crown. Their crown was the greatest the world could bestow, but it was fading, and is already withered many a hundred years. The crown of the Christian flourishes on his head with unfading freshness, and will bloom through eternity. Its glory will be witnessed not by the people only of one age, but by all the principalities in Heaven.—W. B. O.

SERMONS AND OUTLINES

PRECIOUS DEATH

By A. C. Dixon, D.D.

Precious in the sight of the Lord is the death of his saints.—Ps. cxvi: 15

As we see death, it means decay, removal, absence. These are things which we do not prize. They are the "present affliction," which is "always grievous." But as God sees death, He beholds something really precious to Him and, we may justly infer, precious to us, for whatever is against us cannot be precious to our Father.

We are looking at the wrong side of the tapestry, where all is tangle and confusion. God sees the right side, where the design is intelligent and the colors harmonious. We look at the back of the canvas; God alone sees the painting wrought by a master hand. We are without the veil, and see but the dim light through the curtain; within is the shechinah glory. We stand in the dark, believing and hoping; God is in the light, seeing and knowing.

It may be of profit to us to inquire, Why is the death of a saint precious in the sight of the Lord?

I. Because to God death means the opportunity to supply every need of His child. Health means conscious strength. While we are well, we may feel that we are equal to taking care of ourselves. Dying means absolute helplessness. Such is God's opportunity. When physicians give up the case, He takes it up. After human help has failed, the Lord delights to be to us all that we need. When loving words fail to comfort, "His rod and his staff, they comfort." His voice in the dark is music to our souls. When we are too weak to speak to Him in prayer, He speaks to us in promise. Our weakness in the dying moment is precious to God, for it gives Him the opportunity of doing all for us.

II. To God death means the most intimate communion. He rejoices to have all to Himself those whom He loves. He said of Israel, "I will allure her and bring her into the wilderness, and speak comfortably unto her." No one else can help us die. Through the valley we must go alone—yet not alone, for Jesus accompanies. For once He has us all to Himself. While living, we may have experiences that isolate us from others: sorrows or joys which no one upon earth can appreciate. Only He can enter into them with us. At such times God delights to be alone with His people. He makes the wilderness a garden and the desert place a fountain of living water. Those of us who have experienced something of this kind may dimly imagine the more blessed experience when, in the hour of death, the Christian has God all to himself, and the joy which he

feels is but a tithe of the joy which the Lord Himself must derive from such intimate communion with His children.

III. To God death means rest. Jesus said, "Come unto me, all ye that labor, and I will give you rest." It was His delight to quiet the heart and give rest to the weary mind. The voice from heaven said, "Blessed are the dead which die in the Lord; they rest from their labors." "There remaineth a rest to the people of God." To us death looks like a rest of the body—the lifeless form no longer suffers; it sleeps until the waking on the resurrection morning. God sees the rest of soul, and the event which introduces His children into this restful state is precious to Him.

IV. To God death means larger life. Christ came to give life, and to give it more abundantly. Whatever imparts and increases the life of God's people is of great value. While to us death seems to be the cessation of life, to God it is an increase of life.

"Death is the crown of life.
    Were death denied, poor man would live in vain;
    Were death denied, to live would not be life;
    Were death denied, even fools would wish to die.'"

To us death is contraction. As we grow older memory fails, sight fails, hearing fails, strength fails. Our world narrows, and to the eye of sense death is the climax of successive failures. It is the final contraction into the narrow grave. Paul looked through God's eyes when he wrote, "The time of my departure is at hand." The word "departure" is a nautical term, which means lifting anchor and sailing out into the broad sea. Death is enlargement of life and opportunity. The last words of Drummond Burns were, "I have been dying for years, now I shall begin to live." It is passing from the land of the dying into the land of the living.

"Death is another life. We bow our heads
At going out, we think; and enter straight
Another golden chamber of the King's,
Larger than this we leave, and lovelier."

V. To God death means joy. All through the Bible we are exhorted to "Rejoice, rejoice evermore!" The joy of His children is precious to God.

We are apt to fear dying more than death. What death will bring we anticipate with pleasure, while we shrink from the pain and mystery of the dying moment; and yet even in this many are agreeably disappointed. Dying may be rapture.

Dying, Rutherford exclaimed: "I feed on manna; oh, for arms to embrace Him!"

President Wingate, of Wake Forest College, whispered to his wife with his last breath, "I thought it would be sweet, but I did not think it would be so sweet as this."

But however great the joy of dying, the joy of death is greater, for

"It is the key
That opens the palace of eternity."

It is passing from shadow into sunshine; from the discords of earth into the music of the celestial harps; from contraction into everlasting expansion.

Oh, the joy of meeting and greeting! Death is still a gathering unto our people. To know that Christ is with us thrills our hearts. To behold Him as He is and be like Him will give such rapture that mortal frame could not endure it. Hope has its joy; hope realized will be ecstasy. If the joys of anticipation are so great, what will be the joys of realization? Pope's picture of the dying Christian is not overdrawn, and marks with vivid outlines the transition between earth and heaven:

"Hark! they whisper; angels say,
'Sister spirit, come away!'
What is this absorbs me quite,
Steals my senses, shuts my sight,
Drowns my spirit, draws my breath?
Tell me, my soul, can this be death?

"The world recedes, it disappears!
Heaven opens on my eyes! my ears
    With sounds seraphic ring:
Lend, lend your wings! I mount! I fly!
O grave! where is thy victory?
    O death! where is thy sting?"

VI. To God death means ministry to the living. Death is a dusky servant of the King. Through death Jesus entered the family of the Jewish ruler, and the death of our friends often leads us to invite this Man of Sorrows to our homes. The departure of loved ones opens a window of heaven, and gives us a glimpse into the beyond; and in leaving us, they, in a very true sense, come to us. We appreciate them as we never did before; we see their virtues and forget their faults; they are to us transfigured, while everything about them shines with a peculiar glory. The most precious treasures in every family are its deaths. Like angels, they come to us daily from the past, making us more heavenly-minded, and we look for our loved ones toward the future, for "them that sleep in Jesus will God bring with him."—H. R.

RECOGNITION OF OUR FRIENDS IN HEAVEN

By J. W. Chapman, D.D.

Then shall I know even as also I am known.—1 Cor. xiii: 12

It would seem to us, if this were the first time we had ever listened to these words, as if they would answer the question which has been in our minds all the days of our lives; the question which we have so often asked each other: Shall we know each other there? Said an old saint to her husband, who for threescore years and ten had journeyed by her side: "Do you suppose we shall know each other when we meet on the other shore?" And the old man who had been seventy years by her side, and more than that in the kingdom of God, answered her in these words: "I am very sure I shall not know less in the next world than this, and I am sure we shall know each other in the better land."

I am sure that in this world we do not know each other. You do not know your own child. Every day as you look into her face, and as you study the little life, you find that there is more in it than you ever imagined. The Word of God makes this plain to us, for we are told that "now we see as through a glass dimly." We behold only the shadow of ourselves and our friends. Then we are told just in the next verse, of the time to come "we shall see face to face," and more than that, we are told "we shall

know even as also we are known." It is a wondrous question. Shall we know each other on the other shore? There are very few of us but what have at some time journeyed to a tomb. As I look around on the right hand and on the left I can see many a one wearing the evidence of mourning, and so as this question comes to us to-night, every heart almost seems to throb right in it. It makes the lips tremble, it moves the heart, and the face is flushed and then grows pale; and we put the question to each other, then breathlessly listen for the answer. How many times we have heard it said, "I wonder if it is true that we shall know each other in the better land?" I have had so many letters during the course of my ministry asking me to preach concerning this subject, that I want to answer the question in a satisfactory manner, to myself at least.

How much more Heaven would seem to be to us if we could only answer the question in the affirmative. In the East we are told that when a friend dies and is buried, they bring to the grave a cage of birds (always singing birds), and there they open the cage, and just as the coffin is being lowered into the tomb, the birds come out singing as they go. There has never been a Christian buried but what the birds of Paradise have been singing their sweetest songs about us, sweeter than any birds of earth, altho we are told that the nightingale is the very queen of birds, and its song is as the very music of Heaven.

Can you tell me what Heaven is? It may be said it is a place not made with hands; a city the census of which has never been recorded; a city through whose streets no rush of toil or travel is heard; a city without griefs or graves, marriages or mournings, without sorrows or sins; a city whose glory is that it has Jesus for a King, the angels for its guards, and the saints of God for its inhabitants; a city whose walls are salvation and whose gates are praise. This is true, and yet this does not satisfy you, and I am sure that it does not satisfy me. We are told that Heaven is a place where all the fulness of glory dwells. Can you give me a definition of what the glory of Heaven is? My idea of the glory of Heaven might differ from yours. I can go to the tent of an Indian and the things he prizes are very few and simple. Just a few eagle feathers, reminding him of the war he has engaged in; an old tomahawk, which he swings around his head and then sends flying to the mark; a bow and arrow which his father had given him, and which he has had ever since he was sent into the field of life.

Now if I were to take these things which are the glory of the Indian, and take them to a shepherd's hut, he would look at them and say, "Why these things are not worth a moment's consideration." He has a few things which he delights in, but if I were to take the things which he has and go over to the house of a rich man, whose walls are covered with paintings and whose halls are filled with statuary, he would look upon the things of the peasant, and turn away with disgust upon his face, and say they were not worth the room they occupied; and yet if I were to take the things in which the rich man finds his glory and carry them to the palace of the king, they would be as nothing to him. An empire has exhausted itself in contributing to his wealth and splendor, and he too would say, "Why these things are not worth the room they take up;" and yet if we were to take the things wherein the king glories into the City above, they would be as nothing compared to the glory of that City; the City whose streets are gold, whose gates are pearl, whose foundation stones are jewels. Can you imagine the wonderful glory that awaits us in the skies?

When Paul was caught up into the Heaven above, he said he had heard things not lawful for him to utter; a better translation would be that he had heard things it would not be possible for him to utter; there was no language to describe his vision. If he had seen the things he could not possibly describe, we can only say to those that ask of us, as Bunyan once told an old woman who was asking him about that beautiful City. "Madam," said he, "I cannot tell you about the city, the only advice I can give you is to live the life that is hid with Christ in God, and go for yourself to behold its splendor." And yet, if this is true, it is a good thing for us to think about Heaven. I have been told that when artists sit for a long time painting pictures their eyes sometimes get below the proper tone or pitch, so they get a number of little bright pebble stones, and place them on the easel, and every little while they will look at these stones before them, and in this way they can always keep the pitch or tone of the eye just right. Thinking of Heaven is to the Christian what the tuning fork is to the great orchestra. They get below the pitch sometimes and it is then necessary to go back to the tuning fork to get the right tone and the right pitch. No man can think of Heaven but for a little time, without it making him a purer and better man. Then another reason, too, why it is a good thing to think of Heaven is that some of you have friends up in the skies. I remember one time calling upon one of the families in my Church in Albany. The mother had never traveled much out of the place where she lived in this country, excepting that she had come from England, for they were English people; yet when I sat down she began to tell me something about the Sandwich Islands, and the islands of the sea, and of places I knew only by name; and I said, "Why, how is it that you know so much about these places?" "Why," she said, "I have a son who travels all over the islands of the sea," and she said, "I surely ought to be interested in the places where my boy goes."

At one time a peasant in an English town lost his little boy. He was taken up with the things of time, and the Bible was a strange book to him until the boy died; but after the boy died, every night just as soon as he returned from his labor, he would be found with the tallow dip bending close over the Book, poring over its pages whenever he could find time. His friends asked him why he was doing so. "Why," said he, "I am trying to find out about the place where my boy has gone in order that I may know all about it." My friends, it is a good thing for you and for me to know about Heaven, because of the number of friends that have gone up into the skies. And yet we have but a faint glimpse and foretaste of Heaven. We read in history that when the people of the northern barbarians, the Huns and the Goths, had once tasted of the rare wines of Italy, they never would be satisfied until they had taken up their abode in that land.

You will remember that when Columbus was coming towards this country, he had a foretaste of it before he ever came in sight of land, for he could see it in the sea-weed, and in those little pieces of bush, with the bright berries on them; then he said to those who were with him, "This is the very first vision of the land towards which I am now leading you."

Let me put this question to you: How do you spell Heaven? I imagine I hear you saying: Well the first letter is H, and the second e, and the third a, and the next v, and the next e, and the last n. But this is not the way I spell it. The better way to spell Heaven is to take the faces of my beloved dead, and view first one here, and one there, another there, until, as I look up into the faces so dear to me so long ago, I have before me the sweetest picture I can think of, and the view which will greet me the moment I enter the city. An eminent divine once said, " The first idea I had of Heaven was a great city, with walls and spires, and a great many angels, but not one person I knew. Then one of my little brothers died, and then I thought of Heaven as a great city, with walls and spires and one little fellow that I knew." Then a second brother died, then the third and fourth, then one of his friends died, and he began to know a little about it, but never until he let one of his own children go up into the skies had he any idea as to what Heaven was like. Then the second and the third and the fourth child was taken away from him and he said, " There came a time when I lived more with them and with God than here on the earth." So the best view of Heaven comes to you and to me, when we have loved ones in that city of light.

And now comes the question, Shall we know each other there? When I see my mother, I believe I shall know her just as surely as I knew her in this world, and that statement is not denied once in the Book, but its truth is implied over and over again, and I think this is about the strongest evidence that could possibly be given to us. A friend of mine who had been traveling in the Alps was telling me about them, and I had never known him to have such power of description, yet he told me, as we sat there, of the sunrise he had witnessed, and I think I have never heard anything so beautiful. His eyes filled with tears; his face was shining as he became more and more interested in his theme, and he sat there and told me all about the sunrise; yet he never stopped a moment to prove to me that the Alps existed, that was all implied in the same way the answer to this great question is implied in this Book. Suppose you heard such statements as these for the first time: " And Abraham died and was gathered unto his people;" " Jacob died and was gathered unto his people;" " Moses died and he was gathered unto his people;" what would you think? Why, if we take the Book and read just as it is, there would be no question but what we shall know each other. What would be the use of gathering all the saints of the Old Testament to their people if they did not know each other in that better land?

There is a sick child in the palace of the king; he is tossing to and fro on the bed that might have been made of gold. The watchers stand on either side, watching the little heart almost as it beats away the life in that little body; and above the breathing of that little boy can be heard the sobs and the moans of the king in another room. His boy is dying; his hands are getting colder, and his feet are already like ice, and some one says, " Go and call the king." Then some one goes to the door where the king is, and they are afraid to go in to tell him. Suddenly the little heart flutters, and then stops and the pulses beat rapidly and are still; the eyes are set and they close them gently; fold the hands over the breast, and then they go and stand like sentineis outside the room where the king is still crying out in his agony. At last he comes forth, and as soon as he sees the people he knows that his boy is dead, so he cried, " Is he dead? Is he dead? " and they say, " Long live the king, but the boy is dead." Then they suppose he will turn away in rage and anger, but instead, he immediately goes into one of the chambers and changes his raiment, and then up into the sanctuary to worship, and they hear him say, " The boy is gone, and he can never come back to me; " and they hear him say, " But I shall go to him, I shall go to him."

Why beloved, the Holy Ghost wrote it in the book, and do you believe that the Holy Ghost would have written it in this Book to have deceived all the ages? Did not I comfort my own heart with that thought when we held in our arms the boy that was more precious to us than life itself? We were comforted with this thought. He never can come to us, but thanks be unto God, we can go to him, because the mouth of the Lord hath spoken it. What would be the use of David going to his boy if he did not know him in the other world. Then when you come to the New Testament, why, it is like a great harbor, which is covered over and over with beautiful vines; and as we stand before it, and look up, the most wonderful fruit hangs down, and this fruit is for the healing of broken hearts the wide world round.

Let me give you two or three places where it is implied. The mount of Transfiguration, where the Master was seen as you and I shall see Him when we reach the other side, with His face shining like an angel's, and His garments whiter than any fuller could make them; and then Moses and Elias standing, and Peter and James and John, who had never until then seen either Moses or Elias, and I doubt if they had ever seen a representation of them, yet they knew them the moment they looked on the transfiguration scene; and Peter said, " Why, this is Moses and Elias." They knew each other and Peter knew them.

I think there is a change comes to us in this world, but a person never changes so much but what we know him. I remember my friend Mr. Brown, of Indianapolis, a man who was an infidel, and who looked like one, and yet when I saw him in Cincinnati he was so changed by the indwelling of the Spirit, but I knew him. It will be a change for you and for me when we walk the streets of the City; but my friends, I am sure we shall know each other there.

Second. The scene at Bethany. Mary and Martha are weeping; their hearts are almost broken because their brother is dead, as they cry out to the Master saying, "If thou hadst only been here our brother had not died." I can see Him as He places His hand on the shoulder of the mourner, saying, "Weep not, for ye shall see him on the resurrection morning." Do you believe that the Lord Jesus for a single moment would have deceived those sisters, when He said, "Thy brother shall rise again?"

Why, He is saying, "Don't you weep, you are going to meet your loved ones in the streets of the wonderful city." I think He said it for you and for me. He comforted Mary and Martha because of the fact that He knew I was going to weep. When I was in the city of Cincinnati, I picked up a shell and held it to my ear, and I could hear the roar of the sea, altho I was a thousand miles away. And so Jesus Christ put as it were the shell to His ear, and He heard me sobbing and moaning, and He said to the sisters, and through the sisters said to me, "Don't you weep, your children shall rise again in the resurrection morning, and you shall know each other there." Take the Bible description of death, and you will find that it is only a sleep. Don't you think we always wake from our sleep with clearer vision and stronger life?

Rutherford says:

"I shall sleep sweet in Jesus,
And in His likeness rise.
To know and to adore Him,
To see Him with these eyes.
'Tween me and resurrection
But Paradise doth stand,
And glory shadeless shineth
In Immanuel's land."

What do you think He meant when He said, "And where I am there ye shall be also?" I think He meant to say, "I am your Brother, God is your Father, and we are like a great family, and you shall know each other there."

What do you think He meant by appearing so many times after the resurrection? Walking with the disciples to Emmaus, talking with them until they knew Him, and then appearing to them again on the sea, saying, "Children, have ye any meat?" It was the appearance on earth of one who had been in Heaven. What did it mean? I think that Christ wanted us to understand that if we knew each other in this world, nothing could keep us from knowing each other in the better land. Think of the Bible description of Heaven. "The Father's house," great family circle," and as Spurgeon has said, "What kind of a family circle would it be in Heaven, if we did not know each other?"

Just in concluding let me say, that I believe it, because if I did not, it must be that the power of memory would leave me as I passed into the other world. A man in Chicago came home one night and as his wife met him at the door she said to him. "The doctor has been here, and he says the boy has had a change for the worse, and that he is dying, and you must go in and tell him." So the father went in, and as he stood looking into the face of his boy he said, "My boy, the doctor has been here to-day, and he says that before the morning you will be with Jesus Christ." And then, strong man that he was, he turned his face away and sobbed and wept; then the little fellow took his hand, and said to him, "Don't you cry about it, because the very moment that I see Jesus Christ I'll tell Him that just as soon as I can remember anything about you, you told me about Him, and tried to lead me to know Him," and friends, I can say that about my own father, and do you think that when that boy reaches the other shore he will forget his father? Do you think that, when I tread the streets of gold, I can forget my good mother, who exerted her love and her sweet influence over me, until she led me into the very kingdom of God? I could not preach with the same power if I did not believe the answer to this question as I have already stated it. I long to meet my mother and to know her in the other world, and nothing else could satisfy my longing. When I have a longing for water God quenches my thirst. If I long for food, He satisfies my hunger; and when I long for immortality, it is the strongest evidence that I am immortal. The longing that I have to know my friends in the skies to me is the strongest evidence that I shall know them.

The last lesson—because so many that have died have seemed to catch a glimpse of the other world. I think the mother of Dr. Cuyler had one, when looking around into the faces of her family she told them all good night, then took the candle in her hands and started to her room, but came back again and said "Good night" to them all, standing at the door just for a little time, with the light upon her beautiful face, then went up to her own room to her couch, and in the morning they found her with her eyes closed, her heart still, and she had gone out into the other world to wake in the morning, and in the morning she was to know them all as she knew them in the eventide. Like the mother of one of the members of a former church of mine, who, as she was coming down towards the end of life's journey, seemed to think that she was a child once more, and as she said "Good night" to them all, she said, "I will see you in the morning," and the next day her eyes were closed, her heart had ceased its beating. Do you think she will see them in the morning? I think so with all my soul. Do you believe it? I can think of another member, who said to those around her just as her heart was beating away its life, "Turn the bed around, so that I can die with my face towards Bethany, the place which has seemed most like Heaven to me." I think that there were angels hovering round her, and as she knew those about her just as she was about to see Jesus Christ, I think she would know them after she had looked into His wondrous face.

Carlyle has said:

"It is an old belief that on some solemn shore.
Beyond the sphere of grief, dear friends shall meet once more,
Beyond the sphere of time, and death and its control,
Serene in changeless prime of body and of soul.
This hope we still would keep, this faith we'll not forego,
Unending be the sleep, if not to waken so."

Are you going there? I put the question to you.

A man was dying in one of the hospitals. The attendants thought he was dead, but they saw him move his arm, and raise it in the air. He had not spoken for more than an hour, and those who were near him heard him saying, "Here sir, here, sir." Then he was still, and they bent down over him and said, "Is there anything we can do for you?" Looking up, with his face shining, he said, "No, they were calling the roll in Heaven, and I was only answering to my name." Is your name written there? Your mother's name is recorded; your child's name is written down; and your loved one's names are recorded there. Is yours there? I can say, through Jesus Christ, my name is **written there. Listen:**

"Into the harbor of Heaven I'll glide
Home at last, home at last.
Softly I'll drift o'er the bright silver tide,
For I'm home at last.
Glory to God all my trials are o'er,
I'll stand then secure on that beautiful shore,
Glory to God, I shall shout evermore,
Home at last, home at last.

"Then shall I know even as also I am known." "Thanks be unto God who giveth us the victory."—U. G. N.

THE PALMS AND ROBES

By T. DeWitt Talmage, D.D.

After this I beheld, and, lo, a great multitude which no man could number, of all nations, and kindreds, and people, and tongues, stood before the throne, and before the Lamb, clothed with white robes, and palms in their hands; and cried with a loud voice, saying, Salvation to our God which sitteth upon the throne, and unto the Lamb.—Rev. vii: 9, 10

It is impossible to come in contact with anything grand or beautiful in art, nature, or religion, without being profited and elevated. We go into the art-gallery, and our soul meets the soul of the painter, and we hear the hum of his forests and the clash of his conflicts, and see the cloud-blossoming of the sky and the foam-blossoming of the ocean; and we come out from the gallery better men than when we went in. We go into the concert of music and are lifted into enchantment; for days after, our soul seems to rock with a very tumult of joy, as the sea, after a long stress of weather, rolls and rocks and surges a great while before it comes back to its ordinary calm.

On the same principle *it is profitable to think of Heaven*, and look off upon that landscape of joy and light which St. John depicts; the rivers of gladness, the trees of life, the thrones of power, the comminglings of everlasting love. I wish this morning that I could bring Heaven from the list of intangibles, and make it seem to you as really it is—the great fact in all history, the depot of all ages, *the parlor of God's universe.*

This account in my text gives a picture of heaven *as it is on a holiday.* Now if a man came to New York for the first time on the day that Kossuth arrived from Hungary, and he saw the arches lifted, and the flowers flung in the streets, and heard the guns booming, he would have been very foolish to suppose that that was the ordinary appearance of the city. While, my friends, Heaven is always grand and always beautiful, I think my text speaks of a gala day in **Heaven.**

It is a time of great celebration—perhaps of the birth or the resurrection of Jesus; perhaps of the downfall of some despotism; perhaps because of the rushing in of the millennium. I know not what; but it does seem to me in reading this passage as if it were *a holiday in Heaven;* after this I beheld, and, lo, a great multitude, which no man could number, of all nations, and kindreds, and people, and tongues, stood before the throne, and before the Lamb, clothed in white robes, and palms in their hands; and cried with a loud voice, saying, "Salvation to our God which sitteth upon the throne, and unto the Lamb."

I shall speak to you of the glorified in Heaven—their number, their antecedents, their dress, their symbols, and their song.

I. But how shall I begin by telling you of the numbers of those in Heaven?

I have seen a curious estimate by an ingenious man who calculates how long the world was going to last, and how many people there are in each generation, and then sums up the whole matter, and says he thinks there will be twenty-seven trillions of souls in glory. I have no faith in his estimate. I simply take the plain announcement of the text—it is "a great multitude, which *no man can number.*"

Every few years in this country we take a census of the population, and it is very easy to tell how many people there are in a city or in a nation; but who shall give the census of the great nation to be saved? It it quite easy to tell how many people there are in different denominations of Christians —how many Baptists and Methodists and Episcopalians and Presbyterians; of all the denominations of Christians we could make an estimate.

Suppose they were gathered in one great audience-room; how overwhelming the spectacle! But it would give no idea of the great audience-room of heaven—the multitudes that bow down and that lift up their hosannas. Why, they come from all the chapels, from all the cathedrals, from all sects, from all ages; they who prayed in splendid liturgy, and those who in broken sentences uttered the wish of broken hearts —from Grace Church and Sailor's Bethel, from under the shapeless rafters and from under high-sprung arch—" a great multitude, that *no man can number."*

One of the most impressive things I have looked upon is an army. Standing upon a hillside you see forty thousand or fifty thousand men pass along. You can hardly imagine the impression if you have not actually felt it. But you may take all the armies that the earth has ever seen—the legions under Sennacherib and Cyrus and Cæsar and Xerxes and Alexander and Napoleon, and all our modern forces, and put them in one great array, and then on some swift steed you may ride along the line and review the troops; and that accumulated host from all ages seems like a half-formed regiment compared with the great array of the redeemed.

I stood one day at Williamsport, and saw on the opposite side of the Potomac the forces coming down, regiment after regiment, and battalion after battalion. It seemed as tho there were no end to the procession. But now let me take *the field-glass of St. John* and look off upon the hosts of Heaven —thousands of thousands, ten thousand times ten thousand, one hundred and forty and four thousand, and thousands of thousands, until I put down the field-glass and say " I cannot estimate it—a great multitude that no man can number."

You may tax your imagination, and torture your ingenuity, and break down your powers of calculation in attempting to express the multitudes of the released from earth and the enraptured of Heaven, and talk of hundreds of hundreds of hundreds; of thousands of thousands of thousands; of millions of millions of millions; of quadrillions of quadrillions of quadrillions; of quintillions of quintillions of quintillions; until your head aches and your heart faints, and exhausted and overburdened you exclaim: " I cannot count them—a great multitude that no man can number."

II. But my subject advances, and tells you of their antecedents " of all nations and kindreds and tongues." Some of them spoke Scotch, Irish, German, English, Italian, Spanish, Tamil, Choctaw, Burmese. After men have been long in the land you can tell by their accentuation from what nationality they came; and I suppose in the great throng around the throne it will not be difficult to tell from what part of the earth they came.

These reaped Sicilian wheatfields and those picked cotton from the pods. These under blistering skies gathered tamarinds and yams. Those crossed the desert on camels, and those glanced over the snow drawn by Siberian dogs, and these milked the goats far up on the Swiss crags. Those fought the walrus and white bear in regions of everlasting snow, and these heard the song of fierywinged birds in African thickets. They were white. They were black. They were red. They were copper color. *From all lands, from all ages.* They were plunged into Austrian dungeons. They passed through Spanish inquisitions. They were confined in London Tower. They fought with beasts in the amphitheater. They were Moravians. They were Waldenses. They were Albigenses. They were Scotch Covenanters. They were Sandwich Islanders.

In this world men prefer different kinds of government. The United States want a republic. The British Government needs to be a constitutional monarchy. Austria wants absolutism. But when they come up from earth, from different nationalities, they will prefer one great monarchy—King Jesus ruler over it. And if that monarchy were disbanded, and it were submitted to all the hosts of Heaven who should rule, then by the unanimous suffrages of all the redeemed, Christ would become the president of the whole universe.

Magna chartas, bills of right, houses of burgesses, triumvirates, congresses, parliaments, nothing in the presence of Christ's scepter, swaying over all the people who have entered upon that great glory. Oh! can you imagine it? What a strange commingling of tastes, of histories, of nationalities, " of all nations and kindreds and people and tongues."

III. My subject advances and tells you of the dress of those in Heaven. The object of dress in this world is not only to veil the body, but to adorn it. The God who dresses up the spring morning with blue ribbon of sky around the brow, and earrings of dewdrops hung from the tree branch, and mantle of crimson cloud flung over the shoulder, and the violeted slippers of the grass for her feet—I know that that God does not despise beautiful apparel.

Well, what shall we wear in Heaven? " I saw a great multitude clothed *in white robes."* It is white! In this world we had sometimes to have on working apparel. Bright and lustrous garments would be ridiculously out of place sweltering amid forges, or mixing paints, or plastering ceilings, or binding books. In this world we must have the working-day apparel sometimes, and we care not how coarse it is. It is appropriate; but when all the toil of earth is past, and there is no more drudgery and no more weariness, we shall stand before the throne robed in white.

On earth we sometimes had to wear mourning apparel—black scarf for the arm, black veil for the face, black gloves for the hands, black band for the hat. Abraham mourning for Sarah; Isaac mourning for Rebecca; Rachel mourning for her children; David mourning for Absalom; Mary mourning for Lazarus. Every second of every minute of every hour of every day a *heart breaks*.

The earth from zone to zone and from pole to pole is cleft with sepulchral rent; and the earth can easily afford to bloom and blossom when it is so rich with moldering life. Graves! graves! graves! But when these bereavements have all passed, and there are no more graves to dig, and no more coffins to make, and no more sorrow to suffer, we shall pull off this mourning and be robed in white. I see a soul going right up from all this scene of sin and trouble into glory. I seem to hear him say:

" I journey forth rejoicing
From this dark vale of tears,
To heavenly joy and freedom,
From earthly care and fears.

" When Christ our Lord shall gather
All His redeemed again,
His kingdom to inherit—
Good-night till then.

" I hear my Savior calling;
The joyful hour has come
The angel guards are ready
To guide me to our home.

" When Christ our Lord shall gather
All His redeemed again,
His kingdom to inherit—
Good-night till then."

IV. My subject advances, and tells you of the symbols they carry. If my text had represented the good in Heaven as carrying cypress branches, that would have meant sorrow. If my text had represented the good in Heaven as carrying nightshade, that would have meant sin. But it is *a palm branch* they carry, and that is victory.

When the people came home from war in olden times, the conqueror rode at the head of his troops, and there were triumphal arches, and the people would come out with branches of the palm-tree and wave them all along the host. What a significant type these of the greeting and of the joy of the redeemed in Heaven! On earth they were condemned of synagogs, and were put out of polite circles. They had infamous hands strike them on both cheeks. Infernal spite spat in their faces. Their back ached with sorrow.

Their brow reeled with unalleviated toil. *How weary they were!* Sometimes they broke the heart of the midnight in the midst of all their anguish, crying out, " O God! " But hark now to the shout of the delivered captives; as they lift their arms from the shackles they cry out, " Free! Free! " They look back upon all the trials through which they have passed, the battles they have fought, the burdens they carried, the misrepresentations they suffered, and because they are delivered from all these they stand before God waving their palms.

They come to the feet of Christ and they look up into His face, and *they remember His sorrows,* and they remember His pain, and they remember His groans, and they say: " Why, I was saved by that Christ. He pardoned my sins, He soothed my sorrows; " and standing there they shall be exultant, waving their palms.

That hand once held the implements of toil or wielded the sword of war; but now it plucks down branches from the tree of life as they stand before the throne waving their palms. Once He was a pilgrim on earth; He crunched the hard crusts—He walked the weary way: but it is all gone now, the sin gone, the weariness gone, the sickness gone, the sorrow gone. As Christ stands up before the great array of the saved and recounts His victories, it will be like the rocking and tossing of a forest in a tempest, as all the redeemed arise up, host beyond host, rank beyond rank, waving, *waving their palms.*

V. My subject makes another advancement, and speaks of the song they sing. Doctor Dick, in a very learned work, says that among other things in Heaven he thinks they will give a great deal of time to the study of arithmetic and the higher branches of mathematics. I do not believe it. It would upset my idea of Heaven if I thought so; I never liked mathematics; and I would rather take the representation of my text, which describes the occupation of heaven as being that of *joyful psalmody.* " They cried with a loud voice, saying, Salvation unto our God."

In this world we have secular songs, nursery songs, boatmen's songs, harvest songs, sentimental songs; but in Heaven we will have taste for only one song, and that will be the song of salvation from an eternal death to an eternal Heaven, through the blood of the Lamb that was slain.

I see a soul coming up to join the redeemed in heaven. As it goes through the gates, the old friends of that spirit come around it and say: " What shall we sing? " and the newly-arrived soul says: " *Sing salvation;* " and after a while an earthly despotism falls, and a scepter of iniquity is snapped, and churches are built where once there were superstitious mosques, and angel cries to angel: " How shall we celebrate this victory? " and angel cries to angel: " Let us sing; " and the answer is: " What shall we sing? " another voice says: " Let us sing *salvation.*"

After a while all the Church on earth will rush into the outspread arms of the Church of heaven, and while the righteous are ascending, and the world is burning, and all things are being wound up, the question will be asked: " What shall we sing? " and there will be a voice " like the voice of many waters, like the voice of mighty thunderings," that will respond: " Sing salvation."

In this world we have plaintive songs—songs tremulous with sorrow, songs dirgeful for the dead; but in Heaven there will be no sighing of winds, no wailing of anguish, no weeping symphony. The tamest song will be halleluiah—the dullest tune a triumphal march. Joy among the cherubim! Joy among the seraphim! Joy among the ransomed! Joy forever!

On earth the music in churches is often poor, because there is no interest in it, or because there is no harmony. Some would not sing; some could not sing; some sang too high; some sang too low; some sang by fits and starts; but in the great audience of the redeemed on high all voices will be accordant, and the man who on earth could not tell a plantation melody from the "Dead March in Saul" will lift an anthem that the Mendelssohns and Beethovens and the Schumanns of earth never imagined; and you may stand through all eternity and listen, and there will not be one discord in that great anthem that forever rolls up against the great heart of God. *It will not be a solo;* it will not be a duet; it will not be a quintette; but an innumerable host before the throne, crying, "Salvation unto our God and unto the Lamb." They crowd all the temples; they bend over the battlements; they fill all the heights and depths and lengths and breadths of Heaven with their hosannas.

When people were taken into the temple of Diana it was such a brilliant room that they were always put on their guard. Some people had lost their sight by just looking on the brilliancy of that room, and so the janitor when he brought a stranger to the door and let him in would always charge him, "Take heed of your eyes."

Oh! when I think of the song that goes up around the throne of God, so jubilant, many-voiced, multitudinous, I feel like saying, "Take heed of your ears." It is so loud a song. It is so blessed an anthem. They sing a rock song, saying, "Who is He that sheltered us in the wilderness and shadowed us in a weary land?" And the chorus came in: "Christ the shadow of a rock in a weary land."

They sing a *star song,* saying, "Who is He that guided us through the thick night, and when all other lights went out, arose in the sky the morning-star, pouring light on the soul's darkness?" And the chorus will come in: "Christ, *the morning-star,* shining on the world's darkness." They will sing a *flower song,* saying, "Who is He that brightened all our way, and breathed sweetness upon our soul, and bloomed through frost and tempest?" and the chorus will come in, "Christ, the lily of the valley, blooming through frost and tempest." They will sing a *water song,* saying, "Who is He that gleamed to us from the frowning crag, and lightened the darkest ravine of trouble, and brought cooling to the temples, and refreshment to the lip, and was a fountain in the midst of the wilderness?" and then the chorus will come in, "Christ, the fountain in the midst of the wilderness."

My friends, will you join that anthem? Shall we make rehearsal this morning? If we cannot sing that song on earth, we will not be able to sing it in Heaven. Can it be that our good friends in that land will walk all through that great throng of which I speak, looking for us and not finding us? Will they come down to the gate and ask if we have passed through, and not find us reported as having come? Will they look through the folios of eternal light and find our names unrecorded? Is all this a representation of a land *we shall never see?*—of a song *we shall never sing?*—C. H.

THE FIRST FIVE MINUTES AFTER DEATH

By Henry P. Liddon, D.D.

I Cor. xiii: 12

I. At our entrance on another state of existence we shall know what it is to exist under entirely new conditions. What will it be to find ourselves with the old self—divested of that body which has clothed it since its first moment of existence—able to achieve, it may be, so much,—it may be, so little; living on, but under conditions which are so entirely new. This experience alone will add no little to our existing knowledge, and the addition will have been made during the first five minutes after death.

II. And the entrance on the next world must bring with it a knowledge of God such as is quite impossible in this life. His vast, His illimitable life, will present itself to the apprehension of our spirits as a clearly consistent whole—not as a complex problem to be painfully mastered by the efforts of our understandings, but as a present, living, encompassing Being who is inflecting Himself upon the very sight, whether they will it or not, of His adoring creatures. "Thine eyes shall see the King in his beauty"—they were words of warning as well as words of promise.

III. At our entrance on another world we shall know ourselves as never before. The past will be spread out before us and we shall take a comprehensive survey of it. One Being there is who knows us now, who has always known us. Then, for the first time, we shall know ourselves even as also we are known. We shall not have to await the Judge's sentence; we shall read it at a glance, whatever it be, in this new apprehension of what we are.—S. B., vol. ix., p. 349.

THE REDEMPTION OF THE BODY

By F. D. Maurice, D.D.

Phil. iii: 20, 21

I. St. Paul valued his privilege of being a citizen of the greatest city upon earth. The Philippians had reason to know that he valued it. He had made them understand by his conduct that citizenship is a great and honorable thing. Men are bound together as citizens of a city, as members of a nation, by God Himself. But St. Paul tells the Philippians that he was the citizen of another country too: " Our citizenship is in Heaven." We have friends and fellow-sufferers upon earth; our work is upon earth; we live to do good to the earth; but our home is with God. He has bought us at a great price that we might be freemen of Christ, and might always fly to Him and plead our cause before Him! He has made for us a new and living way into His presence through the flesh and blood of His Son; and we have a right to walk in that way, and not to be taking the downward way, the way of death.

II. St. Paul had the greatest reverence for his own body and for the bodies of his fellow-creatures that any man could have. For he believed that the Lord Jesus Christ, the Savior, had taken a body such as ours, and had eaten earthly food, and had drunk of earthly water and wine, and had given that body to die upon the cross, and had raised it out of the grave. and had ascended with it to the right hand of His Father. Therefore when St. Paul recollected his citizenship in Heaven, when he claimed to be a member of Christ's body and prayed in His name to His Father and our Father, he could not but think how this body, which is so curiously and wonderfully made, has a hidden glory in it, which, when Christ appears in His glory, shall be fully made manifest. Everything seems to be threatening it with death, but Christ, in whom is the fulness of life. has overcome death and is stronger than death. He has raised up my spirit, that was sinking lower and lower, to trust in Him and hope in Him; He will raise up this body too. Nothing shall be lost of all that God has given us, for Christ has redeemed it. Only death and corruption shall perish, for they have assaulted God's glorious handiwork. What God has created God will preserve.— S. B., vol. x., p. 344.

THE INTERMEDIATE STATE

By John H. Newman, D.D.

Rev. vi: 11

I. In this passage we are told that the saints are at rest. " White robes were given unto every one of them; and it was said unto them, that they should rest yet for a little season." The great and anxious question that meets us is, What is to become of us after this life? We fear for ourselves, we are solicitous about our friends, just on this point. Now here Scripture meets our need. It is enough, surely, to be in Abraham's bosom, in our Savior's presence; it is enough, after the pain and turmoil of this world, to be at rest.

II. Next, in this description it is implied that departed saints, tho at rest, have not yet received their actual reward. " Their works do follow them," not yet given in to their Savior and Judge. They are in an incomplete state in every way, and will be so till the day of judgment, which will introduce them to the joy of their Lord. (1) They are incomplete inasmuch as their bodies are in the dust of the earth, and they wait for the resurrection. (2) They are incomplete as being neither awake nor asleep; they are in a state of rest, not in the full employment of their powers. (3) There is an incompleteness also as regards their place of rest. They are " under the altar," not in the full presence of God, seeing His face and rejoicing in His works, but in a safe and holy treasure-house close by, like Moses " in a cleft of the rock," covered by the hand of God and beholding the skirts of His glory. (4) The intermediate state is incomplete as regards the happiness of the saints. The blessed in their disembodied state admit of an increase of happiness, and receive it. " They cried out in complaint, and white robes were given them; they were soothed and bid wait a while."

III. Nor would it be surprising if, in God's gracious providence, the very purpose of their remaining thus for a season at a distance from Heaven were that they may have time for growing in all holy things and perfecting the inward development of the good seed sown in their hearts. As we are expressly told that in one sense the spirits of the just are perfected on their death, it follows that the greater the advance each has made here, the higher will be the line of his subsequent growth between death and the resurrection. —S. B., vol. xii., p. 301.

NO MORE TEARS

God shall wipe away all tears from their eyes.—Rev. vii: 17

What are tears? Little drops—salt—like water. Where seen? In eye, on cheek, on pillow, copy-book, mother's lap.

What cause tears? Sudden pain (a fall, a knock)—sickness, death of dear ones, passion, disappointment, penitence, sympathy, sorrow for others' sins (like David, Psa. cxix: 136).

All cry, good as well as bad—even Jesus (Luke xix: 41; John xi: 35). Why? Whence comes all the trouble that brings tears? *Sin.* Every sorrow caused by some sin. Christ's sorrow by our sin.

How happy and bright a child that seldom cries! Suppose *never*—how happy! *There is a place where no tears.* Where? At home—in church—in green fields—in Queen's palace? Tears everywhere in this world. *Heaven.* There all faces bright—all hearts happy. Voices not crying, not complaining, but singing for joy.

Why? *Because God wipes all tears away.* You like mother to do so, it shows her love; how loving must God be!—more even than a mother (Isa. xlix: 15). Sometimes mother can't wipe away your tears, for she can't stop sickness—can't prevent disappointment. How can God wipe *all* away? Because He takes away what brings tears—*sin.* How?

1. Washed away by the blood of lamb.
2. Driven away by Spirit in heart.
3. Put away forever from Heaven and all who are there.

Whose eyes? "Their"—the great multitude (ver. 9)—Abel, Moses, David, Peter—white and black, old and young, kings and beggars. *Shall we be among them?*

On earth, much crying—in Heaven, no crying—another place, where *nothing but crying.* How escape *that?* Ask God to take away all sin for Christ's sake, *then* all tears go away too.—P. M.

SUGGESTIVE THOUGHTS AND ILLUSTRATIONS

DEATH, Beautiful.—*Is. lxi: 3.* Death, like autumn, is sad, spectral, and seemingly ruinous, and yet like it also, what unearthly beauty shines through it. What light of faith, and tenderness of love in the eyes, in the words of the passing saint. How the struggle with death, the burnings of disease, transfigure the countenance into a heavenly glow of patience, and hope, and self-sacrifice that betoken the nearness and glory of a better life. "They are not," for God has taken them.—C. G.

DEATH, Happiness After.—She is gone! No longer shrinking from the winter wind, or lifting her calm pure forehead to the summer's kiss; no longer gazing with her blue and glorious eyes into a far-off sky; no longer yearning with a holy heart for Heaven; no longer toiling painfully along the path, upward and upward, to the everlasting rock on which are based the walls of the city of the Most High; no longer here; she is there; gazing, seeing, knowing, loving, as the blessed only see, and know, and love. Earth has one angel less and Heaven one more, since yesterday. Already, kneeling at the throne, she has received her welcome, and is resting on the bosom of her Savior. If human love hath power to penetrate the veil (and hath it not?), then there are yet living here a few who have the blessedness of knowing that an angel loves them.—F. II.

DEATH IS GAIN.—Precious, in the sight of the Lord is the death of His saints, because *it brings them near to God.* How strange, indeed how absurd, this life would be if death ended all! Think of a man like Gladstone, who lived under a high sense of duty, whose life was one of prayer, who sang "Praise to the Holiest in the height" amid the suffering of his last days; his whole life a trust in God, a serving God, a striving after God, and, finally, a longing to be free and get away to God,—just imagine all this ending in nothingness! Why, it reminds one of the famous Amblongus pie of the nonsense book. It was a pie of most elaborate construction. Particular directions were given as to the making of it, what was to be put in, and in what quantities. It was to be very carefully compounded, and most scientifically baked, and then the final instructions were to "open the window and pitch it out as fast as possible." Just as laughable, so to speak, is the idea of a man, trained to high thought and holy feeling and submissive will, being, at the last, simply "cast as rubbish to the void."—E. Times.

DEATH OF LITTLE NELL.—She was dead. There, upon her little bed, she lay at rest. The solemn stillness was no marvel now. She was dead. No sleep so beautiful and calm, so free from trace of pain, so fair to look upon. She seemed a creature fresh from the hand of God, and waiting for the breath of life; not one who had lived and suffered death. Her couch was dressed with here and there some winter berries and green leaves, gathered in a spot she had been used to favor.

"When I die, put near me something that has loved the light, and had the sky above it always." She was dead. Dear, gentle, patient, noble Nell, was dead. Her little bird—a poor slight thing the pressure of a finger would have crushed—was stirring nimbly in its cage; and the strong heart of its child-mistress was mute and motionless for ever. Where were the traces of her early cares, her sufferings, and fatigues? All gone. Sorrow was dead indeed in her, but peace and perfect happiness were born; imaged in her tranquil beauty and profound repose. And still her former self lay there, unaltered in this change. Yes. The old fireside had smiled upon that same sweet face; it had passed, like a dream, through haunts of misery and care; at the door of the poor school-master on the summer evening, before the furnace-fire upon the cold wet night, at the still bedside of the dying boy, there had been the same mild, lovely look. So shall we know the angels in their majesty, after death.—CHARLES DICKENS.

DEATH OF LITTLE PAUL.—" Now lay me down," he said; " and Floy, come close to me, and let me see you!" Sister and brother wound their arms around each other, and the golden light came streaming in, and fell upon them, locked together. " How fast the river runs between its green banks and the rushes, Floy! But it's very near the sea. I hear the waves! They always said so!" Presently he told her that the motion of the boat upon the stream was lulling him to rest. How green the banks were now, how bright the flowers growing on them, and how tall the rushes! Now the boat was out at sea, but gliding smoothly on. And now there was a shore before him. Who stood on the bank? He put his hands together, as he had been used to do, at his prayers. He did not remove his arms to do it; but they saw him fold them so, behind her back. " Mamma is like you, Floy. I know her by the face! But tell them that the print upon the stairs at school is not divine enough. The light about the head is shining on me as I go!" The golden ripple on the wall came back again, and nothing else stirred in the room. The old, old fashion! The fashion that came in with our first garments, and will last unchanged until our race has run its course, and the wide firmament is rolled up like a scroll. The old, old fashion—Death! Oh thank God, all who see it, for that older fashion yet, of immortality! And look upon us, angels of young children, with regards not quite estranged, when the swift river bears us to the ocean!—CHARLES DICKENS.

DEATH, The Entrance into Life.—*1 Cor. iii: 21, 22.* I once went, with a large party of friends, into a beautiful cave. The passage into the cave was, in places, quite difficult. At one place we had to crawl along through an opening very close and narrow, and in doing so felt the dread of suffocation. When the end of this narrow passage was reached, a spacious room was before us, brilliantly illuminated by the torches of the many who had preceded us, dome and floor and walls glittering like the palace of a king, with stalactites and stalagmites. The sight was beautiful beyond expression. And I thought, so is death but a dark and narrow passage into the unspeakable glories and beauties of Heaven. What must be our rapture when the soul emerges from the stifling atmosphere and the appalling darkness of the tomb into the city of God, with its gold-paved streets and jasper walls!—C. G.

HEAVEN AND EARTH BRIDGED.—*Gen. xxviii: 12.* When they began to build a great wire suspension bridge over a wide river, a kite was sent across with the first fine wire. This was fastened, and then on it other wires were drawn across, until the great bridge hung in the air, and thousands were passing over it. From many a home a loved one, borne to Heaven, carries the first heavenward thought of a worldly household. But from that moment, and on that slender thread, their thoughts, affections, and longings go continually heavenward, until there is a broad golden bridge hung between their home and God's house, and prayer and love are constantly passing over.—S. S. T.

HEAVEN AND EARTH, The Things in.—*Eph. i: 3, 10.* Both the spheres of Heaven and earth have become places of sin, when a part of the angels fell into sin from God (1 John iii: 8; James ii: 19; 2 Pet. ii: 4; Jude 6). Thence it came to earth (2 Cor. xi: 3) in even greater dimensions (1 Cor. x: 20, 21). Thus the state originally appointed by God, and the development He wished to be without disturbance, ceased (Rom. viii: 18, 24), so that a renewing of the heavens and of the earth, was taken into view (2 Pet. iii: 13). The center of this renewal is Christ and His redeeming work (Col. i: 20), which, however, has its development also as before His appearance up to the fulness of time, so afterward up to His second Advent, when the restitution of all things (Acts iii: 21), the palingenesia (Matt. xix: 28) will be introduced (2 Pet. iii: 10-13).—A. P. L.

HEAVEN A PLACE.—*John xiv: 2.* It is certain that there must be some place in the upper worlds where the beauties and wonders of God's works are illuminated to the highest transparency by His power and holy majesty; where the combination of lovely manifestations as seen from radiant summits, the enraptured gaze into the quiet valleys of universal creation, and the streams of light which flow through them must move the spirits of the blest in the mightiest manner to cry out, Holy! holy! holy! And there is the holiest place in the great temple! It is there because divine manifestations fill all spirits with a feeling of His holiness. But still rather, because there He reveals Himself through the holiest one of all, even Jesus Himself.—A P. L.

HEAVEN, Doctrine of.—*John xiv.* The doctrine of Heaven was not intelligible to believing hearts until the disciples were forced to learn experimentally that the earthly world was no longer a resting place for the Lord and for them, that they were cast out of the world.—A. P. L.

HEAVEN, Names Written in.—They that are written in the eternal leaves of heaven shall never be wrapped in the cloudy sheets of darkness. A man may have his name written in the Chronicle, yet lost; written in durable marble, yet perish; written on a monument equal to a Colossus, yet be ignominious; written on the hospital gates, yet go to hell; written on his own house, yet another come to possess it. All these are but writings on the dust, or in the water, when the characters perish as soon as they are made. They no more prove a man happy than the fool could prove Pontius Pilate a saint, because his name was written in the Creed. But they that are written in heaven are sure to inherit it.—A. P. L.

HEAVEN OUR HOME.—*John xiv.* These sayings inculcating faith in the Heavenly home. I. The saying addressed to Thomas. II. The saying addressed to Philip. III. The saying addressed to Judas Lebbaeus. Or, our heavenly home is sure to us. (1) In spite of the contradiction of an outward reality full of distress and death. (2) In spite of the want of phenomena evident to the senses.

I know nothing against Christianity except its want of evidence. (3) In spite of the denial of the hostile world, which even by its hate, as a germ and sign of hell, must testify of love as the seed and sign of heaven. —A. P. L.

HEAVEN, Preparation for.—(1) Jesus is now going thither. (2) The Jews, as Jews can never come thither. (3) The disciples cannot now come thither. A decided indication of our need to ripen for heaven by a Christian life. Heaven is to be gained by a ladder, not by a leap, step by step, not by a bound.—A. P. L.

JOY, Eternal.—The sufferings of the just may well be likened to fleeting shadows or passing dreams. As soon as the bright morning of eternity begins to dawn, the shadows of mortality are forever dissipated; and they forget at once, in the glorious light of God's majesty, the tribulations which they have endured for His cause. The unspeakable joys of which they partake so absorb all their faculties, that there is no room left for sorrow or suffering. If, indeed, their past trials are remembered by them, it is but to swell with fresh rapture, and to tune their voices to louder anthems in the praise of Him who has given them, in exchange for the cross, such an exceeding and eternal weight of glory.— F. II .

POETRY

At The End

By Danske Dandridge

Fearlessly into the Unknown
Go forth, thou little soul.
Launch out upon the trackless sea,
Nor wind nor stars to pilot thee,
Alone, alone, alone!

Thine is a helpless plight,
Thou canst not turn thy helm,
Nor reach the harbor any more;
Thou driftest to an unguessed shore.
Dark, dark the night.

Yet launch and take no care;
For what can care avail?
In the dark void, the awful space,
Where wand'rest thou to find thy place,
Thy God is even there.—I.

The Dead

By Richard Henry Stoddard

Pluck not flowers from graves,
For those which June has shed
Profusely there are precious;
The largess of the dead!

Tread lightly o'er their dust,
And speak with bated breath,
Lest you disturb the silence
And sanctity of Death—

The pure and perfect peace,
The sleep where dreams are not;
No evil thing remembered,
And no good thing forgot!—I.

Companioned

By Lilian Whiting

(*In Memoriam—C. R. S.*)

" Hath God new realms of lovely life for thee
In some white star, the soul of eve, or morn?"

Through days and dreams, I seem to walk with one
Whose feet must shun
Henceforth the paths of earth; for whom the sun
Rises in unknown realms I cannot trace;
And still there is to me no vacant place.
Before me comes upon the air her face.
In the deep, luminous, and wondering eyes
I read the rapture of a glad surprise;
A tender hand is clasped within my own,
And on the air there vibrates still her tone.

O Friend! on whom the Vision shines to-day,
What mystic sway
Hath wrought its spell o'er thee? What fair desire,
As o'er that sea of glass with mingled fire
Thy way hath sped—what fair desire
Is born within thy soul? What strange, sweet dreams

Transfigure thy new life, in wondrous gleams
Of rose, and gold, and pearl, through starry
  space?
Not vainly do I ask. Thy tender grace
Answers my love, and brings the new life
  near;
And all our baffled meanings grow more
  clear.—I.

Goodnight

BY MAY CHRISTIE

Goodnight! Sweet sleep!
Come, wandering, way-worn sheep;
God is thy Home, He longs to have thee
  come.
  Goodnight! Sweet sleep!

Goodnight! Sweet sleep!
Oh, leave the mountains rough and steep!
In God is peace which evermore shall cease.
  Goodnight! Sweet sleep!

Goodnight! Sweet sleep!
Thy tear-filled eyes no more need weep;
God is Thy Friend, and will all danger fend.
  Goodnight! Sweet sleep!

Goodnight! Sweet sleep!
He in His tender care will keep
Thee safe from harm with His almighty arm.
  Goodnight! Sweet sleep!

Goodnight! Sweet sleep!
So o'er thy frame will slumber creep,
And thou'lt find rest upon thy Savior's
  breast.
  Goodnight! Sweet sleep!

Goodnight! Sweet sleep!
And dreaming, thou wilt hear the sweep
Of angel wings, and strains from golden
  strings.
  Goodnight! Sweet sleep!—I.

Heaven

BY F. W. FABER

Oh what is this splendor that beams on me
  now,
  This beautiful sunrise that dawns on my
    soul,
While faint and far off land and sea lie below,
  And under my feet the huge golden clouds
    roll?

To what mighty king doth this city belong,
  With its rich jeweled shrines, and its
    gardens of flowers,
With its breaths of sweet incense, its meas-
    ures of song
  And the light that is gilding its numberless
    towers?

See! forth from the gates, like a bridal array,
  Come the princes of heaven, how bravely
    they shine!
'Tis to welcome the stranger, to show me the
    way,
  And to tell me that all I see round me is
    mine.

There are millions of saints, in their ranks
    and degrees,
  And each with a beauty and crown of his
    own;
And there, far outnumbering the sands of the
    seas,
  The nine rings of Angels encircle the throne.

And oh if the exiles of earth could but win
  One sight of the beauty of Jesus above,
From that hour they would cease to be able
    to sin,
  And earth would be Heaven; for Heaven
    is love.

But words may not tell of the Vision of
    Peace,
  With its worshipful seeming, its marvelous
    fires;
Where the soul is at large, where its sorrows
    all cease,
  And the gift has outbidden its boldest de-
    sires.

No sickness is here, no bleak bitter cold,
  No hunger, debt, prison, or weariful toil;
No robbers to rifle our treasures of gold,
  No rust to corrupt, and no canker to spoil.

My God! and it was but a short hour ago
  That I lay on a bed of unbearable pains;
All was cheerless around me, all weeping and
    wo;
  Now the wailing is changed to angelical
    strains.

Because I served Thee, were life's pleasures
    all lost?
  Was it gloom, pain, or blood, that was
    Heaven for me?
Oh no! one enjoyment alone could life boast,
  And that, dearest Lord! was my service of
    Thee.

I had hardly to give; 'twas enough to re-
    ceive,
  Only not to impede the sweet grace from
    above;
And, this first hour in Heaven, I can hardly
    believe
  In so great a reward for so little a love.

Heaven

BY THOMAS MACKELLAR

There is a land immortal,
  The beautiful of lands;
Beside its ancient portal
  A silent sentry stands:
He only can undo it,
  And open wide the door;
And mortals who pass through it
  Are mortals evermore.

That glorious land is heaven,
  And Death the sentry grim:
The Lord thereof has given
  The opening keys to him;
And ransom'd spirits, sighing
  And sorrowful for sin,
Pass through the gate in dying,
  And freely enter in.

Tho dark and drear the passage
  That leads unto the gate,
Yet grace attends the message
  To souls that watch and wait;
And at the time appointed
  A messenger comes down,
And guides the Lord's anointed
  From cross to glory's crown.

Their sighs are lost in singing;
  They're blesséd in their tears:
Their journey heavenward winging,
  They leave on earth their fears.
Death like an angel seeming,
  "We welcome thee!" they cry:
Their eyes with rapture gleaming,
  'Tis life for them to die.—P. J.

In Heaven

By Bell Stuart

"There shall be no night there."
  I wonder will we sometimes say,
"Do you remember how the darkness
    checked
  The hurrying day?
The soft, cool darkness, bringing time to
    love
  And time to pray?

"Do you remember how the twilight came,
  By wandering breezes fanned,
How all the flowers talked in plainer speech
  On every hand,
With fragrant voices that our souls were then
  Too dull to understand?

"And ere the twilight fell, that blazing west
  That gave to us the clue
Of colors builded into heavenly walls,
  Even then we knew
Those tints but faintly hinted at the sights
  Which now we view."

And if there falls no night in Heaven
  Must we the mornings miss?
Or are these too but hints of brighter things?
  What unimagined bliss
Has been prefigured in this earthly joy,
  A dawn like this?

A whispering breeze has waked the sleeping
    leaves
  With the birds' first twittering call,
The dew washed earth turns to the climbing
    sun,
  The stars grow small,
Soon o'er the grass with westward pointing
    hands
  Long shadows fall.

How will it seem when day and night no
    more
  Measure the hours that fly,
When changing seasons mark no more the
    years
  That hurry by,
When time itself shall cease and be
  Eternity?

In that eternal summer shall we sometimes
    miss
  The miracle of spring?
No August ripeness wears the tender flush
  That May-times bring;
To June's first roses, richer touch and grace
  Of freshness cling.

The vision reads, "And there was no more
    sea,"
  The sights we love so well—
The flashing spray, the white-fringed tum-
    bling surf,
  The rolling swell—
Its many voices, singing truth our lips
  Can never tell.

Yet as a child with ignorant delight,
  Follows a funeral train,
Drawn by the notes that break the heart
    bereft—
  The sad refrain
Makes one whose grief was healed feel the
    old loss
  Made new again—

So could we read the message of the sea,
  But grasp its mystery,
But know the meaning of its music deep,
  It well might be
If we could understand, we could not bear
  To hear the sea.

Suppose the children lived apart from us,
  Not knowing of our joys,
And one should tell them, "When you grow
    to be
  No longer girls and boys
Your hands must put away these childish
    things
  And have no toys."

"No toys!" the disappointed little hearts
  Might grieving say,
"No rocking horse! No dolls! When we
    are grown
  What *can* we play?
If this is true then we will not grow up,
  But children stay."

Ah, little hearts, as childishly we ask
  Shall we earth's beauties crave
When we have grown to Heaven's high
    estate;
  Does manhood brave
Sigh for the wooden horse that once
  Such pleasure gave?

"No dolls!" for her whose heart exulting
    knows
  The bliss of motherhood?
So when we reach the fulness of that great
    Undreamed of good,
We may forget these sights, nor ask to have
    them
  If we could.—I.

To Some in Heaven

By Will Carleton

Beloved, who have heard a call too sweet to
    hear and stay
Where earthly suns and shadows fall, whose
    feet have trodden the way,

Beyond these hills and vales of ours, to
    where the towers rise
Of that fair house God builds for us, that
    home beyond the skies,

Beloved, can you sometimes see, when swing
    the gates ajar,
And happy souls brought safe to heaven find
    entrance where you are,
Through just a little, little rift, the homes
    you left behind,
Or in the joyous life of heaven, are we quite
    out of mind?

Oh, darlings, when you fell asleep, you looked
    so hushed and calm!
The very silence round you, dears, was
    sweeter than a psalm;
Your brows forgot the care-lines, and your
    hands were folded still,
As if you knew all secrets of the Father's
    tenderest will!

And tho we saw you tranquil in that dream-
    less radiant peace,
Ere closed the grave-gloom over you—our
    mourning does not cease;
Our tears drop slowly in the night, our ach-
    ing eyes are blurred,
We cry for you in anguish, and you answer
    not a word.

We have put away your playthings, our little
    children sweet,
And the house is very empty, and the rooms
    are very neat;
But we'd give our best possessions, to hear
    you at the door,
And to see your dolls and toys again, in a
    litter on the floor.

We have done the things you bade us, our
    mothers fond and true,
We never kneel to say our prayers, without
    a thought of you;
O, comrades of the journey, beloved who
    could not stay,
Do you in heaven remember us yet on the
    earthly way?

Beloved, this we beg you: won't you pray to
    God for this:
That we may grieve less bitterly; that even
    as we miss
Your presence and your voices, there may
    reach us from above
A gracious balm of comfort from your own
    unceasing love?—E. W.

The Life Beyond

By Dr. S. F. Smith

To feel the mild, delicious clime,
    Where summer never fades;
To breathe the glorious atmosphere,
    Which sickness ne'er invades;

To reach at last that happy land,
    Where tears are never known;
To see the wondrous face of Him
    Who sits upon the throne;

All the great souls of all the years,
    In heaven's high courts to meet;
All kindred spirits, glorified,
    To join in converse sweet;

To burst the chrysalis, and soar
    On love's triumphant wing;
To swell the hymns of mighty praise
    The ransomed armies sing;

To wear the robes of saints in light;
    To shine as shines the sun;
To hear the Savior's welcome voice
    Pronounce the glad "Well done!"

And oh, the crowning heights of bliss,
    Where all the glories blend,
To know the bliss, the light, the love,
    Shall never, never end!

Beyond the shades of sin and wo,
    With joyful speed to fly,
And in God's loving arms to rest—
    Oh, it is gain to die!—G. R.

The Loved Not Lost

By John G. Whittier

How strange it seems, with so much gone
Of life and love, to live still on!
Ah, brother, only I and thou
Are left of all that circle now—
The dear home faces whereupon
The fitful firelight paled and shone.
Henceforward, listen as we will,
The voices of that hearth are still;
Look where we may, the wide world o'er,
Those lighted faces shine no more.
We tread the path their feet have worn,
We sit beneath their orchard trees,
We hear like them the hum of bees,
And rustle of the bladed corn;
We turn the pages that they read,
Their written words we linger o'er;
But in the sun they cast no shade,
No voice is heard, no sign is made,
No step is on the conscious floor!
Yet Love will dream, and Faith will trust,
(Since He who knows our need is just.)
That somehow, somewhere, meet we must!
Alas! for him who never sees
The stars shine through his cypress trees!
Who, hopeless, lays his dead away,
Nor looks to see the breaking day
Across the mournful marbles play!
Who hath not learned, in hours of faith,
The truth to flesh and sense unknown,
That Life is ever Lord of death,
And Love can never lose its own!

The City of Rest

By James Buckham

In love was it founded and pity,
    That home at the heart of the grasses,
    Where sleep never wearies nor passes,
But lies with God's peace in his breast,—
    In love for the spent and the dying,
    In pity for sorrow and sighing,
A home for the homeless, a city,
    A welcoming city, of rest.

There never a trouble shall find them;
There, under God's dew and man's weeping,
The sick and the weary are sleeping.
Nor burdened, nor worn, nor distressed.
The earth folds them close, like a mother,
And none is more dear than another,
For God in His love has assigned them
One home in the city of rest.

They sleep, but their eyes are not holden.
They joy in the daisies and clover.
Yea, when the loved faces bend over,
They smile, knowing silence is best.
They see nature's beauty and splendor,
They hear all the bird-music tender;—
Ah! rose-lit the windows and golden
That look from the city of rest.

'Tis sweet at the last, when God calls us,
To go to the city of slumber.
Oh! think of the infinite number
To whom that long surcease is blest!
Release from the ache and the sorrow,
No slaving to-day or to-morrow—
Ah! call it not death that befalls us,
But peace, in the city of rest!—Y. C.

Over the River

Over the river they beckon to me—
Loved ones who've crossed to the further
side;
The gleam of their snowy robes I see,
But their voices are drowned in the rush-
ing tide.

There's one with ringlets of sunny gold,
And eyes the reflection of heaven's own
blue—
He crossed in the twilight gray and cold,
And the pale mist hid him from mortal
view.

We saw not the angels that met him there;
The gate of the city we could not see—
Over the river, over the river,
My brother stands waiting to welcome me!

Over the river the boatman pale
Carried another—the household pet;
Her brown curls waved in the gentle gale—
My darling child! I see her yet!

She crossed on her bosom her dimpled hands,
And fearlessly entered the phantom bark—
We watched it glide from the silver sands.
And all our sunshine grew strangely dark.

We know she is safe on the other side,
Where all the ransomed and angels be;
Over the river, the mystic river,
My childhood's idol is waiting for me.

For none return from those quiet shores,
Who cross with the boatman cold and pale;
We hear the dip of the golden oars,
And catch a glimpse of the snowy sail.

And lo! they have passed from our yearning
hearts,
They cross the stream and are gone for aye;
We may not sunder the vail apart
That hides from our vision the gates of day.

We only know that their barks no more
Will sail with us o'er life's stormy sea;
Yet somewhere, I know, on the unseen shore,
They watch, and beckon, and wait for me.

And I sit and think, when the sunset's gold
Is flushing river, and hill, and shore,
I shall one day stand by the water cold,
And list for the sound of the boatman's
oar;

I shall watch for a gleam of the flapping sail;
I shall hear the boat as it nears the strand;
I shall pass from sight with the boatman pale,
To the better shore of the spirit land;

I shall know the loved who have gone before,
And joyfully sweet will the meeting be—
When over the river, the mystic river,
The Angel of Death shall carry me.—C. H.

The Silence of the Departed

By Joel Swartz.

The lips of the vanished in silence are
sealed,
And sealed are the portals through which
they have passed;
No whisper, no token has ever revealed
What followed that moment we knew as
their last.

O, where do the sleepers awaken again?
Where blushes the morning that crimsons
their sky?
To us who, alas, in these shadows remain
They cannot or will not return to reply.

When rings o'er the harbor the last evening
bell,
And twilight has drawn down the last curtains of day,
And pale lips have uttered the final farewell,
O, whither then opens the vanished one's
way?

So candid, so affable were they when here,
That if their fond spirits are still in our
range,
Their stillness, their silence. wherever their
sphere.
To sorrow and ignorance are painful and
strange.

It may be our air is so murky and dense,
That it yields to no touch the vanished can
give;
Or may be, so dull is our bodily sense,
That we are as dead to the spirits who live.

The caterpillar's web, whose soft, silver fold,
Is wrapt round the leaves of the sweet-
budding spring,
May shut in the worms but it shuts out the
gold
Which sparkles and burns on the butterfly's wing.

Perhaps it is well, if somehow we could find
The vanished of earth in their loftier
sphere,
That might the sweet ties of the present un-
bind
And hinder the duties imperative here.

It may be the burdens we properly bear,
Would pass to their shoulders, so true to
the last;
O, how could we ask them our journey to
share,
Return and retrace the desert they have
passed?

But are they not near us, a witnessing cloud,
With sympathies sweet and interest in-
tense,
And close to the race-course invisibly crowd
Where hang the great issues of life in
suspense?

Ah yes; let us think, were our senses unsealed,
The mountains around us would kindle
with fire;
Bright hands would reach forward assistance
to yield,
And whispers of hope our courage inspire?

And high over all, at the end of the race,
Our conquering captain in glory should
stand,
With cheer for our hearts in the smiles of
His face,
And crowns for our heads in His nail-
pierced hand.

Accept, brother pilgrim, this world as thy
home,
And labor to make it the brightest and best;
Yet ready to answer the call, " Welcome,
come,
And hear through the silence the songs of
the blest!"—P. J.

Thou Art Gone

By Reginald Heber

Thou art gone to the grave! but we will not
deplore thee,
Tho sorrows and darkness encompass the
tomb;
The Savior hath passed through its portals
before thee,
And the lamp of His love is thy guide
through the gloom.

Thou art gone to the grave! we no longer
behold thee
Nor tread the rough paths of the world by
thy side;
But the wide arms of mercy are spread to
enfold thee,
And sinners may hope, for the Sinless hath
died.

Thou art gone to the grave! and, its mansion
forsaking,
Perchance thy weak spirit in doubt lingered long;
But the sunshine of glory beamed bright on
thy waking,
And the sound thou didst hear was the
seraphim's song.

Thou art gone to the grave! but we will not
deplore thee,
Since God was thy ransom, thy guardian,
and guide:
He gave thee, He took thee, and He will restore thee,
And death has no sting, since the Savior
hath died.

THANKSGIVING DAY

(November)

WHEN, after the ingathering of the first harvest in a new world, Governor Bradford sent four men out to shoot wild fowl that the infant colony "might after a more special manner rejoice together," he little dreamed to what that pious act would grow. For many years the autumnal "feast of ingathering" was merely an occasional festival, as unexpected prosperity or unhoped-for aid in adversity moved our Pilgrim ancestors to a special act of praise. It was not until our Revolutionary War that the Feast became national, and after 1784 it was only occasionally observed except in New England. It was our civil war which brought the people to a new sense of national oneness, and since 1863, the President of the United States has annually issued a Thanksgiving proclamation. But what President or prophet in 1864 could have dreamed that a quarter century later the lines of such a proclamation would go out into all the world, that islands in the Southern Sea, and in the broad Pacific Ocean should be summoned with us to observe a day of joyful thanksgiving?

On such a day as this, when in Cuba and Hawaii and the Philippines there are hearts uplifted with thankfulness that the United States Government exists and is theirs, the thoughtful mind cannot but occupy itself with the question, To what end is this vast and marvelous expansion of a government which a century and a half ago was not even a prophecy? To many it will seem but the action of a natural law—the law of Progress; but are there not an elect few at least who will recognize in it the workings of another natural law—that of Redemption?

For these two laws are equally natural and equally imperative. They rule in different spheres, but they rule none the less. And happy is that nation which has entered the higher sphere in which the law of Progress is perceived to be simply the means by which the law of Redemption shall prevail.

In all ages of the world there have been men whose function it was to redeem. Prophets, poets, law-givers, martyrs have been aware of this high calling, not as something exceptional, singling them out from all the world, but as something inevitable and universal, their singularity being but a symbol of that which should one day be the rule. From time to time there have been nations which at least fitfully and as by a flash of insight perceived that they were called to redeem the world. Israel was such a nation; from first to last, amid all its darkness, errors, shortcomings, the conviction that it was called to a work of Redemption has been an integral element in the Hebrew character, and by virtue of it the Jewish people through vicissitudes unparalleled, have remained a people. France was such a nation for the brief wild period of the Revolution; its inspiring spirit was the conviction that it was set for the redemption of society, its worst blunders, blunders that were nothing short of crimes, were but a startling proof of the vital truth that the mission of Redemption must have as its basis religious and not political sanctions.

That is the truth that our nation needs to learn to-day. Already it is profoundly impressed with its calling to something other than mere Progress; already the prophetic vision that its progress is in order to Redemption is dawning upon the national consciousness. May the profound conviction that the work of Redemption is possible only in alliance with God be the gift of this Thanksgiving Day!—E.

THE FIRST THANKSGIVING IN AMERICA

By HENRY AUSTIN

The first Thanksgiving! This is a theme, which even a flippant writer would perforce be compelled to approach with a feeling akin to reverence.

The Signifi- cance of Thanks- giving Even John Boyle O'Reilly, a man not born in the faith of our Pilgrim fathers, but representing an antagonistic creed, spoke always throughout his life with a certain enthusiasm in regard to this great original of a now historic and national ceremony.

For the festival of Thanksgiving to-day, tho an American institution and a matter of proclamation on the part of the administration, is a thing that goes deeper than its national significance, and finds its firm root, not merely in the affections and the customs of one people, but in that potent imagination everywhere that speaks the aspirations of mankind, and voices in no vague tones the triumph of common humanity.

To us individually Thanksgiving signifies a reunion of kinsfolk under the natal roof, at the hearthstone, which is the heartstone, and this reunion is for a joyous discussion of especially good cheer and a gentle rewelding of the old associations of consanguinity.

But to us collectively as a people Thanksgiving means more. It stands to-day for what it stood in that almost primeval wilderness when the forlornly brave little band which came over on the *Mayflower* celebrated their gratitude to Him who had preserved them from the perils of the deep; when they performed the rites of hospitality to the savages whose minds had been inclined toward them in kindness; and when, furthermore, they gave shape and example to that spirit of cooperation and fraternal love which was destined to ripen in the following century into a republic broad-based on the rights of every man.

And now that we realize the wide significance in a historical way of the first Thanksgiving, let us understand it in detail and behold it in all the vitality of a picture as an event by itself.

The festival began about a year after the landing of the Pilgrims on Plymouth rock, for it was on November 21, 1620, that the *Mayflower* with one hundred and two Pilgrims cast anchor off Cape Cod.

The May- flower Their voyage had taken about ten times the time which a crossing of the Atlantic now consumes, and the poem of Mrs. Hemans, that so many of us learned by heart in childhood, was no exaggeration of the storm and gloom which had companioned their flight across the sea and their landing where "the breaking waves dashed high."

The first half of their first year on the roaring ocean edge of the wilderness had been a period of deaths, of haunting doubts, of constant hardships, and of danger; tho not danger in any large degree from the hostility of the natives, because it is a curious fact that the New England Indians were originally well-disposed toward the white men.

It is of record that, shortly after their first landing, one of their exploring parties received the sudden salute of a flight of arrows from ambush; but these arrows did not kill anybody and evidently were intended solely as a salute, or to apprise the strangers of the presence of the owners of the land.

Relations with the Indians

Friendly relations were established with the Indians at the start and might have continued undisturbed, had the government of the colony been supremely single, instead of general, or had the subsequent additions to the colony been of equally high character and benevolent intent with the first comers.

Their Indian friends had taught the Pilgrims how to plant and fertilize corn, and it is interesting to note that for this fertilization the bones of shad and other fish that abounded along the coast were used.

The first year of the Pilgrim settlement, in spite of that awful first winter when nearly half of them perished, had therefore been comparatively successful. They had planted themselves well, and it is easy to understand why this fact should have appealed to the pious mind of their second governor, William Bradford, as an especial reason for proclaiming a season of thanksgiving.

Governor Bradford

The exact date of this first Thanksgiving, which also might be considered as in some sense a natural evolution from the old harvest festivals of England, is not certain; but from the fact that it was an open-air feast, it is evident that it must have occurred in that lovely period of balmy calm, cool air, and soft sunshine, which is called Indian summer, and which may be considered to range between the latter week of October and the latter week of November.

Edward Winslow, whose name stands third as a signer to the original compact in the cabin of the *Mayflower* and who was thrice made governor, 1633, 1636, and 1644, writes an account of it, supposedly to one George Morton, under date of December 11, 1621. This account runs as follows:

"You shall understand that, in the little time that a few of us have been here, we have built seven dwelling-houses and four for the use of the plantation, and have **A Pilgrim** made preparation for divers **Father's** others. **Account** "We set the last spring some twenty acres of Indian corn and sowed some six acres of barley and peas, and, according to the manner of the Indians, we manured our ground with herrings or rather shads, which we have in great abundance, and take with great ease at our doors.

"Our corn did prove well; and, God be praised, we had a good increase of Indian corn, and our barley indifferent good, but our peas not worth the gathering, for we feared they were too late down. They came up very well and blossomed; but the sun parched them in the blossom.

"Our harvest being gotten in, our governor sent four men on fowling, that so we might, after a special manner, rejoice together after we had gathered the fruit of our labors.

"They four in one day killed as many fowl as, with a little help beside, served the company almost a week, at which time, amongst other recreations, we exercised our arms, many of the Indians coming amongst us, and among the rest their greatest king, Massasoit, with some ninety men, whom for three days we entertained and feasted; and they went out and killed five deer, which they brought to the plantation, and bestowed on our governor, and on the captain and the others.

"And, altho it is not always so plentiful as it was at this time with us, yet by the goodness of God, we are so far from want, that we wish you partakers of our plenty."

Certes, from this frank, straightforward letter, the four men sent out as gunners, or fowlers, for this was the word used in that day, by Governor Bradford, were veritable Nimrods, men of mark as marksmen; or else the New England forest was more plentifully supplied with game than even the woods of Maine, New Hampshire, and Vermont are to-day.

That they killed many wild turkeys which the women in dressing probably stuffed with beechnuts and that they brought home wood pigeons and partridges in abundance, is clear.

But it seems they must have lacked deer, since the Indian nobles in the train of King Massasoit volunteered to go out and bring in the venison.

The Indians, of course, knew the haunts of the deer far better than the pilgrim fowlers. What a cheerful spectacle it must have been, when their Indian guests **White** reappeared carrying a many- **Man and** branched buck, slung downward **Red Man** on a pole, or a pretty little doe, possibly hung across the stalwart shoulders of some giant red man who, in endurance and activity, could have easily eclipsed one of our modern professional athletes!

Shall one doubt that the Pilgrim gravity of demeanor was for a moment dispelled, when the Indians returned with their delicious contribution to the fraternal feast, and that a welcoming cheer arose from the throat of many of the deep-lunged Englishmen, or that the younger of the women may have clapped their hands and beamed upon their red brothers with smiling eyes of Saxon blue?

There was no prejudice then in English breasts against a man on account of the color God had given him. That feeling was to come later in some of the descendants of the English toward another dark-skinned race.

The men and women of the *Mayflower* met the copper-colored semi-savage as a man and brother on equal footing, tho, of course, a pagan whose soul had to be saved.

And the religious exercises that accompanied every day of that first Thanksgiving season were doubtless intended to serve the double purpose of expressing their own gratitude to God and of impressing on the minds of the strangers in enjoyment of their hospitality the beauty and truth of a worship more suitable to the diversified human mind than the Indian's simple deism.

Between the feastings, in generous emulation like the athletes of olden Greece or the knights in medieval tourneys, many of the dusky suite of King Massasoit contended with the younger Pilgrims in various games and races or in feats of strength and agility. Perhaps Massasoit himself unbent from his kingly dignity to show how straight he could send an arrow at some improvised target. Maybe, some Puritan maiden, remembering her bowman ancestors at Hastings, laughingly tried her hand on an Indian bow.

Possibly, too, in the military drill and evolutions which Miles Standish, with his little regiment of twenty, went through, there was **Games** a sagacious intention on the part **and** of that stout little warrior to give **Feasting** the Indians an idea what a formidable foe the white man might be if provoked.

The feasting through those balmy days, and with such an army of unexpected guests, was doubtless mostly out in the open and the cooking done at huge fires.

Naturally, the deer, like the oxen of England at the old popular feasts, or like animals at our Southern barbecues, was in some cases roasted whole, tho it is likely that, as they had barley flour, the cunning hands of the Puritan women composed some delicious venison pasties, and possibly some pies and puddings with wild fruit.

Fish, broiled to a rare brown turn; clams, roasted or stewed, and oysters, also brought in by the Indians and believed to be the first ever eaten by the Pilgrims, were likewise among the dainties.

Some "fire-water," too, it is fair to infer, was passed about, for our Pilgrim fathers, there is abundant evidence to prove, tho temperate, were not teetotalers.

Whether the Indians sat on settles, at rude tables improvised for the occasion, or whether most of them stretched along the ground in the Roman fashion of **The** dining, is a question for imagina- **Dinner** tion to decide.

To their king, Massasoit, it is presumable that a seat of honor must have been offered, and it would be a satisfaction of the mind to know whether were present on this occasion his two sons, Metacom and Wamsutta, or Philip and Alexander, as they were afterward styled, who, in the unfraternal years to follow, fell victims to the cruelty and greed of the white man.

The eye of imagination beholds at this feast the Puritan women handing about to their guests bowls of delicious food with a grave and simple courtesy that must have made its impression on the Indian mind. Perhaps the memory of their grace and graciousness lingered long. We know that, in the frightful wars that subsequently occurred, the New England Indians, as a rule, treated well the white women who fell into their hands. There is the testimony of Mrs. Rowlandson, that even when held in captivity by King Philip, who had the deepest of reasons to hate the white man, she was always an object of most courteous consideration. The King even paid her a shilling for making a shirt for his little boy.

And the ear of imagination hears in that first season of Thanksgiving, along with the solemn music of the stern Pilgrim hymns, the ripple of feminine merriment and the deep laughter of the soldiers of Miles Standish.

And if Massasoit and his ninety men did not forget momentarily their racial gravity and join audibly in this laughter, it still must be believed that their hearts laughed and leaped in their bosoms and their dark eyes brightened in conviviality and friendship. That friendship, hallowed by Thanksgiving hospitality, continued unbroken, tho occasionally disturbed, for about half a century.

Contrary to the line in Mrs. Hemans', for poetry abhors the exactness of history, every day there was heard " the roll of the stirring drum; " but it summoned not to battle, simply to prayer; and at every set of sun, again with prayer and song, the gratitude of all hearts was poured forth.

And one of the leading cooks of this wonderful woodland banquet was none other than Priscilla, whom Captain Standish made **Priscilla** the grand mistake of wooing **the** through another man, instead of **Cook** trying to take her heart like a true soldier by storm face to face.

She it was who presided over the largest kitchen, for some of the cooking of especial dishes was done inside.

What a picture is here for some historical painter: Priscilla at the fire or flitting through the throng outside with some dainty offering for Massasoit, while the eyes of all younger men follow her footsteps!

And what a noble, inspiring picture is the whole scene—a picture of piety, of human brotherhood, and of poetry, for which the universal heart of man, when realizing its profound significance, must gladly and proudly give thanks.—I. A.

FIRST NATIONAL THANKSGIVING PROCLAMATION

The following is the first national proclamation issued by George Washington, first President of the United States. It is dated January, 1795, and will be read with interest, especially in view of the fact that some persons would have us believe that a national Thanksgiving proclamation is a recent invention in our country:

PROCLAMATION

When we review the calamities which afflict so many other nations, the present condition of the United States affords much matter of consolation and satisfaction. Our exemption hitherto from foreign war, an increasing prospect of the continuance of that exemption, the great degree of internal tranquillity we have enjoyed, the recent confirmation of that tranquillity by the suppression of an insurrection * which so wantonly threatened it, the happy course of our public affairs in general, the unexampled prosperity of all classes of our citizens, are circumstances which peculiarly mark our situation with indications of the divine beneficence toward us. In such a state of things it is in an

especial manner our duty as a people, with devout reverence and affectionate gratitude, to acknowledge our many and great obligations to Almighty God, and to implore Him to continue and confirm the blessings we experienced.

Deeply penetrated with this sentiment, I, George Washington, President of the United States, do recommend to all religious societies and denominations, and to all persons whomsoever, within the United States, to set apart and observe Thursday, the 19th day of February next, as a day of public thanksgiving and prayer, and on that day to meet together and render sincere and hearty thanks to the great Ruler of nations for the manifold and signal mercies which distinguish our lot as a nation; particularly for the possession of constitutions of government which unite and, by their union, establish liberty with order; for the preservation of our peace, foreign and domestic; for the reasonable control which has been given to a spirit of disorder in the suppression of the late insurrection, and generally for the prosperous condition of our affairs, public and private, and

* The Whisky Insurrection in Western Pennsylvania.

at the same time humbly and fervently beseech the kind Author of these blessings graciously to prolong them to us; to imprint on our hearts a deep and solemn sense of our obligations to Him for them; to teach us rightly to estimate their immense value; to preserve us from the arrogance of prosperity, and from hazarding the advantages we enjoy by delusive pursuits, to dispose us to merit the continuance of His favors by not abusing them, by our gratitude for them, and by a corresponding conduct as citizens and as men to render this country more and more a safe and propitious asylum for the unfortunate of other countries; to extend among us true and useful knowledge; to diffuse and establish habits of sobriety, order, morality, and piety, and finally to impart all the blessings we possess or ask for ourselves to the whole family of mankind.

In testimony whereof, I have caused the seal of the United States of America to be affixed to these presents, and signed the same with my hand. Done at the city of Philadelphia the first day of January, 1795.

GEORGE WASHINGTON.

By the President:

EDM. RANDOLPH.   —P. M.

FOR ALL THE PEOPLE

Of the religious festivals of the year Thanksgiving Day is the only one that is for all the people. Christmas and Easter and the whole series of Church festivals are for Christians only. The Jews have their Rosh Hashana and their Passover, and that day of festivity on which it is, or was, the rule to drink wine until they could not distinguish "Bless Mordecai" from "Curse Haman." The Mohammedans among us have their Ramadan, and the Chinese have their feast days also, if we only knew what they are. Each religion has its own; but there is one Thanksgiving Day for all, when all, of whatever faith, can in their own way call on God and praise Jesus, Moses, Mohammed or the Buddha after their own several rites; for Thanksgiving Day appeals to us all without distinction as worshipers of our God, just as Independence Day appeals to all of us, of whatever political faith, as lovers of our country.

The same mercies to households and individuals demand gratitude to God as on other years. As many times before, there have been new households, enlarged families, dearer ties, increased affections, comfortable homes, plentiful tables, abundant harvests, a beneficent government, free schools, and religious liberty. And with more emphasis than might be necessary, those who this week put our thanksgiving into verse remind us that the losses, the trials, the sufferings of the year (1899) need not quench our gratitude; for these, too, are included in the wise providence of a loving Father, and those bereavements which bring the most tears add most to our treasures in Heaven.

There is much to be grateful for in the national history of the year. We have brought to an end our war with Spain, with little loss to us and great gain to those for whose sake we took the sword. Of our new possessions those that were nearest to us and knew us best have accepted with joy their new conditions. Only in the Philippines has a faction resisted. Whatever may have been our sense of past duty, it is the privilege of all to thank God that He has given us the unexpected and unsought opportunity to relieve much oppression and to extend the blessings of good government and fair freedom to many millions of people. It is a wonderful opportunity, and no people on the face of the globe has a stricter sense of duty to those under their power. Far are we from being perfect, if tried by the highest standard, but where shall we find a nation which less desires to rule and more desires to rule justly and to give liberty to all?

For one great event that transcends the bounds of any one country and embraces the whole world we must render thanks this day to Almighty God. For the first time in the history of the earth all its great nations have come together in council, and have consulted how they shall go to war no more. This may not end all wars, but it will suppress most of them. It puts the ban on war. It requires nations in dispute to seek some other arbitrament. It makes war a shame. It smooths the way for the reduction of armies and armaments. It sings the song of the angels of Bethlehem about the cradle of the Prince of Peace. We, of this generation, have lived to see—and have hardly known it—what may be the greatest epoch in the world's history since Jesus came to earth. For such mercies what soul, what household, will not raise its thanksgiving to God?—In.

THANKSGIVING THOUGHTS

BY E. S. MARTIN

When the President proclaims to us, as he does every year, that Thanksgiving is at hand and that it behooves us to observe it, he gives us reasons why our hearts should be grateful and our spirits reverent. The crops have been good, he says, and work has been plenty, we have been prospered and have grown richer; pestilence has not vexed us; a fair degree of success has attended our aims; we have been able to perform in good measure what has seemed to us to be our national duty, and our credit as a people stands high among the nations of the world. These are all sound reasons for thankfulness, but they have need to be supplemented, if, as individuals, we are to bring to Thanksgiving all the feelings and sentiments that it ought to excite. To be thankful for health and prosperity, if we happen to be in the enjoyment of those blessings, is reasonable and right, but it is not enough. We should go deeper than that, and considering what is the true purpose of our stay on earth, should be thankful for every experience that promises to make for that purpose's most complete fulfilment. For crushing blows and devastating bereavements it is not in us to be thankful, and we are apt to verge on hypocrisy, or on hysterics, if we attempt it. It is enough surely, if we endure such distress with fortitude and what tranquillity we may.

To the eye that takes large views and sees, however dimly, the purposes of the Almighty fulfil themselves on earth, it may be evident that whatever is, is right, because whatever is, results from the operation of laws that are essential to the well being of the universe. That folks who fall get hurt is due to a law of gravity which apparently is necessary to our existence. We should be thankful that the law holds, but the fall may easily be a grievous thing and fit to be lamented. There are such things as disasters, and when they befall there is no occasion for us to try to be thankful for them. But by no means all that disappoints our hopes and thwarts our wishes is disastrous. A great deal that troubles us turns out in the end to be for our good. Distasteful tasks that we are constrained to execute may prove unexpectedly wholesome and profitable to us. Losses and setbacks which try us sorely, may rouse us from dangerous ease and drive us into beneficent inactivity. Which of us that has lived long enough and well enough to compass any measure of true success, but can look to trials and reverses which have seemed in the end to be the very making of him. Who can look about and not see blight, distortion and disappointment that are traceable to prosperity too easily won, or to some quip of fortune which seemed when it came to be the acme of good luck.

The wisest of us cannot see far into the future, nor discern remote results. While we are trying to be thankful we shall do well to be thankful not only for what we have received and for what we have been spared, but for much that has been denied us. So many things we want that would not be good for us if we got them! Wanting them may be well enough, for every lawful want is a spur and helps to keep us moving, but attainment is another matter. So much the better for us if, while we try hard, and keep trying, to get what we want, we are pious-minded enough to be thankful for what we get even tho it falls short of our expectations.

The blessings we are used to, become so much the habit of our lives that we are apt to take them for granted and to fail to be stirred by them to any positive emotion of thankfulness. There are those who, ever mindful of the unequal measure in which privilege, opportunity and all material goods are distributed in this world, are always consciously grateful for the ordinary, every-day comforts; for food and shelter and decent surroundings and a peaceful life. But most of us, differently constructed, are prone to consider that all we are used to have is ours by a natural right, and that on the whole it is rather a hardship that we cannot contrive to have an ever-increasing share of sugarplums allotted to us. We that are of that disposition must try at Thanksgiving to come to a fuller appreciation of our more recondite blessings, as well as of those which we accept as matters of course. As Riley puts it in his Thanksgiving poem—

Let us be thankful, thankful for the prayers
    Whose gracious answers were long, long delayed,
That they might fall upon us unawares,
    And bless us, as in greater need we prayed.

What do we want most? To be good people according to our lights and our abilities; to do right; to grow in grace; to develop character and strength and unselfishness; to love and to be loved, and as far as lies in us to promote righteousness on this earth. These aspirations are not too lofty for us. The goal they point to is really that toward which we would direct our courses. Nearly all of us are full of selfish desires; we want more things, more money, more fame, more of what we call the good things of life. But after all, imperfect as we are, and conflicting as our various aspirations may be, few of us would deliberately and consciously barter spiritual and intellectual valuables for material ones. We want what is justly our due, but if greediness and harsh exactions are the price of riches we would rather be less rich; if self-seeking and egotism are the price of fame we would rather continue somewhat obscure. In so far as our scruples are sound and well founded we hold them to be beyond price, and would not deliberately sacrifice them for apparent advancement. We are wise in these preferences, for what we are after is not so much the means to buy happiness, as happiness itself, and the basis of that we know is the love and contentment which dwell in a clean heart. What we have reason to fear is not that we shall consciously choose the baser part; it is the thin end of the wedge which in time might separate us from our ideals.

Let us be thankful then for all the right choices we make when we have to choose; for all the unseen influences that help us to choose right; for whatever withholds us, or diverts from a course that is not our true course; for any denial of apparent advantage or present ease which constrains us towards the fulfilment of a nobler destiny. It sometimes seems as if in our immediate time humility was not in so great request as its traditional reputation as a virtue entitles it to be. We Americans are inclined to proclaim that we are the salt of the earth, and a fit pattern for all who dwell therein. We have excuse perhaps; but for all that, pride has been known to be the precursor of painful experiences. It is well that we should be humble in our thanksgivings, and that our gratitude should neither show itself in exultation over our prosperity, nor in expectation of benefits to come, but in the hope of such leadings and inspirations as may make us fit instruments of God's work on earth.—In.

THANKSGIVING

By James M. Ludlow, D.D.

A Nation's Thanksgiving! What a beautiful sentiment! Seventy millions of people at the call of their Chief Magistrate forsaking their secular pursuits and crowding the temples to sing and pray their gratitude to the Deity! Alas! a sentiment as empty as most of the temples will be on Thursday! The holy day is chiefly a holiday. The race, the game, the matinee, the feast—these our thanksgiving liturgy!

Perhaps God will forgive us. We parents take the hilarity of the children—if they are little or thoughtless—in lieu of " Thank you."

Yet he asks our thanks. A neighbor found his recreation during the hot summer in refurnishing his home to delight his loved ones on their return from vacation. The parlor gleamed with new pictures, and every chamber had its souvenir of thoughtfulness. He said: " It paid to see their enjoyment. But one thing broke me all up. My little dot climbed into my lap and kissed me and said, 'Papa, you was weal good, wasn't you?' She was the only one that said so. Bless her heart! "

The least thing you or I can do to show that we are thankful is to *say so*. If you are a Christian, that means a confession of your faith in the goodness of God. If you are not a Christian and only a deist, then emulate, if you do not imitate, the boy Goethe, who made a tiny altar, put on it some combustibles, and placed it in the window where the sun's rays would make them flash.

Try also to *feel grateful*. A class of deaf mutes was asked for a definition of gratitude. One wrote, " Gratitude is the memory of the heart." Noah Webster could not beat that. To kindle a sense of thankfulness we have only to think. Rubbing will set dry sticks on fire; certainly heart fibers will do as much under the friction of purposeful remembrance. An old man could not come to Church, so he spent the morning in recollecting the events of his life. It was his last worship on earth. Two days later he was gone. Some of us are going out of life like boorish guests who depart without thanking their host.

Do something to show your gratitude. Has the year been prosperous? Help somebody who is in need. Has your faith comforted you? Tell it to somebody who is staggering under his load without your assurance of the divine love. Edwin Booth, after a terrible bereavement, wrote to a friend: " Oh, that I could give you the full companionship of the love of God as I have felt it since Mary's death, the peace that has filled my soul, and the strength that has flowed steadily into it since that terrible day! " Did he give the companionship of God? Nay, that is for God himself to give; but he led the way into the house of comfort where God always lives and waits to bless all who will become guests of his affection. Are you grateful for 1899? Try to lift somebody else into the sunshine. Sir John Lubbock tells us that ants will drop the load of sweetness they are conveying to the nest and carry in any wounded or sick ant. " Go to the ant, thou sluggard, consider her ways, and be wise."

Especially *keep the vows* of the year. King Richard Cœur de Lion used to tell his comrades this story, as we find it in old Roger of Wendover's Chronicles: A pit had been dug to entrap wild beasts. A rich Venetian while hunting fell into it. He found at the bottom a lion and a serpent. Seeing that he was a companion in misery they did not harm him. A poor woodcutter going by, the Venetian begged his assistance in escaping, promising to give him a rich reward. When the ladder was let down the lion and the snake got out first, and crouching at the woodcutter's feet roared and hissed their gratitude. Afterward the lion brought to the woodcutter's cottage a dead goat; the serpent brought a precious stone, and laid it on his deliverer's dinner plate. The Venetian failed to remember the poor man, until the judges of Venice, shamed by the story of the grateful beasts, compelled their townsman to fulfil his promise even to the extent of half the rich man's fortune. A yarn? Yes, but one of those yarns that Great-hearts like to tell. Your experience, my friend, during the year past has been exceptional if you have not cried out a promise from the bottom of some pit. Give your *whole life* in gratitude to God, who has given you everything. At the temple of Æsculapius those who were healed always left some testimonial to the divine healer. Where life had been saved it was customary for the beneficiary to present his full statue in stone, wood, ivory, or silver. The custom shows a premonition in noble souls of the duty which the apostle enjoins of making one's self a living sacrifice to Him " in whom we live and move and have our being."

The shadows of the falling year remind us of the time when our *earthly joys will be gone.* Would you perpetuate them? George Eliot says of these passing delights: "Tho perishable as to their actual existence, they will be embalmed to eternity in the precious spices of gratitude." No gift of God has only present value. The happiness it brings now is only the glisten on the coin; the real metal does not perish if its luster passes off. It may be reminted for our use in another realm of being, but its value is in the fact that it was mined for us from the heart of the Infinite.

Thanksgiving Day is only our annual time for saying grace at the table of eternal goodness.—I.

THANKSGIVING MEMORIES AND HABITS

By William Adams, D.D.

The beginning of this world's history was a song; its end will be a doxology. The secret of all rational contentment is revealed in that inspired direction which ought to be written on every heart, as a compendious rule of life. "Be careful of nothing; but in *everything,* by prayer and supplication, *with thanksgiving,* let your requests be made known unto God. And the peace of God, which passeth all understanding, shall keep your hearts and minds through Christ Jesus." In the cathedral of Limerick there hangs a peal of bells which was manufactured for a convent in Italy, by an enthusiast who fixed his home for many years near the convent cliff to enjoy their daily chimes. In some political convulsion the bells and their manufacturer were swept away to another land. After a long interval, the course of his wanderings brought him to Ireland. On a calm and beautiful evening, as the vessel which bore him floated along the broad stream of the Shannon, he suddenly heard the bells peal forth from the cathedral tower. They were the long-lost treasures of his memory. Home, happiness, friends, all early recollections were in their sound. Crossing his arms on his breast, he lay back in the boat. When the rowers looked round, they saw his face still turned to the cathedral—but his eyes had closed forever on the world. Such a tide of memories had swept over the sympathetic cords of his heart, that they snapped under the vibration. Who has not experienced the power of association in its milder and happier forms? The return of an anniversary, the melody of a tune, the swinging of a church bell, will set memory in motion, and unveil the pictures which hang on her sacred walls. Because memory is clad in sober and russet garb, many associate her form with sadness. But it is a sadness from which we never wish to be divorced. Peace, quietness, and "cherub contemplation," come in her train. Memory is the mother of gratitude. Mirth and frivolity are born of present excitements; but there cannot be deep and serene happiness in the absence of all memories of the past.

The bare mention of the word, the Old Thanksgiving Day—what a power it has it to revive the pleasantest reminiscences, and recall the brightest scenes of other days in many hearts! It transports them to the home of their childhood. It takes them at once into the presence of the father and mother who, it may be, for many years have been sleeping in the grave. It recalls their smiles of affectionate greeting, their tones of cheerful welcome; tones and smiles such as only they could give. Every image of peace, contentment, competence, abundance, and joy, comes back spontaneously on each return of the grateful festival. It is a day not indeed heralded and emblazoned, like the corresponding festivals in our ancestral land, in all the pomp and glory of song. It has not been celebrated, like Christmas, by the imperial song of Milton, the dove-like notes of Herbert, or the classic beauty of Keble. Connected with it are no superstitious rites handed down from time immemorial; no revellings in baronial halls; no decorations of churches or houses with garlands or evergreens; no wassailings; no shoutings; no carols; no riotous dissipation.

Simpler in its nature, humbler in its pretensions, better suited to a people of a more recent origin, it is set apart to the exercise of those home-bred affections, those "honest fireside delights," which are greener than laurel or fir-tree, and which, from a natural affinity, most closely harmonize with the sweet sanctities of our holy religion. As the day drew on, anticipation was busy in the young and old. The aged pair, from beneath whose shelter their children, one after the other, had gone forth into the world, leaving them alone, looked forward with delight to the prospect of being surrounded once more by their numerous progeny on a day of gladness; and children separated widely apart, and already grown familiar with life's perplexities and cares, hailed with pleasure the "yearly sacrifice," when they should all rally again around the paternal hearth, and renew their faith and affection among the long-cherished scenes of their childhood. Happy was the venerable sire, who went up that day to the house of God, in company with his children and children's children, and who sat down to the table of plenty with his household, in health, peace, and contentment. If any were detained from the gathering by stern necessity places were prepared for them as if they were present, in order that all might feel how closely they were linked by invisible sympathies; and the absent ones, wherever on sea or land they roamed, were as "a bird wandering from its nest," or crippled in the time of migration, looking far away, and longing to join himself unto his fellows.

Tho this particular day has been designated by the civil authorities, it should be borne in mind that in the one only national organization which had God for its author, several days in the year were set apart by Divine institution for religious festivities. Spring, summer, and autumn had each its festal symbolism; the most joyous of which, called the Feast of Tabernacles, was an annual Thanksgiving—not only in memory of ancestral favors, but for the ingathering of the harvests. Nothing can be conceived more beautiful than the manner of its observance. Booths were erected in the open air, with branches from the palm and willow, within which families were gathered, to eat together before the Lord; so that the occasion was sacred to the reunion of friends, the enjoyment of hospitality, the interchange of kindness, the expression of generous regard for the stranger, the widow, and the fatherless. Nor was it lawful for a Jew so much as to taste of ear or parched corn, or bread of the new harvest, till a nation had borne a sheaf of barley or wheat and waved it before God, in token of their gratitude. Are we charmed by the picture which the imagination paints of that national spectacle when the glens of the vine and olive gave forth their happy inhabitants, to flow together into the court of the Lord, with chanting of psalms and waving of sheaf and branch? But when did the sun ever look down upon such a scene as has been spread often beneath his eye on this Western Continent, a land unknown and undreamed of when Hebrew feasts were instituted, when many States have agreed to devote one and the same day for Thanksgiving to our common Father for His abundant goodness? What millions of well-clad, well-fed, well-taught, and, if they would but believe it, happy people, within the temples of religion, and the homes of health, comfort, and plenty!

As the mind travels over the extended scene, it rests not so much on metropolitan affluence, on gatherings in stately mansions and tapestried walls, where sumptuous fare is of daily occurrence, as on the humbler habitations of rural life, where man is brought by earth, sky, and season, in closer contact with God. Toil is at rest and contented with its rewards. Plow and flail are exchanged for recreation. If nature is more silent than in earlier months, when birds and beasts are full of jocund music and life, it is the silence of peaceful contentment. The rich autumn sunlight bathes the sere and yellow stalks and husks of corn still standing in the field, reduced to the undress of the year, yet testifying of the golden wealth they have yielded to man; barns bursting with plenty; the cattle chewing the cud with mute thankfulness; families reassembled in the old homestead; mirth in the voices of the young, and placid delight warming the ashy hue of age; what images of serene satisfaction are those which are presented by this day of happy memories!

Thanksgiving Day has a history attached to it. Like the Latin word "virtus," it is a history which runs through the entire life of a people. We cannot afford to lose reverence for ancestral memories. It is to be regretted that Mr. Irving, our American Goldsmith, has expended so much time in the prolix exaggeration of the peculiar habits of the early Dutch colonists. When Diedrich Knickerbocker extends an extravaganza through two volumes over that portion of our history, we confess to a feeling somewhat painful, mingling with the keenest relish of the humorous. We need more, not less of filial respect and gratitude in our national character.

Shem and Japheth, with their mantle of charity, did a nobler service than their brother who laughed at the shame of their common parentage. In that transition period through which we are passing, it is well to think of the primitive strength which is beneath us, and upon which a fruitful surface invites and rewards our toil. The origin of this day was with a people who were exiles for the sake of truth and liberty, and who gave a soul to the scattered colonies of the Western Hemisphere. "Te Deums" had been chanted in the cathedrals of the Old World by royal decree, at the birth of princes, the coronation of kings, and the issue of great battles; but the voluntary appointment of a day, by a whole people, for the distinctive purpose of rendering thanks to the Almighty for His manifold blessings, civil and religious, national and domestic, marks an epoch in history—Thanksgiving Day is the festival of religious liberty. Removed to a distance from all tyranny, passing from suffering, which called for brave defiance and patience, into success and enlargement which inspired gratitude, religion, finding its freedom in New World, poured out its carols at the very gate of heaven.

Among the many proclamations issued by the Governors of the several States in the autumn of 1857, appointing the Thanksgiving for that year, was one couched in these words:

"Since I have been in office, I have, in each year, as Governor of the State, without any authority of law, but sustained by ancient custom, appointed a day of thanksgiving. Thursday, the 19th day of November, is the day now appointed, and I trust it will be observed. There is, certainly, some superruling Providence which has brought us into existence, and which will ultimately accomplish the ends for which we were created, not only as individuals, but as a people. Nothing can, therefore, be lost by recognizing the obligation which we owe to the Supreme Being—by it much being gained."

With all respect to magistracy, I call that an extraordinary document. He is not altogether confident about it, but on the whole is inclined to think that "some super-ruling Providence" may be addressed with thanks, especially since nothing can be lost, and something may be gained by the act! The idea of "making something" out of Thanksgiving carries our national propensity quite to a ludicrous extreme; and the words "loss" and "gain," if they do not convey the nicest sense of religious obligation, certainly suggest an eye to the "main chance," as an apology for the rendering of thanks!

We are certainly a most astonishing nation! We are very tenacious of our old British privilege of *grumbling*. If weather and business and politics kept along smooth and prosperous all the time, very many would be thrown out of occupation. Croaking is their profession, and making themselves unhappy is their habit. A man ought to have a very steady head who reads nothing but American newspapers. He becomes familiar with excitement and apprehension, and is all the while wondering what will come to pass next. Mr. Miller,* who, a few years ago, broached the theory that the world was near its end, and like "Judas of Galilee, in the days of the taxing drew away much people after him," could have succeeded with this notion nowhere else so well as in these United States of America. Such things are indigenous to our soil. In a country like our own stretching over so many degrees of latitude and longitude, through such varieties of climate, hot and cold, dry and wet, with such diversities of interest and manners among a heterogeneous population, and with such artificial facilities for flashing the report of everything which occurs on a vast continent backwards and forwards, and bringing it, every few minutes, upon the retina of every man's eye—why one might be excused who should live in a constant expectation of the world's catastrophe! Rumors of a comet whisking its fiery tail among the stars and certain to demolish our planet upon such a day of the calendar; a tornado upsetting houses, fences and forests; corn in the last of June, all over the West, not more than three inches high, when it should have been as many feet, alarming the country with the certainty of a famine; now a drought which bakes the furrows and burns up the pastures; now rains, excessive and continuous beyond all the memories of the "oldest inhabitant;" a tremendous inundation of the Mississippi; a cold snap in May, which kills all the fruit; a popular election, when the very foundations of society are moved, the sea upturning its discolored depths; mobs in Baltimore and New York, bringing out the military; senators, counselors, judges—names so venerable in the beginning,—accused of corruption and venality; good old philanthropic and ecclesiastical bodies rent asunder; Shem, Ham, and Japheth pelting one another with hard recriminations, and the air filled with all the menaces and terrors of the old prophets; today, a plethora of money, eager to buy up the whole continent, and all the islands and countries which lie adjacent thereto; and tomorrow, a "panic" before which the bags of gold in all the bank vaults collapse and shrivel up, like those of wind which Eolus sent to Homer's hero; verily, one might think the world was coming to an end, twenty times in the course of a twelvemonth!

But in some way, I know not how it is, we get along marvelously well. The sun rises and sets; the stars are not jostled out of their steady orbits; the months are not thrown out of step in their orderly procession; the seasons follow each other serenely and honestly; the sign of the covenant is in the heavens, bright and beautiful as when the mothers from the ark lifted their babes aloft to "bless the bow of God;" all the heathenish signs in the Zodiac do not prevent the mighty monarch of day from bringing the year about, "filling our hearts with food and gladness;" and on Thanksgiving Day, in the golden autumn, multitudes of people, in the temples of religion and in their homes, meet together with more reason and occasion for gratitude—if they were wise enough to know it—than any nation upon the face of the earth. "The Lord hath done great things for us, whereof we are glad." If there is one peril more than another which threatens our prosperity, it is that indifference to our mercies which might provoke God to withdraw them. May God incline us more and more to that unambitious, unselfish, contented, cheerful, thankful temper, which is at once a medicine and a feast, an ornament and a protection.

One of the chief advantages, we are told, of the national festivity of the Hebrew, was that, by friendly intercourse between different tribes, it promoted a spirit of common patriotism. If Thanksgiving would but be observed in a becoming spirit, how much would it accomplish in the way of purifying and strengthening the sentiment of nationality, which was fostered by ancestral memories, cemented by the blood of our fathers, and wrought into the structure of our continent by the hand of God, in the flow of rivers, the clasp of lakes and ridges, and the embracing arm of an unbroken seaboard.

An excellent minister of my acquaintance is in the habit of selecting the texts of his Thanksgiving sermons out of the book of Lamentations. The elegies of the weeping prophet are a part of the Sacred Volume, and frequent enough are the occasions when they may be used with utmost pertinency. But it so happens that "Thanksgiving"—the only day in our calendar of the kind—is the one in which dirges are not so appropriate as carols. Its true design is not to furnish the pulpit with an opportunity for pelting the civil magistracy, nor for indulging in lugubrious complaints and apprehensions as to the condition and prospects of political affairs; but specifically to rehearse those acts of the Divine goodness which should inspire us with gratitude and incline us to a cheerful expression of thanks. That man who, in the worst condition of affairs, cannot discover material enough for praise, is already in a morbid and most deplorable state.

This festival was first appointed by a people proverbially parsimonious in the designa-

*William Miller, founder of the sect called Millerites.

tion of holidays. With the exception of "Election Day," and the "Fourth of July," it was the one only holiday of the year. "New Year" came and passed in the New England States with no recognition, save in the presence of a new primer, and a vague impression that it was the time for a boy to make good resolutions. But the last Thursday in November gathered to itself all fragrant and pleasant associations. What extraordinary sermons, what extraordinary anthems, on that day in the old "Meeting House"!* Without reproof, one could smile, on that day, at the wonderful performances of the choir in those old fugue tunes in which the several parts were perpetually chasing each other in a hard race, till they came in at the close, with a general making up on satisfactory terms; and even at the sermon too,

when the minister—that man of black—did not seem so ghostly as in other days, but descending from high mysteries, talked of passing events and familiar things, in a style which kept his hearers awake without the aid of physical appliances; and so the day which went forth with joy was led in at night with peace.

The reader will infer that the foundations of the author's mind were laid in happy memories and associations with the Day and the Habit of Thanksgiving.

Sufficiently compensated will he be if anything shall be found in these pages, which may serve as a few grains of frankincense on that oblation which, he trusts, will burn pure and bright on all our altars and our hearths, on each return of Thanksgiving Day.

SERMONS AND OUTLINES

MAKING OUR OWN WORLD

By Maltbie D. Babcock, D.D.

The people therefore, that stood by, and heard it, said that it thundered; others said, An angel spake to him.—John xii: 29

A verse from one of the songs of boyhood runs:

"This world is not so bad a world
As some would like to make it;
But whether good, or whether bad,
Depends on how you take it."

What you make of the world is, practically, what you think of it and what you do with it. There is a difference in the opinions and behavior of people. From the same facts they reach different philosophies; from the same premises, different conclusions. Some said it thundered; others said, An angel spake unto Him—one fact, but two opinions; one sound, but two interpretations. Where lay the difference? It must have been in the people.

Fichte says, what system of philosophy you hold depends wholly on what manner of man you are. Philosophy means, in effect, your theory of life—Epicurean, Stoic, Utilitarian, Necessitarian. Kant speaks of the "*Ding an sich*"—the thing in itself. But who can tell what that is? The moment I behold anything, it is colored by my powers of perception and interpreted by my personality. There was a sound that day in Jerusalem; but who knows what it was in itself? To one man, thunder; to another, an angel's voice; to Jesus Himself, the voice of His Father. What is music in itself, if there were no one to hear it? I remember listening to a string quartet concert with a friend. I cannot describe the pleasure it was to me. Asking my friend afterward what he thought

of the concert, he said, "It was one long squeak to me." Mr. Lowell, in an English address, said: "The proverb, 'Truth lies at the bottom of the well,' comes about because whoever looks down to see her sees his own image, and is sure, not only that he has seen the goddess, but that she is far better looking than he had imagined." Metaphysicians call this, not perception, but apperception. It is the fact colored by the mind. It is the sound as I hear it, the sight as I see it. It is a landscape through the glass of my mind—distorted, if the glass is poor; clear, if the glass is good. In the first scene of Julius Cæsar, Decius says, "Here lies the east." "No," says Casca, with heart full of conspiracy. Cinna agrees with Decius, and points to the gray dawn in the east. Again Casca says, "No, there in the south, where I point my sword, the sun will rise," thinking of revolution and a new political day. "As a man thinketh in his heart, so is he," and so he sees; and the world is not what it is in itself, but what it is to us,—colored and interpreted by what we import, impart. Wordsworth is accurate when he speaks of

"The mighty world of eye and ear,
Both what they *half create*, and half perceive."

He laments:

"I heard a thousand blended notes,
While in a grove I sate reclined,
In that sweet mood when pleasant thoughts
Bring sad thoughts to the mind.

* This name for a church is not of New England origin, as is generally supposed, for the classic Addison uses it in the *Spectator*.

" To her fair works did Nature link
The human soul that through me ran;
And much it grieved my heart to think
What man has made of man.

" Through primrose tufts, in that green
bower,
The periwinkle trailed its wreaths;
And 'tis my faith that every flower
Enjoys the air it breathes.

" The birds around me hopped and played;
Their thoughts I cannot measure;
But the least motion which they made,
It seemed a thrill of pleasure.

" The budding twigs spread out their fan,
To catch the breezy air;
And I must think, do all I can,
That there was pleasure there.

" If this belief from heaven be sent,
If such be Nature's holy plan,
Have I not reason to lament
What man has made of man? "

Again and again he complains over the
dulling and deadening of our sensibilities,
and of the materializing of our common life.

" The world is too much with us; late and
soon,
Getting and spending, we lay waste our
powers:
Little we see in Nature that is ours."

Why do we not see " Earth crammed with
heaven, and every common bush afire with
God? " Why is " a primrose on a river's
brim " a yellow primrose to us, and nothing
more, when to another it gives " thoughts
that do often lie too deep for tears "? Why
do we only hear it thunder, when some one
else hears an angel? Why cannot I see the
violet hue in the shadows of the fence rails?
Artists do. " I do not see these things in
Nature that you see," said a man to Turner
as they stood before one of his pictures.
"Don't you wish you could? " was the response. It looks as tho the explanation of
differences was inside, not outside, and a
man's temperament was his fate.
I. What, then, have I to do with this? If
the differences is in people, so that one hears
it thunder and another hears an angel's voice,
what have I to do with it all? I am what I
am. How can I be held responsible? " Can
the blind see or the deaf hear? " The whole
problem, brethren, is solved by the word
attention. It is attention that makes the difference between seeing and looking, between
hearing and listening. Seeing plus attention
equals looking. Hearing plus attention equals
listening. What you see and hear may be
wholly out of your control now, but not so
with your looking and listening. Moral responsibility and moral power meet in your
will. You can choose to look up, not down;
to the right, not to the left; not because it is
natural to you or pleasant, but because God's
word tells you it is right. What is your neck
for, but to govern your looking and listening? You may see wine red in the cup, but

you can look another way. You may hear
the voice of temptation, but resolve to listen
to the voice of God. So, with your God-
given will, you may dispose yourself in opposition to your disposition. This can be done.
No man is the slave of his disposition in a
world where the Divine will and the human
will together can do eventually what they
please. Temperament is wax before the
human will and God. Natural traits are
powerless before moral decisions. You are
not responsible for the disposition you are
born with, but for the disposition you die
with. It can be changed. Family characteristics may be chosen or repudiated by the determination of the character-builder. Heredity is powerful; but human choice has God
within reach.
With God all things are possible; Saul becomes Paul; human nature is changed. A
man can be born again—can become a new
creation. " Instead of the thorn shall come
up the fir-tree, and instead of the brier shall
come up the myrtle-tree, and it shall be to the
Lord for a name, for an everlasting sign." A
sign—of what? That God can cross the sign
and line of your nativity; that by the Holy
Spirit you can be regenerated; that, tho you
were born under a mercurial, a saturnine, or
martial star, you may be born again under
the star of Bethlehem, with another disposition, divine, and loyal to God, with a new
heart that sees God, with a new heart
that hears His voice.
II. This is the first, great, and Divine possibility, and the second is like unto it and involved in it. You can change your point of
attention, and create or destroy your faculties, govern your senses, and determine what
you shall see and hear. Christ taught this
truth again and again: he gains that uses.
he loses that neglects; seek God first, and
things become incidental; seek the world
first, and God becomes vague and remote.
Attention develops; neglect disintegrates. If
I were by nature like a fly that feasts on carrion, and should resolve to follow the flight
of the bees, and seek only fragrance and nec-
tar, my love for the foul would lessen, my
faculties gradually be transformed, and
honey and wax, sweetness and light, would
become the income and output of my life.
Beloved, every Christian of us has both natures; the old instinct for decay, the new
impulse for soundness; the old instinct rejoicing in iniquity, the new impulse in the
truth. On the left is death, on the right is
life. The depressing and the encouraging are
side by side. Scandal and records of sin are
opposed to kindness, and hope, and words of
good report; on the one hand debits and
things that hurt—on the other credits and
things to be thankful for; voices of temptation—high calling from God; our personal
wrongs—our imperial duties; carrion—clover. To which will you choose to look and
listen, despite what you now ordinarily see
and hear? " His servants," said Jesus, " are
ye who carries you away *by force?* " No.
" to whom ye yield yourselves." Which way
will you *look?* You can decide: it will

affect your seeing. To what will you *listen?* You can decide: it will affect your hearing. You begin saying: "As I am, I see and hear." True. It only thunders to the dull or guilty soul; while the ethereal and aspiring spirit hears angel voices. As we are, we do, say, think, hear, see. But you can reverse the process: As you look and listen, will you see and hear, think, say, do, become.

The men who heard it thunder could not help it that day. But if they discovered that others heard angels' voices; if they said, "why cannot I?" if they began to look for God, began to listen for angels, some day glimpses of God came to them; some day heavenly music blessed them. "If with all your hearts ye truly seek me, ye shall also surely *find* me." Every one that seeketh, findeth; for God is the God of the hungry and thirsty soul, and satisfieth the desire of every living thing.

Beloved, what Thanksgiving Day is to us, what voices speak to us to-day, depends upon what we have been looking for and listening to in the days that are gone. If to-day you find yourself inclined to murmur, seeing much that is hard to bear, seeing little to be thankful for; if you find fault instead of saying grace; if you groan and cannot sing; if, as Whittier says,

"You see the cloud which overhangs
A world of sin and loss;
I hear the Lord's beatitudes,
His prayer upon the cross;"

if, in a word, you see only the dark side, I am sorry. But it can be helped, swiftly, to-day, by an act of faith; more slowly in the year to come by obedience to God's laws. God can immediately open your eyes. You remember Elijah and the terrified young man who thought they were friendless and helpless. "Lord, open thou the young man's eyes!" prayed the prophet, and lo, the mountains were full of chariots and horsemen!

Like a piece of cold iron in sand and metal filings, which brings no iron out, you see no especial mercies. But wind a coil of wire about the iron, and the invisible current so inspires it that every scrap of iron leaps to meet it. You, too, can be so filled with the Spirit of Jesus to-day that God's benefits will swiftly greet your eyes and cluster about your heart.

But for the future, I appeal to you, friends under the clouds, friends of the minor key, knights of the rueful countenance, missing the voice of angels, hearing only the thunder, see what can be done by your will and God's in a year. Make three resolutions.

1. Resolve *to do*—the seraphic rather than the stormy thing; do the thoughtful thing, and cause a thankful response; it will affect the air outside you and change the tone and temper of your mind. We are only just learning the supreme interest of the mind in the hand. Train your hand to be kind and it will soon react upon your heart and make it sensitive to God's mercies. Being kind to others will awaken you to the Being "kinned" to you. "One who loves his fellow men" will find himself "one whom love of God has blest."

2. Resolve to *say*—thankful words. However you feel, you are not obliged to talk. It is seldom your duty to say, "What disagreeable weather!" "What a poor breakfast!" "What a homely person!" "What a headache I have!" There is always an appreciative word that can be uttered. As a rule, we say what we choose. Why not choose what we say by the rule of love? We say what comes naturally, and excuse ourselves by temperament. Let our temperament keep silence before a heart that will tell of God's faithfulness and speak good things of the Lord. It is not wrong for a shadowed heart to prompt sunny words. Even a cat will curl up in the only spot of sunshine in a room. Carlyle came down one morning with his "waes" and lamentations: "If I could but have had that dog by the hind legs within reach of a stone wall!" Walter Scott once had just such a night. "Did you hear that dog?" he was asked. "Yes, poor cur, he kept me awake. I was sorry for him; he, no doubt, has his troubles too." Let our speech be with grace, not groaning. The discouraging note can be left in silence, the loving thought can be uttered; it will help our heart to hope.

3. Resolve to *look*—for causes of thankfulness. "Seek and ye shall find," is a principle as well as a promise. Look for trouble, for sin, shame, ash-heaps, broken dishes; you will find them. Look for goodness, good people, good apples; you will find them. The Pharisees saw in Matthew a despised publican, and their pride was gratified. Jesus saw in Matthew a man, a possibility, and His love was gratified. Look for the good in people, in history, in the providence of God. Look for the goodness of the Lord in your own life. The dross and slag of life accumulate; smoke is in the air; flakes of soot fall softly upon us; life can easily seem a poor affair. But life is full of dignity, grace, and joy, full of opportunity for goodness and kindness. Will you wait till the sunset hour gilds its passing? Will you wait till death stirs your imagination and you see, but too late, how much beauty and half-appreciated joy there was in life; how much you had of blessing, in how many ways you could have been a blessing? Look for God's goodness to-day. Only so will you come to see life in its fulness. The disagreeable may be forced upon you; but your mind will instinctively find an offset. Sweet uses will shine out of adversity. You will find "Tongues in the trees, books in the running brooks, sermons in stones, and good in everything." In every storm you will hear your Savior's voice, "It is I." Every day will have sufficient testing; but the word of Jesus will hold good, "My grace is sufficient for thee." You will see the sterner side of life, the rocklike structure of righteousness with the Puritan; but also life's gentler side with the Mystic, the green pastures and still waters of Peace. In your life mercy and truth shall meet, righteousness and peace shall kiss each other. The world

of law shall yet to you be a world of love. You shall hear it thunder at Sinai; but you shall hear the angel voices at Bethlehem singing the glory of the God of love, heralding to all mankind tidings of peace and good will.

" Old friends, old scenes, will lovelier be,
As more of Heaven in each we see:
Some softening gleam of love and prayer
Shall dawn on every cross and care.

" As for some dear familiar strain
Untired we ask, and ask again,
Ever in its melodious store,
Finding a spell unheard before;

" Such is the bliss of souls serene,
When they have sworn to steadfast mean,
Counting the cost, *in all to espy*
Their God, in all themselves deny."
—H. R.

OUR COUNTRY

By J. P. Newman, D.D.

He hath not dealt so with any nation.—Psalm cxlvii: 20

This psalm is a beautiful ascription of praise to Almighty God for national benedictions. It is a recognition of the fact that He makes a distinction between individuals, between communities and nations, by the bestowment of His blessings, and there is no fact more patent than this, that we differ in our gifts and blessings; and what is true of us as individuals is also true of the nations of the earth. The Psalmist therefore recognizes this great fact, that national blessings come from the Almighty, and are given in recognition of national fidelity to His government, obedience to His laws, and are given for a special purpose, to be used not for selfish gratification, but for our own happiness and that of others. The Psalmist ascends from the individual, crowned with innumerable mercies, to the Jewish commonwealth, and after reciting the marvelous history of that people, enumerating God's wonderful interpositions therein, and recounting the blessings enjoyed, he then exclaims in the language of the text, " He hath not dealt so with any nation."

Let me, therefore, call your attention calmly, and I trust gratefully, to the national blessings which at this time call for our gratitude. And it seems to me that if we recognize the truth stated by St. Paul when he stood on Mars Hill, that God hath ordained the habitations and the boundaries of nations, we must acknowledge that in His infinite wisdom and goodness He has selected for us the most desirable, the most beautiful portion of this earth. No matter whether we take the geographical location, or the climate, or our mineral and agricultural capacities, the variety of our climates, our longitude and latitude—no matter from what standpoint we view our location, we must confess, without self-conceit or national vanity, that this national location is the most desirable on the face of the earth. It is far from the frozen regions of the north, it is far from the burning suns of the south, but sweeping over the lovely regions of a temperate zone, it lies too far south to be bound in by perpetual chains of frost, and too far north for its social character to sink under the enervating influences of a tropical sun. It is therefore on that side

of the equator destined by Providence to be the great receptacle of humanity; it is in the latitude and longitude where the great nations of the earth have dwelt in prosperity and in power.

Here it is possible to find within our own region all the climates of the earth; the climate of the tropics, the climate of the temperate zone, and the climate of the polar region, and with these peculiarities of climate it is also possible for us to find the fruits of all climates and of all countries. Indeed, a richer inheritance was never portioned out to any people, Palestine not excepted. Tho I consider Palestine a world in miniature, worthy the gift of God and worthy the acceptance of a chosen people, yet it is a narrow strip of land; you could place it inside of one of our counties, and especially if we take counties of the great Western States beyond the Mississippi.

And then, in addition to these great geographical advantages, we ought to remember that God hath graciously favored us in our ancestry. Our ancestors were never vassals; our ancestors were English gentlemen, occupying high social positions; persons of wealth and of intelligence; they were the men who stood abreast with the foremost men of every nation, and we must look upon them, not as some of the English looked upon them in the days of the Revolutionary war, as felons banished from their country, but we must look upon them as English gentlemen; and had England been wise and allowed Patrick Henry or George Washington, or both, to represent the colonies in the parliament of Great Britain, there would have been no Revolution, and these vast States to-day would have been the richest possession of the English Crown. But our fathers were men of renown and determination, who fully appreciated their rights, which they declared for themselves and for their posterity, that where there is no representation there shall be no taxation. Denied representation, they withheld taxation; they asserted the rights of freemen; they announced the ultimate principles of human rights, and thus inaugurated the grandest political era in the annals of time.

If from our ancestors we look out upon our population, made up of the nationalities of the earth, to be in the second, certainly in the third generation, harmonized unities, and Americanized—if we look out upon our population we must be satisfied therewith. It must awaken gratitude in the national heart that the Almighty has so ordained that while this country's population was to be made up so largely of emigrants, yet the emigrants were not to be the offscouring of the earth, were not to be the aged and the decrepid, were not to be the poverty-stricken; but they were to be the children, the youth, the manhood, the womanhood of the best populations of the great Caucasian race; in other words, of the descendants of Japheth, that branch of the human race which to-day is advancing to supreme power over Ham on the one side, and over Shem on the other.

The foreign element in our population is too frequently denounced, but I beg of you, citizens, to analyze it, if your attention has never been turned to the wealth of the emigrants, the amount of money which each foreigner brings into this country. Usually those who come are thrifty; whether they are farmers or artisans, they are not paupers, but they represent what may be called the bone and the sinew of the Old World; and I do not wonder that Bismarck in his astute sagacity favors * the enactment of laws against emigrating from Germany here, because he knows that those of Germany who come to this country represent national wealth in their capacity for industry as well as in their capacity for the legislation of a great country. I do not wonder that Lord Beaconsfield is alarmed; and that in his poetic fancy he even stepped beyond the truth. I will not say beyond the truth intentionally, for it seems that there was a Canadian who went over there, and, if he did not misrepresent the facts, he certainly led the prime minister astray; and therefore I do not wonder that in the exercise of his poetic imagination he should paint such a picture as might deter the artisans and the farmers of Great Britain from coming to this country. The crowned heads of Europe may well hold up their hands in anxiety, for they see that the class of people who are looking toward America are the people who contribute most largely to a nation's wealth.

It is true, as I have intimated, there is danger in the stranger, danger in the foreigner who comes with antagonistic ideas and who comes with selfishness, for selfishness underlies emigration. It is so in all the past. The Hebrews went into Egypt for corn; the Spaniards went into Mexico and South America for gold, and the only emigrants in the history of the world who did not emigrate from selfishness, were those few Puritans who landed on a barren rock in mid-winter, who came for God and for conscience.

Then we are to rejoice in this great fact that we have a transforming power inherent in our national mind, so that in the second,

certainly in the third generation, the foreigners who come here are no longer foreigners, no longer Italian, nor French, nor German, nor Irish, nor Scotch, but have become Americans. . . .

And then we are to remember the relative position in which we are placed by the mercy of Almighty God, and tho it is not pleasant at any time to draw distinctions, there seems to be something of duty therein; in view of the object to be accomplished it may be proper for us to place in juxtaposition our nation with the other nations of the earth, and see how exalted, how desirable our position, as a people, when contrasted with theirs. For instance, let us go into South America, a country of indefinite capability; a country with friendly skies and an inexhaustible soil, that should be rich and prosperous and virtuous. Go there and behold South America like a mosaic pavement as to governments, or like a potter's vessel broken into a thousand fragments; petty states pitted against each other; family broils, wars and famines, and pestilence reigning there. And if we turn from South America to Mexico, that has in part thrown off the incubus of Rome under which she lived and suffered so long; Mexico that seeks to strike for herself and for God; Mexico, that with her capabilities should be a grand republic, and yet how disordered; how broken into parts: and how difficult to harmonize, unify, and bring into unison the distracting elements of that country.

If we turn from our own continent and cross the briny deep, if we go to mother England, mother of us all, what a sad condition England is in to-day with her great constitution, with her Christian creed, with her flag on every sea, under every sky; with her great parliament, with her distinguished ministry, with her rapt poets, her eloquent orators, her splendid scholars; England, the mistress of the seas; England, whose civilization is everywhere—England, that to-day should be the freest and the happiest nation on the globe! But look at England! Oppressed in her finances, her laboring classes crying for bread, her farmers stretching out their hands in prayer for aid, her artisans packing up their tools and gathering together their families and turning their faces to Columbia's land; and then in her politics so divided, in her finances so embarrassed; with a war in Afghanistan, with a war in Africa, and see her preparations for a war with all Europe!

Then cross the channel and enter France; go to the land of Lafayette. True, there is a republic, true the Jesuits have been dethroned, true, France has developed a financial capacity of which we had not dreamed; but France is not firm, is not certain. . . .

And then if we pass into Russia, with her exchequer exhausted, with a fearful war upon her hands, her armies everywhere, but not competent to conquer; with two parties in the kingdom—the German party and the Russian party; with the Czar, the father, at the head of the German party, and the son at the head of the Russian party. Russia to-day is divided against herself, and is preparing, as she never prepared before, for the bloodiest conflict anticipated in the annals of time. And besides this, Russia with her students—young men who refuse to bow to despotism—banished to Siberia, whose perpetual snows are stained with the blood from their exposed bodies; and even womanhood—helpless, innocent, beautiful—treads those icy paths.

And from Russia let us turn to Germany—grand old Germany—with a Christian prince on the throne, and by his side a Christian empress, with Moltke, who draws the sword only for victory—Moltke, who bows morning and evening around his family altar; and with Bismarck, the great statesman. Germany—grand in her history; grand in her Protestantism; grand in her resources. But, alas! in an evil hour Bismarck has joined hands with the Ultramontanists. Alas! Prussia is jealous—jealous, they say, of Russia; jealous, they say, of France. Germany to-day is on a war-footing, and the people are taxed to death to support a standing army. The same is true of Austria—Austria, where the House of Hapsburg has reigned so long. Francis Joseph now sleeps with a drawn sword under his pillow, and the armies of Hapsburg are ready to march at the sound of the bugle.

If we pass into the vine-clad plains of Piedmont and down into Italy, and stand before the Quirinal Palace, in the Eternal City, there we find the youthful king, son of Victor Emanuel; *he* has drawn the sword, and all Italy, from Monte Rosa to where Vesuvius sends her incense up to God—all Italy is armed for the coming strife.

Then, if we turn to Spain, whose youthful prince is soon to lead to the bridal altar a beautiful Austrian princess, there in Spain to-day is rebellion; the provinces are rising and in league with the Catholic power against the Republican orators. The land of Castile to-day is in the throes of war. Look, then, to the great Asiatic regions; compare Asia with America. The Porte to-day is bankrupt; he is surrounded with ministers forming his cabinet, who are as so many leeches on the body of the empire, sucking the very life-blood of its wealth; and with an army defeated everywhere, but, like the locusts of Egypt, eating out the very life of the empire; and with an empire which, with its friendly skies and rich soil, should be the richest in Asia, is famine-stricken to-day.

There is war in Afghanistan: England trembles on her throne in India. Famine in China; war in Japan. It is not, therefore, with any pleasure—indeed it is with sadness—that I paint a picture of the national condition of the world so sad as this.

But from this side of the picture let us look to our own land; here, where the rose of health is upon the national cheek; here, where with peace the bounty of God has blessed us as never in the past; here, where the Government stands secure; where the laws are executed; where peace reigns, with a standing army of twenty or twenty-five thousand to defend fifty millions of people—and these twenty or twenty-five thousand men scattered on the frontiers. In this country peace reigns; public sentiment controls; public conscience is enthroned; and here there is an invisible, omnipresent Power controlling the intellect, controlling the passions, controlling the will, of the American. And never before in the history of the world, never before in the history of this nation, has the Almighty so smiled upon the husbandmen; never was the shout of the harvesters more gleeful; never was the harvest moon so large and so rich as in this year. The corn crop of last year (1878) was 1,290 millions of bushels; this year it is 1,000 millions of bushels, or more than three hundred millions increase. This is reliable, for I received these statistics directly from the Agricultural Bureau in Washington. And it is said that the corn raised this year is worth five hundred and ninety-five millions of dollars, and worth to the farmer five hundred millions of dollars. The wheat crop of last year was 420 millions of bushels; this year, 449 millions of bushels—the increase about thirty millions; worth to the farmer four hundred and fifty millions of dollars. The oat crop this year is 365 millions of bushels, worth one hundred and thirteen millions, netting the farmer ninety millions of dollars. The rye crop is twenty-four millions of bushels, netting the farmer eleven millions of dollars. The barley crop is forty millions of bushels, worth about twenty-eight millions of dollars. And the same proportion holds as to buckwheat, potatoes, hay, etc. The cotton crop this year amounts to five millions of bales, worth two hundred and forty-four millions of dollars, and worth to the planters of the South, after all expenses are paid, one hundred and ninety millions of dollars. The grand total of our products this year is valued at two thousand one hundred and fifty-two millions of dollars, netting the farmers and the planters, after expenses are paid, about one thousand seven hundred and fifty millions of dollars. And it is said, taking into account these crops that I have mentioned, together with other crops not mentioned, that our farmers will realize this year from three to three thousand five hundred millions of dollars for their crops.

These figures are almost incomprehensible, but they are grand and reliable. Now I say that a people thus blessed should shout the harvest-home; they should recognize Him who is the God of the harvest; recognize Him who holds in His fists the winds; who calls forth the clouds and waters the earth, and then disperses the clouds and calls forth the genial and invigorating sun to shine upon the latent energies of the earth, so that these harvests shall shine in glory before the face of God and the face of man.

Citizens—American citizens,—I take it that you are not farmers—that you are merchants; you are mechanics; you are bankers;—but, merchants, mechanics, bankers, what were you without the farmer? It is the farmer that stands back of all prosperity and of all happiness. If the farmer fails, you fail; and therefore you should join hands with the farmer and shout the harvest-home, and return thanks to God, saying, " He hath not dealt so with any other people! "

And it is also stated in these statistics from our distinguished statistician in Washington, that we shall be enabled to export this year two hundred and twenty-five million bushels of grain; and also that we cannot meet the demand. Now I take it that Providence has not merely a financial object in this. He has another object: He can put two hundred millions of the human race on this continent, and proposes to call them here, where corn is abundant, and where the wheat invites them. We, for a time, must send our grain abroad, and gold will return; but I prophesy that this vast agricultural yield this year is an invitation to Europe to come to our shores.

And there is another fact worthy of our consideration, of a moral and intellectual nature: This is a Christian nation. Some infidels deny this. But look at the facts in proof that this is a Christian nation. Our population now is about fifty millions. We have seventy thousand churches under our flag, worth four hundred millions of dollars. We expend annually eighty millions for churches, and we have the money to do it. We have provided over thirty millions of sittings in our churches—room enough for all; and if you take out the children, and also take out the sick and the aged, here is church room enough for the vast population of this country, and all the adults can go and within God's house hear the Word of the Lord.

There are more than seventy thousand ministers. Now, compare this number with the number of lawyers, forty thousand; with the number of physicians, sixty-two thousand. And then, to indicate our intellectual advancement, there are in this country one hundred and eighty-three thousand schoolteachers: we have one hundred and thirty thousand public schools, and support the same at a cost of one hundred millions a year. There you gain an idea of the average intelligence of our citizenship. Remember this, that we have six thousand newspapers, and those newspapers have a circulation of twenty-two millions; and for these newspapers our people spend in the neighborhood of sixty-four millions of dollars a year. What a comment upon the average intelligence of the American people! And no such average can be found elsewhere; no such array of facts and figures as to churches, ministers, lawyers, physicians, schoolteachers, newspapers; and especially no such array of facts as to public schools, the glory of this Republic; and God preserve unto us, and to the generations to come, our public schools, which stand hard by the Churches of the living God!

Now, it becomes us, in view of all these remarkable facts, to look for a moment how we may express our thanks to Almighty God. I hold that it is by the full realization and appreciation of these blessings, and by the determination to transmit the same to posterity. Let me ask, what are the theories among public men as to the secret of this marvelous success? The statesman in his vanity ascribes it to statesmanship; but the statesman should remember that there is nothing in statecraft independent of itself; there is nothing in statecraft competent to produce such results, and competent to preserve a nation as we have been preserved. Our splendid government, the result of the ripened wisdom of a hundred years, would go to pieces like a rope of sand were it not for other vitalizing influences. It is not, therefore, in statesmanship. Why, there is not a statesman to-day in this country worthy to be compared with the forefathers. We are weak in this; our public men are second-rate men. And I am sorry to say that even men who claim to be senators, who claim to be statesmen, condescend to mingle in party politics, and are themselves the biggest politicians in the country. Washington, Webster, and Clay would have looked with loathing upon such a character, and with contempt upon senators who seek to control a ward election. No, gentlemen, it is not in the statesmanship of this country. It is in something else.

The scholar ascribes it to our culture, our public schools, the average intelligence. But then I must remind you that Lord Bacon said that " in knowledge without love there is something of malignity; " I must remind you of the saying of Coleridge, that in the mere products of the understanding there is death; and had I the time, I might recite to you facts of cultured minds, cultured communities, that have gone to ruin because of moral corruption. The strength of this Republic is, therefore, not in our common schools, as it is not in our statesmanship; but it is in a Divine Christianity. And only as Christianity is received as a fact, practical, necessary, sublime; only as Christianity is incorporated in your conscience and will, and sanctifies your hearts, and your fortunes, and your desires, does it become a saving power. This is the saving power of the nation. We are in danger to-day from the insubordination of civil legislation. Here is the rock on which we may split. Now and then a grave minister, now and then a bishop, will prophesy that this Republic will go as Venice went, as Greece went; now and then a statesman is gloomy, and says we are hastening to the rocks. Yes, we will hasten to the rocks, and the proud ship of state will founder there, if our civil legislation is insubordinate to the legislation of high Heaven. Just as the legislation of the several States of this Union must always harmonize with our national legislation, so must our national legislation always harmonize with the legislation of Heaven; and wherever there is an infringement of the Divine law, God's wrath is aroused, and one of the saddest spectacles to-day in this Republic is that a million and a half of American citizens are deprived of the right of American citizenship; that a million and a half of citizens who have all the rights and immunities of citizenship, yet are under duress, and dare not exercise a freemen's right, dare not say at the polls who shall be their legislator, their governor, or their president.

The Almighty sympathizes, always, with the oppressed; and while we to-day are happy in our abundant and glorious harvest, north and south, yet His eye is upon that million and a half of citizens deprived of their rights, and I warn you, I do not care what your politics are—I never bring these things into the pulpit; I am now speaking as God's messenger, as His minister; I am voicing His thoughts to you—and I warn you, citizens, if there is not a correction of this evil that cries to heaven, that the God of justice will arise in His wrath, and that wrath will break forth. Then let us have a republican government everywhere, in Massachusetts and South Carolina, in New York and in Louisiana. Let the citizen be free, whether he is yellow, white, or black. *Let him be free.* **God** demands it, and he *shall* be free!

Now, there is another danger, and that comes from the abuse of the blessings which we enjoy so lavishly. Our danger is now at this point—excessive luxury. And how strange it is that after the terrible ordeal through which we have passed of financial depression and suffering, yet we are as light-hearted as ever; and with this abundant harvest, with this increase of foreign trade, with this income of gold, there is to be a rebound, and with this rebound we will be vain, proud, and pompous—we will resort to our old habits of luxury. Then God will come again and smite us as He has smitten, and the splendid fortunes will totter to their fall; millionaires will become beggars again, and a cry will go up—the cry of bankruptcy and of poverty. This, I say, is our danger. Fellow-citizens! Remember that this abun-

dant harvest is given for gratitude, and to bless those who are in need.

And our danger comes also from an abuse of our religious duty. That religious liberty is in danger above all from the infidel, who declares there is no God, that the Bible is no longer the guide of our conscience—the infidel that would destroy our altars, that would hush the chiming of the church-bells, that would abolish our Sabbaths and exile our pastors, that would, in a word, abolish religion from the face of the nation. These men are not to be tolerated, and not to be supported. . . .

But I must release you. It seems to me that these thoughts are sufficient to awaken your gratitude. Let me, however, in conclusion, cast the horoscope and prophesy of the coming future of my beloved country. Poets have sung of the "parliament of nations, the federation of the world," and that great soldier who drew his sword only to conquer, who has visited all lands, and who to-day is a citizen of the world—that great soldier is the John the Baptist of this "parliament of nations, this federation of the world," in proclaiming everywhere a citizenship intelligent, cultured, Christian, and we are to follow in his glorious wake in our mission to the nations of the world. I do not look for a universal republic, but I dream of this parliament of nations, when wars shall cease, when the drum shall be silent, when the cannon shall be heard no more, when the sword shall be sheathed. I dream of this federation of the world, when the nations shall gather somewhere—on the banks of the Potomac, or on the banks of the Thames, or on the banks of the Tiber. And in this parliament of nations all men shall be brothers; war shall be abolished, and Jesus Christ proclaimed the Savior of mankind, the Prince of peace, and the Lord of lords. Then will go forth these beautiful words of the Psalmist, "He hath not dealt so with any other nation."—H. R.

OWE NO MAN ANYTHING*

By Henry C. Potter, D.D.

Owe no man anything, but to love one another.—Romans xiii: 8

We cannot return to such a feast as that which assembles us in this place this morning without thoughts that revert to its origin and to the circumstances which gave to it its character. I speak to those whose lineage traces its way back to various sources—English, Scotch, Dutch, French and German. But there is no one of us, however remote our ancestries from one another, who does not feel that we have nothing more distinctively American than this day, and that, however peculiarly New England-like many of its original characteristics may have been, it is the relic of an age and a spirit which be-

longed in greater or less degree to all our forefathers alike.

That spirit disclosed itself in certain conspicuous characteristics which stand out in strong relief. As we read the history of our ancestors, whether they were the founders of New England or the founders of the New Netherland, we find it distinguished everywhere by energy, probity, frugality, and domestic concord. Underneath the charming pictures which Irving has drawn in his KNICKERBOCKER'S HISTORY OF NEW YORK, you may trace the influence of that earlier, simpler age of which he there tells the story.

*This sermon is an outline only.

The old burgher and his vrow; the primitive and orderly habits of the house and the people; the universal contempt for trickery and equivocation; the sturdy virtue that scorned a dishonest advantage and hated debt as the worst of slaveries; the family unity that bound the household, master and servant, husband and wife, parent and child in a common industry, unity, and economy—these are the lineaments of that earlier life which laid the foundations of this New York of ours, and opened the avenues of its future prosperity. If we should be bidden to-day to keep a thanksgiving now as our fathers kept it then, we should doubtless smile with a fine sense of superiority at the contrast which our own houses and habits would usually present. "The fire-place of patriarchal dimensions," so Irving has sketched the scene, "gave welcome to the whole family, old and young, master and servant, black and white —nay, even the very cat and dog enjoyed a community of privilege and had each a right to a corner."

The old Dutch china was passed on from generation to generation, and the viands upon the table and the garments upon the persons of the guests gave scant token of elaborate forethought or unusual cost.

How tasteless and even wearisome we might easily account it! And yet these things were the expressions of the social and domestic life of a people who lived resolutely within their means, who neither ate nor drank nor wore what they had not paid for, whose life was no miserable struggle to escape from tradesmen and creditors, who were bitten by no tarantula madness to rival the extravagances and imitate the fashions of foreign life, who feared God and obeyed the law, and bred in their children the same virtues.

And as of these, so of those others, our New England ancestry, from whom many among us here gathered this morning are doubtless sprung. They lie to-day sleeping among their own austere Northern hills, beneath the shadow of the white clapboard meeting-house, and too often, I fear, we shall look in vain for their successors. Among them were men whom Horace Bushnell aptly calls "the sturdy kings of Homespun, who climbed among the hills with their axes to cut away room for their cabins, and for family prayers, and so for the good future to come."

How simple, nay, even how severe, as it seems to us, were their modes of thought and habits of life and customs of recreation! There must be some here who have memories of those plain New England homes and of the men and manners that adorned them. There was simplicity, there was drudgery, if you choose, but there was health and virtue and integrity. Facing all weather, cold and hot, wet and dry, wrestling with the plow on the stony-sided hills, digging out the stones with hard lifting and persistent prizing, dressing the flax, threshing the rye, dragging home in the deep snow the great wood-pile for the winter's consumption, they knew no tedium and no discontent. And even so the mothers spent their nervous impulse through their

muscles, and had so much less need of keeping down the excess or calming the unspent lightning by doses of anodyne. In the play of the spinning-wheel they spun fiber within, and wove daily something strong and wholesome in the patterns of womanly love and service. But, best of all, around all this simpler life there was a closely-girded habit of economy.

And yet they had their ways and hours of recreation, and, dry and angular as their life now seems to us, brightened it often with mirth and good cheer. Who that has ever seen an oldfashioned New England fireside, or heard its story from someone who long ago had a place beside it, will ever forget it? The home circle gathered about the high fire-place; the sleighload of guests from the neighboring village; the quaint old songs; the elders discussing the minister's sermons, and scenting a heresy with a keenness which had at least the virtue that it cared for the difference between truth and error; the simple fare and simpler furniture; the old Bible brought reverently to be read before the friends withdrew; the hymn sung to Coronation, or Duke Street, or old Warwick; the homely prayer, with its unpolished phrase and rugged fervor—it was thus that our fathers, some of them, kept their thanksgiving days, and rounded the quiet lives of which those days were so cherished and conspicuous a feature. Here, again there is a fine field, if we choose to enter it, for our own more modern scorn or criticism. How narrow and intolerant, and even full of cant, sometimes were those earlier and hardier worthies! What stern and even cruel ideas they had about God and little children, and the unpardonable quality of sin! Well, there were some sins that they did find it hard to forgive—sins against home and kindred; sins against common honesty; sins of extravagance and self-indulgence, of ungoverned ambition and personal unfaithfulness—upon those they had certainly but scant and stinted mercy. But they paid their debts and kept their word. They ruled their own houses and had their children in subjection. A household then was a united and homogeneous community, in which the love and trust that reigned within were prophecies of the peace and contentment that were shed abroad. It was rugged, that elder American life of ours, but at least it was, on the whole, healthy and upright and kindly.

But at any rate, whatever may have been its characteristics, we are far enough away from them now. No nation in the world has ever known, I venture to affirm, so radical a revolution in its social and domestic habits as has this people in so short a space of time. The love of display, the craving for luxuries, the eagerness to have and wear and eat and drink what one's neighbors have and wear and eat and drink, the widespread disposition to make life more ornate and less rugged, more smooth and less self-denying— these are tendencies and desires concerning which there can be no dispute nor any serious question. Explain it as you choose—say that the austerities of the fathers have provoked the luxury of the children; appeal to the age as placing greater luxury within easy range of a greater number—*the fact remains* that, on the whole, our habits are not simple, our training is not frugal. our social customs are not plain or inexpensive.

Such a fact might surely be regarded with something of solicitude if it indicated no more than the advent of an age of self-indulgence. For, whatever may be said in favor of profuseness and luxury, it will not be denied that luxury is enervating. We do not need to go back to Rome to see that national luxury paved the way for national dishonor. France discovered it in the reigns of the Louis's. England experienced it in the time of Charles. Costliness of living and unlimited personal indulgence mean enfeebled manhood and decaying intelligence.

But in our case it means something more and *worse*. It means the growth of a relaxed sense of individual honor and of common honesty. It means a disposition that will have luxuries by paying for them *if it can*, but which will have them *anyhow*. And so with us, such an age has come to mean an age in which the mere externals of living have become so precious to some persons that, rather than forfeit or forego them they will betray a trust and defraud a creditor. To think lightly of debt and the personal and business discredit which come or ought to come with it; to be loose in matters of trust, and reckless or unscrupulous in dealing with the interest of others; to maintain a scale of living which is consciously beyond one's means, and yet to go any length and run any risk rather than abridge or relinquish it—these things are so frequent, if not so familiar, as almost to have lost the power to shock us.

And yet is there any degradation more abject, any slavery more absolute, than they are sure mentally to involve? Every now and then the community stands aghast at some tragedy of horror, in which a poor wretch, daring rather to face his Maker than his creditors, jumps into the dock or blows his brains out. A dozen of his fellows, hastily gathered and as hastily dismissed, register their verdict of "suicide occasioned by financial difficulties," and the great wave of human life rolls on and over, and the story is soon forgotten. Whereas, if we firmly realized what such things *meant*, we would empanel as the jury every youth who is just setting out in life, every husband who has just led home a young wife, every woman who is a mother or a daughter in so many thoughtless households, and cry to them: "See! Here is the fruit of extravagant living and chronic debt! Here is the outcome of craving for what you cannot pay for and of spending what you have not earned! Would you be free and self-respecting and undismayed, no matter how scanty your raiment or bare your larder, hear the apostle's words to that Rome that had such dire need

to heed them, '*Owe no man anything, but to love one another.*'"

Yes, honest dealing and mutual love. Believe me, brethren, the two things are closer together than we are wont to imagine. Said a foremost physician in one of our foremost cities not long ago, when asked how far the facility with which American constitutions break down was occasioned by *overwork:*

"It is not overwork that is killing the American people, neither the people who work with their brains nor those who work with their hands. I see a great many broken-down men and broken-down women. I am called to treat scores of people with shattered brains and shattered nerves, but they are not the fruits of overwork. The most fruitful sources of physical derangement and mental and nervous disorders in America are *pecuniary embarrassments and family dissensions.*"

For, as I have just intimated, far oftener than we imagine the two things lie close together. The father crowded beyond endurance by the strain to maintain a scale of living long ago pitched too high; the mother consciously degraded by the petty evasions and domestic dishonesty that draws money for wages and marketing and spends it for dress; the sons and daughters taught prodigality by example and upbraided for it in speech—what can come to such a home or family circle but mutual recrimination and personal alienation, and chilled and embittered feelings? How can love reign in a household where mutual confidence and mutual sacrifice, where the traits that inspire respect and kindle affection, are equally and utterly wanting? It seems as if it were a matter extremely remote from any domestic or social interchange of the affections whether two people, or indeed a whole community, made it a rule to pay their debts; but, in fact, *not* to pay one's debts is as sure and as short a road as can be found to the extinction of confidence, the destruction of respect, and the *death of love*.

Where now shall we look for a correction? I answer, in a higher ideal of the true wealth or weal of the nation, and so of the individuals who severally comprise it. It was Epictetus who said, long ago, "You will confer the greatest benefit upon your city, not by raising the roof, but by exalting the souls of your fellow-citizens; for it is better that great souls should live in small habitations than that abject slaves should burrow in great houses." The words send our thoughts back again to those memories of our forefathers with which I began this discourse. Recall for a moment their simple beginnings. "They brought hither in their little ships," as some one has described them,* "not money, nor merchandise, nor array of armed force, but they came freighted with religion, learning, law, and the spirit of men. They stepped forth upon the shore, and a wide and frowning wilderness received them. Strong in God and in their own heroic patience, they

* Bushnell.

began their combat with danger and hardship. Disease smote them, but they fainted not; famine stalked among them, but they feasted on roots with a patient spirit. They built a house for God and then their houses for themselves. They established education and the observance of a stern but august morality, and then legislated for the smaller purposes of wealth and convenience. They gave their sons to God, through Him to virtue, and through virtue to the State. So they laid the foundation. . . . What addition, we are now tempted to ask, could any amount of wealth or luxury have made to the real force of these beginnings? Having a treasure in her sons, what is there beside, whether strength, growth, riches, or anything desirable, which a State can possibly fail of? Wealth is but the shadow of men; and lordship and victory, it has been nobly said, are but the *pages* of justice and virtue."

——" What! are numbers knit,
By force or custom? man who man would
　　be—
Must rule the empire of himself, in it
Must be supreme, establishing his throne
　Of vanquished will, quelling the anarchy
Of hopes and fears, being himself alone!"

And this is what, in their frugal lives, their sturdy simplicity, their honest dealings, our fathers taught us. Oh, then, as we remember on such a day as this how much we have to thank *them* for as well as to thank God for, let us resolve that we will not be unworthy of a lineage so noble, a race so true. In those questions of the hour which are so much the echo of the questions of our personal conscience, let us lift up our voices for the payment of every honest debt in honest coin. Let us resolve that, so far as in us lies, the nation shall have a clean and righteous record in its dealings with those who, whether here or there, are its creditors, and that this may come to pass, let us begin by dealing justly with those creditors who are ours. Let us pay every debt but the debt which we can never wholly pay, whether to God or our neighbor, which is the debt of love. But let us gladly own that debt, and be busy every day of our lives in making at least *some small payment on account.* As we gather about the family board to-day let us remember the houseless and homeless and unbefriended, and be sure that we have done something to make sunshine in their hearts, no matter what November gloom may reign without. And as we grasp the hand and look into the eyes of friend and kinsman, be this the greeting we give: " Brother, whatever else our homes provide to-day of plenty and good cheer, let us provide things *honest in the sight of all men*," and then, in the name of that Master whom we serve and who has loved us with such a great exceeding love, " let all bitterness and wrath and anger and clamor and evil-speaking be put away from us with all malice; and let us be kind to one another, tender-hearted, forgiving one another," whatever the old wound that aches and burns to-day, " even as God for Christ's sake hath forgiven us."—H. R.

A FIVEFOLD THANKSGIVING

America has just turned a new and wonderful page in her history. Reasons for thanksgiving (1899) :—

I. SPIRITUAL IDEALS HAVE BEEN BROUGHT TO THE FRONT.—The American people have been accused of being a nation of mercenaries, money-gatherers, but we have discovered that there are other things far more dear to us than stocks and bonds. We are a nation of prayer, of self-sacrifice and of Christian ideals. Expand. Another fact underscored is:—

II. THE GROWTH OF THE DEMOCRATIC SPIRIT.—We represent this spirit before the world at its best. Spain represents the opposite spirit at its worst. The third grand result which has been promoted by the war is :—

III. THE CLOSING UP OF THE OLD ANGLO-SAXON FEUD.—England our friend. Quote expressions of this sentiment. See verses of the poet Laureate in June *Cut Gems* (p. 484).

IV. THE WELDING TOGETHER OF OUR OWN NATION IN A STRONGER UNION THAN WAS EVER KNOWN BEFORE.—Compare the Massachusetts Sixth going through Baltimore in April, 1861, and the same named regiment passing through in May, 1898. Procession of citizens headed by mayor, children pelted the soldiers with flowers. Grand reception, feasted, given an American and Cuban flag and this note :

" Maryland's greeting to Massachusetts. Baltimore and Boston clasp hands. God speed the historic Massachusetts Sixth. A united country honors the men who are rallying to her defense. May the memory of 1861 be effaced by the welcome of 1898. Do we love you? Dewey? " Let the bloody shirt be laid away among the archeological curiosities Mason and Dixon's line has been wiped out.

" No North, no South, no East, no West,
　But one great land with freedom blest."

Last, but not least, we have reason to look with grateful eyes on :
V. THE GROWING UNITY OF THE WORLD.—Grand openings for Christian civilization in conquered territories, in Spain, in Africa, in China. Czar's call for disarmament of the nations.—S. R.

THE HOME GATHERING

By William Adams, D.D.

For there is a yearly sacrifice there for all the family.—1 Sam. xx: 6

This was a time-honored custom in the family of Jesse, apparently maintained by his children even after Jesse was dead.

The coming of winter emphasizes the joys of home. It is well that we have our annual home-gathering when we are called to give thanks for our blessings.

There is a great variety in our household affections:

1. The love of a father for a child; gratitude and awe at his own relation to an immortal spirit; pity for helpless infancy; pride in the possibilities of the child.

2. The love of a mother; who offered her own life for the new life; glorying in unlimited expression of love; pitying and loving to the last what the world counts worthless; when death strikes her child, refusing to be comforted.

3. The love of children for their parents; of slow growth, hidden at first by weeds of wilfulness; not perfected till the child becomes a parent; but even in childhood a beautiful compend of gratitude, reverence, and trust.

4. The love between brothers and sisters: independent, but looking back to the same source; sharing pillow and table, and intertwining sympathies and affections; manliness in the brother; gentle beauty in the sister, as in complete companionship she insensibly assimilates to herself the man that is to be.

5. The love of husband and wife; two independent lives so harmonizing as to become the symbol of Christ's love for His Church; the relic of Paradise, which softens life's asperities, and helps its purposes by joy.

6. The relation between grandparents and their descendants; reaching down with peculiar tenderness; most useful in offering to the young an object of respect, reverence, and love.

For these affections let us give thanks. These are the possessions of poor and rich, dearer in adversity.

Christianity refines and enlivens the domestic affections, giving us a true home, where children may grow strong before they go out into hard life; the memory of which is a comfort and inspiration; where mature manhood learns its best lessons of simplicity, humility, trust in Providence.

As the ancients threw the gall of the nuptial sacrifices far behind the altar, we should banish all bitterness from home.

Mixed with sweet thoughts may be sad memories, and there may be a vacant chair; but this may be only as at night we go to our different chambers to meet again in the morning.—H. R.

THANKSGIVING

Praise ye the Lord.—Psalm cl: 1

The first word is *Halleluiah,* here rendered, "Praise ye the Lord," Not all are equally happy or comfortable; but all have occasion for gratitude. Pain, poverty, bereavement, homelessness, friendlessness—these are "ills that human flesh is heir to;" nevertheless the catalog of our mercies is longer. The old song strikes a true note:

"Don't be sorrowful, darling; don't be sorrowful, pray;
For taking the year together, my dear,
There isn't more night than day."

First, as to Personal Mercies. God's providence has been round about us. He has held us in His arms at night as mothers hold their children. He has guided us by day amid dangers like flying arrows. Our lives are spared; we have, at the worst, enough of this world's good to keep soul and body together. For such commonplace mercies let us thank God.

And then the blessings of His grace. We are familiar with the Gospel. If we have accepted its conditions of life, let us call upon our souls and all that is within us to praise God. If we are not Christians, let us nevertheless be thankful that we are on Mercy's ground. God's hands are stretched out still. The river of life is flowing past our feet; we may dip and drink if we will. How many have died impenitent; how many are just now dying in despair! But heaven's gates are open before us. "Oh, that men would praise the Lord for his goodness and for his wonderful works to the children of men!"

Second, as to National Blessings. God hath not dealt so with any people. Our brief history is the marvel of all time. Let us thank God for our heritage and pray against pride. A distinguished foreigner, on returning from a visit to this country, said: "The only fault I have to find with the Americans is that they are so beastly prosperous." In spite of all representations to the contrary, our people are better fed, clothed, and sheltered than any other. We are the richest of nations. Our wealth is most equally distributed. The rich are growing richer, and the poor are growing richer, too.

Just now, while we are remembering the divine goodness, let us not forget to thank God for the recent war with Spain. It is a great thing for a nation to be divinely chosen to vindicate justice and humanity. How reluctant we were to enter upon the task! We preached on the horrors of war; we prayed: "O Lord, give us peace in our time!" We hoped that our President and his counselors would make all possible concessions, and that Spain would be reasonable, and that our politicians would not lose their heads. Then down went the *Maine;* and the die was cast. It is easy to see, now, that God all along meant us to champion the oppressed Cubans. A nation that had distinguished itself for oppression during four hundred years needed a sound thrashing; and we were apparently called to administer it. Now thank God for the outcome. Cuba and Porto Rico are free. The Philippines are probably free. It has cost us something to bring this about; but nobody doubts the wisdom of the investment. Our country is wiser, richer, nobler, for assuming the responsibility which God laid upon it.

And blest be God for peace; peace with honor and with increase of righteousness. One thing is perfectly clear in the light of recent events: to wit, *ours is a Christian nation with a Christian calling.* It looks as if God intended us to be the center of a great evangelizing influence. "We have the men, we have the ships, we have the money too." The last census shows that no less than twenty-two millions of our countrymen are connected with some sort of religious organization. What an army of crusaders! If the Churches of America were to realize their latent energies for the propagation of the Gospel at home and abroad, how speedily would the kingdoms of this world become the kingdoms of our Lord and of His Christ! Thus it appears we have abundant reasons to lift our hearts and voices in the rejoicings of Thanksgiving Day. "Oh, praise the Lord, for he is good, for his mercy endureth forever!"—H. R.

GOD'S PROVIDENCE AND THE OPEN DOOR *

Whoso stoppeth his ears at the cry of the poor, he also shall cry himself, but shall not be heard.—Prov. xxi: 13
I know thy works: behold, I have set before thee an open door, and no man can shut it: for thou hast a little strength, and hast kept my word and hast not denied my name.—Rev. iii: 8

Consider first the fact that God has set before His Church the open door of a world, in great measure, physically subjugated.

There is no more significant historic phrase in the New Testament than that phrase, so often recurring, especially in St. Paul's epistles, "the fulness of the times."

Get one aspect of its meaning. At the time of the advent, birth, life, death, glorious resurrection, and ascension of Christ, and for some time thereafter, the then known and habitable world was held in the peace-compelling grasp of the Roman Empire. That empire had changed the Mediterranean Sea into a kind of inland lake, bordered on all its sides by peaceful provinces, centralized into and under the acknowledged authority of the Roman Emperor. From the golden mile-post in the Forum went raying out ways like the Appian, almost as straight as any modern railway, and almost as disdaining of mountains and of valleys. Those roads were the track-ways of a mighty and interchanging domestic commerce. They were also unhindered passageways for the carrying of imperial edicts and for the swift marching of the Roman legions. Also these roads were the avenues of travel. And these highways were an important element in the "fulness of the times." For, also, along these roads apostles and other heralds of the cross could speed, carrying the good news of God. Such an evangelizing career as that of the Apostle Paul had been impossible had not the Roman Empire laid at his feet such ways of swift, easy, various access.

Our world to-day is a much larger and more various one than that of the ancient Roman Empire. Yet our world is a much more thoroughly subjugated one, in all physical directions. Think what the discovery of the magnetic needle has accomplished, prompting to the farthest-reaching voyages. Think what steam has done. Think what electricity has done. Think of the printing-press.

Now—and here is a wonderful fact—all these vast powers of magnetism, steam, electricity, etc., have not been chiefly given into the hands of nations, heathen or Mohammedan, nor prevailingly Romanist, but into the hands of nations Protestant, of a free Bible, of free churches. And, just as in that ancient fulness of the time the ancient Church found the ways made and open for her feet that she might propagate her Lord's Gospel, so now, in this modern fulness of the times, the modern Church stands before the open door of a largely subjugated physical world, with steel, steam, and electricity making easy intercommunication for her.

Consider, second, the governments of the world have set open doors for the feet of

* For further suggestion along the line of this topic and for most admirable elaboration of these hints and of others like them, attention is called to CHRIST'S TRUMPET CALL TO THE MINISTRY, by Daniel S. Gregory, D.D., LL.D., published by Funk & Wagnalls Company.

the Church of Christ. In almost every land beneath the stars the missionary is now safe and protected.

Consider, third, the open door God has set before His Church in the wealth He has given her. It has been accurately computed that the fourteen million members of the Evangelical Churches in the United States have a gross income of $2,000,000,000.

For such vast openings on every side, for such munificent material, surely all Christians should render to God thanksgiving, and set themselves at using for His sake what God has given so abundantly.—H. R.

MERCIES

By E. Mellor

Lam. iii: 22-23

I. There is no greater evil committed by any of us than a practical forgetfulness of the *common* mercies of life: mercies, which because of their commonness, cease to be regarded as mercies. The Psalmist calls upon us to "forget not all God's benefits," and he thus indicates our perpetual danger, a danger which he himself felt, and against which he had to guard his own soul. There are two great causes which may be said to account for our forgetfulness of the mercies of God, which are new every morning. The first is that the hand of the Giver is invisible; and the second is that they come to us with such marvelous regularity.

II. Notice a few of the common mercies which we are most prone to forget: (1) Take, as the first illustration, sleep. There are thousands who never kneel down and thank God for sleep. I do not think that any man who finds sleep an easy thing has ever calculated rightly its inestimable value. It is when pain or overwork chases sleep away, when he lies upon his bed and waits for its coming but it comes not, when he begins to dread the nights lest he should have the same wretched experiences again and again—a fear which prepares the way for its own fulfilment —it is then that he begins to learn what is meant by sleep, and what high rank it takes among the common mercies of life. It is a mercy which no money can buy, which no rank can command. (2) Our reason. When we consider how closely the reason is allied with the brain and with the whole nervous system, it is a surprising circumstance that insanity is not a more widespread evil than it is. The possession of reason should stir us up to daily thanksgiving to Him whose mercies are new to us every morning. (3) The power of motion and action, and speech, is another mercy which is new every morning. We live not upon old mercies, but upon new ones fresh from the Divine hand, fresh from the Divine heart.—S. B., vol. iv., p. 270.

THANKSGIVING AND THANKSLIVING

By E. J. Banks

Eph. v: 15-20

Thanksgiving *without* thanksliving comes under condemnation both from the prophets and the Lord Jesus. Isaiah says (xxiv: 13), "The Lord said . . . this people draw nigh with their mouth, and with their lips do honor me, but have removed their heart far from me." And our Savior's complaint was, "Why call ye me, Lord, Lord, and do not the things which I say?" (Luke vi: 46).

Eph. v: 15-20. Here we have the *thanksliving* shown in the first verses, and the *thanksgiving* described in the last. Verse 15. "Look carefully how ye walk," let your walk be accurate, exact (verses 9, 10), not as unwise, but wise. Thus shall we bring honor to Him whose name we bear—this will be the thanksgiving He will prize. Verse 16. Seizing every opportunity, because the days will soon be past, and the evil of the times calls for urgency. Verse 17. "Be not foolish." It is the height of foolishness not to understand our Lord's will, or to know the Lord's will and do it not (Luke xii: 47; 1 Thess. iv: 3; v: 18). Verse 18. The world seeks its exhilaration from the use of strong drinks; the Christian gets it from being filled with the Spirit, and should honor his God by abstaining from that which the worldling needs. God's Holy Spirit will not dwell in a mind which is unbalanced by excitement produced by excess. Throughout this whole passage there is the contrast between the life of a heathen and that of a Christian. Verse 19. The indwelling Spirit so fills our hearts with unrestrainable joy that we must give vent to our feelings with our voice. True thanksgiving thus expresses itself in sacred song (Col. iii: 15-17). Verse 20. Thanksgiving for the trials as well as the joys, for the pain as well as the pleasure, in time of adversity as well as prosperity. Thanksliving by our grateful acceptance of all that comes, be it weal or wo, knowing it is from the hand of a loving Heavenly Father. The only medium through whom our thanks can be offered is the Lord Jesus (Acts iv: 12).—P. M.

THANKSGIVING THEMES AND OUTLINES

[From the *Homiletic Review*]

Christian Citizenship.—*Jer. xxxi: 38. Behold the days come, saith the Lord, that the city shall be built to the Lord.*

This Puritan festival shows us:

I. Our nation founded in the fear of God; rulers devout, and Church members worshiping with guns over their shoulders.

II. A good citizen above the selfish and stupid indifference which lets politicians rule for him.

III. That civic character, the revival of which is our hope. If we are indeed awakening to a civic revival, it is ground for devout thanksgiving.

Christ the Crown of Our Blessings.—*2 Cor. ix: 15. Thanks be to God for his unspeakable gift.*

The heathens have their autumn festivals: the universal Father has not left Himself without witness even to them, "filling their hearts with food and gladness." But Christ alone crowns the natural revelation of the Father; assures us we are at home in our Father's house; and wakes in us the confident gladness of children accepted.

Gains That the People Have Made.—*Psalm xxx: 14. Offer unto God thanksgiving.*

If in the spirit of reverence for our fathers we climb the heights of thanksgiving for an outlook upon the tendencies of the Republic, we shall discern a scene of great beauty in the plains below:

1. The glorious fruitfulness of our land. See in the markets of the city what God has given us for food. Travel over valleys and plains, and see how the great harvests make pessimism impossible.

2. The high courage, hope, and good cheer of the people. Enterprise and thrift in the North; wonderful paying off of mortgages in the West.

3. The advance of the working people into better conditions. Never were the common people so bountifully fed, so beautifully housed, so comfortably clad.—NEWELL DWIGHT HILLIS, D.D.

God Abides Restfully with a Thankful People.—*Psalm xxii: 34. Thou that inhabitest the praises of Israel."*

As God accepts the prayers of His people, rising to Him like sweet incense, so He is satisfied in our thanksgivings; and makes them His abode.

God, Heaven and Earth Harmonized in the Praise of.—*Habak. iii: 3. His glory covered the heavens, and the earth was full of his praise.*

His heavenly glory is undimmed; discerning eyes may always see it. As we secure His earthly praise, we fulfil the vision of the prophet that the earth too shall praise Him.

God, Nature Praises.—*Psalm lxix: 34. Let the heaven and earth praise him.*

In a season of natural bounty we are drawn "near to nature's heart"; we catch the expression of the glad season, make it the utterance of our hearts, and call upon nature to enter into the higher emotions which strictly belong only to intelligent souls.

Gratitude to One Another.—Am I sufficiently thankful to my fellow men? There must be now living hundreds, yes, thousands, of my fellow beings—mechanics, manufacturers, artists, merchants, and sailors—to whom I am indebted for the things about me that minister to my bodily comfort, to my intellectual growth, and to my spiritual enjoyment.

1. I might be a better man if I took my pad and began with the articles nearest to me—the Turkish rug under my feet, and the easy-chair in which I am sitting, one sent me from Asia, and one given in New York—and then made an inventory not only of the things that are presents, but of those things for which I have paid money, but which no money could have procured if my fellow men had not wrought to produce them.

2. I ought to be profoundly thankful that I live as a member of our great thinking, working, pushing humanity. I ought to be thankful that I did not live in any preceding century, but that I live now, when any man can do more for himself and his fellow man in any one week than he could have accomplished any month eighty years ago. Plainly, then, I ought to be thankful to my fellow men who lived in the preceding centuries, and who so wrought as to make it possible for my generation to do more for society in the last fifty years than others have been able to do in any five preceding centuries.

3. I have had some terrible battles to fight and some bitter cups to drink; but I ought this day to be thankful that ever I was born, even when I regard only the past. When I think how that past has put me on the road toward the future in which there may be thousands of blessed hours in this world, and in which I know there is a place being prepared for me as I pass out of this mansion to the Father's house, I ought to be profoundly thankful.—M R.

Paul's Idea of Enough.—*1 Tim. vi: 18. Having food and raiment let us be therewith content.*

"Raiment,"—"covering" (R. V.). "Be content"—"have enough" (marginal reading).

The apostle, living in his own hired house, and paying his rent from the proceeds of tent-making, was as independent a gentleman as walked the streets of Rome. He differed from most people in that he was wise enough to see that, in order to get on top, it was folly to begin by getting under the mass of worldliness and then try to burrow up. He balanced his mind with a sublime philosophy and sat down above the world, with as little care for the shape secular things assumed as a king has for the mere carvings of his throne.

Fichte, the German philosopher, wrote: "Since I could not alter what was without me, I resolved to try to alter what was within me."

Descartes laid down as one of the practical rules of life: "I must not seek to gratify my desires so much as I seek to restrain them."

Sir Thomas More wrote in his journal: "I make it my business to wish as little as I can, except that I were wiser and better."

Plato taught his disciples: "We should not demand that things be as we wish, but we should wish that things should be as they are."

Horace said of the money-scrambling Romans: "What they have, that they are." The Christian idea is just the reverse; a man really possesses, enjoys the world, in accordance with what *he is* in himself. Faith makes the whole world "Our Father's house;" takes away every solicitude for the future, for we are "heirs of God." A good conscience before God brightens everything with the reflection from our hearts of "the light of his countenance."

Praise Gives God Glory.—*Psalm l: 23.* *Whoso offereth praise glorifieth me.*

Glorify is kindred with *declare:* to glorify God is to declare or manifest Him; and what men most need to know of Him is that goodness which wakens our hearts to praise. When they hear sincere praise from our lips, they have evidence that He has been good to us, and so He is glorified as the harvest glorifies the fertile fields.

Remembrance.—*Psalm xxxviii: Title.* *To bring to remembrance;* and *I Chron. xvi: 4. And he appointed certain of the Levites to minister before the ark of the Lord, and to record (bring to remembrance), and to thank and praise the Lord God of Israel.*

The annual appointment is based upon our danger of losing right feelings we once had. We stay for a little the attention of common cares, and remind one another of what we are losing, and open our hearts to its renewal and strengthening.

"Lord God of Hosts, be with us yet,
Lest we forget—lest we forget!"
KIPLING.

Tears Mingled with Thanksgiving.—*Ezra iii: 13. The people could not discern the noise of the shout of joy from the noise of the weeping of the people.*

1. Thanksgiving is preëminently the family day; and as we rejoice in our family reunions there are few circles where some break has not come. The joy of gathering is mixed with the sorrow of some absent.

2. Thanksgiving is the day of the bountiful harvest. We sit at tables of plenty, we dwell in happy communities, in a land richer than any other; but there are regions famine-struck, there are starving poor, there is pinching want.

3. Thanksgiving "crowns the year," is the culminating-point where we look back at a time on the whole blest with great favor from God; but the year has had its trials which we are glad to be past. We would not live the year over again. Our glad thankfulness in its blessings is mingled with a rueful gladness that some of its experiences are over, and not to be endured again.

4. A truly happy and devoutly thankful spirit does not doubt that the best thing about our thankfulness here is its power to look toward the *un*mingled thanksgivings of heaven:

"To where beyond these shadows there is peace."

Thankful Deeds.—But how shall we give thanks? Words are good and necessary; but deeds are imperative. "As ye did it unto these my brethren, ye did it unto me." Let us first look around us upon our immediate neighbors. Possibly some of them may give us opportunity for thankfulness by deeds. All of them will afford us opportunity for thankfulness by kindness. Very often those who have no lack of food are starving for encouragement and sympathy. And there may be cases in which this will cost us a greater sacrifice than we could make in money. One can put thankfulness to God into his manner by saying "Good-morning" to a neighbor. Indeed, one does not need to go out of his own household to find a way of thanking God by words not addressed to Him, and by deeds that are for Him only as they may be for his sake.—*In.*

Thankful Thoughts.—*I Chron. xvi: 8. Give thanks unto the Lord, call upon his name, make known his deeds among the people:*

1. Thanksgiving in spite of sorrow. The autumn is a time of decay, as well as of harvest. There is a minor key struck in the soul as the summer dies; yet there is rest in the gathered fruits, and we feel that all things work for our good.

2. There is more light than shadow. There is the light of home, country, love, and worship.

3. The harvest came with toil. God watched it and gave the increase; but only to the faithful worker. The idler has a harvest of weeds.

4. What harvest have we gathered? Is it ripened purpose, or vacant irresolution?

5. It is right to rejoice in God's gifts. If we have not deserved them, we may.

Thanks for What, Give.—1. For a bountiful harvest.

2. For a national prosperity.

3. For religious prosperity.

4. For a united people.

5. For growing sympathy between the two great English-speaking nations.

6. For the removal of an oppressive government from the Western hemisphere.

7. For the courage, heroism, and patriotism of the American people.

8. For a splendid national outlook.—C. A.

Thanksgiving Day Harpstrings.—*Ps. civ: 33, 34. I will sing unto the Lord as long as I live; I will sing praises to my God while I have my being. My meditation of him shall be sweet.—Acts xxviii: 15: Whom when Paul saw, he thanked God and took courage.*

THANKSGIVING DAY is the harp of the American home year. In order that we may awaken its proper music let us touch some of the strings of our text.

1. Meditation on the GOODNESS OF GOD: "My meditation of him shall be sweet."

That note will lead to the second.

2. GRATITUDE: "I will sing *praises* to my God."

Gratitude naturally bursts forth in song.

3. SONG: "I will *sing* unto the Lord."

All these strings lead to a result.

4. COURAGE: "He thanked God and took courage."

If we touch all these harpstrings to-day it will be a happy and fruitful Thanksgiving. —LOUIS ALBERT BANKS, D.D.

Thanksgiving Day, How Shall We Spend Our.—*Psalm cxvi: 12. What shall I render unto the Lord for all his benefits toward me?*

How shall we spend our day of Thanksgiving?

1. Spend it joyously. Nehemiah said: "The day is holy to the Lord your God; mourn not, nor weep. . . . Neither be ye sorry, for the joy of the Lord is your strength."

2. Spend it religiously. Read such a psalm of gratitude as the 103d, or of confidence as the 91st, or such comforting words as John xiv. Speak your gratitude to God, and sing to His praise.

3. Spend it helpfully. Specially try to serve every one you touch during the day. Speak gently to those of your family. Make the household glad. Reach out to the poor and the lonely. You may help one ready to fall.

Thanksgiving Day, the Home Festival.—1. If there has been a decline in the strictly religious observance of the holiday, it is no less than in the past a home festival. If the sons are too distant from the ancestral homestead to travel back, they yet make in each several household a center of simple hospitality.

2. We do not forget industrial oppression, growing monopolies, and municipal corruption; but the large majority of our population maintain the home. We are a nation of homes. We do not believe that the divine institution of the family is decaying in our land.

3. Yet vigilant protection of the home is necessary. We must fight easy divorce and sins against the family; exalt the positive value of home and rouse parental responsibility and filial loyalty; guard against trifling discords which grow into disruption of the family; beware of so crowding Sunday with religious work that home rest and association suffers.

4. In serving the home we serve the nation, (*a*) in rearing good citizens, (*b*) in maintaining high social ideals. Patriotism is close kin to family affection.—ST.

Thanksgiving for Christian Men.—*1 Cor. i: 4-7. I thank my God always on your behalf, for the grace of God which is given you by Jesus Christ; that in everything ye are enriched by him, in all utterance, and in all knowledge; even as the testimony of Christ was confirmed in you; so that ye come behind in no gift; waiting for the coming of our Lord Jesus Christ.*

1. It is reason for national thanksgiving that so many of our public men—president, admirals, generals—are God-fearing men.

2. Such men are the strength of every town and Church. They make banks trustworthy, courts incorruptible, and business honorable and truly prosperous.

3. The growth of this highest class is a feature of our time, and calls out our thanksgivings, as it called out Paul's.

4. Their character is a blessed confirmation of the truth of the Gospel.

5. They forbid vain hero-worship, and carry our regard on to those principles of right and blessing which will triumph completely in the coming of the Lord.

Thanksgiving for Common Blessings, The Common Duty of.—There are certain blessings which are enjoyed alike by Protestant and Catholic, Republican, Democrat, Populist, and Prohibitionist: the sovereignty of the people, the supremacy of law, the common sense of patriots, the universal submission to the authority of the majority, the respect for the rights of the minority.

God takes care that neither corruption, nor monopolies, nor the liquor traffic thwart the destiny of the nation. We may trust that He will preserve and maintain the essentials of our national life.

That He has maintained them so far, and so gives assurance for the future, is reason why all, of whatever religious or political faith, should join to give Him thanks.

Thanksgiving for Everything.—*Ephes. v: 20. Giving thanks always for all things.*

1. When the day has been contrary to my wishes and expectations, I will thank God for the love that considered my welfare rather than my desires. I will try to make the day bright with pleasant words, and I will thank God that I can brighten the lives of others.

2. If I am sick, I will make as little trouble as possible, and try to forget my pain in speaking a good word, and thank God that "all things work together for good."

3. I will thank God for the joys of others; for the prosperity of my neighbors.

4. I will thank God for past good things for which He has never been thanked.

5. Along with my thanksgivings I will pray earnestly; (*a*) for a deeper and wider appreciation of His goodness; (*b*) for help to tell the good to all, saying nothing about the evil; (*c*) for faith to see good in everything; (*d*) for help to magnify the good and make the evil as small as possible.—From a sermon by Rev. George W. Dell.

Thanksgiving for Fresh Affections.—*2 Tim. i: 3. I thank God that without ceasing I have remembrance of thee.*

No doubt God keeps our hearts warm by giving us lovable friends, and surrounding us with happy influences. But He also moves within our hearts, and quickens us to appreciate what is good and lovable. Sometimes He opens our hearts with gladness, and sometimes with sorrow, and the chief value of these is in their effect within us.

Our affections apart from God may mislead us, but if we take them to Him in prayer they will always help us. This is a day for the sanctifying in worship of all that is in our hearts.

Loving affections brought gratefully before God make our present life most like heaven, and lift us above the world's temptations as well as sorrows.

This thought is the touch of nature that makes all the world kin, and so this festival breaks down the barriers between rich and poor.

Thanksgiving for God's Wise and Strong Rule.—*Rev. xi: 17. We give thee thanks, O Lord God Almighty, which art and wast and art to come, because thou hast taken to thee thy great power and hast reigned.*

Thanksgiving Granted Us Through the Gospel.—*Rom. i: 8. I thank my God through Jesus Christ.*

We have substantial reason for heart-felt gratitude to God as we know Christ.

This is not only for our personal assurance of pardon and eternal life, but to-day especially for the social value of the gospel, which gives us (1) Christian home, (2) Christian civilization, and (3) a Christian state.

Thanksgiving, Paul's in Trial.—*Acts xxvii: 35. He gave thanks in the presence of them all.*

It was a mere grace at meat, but full of meaning to the shipwrecked crew.

A brave soul is not blinded by present evil, but sees the deeper good and blessing.

Thanksgivings, Christ's.—*(a) Matt. xv: 36. And he took the seven loaves and the fishes, and gave thanks, and brake them, and gave to his disciples, and the disciples to the multitude.*

The thanksgiving at daily meat, like the autumnal thanksgiving, is an expression of habitual gratitude for God's care.

(b) Luke xix: 37. The whole multitude of the disciples began to rejoice and praise God with a loud voice for all the mighty works which they had seen.

This was one thanksgiving day in the life of Jesus on earth, tho it was also dashed with tears as He wept over the city.

Thanksgiving Spirit, The.—*Prov. xvii: 22. A merry heart doeth good like a medicine.*

It is customary to deliver political discourses on Thanksgiving Day; but instead of politics we offer both a prescription and a provision.

1. The value of a cheerful spirit. Not jollity, but joy; not the gladness dependent on outward circumstances, but the sunshiny frame which comes from health of heart.

i. It helps bodily health. A good dose of divine grace, with a few grains of gratitude for His mercies, and a frequent bracing walk of benevolence in helping other people, is better than all the drugs of the apothecary.

2. It is a clarifier and invigorator of the mind. Many giants in the Christian Church have been men of exuberant cheerfulness. Luther, Lyman Beecher, Spurgeon, Phillips Brooks, Newman Hall, and Guthrie are examples.

3. It lubricates the wearing machinery of business and daily care. The cheerful heart is a " continual feast "—Thanksgiving Day every day in the year.

II. How attain this spirit?

1. Look at your mercies with both eyes; your troubles with only one eye.

2. Learn Paul's secret. " In whatsoever state I am, therewith to be content."

3. Be useful. Light somebody's torch, and your own will burn brighter.

4. Make God your trustee. Believe in His care of your welfare.—From a sermon by T. L. Cuyler, D.D., LL.D.

Thanksgiving, We Go on with New Heart from.—*Acts xxviii: 15. He thanked God and took courage.*

A certain sense of fulness and strength we need as a starting-point for every new advance. We thank God that we have finished the sea journey, and now we can undertake the land journey. We thank God that we have seen the brethren, and now we can move forward to help them and perhaps lead them.

SUGGESTIVE THOUGHTS AND ILLUSTRATIONS

BASKETS, The Two.—Our petitions for favors are likely to greatly outnumber our thanks for blessings received. There is an old legend that tells of two angels sent to earth, each with a basket, the one to gather up the prayers of the people, and the other their thanksgiving. When they returned, they grieved to find that the first was filled to overflowing, while the other was nearly empty. Our blessings are usually equal to our needs, and far outnumber our misfortunes.

BLESSEDNESS.—When we give up looking for happiness, we find blessedness.—CARLYLE.

BLESSINGS, Private.— . . . The private blessings—the blessings of immunity, safeguard, liberty and integrity—which we enjoy, deserve the thankfulness of a whole life.—J. COLLIER.

BLESSINGS, Vicarious.—" David said, Mephibosheth . . . Fear not; for I will show thee kindness for Jonathan thy father's sake, and will restore thee all the land of Saul thy father, and thou shalt eat bread at my table continuously."—2 Sam. ix: 6, 7.

BLESSING, The Perspective of.—*Eph. iii: 17-19.* We get the perspective of nature objects and the visible world because of light and the three dimensions of space—length, breadth, and thickness. So the favors and blessings of God become impressive and substantial to faith when the light of His saving love shines in our hearts, " to give the light of the knowledge of the glory of God in the face of Jesus Christ." Then also are we " able to comprehend with all saints what is the breadth and length and depth and height " of the blessings of the kingdom of God, and of Christian civilization.—C. G.

CONTENT AND DISCONTENT.—Contentment furnishes constant joy. Much covetousness, constant grief. To the contented, even poverty is joy. To the discontented, even wealth is a vexation.—MING SUM PAOU KEEN. *In Chinese Repository.* (Trans. by Dr. Milne.)

CONTRAST, A Historic.—Our first Thanksgiving Day in this country was that appointed by Governor Bradford, of Massachusetts, in 1623. Contrast common life then with that we enjoy in 1886.

Henry VIII. was upbraided for wanton extravagance in having a bed-tick stuffed with feathers.

Saw-mills enabled common people to have wooden floors, instead of stone or earth, about 1666.

Anthracite coal utilized for warming and manufacturing purposes in 1770.

Coal-gas light, 1792.

Electric light, 1874.

Stoves, The Franklin, 1745.

Cotton goods—muslins, calicoes—used by English not before the eighteenth century. Common dress of men made of leather.

Glass mirrors in England, 1673.

Watches, 1658.

Coffee, 1641.

Tea, 1666.

Potatoes not commonly used before 1754.

Meats not within the ordinary purse-limit until the eighteenth century. Says Macaulay: " It is the fashion to place the golden age of England in times when noblemen were destitute of comforts, the want of which would be intolerable to a modern footman; when farmers and store-keepers breakfasted upon loaves, the very sight of which would raise a riot in a modern workhouse."

Sewing machines, 1849.

Newspapers introduced by Roger L'Estrange in 1663.

Medicine—" Starve 'em and bleed 'em " practice until recently.

Anesthetics, 1844.

Death-rate in seventeenth century, one in every 17 persons annually; in nineteenth century, one in 40. Macaulay says of the former period: " Men died faster in the purest country air than they now do in the most pestilential lanes of our towns, and men died faster in the lanes of our towns than they now do on the coast of Guinea."

Production to the acre in seventeenth century averaged less than seven bushels. The advance of agricultural knowledge has advanced the average to thirty bushels.

The majority of occupations now followed were unknown two centuries ago; estimate the limitation of enterprise.

Recent inventions have given to each person a help in the way of comfortable living equal to a half a dozen servants who should labor gratuitously.

Traveling—Coaching in seventeenth century *versus* steam-rail and steam-boat.

Old writers speak of the incessant danger from traveling. Statistics show that a man may now ride 100,000 miles every year for forty years without chance of injury.

Men formerly limited for life to their neighborhood; the world now open for inspection.

Pianos, 1717.

Studies in science, art, etc.

Respect for Clergy. Lord Clarendon complained that in his day there was such confusion of rank that damsels of much culture had married clergymen. Queen Elizabeth gave special command that servant-girls should not marry ministers without the consent of the master or mistress. A " young

Levite's " salary was called fair at ten pounds a year.

To carry out this contrast, read Macaulay's History, Chapter III., and Ludlow's Chart, page, " Useful Arts."—H. R.

GRATEFUL MAN, The.—Qui gratus futurus est statim dum accipit de reddendo cogitet.

Let the man, who would be grateful, think of repaying a kindness, even while receiving it.—SENECA.

GRATITUDE.—Gratitude is the fairest blossom which springs from the soul; and the heart of man knoweth none more fragrant.—HOSEA BALLOU—*MS. Sermons.*

Gratitude is expensive.—GIBBON—*Decline and Fall of the Roman Empire.*

HEART, The Thankful.—Gratus animus est una virtus non solum maxima, sed etiam mater virtutum omnium reliquarum.

A thankful heart is not only the greatest virtue, but the parent of all the other virtues.—CICERO.

RELIGION, A Phase of.—It's part of my religion to look well after the cheerfulness of life, and let the dismals shift for themselves, believing with good Sir Thomas More that it is wise to be " merrie in God."—LOUISA MAY ALCOTT.

THANKFULNESS.—Our whole life should speak forth our thankfulness; every condition and place we are in should be a witness of our thankfulness. This will make the times and places we live in better for us. When we ourselves are monuments of God's mercy, it is fit we should be patterns of His praises, and leave monuments to others. We should think it given to us to do something better than to live in. We live not to live: our life is not the end of itself, but the praise of the giver.—R. LIBBES.

THANKFULNESS, Christian.—Rev. T. Collins writes of an invalid thankful for intervals of ease, but doubtful of God's mighty mercy in Jesus. He said to him, " Thomas, suppose I plunged into the Severn to save you from drowning, got you out, led you home, and parting on your door step gave you a lozenge. What would rise to your mind ever after when you thought of me, the lozenge? " " The lozenge? O no sir! the rescue! " " Well, let it be so concerning Jesus. You tell me of just one of His little gifts. Speak as Paul did of His dying love. Say ' He loved me, and gave himself for me.' Think of that till it sets your soul on fire; think of that till a passion for Him swells within you."—F. II.

THANKFULNESS, Emblem of.—The circulations of the ocean constitute a plain and permanent picture of these relations between a human soul and a redeeming God. The sea is always drawing what it needs down to itself, and also always sending up of its abundance into the heavens. It is always getting, and always giving. So, when in the covenant the true relation has been constituted, the redeemed one gets and gives, gives and gets; draws from God a stream of benefits, sends up to God the incense of praise.—ARNOT.

THANKFULNESS TO BE DECLARED.—*Luke xvii: 16.* It is not enough to feel thankful to God. He wants us to tell our thankfulness. It was the cleansed leper who returned and gave thanks for his cure, and not the nine who went on without a word, who best pleased his healer. No doubt that the others felt grateful that they had been cured, and could again enter their homes and sanctuary, but they grieved Him who so richly blessed them because the gratitude did not have a tongue. God is not satisfied with emotions only. He would have feelings clothed in language, sentiments embodied in words and life. It is not the love the husband feels but that which he tells that encourages the worn wife. As it is not the knowledge we possess but that which we make known to others that makes the world the wiser, so it is not the grateful feeling but the gratefulness revealed that inspires the one who bestows the favor. It is the mouth that is opened to praise that oftenest tastes Heaven's sweets, and the hand that carries thanks that is fullest laden with love's choicest gifts.—REV. W. W. DAWLEY.

THANKFUL, Not Brutish But.—Thanksgiving is the natural outcome of thoughtgiving. " Thank " and " think," the philologists say, are the same word at bottom. It is the careless, heedless attitude which is thankless. When mere habit and wont have brought us to take without thinking, we easily take without thanking, as we lose sight of the Giver in the very constancy of His gifts. The Psalmist, in the grand psalm which begins, " It is a good thing to give thanks unto the Lord! " specifies the reasons for thanksgiving in what God is, and in what He does for us, but adds, " A brutish man knoweth not; neither doth a fool understand this."

So, in the brutish and foolish moods of the mind, we do not feel how good it is to give thanks. We do not see into the grand economies of nature and of grace; but, if we think, we can see that God incessantly gives Himself, His life, His help, His watchfulness, to everything that hath life; and most of all to man, in whom the power to receive is the greatest. Think, and be thankful!—S. S. T.

THANKS ARE DUE, Where.—Gratia pro rebus merito debetur inemtis.

Thanks are justly due for things got without purchase.—OVID.

THANKSGIVING.—Thanksgiving makes our prayers bold and strong and sweet; feeds and enkindles them as with coals of fire.—LUTHER.

THANKSGIVING.—Let us give thanks to God upon Thanksgiving Day. Nature is beautiful, and fellow-men are dear, and duty is close beside us, and God is over us and in us. We want to trust Him with a fuller trust, and so at last to come to that high life where we shall "be careful for nothing, but in everything, by prayer and supplication, with thanksgiving, let our request be made known unto God;" for that, and that alone, is peace.—Phillips Brooks.

THANKSGIVING.—I said, "I will give thanks unto the Lord." Then like a peep with a candle into an empty barrel, I saw my own heart a startling void. I could sing and smile and work, I could pray and give and weep, but I could not give thanks unto the Lord. The "I received" would always seem to weigh more than the "Thou hast given." I counted the mercies over one by one, until lost in the maze of their plenitude; I said to my heart, "Heart of mine, the appliances are all invented, and every wheel and spring fits into its own little place, now give, give, *give thanks.*" But the result was like the voice of a consumptive, or the pale, cold face of the dead. I thought of God. It was National Thanksgiving Day, and I said, "He is all good, and He is good unto all. Each little providence is jeweled with His goodness." I heard the Thanksgiving anthems, I heeded the words of the preacher's message. I greeted my friends with joy and remembered my enemies with kindness, but thanksgiving—real, deep, heartfelt thanksgiving—it eluded my grasp. I could not attain it.

Then I mused: "Shall trouble come, shall God sends losses and bereavements to break the fallow nature up and cause the seeds of grace to sprout and grow?" A voice of holy sweetness whispered, "In everything give thanks, for this is the will of God in Christ Jesus concerning you." Then those three phrases chanted up and down the pathway of my soul. "The will of God," "In Christ Jesus," "Concerning you." I heard their music until I could no more forbear to cry, "O God, Thy will be done!" Now found I why my deep concern had been. The Holy Spirit had so patiently been pressing the key to gratitude into my hand that He had kept my attention to the precious theme, and when I cried, "Thy will be done," He entered, O precious wonder, He entered in, and He filled my life. Then the dear response came flooding all my being. The heart stood giant while the words seemed really dwarf. Then I said, reverently, exultantly, "Bless the Lord, O my soul, *and all that is within me,* bless His holy name."—Rev. Henry Ostrom.

THANKSGIVING CRESCENDO.—*Lam. iii: 22; Ps. ciii:1-5.* Carlyle has somewhere said, that a man should put himself at zero, and then reckon every degree ascending from that point as an occasion for thanks. Precisely on this scale do the Scriptures compute our mercies. Demerit places us at the very nadir. Every step we take from the point where conscious unworthiness would consign us, should call for an offering of gratitude, whatever envied heights may tower unreached, above us. "It is of the Lord's

mercies that we are not consumed." "Why should a *living* man complain?" So begins the anthem of thanks, at its lowest note of all, "We are alive—we are not consumed." We are all of us far, far above the extremest point; therefore, let each, from the place where he stands, strike in with his own melody, till the accumulated song rises higher and higher, like the lark circling towards the skies. "Bless the Lord, O my soul, who forgiveth all thine iniquities, who healeth all thy diseases, who redeemeth thy life from destruction, who satisfieth thy mouth with good things, who crowneth thee with loving kindness and tender mercies."—Wm. Adams, D.D.

THANKSGIVING DAY MEDITATION, A.—Wants a night's lodging, does he? We do not keep an inn. Let him go on to the next town! Probably he has no money. We have no place where he can lie. He would be frozen to death in the old barn, and the spare bedroom is not to be thought of.

An old man, his clothes in tatters. The snow and ice lie thickly over the ground. As he turned away he asked only if there were many houses near, if they stood close together. As he leaves I see that he is footsore and weary. He does not look back. I may not leave the fireside to follow him. He passes away. He has not returned.

But he returns in the night watches, entering through the barred door. He is with me; yet not he, but another; no longer the Beggar, but the Accuser. He will not leave me in the morning. Shall I ever be rid of him? His sad eyes tell me that I have done a vile thing. O my heart, is it not so? Did not He who made me make this wretch also? "Of one blood." This, perhaps, a better man than I am.

But in those clean sheets—a beggar! My spare room is altogether too good for him, who did not know where to lay his head. There are moneys in my house needed for my children, some portable valuables also, heirlooms and relics. Suppose the stranger should rob me!

It would be an ill thing if I, now at least hospitably inclined, should be soured against my fellows. And, if he turned out well and in the morning went on his way blessing me and telling of my goodness, might not that bring more needy visitors, among them some unworthy, who would impose upon my weakness? Does it not become a man to be prudent, careful first of his own household? So the wayfarer remains in the darkness and the cold. He need not perish if he can find one more charitable and less prudent.

After all I am a good citizen and a kindly man, paying my proportion and gladly giving more. Why did this man come to my doorstep? The state should care for the poor, the rich giving of their abundance.

"Whatsoever ye would that men should do unto you, that do ye unto them!"

On a winter night, the man scarce seen in darkness, I turned my brother from my door, afraid to let him in, afraid of personal consequences. Take that sad look from me! It tells me I am a coward. "Afraid!" is in its rebuke.

A savage would have been hospitable. A poor man might have shared his bed with him. But I am a gentleman and have goods. God help me! For I too am in the cold, and the night is dreary, and the way is long and unknown. Out in such darkness and inclemency that I dare not and cannot help my brother. Hast Thou redeemed us yet, O Christ.—W. J. LINTON. (I.)

THANKSGIVING DINNER, An Old.— How well I remember that old Thanksgiving dinner! Father at one end, mother at the other end, the children between wondering if father will ever get done carving the turkey. O, that proud, strutting hero of the barnyard, upside down, his plumes gone and minus his gobble! Stuffed with that which he can never digest. The day before, at school, we had learned that Greece was south of Turkey, but on the table we found that turkey was bounded by grease. The brown surface waited for the knife to plunge astride the breast-bone, and with knife sharpened on the jambs of the fire-place, lay bare the folds of white meat. Give to the disposed to be sentimental, the heart. Give to the one disposed to music, the drumstick. Give to the one disposed to theological discussion, the "parson's nose." Then the pies! For the most part a lost art. What mince pies! in which you had all confidence fashioned from all rich ingredients, instead of miscellaneous leavings which are only short of glorified hash! Not mince pies with profound mysteries of origin! But mother made them, sweetened them, flavored them, and laid the lower crust and the upper crust, with here and there a puncture by the fork to let you look through the light and flaky surface into the substance beneath.—T. DE WITT TALMAGE, D.D.

THANKSGIVING, Enter His Gates With.—*Ps. c: 4.* There is a self-opening gate which is often used in country roads. It stands fast and firm across the road as a traveler approaches it; it won't open. But if he will drive right at it, his wagon wheels press the springs below the roadway, and the gate swings back to let him through. So the spirit of thanksgiving pushes the way of all approach to God's favor, through all the gates of privilege, with all the assurance of faith that no good thing of blessing and of knowledge and power shall be withheld. Try it.—C. G.

THANKSGIVING, Public.—*Ps. xxxiv: 3.* Why not confine our thanksgiving to specific individual blessings or to the privacy of our homes and hearts? Why should there be public or national thanksgiving? As well might we ask why not let the great musical conceptions of master composers be confined to their own enjoyment or to their own private rendering? Why gather instruments of various capacity, players of great skill, an audience of fine musical taste and sympathy? We answer, the musical ideas themselves require an adequate instrumentation and skill, in order to their full interpretation and communication. Thus all musical souls are or may be lifted up to the high level of joy of the master composer himself.

So our blessings being divine, human, historic, international, voluminous, public, they require an adequate recognition and celebration. The great souls that are best able to catch the magnificent harmonies of God's character and providence, in the very nature of praise and worship, are the ones to communicate their heavenly joy to others, crying with the psalmist, " Let the people praise the Lord, let all the people praise him; O magnify the Lord with me, and let us exalt his name together."—See Ps. ciii: 20-22.—C. G.

THANKSGIVING, Reason for.—When our national independence had been triumphantly achieved, the colonies held general jubilee. King George, who had been sadly worsted in the conflict, thinking himself quite as pious as his disloyal subjects, and not to be outdone in godliness by such rebels against the divine right, appointed also a day of thanksgiving for the restoration of peace to his long-disturbed empire. In the vicinity of the monarch's residence, then Windsor Castle, dwelt a most estimable member of the Church, who shared his sovereign's intimacy, and conversed with him freely. On this occasion the worthy divine ventured to say, " Your Majesty has sent out a proclamation for a day of thanksgiving. For what are we to give thanks? Is it because your Majesty has lost thirteen of the fairest jewels from your crown?" " No, no," replied the monarch, " not for that." " Well, then, shall we give thanks because so many millions of treasure have been spent in this war, and so many millions added to the public debt?" " No, no," again replied the King. " not for that." " Shall we, then, give thanks that so many thousands of our fellow-men have poured out their life-blood in this unhappy and unnatural struggle between those of the same race and religion?" " No, no," exclaimed the King for the third time, " not that." " For what, then, may it please your Majesty are we to give thanks?" asked the pious divine. " Thank God!" cried the King, most energetically, " thank God it is not any worse." Yes, and here is a reason for thankfulness in all circumstances, since it is never so bad with us as it might be; and even if God be pouring out the vials of His anger, yet, blessed be His name, He never empties them to the uttermost!—DR. CHARLES WADSWORTH.

THANKSGIVING SERVICE.—*How to keep a feast day.*—" Go your way, eat the fat, and drink the sweet, and send portions unto them for whom nothing is prepared: for this day is holy unto our Lord," etc.—Neh. viii: 10, 11. 1. The universal custom in Scripture times, and with all nations since, to give grateful offerings to the great Protecting Power on holy days. 2. Our special reasons for thankfulness. He has provided for us the "fat" and "sweet." 3. God delights to have us express our thankfulness by relieving the distress of others. "Send portions for them for whom nothing is prepared"—the sadly afflicted people of the South—the poor in our midst. 4. A day of rejoicing. They grieved not but made great mirth.

See the thanksgiving sermons:
"The crowning of the year," by Dr. Ryllance, in *Complete Preacher,* January Number, 1878.
"Divine Forces in Human History," by Prof. Nelson, in same, March Number, 1878.
"The Hard Times God's Pruning Knife," by Dr. Wadsworth, in the *Metropolitan Pulpit and Homiletic Monthly,* January Number, 1878.—H. R.

THANKSGIVING THEMES.—THANKS-GIVING IN PERILOUS TIMES.—*Dan. vi: 10.* When Daniel knew that the writing was signed, he went into his house, and his windows being open in his chamber towards Jerusalem, he kneeled three times a day, and prayed and gave thanks before his God, as he did aforetime.

AN APPEAL TO GRATITUDE.—*1 Sam. xix: 4, 5.* And Jonathan spake good of David unto Saul his father and said . . . For he did put his life in his hand and slew the Philistine, and the Lord wrought a great salvation for all Israel: thou sawest it and didst rejoice; wherefore then wilt thou sin against innocent blood to slay David without a cause?

FORGOTTEN MERCIES REMEMBERED.—*Gen. xli: 9-12.* Then spake the chief butler unto Pharaoh, saying, I do remember my faults this day . . . there was there with us a young man, a Hebrew . . . and he interpreted to us our dreams.

GRATITUDE PROCLAIMED.—*Mark v: 20.* And he departed [the man out of whom Christ had cast an unclean spirit], and began to publish in Decapolis how great things Jesus had done for him, and all men did marvel.

THE MOST UNPROMISING SOMETIMES THE MOST THANKFUL.—*Luke xvii: 15, 16.* And one of them [the ten lepers whom Christ had healed] when he saw that he was healed, turned back and with a loud voice, glorified God, and fell down on his face at his feet, giving him thanks; *and he was a Samaritan.*

WITH THE SPIRIT OF SONG.—*Psalm xcv: 2.* Let us come before his presence with thanksgiving, and make a joyful noise unto him with psalms.

WITH CHARITY.—*Psalm xli: 1.* Blessed is he that considereth the poor.

RISING SUPERIOR TO OUR TROUBLES.—*Psalm cxix: 62.* At midnight will I rise to give thanks unto thee. Compare the mingled thanksgiving and weeping in Ezra iii: 11-13.

NOT IN A SELF-RIGHTEOUS SPIRIT.—*Luke xviii: 11.* Lord, I thank thee that I am not as other men, . . . or even as this publican.

THE UNIVERSALITY OF MERCY IN THE EXPERIENCE OF CHRISTIANS.—*Eph. v: 20.* Giving thanks always for all things unto God and the Father in the name of the Lord Jesus Christ.

THE HOLINESS OF GOD AN INSPIRATION TO GRATITUDE.—*Psalm xcvii: 12.* Rejoice in the Lord, ye righteous: and give thanks at the remembrance of his holiness.

THE DIVINE AGENCY IN NATIONAL DEVELOPMENT.—*Isa. xxvi: 15.* Thou hast increased the nation, O Lord, thou hast increased the nation: thou art glorified: thou hast removed it far unto all the ends of the earth [or hast extended it unto, etc.].

THE SECRET OF MUNICIPAL AND NATIONAL STABILITY.—*Isa. xxvi: 1, 2.* We have a strong city; salvation will God appoint for walls and bulwarks. Open ye the gates that the righteous nation which keepeth the truth enter in.—H. R.

THANKSGIVING THOUGHTS.—"They that cannot have what they like should learn to like what they have." A tough lesson but well worth learning.—SPURGEON.

To receive honestly is the best thanks for a good thing.—GEORGE MACDONALD—MARY MARSTON. Ch. V.

Christians thank God that He hath created them after His own image; that He hath called them out of the common crowd of this world and made them Christians; that among those that bear the name of Christ He hath made them faithful ones, like a few quick-sighted men among a company of blind ones; like the light in Goshen, when all Egypt was dark besides, or like Gideon's fleece, only watered with the dew of heaven, while the rest of the earth was dry and destitute of His favor; great cause of thankfulness indeed!—H. SPENCER.

As flowers carry dewdrops, trembling on the edges of the petals, and ready to fall at the first waft of wind or brush of bird, so the heart should carry its beaded words of thanksgiving, and at the first breath of heavenly flavor, let down the shower perfumed with the heart's gratitude.—BEECHER.

I thank God that I was born a man, and not a beast; that I was born a Grecian and not a barbarian.—PLATO.

There is this difference between a thankful and an unthankful man: the one is always pleased in the good he has done, and the other only in what he has received; but there are some men who are never thankful.—A. MONOD.

Non est diuturna possessio in quam gladio ducimus; beneficiorum gratia sempiterna est. That possession which we gain by the sword is not lasting: gratitude for benefits is eternal.—QUINTUS CURTIUS RUFUS.

Inasmuch as we are sinners, and have forfeited the blessings which we daily receive, what can be more suitable than that we should humbly thank that Almighty Power from whom comes such an inexhaustible supply of goodness to us so utterly undeserving?—FRANCIS WAYLAND.

TROUBLE.—Some folks are so fond of trouble they can't enjoy honey for thinking of what might have happened if the bee had stung 'em.—*Selected.*

POETRY

A Harvest Canticle

By Theron Brown

What is bounty but love in the giver,
That waits for no plea to bestow,
The evergreen boon of the river,
To the fields that are blessed by its flow?
Does the light when the morning uncloses,
Count the leagues of its flight on the plain?
Does the sky call the roll of the roses
That hold up their lips for its rain?

God is never at loss with His plenty,
And Nature, His handmaid, no more
Ripens sweets for the feast of the dainty
Than bread for the fare of the poor.
'Tis a loan with no burden thereafter,
'Tis a grace never measured nor weighed;
If the banquet turns weeping to laughter
The debt of the eater is paid.

O Goodness so grand in its doing!
Are there gluttons who starve at its board;
Craven souls, whose insatiable suing
Has poisoned the comforts they hoard,
Who, insane with the joy of receiving,
Are glad for no sake but their own,
Who are deaf to the song of Thanksgiving
And tongueless to utter its tone?

Give us want, give us nothingness rather
Than this; better never be born
Than to harvest the fields of our Father
And leave Him unthanked for the corn,
The just will pay measure for measure
And the selfish give love for a fee;
But they squander an infinite treasure
Who sin against love that is free.—I.

In Glad Content

By Frank L. Stanton

The world, they say, is gettin' old an' weary
as can be;
But write me down as sayin' it's good enough
for me!
It's good enough, with all its grief, its pleasure, an' its pain;
An' there's a ray of sunshine for every drop
o' rain!

They stumble in the lonesome dark, they cry
for light to see;
But write me down as sayin' it's light enough
for me!
It's light enough to lead us on from where
we faint an' fall,
An' the hilltop nearest heaven wears the
brightest crown o' all!

They talk about the fadin' hopes that mock
the years to be;
But write me down as sayin' there's hope
enough for me!
Over the old world's wailin' the sweeter
music swells;
In the stormiest night I listen an' hear the
bells—the bells!

This world o' God's is brighter than we ever
dream or know;
Its burdens growin' lighter—an' it's Love that
makes 'em so!
An' I'm thankful that I'm livin' where Love's
blessedness I see,
'Neath a heaven that's forgivin', where the
bells ring " Home " to me!— C. E. W.

Five Kernels of Corn

By Hezekiah Butterworth

(A Thanksgiving Tradition.)

"Out of small beginnings great things have been
produced, as one small candle may light a thousand."
—Gov. Bradford.

I

'Twas the year of the famine in Plymouth of
old,
The ice and the snow from the thatched roofs
had rolled.
Through the warm purple skies steered the
geese o'er the seas,
And the woodpeckers tapped in the clocks
of the trees;
The boughs on the slopes to the south winds
lay bare,
And dreaming of summer the buds swelled
in air,
The pale Pilgrims welcomed each reddening
morn;
There were left for rations but Five Kernels
of Corn.
    Five Kernels of Corn!
    Five Kernels of Corn!
But to Bradford a feast were Five Kernels
of Corn!

II

" Five Kernels of Corn! Five Kernels of
Corn!
Ye people be glad for Five Kernels of Corn! "
So Bradford cried out on bleak Burial Hill.
And the thin women stood in their doors
white and still.
" Lo the Harbor of Plymouth rolls bright in
the spring,
The maples grow red, and the wood robins
sing,
The west wind is blowing, and fading the
snow,
And the pleasant pines sing, and arbutuses
blow.
    Five Kernels of Corn!
    Five Kernels of Corn!
To each one be given Five Kernels of Corn! "

III

O Bradford of Austerfield, haste on thy way,
The west winds are blowing o'er Province-
town Bay,
The white avens bloom, but the pine domes
are chill,
And new graves have furrowed Precisioners'
Hill!

" Give thanks all ye people, the warm skies
   have come,
The hilltops are sunny, and green grows the
   holm,
And the trumpets of winds, and the white
   March is gone,
And ye still have left you Five Kernels of
   Corn.
          Five Kernels of Corn!
          Five Kernels of Corn!
Ye have for Thanksgiving Five Kernels of
   Corn! "

IV

" The raven's gift eat and be humble and
   pray,
A new light is breaking, and Truth leads
   your way.
One taper a thousand shall kindle: rejoice
That to you has been given the wilderness
   voice! "
O Bradford of Austerfield, daring the wave,
And safe through the sounding blasts leading
   the brave,
Of deeds such as thine was the free nation
   born,
And the festal world sings the " Five Kernels
   of Corn."
          Five Kernels of Corn!
          Five Kernels of Corn!
The nation gives thanks for Five Kernels of
   Corn!
To the Thanksgiving Feast bring Five Ker-
   nels of Corn!
                        Y. C.

November's Gift

By Emma C. Dowd

However flowerless the ways
   Of grim November,
However dull and drear her days,
   We should remember
One happy time she sets apart
   For royal living,
A gift to cheer and bless each heart,—
   It is Thanksgiving!—Y. C.

All the People Praise Him

By Will Carleton

Let all pleasures be more pleasant, let all
   griefs with help be nerved,
Let all blessings praise their sources, with the
   thanks that are deserved!
Every spirit should look heavenward, every
   heart should tribute pay,
To the Soul of souls that treats us to the
   Grand Old Day!

Thanks be to God

By Frances Ridley Havergal

Thanks be to God! to whom earth owes
   Sunshine and breeze,
The heath-clad hill, the vale's repose,
   Streamlet and seas,
The snowdrop and the summer rose,
   The many-voicéd trees.

Thanks for the darkness that reveals
   Night's starry dower;
And for the sable cloud that heals
   Each fevered flower;
And for the rushing storm that peals
   Our weakness and Thy power.

Yet thanks that silence oft may flow
   In dewlike store;
Thanks for the mysteries that show
   How small our lore;
Thanks that we here so little know,
   And trust Thee all the more.

Thanks for the gladness that entwines
   Our path below;
Each sunrise that incarnadines
   The cold, still snow;
Thanks for the light of love, that shines
   With brightest earthly glow.

Thanks for the sickness and the grief
   That none may flee;
For loved ones standing now around
   The crystal sea;
And for the weariness of heart
   That only rests in Thee.

Thanks for Thine own thrice-blessed Word
   And Sabbath rest;
Thanks for the hope of glory stored
   In mansions blest;
And for the Spirit's comfort poured
   Into the trembling breast.

Thanks—more than thanks—to Him ascend
   Who died to win
Our life, and every trophy rend
   From death and sin;
Till, when the thanks of earth shall end,
   The thanks of heaven begin.—C. E. W.

Thanks for Sorrows and Joys

By Will Carleton

We thank Thee, O Father, for all that is
   bright—
The gleam of the day and the stars of the
   night,
The flowers of our youth and the fruits of
   our prime,
And the blessings that march down the pathway of time.

We thank Thee, O Father, for all that is
   drear—
The sob of the tempest, the flow of the tear;
For never in blindness, and never in vain,
Thy mercy permitted a sorrow or pain.

We thank Thee, O Father of all, for the
   power
Of aiding each other in life's darkest hour;
The generous heart and the bountiful hand
And all the soul-help that sad souls under-
   stand.

We thank Thee, O Father, for days yet to be;
For hopes that our future will call us to Thee.
Let all our eternity form, through Thy love,
One Thanksgiving Day in the mansions
   above.—W. C. M.

A Song of the Thankful Time

BY ROSE HARTWICK THORPE

We think of Thanksgiving at seeding time—
In the swelling, unfolding, budding time,
When the heart of nature and hearts of men
Rejoice in the earth grown young again.
We dream of the harvest, of field and vine,
And granaries full, at Thanksgiving time.

We think of Thanksgiving in growing time—
In the time of flowers, and in vintage prime;
When the palms of the year's strong hands
    are filled
With fruitage, with grain and with sweets
    distilled.
With the dream of hope is a truth sublime,
Then our hearts make room for the thankful
    time.

We think of Thanksgiving in harvest time—
In the yielding, gathering, golden time;
When the sky is fringed with a hazy mist,
And the blushing maples by frost lip kissed;
When the barns are full with the harvest
    cheer,
And the crowning, thankful day draws near.

We think of Thanksgiving at resting time—
The circle completed is but a chime
In the song of life, in the lives of men;
We harvest the toils of our years, and then
We wait at the gate of the King's highway,
For the dawn of our soul's Thanksgiving
    Day.—Y. L. J.

Give Thanks

BY CARLOTTA PERRY

For sweet hopes born and for sorrows dead;
For true songs sung and for fond words said;
For the ready cup, for the daily bread;

For the race that the faithful feet have run;
For the bitter strife, for the battle won;
For brave deeds planned and for brave deeds
    done;

For the truth that liveth forevermore;
For mercy's graciously open door;
For the light that shines from the other
    shore,—

Give thanks, give thanks! Lo! the Spirit
    saith,
Let everything that hath voice or breath
Give thanks for life—for life and death.

In Everything Give Thanks

BY ZITELLA COCKE

" In everything give thanks "—nay, Lord,
To bleeding hearts dost speak that word?
Not in the trial's furnace glow,
Not in the crucible of wo,
May sweet incense of thanks arise .
Durst we but lift our streaming eyes,
Thy help, Thy pity to implore,
Almighty Lord, what can we more?

" In everything give thanks "—yea, Lord,
The chastened soul adores Thy word.
Ay, swing the heavenly censers low,
Receive the heart's rich overflow
Of glad thanksgiving for the pain,
The loss, which wrought its surer gain,
The cross, which proves its claim and share
With Thee, O Lord and Christ, joint heir!—I.

Giving Thanks

BY ELIZABETH LORD CONDIT

A little strength was lost each day,
A little hope dropped by the way,
The feet dragged slowly up the road,
The shoulders bent beneath their load,
Courage seemed dying in the heart,
The will played but a feeble part.
        Night brought no ease
        Day no surcease
From heavy cares or wearying smart,
    Then why give thanks?

Somehow strength lasted through the day,
Hope joined with courage in the way;
The feet still kept the up-hill road,
The shoulders did not drop their load,
An unseen power sustained the heart
When flesh and will failed in their part.
        While God gave light
        By day and night
And also grace to bear the smart.
    For this give thanks.

Thanks for the daily bread which feeds
The body's wants, the spirit's needs;
Thanks for the keen, the quick'ning word,
" He only lives who lives in God,"
Whether his time on earth is spent
In lordly house or labor's tent.
        Thanks for the light
        By day and night
Which shows the way the Master went.
    —And He gave thanks.—I.

Thanksgiving

BY MRS. L. B. HALL

Along the hills that autumn's grace
    Hath lit with sudden tints of flame,
One comes, with sweet, uplifted face,
    Singing her praises to His name,
Whose hand the ready blessings heap,
Whose endless love a world doth keep.

A spirit of thanksgiving, born
    Of grateful people, blessed of God,
Whose barns He fills with golden corn;
    Whose level fields of lifeless sod,
His sunshine and His fragrant rains,
Have quickened into fruitful plains.

E'en should the angry clouds uplift
    Dark faces on the trembling days,
The seeming, ill is yet God's gift;
    Out of the shadows lift His praise.
Calm as the child who, smiling, hears
The footsteps of advancing years.

Above is God, come joy or ill,
  Come life or death, come want and wo,
Changeless His love exists, and still
  Boundless His great compassions flow,
O people, by His mercy crowned,
Through thy full lives His praises sound!
                                        P. J.

Thanksgiving

Lord, for the erring thought
Not into evil wrought;
Lord, for the baffled will
Betrayed, and baffled still;
For the heart from itself kept
Our thanksgiving accept.

For ignorant hopes that were
Broken to our blind prayer;
For pain, death, sorrow, sent
Unto our chastisement;
For all loss of seeming good
Quicken our gratitude.—C. G.

Thanksgiving

By Hattie Whitney

Happy the days when the cowslips tipped their
    caps to the friendly sun,
Happy the days when the merry work of the
    year was just begun,
And happy days are these, my love, when the
    work of the year is done.

Sweet was the time when showers of scent
    from the lilac tops were tossed,
And sweet when the dancing feet of spring
    in the summer paths were lost;
And cheerisome times are these, my love,
    when the air is sharp with frost.

The summer wrought with a diligence, and
    her needle flashed amain,
Her thread was red with the rosy sun, and
    white with the pearls of rain;
And her needle is thrust in a folded case—
    the thread is snapped in twain.

The sun is faded—Heigho! What then? For
    the fire's heart is clear,
And cellar and storehouse are brimming full
    —and have ye then no cheer?
So let her sit in the chimney light and rest
    her—the tired year.

Who would wish for the light to last till it
    dazzled the weary eye?
Live and give, and carol away—when the
    winds are piercing and high,
And let the soul of the rose live on, when
    its day has drifted by.

The grass will dry and the fruit will fall,
    and the sun will slip away,
But the "merry heart," it "doeth good,"
    when the days are short and gray,
And the soul that sings in the storm shall
    find the true Thanksgiving day.
                                        Y. C.

Thanksgiving

By Paul Laurence Dunbar

Don't talk to me of solemn days
  In autumn's time of splendor,
Because the sun shows fewer rays
  And these grow slant and slender.

Why, it's the climax of the year—
  The highest time of living!
Till naturally its bursting cheer
  Just melts into thanksgiving.—C. G.

Thanksgiving

By Zoeth Howland

We're thankful for the winter frost
  That made the snowflakes fall,
For every snowball that we tossed,
  And sleds and skates and all.
We're thankful for the flowers we found
  In May-time, long ago;
Spring-beauty peeping from the ground,
  And bloodroot white as snow.
We're thankful for the holidays
  That came with summer heat,
And all the happy summer plays
  In grandma's garden sweet.
We're thankful for the autumn's store,
  When fields are bare and gray,
And all the year that brings once more
  Our dear Thanksgiving Day.—Y. C.

Thanksgiving

By Mary F. Butts

That fields have yielded ample store
Of fruit and wheat and corn,
That nights of restful blessedness
Have followed each new morn;
That flowers have blossomed by the paths
That thread our working days,
That love has filled us with delight,
We offer heartfelt praise.

What shall we say of sorrow's hours,
Of hunger and denial,
Of tears, and loneliness, and loss,
Of long and bitter trial?
Oh, in the darkness have not we
Seen new, resplendent stars?
Have we not learned some song of faith
Within our prison bars?

Not only for the Earth's rich gifts,
Strewn thick along our way,
Her looks of constant loveliness,
We thank our God to-day;
But for the spirits subtle growth,
The higher, better part,
The treasures gathered in the soul—
The harvest of the heart.—Y. C.

Thanksgiving

By J. Zitella Cocke

One cycle more, with rich fruition crowned,
Hastes to fulfilment of its perfect round,—
Great year of wonder, and of vast emprise!—
For all its gifts, ay, let Thanksgiving rise,

The hero's prowess—bloodless victory won;
The martyr's patience, sternest duty done,—
Yet, loftier pæans still, for war's surcease,—
For God's best gift,—the precious boon of
   peace!

For garnered opulence of flock and field,
Joys ever new, revolving seasons yield,—
For those bright presences of radiant night,—
The garment-hem of Glory Infinite,—
Blithe speech of birds, and bloom of sunny
   bower,
Health, home, and love,—the best of earthly
   dower,—
Yet in this gracious time of strife's release,
Thank God, ye people, for His gift of peace!
                     Y. C.

Thanksgiving

BY WILLIAM LAMBIE

Good crops all gathered in the barn,
All safe from rain and snow and harm,
Bring joy and pleasure on the farm.

Thanksgiving for sweet buds and flowers,
For balmy winds and sunny showers,
Through all the rich, grand summer hours:

For health and friends coming kindly,
For the crops that grow so finely,
For all blessings sent divinely;

For autumn with her glories on,
Now all the golden leaves are gone,
The fields are desolate and lone.

Over the cribs heaped full of corn
We hear the robins peep at morn
Farewell before the winter's storm.

Gathering round abundance spread,
Asking for blessings on our head,
For health and peace and daily bread.

With all the harvest treasure stored,
And young and old around the board,
To praise the goodness of the Lord.

Gay young toddlers run round the floor,
With Willie in a glad uproar
In the first boots he ever wore.

Old age enjoying youthful mirth,
In useful lives of honest worth,
Making the best of life and earth.—E.

Thanksgiving

BY JOEL BENTON

Bloom of spring and summer's glow
Joyful come and swiftly go;
Not a hint you find to-day
Of the aureole of May.

Dead are all the flowers of June,
Changed the cooing brooklet's tune;
Summer's singing birds have flown
To some far off, tropic zone.

The gorgeous show October gave
Nature would not pause to save;
But, hastening on, the rapid year
Stands in desolation drear.

How the North wind moans and grieves
Over carpets of dead leaves;
But in cellar, barn, and bin
Harvests rich are gathered in.

War's grim face, a specter drear,
Trembling, feels its finish near;
It came that Tyranny might cease
And Justice bring enduring peace.

Thanks fill the hearts for halcyon skies,
And bettered human destinies;
For the swift years, which, as they fly
Lift up mankind in passing by.—I.

Thanksgiving

BY MRS. M. E. LEONHARDT

Our heartful thanks we offer Thee,
   Our Father, God,
For all the blessings full and free,
   By Thee bestowed.

For the year's great prosperity,
   Our praise ascends,
And sweeter comforts lent by Thee—
   A home and friends.

The full and plenteous harvest store,
   And fruitage fair,
All with unnumbered tokens more,
   Thy love declare.

For blessings of each passing hour—
   Things fair to see—
The sunshine and refreshing shower,
   As sent by Thee.

For all of nature's beauties bright,
   In grand array—
All the fair glory of the night,
   And fairer day.

And Thou wilt be our sure defense,
   When death draws near—
E'en pain assumes a sweeter sense,
   If Thy grace cheer.

And so our thanks to Thee we bring,
   And filial love—
And join with heart and voice, to sing
   With saints above.—P. J.

Thanksgiving Day

BY SUSAN COOLIDGE

For what do we thank Thee, O Father and
   King,
  As through highroads and streets and leaf-
     scattered ways,
Thy people come flocking in reverence to
   bring,
  At the close of the year, the year's harvest
    of praise?

So many, so various the gifts of Thy hand,
  Some sweet, some bitter, some dark, and
    some bright,
The cross to upbear and the staff of com-
    mand,
  The weariful march and the dance of
    delight.

The joy so intense that it pierced like a pain,
  The sorrow so deep that it grew wholly
    sweet,
The love that was crowned and the love that
    was vain,
  The strength and the hope that were born
    of defeat.

Shall we thank Thee for these and not thank
    Thee for those?
  Shall we love Thee for blessings and chide
    Thee for ill?
And chafe at Thy thorn while we seize on
    Thy rose,
  And praise while our hearts are unsatis-
    fied still?

No, we bless Thee for all, for in all we have
    Thee,
  And all is from Thee; who can never do
    wrong,
And feeble and faint tho our utterance be,
  No murmur discordant shall sadden our
    song.

For life then, for death then, for good and
    for ill,
  For storm as for sunshine, for harvest and
    blight,
In glad days, in sad days, we worship Thee
    still,
  The Lord of the darkness, the Lord of
    the light.

A Psalm Meet for Thanksgiving Day

By Henry van Dyke

O Thou whose boundless love bestows
  The joy of life, the hope of heaven;
Thou whose unchartered mercy flows
  O'er all the blessings Thou hast given;
Thou by whose light alone we see;
Thou by whose truth our souls set free
Are made imperishably strong;
Hear Thou the solemn music of our song.

Grant us the knowledge that we need
  To solve the questions of the mind;
Light Thou our candle while we read,
  And keep our hearts from going blind;
Enlarge our vision to behold
The wonders Thou hast wrought of old;
Reveal Thyself in every law,
And gild the towers of truth with holy awe.

Be Thou our strength when war's wild gust
  Rages around us, loud and fierce;
Confirm our souls and let our trust
  Be like a wall that none can pierce;
Give us the courage that prevails,
The steady faith that never fails,
Help us to stand in every fight
Firm as a fortress to defend the right.

O God, make of us what Thou wilt;
  Guide Thou the labor of our hand;
Let all our work be surely built
  As Thou, the architect, hast planned;
But whatsoe'er Thy power shalt make
Of these frail lives, do not forsake
Thy dwelling. Let Thy presence rest
Forever in the temple of our breast.

A Sacramental Thanksgiving Hymn

By T. M. Niven

Hosannas let us sing
  To our Redeemer, God,
Who offered up His life,
  And freely shed His blood;
That we by Him might ransom'd be
From the Law's curse and penalty.

Hosannas sing aloud
  To him who left His throne,
And in a human garb
  "The wine-press trod alone."
'Twas God and man, the two in one,
That must undo what sin had done.

Hosannas we will raise
  To Him to whom we owe
Our hopes of heaven above,
  Our mercies here below.
To Him our all we consecrate,
Tho 'tis but small for love so great.

Hosannas shout aloud
  While we're sojourning here:
His Spirit and His Word
  Will make our pathway clear.
In Guide so safe we will confide,
Nor life nor death from Christ divide.

Hosannas we'll repeat
  While we on earth remain;
But in the Church above
  We'll join the glad refrain
To Him who washed us in His blood,
"And made us Kings, and Priests to God."

Hosannas, Jesus, come,
  Thy pledge we've had to-day
Which should our faith confirm,
  And all our doubts allay.
Lord Jesus, come, Thy foes subdue,
The curse remove, make all things new.—E.

A Song of Thanksgiving

By Clinton Scollard

Thanksgiving! Thanksgiving! Of yore,
  In the youth of the nation,
When the harvest had yielded its store
  There was feast and oblation.
Or when danger had lifted its hand
  From the lips of the living
There rang through the length of the land
  A Thanksgiving! Thanksgiving!

Our home was a wilderness then
  With the floods to enfold it;
To-day with its millions of men,
  We rejoice to behold it.

From the sea to the surge of the sea,
  We have all for treasure;
We are blest in the promised To-be
  In a manifold measure.

War flaunts not a red pennon now,
  For the olive is regal;
Like the birds that are twin, on one bough
  Sit the dove and the eagle.
The clash of the conflict that cleft
  We in sorrow remember,
But the fire of the great feud has left
  In the ash scarce an ember.

For the fruit of the time of our toil;
  For whate'er we have fought for;
Whether born of the brain or the soil
  Be the meed we have sought for;
For the gifts we have had from His hand
  Who is Lord of the living,
Let there ring through the length of the land
  A Thanksgiving! Thanksgiving!
                                    —L. H. J.

A Song of Thanksgiving

By Helen Whitney Clark

Give thanks for the year, ere it closes,
  The fruitful and prosperous year;
Give thanks for the summer's red roses,
  That blossomed our pathway to cheer.

Give thanks for the seed-time and harvest
  That brought us the sheaves and the shocks;
Give thanks for the vine and the fig-tree,
  Give thanks for the herds and the flocks.

Give thanks for the spring-time that brought
    us
  Her lap full of May flowers gay;
Give thanks for the song of the robin,
  The thrush and the blue-feathered jay.

Give thanks for the morn's rosy dawning,
  The dew-gems that blaze on her breast;
Give thanks for the night's purple awning
  That folds us in slumber's sweet rest.

Give thanks for the loved ones who gather
  To welcome our coming at night—
Whether mansion or cot be our dwelling,
  Give thanks that our heart-fires are bright.

And if, weary-hearted, we struggle
  Alone through the battle of life,
Give thanks to the Power that leads us
  In safety through peril and strife.

Nature's Thanksgiving

By J. H. Bomberger

The sunlight on the meadows is the smile of
    Christ my Lord;
The raging of the tempest is the thunder of
    His word;
The snow-capped mountain-summits, which
    pierce the upper blue,
Are symbols of His promises unchangeable
    and true.

The silver stars that sparkle in the purple
    depths of night
Are His signals flashing earthward from the
    battlements of light;
The birds whose tuneful melody resounds
    through wood and glen,
Are His messengers of trust and hope to
    weary, baffled men.

The falling rains remind us of the showers
    of His grace;
The clouds, with trailing shadows, are thin
    veils that hide His face:
The changing seasons whisper of His own
    unchanging love,
And everything in nature tells of better
    things above.

The ocean's surging billows with their crests
    of snowy foam,
And the murmuring brooklet's echoes 'mid
    the glades where shadows gloam,
The spotless fleecy mantle spread by winter's
    drifting snow,
The grain-fields turning golden 'neath sum-
    mer's ardent glow.

The winds that chant their music through
    autumn's trees, stripped bare
Of summer's fruits and foliage, when a chill
    is in the air,
All speak the same assurance of a loving
    Father's hand,
To all that Father's children who have
    learned to understand.

For all the world is vocal with the music of
    His praise,
And in mighty swelling chorus breaks forth
    in grateful lays,
And from all those myriad voices comes not
    one discordant strain
To mar the blessed melody of nature's glad
    refrain.—C. E. W.

Thanksgiving Reunion

By Charles Sprague

We are all here!
  Father, mother,
  Sister, brother,
All who hold each other dear;
Each chair is filled, we're all *at home,*
To-night let no cold stranger come;
It is not often thus around
Our old familiar hearth we're found;
Blessed then the meeting and the spot;
For once be every care forgot;
Let gentle peace assert her power,
And kind affection rule the hour:
  We're all—all here.

We're *not* all here!
Some are away—the dead ones dear,
Who thronged with us this ancient hearth,
And gave the hour to guiltless mirth.
Fate, with stern, relentless hand,
Looked in, and thinned our little band;

Some like a night flash passed away;
And some sank, lingering day by day;
The quiet graveyard—some lie there;
And cruel Ocean has his share;
    We're *not* all here.

We *are* all here!
Even they, the dead; tho dead, so dear;
Fond memory, to her duty true,
Brings back their faded forms to view.
How life-like, through the mist of years,
Each well-remembered face appears!
We see them as in times long past,
From each to each kind looks are cast;
We hear their words, their smiles behold;
They're round us as they were of old;
    We *are* all here.

We are all here!
    Father, mother,
      Sister, brother;
    You that I love with love so *dear*.
This may not long of us be said;
Soon must we join the gathered dead;
And by the hearth we now sit round,
Some other circle may be found.
O then that wisdom may we know,
Which yields a life of peace below;
So, in the world to follow this,
May each repeat in words of bliss,
    We're all—all *here*.—E.

A Thanksgiving to God

By Robert Herrick

Lord, Thou hast given me a cell,
    Wherein to dwell;
A little house, whose humble roof
    Is weather proof;
Under the spars of which I lie
    Both soft and dry;
Where Thou, my chamber for to ward,
    Hast set a guard
Of harmless thoughts, to watch and keep
    Me while I sleep.
Low is my porch, as is my fate;
    Both void of state;
And yet the threshold of my door
    Is worn by the poor,
Who thither come, and freely get
    Good words, or meat.
Like as my parlor, so my hall
    And kitchen's small;
A little buttery, and therein
    A little bin,
Which keeps my little loaf of bread

    Unchipt, unflead;
Some brittle sticks of thorn or briar
    Make me a fire,
Close by whose living coal I sit,
    And glow like it.
Lord, I confess too, when I dine,
    The pulse is Thine,
And, all those other bits that be
    There placed by Thee;
The worts, the purslain, and the mess
    Of water-cress,
Which of Thy kindness Thou hast sent;
    And my content
Makes those, and my beloved beet,
    To be more sweet.
'Tis Thou that crown'st my glittering hearth
    With guiltless mirth,
And giv'st me wassail bowls to drink,
    Spiced to the brink.
Lord, 'tis Thy plenty-dropping hand
    That soils my land,
And giv'st me for my bushel sown,
    Twice ten for one;
Thou mak'st my teeming hen to lay
    Her egg each day;
Besides, my healthful ewes to bear
    Me twins each year;
The while the conduits of my kine
    Run cream for wine;
All these, and better, Thou dost send
    Me, to this end,—
That I should render, for my part,
    A thankful heart;
Which, fired with incense, I resign,
    As wholly Thine;—
But the acceptance, that must be,
    My Christ, by Thee.

The Heritage of Thanksgiving

By George T. Packard

Our songs are sweetest for the songs they
    lifted,
Our praises higher for their praises given;
And tho the firelight show their vacant
    places,
    Heart cleaves to heart, in bonds of song
    unriven.

So at the feasts when some will miss our
    faces,
Our notes from far-off days will meet their
    own;
The past and present in one chorus blending
    To swell Thanksgiving hymns around the
    Throne!—Y. C.

ADVENT

ADVENT (Latin, the coming) is a holy season rather than a holy day. It is observed more especially by the Lutheran, English, Protestant Episcopal, Greek and Roman Catholic churches. St. Andrew's Day falls on November 30th, and Advent Sunday is the one nearest, before or after, that day, introducing the Advent season, which lasts four weeks, closing with the Sunday preceding Christmas Day. "Originally, and with stricter verbal propriety than now, the word Advent was taken to mean the time of the birth of Christ—His arrival, or having come, rather than His coming. But the Church has always loved dutifully to cultivate the idea of preparation for seasons of uncommon sanctity; and one effect of this disposition has been to throw back Advent over a season of three or four weeks, intended to be spent as a long Christmas Eve in the contemplation of the incidents of which the approaching festival is commemorative, and in devout and self-questioning anticipation of the Day of Judgment." *

From very early times the coming of Christ (the central thought of Advent) was regarded as fourfold: (1) "His first coming in the flesh;" (2) His coming to Christians at their death; (3) His coming at the destruction of Jerusalem (Matt. xxiv: 30), and (4) His coming at the day of judgment. Only the first and last of these thoughts, however, have received general attention.†

Tradition carries the origin of the observance of Advent as far back as St. Peter. But reliable history takes us back to the fifth century, when it is referred to by Maximus Tourmensis in a homily on the subject. The Synod of Lerida (524 A. D.), speaks of it as a Church appointment, marriages being forbidden from the beginning of Advent until Christmas.

The Nestorians observe a fast of twenty-five days at this season; but with that exception, the Eastern Church has no Advent.

As observed by the Roman Catholic and English Churches, this season was probably introduced into the calendar by Gregory the Great. In the former it is observed by fasting, and by abstaining from public amusements and festivities. As it comes just before the time celebrating our Lord's nativity, it is considered an appropriate time for penitence in preparation for that event. The Protestant Episcopal and English Churches observe it by special services, and it is the beginning of the Church year.

The Rev. A. J. Mason, in a sermon on 1 Thess. v: 2, referring to our Lord's second advent and the final judgment, says: "The date at which the great Advent will take place is entirely unknown to us. It cannot be calculated from the symbolical numbers of St. John; nor can the most spiritual discernment be sure of reading unerringly the signs of its approach. If in reaction from the profane curiosity which delights to make out the day and hour, we hold that it is still far distant, our very thinking so is more of a sign that it is at hand than otherwise; for the one thing certain about the date is that it will throw out all computations, 'for in such an hour as ye think not, the Son of Man cometh,' (Matt. xxiv: 44.) Assuredly Christ will not come till the very moment of the

---

* THE CHURCH SEASONS, page 21. A. H. Grant. New York, Thomas Whittaker.
† As "Christ's coming in the flesh" is emphasized under "Christmas," the selections in this department bear chiefly on His final coming to Judgment.

fulness of the times any more than at the first coming. But if the world does not yet appear ripe for the end, no one can calculate how long or short a time might be needed for the ripening. One day is with the Lord as a thousand years *(2 Pet. iii: 8);* and events might move with an appalling rush if it pleased Him to give the impulse. The ingredients are all in the cup; it only needs the addition of some drop to resolve and precipitate them. There is but one lesson which Our Lord inculcates on every mention of His Coming—always to be watching for it, and never to acquiesce in the belief that it is far away."

CHRIST'S SECOND COMING

By John Hall, D.D., LL.D.

The unrest in some sincere minds regarding the expected appearance of the Messiah, and the conventions of ministers and others from time to time for its discussion renders consideration of the subject appropriate. There is only one passage in the Bible in which is mentioned a period of 1,000 years during which Christ is to reign on earth. What relations has this millennium to the coming of the Lord? The majority of people believe that the Lord would come a second time only as a judge. The minority believe that He would come in His glory and reign 1,000 years. This latter class is known as the pre-millenniumites, because, in order to establish such a religion, the Lord must come before the actual beginning of the millennium. But may not the passages in reference to the coming of the Lord be interpreted in a different way?

It is not advisable to attach too much importance to the utterances upon the subject in the early Christian literature. The early Christians had suffered terrible persecutions from the civil government. It was only natural that they should take refuge in the hope that Christ would come again and give them satisfaction on earth for the trials which they had borne. When the Roman Empire had been converted, these persecutions ended. The enthusiastic hope called out by the persecutions then expired, because the cause had ceased to operate. The Roman Church has been comparatively silent upon the subject. That is easy to explain. The Church of the Dark Ages was not occupied so much with the study of God's holy oracles. The Church has been the main thing with which men concerned themselves. As long as truth was silent, Satan always let it alone. When it became living, then he tried to kill it.

The discussion of the pre-millennium became active again during the Reformation, and a little later, when the persecutions of the Huguenots and Puritans began. The cause was the same as had led to its discussion in the early centuries of the Christian era. It began again in the seventeenth century, and became so general that in Germany even the place of the Lord's coming has been fixed. In comparatively recent years, it has been taken up also by the English-speaking

race. The extreme conception of the subject led to the founding of the Adventists. Even the Mormon movement may be regarded as the outcome of that same fanaticism.

It is not wise to interpret the statements of the Old Testament otherwise than as they are interpreted in the New Testament. It is not wise to take obscure and difficult portions of God's Word, and explain by them the teachings of the Lord. The Book of Revelation is full of mysteries to most people and will continue to be so. Why, then, had they been given? The answer is that it was with the Churches as with the disciples. Jesus said to them that, altho they did not understand Him then, a time would come when they would understand Him. The time would come when, in the light of history, the mysteries would be revealed. It is not wise to insist that all of God's Word should be interpreted literally. If the Hebrew people interpreted literally the statement that the Messiah was to be a king upon a throne, they had reason to object to Jesus. We did not interpret literally the sayings of ordinary intercourse. Words were to be interpreted according to their connection, according to the conditions which gave them birth, and according to their spirit. If the word millennium was to be interpreted literally, there could be no unanimity of interpretation. Was the Lord to come before the Jews had been converted? Was He to come at Jerusalem? Were there to be generations of men living after His millennial reign? These questions might all be asked if the word was to be interpreted literally.

What, then, is meant by the coming of the Lord Jesus? In answering it, the heart and mind must be exercised. First of all, the King of Zion is sometimes spoken of as coming in His grace, in His spirit, in His spirit, not in a visible way. He had promised "to come" to all believers in spirit, to comfort them. All Christians believed in that coming. They prayed for it daily. That, then, is the first coming of the Lord, which is alluded to frequently in the Scriptures. He had promised the Hebrews in the Old Testament that He would "come" where His name was recorded.

Secondly, the King of Zion is coming for administrative purposes. He had said that all power was given to Him in heaven and on earth. He is to carry out the purpose of the Divine Father and defeat the purposes of the devil. In that sense He comes to set up a kingdom. That is not a visible coming either. He meant to found a kingdom by dying on the cross. The administrative character of Christ's coming is referred to also in other places in the Bible. He comes to defend His people.

Thirdly, Jesus comes to take away His beloved people one by one. He comes to relieve suffering. Many a man has said on his deathbed, " Lord, come quickly." When the Lord said to wait until He should come, He had not meant to come in a visible sense, but to come to relieve the suffering of His people. When He said that He would come to " smite the stiff-necked people," He had meant to come in the administrative sense and not in a visible sense. Jesus Christ carried on His work, and in time would develop that millennial period for which Christians hoped. He would thus come in His glory to take to Heaven those who loved Him. That was the second coming. It was a coming for judgment. It was not a coming to set up a throne on earth. It was for " concluding purposes." It was to bring His kingdom in its present form to an end forever. He would then deliver up that kingdom to the Father. If He did not have that kingdom to-day He could not deliver it up. That was the only Second Advent which the Bible taught.—P. T.

THE SECOND ADVENT

ITS PREPARATIONS ACCORDING TO THE APOCALYPTIC FORE-VIEW IN REVELATION XIX, ETC.

By Sir John William Dawson, C.M.G., F.R.S., LL.D.

In interpreting fulfilled prophecy, we have the guiding light of history; but we lose this so soon as we enter the region of the unfulfilled. It is here, therefore, that those who follow the historical method show most difference of opinion; and in treating of this it is, therefore, wise to avoid too much confident assertion, and to cultivate reserve and humility, keeping closely to the terms of the inspired Word. If we are now nearing the close of that vast septenary of chastisement symbolized by the seven vials (Rev. xix), we have next before us events immediately preparatory to the second coming of our Lord, which in many parts of Scripture we are taught to regard as sudden and unexpected, and to be watched for earnestly by Christians. See especially our Lord's comparison of it to the deluge of Noah (Matt. xxiv: 27), and Paul's intimations in the fourth and fifth chapters of his First Epistle to the Thessalonians.

Yet in the more detailed foreview given in the closing chapters of the Revelation of John, we find indicated by remarkable symbols, certain great movements which are to intervene between the closing of the vials and the actual establishment of Christ's kingdom in the world, and which we should now be better able to understand than our predecessors, however gifted.

The first of these (chap. xix) is the opening of heaven and the descent therefrom of a white horse, the symbol of victory, bearing a rider who represents the power and influence of the Son of God Himself, now manifested in a new and more evident aspect. This heavenly rider is called " faithful and true," and is said to judge and make war in righteousness, and to wear many diadems, in anticipation of the vast extent of His rule.

He is said to have a secret name written, which we are afterward told is the " Word of God," the *Logos*, that mysterious and inscrutable name by which Christ is introduced to us in the first chapter of John's Gospel. He is identified with the Savior by being clothed in a garment sprinkled with blood, and with the Son of God by being entitled King of kings and Lord of lords.

He is destined to smite with the sword of the Spirit, proceeding from His mouth, the nations that serve the beast, and to tread the wine-press of the fierceness of the wrath of Almighty God, as well as to rule the disobedient nations with an iron scepter. He is not alone, but is followed by the " armies that are in heaven," mounted on white horses and clad in pure white garments. These armies are not composed of angels, who when introduced in the Revelation are specially designated as such. They must symbolize redeemed and glorified men, and especially those who have been the agents in the production of the revealed Word of God. This, as the sword of the Spirit, has all through the work of redemption been His great weapon, and still continues to be such, even in this grand vision of the appearance of Christ as a conqueror. There seems in this a special appropriateness, for in His absence since the ascent from Olivet, the written Word and the Spirit have been His representatives, and have had to bear all the violent assaults of Satan and the Apostasy. They are thus entitled to be manifested and vindicated when the Divine Word is about to appear as Conqueror of the world.

Even in our own time we have too often seen all the inspired authors of the Bible— from Moses, " the man of God," to John, " the beloved disciple,"—sitting, like Bun-

yan's pilgrims in Vanity Fair, with their feet
fast in the stocks of a cruel and heartless
criticism, and pelted with mire by the rabble
of the ungodly world; but now it is to be
their turn to be exalted, as shown by their
riding in the train of their glorified Master.
If we ask, What does all this import in literal
fact? it clearly means at least the entire victory of the inspired Word of God over its
opponents, and its practical conquest of the
civilized world in anticipation of the advent
of the Son of God Himself.

If we ask, With what bodies do they come?
we can give no definite reply, as we have no
mention here of any resurrection of earthly
bodies. We may, however, refer back to an
earlier period (chap. viii: 9), where we shall
find a multitude of redeemed men, being the
souls of those beheaded in the early heathen
persecutions, and who, tho their earthly
bodies are not raised, have not only distinct
personality, but white robes and palms in
their hands, and have functions of service
assigned to them in the heavenly world. As
the armies here, however, are seen to descend
from Heaven and act on earth, we may suppose them to symbolize a new development of
power and energy on behalf of God by means
of their writings in aid of the mission of their
great leader, the Divine Word.

However this may be, their mission is not
to be unopposed. The beast and the false
prophet gather their forces, physical and political, to maintain their sway. They meet,
however, with a signal defeat, while the vultures are summoned to prey on the flesh of
their armies. It is to be noted here, that
while the beast and the false prophet, which
are the organized forces of evil, are taken
prisoners and cast into the lake of fire, their
individuals followers, from "*chiliarchs*" or
colonels down to the rank and file, are slain
and their flesh given to the vultures, which
may mean their entire withdrawal from the
service of their former masters.

The next act in the great drama (chap. xx)
introduces an angel, who seizes the great
dragon or old serpent, the Satanic head of all
forms of false religion and infidelity, as distinguished from apostate Christianity, and
chains him in the abyss or outer space, beyond nominal Christendom, as a helpless captive, for a thousand years (the millennium),
the description of which is given in the following verses of chap. xx. In the millennial
age Christ is said to reign, and with Him the
souls of the martyrs, whether slain under pagan Rome or the Antichrist; and this is
said to be the "first resurrection," which
some regard as a revival of pure religion, like
that called a resurrection in the case of the
two witnesses in chap. x, while others regard
it as a literal resurrection of all the deceased
saints.

Whichever view we adopt, the religion of
Christ is dominant in this happy period, and
the power of Satan, whether as tempter or
persecutor, is in abeyance for a time. But
" God's mill grinds slowly," and even the development of the Messiah's kingdom has
more than once had to await the growth and

decay of hostile powers. So the thousand
years of peace and prosperity draw to a close,
and perhaps before the end the saints begin
to decline from their first love. Then Satan
is loosed from his prison, and goes forth,
perhaps with renewed energy and new devices, to deceive the nations. The chief seat
of his revived activity seems to be in the remote parts of the world, and among those
barbarous peoples known in ancient times as
Gog and Magog, who may probably during
the thousand years of peace have become very
numerous. He is so successful with these
peoples that he is able to encompass or surround that part of the world occupied by
Christ's people, called here the " Camp of the
Saints," with its capital, the " Beloved City."

It must have seemed to the Seer as if the
power of evil were now to be victorious; but
the long-suffering of God has at length
reached its limit, and He now intervenes
directly to destroy the invaders with fire from
Heaven, while Satan is finally cast into the
lake of fire.

We are next introduced (chap. xx: 11) to
the general judgment and resurrection of the
righteous and wicked. This is so often referred to in Scripture, and so plainly described here, that we may leave it without
other comment than that of the Prophet himself. We may, however, add a few words as
to the practical bearing of these last things
on the present attitude of the Church and the
world.

I. The above intimations of the Prophet
serve to harmonize Christ's great commission
to His disciples, as given in the last chapter
of Matthew and the first chapter of the Acts
of the Apostles, with the frequent injunctions
to watch for the return of Christ, as an event
that might come unexpectedly at any time.
Christ commissions His disciples to evangelize the world, but He did not promise that
they should succeed in wholly converting it
before His return. Still, when He comes it
will be necessary at least that the Gospel
should be universally known, because Christ's
kingdom is not an external one, but founded
in men's hearts; hence it becomes proper that
the revealed Word of God should be His
forerunner at His second coming, and He has
left this preparation in the hands of His people, who are bound to see that all nations
should have the Bible and be able to read it
before Christ comes again.

II. There is thus an urgent call on us for
the universal distribution of the Scriptures
and for missionary effort in advance of the
advent of the Personal Word. On this must
depend in some degree the geographical area
of the Millennial reign itself, and also that
spiritual unity of Christ's people which fits
the Church to be the Bride of the Lamb. It
may also determine the amount of unevangelized population available for the schemes
of Satan at the close of the Millennium.

A little reflection on these points should
convince any thoughtful Christian of the fundamental unity of all the prophetical intimations of the second advent and the final kingdom of God, and of the connections of watch-

ing for Christ's coming and working toward it at the same time; and in both attitudes we can manifest our "love of his appearing."

III. In conclusion, while the Prophet dwells on the beautiful pictures of the new heavens and the new earth and the New Jerusalem, he does not hesitate to warn the finally impenitent of the fate which awaits those who despise God's forbearance and reject the salvation of Christ. But in the remarkable statement in chap. xxii, beginning with the words "he that is unrighteous, let him be unrighteous still," he throws the whole responsibility on themselves. Still even after this he closes with a final invitation to them from the Savior, who calls Himself here the "root and offspring of David, the bright and morning star:" "And the Spirit and the bride say, Come. And he that heareth, let him say, Come. And he that is athirst, let him come: he that will, let him take the water of life freely."

A peculiar solemnity attaches to these closing words—the last Gospel invitation before the Bridegroom finally closes the door of entrance to the marriage feast. If these lines are read by any who have not yet accepted Christ as their Savior, I beg them to remember that the door is still open, but the *time is short.—H. R.*

SERMONS AND OUTLINES

A BLESSED ADVENT SEASON

By Pastor Hermann Kunze

Behold, I will send my messenger, and he shall prepare the way before me: and the Lord, whom ye seek, shall suddenly come to his temple, even the messenger of the covenant, whom ye delight in: behold, he shall come, saith the Lord of hosts, etc.—Mal. iii: 1-4

Advent! He comes, the angel of the Lord, thy Lord and thy King, thy Savior! This is the cry that to-day again resounds from Heaven above and out of the houses of the Lord into our homes and our hearts. How clearly and joyfully it re-echoes in a Christmas spirit on the streets of Zion to-day, the New Year of the Church, when the King of Zion, amid the crying of hosannas and strewing of palms and spreading of garments, enters the great city.

And what a contrast with the sad memories of one week ago, the last Sunday of the old Church year, the memorial day of our beloved dead! Then we heard of the coming of the angel of the Lord, the angel of death, who comes to cut down the human race and convey the souls of men before the judgment-seat of their God.

And yet on both occasions, both amid the echoes of the Advent trumpets and the tolling of the bell in the memorial day of the dead, both on the first Advent day and on the last day, it is the voice of the same Lord that reaches us, of Him who comes to us both as a just Judge and as a Savior, as a righteous Ruler and a Deliverer, in order that, through judgment and grace, He may save our souls and bring the Zion pilgrims home to the Jerusalem above, to what is His Father's house in truth.

And what can my sermon be to-day, on the New Year of the Church, except an Advent-New-Year greeting, a blessing asked down upon you, beloved congregation? My prayer is, "A blessed Advent." We bless you who are of the house of the Lord. The Lord bless your coming in. May His word and His will grow and rule in this congregation; may His image dwell in your hearts and sanctify you, and enable you to become His disciples in truth, so that in the true faith and a holy life you may follow your Advent King unto the final Advent season in the eternity of the blessed.

A Blessed Advent Season.— For this we need.

1. Blessing Advent messengers.

2. Blessed Advent hearts.

Malachi, the last of the Old Testament prophets, stands upon his prophetic outpost. His heart burns within him. Before him he sees the holy temple of his God; before him the people which in olden times the Lord had chosen as His own. The temple had indeed been built up anew, and had arisen out of its ashes in great magnificence; but a curse rested upon the people. The holy places of the Lord are desecrated because the people have broken the covenant, have blasphemed their God, and have pursued the idols of a false righteousness. Then it is that the Lord opens his spiritual eye, and the prophet looks beyond and sees the days to come, and prophesies in the name of the Lord, verse 1: "Behold, I send my messenger, and he shall prepare the way before me: and the Lord, whom ye seek, shall suddenly come to his temple, even the messenger of the covenant, whom ye delight in: behold he shall come, saith the Lord of hosts."

Malachi, himself a messenger of the Lord, as his name signifies, here predicts the coming of two messengers of the Lord. The one he calls the angel, or the messenger who shall prepare the way before the Lord; the other he calls the angel of the covenant. You Advent Christians know them both from the early history of our faith, these two mighty Advent forms. On the one hand is the Advent herald, the voice of the one crying in the wilderness; on the other is the greatest of Advent bringers, the Messiah Himself, the Son who has proceeded from the Father. And these two are the messengers that bring to us the Advent blessings.

1. It was necessary that John the Baptist, with the fire of an Elias, should come to prepare the way before the gentle Prince of Peace, Christ, could enter upon His calling. Thus say the prophets, thus say all the Scriptures, and thus saith our own heart. First comes the Law, with its demand for repentance, which does away with all self-righteousness; then comes the Gospel, with the sweet comfort of its grace and faith. First comes the schoolmaster, then comes the heavenly Master. Judgment and grace—these two are ever the blessed gifts of the Advent messengers to the Church, the home, and the heart.

Let us, then, this day too give a warm welcome to these two blessing Advent messengers.

There he stands, the Advent herald, John, in the desert, the firm prophet, with his brow of iron turned against all unrighteousness and all hypocrisy, the holy priest of the people in the rugged garment of a hermit; the fiery preacher of repentance, but at the same time also proclaiming the near advent of the kingdom of God. This, then, is the double Advent way preached by John, to do away with sin by repentance, and to prepare the heart for the grace that is coming.

This day, at the threshold of the new Church year, the preacher of repentance again appears before the Advent congregation. With one hand he points backward to the sins of the old year, to the transgressions of God's law, to the neglect of the Gospel privileges, to the want of zeal in the doing of the Lord's will, and says, "These things ye have done." With the other hand he points forward to the future, to the righteous Judge, and says, "This is thy reward. The ax has been laid at the roots of the tree; let it be cast into the fire."

In the face of such a settlement all self-deception must fall away; and the mere fact that we are baptized and are Abraham's children, and have gone through the rite of confirmation, will avail us nothing. Nothing remains for us but to say, "Lord, cover up my shortcomings, and direct Thou my life in the future." We hear the words of the Baptist, "Prepare ye the way of the Lord. Make straight in the desert the highway of our God. Every valley shall be exalted, and every mountain and hill shall be made low, and the crooked shall be made straight, and the rough places plain." This is, indeed, hard work, to make the hills and mountains of self-righteousness and self-satisfaction low; to fill up the valleys of weak faith and hearts without courage, and to make these level by the comfort of the Gospel. And yet all this must be done to prepare the way for the entrance of the Savior and the Lord.

But even if we close our ears and hearts to the cry of John, the Lord still has other messengers after John's kind—namely, misfortune and death, two Advent messengers with stern face and rough hands, that testify to us, "Behold, I come quickly, and my reward is with me."

John's disciples are also recognized in days of penance and prayer. This year too these will come and admonish us and say, "Thou art the man!" An Advent preparer thou, too, beloved congregation, shouldst be, to prepare the way all the better in your midst for the entrance of the King of Glory. Every member should help prepare the way, to help put his heart and family in a condition to welcome the Lord constantly.

"Behold, the King comes also to you!" This, again, is an Advent messenger that brings us His blessings. It is the Advent Bringer, the Advent King Himself. When the way has been prepared, when the heart has been made ready by the thunder of God's own law, then comes the Advent Bringer with His sweet gospel of grace and truth. The prophet says, "Soon [suddenly] shall the Lord come whom ye seek;" and yet four hundred years elapsed before the promise became a reality. Here, however, stands John and says, "He is in your midst. Behold the Lamb of God, which taketh away the sins of the world!" And the angel on that holy night sings, "Behold, I bring you tidings of great joy; for unto you is born this day, in the city of David, a Savior." And His disciples rejoice, saying, "And the Word became flesh and dwelt among us (and we beheld his glory, the glory as of the only begotten from the Father), full of grace and truth." Now He has come; the past, the present, and the future all join together in this wonderful Advent King.

Ask you, Who is He? The prophet calls Him "the Messenger (or angel) of the covenant." He is the Mediator of the covenant of grace between God and His people. God has built a tabernacle in Israel, the tabernacle of the Old Testament, the law covenant through Moses. But the covenant of Moses was broken by the people. Then God erected a new tabernacle in the time of the fulfilment—namely, the New Testament. He has erected it through the true angel of the covenant, His Son Jesus Christ. Out of this tabernacle shines forth the true sun of righteousness and grace, and casts its rays beyond the limits of Israel and over all mankind. For "Gospel" is the name of the law of the new covenant; it is the glad tidings of great joy, telling us that God will not have us covenant-breaking people be destroyed in our sins, but that the only-begotten Son has come to seek and to save that which is lost.

In Christ the new covenant of God with mankind has become a living and personal reality, for in Him are found united divinity and humanity. He is the Immanuel, the God with us. Now it is no longer a covenant of hard laws, but of heart-conquering grace; no longer fear, but love. Now we have a Mediator through whom we come to the Father, through whom God and all salvation come to us.

" To his temple," says our text, " the angel of the covenant will come "—*i. e.*, to the Church of the Lord, the corner-stone and foundation of which is Jesus Christ. The temple of the Lord thou art, beloved congregation; this temple thou art, O my soul, for He has saved and delivered thee, and has made thee His own.

Ever does He come to this His temple, and before Him go His words of love and mercy, and with Him come the two Jesus messengers, the Word and Sacraments, whom He sends to deliver all those who are bound; and through Word and Sacrament He Himself enters.

2. And now, since He is again announcing His Advent, and is beginning His judgment in the temple of God, who shall stand when He appears? This is what the text asks: from the text let us hear also the answer. In order to appropriate and appreciate true Advent blessings we must also have Advent hearts, in which Jesus can become an actual reality and a living power. This is done, says our text, in three ways—namely, first, when they seek and desire Jesus in faith; secondly, when they are sanctified and cleansed as by fuller's soap; and thirdly, when they are selected and are purified in the fire of the true Refiner.

First, then, to seek and to desire Jesus in faith. He who seeks Him shall also find Him, for Christ is ever near to the soul. He is to be found in His Word. When the soul thirsts for salvation, then it can quench its thirst at the fountain of God's Word. There it will find the High Priest that atones for its sins; there the Mediator between God and man; there the love of God becomes manifest to the heart. To the Word of God and in the heart of Jesus faith's anchor must cling, and then we are saved.

Alas! that the seekers of Jesus and those who strive to find the Savior are so few. If they would seek Jesus as ardently as they strive after riches and earthly goods, they would soon find Him; and yet He is the greatest of all treasures. May God give us this New Year's gift, that with burning zeal we in this new Church year seek the Lord as never before, and that the love of Christ become a consuming fire in our hearts. Be careful, then, beloved congregation, and let us, as Mary did, diligent and quiet and blessed, sit at the feet of the Lord. Ye children, seek the Lord, for if ye seek Him early ye shall find Him. Ye young men and maidens, learn from the Word of God how a young man and a maiden shall walk acceptably before the Lord. Ye fathers and mothers, do not forsake the assemblages of the saints, for the Lord has given our services the promise that where two or three are gathered together in His name, there He would be in the midst of them. Ye aged men and women, may the fire of faith lighten up and brighten your declining years, so that ye can say, with Simeon, " Lord, now lettest thou thy servant depart in peace, for mine eyes have seen thy salvation."

Out of true faith is born hope. Christ's true believers, indeed, no longer sin purposely and intentionally; but yet they do so out of weakness, being surrounded by a world of temptations without and within. Therefore they cleanse themselves daily by sorrow and repentance for their evil deeds of darkness. But there is a more complete purification than the self-purification of repentance, and that is the sanctification through Jesus Christ. He purifies us also from the dead works of our self-righteousness, and even more, He gives us holy courage and power and strength, that, in following the Lord, we become sanctified, and live as the children of God in righteousness and Christian virtues. Then we learn from Him how to deny ourselves, to adhere to Him in true faith, to become strong in love, joyful in hope.

This heavenly washer has an exceedingly fine soap with which He cleanses us and makes us acceptable to God. The pale water of mere human sympathetic tears does not suffice; He makes use of His Holy Word, which removes all falsehood, and desires, and uncleanness, and wickedness.

Do not, ye saved of the Lord, forget the Word. Without holiness no man shall see God. Strive after this that ye may enter the narrow gate, for the portal is narrow which leads to eternal life. Ever must ye remember with Paul that ye have not yet attained perfection, but that ye strive ever to become more and more Christlike.

But when a man has been cleansed in this way by the blood of redemption, then is he thoroughly and entirely clean. But the Lord will do even more than this for him. This is beautifully expressed in our text, verse 3, " And he shall sit as a refiner and purifier of silver, and he shall purify the sons of Levi and purge them as gold and silver; and they shall offer unto the Lord offerings in righteousness."

There sits the purifier at His work and stirs the fire, and watches closely until the silver makes its appearance. When this has been done, then the metal becomes separated from the dross, and it is pure and perfect.

This is the way which the heavenly smelter adopts in dealing with the souls of men. In His eyes these are the most precious gold and silver; but they are not yet pure. Therefore He stirs the fire to separate all this dross —that of self-righteousness and injustice— and burns these to ashes. Into this fire of purification all the faithful are placed, even the favorites of the Lord. How often do not trials and tribulations and misfortunes overtake us in the providence of our God; but all these have the one purpose and end of purifying our faith, of purging off the unclean elements, and making us ever more worthy to be the holy temples of our God.

Such will be a blessed Advent season to our hearts. Whenever we look in us or around about us we see only and everywhere the Lord Jesus Christ coming as the King and the Savior. Let it ever be said of us, " And they saw none save Jesus alone!" Amen.—H. R.

CHRIST'S SECOND ADVENT

By H. Melvill, D.D.

I have trodden the wine-press alone; and of the people there was none with me; for I will tread them in mine anger, and trample them in my fury; and their blood shall be sprinkled upon my garments, and I will stain all my raiment.—Isaiah lxiii: 3

I. Consider what Scripture reveals to us in regard to Christ's second advent. There is a time appointed in the history of our world, when that very Jesus who appeared on earth, "a man of sorrows and acquainted with grief," shall reappear with all the circumstances of majesty and power, "King of kings and Lord of lords." We are led to expect a day when Christ shall find a home in the remotest hearts and families, and the earth in all its circumference be covered with the knowledge and the power of the Lord. In effecting this sublime revolution, we are taught that the Jews shall be God's mightiest instruments. But it shall not be without opposition, nor without convulsion, that Satan is driven from his usurped dominion. Previously to this great consummation, and in order to the production of this, is to be what Scripture calls the second advent of Christ; and the judgments with which this second coming shall be attended and followed constitute that tremendous visitation which prophecy associates with the last times, and delineates under every figure of wo, of terror, and of wrath.

II. The Redeemer, as exhibited in our text, is returning from the slaughter of His enemies, and He describes Himself as "speaking in righteousness, mighty to save." His actions have just proved Him mighty to destroy, and His words now announce Him mighty to save; so that He is able to confound every foe and uphold every friend. The two grand principles which we expect to see maintained in every righteous government are that none of the guilty shall escape, and that none of the innocent shall perish. And in the reply given to the challenge of the prophet there is a distinct assertion that He who comes with the dyed garments from Bozrah maintains these principles of government, which cannot be maintained but by an Infinite Judge. This agrees admirably with Christ's second advent; for that is the only season at which men living on the earth shall be accurately divided into the evil and good—into those who are to be consumed, and those who are to be untouched by the visitations of wrath.—S. B., vol. iv., p. 199.

HOW TO PROVIDE FOR THE FUTURE

By Rev. Charles Cross

Matt. xxv: 31-46

This description of the general judgment is not a parable but a prophecy, altho to a great extent couched in symbolic language.

I. What to provide for the future:

1. *A good character.*—" The right-hand group will consist of those who have done right and are right, and the left-hand group of those who have done wrong and are wrong" (Jas. Morison). A good character includes righteousness: "The righteous" (verses 37, 46). Character "is moral meetness for everlasting glory" (Jas. Morison). A good character includes fitness for Christ's Kingdom: "Inherit the kingdom" (verse 34). Sheep or goats (verses 32, 33). There are no alpacas. The separation is "with unerring penetration and with infinite equity" (Richard Watson). Similar metaphor in Ezek. xxxiv: 17.

2. *A good record.*—Faith in Christ must be shown by Christ-like works. "Inasmuch as ye have done it," etc. (verse 40). Good works are a manifestation of genuine faith. Dr. Morison says: "Their faith, 'without works,' is the only condition on which they get the benefit of the great propitiation (Rom.

iii: 20-21; iv: 5, 6). But still their faith was never meant to continue without works (Jas. ii: 17). It would be of no worth if it did not work. It was meant to work; and it does work diligently (Gal. v: 6). It effloresces and bears fruit in works (Rom. vi: 22)."

II. How to provide for the future:

1. *A good character.*—By learning to love the right and hate the wrong. Love leads to action. By learning to submit to Christ "the King" (verses 34-40). Let "the King" rule, govern, and influence your life. Be loyal to Him. "They who serve the devil must share with him in the end" (Alford). If you will not submit to the King while you are on earth, you will be a rebel in the next world.

2. *Provide a good record,* by doing good as well as by being good. Study and imitate the character of Christ, "who went about doing good" (verses 35, 36). Cf. Isa. lvii: 7; Ezek. xviii: 7; Jas. i: 27; Heb. xiii: 2; 3 John v: 8; Jas. ii: 15. 16; 2 Tim. i: 16; Prov. xiv: 31, and xix: 17; Matt. x: 42; Mark iv: 41; Heb. vi: 10). "Who would

not run to prisons and hospitals on errands of mercy, if assured that Christ was there? Yet Christ Himself tells us so, and we turn a deaf ear to Him" (P. QUESNEL). "When benevolence is shown to the least of the human brotherhood, because he is a brother and a man, Christ is honored and God is glorified."—JAMES MORISON. (P. M.)

THE PROBLEM ABOUT ADVENT

BY F. D. MAURICE, D.D.

Be ye therefore ready also: for the Son of man cometh at an hour when ye think not.—Luke xii: 40

What is the problem about Advent? You hear of the Son of Man coming. Sometimes you hear of His coming as a thief in the night: sometimes you hear of His returning as a bridegroom from the wedding. In the passage from which my text is taken both these forms of speech are combined. What do they signify; are they merely figures which point to the necessity of preparation for death?

I. The first coming of Christ in great humility imports a continual lordship of His over the being and faculties of man. His purpose, the apostles teach us, was not accomplished till He rose from the dead, and ascended on high, till He had claimed the glory which He had had with His Father before the worlds were. That was the vindication of His title to be Lord. That was the beginning of a society which could be nothing but universal, because it stood in the Name of the Son of God and Son of Man. That was necessary that the promise might be thoroughly accomplished, "The Lord God shall dwell among you, and He shall be your Father, and ye shall be His children." By this language we are able to understand that other language which refers to the coming, or to the appearing and unveiling of the Son of Man after His ascension. We may very well admit that when our Lord says, "In such an hour as ye think not the Son of Man cometh," He gives us all and more than all the warning respecting the hour of death which preachers have ever drawn out of His words. Assuredly it is no contradiction of His other teaching to say that, tho on earth we may fancy ourselves under a law of selfishness, tho here we may act as if we had no ties and relationships to those who surround us, when we close our eyes on the things with which they have been familiar, we pass into a region where we shall know assuredly that the Son of Man is reigning, where it will be impossible any longer to think that we are out of His Presence, or to escape from that Divine law of love which binds man to man, which binds earth and Heaven together. The lie upon which we have acted must then be laid bare, the whole scheme of our existence must be exposed and broken in pieces; we must confess Him who gave Himself for men to be the Lord of all.

II. If this be the idea of Christ's coming, whether to the world or to individuals, which the New Testament sets before us, what is to make us ready for His coming? What is to save us from that sleep into which our Lord warns us that we may fall? What is to arouse us if it has overtaken us? Surely we must be reminded of His Presence with us. The natural notion that what is invisible is unreal; that He does not govern us because our eyes do not see Him; that He does not govern the world because the world fancies that it governs itself, this must be set at nought. We have an assurance that the senses are as little judges of what is true in morals as they are in physics; that self, which appears to be the center round which everything here revolves, is no more really the center than our earth is the center round which the heavenly bodies revolve. What shall give us this assurance? In the Eucharist we declare that our hope is in a Lamb of God which has taken away the sin of the world by the sacrifice of Himself: therefore, we ask that we may be ready when the Son of Man comes to claim us as sacrifices to God; and that we may not be found choosing another master for ourselves, and shutting ourselves up in a hell of selfishness and despair. In the Eucharist we give thanks for a death not for ourselves only, but for the whole world, therefore in it we look forward to a redemption, which shall be not for ourselves only, but for the world, when Christ shall appear without sin, unto salvation.—S. B., vol. vii., p. 199.

FAITH AT OUR LORD'S COMING

BY HOWARD CROSBY, D.D.

Nevertheless when the Son of man cometh, shall he find faith on the earth?—Luke xviii: 8

This is one of the favorite passages of our pre-millenarian brethren, teaching, as they say, that at our Lord's coming there will be very few found believing in Christ. Those of us who reject the pre-millenarian view believe that when our Lord comes again, it will be at the judgment, and that the world will then be full of His glory. We believe that the gospel will conquer the world, and that its preaching is not to be in vain. We find too many passages like Is. xi : 9; " The earth shall be full of the knowledge of the Lord as the waters cover the sea," used in direct connection with Messiah's first coming, the stem of Jesse, the Branch out of his roots, that would have to be explained away, if we adopted the theory that the world is to grow worse and worse till Christ comes again to renew it.

Well, then, what are we to do with this text from Luke? We simply call attention to the context and to the Greek.

Our Lord was teaching His disciples that they ought always to pray and not to faint, and He shows how a woman perseveres even with an unjust judge till she gets justice, and then by contrast He teaches that God's own chosen ones ought certainly to persevere in calling upon God, the *righteous* Judge, to avenge them of their wicked adversaries (compare Rev. vi : 10). It is not an unholy and selfish vengeance that is sought, but the release of the Church from its enemies, the holy action of divine justice against the powers of evil that have ever assaulted the Church and have wrought it such damage.

So much for the context. Now for the Greek. It reads thus: πλὴν ὁ υἱὸς τοῦ ἀνθρώπου ἐλθὼν ἆρα εὑρήσει τὴν πίστιν ἐπὶ τῆς γῆς : Note that πίστιν has the article This shows that the faith mentioned is a faith somewhere described in the context. The definite article here, as so often, has the force of a demonstrative pronoun. If persons have been mentioned before as the main subject, then it often has the force of a possessive pronoun. Here the faith referred to is the faith in God's avenging the Church's enemies. It is not saving faith in God as to personal salvation, and therefore synonymous with piety or godliness. Our Lord does not say, " When the Son of Man cometh, shall he find piety on the earth?" but He says: " When the Son of Man cometh, shall he find in his own chosen ones this confidence of a speedy vengeance on the Satanic forces?" The coming will be a delightful *surprise* to them, for they, tho God's faithful ones, will be halting in this particular confidence.

This is certainly the only meaning that a sound exegesis can derive from the text. Our English rendering has led many astray. The revision has put the true rendering in the margin, altho it would be still better to say " *this* faith" instead of " *the* faith." Our pre-millenarian brethren must give up this text.—H. R.

THE DAY OF THE LORD

By S. A. Brooke

The night is far spent, the day is at hand.—Rom. xiii: 12

It is more than eighteen hundred years since the apostle uttered this exulting cry. We cannot repeat it to-day when once more we come to our Advent time without some sense of hopelessness. For what has come of it? we ask; is the night gone, is the day at hand? Century after century, with the indestructible aspiration of the heart, has this note of joy been taken up, and the aspiration has been disappointed and the joy unreached. The drama of mankind has been charged with so much action, apparently wasted, and so much suffering, apparently squandered, on the ground of this incessant hope, and yet the great end seems no nearer. On and on, stumbling in the night with bleeding feet and wearied brain, the great world has struggled forward, hoping for the dawn. " There is no radiance," it mutters, " on the mountains yet. I hope for ever, that is my doom; but the night is deep, and the day delays. Would to God I could see the morning glow! "

I. St. Paul was wrong when he expected the final close in his own time; but he was right in this—that a new day was near at hand. We are wrong when we think we are near to the last great hour of time; but we are right when our heart tells us that God is coming to bring light to our own souls, to awaken our nation out of wrong into right, to set on foot new thoughts which will renew the life of mankind, for that is His continuous and Divine work. The reason, then, denies the nearness of the time when God will close this era of the world, and denies it on account of the slowness of God's work. In reality God's work is never slow or fast; it always marches at a constant pace; but to our sixty or seventy years it seems of an infinite tardiness. We live and grasp our results so hurriedly, and we have so short a time in which to work, that we naturally find ourselves becoming impatient with God. To work quickly seems to us to work well. But we forget how, even in our little life, we lose the perfection of results by too great rapidity. We seclude no hours of wise quiet, and our thought is not matured. God never makes these mistakes, the mistakes of haste. He never forgets to let a man, a nation, the whole of mankind rest at times, that they may each assimilate the results of an era of activity.

II. But tho that great day is far away, the heart asserts, and truly, that when there is deepest night over nations and the world and men, a day of the Lord is at hand; that a dawn is coming—not the last day nor the final dawn, but the uprising of Christ in light, deliverance, knowledge, and love. The belief is born not only out of our natural hatred of evil and suffering and the desire to be free, but out of actual experience. Again and again have these days of the Lord come, has the night vanished and the sunlight burst on the world, not only in religion, but in the regeneration of societies, in the revolutions of nations, in the rush of great and creative thoughts over the whole of the civilized world. Men sunk in misery, ignorance, and oppression cried to the watchers, and the prophets answered, " The night is far spent," we see the coming day. And never has their answer been left unfulfilled.—S. B., vol. ix., p. 237.

NIGHT AND DAY

Romans xiii: 11

This admonition is addressed to those who know the time, the season. To those who know something by serious meditation of the rapid flight of seasons, and their precious opportunities, of the irrecoverableness of seasons, and of the momentous issues which depend upon the diligent and faithful use of them.

I. THE RETROSPECT OF THE PAST. " The night is far spent."

1. The spiritual night of the world has been passing away, for Christ, the Sun of Righteousness, has arisen upon mankind.

2. The night of time is fast passing; out of its gloom the generations are fast emerging into the free light of eternity.

3. The night of life is nearly spent: it may be so with any; it is manifestly so with the aged. Immortality is near.

II. THE PROSPECT OF THE FUTURE.

1. " The day is at hand." The day breaks, the shadows flee away. Our ignorance, our doubts, our temptations, our fears, are all for a season, and shall soon be left behind. We shall see Him as He is, whom now we see not, tho we trust and love Him.

2. " Our salvation is nearer than when we believed." The figure is of a beleaguered fortress; the garrison is besieged, in straits, feeble, and despondent. Yet relief is planned, and approaches, and now that the morning breaks, and the weary and discouraged defenders look from the walls, and over the camp of their assailants, they behold the banners of the deliverer, and hear the welcome music of His march. So gazes the weary and harassed Church of Christ and so appears to her vision the approach of the Deliverer, the deliverance, at hand.

III. THE DUTY OF THE PRESENT. These things being so, this is no time for the indulgence of sentiment or sloth.

1. It is time to awake out of sleep—of indifference, of inactivity, of unbelief.

2. To cast off the works of darkness—the impediments to active service, the sin which doth so easily beset us.

3. To put on the armor of light. We are as Christians, not only children of light; we are soldiers of light. Let the soldier see to his weapons, the servant to his work, the steward to his trust. Thus, when the Lord cometh, shall He find us prepared to receive and to welcome Him!—H. L. S. E., vol. i., p. 12.

THE CHRISTIAN'S POSITION AND DUTY

Romans xiii: 12

Second advent of Christ great theme of Christian hope.—His first coming longed for, even by the heathen.—When He came, a faithful few welcomed Him.—But He came only to depart, promising to come again.—For the fulfilment of that promise the Church watches.—Christian hopes excited by events which seem to correspond with what Christ foretold should be signs of His coming.—Yet scoffers still cry, " Where is the promise of His coming? "—But the Church knows His promise will be fulfilled.

I. OUR PRESENT POSITION. To estimate force of these words place ourselves in apostle's position.—Writing to Christians, writing under persecution.—Jewish fanaticism and heathen superstition arrayed against them.—" The Christians to the lions," ever ringing in their ears.—How eagerly look for cessation of such a night.—Long for time when fulfilled. Isaiah ix: 18.—In Christ's death and resurrection they found key to explain prophecy.—Their hopes strengthened by what already saw fulfilled.—Rejoice in confirmation of their hope furnished by this epistle.—Europe greatly changed since then. —Christianity has established itself.—Point out benefits it has conferred on mankind. Compare society now with that of Pagan Rome, and may we not say " the night is past, the day has dawned? "—But other considerations contradict this.—What is the real condition of the world now?—Eph. vi: 12.—Darkness the element congenial to it.—Education and science may foretell " a good time coming," but this doomed world is shrouded in a moral night.—Yes, its doom is pronounced.—2 Peter iii: 10.—That sentence confirmed by men's own acts.—John iii: 19.—Desire continuance of darkness, as the thief. —Job xxiv: 17.—What a melancholy picture of the world.—But the apostle says this is fast coming to an end.—Destruction shrunk from by organized beings.—Worldly persons cannot contemplate world's end without a pang.—But disturbs not serenity of believer's confidence.—Before it is to take place, prophecy points to terrible convulsions.—War between France and Germany, overthrow of Papacy.—Seem to stand at close of 1260 days.—Think of solemn events immediately to follow.—" The day is at hand."

II. OUR DUTY ARISING OUT OF IT.—Such a day can afford no satisfaction to sinners.—Slaves of rulers of darkness, doing works of darkness.—We charged to put off these.—What are they?—Evil works, fruit of corrupt minds.—Works wrought from impulse of self-interest, having no reference to God's glory.—Nearness of eternity should operate as motive for increased purity.—Lusts of flesh, are the night-dress of the world.—An indecency about them.—As subject going to sovereign's levee, careful of his dress, so text.—Scripture represents Christian as a warrior.—Armor not worn in times of peace.—The sinner it is that is unarmed.—Satan is armed, but " his goods are in peace " lulled

by opiates.—Not so with those who have been taught " the truth as it is in Jesus."—Need armor against devil, world, and their own hearts.—Need it too for attack.—As Christians without excuse if not buckled on armor.—Charge to us is Josh. i : 9 ; 2 Tim. ii : 1.—Eminently need armor now.—2 Tim. iii : 1.—Is not truth despised, and falsehood rampant?—Is not commerce too often a gigantic system of deceit?—Even clergymen guilty of pitiful evasions, traitors to articles.—In danger of being carried away by the lax morality of present day.—Our profession of Christianity must be no lip service.—Warnings loud and frequent of Master's approach.—

" Faith's ear, with awful, still delight,
Counts them like minute-bells at night,
Keeping the heart awake till dawn of morn,
While to her funeral pile this aged world is borne."

But it is ours to be up and doing.—H. A. C. Y.

PREPARATION FOR THE SECOND COMING OF CHRIST

By Rev. Canon Liddon

Looking for and hasting unto the coming of the day of God.—2 Pet. iii : 12

I. One effect of a true love of our Lord, which expects Him to come to judgment at the last great day, will be TO KEEP THE MIND AND HEART OF MAN FREE FROM DISTRACTING FORMS OF EXCITEMENT. " The day of the Lord " has in all times been to men *believing* in Christ, but not *loving* Him, an occasion of disorderly walking, of idleness, and disobedience.

II. AND AGAIN, A TRUE LOVE OF OUR LORD IN VIEW OF HIS COMING AT THE DAY OF JUDGMENT IS GREATLY CONCERNED TO BE DOING THE BEST IT CAN WITH WHAT HE HAS GIVEN IN THE WAY OF ABILITY AND OF OPPORTUNITY. This is our Lord's own teaching in the parable of the talents. In that parable there is one lesson which we cannot lay too seriously to heart. It is the temptation to do nothing,

to which the man with one talent yielded, and because he had only one talent.

III. ONE OTHER RESULT OF THE LOVE OF OUR LORD, OF WAITING FOR AND HASTING UNTO HIS COMING, WILL BE TO MAKE MUCH OF PRAYER, PRIVATE AND PUBLIC, AS A PREPARATION FOR IT. In one aspect, worship is a mode of accustoming the eye and ear of the soul to the sights and sounds of the coming life.

IV. IT MAY, INDEED, BE ASKED HOW, STRICTLY SPEAKING, WE CAN HASTEN TOWARD THE DAY OF GOD IN ANY OF THE WAYS DESCRIBED? We can make it nearer to us by duty, prayer, love—through which we approach the secret of eternal life, in which a thousand years are as one day.—H. R.

THE BOOKS OPENED

By Rev. A. G. Houghton

Rev. xx : 12

Nothing can be more certain than a universal judgment; whether we consider *(a)* the character of God, *(b)* the powers with which we are endowed : *(c)* the present unequal distribution of things, *(d)* the judgments inflicted on nations and individuals, or *(e)* the general feeling of mankind throughout the world of the *need* of a judgment. If

justice is to be done, reliable evidence must be forthcoming. We cannot know to the fullest extent what this evidence will be, but suggestions are not wanting in the Scriptures of the direction in which we may look for it. Certain books will be opened.

I. THE BOOK OF PROVIDENCE. God is always working to bring about man's highest good. He controls time, matter, and will, with this end in view. When this book is opened it will be shown how many conjunctions of circumstances there have been to secure our salvation.

II. THE BOOK OF MEMORY. The Chinese artist, it is said, has no india-rubber. Every line he sketches must remain. So the actions of life are indelible. And as the actions cannot be obliterated, so the knowledge of them can never be lost. Out of *sight* it may be, but not really out of mind. In the day of judgment when God says, " Son, remember ! " memory will play its part unfettered by the flesh, and every act of our life will come flashing back once more into vividness.

III. THE BOOK OF CONSCIENCE. Every man's soul has something to say about the moral government of God. In the day of judgment conscience will be interrogated and its verdicts on human action recorded. One of the Swedish kings could never bear to lie awake in the night without music playing,

while another king declared that he lived, yet for his misdeeds he died daily. In an opposite strain one of God's servants said, " How pleasant it is to have the bird in the bosom sing sweetly."

IV. THE BIBLE. In view of the open Bible, with its commands and promises the question will be asked, " What did you do with this Book ? " The Bible is the final court of appeal, and to despise or neglect it, knowing its value, is to choose eternal death. Where the Bible is, the individual is without excuse. (See Luke xvi : 29-31.)

V. THE BOOK OF LIFE. This will be opened to see if our names are inscribed therein. As soon as there is any real change of heart toward God, our names are entered there. Wherever else they may be (in the class-book or on the Church roll) if they are not found in the Lamb's Book of Life we are not safe. Let me ask if you are living within sight of the open books? and how it will be with you in the Day of Judgment? (2 Cor. v : 10.) P. M., vol. vii., p. 363.

SUGGESTIVE THOUGHTS AND ILLUSTRATIONS

ADVENT, Christ's Second.—It is described by many figures and in many ways in the Bible. The Bridegroom going forth to meet the Bride, Matt. xxv : 1-13. The Master returning to distribute His awards, Luke xix : 12; Matt. xxiv : 43-51; xxv : 14-30. The Time of Harvest, Matt. xiii : 30; Rev. xiv : 15; and of Vintage, Rev. xiv : 17-20. The Breaking forth and dawn of day (Cant. ii : 17; iv : 6) ; 2 Pet. i : 19. The Marriage Supper of the Lamb, Matt. xxii : 1-14; Rev. xix : 6-9. The Times of Refreshing, Acts iii : 19. The Times of the Restitution of all things, Acts iii : 21. The Times of Separation—when the gospel net shall be brought to shore, Matt. xiii : 47-50; and the Shepherd shall divide the sheep from the goats, Matt. xxv : 31-46. " The day of our Lord Jesus Christ," 1 Cor. i : 8, spoken of emphatically as the one great day (" the day for which all other days were made "). Hence described as " that day " three times in one epistle, 2 Tim. i : 12-18; iv : 8; see also Mark xiii : 32. " That hour," Mark xiii : 32; John v : 28. The very frequent recurrence of the expression " in that day," through the prophets, may be seen by the Concordance. It constantly refers to the great and final day. As an example see Zach. xii : 14, where the expression occurs fifteen times. The day of the manifestation of the Son of God, Rom. viii : 19; 2 Cor. v : 11 (Greek), when " the Chief Shepherd shall appear," and His saints shall appear with Him in glory, 1 Pet. v : 4; Col. iii : 4. The suddenness of Christ's coming is illustrated by the lightning flash, alike sudden, terrible, irresistible, Matt. xxiv : 27. A snare or trap, Luke xxi : 35; surprising the secure and unsuspecting. A thief in the night, Matt. xxiv :

43; 1 Thess. v : 2; Rev. xvi : 15. It will be unlooked for by a gay and scoffing world. " As it was in the days of Noah," and " of Lot," Luke xvii : 26-30. See also Luke xviii : 8; 2 Pet. iii : 3-10. Nevertheless there is a waiting for it. The whole creation is earnestly expecting the great day of liberation (expecting, as the Greek word imports, like one stretching out the neck with longing looks), Rom. viii : 19-22. The Church of Christ is waiting—groaning for complete redemption, Rom. viii : 23. The members of Christ's Church are now, and will be, " looking," " watching," " praying," " waiting " for His appearance—loving the anticipation, and hasting toward it; like the wise virgins waiting for the Bridegroom, Matt. xxv : 1-13; like the wise servant waiting for the Master, Matt. xxiv : 45; Luke xii : 35, 36; like patient laborers waiting for the earth's ripe fruits, Jas. v : 7, 8; like those night watchers who keep their garments, and are not like watchmen sleeping at their posts, Rev. xvi : 15.—BOWES.

ADVENT, Expected.—It is a very remarkable fact, that God's prophecies respecting the Advent of His Son seem to have spread athwart the whole habitable globe, and in the shape of traditional echoes to have been dispersed over all the world. The great promise of a Messiah, which was the grand truth that the Jew clung to in his most desperate fortunes, found itself translated into heathen tongues, and accepted even by heathen men. For instance, the poet Virgil dedicates a poem to Pollis, his patron, in which he says that one would soon be born into the world who, it was expected, would bring in the golden age. Suetonius, an ancient historian, states, too, what is a remarkable proof of the spread of this idea, that a certain and settled persuasion prevailed in the East, that the cities of Judea would bring forth, about this time, a person who should obtain universal empire. And Tacitus, the eloquent historian, but the very incredulous one, who called the Christian religion *execrabilis superstitio,* states that it was contained in the ancient books of the Jewish priests that the East should prevail, and that a power should proceed from Judea that should possess universal dominion. These were scattered lights that went out from Judea, their reuniting center, and gave the heathen an anticipation and persuasion that some great and illustrious deliverer was about to be born in the world.—TRENCH.

ADVENT, Faith in the.—I die in the faith of the speedy accomplishment of those glorious things which are spoken concerning the city of God and of the kingdom of Christ. "Amen. Even so, Lord Jesus! Come quickly!"—INCREASE MATHER.

ADVENT, Glory of the.—There is an account come of the arrival of King George II. and a great rejoicing for it in Edinburgh. I see the fires and illuminations of that city reflected on the skies. O, how will the heavens reflect and shine with illuminations, when the King of Kings, and Lord of Lords, shall erect His tribunal in the clouds, and come in His own glory, and His Father's glory, and in the glory of the holy angels! O, what a heartsome day will that be! When Christ, who is our life, shall appear, then shall we appear with Him in glory. We shall then lift up our heads with joy, because it shall be a time of refreshing from the presence of the Lord.—EBENEZER ERSKINE.

ADVENT, Joy at the.—"I remember," says the writer of Mr. John Janeway's life, "once there was a great talk that one had foretold that doomsday should be on such a day. Altho he blamed their daring folly that could pretend to know that which was hid, yet, granting their suspicion to be true, "What then?" said he; "what if the day of judgment were come, as it will most certainly come shortly? If I were sure the day of judgment were to come within an hour, I should be glad with all my heart. If, at this instant, I should hear such thunderings, and see such lightnings, as Israel did at Mount Sinai. I am persuaded my very heart would leap for joy. But this I am confident of, through infinite mercy, that the very meditation of that day hath even ravished my soul, and the thought of the certainty and nearness of it is more refreshing to me than the comforts of the whole world."—F. II.

ADVENT, Looking for the.—I was told of a poor peasant on the Welsh mountains who, month after month, year after year, through a long period of declining life, was used every morning, as soon as he awoke, to open his casement window toward the east, and look out to see if Jesus Christ was coming. He was no calculator, or he need not have looked so long; he was no student of prophecy, or he need not have looked at all; he was ready, or he would not have been in so much haste; he was willing, or he would rather have looked another way; he loved, or it would not have been the first thought of the morning. His Master did not come, but a messenger did, to fetch the ready one home. The same preparation sufficed for both; the longing soul was satisfied with either. Often when, in the morning, the child of God awakes, weary and encumbered with the flesh, perhaps from troubled dreams, perhaps with troubled thoughts, his Father's secret comes presently across him, he looks up, if not out, to feel, if not to see, the glories of that last morning when the trumpet shall sound, and the dead shall arise indestructible; no weary limbs to bear the spirit down; no feverish dreams to haunt the vision; no dark forecasting of the day's events, or returning memory of the griefs of yesterday.—FRY.

ADVENT, Prayers for the.—The words "Come, Lord Jesus," have often been on the lips of departing believers. They were the last uttered by Burkitt. They were the closing prayer of Bishop Abbott, who died early in the seventeenth century. "It is death: It is death," exclaimed Robert Hall, "Oh, the sufferings of this body!" His wife then asked him, "But you are comfortable in your mind?" He answered, "Very comfortable," adding, "Come, Lord Jesus, come." He then hesitated, as if unable to utter the next word, and one of his daughters added, "Quickly;" whereupon her dying father gave her a look expressive of the utmost delight. Lady Colquhoun seemed to long for her release, and frequently repeated the words "Come, Lord Jesus, come quickly." Dr. Andrew Eliot, of Boston, in his last sickness, expressed unshaken confidence in the doctrines of grace which he had preached, and would frequently breathe the ejaculation, "Come, Lord Jesus, come quickly." Under similar circumstances, the Rev. Dr. Joseph Sewall was sometimes heard to say, with great pathos, "Come, Lord Jesus, come quickly." The last words of the pious Henry Holmes, of Boston, were, "Lord Jesus, come quickly." In their primary sense, as referring to Christ's personal and glorious advent, these words have often dropped from the lips and pens of earnest believers. In a somewhat desponding mood, Martin Luther broke out, "May the Lord Jesus come at once! Let Him cut the whole matter short with the Day of Judgment; for there is no amendment to be expected." The martyr Ridley wrote: "The world, without doubt—this I do believe, and therefore say it—draws toward an end. Let us with John, the servant of God, cry in our hearts unto our Savior, Christ, 'Come, Lord Jesus, come.'"—DR. A. C. THOMPSON.

ADVENT, The Second.—As every student of the Greek New Testament knows, there are three words which are employed with reference to the return to earth of our Savior Jesus Christ. All the three are so frequently used that they have become almost English words. The first of these is *parousia*, which Thayer defines as "the presence of one coming, hence the coming, arrival, advent." He goes on to say that it is "employed in the New Testament especially of *the advent*, that is the future visible return from Heaven of Jesus the Messiah to raise the dead, hold the last judgment, and set up formally and gloriously the kingdom of God." The second word is *epiphaneia* from which we have the English word "epiphany." Thayer says it means "in the New Testament the 'advent' of Christ—not only that which has already taken place, 2 Tim. i: 10; but also that illustrious return from Heaven to earth hereafter to occur, 1 Tim. vi: 14; 2 Tim. iv: 1, 8; Titus ii: 13." He also translates the word in 2 Thess. ii: 8, as meaning "the breaking forth" of His coming. The third word is *apokalupsis*, which we have in English as "apocalypse," or revelation. Thayer states that it means the return of Christ in 2 Thess. i: 7; 1 Cor. i: 7; 1 Peter i: 7, 13; and that in 1 Peter iv: 13 it refers to "the glory, clothed with which he will return."—*Selected*.

ADVENT, The Second.—Did you ever hear the sound of the trumpets which are blown before the judges as they come into a city to open the assizes? Did you ever reflect how different are the feelings which those trumpets awaken in the minds of different men? The innocent man, who has no cause to be tried, hears them unmoved. They proclaim no terrors to him. He listens and looks on quietly, and is not afraid. But often there is some poor wretch waiting his trial, in a silent cell, to whom those trumpets are a knell of despair. They tell him that the day of trial is at hand. Yet a little time, and he will stand at the bar of justice, and hear witness after witness telling the story of his misdeeds. Yet a little time and all will be over,—the trial, the verdict, the sentence; and there will remain nothing for him but punishment and disgrace. No wonder the prisoner's heart beats when he hears the trumpet's sound! So shall the sound be of the archangel's trump.—J. C. RYLE.

ADVENT, Welcoming the.—No man rightly desires Christ's coming, but he that hath assurance of benefit at His coming. To him the day of Christ is as the day of harvest to the husbandman; as the day of deliverance to the prisoner; as the day of coronation to the king; the day of wedlock to the bride; a day of triumph and exultation, a day of freedom and consolation, a day of rest and satisfaction. To him the Lord Jesus is all sweetness, as wine to the palate, and ointment to the nostrils, saith Solomon; honey to the mouth, saith St. Bernard; music in the ear, and a jubilee in the heart. Get assurance of Christ's coming, as a ransomer to redeem you, as a conqueror to subdue all your enemies under you, as a friend to comfort you, as a bridegroom to marry you, and then shall you with boldness and confidence, with joy and gladness, with vehement and

holy longings, say, "Come, Lord Jesus."—GROSSE.

CHRIST TO JUDGE THE WORLD, The Second Coming of.—*And the dead were judged out of those things which were written in the books according to their works.—Rev. xx: 13.* The judgment then to be given will be perfectly fair, for it will be based on the light and opportunities which each one has received. The African savage, the slave in Chinatown, and the heathen at home or abroad, who are groping their way in the darkness of superstition, will not be judged by the same standard as the Christian who walks in the white light of truth. Whoso has been offered the truth and rejects it because he prefers to walk in darkness, will be strictly judged. All will appear before the Son of Man, who reads every heart and will judge aright.

Our whole lives will be judged; not a part only. Do not think we may sin with impunity now if only we repent before we die. Do not suppose we may sow our wild oats in youth without a fearful reaping by and by. Every sin committed enters into the quality of our character, and, even if repented of, lessens our capacity for enjoying the spiritual delights of the future state.—REV. W. H. MORELAND. (H. R.)

DUTY, Faithful to.—During the dark day of 1780, in Connecticut the candles were lighted in many houses, and domestic fowls went to their roost. The people thought the day of judgment had come. The legislature was then in session in Hartford. The house of representatives adjourned. In the council, it was also proposed. Col. Davenport objected, saying, "The day of judgment is either approaching, or it is not. If it is not, there is no cause for adjourning; if it is, I choose to be found doing my duty. I wish, therefore, that candles may be brought."—F. I.

FREEDOM, Watching for.—In the year 1830, on the night preceding the 1st of August, the day the slaves in our West-Indian colonies were to come into possession of the freedom promised them, many of them, we are told, never went to bed at all. Thousands and tens of thousands of them assembled in their places of worship, engaging in devotional duties, and singing praises to God, waiting for the first streak of the light of the morning of that day on which they were to be made free. Some of their number were sent to the hills, from which they might obtain the first view of the coming day, and, by a signal, intimate to their brethren down in the valley the dawn of that day that was to make them men, and no longer, as they had hitherto been, mere goods and chattels,—men with souls that God had created to live forever. How eagerly must these men have watched for the morning!—REV. T. W. AVELING.

JUDGMENT-DAY, Appeal to the.—I am content to wait till the judgment-day for the clearing up of my character; and, after I am dead, I desire no other epitaph than this,

"Here lies George Whitefield." What sort of a man he was the great day will discover. —WHITEFIELD.

JUDGMENT-DAY, Awards of the.— There is a machine in the Bank of England which receives sovereigns, as a mill receives grain, for the purpose of determining wholesale whether they are of full weight. As they pass through, the machinery, by unerring laws, throws all that are light to one side, and all that are of full weight to another. That process is a silent but solemn parable for me. Founded as it is upon the laws of Nature, it affords the most vivid similitude of the certainty which characterizes the judgment of the great day. There are no mistakes or partialities to which the light may trust: the only hope lies in being of standard weight before they go in.—ARNOT.

JUDGMENT-DAY, Certainty of the.— The bringing into judgment is a thing which is known by reason, and is clear by the light of nature; wherefore, in Austria, one of the nobles dying, who had lived fourscore and thirteen years, and had spent all his life in pleasures and delights, never being troubled with any infirmity, and this being told to Frederick the emperor, " From hence," saith he, " we may conclude the soul's immortality; for if there be a God that ruleth this world, as divines and philosophers do teach, and that He is just no one denieth, surely there are other places to which souls after death do go, and do receive for their deeds either reward or punishment; for here we see that neither rewards are given to the good, nor punishment to the evil."—BROOKS.

JUDGMENT-DAY, Disclosures of the. —The philosophic historian is expected not only to tell us that certain events occurred, but also to trace them to their origin, and tell how it was they were brought about; the skilful physician is expected not only to discern the marks of disease, but also to trace it to its source, and tell us what functions are deranged; but, in arguing from the seen and known to the unseen and the unknown, how often, how grievously do they err. A time, however, is coming when there shall be a great bringing together of causes and effects, of motives and actions, and when no mistake shall be made—that time is the judgment-day; then it shall be seen not only what men did, but why they did it.—POWER.

JUDGMENT-DAY, Discoursing on the. —When Jonathan Edwards preached at Enfield, there was " such a breathing of distress," that he was compelled to stop, and request the people to retain their composure. He discoursed on the judgment to come, as if he were standing on " the sides of eternity," and the people heard him as if they were listening to the sound of " the last trump," or to their own sentences of condemnation from the lips of the Son of God.— TURNBULL.

JUDGMENT-DAY, Universal.—As some go to the assizes to receive their judgment and condemnation, and others to give evidence against them; so shall it be at the last day. As, at the bar of an earthly judge, the malefactor is brought out of prison, and set before the judge for examination; so, in that great day, shall every man, without exception, be brought before the Lord to be tried. —CAWDRAY.

JUDGMENT, Indifference to the.— When Channing was a boy of ten years, he heard Dr. Hopkins preach a forcible sermon on the reasonableness of a future judgment. He was deeply impressed, and expected his father, who was a deacon of the Congregational Church, to speak to him about his soul's salvation. He did not utter a word in regard to the sermon, or his danger, but, on reaching home, sat down to read. Dr. Channing says, " I made up my mind that my father did not believe one word that he had heard. He was not alarmed, why should I be? and I dismissed the whole subject from my thoughts." His father's thoughtlessness drove him into the ranks of heterodoxy, and he became the champion of Unitarianism.—F. II.

JUDGMENT, Lesson of the.—A young man who graduated at West Point said, so intense was the feeling and anxiety felt with regard to the final examination at the close of the course, that the first scholar in his class fainted and fell at the first question asked him. He felt that his standing in the profession he had chosen was now at stake, that his future position depended upon the manner in which he acquitted himself. If the loss or gain of a little worldly distinction could so move a man, what must be the feeling of the soul as it stands alone at the bar of God? We shall be judged as individuals. West Point honors are but for the little moment of time here, but the results of this final examination are for eternity. The cadet keeps this examination constantly in view. He studies and drills with the wrestler's earnestness to attain a high standing at the close. How strange that we so lose sight of this solemn hour! There are often mistakes made in worldly judgment, but there will be no mistake there.—S. S. T.

JUDGMENT, Prejudice in. — Nero thought no person chaste, because he was so unchaste himself. Such as are troubled with the jaundice see all things yellow. Those who are most religious, are least censorious. " Who art thou that judgest another man's servant! " Those who are fellow creatures with men, should not be fellow judges with God.—SECKER.

JUDGMENT, Slighting the.—A man would be counted a fool to slight a judge before whom he is to have a trial of his whole estate. The trial we have before God is of otherwise importance; it concerns our eternal happiness or misery; and yet dare we affront Him?—BUNYAN.

JUDGMENT, Storm of.—As that storm roars the loudest which has been the longest gathering, so God's reckoning day with sinners, by being long coming, will be the more terrible when it comes.—GUTHRIE.

JUDGMENT, The Sinner at the.—At the day of judgment, the attention excited by the surrounding scene, the strange aspect of nature, the dissolution of the elements, and the last trump, will have no other effect than to cause the reflections of the sinner to return with a more overwhelming tide on his own character, his sentence, his unchanging destiny; and amidst the innumerable millions who surround him, he will mourn apart. It is thus the Christian minister should endeavor to prepare the tribunal of conscience, and turn the eyes of every one of his hearers on himself.—ROBERT HALL.

JUDGMENT, The Worldling at the.—Chosroes, King of Persia, in conversation with two philosophers and his vizier, asked, "What situation of man is most to be deplored?" One of the philosophers maintained that it was old age, accompanied with extreme poverty; the other, that it was to have the body oppressed by infirmities, the mind worn out, and the heart broken by a heavy series of misfortunes. "I know a condition more to be pitied," said the vizier, "and it is that of him who has passed through life without doing good, and who, unexpectedly surprised by death, is sent to appear before the tribunal of the sovereign Judge."—WHITECROSS.

WORLD, Destruction of the.—The cool night arrived, and, about half-past eight, I was lying half asleep. I fancied I heard a rumbling like distant thunder. I had not heard such a sound for months; but a low, uninterrupted roll appeared to increase in volume, altho far distant. Hardly had I raised my head to listen more attentively, when a confusion of voices arose from the Arab's camp with a sound of many feet; and, in a few minutes, they rushed into my camp, shouting to my men in the darkness, "El bahr! El bahr!" "The river, the river!" We were up in an instant; and my interpreter, Mahomed, in a state of confusion, explained the river was coming down, and that the supposed distant thunder was the roar of the approaching water. Many of the people were asleep on the clean sand of the river's bed: these were awakened by the Arabs, who rushed down the steep bank to save the skull of my two hippopotami that were exposed to dry. Hardly had they descended, when the sound of the river in the darkness beneath told us that the water had arrived; and the men had just sufficient time to drag their heavy burdens up the bank. All was darkness and confusion; everybody was talking, and no one listening; but the great event had occurred,—the river had arrived "like a thief in the night," as it is said the end of the world shall come.—BAKER.

POETRY

Suddenness of the Advent

By H. H. MILMAN

Matthew xxiv: 37-39

Even thus amid thy pride and luxury,
O earth! shall that last coming burst on thee,
That second coming of the Son of man.
When all the cherub-throning clouds shall shine,
Irradiate with His bright advancing sign:
When that Great Husbandman shall wave His fan,
Sweeping, like chaff, thy wealth and pomp away:
Still to the noontide of that nightless day,
Shalt thou thy wonted dissolute course maintain.
Along the busy mart and crowded street,
The buyer and the seller still shall meet,
And marriage feasts begin their jocund strain:
Still to the pouring out the cup of wo;
Till earth, a drunkard, reeling to and fro,
And mountains molten by His burning feet,
And heaven, His presence own, all red with furnace heat.

The hundred-gated, cities, then,
The towers and temples, named of men,
Eternal, and the thrones of kings;
The gilded summer palaces,

The courtly bowers of love and ease,
Where still the bird of pleasure sings:
Ask ye the destiny of them?
Go gaze on fallen Jerusalem!
Yea, mightier names are in the fatal roll,
'Gainst earth and heaven God's standard is unfurled,
The skies are shriveled like a burning scroll,
And the vast common doom ensepulchers the world.

Oh! who shall then survive?
Oh! who shall stand and live?
When all that hath been is no more:
When for the round earth hung in air,
With all its constellations fair,
In the sky's azure canopy:
When for the breathing earth, and sparkling sea,
Is but a fiery deluge without shore,
Heaving along the abyss profound and dark,
A fiery deluge, and without an ark.

Lord of all power, when Thou art there alone
On Thy eternal fiery-wheeled throne,
That in its high meridian noon
Needs not the perished sun nor moon:
When Thou art there in Thy presiding state,

Wide-sceptered monarch o'er the realm of
doom:
When from the sea depths, from earth's
darkest womb,
The dead of all the ages round Thee wait:
And when the tribes of wickedness are
strewn
Like forest leaves in the autumn of Thine
ire:
Faithful and true Thou still wilt save Thine
own!
The saints shall dwell within th' unharm-
ing fire,
Each white robe spotless, blooming every
palm.
Even safe as we, by this still fountain's
side,
So shall the Church, Thy bright and mystic
bride,
Sit on the stormy gulf a halcyon bird of calm.
Yes, 'mid yon angry and destroying signs,
O'er us the rainbow of Thy mercy shines,
We hail, we bless the covenant of its beam,
Almighty to avenge, Almightiest to redeem!

Waiting for the Second Advent

ANONYMOUS

What of the night, watchman, what of the
night?
The wintry gale sweeps by,
The thick shadows fall, and the night-bird's
call
Sounds mournfully through the sky.

The night is dark, it is long and drear,
But who, while others sleep,
Is that little band, who together stand,
And their patient vigils keep?

All awake is the strained eye,
And awake the listening ear:
For their Lord they wait, and watch at the
gate
His chariot-wheels to hear.

Long have they waited—that little band,
And ever and anon
To fancy's eye the dawn seemed nigh,
The night seemed almost gone.

And often, through the midnight gale,
They thought they heard at last
The sound of His train, and they listened
again,
And the sound died away on the blast.

Ages have rolled, and one by one
Those watchers have passed away;
They heard the call on their glad ear fall,
And they hastened to obey.

And in their place their children stand,
And still their vigils keep,
They watch and pray for the dawn of day,
For this is no time for sleep.

What of the night, watchman, what of the
night?
Tho the wintry gales sweep by,
When the darkest hour begins to lower
We know that the dawn is nigh.

Courage, ye servants of the Lord,
The night is almost o'er;
Your Master will come and call you home,
To weep and to watch no more.
*F. II.

Approaching Advent

BY HORATIUS BONAR

Revelation xxii: 20

He is coming; and the tidings
Are rolling wide and far;
As light flows out in gladness,
From yon fair morning-star.

He is coming; and the tidings
Sweep through the willing air,
With hope that ends forever
Time's ages of despair.

Old earth from dreams and slumber
Wakes up and says, Amen;
Land and ocean bid Him welcome
Flood and forest join the strain.

He is coming; and the mountains
Of Judea ring again;
Jerusalem awakens,
And shouts her glad Amen.

He is coming; wastes of Horeb,
Awaken and rejoice!
Hills of Moab, cliffs of Edom,
Lift the long silent voice!

He is coming, sea of Sodom,
To heal thy leprous brine,
To give back palm and myrtle,
The olive and the vine.

He is coming, blighted Carmel,
To restore thy olive bowers.
He is coming, faded Sharon,
To give thee back thy flowers.

Sons of Gentile-trodden Judah,
Awake, behold, He comes!
Landless and kingless exiles,
Re-seek your long-lost homes.

Back to your ancient valleys
Which your fathers loved so well,
In their now crumbled cities
Let their children's children dwell.

Drink the last drop of wormwood
From your nation's bitter cup;
The bitterest but the latest,
Make haste and drink it up.

For He thy true Messiah,
Thine own anointed King,
He comes, in love and glory,
Thy endless joy to bring.

Yes, He thy King is coming
To end thy woes and wrongs,
To give thee joy for mourning,
To turn thy sighs to songs;

To dry the tears of ages,
  To give thee as of old,
The diadem of beauty,
  The crown of purest gold;

To lift thee from thy sadness,
  To set thee on the throne,
Messiah's chosen nation,
  His best-beloved one.

The stain and dust of exile
  To wipe from thy weary feet;
With songs of glorious triumph
  Thy glad return to greet.
                              *F. II.

Advent Hymn

By F. B. D.

1 John iii: 2

" We shall see Him as He is,"
  Not as once He came to earth,
When the angel chorus sang,
  At His lowly human birth.

Seated on the eternal throne,
  On His vesture and His thigh,
Is a name forever writ,
  Holiness to God Most High.

Yet the pierced hand is there,
  And the wound-print in His side,
Whence there flows the healing stream,
  In a never ending tide.

Very God and very man,
  Thus He rose from Judah's plain,
Thus He lives and reigns on high,
  Thus at last He comes again.

Sing we then with joyful song,
  Tho His form on earth we miss,
Be the waiting short or long,
  " We shall see Him as He is."—E.

Prayer for the Advent

By Horatius Bonar

Revelation xxii: 20

The Church has waited long,
  Her absent Lord to see;
And still in loneliness she waits,
  A friendless stranger she.
Age after age has gone,
  Sun after sun has set,
And still, in weeds of widowhood,
  She weeps, a mourner yet.
Come, then, Lord Jesus, come!

Saint after saint on earth
  Has lived and loved and died;
And as they left us one by one,
  We laid them side by side.
We laid them down to sleep,
  But not in hope forlorn;
We laid them but to ripen there,
  Till the last glorious morn.
Come, then, Lord Jesus, come!

The serpent's brood increase,
  The powers of hell grow bold,
The conflict thickens, faith is low,
  And love is waxing cold.
How long, O Lord our God!
  Holy and true and good,
Wilt Thou not judge Thy suffering Church
  Her sighs and tears and blood?
Come, then, Lord Jesus come!

We long to hear Thy voice,
  To see Thee face to face,
To share Thy crown and glory then,
  As now we share Thy grace.
Should not the loving bride
  Her absent bridegroom mourn?
Should she not wear the signs of grief
  Until her Lord return?
Come, then, Lord Jesus come!

The whole creation groans,
  And waits to hear that voice,
That shall restore her comeliness,
  And make her wastes rejoice.
Come, Lord, and wipe away
  The curse, the sin, the stain,
And make this blighted world of ours
  Thine own fair world again.
Come, then, Lord Jesus, come!
                              *F. II.

The First Sunday in Advent

By John Keble

*Now it is high time to awake out of sleep:
for now is our salvation nearer than when
we believed.—Rom. xiii: 11.*

Awake! again the gospel-trump is blown,
  From year to year it swells with louder
    tone,
  From year to year the signs of wrath
    Are gathering round the Judge's path,
Strange words fulfilled, and mighty works
    achieved,
And truth in all the world both hated and
    believed.

Awake! why linger in the gorgeous town,
Sworn liegemen of the Cross and thorny
    crown?
  Up from your beds of sloth for shame,
  Speed to the eastern mount like flame,
Nor wonder, should ye find your King in
    tears,
Even with the loud Hosanna ringing in His
    ears.

Alas! no need to rouse them: long ago
They are gone forth to swell Messiah's show:
  With glittering robes and garlands sweet
  They strew the ground beneath His feet:
All but your hearts are there—O doom'd to
    prove
The arrows winged in Heaven for Faith that
    will not love!

Meanwhile He paces through the adoring
    crowd,
Calm as the march of some majestic cloud
  That o'er wild scenes of ocean war
  Holds its still course in heaven afar:

Even so, heart-searching Lord, as years roll
  on,
Thou keepest silent watch from Thy triumphal throne:

Even so, the world is thronging round to
  gaze
On the dread vision of the latter days,
  Constrained to own Thee, but in heart
  Prepared to take Barabbas' part:
"Hosanna" now, to-morrow "Crucify,"
The changeful burden still of their rude law-
  less cry.

Yet in that throng of selfish hearts untrue
Thy sad eye rests upon Thy faithful few;
  Children and childlike souls are there,
  Blind Bartimeus' humble prayer,
And Lazarus wakened from his four days'
  sleep,
Enduring life again, that Passover to keep.

And fast beside the olive-bordered way
Stands the blest home where Jesus deigned
  to stay,
  The peaceful home, to Zeal sincere
  And heavenly Contemplation dear,
When Martha loved to wait with reverence
  meet,
And wiser Mary lingered at Thy sacred feet.

Still through decaying ages as they glide,
Thou lovest Thy chosen remnant to divide;
  Sprinkled along the waste of years
  Full many a soft green isle appears:
Pause where we may upon the desert road,
Some shelter is in sight, some sacred safe
  abode.

When withering blasts of error swept the
  sky,*
And Love's last flower seemed fain to droop
  and die,
  How sweet, how lone the ray benign
  On sheltered nooks of Palestine!
Then to his early home did Love repair,†
And cheered his sickening heart with his
  own native air.

Years roll away! again the tide of crime
Has swept Thy footsteps from the favored
  clime,
  Where shall the holy Cross find rest?
  On a crowned monarch's mailed breast.‡
Like some bright angel o'er the darkling
  scene,
Through court and camp he holds his heaven-
  ward course serene.

A fouler vision yet; an age of light,
Light without love, glares on the aching
  sight:
  O who can tell how calm and sweet,
  Meek Walton! shows thy green retreat,
When wearied with the tale thy times dis-
  close,
The eye first finds thee out in thy secure
  repose?

Thus bad and good their several warnings
  give
Of His approach, whom none may see and
  live:
  Faith's ear, with awful still delight,
  Counts them like minute-bells at night,
Keeping the heart awake till dawn of morn,
While to her funeral pile this aged world is
  borne.

But what are Heaven's alarms to hearts that
  cower
In wilful slumber, deepening every hour,
  That draw their curtains closer round,
  The nearer swells the trumpet's sound!
Lord, ere our trembling lamps sink down and
  die,
Touch us with chastening hand, and make us
  feel Thee nigh.

Two Advents

By William C. Doane

He came not with His heavenly crown, His
  scepter clad with power:
His coming was in feebleness, the infant of
  an hour;
An humble manger cradled, first, the Virgin's
  holy birth,
And lowing herds companioned there the
  Lord of heaven and earth.

He came not in His robe of wrath, with arm
  outstretched to slay,
But on the darkling paths of earth to pour
  celestial day;
To guide in peace the wandering feet, the
  broken heart to bind;
And bear, upon the painful cross, the sins
  of human kind.

Yet once again Thy sign shall be upon the
  heavens displayed,
And earth and its inhabitants be terribly
  afraid;
For not in weakness clad Thou com'st our
  woes, our sins, to bear,
But girt with all Thy Father's might, His
  vengeance to declare.

The terrors of that awful day, oh! who
  shall understand?
Or who abide when Thou in wrath shalt
  lift Thy holy hand?
The earth shall quake, the sea shall roar,
  the sun in heaven grow pale,
But Thou hast sworn, and wilt not change,
  Thy faithful will not fail.

Then grant us, Savior! so to pass our time
  in trembling here,
That when upon the clouds of heaven Thy
  glory shall appear,
Uplifting high our joyful heads in triumph
  we may rise,
And enter, with Thine angel train, Thy temple, in the skies!

---

* Arianism in the fourth century.   † See St. Jerome's Works, i. 123. Edit. Erasm.
‡ St. Louis in the thirteenth century.

Dies Irae

TR. BY WILLIAM J. IRONS

Day of wrath! O day of mourning!
See once more the cross returning,
Heaven and earth to ashes burning!
O what fear man's bosom rendeth,
When from heaven the Judge descendeth,
On whose sentence all dependeth!

Wondrous sound the trumpet flingeth;
Through earth's sepulchers it ringeth;
All before the throne it bringeth.
Death is struck, and nature quaking,
All creation is awaking,
To its Judge an answer making.

What shall I, frail man, be pleading?
Who for me be interceding,
When the just are mercy needing?
King of majesty tremendous,
Who dost free salvation send us,
Fount of pity! then befriend us!

Think, good Jesus, my salvation
Cost Thy wondrous incarnation;
Leave me not to reprobation!
Faint and weary Thou hast sought me,
On the cross of suffering bought me.
Shall such grace be vainly brought me?

Day of sorrows, day of weeping,
When, in dust no longer sleeping,
Man awakes in Thy dread keeping!
To the rest Thou didst prepare him;
By Thy cross, O Christ, upbear him;
Spare, O God, in mercy spare him.

The Voice of Jesus

ANONYMOUS

I heard the voice of Jesus say
"Go thro', go thro' the gates:
A work of faith, a work of love
For thee outside awaits."
I left my ease, I left my sloth,
I left my trifling care;
I found my work upon the way
And He has met me there.

I heard the voice of Jesus say—
"Prepare for all a road
That wandering feet may gladly turn
And find their way to God."
I sought my task, my lot I found,
I spake of Him the Way
The Truth, the Life, the All in all:
The words He bade me say.

I heard the voice of Jesus say—
"Cast up, cast up the path;
That all who will may enter in
The covert from God's wrath."
The flesh was weak, the toil was long,
But strength was close at hand,
And on the path the wanderers came
A joyous, sheltered band.

I heard the voice of Jesus say—
"The stones afar cast out;
No stumbling blocks to work offense
Leave thou in Zion's route."

The stones lay thick, both great and small
The workers were but few;
I looked above, a helping host
Of angels met my view.

I heard the voice of Jesus say—
"The standard lift on high,
That all may see the Savior, God,
Who came to earth to die."
I spake no more of self or cares.
Of joys or worldly goal:
I spake of Christ, the living Bread,
And He has fed my soul.—E.

The Judgment

BY MARTIN LUTHER

Great God, what do I see and hear!
The end of things created!
The Judge of mankind doth appear
On clouds of glory seated!
The trumpet sounds; the graves restore
The dead which they contained before;
Prepare, my soul, to meet Him!

The dead in Christ shall first arise
At the last trumpet's sounding,
Caught up to meet Him in the skies,
With joy their Lord surrounding:
No gloomy fears their souls dismay,
His presence sheds eternal day
On those prepared to meet Him.

But sinners, filled with guilty fears,
Behold His wrath prevailing:
For they shall rise, and find their tears
And sighs are unavailing:
The day of grace is past and gone;
Trembling, they stand before the throne,
All unprepared to meet Him.

Great God, to Thee my spirit clings,
Thy boundless love declaring,
One wondrous sight my comfort brings,
The Judge my nature wearing.
Beneath His cross I view the day
When Heaven and earth shall pass away,
And thus prepare to meet Him.

The Coming of the King

BY SUSAN COOLIDGE

Slowly the night draws on to dawn;
Slowly the darkness thins and pales;
And faint gray lines, all silver-drawn,
Creep shimmering through the misty veils.
The pallor of the new-born day
Flushes to rose-bloom, deepening slow:
Then, suddenly, a long, bright ray
Of bannered gold waves to and fro,
As signaling a guest: "Make room;
The King is coming!"—Let Him come.

Slowly the dim eyes of the heart,
The heart too young to know the sun,
Tremble, and open with a start,
To find its day of life begun.
Amazed and tremulous, it sees
The glory grow, the passion stir,

And rouses from its childish peace
　To greet the unknown visitor,
Half happy, half amazed and dumb:
"The King is coming!"—Let Him come!

Slowly the closed eyes of the soul,
　The soul which long in sleep has lain,
Open, to find a new control,
　A mastery blent of joy and pain,
Compelling, strenuous, urgent, kind,
　Has dawned upon its drowsy skies,
And starting up from slumber blind,
　With lips made newly eloquent, cries
(Life pulsing in the veins once numb),
"The King is coming! Let Him come!"

Slowly the eyes that love the light
　Perceive that light is on the wane,
And, shivering, through the growing night
　Confront the darkling shade of pain;
Confront a dim-seen, hovering shape,
　With eyes inexorable and dread,
And grasp from which is no escape;
　But still Faith rears her dauntless head,
And cries, tho flesh and heart be dumb,
"The King is coming! Let Him come!"
　　　　　　　　　　　　　G. R.

Come to Us, Lord

By Margaret E. Sangster

Come to us, Lord, as the daylight comes
　When the darkling night has gone,
And the quickened East is tremulous
　With the thrill of the wakened dawn.

Come to us, Lord, as the tide comes in
　With the waves from the distant sea;
Come, till our desert places smile,
　And our souls are filled with Thee.

Come to us, Lord, on our beds of pain,
　And soothe the fevered smart;
Come to our grief and our loneliness,
　And pillow our heads on Thy heart.

Come to us, Lord when the tempter dares
　Our faltering faith to smite;
Come, that the powers of Satan then
　May haste to take their flight.

Come to us, Lord, we watch for Thee;
　We shall never feel surprise,
If sudden we lift our eyes and see
　The dayspring o'er us rise.—C. G.

The New Pentecost

By William E. Barton

*Every man heard them speak in his own
　language.—Acts ii: 6*

"*Multae terricolis linguae, coelestibus una.*"

From lands afar the story
　To-day we gladly hear,
Of Pentecostal glory
　That brings the kingdom near;
How men of every nation
　Hear gladly preached and sung
The message of salvation,
　Each in his native tongue.

O lands that greet the dawning
　Of heaven's glad orb of day,
Too long for this glad morning
　In darkness still ye stay!
From all your plains and highlands
　Let Jesus' praise be rung!
Praise Him, all shores and islands,
　Each in your native tongue!

From every land they gather,
　The thousands round the throne;
Children of one same Father,
　One language there is known.
Yet earthly songs ascending
　All blend in heaven above
With anthems there unending
　In one glad song of love.—C. E.-W.

Our Lord's Return

By Rev. A. N. Raven

*Watch, therefore, for ye know not what hour
your Lord doth come.—Matt. xxiv: 42*

When the morn of life is beaming
And our hearts are full of joy,
And we long for some endeavor
Which shall all our powers employ;
When 'tis sweet to live with dear ones
Round about us in our home,
We should watch as He commanded
For perhaps our Lord will come.

When our sun has reached the zenith
Of its glory and its power,
And the fruits of toil are ripening
From the early bud and flower,
When we stand at life's bright noontide,
Ere decline has yet begun,
We should watch as He commanded
For perhaps our Lord will come.

When the golden sun is sinking
'Neath the rosy-tinted west,
And we're standing on the border
Of the land of peace and rest,
When the eye, undimmed by watching,
Looks toward our eternal home,
We should watch as He commanded
For perhaps our Lord will come.

If we watch for His appearing
We shall never watch in vain,
For He promised His disciples
He would surely come again;
Tho our eyes may not behold Him
Coming with the angel throng,
In our hearts He is begotten
While we watch with prayer and song.

If His coming be at morning,
At the noontide or the night,
May He find His children watching
In the thickest of the fight;
With our faces turned toward Zion
Let us watch and labor on,
Never doubting or discouraged,
Knowing that our Lord will come.

CHRISTMAS

(December)

CHRISTMAS is a Christian festival celebrated in memory of the birth of Jesus Christ. Originally we find the feast was celebrated by the Eastern Church as Epiphania, January 6, and by the Western Church as Natalis, December 25. While December 25 was in all probability not the actual date of Christ's birth, its selection by the Western Church was by no means arbitrary.

Precisely at this season of the year occurred a series of Pagan festivals, closely connected with the civil and social life of the Romans, and from the nature of their observance, easily capable of being spiritualized and made symbolic. This series culminated in the festival of the winter solstice, the birthday of the new sun about to return once more toward the earth. In this feast the transition to the Christian point of view easily presented itself, and hence it came about that in the Christian cycle of holidays December 25 was set to celebrate the birthday of Jesus, the Sun of the spiritual world for the purpose of drawing away Christian people from heathen festivities, and of purifying eventually these heathen customs and ideas.

In the fourth century, through the influence of Chrysostom, it is believed, the Eastern Church transferred its celebration to the same date, and the day being thus uniformly accepted, Christmas became one of the three great annual festivals of the Church.

CHRISTMAS, HISTORIC AND LEGENDARY

For several centuries after the birth of Jesus Christ, Christmas, our happiest season, was to His followers one of heroic ordeal. His birthday was first celebrated in the second century, it is said, by order of Telesphorus, seventh Bishop of Rome, who shortly after suffered martyrdom, the observance of the anniversary of Christ's nativity being one of his offenses. But tho the initiator of the observance died, the observance lived—lived through flame and sword. After two hundred years, in the reign of Diocletian we read of a vast multitude of Christians assembled,—of windows and doors barred by the Pagan emperor's order—of torches applied to the crowded building, and the burning alive of hundreds of worshipers assembled to celebrate the birthday of Christ.

Six hundred years after the martyrdom of the man who is reported to have instituted the Christmas observance, the man to whom tradition assigns the ideas of the Christmas tree suffered a like fate at the hands of the Pagan tribes of Germany.

The legend of St. Boniface and the first Christmas tree has been beautifully told. The scene lives before us:—the wintry night, the swelling hillock crowned with the great oak tree—the "Thunder Oak," sacred to the Pagan god, Thor,—the tongues of ruddy flame, the fountains of ruby sparks from the great fire kindled near the altar at its foot, the curved ranks of white-clad warriors, women and children facing the altar, the hoary High Priest and kneeling child—the victim doomed to die by the blow of the hammer, a sacrifice to Thor, the Hammerer.

Then the coming of Boniface, the blow from the Hammer turned aside by the Cross, the rescue of the boy, the fall of the oak before the mighty blows of the apostle, the story of Jesus simply told and how sin, not human life, is the sacrifice He asks.

" ' And here,' said the apostle, as his eyes fell on a young fir tree, standing straight and green with its top pointing toward the stars, amid the divided ruins of the fallen oak, ' here is the living tree, with no stain of blood upon it, that shall be the sign of your new worship. See how it points to the sky. Let us call it the tree of the Christ-child. Take it up and carry it to the Chieftain's hall, for this is the birth-night of the White Christ. You shall go no more into the shadows of the forest to keep your feasts with secret rites of shame. You shall keep them at home with laughter and song and rites of love.' "

Thus did " the hour of darkness, the power of winter, of sacrifice, and mighty fear " vanish before the glad radiance of redeeming love, and the Pagan oak, whose roots were fed with blood, fall before the fir tree which " points to the stars."—P. Tid.

CHRISTMAS AT BETHLEHEM

By Cunningham Geikie, D.D.

I remember sitting on one of the old marble pillars lying now, for who knows how many centuries, on the open ground beside the Church of the Nativity at Bethlehem, and letting my thoughts wander back till the haze of millenniums sent them home to me again, like Noah's dove, wearied with vain attempts to find anything, in those dim regions, on which to alight. The horizon must have been very much the same ever since the age when the soft white chalky limestone which once covered all Palestine, from Lebanon to the southern desert, fell in a snow-like shower of microscopic particles, through the waters of the then superincumbent ocean, and in the course of untold thousands of years heaped up the strata which gave Lebanon its name,—the White Mountains,—and sealed all Palestine besides under the same pure winding-sheet.

The Horizon near Bethlehem

Since then the chalky sandstone of the coast plain has been deposited, and the curious " nummulite " limestone which runs behind it, sweeping on round what remains of the earlier soft limestone of Lebanon, to the edge of the plateau and off into Egypt, to yield, long eons after, the stone made up of coin-like fossils, which built the Pyramids, and gave the stone itself its name—" nummus." meaning " money." But all these beds are washed away from Central Palestine, excepting at a spot round Kadesh, where Moses encamped so long, about fifty miles south of Hebron. To-day, Bethlehem sits high up. on the flat top of a narrow ridge of this soft limestone, white as milk, when fresh cut. as one sees in the walls of the nicely built, flat-roofed, one-story houses of the village.

The Limestone

When we first hear of this old place, the landscape must have shown the same table-land, sawn into valleys by the winter storms of millions of years ; the hills thus left rounded atop by long weathering ; the valleys small but fertile ; the prospect everywhere one of height beyond height, all running up. however, to nearly the same level, except to the east, where the country sinks in great steps, from ancient volcanic disturbance, towards the Dead Sea ; here, white ; there, brown with thin herbage and shrubs ; and yonder, light yellow. Fifteen miles off, eastward, and more than four thousand feet below Bethlehem, the deep blue waters of the Dead Sea have met the eye ever since man existed, to look down on them, while to the southeast the utterly barren hills of the wilderness of Judea, thickly seamed with fissures and narrow gorges and ravines, have been desolate and uninviting for as long.

The Landscape

We first meet with Bethlehem in human story to find ourselves beside the tents of Jacob, as he bears out, amidst loud wailing, the loved form of Rachel, the joy of his life, to lay her in the grave which one still sees marked by a square, rough-stone, low, domed building, at the side of the road, even then the same as now, just before it turns to the left in a white, scarped bend, to go into Bethlehem. Jesus must often have passed it, never, we may be sure, without a tender thought for her who lay sleeping there, amidst her children, so many centuries.

The Tomb of Rachel

The next picture of this old-world place we have is when Naomi, with her husband and two sons, is forced to leave it, the failure of the rains having made living in it beyond their means, in spite of its name—Bethlehem, " The House of Bread." In Moab, across the Jordan, and behind the Dead Sea, a long journey for the famished villagers, they were to find the humble maintenance which their own mountain home could not, for the time, yield. Then comes the story of the return of Naomi and Ruth, leaving the dear forms of husband and sons in the graves of their temporary land of refuge. But the cloud lifts after they have reached the loved hamlet, with its sweet little valleys on both north and south. and the breezy air of its height, nearly three thousand feet above the sea ; which, however, lies beyond their horizon about forty miles to the west. The episode of Ruth's courtship of Boaz, their marriage, and her connection, in consequence, with the noblest annals of Judah, as ancestress of David, keeps Bethlehem still in our view. Then we see the town fathers—the elders—in terror at the sudden appearance of the judge, Samuel ; but he appeases their fears without telling them his real errand, and leaves, after having anointed David as successor to Saul, whose sons were thus superseded and whose dynasty was forever set aside.

Naomi and Ruth

There is, and could have been, at any time, only one long winding row of houses in Bethlehem, tho a second short street, or rather line of isolated buildings, modest enough, runs parallel with this for a little way, side openings leading from the one to the other. The ridge is too narrow for any change in the limits of the village. We may fancy young David growing up in this sequestered spot ; wandering as a boy into the valleys on each side ; away, east, along that on the north side of it, to the upward slope, to be called, ages after, the Hill of Shepherds, as famous for the vision

The Country of David

of angels on the Christmas that saw the birth of the Savior. Or he may have strayed up the sides of the hills, towards the then Jebusite-town of Jerusalem, or, on the south, down the long-drawn glen that leads towards Hebron, the flowers, the birds, and the butterflies pleasing the child as well then as they do his successors of similar age to-day. To see these little Bethlehemites at play before the Church of the Nativity carried back my thoughts to the time when the boys of Jesse were happy on the same spot, with the same childish light-heartedness, amidst the same landscape; *they* so long vanished; *it* the same as when they were busy with their boyish games!

But the time was to come when a greater than David, tho sprung from his " root," was to make Bethlehem sacred forever by His birth, within its humble bounds.

The Date of Christ's Birth The exact time of the nativity of Christ can never be known, for it has been disputed from the earliest ages of the Church. The twenty-fifth day of December, which was at last accepted as the date on which it should be celebrated, has little in its favor beyond the fact that it was the day on which, in antiquity, the return of the sun from its winter absence was kept, such a festivity, as it well appeared, suiting the feast of the nativity of Him who was to be the Light of the World, the victorious Sun of righteousness, rising on a world long sunk in darkness to restore spiritual day to mankind. It could hardly have been at that season, however, for such a time would surely not have been chosen by the authorities for a public enrolment, which necessitated the population's traveling from all parts to their natal districts, storms and rain making journeys both unsafe and unpleasant in winter, except in specially favorable years. Snow is not at all uncommon at Jerusalem in the winter months, and I have even known it so deep that people lost their way outside the gates, and Bethlehem lies even higher than the Holy City. Then there is no provision for heating houses in Palestine, and the suffering from cold is, in proportion, great, especially to a population accustomed to great heat for most of the year. One knows how wretched even Rome is in winter, and Palestine is much worse during hard weather. Nor is it likely that shepherds would lie out through the night, except during unseasonably fine weather.

But it matters little on what precise day the Savior deigned to take our nature upon Him; the great thing is to commemorate the amazing event on some day accepted by Christians at large.

Mary's journey from Nazareth was a long one, and must have been made easier, we may suppose, as such family journeys are still, by the services of an ass,—the general riding-beast of Palestine since the earliest times. Simple food, of bread, with figs, and perhaps the soft cheese of the country, would be enough; water sufficing for drink, except

where hospitality offered a cup of the wine then made by nearly all households.

We must not, moreover, think of Joseph seeking out an inn at Bethlehem, for inns were unknown among the Jews, and indeed useless, where the only accommodation usually required was **The Events Following the Birth** leave to sleep on the floor, or on one's own mat brought with him —as in the khans we still find over the East. It was a sacred obligation on every Jew to give shelter to his countryman when on a journey, and hence, instead of " an inn," the real sense of the gospel is that there was no room in any house for the weary Nazarene " to loosen " the girth of the ass and make his stay there.

A Hebrew house in those days would be like a peasant's house now: a living-room of four walls and a bare floor, which served for sleeping on at night and for eat-**A Hebrew House** ing on by day. No one sits in the house except in bad weather, so that the open air serves for a gossiping-place, the ground being the usual seat of a cross-legged Oriental to this day. Behind the living part of the house there is a somewhat lower floor, also of mud, this part of the establishment being given over to the household ass, a goat or two, or perhaps a sheep, and to the poultry of the house-mother.

In a place built, like Bethlehem, in many cases, against the soft limestone rock, it often happens that the existence of a cave, where the house was to be, was a great **Where Christ Was Born** attraction, since it offered a ready-made, dry, above-ground cellar, as well as a specially suitable spot for the household animals and for a storeroom. It would seem that Joseph was at last able to get room in some such back portion of a house, and there, we are told, Mary bore her divine Son. A cave, below the high altar of the Church of the Nativity, is now shown as the very place where this august event transpired; a little recess, shaped like a clam-shell, its floor of marble wrought into a star in the center, bearing in Latin the words, " Here Jesus Christ was born of the Virgin Mary." A row of lamps hangs round the outer edge, the right to attend to them being a jealously watched matter, each of the ancient churches, the Greek, the Latin, the Armenian, and, I think, the Coptic, having one or more of these under their care.

The evidence for this site is so strong that I, for one, accept it as sufficient, reaching up, as it does, to within living memory of the days of the apostles. But even if this be an illusion, the fact remains that in this petty village the Savior of the world was made man for our redemption. No wonder that we read of the anthem of the angels, for surely nothing could draw forth the interest of the heavenly population like the exceeding grace God was showing to sinful man.

The scene of the visit to the shepherds is

pointed out as on a rough slope, facing the village, at some distance to the east, Bethlehem lying, far above, on its **The Journey of the Shepherds** mountain-seat. One can follow the shepherds in their journey to see the unspeakable wonder. They would go along the rich valley of Boaz, and then up the terraced hill, by a path still in use; nor is it uninstructive to reflect that, while simple shepherds were led by angels to the manger, the High-Priests and the great of Jerusalem, so near, slept through that most illustrious night of all history, quite, unconscious of what had happened. But we know of it; and may God grant that if we cannot go with the shepherds to Bethlehem, we may, one day, go to the right hand of God, and worship Him there, who that night lay, a little child, in Mary's arms!

CHRISTMAS IN CONSTANTINOPLE

By Cyrus Hamlin, D.D.

There are more kinds of Christmases brilliantly kept in the great Osmanli Capital than in any city of which we have any knowledge. **The Moslems and Christ** It is a day to which even the Moslems are lenient, because, altho hostile to Christians, they honor Jesus; and Mohammedan theology maintained the sinless birth of Mary, the mother of Jesus, centuries before it was adopted in the Romish Church. The message of the angel to Mary, as given in the third Sura of the Koran, is, " O Mary, verily God sendeth thee good tidings, that thou shalt bear the Word, proceeding from Himself. His name shall be Christ Jesus, the son of Mary, honorable in this world and in the world to come, and one of those who approach near to the presence of God." There is no other Christian festival to which the Moslems look with the same regard as to that which celebrates the birth of " Christ Jesus, the son of Mary."

I will sketch, as briefly as possible, the four chief Christmases of the Capital, and they will stand for the observances throughout the Empire.

First comes the Roman Catholic faith, with its numerous large, magnificent churches. The Christmas adorning of these churches **The Christmas of the Roman Catholics** can hardly be excelled in any part of the world. The supply of flowers of every hue and vines of every leaf is inexhaustible. The open gardens still yield a rich variety, and the conservatories of the rich refuse none of their treasures. The large numbers of the clergy, the Brothers of St. Paul, the Sisters of Charity, and crowds of volunteers, soon transform the churches with the most gorgeous array of flowers and vines. The splendid procession of boys and of maidens from the schools and nunneries, the various religious associations with their banners and badges, make the scene a gorgeous one. It is more magnificent than any mere floral exhibition can be; for you see at every step that it is religious. You meet everywhere the Virgin and the Child, in statues, statuettes, and paintings. They are embowered in floral chapels, or in side chapels of the churches. Before them are clouds of incense and crowds of prostrate suppliants.

Theatrical display, religious fervor, and the jovialities of youth are all commingled. But above all this is the music. The Roman Church is never wanting in the attraction of glorious music. The hymns, being in Latin, cannot be enjoyed by a Protestant without the book, and with the book he is astounded at the worship offered to the Virgin.

After church service, which occupies the morning hours, come the Christmas socialities. They are like our Thanksgiving so- **Christmas Pleasures** cialities, with the added excitement of gifts to all the children. Nor are the poor by any means neglected. The evening is devoted to balls, to the theater, and to carousings which often have an unpleasant ending.

As the Greek Church retains the " Old Style," her Christmas comes twelve days **The Christmas of the Greek Church** later. It is quite different from the Christmas of the Latin Church. The clergy of the Latin Church are chiefly Italians and French, educated at Rome. They control the fashions and forms of their Church.

The Greek Church is purely Oriental; and, altho it is making great progress in general cultivation, its Christmas is very different, or at least *was*, some twenty years ago; I have not entered a Greek Church in the midst of its joyous Christmas festivities at a later date. Its devotion to the worship of the Virgin, however, is quite equal to that of the Latin Church.

There is a large, wealthy, and highly cultivated Greek society in Constantinople, and also an immense population of the common people. It is the multitude that governs Christmas. If their churches are less elaborately adorned, it is a matter of necessity. For the crowd is compact, and fills every part. The " congregation joins " in the Christmas hymn. An immense volume of sound is poured forth; but how much artistic music there is, I am not prepared to judge.

Every man and every woman holds a lighted wax taper. You are expected to buy one on entering; and, with this in your hand, your orthodoxy will not be questioned. The smoke and dripping of the candles make the atmosphere nearly suffocating; but everybody is joyous and happy, without a thought of suffocation.

For boys it is, to all intents and purposes, our Fourth of July. They begin soon after midnight to fire off crackers and pistols, but not in the Turkish quarter. They also play shy of the police, except within the courts of the churches, which, being surrounded by high walls, give a free space for "scaring away the devil!" This is the declared purpose of the firing. To interdict it wholly would be religious persecution! The boys evidently "go in" for making a noise. It is their "Fourth," and they improve it.

I once entered the great Greek Church of Galata, in the very height of the celebration, to find a physician. A short cannon was being fired, every few minutes, in the court; and the concussion, under the high walls, was anything but pleasant. Fiery serpents sometimes went hissing among the crowd, to their no small annoyance. As every Greek knew the doctor whom I wanted, I worked through the mass of people, asking for him. At length I found him with a tall candle in his hand, singing as lustily as any of them. I was glad to escape with only a moderate drip of tallow and wax.

After church the social interchanges are very pleasant. Presents of fruit, cake, and flowers are sent from house to house; and the poor are not left without a good dinner. There is perfect *abandon* in the Greek multitude and perfect good nature.

Christmas Pleasures

In the evening the wine-shops are crowded, and there is much drinking and jollity, with, of course, the results which always, in every land, follow excessive drinking.

The Armenian Church has its own Christmas. In general dogma and worship it is the same with the Greek; but it holds to its own language, national customs, and nationality. Its Christmas is more sober. As a race, the Armenians are less given to extravagances. As a social and jolly time, it is equally pleasant with the Greek Christmas.

The Christmas of the Armenian and Bulgarian Churches

And now the Bulgarians, having their own churches and their own language—the Slavic —have their own Christmas as separate as possible from all others. Thus we have four Christmases—the Latin, the Greek, the Armenian, and the Bulgarian—as entirely separate as though a thousand miles intervened. In all these the Virgin Mary is worshiped.

There is one more Christmas, which, in time, accords with the Latin. It is the Protestant Christmas.

Many years ago, outside the Episcopal Church, we paid very little attention to Christmas. But we have changed all that.

The Protestant Christmas

We now enter into the joy of the Christian world, and in a much more reasonable way. In the East, I think, we all keep Christmas, and keep it joyfully. I will describe it as kept in our missionary families. Others—English, German, French —keep it in the same general way.

Dr. Schauffler's house was the central Christmas house for all who could unite their families with his. As a German, he entered into it with all the love and memories of the Fatherland. In preparation one room would be closed and locked some days before Christmas. No child could enter or pry into it. When the children were all away or in bed the mysterious preparations were made.

The Christmas tree stood in the center, reaching the ceiling, its branches adorned with festoons of tinsel, multitudinous tapers, and gifts for every child. The bigger children—all became children then—also had many choice presents for one another. There were little side ways to please the children; a grotto; a castle among the hills, with a lakelet in which white swans were floating. These would remain for days after the tree was taken away, to be the delight of all visitors.

The evening comes. The children, old and young, assemble. First, they repeat Christmas passages which they have learned from the Old and New Testament, also hymns. Christmas songs are sung. Dr. Schauffler talks in his inimitable way to the children, and offers a prayer of thanksgiving. Then the door is opened, and the eager children, almost awe-struck, enter. Exclamations of delight burst from their lips. The scenic wonders are admired, and then the distribution begins, amid shouts of merriment and expressions of gratitude. At length the work is done, and calm succeeds. Perhaps the oldest one present tells a pleasant story of his boyhood. The Doxology is sung, and the happy crowd disperses.

Such Christmases leave memories for all the remainder of this earthly life.—C. U.

CHRISTMAS CUSTOMS THE WORLD AROUND

By WILL M. CLEMENS

There is always something fascinating about the folklore of the seasons; and when such legends are based upon pleasant conceits, they become of double interest. Despite the whirligig of time, the good old traditions linger with us.

Quaint Ideas in England and Scotland

A quaint belief, peculiar to England, holds that any person turning a mattress on Christmas Day will die within a year; but it is praiseworthy to bake bread on Christmas Eve, and loaves baked then will never go moldy.

The Scotch hold it to be very unlucky for any but a dark-haired person to first cross the threshold on Christmas Day, the reason assigned being that Judas had red hair! In parts of Lancashire, and in Worcestershire and Gloucestershire, no one would dream of giving matches, fire, or light out of a house on Christmas Day; but what trouble is to ensue if the rule be violated is not very clear.

Of course bees are not exempt from special observance. They must be wished the compliments of the season in the same way that they are told of births and deaths; and a sprig of holly must adorn the hive, just as white ribbon or crape does duty upon other occasions. Devonshire folk say that the bees sing all night through on Christmas Eve; but as bees are seldom quiet, there is nothing remarkable about that.

All over England and Wales some graceful tradition prevails, not the least touching being the pretty general belief amongst country folk that persons who die upon Christmas Eve are certain of immediate and eternal happiness.

In Germany, on Christmas Eve, the whole household prepares for church, where a simple but impressive service is always held. **In Germany** The worshipers are always armed with lighted candles, and the first comer will find the Church in darkness. He places his lighted candle before him; and, as one after another appears, fresh candles flash out, till the building resembles a large parterre of single flames. The service over, the season is supposed to have fairly begun, and Christmas greetings are heard on every side.

In Sweden and Norway the " Julafred," or peace of Christmas, is publicly proclaimed. Quite early in the day the children hasten to **In Norway and Sweden** the churches, which are appropriately decorated, and later the adults attend. The time out-of-mind custom of telling stories and legends around a blazing hearth is still most popular, and a really good raconteur is ever welcome. Both Norwegians and Swedes are noted for their hospitality, which extends not only to domestic pets but to wild birds:—

" From gable, barn, and stable
Protrudes the birdie's table
Spread with a sheaf of corn."

A like custom of feeding the birds prevails also in Switzerland, Montenegro, and other places.

At Lyons, in France, it has long been the rule for the first infant received at the Foundling Hospital on Christmas Day to be welcomed with special honor. A **In France** handsome cradle is in readiness, softest clothing is provided, and the kindest solicitude is evinced. The object of the ceremony is to mark the contrast between the lot of the Savior and one of the most helpless and forlorn of His creatures on the anniversary of the beginning of the great renunciation. It is a lesson in charity that is not lightly forgotten.

A very singular custom prevails in Servia and Bulgaria amongst the orthodox. If it can possibly be avoided, no one crosses a **In Servia and Bulgaria** strange threshold on the morning of Christmas Day. An early ceremony has to be performed by the head of each household. Before breakfast is thought of, corn is placed in a stocking, and the chief of the family sprinkles a little before the house door, saying, " Christ is born; " to which one of the inmates replies, " He is born indeed." Then the house-father has to " wish," and, advancing to the hearth, where logs are burning in readiness, strikes them till sparks fly out, with a good wish for the horses, another for the cows, another for the goats, and so on through the whole farming stock, winding up with an extra blow for a plenteous harvest. Then the ashes are collected, a coin is placed amongst them, and the whole is hidden, or, in some districts, burned. As for the Yule logs, they are not permitted to smolder quite away, but are carefully garnered, and the burnt ends placed in clefts of the fruit-trees, so as to ensure a bountiful crop.—G. R.

QUEER CHRISTMAS CUSTOMS

Among the Christmas observances that grew up by degrees all over Europe, many of them grotesque and absurd, and some with profuse and unseemly accompaniments, were also not a few of a more pleasing and humanizing kind, and among the rural population the brute creation was included as interested parties. Shakespeare tells how

" Some say that ever, 'gainst that season comes,
Wherein our Savior's birth is celebrated,
The bird of dawning singeth all night long."

Among the fancies of this kind that longest survived in Europe, and even became naturalized in our own prosaic land, was one that the cattle, at one o'clock on Christmas

morning, whenever they were free to do so, would turn their heads to the eastward, and get down upon their knees to worship the King that was born in a stable; and still another, which continued to comparatively recent times, that during the Christmas season the barnyard cocks were accustomed to crow with more than usual force and frequency, both by day and by night.

The early inhabitants of the great Scandinavian peninsula were accustomed to celebrate, at this season, the great festival of their gods. When the people of the peninsula become Christians, altho no less zealous for their Christmas observances, they retained some of the old practices, and are to this day careful to associate with themselves in its festivities every living thing about them.

The author of The Land of the Midnight Sun tells us, in his account of a Christmas in Norway:

"The Christmas feeding of the birds is prevalent in many of the provinces of Norway and Sweden. Bunches of oats are placed on the roofs of houses, on trees and fences, for them to feed upon. Two or three days before, cartloads of sheaves are brought into the towns for this purpose, and both rich and poor buy and place them everywhere. Every poor man and every head of a family had saved a penny or two, or even one farthing, to buy a bunch of oats for the birds to have their Christmas. On this day, on many farms, the dear old horse, the young colt, the cattle, the sheep, the goats, and even the pig receive double their usual amount of food. It is a beautiful custom, and speaks well for the natural goodness of heart of the Scandinavian."

But our matter-of-fact times and modes of thinking are rapidly driving away all of these pleasant illusions, until nations as well as individuals have reason sometimes to sigh to be children again.—S. C.

NOËL

MIDNIGHT MASS AT THE MADELEINE

By Mrs. A. M. Gardiner

The night is set with stars. All the evening the Place de la Madeleine has been thronged with merry Christmas folk, eager to assist at the gorgeous ceremony of the Midnight Mass.

The *place* which surrounds this temple—modeled after the Greek Parthenon—is bounded by the grand boulevards, and is the center-piece of modern Paris. On almost any day, standing here, you may see men and women from every civilized clime; but to-night, under the canopy of the stars, and amid the blaze of electric burners, there is gathered a host that comes but once a year.

It is nearing the solemn hour of midnight, and the people await the opening of the portals. Ah! there is the signal light from within, and, pressing forward, the multitude ascend the marble stairs. There is neither noise nor confusion, and the large concourse is seated without apparent aid or suggestion.

Precisely as the great clock on the boulevard rings on the crisp air its twelve notes, announcing the midnight hour, the lights of the temple flash upon our vision, and, simultaneously, the grand organ thunders triumphant welcome.

The interior of the Madeleine is a work of high art. In form it is a vast parallelogram, without nave or transept. The walls are poetic frescoes. The ceiling, too lofty to be studied from the main floor, reveals its glories of brush and coloring to the few who have received cards for the narrow side galleries, that are opened only on the occasion of high festivals. The altar is studded with burning candles and generous flowers that mingle their perfumes with the holy incense. One hundred surpliced boys chant the measured music that precedes the celebration. The priests, clad in richest vestments, approach the shrine of their devotions. Away to the left of the altar a sound comes floating toward the people. Is it voice of man or spirit that fills the mighty space with a melody that rises and falls in sweetest cadence? We catch a single word, "Bethlehem." It is not spoken. It is a cry, an exultant cry. A chorus of trained singers now breaks forth in that matchless refrain:

"*Venite adoremus, venite adoremus,
Venite adoremus, Dominum.*"

Again the solo is carried with harp and flute from what seems to be the very altar; and, again, responsive from organ-loft, comes the swell of the grand chorus. It is the hymn, "*Adeste Fideles,*" sung for centuries on Christmas morning. It is one of those grand old hymns that is married to *one* melody; we know it everywhere as the Portuguese. And now the gospel recitation of "Peace on earth and good will to men" is harmoniously chanted by the priests. It is the story of "Jesus and His love." How the shepherds watched by night, how the miraculous Star "stood over the place where the young child lay," how the wise men brought gifts of gold, frankincense and myrrh, and how in a manger cradle is fulfilled that glorious prophecy, "Unto us a child is born, unto us a son is given."

Brilliant and subdued is the great congregation. We are in Judea. The soul is hushed in adoration. We have found a common shrine, *Jesus,* unto whom "every knee shall bow." And now the silence opens and the *Benedictus* is sung, standing. Slowly the massive doors swing backward. A refreshing breeze tells us that there *is* an outer world. But we are in no haste to depart. Memories, thick as flowers, cluster around the service, while at every step, some mosaic or a fresco of surpassing beauty challenges the eye. And so, as we come to the very portal we discover that the army of worshipers has departed, and we stand gazing out into the clear-cut atmosphere, beholding a scene down the Rue Royale and out upon the boulevards that can only be witnessed in the early morn of Christmas in the streets of the City of Paris.—I.

SERMONS AND OUTLINES

THE CHIMES

By David James Burrell, D.D.

"For unto us a Child is born, unto us a Son is given, and the government shall be upon his shoulders; and his name shall be called Wonderful, Counselor, the mighty God, the everlasting Father, the Prince of Peace."

"Ring out, wild bells, to the wild sky,
The flying cloud, the frosty night! . . .
Ring out, wild bells!"

Long ago—seven hundred years before the first Christmas—it was the darkest hour of the night—stars fading; people groping like the blind, stumbling, falling; lights out in the sanctuary; no open vision; silence: a prophet standing with his face toward the east, shading his eyes. Hark! The clear note of a bell; again and again; five times it strikes the air. In the distance it is answered by the song of angels. And now the shadows flee before the sun! Welcome the day!

"Joy to the world, the Lord has come!
Let earth receive her King!"

First bell: "His name shall be called Wonderful!" Here is mystery at the threshold of life; as it is written, "Great is the mystery of godliness, God was manifest in the flesh." In Lerolle's "Nativity" a group of rustics stand peering in at the stable door, overawed, agape. So stand we all before this marvel: "The angels desire to look into it." Nor does the wonder cease as the Christ-child grows in wisdom and stature. His life is as unique as His person; His doctrine bewilders; His death is strangest of all. Daniel Webster, on being asked whether he understood Christ, answered: "No, how should I? I could not believe in Him if I understood Him." It is easier for the infinite to be bound with swaddling bands than to come within the compass of a finite mind. Can a man hold the ocean in his palm? God is always wonderful, whether He dwells in glory unapproachable or in a carpenter's shop; whether He thunders from Sinai or sleeps upon His mother's breast.

Second bell: "His name shall be called Counselor!" Many a soul bewildered at life's crossroads gives grateful heed to the sweet reverberation of this bell. The world needs guidance. "We are floating on a raft upon an open sea," said Plato; "whence we came or whither we go we know not." We dream dreams and see visions; we face great problems and entertain glorious hopes; but, What is truth? There is a path which no fowl knoweth and which the vulture's eye hath not seen. Where shall ·wisdom be found? A voice from Heaven answers: "This is my beloved Son. Hear ye him." He teacheth not as the scribes, but with authority. Here is no *if* or *perhaps,* but "verily, verily." Never man spake like this Man. Blessed Counselor! Is sin the burden? He lifts it. Are our eyes blinded with sorrow? He gives the garment of praise for the spirit of heaviness. Are we troubled by "a certain fearful looking for of judgment?" Hear Him: "Let not your heart be troubled, neither let it be afraid." Blessed Counselor, Thou givest liberally and upbraidest not!

Third bell: A deep, majestic note—"He shall be called the mighty God!" If ever the polemic argument for Christ's divinity is in order it is surely not here nor now. There is a better way at Christmas tide. The air is laden with the truth, "Emmanuel, God with us." A bright morning asks no explanation, calls for no analysis of light. It is enough that the shadows flee away, that birds awake, that flowers glisten with the dew, that the sun "flames in the forehead of the sky." What means this gathering at the family board, this laughter of children, this sweet content, this glorious freedom, if not that the Sun of Righteousness—the mighty God—hath risen upon us with healing in His beams?

Fourth bell: "He shall be called the everlasting Father!" The heart longs for a glimpse of the ineffable One; but no man hath ever seen God. He makes Himself visible, however, in the person of His Son. Jesus said:
"If ye had known me, ye should have known my Father also. Philip saith unto him: Lord, show us the Father and it sufficeth us. Jesus saith: Have I been so long time with you and yet hast thou not known me, Philip? He that hath seen me hath seen the Father. Believest thou not that I am in the Father and the Father in me?"

It was observed by Madame de Staël that "if the Founder of Christianity had done no more than to say ' Our Father which art in Heaven,' He would have conferred an inestimable boon upon the children of men."

Fifth bell: "He shall be called the Prince of Peace!" Here is the sweetest note. "Names name Him not," yet Shiloh is best of all. The burden of unrest is upon us. The Master stretches forth His pierced hands over our passions and heartaches, saying "Peace, be still."

"God rest ye, merrie gentlemen,
Upon this Christmas morn;
The God of all good Christians
Was of a woman born."

His name is Shiloh, His blessing is *Salaam,*
His bequest is *shalom,* and His home in the
heavens is Salem, the City of Peace. Peace
alway. "My peace I give unto you." Open
no more, ye gates of Janus; for swords shall
be beaten into plowshares and spears into
pruning hooks. Be loosed of thy terrors, O
Judgment, for Christ has sprung an arch over
the "great gulf fixed." You that were alienated, now hath He reconciled. Midway betwixt earth and Heaven the red-cross banner
meets a flag of truce. Peace, peace forever!
And a merry, merry Christmas! In the

message of the chimes let us rejoice and be
glad. The joy of salvation is ours. The
waste places of our life below blossom as the
rose; each morning brings a new promise of
life, and at every sunset the crimson gates
of Heaven roll back.

> "Ring and swing,
> Bells of joy! On morning's wing
> Send the song of praise abroad!
> Tell the nations that He reigns
> Who alone is God!"
>
>   I.

WHERE WAS CHRIST BEFORE CHRISTMAS?

By David Gregg, D.D.

I. He was in the genealogies. God framed
the history of the world in view of the coming of Jesus Christ. In the very beginning
He chose a family whose line of descent
should run directly from Eden to Bethlehem. This family God took into covenant
with Himself, and the promise of the covenant was that *of its seed Christ should be
born in the fulness of time.* This covenant-
line runs through the whole of the Old
Testament as the golden thread runs through
the beautiful fabric. Everything centers in
this covenant-line. It unifies the Old Testament. It is the cord upon which the pearls
of history are strung. Keep this in mind, and
it will explain a thousand mysteries and perplexities in reading the Old Testament.

Let me illustrate! Dark pages, which we
would not read in public, are in the Holy
Book. They chronicle the worst sins of
humanity—the sin of Lot; the lust of Judah
and Thamar. Why are these pages here?
Ingenuity answers: "To show the truthful-
ness and impartiality of the sacred writers.
Without these shadows, their portrait-narra-
tives would be eulogies and not histories."
It is answered: "These dark incidents are
recorded to reveal the wonderful mercy of
God, and thus create hope for despairing
sinners of every age." These answers have
their value, but they are not sufficient. The
real reason these dark things are in the Book
is this: The Bible is a Messianic record, and
these things pertain to the ancestors of Christ.
The fruit of Lot's sin was Moab. In the line
of Moab, Ruth, the grandmother of David,
was born. Christ is called the Son of David.
As the human ancestry of Christ ran through
the sin of Lot, in like manner also it ran
through the sin of Judah and Thamar. The
fruit of that sin was *Pharez.* When we
come to make up the genealogy of Christ,
we need the name of *Pharez,* else the line
will be broken and the claims of Christ fail
of establishment. Do you not see the reason
for these dark pages in the old Book? They
are necessary to the fulness of the history
of Jesus Christ. They are steps in the march
of events toward Bethlehem. Christ is in

them, and nothing pertaining to Christ can
be omitted from the Bible.

It is an interesting study to trace the different streams of humanity which run into the
human ancestry of the Christ. Here the sinful life of Thamar flows into it; there the
life of Rahab the harlot; yonder the life of
Bathsheba. Different elements from Gentile
quarters as well as from Jewish quarters
enter His humanity, so that He is not the
son of any one tribe, but the son of all tribes.
He is not exclusively the son of the Jew, He
is the son of the Gentile as well. He had
Gentile mothers and brothers and sisters as
well as Jewish mothers and brothers and
sisters. He was a man of the human race,
"the Son of Man."

But what is the use of all this? I answer.
The true humanity of Christ is established;
the grand work which Christ can do for our
human nature is made known. He dwelt in
a human nature representing the human race,
and He exalted that nature to the highest
heavens. Standing in the persence of the
work which Christ did for His own human
nature, we say to ourselves: "What if our
nature has been derived from sinning ancestors, what if we have downward hereditary
tendencies; the Son of God can do for human nature what He did for His own; He
can incarnate Himself in us, and dwell in
us, and make us holy, and at last lift us into
the glory of Heaven."

The genealogies of the Holy Book help us
to understand Christ; hence it is that His
biographers gather and write the genealogies
on the first page of His history. This is what
Matthew and Luke do. The fact that these
genealogies are here should be enough to
teach us that they serve an important use, for
God is a severe economist in writing His
Book. In the past, Christ was, in the genealogies, stepping Bethlehemward. Every time
a new descendant in the covenant-line was
born, the voice of prophecy shouted: "*Christ
is coming!*" As ancestor was added to ancestor, the voice waxed louder and louder.
Thus the shout was repeated and repeated
until at last the angels and the magi and the

shepherds and the watchers in the Temple answered back that shout with the gladder and louder shout, "CHRIST HAS COME!" That is the Christmas shout which to-day Church of God throws to Church of God all through Christendom.

II. He was in the ideal manhood which the Old Testament lifted before the world. We know the power of an ideal manhood, for we see it in the Christ who walks in history, the Emperor of the ages. Humanity is shot through and through with the influence of His beautiful and perfect life. To His earthly life is traceable all that is best in our nineteenth century civilization. My point is this: This life of the New Testament page, which is the transfiguring power in society to-day, was the transfiguring power in society in the Old Testament day. Does the New Testament produce it, the Old Testament forecasts it. It vivifies both pages. On the one page it is history, on the other page it is prophecy. In the New Testament, Christ is an actuality; in the Old Testament, Christ is an ideal. Contemplate Him as an ideal seen in the Old Testament! He was the highest conception in all the literature and thought of the Hebrew people. His predicted career stood for all that was grand and sublime in the moral and spiritual world. Hence out of the Old Testament economy came lives which for nobility and grandeur and sacrifice and power it is hard to match in our age. What produced these characters? The power of the coming Christ. The real essential Christ was in the Old Book. Every attribute of His grand character was there. He was the most intense reality in the kingdom of the Jews. They of the olden times talked of the deeds He would do, and of the sacrifices He would make, and of the burdens He would bear, and of the spirit He would breathe, and of the character He would build up, and of the life He would live. As they talked of these sublime things, they said the one to the other: "Let us incorporate these sublimities into our lives, that we may be Messianic men when the Messiah comes." And this they did. He made Moses. The life of the Hebrew lawgiver was the result of the inspiration of the predicted Messiah. Under this inspiration he "esteemed the reproach of Christ greater riches than all the treasures of Egypt." The face of Christ looked out at the men of old from every holy commandment, and from every spiritual song, and from every sacred type and symbol. By anticipation He was a real, present and practical power in the commonwealth of God. By anticipation His human life was an educational, a molding, a spiritualizing and an uplifting force hundreds of years before it was lived.

III. He was in the Godhead. John gives us light here. He says: "In the beginning was the Word, and the Word was with God, and the Word was God!" According to these words Christ was coeternal with the Father. He antedated time and creation. He made the world, and prior to His advent He was busy building up the providences. He was the active person of the Godhead in dealing with mankind. All revelations from God came through Him. He was *the Word*.

He did not always maintain invisibility; He fellowshiped with man. It was He who walked with Adam in the garden, and communed with him in the cool of the day. Just as in New Testament times He had special friends, Peter and James and John; so in Old Testament times He had special friends, Abraham, Isaac, and Jacob. With Abraham He talked face to face as a friend talks with his friend. He was as tender and as kind to Abraham before His incarnation as He was tender and kind to John after His incarnation. He visited his tent and ate of the kid which he dressed and of the cakes which his wife Sarah baked. He dealt with Jacob much as He dealt with Peter. He bore long with his faults and patiently trained him.

There is a correspondence between the Son of God in the Old Testament and the Son of God in the New Testament. He is the same Son of God in both Testaments. In both Testaments He does similar acts. In Exodus He executes the plagues; in Revelation He pours out the vials; in the Pentateuch He watches over the Old Testament saints; in the Book of the Acts He watches over the New Testament Church. In the days of His flesh He mingles with men; in the days before His incarnation He frequently puts on the form of a man and makes visits to His own; or else He wraps Himself up in the Pillar of Cloud and Fire, and from it talks with men and communicates to them the will of God. "As a Guest, as a nameless presence, as a wrestling angel, as an eye in the wheel of the chariot of Israel, He was among men." On one occasion He was seen by seventy elders; upon two occasions by a man and his wife; then by Joshua, then by Gideon, then by Ezekiel, and then by Daniel.

Christians, stand at Bethlehem and open every door and window of your being Christward. Look backward. Look forward. Magnify Bethlehem. Recount to your souls the things for which it stands. It stands for the "fulness of time." It stands for the fulfilment of glorious predictions. It stands for the realization of those burning hopes which made the heroic men of the past. It stands for the coming of the Son of God Himself into our nature. It stands for the glorious past and for the more glorious future. As the dawn carries in it the full day, it carries in it the salvation of man, and the triumph of the right over the wrong, and the coming millennial glory of the kingdom of Jesus Christ.

When we comprehend the backward and forward reach of Bethlehem, we do not wonder that all that is grand crowds around the Cradle-Manger. It is worthy of all. Let the Star shine. Let the Magi give gifts. Let the Shepherds worship. Let the angel-faces flash out from the great dome overhead. Let the church-bells chime. Let the sacred harps and organs respond to the masterhand that sweeps their strings and flies over their keys, and let them turn the common air into praise.

Let Christmas carols roll over this wide earth, and echo among the stars. Let the great universe of God jubilate. Let everything in Heaven and earth shout, "Hosanna to the Son of David; blessed is he that cometh in the name of the Lord; Hosanna in the Highest." While all this takes place, see to it, O my soul, that thou carriest thyself to Bethlehem, to receive, and to love, and to trust, and to worship. Be thou certainly there; and while there recognize Christ, honor Christ, reincarnate Christ, and call Christ God.—I.

THE MOTHER OF THE CHRISTMAS BABE

When God would give the world a great man—a man of rare spirit and transcendent power, a man with a lofty mission—He first prepares a woman to be his mother. Whenever in history we come upon such a man, we instinctively begin to ask about the character of her on whose bosom he nestled in infancy and at whose knee he learned his life's first lessons. We are sure of finding here the secret of the man's greatness. When the time drew nigh for the incarnation of the Son of God, we may be sure that into the soul of the woman who should be His mother, who should impart her own life to Him, who should teach Him His first lessons and prepare Him for His holy mission, God put the loveliest and the best qualities that ever were lodged in any woman's life.

We need not accept the teaching that exalts the mother of Jesus to a place beside or above her divine Son. We need have no sympathy whatever with the dogma that ascribes worship to the Virgin Mary, and teaches that the Son on His throne must be approached by mortals through His more merciful, more gentle-hearted mother. But we need not let these errors concerning Mary obscure the real blessedness of her character. We remember the angel's greeting, "Blessed art thou among women." Hers surely was the highest honor ever conferred upon any woman.

"Say of me as the heavenly said, 'Thou art
The blessedest of women!'—blessedest,
Not holiest, not noblest,—no high name,
Whose height misplaced may pierce me like a shame,
When I sit meek in heaven!'"

We know how other men, men of genius, rarely ever have failed to give to their mothers the honor of whatever of greatness or worth they had attained. But somehow we shrink from saying that Jesus was influenced by His mother as other good men have been; that He got from her much of the beauty and the power of His life. We are apt to fancy that His mother was not to Him what mothers ordinarily are to their children; that He did not need mothering as other children do; that by reason of His deity indwelling, His character unfolded from within, without the aid of home teaching and training, and the other educational influences which do so much in shading the character of children in common homes.

But there is no Scriptural ground for this feeling. The humanity of Jesus was just like our humanity. He came into the world just as feeble and as untaught, as any other child that ever was born. No mother was ever more to her infant than Mary was to Jesus. She taught Him all His first lessons. She gave Him His first thoughts about God, and from her lips He learned the first lispings of prayer. Jewish mothers cared very tenderly for their children. They taught them with unwearying patience the words of God. One of the rabbis said, "God could not be everywhere, and therefore He made mothers."—F.

CHRISTMAS

By Cardinal Gibbons

To-day the whole Christian world prostrates itself in adoration around the crib of Bethlehem and rehearses in accents of love a history which precedes all time and will endure throughout eternity. As if by an instinct of our higher, spiritual nature, there well up from the depths of our hearts, emotions which challenge the power of human expression. We seem to be lifted out of the sphere of natural endeavor to put on a new life and to stretch forward in desire to a blessedness which, tho not palpable, is eminently real.

If asked to explain the rapturous influence which controls us, we have no other words than the evangel of joy which the angel gave unto earth: "For this day is born unto you a Savior who is Christ the Lord." We rejoice in anticipation of a new outpouring of God's blessed life, for the scope of the Divine Infant's mission is "to enlighten them who sit in darkness and in the shadow of death; to direct our feet into the way of peace." He is in our midst to flood the world with the light of God's truth; to restore to us our lost birthright of joy; to set the discordant wail of humanity to new harmonies; to attune to the music of heavenly hope hearts which for ages had been swept by the wild notes of despair.

The message of Christmas morning is as universal as it is personal and present. It is addressed to each man; it is addressed to all men. It is destined to shape private conduct and to impress and mould the life of society. Divine in its content, it has an earthly relation and significance. Whilst holding out a promise of the greater things which shall be revealed in us hereafter, it is not without action in time and influence upon the world around us.

Indeed we live and move and have our being in the midst of a civilization which is the legitimate offspring of the religion of Christ.

The blessings resulting from our Christian civilization are poured out so regularly and so abundantly on the intellectual, moral, and social world, like the sunlight and the air of heaven and the fruits of the earth, that they have ceased to excite any surprise, except to those who visit lands where the religion of Christ is little known. In order to realize adequately our favored situation, we should transport ourselves in spirit to ante-Christian times and contrast the condition of the Pagan world with our own.

Before the advent of Christ the whole world, with the exception of the secluded Roman province of Palestine, was buried in idolatry. Every striking object in nature had its tutelary divinities. Men worshiped the sun and moon and stars of heaven. They worshiped their very passions. They worshiped everything except God only, to whom alone divine homage is due. In the words of the Apostle of the Gentiles: " They changed the glory of the incorruptible God into the likeness of the image of a corruptible man, and of birds, and of four-footed beasts, and of creeping things. . . . They worshiped and served the creature rather than the Creator, who is blessed forever."

Christ, the Light of the world, proclaimed unto all men in its fulness the truth which had hitherto been hidden in Judea. He taught mankind to know the one true God, a God existing from eternity unto eternity, a God who created all things by His power, who governs all things by His wisdom, and whose superintending providence watches over the affairs of nations as well as of men, " without whom not even a bird falls to the ground." He proclaimed a God infinitely holy, just, and merciful. The idea of the Deity, so consonant to our rational conceptions, was in striking contrast with the low, sensual notions which the Pagan world had formed of its divinities.

The religion of Christ imparts to us not only a sublime conception of God, but also a rational idea of man and of his relations to his Creator. Before the coming of Christ, man was a riddle and a mystery to himself. He knew not whence he came nor whither he was going. He was groping in the dark. All he knew for certain was that he was passing through a brief phase of existence.

The past and the future were enveloped in a mist which the light of philosophy was unable to penetrate. Our Redeemer has dispelled the cloud and enlightened us regarding our origin and destiny and the means of attaining it. He has rescued man from the frightful labyrinth of error in which Paganism had involved him.

The Gospel of Christ, first heralded by angels, has brought not only light to the intellect, but also comfort to the heart. It has given us " that peace of God which surpasseth all understanding; " the peace which springs from the conscious possession of the truth. It has taught us how to enjoy that triple peace which constitutes true happiness as far as it is attainable in this life—peace with God by the observance of His Commandments; peace with our neighbor by the exercise of justice and charity toward him, and peace with ourselves by repressing our inordinate appetites and by keeping our passions subject to the law of reason and our reason illumined and controlled by the law of God.

The message of Christmas Day is intended for all men, for all times, for all conditions of existence. Christ alone of all religious founders has the courage to say to His disciples: " Go, teach all nations." " Preach the Gospel to every creature." " You shall be witnesses to me in Judea and Samaria and even to the uttermost bounds of the earth." Be not restrained in your mission by national or state lines. Let My Gospel be as free and universal as the air of heaven. " The earth is the Lord's and the fulness thereof." All mankind are the children of My Father and My brethren. I embrace all in My charity. Let the whole human race be your audience and the world be the theater of your labors.

These then are in broad outline, some of the grand truths and consoling experiences which " the glad tidings of great joy " reveal in their unfolding. Only by stern adhesion to the principles therein contained can individuals and nations hope to share in that peace which has been promised to men of good will. To violate them is to reverse the order established by God, and disorder is the synonym for sin and strife.

On the other hand, as beauty is the splendor of order, so peace is the tranquillity of order or joy in repose.

Whilst, therefore, we rejoice in our Christian privileges, we should ever remember that by the grace of God our Savior hath appeared to all men, instructing us that, denying ungodliness and worldly desires, we should live soberly and justly and godly in this world, looking for the blessed hope and coming of the glory of the great God and our Savior Jesus Christ, who gave Himself that He might redeem us from iniquity and might cleanse us to Himself a people acceptable and pursuers of good works.—N. Y. W.

CHRISTMAS AND ORIENTAL SCENES

By Canon H. B. Tristram, D.D.

A BETHLEHEM SHEPHERD'S TASK.—"Shepherds abiding in the field, keeping watch over their flocks by night." Very different is the shepherd's life in the East from the prosaic task of the sheep-farmer of western lands. Bethlehem stands on the shoulder of a hill which descends abruptly into a rich, un-fenced, corn plain, stretching eastward. In that plain each villager has his plot, indicated by the well-known stones, placed here and there—the neighbor's landmark. Beyond this tillage land, where Boaz had his reapers, and where Ruth, the Moabitess gleaned, a walk of two miles brings us to the picture land, on the hilly fringe of the wilderness of Judea, where David valiantly watched his father's sheep, and where a thousand years later, the shepherds of Bethlehem received the angelic news of the Messiah's birth. The wide, flat valley then breaks out into white, stony slopes on either side. After the corn-fields end, the whole is treated as common land, where the flocks of the villagers pasture together. But they need the shepherd's constant care. The labyrinth of rocky valleys, or wadies, on all sides, form a convenient lurking-place for the wolf, the jackal, and the thief, tho the lion and the bear of David's time are extinct. It is impossible to trust the flock in the open at night; they are led to some of the many shallow caves with which the hillsides are studded, with a rude, dry stone wall, and a narrow entrance in front. The shepherds themselves, in parties of from three to six or eight, sleep outside. They arrange an oblong circle of stones, which remains from year to year, and place inside a thick layer of brushwood, on which they spread straw for their bed, and lie surrounded by their dogs.

WATCHING BY NIGHT.—These watchful guardians are ever on the alert, and wake the echoes of night as they detect the prowling wolf, or hear the howling of the jackals, on their search for some hapless stray sheep. It was in front of such a cave that the shepherds were keeping watch when the heavenly host accosted them, and roused them to leave their charge for a time, that they might be the first to do homage to the infant Savior. The habits of the shepherds of Bethlehem are still unchanged, a steady, resolute set of men; and we may see to-day their humble *douars*, and the stone circles, in front of many a hillside cave.

"LYING IN A MANGER."—The monks of Bethlehem show a grotto beneath the great Christian Church, lined with marble, which they claim to be the stable where the infant Christ was laid. I believe that this tradition is better grounded than those of most holy places. The caravanserai, or inn, would naturally be where this is, just outside of the little town. It was founded by Chimham, son of Barzillai, in the days of David, and was scarcely likely to be changed up to the time of Roman rule, when the early Christians consecrated it as a Church. There are many natural grottoes on the slope of the hill; and we frequently see in other places that the caves near a caravanserai have been enlarged and used as stables. The stable is very unlike ours. At the end farthest from the door is always an elevated dais or platform, usually made by enlarging the cavern, but leaving the floor of the platform about three or four feet higher than the area. In front of it a long trough is hollowed out, reaching from end to end—the manger. The forage is stored on this platform, out of reach of the cattle, and is pushed into the long manger as required. Here the camel-drivers usually sleep, close to their animals. Now the inn being full, Joseph and Mary would be compelled to avail themselves of this shelter, and to sojourn on the platform. Naturally, when the child was born, the manger would suggest itself as the only cradle available where His mother could tend Him lying by His side and wrapped, as is still the universal Eastern custom, in a series of bandages from head to foot, like a mummy, till the babe looks like some limb newly set and bandaged with surgical skill.—P. T.

A CHRISTMAS DAY PRINCIPLE

By A. P. Stanley

Born in the first century, Christ belongs more to the full development of the nineteenth century than He does to the imperfections of the first.

This, then, is the principle of which the event of Christmas Day is the most striking example; external circumstances are something, but they are not everything. The inward life is the essential thing; but for its successful growth it needs external circumstance. The main element in the foundation—the main pledge for the future progress of Christianity—was the character, the personal character, of its Founder. Had Christ been other than He was, had He been a mere specter or phantasm, however Divine, such as He is represented in some well-known systems, without human affection, or persuasive words, or energetic actions, or constraining will, the course of the empire would have rolled on its way, and His place in history and in the hearts of men would have been unknown.

But being what He was—the impersonation

of goodness and truth, containing within Himself all those elements of character which win, convince, stimulate mankind—His religion, so far as it was derived from Himself, became all-pervading and all-embracing.—S. B., vol. vii., p. 23.

WE THREE KINGS OF ORIENT ARE

By David James Burrell, D.D.

Seek and ye shall find.—Matt. vii: 7
Run ye to and fro, and see now if there be any that seeketh the truth.—Jer. v: 1
For this is good and acceptable in the sight of God our Savior, who will have all men to come unto the knowledge of the truth.—1 Tim. ii: 3, 4
Jesus saith, I am the truth.—John xiv: 6
Now when Jesus was born in Bethlehem of Judea in the days of Herod the king, behold there came wise men from the east to Jerusalem, saying, Where is he that is born king of the Jews? for we have seen his star in the east and are come to worship him.—Matt. ii: 1, 2

The king of Judea was troubled. It was rumored that about this time, in fulfilment of prophecy, a Prince was to be born, who would assume the Jewish throne. Tacitus declares that the opinion was prevalent in the East that the Messiah of Israel was about to appear. Vergil had written his fourth Eclog, in which he announced the near approach of the golden age. A feeling of expectancy was prevalent everywhere. Herod was an old man, but still tenacious of his ill-gotten power. He was an apostate Jew, who long ago had forsaken the religion of his fathers to enter the service of the Roman government. His career had been a brilliant one; a *protégé* of Antony, he had at a very early age, been made governor of Galilee and afterward tetrarch of Judea. He was a man of vast ambition; shrewd, cunning, and of violent passions; not above the trick of a demagog, he was nevertheless possessed of much cleverness and a vast executive ability. To please his royal master, he built the splendid city of Cæsarea. To conciliate the Jews, whom he hated, he rebuilt their temple and splendidly adorned it.

In the porch of this temple the old king was walking on a February morning nearly nineteen hundred years ago. His purple robes sparkled with gems and precious stones; a glorious ruby blazed in his turban; but his restless eyes betrayed a troubled heart. Off yonder, beyond the Kedron, a group of venerable strangers drew near, their long garments covered with dust. They would have attracted attention anywhere. Entering at the eastern or Shushan gate, they climbed the marble stairway of the temple, entered Solomon's porch, and would have passed on into the inner courts but for the admonition of a Levite, who pointed to an inscription on the middle wall of partition, " Let no Gentile or unclean person enter here under penalty of death." Arrested by this rebuff, they said, " We have come from the far East, seeking Him who is born King of the Jews. Tell us where we may find Him." A moment later they were engaged in conversation with Herod. " Whence come ye?" "From the East." "And your errand?" " To find the promised King of the Jews."

" It's a fool's errand; I alone am king of the Jews." " Nay, we cannot be mistaken, for we have come under Divine guidance." And thereupon they told their story—how as they were watching the stars according to their custom, and meditating on the great promise of the coming Deliverer, a new luminary wheeled into view and seemed to beckon to them. Was this a harbinger of that event for which they looked? While they wondered, it moved on toward the West and they arose and followed it. Their hope had been that the Jewish Prince would be found in the Holy City, and they were amazed to find that nothing was here known of Him. The wise men were then detained while at Herod's order the members of the Sanhedrin came together to consult as to the rumored birth of this Prince. They agreed as to the prophecy; the event was to occur in Bethlehem: " And thou Bethlehem, in the land of Judah, are not the least among the princes of Judah, for out of thee shall come a governor that shall rule my people Israel." The wise men were then permitted to resume their journey, with a parting injunction that they should return and report as to the success of their singular quest. As they resumed their journey, lo, yonder in the heavens a star moved along before them, and they followed with great joy.

We may find profit in the contemplation of the deed of these pilgrims on this Christmas Sunday. From time immemorial they have been regarded as kings:

" We three kings of orient are,
  Bearing gifts, we journey afar;
O'er field and fountain, moor and mountain,
  Following yonder star."

In the cathedral at Cologne there is a golden reliquary in which are preserved, in the odor of sanctity, the relics of these men. I said to the venerable monk in attendance, " Do you really believe that these are the relics of the wise men?" " Oh, yes," he replied. " There is no question whatever as to their genuineness; we know their names— Gaspar, Melchior, and Balthazar. The venerable Bede tells all about them." There is, however, considerable doubt—to put it mildly—as to the trustworthiness of the legends which have gathered about these Magi. We have no reason to suppose they were kings, but we know they were truth-seekers; and, as Cromwell said to his daughter, "To be a truth-seeker is to be one of the best sect next to a truth-finder."

I. THE QUEST.—Wisdom is the principal thing, and there is nothing better than to get understanding. All truth is worth having. We blame our children for being inquisitive. But why? John Locke said. "The way to get knowledge is to ask questions." A wiser still has said, "Seek, and ye shall find." The cure for doubt is not a hoodwink, but a telescope. All truth is worth the having, and, therefore, worth the seeking. "Eureka!" cried Archimedes over a certain mathematical discovery. In all the world there is no pursuit so ennobling, so inspiring, and so gladdening as the pursuit of truth. This holds in all the provinces, but especially in the province of spiritual things.

It is related of Edmund of Canterbury, who was deeply interested in secular researches, that one night as he was poring over an ancient parchment, the spirit of his dead mother came to him and made three circles upon the palm of his hand, in token of the Holy Trinity, saying as she vanished, "Be this the purpose of thy life." Three circles do indeed embrace all. The fear of the Lord is the beginning of wisdom—and the end also. God is Alpha and Omega, the beginning and the end. To know Him is life eternal.

A man is in his noblest attitude when confronting the great spiritual verities. In this we are distinguished from the lower orders of life. We are able to touch the tremendous problems and measurably to solve them; and herein is the sweetest of life's delights. Lord Bacon said: "It is a pleasure to stand upon the shore and see ships tossing far away upon the sea; it is a pleasure to stand in the castle window and look down upon the battle and the adventures thereof; but no pleasure is comparable to the standing upon the vantage-ground of truth and beholding spiritual things."

II. THE HARBINGER.—God helps every man who earnestly desires to solve the problem of destiny. To these wise men He gave the guiding star. A vast amount of erudition has been spent in the attempt to get rid of the supernatural on these premises. It is said that a remarkable conjunction of certain planets occurred at about this time. In 1604 Kepler saw in the heavens a phenomenon which occurs only once in nearly a thousand years: Saturn and Jupiter were in conjunction; presently Mars also wheeled into line, thus forming "a fiery Trygon in Pisces." The constellation of Pisces, or the fish, was regarded as symbolical of Judea. The fish was also used by the early Christians as an anagram of Christ. Thus the "fiery Trygon" was identified with the star of Bethlehem. It is a fascinating hypothesis, but unfortunately (1) it did not occur at the precise time of the advent; and (2) being at an altitude of fifty-seven degrees, it could not have paused over a village or a particular home. We are, therefore, led to regard the star as a special messenger—an angel with a torch, as it were—sent to direct these wise men in their earnest quest. So God interposes in behalf of every sincere seeker for truth. "Seek, and ye shall find." Seek, good friend, and you shall find, God is on your side. Be of good courage.

It was many years ago that a butcher's boy went singing ribald songs about the streets of Nottingham. A taste for knowledge brought him to Cambridge University, where he distinguished himself not only for his cleverness as a student but as a reviler of Christ. By the unexpected death of a companion he was brought to think seriously of eternal things; his sins weighed heavily upon him; but at Calvary he found pardon. In the early flush of his conversion he wrote his gratitude in the familiar hymn:

"Once on the raging seas I rode;
  The storm was loud, the night was dark,
The ocean yawned, and rudely blowed
  The wind that tossed my foundering bark.
Deep horror then my vitals froze;
Death-struck, I ceased the tide to stem,
When suddenly a star arose:
  It was the Star of Bethlehem!

"It was my guide, my light, my all;
  It bade my dark forebodings cease,
And through the storm and danger's thrall
  It led me to the port of peace.
Now safely moored, my perils o'er,
  I'll sing, first in night's diadem,
For ever and forevermore,
  The Star, the Star of Bethlehem!"

God never yet left a man in the lurch who sincerely desired to solve the problem of destiny. It is a true saying, "A seeking sinner finds a seeking Savior." Somewhere in heaven the star is set that calls and beckons to the fountain of life.

III. THE TREASURE-TROVE.—The wise men have reached their destination. All the divinely kindled stars lead to Bethlehem. Here is the end of the great quest. The star that guided the Magi rested over a humble cottage. They entered and found the Christ-child—a child upon its mother's breast! Is that all? Ay, all—everything! In this child all the streams of prophecy converge. From this child radiate all the glowing lines of history. On the walls of the palace at Versailles, in a series of magnificent battle scenes, are portrayed the glories of France. In this humble home at Bethlehem all the hopes of Abraham, the dreams of David, and the visions of Isaiah are realized. This cottage is the center of the world.

Are you, friend, seeking the truth? Follow your star. Hearken when God speaks. "There are so many voices, and none of them is without significance." It is easy to quench all lights; to hush all voices; but hearken and give heed. Bethlehem is not far ahead. "Press on!" as Cromwell, the

Lord Protector, said to his daughter, "press on, dear heart, and thou shalt find the satisfying portion. Let nothing cool thy ardor until thou find it."

So here are the Magi opening their packs before the Christ-child. The search is over; the problem of destiny is solved. Here is gold for the King; here is myrrh for the Victor; here is frankincense for very God of very God. We are passing through the days of giving. We are celebrating now the infinite grace that lavished upon us the unspeakable gift, and what shall we render in return? I beseech you, brethren, by His great mercy, that ye present yourselves, a living sacrifice; which is your reasonable service. The best is none too good for God.—H. R.

THE TIME, MANNER, AND PURPOSE OF CHRIST'S ADVENT *

By William M. Taylor, D.D.

But when the fulness of the time was come God sent forth his Son, made of a woman, made under the law, to redeem them that were under the law, that we might receive the adoption of sons.—Gal. iv: 4, 5

These words occur in connection with a labored argument by which the apostle establishes the proposition that they who are of faith are the children of Abraham. The Gospel is thus a reproduction, only in fuller and more intelligible terms, of the promise made to the father of the faithful, and sinners now are to be justified precisely as he was, not by the works of law, but by the hearing of faith. And if that be the case, what is the use of the law? And to his inquiry, "Wherefore, then, serveth the law?" the answer is, "It was added because of transgressions until the seed should come to whom the promise was made." The law was thus not a contradiction of the promise, but an addition to it, designed for its protection until the time came when it could be fully revealed.

Believers have been God's children always, but under the law they were like children in the nursery under the care of the pedagog, who exercised restraint upon them and kept watch over them. When Christ came, however, the pedagog was discharged, and the children, having now arrived at mature age, were transferred from the nursery to the parlor, and admitted to the status of that full-grown sonship whose glorious liberty is elsewhere by the apostle so ravishingly expatiated upon. God's true people were always heirs, according to the promise made to Abraham; but under the law of Moses they were heirs in boyhood, and so subject to tutors and governors. When, however, at the time appointed by the Father, Christ came into the world, He proclaimed the full sonship—in modern phrase, the majority, the coming of age—of the children of God, and gave them their position in the home as that of those who are grown up into spiritual manhood. Thus Paul here views the advent of Christ in its bearing upon those who had been under the Jewish law. But, while we keep his standpoint clearly in sight, we may also make his words the germ of a few thoughts appropriate to this interesting season.

We have here, then, brought before us, in the first place, the period at which Christ appeared when the fulness of the time was come. Now here the question at once presents itself, Why did not the Redeemer appear sooner upon the earth? and few objections have been more persistently made to the whole system of redemption which the Gospel reveals than this: that it was unworthy of God to let four thousand years of the history of the race go by before He sent His Son into the world to deliver men. To the devout Christian it is enough that the time selected was God's time, but one or two statements may be made—first, in opposition to the position taken up by the objector, and, second, in vindication of that which he assails.

It is pertinent to say, then, to one who rejects the Savior on the ground which we have heard, that to refuse to believe on Jesus Christ as the Son of God for any such reason is eminently unphilosophical. The great principle of modern inductive philosophy is that we ought not to object to investigate anything which claims to rest on a basis of fact. No allegation of accident, improbability, or even impossibility, is to keep us from examining phenomena. Now the Gospel sets before us what purports to be a series of facts all tending to show that He in whom they center is the Son of God and the Savior of the world; and what the inquirer has to determine is, Are these alleged facts true? Is Jesus of Nazareth the Word made flesh? And if these questions must, on full and candid investigation, be answered in the affirmative, there is but one course left—viz.: to accept Him as the Redeemer. See where the principle of the objector would carry him in other departments. To be consistent, he must reject the whole system of the Copernican astronomy and all the discoveries of modern science, because of the late date in the history of the world in which they were made. To be consistent, he must reject the relief that chloro-

* Reported.

form or ether would give him in submitting to a serious surgical operation, on the ground that, if it were a real anesthetic, it would have been, under the providence of God, discovered as soon as pain was felt. But, further, it ought to be borne in mind that no mere man is in a position to form any accurate judgment on such a matter as this. We know some little of the history of the past, but we know little or nothing concerning that of the future. For anything that we can tell, there may be hundreds of millenniums yet in store for the human race, and in comparison with these the past six thousand years shall seem but as the morning twilight to the day of which it is the prelude. No idea of the contemplated building can be formed by one who only sees the foundations laid out for it; and when the work of God shall be finished, we may rest assured we shall see the wisdom of the whole. Meanwhile, the proper attitude of our souls in the contemplation of the question I have suggested is that of Paul when he cries: " O the depth of the riches both of the wisdom and knowledge of God! How unsearchable are His judgments, and His ways past finding out!"

Still, while all this is most true, I think I can see one or two good and sufficient reasons why the coming of the Lord was delayed until what Paul here calls the fulness of time. For one thing, some such delay would seem to have been needed for the accumulation of prophetic evidence, so that when the Messiah did come there should be no doubt whatever of His identity. It will be seen in a moment that, if the Son of God was to come in human nature at all, there was need for some special marks by which He should be recognized. It will be admitted, also, that the nature of these marks was conditioned by the limitations of the humanity in which He came. He might, indeed, have enshrouded Himself in majesty, as on Sinai—but, then, that would have been God in His glory; so that His appearance in the flesh necessitated some other kind of evidence, and, as miracles were wrought by other divinely commissioned ones, there was needed something else by which to distinguish the Christ when He came. This something else was prophecy: but prophecy from its very nature requires time to give it weight. The man who takes it upon himself to say what shall be to-morrow, next week, or next year, may very likely be right; yet no one thinks of attributing anything but great human shrewdness to him. When, however, things are described hundreds of years before they come to pass, and a person is minutely and graphically portrayed half a millennium before he appears, the conclusion is irresistible that God has drawn the portrait, and that he who comes and fulfils the conditions of the prediction is all that the prophecy proclaims him to be. The fulfilment thus not only authenticates the messenger who utters the prophecy, but identifies him in whom the prophecy has been fulfilled.

Now, such being the case, the further the date of the giving of the prophecy is from that of its fulfilment, the more cogent and convincing is the evidence it gives; just as the wider the span of the arch, the greater is the skill of the engineer who has constructed it. And so it seems to me that one reason for the delay of Christ's appearance was to allow time for the accumulation of such a body of predictions, all centering in Him, as should make it clear beyond all possibility of cavil that He is the sent of God. Of course, every one sees that, after the predictions had been given, they had to be fulfilled; but my argument is now not, that Christ came when He did in order to fulfil prophecy. I am seeking to go behind the prophecies themselves to the principle upon which they are constructed, and, if I have been correct in supposing that the further the time the giving of a prediction is from the date at which it was to be fulfilled, the stronger is the evidence which it furnishes of the divinity of its origin and the identity of Him to whom it refers. You will see at once how it came that a long lapse of years was needed before the advent of the Christ. But, when He did come, the key which He brought fitted into every ward of the prophetic lock; for it was when the stem of Jesse was to human view a withered root that the Christ sapling sprang out of it; it was when the scepter was fallen from Juda's hand that Shiloh appeared (?); it was when Daniel's seventieth week (?) was hastening to the close that Messiah the Prince came, and came in such a peculiar manner as to interpret as well as to fulfil the primeval and paradisial prophecy that the seed of the woman should bruise the head of the serpent.

But yet another reason for the delay of Christ's appearance might be to make evident the utter inability of men by themselves to find their way back to God. This seems to me to be more than hinted at by Paul in those words written by him to the Corinthians: " For after that in the wisdom of God the world by wisdom knew not God, it pleased God by the foolishness of preaching to save them that believed." It was, therefore, a part of the plan of God to show that the tendency of sin is ever downward, and that without His direct intervention there was no possibility of salvation for mankind. This same truth seems to me to be the prominent feature of Daniel's vision of the four empires, as described in the seventh chapter of his book. These kingdoms, you may remember, were symbolized to him by beasts, to show that earthly power left to itself always runs to brutality. The first was like a lion, but still it had the feet of a man, and a man's heart was given to it. The second was like a bear devouring much flesh. The third was like the fierce and bloodthirsty leopard, and the fourth was a strange and terrible animal, having iron teeth and stamping with its feet everything which it did not destroy with its mouth. Men talk of development theories; that is, the development of worldly power when left to itself—and, observe, it is the development of cruelty. Each of these empires was worse than that which went before it; and the deterioration would have gone on and on, if it had not been for Him like unto the Son of man, who came with the clouds of Heaven, and who received from the Ancient of days dominion and glory and a kingdom, that all peoples, nations, and languages should serve Him. What, I ask, could better describe the history of the Babylonian, the Persian, the Grecian, and the Roman empires? Altho there was an apparent rise in merely intellectual culture from the one to the other, there was at the same time, parallel to that, a constantly increasing immorality; and at the very era of the Advent the cruelty of Rome was at its height. Some there were, even in these old days, that saw with eagerness the truth. The philosophers of Greece, as mere intellectual giants, were among the greatest of men; but, tho they discarded for themselves the polytheism of the vulgar, they could not put anything better in its place. The old faiths were losing their hold, even upon the most thoughtful of heathen. In the words of Milton in his hymn on the Nativity:

" The oracles are dumb,
　No voice or hideous hum
Runs through the archéd roof in words deceiving.
　Apollo from his shrine
　Can no more divine,
With hollow shriek the steep of Delphos leaving.
No mighty trance of breathéd spell
Inspires the pale-eyed priest from the prophetic cell."

Heathenism had proved unequal to the wants of men; and it was when the most thoughtful among the Pagans were turned away from its hollow mockeries and misleading altars that the anthem of the angels broke clear and loud above the slopes of Bethlehem: " Glory to God in the highest! Peace on earth and good will toward men!"

Still again, the coming of the Lord may have been delayed so long a time for the preparation of the world for the diffusion of the Gospel. Geologists tell us that long ages must have elapsed while stratum was rising above stratum on the crust of the earth ere yet it was fit for the abode of man; and much in the same way centuries passed away while each empire rose and fell and left its own stratum of deposit until a fair platform was erected for the Gospel of Jesus Christ. Who does not see that if the Lord had come in the early days—for example, of the kings of Israel—there would have been little opportunity for the propagation of His message of mercy to mankind? Petty states were then continually striving for the mastery over each other, and no one had arisen with resources sufficient to conquer and control the rest. Then, when Babylon had gained the mastery, Palestine became in a remarkable way the battlefield of the world whereon

Persia, and afterward Greece, strove for the supremacy, and there was no point at which the Savior could have come with the opportunity of reaching immediately the race as a whole; but at length Rome built up her territory, and without thinking at all about anything else than the holding of those faraway regions on which she had laid her iron hand, she made such a system of roads that from Parthia, in the east, to Britain, in the west, the man who was privileged to call himself a Roman citizen could go with safety. Nay, more, the language of Greece had well-nigh vanquished the conquerors of the Greeks, and he who was acquainted with that could make himself understood wherever he went. Never before had it been so easy for the heralds of truth to pass from land to land; never before had the world, as a whole, been so accessible; never before had the confusion of tongues been so largely counteracted. Who does not see in all this the fore-arranged hand of God? And when we add that at the moment of the Advent, the Temple of Janus was shut because then, for the first time in many years, peace did reign o'er all the earth, we are constrained again to take refuge in the words of Milton:

" No war, or battle's sound,
　Was heard the world around,
The idle spear and shield were high uphung;
　The hookéd chariot stood
　Unstained with hostile blood,
The trumpet spake not to the arméd throng:
　And kings sat still with awful eye,
As if they surely knew their Sovereign Lord was by."

But we must turn now, in the second place, to consider the Person who came in the fulness of time. He was the Son of God. These words describe His origin and inherent dignity. They are not, as some, even of those who believe in His Deity, would assert, a mere title belonging to His mediatorial office. He did not become God's Son by being sent into the world, but He was sent into the world *because* He was the Son of God. If anything were needed to convince us that this is the correct account of the matter, it is furnished by His own parable of the vineyard, in which, when one deputation of servants after another had been shamefully illtreated by the husbandmen, the lord of the vineyard is represented as last of all sending his son, saying: " They will reverence my son."

But, while we thus claim that the words of the Son of God are descriptive of an eternal and divine relationship, we must beware of robing the idea which they express with all the material dress of a mere earthly significance. It is not to be supposed that everything which is true of a human son as related to his father is true of the Son of God in His filial position in the Godhead. The son of a man derives his existence from his father, and has an existence that began subsequent to that of his parent; but when we speak of the Deity, both of these ideas must be eliminated from sonship. In using the word "son" God has, if I may so express it, accommodated Himself to the limitations of human speech. No earthly term could give us an absolutely correct idea of a divine relationship because no finite mind could coin a word for an infinite idea. Hence the phrase, "God sent forth his Son," does not imply that the Son so sent was in every respect to Him what a man's son is to his father. Sonship on earth is that which comes nearest to it; but, from the very necessities of the case, the ideas of derivation of being and posteriority of existence must be excluded from it, and when that is done there remain identity of nature and intensity of affection. The Son of God, therefore, is a partaker of the Divine nature and essence, and an object of the Divine love and complacency; for, when God introduced Him to man, He said: "This is my beloved Son, hear ye him!"

If you ask me to distinguish or define any further, I declare myself unable to proceed. There is a distinction of some kind between Father, Son, and Holy Spirit in the Godhead. They are three in one sense, but they are not three in the same sense as that in which God is one. And so, while there is mystery, there is no contradiction; and the difficulties which men have found have all arisen, in my judgment, not from the statement of the fact as I now put it, but from the unwise attempts which have been made to explain the mode of the fact. So soon as we step out of the Word of God we find ourselves more and more astray, and by our very efforts to remove perplexity we only the more increase the bewilderment of the inquirer. I content myself, therefore, with the mere statement of the truth as it has been revealed, and refuse to be drawn into any vain inquiry as to those things which have not been made known, probably for the very reason that they could not be made known to our finite intelligences. Sufficient for us it is to be assured that He who came to earth as our Redeemer is the Son of God, partaker with the Father of the Divine essence, and the object of the Father's love and complacency. He brings the help we need. He is not a man merely on a level with ourselves. He is God, and so He is mighty to save. He could have been no deliverer for us if He had not been something different from us.

I know not, for my own part, while I have great regard for the honesty and sincerity of the Unitarians, how they can speak of Jesus as a Savior who denied His Deity, for it is His Deity which gives Him ability to save. If He were only a man, then He is no more to me than any other of the great men of antiquity, and all this Christmas festivity in honor of His birth is only an absurdity. If He were only a man, then He was a deliverer of a race simply as Washington was the father of his country; and churches and the Lord's supper and missions are a huge mistake. If He were only a man, then the story of other men might be supposed to be equally helpful to the human race with His. But, no! no! The instinct of humanity cannot be thus deceived. In its passionate longing for deliverance the soul cries, "O God! my God!" for it recognizes that there can be no help for it except in God. And in the contemplation of Christ, it has even exclaimed, "My God!" No candid man will ever put the Jesus of the Gospel on the same level as a philosopher. There is a difference, not only in degree, but in nature, between the two, and in that difference known and recognized is the quality that fits Him to be the Redeemer.

That which I cling to for support must be something different from myself, and stronger than myself; otherwise, in the time of my necessity I shall be no better than if I were leaning on a broken reed. When in the irresistible whirlwind the waves are breaking over the vessel and sweeping the deck from stem to stern, it will not do for the sailor to stand alone; neither will it do for him to lay hold on his fellow, for they together may be swept into the ocean. Far wiser he who lays hold upon the iron bulwark of the ship, making for the moment the strength of the iron as his own, and is by that upheld; and so, amid the storms of life, it will not do for me to stand alone; it will not do for me even to cling to a fellowman. I must have some one higher and stronger than myself lest I be swept from my foothold; and I find that loftiness, that might, that strength, in the Deity of Christ, and it is because He is my God that He is my Savior.

But, now, let us look at the manner in which the Son of God came into the world: He was made of a woman—made under the law. That is to say, He became a man and a Jew. He took on Him human nature. Now, what does that imply? Not, certainly, that He ceased to be divine, but that, in addition to what He had been before, He became a partaker of flesh and blood. He assumed humanity, that through His manhood He might give to men a manifestation of Deity. He took not only a human body—for that is only a part of manhood; it is only the tabernacle in which the better part of man dwells—but He took human nature into union with His Deity. If you ask me how that is possible, again I reply that I cannot tell any more than I can explain how the soul, of which I am conscious, is united to the body which I know to be not *mind,* but only *mine.* But, while I cannot make the mystery plain, I think I can see that this union of Deity and humanity must have conditioned both. It made it necessary, for one thing, that His humanity should be pure: and so that accounted for the peculiar manner of His birth, wherein for Him the entail of sin was broken, and His very body was a holy thing. It made it necessary also that His Deity should be manifested under certain limitations. That is the very difficulty of the Incarnation, for it was to be manifest through His manhood. That is what Paul refers to when he said: "Tho he was rich, for our sakes he became poor;" and in another connection, that "he made himself of no reputation," or, as it is literally, He *emptied* Himself. His Deity was in some sort veiled by His humanity, and that explains what is said in the Gospel about the limitations of it, as when we are informed that He increased in wisdom, and that He knew neither the day nor the hour of a certain event. The Incarnation to the eyes of men was indeed a revelation of God, but to the eyes of angels it was rather, for the time being, the veiling of Deity—the tabernacle of the flesh curtaining, as it were, the glory of the Godhead. Still through that which to the eyes of angels was a curtain, men saw more of God than they ever did before. Indeed, but for the curtain they could have seen nothing at all of Him.

If you want to look at the sun through a telescope, you must be very careful to put a smoke glass before that which you look through; for, if you do not, the light of the sun through that of the mirror on which you look will strike into your eye and make you utterly blind. And so, in like manner, no man can behold the unveiled God and live. There would come from the unveiling an excess of light that would blast him. But, if we contemplate God as He has veiled Himself in the humanity of Christ, we see Him without being destroyed by it, and the sight of Him imparts salvation to us. Or, as John says: "The Word was made flesh and dwelt among us, and we beheld his glory, the glory as of the only begotten of the Father;" and lo! it was a glory not full of destruction, but rather "full of grace."

But the Savior was also made under the law—that is, He became a Jew. It behooved Him to fulfil all righteousness: and so He was circumcised. He lived under the restrictions of the Mosaic Law, and in all forms of conduct conformed to the discipline under which the children of Abraham were placed. The purpose of this was that He might redeem them that were under the law. He took the place of those whom He came to deliver; and the same principle that required that He should become a man in order to deliver men, made it needful that He should become a Jew in order to redeem the Jews.

The law that is satisfied by a redeemer must be the law that was broken by those whom he wishes to redeem. In the abstract, indeed, law is always the same thing. Law is always that which God requires of His creatures; but for different creatures the law is different, being conformed to the nature which they possess. Thus, if I have any right conception of the nature of angels, I cannot conceive how they can conform, or can be required to conform, to the precepts of the Decalog. These commandments are for creatures with a human nature; and so, when these were broken, the obedience of an angel to the law by which angels were held could not satisfy them. They could be obeyed only by one who is himself human. Hence, if it were needful for our Redeemer

to satisfy the law which we had broken, it was needful for Him to become a man before He could do it. But in the same way the Jewish law was laid by God upon the descendants of Abraham for special reasons, and it was different from that law under which other men were held. Hence, if it were needful for the Redeemer of the Jews to satisfy the law which they had broken, it was needful that He should become a Jew. By His Jewish birth He became subject to the Jewish law, under the curse of which the laws were held; and so through the honoring of the law, He has redeemed both Jew and Gentile from the curse of the law, being made a curse for us, as it is written: "Accursed be every one that hangeth upon a tree."

Now see the glorious result of this, in the closing words of my text: "That we might receive the adoption of sons." As I stated in the outset, this "adoption" means, primarily, not the taking into the family of those who formerly did not belong to it, but the raising to the position of full-grown sonship of those who had formerly been under tutors and governors. Still, as the Gentiles were placed on a footing of equality with Jews—if in Christ, as Paul has told us in the immediate neighborhood of my text, "there is neither Jew nor Gentile"—we may take the words as signifying that the grand outcome of redemption for us is the making of us sons of God by the power of the Holy Ghost. And what does it mean, my brethren, when we say of ourselves that we are *sons of God?* It means that we have been born again by the Holy Ghost, into God's family, having His nature imparted to us; so that, whereas before we were prone to evil and averse to good, we are now inclined to holiness, and turn away from sin. It means that God is now the object of our filial affection —that we are the subjects of His fatherly regard. It means that we hold ourselves under His authority, and that He will provide for us and protect us as His children. It means that we have liberty of fellowship with Him, and walk with Him in the enjoyment of that highest kind of intercourse which the world knows, viz.: the confidential friendship which subsists between the father and the son when the father becomes the companion of the son, and the son grows up to be the associate of the father. It means that His house is our home, round which our highest and holiest and fondest associations cluster, and in which, at last, we are to find our eternal abode.

Sons of God! Sons of God! What an honor, what a passion, what a privilege it is to be the outcome of the Savior's advent to our world, that we might receive the adoption of sons! He came to secure for us God's forgiveness and blessing; and, by taking us by the hand and leading us into the very mercy-seat, to teach us to say, "Our Father." He came to put new life into our devotions, new joy into our hearts, new holiness into our lives, new significance into our trials, and new attraction into our heaven.

This was the object He had in view when He was born into our earth a little babe.

But, O my hearers! it is not accomplished in you until He is born into your hearts. For, look what Paul says in the twenty-sixth verse of the chapter preceding that from which my text is taken: "Ye are all the children of God by faith in Christ Jesus." Through faith, then, Christ is born within us, and we become the sons of God, entering into His family.

And so, after the wide sweep we have taken this morning, we now come again to the old question: "Dost thou believe in the Son of God?" That is for me and thee the question of this recurring anniversary. When Christ was born in Bethlehem a new era in the world's history was rung in, and when, by faith, He shall be born again in your heart a new era in your life shall be begun. "As many as received him, to them gave he power to become the sons of God, even to them that believe in his name."

Wilt thou, my hearer, receive Him now? O, let the joy-bells of thy heart ring out thy soul's great Christmas peal! It is a time of giving of gifts. Ah, yes! and here, my beloved, is God's best gift to thee—sonship, through the birth of Christ within thee. Wilt thou accept it at His hands? Put it not, I beseech thee, away from thy heart, but make room for Jesus there. Ah! you remember how it is written in the beautiful story, that comes up year after year at this joyful season: "And there was no room for him in the inn." How many human hearts there are to-day like that caravansary in the Bethlehem of old! Room for this and that of business, and pleasure, and domestic joy—room for everything but Christ! O, make room, make room this morning, my hearers, for the Christ-child in your heart, no matter what must be dislodged to secure His entrance. Put every intruder out, and let the Christ-child to-day be born within thee. May God add His blessing, and to His name be praise!—H. R.

WHY THE MAGI EXPECTED CHRIST

By James Mulcahey, D.D.

I shall see him, but not now; I shall behold him, but not nigh: there shall come a Star out of Jacob, and a Sceptre shall rise out of Israel.—Num. xxiv: 17

Our lesson has reference to the wise men who came from the East seeking Christ. Who were these men, who had doubtless learned to look through nature up to nature's God, who were moved by appearances in nature to spiritual thoughts? They were not Jews. The East, from which they came was beyond the boundary of the Holy Land—perhaps Arabia or Persia. The Magi were men to whom were entrusted the sacred books. They were the leaders of the people in religion. They studied astronomy. It is not strange that the appearance of a new star attracted their attention, or that they should have connected it with some new revelation from Heaven. There was at this time an expectation that a great deliverer would come. This feeling was widespread among the Eastern nations. Now, whence this expectation? For an answer to this we must look to the prophecy of the text.

Balaam was a soothsayer. He did not scruple even to receive the rewards of his divination. But he was more than a sooth-sayer. He was a prophet and a servant of God. Several times it is declared that the word of the Lord was in his mouth. He had the gift of prophecy. He was constrained to speak as the spirit moved him. This Balaam was of the land of Abram, a land in which there was a knowledge of the true God. Let us listen to this prophecy and its import:

I. Of whom was it made? The words of the text cannot refer to the covenants of David or other kings of Israel. Their solemnity carry the conviction that they refer

to One beyond David. "I shall see him, but not now; I shall behold him, but not nigh." Who is that *Him?* How emphatic and solemn the reference! We cannot doubt but that it refers to Him in whom all prophecy converged, and to whom all the ends of the world shall look for salvation. Is it not likely that the words of a prophet so prominent as was Balaam in the East would have been treasured carefully, and that the star that was to arise out of Jacob would have been anxiously awaited? For centuries the Magi watched for that mystic star.

II. Who were to be blessed in the fulfilment of the prophecy? It was a promise of salvation for the Gentiles. What a longing do the words express! "I shall see him, but not now, I shall behold him, but not nigh." How quickly these wise men arose when the star appeared and entered the land of Jacob!

An important question arises: Why the seeming injustice of selecting a comparatively insignificant people to be the depositaries of sacred truth? Then, why the seemingly greater inconsistency: the rejection of the chosen people for two thousand years, and the keeping of the truth from all but a small fragment of the human race? As the Jews were made to understand that it was because of their narrow misconception of the nature of the religion revealed to them, and their consequent self-complacency, that the Gentiles were kept from a knowledge of the religion God had revealed to them, so we to-day, by our narrow and selfish view of the ends of grace, restrict its blessings. Revelation is a universal, not a partial gift. We are not to understand that we are infallibly guided or that the rest of the world is infallibly wrong. While the means of grace are specially vouchsafed to the Church, yet do they belong to all the world. There is light given to all nations. This is no new doctrine, forced by the inroads of modern liberalism. Saint Clement of Alexandria held, that God had revealed Himself in philosophy to the Greeks, and that He was a Savior enlightening, in manifold ways, all the world.

Two thousand years passed after this prophecy of Balaam before its fulfilment, but the world was not neglected. An educating and disciplining process was all the while carried forward. So is the work of God carried forward to-day throughout the world.

The star still shines in the East. Let us turn our eyes towards it, and welcome the coming of the nations guided by its light.— H. R.

GOD WITH US

By Wayland Hoyt, D.D.

Matt. i: 23

One day, years ago, the people living near Niagara Falls were startled by the cry: "Man in Niagara! Man in Niagara!"

So they all ran, thronging the suspension bridge and crowding the cliffs hard by.

"Where is he? Where is he?" each asked of each, because at first they could not see him. "Poor fellow," they said; "he's gone!"

Then some one cried out: "See; see, yonder—he is hanging on a rock!" pointing as he spoke to a low, waterwashed rock about sixty yards below the great falls on the American side.

Then the question went through all the murmuring crowd: "Can we save him? Can we save him?"

They got a long rope ladder. They hoped they might be able to let it down somewhere in the poor man's neighborhood from one of the overhanging cliffs. They threw the ladder over, but there were some bushes growing out of a crevice down part way in the rocks, and as the rope ladder fell it got tangled in the bushes, and they could not loosen it.

Then they asked this other question: "Who will go down and clear the rope ladder and try to save that man?" It was a terrible question to ask, for it was a terrible thing to do. The man who should dare do it must do so at the greatest risk of his own life.

At last a brave young man stepped forward and said, "I'll go." Carefully he climbed down the rope ladder to the bushes. There he waited for some time seeking to get the ladder clear. With difficulty, he got it clear, and then the rope ladder fell down near to where that imperiled man was clinging for his life to that wet, low rock.

Then this man who had descended from the cliff began himself to go down farther. It was a frightful thing to do. The rope ladder swung and swayed, and below him were the dashing, boiling waters. One loose grasp, one misstep, and nothing in God's world could save him. But he went slowly and steadily down and down.

At last he reached the rock where the drenched, buffeted, weakening man was clinging. Holding with one hand firmly to the swaying ladder and putting one foot as firmly as he could upon the low rocks the waters were dashing over, with the other hand he took hold of the poor fellow, and, saying words of courage to him, got him to take hold of the rope ladder and try to climb up it to the cliffs above.

This brave helper could not carry the poor man up. To attempt that would be altogether beyond his own strength. Nor could he tie the poor fellow to the rope ladder, and let him be dragged up, for so he would be dashed to death against the projecting rocks above, as the rope ladder would sway, now this way and now that.

So this man who had somehow fallen into the wild waters, with nearly all his strength gone through his terrible clinging to that low rock against the awful force of the invading water, took hold of the rope ladder and began to climb. After he had gone up perhaps a hundred feet, he had to stop to rest. Those up there on the cliffs were in great fear lest his small strength should give way entirely and he fall again into the raging waters. "Hold on!" they shouted to him. "Hold on!" But their voices could not be distinctly heard amid the thunder of the mighty falls.

Then the man climbed up another hundred feet, and stopped again to rest. Those on the cliff grew more hopeful now. And the brave helper at the bottom stood there, getting what foothold he might and steadying the ladder.

Then, again, the man began to climb, painfully, laboriously, his strength, which had been tasked so terribly, almost failing him.

Then, at last, he was in reach of the top, and some strong arms, reaching over, seized him and lifted him into safety, amid the tears, and shouts, and eager joy of the multitude.

And the brave helper who had gone down for him and at so great a risk climbed safely to the summit too.

I think the story is a good one for the Christmas time, because it tells, tho in the dimmest and in the poorest way, what our Lord Jesus has done for every one of us.

He was the One who came down from Heaven to us, amid all the storm and danger and death of our sad sins.

HE CAME DOWN TO US. He did not stand, like the people on the cliffs, away off in the far heavens shouting to us to climb up. He was like the brave helper in the story: from the far heavens He Himself came down to us, and all our risk and pain and sorrow and death He took upon Himself.

He is a great deal better to us, too, than was this brave helper, good as he was to the poor man clinging for his life to the wet, treacherous rock. Our Lord Jesus does not simply bring the ladder of escape to us, but He gives us His own strength that we may have strength to climb. Nay, He does more than that, for really we have no strength. If we will only let Him, with a deep trust, like the shepherd in the parable of the lost sheep, He lays us on His own shoulders and carries us up.

So our Lord Jesus is the one who comes to us; and if we will have it so, there is not one of us who may not be saved because He came.

And the Christmas time is the time when we think of the fact and of the way of His coming to us.

Consider, first, *the reality of the Incarnation.* Jesus Christ is actually God with us. As another has most truly and thoughtfully said: "Everything of the Christian religion depends on the truth of the story of Bethlehem. If He who was there born was not really God, then the religion He set up is but *human* religion, and our hopes of a manhood perfected in a God-man are quenched. If He who was there born was not really man, but only phantom flesh, the religion He set up is a *deceitful* religion, leaving to us, it may be, nothing but a phantom God. I say, then, that Christianity from center to circumference is balanced on the solitary pivot of the nativity. Revelation, Mediation, Passion, Crucifixion, Resurrection, Ascension, Parousia, all revolve round Bethlehem's manger."

Consider, second, *how sacred a thing is childhood.* God entered into our human nature as a child; and what higher work than the training of this childhood, dignified thus by the fact that our Lord and Savior was once a little child! Daniel Webster at one time said: "If we work upon marble, it will perish. If we work upon brass, time will efface it. If we rear temples, they will crumble into dust. If we work upon immortal minds, if we imbue them with principles, with the just fear of God and love for our fellow men, we engrave on these tablets something which will brighten for eternity."

Consider, third, since God is thus with us, how certain it is that our Lord Jesus *can enter into the most real and close sympathy with every one of us.*

Consider, fourth, how the Babe in the manger, who is yet God with us, teaches us that *the true life is that of forgetfulness of self.* He, thinking not His equality with God a thing to be grasped at, emptied Himself.—H. R.

CONCEALING CHRIST

BY J. FLEMING

But he could not be hid.—Mark vii: 24

I. THE LORD JESUS IS NOT HID.—The Old Testament contained one promise which like a thread of gold ran through the whole; a promise which was oft repeated, which was embraced by all believers, the blessings of which were grandly unfolded as time rolled on; and which, in the fulness of time was accomplished. It was the Messiah. The Dayspring from on high has visited us. The Sun of Righteousness has arisen with healing in His wings, and therefore the Lord Jesus is not hid. He is plainly seen by those who have eyes to see, and plainly heard by those who have ears to hear, altho He is in the highest heavens.

II. THE LORD JESUS OUGHT NOT TO BE HID.—Who shall declare how wicked is the attempt to hide the Lord Jesus, who said, "I am the light of the world." Do any attempt it? Yes, many have done so. The Scribes and Pharisees saw clearly enough that He was the Christ; yet they tried to hide Him by saying that He wrought miracles by the power of Beelzebub. This our Lord declared, but nothing else, is the unpardonable sin. The Jews wished Christ to be hid, when they quenched His costly life on Calvary; they wished His words to be hid when they beat the apostles, and commanded them not to speak in His Name. Christ *ought* not to be hid.

III. CHRIST CANNOT BE HID.—All things prepare for the coronation of Christ. All things, consciously or unconsciously, are being attuned for the glory of Christ. This is God's mighty purpose which all events are unfolding. All things are for Christ and Christ in all things. He cannot be hid. For Christ the vast machinery of providence is kept in beneficent action; all persons, all things, all events, are under His beneficent rule. Over all men's conscience His purpose must prevail, His cause roll on. "He must reign."—S. B., vol. vi., p. 253.

THE SHEPHERDS OF JUDEA

By Charles H. Hall, D.D.

And there were in the same country shepherds abiding in the field, keeping watch over their flocks by night.—Luke ii: 8

In all ancient history, the shepherd is represented as the embodiment of innocent stupidity. But we think of these shepherds near Bethlehem as ideal shepherds. This is the trick poetry and art have played. In the same way, Mary is taken out of ordinary maidenhood, and has offered to her the incense that formerly was offered to Diana. The fact is, God came down through all the strata of society when He came to redeem man. Ignorance must cease to be the mother of devotion. It is possible so to clothe Christ with the imagination, as to take Him out of the reach of ordinary men. Let us look upon these men as simple shepherds. The record that is given of them will teach us several lessons.

I. It is said they were sorely terrified. Their idea of God was one clothed with terror. When will it be possible for Christians to face without fear the messenger of God in the dark. We cultivate fear. The air is electrical with the divine presence. The heathen thought by smearing their faces with filth to please their gods. Some such idea still lurks in our minds. About this time there were three angelic visitations. (a) The shepherds were frightened out of their wits. (b) Zacharias was troubled at sight of the divine messenger, and became dumb. (c) Mary was, doubtless, surprised, but was not afraid. "Behold the handmaid of the Lord; be it unto me according to thy word." Her nature had been so schooled as to be able to stand, unterrified, on the verge of the supernatural.

II. The shepherds went to find Christ. I give as my fancy that they found Him when they put up their flocks in the sheepfold. Christ was first found in a *sheepfold*. Since then the world has been too apt to seek for Christ only in magnificent temples, etc. The mystery of all mysteries in religion to me is God Himself. He who must have microscopic vision to see me at all, came down, passing thrones of kings—in ancient times all kings were gods, etc. The wonder of Christianity is its simplicity. I tell you, if the Bible had been an imposition, it would have fallen into this trap. The world had been 1,800 years coming up to the idea of democracy embodied in that wonderful effort of human wisdom, the Declaration of Independence. The idea of democracy was in this, *coming to a stable to find Christ.* •

III. The occasion must have turned out as one of joy to the shepherds, as it was to the angels. We are too gloomy in our religion. Four-fifths of Christendom still sing the words of a half-crazy man, asking for the joy he felt when he first knew the Lord. It was once thought out of harmony to celebrate the Lord's Supper on Christmas day. Religion and joy should go hand in hand.

Let us remember—

1. That there is no place so humble but that Christ may be successfully sought there. No home can be inferior to a stable or sheepfold.

2. God is love, and should not occasion fear.

3. Then, also, they who are in God, are in love. They will love all.

I wish you all a Merry Christmas.—H. R.

THE SEASON OF PEACE

By Robert S. MacArthur, D.D., LL.D.

On earth peace.—Luke iii: 14

The whole air at the first Christmastide was tremulous with joy. It was a time for holy song, for inspired pæan, for seraphic song. Let joy come still to our homes and hearts. Christ gives brightness and beauty, gladness and glory, to the whole circle of life and duty. Come, Lord Jesus, there shall be room for Thee in our homes. Once there was none in the inn, but only in the stable; now our best is Thine. Only honor us with Thy beneficent presence!

I. Let us away with strife at this season; now is the time to speak kindly words. Let us not carry into the new year the enmities of the old; let not the harsh notes of contention come into the heavenly song of peace.

II. Christ came to give peace, and from Heaven's throne to-day He bends to give peace to all who trust Him. He was the only person ever born into the world who had His choice as to how He should come. He might have come man, as did the first Adam; He came a babe. He inserted Himself into our race at its lowest and weakest point. If He were to lift the race He must get under it. He glorified the cradle; He beautified boyhood; He sanctified motherhood.

III. But Christ must be born in each heart in order that we may have a true Christmas. Are we rejoicing in the gifts of human love? Shall we be unmindful of Him who is the "unspeakable gift?" Turn not the Christ of God away from the heart's inn; banish Him not to the manger. Heaven's gift is now offered without money and without price. Receive Him with glad welcome!—H. R.

SONG OF THE ANGELS AT THE BIRTH OF CHRIST

By Matthew Simpson, D.D., LL.D.

And suddenly there was with the angel a multitude of the heavenly host, praising God, and saying, Glory to God in the highest, and on earth peace, good will toward men.—Luke ii: 13, 14

What an interest centered in that babe, wrapped in swaddling-clothes, lying in a manger at Bethlehem! Prophets were interested, angels were interested, the ages have been most deeply interested since. The shepherds had, perhaps, some premonition. The seventy weeks of Daniel's prophecy were about fulfilled. It may be, at that very time, they were talking of the coming of Christ. Suddenly their attention was arrested by a strange sight in the heavens. It grew brighter, and took the form of an angel, and then they heard a voice announcing the birth of Christ as glad tidings for *all* people, not to the Jews only. Then *suddenly* the air was filled with angels singing, as if they had come right out from the air. We know not their wonderful song, but part came to mortal ears, "Glory to God in the highest," etc. I know not who those angels were, but I fancy they were the redeemed. Adam was there, Eve was there. Eve, who, in her maternal earnestness, declared at the birth of her first born, "I have gotten a man from the Lord," hoping that that was he who should bruise the serpent's head. Now, in the fulness of time, she had come to witness the birth of the babe who was to be the Savior of her race. David, Elijah, Moses, the patriarchs, I believe, were with that heavenly host. I think, if I had lived before the birth of Christ, and been in Heaven when Christ left His throne to come to earth, I would have asked permission to come down, etc.

This song reveals three things:

1. The glorification of God through the incarnation. God has glory through His vast work in nature, His providence building up and casting down nations, etc.

In the incarnation there was special glory. It was glory to God in the highest. Highest, in that it was above all other glory, in that it extended to all time, and in that it wrought such wondrous good.

2. The great results to the earth. It would result in peace. Strifes, thorns, and thistles were abounding. The earth was torn and bleeding by constant contention. With Christ came peace. The result would be universal peace.

3. The effect on the individual man. "Good will toward men," from one another, from God. Out of this good will would finally spring peace on earth, and glory to God in the highest.

These results are obtained by certain stages.

From what a small beginning the work started. It is illustrated by a mustard-seed, a bit of leaven, a little stone cut from the mountain side. When Christ came, the event made little commotion. He came as a little babe, in an obscure country, among a despised and conquered people, and of a poor family. A star showed the interest of the universe, the singing angels the interest of Heaven, in the birth of that babe. On earth there was but a brief commotion. A little potentate was made jealous for a while. Then all is quiet for thirty years. Kings and governors changed. Most of those who remembered anything of the shepherd's story, and the massacre of the little ones at Bethlehem, had died. At last an unknown man came for baptism at the hands of John, and a voice was heard from Heaven, and then the marvelous work of Christ began. Opposed on every side, crucified at last, and His few disciples scattered, Christ's death gave the triumphant illustration of this good will. The world is no longer an orphan—God is the Father.

Another stage in reaching peace on earth, and the glory to God in the highest, is in this; if a man has good will, he begins to act good will. Christ never showed illwill to an enemy, even. If Christ is in us, we will love all. Now, I tell you from God on the eve of the Christmas day, that he who hates his brother is a murderer. No matter where your name is written on earth, in Church book, or class book, if you bear ill-will to any one, it is not written in Heaven.

Then the Holy Spirit is given, which works in men universal good will.

Now, when this good will is perfect, you have a basis for lasting peace. Permanent peace can come in no other way. Recognize every man as a brother, and war must cease. Then every babbling tongue will sing, Glory to God in the highest.

Let us learn to do good to all people.—H. R.

THE WORD AMONGST US

By Alexander Maclaren, D.D.

The Word dwelt among us.—John i: 14; (with Rev. vii: 15 and xxi: 3)

The word rendered "dwelt" in these three passages is a peculiar one. It is only found in the New Testament—in this Gospel, and in the Book of the Revelation. The word literally means "to dwell in a tent"—or, if we may use such a word, "to tabernacle;" and there is, no doubt a reference to the Tabernacle in which the Divine Presence abode in the wilderness and in the land of Israel before the erection of the Temple. In all three passages, then, we may see allusion to that early symbolical dwelling of God with man.

I. Think, first, of the Tabernacle for earth. The Word was made flesh, and dwelt, as in a tent, among us. St. John would have us think that, in that lowly humanity, with its curtains and its coverings of flesh, there lay shrined in the inmost place the brightness of the light of the manifest glory of God. The manifestation of God in Christ is unique, as becomes Him who partakes of the nature of that God of whom He is the representative and the revealer. Like the Tabernacle, Christ is the dwelling-place of God, the place of revelation, the place of sacrifice, and the meeting-place of God and man.

II. We have the Tabernacle for the heavens. He that sitteth on the throne shall spread his Tabernacle above them," as the word might be rendered. That is to say, He Himself shall build and be the tent in which they dwell; He Himself shall dwell with them in it; He Himself, in closer union than can be conceived of here, shall keep them company during that feast.

III. Look at that final vision which we have in these texts, which we may call the Tabernacle for the renewed earth. "Behold, the Tabernacle of God is with men, and he will tabernacle with them." The climax and the goal of all the Divine working, and the long processes of God's love for, and discipline of. the world are to be this, that He and men shall abide together in unity and concord. That is God's wish from the beginning. And at the close of all things. when the vision of this final chapter shall be fulfilled, God will say, settling Himself in the midst of a redeemed humanity, "Lo! here will I dwell; for I have desired it. This is my rest for ever." He will tabernacle with men, and they with Him.—S. B., vol. vii., p. 363.

THE WORD

By F. D. Maurice

John i: 14

I. "The word was made flesh and dwelt among us." This is St. John's declaration. He does not invent a great many arguments to prove it; he simply says "so it was." This poor fisherman, who was once upon a time sitting in his father's ship on the Lake of Galilee, mending his nets; this man who was infinitely humbler and less self-conceited now than he was then, says out boldly and without hesitation, "This everlasting Word, in whom was life and whose life was the light of men—this Word, who was with God and was God—was made flesh and dwelt among us." And he adds, "We beheld his glory—the glory as of the only-begotten of the Father." We are sure that in this poor man, thus entering into our feelings and circumstances, we beheld the living God. Not some unseen power, some angel or Divine creature who might have been sent down on a message of mercy to one little corner of the earth, or to us poor fishermen of Galilee; it is not such a being whom we saw hidden under this human form; we declare that we saw the glory of the Father, of Him who made Heaven and earth and the sea, of Him who has been and is and is to be.

II. That a meek. humble man, who believed that nothing was so horrible as to trifle with God's Name, should have spoken such words as these, so boldly and yet so calmly, with such a certainty that they were true, and that he could live and act upon them, this is wonderful. But yet, this might have been, and the world might have gone on as if no such sounds had ever been proclaimed in it. What is the case actually? These incredible words have been believed. The question was. Who is the Ruler of the world? The apostle said, "This Jesus of Nazareth is its Ruler." Their word prevailed. The masters of the earth confessed that they were right. Here in England, at the other end of the world, the news was heard and received. Then the day which said, "The Word has been made flesh, and has dwelt among us," became the Queen Day of the year. All the joy of the year was felt to be stored up in it. Every man, woman, and child has a right to be merry upon it. This is the festival which make us know, indeed, that we are members of one body: it binds together the life of Christ on earth with His life in Heaven; it assures us that Christmas Day belongs not to time but to eternity.—S. B., vol. vii., p. 364.

SUGGESTIVE THOUGHTS AND ILLUSTRATIONS

ADVENT, Lessons of the.—1. Christ comes by the gateway of birth, appealing to childhood and motherhood. 2. His humble birth shows the humblest and poorest that poverty need be no curse. 3. His unnoticed arrival shows that "the kingdom of God cometh not with observation." 4. The visit of the Magi shows the affinity of Christianity for disciplined minds. 5. All the manner of His coming shows the unbounded wisdom and love of God, who gives us the Christ we need, poor or rich, children or mature. 6. Christ's coming was the greatest event in the world. 7. His star is shining for you.—REV. S. M. JOHNSON. (H. R.)

ANGELS' CHORUS, The.—The one angel voice has barely time to tell its message, when, as if unable longer to be silent, "suddenly" the "multitude of the heavenly host pours out its praise." I adhere to the old reading which divides the angel chorus into three clauses, of which the first and second may be regarded as the double result of that birth, while the third describes its deepest nature. The incarnation and work of Christ are the highest revelation of God. The wondrous birth brings harmony to earth.—ALEXANDER MACLAREN.

BETHLEHEM.—Bethlehem is a little, lowly hamlet, and Christ was born in a common, lowly stable. The literal story of the Nativity is, or ought to be, engraven deeply on our hearts. Do we pause to consider the symbolism of lowly Bethlehem and the lowly manger? We are disposed to reckon large sacrifices, large acts of beneficence, large deeds of heroism, as the means of grace in the building of a Christlike character. We appreciate the fact that a worker in the slums is more of a hero than the hussar who rode forty miles with a saber cut to carry an important message—and yet—.

Yes the hussar's deed was more interesting, but not more *glorious*, in the best sense of the word, than the tending by night and by day of a man suffering with a loathsome disease. Again, a millionaire banker may heavily endow a cripples' home, and a mother at home may wear the same pair of shoes for eight months that her boy may be taught the best by the best. A thoughtful comparison brings out the more noble deed with the clearness of a cameo; and yet, what heed does the world pay to the widow's sacrifice? Let us remember that the greatest love of all was born in a lowly manger.—O. C. W.

CHRIST APPEARED ON EARTH.—During this month all Christians will be celebrating the advent of our Lord to this world. There was some ground for rational doubts as to whether the promise of His first coming would be *literally* fulfilled. Would the One who deserved the title of Emmanuel—God with us—stoop to be born of a woman? Would He consent to be despised and rejected of men? Would the One who created all, sustained all, and filled and bounded all, stoop to the limitations of a man whose days are as grass and whose greatness is that of the worm? Would He humiliate Himself to be sold by a traitor, to be classed with transgressors and to become a curse because wounded for our transgressions and bruised for our iniquities? And yet, altho it *seemed* so irrational, so improbable and even impossible, not one word of God's promises has failed of fulfilment. Nineteen hundred years ago Jesus was born of a Virgin Mother, the Word who was God became flesh—God was manifested in the flesh, and His glory was seen, "full of grace and truth." He was full of grace to forgive and to save, and full of truth to enlighten, to purify, and to guide. He *has* appeared on earth.—P. J.

CHRIST, Birthday of.—I have always thought of Christmas time, when it has come round apart from the veneration due to its sacred name and origin, if anything belonging to it can be apart from that—as a good time; a kind, forgiving, charitable, pleasant time.—CHARLES DICKENS. *Christmas Carol;* Stave I.

CHRIST, Birth of.—The death of Christ is a great mystery; but His birth is even a greater. That He should live a human life at all, is stranger than that, so living, He should die a human death. I can scarce get past His cradle in my wondering, to wonder at His cross. The infant Jesus is, in some views, a greater marvel than Jesus with the purple robe and the crown of thorns.—CRICHTON.

CHRISTMAS.—The chief charm of Christmas is its simplicity. It is a festival that appeals to every one, because every one can understand it. . . . A genuine fellowship pervades our common life—a fellowship whose source is our common share in the gift of the world's greatest Life which was given to the whole world.—ARTHUR REED KIMBALL.

CHRISTMAS AND BROTHERHOOD. —Last Christmas Day, in New York City, a millionaire was driving down Fifth Avenue in his sleigh, when his high-spirited horse ran away. The sleigh was overturned and the rich man and his coachman rolled in the snow together. As they struggled to their feet and turned to follow the runaway horse, they saw the sleigh strike a poor peddler and knock him into a heap, both runners passing over his body. The millionaire uttered a cry of dismay when he saw the ragged peddler fall in the street, and leaving his valuable trotter to vanish in the distance, he cast himself on his knees by the injured man, and lifted his blood-stained head tenderly in his arms. He got help as soon as possible, and himself assisted in carrying the poor fellow into a fashionable hotel near by, and sent for the doctor. Later he got him a comfortable room in a hospital and ordered that every possible attention should be given him. When the peddler was seen by the reporter at the hospital and told that the man whose horse had run over him was a millionaire, he replied: " A millionaire, is he? Well, all I can say is that he's the whitest man I ever seen in me life, an' I'll never say another word agin millionaires. I tell yer wot, that man is a wonder. Why, he—he—he went down on his marrow-bones in the snow alongside me an' took my head on his knee, same as if I was his brother—an' it all bleedin', too." O brotherhood, how great is thy power! There is no quack way of bridging the so-called gulf between the rich and poor, but with the brotherhood of Jesus Christ, exemplified as in this case, there is no gulf.—H. P.

CHRISTMAS AND MISSIONS.—Two very important events are connected with the Christmas of 1786, and it is also remarkable that they both relate to missions. It was on that day that William Carey, the great Baptist missionary, and Charles Grant, one of the founders of the Church Missionary Society, first formally set forth their views on the subject of missions, and it was on that day also that Dr. Coke and his three companions landed at Antigua, in the West Indies, for the purpose of prosecuting missionary operations there. Surely Dr. Coke and his friends must have regarded it as almost significant that they, the messengers of the gospel of peace and goodwill to men should have reached the scene of their future labors on the day which commemorates the birth of the Prince of Peace.—Rev. W. S. McTavish, B.D.

CHRISTMAS AND MOTHERHOOD.—On that Christmas night God honored motherhood. The angels on their wings might have brought an infant Savior to Bethlehem without Mary's being there at all. But, no; motherhood for all time was to be consecrated, and one of the tenderest relations was to be the maternal relation, and one of the sweetest words, "mother." In all ages God has honored good motherhood. In a great audience, most of whom were Christians, I asked that all those who had been blessed with Christian mothers arise, and almost the entire assembly stood up. Don't you see how important it is that all motherhood be consecrated?—Talmage.

CHRISTMAS CUSTOM, A Beautiful.—There are many pretty customs which are observed at Christmas time in different countries. One of the prettiest of these customs is thus described for us by a traveler in Sweden. He writes:
" One wintry afternoon at Christmastide I had been skating on a pretty lake three miles

from Gothenburg. On my way home I noticed that at every farmer's house there was erected, in the middle of the dooryard, a pole, to the top of which was bound a large, full sheaf of grain.
" ' Why is this? ' I asked my companion.
" ' Oh, that's for the birds,' he answered, ' for the little wild birds. They must have a merry Christmas, too, you know.'
" Yes, so it is; not a peasant in Sweden will sit down with his children to a Christmas dinner, indoors, till he has first raised aloft a Christmas dinner for the little birds that live in the cold and snow without."—A. G.

CHRISTMAS HOMILY, A.—I. " He emptied Himself." This is a truer translation of the first words. Creation involves the incarnation. It implies a love which enables God to cast aside whatever was incompatible with a real humanity.
II. His assumption of humanity meant the assumption of servanthood, for man is dependent.
III. His was no phantom life. All that is essential to humanity, He took upon Him. He knew no sin—but sin was no element in man's original constitution.
IV. His obedience to death was real, because He laid down His life. He was obedient to the law, and took death as part of the experience of life.
V. He took the death of the cross, because He meant death to have no untasted bitterness; all its shame and hate were parts of that burden He came to bear. Even God's wrath against sin He would know, that He might stand in the sinner's place.—Rev. Samuel McComb, A.M. (H. R.)

CHRISTMAS JOY.—The universal joy of Christmas is certainly wonderful. We ring the bells when princes are born, or toll a mournful dirge when great men pass away. Nations have their red-letter days, their carnivals and festivals, but once in the year and only once, the whole world stands still to celebrate the advent of a life. Only Jesus of Nazareth claims this world-wide, undying remembrance. You cannot cut Christmas out of the Calendar, nor out of the heart of the world.—*Anon.*

CHRISTMAS MESSAGES.—A Message of Love.—John iii:16; xiii:1; xiv:23; xv:9; Gal. ii:20; Eph. ii:4, 5; 2 Thess. ii: 16, 17; Tit. iii:4; 1 John iv:8-11; xvi:19; Rev. i:5, 6.
A Message of Life.—John i:4; iii:14-16; vi:35; viii:12; x:10; xi:25; xiv:6; xvii:2, 3; xx:31; Col. iii:4; 2 Tim. i:10; 1 John ii:25; v:20; Rev. xxi:6.
A Message of Peace.—Luke i:79; xix: 41, 42; John xiv:27; xvi:33; Rom. v:1; xvi:20; Eph. ii:17, 18; Col. i:19, 20; 2 Thess. iii:16.
A Message of Salvation.—Isa. xliv:22; Luke i:68, 69, 77; xix:10; John iii:36; Acts iv:12; xvi:31; Heb. ii:3; vii:25; 1 John v:11, 12.
A Message for all Men.—Luke iii:6; John i:9, 29; Acts x:43; Rom. v:6, 8; 1 Tim.

i: 15; ii: 3, 4; Tit. ii: 11; 2 Pet. iii: 9.—A Bible-Study by Miss L. A. WALLINGFORD.

CHRISTMAS, Real Lessons of.—There can be no love for God which is unattended with love for man. The final test of a Christian life is not the worship of God, but always the love of man for man. If the message of Him whose birth we celebrate at Christmas teaches us one thing above all others, it is not that we shall try to do for Him as a person, but that we shall seek to do for one another. That is knowing Jesus and clearly understanding Him.

And wherever this true conception of His life and teaching is reached, there we find men and women thrilled with the passion for giving. The little child wakes on Christmas morning with its heart full to overflowing with gladness, and by every gift in stocking, or beside cradle or bed, is taught anew the old, old lesson of love. Husband and wife, brother and sister, lover and sweetheart, friend and friend, as they receive their gifts are reminded once more that love is not a dream, but a reality—and a reality which grows more vital, more precious and more enduring with years.

The sick, in chair or in bed, as they open their Christmas packages are almost reconciled to loneliness and pain. The friendless, the poor, the outcast, the waifs on the streets; those who have sinned and seem shut out from God and from man, all begin to feel strange thrills of hope and renewed aspiration as they are taken up and enfolded in the richness and fulness of the Divine love as it comes to them through human love or attention on Christmas Day. That is knowing Christmas in its highest and noblest sense; in its truest conception; knowing it in that spirit from which we derive the surest happiness.—EDWARD BOK.

CHRISTMAS STAND FOR PLEASURE, Let.—Let Christmas stand for pleasure, and for the reason that it is especially the Christian day. Then Christianity drops her weeds, and smiles. Then the whole world takes up the refrain—

Religion never was designed
To make our pleasures less.

And even Dr. Doddridge comes singing in,

I live in pleasure when I live to Thee.

The doctor must not fly his own logic. Not to live in pleasure is not to live to Thee. Pure pleasure it must be, no doubt, but that is the pleasure embodied in Christmas. If we were to fancy a wholly Christianized world, it would be a world inspired by the spirit of Christmas—a bright, friendly, beneficent, generous, sympathetic, mutually helpful world. A man who is habitually mean, selfish, narrow, is a man without Christmas in his soul. Let us cling to Christmas all the more as a day of the spirit which in every age some souls have believed to be the possible spirit of human society. The earnest faith and untiring endeavor which see in Christmas a forecast are more truly Christian, surely, than the pleasant cynicism of Atheists, etc., which smiles upon it as the festival of a futile hope. Meanwhile we may reflect that from good natured hopelessness to a Christmas world may not be farther than from star dust to a solar system.—GEORGE WILLIAM CURTIS.

CHRISTMAS, The Twelve Days of.—The New England custom during those early years of the present century to observe Christmas from December 25 to January 5, the twelve days being generally given up to receiving and returning family visits. Contemporary with this custom was the belief, inculcated in the minds of the children, that if they would visit the cow stables at midnight of Christmas eve, they would see the cattle kneel before the mangers.

A poem of the twelve days shows the gift for the first day of Christmas to be a parrot on a juniper tree instead of a "partridge on a pear tree." The verse for the twelfth day, which embodied the entire list of days and "gifts," was as follows:

The twelfth day of Christmas my true love gave to me twelve guns shooting, eleven bears chasing, ten men hunting, nine fiddlers playing, eight ladies dancing, seven swans swimming, six chests of linen, five gold rings, four coffee bowls, three French hens, two turtle doves and a parrot on a juniper tree.—JOHN RODEMEYER, JR. (N. Y. S.)

CHRIST'S NATIVITY.—The earth wondered at Christ's nativity, to see a new star in Heaven; but Heaven might rather wonder to see a new sun on earth (Ps. lxix: 35; Isa. xliv: 23; Matt. ii: 10).—DR. RICHARD CLARKE.

DAY, The Sun of a Better.—What images do I associate with the Christmas music as I see these images set forth on the Christmas tree? Known before all others, keeping far apart from all the others. . . . An angel, speaking to a group of shepherds in a field; some travelers, with eyes uplifted, following a star; a baby in a manger; a child in a spacious temple, talking with grave men; a solemn figure, with a mild and beautiful face, raising a dead girl by the hand; again, near a city gate, calling back the son of a widow, on his bier, to life; a crowd of people looking through the opened roof of a chamber where He sits, and letting down a sick person on a bed, with ropes; the same, in a tempest, walking on the water to a ship; again, on a seashore, teaching a great multitude; again, with a child upon His knee, and other children around; again, restoring sight to the blind, speech to the dumb, hearing to the deaf, health to the sick, strength to the lame, knowledge to the ignorant; again, dying upon a cross, watched by armed soldiers, a thick darkness coming on, the earth beginning to shake, and only one voice heard: "Forgive them, for they know not what they do."—CHARLES DICKENS. *Christmas Stories.*

DWELT AMONG US.—"And the Word became flesh and dwelt among us;" literally "pitched his tent," (ἐσκήνωσεν). Three sorts of men are described in the Bible as living in tents: shepherds, sojourners, and soldiers. The phrase here used has reference to the calling of all these three, and it points to Christ's life on earth as being that of a shepherd, a traveler, and a soldier."— A. ARROWSMITH.

GIFT, The Divine Christmas.—*For unto us a child is born, unto us a son is given, etc.—Isa. ix: 6.*

I. The gift of Christ as a child, a son, (a) a gift of love, (b) of supreme beauty and joy, (c) of universal fitness to our wants, (d) of eternal enrichment, forever increasing in value, (e) ensures all other gifts needful. " How shall he not with him also freely give us all things?"

II. The fitness of Christ's infancy to the world, beauty and pathos of His being committed, a babe, to a human bosom. Our child relation intimates the fruit of the race's soul travail. Christ born in every family where faith is, and in every heart where love welcomes. Marvels of His nature and errand.

III. Gift how received. Many make merry on Christmas while shutting Christ out in the cold. " No place in the inn."

Happy those who welcome Him. Christ formed in us the hope of glory.—H. R.

GIVING AND RECEIVING.—It may indeed be more blessed to give than to receive, but when the former luxury is not within one's honest reach, it is blessed too to receive from those one thoroughly loves.— GEORGE S. MERRIAM.

HEART, The Message to the Blind in.— One Christmas eve a lady was walking in the beautiful city of Berlin, enjoying the pretty sights. She stopped to look at the large window where was laid out the lowly stable in Bethlehem. Before the window stood two little girls, their faces beaming with pleasure, while they talked to another little girl between them, and around whom they had their arms. This dear child was quite blind, and to her poor sightless eyes the pretty window told no story. But the loving little friends told the blind child of the rude stable, the hay, the cows and the sheep, the sweet mother beside the manger in which the Christ-child was sleeping, the open door through which the wandering shepherds were coming and the bright star above which shed a soft silvery light over all and the wise men with rich gifts for the little sleeping babe, who was the Son of God our Savior. The little blind girl listened till her face grew happy and she clasped her hands together, saying again and again, " Ah! that is beautiful."

There are those who have blind hearts, instead of blind eyes, because they do not know the blessed story.—S. E. BULL.

INCARNATE WORD, The.—When the eye gazes on the sun, it is more tormented with the brightness than pleased with the beauty of it; but when the beams are transmitted through a colored medium, they are more temperate, and sweetened to the sight. The Eternal Word, shining in His full glory, the more bright, the less visible is He to mortal eyes; but the Incarnate Word is eclipsed and allayed by a veil of flesh (Heb. x: 20), and so made accessible to us. God, out of a tender respect to our frailty and fears, promised to raise up a Prophet, clothed in our nature (Ex. xx: 18, 19; Deut. xviii; 15-19), that we might comfortably and quietly receive His instructions (Job xxiii: 6, 7; Luke iv: 20-22; John i: 18).—A. P. L.

INCARNATION, Mystery of.—For the sun to fall from its sphere, and be degraded into a wandering atom; for an angel to be turned out from heaven, and be converted into a fly or a worm, had not been such abasement; for they were but creatures before, and so they would abide still. tho in an inferior rank. But for the infinite glorious Creator of all things to become a creature, is a mystery exceeding all human understanding.—JOHN FLAVEL.

POETRY

Bells, Christmas

I heard the bells on Christmas Day
Their old, familiar carols play,
    And wild and sweet
    The words repeat
Of peace on earth, good-will to men!
    H. W. LONGFELLOW—*Flower de Luce.*
                Christmas Bells.

Bethlehem

Dear Bethlehem, the proud repose
Of conscious worthiness is thine.
Rest on! The Arab comes and goes,
    But farthest Saxon holds thy shrine
More sacred in his stouter Christian hold
Than England's heaped-up iron house of gold.
                JOAQUIN MILLER.

Bethlehem Exalted

Hill with the olives and the little town!
If rivers from their crystal founts flow down,

If 'twas the dawn which did day's gold unbar,
Ye were beginnings of the best we are,
The most we see, the highest that we know,
The lifting heavenward of man's life below.
                EDWIN ARNOLD.

Child is Born, Unto us a

To us, who look with anxious gaze
On coming lonely, burdened days—
To us, who cower deep in shame,
Unable e'en to speak His name—
To us, the tempted, who within
Still feel the throb of inbred sin—
To us, sore laden and distressed,
He comes, our comfort, joy and rest.
To all earth's weary, struggling men,
The world's sole Hope seems born again
When breaks the light of Christmas morn.
Lo, " Unto us a Child is born."
                MARY ISABELLA FORSYTH.

Christ Came, How

Not sheltered by a gleaming palace-roof,
Or hedged about with glittering thorns of
  spears,
Or shadowed by a jewel-blazoned court,
Was Jesus born!—no babe could humbler lie
Within the precincts of a hovel-home.
Yet wise men came afar to worship Him,
Their guide a star whose wealth outmatched
  the world.
Thus did He clasp all man in His embrace!
  OTTO SINCLAIR.

Christmas Comes but Once a Year

At Christmas play and make good cheer,
For Christmas comes but once a year.
  THOMAS TUSSER—1515-1580.

Christmas, Eternal

In the pure soul, altho it sing or pray,
The Christ is born anew from day to day;
The life that knoweth Him shall bide apart
And keep eternal Christmas in the heart.
  ELIZABETH STUART PHELPS.

Christmas Joys

We ring the bells and we raise the strain,
We hang up garlands everywhere
And bid the tapers twinkle fair,
And feast and frolic—and then we go
  Back to the same old lives again.
  SUSAN COOLIDGE—*Christmas.*

Christmas Tree, The World

The whole world is a Christmas-tree,
  And stars its many candles be.
Oh! sing a carol joyfully
The year's great feast in keeping.
  S. N.

Courage, Take

Take courage, soul, in grief cast down,
  Forget the bitter dealing;
A Child is born in David's town,
  To touch all souls with healing.
Then let us go and seek the Child,
Children like Him, meek, undefiled.
  HANS CHRISTIAN ANDERSEN.

Day Dawn of the Heart

'Tis not enough that Christ was born
  Beneath the star that shone,
And earth was set that morn
  Within a golden zone.
He must be born within the heart
  Before He finds His throne,
And brings the day of love and good,
  The reign of Christ-like brotherhood.
  MARY T. LATHROP

Glory to the King

Hark! the herald angels sing,
  Glory to the new-born King:
Peace on earth, and mercy mild,
  God and sinners reconciled.
  CHARLES WESLEY.

God, Glory to

Like Him be true, like Him be pure,
  Like Him be full of love;

Seek not thine own, and so secure
  Thine own that is above.
And still, as Christmas-tide draws nigh,
  Sing then of Jesus' birth;
Glory be to God on high,
  And peace to men on earth.—*Selected.*

God, Glory to

Like circles widening round
  Upon a clear blue river,
Orb after orb, the wondrous sound
  Is echoed on forever:
Glory to God on high, on earth be peace,
And love towards men of love—salvation and
  release.
  KEBLE.—*Christmas Day.*

God Rest You

God rest you, merry gentlemen,
  Let nothing you dismay,
For Jesus Christ our Savior
  Was born upon this day,
To save us all from Satan's power
  When we were gone astray.
O tidings of comfort and joy,
  For Jesus Christ our Savior was
Born on Christmas day.
  Old English Carol.

Man Divine, The

But lead me, Man divine,
Where'er Thou will'st; only that I may find
At the long journey's end Thy image there,
And grow more like to it. For art not Thou
The human shadow of the infinite Love
That made and fills the endless universe?
The very Word of Him, the unseen, un-
  known,
Eternal Good that rules the summer flower
And all the worlds that people starry space?
  RICHARD WATSON GILDER.

Mistletoe, The

The mistletoe hung in the castle hall,
The holly branch shone on the old oak wall.
  BAYLY.—*The Mistletoe Bough.*

Month, The

This is the month, and this the happy morn,
Wherein the Son of Heaven's eternal King,
Of wedded maid, and virgin mother born,
Our great redemption from above did bring,
For so the holy sages once did sing,
That He our deadly forfeit should release,
And with His Father work us a perpetual
  peace.
  MILTON.—*On the Morning of Christ's
  Nativity.* St. I.

Prince of Peace, The

And they who do their souls no wrong,
But keep, at eve, the faith of morn,
Shall daily hear the angel-song,
"To-day the Prince of Peace is born."
  JAMES RUSSELL LOWELL.

Salvation Tidings

All hailed with uncontrolled delight,
And gentle voice, the happy night,
That to the cottage, as the crown,
Brought tidings of Salvation down.
  WALTER SCOTT.

Savior, The Presence of the

O Savior! Whom this holy morn
  Gave to our world below;
To mortal want and labor born,
  And more than mortal wo!

If gaily clothed and proudly fed,
  In dangerous wealth we dwell,
Remind us of Thy manger bed
  And lowly cottage cell.

If pressed by poverty severe,
  In envious want we pine,
Oh may Thy Spirit whisper near,
  How poor a lot was Thine.
                REGINALD HEBER.

Season, The Full

Now that the time is come wherein
  Our Savior Christ was born,
The larders full of beef and pork,
  The garners filled with corn;
As God hath plenty to thee sent,
  Take comfort of thy labors,
And let it never thee repent
  To feast thy needy neighbors.
                Selected.

Season, The Joyous

This happy day, whose risen sun
  Shall set not through eternity,
This holy day when Christ the Lord,
  Took on Him our humanity,
For little children everywhere
  A joyous season still we make,
We bring our precious gifts to them,
  Even for the dear Child Jesus' sake.
                PHOEBE CARY.

Shepherds' Singing

Shepherds at the grange,
  Where the Babe was born,
Sang with many a change,
  Christmas carols until morn.
H. W. LONGFELLOW.—By the Fireside.
                A Christmas Carol.

Sin, The Price of

What comfort by Him do we win,
Who made Himself the price of sin,
To make us heirs of glory?
To see this babe all innocence;
A martyr born in our defense;
Can man forget the story?
                BEN JONSON.

Sleep, Holy Babe

Upon Thy mother's breast;
Great Lord of earth and sea and sky,
How sweet it is to see Thee lie
In such a place of rest.

Sleep, Holy Babe,
O take Thy brief repose—
Too quickly will Thy slumbers break,
And Thou to lengthened pains awake
That death alone can close.
                EDWARD CASWELL.

Songs Raise on High

Sound over all waters, reach from all lands,
The chorus of voices, the clasping of hands;
Sing hymns that were sung by the stars of
  the morn,
Sing songs of the angel when Jesus was
  born!
    With glad jubilations
    Bring hope to the nations!
The dark night is ending and dawn has
  begun;
Rise, hope of the ages, arise like the sun,
All speech flow to music, all hearts beat as
  one.
Blow bugles of battle. the marches of peace;
East, west, north and south, let the quarrels
  all cease,
Sing the song of great joy that the angels
  began,
Sing of glory to God, and of good will to
  man!
    Hark, joining the chorus
    The heavens bend o'er us.
                J. G. WHITTIER.

Spheres, The Crystal

Ring out, ye crystal spheres,
Once bless our human ears,
  (If ye have power to touch our senses so:)
And let your silver chime
Move in melodious time,
  And let the bass of Heaven's deep organ
  blow,
And with your ninefold harmony
Make up full consort to the angelic sym-
  phony.
    MILTON.—On the Morning of
        Christ's Nativity. St. 13.

O Little Town of Bethlehem!

By PHILLIPS BROOKS

O little town of Bethlehem!
How still we see thee lie;
Above thy deep and dreamless sleep,
The silent stars go by.
Yet, in thy dark street shineth
The everlasting Light;
The hopes and fears of all the years,
Are met in thee, to-night.

How silently, how silently,
The wondrous gift is given!
So God imparts to human hearts,
The blessings of His Heaven.
No ear may hear His coming,
But in this world of sin,
When meek souls will receive Him still,
The dear Christ enters in.

O holy Child of Bethlehem!
Descend to us, we pray;
Cast out our sin and enter in
Be born in us to-day.
We hear the Christmas angels
The great glad-tidings tell;
Oh come to us, abide with us,
Our Lord Emmanuel.

A Christmas Carol

By Dinah Maria Mulock (Craik)

God rest ye, merry gentlemen; let nothing
you dismay,
For Jesus Christ our Savior, was born on
Christmas Day.
The dawn rose red o'er Bethlehem, the stars
shone through the gray,
For Jesus Christ our Savior, was born on
Christmas Day.

God rest ye, little children; let nothing you
affright.
For Jesus Christ, your Savior, was born this
happy night;
Along the hills of Galilee 'the white flocks
sleeping lay
When Christ, the Child of Nazareth, was
born on Christmas Day.

God rest ye, all good Christians; upon this
blesséd morn
The Lord of all good Christians was of a
woman born;
Now all your sorrows He doth heal, your sins
He takes away;
For Jesus Christ our Savior, was born on
Christmas Day.—I.

Christmas Carol

By Phillips Brooks

The earth has grown old with its burden of
care,
But at Christmas it always is young.
The heart of the jewel burns lustrous and
fair,
And its soul full of music breaks forth on the
air,
When the song of the angels is sung.

It is coming, old earth, it is coming to-night!
On the snowflakes that covered thy sod
The feet of the Christ-child fall gentle and
white,
And the voice of the Christ-child tells out
That mankind are the children of God.

On the sad and the lonely, the wretched and
poor,
The voice of the Christ-child shall fall;
And to every blind wanderer open the door
Of a hope that he dared not to dream of
before,
With a sunshine of welcome for all.

The feet of the humblest may walk in the field
Where the feet of the holiest have trod,
This, this is the marvel to mortals revealed
When the silvery trumpets of Christmas have
pealed,
That mankind are the children of God.

Blessed Christmas Day

By Charles Kingsley

O blessed day which giv'st the eternal lie
To self, and sense, and all the brute within;
O come to us amid this war of life;
To hall and hovel come! to all who toil

In senate, shop, or study! and, to those
Ill-warned and sorely tempted—
Come to them, blest and blessing, Christmas
Day!
Tell them once more the tale of Bethlehem,
The kneeling shepherds, and the Babe Divine;
And keep them men, indeed, fair Christmas
Day!

The Little Christ is Coming Down!

By Harriet F. Blodgett

The little Christ is coming down
Across the fields of snow;
The pine trees greet Him where they stand
The willows bend to kiss His hand,
The mountain laurel is ablush
In hidden nooks, the wind, ahush
And tiptoe, lest the violets wake
Before their time for His sweet sake
The stars, down dropping, form a crown
Upon the waiting hills below,—
The little Christ is coming down
Across the fields of snow.

The little Christ is coming down
Across the city street;
The wind blows coldly from the north,
His dimpled hands are stretching forth,
And no one knows, and no one cares.
The priests are busy with their prayers,
The jostling crowd hastes on apace,
And no one sees the pleading face,
None hears the cry as through the town
He wanders with His small cold feet,—
The little Christ is coming down
Across the city street.—I.

The Christmas Peal

By Harriet Prescott Spofford

Swinging across the belfry tower
The bells rang backward all the hour;
They rang, they reeled, they rushed, they
roared:
Their tongues tumultuous music poured.
The old walls rocked, the peals outswept,
Far up the steep their echoes leapt,
Soaring and sparkling till they burst
Like bubbles round the topmost horn
That reddens to the hint of morn
That halts some trembling star the first.
And all the realms of ice and frost
From field to field those joy bells tossed,
They answered from their airy height;
They thrilled; they loosed their bands for
flight;
They knew that it was Christmas Night!

Where awful absence of sound
The gorge in death's dumb rigor bound,
Below, and deep within the wood,
Windless and weird the black pines stood,
The iron boughs slow-swaying rose
And fell and shook their sifted snows,
And stirred in every stem and branch
To the wild music in the air
From far lone upper regions where
Loose plunged the silver avalanche.
All up and down the valley-side

These iron boughs swayed far and wide;
They heard the cry along the height;
They pulsed in time with that glad flight:
They knew that it was Christmas Night!

You who with quickening throbs shall mark
Such swells and falls swim on the dark,
As crisp as if the clustered rout
In starry depths sprang chiming out,
As if the Pleiades should sing,
Lyra should touch her tenderest string,
Aldebaran his spear-heads clang,
Great Betelgeuse and Sirius blow
Their mighty horns, and Fomalhaut
With wild sweet breath suspended hang—
Know 'tis your heart-beats, with those bells,
Loosen the snow-clouds' vibrant cells,
Stir the vast forest on the height,
Your heart-beats answering to the light
Flashed earthward the first Christmas Night!
H.

Christmas Roses

BY R. J. O.

Pale Winter roses, the white ghosts
Of our June roses,
Last beauty that the old year boasts,
Ere his reign closes!
I gather you, as farewell gift
From parting lover,
For ere you fade, his moments swift
Will all be over.
Kind ghosts ye are, that trouble not,
Nor fright, nor sadden,
But wake fond memories half forgot,
And thoughts that gladden.
O changeless past! I would the year
Left of lost hours
No ghosts that brought more shame or fear,
Than these white flowers!—Sp.

A Christmas Song

BY FLORENCE EVELYN PRATT

Oh, Christmas is a jolly time
When forests hang with snow,
And other forests bend with toys,
And lordly Yule-logs glow.

And Christmas is a solemn time
Because, beneath the star,
The first great Christmas Gift was given
To all men near and far.

But not alone at Christmas time
Comes holiday and cheer,
For one who loves a little child
Hath Christmas all the year.

The Christmas Spectrum

BY AMOS R. WELLS

Seven points hath the Christmas star;
One is the love that shines afar
From God to man; and one is the love
That leaps from the world to the Lord above;
And one is good will on the happy earth;

And one is purity, one is peace,
And two are the joys that never cease,—
God's joy,
Man's joy,—
Aflame in the star of the wonderful Birth.

And the light of God's love is a golden light,
And man's love to man is crimson bright,
And man's love to God is an azure ray,—
Alas, when it flickers and dies away!
And the seven rays through the worshiping
night
Like the flash of all jewels, exult and play,—
God's joy,
Man's joy,—
Yet they shine as one, and the star is white.

Following the Star

BY FREDERIC E. WEATHERLY

It was the eve of Christmas, the snow lay
deep and white;
I sat beside my window and looked into the
night;
I heard the church-bells ringing, I saw the
bright stars shine,
And childhood came again to me, with all its
dreams divine.
Then, as I listened to the bells and watched
the skies afar,
Out of the East majestic there rose one radiant star:
And ev'ry other star grew pale before that
heav'nly glow,
It seemed to bid me follow, and I could not
choose but go.

From street to street it led me, by many a
mansion fair,
It shone through dingy casement on many a
garret bare;
From highway on to highway, through alleys
dark and cold,
And where it shone the darkness was flooded
all with gold.
Sad hearts forgot their sorrow, rough hearts
grew soft and mild,
And weary little children turned in their sleep
and smiled;
While many a homeless wanderer uplifted
patient eyes,
Seeming to see a home at last beyond those
starry skies.

And then methought earth faded; I rose as
borne on wings
Beyond the waste of ruined lives, the press
of human things;
Above the toil and shadow, above the want
and wo:
My old self and its darkness seemed left on
earth below.
And onward, upward shone the star, until it
seemed to me
It flashed upon the golden gates and o'er the
crystal sea.
And then the gates rolled backward, I stood
where angels trod;
It was the Star of Bethlehem had led me up
to God!

The Holy Month

By J. K. Hoyt

Shout now! The Months, with loud acclaim,
Take up the cry and send it forth:
May, breathing sweet, her spring perfumes,
November, thundering from the North;
With hands upraised, as with one voice,
They join their notes, in grand accord;
" Hail to December! " say they all,
" It gave to Earth our Christ the Lord! "
Down from the spheres a peal rang forth;
Angels and men their incense poured;
" Hail to the month! Hail to the day!
Which gave all worlds our Christ the Lord."

Mary in the Cave

By Louise Dunham Goldsberry

Little Child, Little Child, Thy silken head
    lying
        Between my breasts,
Thou art the Promise to the broken reed of
    Israel.
My body cradled Thee, my heart sung o'er
    Thee,
Under the solemn witness stars alone I bore
    Thee—
Oh, what is this that I should be the nursing
    mother
        Of my God!

Little Son, Little Son, I hear the cold winds
    crying
        Around a tree,
And Thou and I, we twain carry a gruesome
    load;
Shut Thy sad eyes, Thy mother's kisses falling
Shall hush to Thee the piteous dead voices
    calling—
Oh, what is this that I shall pluck the nails
    from these sweet hands
        And baby feet!

Little Child, Little Child, the milk dries on
    Thy lips;
        All in my bosom
Thy naked limbs lie warm upon my heart.
Breath to breath we sleep, the clamoring
    world afar,
Thou and I, we twain under the keeping star—
Oh, what is this that Thou art Son and
    Savior,
        My little Child!

The Star in the East

Anonymous

The hearts of all mankind are turned
        Toward lowly Bethlehem;
For in the East the wondrous star, that
    burned,
        In days of old
        Still beckons them.

Back o'er the centuries,
        Storm swept and bare
        It moves, until, behold!
It stands above the manger where
        The young child lies.

Star-Beams

While stars of Christmas shine,
    Lighting the skies,
Let only loving looks
    Beam from your eyes.

While bells of Christmas ring,
    Joyous and clear,
Speak only happy words
    All mirth and cheer.

Give only loving gifts,
    And in love take;
Gladden the poor and sad,
    For love's dear sake.

                            S. N.

The Watchers That Fear

Frank Walcott Hutt

Over the snow-covered hills hear ye the bells
    of the morn,
Speeding the shade of the past, hailing the
    Babe that is born.
Who for the old and the lost droppeth a sor-
    rowful tear?
Who, with a shiver and sigh, welcomes the
    birth of the year?
Glad is the singer whose song praiseth the
    tried and the true:
Sweet is the soul that with smiles lighteth
    the way of the new.
White are the pathways of earth, white for
    thy coming, O Year!
Angels and holy ones, pray, pray for the
    watchers that fear!—C. G.

OLD YEAR DAY

(December 31)

OLD YEAR DAY is to be found neither in the lists of legal holidays nor in the church calendars. The same is true of Old Year Sunday, but, as a matter of fact, in the home, in the church, and in society, Old Year Day, especially the night on which the year goes into the past, and the Sunday following, are receiving greater attention every year. Throughout Christendom, thousands of families sit up, and with story and music and conversation " watch the old year die." " Watch Night " services in the churches are held with growing frequency and deepening interest. And there is scarcely a pulpit in the world in which the thoughts inevitably suggested by the season are not expressed and emphasized on the last Sunday of the year, Old Year Sunday. Poets, essayists, and preachers are invariably stirred by the dying of the old year to the noblest use of their arts and the highest exercise of their talents.

The Holy Scriptures abound in passages appropriate to the thoughts of the day. The most prominent theme is Time: Its flight, value, improvement, loss, irrecoverableness, and end. *(Ps. xxxix: 4-6; Ps. xc. 4, 6, 9, 10; Job vii: 6, 7, 9; Job ix: 25, 26; Ps. xc: 12; Eph. v: 15, 16; Col. iv: 5; Joel ii: 25; Rev. x: 5, 6.)* This line of thought naturally suggests the contemplation of Life: its brevity, frailty, uncertainty, opportunities neglected or improved, purpose, departing youth, advancing old age, and approaching end. *(2 Cor. iv: 18; Ps. ciii: 14-17; Isa xl: 6; 1 Peter i: 24, 25; Job xxix: 2-4; Deut. iv: 32; Job xvii: 11; Eccl. iii: 15; Jer. viii: 20; 1 John ii: 8; Heb. ix: 27.)* The last day of the year, to the thoughtful mind, is also suggestive of the last day of life. *(Heb. ix: 27.)* And Old Year thoughts of time, and life and death lead up to the consideration of the Day of Judgment, Heaven, Hell, Eternity, and that God to whom all His intelligent creatures must give an account. *(John vi: 40; Acts xvii: 31; Rom. ii: 5; 1 Cor. iii: 13; Heb. x: 25; Jude 6; 2 Cor. v: 1; Rev. xv: 2, 3; Matt. xxv: 41; Isa. lvii: 15; 2 Cor. iv: 18; Luke xvi: 9.)* Probably no other holy day, unless we except Easter Sunday, has suggested as profound thought, as eloquent expression, and as earnest and noble living as the last day of the year.

THE NINETEENTH CENTURY

On January 1, 1900, we enter upon the last year of a century that is marked by greater progress in all that pertains to the material well-being and enlightenment of mankind than all the previous history of the race; and the political, social, and moral advancement has been hardly less striking.

The century opened with all Europe in a state of war, and after the delusive and short-lived peace of Amiens (1802), Napoleon as First Consul and then as **Napoleon** Emperor of France, was for thirteen years in almost continual conflict with the great powers. The lesser nations—Spain, Italy, Holland, Belgium, Norway, and Sweden, and some of the German States were submissive under rulers of his choosing, but most of the time Austria, Prussia, Russia, and England were combined against him. His design of invading England was frustrated by the " sea power " and Nelson's victory in Trafalgar in 1805, but on land he seemed invincible until 1812, when he undertook his ill-fated expedition to Moscow, and the English expelled his forces from Spain. Then the tide turned. Through the varying fortunes of the capture of Paris, the retirement to Elba, and the " hundred days," he came to Waterloo in 1815, and spent the remnant of his days until 1821 at St. Helena. The fierce conflict between England and France disturbed the peace of the United States, for it was their interference with trade by Napoleon's Berlin decrees and the English orders in Council, that produced suffering and discontent in this country, and occasioned England's exercise of the right of search, which brought on the war of 1812. In that contest we had some triumphs on the sea and only misfortunes on the land until Jackson's victory at New Orleans made both parties ready to end a war for which neither had much relish.

After the Napoleonic disturbances of boundaries in Europe, the Congress of Vienna, in which Russia, Austria, Prussia, and **The Holy** England had the prevailing **Alliance** voice, undertook to reconstruct the nations nearly upon their old lines and to restore the ancient forms and methods of government. The Roman Empire was gone, and Austria now headed a German confederation; Italy was again dismembered and the Bourbon monarchs returned to the thrones of France and Spain. Austria, Prussia, and Russia formed the Holy Alliance for the maintenance of the peace of Europe and the preservation of existing dynasties. But the subject peoples, who had borne the cost and suffering of twenty-five years of conflict were no longer submissive to the old order of things. The lessons of American independence, the French Revolution, and Napoleon's subversion of ancient traditions were bearing fruit, and a struggle began for constitutional liberty and representative govern- **Spanish** ment. An incidental effect of **Colonies** this, even while the nations of Europe were at war, was the revolt of the American colonies of the weakest of the powers, and between 1810 and 1821 the dependencies of Spain, beginning with Buenos Ayres and ending with Mexico, became independent. In 1822 Brazil broke away from Portugal and became an empire. The disposition of the Holy Alliance to intervene and bring these new-born States to their old allegiance, was checked by the proclamation of the Monroe doctrine in 1823, in which the United States was assured of the sympathy and countenance of Great Brit- **The** ain. While engaged in his ag- **Monroe** gressive warfare in Europe Na- **Doctrine** poleon had sold the vast terri- **and** tory of Louisiana to the United **Purchase** States in 1803, and in 1821 Spain **of** gave up Florida. The first effort **Louisiana** to rise against oppression in Europe was made in Greece in 1821, and after a seven years' struggle England and France came to her rescue and in the naval battle of Navarino broke the Turkish power and set Hellas free. Its independence was acknowledged by the Sultan in 1829. There had also been risings in Italy, but Austria, as the chief power in the Holy Alliance, suppressed them.

The history of Great Britain from Waterloo to the middle of the century was made up chiefly of contests of the people for Con- **Great** stitutional and parliamentary re- **Britain** forms. They had had practically **and** no voice in their Government be- **Reforms** fore. Two-thirds of the members of the House of Commons were chosen by the peers and rich landowners, and spoils and corruption prevailed in the public service. There was no public education, criminal and poor laws were grossly inequitable, prisons were outrageously managed, taxation was oppressive, and labor was in a state of misery. Bold and persistent agitation under able leaders extorted remedial measures from Parliament and resulted in 1832 in the first substantial representation of the people in the House of Commons. The extension of the suffrage gave a new impetus to improvement in legislation and administration, and the Chartist agitation made new demands even after the accession of Victoria in 1837 and the fresh impulse which that event gave to the sentiment of loyalty. The contest for the repeal of the oppressive corn laws and the establishment of free trade culminated in 1846. Meantime England had made great strides in industrial and commercial progress, while the social and moral condition of the people advanced with their gain in political power. The results were fittingly celebrated in the first World's Fair in London in 1851.

The French people, wearied and exhausted by the tremendous drain of Napoleon's costly conquests, fell under the reactionary and op- **France** pressive rule of the Bourbons **and** and bore the burden with in- **Constitu-** creasing discontent until 1830, **tional** when they had gained enough **Govern-** strength and spirit to rise in re- **ment** volt and drive Charles X. from the throne. They won a Constitutional government, and Louis Philippe courted their favor for a time, while they gained a new sense of popular power. But the Government was extravagant and costly and tended to revert to arbitrary ways. The popular mind turned back to the glories of the empire, and when Napoleon's remains were brought to Paris in 1840 there were demonstrations that boded ill for the bourgeois monarchy. Already Louis Napoleon had made his first attempt to provoke an insurrection, and a few years later a second one sent him to prison. The agitation for a larger measure of popular rights went on under such leaders as Arago, Lamartine, Thiers, and the King grew more unpopular, until he was forced to abdicate in 1848, when the shrewd, persistent, and unscrupulous Louis Napoleon found his opportunity and contrived to be elected President of the newly founded republic. He strengthened his power on the nominal basis of universal suffrage, gaining control of the police and the army, until in 1851 he was able to overthrow a hostile Assembly and soon after to set up an Empire, with a new Constitution of his own making. He was crowned as Emperor in December, 1852.

Germany continued to be a loose confederation of more than thirty States, with a growing rivalry between the Kingdom of Prussia and the Empire of Austria for the ascendancy, and a growing struggle of the people for Constitutional privileges. The pol-

**Conti-
nental
Changes**
icy of suppression led to violent outbreaks in 1848, the year of revolution in Paris. Concessions were made in Prussia, but after an attempt to form a new German Empire had failed in 1849, there was a reversion to the policy of repression and a strengthening of the throne and the army to resist popular encroachment upon royal power. In Austria the revolt led to the declaration of the independence of Hungary under the lead of Louis Kossuth, first President of the Hungarian Republic in 1849, but Russia intervened to help the Emperor crush out the movement for self-government. Italy continued to consist of the kingdoms of Sardinia, Naples, and Sicily, and several duchies and principalities, while the Pope ruled at Rome, and Lombardy and Venice were appurtenances of Austria. But the ardor of Massini and the genius of Cavour were preparing the way for a united Italy.

In 1848 there was an insurrection in Naples which was put down by the King, Ferdinand II., and Sardinia tried to force Austria out of Lombardy, but without avail. For a time the popular movements were compelled to subside. The northern nations were comparatively quiescent during the first half of the century, tho Russia was extending her borders both in Europe and Asia. Turkey not only lost Greece in 1829, but ten years later her power over Egypt was broken; otherwise her corrupt and oppressive rule was maintained to the middle of the century.

Away from home Britain's empire had been growing. Canada progressed peaceably toward colonial freedom; Australia, which was

**England
Abroad**
a heritage from Capt. Cook's discoveries, was passing from a region of exploration and a penal colony to a domain of flourishing dependencies; the English foothold in South Africa was a mere vantage ground for the future, and the Indian Empire, which had its beginning before the century opened in a possession exploited by a commercial company, was enlarged by the suppression of native revolts and the annexation of troublesome States. India was a dependency under military government until after the middle of the century. English traders had broken into China before 1840, and their protection led to what is known as the opium war and to the possession of Hongkong; but Japan was not opened to the world's trade until after the expedition of Commodore Perry in 1853.

The third quarter of the century was characterized by new wars, which brought political changes and adjustments that could have

**The
Crimean
War**
been effected by no other means. The Crimean war of 1854-5 grew out of the demand of the Emperor of France for certain privileges for Latin Christians in Palestine, the interference of the Emperor Nicholas in behalf of the Greek Church, and his claim to a protectorate over the Christian population of Turkey. England joined France on the side of Turkey, and Sardinia came in, hoping for advantage for Italy in such an alliance. Russia's advance to the Mediterranean was stopped and Turkey was saved, to maintain the " balance of power " in Europe. Having France as an ally, Sardinia fought Austria, in 1859, and after the battles of Magenta and Solferino, gained Lombardy, while France took Savoy and Nice. Austria and Prussia quarreled over Schleswig and Holstein, which they had torn from Denmark, and came to blows in 1866, when the

**Forming
Empires
and
Kingdoms**
first breech-loading needle gun settled the battle of Sadowa and Austria's pretensions as head of the German system were ended, and the North German Confederation was formed. Cavour, with the help of Garibaldi in Sicily and Naples, had been striving for united Italy; the opportunity of the war of Austria with Prussia was seized, and after Sadowa the Italian nation was formed under Victor Emmanuel, with the capital at Florence. Four years later, when the French bayonets no longer held up the temporal power of the Pope, the Papal States fell into the union and Rome became the capital and Italy was a European power. In 1867 the Empire of Austria-Hungary was formed.

In 1870 Napoleon III., needing distractions to avert opposition to his corrupt and decaying power, provoked the war with Germany, which created the German Empire and the Third French Republic. Other wars in the last half of the century have been waged mainly to force civilization forward. The revolt of Christian provinces against the cruel oppression of Turkey brought on the conflict between Russia and that nation in 1877, when, after the fall of Plevna, Roumelia, Roumania, Bulgaria, Bosnia, Herzegovina, and Montenegro were freed from their vassal state, Servia having been enfranchised long before. England's contests in India and with the fierce peoples beyond its northern borders had their serious episodes, the chief of which was the mutiny of the Sepoy soldiers in 1857, when the greased cartridges of the Enfield rifle roused their superstitious frenzy. After the fierce battles by which the consequent insurrections were quelled, the Government of India was for the first time placed under the British Crown direct.

The history of the United States since the early years of the century has consisted mainly of territorial expansion, industrial and commercial development, and the settle-

**Slavery
in the
United
States**
ment by political agitation and the conflict of arms of the problems entailed upon the Republic by the heritage of slavery. England prohibited the slave trade in 1807, and the United States followed the example, but when the former nation decreed emancipation for slaves with compensation to the owners in 1833, the " in-

stitution " had become too firmly wrought into our industrial and political fabric to be easily dislodged. The anti-slavery agitation began in earnest with the starting of Garrison's *Liberator* in 1831, but the wide cultivation of cotton in the South, the invention of the " gin," the development of the manufactures of cotton in the North, and the demand for the material in England, made the perpetuation of slavery seem an economic necessity and gave a fanatical zeal to its defenders. The annexation of Texas, which had become independent of Mexico in 1836, brought on the Mexican war of 1845, which incidentally increased the slave power. Upon the close of that war, in 1848, the Free Soil Party was formed, and the adoption of the fugitive slave law in 1850 gave a new intensity to the controversy. The publication of Uncle Tom's Cabin in 1852 added fuel to the flames, and the repeal of the Missouri Compromise in 1854 made the conflict irrepressible. Then the Republican Party was formed and the country was politically divided on the slavery question. When Lincoln was elected President, in 1860, and the ordinances of secession were adopted, the passions of the people were wrought **The Civil War** to such a pitch that only war and the destruction of slavery could save the Union. When the Republic had passed through that fiery ordeal her face was set in a new direction. The Nation was reconstructed with new guarantees of freedom and equal rights, and with new difficulties to overcome. They are not all surmounted yet, but the movement has been steadily forward.

In Europe political advancement has continued. England began the reform of her civil service in 1855, and made new extensions of parliamentary franchise in 1867 and again in 1884. Before the last " reform " act, **Continental Advances** provision had been made for the secret ballot and for the punishment of corrupt practices at elections. Notable reforms have been wrought out in the government of cities, and legislation affecting the welfare of the citizen has constantly improved. In spite of drawbacks and turmoils, the French Republic has grown in strength and stability; Germany is constantly forced toward a recognition of the power of public opinion and the dependence of Government upon popular support, and even Russia is not wholly impervious to the enlightening sentiment of the world. While armaments and defenses have been increased, they have become avowedly a means of preserving peace by deterring from war, and the tendency toward a settlement of international disputes by arbitration resulted in a conference at The Hague in 1899, in which all the great powers were represented at the invitation of the Czar of Russia. Small as the practical result seemed to be, it is a promising sign for the new century.

But what characterizes the nineteenth century more than all else is the vast strides in scientific discovery and the application of the **The Advance of Science** forces of nature to the service of man. The wave theory of light, the nebular hypothesis, and the discovery of spectrum analysis have made new revelations in the heavens and exalted our conceptions of time and space. The atomic theory in chemistry, the molecular composition of gas, and the doctrine of the conservation of energy have opened a new avenue to the understanding of the earth. The cell theory of organisms, Lamarck's discoveries as to the progressive development of plants and animals, Darwin's study of the origin of species, the doctrine of evolution, and the tracing of the globe's history in the geological strata, relegate all the science that preceded this century to the same category as the lore of the Chaldeans and the Egyptians. Knowledge of the human frame and its functions and the treatment of its defects and maladies have developed from the rudest germs in this century. The use of anesthetics and antiseptics, improved surgical methods and appliances, and scientific sanitation and hygiene have prolonged life and added to its comforts.

But when we think of the mechanical inventions, the applications of machinery to the saving of human labor and the multiplying of its product, the marvel grows. Friction **Inventions** matches did not exist until 1827. Torches, candles, rushlights, and rude oil lamps were not superseded by the argand burner until 1830, and petroleum and gas as illuminants were still later. The steam engine and the power loom were invented in the last century, but they were primitive devices, and all the vast and complicated machinery of manufacture which so enormously increases man's power of production and of interchange of products has been created since the Napoleonic wars. The first experimental steamboat was launched in 1807, but it was 1838 before successful steam navigation on the ocean began. The first rude railway from Darlington to Stockton, in England, was opened in 1825. The Erie Canal brought the Great Lakes into communication with the ocean, and the first section of the Baltimore and Ohio was completed in 1828. The modern locomotive and railroad train, and the vast system of transportation that reticulates the face of the earth have had their colossal growth within the lifetime of men still surviving. Electricity excited wonder and fear, but performed no service for men before Faraday's discovery of the means of developing it by magnetism, in 1831. It was first used for signalling on railroads in 1837, and it was in 1844 that the first telegraphic message was sent from Baltimore to Washington. A submarine cable was stretched from Dover to Calais in 1851, and the first Atlantic cable was laid in 1858, tho the first to work successfully was that of 1866. The first exhibition of the telephone was ten years later. Electric lighting is not a quarter of a century old, and the application of the subtle fluid as a heating and propelling power is still in its infancy. Daguerre's first discovery of picture making by the sun's rays was made in 1839, and the printing of photographs from negatives dates from 1850. The development of cheap and profuse illustration since has been attended by marvelous improvements in all that pertains to printing and the diffusion of intelligence.

Attending the wonderful advance in the use of labor-saving and product-multiplying machinery and in the means of transportation and interchange, has been the **The Crea-** growth of corporations, by **tion of** which the productive power of **Wealth** capital has been massed, and the development of a vast system of credit and banking whereby 95 per cent. of the exchanges is effected without the use of money, altho the volume of currency in use has enormously increased. The creation of wealth during the present century has been prodigious and goes on with accelerating pace, and in spite of complaints of unfair distribution, its benefits are irresistibly diffused, so that the condition of the mass of the people is immensely improved and continually improving. There is much to do, but the forces that enlighten and elevate humanity have gained tremendous power in the century and are dispelling ignorance, degradation, and misery as never before.

We step upon the threshold of 1900, which leads to the new century, facing a still brighter dawn for human civilization. Through agitation and conflict European nations are working toward an ultimate harmony of interests and purposes, and bringing awakened Asia into the sweeping current of progress. Light has been let into the "Dark Continent" beyond the ancient borders and is rapidly spreading. America is facing westward and beginning to take its part in carrying the regenerating forces of popular government to the uttermost parts of the earth. Notwithstanding the bloody conflicts through which some of the steps of progress must still be made, the "vision of the world" grows clearer toward the time when—

The war-drum throbbed no longer, and the
    battle-flags were furled
In the parliament of man, the federation of
    the world.
There the common sense of most shall hold
    a fretful realm in awe,
And the kindly earth shall slumber, lapt in
    universal law.

            N. Y. Ti.

THE DYING YEAR

By Alexander Macaulay

Sad and solemn are the cadences of the dying year. Only a few months ago, how full of life and vigor was the new year, now grown old and ready to drop into the irrevocable past. It has spent its life on earth, for good and ill, and its footprints are eternal. Nothing can be altered, nothing recalled. It has left its ineffaceable marks, and they cannot be removed. What sights has this year witnessed! Murder has unbared its red right hand, and struck down many a noble man and woman, who might else have seen the dawning of another year. Lives full of worth and beauty have been ruthlessly destroyed, till the very atmosphere seemed to reek with murder; and yet men will insist that human nature is free from depravity, and needs no regeneration.

But if this year has witnessed many soul-harrowing scenes, it has also gazed on many joyous ones. How beautiful was the springtime with all its gladness and rapture and beauty! How pleasant the seaside and mountain rambles of the summer! The songs of birds, the happy voices of children bidding defiance to dull care, the beautiful resignation of old age about to fall into the grave, the happy brides and bridegrooms, would seem to convert life into a glad holiday.

But death disturbs the joyous scene, and we mark the long procession of the departed as they are borne to their last resting-place. And this is life, and these are the years that come and go, and we but wait for the end, wondering what that will be. We greatly wonder, of all that have died, how many were prepared to go. To some, death came slowly, and by perceptible degrees. But others were found amid the daily battle of life, and there struck down. We recall the case of a friend, who was ambitious and eager for distinction in his calling, and had been successful. To him death came without a seeming warning, and he only lived long enough to articulate a few broken sentences indicative of his great disappointment at his sudden taking off. Truly, it behooves us to be ready for the fatal summons.

And nothing can prepare us for the end like a true and benevolent life. Repentance may, and does, save many a seared sinner, but a life that finds little to repent of, save for the little good accomplished, is far fitter for a passage to the skies when sealed by Christ's pardon. "The readiness is all." But the world turns a deaf ear to all these warnings and examples, and plods on in sullen and obstinate defiance, as if men, as of old, bore charmed lives, and would never die. But, nevertheless, the day of the stoutest must come, and with faltering limbs and covered face he will press into the beyond, so dark and dismal and replete with horror to the unready and unwilling participant. The parable of the marriage feast depicts in awful colors the fate of the unprepared. How fairly steeped in horror is the doom of the "guest without a garment." From among the gay throng that are participating in the feast he is suddenly snatched and thrust, without a moment's warning, into "outer darkness," whose indescribable gloom and blackness and dreariness stand in fearful contrast to the warmth, light, glory, and illumination of the heavenly mansion.—In.

SERMONS AND OUTLINES

YESTERDAY AND TO-MORROW

By Newell Dwight Hillis, D.D.

Teach us to number our days.—Ps. xc: 12

Among the half dozen great names of history let us include the name of Moses. If Plato stands for pure thought and Paul for personal liberty, Moses stands for law, patriotism, and religion. The great jurist was of intellect all compact. He fulfilled Emerson's ideal, being at once "strong and true, his every word a cube of stone." Perhaps no single piece of literature outranks Moses' song of the eternity of God and the brevity of man's earthly career. Grown old, wearied by much wandering, lonely midst the multitude, with joy the seer welcomed the signals hung out over the heavenly battlements. For him at last the end had come. In that hour his thought journeyed backwards. How brief and shrunken seemed his life! Looking forward, youth enlarges the years to the size of radiant stars. Looking backward, old age shrinks years to the size of beads strung about the child's neck. Seeking an image of the eternity of God, the seer found it in the glowing sun, unexhausted and inexhaustible, as it pours forth the summers, and the autumns. But as for man's career, his days are swifter than the weaver's shuttle; his years swifter than the arrow, curving as it rises unto its fall. What is man's life? It is a cloud dissolving in the sunshine. It is the summer's brook, swollen by sudden rains and overflowing its banks, but soon running out and leaving the stones bare again. It is a tale that is told. To the seer it seemed like the flight of a bird, like the swift ship passing beyond the horizon, like the night watch before the morning's battle, like the new-mown grass soon withering, like the newly plucked flower swiftly fading. Remembering, therefore, life's brevity, Moses condensed all his wisdom and research into one prayer. Teach us to number our days," for time is short, art is long, and the building of a character more than the building of a cathedral or the enrichment of a city.

Astronomers count the completion of a year an event in nature; but it is not less an epoch in man's life. In the nature of the case, the completion of a vast enterprise like a military campaign or the termination of a voyage made great by its important discoveries, must be accompanied by a certain quickening of the pulse and a glow of mind and heart. When Isaac Newton, in testing his theory of gravitation, approached his final calculations and foresaw the establishment of his theory, the astronomer became so agitated as to be compelled to deliver to his companion computations which he could not compute himself. The successful solution of a lifelong problem overcame his tranquillity and exceeded his strength. By so much as Newton is more than the apple whose weight he computes, by that much is the completion of a year for man toiling hard over his arts, his industries and his homes, more than the completion of a year for forests, trees, and rivers. To the shrub a year means only a leaf; to a vine it means a cluster; to a tree it means a new ring of wood. But to a man a year means friendships won, books mastered, temptations met and vanquished—sometimes, alas! means hearthstones cold, a chair empty, a grave in the churchyard freshly dug! Deeply reverent should be those few golden days that bind together the Christmas and the New Year. Already the months and weeks are buried. Each passing hour should hold some thoughts of what the years take and what the years bring. In the olden time when ambassadors to a foreign country returned home, the king assembled his court, and with solemn pageantry received the commissioners' report. Man also does well in signalizing these days, when memory makes up her records, and closes the books against the great age of revelation.

On this last Sunday of the old year the shortness of life is a thought that warns us against overloading the future. These days, so few and brief, ask man to freight each hour with wise thoughts and right purposes. Too often the youth is slain by his to-morrows. Looking forward, the years stand forth as rich in materials, as forests and quarries for building those cities called ambitions. For youth the morrow will avail for reading many books. For youth the morrow will avail for the economy of thrift that gathers great gain. For youth the morrow will avail for habits and character. Soon the present is eclipsed by the future. As Cervantes says, "youth the morrow will avail for reading in a street called By and By, in a house named Never." Dazzled by the future as by the *ignis fatuus*, the years run out and leave the man an intellectual infant and a moral feebling. To each young heart possessed of great enthusiasm, ambition, aspiration, qualities that enable man to write his greatest books, paint his noblest pictures, win his greatest battles, there comes the seer, whispering that the years are short and that he alone can look joyfully forward who can wisely look back. For to-morrow holds no harvests that those laborers named yesterdays did not sow and culture and garner. To-morrow wins no successes that yesterday did not plan. To-morrow is only the point where yesterday empties out its baskets laden with treasure. The closing year asks each youth to guard against all idle summers, to spend no winters killing time and slaying the very hours that wise men covet so eagerly. Martineau was deeply affected by the thought that hours mean different things to a stone and to a man. Over the dead rocks the unending ages roll, only the years are as tho they were not. But to Him who knelt in Gethsemane a single night availed for the sublimest crisis in history. To the martyr waiting in his dungeon for the tyrant's decision, not knowing whether it will be " To the release," or " To the lions," a night was crowded with thoughts that would fill years for other men. It is the mother, hanging over the dying couch, watching the ebbing pulse and treasuring each whispered word; it is the patriot, Lincoln, snatching from the courier the news of a battle lost or won; it is the wife hurrying to the ship's office to ask the list of the crew lost, or saved, who can best tell us for what an hour avails, and what issues tremble thereupon. To the insect a summer's day of four and twenty hours may seem a career all too long, but to a man searching out the secrets of the rocks, hunting for some new remedy, some new force or tool, to man toiling upon his arts, his reforms, his industries, threescore years and ten are all too short for his many and sublime purposes.

Standing here between the old year and the new, let us dedicate the hour to retrospection and aspiration. The past is valuable alike to the individual and to the race. Indeed, the civilization of to-day does but represent the accumulated treasures of yesterday. Man begins his career an infant, but memory gathers up the experience, the observations and the reflections of the yesterdays and carries them forward unto to-day. Enriched thereby, soon the babe stands forth clothed with all the qualities of a patriot or a statesman. Take away his years and the individual becomes only an infant. Take away the years from society and for the city we have a group of savages. To-day each child is born into the midst of a civilization wondrously rich.

But yesterday gave the youth his language and his laws. Yesterday built the pyramids and the Parthenon. Yesterday fashioned all cathedrals and temples. Yesterday stored the gallery with pictures, the libraries with their books, the factories with their tools. Through our fathers yesterday gave us this new world. Not to-day, but yesterday, subdued the forests, reared the orchards, covered the land with villages and cities. Yesterday gave us the schoolhouse and the church. Yesterday

won all the battles for liberty and religion. Browning calls civilization a temple. But standing under its lofty dome, admiring its wide, high walls and flaming altars, let us remember that we minister in a temple built by other hands and hearts. The enthusiasm mankind feels toward the patriot or hero, the dignity and majesty that belong to the seer or saint, are also explained by the fact that the past years, with their battles and victories, with their heroisms and self sacrifices, have lent wisdom and dignity unto each Grant or Garfield or Burke.

Edward Everett tells us that Daniel Webster retired late and slept soundly the night before his celebrated reply to Haine. The next day the great statesman fronted the Senate, having in his hand only a few headings of his speech. Seeking to explain the calm confidence of the orator, his biographer says: " A full hundred oratorical triumphs behind him lent Webster confidence and intellectual momentum." If we define a great nation as a people with a noble history lying back of it, let us define a great individual as a soul with years many and great lying back of him and lending him their intellectual and moral force. As the gardens of Italy have their treasure through the snows and the mineral stimulants that are washed down from the mountain sides, so man's to-days are made rich and deep because many noble thoughts and purposes out of the yesterdays have poured down into his present.

But not all yesterdays are equally honorable. There is a past that turns the present into a torment and a curse. It is easy to understand that he whose yesterday holds some grievous sin will be slain by that past. For all such, yesterday is an avenger. And it must needs be that Eugene Aram flees from the memory of his black deed. Of necessity, Charles IX. strives to forget the night when, sitting in his palace window, he fired the signal shot for the massacre of St. Bartholomew. For him whose memory holds some dark wrong, " one sight out of yesterday, the murmur of a stream, the ringing of a church bell, the green path in the wood with the sunshine glinting upon it, the light of the moon upon the waters," may, under memory's influence, turn the heart to stone and fill the mind with a consecrated agony of remorse. For all such memory becomes a chamber of horrors. He who has betrayed his trust or his friend, he who has blackened his name with untruth or dishonor, will recall the old year only as Bonaventura recalled the dungeon in which he had been long imprisoned, or as the sleeper recalls the hideous nightmare when he seemed trembling and falling over the precipice.

Once there was a youth who went to Thebes to recover the heritage that was his. Because the boy was beloved of the gods, a celestial friend went with the youth for guiding him upon the way. Going before, this invisible friend made rough places smooth, crooked places straight, and threw the bridge across the deep chasm. But, unfortunately, the youth lost his companion's friendship. He was cruel and haughty. Hurling a stone at a lark with its sweet song, the boy broke the bird's wing. Lifting a stick over his dog, his blow left a bloody mark upon the faithful beast. After that, his invisible friend became as an enemy. Going before, he twisted the grass by the path into wands that tripped the boy and gave him many heavy falls. He cast briars and sharp stones in the way for cutting the pilgrim's feet. He sprinkled deceiving grasses over the bog, and soon the youth was struggling in the black mud. Oh, marvelous story, telling us that our yesterdays are not dead. They will take to themselves feet, and journey forward with us into the new year. No man has a right to look smilingly forward whose sins cause him to look tearfully back.

But some there are whose yesterdays become a curse through misuse. Here is a youth who has been guilty of some error or mistake. Morbid reflection has magnified his wrong. Repentance and forgiveness do not avail to remove the millstone from his neck. Memory slays his hope. It seems impossible for him to become again a candidate for honor and confidence. Strength leaves his arm, courage departs from his heart, ambition forsakes his will. He seems a Peter who, after his restoration, has no eloquence or courage to retrieve himself. He seems a David, whose lips are henceforth dumb. Never again will he soar and see like an eagle.

The past is only a chamber of discontent. In the winter, when the snows fall upon the western cornfields, the grouse come in from the swamps and prairies. Then the farmers' boys go forth to set small steel traps beside the cornstalks. Soon the unthinking bird finds the cruel jaws closing upon foot or thigh. Rising, the trap drags the bird down again. With wings broken and bleeding, the beautiful creature beats its life out upon the frozen ground. Thus men are often imprisoned between the jaws called yesterdays and need a deliverer from their past. But no man has a right to allow the errors of yesterday to slay the hopes and plans of to-morrow. Once a sin has been repented of and forgiven, it should be forgotten. The law of seemliness forbids the householder casting the wastes from the garret, the refuse from the kitchen and pantry, into a hideous heap in the library or parlor. Cities of the Orient have their offal heaps outside the walls. The law of health forbids the preservation of the refuse of life. And that which is unseemly toward the eye and the nostril outwardly does but typify the unseemliness of preserving in memory the sins and errors of yesterday. In the garden the rosebud is sheathed by certain outer leaves. But when the rose blooms the outer covering falls off. The leaves upon the ground, blackened by blight and eaten by worms, have no part with the sweet red rose freshly bloomed. Thus, when God forgives, He forgives utterly. In the beautiful words of the seer, He " casts man's sins behind his back." Why, then, should man remember what the good God forgets? He casts man's sins " into the depths of the sea." Why, then, should memory thrust its hooked pole into the sea to dredge the bottom and bring up

by the locks some pale and drowned memory that God hath plunged into the ocean of forgetfulness? Man's life is not in the past, but in the days to come.

The old year slays others through its failures. The strong wooden bow does not lose its spring when the arrow misses the bull's eye, but strangely enough missing the mark often takes the hope out of the archer's heart. Here is a business man. Events have dealt hardly with him. He has lost his vantage ground, and must needs reconquer the old supremacy that had come to seem his natural right. It has been given him to see his possessions dissolve like snowflakes in a river. The competence gathered by years wastes away in weeks. Where defeat did but dictate a fresh assault for Napoleon's Old Guard, defeat of this man dictates a retreat. He has no heart to open up new activities. As optimism is the cradle of progress, so pessimism is the grave of success and prosperity. Thus, yesterday threatens to slay this man's life and prosperity. And here is the man who realizes that he has lost his opportunity. The time was when books and teachers, when leisure for travel and study all were his. But he committed unto the morrow his scholarship, his politics, his business career, even his conquest of men's good opinion.

But the morrows do for the individual what the passing years do for houses. The days and the nights do not adorn the old homestead. Rather do they dismantle it. The rains put moss upon the shingles. The frosts eat holes in the porch. The sleets cast a verdure of decay over the old home. The summers do not repaint the clapboards, the winters do not beautify the inner walls. Thus the mere passing of time has no power for storing the mind with knowledge or the heart with character. There came a day to Coleridge when he realized that his life was in the past, and the realization brought an awful shock. He had within his mind a full hundred volumes, poems, dramas, philosophies, ethics, but each volume existed only in outline—not one was complete. The realization of the much to do and the little time to do it paralyzed his energies. The future became only the point where his heart broke. Looking backward, also, poor Haydn was slain by the memory of the opportunities forever gone, and in a dark hour he went out of life of his own calling, not waiting for God's angels to bring him the message of release. And here are those who have stormed and sulked through life and froze to death some heart that loved them and made a loved one die as

Travelers have died o'ertaken on an Alpine road,
By night confused and bewildered by the falling snow;
Yet, 'twas in the place she called her home she died,
Frozen by the wintry nature that encompassed her.

Only when it was too late did the man awaken to smite his breast, and curse his selfishness and murmur loving words over the dust lying in the churchyard. Oh, for us all alike, yesterday holds many errors and lost opportunities, holds our mistaken plans, holds also our sins. But the past is irretrievable. Repented of, it cannot be altered by tears and mournings and discontents. Yesterday's mistakes should only lend new force to the bow, sending our aspirations the higher and farther into the future. Yesterday's errors should be stimulants for to-morrow's endeavors.

But as there is an ignoble, so is there a true use of yesterday. The past is a granary holding seed for to-morrow's sowing. The past is a library holding wisdom for to-morrow's emergencies. The past is an armory holding weapons against to-morrow's battles. The past is a chest holding medicines against to-morrow's wounds. For those whose sky is all beclouded yesterday is a place of refuge, sheltering man until the storm be past. Not that any man has ever done enough for society. Not that any man has a right to sit down in a miserly way and count his kindnesses to orphans or his gifts to widows. For all such pinched hearts the worst thing that can happen is for them to do a good deed. The memory of one good deed done prevents some from ever doing another. There are those who, never forgetting themselves the gift of forty years ago, will not allow either God or man to forget it. For all such the past is full of deceit, and its light is like the will-o'-the-wisp, the light of selfishness and decay.

Nevertheless, if weakness or age or blindness overtakes some Milton, then surely the old hero in his weakness has a right to remember his days of strength, when he withstood the tyrant face to face, and did brave deeds. For Kossuth, weary with the weight of ninety years, whose limbs refused to support his weight, whose eyes refused to guide his pen and step, there was a right to all the sweets of retrospection as he went back to the day when, as a patriot, he suffered unto blood and filled the world with his name and fame. The reformer, overtaken by discouragement; the patriot, dispirited by defeat; the citizen through whose life has passed the plow of adversity midst their present discouragement have the privilege of retreating into the past. Each has a right to think of himself as a pilgrim who, in years gone by, carried with him seeds and roots and grains, and cast them out upon the right hand and the left, committing them to nature, that never permits any good thing to be lost; and now, looking back over life's long way, and perceiving that the way of the wilderness has become a place of goodly trees, beneath which weary pilgrims sit, he has a right to shelter himself from life's distresses and ingratitudes, from its adversities and discouragements.

But know, O friends immortal, that the past does not hold man's career, his life is all in the future. Yesterday's victories do but dictate new struggles for to-morrow. The hero's motto must be ours, "He loses his battle who does not thrust his standard farther and farther into the enemy's ranks." Flushed with to-day's success, man may camp down in the tents of satisfaction for one night only; when the morning comes he must take down his tents and go on to new ventures. The forest trees, pushing off their old leaves and enterprising toward new buds and growth, are nature's way of bidding man forget his past successes and encouraging him to open up new furrows and sow larger harvests. No achievement of yesterday, no victory for liberty and humanity gained in the past, no need of service to church or city or state, can ever give man the right to retire from the battle. When Wendell Phillips had helped achieve liberty for the slave, he did not say, "My work is done," but, rather, "Now let us fight intemperance and expel the saloon from the land, and achieve wisdom and happiness for each laborer." When General Grant had toiled for his country by day and by night, through storm and calm, through youth unto age, and death at length threatened him, he did not cease toiling because of past services, but meditated his memoirs and wrote two volumes, holding off death by sheer will force until the last page was completed.

Indeed as men go upward toward greatness they increasingly forget their past achievements, and, like the knights of old, plunge anew into the arena to win victories for humanity. Forgetting what he had done for poetry and song, at eighty, Tennyson meditated a new drama. Forgetting his achievements in prose and verse, at eighty, Holmes wrote "Over the Teacups." Forgetting his services for liberty, for patriotism, for religion, at eighty, Gladstone translated the odes of Horace and then announced a volume on Butler's ANALOGY. Always heroic souls have been unwilling to point to what they did yesterday, in their enthusiasm to achieve new successes for their fellows. Not disease nor age has been able to conquer their passion to serve and help humanity. These heroes seem like mountain streams that run full breasted to the sea, turning the mill wheels up to the last moment before they leap forward into the unlimited sea.

How splendid is the roll of the victories for humanity gained during the past eight and thirty years. This generation has seen liberty widening and including the slave; has seen the schoolhouse open its doors to welcome a race that a century ago had neither language, literature, nor laws; millions of serfs rising up to the dignity of citizens; inventors honored more than were the ancient warriors; the cottage of the peasant enriched with conveniences beyond the palace of the ancient patrician; new methods of travel and speech, increasing the happiness of millions; schoolgirls made wiser than queens once were; nations many and separated coming together to consider the improvement of their arts, industries, and institutions; the religious leaders of all races meeting, not to war about differences, but to meditate upon the divine truths held in common.

Oh, wondrous scene! The gains made by

this single generation seem to equal in number and to surpass in splendor those of the previous thousand years. But the greatness of yesterday comes only to revelators of the greater gains to be achieved to-morrow. There are new tools to be invented, new forces to be discovered, new songs to be written, new laws to be enacted, new reforms for humanity to be achieved. Not until the sound of war and strife has died forever out of the air, not until the pauper and the parasite and the criminal have been expelled from the land, will the work be completed.

Soon we shall say farewell to the old year. Already the months have gone, and only hours remain. The years are forming and disappearing. The months are woven and unraveled. The days are speeding on. Powerless are we to postpone that day when we shall pass forever from the streets and scenes we so dearly love. Soon we shall be like dismantled palaces. As in the harvest-field men cast up the bundles upon the wagons to be drawn to the barns for winnowing and threshing, thus, soon we shall have cast up the last bundle upon the coursers of time and the stars will draw the load into the eternal granary. The years are going. Let the chaff and the evil part of this life pass with them. As men load the wagon with the sweepings of the street, and, carrying it far to the ocean, cast it into the deep abyss, so bring together all your hatreds, weaknesses, unkindnesses, jealousies, all passions, ingratitudes, and embittering memories, and, tying them into one bundle, let the old year sweep them out and drop them into the gulf of oblivion. Expel from your life all sins and sordid aims. Carry into the new year only the choicest thoughts and aspirations. As in the olden days when men approached the Parthenon they cleansed their persons and arrayed themselves in white robes before entering that glorious temple, so cleanse your garments from transgression, clothe yourself with aspirations. Farewell to the past! Welcome and all hail to the future.—B. E.

A MIDNIGHT DOXOLOGY: A WATCH-NIGHT MESSAGE

By Rev. C. J. Greenwood

At midnight I will rise to give thanks unto thee because of thy righteous judgments.—Psalm cxix: 62

Midnight is the time for repose. At that hour Morpheus keeps thousands of eyes sealed. It is the hour when "deep sleep falleth upon man." The busy brain and active muscles relax and the prostrate form presents the "counterfeit rehearsal of death."

There are slumber hours in Christian experience. The spiritual eyes are holden. It is hard work to get up in season for church Sunday morning, too much of an effort to go out to prayer-meeting. Drowsiness paralyzes the spiritual activities. Then is the time to shake off the drowsy feeling by getting down upon the knees and praising God. The act itself will arouse. The reflex blessing will set the heart aflame. The joy will thrill.

Midnight is a time of revel. While thousands sleep, other thousands dissipate. Hell empties itself. The saloon belches forth its volume of sin, sorrow, and suffering. Somebody's boys and girls are on the road to ruin. This is the welcome hour for the thief and murderer. What can we thank God for as we stand before this midnight picture of doom? Thank God that there are churches striving to save those boys and girls. Thank God that there are hundreds of consecrated men and women going about doing good. Thank God for a rescue mission where scores of prodigals and Magdalens are being saved every year. Thank God that there is an opportunity given for you to throw yourself into the heat of battle, and forget your wounds and heartaches in healing the wounds and heartaches of others.

There is midnight in the heart as well as in the sky. Those who visited the Columbian Art Gallery at Chicago in 1893 have not forgotten that pathetic picture by Josef Israel, entitled "Alone in the World." The dear companion stretched upon the humble bed, cold in death, the old man sitting there with head bowed between the wrinkled hands. The stars might have shone o'erhead, but it was midnight in the old man's heart. You and I have sat under some such experience when we could almost feel the darkness, so dense it seemed. In days gone by the sun of prosperity shone in unclouded splendor. How many the stars of promise that looked down from the clear sky! But midnight came. and the clock of adversity tolled the funeral knell of hope.

But after the midnight comes the dawn. How the long hours lengthen as you begin the night-watch beside the sick-bed! But the clock in the tower strikes twelve. Then the hours begin to shorten. You look out of the window for the morning star, the herald of the day. Presently "jocund day stands tiptoe on the misty mountain-tops." After the night of tears comes the dawn of joy. "Weeping may endure for a night, but joy cometh in the morning." Oh, the calm after the fitful storm, the peace after the sighing! Midnight closed in upon your soul. You thought God had withdrawn His presence. How deep the gloom! How the wind beat against the window-pane of your poor heart in fitful gusts! But the winds are dying out now. The clock in the tower has boomed the last stroke. The morning star of hope heralds the dawn of a brighter day.

You men and women in Christ are stronger pillars in Zion's temple because of the midnight experiences. Then—

"Let the dead past bury its dead!
Act—act in the living present!
Heart within, and God o'erhead!"

The Israelites appointed a feast of thanksgiving to God for that midnight deliverance of the first-born. Let this midnight hour be a feast of thanksgiving. The clock that tolls the knell of the dying year is almost done striking. Dawn is breaking on the hills. Let us thank God for our deliverance and His righteous judgments.

Florence Nightingale was called "the angel of the Crimea." At midnight as the soldier lay tossing, burning with the fever, how he listened for the footfall of Florence Nightingale! Whenever the midnight hour of sorrow or suffering comes to us, let us listen for the footfalls of God's angels of mercy.—H. R.

OUR STEWARDSHIP

BY ARCHDEACON PALMER

Give an account of thy stewardship; for thou mayest be no longer steward.—Luke xvi: 2

We are God's stewards our whole life long; each day of our lives, therefore, claims its own account; each year, as it passes, suggests to us naturally such reflections, since we reckon our life by years. To many thoughtful men their own birthdays have been days of solemn self-examination. To many, the last day of the civil year brings a like reminder. Indeed, popular language recognizes in it something of this power.

I. While our life is full of vigor, such anniversaries, however, invite us to look forward as well as backward. The end of an old year is the beginning of a new one. To look back is for a Christian to repent, since the best of us is but a sinner before God; but repentance should bear fruit in new life. And if we have abused God's gifts in the past year, the approaching festival of Christmas with the whole train of holy seasons that follow one after another, and bringing manifold reminders of God's love to man, tell us that there is help in heaven, help ready for us on the earth, if we will even now turn to God and amend our lives. Advent, Christmas, Passiontide, Easter, Ascension Day, are not only thankful commemorations before God of glorious things done for us in past time; they are not only settings forth before man of great events of which we might neglect to read, or read carelessly, in Scripture. They serve to remind us also of a God, ever-living and ever-present, able and willing to renew for us daily those great blessings which our Lord lived and died on earth to win for us all.

II. But as anniversaries multiply upon us, as the years behind us are many, the years to come few in comparison, my text has a meaning for us which deepens continually—

a meaning which cannot but force itself on the attention of those who avoid generally serious thoughts. The end of life is in very deed the end of our stewardship. We know little of the existence appointed for us between death and judgment. Little has been told us, except in brief and momentous outline of that which is to come after the Judgment Day. But we have no reason to think that in either there will be room for further probation for use or misuse of gifts and opportunities. As we draw near to the end of this earthly life our thoughts are apt to retrace the space which we have crossed. We find that we have done little, far less than we might have done, because our own indolence made us decline the task, or private aims warped and marred our public action. And yet another question remains which we put to ourselves as we look back on our past life. How have we done our duty to God in it? Ability to know God and to serve Him is one portion assuredly of our stewardship; and as we draw near to the end of life, we cannot but ask ourselves how we have used it. We alone know—I do not say that we ourselves know perfectly—whether we have sought to draw near to God, to know, serve, and love Him in real earnest. In the retrospect of which I have been speaking, there is more of sadness and less of hope. Little time, little opportunity, remain for amendment. But there is hope for us still. God's love, God's mercy, is inexhaustible. Humbly, trustfully, lovingly, we must cast all our sins before the throne and commit ourselves to God's mercy in the Name of Him who heard and accepted the thief upon the cross.—S. B., vol. vii., p. 248.

REDEEMING THE TIME

Ephesians v: 16

This expression also occurs in Colossians. The connection there is that we are to walk "in wisdom toward them that are without." Here there is virtually the same connection: "walk circumspectly," etc.; with a reason added: "Because the days," etc. The word redeeming means the forestalling of a market—first buying up all the goods of a certain kind, and then getting a large price. The general meaning is, *making the most of every opportunity;* seizing it and putting it to greatest possible account. In a literal sense time cannot be redeemed. Once gone, gone forever. But the *present* may be made the utmost of, and that is the meaning of the injunction here given.

I. SOME REASONS FOR REDEEMING THE TIME.

1. *One reason is that time is so precious in itself.* Would you know the value God sets on time? Look up to the *heavens.* He appointed those stars for "signs," etc., and for *days and years."* And how exactly that great clock keeps time! Look on *Nature*—" unhasting, unresting." Look at the *process of life in your own bodies.* Beat by beat that God who giveth so royally doles out *this* gift second by second.

2. *Another reason is that so much of our time is gone.* The close of the year reminds us that the day is far spent and the night at hand. Gone are the morning hours, forenoon, noon, afternoon. Now this is apt to make men desperate and wasteful rather than diligent. So much gone! So many opportunities! So many resolutions broken, or weakly kept! Is the rest worth minding? But the Bible encourages and urges us to make the most of what remains. "Strengthen the things that remain," as workers in gold preserve and sift their refuse.

3. *Another reason is, that our hold on what remains is so uncertain.* Specially favorable times are very uncertain, such as health, present position, etc. We are like harvesters in a short season and a broken one; like traders in the *heyday* of the market, and our *entire time* is very uncertain. "In such an hour as ye think not," etc.

II. THE GREAT USES FOR WHICH TIME IS TO BE REDEEMED. Some people redeem it for *unworthy* uses. They cut and pare the minutes of honest and honorable work for frivolous pleasure, or worse. As a drunkard will save money for drink, or a foolish woman for absurd display in dress.

1. *The sinner is to redeem time for his own salvation.* Men here and now make the *turning* for future glory or shame. Redeem time as shipwrecked men redeem it when the lifeboat is by the ship's side. "Behold, now is the accepted time," etc. "To-day, if ye will hear," etc.

2. *The child of God is to redeem it for building up a Christlike character.*—Passing opportunities are the stones beside the builder. Under God, and in His strength, we build *for ourselves* our future mansion. You complain of *hardships and afflictions?* They are precious stones; meant to beautify our house with meekness, sympathy, etc. *Temptations?* They are educators, showing us how and where to strengthen the walls of our house.

3. *The servant of Christ is to redeem time for works of love and helpfulness.*—Perhaps you are very busy in your worldly calling. That is a special reason for seizing the minutes which you can become possessed of. It is wonderful what spare half hours and minutes can do. What beautiful work can deft fingers make of parings of silk, inches of wool, etc. Pope wrote his poems on fly-leaves and scraps of paper, etc. In mere snatches of time, how much may be done for the warning, instruction, influencing, comforting and helping of our fellowmen.—H. L. S. E., vol. i., p. 307.

THE LAST DAYS OF THE OLD YEAR

John xvii: 7

What changes time works! How impossible it is to stop time!

When Napoleon the Great led his wearied army to the plains of Waterloo, on the day before the battle, the shadows had lengthened far on toward the evening. It was too late for him to make precisely the disposition he desired and had intended. As the light was fading he pointed toward the setting sun, and said:

"What would I not give to be this day possessed of the power of Joshua, and be enabled to retard thy march for two hours."

Lord Wilmington said of the Duke of Newcastle, once the prime minister of England:

"He loses half-an-hour every morning, and runs after it during all the day without being able to overtake it."

But the sun would not wait at Waterloo; the Duke of Newcastle could not catch his lost half-hour. I heard an admirable definition of time. Time is continuous succession—neither backward, nor to the left hand, nor to the right hand but straight forward. Yes, time is continuous succession, straight forward. And it is impossible to stop the succession forward. You cannot stay time.

And what a really solemn thought it is! Is it not a thought even the stupidest of us cannot help heeding on the last Sunday of the old year?—that time is resistlessly carrying every one of us on somewhither.

As one grows older, the whelming force and rush of time seems swifter. A year—now it is, and then—is gone! and you have helplessly gone with it. A decade of years —why, the whole ten of them seem to pass and take you with them with quicker speed than did a single year when the laggard sun of youth was shining.

Ah, the changing, unstopping, resistless years! What shall we think about them? What shall we say about them? What teaching for us is there in the presence of them, as we stand here in the last week of another year, almost utterly sped away?

Three great truths stand out of our Scripture and its surroundings—truths of comfort, amid the passing years.

1. Amid these changing, unstopping, resistless years, it is the Lord who cares for us.

2. Amid these unstopping, changing, resistless years, it is the Lord only who makes disclosures for us. Mark some of the elements of this disclosure of the Lord: (a) It is a disclosure of life beyond death. Jesus had died, but He had risen. (b) It is the disclosure of identity through death. Tho Jesus was changed, He was still the same. (c) It is the disclosure of recognition beyond death. Tho He had died and risen, Jesus was still cognizant of His disciples. (d) It is a disclosure of a sure friend for us when the years bring us to the change to which they hasten us. Amid the darkness of death the risen Christ shines radiantly forth.

3. It is the Lord, who, amid these changing, unstopping, resistless years demands our service. Lovest thou me? asked Christ of Peter. Then feed, shepherd, my lambs, my sheep. The test of love is service. Ah, it is wise for us to ask: have we yielded such test of love in the past year?—H. R.

THOUGHTS FOR THE OLD YEAR AND THE NEW

Acts vii: 17

Here the steamer in which I was passenger was sailing steadily out into the wide sea. I do not think any man can begin a voyage at sea and not be just a little wondering and questioning. The sea is so uncertain. There are so many contingencies in it of wave and wind and mist and current. You cannot at all tell what the voyage may bring you. You say the steamer is stanch and the captain trustworthy, and these secondary things are right; but I do not think any man, even tho he may not be distinctively religious, can help or would help his thought flying on and up from all these secondary things to Him who is the great, personal, primary, presiding God, and saying to himself, " Well, God is as much for the sea as for the land; I have God to trust in."

And I do not think that any one of us, as we debark from the ship of an old year and embark in the ship of a new, can help a questioning wondering. The future is so uncertain. What tempest shall rise in it; what thick mists shall drop in it; what unusual currents shall sweep in it? Who can tell? But the comforting and steadying thought, after all, is that of the primary and presiding God.

This, then, is what may be brought us by our Scripture, as in the ship of a new year we sail off into the uncertain and untried future—*some thoughts of God.*

I. *In this world of ours, God has a time for things.* " But when the *time* of the promise drew nigh, which God had sworn to Abraham." This world of ours is not a bit of sea-weed, tossed upon the tides of time. This world is steered. An infinite intelligence grasps its helm, controls the winds, orders or permits the tides. God has a time for things. Turn to the history of our world.

" It is incontrovertible that it was predicted ages ago that a chosen man, called yonder out of Ur, of the Chaldees, should become a chosen family, and this a chosen nation; and that in this chosen nation should appear a chosen Supreme Teacher of the race, and that He should found a chosen church, and that to His chosen people, with a zeal for good works, should ultimately be given all nations and the isles of the sea. In precisely this order, world-history has unrolled itself, and is still unrolling. Christianity, at this hour, reads her Scriptures and lifts her anthems in two hundred languages. This great gulf-current has flowed in one direction two thousand, three thousand, four thousand years. Advance to-day is on the side of at least the professedly Christian nations. Islam is losing her grasp. Islam is gasping. A power not ourselves makes for righteousness. It has steadily caused the fittest to survive, and thus has executed a plan of choosing a peculiar people. The survival of the fittest will ultimately give the world to the fit. Are we in our anxiety for the future to believe that this law will alter soon, or to fear that He whose will the law expresses, and who never slumbers nor sleeps, will change His plan to-morrow or the day after? Let us gaze on this gulf-current and take from it heart and hope, harmonious with the heart of Almighty God, out of which the gulf-current beats only as one pulse."

" But when the *time* of the promise drew nigh which God had sworn to Abraham." God has a *time* for things in this world of ours. Over it, through it, around it, there is intelligent purpose. All this is a thought to sail into the uncertain future in the ship of a new year with.

II. *God does not forget His time for things.*

But when the times of the promise *drew nigh.* Read the promise (Gen. xv: 13, 14). When the times of the promise *drew nigh, then*—then the people began to multiply in Egypt; then the oppression of the king who knew not Joseph began to turn the Hebrews' thoughts toward escape and deliverance; then Moses was born; then was given him that strange and necessary culture in the royal court; then were the gateways of miracle opening toward the promised land. God does not forget His time for things.

What better thought with which to leave the old year and begin the new than this of God, who has a time for things and who does not forget His time; and as for the Hebrews generally, so for you and me specifically. For me God has His time; and concerning me He will not forget His time. —H. R.

THE CLOSE OF THE YEAR

By H. Alford, D.D.

To him that overcometh will I grant to sit with me in my throne, even as I also overcame, and am set down with my Father in his throne.—Rev. iii: 21

I. " He that overcometh." Then there is light shining in and struggling with the darkness—a conflict year-long and life-long, which, tho it has its defects, may have its victories also; which, tho its outward aspect is gloomy, may issue in glory, and honor, and immortality. Years bring us another lesson than the lesson of discouragement. Tho much is taken away, much is also gained—gained by that very loss. The past has become for us full of rich and precious store: lessons of self distrust; lessons of charitable thought; lessons of reliance on God. If we have lost bloom, we have gathered ripeness. The future has opened and widened before us. It is no longer the book of dark things, closed and put by till our play is over: the page lies open before us on the desk of life's business; tho much in it is hidden, much is revealed to our inner sight, which solemnizes us, and stirs us to action. It is no longer the great unknown land talked of as a dream and a mystery, but we are plying our voyage thither, standing at watch, and holding the helm. Already we begin to see its tokens float past us, and to scent the gales which come from its fields. And the present —we have learned to distrust it and to question its testimony, have become wiser than to encumber by loading ourselves with its fading flowers; we search for pearls that shall endure.

II. " Who is he that overcometh the world but he that believeth that Jesus is the Son of God? " Here, again, as years pass on, we want more of Him, a firmer reliance on His work and His word, to stand among things visible and endure as seeing the invisible. If we would be gaining this victory, we must labor hard for knowledge and obedience, and every way for a greater realizing of Christ. Our text is not only an implication of the possibility of victory: it is also a promise to the victor. The Author and Finisher of our faith Himself proclaims it, Himself offers to the conquerors a prize, and pledges for it His own word: " To him that overcometh will I grant to sit with me in my throne."—S. B., vol. xii., p. 286.

SUGGESTIVE THOUGHTS AND ILLUSTRATIONS

BEGINNING, Time of.—Emma was a sweet little girl six years old. One day she said to her mother, " Mamma, I mean to begin at the new year to love Jesus."—" But," said her mother, " how do you know you will live till the new year? " Emma sat some moments without speaking. At length she looked up, with tears in her eyes, and said, " Perhaps I shall not. I will begin now; and then, mamma, if God lets me live, I shall be a Christian when the new year begins."—F. I.

BOOK OF LIFE, Enrolled in the.—Some people say they can't tell down here, but must wait till they get to Heaven to know whether their names are written in the Book of Life. I believe it is the privilege of every Christian to know it here. Men in China tell me that the greatest honor that can be paid them there is to write their name in one of their joss houses, in the house of Confucius. Christ says, " Rejoice that your names are written in heaven." I was coming into Liverpool one night with a party of friends, and we found the Northwestern Hotel full, and they told me it had been full for days. I said to my friends, " Let us go over to the Adelphi." "No," they said, "we have a room engaged." "Why," I said, "they told me the house had been full for days, and now you say you have got a room." They said, "We sent our names on ahead and secured a room." "How wise," thought I. Many of you are laying in wood for the bleak winter, and food and clothing. Oh, prepare for the long, bleak night that is coming! See that your names are written in Heaven; send your names on ahead and secure a room. And when sure that our names are written there we should see that those of our children are. A friend said to me "Why talk of books being kept in Heaven." I said, "The Bible has a good deal to say about it." In Daniel xii: 1, "every one was saved whose name was found written in the book." In Philippians iv: 3, Paul speaks of those whose names were written in the book. We ought to live so that not only we but others would know our names are on the record.—Moody.

BOOK OF LIFE, Example of the.—In the public registers all that were born of a particular tribe were entered in the list of their respective families under that tribe. This was the book of life; and when any of these died, his name might be considered as blotted out of the list. "In China, the names of the persons who have been tried on criminal processes are written in two distinct books, which are called the book of life, and the book of death; those who have been acquitted, or who have not been capitally convicted, are written in the former; those who have been found guilty, in the latter. These two books are presented to the emperor by his ministers, and he, as sovereign, has a right to erase any name from either: to place the living among the dead, that he may die: or the dead, that is, the person condemned to death, among the living, that he may be preserved. Thus he blots out of the book of life, or the book of death, according to his sovereign pleasure, on the representation of his ministers, or the intercession of friends."—*Selected.*

BOOK OF LIFE, Legend of the.—St. Julian and his wife Basilissa, resolved to live chaste lives, as if they had not been married. Their bridal chamber became illuminated, and Jesus, standing by them, said. "Thou hast conquered, O Julian!" Then two angels, clothed in white robes, girded with golden zones, having crowns, stood beside their couch. Thereon lay a book seven times brighter than silver, wherein were various names in letters of gold. Julian read there his name and that of his wife, Basilissa. And one of four witnessing elders, who were also there, said, "In that book are written the chaste and the sober, the truthful and the merciful, the humble and the gentle, those whose love is unfeigned, bearing adversities, patient in tribulation, and those who, for the love of Jesus Christ, have given up father, and mother, and wife, and children, and lands for His sake, lest they should impede the progress of their souls to perfection, and

they who have not hesitated to shed their blood for His name, in the number of whom you also have merited to be written."—F. II.

CHILDHOOD, Second.—Rev. Dr. Nott sank into a second childhood that was peculiarly tender. The last hours of his life were particularly impressive. He lay on his bed, blind, and apparently unconscious. His wife sat by his bedside, and sang to him, day by day, the songs of his childhood. He was hushed to repose by them, like an infant on its pillow. Watts' cradle-hymn, "Hush, my dear! lie still and slumber," always soothed him. Visions of home floated before him, and the name of his mother was frequently on his lips. The last time he conducted family devotions with his household, he closed his prayer with the well-known lines, "Now I lay me down to sleep," etc.—B. J.

CONVERSION, Late.—Conversions after forty years of age are very rare; like the scattered grapes on the remotest branches after the vintage is over, there is only one here and there. I have sometimes seen an old withered oak standing with its stiff and leafless branches on the slopes of a woody hill, tho the same refreshing rains and genial sunshine fell on it as on its thriving neighbors, which were green with renewed youth, and rich in flowing foliage: it grew not, it gave no signs of life; it was too far gone for genial nature to assist. The old, blanched, sapless oak is an emblem of the aged sinner.—Dr. Thomas.

DAYS THAT ARE PAST, The.—As "few and evil" they were regarded by even the aged patriarch. But how many fine days among them—days full of means and opportunities, deliverances from evils and blessings from Heaven, the excitements of conscience and the stirrings of the Spirit of God! Who can tell what report they have borne to Heaven?

"Oh! The dark days of vanity! while here,
    How tasteless! and how terrible when
        gone!
Gone! they ne'er go; when past they haunt
        us still;
The Spirit walks of every day deceased,
And smiles an angel, or a fury frowns."
                                        P. T.

END OF A THING.—*Eccles. vii: 8:* Better is the end of a thing than the beginning. The general principle is established that by the condition of our existence here, a conclusion is better than a beginning.

The fruit is better than the blossom; the reaping than the sowing; the enjoyment than the reaping. The second stage of a journey is better than the first; the home itself than all. The victory is better than the march and the battle; the reward than the course of service.

Let us not shrink from a salutary exercise of review and comparison. Have our affections, activities, years, and months, been devoted to God? Without this, no year is good either in its progress or in its end.—John Foster.

FUTURE, The.—The great bell of time is striking. Another year is nearly gone, another milestone on life's journey, another stage of our race for the goal. Let the past go. Its retrospect is gloomy, at the best. Its memory brings pain and discouragement. We want all that is hopeful for the future. We ring bells for the new; we do not toll out our mournful ding-dongs over the old. Let our hearts reciprocate the sentiment of Tennyson's New Year bells:

" Ring out the old, ring in the new."

" Ring out the false, ring in the true."

" Ring in the Christ that is to be."

C. A.

GOODNESS, Perseverance in.—The philosopher, being asked in his old age why he did not give over his practice, and take his ease, answered, " When a man is to run a race of forty furlongs, would you have him sit down at the nine and thirtieth, and so lose the prize? We do not keep a good fire all day, and let it go out in the evening, when it is coldest; but then rather lay on more fuel, that we may go warm to bed." He that slakes the heat of his zeal in old age will go cold to bed, and in a worse case to his grave. Tho the beginning be more than half, yet the end is more than all.—SPENCER.

LIFE, A Delusion of.—It is a sad thing to look at some of the receiving-hulks at the navy-yard; to think that that was the ship which once went so fearlessly across the ocean. It has come back to be anchored in some quiet bay, and so roll this way and that with the tide. Yet this is what many men set before them as the end of life,—that they may reach some haven, where they will be able to cast out an anchor at the bow and an anchor at the stern, and never move again, but rock lazily, without a sail, without a voyage, waiting simply for decay to take apart their timbers.—BEECHER.

THINGS FLEETING.—There are four things that come not back,—the spoken word, the sped arrow, the past life, the neglected opportunity.—*Arabian.*

TIME.—" We, all of us, complain of the shortness of time," saith Seneca, and yet have much more than we know what to do with. We are always complaining our days are few and acting as tho there would be no end of them.

I often consider mankind as wholly inconsistent in a point that bears some affinity to the former. Tho we feel grieved at the shortness of life in general, we are wishing every period of it at an end. The minor longs to be of age, then to be a man of business, then to retire. Thus, altho the whole of life is allowed by everyone to be short, the several divisions of it appear long and tedious. We are lengthening our space in general, but would fain contract the parts of which it is composed.—ADDISON.

TIME.—Think not thy time short in this world, since the world itself is not long. The created world is but a small parenthesis in eternity, and a short interposition, for a time, between such a state of duration as was before, it may be after it.—SIR THOMAS BROWNE (Bohn's edition) vol. iii., p. 143.

TIME A DESTROYER.—I saw a temple reared by the hands of man, standing with its high pinnacle in the distant plain. The streams beat about it, the God of Nature hurled His thunder-bolts against it; yet it stood as firm as adamant. Revelry was in the hall; the gay, the happy, the young, the beautiful, were there. I returned, and, lo! the temple was no more. Its high walls lay in scattered ruin; moss and grass grew rankly there; and, at the midnight hour, the owl's lone cry added to the solitude. The young and gay who had reveled there had passed away. I saw a child rejoicing in his youth, the idol of his mother, and the pride of his father. I returned, and that child had become old. Trembling with the weight of years, he stood, the last of his generation, a stranger amidst all the desolation around him. I saw an old oak standing in all its pride upon the mountain; the birds were caroling in its boughs. I returned, and saw the oak was leafless and sapless: the winds were playing at their pastime through the branches. " Who is the destroyer? " said I to my guardian angel. " It is Time," said he. " When the morning-stars sang together for joy over the new-made world, he commenced his course, and when he has destroyed all that is beautiful on the earth, plucked the sun in his sphere, veiled the moon in blood; yea, when he shall have rolled the heavens and the earth away as a scroll, then shall an angel from the throne of God come forth, and, with one foot upon the land, lift up his hand towards Heaven, and swear by Heaven's Eternal, time was, but time shall be no more."—PAULDING.

TIME CLOSING IN UPON US.—There is a story of a prisoner in a cell with contractile walls. Day by day his space lessens; he saw the whole of that window yesterday, he sees only half of it to-day. Nearer and nearer the walls are drawn together, till they meet and crush him between them. So the walls of time are closing in upon us.—MACLAREN.

TIME, End of.—There was an ancient custom of putting an hour-glass into the coffin of the dead to signify that their time had run out, a useless notification to them. Better put the hour-glass into the hand of every living man and show them the grains gliding steadily out. Soon all will be gone.—F. I.

TIME, Flight of.—When young, our years are ages; in mature life, they are three hundred and sixty-five days; in old age, they have dwindled to a few weeks. Time is, indeed, the messenger with wings at his feet. Yesterday, he took my wife; to-day, my son; to-morrow, he will take me.—MADAME DE GASPARIN.

TIME, Fragments of.—In the Palace of Industry, there were several curious specimens of art, wrought by humble individuals out of such fragments of time as they could secure from their regular occupations. Oh the preciousness of moments! no gold or gems can be compared to them. Yet all have them; while some are thereby enriched, and others leave themselves in poverty. The wealth of time is like gold in the mine, like the gem in the pebble, like the diamond in the deep. The mine must be worked, the pebble ground and polished, the deep fathomed and searched.—J. STOUGHTON.

TIME, Improvement of.—The learned Grotius had for his motto *Hora ruit*. By it he lived, improving every moment; yet so great was his sense of non-improvement, that at his death he cried, " I have wasted my life in incessant toil, and have done nothing."—F. I.

TIME, Influencing.—It is notorious to philosophers, that joy and grief can hasten and delay time. Locke is of opinion, that a man in great misery may so far lose his measure as to think a minute an hour, or, in joy, make an hour a minute.—STEELE.

TIME, Irrecoverable.—A woman in the agonies of despair, cried out to those who sought to comfort her, " Call back time again! If you can call back time again, then there may be hope for me; but time is gone."—F. I.

TIME, Loss of.—We are doomed to suffer a bitter pang as often as the irrevocable flight of our time is brought home with keenness to our hearts. The spectacle of a lady floating over the sea in a boat and waking suddenly from sleep to find her magnificent ropes of pearl necklace by some accident detached at one end from its fastenings, the loose string hanging down into the water, and pearl after pearl slipping off forever into the abyss, brings before us the sadness of the case. That particular pearl which at the very moment in rolling off into the unsearchable deep carries its own separate reproach to the lady's heart; but it is more deeply reproachful as the representative of so many other uncounted pearls that have already been swallowed up irrecoverably while yet she was sleeping, and of many besides that must follow before any remedy can be applied to what we may call this jewelly hemorrhage.—F. I.

TIME, Neglected.—Many sitting up long at play have to go to bed in the dark. Life here is a play whose bed is eternity. Let us, then, give over play before our candle is out, and we, left in darkness, have to take up our bed in hell to all eternity.—SPENCER.

TIME, Never Recovered.—Lost wealth may be restored by industry, the wreck of health regained by temperance, forgotten knowledge restored by study, alienated friendship smoothed into forgetfulness, even forfeited reputation won by penitence and virtue; but who ever looked upon his van-

ished hours, recalled his slighted years, stamped them with wisdom, or effaced from heaven's record the fearful blot of wasted time?—MRS. SIGOURNEY.

TIME, No Leisure.—Dionysius the Silician, employed his time so well, that, being asked by one who wanted to speak with him if he were at leisure, he answered, " Heaven forbid that I should ever have any leisure time! "—SCRAGGS.

TIME, Picture of.—It was wittily said, that by some time was thus pictured of old: *Time to come* had the head of a fawning dog; *time present,* the head of a stirring lion; *time past,* the head of a biting wolf; so teaching, that tho silly souls fancy still their best days are to come, yet, if they bestir not well themselves in their *present* ones, they will be very miserably torn and bitten in their *future.*—BURGESS.

TIME, Redeeming the.—A sibyl came to the king of Rome, and offered to sell unto him three tomes of her oracles, but he, counting the price too high, refused to buy them. Away she went and burned one tome of them. Returning, she asked him whether he would buy the two remaining at the same rate. He refused again, counting her little better than frantic. Thereupon she burned the second tome, and peremptorily asked him whether he would give the sum demanded for all the three for the one tome remaining, otherwise she would burn that also, and he would dearly repent it. Tarquin, admiring her constant resolution, and conceiving some extraordinary worth contained therein, gave her her demand. There are three volumes of man's time—youth, man's estate, and old age—and ministers advise them to redeem this time (Eph. v : 16). But men conceive the rate they must give to be unreasonable, because it will cost them the renouncing of their carnal delights. Hereupon one-third part of their life, youth, is consumed in the fire of wantonness. Again, ministers counsel men to redeem the remaining volumes of their life. They are but derided for their pains. And man's estate is also cast away in the smoke of vanity. But preachers ought to press peremptorily on old people to redeem, now or never, the last volume of their life. Here is the difference: the sibyl still demanded but the same rate for the remaining book, but aged folk (because of their custom in sinning) will find it harder and dearer to redeem this, the last volume, than if they had been chapmen for all three at the first.—THOMAS FULLER.

TIME, Saving.—Said General Mitchell to an army officer who apologized for a little delay, " Only a few moments! I have been in the habit of calculating the value of the thousandth part of a second."—F. I.

TIME, The Flight of.—1. *Psalm xc: 9: We spend our years as a tale that is told.* When a tale is told, its conclusion explains the plot and all that precedes. As we look back from the end of the year do we understand our life, or is it still confused and incomplete?

2. *Gen. xlvii: 8: How old art thou?* Li Hung Chang often asked this usual Oriental question. It is a fitting question to ask thoughtfully at the end of the year.

3. *Jas. iv: 14: We know not what shall be on the morrow. For what is your life? It is even a vapor, which appeareth for a little time, and then vanisheth away.*

4. *1 Cor. vii: 31: For the fashion of this world passeth away.*

TIME, The Treasure.—An Italian philosopher expressed in his motto, " that time was his treasure,"—an estate, indeed, which will produce nothing without cultivation, but which will always abundantly repay the labors of industry, and satisfy the most extensive desires, if no part of it be suffered to lie waste by negligence, to be overrun with noxious plants, or laid out for show rather than use.—DR. JOHNSON.

TIME, Treasuring.—Boyle remarks, " that sand-grains are easily scattered; but skilful artificers gather, melt, and transmute them to glass, of which they make mirrors, lenses, and telescopes. Even so, vigilant Christians improve parenthetic fragments of time, employing them in self-examination, acts of faith, and researches of holy truth; by which they become looking-glasses for their souls, and telescopes revealing their promised heaven." Jewelers save the very sweepings of their shops, because they contain particles of precious metal. Should Christians, whose every moment was purchased for them by the blood of Christ, be less careful of time? Surely its very minutiæ should be more treasured than grains of gold or dust of diamonds.—S. COLEY.

TIME, Trifling with.—Every day, every hour in the day, is a talent of time; and God expects the improvement of it, and will charge the non-improvement of it upon you at last. Cæsar, observing some ladies at Rome to spend a large part of their time in making much of little dogs and monkeys, asked them whether the women in that country had no children to make much of.—F. I.

TIME, Unnoted.—When the famous Baron de Trench came out of his dark dungeon in Magdeburg, where he could not distinguish night from day, and in which the King of Prussia had kept him imprisoned for ten years, he imagined that he had been in it for a much shorter period, because he had no means of marking how the time had passed, and he had seen no new events, and had had even few thoughts. His astonishment was extreme when he was told how many years had thus passed away like a painful dream.—L. GAUSSEN.

TIME, Used.—Among the ancient Indians there were a set of men called gymnosophists, who had a great aversion to sloth and idleness. When the tables were spread for their repasts, the assembling youths were asked by their masters in what useful task they had been employed from the hour of sunrise. One, perhaps; represented himself as having been an arbitrator, and succeeded, by his prudent management, in composing a difference between friends. A second had been paying obedience to his parents' commands. A third had made some discovery by his own application, or learned something by another's instruction. But he who had done nothing to deserve a dinner was turned out of doors without one, and obliged to work while the others enjoyed the fruits of their application.—KNOWLES.

TIME, Use of.—Time is life's freightage, wherewith some men trade, and make a fortune; and others suffer it to molder all away, or waste in extravagance. Time is life's book, out of which some extract wondrous wisdom; while others let it lie uncovered, and then die fools. Time is life's tree, from which some gather precious fruit, while others lie down under its shadow, and perish with hunger. Time is life's ladder, whereby some raise themselves up to honor and renown and glory; and some let themselves down into the deeps of shame, degradation, and ignominy. Time will be to us what, by our use of the treasure, we make it—a good or an evil, a blessing or a curse.—J. STOUGHTON.

TIME, Value of.—Queen Charlotte said: " I am always quarreling with time: it is so short to do something, and so long to do nothing." John Bradford used to say, " I count that hour lost in which I have done no good by my pen or tongue." Seneca taught, that time was the only thing of which it is a virtue to be covetous. Dr. Cotton Mather would express his regret after the departure of a visitor that had wasted his time, " I had rather have given him a handful of money than have been kept thus long out of my study." Henry Martyn won the honorable title, " The man that never wasted an hour." —F. I.

TIME, Waste of.—The amount of time wasted in some men's lives is fearfully large. Not to mention the time which is wasted in sleep, dress, and gossip; look at the time wasted in reveries, absence of mind, air-balloon imaginations, and wild-goose chases, searching for new inventions without finding them; making schemes, and never executing them; writing manuscripts with a view to publish, and never publishing them; brooding over imaginary fears, and never realizing them; indulging in sanguine hopes which never ripen into fruit; battling with expected spectral appearances which never were seen; crossing bridges and streams and forests which never came in the way; meeting objections of opponents which were never raised; preparing defenses of character upon points which were never assailed; quaking, shaking, moaning, groaning, grumbling, over aches, pains, losses, woes, and death, which only existed in the dreams of a diseased brain. —BATE.

TIME, Worth of.—To show us the worth of time, God, most liberal of all other things, is exceedingly frugal in the dispensing of *that;* for He never gives us two moments together, nor grants us a second till He has withdrawn the first, still keeping the third in His own hands, so that we are in perfect uncertainty whether we shall have it or not. The true manner of preparing for the last moment is to spend all the others well, and ever to expect *that.* We dote upon this world as if it were never to have an end, and neglect the next as if it were never to have a beginning.—FÉNELON.

YEAR, Old and New.—A strange scene was witnessed by an English visitor at Odessa on the first day of one Jewish year. Sixty thousand Jews living at Odessa went down to the sea for the purpose of throwing last year's sins therein, to begin the New Year with a clear conscience. They stood in groups closely packed together, looking toward the water, reciting prayers. Some of the people turned their pockets inside out and shook them towards the sea; others merely made a sign of throwing stones into it. This was a public act of confession and contrition. Whether or not it was followed by a better life would depend on how much of sincere penitence there was in the act. —C. G.

YEAR, The End and Opening of a.— *How old art thou?—Gen. xlvii: 8.*

Amidst the fleeting years that are hurrying us to the grave, the judgment and eternity, it is well for us to consider the nature of our progress. How are we growing old? As we grow older we should grow in grace and in the knowledge of our Lord and Savior Jesus Christ. As we grow older it should be true of us as it was of Zacharias and Elizabeth, that we are found " righteous before God, walking in all the commandments and ordinances of the Lord, blameless." As each advancing year brings us nearer to Heaven, so each advancing year should make us more heavenly. As the journey of life brings the pilgrim nearer to the grave, it should, at the same time, bring us nearer to God. As the years multiply, graces should multiply and our treasure in Heaven should increase. As we walk in the path that God has laid out for us, old age will bring with it many spiritual experiences in which we shall be cheered and encouraged by those views of spiritual truth that will bring Heaven very close to us and make it preciously real. You and I may, by the grace of God, choose this path for ourselves; and if hitherto we have not walked in it, we may begin now. How old art thou? Old enough to make a right choice, and may God help you to do it. How old art thou? Old enough to know that without Christ no life finds its perfect relation to God; old enough to know that the Bible points out only one way of salvation; old enough to know that God loves you and wants you.—A. S. GUM-BART, D.D.

YEAR, Wail of the Dying.—Listen to me, ye mortals! for I also am of the race of the ephemerals. I had my sturdy youth, when it seemed that my life would never end; and I dug, and plowed, and planted, and enjoyed my jocund prime and my golden summer; and I decked myself in the garlands of May, and reaped the yellow harvest, and gathered the purple vintage of autumn; but scarcely had I attained the object of my desires, and secured the plenty for which I labored, than I found the shadows lengthening, and the days shortening, and my breath growing short with them, and decrepitude coming upon me, and the days at hand of which I said, " I have no pleasure in them." I have laid up riches, and know not who shall gather them; have planted trees which must shade far distant years, and stored the vintage of which other years must drink.—F. H.

POETRY

Key, the Lost

The key of yesterday
I threw away.
And now, too late,
Before to-morrow's close-locked gate
Helpless I stand—in vain to pray!
In vain to sorrow!
Only the key of yesterday
Unlocks to-morrow.
                    PRISCILLA LEONARD.

Life

Life *is* a battle! How these sayings trite
Which schoolboys write,—and know not
    what they write—
In after years begin to burn and glow.
                    E. C. STEDMAN.

Life

Life is a certainty,
    Death is a doubt;
Men may be dead
    While they're walking about.

Love is as needful
    To being as breath;
Loving is dreaming—
    And waking is death.
                    JOHN BOYLE O'REILLY.

Life, The True

Self reverence, self knowledge, self control,
These three alone, lead life to sovereign
    power.   TENNYSON.

Thanksgiving

Our fathers' God from out whose hand,
The centuries fall like grains of sand,
We meet to-day, united, free,
And loyal to our land and Thee,
To thank Thee for the era done,
And trust Thee for the opening one.
WHITTIER.

Time

When time is flown, how it fled
It is better neither to ask nor tell,
Leave the dead moments to bury their dead.
OWEN MEREDITH—*The Wanderer.* Bk.
IV. *Two out of the Crowd.* St. 17.

Time

Time eftsoon will tumble
All of us together like leaves in a gust,
Humbled indeed down into the dust.
JOAQUIN MILLER—*Fallen Leaves.*
Down into the Dust. St. 5.

Time

Day and night,
Seed-time and harvest, heat and hoary frost
Shall hold their course, till fire purge all
things.
MILTON—*Paradise Lost.* Bk. XI.
Line 898.

Time

The never ending flight
Of future days.
MILTON—*Paradise Lost.* Bk. II.
Line 221.

Time

Time will run back, and fetch the age of
gold.
MILTON—*Hymn on the Nativity.*
Line 135.

Time

Time still, as he flies, adds increase to her
truth,
And gives to her mind what he steals from
her youth.
EDWARD MOORE—*The Happy Marriage.*

Time

This day was yesterday to-morrow nam'd:
To-morrow shall be yesterday proclaimed:
To-morrow not yet come, not far away,
What shall to-morrow then be call'd? To-
day.
OWEN—*To-Day and To-Morrow.*
Bk. III. Line 50.

Time

Let time, that makes you homely, make you
sage.
PARNELL—*An Elegy to an Old
Beauty.* Line 35.

Time

Time, the foe of man's dominion,
Wheels around in ceaseless flight,
Scattering from his hoary pinion
Shades of everlasting night.
Still, beneath his frown appalling,
Man and all his works decay:
Still, before him, swiftly falling,
Kings and kingdoms pass away.
THOMAS LOVE PEACOCK—*The Genius of
the Thames.* St. 42.

Time

Like wind flies Time 'tween birth and death;
Therefore, as long as thou hast breath,
Of care for two days hold thee free:
The day that was and is to be.
OMAR KHAYYAM—Bodenstedt,
Translator.

Time

A handful of red sand, from the hot clime
Of Arab deserts brought,
Within this glass becomes the spy of Time,
The minister of Thought.
H. W. LONGFELLOW—*Sand of the
Desert in an Hour-Glass.*

Time

Art is long and Time is fleeting.
H. W. LONGFELLOW—*A Psalm of
Life.*

Time

It is too late! Ah, nothing is too late
Till the tired heart shall cease to palpitate.
H. W. LONGFELLOW—*Morituri Salu-
tamus.* Line 240.

Time

Even such is Time, that takes on trust
Our youth, our joys, our all we have,
And pays us, but with age and dust;
Who in the dark and silent grave,
When we have wandered all our ways,
Shuts up the story of our days.
SIR WALTER RALEIGH—*Verses Writ-
ten the Night Before His Death*

Time

Come, gone,—gone forever,—
Gone as an unreturning river,—
Gone as to death the merriest liver,—
Gone as the year at the dying fall,—
To-morrow, to-day, yesterday, never,—
Gone once for all.
CHRISTINA G. ROSSETTI—*The Prince's
Progress.* St. 62.

Time

The long hours come and go.
CHRISTINA G. ROSSETTI—*The Prince's
Progress.* St. 1.

Time

Forever haltless hurries Time, the Durable
to gain.
Be true, and thou shalt fetter Time with everlasting chain.
SCHILLER—*The Immutable.*

Time

Fate seemed to wind him up for four-score
years;
Yet freshly ran he on ten winters more:
Till like a clock worn out with eating time.
The wheels of weary life at last stood still.
DRYDEN—*Aedipus.* Act IV. Sc. 1.

Time

"Time goes," you say? Ah no!
Alas, Time stays, we go.
AUSTIN DOBSON.

Years, The

The years have taught some sweet,
Some bitter lessons—none wiser than this—
To spend in all things else,
But of old friends to be most miserly.
JAMES RUSSELL LOWELL.

Year, The

Sin of the year forgiven;
Need of the year supplied;
Mercy of the year enjoyed;
Fears of the year removed;
Hopes of the year fulfilled.
SPURGEON (P. M.).

Year, The Flying

As a dream when night is done,
As a shadow flees the sun,
As a ship whose white sails skim
Over the horizon dim,
As a life complete of days
Vanisheth from mortal ways,
As a hope that pales to fear—
Is the dying of the year.
CHRISTIAN BURKE.

Year, The Going

How stealthily the old year dies!
We may not catch his parting sighs,
Or even on the withered grass
Hear a retreating footstep pass,
And yet we know
This old year has reached his time to go.
MRS. EMMA FRANCES ANDERSON. (Y. C.)

Ending of the Eighteenth Century

BY THEODORE DWIGHT

The following poem, written on New Year's Day, 1801, was republished in the *New York Sun,* and respectfully referred to the President of Wellesley, who had maintained in a communication that the century ended with 1899:

Precisely twelve o'clock last night
The 18th century took its flight,
Full many a calculating head
Has racked its brain; its ink has shed
To prove by metaphysics fine
A hundred means but ninety-nine.
While at their wisdom others wondered,
But took one more to make a hundred.
Strange at the 18th century's close
While light in beams effulgent glows,
When bright illumination's ray
Has chased the darkness far away,
Heads filled with mathematics lore
Dispute if two and two make four.
Go on, ye scientific sages,
Collect your light a few more ages,
Perhaps as swells the vast amount
A century hence you'll learn to count.

The Lost Days

BY SUSAN COOLIDGE

As, each in turn, the Old Years rise and gird
them up to go,
The days, which were their servitors, press
round them sad and slow,
The happy days, the hard days, the bitter
and the dear;
And they front us with reproachful eyes as
they wend forth with the year.

The lost days which except for us so blessed
might have been,
Blighted by our perversity, or shadowed by
our sin.

The vexing days, the moody days, the days
of stress and pain,
The shrill, perverse, unhappy days, we face
them all again.

"Come back, dear days," we cry; "we will
atone for all the wrong;
Your emptiness shall be made full, your discords turned to song."
Only the echo answers; all vain the grieving
sore.
The past is past, the dead is dead, the chance
returns no more.

But, as the sweetest hopes are born of sharp-
est suffering,
And midnight is the womb of day, and winter of the spring,
So, winning blessing from despair, lost opportunity
May serve to make the fruitful soil of harvests yet to be.

For each day heavy made by us, some day
may gather wings,
Be every failure that we mourn the germ of
happier things,
And all the sadness of the past the seed of
hope new-born,
Till out of the defeated night bursts the triumphant morn.

The old years, stern, inexorable, may go their
ways in vain;
The days we marred and mourn shall smile
if from their perished pain
Distills a perfume, shines a gleam, to make
the future way
The brighter and the easier because of yesterday.—C. E. W.

If

BY ELLWOOD ROBERTS

How few there are who value time aright—
That treasure given by the Infinite!
In youth we squander it; in age we grieve
At sight of loss we never may retrieve.
If you and I and all were truly wise,
The fleeting moments we would highly prize.
What sorrow and temptation would we shun!
How many good deeds do now left undone!

The Inn

BY JAMES B. KENYON

How quiet is the mossy inn
Where weary travelers lie,
Unheeding how the morns begin,
And how the sunsets die.

Here are no sounds of reveling,
Here is no flaring light;
Here no fair maids with laughter bring
The tankards foaming bright.

The guests sleep long, the lights are out,
No bustling landlord calls
His serving-men with cheery shout
Along the echoing halls.

Who come to this still inn, abide
　　Through cycles deep and sweet;
And while the seasons o'er them slide,
　　They rest their tired feet.

The Gauge of Life

They err who measure life by years,
　　With false or thoughtless tongue;
Some hearts grow old before their time;
　　Others are always young.
'Tis not the number of the lines,
　　On life's fast filling page,—
'Tis not the pulse's added throbs
　　Which constitute their age.
Some souls are serfs among the free,
　　While others nobly thrive;
They stand just where their fathers stood;
　　Dead even while they live!
Others, all spirit, heart and sense;
　　Theirs the mysterious power
To live in thrills of joy or wo,
　　A twelvemonth in an hour!
Seize, then, the minutes as they pass;
　　The woof of life is thought!
Warm up the colors; let them glow
　　With fire and fancy fraught.
Live to some purpose; make thy life
　　A gift of use to thee:
A joy, a good, a golden hope,
　　A heavenly Argosy!　　　　　G. T.

An Obituary

By Curtis May

Dead Year, upon whose bier I lean!
Dead Year, whose sheeted features lie
Half-formless in the falling snow!
You brought such joys, such sorrows keen,
Such mingled pain and ecstasy,
I cannot lightly let you go;
But pause awhile to shed a tear
That you should lie so low, Old Year.

How blithe you were when first we met!
A flying chorus round you sung,
The snowdrops peeped to see you pass,
And where your hasty foot you set
Deep violets and field daisies hung
Their trembling blossoms on the grass;
And hope, with swiftly-moving wing,
You brought to make eternal spring.

A grass-green kirtle next you wore,
And gathered wild-flowers in the wood,
Sweet odors all around you stole
Forth from the chalice that you bore.
Knee-deep in tangled brakes you stood;
The red sun cast an aureole
About your golden head, Old Year.
And that glad vision brought me cheer.

Then with a sheaf of ripened grain
Laid close against your heaving breast,
And crowned with purple grapes, you came.
I marked the brown and stubby plain,
I marked the forest's waving crest,
With tufts and branches all aflame.
With every feature grown more dear,
I loved you daily more, Old Year.

At last the solemn winter laid
Its diamond crown upon your brow;
The icicles hung on the eaves;
And deep within the beechen glade
The bare trees in the blast did bow
Their heads all shorn of crisp, brown leaves.
You taught me how old age might be
Made grand by simple majesty.

Now garbed and silent for the tomb,
You lie before me still and white.
With burning tears I say, "Good-by,"
And take from out the darkened room
The happy hopes that once were bright,
In guise of tender memory.
What most was precious cannot die,
Old Year, altho so low you lie!—Y. C.

Death of the Old Year

By M. C. C.

Thy life is ebbing fast, thou aged Year!
This night that wintry sun of thine will set
To rise no more. Thy days are told: and
　　yet
It seems but yesterday thou didst appear!
But yesternight we watched, all silent here,
The Old Year's dying hours, while backward
　　rolled
Its story, page by page; and now, behold!
Thy course is run. Even now thy moments
　　wear
The fading hue of death. Farewell, old
　　Friend!
Fain would we linger by thy side awhile,
And gather up thy mem'ries one by one,
While, in the vacant chairs, dear faces smile
Upon us, as of old. But ever on,
Life's current bears us—swifter to the end!
　　　　　　　　　　　　　　　　C. J.

Good-by to the Old Year

By Jennie Elisabeth Gates

Good-by, Old Year! for twelve long months
　　together
We've traveled on, in bright and stormy
　　weather;
I hear thee like a grief-pressed maiden sigh,
As stand we here beneath this wintry sky.

I met thee first as children do, when weep-
　　ing—
Turn from new friends, while for the old
　　they're keeping
Their warmest love, and sigh that they must
　　part
From one they've loved so long with tender
　　heart.

But tho we met in tears, we part both smil-
　　ing;
Sweet memory is thy dying hour beguiling
With tenderest treasures from her store-
　　house brought,
That thy last hour may with her best be
　　fraught.

I little dreamed what sacred gifts were hi-
　　ding
Within thy breast for me—nor that abiding

Within the mists and clouds which veiled my
　　way
A light was shining—leading unto perfect
　　day.

I only saw gray, leaden clouds—unbreaking,
Portending evil—anxious fear awaking;
Nor did I dream that hid 'neath winter's
　　snow
Slept wealth of bloom which must awake
　　and grow.

O dear, tried friend, thou dost forgive my
　　pining;
In thy calm face I see forgiveness shining;
I catch the scent of love from thy last breath,
And thou art true and beautiful in death.

Good-by, Old Year! I whisper in thy hear-
　　ing;
For tolling bell proclaims that we are nearing
The moment when we part, and will no more
Together walk; but I will love thee ever-
　　more;
A wreath of amaranth for thee I'll take,
And wear it on my heart, for thy dear sake.
　　　　　　　　　　　　　　　C. A.

Remember

By Grace Ellery Channing

When comes the sad year to its close,
　　And leaves fall fast about thee, think,
In other gardens Summer glows,
　　And others thirsting, breathe and drink
The perfume of the rose;
Bethink thee, even in thy snows!

And when thy rose is blossoming, know,
　　Tho thine laugh in its rosy crown,
In other gardens, stripped and brown,
　　At other feet, dead leaves fall down:
Dead roses lie beneath the snow.
Remember, when thine bud and blow!—Y. C.

The Glory of Service

By John G. Whittier

Who, looking backward from his manhood's
　　prime,
Sees not the specter of his misspent time?
　　And, through the shade
Of funeral cypress planted thick behind,
Hears no reproachful whisper on the wind
　　From his loved dead?

Yet who, thus looking backward o'er his
　　years,
Feels not his eyelids wet with grateful tears,
　　If he hath been
Permitted, weak and sinful as he was,
To cheer and aid, in some ennobling cause,
　　His fellow-men?

If he hath hidden the outcast, or let in
A ray of sunshine to the cell of sin—
　　If he had lent
Strength to the weak, and in an hour of need,
Over the suffering, mindless of his creed
　　Or home, hath bent,

He has not lived in vain, and while he gives
The praise to Him, in whom he moves and
　　lives,

With thankful heart;
He gazes backward, and with hope before,
Knowing that from his works he nevermore
　　Can henceforth part.

The Last of an Hundred Years

By Emma Herrick Weed

The Old Year stands at the postern gate
　　And gropes for the latch with his fingers
　　　cold.
Without the shades of his kinsmen wait,
　　And twelve from the belfry tower is tolled.
While the shout of acclaim for the young
　　king nears—
" The Year—the last of an hundred years!"

He has doffed his crown and his purple
　　dress;
He has handed over the palace keys:
Unheeded slipped through the teeming press,
　　As a wreck down a hollow of tossing seas.
And the shout is the shout that a dreamer
　　hears—
" The Year—the last of an hundred years!"

A moment he halts—and the dim eyes close;
　　And a goodly company round him throng;
Again through his veins Youth's hot blood
　　flows,
　　It is May in the woods with shimmer and
　　　song!
And he flings about him like golden pence,
The days, in his splendid opulence.

Then the houri, summer, red-lipped, comes by,
　　All sweet as the rose with an hundred
　　　leaves.
There are jasmine stars in a perfumed sky—
　　There are dawns of opal and yellow eves.
And she leans towards him with lilied grace.
And her tresses of amber sweep his face.

A shiver—a whirl of leaves let go—
　　And a wind with a cry like the cry of the
　　　sea:
White dusk of a world with falling snow—
　　And the tramp of the ebb-tide's cavalry!
And now in a trance his senses swim,
And he smiles at the voices calling him.

" All hail to the heir! And again, all hail!"
　Time's great key turns in its massive lock.
A light—like the light of the Holy Grail—
　　Gleams white on the face of the belfry
　　　clock.
Then a silence falls. 'Tis the charméd hour
The crown of the aloe has burst in flower!

Hark to the clang of the postern gate!
　　And the beating of wings adown the night!
He has gone where his shadowy kinsmen
　　wait,
　　In the wind of his passing flares the light!
And comes to his reign of smiles and tears,
The Year—the last of an hundred years!—In.

The Old Year

By Lotta Miller

Of its words of comfort spoken,
Of its joys, give we no token

To the swiftly dying year?
While we sorrow o'er its sadness,
Shall we pass by all its gladness,
    All remembrance of its cheer?
Nay; the sorrows we have known,
And the winds that chill have blown,
    Only make it the more dear,
And we, weeping, say adieu,
As we welcome in the new.

A. M.

Old Year

By W. H. Burleigh

Still on—as silent as a ghost!
    Seems but a score of days, all told,
Or but a month or two at most,
    Since our last New Year's song we trolled.
    And lo! that New Year now is Old.
And here we stand to say " Good-by! "
Brief words—and yet, we scarce know why,
They bring a moisture to the eye,
    And to the heart some quakes and aches;
We speak them very tenderly,
    With half a sob and half a sigh—
" Old Year, good-by! " " Old Year, good-by! "

Death of the Old Year

By Alfred Tennyson

He frothed his bumpers to the brim;
    A jollier year we shall not see.
But tho his eyes are waxing dim,
And tho his foes speak ill of him,
    He was a friend to me.
Old Year, you shall not die;
We did so laugh and cry with you,
I've half a mind to die with you,
    Old Year, if you must die.

*   *   *   *   *   *

His face is growing sharp and thin.
    Alack! Our friend is gone.
Close up his eyes; tie up his chin;
Step from the corpse, and let him in
    That standeth there alone,
    And waiteth at the door;
There's a new foot on the floor,
    My friend,
And a new face at the door,
    My friend,
A new face at the door.

Holidays

If all the year were playing holidays,
To sport would be as tedious as to work.

SHAKESPEARE—*Henry IV.*

LEGAL HOLIDAYS IN THE UNITED STATES

Legal holiday, a day appointed by law to be kept as a holiday, especially with regard to the closing of public offices and the suspension of judicial proceedings and general business. Such appointment usually changes the time for presentment or protest of negotiable paper maturing on such a day to the preceding secular day. In the UNITED STATES legal holidays are usually fixed by State statute, and their number and purposes vary. See the following list, in which the sign * denotes the recognition of holidays:

STATES AND TERRITORIES	JANUARY 1 (a)	FEBRUARY 22 (e)	MAY 30 (m)	JULY 4 (o)	THANKSGIVING DAY	DECEMBER 25 (s)	ARBOR DAY	LABOR DAY (ab)	GENERAL ELECTION
Alabama (f), (t), (r)	*	*	....	*	*	*	*	....	....
Arizona Territory	*	*	....	*	*	*	*	....	*
Arkansas	....	....	....	*	....	*	*	....	....
California	*	*	*	*	*	*	* (q)	*	*
Colorado	*	*	*	*	....	*	* (v)	*	....
Connecticut (r)	*	*	*	*	*	*	*	....	....
Delaware	*	*	*	*	....	*	*	....	....
District of Columbia (ac)	*	*	*	*	*	*	*	....	....
Florida (n)	*	*	....	*	*	*	*	....	*
Georgia (c), (j)	*	*	....	*	....	*	*	....	....
Idaho	*	*	*	*	*	*	*	* (aa)	....
Illinois (d)	*	*	*	*	*	*	*	....	*
Indiana	*	*	*	*	*	*	*	*	*
Iowa	*	....	*	*	*	*	*	*	....
Kansas	*	....	*	*	*	*	* (w)	*	....
Kentucky (b), (g), (r)	....	*	*	*	*	*	*	....	....
Louisiana (b), (g), (r)	*	*	....	*	....	*	*	....	....
Maine	*	*	*	*	*	*	*	*	....
Maryland (r)	*	*	....	*	*	*	*	*	....
Massachusetts (ad)	....	*	....	*	*	*	*	* (x)	....
Michigan	*	*	*	*	*	*	*	....	....
Minnesota (y)	....	*	*	....	*	*	....	....	....
Mississippi	....	....	....	....	....	*	*	*	*
Missouri	*	*	....	*	*	*	*	*	....
Montana	*	*	....	*	*	*	*	....	*
Nebraska	*	*	*	*	*	*	*	* (i)	*
Nevada	*	*	*	*	*	*	*	*	*
New Hampshire	....	*	*	*	*	*	*	....	*
New Jersey	*	*	*	*	*	*	*	*	*
New Mexico Territory	*	....	*	*	*	*	*	....	....
New York (d)	*	*	....	*	*	*	*	*	....
North Carolina (k), (l), (c)	*	*	....	*	*	*	*	....	....
North Dakota	*	*	*	*	*	*	*	....	....
Ohio	*	*	*	*	*	*	*	....	*
Oklahoma Territory	*	*	*	*	....	*	*	....	....
Oregon (z)	*	*	*	*	*	*	*	*	*
Pennsylvania (r)	*	*	*	*	*	*	*	....	*
Rhode Island (u)	....	*	*	*	*	*	* (w)	*	....
South Carolina	*	*	*	*	*	*	*	....	*
South Dakota	*	*	*	*	*	*	....	....	*
Tennessee (j), (r)	*	*	*	*	*	*	*	....	*
Texas (f), (h)	*	*	....	*	*	*	*	....	....
Utah Territory (p), (r)	*	*	*	*	....	*	*	....	*
Vermont	*	....	*	*	*	*	*	....	....
Virginia (c)	*	....	....	†	*	*	*	....	*
Washington	*	*	*	*	†	*	*	....	*
West Virginia	*	*	....	†	*	*	*	....	*
Wisconsin	*	*	....	*	*	*	....	*	*
Wyoming	*	*	*	*	*	*	* (w)	....	....

(a) New Year's Day.—(b) January 8, anniversary of battle of New Orleans.—(c) January 19, Gen. Robert E. Lee's birthday.—(d) February 12, Abraham Lincoln's birthday.—(e) George Washington's birthday.— (f) March 2, anniversary of Texan independence.—(g) March 4. Fireman's anniversary: in New Orleans only.—(h) April 21, anniversary of battle of San Jacinto.—(t) April 22.—(j) April 26, Memorial Day.—(k) May 10, Memorial Day.—(l) May 20, anniversary of signing of Mecklenburg Declaration of Independence.—(m) Decoration (or Memorial) Day.—(n) June 3, Jefferson Davis' birthday.—(o) Independence Day.—(p) July 24, Pioneers' Day.—(q) September 9.—(r) Good Friday.—(s) Christmas Day.—(t) Mardi Gras, or Shrove Tuesday.— (u) State election day (first Wednesday in April).—(v) The third Friday in April.—(w) Date appointed by the Governor.—(x) April 28.—(y) Thanksgiving Day, Good Friday, Christmas, January 1, and July 4 by banks.— (z) Labor Day, first Saturday of June.—(aa) Friday after May 1.—(ab) In most States, the first Monday in September.—(ac) March 4, Inauguration Day.—(ad) April 19.

Fast-days (whenever appointed) and Thanksgiving day are not uniformly specified as legal holidays, but the statutes often implicitly recognize them by adopting as holidays days so proclaimed by the President or the Governor.—ST. D.

LEGAL HOLIDAYS IN THE UNITED KINGDOM OF GREAT BRITAIN AND IRELAND, AND IN CANADA

THE UNITED KINGDOM OF GREAT BRITAIN AND IRELAND

In ENGLAND, IRELAND AND WALES the legal or bank holidays are : Easter Monday, Whit-Monday, the first Monday in August, and December 26 : in SCOTLAND the bank holidays are : New Year's Day, Christmas (if either fall on a Sunday, the following day), Good Friday, and the first Mondays in May and August.—ST. D.

DOMINION OF CANADA

Sunday ; New Year's Day ; The Epiphany*; Good Friday ; The Ascension ; All Saints' Day*; Conception Day*; Easter Monday*; Ash Wednesday*; Christmas Day ; the Birthday, or day fixed by proclamation for Celebration of Birthday of reigning Sovereign ; Victoria Day ; Dominion Day ; Labor Day ; and any day appointed by proclamation for a general fast or thanksgiving.

QUEBEC

New Year's Day; Epiphany*; Ash Wednesday*; Good Friday; Easter Monday; The Ascension*; All Saints' Day; The Conception; Christmas Day; the Anniversary of the Birthday of the Sovereign, or day fixed by proclamation; 1st July, or 2nd July, if 1st is a Sunday; any other day fixed by Royal proclamation, or by proclamation of Governor or Governor-General, as a day of fast or thanksgiving; Labor Day.

NOVA SCOTIA

Sunday ; New Year's Day ; Epiphany ; Ash Wednesday ; Good Friday ; Easter Monday ; Ascension Day ; Victoria Day; Conception Day; Dominion Day ; Christmas Day ; day appointed for the celebration of the Birthday of His Majesty, or any of the Royal Successors ; Labor Day ; All Saints' Day ; and any day appointed by proclamation of Governor-General, or Lieutenant-Governor, as a general holiday, or for general fast or thanksgiving.

MANITOBA

New Year's Day ; Good Friday ; Christmas Day; Victoria Day ; Dominion Day ; Labor Day ; the day appointed for celebration of Birthday of His Majesty or the Royal Successors ; and any day appointed by proclamation for a general thanksgiving or general holiday ; Arbor Day.

BRITISH COLUMBIA

Sunday ; New Year's Day ; Good Friday; Easter Monday ; Victoria Day ; Dominion Day ; Labor Day ; Christmas Day ; the days appointed for celebration of the Birthday of His Majesty, and of His Royal Successors ; any day appointed by proclamation for a general fast or thanksgiving ; and any day appointed by proclamation or order of the Lieutenant-Governor in Council as a holiday.

ONTARIO

Sunday ; New Year's Day ; Good Friday ; Easter Monday*; Christmas Day; Victoria Day ; Dominion Day ; Birthday of His Majesty and His Royal Successors ; Labor Day ; and any day appointed by proclamation of Governor-General, or Lieutenant-Governor as a public holiday or for a general fast or thanksgiving.

NORTHWEST TERRITORIES

Sunday ; New Year's Day ; Ash Wednesday* ; Good Friday ; Easter Monday ; 2nd Friday in May, known as Arbor Day ; Christmas Day ; Birthday of reigning Sovereigns ; Victoria Day ; Dominion Day ; Labor Day ; such days as may, in each year, be proclaimed public holidays for the planting of forest and other trees ; and any other day appointed by proclamation for a general fast or thanksgiving.

Compiled by JAMES BAIN of Toronto Public Library.

Days marked with * are not observed as general holidays, but all Government Offices are closed.

LINCOLN'S BIRTHDAY

(February 12)

IN Connecticut, Illinois, Minnesota, New Jersey, New York, North Dakota, Pennsylvania and Washington (State), February 12 is a legal holiday. It is devoted to the memory of Abraham Lincoln, the sixteenth President of the United States, who was born at Nolin Creek, Kentucky, February 12, 1809.

Not only in the states in which it is a legal holiday is Lincoln's Birthday observed, but in many other states, by special exercises in the public schools, in clubs and societies, and in home circles, the patriotic people keep alive the memory of that plain but wise, witty, and great man, who was in the President's chair during the Civil War of 1860-1865, and by whose issues the Union was preserved and slavery abolished from the United States.

The passing of time so far from detracting from Lincoln's greatness is bringing out its noble proportions and increasing the almost veneration with which he is regarded by the American people. The event in President Lincoln's career which to the end of time will be linked with his name is his issuing, on September 22, 1862, the Emancipation Proclamation, whereby he set free five million negro slaves, and relegated slavery in the United States to the past. He entered upon the war with the declared purpose of saving the Union, with slavery or without it. But in time his antagonism to slavery became more pronounced, until at last it crystallized in his Emancipation Proclamation, a document whose purpose and results were such that it must ever be preserved among the most important and precious of the annals of our people.

Rising, as Lincoln did, from social obscurity through a youth of manual toil and poverty, steadily upward to the highest level of honor in the world, and all this as the fruit of earnest purpose, hard work, humane feeling and integrity of character, he is an example and an inspiration to youth unparalleled in history. At the same time he is the best specimen of the possibilities attainable by genius in our land and under our free institutions.

The work which Abraham Lincoln accomplished should never be forgotten, and will never be forgotten, for it was unselfishly wrought for all men and all time. As George Bancroft truly says: "He finished a work which all time cannot overthrow. He was followed by the sorrow of his country to his resting-place in the heart of the Mississippi Valley, to be remembered through all time by his countrymen, and by all the peoples of the world."

HISTORICAL

MEMORABILIA OF ABRAHAM LINCOLN

FOURTEENTH ELECTED PRESIDENT OF THE UNITED STATES

1809. Feb. 12. Abraham Lincoln born in Hardin Co., Ky.; his father was Thomas Lincoln, a farmer, who married Nancy Hanks.
1816. Family moved to Perry Co., Ind.

1818. Abraham's mother died.
1820. Thomas Lincoln married again.
1825. Became ferryman on the Ohio, receiving $6 per month as salary.

1826. Lincoln's last attendance at school.
1830. Moved to Illinois.
1832. Captain of a company in Black Hawk Indian War.
1832. Ran for office of State assemblyman. Defeated.
1832. Studied law.
1833. Became postmaster at New Salem.
1834. Elected to legislature by Whig Party.
1836. Reelected to legislature.
1837. Admitted to the bar. Business flourished.
1839. Settled in Springfield.
1839. Debate with Douglas.
1842. Married to Miss Mary Todd.
1846. Elected to Congress.
1854. Took decided stand against slavery.
1856. Republican Party of Illinois formed, and Lincoln's eloquent anti-slavery speech delivered.
1858-1859. In the lecture field; no success.
1860, May 19. Lincoln and Hamlin nominated for President and Vice-President of the United States.
1860, Nov. 6. Elected President.
1861, Mar. 4 (Monday). Inaugurated President.

1861, Apr. 12. Bombardment of Fort Sumter.
1861, Apr. 14. Lincoln called out 75,000 militia.
1861, Apr. 19. Proclaimed blockade of Southern ports.
1861, July 21. Union forces defeated at Bull Run. McClellan succeeded Scott at head of Army.
1862. Burnside succeeded McClellan.
1862, Sep. 22 (Monday). Lincoln issued the Emancipation Proclamation, freeing all slaves in the United States.
1863. General U. S. Grant captured Vicksburg, and Meade defeated Lee at Gettysburg.
1864, March. U. S. Grant appointed lieutenant-general of the armies of the United States.
1864. Sherman's march to the sea.
1864, Nov. Lincoln reelected President.
1865, Apr. 9. Lee surrendered to Grant at Appomattox, and the war was closed.
1865, Apr. 4. Lincoln was shot through the head at Ford's Theater, Washington, D. C., at 11:30 P. M., by John Wilkes Booth, an actor.
1865. Apr. 5, at 7:30 A. M., Abraham Lincoln died.

ABRAHAM LINCOLN'S EARLY YEARS

By Charles Carleton Coffin

Denton Offut, merchant, of Springfield, Illinois, in the summer of 1831, wanted to send a lot of corn, pork, and live pigs to market. He could load a flat-boat on the Sangamon, float it to the Illinois, down that stream to the Mississippi, and thence to New Orleans. He could not go himself, but must have somebody whom he could trust. Just how it came about we do not know, but in some way he learned that Abraham Lincoln, who had just driven an ox team from Indiana, and who was living near Decatur, had already made a successful trip down the Mississippi, and that he was honest and could be trusted. Offut had no boat, and must build one. Lincoln was just the man, for he had worked with his father as carpenter, could hew timber, and make mortises.

A few weeks later, Lincoln and John Hanks were at work on the banks of the Sangamon, cutting down trees, sawing planks, and building the boat. They were so diligent that in four weeks from felling the first tree it was completed, launched, loaded with barrels of pork and bags filled with corn, and floating down the Sangamon. It was supposed that the boat would glide over the dam at New Salem, but it grounded instead, and they were obliged to obtain a canoe, carry the corn to the shore, and reload it after getting the boat below the dam. Farther down stream they were to take a herd of pigs. But the animals had no intention of being driven on board. They could not be coaxed by corn strewn on the ground. Lincoln was not to be foiled, and by main strength carried them in his arms one by one upon the boat. The cargo completed, they floated into the Illinois, and with the current of that river to the Mississippi, and thence to New Orleans.

Planters are there from Mississippi and Louisiana to obtain slaves to work in the cotton-fields. The two boatmen saunter into the mart, and behold negro men, women, boys, and girls standing on a bench around the walls of the room, the planters looking into their mouths, as they would look at the teeth of a horse. The auctioneer proclaims their good qualities as he would those of a horse or mule. Maybe they are members of a church—Christians—therefore regarded as more valuable than irreligious slaves. His hammer falls. A husband and wife are forever separated. Children never again will behold their father and mother. Abraham Lincoln goes out from the auction-room with his blood on fire. There is a choking in his throat, a quivering of his lips, as he turns to his fellow-boatman, "If I ever get a chance to hit that thing, I'll hit it hard, by the eternal God!"

Who is he to hit the "thing" a blow? He is a boatman, splitter of rails, teamster, backwoodsman,—nothing more. His poverty is so deep that his clothes were in tatters, and he could hardly appear in public till Nancy Miller made him a pair of trousers. What position of influence or power is he likely to attain to enable him to strike a blow? The "thing" which he would like to hit is incorporated into the frame-work of society, and legalized in half of the States composing the Republic. It is intrenched in Church and State alike, accepted by doctors of divinity as beneficent to the human race, as authorized and blessed by Almighty God., It is a political force, recognized in the Constitution, entering into the basis of representation. Is there the remotest probability that he ever will be able to smite such an institution? Why utter the words? Why raise the right hand toward heaven and swear a solemn oath? Was it that he saw some dim vision of what might come to him through divine Providence in the unfolding years? Was it an illumination of spirit that for the moment forecast an impending conflict between right and wrong in which he would take a conspicuous part? Was it the whispering to him by a divine messenger of the unseen realm that he was to be a chosen one to wipe the "thing" from the earth, and give deliverance from bonds to millions of his fellow-men? If we conclude that the words only fell from his lips by chance, their utterance, taken in connection with what he did in after years in giving freedom to four millions of slaves, is very wonderful.

The pigs, pork, and corn sold and the boat disposed of, Lincoln and Hanks took passage for St. Louis on a steamboat. There were slaves on board. As he saw their abject condition and recalled the scene he had witnessed at New Orleans, he became silent, thoughtful, and sad. Through life he remembered it.—H. Y. P.

LINCOLN'S FOSTER-MOTHER

By Rev. George G. Hepburn

The near return of the 12th of February, the birthday of Lincoln, brings to mind his extraordinary career and his wonderful training, by which means God seemed to have raised him up to guide the destinies of this Nation through the perilous storms of civil war. A short time since, the writer, in passing a day or two in Elizabethtown. Ky., was informed by the hotel proprietor, in the course of a conversation, that Lincoln was born there. In this statement, however, subsequent inquiry found him to be not quite correct. Lincoln was born a little less than twelve miles from Elizabethtown, on a spot well known, and literally in a house built of logs, which was afterwards used as a barn, and then removed a short distance and converted into a slaughter-house. One of the logs of this building was sent by express to New York as a relic by a gentleman visiting that locality some years ago.

I met an aged gentleman, Mr. Haycraft, for forty years a clerk of the county court —Elizabethtown is the county seat of Hardin county—who showed me four letters from Lincoln, one written just after his nomination, in response to one from Mr. Haycraft, two after his election. and one from Washington in the early part of his presidential term. In the first Lincoln began by saying, "I remembered your handwriting, tho I could not recall your face before I looked at the signature," and this notwithstanding they had had no communication for twenty-five years, at which time Lincoln practised law in the county court. After his election Mr. Haycraft invited the President-elect to visit Elizabethtown—the home of his boyhood, and where, in later years, he had practised his profession—en route to Washington, assuring him that his old friends, the boys, would give him a warm reception should he do so. Lincoln facetiously replied to this courteous invitation: "It would give me great pleasure to do so, but perhaps the boys would give me too warm a reception."

Mr. Haycraft related to the writer some interesting reminiscences of Lincoln's early history. Abraham Lincoln was seven or eight years old when his father, Thomas Lincoln, removed from Kentucky to Indiana, where, in a year or two, his mother died. The year following her death his father returned to Elizabethtown to search out, if possible, a former neighbor and friend, Mrs. Sally Johnston, whom, upon inquiry, he found still a widow, and to whom he at once made a proposal of marriage. The quaint manner and homely words used to tell the simple narrative of that brief courtship, if courtship it could be called, together with the pith or point of the story, so pregnant with momentous issues in the future of one who was to have committed to him, one might almost say, the rise or fall of this free government, made a great impression upon the writer. "On entering Mrs. Johnston's humble dwelling," says Mr. Haycraft, "Mr. Lincoln asked if she remembered him. 'Yes,' replied she, 'I remember you very well, Tommy Lincoln; what has brought you back to old Kentucky?' 'Well,' said he, in answer, 'my wife Nancy is dead.' 'Why, you don't say so!' replied Mrs. Johnston. 'Yes,' said Mr. Lincoln, 'she died more than a year ago, and I have come back to Kentucky to look for another wife. Do you like me, Mrs. Johnston?' said Mr. Lincoln. 'Yes,' replied Mrs. Johnston, 'I like you, Tommy Lincoln.' 'Do you like me well enough to marry me?' said he. 'Yes,' she answered, 'I like you, Tommy Lincoln, and I like you well enough to marry you, but I can't marry you now.' 'Why not?' said he. 'Because,' said she. 'I am in debt, and I could never think of burdening the man I marry with debt; it would not be right.' 'What are those debts?' said he— and let it be remembered all this happened at their first interview, on renewing their acquaintance after an absence of several years. She told him of the sums, 'which,' said she,

'I have all down here in my account-book,' going towards a cupboard and taking out a small blank-book. On looking it over he saw that her debts ranged in sums between fifty cents and a dollar and a quarter, amounting in the gross to something less than twelve dollars—not a very startling sum even in those days of small things. He succeeded in putting the little book into his coat pocket without attracting her attention, and went out, looked up the various parties and paid off all those little sums according to the memorandum, and returned in the afternoon with the acknowledgments, by name or with their mark, of payments in full. On returning her account-book to her, she exclaimed, on beholding the evidence of what he had done, 'Why, Tommy Lincoln, have you gone and paid off all my debts?' 'Yes,' he said; 'and will you marry me now?' 'Yes,' said she, and they were married the next morning at nine o'clock,' and Mr. Haycraft, the narrator, told me

that he was present himself at the ceremony.

They started the next day for Indiana. This woman, Mrs. Sally Johnston, was the one who had the training of Abraham Lincoln—for he said that he had no definite recollection of his own mother—and to whom he gave the credit, while he was President of the United States, that he owed to her the principles of integrity which had been the guide of his life, and that she taught him all that he knew about the Holy Bible. Lincoln's unswerving adherence to principle, and to all the obligations which at any time he assumed, gained for him, before he had attained the age of forty years, the soubriquet of "honest old Abe."

It is not too much to say that the world itself owes a very great debt to one who exerted such a molding influence upon the character of the man who, in these latter days, may with truth be said to have directed the course of human history.—C. U.

LINCOLN AND DOUGLAS

By Edson C. Dayton

In an article written for *The New York Evangelist* I observed that Mr. George Bancroft, in his "Memorial Address" delivered before Congress in 1886, conceded to Lincoln a tender conscience but denied him the possession of acute sensibilities.

In applying this negation, he asserted that Lincoln "had no vividness to picture to his mind the horrors of the battle-field or the suffering in hospitals." Is there anything finer in the English language than the Gettysburg speech? Can it be believed that any other living man would have more adequately responded to the inspirations of the place? It is true that he did not indulge in description of the events which there occurred; it is doubtful if his great heart could have felt it other than the severest strain to dwell in public address upon the scenes which had there been witnessed, and so he summed all up when he declared: "The world will little note, nor long remember, what we *say* here; but it can never forget what they *did* here." The word *did* compressed a vast amount of memory and of imagination. That Gettysburg speech also illustrated a tender conscience. . . .

Still another experience on Lincoln's part discloses both a tender conscience and tender feelings. I am indebted for it to Mrs. Granger, of Clifton Springs, a sister of Stephen A. Douglas, and am not aware that it has ever been published. Mr. Bancroft has remarked that the President "was supported in advance by Douglas, who spoke as with the voice of a million." The early rivalry of these two men and their final co-operation, if fully told, would make a touching and instructive chapter in our political

history. Mr. Schuyler Colfax is the authority for the fact that the President offered a Major-Generalship to Douglas, and that his acceptance of it was taken under advisement. The incident which comes from Mrs. Granger shows the dependence in another direction which Lincoln felt and made known.

It seems that Lincoln sent his carriage once at midnight to the residence of Douglas with a request for his presence at the White House. In the interview which followed, Lincoln said, substantially, that there was one man, and only one, who could save Illinois to the Union, and that was Douglas, and he urged upon him a tour of the State with a closing address at Chicago. Rumors of personal assault did not deter him from meeting the engagement. He was acquiring control of his audience when a storm began. He would have desisted and spoken another time, but was pressed to continue by the general cry, "We can hear as long as you can talk." He kept on and became overheated. The result was first a heavy cold, and then typhoid fever, and in less than four weeks from his arrival in the city, the ambitious, but patriotic Douglas was dead. The news was of course telegraphed all over the country. Mrs. Granger, receiving it in her home, prepared at once to attend the funeral of her brother. As she was being driven to the depot, she was thrown from the carriage, her arm was broken, and it was feared that there were internal injuries. Word regarding her condition was at once sent to her husband, who was connected with one of the departments in Washington, and he immediately repaired to the White House to inform Lincoln of the necessary change in his plans; that he would be compelled to go to Clifton Springs instead of Chicago. How like Lincoln it was to say, with tears flowing down his cheeks, that he had been "the cause of it all."

The Lincoln-Douglas senatorial campaign one can go over and over again with increasing enjoyment. There is about Lincoln, and what he, said, a never-failing humor and an everpresent pathos. The second time that he spoke at Springfield (July 17, 1859), he began by enumerating the disadvantages under which his party labored, and one of them was "the relative positions of the two persons who stand before the State as candidates for the Senate. Senator Douglas is of world-wide renown. All the anxious politicians of his party, or who have been of his party for years past, have been looking upon him as certain, at no distant day, to be the President of the United States. . . . On the contrary, nobody has ever expected me to be President!"

A little further on in the same speech, and more in point with my object in writing, is his expression of the spirit in whch it was his hope that the campaign would be carried on: "I set out in this campaign," remarked Lincoln, "with the intention of conducting it strictly as a gentleman. in substance at least, if not in the outside polish. The latter I shall never have, but that which constitutes the inside of a gentleman I hope I understand, and am not less inclined to practise than others."

Lincoln's self-estimate is our estimate of him. We have forgotten the lack of polish, but we can never forget his sincerity, his sensitive conscience, his tender feelings; these inner constituents of a true gentleman he understood and practised.—E.

A REALISTIC ACCOUNT OF LINCOLN'S MURDER

By General Hamlin

Often a person's own experiences upon a certain occasion, told simply and directly, give us a closer and more accurate picture of it than all the stilted formal accounts, which are often somewhat vague.

General Hamlin, oldest son of the late Hannibal Hamlin, was present at the famous Ford's Theater on the occasion of the shooting of President Lincoln, and related what he saw of the mournful affair, in the following vivid manner:

"The night that Mr. Lincoln was murdered, I observed that 'The American Cousin' was to be played, and I took my sister and another lady to the theater. We had seats far down to the front, only a few steps from the stage. Mr. Lincoln came in and proceeded to his box, which was the upper one on the right, but he was not visible to the audience where he sat, having a place back in the box. from which he could better see the stage. Indeed, from where I sat below I could see no person in the boxes.

"Not long before Mr. Lincoln was shot, there was a change of scenes during an act, and it seemed to me that it was the longest time required to change scenes that I had ever observed in a theater. It was so noticeably long that I afterward wondered in connection with the murder if there might not have been some irresolution or perplexity on that stage.

"Not long after, there was a sound somewhat like the slapping of your hands together, sharp, yet not very loud, but loud enough to make me turn my head and wonder what could have made it, and whether it was a pistol.

"The next thing I saw was Booth getting out of Mr. Lincoln's box. I had seen him play on two occasions, and knew his face perfectly well. There never was a more deliberate thing than his stepping out on the sill of the box and leaping from it. He made as pretty a jump as I ever saw. If he had practised that leap, it could hardly have been more elegant. He alighted in a crouching position, like one who had brought his body down to break the shock of the fall.

"While it was a good jump in height, it was not a dangerous one at all,—perhaps from where he leaped to the stage nine to twelve feet. His spur tore a flag, and that seemed to bring him around somehow so that he alighted with his face turned more to the audience than would have been the case had he merely hopped directly downward. He was marble pale. In his right hand he held a knife, and in a theatrical way he stretched it upward and distinctly said the words: 'Sic semper tyrannis.' Then in a very stagey stride, still pale, serious, and intense, he went right across the stage and out. Many people at this stood up, and near me was a naval officer whose name I still remember, who, hearing some one exclaim, 'the President has been shot!' lifted himself up sailor-fashion, by means of the woodwork and decorations of the private box under the President's, and climbed into the box above. He came down the same way into the audience.

"Of course, the audience was dismissed, and as I was going up the street a few minutes afterward, I met a friend in the service who said to me: 'This is terrible news; Mr. Stanton and Mr. Seward, we fear, have been mortally wounded.' At this I went immediately to my office and took the responsibility, as chief of staff of the artillery, of ordering out the field batteries we had around Washington."—E. W.

ADDRESSES

THE ASSASSINATION OF LINCOLN *

By Lord Beaconsfield

There are rare instances when the sympathy of a nation approaches those tenderer feelings which are generally supposed to be peculiar to the individual and to be the happy privilege of private life; and this is one.

Under any circumstances we should have bewailed the catastrophe at Washington; under any circumstances we should have shuddered at the means by which it was accomplished. But in the character of the victim, and even in the accessories of his last moments, there is something so homely and innocent, that it takes the question, as it were, out of all the pomp of history and the ceremonial of diplomacy,—it touches the heart of nations and appeals to the domestic sentiment of mankind. Whatever the various and varying opinions, in this House, and in the country generally, on the policy of the late President of the United States, all must agree that in one of the severest trials which ever tested the moral qualities of man, he fulfilled his duty with simplicity and strength. Nor is it possible for the people of England at such a moment to forget that he sprang from the same fatherland and spoke the same mother tongue. When such crimes are perpetrated, the public mind is apt to fall into gloom and perplexity, for it is ignorant alike of the causes and the consequences of such deeds. But it is one of our duties to reassure the public under unreasoning panic and despondency. Assassination has never changed the history of the world.

I will not refer to the remote past, tho an accident has made the most memorable instance of antiquity at this moment fresh in the minds and memory of all around us. But even the costly sacrifice of a Cæsar did not propitiate the inexorable destiny of his country. If we look to modern times, to times at least with the feelings of which we are familiar, and the people of which were animated and influenced by the same interests as ourselves, the violent deaths of two heroic men, Henry IV. of France, and the Prince of Orange, are conspicuous illustrations of this truth.

In expressing our unaffected and profound sympathy with the citizens of the United States on this untimely end of their elected chief, let us not, therefore, sanction any feeling of depression, but rather let us express a fervent hope that from out of the awful trials of the last four years, of which the least is not this violent demise, the various populations of North America may issue, elevated and chastened, rich with the accumulated wisdom, and strong in the disciplined energy which a young nation can only acquire in a protracted and perilous struggle. Then they will be enabled not merely to renew their career of power and prosperity, but they will renew it to contribute to the general happiness of mankind. It is with these feelings that I second the address to the crown.— W. B. O.

ABRAHAM LINCOLN

By Emilio Castelar

Abraham Lincoln was born in a cabin of Kentucky, of parents who could hardly read; born a new Moses in the solitude of the desert, where are forged all the great and obstinate thoughts, monotonous like the desert, and, like the desert, sublime; growing up among those primeval forests, which, with their fragrance, send up a cloud of incense, and, with their murmurs, a cloud of prayers to heaven; a boatman at eight years in the impetuous current of the Ohio, and at seventeen a woodsman, with ax and arm felling the immemorial trees, to open a way to unexplored regions for his tribe of wandering workers; reading no other book than the Bible, the book of sorrows and great hopes, dictated often by the prophets to the sound of fetters they dragged through Nineveh and Babylon.

A child of Nature, in a word, by one of those miracles, only comprehensible among free peoples, he fought for his country, and was raised by his fellow-citizens to the Congress at Washington, and by the Nation to the Presidency of the Republic; and, when the evil grew more virulent, when those States were dissolved, when the slaveholders uttered their war cry and the slaves their groans of despair—the woodcutter, the boatman. the son of the West, the descendant of Quakers, humblest of the humble before his conscience, greatest of the great before history. ascends the Capitol, the greatest moral height of our time, and strong and serene with his conscience and his thought; before a veteran army, hostile Europe behind him, England favoring the South, France encouraging reaction in Mexico, in his hands

* From a speech in Parliament, 1865.

the riven country; he arms two million men, gathers half a million horses, sends his artillery twelve hundred miles a week from the banks of the Potomac to the shores of the Tennessee; fights more than six hundred battles, renews before Richmond the deeds of Alexander and Cæsar; and, after having emancipated three million slaves, that nothing might be wanting, he dies the very moment of victory—like Christ, like Socrates, like all redeemers, at the foot of his work. His work! sublime achievement over which humanity shall eternally shed its tears, and God His benedictions!—W. B. O.

ABRAHAM LINCOLN

By George H. Smyth, Jr.

Next to Washington, Lincoln stands forth as the grandest patriot in our American life. Washington was the "Father of his Country; "Lincoln was her most loyal son; Washington brought the United States of America into being; Lincoln made that being immortal; Washington unfurled a new flag among the nations of the world; Lincoln made that flag a mighty power among those nations. Dead they yet speak. The good they did will last through time and on through eternity. And so our Nation has most rightly and fittingly made the birthdays of these, her illustrious sons, legal holidays, to inspire us to a purer, nobler, holier manhood.

Abraham Lincoln, like David of old, was divinely led from obscurity up to the very highest place in the land. Away back there in that little log cabin God and His angels watched over that humble birth and guided that precious life until the hour came and the great Emancipator was called "to set at liberty them that were bound." Reared in the forests of poverty, ignorance and darkness, Lincoln cut his way out step by step until at last he stood in the highway of success and fame. He never forgot his humble beginning nor his hard struggle to rise to higher things and he was always ready and willing to help those engaged in that same struggle. Prosperity never changed this noble character. Its strong points were honesty, sincerity, sympathy, fearlessness, perseverance, and a firm belief in the Creator and Governor and Redeemer of mankind.

No institution of learning had the honor of enrolling upon its records the name of Abraham Lincoln; in God's great school his mind was developed and trained for the mighty work he was to do, and earnestly did he apply himself to those lessons, and courageously did he overcome those obstacles and meet those trials which came to him day by day, till at last he who had been faithful unto death received his Master's Crown of Life. And North and South, East and West were bowed together in deepest sorrow when Abraham Lincoln passed from earth to Heaven.

Forever may the fires of our hearts keep warm and bright the memory of this noble man who was

" Rich in saving common sense,
And as the greatest only are—
In his simplicity sublime;
Who never sold the truth to serve the hour,
Nor paltered with Eternal God for power;
Whose life was work, whose language rife
With rugged maxims hewn from life;
Who never spake against a foe.
Let his great example stand
Colossal, seen in every land,
Till in all lands and through all human story
The path of duty be the way to glory."—E.

SELECTIONS FROM ADDRESSES ON LINCOLN'S CHARACTER

COUNTRY, Lincoln's Work for the.— The West, the child of the Union, met the slave-power with determined resistance, and its threat with a defiant assertion of the inherent powers of the Nation, and with the pledge of its young and heroic life for their enforcement.

This double sentiment found its oracle and representative in Abraham Lincoln. He consolidated the Northwest by declaring that the Mississippi shall flow unvexed to the sea. In the great debate with Douglas, his challenge rang through the whole land, a summons to battle.

" A house divided against itself," he said, " cannot stand. I believe the government cannot endure permanently half slave and half free. I do not expect the Union to be dissolved; I do not expect the house to fall; but I do expect it will cease to be divided."

To enforce that expectation, he called a million men to arms, he emancipated four millions of slaves by presidential proclamation; and, when the victory was won for liberty and unity, this most majestic figure of our time, clothed with the unlimited power of a triumphant government, stood between the passions of the strife and commanded peace and forgiveness. When he fell by the hands of the assassin, the hundred years' struggle for national existence was ended. He throttled sectionalism and buried it. The republic, for which half a million men had died and a million been wounded, was so firmly bedded in the hearts, the minds, and the blood of the people, that the question of dissolution will never more form part of the schemes of its politicians, or require the wisdom of its statesmen, or the patriotism of its people.—From an Address by CHAUNCEY M. DEPEW, February 12, 1888.

FAITH, Lincoln's Change of.—Inaction kills belief, while action nourishes it. Lincoln's life gives a notable example of this truth. In his pioneer days he was a skeptic. Both Lamon and Henderson say, that up to the time Lincoln went to Washington as President, he was not a professing believer in any Christian faith. But during the days of the war, when Lincoln bore tremendous burdens of action and anxiety, embodying and enforcing the will of the nation, he became thoroughly religious. It is told that in 1864, when the tension was at its highest, and Lincoln's life was like the action of the heart of the whole people in that time the President was found more than once on his knees in prayer.

Lincoln's faith did not come to him by reasoning, but in the stress and strain of life. He laid hold upon great truths with the grip of a hungering and thirsting nature. It is in this way, I believe, that the strongest faith is attained. With his whole nature stretched to its highest tension, no man can avoid conviction. So long as he merely rests, remains inactive, passive, he may get along without a faith; but when his soul is awakened and his feeling is aroused, *believe* he must.—P. S. M.

HERO OF OUR TIME, The Great.—The story of the life of Abraham Lincoln savors more of romance than of reality. It is more like a fable of ancient days than a story of a plain American of the nineteenth century. The names of Washington and Lincoln are inseparably associated. . . . Washington could not tell a story. Lincoln always could. . . . But his heart was not always attuned to mirth; its chords were often set to strains of sadness. Yet throughout all his trials, he never lost the courage of his convictions. When he was surrounded on all sides by doubting Thomases, by unbelieving Saracens, by discontented Catalines, his faith was strongest. As the Danes destroyed the hearing of their war horses in order that they might not be affrighted by the din of battle, so Lincoln turned a deaf ear to all that might have discouraged him, and exhibited unswerving faith in the justice of the cause and the integrity of the Union.

It is said that for three hundred years after the battle of Thermopylæ, every child in the public schools of Greece was required to recite from memory the names of the three hundred martyrs who fell in the defense of that pass. It would be a crowning triumph in patriotic education, if every school-child in America could contemplate each day the grand character and utter the inspiring name of Abraham Lincoln.

He has passed from our view; we shall not meet him again till he stands forth to answer to his name at roll-call when the great of the earth are summoned on the morning of the last great reveille. Till then (*apostrophizing Lincoln's portrait*)—till then, farewell, gentlest of all spirits, noblest of all hearts! A child's simplicity was mingled with the majestic grandeur of his nature. You have handed down unto a grateful people the richest legacy which man can leave to man—the memory of a good name, the inheritance of a great example.—From an Address by HORACE PORTER, Feb. 12, 1889.

POWER, The Secret of His.—What were the traits of character which made him leader and master, without a rival, in the greatest crisis in our history? What gave him such mighty power? Lincoln had sublime faith in the people. He walked with and among them. He recognized the importance and power of an enlightened public sentiment, and was guided by it. Even amid the vicissitudes of war, he concealed little from public review and inspection. In all he did he invited rather than evaded examination and criticism. He submitted his plans and purposes, as far as practicable, to public consideration, with perfect frankness and sincerity. . . . He had that happy peculiar habit, which few public men have attained, of looking away from the deceptive and misleading influences about him—and none are more deceptive than those of public life in our capitals—straight into the hearts of the people. He could not be deceived by the self-interested host of eager counselors who sought to enforce their own particular views upon him as the voice of the country. He chose to determine for himself what the people were thinking about and wanting him to do; and no man ever lived who was a more accurate judge of their opinions and wishes.—From an Address by WILLIAM McKINLEY, February 12, 1895.

PROVIDENCE AND LINCOLN.—If I have any purpose, it is to strengthen the belief in a Divine Providence; and if I have any further purpose in this time of wars and rumors of wars, it is to show that God Almighty has made nations for higher purposes than mere money making. I am to speak of Abraham Lincoln, the simplest, serenest, sublimest character of the age. Seventy millions of people join in commemorating his greatness. It is not my purpose to review his life; that is too much a part of history. That history should be taught in every public American school and preached from every Christian pulpit. The story of Abraham Lincoln, citizen, President, liberator and martyr, should be in the heart of every American child.—SENATOR JOHN M. THURSTON.

SERMONS

LINCOLN AS A TYPICAL AMERICAN *

BY PHILLIPS BROOKS, D.D.

While I speak to you to-day, the body of the President who ruled this people, is lying, honored and loved, in our city. It is impossible, with that sacred presence in our midst, for me to stand and speak of ordinary topics which occupy the pulpit. I must speak of him to-day; and I therefore undertake to do what I had intended to do at some future time, to invite you to study with me the character of Abraham Lincoln, the impulses of his life and the causes of his death. I know how hard it is to do it rightly, how impossible it is to do it worthily. But I shall speak with confidence, because I speak to those who love him, and whose ready love will fill out the deficiencies in a picture which my words will weakly try to draw.

We take it for granted, first of all, that there is an essential connection between Mr. Lincoln's character and his violent and bloody death. It is no accident, no arbitrary decree of Providence. He lived as he did, and he died as he did, because he was what he was. The more we see of events, the less we come to believe in any fate or destiny, except the destiny of character. It will be our duty, then, to see what there was in the character of our great President that created the history of his life, and at last produced the catastrophe of his cruel death. After the first trembling horror, the first outburst of indignant sorrow, has grown calm, these are the questions which we are bound to ask and answer.

It is not necessary for me even to sketch the biography of Mr. Lincoln. He was born in Kentucky fifty-six years ago, when Kentucky was a pioneer State. He lived, as a boy and man, the hard and needy life of a backwoodsman, a farmer, a river boatman, and, finally, by his own efforts at self-education, of an active, respected, influential citizen, in the half organized and manifold interests of a new and energetic community. From his boyhood up he lived in direct and vigorous contact with men and things, not as in older states and easier conditions with words and theories; and both his moral convictions and intellectual opinions gathered from that contact a supreme degree of that character by which men knew him; that character which is the most distinctive possession of the best American nature; that almost indescribable quality which we call, in general, clearness or truth, and which appears in the physical structure as health, in the moral constitution as honesty, in the mental structure as sagacity, and in the region of active life as practicalness. This one character, with many sides, all shaped

by the same essential force and testifying to the same inner influences, was what was powerful in him and decreed for him the life he was to live and the death he was to die. We must take no smaller view than this of what he was.

. . . .

It is the great boon of such characters as Mr. Lincoln's, that they reunite what God has joined together and man has put asunder. In him was vindicated the greatness of real goodness and the goodness of real greatness. The twain were one flesh. Not one of all the multitudes who stood and looked up to him for direction with such a loving and implicit trust can tell you to-day whether the wise judgments that he gave came most from a strong head or a sound heart. If you ask them, they are puzzled. There are men as good as he, but they do bad things. There are men as intelligent as he, but they do foolish things. In him, goodness and intelligence combined and made their best result of wisdom. For perfect truth consists not merely in the right constituents of character, but in their right and intimate conjunction. This union of the mental and moral into a life of admirable simplicity is what we most admire in children; but in them it is unsettled and unpractical. But when it is preserved into manhood, deepened into reliability and maturity, it is that glorified childlikeness, that high and reverend simplicity, which shames and baffles the most accomplished astuteness, and is chosen by God to fill His purposes when He needs a ruler for His people, of faithful and true heart, such as he had, who was our President.

Another evident quality of such character as this will be its freshness or newness, if we may so speak; its freshness or readiness,—call it what you will,—its ability to take up new duties and do them in a new way, will result of necessity from its truth and clearness. The simple natures and forces will always be the most pliant ones. Water bends and shapes itself to any channel. Air folds and adapts itself to each new figure. They are the simplest and the most infinitely active things in nature. So this nature, in very virtue of its simplicity, must be also free, always fitting itself to each new need. It will always start from the most fundamental and eternal conditions, and work in the straightest, even tho they be the newest ways, to the present prescribed purpose. In one word, it must be broad and independent and radical. So that freedom and radicalness in the character of Abraham Lincoln were not

* Delivered in Philadelphia as a Funeral Oration.

separate qualities, but the necessary results of his simplicity and childlikeness and truth.

Here then we have some conception of the man. Out of this character came the life which we admire and the death which we lament to-day. He was called in that character to that life and death. It was just the nature, as you see, which a new nation such as ours ought to produce. All the conditions of his birth, his youth, his manhood, which made him what he was, were not irregular and exceptional, but were the normal conditions of a new and simple country. His pioneer home in Indiana was a type of the pioneer land in which he lived. If ever there was a man who was a part of the time and country he lived in, this was he. The same simple respect for labor won in the school of work and incorporated into blood and muscle; the same unassuming loyalty to the simple virtues of temperance and industry and integrity; the same sagacious judgment which had learned to be quick-eyed and quick-brained in the constant presence of emergency; the same direct and clear thought about things, social, political, and religious, that was in him supremely, was in the people he was sent to rule. Surely, with such a type-man for ruler, there would seem to be but a smooth and even road over which he might lead the people whose character he represented into the new region of national happiness, and comfort, and usefulness, for which that character had been designed.

· · · · · ·

The cause that Abraham Lincoln died for shall grow stronger by his death, stronger and sterner. Stronger to set its pillars deep into the structure of our Nation's life; sterner to execute the justice of the Lord upon his enemies. Stronger to spread its arms and grasp our whole land into freedom; sterner to sweep the last poor ghost of slavery out of our haunted homes.

· · · · · ·

So let him lie here in our midst to-day, and let our people go and bend with solemn thoughtfulness and look upon his face and read the lessons of his burial. As he paused here on his journey from the Western home and told us what, by the help of God, he meant to do, so let him pause upon his way back to his Western grave and tell us, with a silence more eloquent than words, how bravely, how truly, by the strength of God, he did it. God brought him up as He brought David up from the sheep-folds to feed Jacob, His people, and Israel, His inheritance. He came up in earnestness and faith, and he goes back in triumph. As he pauses here to-day, and from his cold lips bids us bear witness how he has met the duty that was laid on him, what can we say out of our full hearts but this:—" He fed them with a faithful and true heart, and ruled them prudently with all his power."

THE SHEPHERD OF THE PEOPLE! that old name that the best rulers ever craved. What ruler ever won it like this dead President of ours? He fed us faithfully and truly. He fed us with counsel when we were in doubt, with inspiration when we sometimes faltered, with caution when we would be rash, with calm, clear, trustful cheerfulness through many an hour, when our hearts were dark. He fed hungry souls all over the country with sympathy and consolation. He spread before the whole land feasts of great duty and devotion and patriotism, on which the land grew strong. He fed us with solemn, solid truths. He taught us the sacredness of government, the wickedness of treason. He made our souls glad and vigorous with the love of liberty that was in his. He showed us how to love truth and yet be charitable— how to hate wrong and all oppression, and yet not treasure one personal injury or insult. He fed *all* his people, from the highest to the lowest, from the most privileged down to the most enslaved. Best of all, he fed us with a reverent and genuine religion. He spread before us the love and fear of God just in that shape in which we need them most, and out of his faithful service of a higher Master, who of us has not taken and eaten and grow strong? " He fed them with a faithful and true heart." Yes, till the last. For at the last, behold him standing with hand reached out to feed the South with mercy, and the North with charity, and the whole land with peace, when the Lord who had sent him called him, and his work was done!

He stood once on the battlefield of our own State, and said of the brave men who had saved it, words as noble as any countryman of ours ever spoke. Let us stand in the country he has saved, and which is to be his grave and monument, and say of Abraham Lincoln what he said of the soldiers who had died at Gettysburg. He stood there with their graves before him, and these are the words he said:

" We cannot dedicate, we cannot consecrate, we cannot hallow this ground. The brave men who struggled here have consecrated it far beyond our power to add or detract. The world will little note nor long remember what we say here, but it can never forget what they did here. It is for us the living rather to be dedicated to the unfinished work which they who fought here have thus far so nobly advanced. It is rather for us to be here dedicated to the great task remaining before us, that from these honored dead we take increased devotion to that cause for which they gave the last full measure of devotion; that we here highly resolve that these dead shall not have died in vain; and this nation, under God, shall have a new birth of freedom; and that government of the people, by the people, and for the people, shall not perish from the earth."

May God make us worthy of the memory of Abraham Lincoln!—W. B. O.

EFFECT OF THE DEATH OF LINCOLN *

By Henry Ward Beecher

Again a great leader of the people has passed through toil, sorrow, battle, and war, and come near to the promised land of peace, into which he might not pass over. Who shall recount our martyr's sufferings for this people? Since the November of 1860, his horizon has been black with storms.

By day and by night, he trod a way of danger and darkness. On his shoulders rested a government dearer to him than his own life. At its integrity millions of men were striking at home. Upon this government foreign eyes lowered. It stood like a lone island in a sea full of storms, and every tide and wave seemed eager to devour it. Upon thousands of hearts great sorrows and anxieties have rested, but not on one such, and in such measure, as upon that simple, truthful, noble soul, our faithful and sainted Lincoln. Never rising to the enthusiasm of more impassioned natures in hours of hope, and never sinking with the mercurial, in hours of defeat, to the depths of despondency, he held on with unmovable patience and fortitude, putting caution against hope, that it might not be premature, and hope against caution, that it might not yield to dread and danger. He wrestled ceaselessly, through black and dreadful purgatorial years, wherein God was cleansing the sin of His people as by fire.

At last, the watcher beheld the gray dawn for the country. The mountains began to give forth their forms from out the darkness, and the East came rushing toward us with arms full of joy for all our sorrows. Then it was for him to be glad exceedingly that had sorrowed immeasurably. Peace could bring to no other heart such joy and rest, such honor, such trust, such gratitude. But he looked upon it as Moses looked upon the promised land. Then the wail of a nation proclaimed that he had gone from among us. Not thine the sorrow, but ours, sainted soul. Thou hast, indeed, entered the promised land, while we are yet on the march. To us remain the rocking of the deep, the storm upon the land, days of duty and nights of watching; but thou art sphered high above all darkness and fear, beyond all sorrow and weariness. Rest, O weary heart! Rejoice exceedingly,—thou that hast enough suffered! Thou hast beheld Him who invisibly led thee in this great wilderness. Thou standest among the elect. Around thee are the royal men that have ennobled human life in every age. Kingly art thou, with glory on thy brow as a diadem. And joy is upon thee for evermore. Over all this land, over all the little cloud of years that now from thine infinite horizon moves back as a speck, thou art lifted up as high as the star is above the clouds that hide us, but never reach it. In the goodly company of Mount Zion thou shalt find that rest which thou hast sorrowing sought in vain; and thy name, an everlasting name in heaven, shall flourish in fragrance and beauty as long as men shall last upon the earth, or hearts remain, to revere truth, fidelity, and goodness.

Never did two such orbs of experience meet in one hemisphere, as the joy and the sorrow of the same week in this land. The joy was as sudden as if no man had expected it, and as entrancing as if it had fallen a sphere from heaven. It rose up over sobriety, and swept business from its moorings, and ran down through the land in irresistible course. Men embraced each other in brotherhood that were strangers in the flesh. They sang, or prayed, or deeper yet, many could only think thanksgiving and weep gladness.

That peace was sure; that government was firmer than ever; that the land was cleansed of plague; that the ages were opening to our footsteps, and we were to begin a march of blessings; that blood was staunched, and scowling enmities were sinking like storms beneath the horizon; that the dear fatherland, nothing lost, much gained, was to rise up in unexampled honor among the nations of the earth—these thoughts, and that undistinguishable throng of fancies, and hopes, and desires, and yearnings, that filled the soul with tremblings like the heated air of midsummer days—all these kindled up such a surge of joy as no words may describe.

In one hour, joy lay without a pulse, without a gleam or breath. A sorrow came that swept through the land as huge storms sweep through the forest and field, rolling thunder along the sky, disheveling the flowers, daunting every singer in thicket or forest, and pouring blackness and darkness across the land and up the mountains. Did ever so many hearts, in so brief a time, touch two such boundless feelings? It was the uttermost of joy; it was the uttermost of sorrow—noon and midnight, without a space between.

The blow brought not a sharp pang. It was so terrible that at first it stunned sensibility. Citizens were like men awakened at midnight by an earthquake, and bewildered to find everything that they were accustomed to trust wavering and falling. The very earth was no longer solid. The first feeling was the least. Men waited to get strength to feel. They wandered in the streets as if groping after some impending dread, or undeveloped sorrow, or some one to tell them what ailed them. They met each other as if each would ask the other, "Am I awake, or do I dream?" There was a piteous helplessness. Strong men bowed down and wept. Other and common griefs belonged to some one in chief; this belonged to all. It was

* Delivered in Brooklyn April 16, 1865.

each and every man's. Every virtuous household in the land felt as if its first-born were gone. Men were bereaved and walked for days as if a corpse lay unburied in their dwellings. There was nothing else to think of. They could speak of nothing but that; and yet of that they could speak only falteringly. All business was laid aside. Pleasure forgot to smile. The city for nearly a week ceased to roar. The great Leviathan lay down, and was still. Even avarice stood still, and greed was strangely moved to generous sympathy and universal sorrow. Rear to his name monuments, found charitable institutions, and write his name above their lintels, but no monument will ever equal the universal, spontaneous, and sublime sorrow that in a moment swept down lines and parties, and covered up animosities, in an hour brought a divided people into unity of grief and indivisible fellowship of anguish.

This Nation has dissolved—but in tears only. It stands four-square, more solid today than any pyramid in Egypt. This people are neither wasted, nor daunted, nor disordered. Men hate slavery and love liberty with stronger hate and love to-day than ever before. The government is not weakened; it is made stronger. How naturally and easily were the ranks closed! Another steps forward, in the hour that one fell, to take his place and his mantle; and I avow my belief that he will be found a man true to every instinct of liberty; true to the whole trust that is reposed in him; vigilant of the Constitution; careful of the laws; wise for liberty, in that he himself, through his life, has known what it was to suffer from the stings of slavery, and to prize liberty from bitter personal experiences.

Where could the head of government of any monarchy be smitten down by the hand of an assassin, and the funds not quiver or fall one-half of one per cent? After a long period of national disturbance, after four years of drastic war, after tremendous drafts on the resources of the country, in the height and top of our burdens, the heart of this people is such that now, when the head of government is stricken down, the public funds do not waver, but stand as the granite ribs in our mountains.

Republican institutions have been vindicated in this experience as they never were before; and the whole history of the last four years, rounded up by this cruel stroke, seems, in the providence of God, to have been clothed now, with an illustration, with a sympathy, with an aptness, and with a significance, such as we never could have expected nor imagined. God, I think, has said, by the voice of this event, to all nations of the earth: "Republican liberty, based upon true Christianity, is firm as the foundation of the globe."

Even he who now sleeps has, by this event, been clothed with new influence. Dead, he speaks to men who now willingly hear what before they refused to listen to. Now his simple and weighty words will be gathered like those of Washington, and your children

and your children's children shall be taught to ponder the simplicity and deep wisdom of utterances which, in their time, passed, in party heat, as idle words. Men will receive a new impulse of patriotism for his sake, and will guard with zeal the whole country which he loved so well. I swear you, on the altar of his memory, to be more faithful to the country for which he has perished. They will, as they follow his hearse, swear a new hatred to that slavery against which he warred, and which, in vanquishing him, has made him a martyr and a conqueror. I swear you, by the memory of this martyr, to hate slavery with an unappeasable hatred. They will admire and imitate the firmness of this man, his inflexible conscience for the right, and yet his gentleness, as tender as a woman's, his moderation of spirit, which not all the heat of party could inflame, nor all the jars and disturbances of his country shake out of place. I swear you to an emulation of his justice, his moderation, and his mercy.

You I can comfort; but how can I speak to that twilight million to whom his name was as the name of an angel of God? There will be wailing in places which no minister shall be able to reach. When, in hovel and in cot, in wood and in wilderness, in the field throughout the South, the dusky children, who looked upon him as that Moses whom God sent before them to lead them out of the land of bondage, learn that he has fallen, who shall comfort them? O, thou Shepherd of Israel, that didst comfort Thy people of old, to Thy care we commit the helpless, the long-wronged, and grieved.

And now the martyr is moving in triumphal march mightier than when alive. The Nation rises up at every stage of his coming. Cities and States are his pall bearers, and the cannon beats the hours with solemn progression. Dead, dead, dead, he yet speaketh. Is Washington dead? Is Hampden dead? Is David dead? Is any man that was ever fit to live dead? Disenthralled of flesh, and risen in the unobstructed sphere where passion never comes, he begins his illimitable work. His life now is grafted upon the infinite, and will be fruitful as no earthly life can be.

Pass on, thou that hast overcome. Your sorrows, O people, are his peace. Your bells and bands and muffled drums sound triumph in his ear. Wail and weep here; God made it echo joy and triumph there. Pass on.

Four years ago, O Illinois, we took from your midst an untried man, and from among the people. We return him to you a mighty conqueror. Not thine any more, but the Nation's; not ours, but the world's. Give him place, O ye prairies. In the midst of this great continent his dust shall rest, a sacred treasure to myriads who shall pilgrim to that shrine to kindle anew their zeal and patriotism. Ye winds that move over the mighty places of the West, chant his requiem. Ye people, behold a martyr whose blood, as so many articulate words, pleads for fidelity, for law, for liberty.—W. B. O.

THE RELIGIOUS CHARACTER OF ABRAHAM LINCOLN

By B. B. Tyler, D.D.

In 1865, the bullet of an assassin suddenly terminated the life among men of one who was an honor to his race. He was great and good. He was great because he was good. Lincoln's religious character was the one thing which, above all other features of his unique mental and moral as well as physical personality, lifted him above his fellow men.

Because an effort has been made to parade Abraham Lincoln as an unbeliever, I have been led to search carefully for the facts in his life bearing on this point. The testimony seems to be almost entirely, if not altogether, on one side. I cannot account for the statement which William H. Herndon makes in his life of the martyred President, that, "Mr. Lincoln had no faith." For twenty-five years Mr. Herndon was Abraham Lincoln's law partner in Springfield, Ill. He had the best opportunities to know Abraham Lincoln. When, however, he affirms that "Mr. Lincoln had no faith," he speaks without warrant. It is simply certain that he uses words in their usually accepted signification, altho his statement concerning Lincoln is not true.

Abraham Lincoln was a man of profound faith. He believed in God. He believed in Christ. He believed in the Bible. He believed in men. His faith made him great. His life is a beautiful commentary on the words, "This is the victory that overcometh the world, even our faith." There was a time in Lincoln's experience when his faith faltered, as there was a time when his reason tottered; but these sad experiences were temporary, and Abraham Lincoln was neither an infidel nor a lunatic. It is easy to trace in the life of this colossal character a steady growth of faith. This grace in him increased steadily in breadth and in strength with the passing years, until it came to pass that his last public utterances show forth the confidence and the fire of an ancient Hebrew prophet.

It is true that Lincoln never united with the Church, altho a lifelong and regular attendant on its services. He had a reason for occupying a position outside the fellowship of the Church of Christ as it existed in his day and in his part of the world. This reason Lincoln did not hesitate to declare. He explained on one occasion that he had never become a churchmember because he did not like and could not in conscience subscribe to the long and frequently complicated statements of Christian doctrines which characterized the confessions of the Churches. He said: "When any Church will inscribe over its altar as its sole qualification for membership the Savior's condensed statement of the substance of both law and gospel, 'Thou shalt love the Lord thy God with all thy heart, and with all thy soul, and with all thy mind, and thy neighbor as thyself,' that Church will I join with all my heart and soul."

Abraham Lincoln in these words recognizes the central figure of the Bible, Jesus of Nazareth, as "the Savior." He recognizes God as the supreme Lawgiver, and expresses readiness, while eschewing theological subtleties, to submit heart and soul to the supreme Lawgiver of the universe. His faith, according to this language, goes out manward as well as Godward. He believed not only in God, but he believed in man as well, and this Christianity, according to Christ, requires of all disciples of the great Teacher.

About a year before his assassination Lincoln, in a letter to Joshua Speed, said: "I am profitably engaged in reading the Bible. Take all of this book upon reason that you can and the balance on faith, and you will live and die a better man." He saw and declared that the teaching of the Bible had a tendency to improve character. He had a right view of this sacred literature. Its purpose is character building.

Leonard Swett, who knew Abraham Lincoln well, said at the unveiling of the Chicago monument that Lincoln "believed in God as the supreme ruler of the universe, the guide of men, and the controller of the great events and destinies of mankind. He believed himself to be an instrument and leader in this country of the force of freedom."

From this it appears that his belief was not merely theoretical, but that it was practical. He regarded himself as an instrument, as Moses was an instrument in the hands of almighty God, to lead men into freedom.

It was after his election, in the autumn of 1860, and but a short time before his inauguration as President of the United States, that in a letter to Judge Joseph Gillespie, he said: "I have read on my knees the story of Gethsemane, where the Son of God prayed in vain that the cup of bitterness might pass from Him. I am in the garden of Gethsemane now, and my cup of bitterness is full and overflowing."

From this it is clear that he believed the Jesus of the Gospels to be "the Son of God." And what a sense of responsibility he must at the time of writing this letter have experienced to cause him to declare, "I am in the garden of Gethsemane now, and my cup of bitterness is full and overflowing!" Only a superlatively good man, only a man of genuine piety, could use honestly such language as this. These words do not indicate unbelief or agnosticism. If ever a man in public life in these United States was removed the distance of the antipodes from the coldness and bleakness of agnosticism, that man was Abraham Lincoln. This confession of faith, incidentally made in a brief letter to a dear friend, is not only orthodox according to the accepted standards of orthodoxy, but, better, it is evangelical. To him the hero of the Gospel histories was none other than "the Son of God." By the use of these words did Lincoln characterize Jesus of Nazareth.

Herndon has said in his life of Abraham Lincoln that he never read the Bible, but Alexander Williamson, who was employed as a tutor in President Lincoln's family in Washington, said that "Mr. Lincoln very frequently studied the Bible with the aid of Cruden's Concordance, which lay on his table." If Lincoln was not a reader and student of the inspired literature which we call the Bible, what explanation can be made of his language just quoted, addressed to Judge Gillespie, "I have read on my knees the story of Gethsemane, where the Son of God prayed in vain that the cup of bitterness might pass from Him"?

I have admitted that in Lincoln's experience there was a time when his faith faltered. It is interesting to know in what manner he came to have the faith which in the maturity of his royal manhood and in the zenith of his intellectual powers he expressed. One of his pastors—for he sat under the ministry of three men, chiefly in Springfield, Ill.—Rev. James Smith, has told in what way Lincoln came to be an intelligent believer in the Bible, in Jesus as the Son of God, and in Christianity as Divine in its origin, and a mighty moral and spiritual power for the regeneration of men and of the race. Mr. Smith placed before him, he says, the arguments for and against the Divine authority and inspiration of the Scriptures. To the arguments on both sides Lincoln gave a patient, impartial, and searching investigation. He himself said that he examined the arguments as a lawyer investigates testimony in a case in which he is deeply interested. At the conclusion of the investigation he declared that the argument in favor of the Divine authority and inspiration of the Bible is unanswerable.

So far did Lincoln go in his open sympathy with the teachings of the Bible that on one occasion, in the presence of a large assembly, he delivered the address at an annual meeting of the Springfield, Illinois, Bible Society. In the course of his address he drew a contrast between the decalog and the most eminent lawgiver of antiquity, in which he said: "It seems to me that nothing short of infinite wisdom could by any possibility have devised and given to man this excellent and perfect moral code. It is suited to men in all the conditions of life, and inculcates all the duties they owe to their Creator, to themselves, and their fellow men."

Lincoln prepared an address, in which he declared that this country cannot exist half-slave and half-free. He affirmed the saying of Jesus, "A house divided against itself cannot stand." Having read this address to some friends, they urged him to strike out that portion of it. If he would do so, he could probably be elected to the United States Senate; but if he delivered the address as written, the ground taken was so high, the position was so advanced, his sentiments were so radical, he would probably fail of gaining a seat in the supreme legislative body of the greatest republic on earth.

Lincoln, under those circumstances, said: "I know there is a God, and that He hates the injustice of slavery. I see the storm coming, and I know that His hand is in it. If He has a place and a work for me, and I think He has, I believe I am ready. I am nothing, but truth is everything. I know I am right, because I know that liberty is right, for Christ teaches it, and Christ is God."

And yet we are asked to believe that a man who could express himself in this way and show this courage was a doubter, a skeptic, an unbeliever, an agnostic, an infidel. "Christ is God." This was Lincoln's faith in 1860, found in a letter addressed to the Hon. Newton Bateman.

Lincoln's father was a Christian. Old Uncle Tommy Lincoln, as his friends familiarly called him, was a good man. He was what might be called a ne'er-do-well. As the world counts success, Thomas Lincoln, the father of Abraham Lincoln, was not successful, but he was an honest man. He was a truthful man. He was a man of faith. He worshiped God. He belonged to the church. He was a member of a congregation in Charleston, Ill., which I had the honor to serve in the beginning of my ministry, known as the Christian Church. He died not far from Charleston, and is buried a few miles distant from the beautiful little town, the county seat of Coles county, Ill.

During the last illness of his father, Lincoln wrote a letter to his step-brother, John Johnston, which closes with the following sentences: "I sincerely hope that father' may recover his health. but at all events tell him to remember to call upon and confide in our great, and good, and merciful Maker, who will not turn away from him in any extremity. He notes the fall of the sparrow, and numbers the hairs of our heads, and He will not forget the dying man who puts his trust in Him. Say to him that if we could meet now it is doubtful whether it would not be more painful than pleasant, but that if it be his lot to go now he will soon have a joyful meeting with loved ones gone before, and where the rest of us, through the mercy of God, hope ere long to join them."

From this it appears that Lincoln cherished a hope of life everlasting through the mercy of God. This sounds very much like the talk of a Christian.

Altho Lincoln was not a church member, he was a man of prayer. He believed that God can hear, does hear, and answer prayer.

Lincoln said in conversation with General Sickles concerning the battle of Gettysburg, that he had no anxiety as to the result. At this General Sickles expressed surprise, and inquired into the reason for this unusual state of mind at that period in the history of the war. Lincoln hesitated to accede to the request of General Sickles, but was finally prevailed upon to do so, and this is what he said:

"Well, I will tell you how it was. In the pinch of your campaign up there, when everybody seemed panicstricken, and nobody could tell what was going to happen, oppressed by the gravity of our affairs, I went into my room one day and locked the door, and got down on my knees before Almighty God, and prayed to Him mightily for victory at Gettysburg. I told Him this was His war, and our cause His cause, but that we could not stand another Fredericksburg or Chancellorsville. And I then and there made a solemn vow to Almighty God that if He would stand by our boys at Gettysburg I would stand by Him. And He *did* and I *will*. And after that (I don't know how it was, and I can't explain it) but soon a sweet comfort crept into my soul that things would go all right at Gettysburg. and that is why I had no fears about you."

Such faith as this will put to the blush many who are members of the church.

It was afterward that General Sickles asked him what news he had from Vicksburg. He answered that he had no news worth mentioning, but that Grant was still " pegging away" down there, and he thought a good deal of him as a general. and had no thought of removing him notwithstanding that he was urged to do so; and " besides," he added, "I have been praying over Vicksburg also, and believe our Heavenly Father is going to give us victory there too, because we need it, in order to bisect the Confederacy and have the Mississippi flow unvexed to the sea."

When he entered upon the task to which the people of the United States had called him, at the railway station in Springfield on the eve of his departure to Washington to take the oath of office, he delivered an address. It is a model. I quote it entire. It is as follows:

"My friends, no one not in my position can realize the sadness I feel at this parting. To this people I owe all that I am. Here I have lived more than a quarter of a century. Here my children were born, and here one of them lies buried. I know not how soon I shall see you again. I go to assume a task more than that which has devolved upon any other man since the days of Washington. He never would have succeeded except for the aid of Divine Providence, upon which he at all times relied. I feel that I cannot succeed without the same Divine blessing which sustained him, and on the same almighty Being I place my reliance for support. And I hope you, my friends, will all pray that I may receive that Divine assistance, without which I cannot succeed, but with which success is certain. Again, I bid you an affectionate farewell."

At the time of Lincoln's assassination these words were printed in a great variety of forms. In my home for a number of years, beautifully framed, these parting words addressed to the friends of many years in Springfield, Ill., ornamented my humble residence. And yet one of his biographers refers to this address as if its genuineness may well be doubted. At the time of its delivery it was taken down and published broadcast in the papers of the day.

But it would be wearisome to you to recite all the evidences bearing on the religious character of Abraham Lincoln. John G. Nicolay well says: "Benevolence and forgiveness were the very basis of his character; his world-wide humanity is aptly embodied in a phrase of his second inaugural: 'With malice toward none, with charity for all.' His nature was deeply religious, but he belonged to no denomination; he had faith in the eternal justice and boundless mercy of Providence, and made the Golden Rule of Christ his practical creed."

In this passage Mr. Nicolay refers especially to Lincoln's second inaugural address. This address has the ring of an ancient Hebrew prophet. Only a man of faith and piety could deliver such an address. After the struggles through which the country had passed Lincoln's self-poise. his confidence in God, his belief in and affection for his fellow men, remained unabated. In Lincoln's second inaugural address he used these words:

"Neither party expected for the war the magnitude or the duration which it has already attained: neither anticipated that the cause of the conflict might cease when or even before the conflict itself should cease. Each looked for an easier triumph, and a result less fundamental and astounding. Both read the same Bible and pray to the same God, and each invokes His aid against the other. It may seem strange that any men should dare to ask a just God's assistance in wringing their bread from the sweat of other men's faces; but let us judge not, that we be not judged. The prayers of both could not be answered; that of neither has been answered fully.

"The Almighty has His own purposes. 'Wo unto the world because of offenses, for it must needs be that offenses come; but wo to that man by whom the offense cometh.' If we shall suppose that American slavery is one of those offenses which, in the providence of God, must needs come, but which, having continued through His appointed time, He now wills to remove, and that He gives to both North and South this terrible war. as the wo due to those by whom the offense came, shall we discern therein any departure from those divine attributes which the believers in a living God always ascribe to Him? Fondly do we hope, fervently do we pray, that this mighty scourge of war may speedily pass away. Yet, if God wills that it continue until all the wealth piled by the bondsman's two hundred and fifty years of unrequited toil shall be sunk, and until every drop of blood drawn with a lash shall be paid with another drawn by a sword, as was said three thousand years ago, so still it must be said. 'The judgments of the Lord are true and righteous altogether.'

"With malice toward none, with charity for all, with firmness in the right as God gives us to see the right, let us strive on to finish the work we are in; to bind up the Nation's wounds; to care for him who shall have borne the battle, and for his widow and his orphan—to do all which may achieve and cherish a just and lasting peace among ourselves and with all nations."

The spirit of this address, under the circumstances, is intensely Christian, and it is one of the most remarkable speeches in the literature of the world.

When Lincoln was urged to issue his Proclamation of Emancipation he waited on God for guidance. He said to some who urged this matter, who were anxious to have the President act without delay: "I hope it will not be irreverent for me to say that, if it is probable that God would reveal His will to others on a point so connected with my duty, it might be supposed He would reveal it directly to me, for, unless I am more deceived in myself than I often am, it is my earnest desire to know the will of Providence in this matter, and if I can learn what it is, I will do it."

Stoddard, in his LIFE OF LINCOLN, gives attention beyond any of his biographers to the religious side of Lincoln's character. Commenting on the inaugural from which I have quoted, Mr. Stoddard said:

"His mind and soul had reached the full development in a religious life so unusually intense and absorbing that it could not otherwise than utter itself in the grand sentences of his last address to the people. The knowledge had come, and the faith had come, and the charity had come, and with all had come the love of God which had put away all thought of rebellious resistance to the will of God leading, as in his earlier days of trial, to despair and insanity."

I wish to call special attention to Lincoln's temperance habits. He was a teetotaler so far as the use of intoxicating liquors as a beverage was concerned. When the committee of the Chicago convention waited upon Lincoln to inform him of his nomination he treated them to ice-water and said:

"Gentlemen, we must pledge our mutual healths in the most healthy beverage which God has given to man. It is the only beverage I have ever used or allowed in my family, and I cannot conscientiously depart from it on the present occasion. It is pure Adam's ale from the spring."

Mr. John Hay, one of his biographers, says: "Mr. Lincoln was a man of exceedingly temperate habits. He made no use of either whisky or tobacco during all the years that I knew him."

Abraham Lincoln was a model in every respect but one. It was a mistake on the part of this great and good man that he never identified himself openly with the Church. I know what can be said in favor of his position. It is not, however, satisfactory. If all men were to act in this matter as Lincoln did, there would be no Church. This is obvious. Hence the mistake which he made. Otherwise, as to his personal habits; as to his confidence in God; as to his faith in man; as to his conception and use of the Bible; as to his habits of prayer; as to his judicial fairness; as to his sympathy with men—in all these respects, as in many others, Abraham Lincoln is a character to be studied and imitated.—H. R.

SUGGESTIVE THOUGHTS

ANECDOTE, An.—When Lincoln was a young man he developed that liking for telling stories which will be remembered as long as his courage and statesmanship. He is said to have kept a grocery store audience spellbound with his story-telling and his jokes, on court days, until midnight.

However, as Lincoln found time about these days to master and practise the law, and to delve into literature and perfect his skill in the use of the English language, he could hardly have wasted much time in this amiable diversion.

A senator of the United States recently related an incident which illustrates Lincoln's aptness in quaint and vigorous allegory. The senator said that Lincoln's son had given him copies of two letters, both addressed to a certain corps commander of the Army of the Potomac on the eve of a forward movement, one of them written by General Halleck, chief of staff, and the other by President Lincoln.

General Halleck's letter was full of formal and military technical terms, and contained a warning couched in this fashion:

"In undertaking to place your command on the opposite shore of the Rappahannock River, you will exercise extreme caution in affording full protection to advance, rear and flanks, in order that the enemy may not be encouraged to make an attack while your forces are separated in the act of crossing."

This was good advice. Lincoln gave it to the same commander in the note which he wrote to him; but this was the form in which he expressed it:

"Look out, when you cross the river, that you don't hang yourself up in the middle like a steer on a fence, neither able to hook with your horns nor kick with your hoofs."

Lincoln's comments on men and things during his presidency often had a piquancy which forced them deep into men's minds. This very quality of distinct and concise utterance undoubtedly saved many hours of time which might otherwise have been spent in explanations. It was well adapted, too, to the rough and perilous times of the Civil War.—Y. C.

CAMP, Lincoln in.—On the morning after the battle of Bull Run the Army of the Potomac was in a sorry condition. Officers were looking after their men, and men were looking after their officers. A cold, drizzling rain was falling, tents and rations were wanting, and worse yet, the army had been beaten, and had not had time to recover itself. The chronicler of the Seventy-ninth New York Regiment pictures the scene as he saw it, and in the same connection relates a characteristic anecdote of President Lincoln.

During the forenoon a few of us had gathered in a barn, where we sat nursing our woes. "I want to go home" was pictured on every countenance.

Colonel Sherman—the future general-in-chief of the army—came in while we were talking, accompanied by two or three members of his staff, and in what appeared to us a gruff and unsympathetic tone, wanted to know what we were doing here.

"Keeping out of the rain," was the reply. "We have no tents, and few of us have blankets; and we have nothing to eat."

"Well, you had better go down in the woods and build bush huts. I want to put my horses in here."

We were in no condition to remonstrate, but we had our opinion of an officer who would turn men out of shelter for the purpose of giving it to dumb brutes.

Colonel Sherman's object was no doubt a good one. He knew that brooding over our troubles would do us more harm than good. But he might have advised us in a more kindly manner.

Next morning we moved to a better situation, and in the afternoon were honored by a visit from the President. As his carriage drove up we noticed Colonel Sherman occupying a seat by his side.

There was no formal reception given the President; he merely drove through the camp, and as he stopped before each regiment the men gathered round his carriage and listened to a few words of sympathy and encouragement.

"Now, boys, keep up a good heart, and all will yet be well," was his concluding sentence.

As he motioned the driver to go on, one of our men thought it a good opportunity to get even with Colonel Sherman.

"Mr. President," said he, "we don't think Colonel Sherman has treated us very well;" and he went on to relate the incident of the barn.

President Lincoln listened patiently till the story was ended, and then, half-turning toward Colonel Sherman, who had sat like a statue during the recital, he said:

"Well, boys, I have a great deal of respect for Colonel Sherman, and if he turned you out of the barn I have no doubt it was for some good reason. I presume he thought you would feel better if you went to work and tried to forget your troubles."

With a bow and a wave of his hand he told the driver to go on to the next camp.

It was wonderful how much good that thoughtful visit of the President worked in the minds of the men. In the grave, serious, yet kindly face of Lincoln we each saw a sympathizing friend, and our own burden became lighter as we reflected on the terrible load our chief magistrate was carrying on his own heart.—Y. C.

FREEDOM'S MEMORIAL.—The name of Mrs. Charlotte Scott, a colored woman, which at one time was doubtless upon the lips of every man and woman in the United States, is now read by the thousands who annually visit the Lincoln statue in Lincoln Park. Inscribed upon one of the bronze tablets resting upon the base is the following:

FREEDOM'S MEMORIAL.
In grateful memory of
ABRAHAM LINCOLN
This monument was erected
By the Western Sanitary Commission
Of St. Louis, Mo.,
With funds contributed solely by
Emancipated citizens of the United States,
Declared free by his proclamation
January 1, A. D. 1863.

The first contribution of five dollars was made by Charlotte Scott, a freed woman of Virginia, being her first earnings in freedom, and consecrated by her suggestion and request on the day she heard of President Lincoln's death to build a monument to his memory.

The woman whose name is thus honored died at her home, Reusens, a little railroad station about four miles from Lynchburg, Va., in the 109th year of her age. As stated in the inscription, she was the first to contribute to the erection of a monument to Abraham Lincoln, and at that time lived in Marietta, Ohio. It is said that when she heard of the assassination of the President, she exclaimed: "Lord, have mercy—and Massa Lincoln is killed! He ought to have a monument, and I am going to give the last cent I have for it;" and immediately contributed—perhaps through Professor J. M. Langston, who was living in Marietta at the time and knew her intimately—the sum of $5. The "St. Louis Commission," as it is known, was soon afterward formed, and taking this $5 as a nucleus, collected the fund for the erection of the famous emancipation group that now adorns Lincoln Park.—W. S.

LINCOLN.—His was a vigorous mind. He possessed that quality we call genius.

Franklin had it and lassoed the lightnings. Webster had it, and expounded the Constitution. Morse had it, and sent electricity with his messages. Edison has it, and machinery talks for him. Longfellow and Holmes and Whittier had it. Heaven robed them with a mantle of song. They made the land "a nest of singing birds." Clay and Phillips and Beecher had it, and their words "fell like the winter's snows." Lincoln had it, and his passion for thought and learning consumed him. He sought both truth and power to pen and voice truth. His genius and training sent him forth equipped as an eloquent orator, an able advocate, a skilful debater, an illustrious statesman. "He won that high honor all great leaders have coveted. He was the shepherd of his people. He fed the North with charity, the South with mercy, and the whole land with peace." —REV. CHARLES E. ALLISON. (P. M.)

LINCOLN AND THE BIBLE.—Except the instructions of his mother, the Bible more powerfully controlled the intellectual development of the son than all other causes combined. He memorized many of its chapters and had them perfectly at his command. Early in his professional life he learned that the most useful of all books to the public speaker was the Bible. After 1857 he seldom made a speech which did not contain quotations from the Bible.—L. E. CHITTENDEN.

LINCOLN'S FIGHT.—When Abraham Lincoln was twenty-five years old, his life appeared to have been a failure. He had retired from keeping a country store and from surveying land, loaded with debt. Nominated for the Legislature of Illinois, he had been badly defeated. But at the age of twenty-five he was again nominated, and this time he was elected. He was re-elected three times, and in 1840 devoted himself to the practise of law. L. E. Chittenden, in his PERSONAL REMINISCENCES, expresses the opinion that the turning-point in Lincoln's career was a fight, and that his success in life dates from his winning it.

In those primitive days Lincoln was looked upon as the champion of New Salem, being the tallest and strongest man in the township, its best wrestler and jumper. He was not a fighting man, but the bragging of his townsmen caused him to be challenged by the champion of Clary's Grove, the neighboring village—one Jack Armstrong, a good-natured giant.

The contest to determine who was the better man had only two rules. There was to be "no grasping or hitting below the belt," and he who should first "down" the other man was to be the victor.

The male population of the two villages gathered to see the two men strive for the honor of their respective localities.

Armstrong was supposed to be invincible as a wrestler. Grasping Lincoln's body, he tried to throw him. Lincoln kept himself upright, tho Armstrong moved him from right to left, forward and backward, and tried in vain to trip him.

Excited by his failure and by the shouts of his friends, Armstrong grasped Lincoln far below the hips—a foul hold. Lincoln protested against the unfairness, but his adversary, disregarding the remonstrance, tried to throw him.

Then Lincoln, whose arms were unusually long, shot out his right arm, caught Armstrong by the throat, forced him to release his hold, and holding him at arm's length, shook him as a terrier shakes a rat. The Clary's Grove boys, seeing that their champion was beaten, rushed to assist him. "No, no, boys!" shouted honest Jack, in spite of the grasp on his throat. "Abe Lincoln has whipped me fair and square! He's the best man. If he'll let me up, the man that wants to whip him has first got to whip Jack Armstrong."

This manly expression ended the contest. The two men became warm friends. Armstrong's house was one of Lincoln's homes. Armstrong's wife became his good angel; her children climbed up his knees and kissed the sadness away from his melancholy face. Armstrong helped to elect him to the Legislature, and years after Lincoln successfully defended one of the sons who had sat on his knee, when tried for murder.—Y. C.

WORK, One's.—I know there is a God and that He hates injustice and slavery. I see the storm coming and I know that His hand is in it. If He has a place and work for me—and I think He has—I believe I am ready. I am nothing, but truth is everything. I know I am right because I know that liberty is right, for Christ teaches it, and Christ is God.—ABRAHAM LINCOLN.

POETRY

Abraham Lincoln

BY JOEL BENTON

Some opulent force of genius, soul and race,
  Some deep life-current from far centuries
Flowed to his mind, and lighted his sad
    eyes,
And gave his name, among great names, high
    place.

But these are miracles we may not trace—
  Nor say why from a source and lineage
    mean
He rose to grandeur never dreamt or seen,
Or told on the long scroll of history's space.

The tragic fate of one broad hemisphere
  Fell on stern days to his supreme con-
    trol,

All that the world and liberty held dear
Pressed like a nightmare on his patient
 soul.
Martyr beloved, on whom, when life was
 done
Fame looked, and saw another Washington!
 I.

Lincoln

By John Vance Cheney

The hour was on us; where the man?
The fateful sands unfaltering ran,
And up the way of tears
He came into the years,

Our pastoral captain. Forth he came,
As one that answers to his name;
Nor dreamed how high his charge,
His work how fair and large,—

To set the stones back in the wall
Lest the divided house should fall,
And peace from men depart,
Hope and the childlike heart.

We looked on him; " 'Tis he," we said,
" Come crownless and unheralded,
The shepherd who will keep
The flocks, will fold the sheep."

Unknightly, yes; yet 'twas the mien
Presaging the immortal scene,
Some battle of His wars
Who sealeth up the stars.

Not he would take the past between
His hands, wipe valor's tablets clean,
Commanding greatness wait
Till he stand at the gate;

Not he would cramp to one small head
The awful laurels of the dead,
Time's mighty vintage cup,
And drink all honor up.

No flutter of the banners bold
Borne by the lusty sons of old,
The haughty conquerors
Set forward to their wars;

Not his their blare, their pageantries,
Their goal, their glory, was not his;
Humbly he came to keep
The flocks, to fold the sheep.

The need comes not without the man;
The prescient hours unceasing ran,
And up the way of tears
He came into the years,

Our pastoral captain, skilled to crook
The spear into the pruning hook,
The simple, kindly man,
Lincoln, American.
 In.

Abraham Lincoln

By Florence Evelyn Pratt

Lincoln, the woodsman, in the clearing stood,
Hemmed by the solemn forest stretching
 round;
Stalwart, ungainly, honest-eyed and rude,
The genius of that solitude profound.

He clove the way that future millions trod,
He passed, unmoved by worldly fear or
 pelf;
In all his lusty toil he found not God,
Tho in the wilderness he found himself.

Lincoln, the President, in bitter strife,
Best-loved, worst-hated of all living men,
Oft single-handed, for the nation's life
Fought on, nor rested ere he fought again.
With one unerring purpose armed, he clove
Through selfish sin; then overwhelmed
 with care,
His great heart sank beneath its load of love:
Crushed to his knees, he found his God in
 prayer.
 Y. C.

Lincoln

By Maurice Thompson

His was the tireless strength of native truth,
The might of rugged, untaught earnest-
 ness.
Deep-freezing poverty made brave his youth,
And toned his manhood with its winter
 stress.
 Y. C.

Abraham Lincoln

THE LIFE MASK

At the National Museum in Washington

By Stuart Sterne

Ah, countless wonders, brought from every
 zone,
Not all your wealth could turn the heart
 away
From that one semblance of our common
 clay,
The brow whereon the precious life, long
 flown,
Leaving a homely glory all its own,
Seems still to linger with a mournful play
Of light and shadow!—His, who held a
 sway
And power of magic to himself unknown.
Through what is granted but God's chosen
 few,
Earth's crownless, yet anointed kings,—a
 soul
Divinely simple and sublimely true
In that unconscious greatness that shall bless
This petty world while stars their courses
 roll,
Whose finest flower is *self-forgetfulness.*
 C. M.

The Cenotaph

By James T. Mackay

And so they buried Lincoln? Strange and
 vain!
Has any creature thought of Lincoln hid
In any vault, 'neath any coffin-lid,
In all the years since that wild spring of
 pain?
'Tis false,—he never in the grave hath lain.
You could not bury him altho you slid
Upon his clay the Cheops pyramid
Or heaped it with the Rocky Mountain
 chain.

They slew themselves; they but set Lincoln
free.
In all the earth his great heart beats as
strong,
Shall beat while pulses throb to chivalry
And burn with hate of tyranny and wrong.
Whoever will may find him, anywhere
Save in the tomb. Not there,—he is not
there.

C. M.

The Proclamation

By John G. Whittier

Saint Patrick. slave to Milcho of the herds
Of Ballymena, wakened with these words:
" Arise, and flee
Out from the land of bondage, and be free! "

Glad as a soul in pain, who hears from heaven
The angels singing of his sins forgiven,
And, wondering, sees
His prison opening to their golden keys,

He rose, a man who laid him down, a slave,
Shook from his locks the ashes of the grave,
And outward trod
Into the glorious liberty of God.

He cast the symbols of his shame away;
And, passing where the sleeping Milcho lay,
Tho back and limb
Smarted with wrong, he prayed, " God par-
don him! "

So went he forth; but in God's time he came
To light on Uilline's hills a holy flame;
And, dying, gave
The land a saint that lost him as a slave.

O dark, sad millions, patiently and dumb,
Waiting for God, your home, at last, has
come,
And freedom's song
Breaks the long silence of your night of
wrong.

Arise and flee! shake off the vile restraint
Of ages; but, like Ballymena's saint,
The oppressor spare,
Heap only on his head the coals of prayer.

Go forth, like him! like him return again,
To bless the land whereon in bitter pain
Ye toiled at first,
And heal with freedom what your slavery
cursed.

Abraham Lincoln

By James Russell Lowell

Such was he, our Martyr-Chief,
Whom late the nation he had led,
With ashes on her head,
Wept with the passion of an angry grief;
Forgive me, if from present things I turn
To speak, what in my heart will beat and
burn,
And hang my wreath on his world-honored
urn.
Nature, they say, doth dote,
And cannot make a man

Save on some worn-out plan,
Repeating us by rote:
For him her Old World molds aside she
threw,
And, choosing sweet clay from the breast
Of the unexhausted West.
With stuff untainted shaped a hero new,
Wise, steadfast in the strength of God, and
true:
How beautiful to see
Once more a shepherd of mankind indeed,
Who loved his charge, but never loved to
lead;
One whose meek flock the people joyed to be,
Not lured by any cheat of birth,
But by his clear-grained human worth,
And brave old wisdom of sincerity!
They knew that outward grace is dust;
They could not choose but trust
In that sure-footed mind's unfaltering skill,
And supple-tempered will
That bent like perfect steel to spring again
and thrust.
His was no lonely mountain-peak of mind,
Thrusting to thin air o'er our cloudy bars,
A sea-mark now, now lost in vapors blind;
Broad prairie rather, genial, level-lined,
Fruitful and friendly for all human kind,
Yet also nigh to heaven and loved of loftiest
stars.
Nothing of Europe here,
Or, then, of Europe fronting mornward still
Ere any names of Serf and Peer
Could Nature's equal scheme deface;
Here was a type of the true elder race,
And one of Plutarch's men talked with us
face to face.
I praise him not; it were too late;
And some innative weakness there must be
In him who condescends to victory
Such as the Present gives, and cannot wait,
Safe in himself as in a fate.
So always firmly he:
He knew to bide his time,
And can his fame abide,
Still patient in his simple faith sublime,
Till the wise years decide.
Great captains, with their guns and drums,
Disturb our judgment for the hour,
But at last silence comes;
These all are gone, and, standing like a
tower,
Our children shall behold his fame,
The kindly—earnest, brave, foreseeing
man,
Sagacious, patient, dreading praise, not
blame,
New birth of our new soil, the first Ameri-
can.

The Moral Warfare

By John G. Whittier

When Freedom, on her natal day,
Within her war-rocked cradle lay,
An iron race around her stood,
Baptized her infant brow in blood;
And, through the storm which round her
swept,
Their constant ward and watching kept.

Then, where our quiet herds repose,
The roar of baleful battle rose,
And brethren of a common tongue
To mortal strife as tigers sprung,
And every gift on Freedom's shrine
Was man for beast, and blood for wine!

Our fathers to their graves have gone;
Their strife is past—their triumph won;
But sterner trials wait the race
Which rises in their honored place,
A moral warfare with the crime
And folly of an evil time.

So let it be. In God's own might
We gird us for the coming fight,
And, strong in Him whose cause is ours
In conflict with unholy powers,
We grasp the weapons He has given,—
The Light, and Truth, and Love of Heaven.

O Why Should the Spirit of Mortal Be Proud

(President Lincoln's Favorite Poem.)

By William Knox

O why should the spirit of mortal be proud?
Like a fast-flitting meteor, a swift-flying cloud,
A flash of the lightning, a break of the wave,
Man passeth from life to his rest in the grave.

The leaves of the oak and the willow shall fade,
Be scatter'd around, and together be laid:
And the young and the old, and the low and the high,
Shall molder to dust and together shall lie.

The infant a mother attended and loved,
The mother that infant's affection who proved,
The husband that mother and infant who blessed—
Each, all, are away to their dwellings of rest.

The maid on whose cheek, on whose brow, in whose eye,
Shone beauty and pleasure—her triumphs are by:
And the memory of those who loved her and praised,
Are alike from the minds of the living erased.

The hand of the king that the scepter hath borne,
The brow of the priest that the miter hath worn,
The eye of the sage, and the heart of the brave,
Are hidden and lost in the depths of the grave.

The peasant whose lot was to sow and to reap,
The herdsman who climb'd with his goats up the steep,
The beggar who wandered in search of his bread,
Have faded away like the grass that we tread.

The saint who enjoyed the communion of heaven,
The sinner who dared to remain unforgiven,
The wise and the foolish, the guilty and just,
Have quietly mingled their bones in the dust.

So the multitude goes, like the flower and weed,
That wither away to let others succeed;
So the multitude comes, even those we behold,
To repeat every tale that has often been told.

For we are the same that our fathers have been,
We see the same sights our fathers have seen;
We drink the same stream, and view the same sun,
And run the same course that our fathers have run.

The thoughts we are thinking our fathers would think;
From the death we are shrinking from, they too would shrink;
To the life we are clinging to, they, too, would cling;
But it speeds from the earth, like a bird on the wing.

They loved, but that story we cannot unfold;
They scorn'd, but the heart of the haughty is cold;
They grieved, but no wail from their slumbers will come;
They joy'd, but the voice of their gladness is dumb.

They died—ay! they died; and we things that are now,
Who walk on the turf that lies over their brow,
Who make in their dwelling a transient abode,
Meet the changes they met on their pilgrimage road.

Yea! hope and despondency, pleasure and pain,
Are mingled together in sunshine and rain,
And the smile and the tear, the song and the dirge,
Still follow each other, like surge upon surge.

'Tis the wink of an eye, 'tis the draught of a breath,
From the blossom of health to the paleness of death,
From the gilded saloon to the bier and the shroud—
O why should the spirit of mortal be proud?

Funeral of Lincoln

By Richard Henry Stoddard

Peace! Let the long procession come,
For, hark!—the mournful, muffled drum,
The trumpet's wail afar;
And see! the awful car!

Peace! Let the sad procession go,
While cannon boom, and bells toll slow.
    And go thou sacred car,
    Bearing our wo afar!

Go, darkly borne, from State to State,
Whose loyal, sorrowing cities wait
    To honor all they can,
    The dust of that good man!

Go, grandly borne, with such a train
As greatest kings might die to gain:
    The just, the wise, the brave
    Attend thee to the grave!

And you, the soldiers of our wars,
Bronzed veterans, grim with noble scars,
    Salute him once again,
    Your late commander,—*slain*.

.   .   .   .

So sweetly, sadly, sternly goes
The fallen to his last repose.
    Beneath no mighty dome,
    But in his modest home,

The churchyard where his children rest,
The quiet spot that suits him best,
    There shall his grave be made,
    And there his bones be laid!

And there his countrymen shall come,
With memory proud, with pity dumb,
    And strangers, far and near,
    For many and many a year!

For many a year and many an age,
While History on her ample page
    The virtues shall enroll
    Of that paternal soul!

WASHINGTON'S BIRTHDAY

(February 22)

THE traveler in Germany, leaving Cologne on the Rhine steamer, sees a few ordinary houses near the pier. But as the city recedes in the distance, the Cathedral spires are seen, then its roof, and then its body, apparently growing larger with the increase of distance. All ordinary houses are soon unnoticed, and the Cathedral seems to stand alone in sublime harmony and vastness of proportions, silhouetted against the blue background of the sky. Similarly, in the eyes of his contemporaries, George Washington was a great man; but it has been only as he has receded down the stream of history that the greatness and symmetry of the proportions of his achievements and character have been realized: his physical strength and fearlessness, his mental penetration, prudence and power; his moral integrity, and religious devotion.

George Washington, Commander-in-Chief of the Continental forces in the war of the American Revolution, and the first President of the United States, was born February 22, 1732, in Westmoreland County, Virginia. He was the oldest son of Augustine Washington, by his second wife, Mary Ball. The story of his steady rise, by dint of hard work and faithfulness, to the position of "First in War, First in Peace, and First in the Hearts of his Countrymen," is a twice-told tale. Every year since the successful close of the Revolution, has seen a growth in the respect and affection in which Washington has been held, not only by his countrymen, but by the wise and good men of every land.

Washington's Birthday in the process of time has been made a legal holiday by the various states, until now, except in Mississippi, it is such in every state in the Union, and in the District of Columbia. It is an anniversary when, in our homes and public schools, and at banquets under the auspices of social and political societies, the people delight to recall the simple greatness of his character, and the far-reaching influence of his deeds; and to learn the lessons that he lived to teach his country and his race. He ever stands for mankind as the incarnation of the holy sentiment of patriotism. This is why at gatherings assembled to honor his memory on his birthday, among the words spoken in his praise, some of the most enthusiastic are those of the representatives of the governments of China and Japan, as well as of the European nations.

Rufus Choate, in his eloquent eulogy of Washington, well expresses the sentiments of all loyal Americans, as he exclaims:

"The birthday of the 'Father of his Country!' May it ever be freshly remembered by American hearts! May it ever reawaken in them a filial veneration for his memory; ever rekindle the fires of patriotic regard for the country which he loved so well, to which he gave his youthful vigor and his youthful energy, during the perilous period of the early Indian warfare; to which he devoted his life in the maturity of his powers, in the field; to which again he offered the counsels of his wisdom and his experience, as president of the convention that framed our Constitution; which he guided and directed while in the chair of state, and for which the last prayer of his earthly supplication was offered up, when it came the moment for him so well, and so grandly, and so calmly, to die. He was the first man of the time in which he grew. His memory is first and most sacred in our love, and ever hereafter, till the last drop of blood shall freeze in the last American heart, his name shall be a spell of power and of might."

WASHINGTON'S BIRTHDAY: EARLY CELEBRATIONS

By Frank W. Crane

The celebration of Washington's Birthday, like the Fourth of July, is an event which, it is a pleasure to say, has lost none of its patriotic sentiment with the advance of years and the rapid and wonderful growth of our country. As long as the name America shall stand for the principles put forth in the Declaration of Independence, the twenty-second day of February ought always to be remembered, and the indications are that its future will be happy in this respect.

It is rather a singular fact that in Washington's voluminous correspondence there is hardly any mention of his birthday and the many honors paid to him on its **The First** occurrence. About the only no-**Celebra-** tice is found in a letter written **tion** to Count de Rochambeau, in 1781. The occasion of Washington's reply is of particular interest in American history, as it marks the first notable celebration of his birthday, and that, too, by Frenchmen. The credit belongs wholly to Count de Rochambeau, and it was a graceful acknowledgment of the friendship between the two countries for the French officers to observe the birthday of the American army's commander with every evidence of patriotic ardor. The French count had been in America barely six months, and was stationed with his force at Newport, R. I. He had, however, met Washington, and a warm friendship had sprung up between them. At that time the old calendar system was still generally adhered to, and Washington's Birthday, therefore, was February 11; but about 1790 the 22d of the month was universally observed. Count de Rochambeau's letter to General Washington, acquainting him of the celebration at Newport, must have been a genuine and cheerful surprise. It was dated from Newport, February 12, 1781, and among other things the count says: "Yesterday (Sunday) was the anniversary of your Excellency's birthday. We have put off celebrating that holiday till to-day, by reason of the Lord's Day, and we will celebrate it with the sole regret that your Excellency be not a witness of the effusion and gladness of our hearts.'"

Washington received this letter in his winter quarters at New Windsor, N. Y., from which place he was closely watching the movements of the enemy, anxiously awaiting the time to strike a decisive blow, which opportunity came the following October at Yorktown. The reply of Washington, dated February 27, is interesting from this allusion to the celebration: "The flattering distinction paid to the anniversary of my birthday is an honor for which I dare not attempt to express my gratitude. I confide in your Excellency's sensibility to interpret my feelings for this and for the obliging manner in which you are pleased to announce it."

After the Revolution the people had more leisure to think of holiday celebrations, and the highest honors were paid alike to Washington's Birthday and the Fourth **Early** of July. In a certain measure **Celebra-** the natal day of Washington **tion in** took the place of the King's **New York** Birthday, which had always been observed with varying degrees of festivity. These royal holidays being relegated to abject insignificance with the retirement of the British from our shores, it was but natural that the birthday of America's great leader should occupy a position of national prominence. The citizens of New York, just as soon as they regained control of their town, did not lose any time in manifesting a proper regard both for the day and the man. The first popular celebration of the day in this city was in 1784, less than three months after the departure of the British. Altho a large part of the city was in ashes, as the result of the great fire in 1776, these scenes of desolation were for the time forgotten in the happier events of the day. Church bells rang out their joyful peals, flags and bunting decorated the houses, while from the old fort on the Battery, patriotic salutes were fired at frequent intervals. In the evening an entertainment was given on board an East Indian ship in the harbor "to a very brilliant and respectable company." A discharge of thirteen cannon was fired, and all the exercises of the day, we are informed, were characterized "with that hilarity and manly decorum ever attendant on the Sons of Freedom."

It is interesting to notice the important part played by the number thirteen in all of these early celebrations. The salutes were always thirteen in number, and **Birthday** thirteen toasts were invariably **Dinners** drunk at the banquets. Later, as new states were added, the number increased proportionately, but gradually this custom of having a toast for each state died out, possibly because the drinking capacities of the diners were unable to keep pace with the rapid increase of additions to the political body. The members of prominent clubs and societies could always look forward to at least two sumptuous dinners every year, on Washington's Birthday, and the Fourth of July. Toward the closing years of the last century, when party feeling ran high, these dinners partook of a strong political stamp, and, while patriotism and the welfare of the Union were toasted in highly colored phrases, the men and opinions of the opposite party were denounced in violent and sometimes vituperative language. No better idea of the social customs and amusements of our eighteenth-century ancestors can be obtained than by a study of their holiday celebrations, and the many incidents of Washington's Birthday recorded in the papers of the time are full of amusing as well as historical interest.

One of these celebrations of over a century ago that should appeal with peculiar interest to New Yorkers was that given by Tammany **Tammany** Hall in 1790. The Society of St. **Celebra-** Tammany had organized the pre- **tion** vious year, and its members nobly improved the opportunity of paying their respects to the man who, as first President of the United States, was then living in New York City. The loyal Tammanyites, moreover, adopted a resolution that Washington's Birthday should always be remembered by the society. The account of this interesting event as published in the New York *Gazette* a few days after the affair is as follows:

"At a meeting of the Society of St. Tammany. at their wigwam in this city, on Monday evening last, after finishing the ordinary business of the evening, it was unanimously resolved: That the 22d day of February be from this day and ever after commemorated by this society as the birthday of the Illustrious George Washington, President of the United States of America. The society then proceeded to the commemoration of the auspicious day which gave birth to the distinguished chief, and the following toasts were drunk in porter, the product of the United States. accompanied with universal acclamations of applause:

"'1. May the auspicious birthday of our great Grand Sachem, George Washington, ever be commemorated by all the real sons of St. Tammany.

"'2. The birthday of those chiefs who lighted the great Council Fire in 1775.

"'3. The glorious Fourth of July, 1776, the birth of American Independence.

"'4. The perpetual memory of those Sachems and warriors who have been called by the Kitchi Manitou to the Wigwam above since the Revolution.

"'5. The birth of the Sachems and warriors who have presided at the different Council Fires of the thirteen tribes since 1776.

"'6. Our Chief Sachem, who presides over the council fire of our tribe.

"'7. The 12th of May, which is the birthday of our titular saint and patron.

"'8. The birth of Columbus, our secondary patron.

"'9. The memory of the great Odagh 'Segte, first Great Sachem of the Oneida Nation, and all its successors.

"'10. The friends and patrons of virtue and freedom, from Tammany to Washington.

"'11. The birth of the present National Constitution, 17th of September, 1787.

"'12. The Sachem and warriors who composed that council.

"'13. May the guardian genius of freedom pronounce at the birth of all her sons—Where Liberty dwells, there is his country.'

"After mutual reciprocations of friendship on the joyous occasion, the society adjourned with their usual order and harmony."

The year 1790 seems to have called out a particularly large number of elaborate celebrations, undoubtedly due to the fact that **Celebra-** Washington had been inaugu- **tion in** rated President in April of the **1790** previous year, and his birthday of 1790 was the first time that it had been possible for the people to honor him as their chief executive. The newspapers, for weeks after the occurrence, were full of accounts detailing at considerable length the methods employed by residents of other localities in remembering the day, the toasts they drank, and the sentiments they expressed. The New York *Daily Advertiser* copies the following account from a Philadelphia paper, the day being celebrated there according to the old style:

"Thursday, the 11th, being the birthday of His Excellency, George Washington, President of the United States of America, the Volunteer Company of Artillery and two companies of infantry paraded and fired a *feu de joie*. Posterity will long remember the day which gave to America its political savior. They will not celebrate it as the birthday of a monarch whose annals can say no more than that he was born. that he succeeded his father, and, dying, left his kingdom to his son, or perhaps contain a long catalog of those black vices which disgrace human nature. No—they will, with grateful hearts, return thanks to the Divine Being who raised up a man to rend asunder the shackles of slavery endeavored to be imposed upon a free people, and, after delivering them from the tyrants of a powerful nation, to save them from destruction from a greater, which they little suspected—danger from themselves. They will rehearse his virtues to their attentive offspring, exhorting them to the practise of them, and endeavor to set them the glorious example."

The Philadelphians of 1792 were honored by the company of the President himself, at a ball given by the New Dancing Assembly, **Celebra-** in Chestnut Street. Mrs. Wash- **tion in** ington was also there, Vice- **1792** President John Adams, the French Minister. and many other prominent officials. The ladies added largely to the pleasure of the evening by the originality of their ideas in arranging various patriotic sentiments, wrought in gold letters, in their headdresses. After the dance there was a supper, at which the President and his wife remained, but when half the toasts had been given the former rose, drank the health of the company, and, with Mrs. Washington, retired. Some of the toasts on this occasion were:

" The land we live in. May temperance and industry continue to be characteristics of its inhabitants; patriotism form the cement of the Union, and its hospitality open an universal asylum for the oppressed and meritorious.

" The daughters of Columbia. May their virtues insure respect, their charms awaken love, and Hymen crown them with domestic bliss.

" Peace and friendship between the United States and all the powers on earth."

The observance of the day in New York City in 1798 is thus described in one of the newspapers: " Yesterday the great, the virtuous, the beloved Washington **New York** entered his sixty-fifth year. The **1798** citizens of New York observed it with a dignified temperance, a becoming zeal! At ten o'clock a salutatory discharge of cannon was fired, and in the evening upwards of four hundred ladies and gentlemen attended a grand ball and supper at the Tontine City Assembly rooms, Broadway. Washington's full-length portrait was exhibited at the same place in the evening, which showed to great advantage."

That the college students of the time were not unmindful of the return of patriotic anniversaries is shown from an interesting newspaper description telling **At** how the boys of Harvard College **Harvard** lege honored the day in 1798: **College** " The sons of our University never let slip any opportunity of doing honor to the character they so much admire. In one of the circles met to celebrate the birthday of the Hero of Mount Vernon, among other toasts was the following: George Washington. A man brave without temerity, laborious without ambition, generous without prodigality, noble without pride, and virtuous without secrecy. Three cheers in pantomime for fear of disturbing the peace."

This fear of disturbing the peace on special occasions is surely not shared by the Harvard students of the present time, or, indeed, by the students of any other college, judging from their proclivity to exuberant outbursts of feeling on almost every possible occasion.

The 22d day of February, 1800, was celebrated in a very different way from that of the previous years. The death of America's great patriot was still too fresh **February** in the minds of the people to **22, 1800** allow of extravagant demonstrations of festivity. The beloved Washington died December 14, 1799, in his beautiful home at Mount Vernon, and, in due sense of their great loss, the day of his birth

was in 1800 generally observed as a day of mourning. President Adams issued a proclamation in accordance with a resolution of Congress, " That it be recommended to the people of the United States to assemble on the 22d day of February next, in such numbers and manner as may be convenient, publicly to testify their grief for the death of General George Washington, by suitable eulogies, orations, and discourses, or by public prayers; and that the President be requested to issue a proclamation for the purpose of carrying the foregoing resolution into effect."

The New York State Society of the Cincinnati paid fitting honors to their departed chieftain by marching in solemn procession to the New Dutch Church. They were accompanied by the mayor, many other officials, and the clergy of the city. The Rev. Mr. Linn delivered a eulogy on General Washington, and so expressive was it of noble and patriotic sentiments that the New York *Gazette and General Advertiser* in printing a portion of the address also says: " This oration exceeds all praise. All were overwhelmed with grief, all in tears! The message from the tomb of Washington was original, bold, and striking. Ye Cincinnati, his companions in arms, and sharers in his glory, what scenes does this day bring to your remembrance! In imagination you suffer all the toils and fight the battles over again. Before you moves the majestic and graceful man; graceful when he steps, more graceful when he mounts the prancing steed. Serene at all times, most serene in misfortunes and dangers. The cares of America appear on his brow, and he wears her defense by his side. Ah, had he been captured by the enemy, your gleaming swords would have been drawn for his rescue. Or had he been exposed in the front of battle, you would have shielded him with your bodies. And had he fallen, a thousand victims had avenged his death. Against natural death you could interpose no shield. Seek not to restrain your tears. 'Tis soldierlike now to weep. True courage and sensibility are intimately connected. Your General, your Father, and your Friend, is no more. The last time he and his band of brothers were all together, you followed him with pensive countenances to the banks of the Hudson, and on his entering the barge he turned towards you, and by waving his hat bade you a silent adieu. He now bids you an adieu forever. Imitate him in his love of country, in all his public and private virtues, and then, like him, you will live beloved and die lamented."

Many other orations were given of a similar nature, not only in New York but in other cities throughout the country. The people on this occasion showed their patriotism, not by outward gaieties, but in attending the numerous church exercises and suitably remembering the death of their great leader— George Washington.—O.

HISTORICAL

MEMORABILIA OF WASHINGTON

COMPILED BY H. B. CARRINGTON, LL.D.

1732, February 22 (February 11, O. S.), Born.

1748. Surveyor of lands at sixteen years of age.

1751. Military inspector and major at nineteen years of age.

1752. Adjutant-general of Virginia.

1753. Commissioner to the French.

1754. Colonel, and commanding the Virginia militia.

1755. Aide-de-camp to Braddock in his campaign.

1755. Again commands the Virginia troops.

1758. Resigns his commission.

1759, January 6. Married.

1759. Elected member of Virginia House of Burgesses.

1765. Commissioner to settle military accounts.

1774. In First Continental Congress.

1775. In Second Continental Congress.

1775, June 15. Elected commander-in-chief.

1775, July 2. In command at Cambridge.

1776, March 17. Expels the British from Boston.

1776, August 27. Battle of Long Island.

1776, August 29. Masterly retreat to New York.

1776, September 15. Gallant, at Kipp's Bay.

1776, October 27. Battle of Harlem Heights.

1776, October 29. Battle near White Plains.

1776, November 15. Enters New Jersey.

1776, December 5. Occupies right bank of the Delaware.

1776, December 12. Clothed with "full power."

1776, December 14. Plans an offensive campaign.

1776, December 26. Battle of Trenton.

1777, January 3. Battle of Princeton.

1777, July. British driven from New Jersey during.

1777, July 13. Marches for Philadelphia.

1777, September 11. Battle of Brandywine.

1777, September 15. Offers battle at West Chester.

1777, October 4. Battle of Germantown.

1778. Winters at Valley Forge.

1778, June 28. Battle of Monmouth.

1778. British again retire from New Jersey.

1778.* Again at White Plains.

1779. At Middlebrook, New Jersey, and New Windsor.

1780. Winters at Morristown, New Jersey.

1781. Confers with Rochambeau as to plans.

1781. Threatens New York in June and July.

1781. Joins Lafayette before Yorktown.

1781, October 19. Surrender of Cornwallis.

1783, November 2. Farewell to the army.

1783, November 25. Occupies New York.

1783, December 4. Parts with his officers.

1783, December 23. Resigns his commission.

1787. Presides at Constitutional Convention.

1789, March 4. Elected President of the United States.

1789, April 30. Inaugurated at New York.

1793, March 4. Re-elected for four years.

1796, September 17. Farewell to the people.

1797, March 4. Retires to private life.

1798, July 3. Appointed commander-in-chief.

1799, December 14. Died at Mount Vernon.—Col. S.

A GLIMPSE OF WASHINGTON'S BIRTHPLACE

BY GRACE B. JOHNSON

Seldom visited and almost unknown is the Wakefield Farm in Virginia, the birthplace of our first president. Recent attempts have been made to popularize the place, but there is little to attract the ordinary traveler; and its distance from a city makes excursions impracticable.

Lying on the Potomac River about seventy miles below the city of Washington, one edge of the estate reaches down a steep, wooded bank to dip into the water, while, stretching back, it rambles on in grassy meadows and old stubble-fields to the corn-lands and orchards of the adjoining plantations. Skirting

*On the return of Washington to White Plains, after an absence of two years, he took occasion to contrast the two periods thus, writing: "The hand of Providence has been so conspicuous that he must be worse than an infidel that lacks faith, and more than wicked that has not gratitude enough to acknowledge his obligation."

the land at one side is Pope's Creek, formerly Bridges' Creek, which in Washington's time was used as the main approach to the estate. On this side there is an easy, undulating slope; but this entrance has been abandoned. Only at high tide can small boats enter the creek, and another way had to be adopted. An iron pier nearly two miles away has been built, and is the landing-place for large and small craft.

All is quiet here now. There is only the rustle of the leaves, the drowsy hum of insects, and the interrupted discourse of the preacher-bird in the clump of trees near which stood the first home of Washington, to break the stillness on a summer day. No one lives here. Indeed, no one has lived here since the fire which destroyed the house and negro cabins, in Washington's boyhood.

But here the baby life was spent, in the homestead founded by his great-grandfather, John Washington, who came from England in 1657.

Only a heap of broken bits grown over with catnip showed the place of the great brick chimney the first time I visited the farm; and the second time these, too, were gone. Now a plain, graceful shaft, bearing the simple inscription, "Washington's Birthplace," and below, "Erected by the United States, A. D. 1895" marks the place.

From the monument, through the trees, can be seen the gleaming river, rippling its way silently to the bay, and over all rests the same brooding sense of peace and quietness which one feels at Mt. Vernon or at Arlington, the city of our nation's dead.—C. E. W.

SOMETHING OF GEORGE WASHINGTON'S BOYHOOD

George Washington was born at a time when savagery had just departed from the country, leaving freshness and vigor behind. The Indian had scarcely left the woods, and the pirate the shore near his home. His grandfather had seen his neighbor lying tomahawked at his door-sill, and his father had helped to chase beyond the mountains the whooping savages that carried the scalps of his friends at their girdle. The year his brother was born, John Maynard's ship had sailed up the James River with the bloody head of Blackbeard hanging to the bowsprit.

He had only one uncle, a brother Lawrence and a cousin Augustine, all older than he, but the youngest of his older brothers was twelve years of age when George was born, while his cousin Augustine was only four years older, and his cousin Lawrence six years older than himself. When he was seven years old his sister Betty was a little lass of six. Two brothers, Samuel and John, were nearing their fourth and fifth birthdays. Charles, his baby brother, was still in his nurse's arms. Early the shadow of death crossed his boyish path, for his baby sister, Mildred, born soon after he was seven, died before he was nine.

The first playmate Washington had, out of his own immediate family, was another Lawrence Washington, a very distant cousin, who lived at Chotauk on the Potomac, and who, with his brother, Robert Washington, early won Washington's regard, and kept it through life. When Washington made his will he remembered them, writing, "to the acquaintances and friends of my juvenile years, Lawrence Washington and Robert Washington, I give my other two gold-headed canes having my arms engraved on them."

It was at Chotauk, with Lal and Bob Washington that George Washington first met with traffic between the old world and the new. There was no money used except tobacco notes, which passed among merchants in London and Amsterdam as cash. Foreign ships brought across the ocean goods that the Virginians needed, and the captains sold the goods for these tobacco notes. Much of Washington's time was spent with these boys, and when he grew old he recalled the young eyes of the Chotauk lads, as they, with him, had stood on the river-bank vainly trying to see clearly some object beyond vision, and in memory of the time he wrote in his will, " To each I leave one of my spy-glasses which constituted part of my equipage during the late war."

Of Washington's first school there is no record or tradition other than that gathered by Parson Weems. He says: " The first place of education to which George was ever sent was a little old field school kept by one of his father's tenants, named Hobby, an honest, poor old man, who acted in the double capacity of sexton and schoolmaster. Of his skill as a grave digger tradition is silent; but for a teacher of youth, his qualifications were certainly of the humbler sort, making what is generally called an A, B, C schoolmaster. While at school under Mr. Hobby he used to divide his playmates into parties and armies. One of them was called the French and the other American. A big boy named William Bustle commanded the former; George commanded the latter, and every day with cornstalks for muskets and calabashes (gourds) for drums, the two armies would turn out and march and fight." —E.

CHARACTERISTICS OF WASHINGTON

Washington began to be a soldier in his boyhood. During the British campaign against the West Indies, Lawrence Washington, George's half-brother, made **Von** the acquaintance of a Dutchman, **Braam** named Jacob von Braam, who **and Wash-** afterwards came to Virginia. **ington** These young men were great heroes to the ten-year-old George. Von Braam took the lad in hand and began his military education. He drilled him in the manual of arms and sword exercise, and taught him fortification and engineering. All the theory of war which Washington knew was gained from von Braam; the practise he was soon to gain in the field.

Many stories are told which show Washington's athletic skill. During a surveying expedition he first visited the Natural Bridge in Virginia. Standing almost di-**Washing-** rectly under it he tossed a stone **ton's Ath-** on top, a distance of nearly five **letic Skill** hundred feet. He scaled the rocks and carved his name far above all others. He was said to be the only man who could throw a stone across the Potomac River. Washington was never more at home than when in the saddle. "The general is a very excellent and bold horseman," wrote a contemporary, "leaping the highest fences and going extremely quick, without standing on his stirrups, bearing on his bridle or letting his horse run wild."

After his first battle Washington wrote to his brother, "I heard the bullets whistle about me, and, believe me, there is something charming in the sound." But years after, when he had learned all there was to know of the horrors of war, he said, sadly, "I said that when I was young."

Punctuality was one of Washington's strong points. When company was invited to dinner he made an allowance of only five minutes for variation in watches. **Punctu-** If the guests came late he would **ality** say: "We are too punctual for you. I have a cook who does not ask if the company has come, but if the hour has come."

In a letter to a friend he wrote: "I begin my diurnal course with the sun; if my hirelings are not in their places by that time I send them messages of sorrow for their indisposition."

A letter to his sister, Betty, shows his businesslike manner: "If your son Howell is with you and not usefully employed in your own affairs and should incline to spend a few months with me in my office as a writer (if he is fit for it), I will allow him at the rate of 300 a year, provided he is diligent in discharging the duties of it from breakfast till dinnertime. . . . I am particular in declaring beforehand what I require, so that there may be no disappointment or false expectations on either side."

Washington's relations with his stepchildren show a very pleasant side of his character. We find him ordering from London such articles as "10 shillings' worth of toys, **His Step-** 6 little books for children begin-**children** ning to read, 1 fashionable-dressed baby to cost 10 shillings, and a box of gingerbread toys and sugar images, or comfits." Later he sent for "1 very good spinet," for Patsey, as Martha Parke Custis was called.

His niece, Hariot, who lived in the Washington home from 1785 to 1796, was a great trial to him. "She has," he wrote, "no disposition to be careful of her clothes, which she dabs about in every hole and corner, and her best things always in use, so that she costs me enough."

One of the characteristics of a truly great man is his readiness to ask pardon. Once when Nelly Custis, Mrs. Washington's granddaughter, was severely reprimanded for walking alone by moonlight in the grounds of Mount Vernon, Washington tried to intercede for the girl.

"Perhaps she was not alone; I would say no more," he said.

"Sir," said Nelly Custis, "you have brought me up to speak the truth, and when I told grandmamma that I was alone, I hoped that you would believe me."

"My child," said Washington, bowing in his courtly fashion, "I beg your pardon."

Stuart, the portrait painter, once said to General Lee that Washington had a tremendous temper, but that he had it under **His** wonderful control. While di-**Temper** ning with the Washingtons, General Lee repeated the first part of Stuart's remark. Mrs. Washington flushed, and said that Mr. Stuart took a great deal upon himself. Then General Lee said that Mr. Stuart had added that the President had his temper under wonderful control. Washington seemed to be thinking for a moment, then he smiled and said, "Mr. Stuart is right."

The popular idea that Washington never laughed is well-nigh exploded. Nelly Custis said, "I have sometimes made him laugh most heartily from sympathy **His Smile** with my joyous and extravagant spirits."

When the news came from Doctor Franklin in France that help was promised from that country, General Washington broke into a laugh, waved his cocked hat, and said to his officers, "The day is ours!" Another story is to the effect that while present at the baptism of a child of a Mr. Wood he was so surprised to hear the name given as George Washington that he smiled. Senator Maclay tells of his smiling at a state dinner, and even toying with his fork. Various sources testify that a smile lent an unusual beauty to his face.

At one time, as Washington entered a shop in New York, a Scotch nursemaid followed him, carrying her infant charge. " Please, sir, here's a bairn was named after you."
" What is his name? " asked the President.
" Washington Irving, sir."
Washington put his hand upon the child's head and gave him his blessing, little thinking that " the bairn " would write, as a labor of love, a life of Washington.

While at his Newburgh headquarters the general was approached by Aaron Burr, who stealthily crept up as he was writing and looked over his shoulder. Altho **Other** Washington did not hear the **Character-** footfall, he saw the shadow in **istics** the mirror. He looked up, and said only, "*Mr. Burr!*" But the tone was enough to make Burr quail and beat a hasty retreat.

A man, who, well for himself, is nameless, made a wager with some friends that he could approach Washington familiarly. The President was walking up Chestnut Street, in Philadelphia, when the would-be wag, in full view of his companions, slapped him on the back and said, " Well, old fellow, how are you this morning? " Washington looked at him, and in a freezing tone asked, " Sir, what have I ever said or done which induces you to treat me in this manner? "

Altho Washington appreciated the good things of life, he would not tolerate extravagance. His steward at one time purchased the first shad of the season, knowing it to be a favorite dish of Washington's. " How much did you pay for it? " asked Washington.
" Three dollars."
" Take it away; I will not countenance such extravagance in my house."

After Washington's retirement from the presidency, Elkanah Watson was a guest at Mount Vernon. He had a serious cold, and after he retired he coughed se- **Thought-** verely. Suddenly the curtains **fulness** of his bed were drawn aside and there stood Washington with a huge bowl of steaming herb tea. " Drink this," he said, " it will be good for that cough."

Washington possessed in a peculiar degree the great gift of remembering faces. Once, while visiting in Newburyport, he saw at work in the grounds of his host an old servant whom he had not seen since the French and Indian war, thirty years before. He knew the man at once and stopped and spoke kindly to him.

Any collection of anecdotes about Washington is sure to refer to his extreme modesty. Upon one occasion, when the speaker of the Assembly returned thanks **Modesty** in glowing terms to Colonel Washington for his services, he rose to express his acknowledgments, but he was so embarrassed that he could not articulate a word. " Sit down, Mr. Washington," said the speaker, " your modesty equals your valor, and that surpasses the power of any language which I possess."

When Adams suggested that Congress should appoint a general, and hinted plainly at Washington, who happened to sit near the door, the latter rose, " and, with his usual modesty, darted into the library room."

Washington's favorite quotation was Addison's " 'Tis not in mortals to command success," but he frequently quoted Shakespeare.

His taste for literature is indicated by the list of books which he ordered for his library at the close of the war: LIFE OF CHARLES THE TWELFTH, LIFE OF LOUIS **Taste for** THE FIFTEENTH, LIFE AND REIGN **Literature** OF PETER THE GREAT, Robertson's HISTORY OF AMERICA, Voltaire's LETTERS, Vertol's REVOLUTION OF ROME, REVOLUTION OF PORTUGAL, Goldsmith's NATURAL HISTORY, CAMPAIGNS OF MARSHAL TURENNE, Chambaud's FRENCH AND ENGLISH DICTIONARY, Locke on the HUMAN UNDERSTANDING, and Robertson's CHARLES THE FIFTH. " Light reading," he wrote to his step-grandson, " (by this I mean books of little importance) may amuse for the moment, but leaves nothing behind."

Altho always very particular about his dress, Washington was no dandy, as some have supposed. " Do not," he wrote to his nephew, in 1783, " conceive that **His Dress** fine clothes make fine men any more than fine feathers make fine birds. A plain, genteel dress is more admired and obtains more credit than lace or embroidery in the eyes of the judicious and sensible."

Sullivan thus describes Washington at a levee: " He was dressed in black velvet; his hair full dress, powdered and gathered behind in a large silk bag, yellow gloves on his hands; holding a cocked hat, with a cockade in it, and the edges adorned with a black feather about an inch deep. He wore knee and shoe buckles, and a long sword. . . . The scabbard was of white polished leather."

After Cornwallis's surrender at Yorktown, Washington said to his army: " My brave fellows, let no sensation of satisfaction for the triumphs you have gained induce you to insult your fallen enemy. Let no shouting, no clamorous huzzaing increase their mortification. It is sufficient for us that we witness their humiliation. Posterity will huzza for us."

While there are many stories which show Washington's straightforwardness, here is one which shows much diplomacy. He was asked by Volney, a Frenchman and a revolutionist, for a letter of recommendation to the American people. This request put him in an awkward position, for there were good reasons why he could not give it, and other good reasons why he did not wish to refuse. Taking a sheet of paper, he wrote:

" C. Volney needs no recommendation from
" GEO. WASHINGTON."

F.

PROVIDENTIAL EVENTS IN THE LIFE OF WASHINGTON

By Irving Allen

At this season of the anniversary of Washington's birth it seems especially appropriate to recall certain singular circumstances in the life of the greatest of Americans—events remarkable in themselves in whatever light they may be viewed; whether, in accordance with the tenets of modern Spiritism and, to a certain extent, in harmony with the doctrines of Swedenborg and his followers, we accept them as proofs of the intervention in human affairs of departed spirits; or if, on the other hand, we adopt the simple teachings of the Sacred Scriptures, and acknowledge the truth of the doctrine of direct providential dealings with men and their affairs.

Authentic history records no less than six marvelous instances in which the life of Washington was saved under circumstances seemingly little less than miraculous. The first of these wonderful escapes from impending peril occurred during the period of Washington's sole recorded absence from the American continent—when he accompanied his brother Lawrence, then fatally ill with consumption, to the Barbadoes.

They sailed in September of 1751, George being then in the twentieth year of his age. Before the brothers had been a fortnight in the island the younger, the future hero of the Revolution, was attacked with smallpox in its "natural" and virulent form. This disease was not then the fangless monster with which we are familiar, but was terrific in its assaults and almost invariably fatal; yet Washington recovered in something less than three weeks, and retained through his life but slight marks of the malady.

One of General Washington's biographers well says, in reference to this incident, in the life of the first President, that "it may well be doubted whether in any of his battles he was in equal danger. If the disease entered an army, it was a foe more to be dreaded than embattled hosts. . . . But it belongs to that class of diseases of which, by a mysterious law of our nature, our frames are, generally speaking, susceptible but once. . . . Thus it came to pass that, in the morning of his days, Washington became (humanly speaking) safe from all future danger from this formidable disease."

The reader of American history will remember that the smallpox appeared among the British troops in Boston in the fall of 1775; that it ravaged our army in Canada in the following spring; that it prevailed the same year at Ticonderoga, and in 1777 at Morristown. Regarding this last occasion of its appearance, Washington said, in a letter to Governor Henry, of Virginia, where vaccination was not permitted:

"You will pardon my observations on smallpox, because I know it is more destructive to the army than the enemies' sword and because I shudder whenever I reflect upon the difficulties of keeping it out."

This was the tremendous peril from which Washington was comparatively safe after his twentieth year. "If," says a very eminent writer, "to refer this to an overruling Providence be a superstition, I desire to be accounted superstitious."

The next imminent danger to which Washington was exposed, and from which his escape was well-nigh miraculous, was on the occasion of his historic expedition to the headquarters of the French Governor at Venango, in 1753. The journey itself, in the winter season, of five or six hundred miles through an unsettled country, most of it constantly traveled by natives at enmity with the English, was one continued story of danger and escape. It was but two years after this trip of Washington's to Venango that English soldiers—surrendered prisoners of war—were tortured to death by the savage natives within sight of Fort Duquesne. On his return from the fulfilment of his mission, Washington traversed the forest with a single companion and an Indian guide. Just at nightfall, on one of the days of their perilous journey, their savage attendant suddenly turned, and, at a distance of but fifteen paces fired on Washington, happily without evil result.

After this alarming experience the two companions pursued their way alone, footsore and weary, through the woods, with the sure knowledge that the savages were on their trail. Reaching the Alleghany River on a night of December, they found it encumbered with drifting ice, and only to be crossed by means of a raft which, with only "one poor hatchet," cost them an entire day's labor to construct. When crossing the river, Washington, while using the setting pole, was thrown violently into the water at a depth of ten feet, and saved his life by grasping a log. They spent the night, in their frozen clothing, on a lit·le island on which, had they been forced to stay till sunrise, they would, beyond question, have fallen into the hands of the Indians; but the intense cold which froze the feet of Washington's companion, also sealed the river and enabled them to escape on the ice. A devout poet, writing of this journey of the youthful Washington, thus expresses his faith in the designs of Providence,

" To exercise him in the Wilderness;
There shall he first lay down the rudiments
Of his great warfare, ere I send him forth
To conquer."

The year following the mission to Venango (1754) Colonel Washington was sent in command of a small force in the same direction; **Another Mission** but by reason of the greatly superior strength of the enemy, the expedition resulted in a calamitous retreat. By a singular coincidence, the compulsory evacuation of the English stronghold—"Fort Necessity," as it was called—occurred on the *Fourth of July*, 1754—a date afterward made forever glorious, in great measure by the inestimable services of the young commander of this earlier and ill-fated military expedition. But such was the ability, energy, and power evinced by its youthful commander, that the disaster resulted in his own greatly enhanced reputation as a born leader of men.

In the following year (1755), a gigantic effort was made by England to recover lost ground, and to repair the military misadventures of 1754. The history of **Braddock and Wash- ington** Braddock's disastrous expedition is familiar to every schoolboy in the land. At this period, Colonel Washington had retired from the army in disgust at the unjust regulations which gave undue preference to officers holding commissions from the Crown over abler men—some of them their seniors of the same rank—in the service of the provinces. He was, however, at length induced —in great measure from motives of the purest patriotism, and partly, no doubt, from his strong leaning toward a military career— to accept a position on the staff of the commanding General, Braddock, a soldier of courage and large experience, but, as events afterward proved, a haughty, self-willed and passionate man.

During the passage of Braddock's forces through the Alleghany Mountains, Washington was attacked by so violent and alarming a sickness that its result was for a time extremely uncertain; on his partial recovery the General caused him to move with the reserve, which proceeded slowly with the heavy artillery and baggage. In this position Washington remained two weeks, returning to the General's headquarters on the eighth of July, the day preceding the fatal battle of the Monongahela.

On the morning of this day—forever and sadly memorable in American annals—Washington mounted his horse, weak and worn by sickness, but strong in hope and courage. These are his own words, uttered in other and better days:

"The most beautiful spectacle I had ever beheld was the display of the British troops on that eventful morning. . . . The sun gleamed from their burnished arms, the river flowed tranquilly on their right, and the deep forest overshadowed them with solemn grandeur on the left."

It is needless to repeat here the tale of that day of defat and slaughter. His- **Braddock's Defeat** torians have recorded its events, and poets have sung its story. Throughout the action Washington was in the thickest of the fight. "I

expected every moment to see him fall," wrote Dr. Craik, his physician and friend. It was during this disastrous battle that Washington escaped perhaps the most imminent peril of his life. In company with Dr. Craik, in the year 1770, he descended the Ohio River on a journey of observation to the Great Kanawha, and it was there that an incident occurred, which is thus described by Irving:

"Here Washington was visited by an old sachem, who approached him with great reverence and addressed him through Nicholson, the interpreter. He had come, he said, a great distance to see him. On further discourse, the sachem made known that he was one of the warriors in the service of the French, who lay in ambush on the banks of the Monongahela, and wrought such havoc to Braddock's army. He declared that he and his young men had singled out Washington, as he made himself conspicuous riding about the field of battle with the General's orders, and fired at him repeatedly, but without success; whence they concluded that he was under the protection of the Great Spirit, that he had a charmed life, and could not be slain in battle."

Washington himself wrote thus to his brother:

"By all the powerful dispensations of Providence, I have been protected beyond all human probability and expectation; for I had four bullets through my coat and two horses shot under me; yet I escaped unhurt, altho death was leveling my companions on every side."

His marvelous preservation was the subject of general remark; Mr. Davies—later, President of Princeton College, used these words in an address a few weeks after the Braddock defeat:

"That heroic youth, Colonel Washington, whom I cannot but hope Providence has hitherto preserved in so signal a manner for some important service to his country."

The next apparently providential intervention in the affairs of the hero of the Revolution is connected with very different scenes **Escape from a Marriage** from those of battle and carnage; it may, perhaps, be fairly described as a narrow escape from a marriage which, while it might have proved a happy alliance in so far as Washington himself was concerned, would almost certainly have resulted in the loss of his inestimable services to his country.

Washington's attachment to Mary Philipse is a fact beyond reasonable question; his offer of marriage to that young lady is somewhat traditional. It is certain, however, that during his necessary absence on military duty, Captain Morris, his associate aid-de-camp in the Monongahela engagement, became a successful suitor for the hand of Miss Philipse.

What is far less generally known is the fact that, had Washington been successful in his early matrimonial aspirations, he would certainly have remained a loyal adherent of the royal cause, and would thus have been lost to his native land. Evidences of the justice of this theory are by no means lacking. The relatives and friends of the lady were nearly all devoted to the cause of England; Washington was the associate of many of them; and Captain Morris, his successful rival, remained in the British service during his life. There can be, I think, little doubt that, in the event of his marriage with Miss Philipse, Washington, like Captain Morris, would have returned to England and been forever lost to America. Mrs. Morris survived her illustrious admirer twenty-five years, dying about the year 1825.

A striking historical fact—as strange as it is authentic—is the treatment of Washington by the English Government after the death of Braddock. Had General Brad-
Washing- dock survived his terrible mis-
ton Un- fortune the result might well
rewarded have been very different; for it is matter of history that the youthful officer had the undivided confidence of his commander. But by the British Ministry, and even by the King himself, the young hero of the fatal battle was treated with scarcely disguised contempt and neglect. In a letter to the British War Minister, Governor Dinwiddie speaks of Colonel Washington as a man of great merit and resolution, adding:
" I am confident that, if General Braddock had lived, he would have recommended him to the royal favor, which I beg your interest in recommending."
The sole results were a half-rebuke from the King, and a malicious fling from the lips of Horace Walpole. For more than three years Washington labored incessantly, by personal effort and by means of influential intercessors, to secure a royal commission. In view of what the world knows now of Washington's well-nigh matchless ability as a soldier, and remembering especially the reputation he had already acquired—amazing in so youthful an officer—his persistent neglect by the military authorities " at home," and particularly the stubborn and doltish determination on the part of the King to ignore the man and his almost unexampled services, suggests the theory that the heart of King George, of England, was as truly and providentially " hardened " as was that of his royal prototype Pharaoh, of ancient times. For, finding that all his efforts were ineffectual, and believing that the chief object of the war was attained by the capture of Fort Duquesne and the final defeat of the French on the Ohio, the young hero retired, after five years of arduous and ill-requited service, in the words of a great writer of our own land and time:
" The youthful idol of his countrymen, but without so much as a civil word from the fountain of honor. And so, when after seventeen years of private life he next appeared in arms, it was as the ' Commander-in-Chief of the Army of the United Colonies, and of all the forces now raised, or to be raised, by them.' "
The same writer elsewhere remarks:
" Such was the policy by which the Horse Guards occasionally saved a Major's commission for a fourth son of a Duke, by which the Crown lost a continent; and the people of the United States gained a place in the family of nations. The voice of history cries aloud to powerful Governments, in the administration of their colonies: ' Discite justitiam moniti.' "

The last of the six marvelous escapes of our hero from impending and fatal disaster occurred during the historic night march of
Washington and the American
A Furious Army on Princeton, where, on
Conflict the third of July, 1776, he compassed the entire destruction of one regiment of the enemy, and captured or forced to ignoble retreat two others. This battle was the subject of one of Colonel Trumbull's most famous paintings; and it was during this engagement—as Washington himself told the illustrious artist—that he was in greater peril than even at the time of Braddock's defeat.

In the height of the battle the two armies were for a brief season in furious conflict, and Washington between them within range of both fires. Washington Irving writes:
" His Aid, Colonel Fitzgerald, losing sight of him in the heat of the fight when enveloped in smoke and dust, dropped the bridle on the neck of his horse and drew his hat over his eyes, giving him up for lost. When he saw him, however, emerging from the cloud, waving his hat, and beheld the enemy giving way, he spurred up to his side: ' Thank God,' cried he, ' your Excellency is safe!' ' Away, my dear Colonel, and bring up the troops,' was Washington's reply; ' the day is our own.' "

Trumbull's immortal picture shows us the hero of that decisive battle standing on the memorable day of Princeton by the side of his white war-horse. Says an eloquent writer:
• " Well might he exult in the event of the day, for it was the last of a series of bold and skilful maneuvers and successful actions, by which, in three weeks, he had rescued Philadelphia, driven the enemy from the banks of the Delaware, recovered the State of New Jersey, and, at the close of a disastrous campaign, restored hope and confidence to the country."

Such are the six memorable events which it well becomes the American people to recall with devout gratitude and awe, realizing anew the Providence that watches alike over human beings and the affairs of nations, and recognizing the solemn truth that ever, as, signally, in those times that tried the souls of men,

" God fulfils Himself in many ways."

I.

WASHINGTON'S INAUGURATION

By Edward Everett Hale

On the fourth of March, 1789, Elbridge Gerry, who had been chosen to the Senate of the United States, wrote thus from New York to John Adams:

"My dear Friend:—I find, on inquiry, that you are elected Vice-President, having three or four times the number of votes of any other candidate. Maryland threw away their votes on Colonel Harrison, and South Carolina on Governor Rutledge, being, with some other states which were not unanimous for you, apprehensive that this was a necessary step to prevent your election to the chair. On this point they were mistaken, for the President, as I am informed from pretty good authority, has a unanimous vote. It is the universal wish of all that I have conferred with, and indeed their expectation, that both General Washington and yourself will accept; and should either refuse, it will have a very disagreeable effect. The members present met to-day in the City Hall, there being about eleven Senators and thirteen Representatives, and not constituting a quorum in either house, they adjourned till to-morrow.

"Mrs. Gerry and the ladies join me in sincere regards to yourself, your lady, Colonel and Mrs. Smith, and be assured I remain, etc.　　　　　　　E. Gerry."

So slow was the movement of news in those days, and so doubtful, even after the election, were all men as to its results, Adams would not start from Braintree, his home, till he knew he was elected, nor Washington from Mt. Vernon. Charles Thompson, the Secretary of the old Congress, arrived at Mt. Vernon on the fourteenth of April and communicated to Washington the news of his election. No quorum of the House of Representatives had been formed until the first of April, nor of the Senate until the sixth. These bodies then counted the electoral vote, with the result predicted by Gerry in his letter written two days before. Washington waited a day before starting to the seat of Government. On the sixteenth of April he started for New York. He writes in his diary:

"About ten o'clock I bade adieu to Mount Vernon, to private life and to domestic felicity; and with a mind oppressed with more anxious and painful sensations than I have words to express, set out for New York in company with Mr. Thompson and Colonel Humphries, with the best dispositions to render service to my country in obedience to its call, but with less hope of answering its expectations."

The journey began with a public dinner at Alexandria. Said the gentlemen of Alexandria in their address to him:

"Farewell! . . . Go! . . . and make a grateful people happy, a people who will be doubly grateful when they contemplate this recent sacrifice for their interest."

And Washington in his reply said:

"At my age, and in my circumstance, what prospects or advantages could I propose to myself, for embarking again on the tempestuous and uncertain ocean of public life?"

The journey went on with similar interruptions. The rule so often laid down by the Virginians afterward that that is the best government which governs least was certainly well kept until the thirteenth of April. To this hour the adventurous cyclist, stopping at some wayside inn to refresh himself, may find upon the wall the picture of the maidens and mothers of Trenton in New Jersey. Here Washington met a deputation sent to him by Congress. A triumphal arch had been erected, and a row of young girls dressed in white, a second row of young ladies, and a third of their mothers awaited him. As he passed, the girls scattered flowers, and sang the verses which Judge Marshall has preserved:

"Welcome, mighty chief, once more
Welcome to this grateful shore;
Now no mercenary foe
Aims again the fatal blow—
Aims at thee the fatal blow.

"Virgins fair and matrons grave,
These thy conquering arm did save.
Build for thee triumphal bowers,
Strew, ye fair, his way with flowers—
Strew your Hero's way with flowers."

His progress through New Jersey was everywhere accompanied by similar festivities—"festive illuminations, the ringing of bells, and the booming of cannon." He had written to Governor Clinton that he hoped he might enter New York without ceremony; but this was hardly to be expected. A committee of both Houses met him at Elizabethtown; he embarked in a splendid barge manned by thirteen pilots, masters of vessels, and commanded by Commodore Nicholson; other barges and boats fell in in the wake, and a nautical procession swept up the Bay of New York. On board two vessels were parties of ladies and gentlemen, who sang odes as Washington appeared. The ships in the harbor were dressed in colors and fired salutes as he passed. On landing at Murray's Wharf he was welcomed by Governor Clinton and General Knox. It is of the landing at this point that the anecdote is told that an officer asked Washington's orders, announcing himself as commanding his guard. Washington, with his ready presence of mind, begged him to follow any directions he had already received in the arrangements, but said that for the future the affection of his fellow-citizens was all the guard that he required.

At the end of the day, in his diary, the sad man says:

" The acclamations of the people filled my mind with sensations as painful as pleasing."

It was some days before the formal inauguration. The two houses of Congress did not know by what title they should address him, and a committee had been appointed to discuss this subject. It was finally agreed that the address should be simply, " To the President of the United States "—a form which has remained to the present day.

The inauguration finally took place on the thirtieth of April.

On the thirtieth, at last all things were ready, and the inauguration went forward. The place was at what they then called Federal Hall, in New York, and Chancellor Livingstone administered the oath:

" I do solemnly swear that I will faithfully administer and execute the office of President of the United States, and will, to the best of my ability, preserve, protect and defend the Constitution of the United States,"

A salute of thirteen guns followed, amid the cheers of thousands of people. Washington then delivered his inaugural speech to both houses in the Senate Chamber. After this ceremony he walked to St. Paul's Church, where the Bishop of New York read prayers. Maclay, who was a Senator in the first Congress, says:

" He was agitated and embarrassed more than he ever was by the leveled cannon or pointed musket. He trembled, and several times could scarce make out to read his speech, tho it must be supposed he had often read it before."

Fisher Ames says:

" He addressed the two houses in the Senate Chamber. It was a very touching scene, and quite of a solemn kind. His aspect, grave almost to sadness, his modesty, actually shaking, his voice deep, a little tremulous, and so low as to call for close attention."

John Adams had taken his place as President of the Senate two days before. As he did not always in after life speak any too cordially of Washington, it is worth noting that at this critical period he said that he congratulated the people of America on " the prospect of an executive authority in the hands of one whose portrait I shall not pretend to draw. . . . Were I blessed with powers to do justice to his character, it would be impossible to increase the confidence or affection of his country, or make the smallest addition to his glory. This can only be effected by a discharge of the present exalted trust on the same principles, with the same abilities and virtues which have uniformly appeared in all his former conduct, public or private. May I nevertheless be indulged to inquire, if we look over the catalog of the first magistrates of nations, whether they have been denominated presidents or consuls, kings or princes, where shall we find one whose commanding talents and virtues,

whose overruling good fortune, have so completely united all hearts and voices in his favor? who enjoyed the esteem and admiration of foreign nations and fellow-citizens with equal unanimity? Qualities so uncommon are no common blessings to the country that possesses them. By these great qualities and their benign effects has Providence marked out the head of this Nation, with a hand so distinctly visible as to have been seen by all men, and mistaken by none."

Whether, on this occasion, there were too much ceremony was a question discussed at the time, in connection with the heated discussion as to the etiquette of the new Administration. There is a correspondence between Washington and an old friend, Stuart, of Virginia, who had told him that the people of that State accused him of " regal manners."

Washington's reply, with his usual good sense, answers a good many questions which are bruited to-day. Dr. Albert Shaw, in the *Review of Reviews,* once brought some of these questions forward. " How far is it right for the people of a free state to kill their magistrates by inches? " This is the question reduced to its simplest terms. It was generally understood, when the late Governor Greenhalge died in Massachusetts, that his career, invaluable to the people of that State and of the country, had been cut off untimely by a certain etiquette, which obtains in Massachusetts, that whenever there is a public dinner the Governor of the State must be present and make a speech. With reference to a somewhat similar notion, Washington says:

" Before the present custom was established I was unable to attend to any business whatever. Gentlemen, consulting their own convenience rather than mine, were calling from the time I rose from breakfast, often before, until I sat down to dinner. To please everybody was impossible. I therefore adopted that line of conduct which combined public advantage with private convenience."

In another place he says:

" Had I not adopted the principle of returning no visits, I should have been unable to have attended to any sort of business."

It is interesting now to see that John Adams wore a sword on occasions of ceremony in New York, as late as this period. Does anybody know when the custom of wearing swords, as a part of a dress ceremony, was abandoned in America? It still obtains in Europe; and the two buttons on the back of every dress-coat are a survival of the custom. They were originally needed to support the belt which sustained the sword.

In contrast with the simple ceremonies at which a sensitive democracy took exception, we find now that a great nation consider no honors too profuse for the ceremonies which attend the inauguration of its chief magistrate.—I.

THE DEATH OF WASHINGTON

By J. E. RANKIN, LL.D.

According to all the laws of nature and of God no man was better entitled to a long life than Washington; and, altho he died years ago, the tragedy of his untimely and unnecessary death may even yet arouse pity and indignation.

The strength of his physique, his long life of physical activity and hardy endurance, his moderation in eating and drinking, and orderliness in all the other details of his life, gave him an unusually strong claim to fourscore years at least. But he died at sixty-eight.

Three days after a slight and not unusual exposure this great man faced death for the last time. On Thursday, December twelfth, 1799, which was rainy, sleety, and wintry, Washington, wrapped in his greatcoat, was out all day on his horse, overseeing his estate. When he came in he did not dress for dinner, but attended to some correspondence, which he would not send to the post-office on account of the inclement weather. It was noticed then that his neck was wet from the snow which still clung to his hair. The next day it snowed and Washington remained in the house until afternoon, when he went out to mark some trees that were to be cut down for the improvement of the lawn. When he came in he was hoarse, but he did not consider it serious.

He was subject to such attacks, he said. "It is only a cold; let it go as it came." Saturday morning, between two and three o'clock, he awoke Mrs. Washington, and complained of a severe chill. Even then he could speak only with great difficulty. But he would not allow her to call a servant, lest she should take cold. At dawn, at his own suggestion, he was bled by one of the overseers on the plantation, himself insisting on a free discharge from the incision made. Between nine and ten o'clock Doctor Craik, his old army surgeon, came and bled him again. About eleven another physician came, and he was bled a third time. At three o'clock other doctors came, and he was bled a fourth time. Thus between daybreak and three o'clock Saturday afternoon the distinguished patient was bled four times. At ten o'clock the end came

A little skilful nursing in the beginning, a little professional common sense, would have saved his life, speaking, of course, after the manner of men. "The life of the flesh is the blood thereof," and enough blood was taken from him to exhaust his vital force. so that it is no wonder he felt a presentiment of coming death. His chief concern seemed to be for those about him. He several times apologized for dying so hard, as tho he were there to die instead of to be ministered unto and saved. He suffered much, but he kept his composure to the end. and the great military leader, who had been in one hundred battles and never had been wounded, met his last foe without fear. Several times he said, "I am not afraid to die," and when at last he did yield his spirit to his Maker it was done willingly, "in the name of God."—N. Y. O.

AT THE ENGLISH TOMBS OF THE SIRES OF AM-ERICA'S FIRST PRESIDENT

By PROFESSOR WILBUR F. STEELE

In the still shades of Mount Vernon, as upon holy ground, does a nation pay uncovered reverence at the tomb of our American St. George. Similarly in the home of the British St. George with related interest does an exiled son of the Revolution turn aside to the English tombs of Washington's sires.

During most of two centuries were expulsion and repulsion the dominant forces between the lands. Apart with might and moment did the continents gravitate. The myriad ties of blood and friendship were stretched and strained, until at last they snapped asunder in the sea. Largely did family communion and knowledge of relationship cease.

But during the past generation or two the force of attraction has asserted itself, with the result that the ties once broken and lost are now being found and knitted together again. In churchyards, enriched by the dust of pre-Puritan parents, through the vista there wells the abba cry, "All hail! thou English sire!" Nor is it fancy alone that makes audible the response, "All hail! thou American son!"

In revealing the continuity of our individual life, at first English and later American, none has been more helpful than Henry F. Waters, our eminent genealogist, for years delving in English archives. But our greatest debt is due to his moral proof some ten years ago of the exact English ancestry and antecedents of our great general and first President.

Suspected, alleged, debated, denied, had it been for nearly a century. But in the presence of the link discovered by him all cavil has ceased. Utilizing his identifications, these scenes were visited, and other material brought into requisition.

The places fully identified are Sulgrave and Great Brington, in Northamptonshire. The better to follow the account, the line is here tabulated. As customary, the American emigrant is indicated by the figure (1) following. From him the line is reckoned both ways, his ancestors being starred:

JOHN (6*)	WASHINGTON, of County Lancaster.
LAWRENCE (5*)	WASHINGTON, Mayor of Northampton and Grantee af Sulgrave in the thirtieth year of Henry VIII. Died Feb. 19, in the twenty-sixth year of Elizabeth. Buried at Sulgrave.
ROBERT (4*)	WASHINGTON, of Sulgrave, which property "he and his son Lawrence sold" early in the reign of James.
LAWRENCE (3*)	WASHINGTON, of Sulgrave and Brington, whither he removed. Buried at Great Brington, Dec. 15, 1616.
REV. LAWRENCE (2*)	WASHINGTON, M. A., Fellow of Brasenose College, Oxford; Rector of Purleigh. Essex, 1633-43. Died before 1655.
JOHN (1)	WASHINGTON; not far from 1657 emigrated to Virginia with his younger brother, Lawrence.
LAWRENCE (2)	WASHINGTON, died 1697.
AUGUSTINE (3)	WASHINGTON, died April 12 1743, aged 49.
GEORGE (4)	WASHINGTON, born Feb. 11, 1732; died Dec. 14, 1799.

At the dissolution of the Roman Catholic monasteries and the confiscation of their possessions in 1539, Lawrence (5*) Washington received from Henry VIII. a large tract of land formerly owned by the priory of Canons Ashby. He had been the successful mayor of Northampton, and now arose to be one of the aristocracy.

His domain embraced several square miles, including the village of Sulgrave. which is eight miles northeast of Banbury, famed afar in nursery rhyme for its cross. In it is the ancient church of St. James. It is the duplicate of any of the hundreds, if not thousands, of little stone churches with which the Normans dotted the land of their conquest. About it "the rude forefathers of the hamlet sleep;" within it, the aristocracy of the holding.

At the east end of the aisle is a brass inscription to "Lawrence Washington, ob. 1584." with effigies of himself and wife and eleven children.

Extremely interesting to note in these rural places of worship are the benefactions of which the Church is the almoner. They are usually tabulated on the wall. Those distributable annually by the Sulgrave Church are as follows:

£9, for education, which is given away in prizes to the children.

£10, to be used for apprenticing youth of the parish.

£14, for beef to be given on St. Valentine's Day.

£11, 16s., for bread to be given in threepence loaves, one third to the poorest of the poor, and the remainder to the poor attending church on Sundays.

£3, for coats and caps.

£5, 4s., in money on St. Thomas's Day.

£1, 1s., for a sermon, and £1, 15s., for the trustees on St. Valentine's Day.

Upon the death of Lawrence (5*) this holding fell into the hands of his son, Robert (4*) Washington, concerning whom it is euphemistically recorded that he and his son, Lawrence (3*), "sold" it. In plainer speech, it was taken from them and given to such as might the more faithfully or profitably serve the crown.

To at least the impoverished Lawrence (3*) did the distantly related Earl of Spencer provide shelter by placing at his disposal a small establishment in Little Brington, some fifteen miles eastward.

In the adjoining Great Brington Church lies buried this Lawrence (3*), with a stone and inscription, a moment's glance at which shows the identity of his arms with those of George Washington, as displayed on his book plate. No doubt exists that they are immortalized the world over in the design of the ever-growing "old glory." It crimsons the cheek, however, and maddens the soul to behold the barbaric vandalism of idiotic Americans who have consigned their names to lasting infamy by cutting them and rude representations of our flag into the soft stones all over the sacred edifice.

Son of this Lawrence (3*) was the Rev. Lawrence (2*) Washington, M.A., sometime Fellow of Brasenose College. As later rector of Purleigh from 1633, he was ejected from his living by the Parliamentarians in 1643 as an incorrigible Royalist. Of his death and entombment the records are unknown.

Some time after his death, or about 1657, his humiliated and hopeless but genteel sons, John (1) and Lawrence, sought to repair their fortunes across the sea. For reasons the most obvious they emigrated, not to Puritan New England, but to Cavalier Virginia. Hence a perfect duplicate of the life, society, and estate of an English lord or gentleman or esquire is that which reappeared upon the bank of the Potomac. The broad miles of estate, the subject tenantry, the gentlemanly leisure and library, the coach and four to the little Episcopal Church in Alexandria, in fact, many of the deeper trends in our national life, are all explained by the knowledge of this ancestry, surroundings, history, and ideals.

And not least suggestive is the remarkable union at Cambridge of Washington as commander-in-chief and the New England troops in the Revolution—the sons of both self-expatriated Royalist and Puritan.—C. W.

ENTOMBMENT OF GEORGE WASHINGTON

By Will Carleton

One hundred years ago this month (Dec., 1899), the man whom American history loves to honor most of all, died and was buried.

A multitude of persons assembled, from many miles around, at Mount Vernon, the choice abode and last residence of the illustrious chief. There were the groves—the spacious avenues, the beautiful scenes, the noble mansion—but the august inhabitant was now no more.

In the long and lofty portico, where oft the hero walked in all his glory, now lay the shrouded corpse. The countenance was still composed and serene. There those who paid the last sad honors to the benefactor of his country, took an impressive—a farewell—view.

On the ornament at the head of the coffin, was inscribed " Surge ad Judicium "—about the middle of the coffin, " Gloria Deo "—and on the silver plate,

GENERAL GEORGE WASHINGTON,

Departed this life on the 14th December, 1799, æt. 68.

Between three and four o'clock, the sound of artillery from a vessel in the river, firing minute guns, awoke afresh the solemn sorrow—the corpse was removed—a band of music with mournful melody was heard, and the procession was formed and moved on in the following order:

Cavalry; infantry; guard, with arms reversed; music; clergy; the General's horse, with his saddle, holsters, and pistols; corpse; mourners; Masonic brethren; citizens.

When the procession had arrived at the bottom of the elevated lawn, on the bank of the Potomac, where the family vault was placed, the cavalry halted, the infantry marched toward the mount and formed their lines—the clergy, the Masonic brothers, and the citizens descended to the vault, and the funeral service of the Episcopal Church was performed. The firing was repeated from the vessel in the river, and the sounds echoed from the woods and hills around.

Three general discharges by the infantry, the cavalry and eleven pieces of artillery, which lined the banks of the Potomac back of the vault, paid the last tribute to the entombed Commander-in-Chief of the armies of United States and to the departed hero.

The sun was setting, when the ceremonies concluded; but the dead man's fame had not, nor has it yet, reached its meridian.—E. W.

ADDRESSES

AT THE DEDICATION OF WASHINGTON MONU-MENT

By John W. Daniel

[Delivered in the Hall of the House of Representatives, February 21, 1885]

Mr. President of the United States, Senators, Representatives, Judges, Mr. Chairman, and My Countrymen:—

Alone in its grandeur stands forth the character of Washington in history; alone like some peak that has no fellow in the mountain range of greatness.

" Washington," says Guizot, " Washington did the two greatest things which in politics it is permitted to man to attempt. He maintained, by peace, the independence of his country, which he had conquered by war. He founded a free government in the name of the principles of order and by re-establishing their sway." Washington did, indeed, do these things. But he did more. Out of disconnected fragments, he molded a whole, and made it a country. He achieved his country's independence by the sword. He maintained that independence by peace as by war. He finally established both his country and its freedom in an enduring frame of constitutional government, fashioned to make liberty and union one and inseparable. These four things together constitute the unexampled achievement of Washington.

The world has ratified the profound remark of Fisher Ames, that " he changed mankind's ideas of political greatness." It has approved the opinion of Edward Everett, that he was " the greatest of good men, and the best of great men." It has felt for him with Erskine, " an awful reverence." It has attested the declaration of Brougham that " he was the greatest man of his own or of any age." . . .

Conquerors who have stretched your scepters over boundless territories; founders of empires who have held your dominions in the reign of law; reformers who have cried aloud in the wilderness of oppression; teachers who have striven to cast down false doctrine, heresy, and schism; statesmen whose brains have throbbed with mighty plans for the amelioration of human society; scar-crowned vikings of the sea, illustrious heroes of the land, who have borne the standards of siege and battle, come forth in bright array from your glorious fanes, and would ye be measured by the measure of his stature? Behold you not in him a more illustrious and more venerable presence? Statesman, soldier, patriot, sage, reformer of creeds, teacher of truth and justice, achiever and preserver of liberty, the first of men, founder and savior of his country, father of his people—this is he, solitary and unapproachable in his grandeur!

Oh, felicitous Providence that gave to America our Washington!

High soars into the sky to-day, higher than the pyramid or the dome of St. Paul's or St. Peter's—the loftiest and most imposing structure that man has ever reared—high soars into the sky to where—" Earth highest yearns to meet a star " the monument which " We the people of the United States " have uplifted to his memory. It is a fitting monument, more fitting than any statue. For his image could only display him in some one phase of his varied character. So art has fitly typified his exalted life in yon plain, lofty shaft. Such is his greatness, that only by a symbol could it be represented. As Justice must be blind in order to be whole in contemplation, so History must be silent that by this mighty sign she may disclose the amplitude of her story.

. . . .

No sum could now be made of Washington's character that did not exhaust language of its tributes and repeat virtue by all her names. No sum could be made of his achievements that did not unfold the history of his country and its institutions—the history of his age and its progress—the history of man and his destiny to be free. But, whether character or achievement be regarded, the riches before us only expose the poverty of praise. So clear was he in his great office that no ideal of the leader or ruler can be forced that does not shrink by the side of the reality. And so has he impressed himself upon the minds of men, that no man can justly aspire to be the chief of a great, free people, who does not adopt his principles and emulate his example. We look with amazement on such eccentric characters as Alexander, Cæsar, Cromwell, Frederick, and Napoleon, but when Washington's face rises before us, instinctively mankind exclaims: " This is the man for nations to trust and reverence, and for rulers to follow."

Drawing his sword from patriotic impulse, without ambition and without malice, he wielded it without vindictiveness, and sheathed it without reproach. All that humanity could conceive he did to suppress the cruelties of war and soothe its sorrows. He never struck a coward's blow. To him age, infancy, and helplessness were ever sacred. He tolerated no extremity unless to curb the excesses of his enemy, and he never poisoned the sting of defeat by the exultation of the conqueror.

Peace he welcomed as a heaven-sent herald of friendship; and no country has given him greater honor than that which he defeated; for England has been glad to claim him as the scion of her blood, and proud, like our sister American States, to divide with Virginia the honor of producing him.

Fascinated by the perfection of the man, we are loathe to break the mirror of admiration into the fragments of analysis. But, lo! as we attempt it, every fragment becomes the miniature of such sublimity and beauty that the destructive hand can only multiply the forms of immortality.

Grand and manifold as were its phases, there is yet no difficulty in understanding the character of Washington. He was no Veiled Prophet. He never acted a part. Simple, natural, and unaffected, his life lies before us—a fair and open manuscript. He disdained the arts which wrap power in mystery in order to magnify it. He practised the profound diplomacy of truthful speech—the consummate tact of direct attention. Looking over to the All-Wise Disposer of events, he relied on that Providence which helps men by giving them high hearts and hopes to help themselves with the means which their Creator has put at their service. There was no infirmity in his conduct over which charity must fling its veil; no taint of selfishness from which purity averts her gaze; no dark recess of intrigue that must be lit up with colored panegyric; no subterranean passage to be trod in trembling, lest there be stirred the ghost of a buried crime.

A true son of nature was George Washington—of nature in her brightest intelligence and noblest mold; and the difficulty, if such there be, in comprehending him, is only that of reviewing from a single standpoint the vast procession of those civil and military achievements which filled nearly half a century of his life, and in realizing the magnitude of those qualities which were requisite to their performance—the difficulty of fashioning in our minds a pedestal broad enough to bear the towering figure, whose greatness is diminished by nothing but the perfection of its proportions. If his exterior —in calm, grave, and resolute repose—ever impressed the casual observer as austere and cold, it was only because he did not reflect that no great heart like his could have lived unbroken unless bound by iron nerves in an iron frame. The Commander of Armies, the Chief of a People, the Hope of Nations could not wear his heart upon his sleeve; and yet his sternest will could not conceal its high and warm pulsations. Under the enemy's guns at Boston he did not forget to instruct his agent to administer generously of charity to his needy neighbors at home. The sufferings of women and children, thrown adrift by war, and of his bleeding comrades, pierced his soul. And the moist eye and trembling voice with which he bade farewell to his veterans bespoke the underlying tenderness of his nature, even as the storm-wind makes music in its undertones.

Disinterested patriot, he would receive no pay for his military services. Refusing gifts, he was glad to guide the benefaction of a grateful State to educate the children of his fallen braves in the institution at Lexington which yet bears his name. Without any of the blemishes that mark the tyrant, he appealed so loftily to the virtuous elements in man, that he almost created the qualities of which his country needed the exercise; and yet he was so magnanimous and forbearing to the weaknesses of others, that he often obliterated the vices of which he feared the consequences. But his virtue was more than this. It was of that daring, intrepid kind that, seizing principle with a giant's grasp, assumes responsibility at any hazard, suffers sacrifice without pretense of martyrdom, bears calumny without reply, imposes superior will and understanding on all around it, capitulates to no unworthy triumph, but must carry all things at the point of clear and blameless conscience. Scorning all manner of meanness and cowardice, his bursts of wrath at their exhibition heighten our admiration for the noble passions which were kindled by the aspirations and exigencies of virtue.

Invested with the powers of a Dictator, the country bestowing them felt no distrust of his integrity; he, receiving them, gave assurance that, as the sword was the last support of Liberty, so it should be the first thing laid aside when Liberty was won. And keeping the faith in all things, he left mankind bewildered with the splendid problem whether to admire him most for what he was or what he would not be. Over and above all his virtues was the matchless manhood of personal honor to which Confidence gave in safety the key of every treasure— on which Temptation dared not smile, on which Suspicion never cast a frown. And why prolong the catalog? "If you are presented with medals of Cæsar, of Trajan, or Alexander, on examining their features you are still led to ask what was their stature and the forms of their persons; but if you discover in a heap of ruin the head or the limb of an antique Apollo, be not curious about the other parts, but rest assured that they were all conformable to those of a god."

. . . .

"Rome to America" is the eloquent inscription on one stone of your colossal shaft —taken from the ancient Temple of Peace that once stood hard by the Palace of the Cæsars. Uprisen from the sea of Revolution, fabricated from the ruins of battered Bastiles, and dismantled palaces of unrighteous, unhallowed power, stood forth now the Republic of republics, the Nation of nations, the Constitution of constitutions, to which all lands and times and tongues had contributed of their wisdom, and the priestess of Liberty was in her holy temple.

When Marathon had been fought and Greece kept free, each of the victorious generals voted himself to be first in honor, but all agreed that Miltiades was second. When the most memorable struggle for the rights of human nature of which time holds record was thus happily concluded in the muniment of their preservation, whoever else was second, unanimous acclaim declared that Washington was first. Nor in that struggle alone does he stand foremost. In the name of the people of the United States, their President, their Senators, their Representatives, and their Judges do crown to-day with the grandest crown that veneration has ever lifted to the brow of Glory, him whom Virginia gave to America, whom America has given to the world and to the ages, and whom mankind with universal suffrage has proclaimed the foremost of the founders of empire in the first degree of greatness; whom Liberty herself has anointed as the first citizen in the great Republic of Humanity.

Encompassed by the inviolate seas, stands to-day the American Republic which he founded—a freer, Greater Britain—uplifted above the powers and principalities of the earth, even as his monument is uplifted over roof and dome and spire of the multitudinous city.

Long live the Republic of Washington! Respected by mankind, beloved of all its sons, long may it be the asylum of the poor and oppressed of all lands and religions— long may it be the citadel of that Liberty which writes beneath the eagle's folded wings, "We will sell to no man, we will deny to no man, right and justice."

Long live the United States of America! Filled with the free, magnanimous spirit, crowned by the wisdom, blessed by the moderation, hovered over by the guardian angel of Washington's example, may they be ever worthy in all things to be defended by the blood of the brave, who know the rights of man and shrink not from their assertion; may they be each a column, and all together, under the Constitution, a perpetual Temple of Peace, unshadowed by a Cæsar's palace, at whose altar may freely commune all who seek the union of liberty and brotherhood.

Long live our country! Oh, long through the undying ages may it stand far removed in fact as in space from the Old World's feuds and follies; alone in its grandeur and its glory, itself the immortal monument of him whom Providence commissioned to teach man the power of truth and to prove to the nations that their redeemer liveth.— W. B. D.

WASHINGTON'S RELIGIOUS CHARACTER

By William McKinley

[In an Address, February 22, 1898.]

Tho Washington's exalted character and the most striking acts of his brilliant record are too familiar to be recounted here, yet often as the story is retold, it engages our love and admiration and interest. We love to record his noble unselfishness, his heroic purposes, the power of his magnificent personality, his glorious achievements for mankind, and his stalwart and unflinching devotion to independence, liberty, and union. These cannot be too often told or be too familiarly known.

A slaveholder himself, he yet hated slavery, and provided in his will for the emancipation of his slaves. Not a college graduate, he was always enthusiastically the friend of liberal education. . . .

And how reverent always was this great man, how prompt and generous his recognition of the guiding hand of Divine Providence in establishing and controlling the destinies of the colonies and the Republic. . . .

Washington states the reasons of his belief in language so exalted that it should be graven deep in the mind of every patriot:

"No people can be bound to acknowledge and adore the invisible hand which conducts the affairs of man more than the people of the United States. Every step by which they have advanced to the character of an independent nation seems to have been distinguished by some token of providential agency; and in the important revolution just accomplished in the system of their united government, the tranquil deliberations and

voluntary consents of so many distinguished communities from which the events resulted cannot be compared with the means by which most governments have been established, without some return of pious gratitude, along with an humble anticipation of the future blessings which the same seems to presage. The reflections arising out of the present crisis have forced themselves strongly upon my mind. You will join with me, I trust, in thinking that there are none under the influence of which the proceedings of a new and free government are more auspiciously commenced."

In his Farewell Address, Washington contends in part: (1) For the promotion of institutions of learning; (2) for cherishing the public credit; (3) for the observance of good faith and justice toward all nations. . . .

At no point in his administration does Washington appear in grander proportions than when he enunciates his ideas in regard to the foreign policy of the government:

"Observe good faith and justice toward all nations; cultivate peace and harmony with all; religion and morality enjoin this conduct. Can it be that good policy does not equally enjoin it? It will be worthy of a free, enlightened, and, at no distant period, a great nation, to give to mankind the magnanimous and too novel example of a people always guided by an exalted justice and benevolence."

THE MAJESTIC EMINENCE OF WASHINGTON

By Chauncey M. Depew

[In an Address, February 22, 1888.]

"Time's noblest offspring is the last."

As the human race has moved along down the centuries, the vigorous and ambitious, the dissenters from blind obedience and the original thinkers, the colonists and state builders, have broken camp with the morning, and followed the sun till the close of day. They have left behind narrow and degrading laws, traditions, and castes. Their triumphant success is putting behind every bayonet carried at the order of Kaiser or Czar; men who, in doing their own thinking, will one day decide for themselves the problems of peace and war.

The scenes of the fifth act of the grand drama are changing, but all attention re-

mains riveted upon one majestic figure. He stands the noblest leader who ever was entrusted with his country's life. His patience under provocation, his calmness in danger, and lofty courage when all others despaired, his prudent delays when delay was best, and his quick and resistless blows when action was possible, his magnanimity to defamers and generosity to his foes, his ambition for his country and unselfishness for himself, his sole desire of freedom and independence for America, and his only wish to return after victory to private life, have all combined to make him, by the unanimous judgment of the world, the foremost figure of history.

ESTIMATES OF WASHINGTON

More than all, and above all, Washington was master of himself. If there be one quality more than another in his character which may exercise a useful control over the men of the present hour, it is the total disregard of self when in the most elevated positions for influence and example.—CHARLES FRANCIS ADAMS.

Let him who looks for a monument to Washington look around the United States. Your freedom, your independence, your national power, your prosperity, and your prodigious growth are a monument to him.—KOSSUTH.

To add brightness to the sun or glory to the name of Washington is alike impossible. Let none attempt it. In solemn awe pronounce the name, and in its naked, deathless splendor leave it shining on.—ABRAHAM LINCOLN.

More than any other individual, and as much as to one individual was possible, has he contributed to found this, our wide spreading empire, and to give to the Western World independence and freedom.—CHIEF JUSTICE MARSHALL.

George Washington, the brave, the wise, the good. Supreme in war, in council, and in peace. Washington, valiant, without ambition; discreet, without fear; confident, without presumption.—DR. ANDREW LEE.

For a thousand years no king in Christendom has shown such greatness or given so high a type of manly virtue.—THEODORE PARKER.

Just honor to Washington can only be rendered by observing his precepts and imitating his example.—HON. ROBERT CHARLES WINTHROP, LL.D

WASHINGTON'S SERVICE TO EDUCATION

By CHARLES W. E. CHAPIN

Washington's ideas concerning education have the approval of educators of our day. He was in advance of his age; it is a question if we have quite caught up with him. Of the two plans of his mature years and ripened experience, one has been realized, the West Point idea, which brings together from every state and territory of the Union, young men to be trained for military service; that other plan of a National University with schools of administration and statesmanship is yet being considered.

Washington shared neither the least nor the most of the educational advantages of his colony. The elder brothers, Lawrence and Augustine, had realized their father's hopes and had been sent to England for their schooling as he had been for his, but the early death of the father defeated that plan for George, so he obtained the early preparation for his life work from the "home university," over which Mary Washington presided, a loving and wise head. At times George was with his brother Augustine at Bridges Creek, to be near the best parish school, and then he was at home; but all the time he was advancing rapidly in that school of men and affairs. "He was above all things else, a capable, executive boy," says Woodrow Wilson in his biography. "He loved mastery, and he relished acquiring the most effective means of mastery in all practical affairs. His very exercise books, used at school, gave proof of it." As he did these things with care and industry, so he followed with zest the spirited diversions of the hunt and the life in fields and forests. Very early he put his knowledge of the surveyor's art to practical test and applied the chain and

logarithm to the reaches of the family lands. His skill came to the notice of Lord Fairfax, who wished to know the extent of the lands he had inherited in the New World. Washington, tho but sixteen, was equal to the task; in a month's time, after fording swollen streams and penetrating the forests, he presented to Lord Fairfax, maps and figures which showed him the extent and boundaries of his estate. For three years Washington followed this fascinating yet perilous work, and then being strongly recommended by Lord Fairfax, and himself being able to show in clear, round style his mastery of the art and science of surveying, he received in 1788 from the President of William and Mary College the appointment as official surveyor for Culpeper County; such a certificate was equivalent to a degree of civil engineering in those days.

Thus from an institution of higher learning. George Washington received the first public recognition of service and of merit. It was the turning point in his life; it opened up fully the path to those experiences which equipped him for that efficient service in the French and Indian War, and the Revolution.

The honorable position of Chancellor had been held by the Bishops of London from the foundation of the College in 1693 to the Revolution. The old statute defining the duties of the office is interesting: "The Chancellor is to be the Mæcenas, or patron of the College; such a one as by his favor with the King and by his interest with all other persons in England may be enabled to help in all the College affairs. His advice is to be taken, especially in such arduous and momentous affairs as the College shall have to do in England. If the College has any petitions at any time to the King, let them be presented by the Chancellor." We can imagine a grim smile on Washington's countenance as he read the provisions made concerning the functions of his office, especially that of conferring with the King. In his letter to Samuel Griffin, Esq., Rector of the College, accepting his appointment, he says: "Influenced by a heartfelt desire to promote the cause of science in general and the prosperity of the College of William and Mary in particular, I accept the office of Chancellor in the same and request you will be pleased to give official notice thereof to the learned body who have thought proper to honor me with the appointment. I confide fully in their strenuous endeavors for placing the system of education on such a basis as will render it most beneficial to the State and the Republic of letters, as well as to the more extensive interests of humanity and religion." This call to the leadership of education in his own State antedated his election to the Presidency of the new Republic by a year. and he continued in that service to the College of William and Mary until the close of his life.

About the close of the Revolution, the State of Maryland began to broaden its educational institutions. The School of Kent County at Chestertown was placed in 1780 under the charge of the Rev. Dr. William Smith, the minister of the parish. who had been President of the College of Philadelphia until its charter was revoked. Dr. Smith conducted the Academy at Chestertown with great energy and ability, and in 1782 the visitors of the Academy asked that it be made a college; the legislature made provision that when a total endowment of five thousand pounds currency should be provided for the school, it should be incorporated into a college, with enlarged courses of study and suitable professors, and should be denominated Washington College "in honorable and perpetual memory of his excellency, General Washington, the illustrious and virtuous Commander-in-Chief of the armies of the United States." In five months the energetic trustees raised $14,000; Washington contributed fifty guineas. The College was at once incorporated and in the following year, at its first commencement, its endowment had increased to $28,000. It was the first college in Maryland; Washington was elected as a member of the first Board of Visitors, but being with the army at Newburgh was unable to take his place on the Board until the second commencement of the College in 1784. Five years later, the College bestowed upon Washington the degree of Doctor of Laws; his letter of acknowledgment expressed the sentiment that, "in civilized societies the welfare of the state and the happiness of the people are advanced or retarded in proportion as the morals and education of the youth are attended to. I cannot forbear on this occasion to express the satisfaction which I feel on

seeing the increase of our seminaries of learning through the extensive country, and the general wish which seems to prevail for establishing and maintaining these valuable institutions." The old College has suffered by fire and the vicissitudes of fortune, yet it has lived through the years and is to-day doing a prosperous and noble work.

The Potomac and Virginia Company and the James River Company were among those organizations for transportation which Washington aided for the opening up of the country. There was a recognition of his services to the country and the legislature of Virginia in 1785, through Patrick Henry, then Governor, who gave Washington fifty shares in the Potomac and Virginia Company and one hundred shares in the James River Company. Washington replied that he had resolutely shut his hand against every pecuniary recompense during the revolutionary struggle; and that he could not change that position. He added, that, if the legislature would allow him to turn the gifts from his own private emolument to objects of a public nature, he would endeavor to select objects which would meet the most enlightened and patriotic views of the Assembly of Virginia. The proposition met with hearty approval, and Washington held the stock in both companies, awaiting the time when proper and worthy objects should be found for the benefactions.

In 1785 he proposed to Edmund Randolph and Thomas Jefferson that the revenue of the stock in those companies be used for the establishment of two schools, one upon each river, for the education of poor children, particularly those whose parents had fallen in the struggle for liberty. The idea was a noble one, yet Washington's call to the large service of the College of William and Mary as its Chancellor, and to the country as its President, prevented him from carrying it out. He carried out the spirit of his idea by giving fifty pounds a year for the instruction of poor children in Alexandria and by making large provision for the education of the sons of soldiers. In 1783 he honored a Princeton commencement by his presence and bestowed upon the College a gift of fifty pounds. A tour through Georgia in 1790, gave him opportunity to visit and approve of the Academy at Augusta. About the same time the indomitable Kirkland, missionary to the Iroquois, was trying every source of influence and money in behalf of an academy in Oneida County, New York, to be located near the old Property Line, where both the sons of the settlers and the children of the forest might be educated. His visit to Philadelphia secured a generous benefaction from Washington and at the same time his influence and that of others, so that Congress appropriated $15,000 yearly to "instruct the Iroquois in agriculture and the useful arts." Washington had now matured his idea of a national university. He was ready to lay it before the country and to be the first contributor to its endowment. Virginia was taking new interest in its schools and the influence of William and Mary College was widening: there was a demand for more thoroughly equipped academies. The school at Augusta, which the Revolution had been the means of christening Liberty Hall, had become prominent. In 1796 Washington settled upon Liberty Hall as the proper recipient of the one hundred shares in the James River Company to augment its endowment. In accepting the gift the name of the academy was changed and the trustees were able to sign themselves, "the trustees of Washington Academy, late Liberty Hall." Washington was greatly touched by the honor and ascribed his ability to make the donation to "the generosity of the Legislature of the Commonwealth of Virginia."

The institution prospered. About 1802 a new charter was granted with larger powers, under the name of Washington College. John Robinson, a soldier of the Revolution under Washington, gave, in emulation of his illustrious commander, his entire estate to Washington College; from it the trustees realized $40,000 toward the endowment. The stock of the James River Company which Washington transferred to the College to-day yields an income of six per cent. on $50,000, and, after prospering years, the College has now a productive endowment of $600,000 and a property worth $800,000. The country has passed through many critical periods since Washington's day and the Union is stronger than ever. The old College is a witness to the all-healing power of time and kinship, for its name has again been added to: it is Washington and Lee University now; and thus is joined with the name of Father of His Country the name of one whom the South has ever loved, whom the North long since forgave, and whose memory the country will ever cherish.

The Revolutionary War was a costly experiment of education in military affairs in the field; it cost heavily in blood and treasure. Washington realized that preparation for service in the army must be had in military schools.

From the very beginning of the war until the end of his life, by official message and by letter, Washington urged the importance of military instruction. In his message to Congress in 1796 he said: "The institution of a military academy is recommended by cogent reasons. However pacific the general policy of a nation may be, it ought never to be without an adequate stock of military knowledge for emergencies. In proportion as the observance of pacific maxims might exempt a nation from the necessity of practising the rules of the military art, ought to be its care in preserving and transmitting by proper establishments the knowledge of that art. A thorough examination of the subject will evince that the art of war is extensive and complicated; that it demands much previous study; and that the possession of it in its most important and perfect state is always of great moment to the security of a nation." Congress did make provision for the carrying out of many of the President's recom-

mendations; it created a new grade in the army, that of *Cadet,* to which young men exclusively were admitted, and money was appropriated for their education in the science of war that they might be prepared for positions of command. But Congress delayed the potential part of the plan; it did not collect the regiment of artillerists and engineers at a single station, nor did it erect buildings for the uses of education.

The idea did not die; in 1802 Congress made the first of those provisions for a military academy with the plan and scope which Washington had so persistently urged. West Point was chosen as the place of its location. That academy has more than once demonstrated the wisdom of the far-seeing Washington.

West Point is the realization of Washington's plans for a national school of military instruction. To-day it represents to the country the important features of that plan for a National University. By his last will and testament, Washington bequeathed the fifty shares of stock in the Potomac Company to the establishment of a National University in the central part of the United States; he made provision that until such a university should be founded the fund should be self-accumulating by the use of the dividends in the purchase of more stock, to still further augment the endowment fund. In the transfers and changes of commercial life apparent record of that stock has been lost, yet that last will bequeathed an ideal which in indirect ways is still inspiring our national educational system.

Let us take our place by the side of a student of our national history and institutions, as after a walk through the buildings and across that noble plain at West Point he sits down to meditate, on the granite steps of "Battle Monument." He is where the history of yesterday abides, but about him is represented the strength and life of the Nation in the strong military figures of officers, cadets and soldiers from every section of our country. He feels the wisdom of that great desire of Washington's that the life and thought of the widely separated sections of the rising empire should become homogeneous and unified by the meeting of the young men of the land in a central school, during the years of training for the country's service at arms. This student of history would feel how that hope had been fulfilled by the loyal service which the sons of West Point to so large a degree rendered the Union in its days of peril; and with deep gratitude would he acknowledge that enthusiastic loyalty with which the North and South, the East and West as represented at West Point and throughout the country rushed to its service to release those islands of the sea from the thraldom and tyranny of a medieval monarchy.

Then the vista of the future would open before him and he would see that larger hope and plan of Washington's realized in the city of his name. There in that center of the Nation's life he would see young men assembling in the national schools of administration, commerce, consular service and finance to study questions of government and international relations. He would see reaching to all the lands of earth a peace more beautiful than that of the river below him; and wider and deeper than that Western ocean where now is flying our flag of hope and promise.—E.

WASHINGTON'S VIEW OF DIVINE PROVIDENCE

By J. M. Buckley, D.D.

George Washington's father, Augustine, married twice; of the first marriage there were four children, of the second, six, of whom he who was to be The Father of His Country was the firstborn.

Much has been said about his mother, Mary Washington, and it is impossible to say too much; for never was the mother of a great man worthy of more honor than she. Like the woman in the Scripture of whom Jesus said, " She hath done what she could," her praise should be perpetual. Augustine Washington died when George Washington was but eleven years old, yet before that time his father had made a deep impression upon him. When the boy was four years old his cousin brought him a fine apple; his father had great difficulty to prevail on him to divide it with his brothers and sisters, but at last succeeded by promising that if he would but do it the Almighty would give him plenty of apples the next fall. On a fine morning Mr. Washington took George by the hand and, accompanied by a guest, led him to the orchard. In subsequent years this lady said that, so far as they could see, the earth was strewed with fruit, yet the trees were still bending under the weight of apples. Mr. Washington reminded the child of the difficulty he had in inducing him to divide that one apple with his brothers and sisters, and said to him, " Look up, my son, and see how richly the Almighty has made good my promise to you." According to the narrator, who was present, he said, " Pa, forgive me this time and see if I am ever so stingy any more."

His father employed a similar method in teaching him that the fear of the Lord is the beginning of knowledge. On a properly prepared bed in his garden, Augustine Washington traced with a stick the letters of his son's name, and sowing seed in them he covered it over and smoothed the ground with a roller. In a short time the plants came up in a way to display legibly the words " GEORGE WASHINGTON." It was not long before this vegetable wonder caught the eye of the child. Again and again he read his name springing up from the earth in letters fresh and green. He could not understand it. He sought his father, who puzzled him pleasantly for a while, but at last showed him how he had made the letters with his stick, sowed the seed in the furrows and how the warm earth had caused them to spring up From that he proceeded to teach him of the Infinite intelligence. He began by

showing him that his name inscribed on the earth was an effect, for this effect there must be a cause; that this cause must have been intelligent appeared from the design manifested in the work. George Washington never forgot this, and used to speak of it when such vegetable printing had become common. So that tho the care of her firstborn devolved entirely on Mrs. Washington, after he was eleven years of age, the recollections of his father were pleasant, and the impressions made upon his memory were inseparably connected with that Providence which had removed him.

At every period of his life he spoke of the Providence of God in a most reverential way. In 1754 he wrote that they " would have starved if Providence had not sent a trader from the Ohio to our relief." In' a letter to his brother after Braddock's defeat he wrote, " By the All-Powerful Dispensations of Providence I have been protected beyond all human probability or expectation; for I had four bullets through my coat and two horses shot under me; I escaped unhurt, altho death was leveling my companions on every side of me."

When he wrote to Lieutenant-General Gage of the British Army, he said, " May that God to whom you appeal judge between America and you." And when he wrote to his officers just before the attack upon the enemy in Boston, he said. " The success, I well know, depends upon the All-Wise Dispenser of events." Writing of the evacuation of Jersey by the British troops, on the 4th of July, 1777, he declared it to be " a peculiar mark of Providence." The capitulation of Burgoyne's army he declared to be " a signal stroke of Providence." In 1779 he said his only hope was that Providence who had " so often taken us up when bereft of every other hope," and declared that " the many remarkable interpositions of the Divine Government in the hours of our deepest distress and darkness have been too luminous to suffer me to doubt the happy issue in the present conflict." Again he speaks of God as the Great Director of Events, and as the Supreme Dispenser of all good.

In 1778 he wrote to General Nelson of Virginia :
" The hand of Providence has been so conspicuous in all this that he must be worse than an infidel that lacks faith, and more than wicked that has no gratitude enough to acknowledge his obligations. But it will be time enough for me to turn preacher when

my present appointment ceases; and therefore I shall add no more on the doctrine of Providence."

But never once did he imagine that a miracle would be performed, and, therefore, he worked as energetically and guarded against attack as cautiously as if dependent wholly upon himself.

How noble his expression, "If we make freedom our choice we must obtain it by the blessing of Heaven on our united and vigorous efforts!"—C. A.

SERMONS

GEORGE WASHINGTON AS AN EXAMPLE TO-DAY

By James T. Bixby, D.D.

Behold I have given him for a witness to the people, a leader and commander to the people.—Isa. lv: 4

I present to you the character of Washington as a noble model for your imitation. I do not mean that if you can make such a character yours, you shall therefore sit in the presidential chair in which he sat, or shall win quick and brilliant success of any kind—in politics, war, or business. The man who should take Washington for his pattern would not feel at liberty to doctor his groceries, or under-measure his cloth, or borrow, unbeknown to any one, the funds committed to his charge. He would have small personal acquaintance with rings, and would stand little chance of getting a government contract.

I doubt very much if he could be elected to Congress, unless he had some lieutenant who knew more about "pulling wires" than he did; and if he should somehow be elected, he would be very useless in distributing patronage, very awkward at log-rolling, and would not draw very well inside the party traces. He would be too foolishly prudish to take a slice for himself out of fat contracts, and I doubt if anyone would think it worth while to present him a block of stock in expectation thereby of securing his vote in favor of a government subsidy.

Nevertheless he who should renew among us a character like Washington would win a greater reward than any of our modern adventurers. If he would have no resounding notoriety, he would have the sweet whisper of the still small voice. If he would not have so full a pocket, he would possess a richer soul. He would have that which our country most needs in its sons to-day.

The free institutions which our fathers planted, and for which they contended so sturdily, will be of no benefit to us unless they are kept in the hands of honest stewards, and are supported constantly by true and upright citizens. When we convert politics into a mere game of intrigue and self-advantage, unhallowed by a single great and unselfish interest, then we may be sure that our worst passions are busy forging our fetters.

If these fetters are hid under silken decorations, they bind no less securely. The only foundations of orderly and free society are in better men—not only in high places, but low places—not fewer Chinamen in this country, but more self-reliant Americans. We want more statesmen, who, amid the outcries of the rabble, can hold true to the principles of our republican government; equal rights to all, whether white or black, red or yellow of skin. A single true, devoted citizen is more precious than 1,000 time-servers, or all the gold in the mines of Nevada.

God be thanked that in General Washington we have the picture of one such man, set where it cannot be hid, in the glorious frame of our country's early history, as an example to the Americans of to-day! May it find no small number who, living by the same great principles, may, in no long time, work in our land a moral revolution—a regeneration into a purer, sweeter, and nobler life.—P. M.

A GREATNESS GREATER THAN MIGHTINESS

He that is slow to anger is better than the mighty; and he that ruleth his spirit than he that taketh a city.—Prov. xvi: 32

In all history there is not, aside from Jesus, a more striking illustration of the truth of the text than that furnished by the life of George Washington.

1. He "ruled his spirit;" ruled it under circumstances of extraordinary provocation; ruled it in times of extreme darkness, under censures severe, and in the face of temptations such as assail few men. But he came forth from the fiery furnace without even "the smell of fire on his garments!" The student of history knows about the "Newburgh" intrigue to make him a king when the order came from Congress to disband the army unpaid; about the terrible winter which he spent with his army at Valley

Forge, bearing in silence a nation's reproach and complaint for seeming failure; his incorruptibility in war and in peace; his virtues in private life, and his distinguished career as the first President of the United States, only too happy to retire to the peaceful shades of Mt. Vernon at its close. Had not God endowed Washington with this virtue in large measure, how different had been our career as a nation!

2. It was the habitual exercise of this high moral quality that constitutes Washington's real greatness, and which enabled him to achieve what he did for his country and the world. He has had his equals as a military leader, as a statesman, as an executive; but there has been but *one Washington!* This is the verdict of history! He "ruled his spirit;" he conquered himself. He was not elated by prosperity, nor depressed by defeat. He "possessed" his soul in patience."

3. It was more than a *natural* gift; the *grace of God* had much to do with it. That Washington was truly religious, is beyond a doubt. Rev. Albert Barnes relates the following touching incident which illustrates it: "In the darkest season of the American Revolution, the commander-in-chief of our armies was observed to retire each day to a grove in the vicinity of the camp. It was at the Valley Forge. A series of disasters had disheartened the army, and the sky was overcast with a dark cloud, and distress and anxiety pervaded the Nation. The army was in want of the comforts, and almost of the indispensable necessaries of life, and disaffection was spreading in the camp. Curiosity prompted an individual to follow the commander-in-chief, and to observe him. The *father of his country was seen on his knees supplicating the God of hosts in secret prayer.* With an anxious, burdened mind, a mind conscious of its need of heavenly support and devotion, he went and rolled these mighty burdens upon the arm of Jehovah. Who can tell how much the liberty of this Nation is owing to the answer to the secret prayer of Washington at the Valley Forge?"

CONCLUSION.—The lesson is specially pertinent to our times and Nation. What a hallowed influence would flow down upon 50,000,000 of people from the high places of authority and position, if our public men would but follow the illustrious example of "the father of his country"! Alas, how few of this class rule their spirits! The lust of the flesh, the lust of office, the lust of party, corrupts, sways, sacrifices, makes shipwreck of virtue, integrity, character, and the public weal.—H. R.

SUGGESTIVE THOUGHTS

ABUSE OF WASHINGTON, The.—On his last day in office Washington wrote to Knox comparing himself to "the weary traveler who sees a resting-place, and is bending his body to lean thereon. To be suffered to do this in peace," he added. "is too much to be endured by some." Accordingly, on that very day a Philadelphia newspaper dismissed him with a final tirade, worth remembering by all who think that political virulence is on the increase:

"'Lord, now lettest thou thy servant depart in peace, for mine eyes have seen thy salvation!' was the exclamation of a man who saw a flood of blessedness breaking in upon mankind. If ever there was a time that allowed this exclamation to be repeated, that time is the present. The man who is the source of all our country's misery is this day reduced to the rank of his fellow-citizens, and has no longer the power to multiply the woes of these United States. Now more than ever is the time to rejoice. Every heart which feels for the liberty and the happiness of the people must now beat with rapture at the thought that this day the name of Washington ceases to give currency to injustice and to legalize corruption. . . . When we look back upon the eight years of Washington's administration, it strikes us with astonishment that one man could thus poison the principles of republicanism among our enlightened people, and carry his designs against the public liberty so far as to endanger its very existence. Yet such is the fact, and if this is apparent to all, this day they should form a jubilee in the United States."—T. W. HIGGINSON.

INAUGURAL, From Washington's.—It would be peculiarly improper to omit, in this first official act, my fervent supplications to that Almighty Being who rules over the universe, who presides in the councils of nations, and whose providential aids can supply every human defect, that His benediction may consecrate, to the liberties and happiness of the people of the United States, a government instituted by themselves for these essential purposes, and may enable every instrument employed in the administration to execute with success the functions allotted to its charge. In tendering this homage to the Great Author of every public and private good, I assure myself that it expresses your sentiments not less than my own, nor those of my fellow citizens at large less than either.

No people can be bound to acknowledge and adore the invisible hand which conducts the affairs of men more than the people of the United States. Every step by which they have advanced to the character of an independent nation seems to have been distinguished by some token of Providential agency; and the important revolution just accomplished in the system of their united government, the tranquil deliberations and voluntary consent of so many distinct communities from which the event has resulted, cannot be compared with the means by which most governments have been established, without some return of pious gratitude, along with an humble anticipation of the future blessings which the past seems to presage.

MOTHER, Washington's.—Mary Washington, the mother of the first President of the United States, died just after her son had reached the highest honors of his career. At the time of his election to the presidency she was living very quietly and modestly, as she had done for some years before, at Fredericksburg, Va.

She died in 1789, and was buried in a family burial-ground near Fredericksburg. For forty-four years her grave remained unmarked by any monument or headstone.

Mary Washington was a noble and Christian woman, and to her careful training and her example of earnestness and virtue the great qualities of the " Father of His Country," were no doubt due in no small measure.

Recognizing the real eminence of such a woman, and the fitness of honoring her burial-place with an appropriate memorial, a wealthy citizen of New York undertook the erection of a large monument of stone upon the spot, and the corner-stone of this memorial was laid with ceremony in 1833 by President Andrew Jackson.

The projector of the monument lost his fortune, however, and the monument was not finished. The foundation alone stands, with broken sections of stone lying about it. A writer in speaking of it recently, said, " Cattle graze about the base; it is discolored by time and weather; the relic-hunter's hammer has been busy with the chiseled edges; the shaft lies prone and half-buried in the earth."

Certain public-spirited ladies have undertaken to collect the funds necessary for the completion of this structure, and it is to be hoped that, as the long delay in the work gives an opportunity for making a better design than the original, which was sadly lacking in dignity and good taste, their efforts may be crowned with success.—Y. C.

MOUNT VERNON TRIBUTE, The.—

Washington

THE DEFENDER OF HIS COUNTRY, THE FOUNDER OF LIBERTY,

THE FRIEND OF MAN.

HISTORY AND TRADITION ARE EXPLORED IN VAIN FOR A PARALLEL TO HIS CHARACTER.

IN THE ANNALS OF MODERN GREATNESS,

HE STANDS ALONE,

AND THE NOBLEST NAMES OF ANTIQUITY LOSE THEIR LUSTRE IN HIS PRESENCE. BORN THE BENEFACTOR OF MANKIND, HE UNITED ALL THE QUALITIES NECESSARY TO AN ILLUSTRIOUS CAREER.

NATURE MADE HIM GREAT;

HE MADE HIMSELF VIRTUOUS. CALLED BY HIS COUNTRY TO THE DEFENCE OF HER LIBERTIES, HE TRIUMPHANTLY VINDICATED THE RIGHTS OF HUMANITY, AND ON THE PILLARS OF NATIONAL INDEPENDENCE LAID THE FOUNDATIONS OF A GREAT REPUBLIC. TWICE INVESTED WITH THE SUPREME MAGISTRACY, BY THE UNANIMOUS VOICE OF A FREE PEOPLE, HE SURPASSED IN THE CABINET

THE GLORIES OF THE FIELD,

AND VOLUNTARILY RESIGNING THE SCEPTRE AND THE SWORD, RETIRED TO THE SHADES OF PRIVATE LIFE. A SPECTACLE SO NEW AND SO SUBLIME WAS CONTEMPLATED WITH THE PROFOUNDEST ADMIRATION; AND THE NAME OF

WASHINGTON,

ADDING NEW LUSTRE TO HUMANITY, RESOUNDED TO THE REMOTEST REGIONS OF THE EARTH. MAGNANIMOUS IN YOUTH,

GLORIOUS THROUGH LIFE,

GREAT IN DEATH,

HIS HIGHEST AMBITION THE HAPPINESS OF MANKIND, HIS NOBLEST VICTORY THE CONQUEST OF HIMSELF, BEQUEATHING TO POSTERITY THE INHERITANCE OF HIS FAME,

AND BUILDING HIS MONUMENT IN THE HEARTS OF HIS COUNTRYMEN,

HE LIVED THE ORNAMENT OF THE EIGHTEENTH CENTURY, AND DIED REGRETTED BY A MOURNING WORLD.

[The author of this inscription is not known. It has been transcribed from a manuscript copy written on the back of a picture-frame, in which is set a miniature likeness of Washington, and which hangs in one of the rooms of the mansion at Mount Vernon, where it was left some time after Washington's death.—H. B. CARRINGTON, LL.D.—Col. S.]

NATION, Prayer for the.—During the Revolutionary War, General Washington's army was reduced at one time to great straits, and the people were greatly dispirited. One of them who left his home with an anxious heart, one day, as he was passing the edge of a wood near the camp, heard the sound of a voice. He stopped to listen, and looking between the trunks of the large trees, he saw General Washington engaged in prayer. He passed quietly on, that he might not disturb him; and on returning home, told his family, " America will prevail," and then related what he had heard and seen.— F. II.

SWEARING, Washington.—The deep reverence of General Washington was pained by the swearing of his soldiers. In a general order, issued August 3, 1776, he said:—

The General is sorry to be informed that the foolish and wicked practise of profane cursing and swearing, a vice hitherto little known in an American army, is growing into fashion. He hopes the officers will, by example as well as influence, endeavor to check it, and that both they and the men will reflect that we can have little hope of the blessing of Heaven on our arms, if we insult it by our impiety and folly. Added to this, it is a vice so mean and low, without any temptation, that every man of sense and character detests and despises it.—C. E. W.

WASHINGTON AS HE LOOKED.—According to Captain Mercer, the following describes Washington when he took his seat in the House of Burgesses in 1759:

" He is as straight as an Indian, measuring six feet two inches in his stockings, and weighing one hundred and seventy-five pounds. His head is well shaped, tho not large, and is gracefully poised on a superb neck, with a large and straight rather than a prominent nose; blue-gray penetrating eyes, which are widely separated and overhung by heavy brows. A pleasing, benevolent, tho commanding countenance, dark-brown hair, features regular and placid, with all the muscles under control, with a large mouth, generally firmly closed."

Houdon's bust accords with this description.—C. E. W.

WASHINGTON, Said By.—To be prepared for war is one of the most effectual means of preserving peace.

There is a rank due to the United States among nations which will be withheld, if not absolutely lost, by the reputation of weakness.

The propitious smiles of Heaven can never be expected on a nation that disregards the eternal rules of order and right, which Heaven itself has ordained.

The very idea of the power and right of the people to establish government presupposes the duty of every individual to obey the established government.

If there was the same propensity in mankind for investigating the motives, as there is for censuring the conduct, of public characters, it would be found that the censure so freely bestowed is oftentimes unmerited and uncharitable.

Where is the man to be found who wishes to remain indebted for the defense of his own person and property to the exertions, the bravery, and the blood of others, without making one generous effort to repay the debt of honor and gratitude?

There is no truth more thoroughly established than that there exists in the economy and course of nature an indissoluble union

between virtue and happiness, between duty and advantage, between the genuine maxims of an honest and magnanimous policy and the solid rewards of public prosperity and felicity.

Against the insidious wiles of foreign influence the jealousy of a free people ought to be constantly awake.

It is our true policy to steer clear of permanent alliances with any portion of the foreign world.

The great rule of conduct for us in regard to foreign nations is to have with them as little political connection as possible.

There can be no greater error than to expect or calculate upon real favors from nation to nation.

Why, by interweaving our destiny with that of any part of Europe, entangle our peace and prosperity in the toils of European ambition, rivalship, interest, humor or caprice?

The name American must always exalt the just pride of patriotism.

To the efficacy and permanency of your union a government for the whole is indispensable.

Every attempt to alienate any portion of our country from the rest should be indignantly frowned upon.

Let us impart all the blessings we possess, or ask for ourselves, to the whole family of mankind.

Let us erect a standard to which the good and honest may repair.

'Tis substantially true that virtue or morality is a necessary spring of popular government.

Labor to keep alive in your breast that little spark of celestial fire, conscience.

It is incumbent upon every person of every description to contribute to his country's welfare.

It would be repugnant to the vital principles of our government virtually to exclude from public trusts, talents and virtue, unless accompanied by wealth.

Give such encouragements to our own navigation as will render our commerce less dependent on foreign bottoms.

I have never made an appointment from a desire to serve a friend or relative.

———

In contemplating the causes which may disturb our Union, it occurs as a matter of serious concern that any ground should have been furnished for geographical discriminations.

———

If a man cannot act in all respects as he would wish, he must do what appears best, under the circumstances he is in. This I aim at, however short I may fail of the end.

———

I never say anything of a man that I have the smallest scruple of saying to him.

———

The liberties of the country are safe,—on receiving news of the battle of Bunker Hill.

WASHINGTON'S FIRST GOVERNMENT OFFICE.—Washington's first government service was rendered in the capacity of official surveyor of Culpeper County at a salary of fifty pounds—two hundred and forty-three dollars—a year. During this time he had to travel over " ye worst Road that ever was trod by Man or Beast." Sometimes he lay on straw, which " once catched fire," sometimes under a tent without covers, sometimes he was driven from the tent by the smoke.—C. E. W.

WASHINGTON, Tribute to.—I mean no disrespect to our own royal family, but, when compared with General Washington, the princes and potentates of Europe seem mean and contemptible. . . . Without one suspicion of his integrity, without one stain upon his character, he has made himself the first man in the world.—CHARLES JAMES FOX, in the British Parliament.

POETRY

Washington

For tho the ears their golden round
  O'er all the lavish region roll,
  And realm on realm, from pole to pole,
In one beneath thy Stars be bound,—
  The far off centuries as they flow,
  No whiter name than this shall know!
    —FRANCIS T. PALGRAVE.

———

Where may the wearied eye repose,
  When gazing on the great,
Where neither guilty glory glows
  Nor despicable state?
Yes one—the first, the last, the best,
The Cincinnatus of the West,
  Whom envy dared not hate,—
Bequeathed the name of Washington,
  To make men blush there was but one!
    —BYRON.

———

By broad Potomac's silent shore,
  Better than Trojan, lowly lies,
  Gilding her green declivities
With glory now and ever more;
  Art to his fame no aid hath lent;
  His country is his monument.
    —ANONYMOUS.

The Birthday of Washington Ever Honored

BY GEORGE HOWLAND

Welcome, thou festal morn!
Never be passed in scorn
  Thy rising sun,
Thou day forever bright
With Freedom's holy light,
That gave the world the sight
  Of Washington.

Unshaken 'mid the storm,
Behold that noble form,—
  That peerless one,—
With his protecting hand,
Like Freedom's angel, stand,
The guardian of our land,
  Our Washington.

Traced there in lines of light,
Where all pure rays unite,
  Obscured by none;
Brightest on history's page,
Of any clime or age,
As chieftain, man, and sage,
  Stands Washington.

Name at which tyrants pale,
And their proud legions quail,
  Their boasting done,
While Freedom lifts her head,
No longer filled with dread,
Her sons to victory led
  By Washington.

Now the true patriots see,
The foremost of the free,
  The victory won,
In Freedom's presence bow,
While sweetly smiling now
She wreathes the spotless brow
  Of Washington.

Then, with each coming year,
Whenever shall appear
  That natal sun,
Will we attest the worth
Of one true man to earth,
And celebrate the birth
  Of Washington.
    Col. S.

Holden's Ode to Washington

Great Washington the hero's come,
Each heart exulting hears the sound,
Thousands to their deliverer throng
And shout him welcome all around.

CHORUS:

Now in full chorus join the song,
And shout aloud great Washington!

Then view Columbia's favorite son,
Her father, savior, friend, and guide;
There see the immortal Washington!
His country's glory, boast and pride!

CHORUS.

When the impending storm of war,
Thick clouds and darkness, hid our way.
Great Washington our polar star,
Arose; and all was light as day.

CHORUS.

Through countless dangers, toil, and cares
Our hero led us safely on—
With matchless skill directs the wars
Till victory cries—The day's his own.

CHORUS.

But soon Columbia called him forth,
Again to save her sinking fame;
So to the helm, and by his worth,
To make her an immortal name.

CHORUS.

'Twas on yon plains thy valor rose,
And ran like fire from man to man,
'Twas here thou humbled Paria's foes,
And chased whole legions to the main.

CHORUS.

His country saved, the contest o'er,
Sweet peace restored, his toil to crown,
The warrior to his native shore
Returns, and tills his fertile ground.

CHORUS.

Not yet alone through Paria's shores,
·Has fame her mighty trumpet blown;
E'en Europe, Afric, Asia hears,
And emulate the deeds he's done.

CHORUS.
C. A.

Washington at Valley Forge

BY REV. CANON R. G. SUTHERLAND

With his lean, ragged levies, undismayed
He crouched among the vigilant hills; a
show
To the disdainful, heaven-blinded foe.
Unlauded, unsupported, disobeyed,
Thwarted, maligned, conspired against, be-
trayed—
Yet nothing could unheart him. Wouldst
thou know
His secret? There, in that thicket, on
the snow
Washington knelt before his God, and
prayed.

Close in their lair for perilous months and
days
He held in leash his wolves, grim, shelter-
less,
Gaunt, hunger-bitten, stanch to the uttermost;
Then, when the hour was come for hardi-
ness,
Rallied, and rushed them on the reeling
host;
And Monmouth planted Yorktown's happy
bays!—
C. E. W.

Washington-Month

BY WILL CARLETON

February—February—
How your moods and actions vary
Or to seek or shun!
Now a smile of sunlight lifting,
Now in chilly snowflakes drifting;
Now with icy shuttles creeping
Silver webs are spun.
Now, with leaden torrents leaping,
Oceanward you run,
Now with bells you blithely sing,
'Neath the stars or sun;
Now a blade of burdock bring
To the suff'ring one;
February—you are very
Dear, when all is done:
Many blessings rest above you,
You one day (and so we love you)
Gave us Washington.
E. W.

Washington's Name in the Hall of Fame

BY MARGARET E. SANGSTER

Republics are ungrateful, but ours, its best-
loved son
Still keeps in memory green, and wreathes
the name of Washington.
As year by year returns the day that saw
the patriot's birth,
With boom of gun and beat of drum and
peals of joy and mirth,
And songs of children in the streets and
march of men-at-arms,
We honor pay to him who stood serene 'mid
war's alarms;
And with his ragged volunteers long kept
the foe at bay,
And bore the flag to victory in many a
battle's day.

We were a little nation then; so mighty
have we grown
That scarce would Washington believe to-
day we were his own.
With ships that sail on every sea, and sons
in every port,
And harvest-fields to feed the world, wherever food is short,
And if at council-board our chiefs are now
discreet and wise,
And if to great estate and high, our farmers'
lads may rise,

We owe a debt to him who set the fashion
of our fame,
And never more may we forget our loftiest
hero's name.

Great knightly soul who came in time to
serve his country's need,
To serve her with the timely word and with
the valiant deed,
Along the ages brightening as endless cycles
run
Undimmed and gaining luster in the twentieth century's sun,
First in our Hall of Fame we write the
name all folk may ken,
As first in war, and first in peace, first with
his countrymen.   —C. H.

To the Shade of Washington

By RICHARD ALSOP

Exalted chief, in thy superior mind
What vast resource, what various talents
joined!
Tempered with social virtue's milder rays,
There patriot worth diffused a purer blaze;
Formed to command respect, esteem, in-
spire,
Midst statesmen grave, or midst the social
choir,
With equal skill the sword or pen to wield,
In council great, unequaled in the field,
Mid glittering courts or rural walks to
please,
Polite with grandeur, dignified with ease;
Before the splendors of thy high renown
How fade the glowworm lusters of a crown.
How sink diminished, in that radiance lost,
The glare of conquest; and of power the
boast.
Let Greece her Alexander's deeds proclaim;
Or Cæsar's triumphs gild the Roman name;
Stripped of the dazzling glare around them
cast,
Shrinks at their crimes humanity aghast;
With equal claim to honor's glorious meed.
See Attila his course of havoc lead!
O'er Asia's realms, in one vast ruin hurled.
See furious Zingis' bloody flag unfurled.
On base far different from the conqueror's
claim
Rests the unsullied column of thy fame;
His on the woes of millions proudly based,
With blood cemented and with tears de-
faced;
Thine on a nation's welfare fixed sublime,
By freedom strengthened and revered by
time.
He, as the Comet, whose portentous light
Spreads baleful splendor o'er the glooms of
night,
With chill amazement fills the startled breast.
While storms and earthquakes dire its course
attest,
And nature trembles, lest, in chaos hurled,
Should sink the tottering fabric of the world.
Thou, like the Sun, whose kind propitious
ray
Opes the glad morn and lights the fields of
day,
Dispels the wintry storm, the chilling rain,

With rich abundance clothes the smiling
plain,
Gives all creation to rejoice around,
And life and light extends o'er nature's ut-
most bound.
Tho shone thy life a model bright of praise,
Not less the example bright thy death por-
trays,
When, plunged in deepest wo, around thy
bed,
Each eye was fixed, despairing sunk each
head,
While nature struggled with severest pain,
And scarce could life's last lingering powers
retain:
In that dread moment, awfully serene,
No trace of suffering marked thy placid
mien,
No groan, no murmuring plaint, escaped thy
tongue,
No lowering shadows on thy brow were
hung;
But calm in Christian hope, undamped with
fear,
Thou sawest the high reward of virtue
near,
On that bright meed in sweet trust reposed,
As thy firm hand thine eyes expiring closed,
Pleased, to the will of heaven resigned thy
breath,
And smiled as nature's struggles closed in
death.—*Selected.*

Washington

By JAMES RUSSELL LOWELL

[Extract from " Under the Old Elm."]

O, for a drop of that Cornelian ink
Which gave Agricola dateless length of days,
To celebrate him fitly, neither swerve
To phrase unkempt, nor pass discretion's
brink,
With him so statue-like in sad reserve,
So diffident to claim, so forward to deserve!
Nor need I shun due influence of his fame
Who, mortal among mortals, seemed as now
The equestrian shape with unimpassioned
brow,
That paces silent on through vistas of ac-
claim.

What figure more immovably august
Than that grave strength so patient and so
pure,
Calm in good fortune, when it wavered,
sure,
That mind serene, impenetrably just,
Modeled on classic lines so simple they en-
dure?
That soul so softly radiant and so white
The track it left seems less of fire than
light,
Cold but to such as love distemperature?
And if pure light, as some deem, be the
force
That drives rejoicing planets on their course,
Why for his power benign seek an impurer
source?

His was the true enthusiasm that burns
    long,
        Domestically bright.
Fed from itself and shy of human sight,
The hidden force that makes a lifetime
    strong,
And not the short-lived fuel of a song.
Passionless, say you? What is passion for
But to sublime our natures and control
To front heroic toils with late return,
Or none, or such as shames the conqueror?
That fire was fed with substance of the soul
And not with holiday stubble, that could
    burn,
Unpraised of men who after bonfires run,
Through seven slow years of unadvancing
    war,
Equal when fields were lost or fields were
    won,
With breath of popular applause or blame,
Nor fanned or damped, unquenchably the
    same,
Too inward to be reached by flaws of idle
    fame.
Soldier and statesman, rarest unison;
High-poised example of great duties done
Simply as breathing, a world's honors worn
As life's indifferent gifts to all men born;
Dumb for himself, unless it were to God,
But for his barefoot soldiers eloquent,
Tramping the snow to coral where they trod,
Held by his awe in hollow-eyed content;
Modest, yet firm as Nature's self; unblamed
Save by the men his nobler temper shamed;
Never seduced through show of present good
By other than unsetting lights to steer
New-trimmed in Heaven, nor than his stead-
    fast mood
More steadfast, far from rashness as from
    fear;
Rigid, but with himself first, grasping still
In swerveless poise the wave-beat helm of
    will;
Not honored then or now because he wooed
The popular voice, but that he still with-
    stood;
Broad-minded, higher-souled, there is but
    one
Who was all this and ours, and all men's,
    —Washington.

Minds strong by fits, irregularly great,
That flash and darken like revolving lights,
Catch more the vulgar eye unschooled to
    wait
On the long curve of patient days and
    nights
Rounding a whole life to the circle fair
Of orbed fulfilment; and this balanced soul,
So simple in its grandeur, coldly bare
Of draperies theatric, standing there
In perfect symmetry of self-control,
Seems not so great at first, but greater
    grows
Still as we look, and by experience learn
How grand this quiet is, how nobly stern
The discipline that wrought through life-
    long throes
That energetic passion of repose.

A nature too decorous and severe,
Too self-respectful in its griefs and joys,
For ardent girls and boys
Who find no genius in a mind so clear
That its grave depths seem obvious and
    near,
Nor a soul great that made so little noise.
They feel no force in that calm-cadenced
    phrase,
The habitual full-dress of his well-bred
    mind,
That seems to pace the minuet's courtly maze
And tell of ampler leisures, roomier length
    of days.
His firm-based brain, to self so little kind
That no tumultuary blood could blind,
Formed to control men, not amaze,
Looms not like those that borrow height of
    haze:
It was a world of statelier movement then
Than this we fret in, he a denizen
Of that ideal Rome that made a man for
    men.
The longer on this earth we live
And weigh the various qualities of men,
Seeing how most are fugitive,
Or fitful gifts, at best, of now and then,
Mind-wavered corpse-lights, daughters of
    the fen,
The more we feel the high stern-featured
    beauty
Of plain devotedness to duty,
Steadfast and still, nor paid with mortal
    praise,
But finding amplest recompense
For life's ungarlanded expense
In work done squarely and unwasted days.
For this we honor him, that he could know
How sweet the service and how free
Of her, God's eldest daughter here below,
And choose in meanest raiment which was
    she.

Placid completeness, life without a fall
From faith or highest aims, truth's breach-
    less wall,
Surely if any fame can bear the touch,
His will say "Here!" at the last trumpet's
    call,
The unexpressive man whose life expressed
    so much.

Never to see a nation born
Hath been given to mortal man,
Unless to those who, on that summer morn,
Gazed silent when the great Virginian
Unsheathed the sword whose fatal flash
Shot union through the incoherent clash
Of our loose atoms, crystallizing them
Around a single will's unpliant stem
And making purpose of emotion rash.
Out of that scabbard sprang, as from its
    womb,
Nebulous at first but hardening to a star,
Through mutual share of sunburst and of
    gloom,
The common faith that made us what we
    are.

That lifted blade transformed our jangling
    clans,
Till then provincial, to Americans,
And made a unity of wildering plans;
Here was the doom fixed: here is marked
    the date
When this New World awoke to man's es-
    tate,
Burnt its last ship and ceased to look be-
    hind:
Nor thoughtless was the choice; no love or
    hate
Could from its poise move that deliberate
    mind,
Weighing between too early and too late
Those pitfalls of the man refused by Fate:
His was the impartial vision of the great
Who see not as they wish, but as they
    find.
He saw the dangers of defeat, nor less
The incomputable perils of success;
The sacred past thrown by, an empty rind;
The future, cloud-land, snare of prophets
    blind;
The waste of war, the ignominy of peace;
On either hand a sullen rear of woes,
Whose garnered lightnings none could guess,
Piling   its   thunder-heads   and   muttering
    "Cease!"
Yet drew not back his hand, but gravely
    chose
The seeming-desperate task whence our new
    nation rose.

A noble choice and of immortal seed!
Nor deem that acts heroic wait on chance
Or easy were as in a boy's romance;
The man's whole life precludes the single
    deed
That shall decide if his inheritance
Be with the sifted few of matchless breed,
Our race's sap and sustenance,
Or with the unmotived herd that only sleep
    and feed.
Choice, seems a thing indifferent; thus or
    so.
What matters it? The Fates with mocking
    face
Look on inexorable, nor seem to know
Where the lot lurks that gives life's fore-
    most place.
Yet Duty's leaden casket holds it still,
And but two ways are offered to our
    will,
Toil with rare triumph, ease with safe dis-
    grace,
The problem still for us and all of human
    race.
He chose, as men choose, where most danger
    showed,
Nor ever faltered 'neath the load
Of petty cares, that gall great hearts the
    most,
But kept right on the strenuous up-hill road,
Strong to the end, above complaint or boast;
The popular tempest on his rock-mailed
    coast
Wasted its wind-borne spray,
The noisy marvel of a day;
His soul sate still in its unstormed abode.

Washington

BY ELIZA COOK

Land of the West! tho passing brief the
    record of thine age,
Thou hast a name that darkens all on his-
    tory's wide page!
Let all the blasts of Fame ring out,—thine
    shall be loudest far;
Let others boast their satellites,—thou hast
    the planet star.
Thou hast a name whose characters of
    light shall ne'er depart;
'Tis stamped upon the dullest brain, and
    warms the coldest heart;
A war-cry fit for any land where freedom's
    to be won;
Land of the West! it stands alone,—it is thy
    Washington!

Rome had its Cæsar, great and brave, but
    stain was on his wreath;
He lived the heartless conqueror, and died
    the tyrant's death.
France had its eagle, but his wings, tho lofty
    they might soar,
Were spread in false ambition's flight, and
    dipped in murder's gore.
Those hero-gods, whose mighty sway would
    fain have chained the waves—
Who flashed their blades with tiger zeal to
    make a world of slaves—
Who, tho their kindred barred the path, still
    fiercely waded on,
Oh, where shall be *their* "glory" by the
    side of Washington!

He fought, but not with love of strife; he
    struck but to defend;
And ere he turned a people's foe, he sought
    to be a friend;
He strove to keep his country's right by
    reason's gentle word,
And sighed when fell injustice threw the
    challenge sword to sword.
He stood the firm, the wise, the patriot, and
    the sage;
He showed no deep, avenging hate, no burst
    of despot rage;
He stood for Liberty and Truth, and dar-
    ingly led on
Till shouts of victory gave forth the name
    of Washington.

No car of triumph bore him through a city
    filled with grief;
No groaning captives at the wheels pro-
    claimed him victor-chief;
He broke the gyves of slavery with strong
    and high disdain,
But cast no scepter from the links when
    he had rent the chain.
He saved his land, but did not lay his soldier
    trappings down
To change them for a regal vest and don a
    kingly crown.
Fame was too earnest in her joy, too proud
    of such a son,
To let a robe and title mask her noble Wash-
    ington.

England, my heart is truly thine, my loved,
　　my native earth,—
The land that holds a mother's grave and
　　gave that mother birth!
Oh, keenly sad would be the fate that thrust
　　me from thy shore,
And faltering my breath that sighed, "Fare-
　　well for evermore!"
But did I meet such adverse lot, I would not
　　seek to dwell
Where olden heroes wrought the deeds for
　　Homer's song to tell.
"Away, thou gallant ship!" I'd cry, "and
　　bear me safely on,
But bear me from my own fair land to that
　　of Washington."
　　　　　　　　　　　　　　　　　　C. O.

Washington

By Mrs. Mary Wingate

O noble brow, so wise in thought!
O heart, so true! O soul unbought!
O eye, so keen to pierce the night
And guide the "ship of state" aright!
O life, so simple, grand and free,
The humblest still may turn to thee.
O king, uncrowned! O prince of men!
When shall we see thy like again?

The century, just passed away,
Has felt the impress of thy sway,
While youthful hearts have stronger grown
And made thy patriot zeal their own,
In marble hall or lowly cot,
Thy name hath never been forgot.
The world itself is richer, far,
For the clear shining of a star.
And loyal hearts in years to run
Shall turn to thee, O Washington.
　　　　　　　　　　　　　　　　　　C. H.

Washington's Statue

By Henry Theodore Tuckerman

The quarry whence thy form majestic sprung
　　Has peopled earth with grace,
Heroes and gods that elder bards have sung,
　　A bright and peerless race;
But from its sleeping veins ne'er rose before
　　A shape of loftier name
Than his, who Glory's wreath with meekness
　　wore,
　　The noblest son of Fame.
Sheathed is the sword that Passion never
　　stained;
His gaze around is cast,

As if the joys of Freedom, newly gained,
　　Before his vision passed;
As if a nation's shout of love and pride
　　With music filled the air,
And his calm soul was lifted on the tide
　　Of deep and grateful prayer;
As if the crystal mirror of his life
　　To fancy sweetly came,
With scenes of patient toil and noble strife,
　　Undimmed by doubt or shame;
As if the lofty purpose of his soul
　　Expression would betray,—
The high resolve Ambition to control,
　　And thrust her crown away!
O, it was well in marble firm and white
　　To carve our hero's form,
Whose angel guidance was our strength in
　　fight,
　　Our star amid the storm!
Whose matchless truth has made his name
　　divine,
　　And human freedom sure,
His country great, his tomb earth's dearest
　　shrine,
　　While man and time endure!
And it is well to place his image there
　　Upon the soil he blest:
Let meaner spirits, who its councils share,
　　Revere that silent guest!
Let us go up with high and sacred love
　　To look on his pure brow,
And as, with solemn grace, he points above,
　　Renew the patriot's vow!
　　　　　　　　　　　　　　　　　　A. A.

George Washington

By John Hall Ingham

This was the man God gave us when the hour
Proclaimed the dawn of Liberty begun;
Who dared a deed, and died when it was
　　done:
Patient in triumph, temperate in power,—
Not striving like the Corsican to tower
To Heaven, nor like great Philip's greater
　　son
To win the world and weep for world's
　　unwon.
Or lose the star to revel in the flower.
The lives that serve the eternal verities
Alone do mold mankind. Pleasure and
　　pride
Sparkle awhile and perish, as the spray,
Smoking across the crests of cavernous seas
Is impotent to hasten or delay
The everlasting surges of the tide.
　　　　　　　　　　　　　　　　　　A. A.

ARBOR DAY

IT is not long since some of our treeless Western states, desiring to promote the culture of trees, appointed a day early in spring for popular tree planting. But up to 1883 no state had advanced this movement by the institution of an Arbor Day to be celebrated and observed in schools. Ohio was the first state to move in this matter and to interest the schools in this work. Cincinnati's Arbor Day in the schools in the spring of 1883 will be remembered by all who took a part in the talks and lessons on trees during the morning hours, and in the practical work during the afternoon. The other states of the East, which all have suffered more or less by the wanton destruction of their primeval forests, soon followed in the wake of the Buckeye State, and our own Empire State celebrated for the first time in the spring of 1889 the Arbor Day in the public schools.

Many considered this scheme impracticable for large cities where trees are a rare sight and where no opportunity is given for practical planting. But the logic of events has now removed any doubts and secured a general appreciation of this subject. To every patriotic American this is the most satisfactory, as in public schools should be introduced what labor shall appear in the nation's life. The foundation of the great deeds the Germans have achieved in every discipline of art, science, industries, and even in warfare, is due to the " schoolmaster." And if we train the youth into a love for trees, the next generation will see realized what we scarcely hope to initiate, the preservation of forests not only for climatic and meteorological purposes, but also for their value in the economy of the Nation.

Children may not be able to understand the importance of trees in their aggregation as forests; however, they will, if allowed to assemble in a grove or park, be inspired with the idea that trees are one of the grandest products of God when they hear that without them the earth could never have produced the necessaries of life, and that with their destruction we could not keep up the sustained growth of the plants that feed man and animals. There is no more suitable subject for practical oral lessons, now common in most of our schools, than the nature of plants, and especially that of trees and the value of tree-planting. Such lessons occupy only a little time, taking the place of a part of the " Reader." They tend to form the habits of accurate observation of common things which are of vast importance in practical life. These lessons will lead our youth to admire and cherish trees, thus rendering a substantial service to the State as well as to the pupils by making them practical arborists.

Wherever the opportunity is given, children should be encouraged to plant or help in planting a tree, shrub or flower, actually practicing what they have learned in the study of the growth and habits of plants. They will watch with pride the slow but steady development of a young tree, and find a peculiar pleasure in its parentage. Such work has not only an educational effect upon the juvenile mind, but its esthetic influence cannot be overestimated. Tree planting is a good school for discipline in foresight, the regard for the future being the leading element in this work. Young people are mostly inclined to sow only where they can soon reap; they prefer the small crop in hand to a great harvest long in maturing. But when they are led to obtain a taste for trees, the grandeur of thought connected with this important line of husbandry will convince them that a speedy reward of labor is not always the most desirable motive in the pursuits of our life, and is not worthy of aspiring men. For patiently to work year after year for the attainment of a far-off end shows a touch of the sublime, and implies moral no less than mental heroism.—NICHOLAS JARCHOW, LL.D. (I.)

HISTORICAL

ARBOR DAY IN SCHOOLS

By B. G. NORTHRUP

J. Sterling Morton, once Secretary of the United States Department of Agriculture, originated Arbor Day in Nebraska in 1872. His able advocacy of this measure was a marvelous success the first year, and still more each succeeding year. So remarkable have been the results of Arbor Day in Nebraska, that its originator is gratefully recognized as the great benefactor of his State. Proofs of public appreciation of his grand work I found wherever I have been in that State. It glories in the old misnomer of the geographies, " The Great American Desert," since it has become so habitable and hospitable by cultivation and tree planting. Where twenty years ago, the books said trees would not grow, the settler who does not plant them is the exception. The Nebraskans are justly proud of his great achievement and are determined to maintain its pre-eminence.

Arbor Day for economic tree planting and Arbor Day in schools differ in origin and scope. Both have been erroneously attributed to me, tho long ago I advocated tree planting by youth, and started the scheme of centennial tree planting, offering a dollar prize in 1876 to every boy or girl who should plant, or *help in planting,* five " centennial trees; " still the happy idea of designating a given day when all should be invited to unite in this work belongs solely to ex-Governor Morton. His great problem was to meet the urgent needs of vast treeless prairies. At the meeting of the American Forestry Association, held at St. Paul in 1883, my resolution in favor of observing Arbor Day *in schools* in all our states was adopted, and a committee was appointed to push that work. Continued as their chairman from that day to this, I have presented the claims of Arbor Day personally, or by letter, to the Governor, or State School Superintendent in all our states and territories.

My first efforts were not encouraging. The indifference of state officials who, at the outset, deemed Arbor Day an obtrusive innovation, was expected and occasioned no discouragement. My last word with more than one governor was: " This thing is sure to go. My only question is, Shall it be under your administration or that of your successor? " Many state officials who at first were apathetic, on fuller information have worked heartily for the success of Arbor Day. The logic of events has answered objections. Wherever it has been fairly tried it has stood the test of experience. Now such a day is observed in forty states and territories, in accordance with legislative act or recommendation of State agricultural and horticultural societies or the State grange, or by special proclamation of the Governor or recommendation of the State School Superintendents, and in some states by all these combined. It has already become the most interesting, widely observed and useful of school holidays. It should not be a legal holiday, tho that may be a wise provision for the once treeless prairies of Nebraska.

Popular interest in this work has been stimulated by the annual proclamations of Governors and the full and admirable circulars to state and county school superintendents sent to every school in the state. The fact that Bergen is the " banner " county of New Jersey, if not in the country, for Arbor Day work is due to the enthusiasm of John Terhune, County Superintendent. His Arbor Day program for 1893, the best he has ever issued, contains, in addition to the Governor's proclamation, a paper by the State School Superintendent, A. B. Poland, and one on " Trees," by J. Sterling Morton, together with selections in prose and verse for recitations—a handsome pamphlet of thirty pages.

Arbor Day has fostered love of country. It has become a patriotic observance in those Southern states which have fixed its date on Washington's Birthday. Lecturing in all these states, I have been delighted, to find as true loyalty to the Stars and Stripes in them as in the North. This custom of planting memorial trees in honor of Washington, Lincoln and other patriots, and also of celebrated authors and philanthropists, has become general. Now that the national flag with its forty-five stars floats over all the school-houses in so many states, patriotism is effectively combined with the Arbor Day addresses, recitations, and songs. Among the latter "The Star Spangled Banner" and "America" usually find a place. Who can estimate the educating influence exerted upon the millions of youth who have participated in these exercises? This good work has been greatly facilitated by the eminent authors of America who have written so many choice selections in prose and poetry on the value and beauty of trees, expressly for use on Arbor Day. What growth of mind and heart has come to myriads of youth who have learned these rich gems of our literature and applied them by planting and caring for trees, and by combining sentiments of patriotism with the study of trees, vines, shrubs, and flowers, and thus with the love of Nature in all her endless forms and marvelous beauty!

An eminent educator says: "Any teacher who has no taste for trees, shrubs or flowers is unfit to be placed in charge of children." Arbor Day has enforced the same idea, especially in those states in which the pupils have cast their ballots on Arbor Day in favor of a State tree and State flower. Habits of observation have thus been formed which

have led youth in their walks, at work or play, to recognize and admire our noble trees, and to realize that they are the grandest products of Nature and form the finest drapery that adorns the earth in all lands. How many of these children in maturer years will learn from happy experience that there is a peculiar pleasure in the parentage of trees —forest, fruit or ornamental—a pleasure that never cloys but grows with their growth.

Arbor Day has proved as memorable for the home as the school, leading youth to share in dooryard adornments. Much as has been done on limited school grounds, far greater improvements have been made on the homesteads and the roadsides. The home is the objective point in the hundreds of village improvement societies recently organized. The United States Census of 1890 shows that there has recently been a remarkable increase of interest in horticulture, arboriculture, and floriculture. The reports collected from 4,510 nurserymen give a grand total of 3,386,855,778 trees, vines, shrubs, roses, and plants as then growing on their grounds. Arbor Day and village improvement societies are not the least among the many happy influences that have contributed to this grand result.—I.

ARBOR DAY AT THE INDIAN SCHOOL

By B. G. Northrop

The Arbor Day celebration held in the Indian School at Carlisle, Pa., was to me the most attractive and significant of the many such observances I have attended during the last dozen years. Thorough preparation had been made by the teachers and scholars. Besides the exercises of the choir, the band, and the "concert exercises" of a large number of younger students, forty-nine took individual parts. Not one needed any prompting. The gems of poetry and prose were selected from our leading authors, so many of whom have enriched our Arbor Day literature expressly for use on such occasions. One of these paid a merited tribute to Secretary J. Sterling Morton, the father of Arbor Day, for economic tree planting, through whose influence the treeless plains of the trans-Missouri States have been especially enriched. Says ex-Gov. R. W. Furnas: "In Nebraska alone many thousands of acres have been clad with millions of trees, converting them from bleak, worthless prairie land into forests and groves and fruitful orchards. Records show that the number of our planted trees runs into billions." Mr. Morton is justly regarded as the greatest benefactor of his State. Hence the Legislature in 1895 passed a resolution "That Nebraska shall hereafter be known and referred to as the 'Tree Planters' State.'"

Many manuals for Arbor Day observance have been issued by the United States Department of Education, State Superintend-

ents of schools, and by private parties. But the best work on this subject has been published by the United States Department of Agriculture. It ought to be sent broadcast over the country.

At the Indian School during one celebration about one hundred trees were planted by the boys and girls on the campus, and one each in honor of their guests of a kind chosen by them. Dr. Hailman chose a Norway maple, "because of his sympathies with those who work their way up by struggling against difficulties." Mr. Northrop selected "the American white ash as a rapid grower, and for the value of its lumber, combining lightness, elasticity, and strength more than any other wood in the world."

Arbor Day is now observed in all our states and territories, except Delaware, Utah, and Indian Territory, and in individual towns in two of these. It has been observed in Great Britain, France, and Northern and Southern Africa.

I had the pleasure in 1895 of helping on this movement in the Hawaiian Islands and in Japan. The third day of November, the Emperor's birthday, is now the Arbor Day of Japan, when the children plant memorial trees in his honor.

The sentiment at Carlisle seems to be that Arbor Day is the most interesting and valuable, as well as widely observed of all our holidays, excepting Christmas and Easter.

For many years I have frequently visited

this grand Indian School, and with growing appreciation of its efficiency and usefulness, and with admiration of the tact and wisdom of Captain Pratt. Having been one of the trustees of the Hampton Institute in its early history, and having visited the Indian schools in the Indian Territory, I say, What General Armstrong was for the colored race, Captain Pratt is for the Indians of America.—E.

DESCRIPTIVE

PLANTING AND PRUNING TREES

By Joseph Meehan

If it were better known how successful the early planting of trees in the fall is, I am sure we would see many more trees planted in September and October than we now do. I have tried for many years to get persons to plant in late September in preference to waiting longer, and I am sure that those who have followed my advice have been more than usually successful with their trees. But it is such uphill work to get many persons to believe that it is proper to plant before leaves fall off, that but little progress has been made.

In regard to waiting for the leaves to fall, I have often shown them trees in full leaf which would be stripped of their leaves in a night by frost; and I have put the question to them if it mattered to the tree whether I stripped the leaves or Jack Frost did it. For my part, I would prefer to plant deciduous trees in early October rather than at any other time. It has been within my experience several times to see large blocks of trees dug up in early October, to be replanted. When such work is in progress, it is customary to heel the trees in for a while as they are dug, until the replanting commences. Very often the trees remain heeled in for two or three weeks or more. At the end of this time, those who are in doubt as to the wisdom of early planting should see these trees. Not only are the tops invariably fresh and plump, but as each one is taken from the ground a mass of new fibrous roots is to be seen, which have been produced by the warm soil of the season.

I have referred before in my writings to my success some years ago in planting a small orchard of fruit trees in late September. The collection consisted of pears, quinces, cherries, and plums. The leaves were stripped off, the trees pruned, planted, and watered, and, tho the weather was dry and hot, I did not lose a tree. I advocate this early planting, knowing as I do that new roots are formed at once, and by the time winter comes it does not find newly planted trees, but, practically established ones, for the new roots are there to carry it safely through the winter. In fact, after the arrival of the first of September I never fear to plant trees, for none are ever lost by it. Evergreens are taken first, followed by deciduous trees. From October first we count on two months of open weather, and sometimes we have more than this, so that there is a good chance for the tree to establish itself.

The question is often asked, how much should a transplanted tree be pruned? and it is indeed a difficult one to answer, so much depending on the kind of tree. Trees with numerous small roots need but little pruning, except for the purpose of shaping them. Maples among trees, and nearly all shrubs, are in this class. On the other hand, oaks, magnolias, hickories, and tulip poplars will serve as subjects to illustrate those with but few roots, which will need close pruning. Even the pin-oak, which has more small roots than many other oaks, is the better for good pruning. When it is black, white, or any other oak (save the swamp white, which, with the pin, is easier to transplant than some others) even closer pruning is exercised. Hickories are extremely hard to transplant. If they are seedlings six to eight feet high, and have never been transplanted, nothing should be left but the main stem. It will be better to dig under them a year in advance, chopping off the taproot at about one foot underground, and pruning the tops at the same time. Having mentioned magnolias and tulip poplars, I should say that these and all fleshy-rooted trees are safely planted in the spring only. They rarely survive when set in the fall.

It is well understood that roots must be in close contact with soil; they have to draw their moisture from it. A tree, the roots of which are not in contact with soil, cannot long survive. It is necessary that care be exercised to get the soil well under the roots as well as over them. Use fine soil immediately about the roots, and work it in so that it be firmly placed—that no hollows exist under the roots. Then cover in with the same fine earth above them, and, as soon as a sufficient thickness exists that bruising of the roots will not occur, use a rammer to pound the soil in. When the hole is nearly filled pour in a bucket or two of water. This places within easy reach of the roots what they look for—moisture—and, at the same time, carries the soil solidly about them. Watering is more important when early planting is followed than it is later, as there is more evaporation going on then, than later, and the soil is often quite dry.—Cul.

THE USE OF DYNAMITE IN TREE PLANTING

By Charles P. Nettleton

In some of the hilly districts of California, where the subsoil is within a foot or two of the surface, if not positively rock, it is prepared for tree planting by the use of dynamite. It may make farmers in the Western States (as we call all the states from Ohio to Idaho) open their eyes in amusement to hear of blasting the soil in order to give trees a good area to grow in; but it has been done again and again on rocky land, where, as it seemed, only a mortgage could grow. Various reports in the agricultural papers of the Coast have appeared, written by men who wanted to experiment, and also by those who could not afford to let what was perhaps a large portion of their land lie idle.

From a paper read before the Oregon Horticultural Society I took liberal extracts relative to the practise and benefits derived from it.

The use of dynamite has passed the experimental stage, and is now used extensively in many parts of the country. It can be handled with perfect safety, and the total expense of preparing an acre of ground in this way is but a small item at most. The kind to use is the thirty per cent. grade, which is considered strong enough for nearly all lands. Use one-half pound for each charge, unless the land be rocky, when from one and a half to two sticks to the charge should be used. In preparing the charge take a fuse six feet long, and on one end attach a fulminating cap. First make a hole in the end of a stick of dynamite with some small stick, say a pencil; in this hole place the cap, and with a string tie the fuse and cap firmly to the stick of dynamite, to hold cap and fuse in place.

To prepare the ground for the charge, take a crowbar or a two-inch auger with a seven-foot shaft, and make a hole in the ground six feet deep. Place the stick of dynamite in the hole, then pour in dry sand and fill it up. If no sand can be had, any soil will do, if tamped somewhat hard with a wooden stick. Fire the charge in the usual way. The explosion will loosen the ground some distance below the bottom of the hole and for many feet on all sides. There is little or no danger, as the ground only heaves a trifle and little or no earth is thrown into the air. The ground, however, will be shaken for from fifteen to thirty feet on all sides.

After the dynamite has exploded, take a shovel and dig a hole sufficiently large to put the tree in, fill the excavation with surface soil and some fertilizer that will aid the tree in growing and also assist in retaining the moisture about the roots of the tree.

The water from rains on the irrigating ditch will now go down as far as the ground is loosened, and will be retained there until used by the tree-roots or until it comes to the surface and evaporates. The surface evaporation can, however, be held in check by frequent and thorough cultivation of the soil.

As the roots reach out in this now loosened soil, they will always find sufficient moisture to make a vigorous growth, and thus in one season the roots will make a growth of two or three times what they would in hard or compact soil where the water could not penetrate on account of hardpan, or the hard-baked soil of dry seasons. This large growth of roots will make it impossible for the tree to be blown over. The tap-root will sometimes go down several feet the first season. We have often seen limbs make a growth of several feet during the season, and it is just as possible for the roots to do the same thing if the conditions are right for it.

The direct results of the dynamite method are larger and more even fruit and earlier ripening. This is easily accounted for by knowing that the water in the spring does not settle round the body of the tree as it does in more compact soils, and as the moisture is spread all through the ground, it is fed to the tree more evenly and for a longer period. Many trees are killed or injured by the water settling round the trunks of the trees; pit fruits especially are easily injured in this way. The soil loosened by dynamite allows the water to settle, and at the depth of six to ten feet, the water in many soils would find a natural outlet.—I.

TREE TREATMENT

By E. P. Powell

I have tried in various ways to call the attention of Americans to the importance of the correct system of tree training. A few years ago we had our ideal tree forms. There was a pear tree ideal, after which every one was expected to shape his trees; but it slowly began to be understood that every kind of pear has its own individuality, and you cannot make them grow alike without deforming them. Then it got further to be understood that even two pear trees of the same kind do not wish to grow exactly alike. It is necessary to throw away your ideal shapes altogether. Nature has no love for uniformity. There is, however, a very general similarity in the growth of Seckels, as also in the growth of Sheldons, and of Anjous and other sorts; so that we can distinguish varieties by their manner of distributing and spreading limbs. What is true of pears is true of all other trees. Note the sharp contrast in growth between a Northern Spy and a Greening. But the ordinary tree pruner does not find this out. He goes into an orchard on general principles, makes the trees as nearly alike as he can, and, after three or four prunings, the orchard is worthless. Maple trees and elms are our most common street trees. The effort is almost sure to be to make the rows consist of trees as nearly uniform as possible. This ends in mutilation, and the death of a large part of the trees by the age of fifty years. I have seen all the avenues of a village taken possession of by the temporary authorities and pruned, with the sole idea of lifting the foliage five or six feet higher. Those who know and love trees know this is to cut off the most vital limbs, and certainly begin decay if not render the trees for the most part monstrosities.

The fact is, no part of horticulture or arboriculture is so important as pruning; and pruning should be the most intelligent of arts. It is a sad sight to find that very few of our shade trees are healthy. Go into the adjacent lots where pruners, especially the professionals, have not been admitted, and you find everywhere the most beautiful specimens of utterly sound trees; but along our highways disease is the rule. I am, for this reason, glad to see that the trustees of the Massachusetts Society for the Promotion of Agriculture have published an edition of a very little book, by Count des Cass on PRUNING FOREST AND ORNAMENTAL TREES. The editing is done by Professor Sargent, of Harvard, and is, of course, done intelligently and sympathetically. The book does not undertake to create a uniform system, but to lay down a few general laws; and, perhaps of more importance, to show where the damage is generally done. He does not hesitate to lay the blame for our sick and unsightly trees where it belongs, to careless or ignorant treatment with the saw, or to entire neglect of all pruning. In France there are many horticulturists who protest against all pruning, especially in forest growing. Des Cass says:

" Opponents of pruning maintain that the scars caused by pruning indicate internal defects in the wood, and that trees so scarred cannot be sold. But it is the method which is faulty; and such objections must disappear before more scientific and rational treatment."

On the contrary, he believes that a system of forest management that discards pruning is disastrous. He is speaking of the timber trees; those grown for timber solely. This phase of the question is of less importance in this country, but of growing importance. We are slowly beginning to plant forests. If I wished to begin life on the very surest basis

for becoming wealthy as an agriculturist. I would plant forests. We should have millions of acres of farm forests planted at once. The value of timber is enormously increased and increasing. The owner of timber hereafter has no speculative crop; he is sure of his income. For this reason a thorough study of pruning is very important. Shall we leave Nature to direct or shall we not? I believe we can see everywhere proofs of the principle laid down by the Count that trees left to themselves do not grow up sufficiently to prevent the too large spread of lower limbs. This expends vitality on wasted growth and prevents the formation of salable lumber. In a dense forest the crowding and pushing for light keeps the lower limbs pruned until a height of thirty to forty feet or more is reached. But in our artificial growth of forests we cannot rely on such crowding. Our trees must be set at some distance from each other. Then it becomes true that the lower branches grow disproportionately large, and absorb too much sap, to the detriment of the upper part of the tree. Then again we have to count on accidents and injuries doing a great deal of unforeseen breakage.

Without intelligent pruning health will quickly be destroyed. Count Cass's fundamental law is to cut close to the trunk, and perfectly even with it. The reason for this is simple. Sap first mounts from the roots to the leaves, where it is elaborated and then sent back in part to the roots. Roots take up water from the soil together with various substances in solution. After going to the leaves, where it meets carbonic acid gas, the sap goes down to deposit the concentric layer of wood. The wound made must therefore be such that the descending sap can gradually cover over. Of course stumps and prongs of decayed or broken limbs involve of necessity, if not removed, a decay into the solid trunk.

The illustrations given by the Count are constant and complete. The little monograph should be in all hands, and it will be worth millions of dollars to American forestry or orcharding. Still I do not believe in his ideal forms for special trees, carried to the extent which he carries them. The general principle unquestionably is, however, that the length of trunk in a young tree should be equal to one-third of the entire height of the tree; that the head, in a very general way, should be elongated ovoid in form, with the center of gravity sufficiently low to keep the tree upright. The lower branches shortened, to prevent excessive development of the leader, should afford sufficient leaf surface to elaborate the sap necessary to insure rapid growth. Of middle-aged trees, the trunk should equal about two-fifths of the entire height of the tree, while a mature tree should have a trunk of about one-half the full tree height.

There is no question of the impatience of American agriculturists in discussing any system of forest culture, or giving the subject any thought whatever; in this I believe they are short-sighted, and that shortly they will be compelled to change. Our agriculture is unnecessarily unprofitable. We have not learned our resources, and are stubbornly unwilling to learn them. But certainly in the treatment of orchard and street trees, we should be willing to listen to good counsel. The last orchard I saw pruned left every sucker on the limbs protruding half an inch, while the larger limbs removed were cut at a slant outward. I need not refer to the laws laid down by the Count to demonstrate that this was really worse than no pruning at all. The stubs could not heal over, but assuredly would lead to diseased holes in the wood. The stubs of suckers were a mass of buds, all of which would be stimulated to growth and there would be from three to ten new suckers for every one removed by the careless pruner. This is not an exceptional case, I regret to say. In fact, nearly all trees suffer from such blunders. The pruner in this case was a professional. The sucker should be cut smooth to, and slightly into the bark. This is equally true when it starts at the base of the tree.

But, after all, the real key to good arboriculture is to keep our trees so well in hand that they will never need large limbs removed; and, as for suckers, they should be removed when so small as to be shoved off with thumb and finger. Our enjoyment of our rural homes can be easily combined with a good deal of this anticipative foresight. I think one-half of my own pruning is done as I walk about enjoying the shade, flowers, and fruits. Each tree and bush should become a study on such occasions; and a pinch here or there will remove a large part of the incipient waste wood. The real height of success is attained where no force goes to waste. It is folly to plant a tree unless we are prepared to study it and care for it. While uniformity is to be avoided, cleanliness, wholesomeness, vigor, and beauty are all to be secured.

Practical aboriculture must ultimately become a part of our country school curriculum. Arbor Day means a great step in that direction. The children of America, at least, begin to comprehend the patriotic as well as economic duty of planting trees; must they not also be taught to care for them? The little book by Count des Cass will serve as a textbook when the day comes that the subject is recognized in the light of its full importance.—I.

CRIMINAL TREATMENT OF TREES

The Rev. Mr. Egleston once called attention, in a forcible and sensible way, to the reckless and criminal treatment of our forests in general and of our good friends the trees in particular. His simple statement that nothing in nature except a man is more valuable than a tree, reminds one of the late Edward Jaffray's judgment that only killing a man was worse than cutting down a tree. The Laurel Hill Association seems likely to become foremost among societies for the prevention of cruelty to trees. The need of active measures to defend these preservers of our springs, these guardians of our rivers, these shelterers of our fields and gardens, from wanton outrage and careless, thriftless despoiling, is forcing itself on public attention, a cry of protest that gains force from the desolating fires among the Western pines, and the miserable pillage of our own Adirondack preserves.

Arbor Day in the public schools is doing something toward the replenishing of treeless regions, restoring forest trees to their former habitation, and also toward the extermination of savagery toward all tree growth from the boys of this generation. Heredity from the slayers of trees in their fight with the primeval woods, will require heroic treatment. A boy with a hatchet is still a desolater, and with an axe he is a scourge second only to the forest burner; when he grows to manhood his greed is proof against all sentiment or suggestion of remoter consequences.

For centuries now the matchless forests of this country have been faced with the cry of " Kill! Kill! " There has been no mercy and no recourse. Slaughter has waged unhindered and unrebuked. Timber forests, with unlimited supply under care and culture, have been ruined. The waste has been more than the product. For bark, for charcoal and firewood, for fence posts and railroad ties, for lumber and shingles, for spars and ship timbers, for wooden ware, matches, and even toothpicks, the woods have been flayed alive. We have wasted our inheritance until the resulting shame is beginning to show. Forest laws that are sharp and usable as axes are demanded. The ownership of woodland must not carry the right to abuse it. Lands that are important water preserves should be protected the same as public reservoirs. Private ownership which has proved detrimental to public interests should be suppressed by public purchases. All possible restraints must be put on the marauders and incendiaries of the woods. For toleration of this criminal treatment of trees has reached its limit. The sentiment of our people is ready to sustain the hand of justice in the defense of these true friends of man.

And this correction of an evil will prove a change of heart in our people. The freedom and needs of our civilization have in this particular blunted our sensibilities. We have become callous to some serious affronts and wrongs. A whole village has been known to stand by, while a century-old tree, the pride and beauty of a street, has been killed to widen a road or to make room for some petty building. Such outrages have been perpetrated with a coolness that confessed to unconsciousness of wrong. The remedy for such things is education. Somebody must teach our people the rights and the dignity of a tree. They know its money value, but there is something more they need to know and to feel. There is a sanctity in natural growth which goes up to the sublimity of the great mountains. To violate this is to degrade ourselves. To despise or to degrade the splendid things about us is to prove ourselves unworthy of them. The Palisades of the Hudson can be made a signboard or a stone quarry, but the people who would so use them, or who would suffer such desecration of them, would sink as low in the scale of man as they would fall in the esteem of the world. This world is something more than a workshop. And a sin against the sanctity of any created thing is a sin against our own souls.—E.

FORESTRY IN NEW YORK

By William Hoyt Coleman

The Annual Report of the Forest Commission of the State of New York for 1894 —Col. William F. Fox, Superintendent— is interesting and valuable as marking progress in a branch of agricultural science comparatively new in this country yet of vital importance to our future prosperity. The report, in fact, is the last which we shall have from the Commission, as it has since been united with the Fisheries and Game Commission.

The Forest Commission has two great duties in hand, the preservation of watersheds and renewal of timber supplies. Heretofore the relation of these things to each other and to the general prosperity of the State has not been understood or studied. Lumbermen have cut away timber wherever it paid to do so, without regard to effects on rivers and streams, or even future supplies for their own business. A third and rapidly growing interest was also affected, that of the great summer travel to the woods and mountains, involving expenditure of millions of dollars. A cry went up that once beautiful localities were so no longer. Wooded mountains had been stripped bare; cool, shaded streams now lay open to the sun, their waters choked with sawdust from the mills, and the fishing spoiled. It was time to act, the streams failing, the timber supply growing less, natural scenery ruined. So in this State and in others *forestry* came into being as a practical science.

The forest region of New York is chiefly in the northern section and along the Catskills and their spurs. The former covers an area of 3,588,803 acres, of which the State owned in 1893 over 731,000 acres. It was proposed to establish a reservation or park of over 2,807,000 acres, buying up such sections as could be profitably handled as timber lands and become a permanent paying investment. Settled farms, villages, etc., on this reservation would not be disturbed, nor would any effort be made to buy hotel property, private parks, etc. These would naturally cooperate with the work of the Commission. These private preserves are estimated to aggregate 940,000 acres, and there is also a water area of 57,104 acres. There remains to be purchased about 1,200,000 acres,

composed of 677,955 acres of lumbered forest (cut over) and 522,045 acres of primeval forest, having an assessed valuation of $1,500,000. The lumbered lands are valued at $1.50 per acre, the virgin forest at $8. The uncut timber lands yield, on an average, 3,000 feet of logs to the acre, worth $1.50 per 1,000 feet on the stump. The estimated value of these lands was about $3,516,000, and the Commission recommended their purchase outright by an issue of bonds, believing that the saving in the end would amply warrant the present outlay. But our legislators, while freely voting vast sums for city speedways, public buildings, world's fairs, etc., could not be made to see how wise this forestry investment would be, nor how far-reaching and beneficial would be its effects. So the Commission must do the best it can with the meager sums doled out, while delay results in further diminution of the forest area and enhanced prices for the remainder.

The wooded area of the Catskill preserve is fully three-fifths of the Adirondack, and includes over 2,000,000 acres of forest lands in Ulster, Delaware and Sullivan counties, of which the State owns 49,332 acres, in scattered tracts, and the purchase of 100,000 acres more in the vicinity would be highly desirable, the summer population of the Catskill range being larger than that of the Adirondacks, the location being accessible to thousands whose means debar them from the remoter resort. Included in the Catskill lands is a deer park, stocked with over fifty deer, taken from the Adirondacks. In summer these are turned loose to browse in the woods. As some confusion exists regarding the distinction between the Adirondack Park and the Forest Preserve, it may be well to say here that the former is composed of lands owned or to be acquired, in six counties of northern New York, including islands in Lake George, and the latter lands in sixteen counties, some of them the same, but not always the same territory. On the Preserve the duties of the Commission are to preserve the timber and make sales of the marketable part (?). Full authority is given to protect against fire and timber stealers. to proceed against individuals. railroads, and other corporations guilty of trespass or carelessness. On the Park, in addition to these duties, the

Commission is to make provision for campers, and to lease lands for camping purposes.

" The Park is to be forever reserved, maintained, and cared for as ground open for the free use of all the people for their health and pleasure, and as forest lands necessary to the preservation of the headwaters of the chief rivers of the State, and a future timber supply, and shall remain part of the forest preserve. . . . On the expiration of the terms of office of the Forest Commissioners appointed pursuant of this chapter (amendment of 1893), the Forest Commission shall cease and determine, and all its powers and duties shall devolve on the Commissioner of Agriculture."

The chief cause of forest waste is undoubtedly from fire, and the fires in too many cases are caused by men's carelessness. The Report of 1894 does well to bring together, covering over sixty pages, the details of widespread destruction not only of forests but of towns, villages and human life in the summer and fall of 1894. It is a terrible record, the reading of which should drive every state to take every precaution possible against the beginnings of such awful endings. New York was the first state to deal with this element of forest destruction. The law of 1885, establishing a forest commission, contained the essential features of the present one for the prevention of forest fires. Maine followed, adopting essentially the same law.

New Hampshire followed, and more recently New Jersey and Pennsylvania have taken active measures, and so have some of the Western States. For ten years past, the forest regions of New York have been continuously and faithfully posted with notices— over 10,000 in a season—containing the rules of the Commission telling every resident what to do or not do in the matter of fire. Each town has a firewarden who has authority to call out help to extinguish fires. A farmer may not burn over a fallow or piece of brush land without notifying the warden. As a result, the people have been educated in regard to the use of fire; carefulness has taken the place of carelessness, and the indifference of former years has been succeeded by a lively interest. In spite of the sultry season of 1894 there was no increase in the number of fires, and most of these were in woodlands and barrens scattered through the farming districts. Those in the Adirondack and Catskill districts were few in number and did little damage.

.   .   .   .   .   ,   .

In view of the uncertain character of our legislation, the future of our State forestry efforts will be studied with interest mingled with apprehension; but let us hope for the best. This Report, and also the one for 1893, are freely illustrated with full-page engravings of Adirondack life and scenery.*—I.

OUR FORESTS

It is estimated, by those whose special study of the subject seems to have fitted them to judge, that the number of acres of land in the United States now covered with wood growth is about four hundred and fifty millions. Of this area, about seventy million acres belong to the United States government. The rest is the property of individuals, except a small amount which belongs to states of the Union.

Of the entire forest area, it was ascertained that more than ten million acres were burned over in the census year 1880. It is not probable that the annual destruction by fire has fallen off since that year.

It is estimated that twenty-five million acres of woodland are cut off each year. At this rate of destruction, the woodlands ot the United States must speedily disappear if it were not the fact that while the woods in many places are being wantonly burned or cut away, they are also growing, not only in a great many sites where they have just undergone destruction, but in many places which have been clear of timber.

But altho woods grow spontaneously in

many parts of the country and so freely that there is little fear that there will be a net loss of timber east of the one-hundredth meridian, or a general unfavorable effect upon soil or climate in that region, the new growth, in the forests of the country, does not by any means keep pace with the destruction.

It is estimated that while twenty-four thousand millions of cubic feet of wood are consumed annually in the United States, the wood that grows each year on the present forest area of the country is not more than twelve thousand millions of cubic feet.

It is reasonably certain that, whether tree growths as a whole increase or diminish, the great forests of the country must disappear unless something is done to check their destruction.

What the effect upon the far Western or more arid section of the country would be if the mountain forests were entirely swept away—as they must be under present conditions, since in that region the woods do not ordinarily spring up again when cut down— can be anticipated by observing the effect

* In 1885 the State of New York appointed a Forest Commission with a view to the preservation of the forests. Since then the law has been modified several times. It now provides for a " Forest, Fish and Game Commission," whose business it is to enforce the fish and game laws and to take care of the Adirondack Park and the State Forest Preserve. In 1897 the Legislature authorized the expending of $1,000,000 for lands in the Adirondacks as an addition to the Park and Forest Preserve; in 1898, $500,000; and, in 1899, $900,000 were added for the same purpose. The State has founded a State College of Forestry at Cornell University, giving it charge of 30,000 acres of land as a demonstration forest in the Adirondack Mountains.

upon the water flow in New York State of the partial destruction of the Adirondack forests.

It is officially reported that the cutting away of woods in the Adirondack region has diminished the reliable water supply in the Mohawk and Hudson Rivers by from thirty to fifty per cent. The loss begins to affect unfavorably navigation in the New York canals and rivers.

In the Rocky Mountain and Pacific Coast regions, the drying up of the sources of water supply by the cutting away of the mountain forests seriously endangers the supply of water for the irrigation of the plains below, and thus menaces the habitability of those regions.

Further east the question is equally a practical one tho not as threatening. The practise is to destroy without replacing. We commonly trust to the unaided operations of nature to put back the wood growths we take; but nature does not always put them back.

The experience of the Old World has proved that a steady and profitable supply of wood may be drawn from forests, and a revenue from them derived by those who own them, and the forests maintained in good growth at the same time, to supply still further revenue and to exercise their equalizing and preserving influence on climate, rainfall, and water supply.

This lesson of profit and loss should not be a hard one for the practical American people to learn, and there are many indications, both in the direction of private enterprise and in projects for legislation, that they are learning it.

President Benjamin Harrison, during his administration (in 1890), sent to Congress a special message calling attention to the necessity of preserving the forests on the public domain, and urging early legislation to prevent the destruction of forest areas.

The legislation which is most actively urged provides for the withdrawal of public forest lands from sale or preemption, and the protection of the forests from destruction by fires and by the depredations of those who take the public timber without paying for it.—Y. C.

PROPERTIES OF TREES

By James Knapp Reeve

Many of our common forest trees have other properties and uses besides that of supplying timber; some of them have distinct medicinal properties, while others supply various by-products of more or less value. When forestry has become a more clearly defined industry with us, we shall appreciate these uses more than we do now. At present our trees are utilized in this way, if at all, only in the most desultory manner. I shall not try to give here any complete compendium of such uses, but merely mention some of the most ordinary of them.

From the inner bark of the blue ash, a tree found principally upon the bottoms of the Mississippi and Illinois Rivers, a blue color is extracted which is used by the people of those regions as a dyestuff.

A fluid extract of the inner bark of the butternut is used in cases of dysentery, habitual constipation, and other bowel complaints, and as a gentle cathartic, operating without producing debilitating effects. Various other preparations of the butternut are used in domestic practise for the ailments of children, especially in throat complaints.

A fluid extract from the bark of the wahoo or winged elm, is used as a tonic, alterative and laxative, and is especially beneficial in hepatic derangements, whether accompanying or preceding intermittents, or occurring independently of malaria. In constipation, due to hepatic torpor, it is highly recommended.

The wood and heart of the yellow locust furnishes a coloring matter which is used in dyeing.

The pine produces pine-tar, resin, and pitch; and throughout all the long-leaved pine region of the South, a considerable industry in the manufacture of these substances is carried on.

The wood of the osage orange yields a yellow dyestuff; and the inner bark of the tree is so very fine and white that it has been suggested that the fiber might be employed in making cloth.

The bark of the horse chestnut yields a yellow dye and in Ireland the nuts are used to whiten linen. They are first rasped into the water and allowed to macerate for a time, and when applied to the linen, the saponaceous matter exudes from the raspings and acts as a bleach.

From the bark of the catalpa is produced a tonic which is powerfully antiseptic. It is claimed to be a sure antidote for the bite of snakes. The flowers of this tree are also valuable as a remedy for asthma.

The wood of the white willow is used extensively in the production of gunpowder, and for tanning purposes also.

From the small branches of the white spruce is extracted a concentrated essence from which spruce beer is manufactured.

A fluid extract prepared from the leaves of the arbor-vitæ is used in the treatment of malarial diseases; the saturated tincture is used in the treatment of pulmonary hemorrhage, and is also applied to cancerous ulcerations, warts, etc. The Indians employ a salve made from the leaves for the relief of rheumatism. By distillation the leaves yield a volatile oil which has been used as a vermicide, and the distilled water has been used in the treatment of dropsy.

The eucalyptus has become so well known as an antiseptic and disinfectant that its common name in some places is the fever-tree. It has been extensively planted about the city of Valencia, Spain, for the purpose of counteracting the malarial fever, from which the people suffered severely. The leaves and small branches are steeped in hot water for preparing baths for the treatment of neuralgia and rheumatism. The oil is used as a scent for cigars, and finds medicinal employment in various ways.

A preparation of the bark of the barberry is used as a purgative and tonic. The berries from this tree, gathered while green and pickled in vinegar, are used as a substitute for capers. A yellow dye is procured from the inner bark of both the stem and roots, and its astringent principle is so abundant that it is sometimes used in tanning leather, which it dyes a fine yellow.

An extract from the roots of the holly-leaved barberry is used in the treatment of bilious fever.

A juice expressed from the berries of the buckthorn is used as a dye or stain, and also as a vegetable paint. The berries are also strongly purgative, but not much used in medicine on account of their severity.

The American silver fir (balm of Gilead) is the source of the remedy known as Canada balsam.—I.

"UNTER DEN LINDEN"

By William Whitman Bailey

It is said of the European linden, or lime, so common as a shade-tree in our streets, that it is always dropping something. In early spring it is the pretty bud-scales that are shed and litter the pavement; in late June the abundant flowers fall and look like snuff on the pathway; in July the air is full of the miniature fruit dislodged by every breeze; later still the ripened berries fall with their scale; and last of all the leaves, by that time clothed with fungi, are cast off and make a slippery, mucilaginous mess. This tree, then, cannot be called a clean one. Our native linden is much handsomer, indeed a noble tree, tall, stately and with ample foliage; yet it is rarely seen in cultivation.

After the above arraignment of the linden, it is only fair to state its virtues. A tree so loved of the poets must have its excellencies. Tennyson is never tired of singing the praises of the "ruby-budded lime." He seems constantly to see its golden flowers noisy "with bees and breeze from end to end."

It is of interest to note also that the famous Swedish naturalist, Linnæus, derived his name from this tree, a noble specimen of which stood on the ancestral estate.

But decidedly the most interesting thing about the tree is the manner in which it distributes its fruit. The flowers are borne on a somewhat long peduncle, soldered for half its length to the linear-oblong scale or brast. After the flowers drop and the berries begin to ripen, the scale is subject to two different tortions. In the first place it twists upon itself in a semi-spiral or corkscrew-like form. Then the whole scale bends backward into a bow. The result is a natural propeller wheel. It will be observed on any breezy day, when the fruit is heavy enough, that the freighted scale, detached from the tree by the wind, flutters earthward with a peculiar gyrating or volatory movement. The whole contrivance revolves so rapidly on its axis that, by an optical illusion, it resembles, while flying, a funnel. Or again, it may be compared in this fancied shape to an open lily-bell. If the observer is more remote from these flying scales, they bear a marvelous resemblance to butterflies.

The observer will at once note that the apparent object of the ingenious mechanism is to deflect the fruit from the immediate vicinity of the parent tree. The flight is always centrifugal. It is a fascinating phenomenon, which one never tires of watching. The same gyratory movement is seen in the seeds of pine and sycamore.—I.

THE GREATEST FOREST IN THE WORLD

"Where is the greatest forest in the world?"

The question was asked in the Forestry section of the American Association for the Advancement of Science, at an annual meeting in Brooklyn. The importance of forests for equalizing the climate and the rainfall of the globe was under discussion, and the purpose of the question was to show where the great forest tracts of the world are situated.

One member, replying offhand, was inclined to maintain that the greatest continuous tract of forest lies north of the St. Lawrence River, in the Provinces of Quebec and Ontario, extending northward to Hudson Bay and Labrador; a region measuring about seventeen hundred miles in length from East to West, and a thousand miles in width, North and South.

A professor from the Smithsonian Institution rejoined that a much larger continuous area of timber lands was to be found, reckoning from those in the State of Washington northward through British Columbia and Alaska. But he limited his statement to North America, for he added that, in his opinion, the largest forest in the world occupied the valley of the Amazon, embracing much of northern Brazil, eastern Peru, Bolivia, Ecuador, Colombia and Guiana; a region at least twenty-one hundred miles in length by thirteen hundred in breadth.

Exception was immediately taken to this statement by several members who have computed the forest area of Central Africa in the valley of the Congo, including the headwaters of the Nile to the north-east, and those of the Zambesi on the south. According to their estimates, Central Africa contains a forest region not less than three thousand miles in length from north to south, and of vast, altho not fully known width, from east to west. Discussion, in which the evidence afforded by travels and surveys was freely cited, seemed favorable to the defender of the Amazonian forests.

Later in the day the entire question was placed in another light, by a member who was so fortunate as to be able to speak from some knowledge of still another great forest region of the globe. This gentleman gave a vivid picture of the vast, solemn *taigas* and *urmans,* the pine, larch and cedar forests of Siberia.

It appears that Siberia, from the plain of the Obi River on the west to the valley of the Indighirka on the east, embracing the great plains, or river valleys, of the Yenisei, Olenek, Lena and Yana rivers, is one great timber belt, averaging more than a thousand miles in breadth from north to south,—being fully seventeen hundred miles wide in the Yenesei district,—and having a length from east to west of not less than forty-six hundred versts, about three thousand miles.

Unlike equatorial forests, the trees of the Siberian *taigas* are mainly conifers, comprising pines of several varieties, firs and larches. In the Yenisei, Lena, and Olenek regions, there are thousands of square miles where no human being has ever been. The long-stemmed conifers rise to a height of a hundred and fifty feet or more, and stand so closely together that walking among them is difficult.

The dense, lofty tops exclude the pale Arctic sunshine, and the straight, pale trunks, all looking exactly alike, so bewilder the eye in the obscurity, that all sense of direction is soon lost. Even the most experienced trappers of sable dare not venture into the dense *taigas* without taking the precaution of "blazing" the trees constantly with hatchets as they walk forward. If lost there, the hunter rarely finds his way out, but perishes miserably from starvation or cold. The natives avoid the *taigas,* and have a name for them which signifies "places where the mind is lost."

The discussion was closed very appropriately by Professor Fernow, of Washington, with an illustrated lecture which showed how, in the earlier ages, forests had covered all the continental areas, and had rendered the climate equable to a degree now unknown.

At first human beings battled with the forest in a fitful manner, making small clearings for themselves; but gradually, by the aid of fire and of their own increasing numbers, they have so far prevailed in the struggle for supremacy that the forests are hopelessly conquered. But grave evils follow their extermination; and now the question is, how to foster, protect and preserve them.—Y. C.

AN ACT TO ENCOURAGE ARBORICULTURE

Approved April 30th, 1888

The People of the State of New York, represented in Senate and Assembly, do enact as follows:

SECTION I. The Friday following the first day of May in each year shall hereafter be known throughout this State as Arbor Day.

§ 2. It shall be the duty of the authorities of every public school in this State, to assemble the scholars in their charge on that day in the school building, or elsewhere, as they may deem proper, and to provide for and conduct, under the general supervision of the City Superintendent or the School Commissioner, or other chief officers having the general oversight of the public schools in each city or district, such exercises as shall tend to encourage the planting, protection, and preservation of trees and shrubs, and an acquaintance with the best methods to be adopted to accomplish such results.

§ 3. The State Superintendent of Public Instruction shall have power to prescribe from time to time, in writing, a course of exercises and instruction in the subjects hereinbefore mentioned, which shall be adopted and observed by the public school authorities on Arbor Day, and upon receipt of copies of such course, sufficient in number to supply all the schools under their supervision, the School Commissioner or City Superintendent aforesaid, shall promptly provide each of the schools under his or their charge with a copy, and cause it to be adopted and observed.

P. T.

SUGGESTIVE THOUGHTS

ARBOR DAY.—The school children of New York State planted more than 200,000 trees within ten years from the time Arbor Day was recognized. Few similar efforts in years have been more thoroughly commendable than the effort to get our people practically to show their appreciation of the beauty and usefulness of trees.

ARBOR DAY'S OBSERVANCE, For.—The primary purpose of the Legislature in establishing "Arbor Day," was to develop and stimulate in the children of the Commonwealth a love and reverence for Nature as revealed in trees and shrubs and flowers. In the language of the statute, "to encourage the planting, protection and preservation of trees and shrubs" was believed to be the most effectual way in which to lead our children to love Nature and reverence Nature's God, and to see the uses to which these natural objects may be put in making our school grounds more healthful and attractive.

The object sought may well command the most thoughtful consideration and the painstaking efforts of school officers, teachers, and pupils in every school district, and in every educational institution, and of all others who are interested in beautifying the schools and the homes of the State.

It will be well not only to plant trees and shrubs and vines and flowers where they may contribute to pleasure and comfort, but also to provide for their perpetual care, and to supplement such work by exercises which will lead all to a contemplation of the subject in its varied relations and resultant influences. It is fitting that trees should be dedicated to eminent scholars, educators, statesmen, soldiers, historians or poets, or to favorite teachers or pupils in the different localities. On this occasion, however, it would be especially appropriate to dedicate one tree in each district to Washington.

The opportunity should not be lost, which is afforded by the occasion, for illustrating and enforcing the thought that the universe, its creation, its arrangement, and all of its developing processes, are not due to human planning or oversight, but to the infinite wisdom and power of God.

Our school exercises, and particularly those of an unusual character, should be interspersed with selections, songs, and acts which will inspire patriotism.—A. S. DRAPER, Superintendent of Public Schools, Albany, N. Y.

FLOWERS, Concerning National.—Lovers of flowers have often wondered why we as a nation have no floral emblem, and at this season, in recent years, efforts have been made to supply our deficiency in this respect. Various flowers, such as the golden-rod and the Mayflower, have been proposed for the place of honor, but somehow none of them has been so widely accepted as to stand for America in the familiar way in which the rose and the lily stand for two nations across the sea.

Now there are several reasons why America has no floral emblem, but I think the principal reason is this. There is no flower that has touched at any particular point our national history. The Mayflower comes the nearest to having this requirement, being associated in name with the ship that brought the Pilgrim Fathers to our shores; but unfortunately it is so humble a little flower that the composite mind of our broad and mighty Nation tacitly refuses to accept it as a national emblem. If we are to choose a national flower in a purely arbitrary way, the cool, matter-of-fact, composite mind demands a certain congruity between our emblematic flora and fauna, and the screaming eagle and the modest little Mayflower would certainly not be very well matched.—GEORGE H. WESTLEY.

FORESTS, The Destruction of.—*Was the Lord displeased against the rivers?*—*Hab. iii: 8.* The earth was made for our dwelling-place, and we are to have dominion over it. It is to be helpful to us, not hurtful. If hurtful, it is because we do not understand the laws that govern it and us; or, if we understand these laws, we do not observe them.

We secure dominion over the forces of nature only through recognition of the laws that govern them. The floods that have made so great havoc in Europe and America this season are the natural results of violated law.

I. The forests of the hills and mountains are God's natural check on the overflow of streams. [See George P. Marsh on "The Earth as Modified by Human Action."]

II. As a nation, we are guilty of violation of this law for protection of the valleys. The plunder of the leafy wealth of the hills has been most wanton. The penalty has been visited upon the valleys.

III. The protection must be secured through the dissemination of knowledge upon the subject, and through the state and national law. Otherwise the floods will augment each year until they become immeasurable calamities.—H. R.

OAK TREE, The Old, and Its New Memorial Stone.—In the old town of Charlemont, Franklin County, stands an ancient oak which antedates all memory of "first settlers" and of those before them. It has a huge, shapely trunk, and once reached its branches to points more than fivescore feet apart.

For a series of years a society called the "Oak Tree Society" has, with the inhabitants, held a kind of town and church history meeting under it. Last year the "Pocumtuck Valley Memorial Association" united their "Field Day Meeting" with the yearly gathering there. It was then proposed to affix a bronze tablet to the tree, telling its story and worth to us. This was afterwards changed to a boulder, or huge stone, to lie at its base.

The stone was unveiled and dedicated. Scripture (Psalm xliv: 1-8) and prayer were followed by the presentation and unveiling of the work by the President. An address of acceptance on behalf of the Oak Tree Society, of the inhabitants of the town, and for all people, was made. The legend reads:

THE HISTORIC OAK:
THE TREE OF COUNSEL AND OF WORSHIP
To OUR FATHERS;
REVERED AND CHERISHED BY US
THEIR CHILDREN.
1765—1893.

Tradition tells of Town Meetings and Sabbath worship held in early days of the town beneath its capacious shade.

The grand old 78th Psalm, "Let children hear the mighty deeds," was sung; a poem "The Old Farm Home;" addresses, recitations, and "America," sung by the assembly, filled the day.

So another "bond to the past" holds these inhabitants by new historic, ancestral, and pious (literally) sympathies to the evergreen homeland among the hills.—REV. LYMAN WHITING, D.D. (E.)

SCRIPTURE SELECTIONS.—"And God said let the earth bring forth the fruit tree yielding fruit after its kind; and the earth brought forth the tree yielding fruit; and

God saw that it was good. And out of the ground made the Lord God to grow every tree that is pleasant to the sight and good for food." Gen. i: 11.

And Abraham said to the three angels: "Rest yourselves under the tree;" and he stood by them under the tree, and they did eat. Gen. xviii: 4.

The tree of the field is man's life. "Then shall all the trees of the wood rejoice before the Lord."—Psa. xcvi: 12. "The trees of the Lord are full of sap, the cedars of Lebanon which he hath planted; where the birds make their nests; as for the stork, the fir trees are her house."—Psa. civ: 17.

"Blessed is the man whose delight is in the law of the Lord; he shall be like a tree planted by the rivers of water, that bringeth forth its fruit in due season; his leaf shall not wither; and whatsoever he doeth shall prosper." Psa. i: 3.

Of Wisdom, the wise man saith: "She is a tree of life to them that lay hold upon her, and happy is every one that retaineth her." Prov. iii: 18. And again, "The fruit of the righteous is a tree of life." Prov. xi: 30. While "Hope deferred maketh the heart sick, when the desire cometh it is a tree of life." Prov. xiii: 12. And "A wholesome tongue is a tree of life." Prov. xv: 4.

And the angel carried me away in the spirit, and showed me that great city the New Jerusalem: "In the midst of the street of it, and on either side of the river was the tree of life which bare twelve manner of fruits, and yielded its fruit every month; and the leaves of the tree were for the healing of the nations." Rev. xxii: 2. And He said: "To him that overcometh, I will give to eat of the tree of life which is in the midst of the paradise of God." Rev. ii: 7.—P. T.

POETRY

Flowers, The Mystery of.

There was never mystery
But 'tis figured in the flowers;
Was never secret history
But birds tell it in the bowers.
RALPH WALDO EMERSON.

Pine Needles

If Mother Nature patches
The leaves of trees and vines,
I'm sure she does her darning
With the needles of the pines.

They are so long and slender;
And sometimes, in full view,
They have their thread of cobwebs,
And thimbles made of dew.
WILLIAM H. HAYNE.

Plants, He Who

He who plants a tree, he plants love;
Tents of coolness spreading out above
Wayfarers, he may not live to see.

Gifts that grow are best;
Hands that bless are blest;
Plant-life does the rest!
Heaven and earth help him who plants a tree,
And his work his own reward shall be.
·LUCY LARCOM.

Plant Trees

We plant the pine and fir tree,
And all that wear green branches.
To give us hope of spring time,
Tho snows are over all;
The maple is for bird songs,
The elm for stately branches,
Whose long, protecting shadows
Through summer noontides fall.
LILIAN E. KNAPP.

Trees

Yon sturdy oak whose branches wide
Boldly the storms and winds defy,
Not long ago an acorn small
Lay dormant 'neath a summer sky.
Selected.

Trees, The.

Could we but read your steadfast lives
        aright,
And hear your message, as true hearts may
        hear,
In you our life might find its meaning clear,
" Rooted in clay, we lift our heads toward
        light."

J. O. RANKIN. (Y. C.)

Arbor Day Song

By Mary A. Heermans.

Of nature broad and free,
Of grass and flower and tree,
        Sing we to-day.
God hath pronounced it good,
So we, His creatures would
Offer to field and wood
        Our heartfelt lay.

To all that meets the eye,
In earth, or air, or sky,
        Tribute we bring.
Barren this world would be,
Bereft of shrub and tree;
Now gracious Lord to Thee
        Praises we sing.

May we Thy hand behold,
As bud and leaf unfold,
        See but Thy thought;
Nor heedlessly destroy,
Nor pass unnoticed by;
But be our constant joy
        All Thou hast wrought.

As each small bud and flower
Speaks of the Maker's power,
        Tells of His love;
So we, Thy children dear,
Would live from year to year,
Show forth Thy goodness here,
        And then above.

Forest Hymn

By William Cullen Bryant

The groves were God's first temples, ere
        man learned
To hew the shaft, and lay the architrave,
And spread the roof above them,—ere he
        framed
The lofty vault, to gather and roll back
The sound of anthems; in the darkling wood,
Amidst the cool and silence, he knelt down,
And offered to the Mightiest solemn thanks
And supplication. For his simple heart
Might not resist the sacred influences
Which, from the stilly twilight of the place,
And from the gray old trunks that high in
        heaven
Mingled their mossy boughs, and from the
        sound
Of the invisible breath that swayed at once
All their green tops, stole over him, and
        bowed
His spirit with the thought of boundless
        power
And inaccessible majesty. Ah, why

Should we, in the world's riper years, neglect
God's ancient sanctuaries, and adore
Only among the crowd, and under roofs
That our frail hands have raised? Let me,
        at least,
Here in the shadow of this aged wood,
Offer one hymn,—thrice happy if it find
Acceptance in His ear.

Father, Thy hand
Hath reared these venerable columns. Thou
Didst weave this verdant roof. Thou didst
        look down
Upon the naked earth, and forthwith rose
All these fair ranks of trees. They in Thy
        sun
Budded, and shook their green leaves in Thy
        breeze,
And shot towards heaven. The century-
        living crow,
Whose birth was in their tops, grew old and
        died
Among their branches, till at last they stood,
As now they stand, massy and tall and dark,
Fit shrine for humble worshiper to hold
Communion with his Maker. These dim
        vaults,
These winding aisles, of human pomp or
        pride,
Report not. No fantastic carvings show
The boast of our vain race to change the
        form
Of Thy fair works. But Thou art here.—
        Thou fill'st
The solitude. Thou art in the soft winds
That run along the summit of these trees
In music; Thou art in the cooler breath
That from the inmost darkness of the place
Comes, scarcely felt; the barky trunks, the
        ground,
The fresh, moist ground, are all instinct with
        Thee:
Here is continual worship;—nature, here,
In the tranquillity that Thou dost love,
Enjoys Thy presence. Noiselessly around,
From perch to perch, the solitary bird
Passes; and yon clear spring that, midst its
        herbs,
Wells softly forth, and, wandering, steeps the
        roots
Of half the mighty forest, tells no tale
Of all the good it does. Thou hast not left
Thyself without a witness, in these shades,
Of Thy perfection. Grandeur, strength, and
        grace
Are here to speak of Thee. This mighty
        oak,—
By whose immovable stem I stand and seem
Almost annihilated,—not a prince,
In all that proud old world beyond the
        deep,
E'er wore his crown as loftily as he
Wears the green coronal of leaves with
        which
Thy hand hath graced him. Nestled at his
        root
Is beauty, such as blooms not in the glare
Of the broad sun. That delicate forest
        flower,
With scented breath, and look so like a
        smile,

Seems, as it issues from the shapeless mould,
An emanation of the indwelling life,
A visible token of the upholding Love,
That are the soul of this wide universe.

My heart is awed within me when I think
Of the great miracle that still goes on,
In silence, round me,—the perpetual work
Of Thy creation, finished, yet renewed
Forever. Written on Thy works, I read
The lesson of Thy own eternity.
Lo! all grow old and die; but see again,
How on the faltering footsteps of decay
Youth presses,—ever gay and beautiful
    youth
In all its beautiful forms. These lofty trees
Wave not less proudly that their ancestors
Molder beneath them. O, there is not lost
One of Earth's charms! Upon her bosom
    yet,
After the flight of untold centuries,
The freshness of her far beginning lies,
And yet shall lie. Life mocks the idle hate
Of his arch-enemy,—Death,—yea, seats him-
    self
Upon the tyrant's throne, the sepulcher,
And of the triumphs of his ghastly foe
Makes his own nourishment. For he came
    forth
From Thine own bosom, and shall have no
    end.

There have been holy men who hid them-
    selves
Deep in the woody wilderness, and gave
Their lives to thought and prayer, till they
    outlived
The generation born with them, nor seemed
Less aged than the hoary trees and rocks
Around them;—and there have been holy
    men
Who deemed it were not well to pass life
    thus.
But let me often to these solitudes
Retire, and, in Thy presence, reassure
My feeble virtue. Here its enemies,
The passions, at Thy plainer footsteps
    shrink,
And tremble, and are still. O God! when
    Thou
Dost scare the world with tempests, set on
    fire
The heavens with falling thunderbolts, or
    fill,
With all the waters of the firmament,
The swift dark whirlwind that uproots the
    woods
And drowns the villages; when, at Thy call,
Uprises the great deep, and throws himself
Upon the continent, and overwhelms
Its cities,—who forgets not, at the sight
Of these tremendous tokens of Thy power,
His prides, and lays his strifes and follies by?
O, from these sterner aspects of Thy face
Spare me and mine, nor let us need the
    wrath
Of the mad, unchained elements, to teach
Who rules them. Be it ours to meditate
In these calm shades, Thy milder majesty,
And to the beautiful order of Thy works
Learn to conform the order of our lives.

How the Leaves Came Down

By Susan Coolidge

"I'll tell you how the leaves came down,"
    The great Tree to his children said,
"You're getting sleepy, Yellow and Brown,
Yes, very sleepy, little Red,
    It is quite time you went to bed."

"Ah," begged each silly pouting leaf,
"Let us a little longer stay:
Dear Father Tree, behold our grief;
'Tis such a very pleasant day,
    We do not want to go away."

So, just for one more merry day,
To the great Tree the leaflets clung;
Frolickt and danced, and had their way;
Upon the autumn breezes swung
    Whispering, all their sports among,

"Perhaps the great Tree will forget
And let us stay until the spring
If we all coax and beg and fret."
But the great Tree did no such thing;
    He smiled to hear their whispering.

"Come, children all, to bed," he cried,
And ere the leaves could urge their prayer,
He shook his head, and far and wide,
Fluttering and nestling everywhere,
    Down sped the leaflets through the air.

I saw them, on the ground they lay,
Golden and red, a huddled swarm,
Waiting till one from far away,
White bed-clothes heaped upon her arm,
    Should come to wrap them safe and warm.

The great bare Tree looked down and
    smiled,
"Good night, dear little leaves," he said,
And from below, each sleepy child,
Replied, "Good night," and murmured
"It is so nice to go to bed."

Planting the Oak

By F. L. Mace

Glad memories of the joyous youth
    Through all your songs repeat,
Who plucked the acorn from the twig
    Blown lightly to its feet,

And gayly to his fellows cried:
    "My destiny behold!
This seed shall keep my memory green
    In ages yet untold.

"I trust it to the sheltering sod,
    I hail the promised tree!
Sing, unborn oak, through long decades,
    And ever sing of me!"

To a Pine Sapling

By W. B. Allen

What song is in thy heart,
    Thou puny tree?
Weak pinelet that thou art—
Trembling at every shock,
Thy feebleness doth mock
    Thy high degree.

Nay, wherefore scoff at thy
  Dimensions small?
For, folded close, I spy
A wee, wee bud, scarce seen
Within its cradle green,
  And, after all,

In ages yet to come,
  Thy stately form,
No longer dwarfed and dumb,
But chanting to the breeze
Sublime, sweet melodies,
  Shall breast the storm!

Planting the Apple Tree

By William Cullen Bryant

Come, let us plant the apple tree.
Cleave the tough greensward with the spade;
Wide let its hollow bed be made;
There gently lay the roots, and there
Sift the dark mold with kindly care,
And press it o'er them tenderly.
As 'round the sleeping infant's feet
We softly fold the cradle sheet,
So plant we the apple tree.

The Elm Tree

By S. B. B. Merrifield

The farmer stood by the carriage house
    door,
Surveying with pride his domain o'er.
" I wish I had planted one more tree,
Just here on this side, by the vines,"
    thought he.

Then he brought to the spot that sweet
    spring day
A young, strong, elm, from over the way,
And placed it there by the carriage house
    door,
Just where it was needed so much before.

Lo, the years went by, till ninety were
    told—
One sows, nor reaps, 'tis the story old—
When a farmer, young, stood by the door,
Surveying with pride his domain o'er.

Said he, " The most beautiful thing I see
Is this grand o'er-arching, old elm tree.
Who planted it, boy? Would that I knew!
He did it for me, he did it for you.
His name we must read
In the loving deed."

The Maple Tree

When on the world's first harvest-day,
  The forest trees before the Lord
Laid down their autumn offerings
  Of fruit in golden sunshine stored,

The maple only, of them all,
  Before the world's great harvest King
With empty hands and silent stood—
  She had no offering to bring

For in the early summer time,
  While other trees laid by their hoard,
The maple winged her fruit with love,
  And sent it daily to the Lord.

There ran through all the leafy wood
  A murmur and a scornful smile
But silent still the maple stood,
  And looked unmoved to God the while.

And then, while fell on earth a hush
  So great it seemed like death to be,
From his white throne the mighty Lord
  Stooped down and kissed the maple tree.

At that swift kiss there sudden thrilled
  In every nerve, through every vein
An ecstasy of joy so great
  It seemed almost akin to pain.

And there before the forest trees,
  Blushing and pale by turns she stood;
In every leaf, now red and gold,
  Transfigured by the kiss of God.

And still when comes the autumn time,
  And on the hills the harvest lies,
Blushing the maple tree recalls
  Her life's one beautiful surprise.
                                    Selected.

The Trees

Gensque virûm truncis et duro robore nata.
                              Æneid viii: 315.

By Samuel V. Cole

There's something in a noble tree—
  What shall I say? a soul?
For 'tis not form, or aught we see
  In leaf or branch or bole.
Some presence, tho not understood,
  Dwells there always, and seems
To be acquainted with our mood,
  And mingles in our dreams.

I would not say that trees at all
  Were of our blood and race,
Yet, lingering where their shadows fall,
  I sometimes think I trace
A kinship, whose far-reaching root
  Grew when the world began,
And made them best of all things mute
  To be the friends of man.

Held down by whatsoever might
  Unto an earthly sod,
They stretch forth arms for air and light
  As we do after God.
And when in all their boughs the breeze
  Moans loud, or softly sings,
As our own hearts in us, the trees
  Are almost human things.

What wonder in the days that burned
  With old poetic dream,
Dead Phaeton's fair sisters turned
  To poplars by the stream?
In many a light cotillion stepped
  The trees when fluters blew;
And many a tear, 'tis said, they wept
  For human sorrow too.

Mute, said I? They are seldom thus;
  They whisper each to each,
And each and all of them to us,
  In varied forms of speech.

" Be serious," the solemn pine
Is saying overhead;
" Be beautiful," the elm tree fine
Has always finely said.

" Be quick to feel," the aspen still
Repeats the whole day long;
While from the green slope of the hill,
The oak tree adds, " Be strong."
When with my burden, as I hear
Their distant voices call,
I rise, and listen, and draw near,
" Be patient," say they all.
                                        Y. C.

Three Historic Trees

BY R. C. ADAMS

A royal charter was obtained
In sixteen sixty-two;
The colonies of Connecticut
A bond of union drew.
When Andros came with sixty men
The charter to revoke,
Brave Captain Wadsworth hid it safe
Within the Charter Oak.

[This Charter Oak was blown down in
1856. The Vice-President's chair at Washington is made from wood from this famous
old oak.]

Penn a treaty with Indians made,
'Neath a spacious, tall elm tree.
These were the words of the Indian chief
In sixteen eighty-three:
" While sun, moon, and stars endure,
In peace we'll live with thee."
Near Philadelphia, these famous words,
He spoke 'neath an old elm tree.

[The elm tree was blown down in March,
1810. It was then 283 years old. For years
it had been an object of veneration. Benjamin West commemorated the scene in a
famous painting. Parts of the tree were
sent to members of the Penn family.]

I speak of that elm at Cambridge,
Where Washington took command;
And that vast army true and brave,
Won liberty for our land.
With muskets clean and courage true,
In seventeen seventy-five,
Our men marched valiantly to fight,
For liberty each did strive.   J. E.

Our Horse-Chestnut Trees

BY SARAH KNOWLES BOLTON

We have planted on our hillside
Three graceful chestnut trees,
Which will swing their pink-white clusters
To every passing breeze
Long after he who gave them
And we who love their shade
Shall be on a distant hillside,
Among the silent laid.

Perhaps beneath their branches
Some child will sing at play;
Perhaps some lover's tale be told
Some golden autumn day,

When the grapes are growing purple,
And the far-off lake is blue,
And two are enough in all the world—
Forever old, yet new.

And here some man or woman,
White-haired and bent with age,
When the moon comes over the hilltop,
And floods the closing page
Of the book of life, near finished,
May rest in well-earned ease,
And thank his God and the giver
For the noble chestnut trees.
                                        I.

Woodman, Spare That Tree

BY GEORGE R. MORRIS

The following history of this poem will
be interesting. Mr. Morris, in a letter to a
friend, dated New York, February 1, 1837,
gave in substance this account: Riding out
of town, a few days since, in company with a
friend, an old gentleman, he invited me to
turn down a little romantic pass, not far
from Bloomingdale. " Your object?" inquired I. " Merely to look once more at an
old tree planted by my grandfather long
before I was born, under which I used to
play when I was a boy, and where my sisters played with me. There I often listened
to the good advice of my parents. Father,
mother, sisters—all are gone; nothing but
the old tree remains." And a paleness overspread his fine countenance, and tears came
to his eyes. After a moment's pause, he
added: " Don't think me foolish. I don't
know how it is; I never go out but I turn
down this lane to look at that old tree. I
have a thousand recollections about it, and
I always greet it as a familiar and well-
remembered friend."

These words were scarcely uttered when
the old gentleman cried out, " There it is!"
Near the tree stood a man with his coat off,
sharpening an ax. " You're not going to
cut that tree down, surely?" " Yes, but I
am tho," said the woodman. " What for?"
inquired the old gentleman, with choked
emotion. " What for? · I like that! Well, I
will tell you. I want the tree for firewood."
" What is the tree worth to you for firewood?" " Why, when down, about ten
dollars." " Suppose I should give you that
sum," said the old gentleman, " would you
let it stand?" " Yes." " You are sure of
that?" " Positive." " Then give me a bond
to that effect." We went into the little cottage in which my companion was born, but
which is now occupied by the woodman. I
drew up the bond. It was signed, and the
money paid over. As we left, the young
girl, the daughter of the woodman, assured
us that while she lived the tree should not
be cut. These circumstances made a strong
impression on my mind, and furnished me
with the materials for the song I send you.

Woodman, spare that tree!
Touch not a single bough!
In youth it sheltered me,
And I'll protect it now.

'Twas my forefather's hand
　　That placed it near his cot,
There, woodman, let it stand;
　　Thy ax shall harm it not.

That old familiar tree
　　Whose glory and renown
Are spread o'er land and sea—
　　And wouldst thou hack it down?
Woodman, forbear thy stroke!
　　Cut not its earth-bound ties;
O, spare that aged oak,
　　Now towering to the skies!

When but an idle boy
　　I sought its grateful shade;
In all their gushing joy,
　　Here, too, my sisters played.
My mother kissed me here;
　　My father pressed my hand—
Forgive the foolish tear,
　　But let that old oak stand.

My heart-strings round thee cling,
　　Close as thy bark, old friend;
Here shall the wild bird sing,
　　And still thy branches bend.
Old tree, the storm still brave!
　　And woodman, leave the spot!
While I've a hand to save
　　Thy ax shall harm it not.
　　　　　　N. B. A. D. M. (1898).

The Elm

By N. S. Dodge

Hail to the elm! the brave old elm!
　　Our last lone forest tree,
Whose limbs outstand the lightning's brand,
　　For a brave old elm is he!

For fifteen score of full-told years
　　He has borne his leafy prime,
Yet he holds them well, and lives to tell
　　His tale of the olden time!

Then hail to the elm! the green-topped elm!
　　And long may his branches wave,
For a relic is he, the gnarled old tree,
　　Of the times of the good and brave.
　　　　　　　　　Selected.

For Arbor Day

By Edith M. Thomas

Let dead names be eternized by dead stone,
　　Whose substance time cannot increase nor
　　　　mar;
Let living names by living shafts be known,
　　That feel the influence of sun and star.
Plant thou a tree, whose griefless leaves shall
　　　　sing
　　Thy deed and thee, each fresh unfolding
　　　　spring.
　　　　　　　　　Selected.

EMPIRE DAY*

(May 24)

D URING the latter half of the last century few things did more to foster British unity and patriotism than the observance of the Queen's Birthday. Every year on May 24, not only in the British Islands but also in India, Australia, Canada, and the other colonies and dependencies, the theme of conversation, essay and oration was "The Queen, God Bless Her!" No sovereign was ever more widely loved by the people at home and abroad; few, if any, have been more respected or more influential in advancing the interests of the nation and of humanity.

Among the noted buildings visited by the traveler in England, not least interesting is Kensington Palace, which was built, in its earliest parts, by William III., whose wife, Mary, as well as the King himself, died there. The most interesting room in the palace is one which was occupied by the Duke and Duchess of Kent, the parents of Queen Victoria. A tablet on the wall reads:

IN THIS ROOM

QUEEN VICTORIA

was born

May 24th, 1819.

The Queen died at Osborne Palace, January 22, 1901, thus having passed eighty-one anniversaries of her birth, and having reigned from June 28, 1838, a period of sixty-three years, lacking five months. This was the longest reign in English history.

By her simplicity, sympathy, and good sense, Queen Victoria won the affection of her people, who observed her birthday with increasing devotion to her and to the British Empire to the end of her long and beneficent life and reign. In palaces and castles, in mansions and homes, in churches and public halls, on land and water, the Queen's Birthday was looked forward to with the greatest interest and celebrated with glowing enthusiasm. It came at last to correspond very closely to our Independence Day in the manner of its celebration: in its social functions, banquets, orations, school exercises, processions, fireworks, out-of-door sports, decorations, and military salutes by the army and navy.

And now that Edward VII. is King, May 24 each year is still to be kept as a holiday, a day which for many years to come will not only elicit words of praise for Victoria and the "Victorian Era," but also serve as a day of happy and reasonable glorification of that great Empire on whose possessions the sun never sets.

* When this work was commenced, Queen Victoria was living. Since her death, in Canada and other parts of the British Empire, May 24 has been made a statutory holiday, to be known as Victoria Day. The birthday of King Edward VII. is November 9. Under all the circumstances, it seems best to the compiler to include under the general head of Empire Day, literature relating to the late Queen Victoria, King Edward VII., and the British Empire.

THE QUEEN'S BIRTHDAY *

By George W. Ross, LL.D.

A national holiday, while the occasion for recreation and pleasure-seeking, should be used by the teacher for impressing upon the minds of his pupils such facts and circumstances as would foster a national spirit. The birthday of Her Majesty, Queen Victoria furnishes an excellent opportunity for this purpose.† As memory is always aided by association, the events which transpired during her reign might be clustered around the holiday to which the pupils so eagerly look forward; and thus a more intelligent conception obtained of the greatness of the Empire and of the grounds on which loyalty to the Sovereign is founded.

To this end the teacher should spend half an hour every afternoon, for two or three weeks before the Queen's Birthday, in familiar conversations on the most important events of Her Majesty's reign (or, of English History). The extent of the British Empire might be shown upon the map and its vast area impressed upon the memory by comparisons with the extent and population of other important countries.

.   .   .   .

The essential unity of the Empire should be duly emphasized. Notwithstanding the number of its colonies and their distance from the capital and from each other, they all acknowledged the sovereignty of one Queen—a Queen whose personal qualities, apart from the dignity of her position, won for her the unqualified affection and allegiance of her subjects and the respect of all the nations of the world.

The teacher might point out that the flag which floats from the schoolhouse on Her Majesty's Birthday is a symbol of national unity, and that in every colony of the Empire, in Australia, in South Africa, in Hindostan,—on every fortress guarded by British soldiers and on every ship manned by British sailors, the same flag proclaims universal allegiance to one Sovereign and universal fealty to one Empire.

The teacher might then give a brief sketch of the monarchical form of government as compared with an absolute monarchy or a republic, explaining clearly that under a limited monarchy the Queen acted on the advice of Parliament, and that she was as much bound by the Constitution of the country as any of her subjects. Reference might be made to the impartiality with which she discharged her functions as a sovereign, to the great measures passed during her reign, such as the Repeal of the Corn Laws, the Extension of the Franchise, acts for the improvement of the laboring classes, the different reform bills, the Education Act, etc.

Then might follow a number of familiar talks or essays on:

(1) *The great wars of the Victorian Era*—Such as the Russian War, the Indian Mutiny, the Egyptian War, the War of the Soudan, etc.

(2) *The great statesmen of her reign*—Sir Robert Peel, Daniel O'Connell, John Bright, Richard Cobden, the Duke of Wellington, Lord Beaconsfield, Lord Salisbury, W. E. Gladstone, etc.

(3) *The great philosophers and literary men of her reign*—Darwin, Murchison, Sir Humphrey Davy, Sir John Simpson, Wordsworth, Browning, Tennyson, Matthew Arnold, Thomas Carlyle, Ruskin, etc.

(4) *The material and scientific improvements of her reign*—Railroads, steam navigation, gas, electricity, the reaping machine, penny postage, etc.

(5) *The great educational and moral reforms of her reign*—Mechanics' institutes, free libraries, free schools, compulsory education, industrial schools, missionary enterprises, factory laws, limitations of capital punishment, hospitals and charities, etc.

(6) *The progress of Canada during her reign*—The railways and canals built, the telegraph, telephone, free schools, the British North America Act of 1867, the ballot, the opening of the Northwest, etc.

An entertainment might be given on the afternoon preceding the Queen's Birthday, to which the parents and friends of the pupils should be invited. In such cases a program might be prepared. This program might be varied as the judgment of the teacher and the circumstances render necessary.

OUR EMPIRE AND EMPRESS AND OUR EMPIRE DAY

Of the many millions of patriots who speak in no uncertain manner of the might of Britain and who are wont to say that the sun never sets on her Empire, comparatively few understand the sentiment to which they give expression. They know that British possessions and colonies form a complete girdle of the globe; that sons of the Empire

* PATRIOTIC RECITATIONS. George W. Ross, LL.D. Toronto: Warwick Bro's & Rutter.
† That the Queen's death will not result in a discontinuance of May 24 as a holiday, is indicated by the following Associated Press item, which appeared in the newspapers of America, May 25, 1901: "London, May 24. There was a general observance of Queen Victoria's Birthday to-day. The Law Courts and Government offices were closed, the pupils of the various schools had a holiday, and there were the usual ringing of bells and the firing of salutes at Windsor and at the military and naval stations. There were special observances of the day in Australia, at the Cape, and in India."

are to be found everywhere and that Great Britain possesses a most enviable position as the greatest power for civilization that has ever existed, but they cannot present, without previous study and investigation, facts and figures which are the proof of Britain's greatness. When Postmaster-General Mulock adopted as suitable for the lettering of Canadian postage stamps, the well known words of Lewis Morris: "A vaster Empire than has been," it was with a purpose of giving to Canadians an impression of the potency of the British Empire. That Canadians have of late years experienced a wonderful and pleasing awakening is undoubtedly true, and especially since the outbreak of the trouble in South Africa have we been brought into a close realization and appreciation of the strength of Great Britain and the wisdom of her statesmen. It is not without the greatest satisfaction and pride that we proclaim ourselves Canadians, subject to Her Gracious Majesty, Queen Victoria, whose devotion to her has undergone a crucial test and has been proven no idle vaunt.

The facts which can be adduced to show the growth of the Empire are most worthy of consideration. In 1871 the Empire embraced a territory of 11,500,000 square miles or including Egypt and the Soudan, 13,-000,000. In this territory was a population of about 407,000,000, which would be increased to over 420,000,000, if Egypt and the Soudan were included. It may be a surprise to some to know that this is one-fourth of the population of the whole earth.* Of course, all people who enjoy the freedom that the Union Jack bespeaks, are not English speaking, but of those above mentioned 50,000,000 are of English speech and race—and it does not seem like a boast to say of the ruling race— they being included in the United Kingdom, British North America and Australasia. The remaining 350,000,000, or thereabouts, are what might be called subject races, being for the most part in India and Africa. To go back to 1871, the increase in area and population of this Empire—excluding Egypt and the Soudan—amounted to 2,854,000 square miles of area, or more than one-fourth of the whole, and to 125,000,000 of a population, which is also more than one-fourth of the whole. Using the term ruling race again, it may be said that in this increase of population they amounted to about 12,500,000, or about one-fourth of the number in 1897, and the increase in the subject races was 112,-000,000, or nearly one-third of the numbers

in 1897, and now that the question of expansion is so prominently before the thinking people everywhere, it may be mentioned that the increase in subject races was due largely, but by no means exclusively, to annexation. The present revenue (1900) of the different parts of this Empire, added together, amounted at that time to £257,653,000, and the imports and exports to £1,375,000,000. The increase since 1871 has amounted to £115,143,000 for revenue, or more than forty per cent. of the present total, while the increase in imports and exports amounted to £428,000,000, about one-third of the present total. It is interesting also, to look at the increase in population in the principal self-governing parts of the Empire, in which Canada cuts no unimportant figure. This increase from 1871 to 1897 has been as follows: United Kingdom, 8,350,000; Australia, 2,500,000; and Canada 1,500,000. Australia showing much the largest relative increase. The subject populations have increased by 2,750,000 in South Africa, 33,-150,000 in other parts of Africa, 72,900,000 in India, and 3,750,000 in other possessions, a total addition of 112,550,000 to what Rudyard Kipling so aptly called "the white man's burden" in a quarter of a century. To simply belong to such an Empire is an education, but it seems that it would take more than a lifetime to secure such an education that would cover a fair understanding of the countries and races which comprise the Empire and to a recognition of the responsibilities that are involved.—B. C. E. (May 23, 1900.)

[In the record of the world's history, never did nation occupy the proud position of Great Britain and her world-embracing colonies and dependencies. Gibbon, in his DE-CLINE AND FALL, sketches with a master's hand the extent of the Roman Empire, when at the zenith of its greatness, stretching as it did from beyond the Euphrates in the east to the Pillars of Hercules in the west, a distance of three thousand miles; and from the arid sands of the Libyan desert in the south to the eternal snows of Sarmatia in the north, a distance of two thousand miles, embracing the fairest portions of the then habitable world. Yet the mighty expanse of the Roman Empire constituted in area only one-fourth part of the British Empire of to-day. Its population of 120,000,000 being only one-half that of India, one of its dependencies.— SILAS ALWARD.]

*The total area of the British Empire was estimated in 1899 at 11,726,217 square miles, and the total population at 385,728,293. The estimated population of England and Wales on June 30, 1899, was 31,742,588 of Scotland 4,281,850; of Ireland, 4,535,516; total United Kingdom, 40,559,954. The British protectorates in Africa have (1901) an estimated area of 2,160,000 square miles, with 35,000,000 population; protectorates in the Pacific, 800 square miles, with 30,000 population; protectorates in Asia, 120,400 square miles, with 1,200,000 population; total area of protectorates 2,281,200 square miles, with 36,230,000 population.
The expenditure of the British Empire for 1901 was estimated at £26,000,000 for debt charges, £27,532,000 for the navy, £61,499,000 for the army, £22,839,000 for the civil services, and £16,221,000 for the revenue departments; total, £154,082,000. On the basis of the existing taxation the revenue was estimated at £21,900,000 from customs, £31,800,000 from excise, £13,000,000 from death duties, £8,400,000 from stamps, £800,000 from the land tax, £1,650,000 from the house duty, £18,800,000 from the income tax, £13,800,000 from the post-office, £3,550,000 from telegraphs, £450,000 from Crown lands, £850,000 from Suez canal shares, etc., and £1,900,000 from miscellaneous sources; total, £116,900,000. This left an estimated deficit of £37,182,000 for the year, which is being provided for by taxation and by the creation of bonds. [The figures in this note have been compiled from Appleton's ANNUAL CYCLOPEDIA for 1900.—ED.]

HISTORICAL
SOVEREIGNS OF ENGLAND *

Saxon Line

	Began to reign A. D.
Egbert	800
Ethelwulf (son)	836
Ethelbald (son)	857
Ethelbert (brother)	860
Ethelred I. (brother)	866
Alfred *the Great* (brother)	871
Edward *the Elder* (son)	901
Athelstan (son)	925
Edmund I. (brother)	940
Edred (brother)	946
Edwy *the Churl* (nephew)	955
Edgar (brother)	957
Edward *the Martyr* (son)	975
Ethelred II., *the Unready* (half-brother)	978
Edmund II., *Ironside* (son)	1016

Danish Line

Canute *the Dane* (son of Sweyn, a Viking)	1017
Harold I., *Harefoot* (son)	1036
Hardicanute (half-brother)	1039

Saxon Line (Restored)

Edward *the Confessor* (son of Ethelred II.)	1041
Harold II., *the Dauntless* (son of Earl Godwin)	1066

Norman Line

William I., *the Conqueror*	1066
William II., *Rufus* (son)	1087
Henry I., *Beauclerc* (brother)	1100
Stephen *Earl of Boulogne* (nephew)	1135

Plantagenet Line

Henry II., *Curtmantle* (son of Henry I. by Matilda)	1154
Richard I., *Cœur de Lion* (son)	1189
John *Sansterre* or *Lackland* (brother)	1199
Henry III., *Winchester* (son)	1216
Edward I., *Longshanks* (son)	1272
Edward II., *Caernarvon* (son)	1307
Edward III., *Windsor* (son)	1327
Richard II., *Bordeaux* (grandson)	1377

House of Lancaster

Henry IV., *Bolingbroke* (son of John of Gaunt)	1399

House of Lancaster

	Began to reign A. D.
Henry V., *Monmouth* (son)	1413
Henry VI., *Windsor* (son)	1422

House of York

Edward IV., *the Rose of Rouen* (son of Richard, Duke of York)	1461
Edward V. (son)	1483
Richard III., *Crookback* (uncle)	1483

Tudor Period

Henry VII.	1485
Henry VIII. (son)	1509
Edward VI. (son)	1547
Mary I. (half-sister)	1553
Elizabeth (half-sister)	1558

Stuart Line

James I. of England or VI. of Scotland (Union of the two crowns; legislative union took place May 1, 1707)	1603
Charles I.	1625

Commonwealth

(During which Oliver Cromwell ruled as Lord Protector, 1653-1658, being succeeded by Richard Cromwell, his son, 1658-1659; a year of anarchy follows)	1649

Stuart Line (Restored)

Charles II. (son of Charles I.)	1660
James II. (brother)	1685
William III. (nephew) and Mary II. (daughter of James II.)	1688
Anne (daughter of James II.)	1702

House of Brunswick or Guelph Line

George I. (great grandson of James I.)	1714
George II. (son of preceding)	1727
George III. (grandson of George II.)	1760
George IV. (son of George III.)	1820
William IV. (brother of preceding)	1830
Victoria (niece of William IV.)	1837
Edward VII. (son of Victoria)	1901

S. S. D.

BRIEF RECORD OF QUEEN'S LIFE

Victoria Alexandrina, Queen of Great Britain and Ireland and Empress of India, was the only child of the Duke of Kent, third son of George III., and of Louisa Victoria, Princess of Saxe-Coburg, sister of Leopold I., King of the Belgians. The chief

*The British Sovereign has, from very early times, been advised in the Conduct of the Government by a Committee of his Privy Council, known as the Cabinet.

incidents in her life and reign and the principal members of the royal family were as follows

PERSONAL HISTORY

1819, May 24.—Born at Kensington palace, London.

1820, January 23.—Death of her father, the Duke of Kent. Brought up by her mother and the Duchess of Cumberland.

1837, June 20.—Succeeded her uncle, William IV.

1838, June 28.—Crowned at Westminster Abbey.

1840, February 10.—Married to Prince Albert of Saxe-Coburg-Gotha.

1861, March 16.—Death of her mother, the Duchess of Kent.

December 14.—Death of the Prince Consort.

1869.—Publication of "Leaves from the Journal of Our Life in the Highlands."

1877, January 1.—Proclaimed Empress of India.

1885.—Publication of "More Leaves from the Journal of Our Life in the Highlands."

1887.—Jubilee celebration—fifty years a Queen.

1892.—Death of the Duke of Clarence.

1896, September.—Visit of Czar and Czarina of Russia to the Queen at Balmoral.

1897.—Jubilee celebration—sixtieth year of her reign.

1901, January 22.—Died at Osborne palace.

CHIEF PUBLIC EVENTS

1840.—Adoption of penny postage.

1845.—Repeal of the Corn laws. Resignation of Peel.

1850.—Clayton-Bulwer treaty.

1855.—Crimean war.

1858.—The Indian mutiny. Possessions of East India Company transferred to the crown.

1867.—Lord Derby's reform bill.

1868.—Irish Church disestablishment.

1870.—The education bill.

1871.—Abolition of army purchases and of university religious tests.

1872.—Treaty of Washington and the Geneva award on the Alabama claims.

1878.—The congress of Berlin. Acquisition of Cyprus.

1878-'80.—The Afghan war.

1881.—Annexation of the Transvaal.

1883.—English occupation of Egypt. Act for prevention of corrupt and illegal practises at parliamentary elections.

1885-'86.—The third reform bill and the redistribution bill; the Irish home rule and land bill; and their defeat.

1886-'93.—Behring sea controversy.

1891.—The free education bill.

1894.—The retirement of W. E. Gladstone. Opening of the Manchester ship canal.

1898.—Recovery of the Soudan.

1899.—Boer War in South Africa.

1900.—Lord Roberts proclaimed the annexation of the Transvaal Republic to the British Empire.

1901.—Queen Victoria died. Edward VII. became the King.

N. Y. T.

QUEEN VICTORIA AND HER REIGN

By Sir John Bourinot

(Clerk of the Canadian House of Commons)

William IV., King of England, died a little after two o'clock on the morning of June 20, 1837, and was instantaneously succeeded by his niece, the Princess **Beginning** Alexandrina Victoria, the only **of Reign** daughter of Prince Edward, Duke of Kent and Strathearne, in the absence of a male heir to the Crown. It was, however, not until eleven o'clock on the same day that the young Queen, then only eighteen years of age, formally met in Kensington Palace the great notables of her council, the representatives of the Witan or Commune Concilium of ancient times, who always assembled to choose and proclaim a new sovereign. Her conduct on this solemn occasion, when she was first called upon to perform a high function of State, has been graphically described in Greville's Memoirs. It was then she first gave some evidence to the world that she possessed those personal qualities which gave her for over sixty years such a preeminence among the Sovereigns of Great Britain. Sir Robert Peel expressed his amazement "at her manner and behavior, her modesty, and at the same time her firmness." When she had addressed the notables and the Privy Councilors had taken the oath of allegiance, she held her first Council, legally organized after such preliminaries and "presided with as much ease as if she had been doing nothing else all her life." In fact, according to the clerk of the Council present, she acted "with every sort of good taste and good feeling as well as good sense, and as far as it has gone nothing could be more favorable than the impression she has made and nothing can promise better than her manner and conduct.

The British people of all classes heard with deep satisfaction of the favorable opinions that were evoked by the admirable manner in which their youthful Sovereign, educated in a seclusion almost as close as that of a convent, had acquitted herself of the trying occasion just mentioned. Monarchy had been on its trial ever since the beginning of the century, even in England, where the sense of the great mass of the people is naturally favorable to such rule. George III. had been an arrogant Sovereign, and the closing year of his life had been clouded by insanity. His son was a thoroughly despicable creature, without honor or morals, and, whether Prince Regent or King, he was too often a source of humiliation to a people anxious to love and respect their Sovereign. William IV. always found it extremely difficult to be a gentleman, and when he ascended the throne at the mature age of sixty-five, and attempted to assume habits and manners in harmony with his regal station, he never succeeded in getting rid of a natural boorishness and failed to acquire the esteem and affection of the great mass of the English people.

The accession of Queen Victoria to the throne was the commencement of a new epoch in the evolution of constitutional and parliamentary institutions. The **Leading** young Sovereign was destined to **Character-** add luster and dignity to the **istics of** Crown, to establish on durable **the Victo-** foundations the great principles **rian Era** of parliamentary government, as they now obtain, and, above all, to win the love and respect of her subjects throughout an ever-extending empire by her exhibition of qualities which proved her to be a noble woman as well as a great Queen. Queen Victoria reigned for sixty-three years and seven months, during which the Empire has grown in all the essential elements of greatness.

I do not presume within the compass of this short article to do more than limn briefly the leading characteristics of an era so memorable in the history of England. Other periods of England's annals were signalized by more brilliant achievements of her army and navy. The victories of Marlborough, Nelson, Wolfe, and Wellington were won against the greatest military and naval power of the world. The Crimean campaign alone brought her into conflict with a first-class European power, and even in this case she did not fight single-handed but as an ally of other nations. The war was even for a while fraught with humiliation to the English people, since it showed the weakness of her military administration, and it closed too soon to enable her army to give to the world conclusive evidence that England was still a great military power. Her wars have been fought in Persia, Afghanistan, Abyssinia, China, and the Soudan, while in India her Empire was threatened by the warlike Sikhs and vindictive native troops, who mutinied and perpetrated the most cruel deeds, which were punished with a relentless hand. It was in India that England's one great general of the era, Lord Roberts, first won fame.

The fiercest conflict has been raging with the small but remarkably brave community of Boers in South Africa, where, as in the Crimean campaign, the existence of defects in military organization, and in the methods of coping with such conditions of warfare as presented themselves suddenly in that southern land, temporarily staggered the English people, hopeful of an easy victory over a foe relatively insignificant in numbers. Nevertheless, while it is true that tho there have been no such great battles as Blenheim or Ramillies or Waterloo or the Nile to emblaze on the imperial escutcheon, yet as many deeds of heroism have been performed during the Victorian era as ever distinguished the most memorable epochs of England's wars. Memories come up of the brilliant charge of the Light Brigade at Balaklava when the six hundred "rode boldly and well into the jaws of death;" of the heroic defense of Lucknow by Lawrence, Havelock, and Inglis—the latter a Canadian; of the equally memorable defense of Kars by Williams, also a Canadian, who, in the language of Palmerston, "displayed a courage, an ability, a perseverance under difficulties never before exhibited in British military history." The wars in the Soudan and South Africa also afford illustrations of English and Colonial courage.

But I do not wish to bring into too bold relief the military features of the Victorian era. The blessings of peace must be the **A Stanch** most enduring memorials of the **Friend of** reign of a great Queen, to whom **the United** war was always repugnant, and **States** whose influence was always constitutionally used to maintain amicable relations with other peoples, whenever compatible with the honor, the dignity, and the security of the Empire, whose interests she never failed to recognize as paramount to any personal sentiment. It is a historical fact that it was largely through her benign influence that the critical relations, which more than once existed between England and the United States during the war of the latter with the South, reached a peaceful solution, and the world was happily spared the sorry spectacle of a conflict between kindred peoples. It is also well known that she was anxious to preserve peace with the Transvaal until President Krüger issued his definite ultimatum, and that the disasters which befell her troops during the war that ensued tended to increase the weight of sorrow caused by personal bereavements.

Even tho in literature the Victorian era cannot present such great names as made the days of Elizabeth and Anne especially famous, still the Queen's reign has **Victorian** been conspicuous for a de- **Literature** cidedly distinctive literature of its own, especially for the works of Macaulay, Carlyle, Ruskin, Tennyson, Browning, Dickens, Thackeray, Charlotte Brontë and George Eliot. The great circulation of newspapers and periodicals is also a very noteworthy feature of a reign remarkable for the spread of popular education and the increasing desire of the masses for information on various branches of knowledge. In the study of science the era is superior to all its predecessors, especially for a practical application of discoveries to human health, comfort, convenience, and methods of communication. The investigations of Wheatstone, Faraday, Brewster, Herschel, and Owen entitle them to the highest place in the domain of practical science, while the novel theories of Darwin and his famous disciples, Huxley and Tyndall, have revolutionized the old traditionary belief with respect to the origin of species.

It is well known that Her Majesty deeply sympathized with all efforts of philanthropy which promised to effect the amelioration of the condition of the poor and humble worker. She was always interested in the triumphs of her era in art, literature, and science, and it is one of its characteristic features that never before in English history has the royal prerogative been so freely used to distribute honors, peerages, privy councillorships, baronetcies, and knighthoods among men who have won distinction throughout the empire in these departments of thought and culture.

During her memorable reign the Queen had for advisers many famous statesmen, the greatest of whom preceded her to the grave.

Famous Statesmen The reader will at once recall Lord Melbourne, somewhat cynical and flippant, but wise and kindly in his relations with the young, inexperienced Queen; the "Iron Duke," whose cardinal principle as a statesman was to carry on the Queen's government, whatever else betided; Sir Robert Peel, cold, dignified, but ever alive to the interests of the British people; Lord John Russell, who, some satirist suggested, had such supreme confidence in himself that he was quite ready at any moment to take command of the Channel fleet; Lord Aberdeen, who was styled by Byron "The Travel'd Thane, Athenian Aberdeen," whose weakness as a statesman was conspicuous in the management of the Crimean campaign, which brought about his downfall; Lord Palmerston, who, despite his failure to achieve any great feat of statesmanship, became the most popular Prime Minister since the time of Wellington, by dint of a certain jauntiness of demeanor, an audacity of purpose, a sense of humor, and a readiness of resource at critical moments; the Earl of Derby, who was well named "The Rupert of Debate;" Disraeli, a brilliant political satirist, an able and dextrous parliamentary debater, a clever writer of political novels and a statesman who often thought more of the interests of the State than of his party; Mr. Gladstone, a great student of books, the possessor of a remarkable store of knowledge, a debater fertile in resource, ready in reply, but gifted with too great fluency of language, a statesman who leaned from Toryism into a very decided Liberalism and ended his political life with the rupture of his own party.

To all of these statesmen Queen Victoria as a British constitutional Sovereign gave her full confidence as long as they possessed the support of Parliament and the people. In fact, her consistent, discreet action in connection with successive Ministries of the two opposing political parties largely tended to give complete recognition to those principles of parliamentary government which are now established beyond dispute in the parent state and all the self-governing dependencies of the Crown. Unlike the Georges, she had no "Queen's Friends" to disturb the harmonious relations which should always exist between the sovereign and her duly accredited constitutional advisers. Even her beloved husband, the Prince Consort, never affected or set up any separate province or authority of his own, never took up a position behind the throne and in no wise assumed any responsibility for any assistance he might give her in coming to a conclusion on subjects submitted to her judgment by her lawful advisers.

But while the Queen, like all constitutional monarchs, performed all executive acts through responsible ministers, it must not be supposed that her royal functions were purely ornamental. On the contrary, so high an authority as Mr. Gladstone has told us that "no head of a department performs more laborious duties than those which fall to the sovereign of this country. In fact, such complete mastery of what has occurred in this country, and of the important subjects of state policy, foreign and domestic, during her reign, was possessed by the Queen that he must be a wise man who could not profit by her example."

No feature of the Queen's reign has been more remarkable than the extension of her Empire and the development of constitutional and local self-government in the great dependencies **Development of the British Colonies** of the Crown. When she ascended the throne, Australia was chiefly known as a refuge for convicts. New Zealand was not yet recognized as a colony, Canada was in a state of political ferment which ended in rebellion, and India was still ruled by a great company. Sixty years later, in the streets of the metropolis of the British Empire there was witnessed a spectacle which the world never saw before, whose illustrations of the happiness and prosperity of the Empire far surpassed any exhibition which the Cæsars of Imperial Rome ever gave to their citizens in the ages when all the world came to pay her tribute. In this imperial procession nearly half the American continent was represented—Acadia and Canada, first settled by France, the Northwest prairies, first traversed by French-Canadian adventurers, the Pacific Coast, first seen by Cook and Vancouver. There, too, marched men from Bengal, Madras, Bombay, Jeypore, Hyderabad, Kashmir, Punjaub—from all sections of that great empire of India, which was won for England by Clive and the men who, like Wolfe, became famous for their achievements in the days of Pitt.

It was a procession which illustrated the content and development of the many colonies and dependencies which cover in the aggregate eleven millions of English square miles and are peopled by four hundred millions of souls representing many races and every color and creed. It was a great object lesson to the world of the blessings of peace, and of the prosperous development of colonies under the liberal system of government which has been one of the characteristic features of the Victorian era. Since that memorable "Diamond Jubilee" the dependencies have been called upon to give expression of their love for the Queen, and of their determination to maintain the unity and security of the Empire, by sending their sons to fight in South Africa alongside of troops from the parent isles. The entrance of the Australian Commonwealth into the rank of federal states is also another illustration of the beneficent influences of the reign of a Queen who passed away almost simultaneously with the accomplishment of this memorable event in colonial history.

I cannot close this story of the Victorian era without saying that while the greatness of the Queen as a constitutional sovereign has won the respect and confidence of all classes and strengthened the throne, her lovable qualities as wife and mother have always touched a sympathetic chord which has brought her closer to the hearts of the people. All the world has known of her great love for her noble husband, Prince Albert, during twenty-one years of the happiest married life, and how, when these ties were severed, she mourned him during many years of seclusion from stately court festivities and ceremonies. Her affection for her children and grandchildren was unbounded. Her greatest happiness was in her home life and, amid the cares and responsibilities of her royal station, she never forgot to show the kindliness and affection of a true woman.

As I close this short review of the reign of the great Queen I hear the city bells yet tolling because of her death. A few hours later a royal proclamation will announce in all parts of the British Empire, amid the roar of cannon, the accession of Albert Edward. By the English law, the throne can never be vacant. George or William or Victoria may die, but a King or Queen ever reigns. The accession of an heir to the crown is instantaneous, tho the coronation of the new sovereign, being merely a confirmation of the royal title, is generally delayed for some time—a year in the case of the late Queen—to allow a proper period for national mourning before the great ceremonies and festivals attendant on such occasions.

"The Queen is Dead— Long Live the King!"

With the accession of a new sovereign there is practically no derangement of the machinery of government. A few formalities—the taking of a new oath of allegiance by all officials, for instance—have to be carried out without delay, but the executive authority everywhere is continuous, and in the parent state and in all the dependencies of the crown remains in existence. The imperial legislature alone is obligated to meet immediately.

The Victorian era has closed, and a new epoch, with all its doubts and possibilities, commences with the twentieth century. British subjects everywhere believe that the noble example of his illustrious mother will influence the character and conduct of her son on the throne which she long adorned. As loyal subjects of the crown we give our loyal allegiance to the King, while at the same time we mourn the loss of a great Queen and a noble woman, whom all generations to come throughout the British Empire will ever call blessed.—Col. W.

EDWARD VII., KING OF ENGLAND

By Arnold White

King Edward VII. was born at Buckingham Palace, November 9, 1841. He was specially educated to occupy the throne, and underwent a course of training at the hands of numerous tutors, and passed through a portion of the curriculum at Edinburgh, Oxford, and Cambridge. Kingsley taught him history; Lyon Playfair, afterwards Lord Playfair, chemistry; Dean Stanley, theology; the Duke of Newcastle, politics; Doctor Schmitz, Roman history; Mr. Fisher, law and history. A good many people at the time thought the young prince was being overeducated. The popular conviction was well expressed in some lines that appeared in *Punch* in 1859:

Early Years of the King

Dipped in gray Oxford mixture (lest that prove a fixture),
The poor lad's to be plunged in less orthodox Cam.,
Where dynamics and statics, and pure mathematics,
Will be piled on his brain's awful cargo of Cram.

Edward was always fond of fiction—English, French, and German—and at this period formed a liking for Sir Walter Scott, which he never lost. Books of stirring incident by land and sea, naval battles, especially those relating to English history and works of imagination, like Arnold Forster's In a Conning-Tower, possessed great attraction for the Prince.

The part of his education which has left the greatest impression upon his mind and character was that derived from the tour in Canada and the United States, which was made in 1860. The first place on which he set foot in the British Empire outside the United Kingdom was at St. John's, Newfoundland. The reason of the visit was that during the Crimean war, Canada had come to the help of the mother-country and had levied and equipped a regiment of foot. In return the Queen was asked to visit what is now the Dominion, but so long a journey was considered unadvisable for the monarch to undertake. The Queen was then invited to appoint one of her sons as Governor-General, but they were little more than children, and the proposal was negatived. A compromise was effected by a promise that the Prince of Wales should visit Canada in the Queen's stead. The promise was fulfilled when the Prince of Wales was seventeen, and in July, 1860, H.M.S. *Hero,* escorted by the *Ariadne,* now a store hulk at Portsmouth employed by the torpedo department, conveyed the Prince to North America. When the visit to Canada was

Visit to America over, the Prince crossed to the United States on the night of the 20th of September, leaving behind him his titular rank and appearing on republican soil as Lord Renfrew. At Detroit the Prince and his companions could not get to their hotel owing to the crowds. The city was illuminated. If George Washington had come to life, it was alleged, there could not have been greater enthusiasm or curiosity displayed by the people. On visiting Washington during the presidency of Mr. Buchanan, the Prince staid at the White House for five days, and made the pilgrimage to Mount Vernon and the tomb of Washington. The *Times* correspondent of the period described the scene as follows:

"Before this humble tomb, the Prince, the President, and all the party stood uncovered. It is easy moralizing on this visit, for there is something grandly suggestive of historical retribution in the reverential awe of the Prince of Wales, the great-grandson of George III., standing bareheaded at the foot of the coffin of Washington. For a few moments the party stood mute and motionless, and the Prince then proceeded to plant a chestnut by the side of the tomb. It seemed, when the royal youth closed in the earth around the little germ, that he was burying the last faint trace of discord between us and. our great brethren in the West."

There have been a few traces of discord since then, but perhaps the anticipations of the leading journal were only premature. During the Prince's visit in the States, political feeling was running high, and after a good deal of discussion it was decided that he should visit the slave states. He went a short tour to Richmond, but a great slave sale, which had been advertised to be held during the time at which the Prince was to be present at Richmond, was postponed so as not to offend British susceptibilities. He was taken to one plantation, but flatly refused to leave his carriage in order to visit the negro quarters. When the Prince left Washington for the South, President Buchanan wrote a letter to the Queen, in which he spoke of his departing guest in the following terms: "In our domestic circle he has won all hearts. His free and ingenuous intercourse with myself evinced both a kind heart and a good understanding." Three thousand guests were asked to meet him on his return north to New York. All the ladies wore crinolines in those days, but many of them were important people, and therefore arrived at a time of life when dancing had become a reminiscence and ceased to be a pleasure. They represented the solid element in New York society. So solid, in fact, that the floor gave way, and it is a wonder that no serious accident took place. At Albany and Boston the Prince had the honor of meeting Longfellow, Oliver Wendell Holmes, and Emerson. He visited Harvard College, planted two trees at Mount Auburn, and drove out to Bunker Hill. On the 20th of October the Prince reembarked on board the *Hero,* and on the way home was reduced to salt provisions, as the voyage was greatly retarded by heavy weather. On the 15th of November he arrived, and from that day to this he has preserved a lively and sincere liking for the American people, which has been repeatedly evinced, not always to the satisfaction of some of his former subjects, jealous of cousinly influence.

The next event in the Prince's life was his return to Cambridge, where he was a young undergraduate member of Trinity College.

Back at College He was not allowed much freedom, and his governor, Colonel Bruce, had strict orders from the Queen not to allow him to make journeys unaccompanied. On one occasion the Prince made a dash up to London by himself. Both his absence and his destination were discovered before he could reach town, and the enterprising young man was surprised and mortified on his arrival at Paddington Station at being met by the station-master and royal servants, who had been sent from Buckingham Palace for the purpose. Shortly after this interesting event, the Prince was summoned to the bedside of his dying father. Only a few days before, Prince Albert had visited the Prince of Wales at Cambridge, and had caught the cold from which he never recovered. The Prince of Wales was deeply attached to his father, and the only occasion on which his fortitude has deserted him was after Prince Albert's coffin had been lowered into the vault, and the eldest son of the dead Prince, advancing to take a last look, burst into a flood of tears which he was unable to conceal.

At this period of his life, broad-minded Arthur Stanley, Dean of Westminster, and Laurence Oliphant exercised a deep influence

Trip to the Holy Land

over his character. With Doctor Stanley the Prince visited the Holy Land, and together they reached the closely guarded cave of Machpelah. Even to royal personages, the mosque of Hebron had remained absolutely barred for nearly seven hundred years, and the Turkish official in charge declared that " for no one but for the eldest son of the Queen of England would he have allowed the gate to be opened; indeed, the princes of any other nation should have passed over his body before doing so." The Prince of Wales, with characteristic kindness, made Doctor Stanley's entrance with himself a condition of his going in at all, and when Stanley thanked him for the great opportunity, the young man answered with some point, " High station, you see, sir, has, after all, some merits, some advantages." Since then the Marquis of Bute has entered the cave, and, I believe, a few others.

In the Cathedral of Worms during the Prince's foreign tour in 1861 he met his future wife for the first time. At Heidelberg he met her again when staying with his sister, the Crown-Princess of Prussia. In September, 1862, they were betrothed.

Married

Before the Prince had seen his future wife, he was much attracted to her by a photograph which had been shown him by a friend. Actual negotiations were impending with a view to a contract of marriage with a German princess, but after he had seen the beautiful Dane, the project of a Teutonic alliance was immediately abandoned. I remember the landing of the Princess Alexandra and her passage through the streets of London on the 7th of March, 1863. From Whitechapel to Piccadilly the metropolis was lavishly decorated, and the streets were crammed, as thirty-four years later they were crowded to do honor to the Princess's mother-in-law. The Queen's recent bereavement was the one blot upon the happy day. A photograph is in existence depicting the Princess in pure white, orange blossoms in her hair, and the crinoline of the period, standing by the Queen swathed in dense crape from head to foot, with the Prince of Wales, slim, frock-coated, and rather gloomy, standing between his mother and a great white bust of his father, placed on a pedestal, at which the Queen is gazing, thinking, no doubt, of her own wedding-day.

Early in the following January the Princess of Wales was skating at Virginia Water, near Windsor, when she was obliged to quit the ice, and the same day the news was published that an heir-presumptive to the British throne was born. The great rejoicings over the event were marred by the war between Denmark and Prussia. At breakfast, one morning, it is related, a tactless equerry read out a telegram announcing the success of the German forces. The Princess of Wales burst into tears, while the Prince, solicitous for his wife, rated the equerry in vernacular English. Sympathy with Denmark, and dislike of Germany pervaded society at this time, and antipathy to the Teuton smolders until this day, notwithstanding identity of interest in certain vexed questions of European politics, and the recent understanding as to Delagoa Bay and Egypt. The influence of the Princess of Wales in creating sympathy for Denmark extended to her young brothers and sisters-in-law. It is related that about this period a royal guest at Windsor asked Princess Beatrice what she would like for a present. A whispered consultation with the Princess of Wales took place, when the little Princess Beatrice spake valiantly with her tongue and said that she would like to have Bismarck's head on a charger.

Perhaps the most marked characteristic of King Edward during the whole of his life has been his phenomenal activity of mind and body. His keen interest in firemen and fires is indicative of this quality. It is remembered in court circles that the assemblage of 6,000 men of the fire department of New York during his American visit gave the Prince of Wales greater pleasure than any other sight. Like the late Duke of Sutherland, the King formerly was a first-rate amateur fireman. He attended during many years of his life most of the great London fires.

Travel

In 1869 the Prince of Wales, accompanied by his wife, paid a visit to Egypt, and ascended the Nile as far as the ruins of Carnac. The Suez Canal formed one of the most interesting points of the tour. M. de Lesseps received and escorted them. It may now be recalled that the Prince of Wales performed the important ceremony of opening the sluices of the dam across the then finished portion of the canal, thus letting the waters of the Mediterranean into the empty basin of the bitter lakes. In 1871 the Prince paid an incognito visit to the battlefield of Sedan. He was accompanied by General Teesdale. The French susceptibilities were highly inflamed at the time, and it was important that his identity should not be suspected. Putting up at a hotel, the time came to pay the bill, when General Teesdale, the Prince's aide-de-camp, found that he had no cash. The Prince was in the same condition. It was impossible to telegraph, as the identity of the party would have been discovered by the French, and it would have been universally believed that the Prince was visiting Sedan in order to exhibit his elation at his brother-in-law's victories. After a good deal of discussion the Prince's watch and that of his aide-de-camp were taken by the latter to the local pawn-shop, and the necessary funds were thus raised to rescue his Royal Highness from an awkward predicament.

Illness

The month of December is notoriously unlucky to the reigning house of England. In November, 1871, the Prince, his groom, and Lord Chesterfield, who had all been on a visit to Lord Lundesburgh, at Scarborough, were stricken with typhoid fever. The peer and the groom died, and for many days the issue was considered exceedingly doubtful in the case of the Prince. No such public expression of emotion had ever taken place since the death of Princess Charlotte in 1817. The bulletins were watched with breathless interest. Sir William Jenner and the late Sir William Gull exhausted themselves in their efforts to save the Prince. Strange remedies were tried. A sheep was killed, and its warm and smoking fleece was wrapped round the pallid and nerveless body of the Prince. When he was actually *in extremis* one of his medical attendants rubbed his patient's body with a large quantity of old champagne brandy until returning animation rewarded his efforts. The turning-point in the illness took place when the Prince asked for a tankard of British ale. This he drank, and never looked back afterwards. A great national thanksgiving was held at St. Paul's, which was attended by the Prince, but a private service of thanksgiving was held in the abbey, which was described by Dean Stanley in a letter to an intimate correspondent which has since seen the light. One passage is still of interest. The Dean wrote: " It was one of those rare occasions on which I was able to say all that I wished to say."

King Edward's catholicity is the object both of censure and praise. The King profoundly believes that while it is not to be expected that every one in the world should believe the same thing, every one should believe something, and should act up to his religious belief. His catholicity is well illustrated by the following extract from a letter of Archbishop Magee, written in December, 1873. He is speaking of a visit to Sandringham from Saturday to Monday: " Just returned from church where I preached for twenty-six minutes (Romans viii : 28). The church is a very small country one, close to the grounds. The house, as I saw it by daylight, is a handsome country house of red stone with white facings, standing well and looking quietly comfortable and suitable. I find the company pleasant and civil, but we are a curious mixture. Two Jews, Sir A. Rothschild and his daughter; an ex-Jew, Disraeli; a Roman Catholic, Colonel Higgins; an Italian duchess, who is an English woman, and her daughter brought up as a Roman Catholic and now turning Protestant; a set of young lords, and a bishop. The Jewess came to church; so did the half-Protestant young lady. Dizzy did the same, and was profuse in his praises of my sermon. We are all to lunch together in a few minutes, the children dining with us. They seem, the two I saw in church, nice, clever-looking little bodies, and very like their mother." The daughter of Sir Anthony Rothschild referred to is the present Lady Battersea, better known as Mrs. Cyril Flower.

Death has removed nearly the whole of the King's warmest and most intimate friends. The loss of Laurence Oliphant, who fell under the influence of the fanatic Harris in later life, was a great calamity. Oliphant is deeply mourned by the King to this day. In 1875 the death of Canon Kingsley came as a great blow.

In 1875 the Prince of Wales went to India. The House of Commons voted a sum of $300,000 for the personal expenses of the party. The Admiralty set aside **Goes to** $260,000 as the expenses of the **India** voyage of the *Serapis* to and from India. The appropriation was not unanimously carried in the House of Commons. Mr. Fawcett, a blind member, whose favorite title was that of Member for India, objected to the vote. Thirty-three members agreed with him. Disraeli, was then Prime Minister, and in supporting the vote, his Oriental imagination revelled in depicting the pomp with which the Prince would be surrounded and the pageants that would adorn his progress. Lord Charles Beresford was the life of the party, and many were the escapades contributed to the enjoyment of the Prince and the suite by one who is now a grave Rear-Admiral in the British navy. Sir Bartle Frere, the Duke of Sutherland, and Earl Grey also accompanied the Prince.

In Ceylon the party went up country to see the process of elephant-catching, and also to give the Prince his first experience of big-game shooting. The shikari of **Elephant-** the party was Mr. F. C. Fisher, **Catching** now the chief commissioner of one of the most important provinces in Ceylon. The first time that a sportsman goes up to an elephant in the jungle is trying to the nerves. The elephant is almost indistinguishable from the trunks of the trees and the undergrowth, and at the distance of a few yards he is almost invisible. Nothing but the constant flapping of his ears reveals his position to the tyro. The facility with which an elephant can make his way through the bamboo undergrowth of a Ceylon jungle almost impenetrable to a biped gives him a distinct advantage over a sportsman. To kill an elephant under such circumstances requires coolness and an exact aim. The etiquette of elephant-shooting in Ceylon requires that he shall only be hit in the head, body shots being likely to maim without stopping the animal. The Prince of Wales was charged by an elephant under these circumstances, and displayed as much coolness and skill as if he had been engaged in the sport all his life. So much so that even a shikari of Mr. Fisher's standing expressed the warmest admiration for the Prince's skill, courage, and self-control.

Descriptions of the Prince's visit to India have been repeatedly published, but there is one unrecorded incident that may be recounted, which throws a light upon the Prince's tact and presence of mind. It was related to me by an eye-witness, a high official in the Indian government. It is well known that the Indian princes are constantly striving among themselves to obtain greater recognition from the Indian government in the form of an addition to the number of guns to which they are entitled as a salute.

To accomplish this end they do not hesitate on occasion to encroach on the rights of others. The Prince was not supposed to hold durbars, but his ceremonial receptions were in every way as impressive and remarkable as if they had carried full official significance. At one of these receptions a great number of native princes and rajahs paid their respects in person to the future Emperor of India. The Prince stood on a small carpet upon which no other person was supposed to tread. The late Maharajah Sindia, desirous of impressing the multitude with his importance and virtual equality with the son of the Queen of England, gradually edged his way upon the carpet as he exchanged compliments with the Prince. Sir Bartle Frere whispered a few words to the Prince of Wales, on which the latter quietly, but **Diplomacy** with the greatest dignity, before thousands of eagerly watching eyes, stretched out his hand and gently edged the Oriental to his proper place. The act was so quietly done and with such simple dignity that the newspaper correspondents present took no notice of the incident. The fact, however, of Sindia being made to retire from the carpet on which the Prince stood was whispered throughout the bazars of India, and according to my informant produced a greater effect on native opinion than many a bloody victory had done in the past.

The effect of the Prince's visit to India amply fulfilled the expectations of those who were responsible for its conception.

The influence of travel upon men in high place is generally admitted to enlarge the sympathies and widen the outlook. Altho **The** King Edward has visited India **Prince's** and Canada, he has never seen **Tastes** Australia or the Cape. I have already referred to his taste in literature, but it is difficult not to associate his foreign travels with the contents of the shelves of that section of the Sandringham libraries which were the special favorites of his Royal Highness. One who had the opportunity of inspecting the books declares that the history of our own country, and especially the history of our own time, form the majority of the volumes. The Indian mutiny occupies several shelves. The King has made a practise of buying official reports, memoirs, novels, and every new work connected with the public and private administration of India. The bibliography of the Crimean war is also well represented in his library. Colonial history and blue books, works of sea power, and the naval prowess of British admirals, dead and gone, also give evidence of the King's tastes.

People whose point of contact with the King when he was Prince of Wales was restricted to the Terrace at Homburg or at crowded receptions in London have sometimes drawn a contrast between him and Prince Albert, his father. The truth of the matter is that a strong affinity exists between the subject of this paper and men of serious and even Puritanic type. With his father,

Prince Albert, he has far more in common than is generally supposed. The late Prince-Consort virtually invented Exhibitions. As Prince of Wales, the King developed the idea, and by so doing has contributed enormously to the enjoyment and instruction of large masses of his fellow-countrymen, and indeed of the civilized world. As executive president of various British commissions he has carried out his father's wishes in a manner that would have delighted that great and good man had he survived to watch his son's success in combining affability with business sense and shrewdness.

It should never have been forgotten, when listening to stories of Prince Albert Edward of Wales, that when anything was said to his discredit, he alone, of all Englishmen, was unable to reply. Since he arrived at man's estate he has been the target of slander and of reckless and malignant aspersion by people of whom the Psalmist wrote, " The poison of asps is under their tongues." I have very strong reason to believe that the malignant stories circulated about the Prince of Wales are absolutely false. In the Tranby Croft baccarat case, which attracted so much attention a few years ago, the Prince was severely blamed in some quarters for carrying with him cards and markers. It is, I believe, a fact that they were the gifts of the Princess of Wales. Many people object to card-playing, but others do not, and, after all, how many people in the Prince of Wales' place would have made as many friends and as few enemies as the King has done?

Many of Prince Albert Edward's duties were unspeakably distasteful, and after the death of the Duke of Clarence an increase in **The** the burden of state fell upon **Prince's** him. His correspondence was **Duties** enormous. The social duties of the crown largely devolved upon the Prince and Princess of Wales, while in other respects they had the disadvantages of private station. Marlborough House was taxed at $5,000 a year for the rates of the Parish of St. Martin, while the Prince's telegraph bill is said to have been over $5,000 a year. Neither letters nor telegrams are franked, and the demand on his purse for charities has always been enormous. Local ceremonies in all parts of the kingdom have required his presence under varying conditions, and if they have been at times irksome the fact has been considerably and successfully concealed. Here is an instance: In 1894 the Prince and Princess of Wales attended the musical carnival of the Welsh known as the Eisteddfod, held at Carnarvon. They were received with much enthusiasm and were initiated into the Druidic rites, the Prince of Wales under the name of Iorweth Dywysog (Edward the Prince), the Princess of Wales as Hoffder Prydain (Britain's delight), and the Princess Victoria of Wales as Buddug (Boadicea). Fancy one's daughter being publicly hailed as Buddug!

Those who read the King's character only

by the glittering light of fashionable society fall into error. During the whole of his lifetime he has lived under the shadow of the greatest responsibility that can fall to the lot of any man—to be King of England. A better King than Edward VII. will be it is possible to conceive, because he is not perfect, and does not pretend to be. He loves England, hates humbug, enjoys sport, the play, music, and a good dinner, and is thought none the less of by his countrymen on that account.

The common-sense distinctive of Queen Victoria descends to her eldest son, and if his ideals are sometimes considered to fall short of the standard set up for other people by the unco guid, it is not that the King does not believe them, but that he does not talk about them. It is impossible in the nature of things that Edward's reign will be a long one. It is satisfactory to know, however, that the scepter so worthily held by a good woman has passed into the hands of an English gentleman.—H. W.

ADDRESSES

THE RACES AND CLASSES OF ENGLAND *

By Lord Beaconsfield

After all, the test of political institutions is the condition of the country whose fortunes they regulate; and I do not mean to evade that test. You are the inhabitants of an island of no colossal size; which, geographically speaking, was intended by nature as the appendage of some continental empire—either of Gauls and Franks on the other side of the Channel, or of Teutons and Scandinavians beyond the German Sea. Such, indeed, and for a long period was your early history. You were invaded; you were pillaged and you were conquered; yet amid all these disgraces and vicissitudes there was gradually formed that English race which has brought about a very different state of affairs. Instead of being invaded, your land is proverbially the only " inviolate land "—" the inviolate land of the sage and free." Instead of being plundered, you have attracted to your shores all the capital of the world. Instead of being conquered, your flag floats on many waters and your standard waves in either zone. It may be said that these achievements are due to the race that inhabited the land, and not to its institutions. Gentlemen, in political institutions are the embodied experiences of a race. You have established a society of classes, which gives vigor and variety to life. But no class possesses a single exclusive privilege, and all are equal before the law. You possess a real aristocracy, open to all who desire to enter it. You have not merely a middle class, but a hierarchy of middle classes, in which every degree of wealth, refinement, industry, energy, and enterprise is duly represented.

And now, gentlemen, what is the condition of the great body of the people? In the first place, gentlemen, they have for centuries been in the full enjoyment of that which no other country in Europe has ever completely attained—complete rights of personal freedom. In the second place, there has been a gradual and therefore a wise, distribution on a large scale of political rights. Speaking with reference to the industries of this great part of the country, I can personally contrast it with the condition of the working classes forty years ago. In that period they have attained two results—the raising of their wages and the diminution of their toil. Increased means and increased leisure are the two civilizers of man. That the working classes of Lancashire and Yorkshire have proved not unworthy of these boons may be easily maintained; but their progress and elevation have been, during this interval, wonderfully aided and assisted by three causes, which are not so distinctively attributable to their own energies. The first is the revolution in locomotion, which has opened the world to the working man, which has enlarged the horizon of his experience, increased his knowledge of nature and of art, and added immensely to the salutary recreation, amusement, and pleasure of his existence. The second cause is the cheap postage, the moral benefits of which cannot be exaggerated. And the third is that unshackled press which has furnished him with endless sources of instruction, information, and amusement.—W. B. O.

ROMAN AND BRITISH IMPERIALISM COMPARED †

By John Bright

My Calcutta critic assured me that Rome pursued a similar policy (as ours) for a period of eight centuries, and that for those

eight centuries she remained great. Now, I do not think that examples taken from pagan, sanguinary Rome are proper models for the

* From Lord Beaconsfield's address on " The Meaning of Conservatism."
† Extract from an address on " Morality and Military Greatness."

imitation of a Christian country, nor would I limit my hopes of the greatness of England even to the long duration of eight hundred years.

But what is Rome now? The great city is dead. A poet has described her as " the lone mother of dead empires." Her language even is dead. Her very tombs are empty; the ashes of her most illustrious citizens are dispersed.

" The Scipios' tomb contains no ashes now." Yet I am asked, I, who am one of the legislators of a Christian country, to measure my policy by the policy of ancient and pagan Rome!

I believe there is no permanent greatness to a nation except it be based upon morality. I do not care for military greatness or military renown. I care for the condition of the people among whom I live. There is no man in England who is less likely to speak irreverently of the crown and monarchy of England than I am; but crowns, coronets, miters, military display, the pomp of war, wide colonies, and a huge empire are, in my view, all trifles, light as air, and not worth considering, unless with them you can have a fair share of comfort, contentment, and happiness among the great body of the people. Palaces, baronial castles, great halls, stately mansions, do not make a nation. The nation in every country dwells in the cottage; and unless the light of your Constitution can shine there, unless the beauty of your legislation and the excellence of your statesmanship are impressed there on the feelings and condition of the people, rely upon it you have yet to learn the duties of government.

I have not, as you have observed, pleaded that this country should remain without adequate and scientific means of defense. I acknowledge it to be the duty of your statesmen, acting upon the known opinions and principles of ninety-nine out of every hundred persons in the country, at all times, with all possible moderation, but with all possible efficiency, to take steps which shall preserve order within and on the confines of your kingdom. But I shall repudiate and denounce the expenditure of every shilling, the engagement of every man, the employment of every ship, which has no object but intermeddling in the affairs of other countries, and endeavoring to extend the boundaries of an empire which is already large enough to satisfy the greatest ambition, and I fear is much too large for the highest statesmanship to which any man has yet attained.

The most ancient of profane historians has told us that the Scythians of his time were a very warlike people, and that they elevated an old simitar upon a platform as a symbol of Mars,—for to Mars alone, I believe, they built altars and offered sacrifices.

To this simitar they offered sacrifices of horses and cattle, the main wealth of the country, and more costly sacrifices than to all the rest of their gods. I often ask myself whether we are at all advanced in one respect beyond those Scythians. What are our contributions to charity, to education, to morality, to religion, to justice, and to civil government, when compared with the wealth we expend in sacrifices to the old simitar? Two nights ago I addressed in this hall a vast assembly composed, to a great extent, of your countrymen, who have no political power, who are at work from the dawn of the day to the evening, and who have therefore limited means of informing themselves on these great subjects. Now I am privileged to speak to a somewhat different audience. You represent those of your great community who have a more complete education, who have on some points greater intelligence, and in whose hands reside the power and influence of the district. I am speaking too within the hearing of those whose gentler nature, whose finer instincts, whose purer minds, have not suffered as some of us have suffered in the turmoil and strife of life. You can mold opinion, you can create political power;—you cannot think a good thought on this subject and communicate it to your neighbors, you cannot make these points topics of discussion in your social circles and more general meetings, without affecting sensibly and speedily the course which the government of your country will pursue.

May I ask you then, to believe, as I do most devoutly believe, that the moral law was not written for men alone in their individual character, but that it was written as well for nations, and for nations great as this of which we are citizens. If nations reject and deride that moral law, there is a penalty which will inevitably follow. It may not come at once, it may not come in your lifetime; but rely upon it, the great Italian is not a poet only, but a prophet, when he says:—

" The sword of heaven is not in haste to smite,
Nor yet doth linger."

We have experience, we have beacons, we have landmarks enough. We know what the past has cost us, we know how much and how far we have wandered, but we are not left without a guide. It is true we have not, as an ancient people, had Urim and Thummim,—those oraculous gems on Aaron's breast,—from which to take counsel, but we have the unchangeable and eternal principles of the moral law to guide us, and only as far as we walk by that guidance can we be permanently a great nation, or our people a happy people.

SUGGESTIVE THOUGHTS

AMERICA, Great Britain and.—Let all good citizens in both England and America, all who desire the world's progress, strive to preserve peace and international good-will.

I appeal to you by the unity of our race—for, with two governments we are one people; by the unity of the grand old language we alike speak, with the thrilling names of father, mother, home, dear to us alike; by our common literature, our Shakespeare, who is your Shakespeare, our Milton, who is your Milton, our Longfellows and Tennysons, side by side in all our libraries; I appeal to you by the stirring memories of our common history,—by those ancestors of both our nations, who proved their prowess at Hastings, whether as sturdy Saxons defending the standard of King Harold, or as daring Normans spurring their chivalry to the trumpet of Duke William,—and who, afterward united on a better field, wrung from a reluctant tyrant that great charter which is the foundation of our liberties on both sides of the Atlantic; I appeal to you by the stirring times when those common ancestors lighted their beacons on every hill, and rallied around a lion-hearted Queen, and launched forth—some of them in mere fishing vessels—against the proud Armada that dared to threaten their subjugation; I appeal to you by the struggles of the Commonwealth, by the memories of those who put to rout the abettors of tyranny—Cromwell, Hampden, Sir Harry Vane; I appeal to you by those Pilgrim Fathers here, and by those Puritans and Covenanters who remained behind, by whose heroic sufferings both nations enjoy such freedom to worship God; I appeal to you by the graves in which our common ancestors repose,—not only, it may be, beneath the stately towers of Westminster, but in many an ancient village churchyard, where daisies grow on the turf-covered graves, and venerable yew-trees cast over them their solemn shade; I appeal to you by that Bible—precious to us both; by that gospel which our missionaries alike proclaim to the heathen world, and by that Savior whom we both adore, never let there be strife between nations whose conflict would be the rushing together of two Niagaras, but whose union will be like the irresistible course of two great rivers flowing on majestically to fertilize and bless the world.

Never let our beautiful standards—yours of the stars and stripes, suggesting the lamps of night and the rays of day, and ours of the clustered crosses, telling of union in diversity, and reminding of the One Great Liberator and Peace-Maker, who, by the cross, gave life to the world—never let these glorious standards be arrayed in hostile ranks; but ever may they float side by side, leading on the van of the world's progress.

Oh, I can imagine that if we, the hereditary champions of freedom, were engaged in strife, all the despots of the earth would clap their hands, and all the demons in hell would exult, while angels would weep to see these two nations wasting the treasure and shedding the blood that should be reserved for the strife against the common foes of freedom.

Never give angels such cause of lamentation, never give despots and demons such cause for rejoicing; but ever Great Britain and America—the mother and the daughter, or, if you prefer it, the elder daughter and the younger—go forth hand in hand, angel guardians together of civilization, freedom, and religion, their only rivalry, the rivalry of love.—NEWMAN HALL.

BRITISH EMPIRE, The.—There is not a country in the history of the world that has undertaken what England in its traditional established policy and position has undertaken. There is no precedent in human history for a formation like the British Government. A small island at one extremity of the globe peoples the whole earth. But it is not satisfied with that; it goes among the ancient races of Asia and subjects 240,000,000 of people to its rule there. Along with all this, it distributes over the world a commerce such as no imagination ever conceived in former times, and such as no poet ever painted. And all this it has to do with a strength that lies within the narrow limits of these shores—not a strength that I disparage; on the contrary I wish to dissipate if I can the idle dreams of those who are always telling you that the strength of England depends upon its prestige, upon its extending its empire upon what it possesses beyond these shores. Rely upon it, the strength of Great Britain and Ireland is within the United Kingdom. Whatever is to be done in defending and governing those vast colonies with their teeming millions, in protecting that unmeasured commerce, in relation to the enormous responsibility of India—whatever is to be done must be done by the force to be derived from you and your children, from you and your fellow-electors. And why? They are between some three and thirty millions of persons. They are a population less than the population of France, of Austria, of Germany or of Russia; but the populations of France, Austria, Germany, and Russia are quite able enough to settle their own matters within their own limits. We have undertaken to settle the affairs of a fourth or nearly a fourth of the entire human race scattered over the world; and is not that enough for the ambition of Lord Beaconsfield? It satisfied Mr. Pitt, Mr. Canning; it satisfied Sir Robert Peel; it satisfied Lord Palmerston, Lord Russell, and the late Lord Derby; and why cannot it satisfy, I wish to know, Lord Beaconsfield and his colleagues? It seems to me they are all very much of one mind. They move with harmony among themselves. Is it not enough to satisfy the ambition of the members of the present Government? Strive as you will—I speak after the experience of a lifetime, of which a fair portion has been spent in office—strive and labor as you will in Parliament and office, human strength and human thought are not equal to the discharge of the whole duties appertaining to government in this great, wonderful, and world-wide Empire.—W. E. GLADSTONE.

BRITISH POWER.—The proudest position Great Britain could occupy is that the overshadowing power and influence which she has so long possessed in giving shape to the destinies and relations of nations has always been exercised with a view to the amelioration of the condition of mankind; that she has the will as well as the power to maintain, in a great measure, the peace of the rest of the world, and that prosperity, peace, and contentment have followed her flag all over the earth, upon whatever soil it has ever been planted. I hope its march of triumph will never be interrupted until it shall become the one absorbing and powerful instrumentality in the hands of Providence for the prevention of war, the extension of commerce, and the promotion of the arts of peace.—ALEXANDER MACKENZIE.

CHURCH OF ENGLAND, The Head of the.—The head of the Church of England is the ruling monarch, who exercises actual authority as such by choosing the archbishops and nominating the bishops. According to the canon law the Church is governed under the monarch, by archbishops, bishops, deans, archdeacons, and the rest that bear office in the same.—*Selected.*

CONSTITUTION, English National.—The favorite principle of Robertson, of Brighton, that the whole truth in the realm of the spiritual consists in the union of two truths that are contrary but not contradictory, applies to the social and political realms. What two contrary truths then lie at the basis of a complete national constitution? First, that the will of the people is the will of God. Second, that the will of God must be the will of the people. That the people are the ultimate fountain of all power is one truth. That government is of God and should be strong, stable, and above the people, is another. In other words, the elements of liberty and of authority should both be represented. A republic recognizes only the first. In consequence, popular appeals are made to that which is lowest in our nature, for such appeals are made to the greatest number and are most likely to be immediately successful. The character of public men and the national character deteriorate. Neither dignity, elevation of sentiment, nor refinement of manners is cultivated. Still more fatal consequences, the ark of the nation is carried periodically into party fights. For the time being, the citizen has no country; he has only his party, and the unity of the country is constantly imperiled. On the other hand, a despotism it based entirely on the element of authority.

To unite those elements in due proportions has been and is the aim of every true statesman. Let the history of liberty and progress, of the development of human character to all its rightful issues, testify where they have been more wisely blended than in the British Constitution.

We have a fixed center of authority and government, a fountain of honor above us that all reverence, from which a thousand gracious influences come down to every rank; and along with that fixity we have, instead of a cast-iron yoke for four years, representative institutions so elastic that they respond within their own sphere to every breath of popular sentiment. In harmony with this central part of our Constitution, we have an independent judiciary instead of judges—too often the creatures of wealthy adventurers or the echoes of passing popular sentiment. And more valuable than the direct advantages are the subtle, indirect influences that flow from our unbroken connection with the past, the dynamical tho imponderable forces that determine the tone and mold the character of a people.

" In our halls is hung armory of the invincible knights of old."

Ours are the graves of our forefathers and a historical continuity that is the best safeguard against revolutionary fever; ours the names " to which a thousand memories call; " ours is the flag that symbolizes the highest thoughts that have ever descended from Heaven to earth, ours the Queen whose virtues transmute the sacred principle of loyalty into a personal affection.—PRINCIPAL GRANT.

CROWN, The, in the Constitution.—" In my judgment," said Mr. Balfour (after Queen Victoria's death), in moving the vote of condolence in the House of Commons, " the importance of the Crown in our Constitution is not a diminishing but an increasing factor. It is increasing and must increase." Mr. Balfour may be right, but even if the influence of the crown on the Constitution does not increase and merely remains at the high-water mark to which it was advanced by the Queen, it is high time we recognized the immense importance of the monarch in the councils of the Empire. The Sovereign has been described as the permanent under-secretary of the Prime Minister, but I prefer my own definition, which is that the Queen made herself the permanent editor of the realm. While she never dictated, she influenced, and altho she never arrogated to herself a prerogative of command, she exercised constantly the far more subtle and influential power of expostulation and argument. It is, of course, impossible for Edward VII. to succeed to the immense inheritance of experience and personal prestige which made the Queen, according to the testimony of all her ministers, so potent in foreign and imperial affairs.—W. T. STEAD. (R. R.)

DRUM-BEAT, Morning.—A power (Great Britain) which has dotted over the surface of the whole globe with her possessions and military posts; whose morning drum-beat, following the sun, and keeping company with the hours, circles the earth daily with one continuous and unbroken strain of the martial airs of England.—DANIEL WEBSTER.

EDWARD VII., As a Social and Political Factor.—As a social factor in England the Prince has always been supreme. Ward McAllister called him " the great social dictator." It was largely through his influence that many Americans gained entrance to the inner circles of the Court of St. James, among them Lily Langtry, dubbed the " Jersey Lily." The Prince's predilection for Americans was bitterly resented in certain court circles and his London residence was nicknamed " The White House." In politics Albert Edward, notwithstanding his natural reticence on all political subjects, has long been regarded as a Liberal. He favored Gladstone and his Home Rule projects, and has ever shown himself a close friend of Lord Rosebery. It is largely due to him that the former social ostracism of Jews in England has given way to an enlightened tolerance, thanks to which Lord Rothschild, Barney, and others have become familiar figures in London society. This liberal attitude of Albert Edward is declared by some of his detractors to be not wholly disinterested.

Still, it is believed in England that the court under Albert Edward's rule will be almost as sedate as it was under the late Sovereign. Queen Alexandra is as strict in matters of propriety as was Queen Victoria. —EDWARD EMERSON, JR. (Col. W.)

ENGLAND, America's Relations to.— Who does not feel, what reflecting American does not acknowledge, the incalculable advantages derived by this land out of the deep fountains of civil, intellectual, and moral truth, from which we have drawn in England? What American does not feel proud that his fathers were the countrymen of Bacon, of Newton, and of Locke? Who does not know that, while every pulse of civil liberty in the heart of the British Empire beat warm and full in the bosom of our ancestors, the sobriety, the firmness, and the dignity, with which the cause of free principles struggled into existence here, constantly found encouragement and countenance from the friends of liberty there? Who does not remember that, when the pilgrims went over the sea, the prayers of the faithful British confessors, in all the quarters of their dispersion, went over with them,

while their aching eyes were strained till the star of hope should go up in the western skies? And who will ever forget that, in that eventful struggle which severed these youthful republics from the British Crown, there was not heard, throughout our continent in arms, a voice which spoke louder for the rights of America than that of Burke, or of Chatham, within the walls of the British Parliament, and at the foot of the British Throne.

I am not—I need not say I am not—the panegyrist of England. I am not dazzled by her riches, nor awed by her power. The scepter, the miter, and the coronet,—stars, garters, and blue ribbons,—seem to me poor things for great men to contend for. Nor is my admiration awakened by her armies, mustered for the battles of Europe; her navies, overshadowing the ocean; nor her Empire, grasping the farthest East. It is these, and the price of guilt and blood by which they are too often maintained, which are the cause why no friend of liberty can salute her with undivided affections. But it is the cradle and the refuge of free principles, tho often persecuted; the school of religious liberty, the more precious for the struggles through which it has passed; the tombs of those who have reflected honor on all who speak the English tongue; it is the birthplace of our fathers, the home of the Pilgrims; it is these which I love and venerate in England. I should feel ashamed of an enthusiasm for Italy and Greece, did I not also feel it for a land like this. In an American, it would seem to me degenerate and ungrateful to hang with passion upon the traces of Homer and Virgil, and follow, without emotion, the nearer and plainer footsteps of Shakespeare and Milton. I should think him cold in his love for his native land who felt no melting in his heart for that other native country which holds the ashes of his forefathers.— EDWARD EVERETT.

FAMILY, The Royal.—Queen Victoria had the following children:

1. Princess Victoria, born on November 21, 1840; married January 25, 1858, Frederick I. of Germany; died August 5, 1901; mother of the present German Emperor.

2. Albert Edward, Edward VII., born on November 9, 1841; married on March 10, 1863, Princess Alexandra, eldest daughter of King Christian IX. of Denmark; succeeded to the crown on the death of his mother, January 22, 1901. Their eldest son is George, Duke of Cornwall and Duke of York, born January 3, 1865. His son is Edward Albert, born June 23, 1894.

3. Prince Alfred, Duke of Edinburgh (Duke of Saxe-Coburg-Gotha), born August 6, 1844. He married on January 23, 1874, the Grand Duchess Marie of Russia, only daughter of the Czar Alexander II; died July 30, 1900.

4. Princess Helena, born May 25, 1846; married on July 5, 1866, Prince Christian of Schleswig-Holstein.

5. Princess Louise, born March 18, 1848; married March 21, 1871, John, Marquis of Lorne, who became Duke of Argyle April 24, 1900.

6. Prince Arthur, Duke of Connaught, born May 1, 1850, and married March 13, 1879, Princess Louise of Prussia.

7. Prince Leopold, Duke of Albany, born in 1853; married in 1882 Princess Helena of Waldeck; died in 1884.

8. Princess Beatrice, born April 14. 1857; married July 23, 1885, Prince Henry, son of Prince Alexander of Hesse.—*Selected*.

GUELPH, The Ubiquitous.—Of the forty monarchical countries at present found on the map of Europe, thirty-three are governed by members or descendants of German families. Of these, twenty-two are in the German Empire and eleven outside of Germany—namely, Belgium, Bulgaria, Denmark, England, Greece. Lichtenstein, the Netherlands, Austria-Hungary, Portugal, Roumania, and Russia. The reigning families of Spain, Sweden, Italy, and Monaco are of Romanic origin, altho those of Savoy and Spain, while Bourbon, are strongly mixed with German blood. Of Slavic origin are only the house of Petrowitch-Njegosh, reigning in Montenegro, and that of Obrenovich, reigning in Servia; this last also is not of unmixed blood. The Sultan is of Turanian origin. The forty rulers in Europe are derived from twenty-six different families, and of them seventeen are German.—*Selected*.

LUCK, The Queen's.—To the dark, half-savage races under the British crown, Queen Victoria was a " totem," a superhuman being. They imagined her an essential part of the British system. To most of her Asiatic subjects, she was Queen of Kings. The Mohammedans thought her in a special degree favored by God and predestined to wide authority and the brightest fortune. Lord Cromer once remarked that belief in the Queen's luck greatly facilitated his task in Egypt. Mr. Clinton Dawkins, the late Financial Secretary of Egypt, has told me that all over the East people said: " The Queen is visibly the favorite of God: Since this is so, why struggle against Him? " The idea that Allah was with her struck Mehemet Ali as early as 1840. It prompted him to accept the terms Sir Charles Napier offered.—Mrs. Crawford. (T. C. R.)

REIGN OF VICTORIA, The Long.—Queen Victoria has not only outreigned all the sovereigns of Europe who were on the throne when she succeeded, but she has seen the end of sixteen reigns which began after hers. She has been contemporary with five sovereigns in Prussia, four in Russia and two in Austria. In the case of France she has seen the reign of Louis Philippe, the Republic of 1848, the Empire and the Republic of 1870. —London Spectator.

REPLY, Victoria's.—An African prince who was sent on an embassy with costly presents for Queen Victoria. from an Ethiopian court, preferred a modest request that England's beloved Sovereign would tell him the secret of England's greatness and glory. Her majesty did not, like Hezekiah, show the ambassador her diamonds and her precious jewels, and her rich ornaments, but, handing him a beautifully bound copy of the Bible, said, " Tell the Prince that this is the secret of England's greatness."—C. A.

SUPREMACY OF THE SEA AND BRITISH ARROGANCE.—Why should we fear a great nation on the American continent. Some fear that a great nation would be arrogant and aggressive. But that does not at all follow. It does not depend altogether upon the size of a nation. but upon its qualities, and upon the intelligence, instruction, and morals of its people. You fancy that the supremacy of the sea will pass away from you; and the noble lord, tho wiser than many others, will lament that " Rule Britannia." that noble old song, should become antiquated at last.

Well, but if the supremacy of the sea excites the arrogance of this country, the sooner it becomes obsolete the better. I don't believe it to be for the advantage of this country or of any other that any one nation should pride itself upon what it terms the supremacy of the sea, and I hope the time is come—and I believe it is—when we shall find that law and justice shall guide the councils and direct the policy of the Christian nations of the world.

.   .   .   .   .   .

I believe, however, that in the centuries which are to come it will be the greatest pride and the highest renown of England that from her loins have sprung a hundred—it may be two hundred—millions of men to dwell and to prosper on the continent which the old Genoese gave to Europe. Now, sir, if the sentiment which I have heard to-night shall become the sentiment of the Parliament and people of the United Kingdom, and if the moderation which I have described shall mark the course of the government and people of the United States, then, notwithstanding some present irritation and some fresh distrust,—and I have faith, mind, both in us and in them,—I believe that these two great commonwealths may march on abreast, parents and guardians of freedom and justice, wheresoever their language shall be spoken and their power shall extend.—John Bright. (From an address on " Will the United States Subjugate Canada? " 1865.)

UNION JACK, The.—On April 12, 1606, exactly 295 years ago, the Union Jack, Great Britain's flag, made its appearance. It was James I. who added the Scottish cross of St. Andrew, in consequence of differences having arisen between English and Scottish ships at sea, and it was he who gave the flag its name. James generally signed his name " Jacques," and some think this originated the term " Jack;" it may, however, have been from the Spanish for coat, " Jaco," as knights wore a little coat or jacket over their armor with distinguishing marks on them. The cross of St. George was introduced as England's battle flag by Richard I. when he returned from Palestine.—*Selected.*

VICTORIA, Queen.—Queen Victoria led a noble life. She personified all that is best in the British character. Firm to obstinacy, tender-hearted and affectionate without being emotional, tranquil in action, reasonable in idea, tho without claim to genius or transcendent ability, the Queen will live in history by force of her character. Great knowledge and an iron will gave to the Queen an influence in the control of public affairs which was, in fact, more akin to that of the Stuarts than to the constitutional conditions which are the theoretical foundation for the House of Hanover. While sticklers for constitutional nicety grumbled at and resented the Queen's overwhelming influence in public affairs, and were indignant at her Majesty's use of the German language, and at her predilections for her German relatives, they loved her as well and faithfully as ever a free people loved a great ruler and a good woman.—Arnold White. (H. W.)

VICTORIA'S MOTHER, Queen.—Perhaps much of the good of Queen Victoria's long reign was due to her being blessed with such a wise mother.

The Duchess of Kent, realizing the responsibilities her daughter was soon to assume, made it the study of her life to bring the future Queen up in such a way that she should rule her subjects in the fear of the Lord.

Of so deeply a religious character was that training, that faith was the foundation of Queen Victoria's career as a woman and a sovereign. That faith was taught her by the influence of her mother, who felt it to be the most important element of character. To know the King of all the earth and have faith in Him, was taught the little Victoria in her earliest years. When she was crowned Queen her first request of her subjects was this one: " I ask your prayers in my behalf." Having had such a good mother herself, she was an exemplary mother to her own children. True motherhood has never been overshadowed by the glories which crowned her as a Queen.—E.

VICTORIA'S, Queen, Irish Descent.—Queen Victoria's descent has been traced back to Turlough O'Conor, King of Ireland, A. D., 1400, as follows:

Turlough O'Conor, King of Ireland.
|
Cathal Red-Hand O'Conor, King of Connaught.
|
Odo O'Conor, King of Connaught.
|
Una O'Conor.
|
Hodierna de Gernon.
|

Richard de Burgh, Lord of Connaught.
|
Walter de Burgh, Lord of Connaught and Earl of Ulster.
|
Richard de Burgh, Lord of Connaught and Earl of Ulster.
|
William de Burgh, Lord of Connaught and Earl of Ulster.
|
Elizabeth de Burgh.
|
Philippa Plantagenet.
|
Edmund Mortimer, Earl of March.
|
Roger Mortimer, Earl of March.
|
Anne Mortimer.
|
Richard Plantagenet, Duke of Cambridge.
|
Richard Plantagenet, Duke of York.
|
Edward IV.

Queen Victoria's descent to Edward IV. is as follows: Edward, Duke of Kent; George III., Frederick, Prince of Wales; George II., George I., Sophia, Elizabeth, James I., Mary Queen of Scots, James V. of Scotland, Margaret Elizabeth, wife of Henry VII.; Edward IV. She was consequently twenty-nine in descent from the great Irish kings.—*Selected.*

VICTORIA'S REIGN.—A notable chapter of human history was closed when the Queen breathed her last. It was given her to be the central figure in an epoch through which moved a procession of illustrious personages, and which was thronged with notable and fruitful events. At the mention of her name, there instinctively comes to mind the length of her reign, the vast extent of her influence, the march of discovery, the brilliance of letters, the imposing strength of statesmanship, the uplifting of the race, the drawing together of the nations, the mighty and triumphant advance of the world. But her unique and illustrious personality outshines the circumstances amid which she moved. The peoples of the earth bow at her bier to-day, not because of what she did, but of what she was. The realm she ruled was far wider than the geographical limits of the British Empire. Whoever recognizes royalty of character counted himself among her subjects. Whoever does homage to noble Christian womanhood yielded her the allegiance of his heart. . . . America has shared the benediction of her life. America joins in the universal tribute of affectionate sorrow at her passing away. He who would not lower the flag has lowered himself. For the people of God to fail to acknowledge the presence and dominance of His Spirit in a life so signally dowered with His gifts, so conspicuously raised up to do His work, and so long and so faithfully devoting its energies to His service, would be for God's people to fail in loyalty to their King.—Howard Duffield.

POETRY

On the Birth of Alfred Edward

Huzza! we've a little Prince at last,
A roaring Royal boy;
And all day long the booming bells
Have rung their peals of joy.—L. Pu.

God Save the King

BY HENRY CAREY

God save our gracious King!
Long live our noble King!
God save the King!
Send him victorious,
Happy and glorious,
Long to reign over us—
God save the King!

O Lord our God, arise!
Scatter his enemies,
And make them fall,
Confound their politics,
Frustrate their knavish tricks;
On him our hopes we fix,
God save us all!

Thy choicest gifts in store
On him be pleased to pour;
Long may he reign.
May he defend our laws,
And ever give us cause
To sing with heart and voice—
God save the King!

To the Queen

BY ALFRED TENNYSON

Revered, beloved—O you that hold
A nobler office upon earth
Than arms, or power of brain or birth
Could give the warrior kings of old,

Victoria,—since your Royal grace
To one of less desert allows
This laurel greener from the brows
Of him that uttered nothing base;

And should your greatness, and the care
That yokes with empire, yield you time
To make demand of modern rhyme
If aught of ancient worth be there;

Then—while a sweeter music wakes,
And thro' wild March the throstle calls,
Where all about your palace-walls
The sunlit almond-blossom shakes—

Take, Madam, this poor book of song;
For tho the faults were thick as dust
In vacant chambers, I could trust
Your kindness. May you rule us long,

And leave us rulers of your blood
As noble till the latest day!
May children of our children say,
" She wrought her people lasting good;

" Her court was pure; her life serene;
God gave her peace; her land reposed:
A thousand claims to reverence closed
In her as Mother, Wife, and Queen;

" And statesmen at her council met
Who knew the seasons, when to take
Occasion by the hand, and make
The bounds of freedom wider yet

" By shaping some august decree,
Which kept her throne unshaken still,
Broad based upon her people's will,
And compassed by the inviolate sea."
MARCH, 1851.

The Queen

BY JOSEPH HOWE

Queen of the thousand isles! whose fragile
form,
'Midst the proud structures of our Father-
land,
Graces the Throne, that each subsiding
storm
Which shakes the earth, assures us yet shall
stand.
Thy gentle voice, of mild yet firm com-
mand,
Is heard in every clime; on every wave,
Thy dazzling scepter, like a fairy wand,
Strikes off the shackles from the struggling
slave,
And gathers, 'neath its rule, the great, the
wise, the brave.

But yet, 'midst all the treasures that sur-
round
Thy royal halls, one bliss is still denied,—
To know the true hearts at thy name that
bound,
Which ocean from thy presence must divide,
Whose voices never swell the boisterous tide
Of hourly homage that salutes thy ear;
But yet who cherish with a Briton's pride,
And breathe to infant lips, from year to
year,
The name thy many virtues taught them to
revere.

How little deem'st thou of the scenes re-
mote,
In which one word, all other words above,
Of earthly homage seems to gaily float
On every breeze, and sound through every
grove—
A spell to cheer, to animate, to move—
To bid old age throw off the weight of
years,
To cherish thoughts of loyalty and love,
To garner round the heart those hopes and
fears
Which, in our western homes, Victoria's
name endears.

'Tis not that, on our soil, the measured tread
Of armed legions speaks thy sovereign sway,
'Tis not the huge leviathans that spread
Thy meteor flag above each noble bay,
That bids the soul a forced obedience pay!
—The despot's tribute from a trembling
    thrall—
No! At our altars sturdy freemen pray
That blessings on Victoria's head may fall,
And happy household groups each pleasing
    trait recall.

Wahonomin

[Indian Hymn to the Queen.]

By GEORGE F. SCOTT

Great mother! from the depths of forest
    wilds,
From mountain pass and burning sunset
    plain,
We, thy unlettered children of the woods,
Upraise to thee the everlasting hymn
Of nature, language of the skies and seas,
Voice of the birds and sighings of the pine
In wintry wastes. We know no other tongue,
Nor the smooth speech that, like the shining
    leaves,
Hides the rough stems beneath. We bring
    our song,
Wood-fragrant. rough, yet autumn-streaked
    with love,
And lay it as a tribute at thy feet.

The Dying Queen

By RANDALL N. SAUNDERS

The world to-day is wrapt in gloom:
    The nations mourn that she,
Who held in hand an empire's doom,
    Is launching on that sea
        Where ruler, subject, at the test,
        Sails forth to find that all the best
        Is that the one who ruleth best
SHALL BE!
She ruled, and nations held their breath:
She ruled, and worlds will mourn her death.

                        L. W.

Death

*[Her Majesty, the Queen of England, died
on Tuesday, January 22, 1901, at 6: 30
p. m.]*

Grief, and the ache of things that pass and
    fade,
    The stately pomp, the pall, the open grave,
    These and the solemn thoughts which
        cannot save
Our eyes from tears, nor make us less afraid
Of that dread mystery which God has
    made:—
    How many thousand thousand men who
        wave
    Speechless farewells, with hearts for-
        lornly brave,
Know well the mockery of Death's parade?

This cannot help us to transgress the bounds,
    Nor give us wings to overpass the steep
    Ramparts of Heaven which God's angels
        keep:

Wide is the "great gulf fixed:" for us, the
    mounds
Of fresh-turned earth; above, sweet peace
    surrounds
The painless patience of eternal sleep.

                        F. R.

Victoria the Good

By SIR THEODORE MARTIN

Stifle the throbbing of this haunting pain,
    And dash this tearful sorrow from the
        eyes!
She is not dead! Though summoned to
    the skies,
Still in our hearts she lives, and there will
    reign;
Still the dear memory will the power retain
    To teach us where our foremost duty lies,
    Truth. justice, honor, simple worth to
        prize,
And what our best have been to be again.

She hath gone hence, to meet the great, the
    good,
    The loved ones, yearn'd for through long
        toilsome years,
To share with them the blest beatitude,
    Where care is not, nor strife, nor wasting
        fears,
Nor cureless ills, nor wrongs to be with-
        stood;
    Shall thought of this not dry our blinding
        tears?

                        N. C.

Britannia

By A. McLACHLAN

All hail, my country! hail to thee,
Thou birthplace of the brave and free,
Thou ruler upon land and sea,
    Britannia!

No thing of change, no mushroom state,
In wisdom thou canst work and wait,
Or wield the thunderbolts of Fate,
    Britannia!

Oh, nobly hast thou played thy part!
What struggles of the head and heart
Have gone to make thee what thou art,
    Britannia!

Great mother of the mighty dead!
Sir Walter sang and Nelson bled
To weave a garland for thy head,
    Britannia!

And Watt, the great magician, wrought.
And Shakespeare ranged the realms of
    thought,
And Newton soared, and Cromwell fought,
    Britannia!

And Milton's high seraphic art,
And Bacon's head and Burns' heart
Are glories that shall ne'er depart,
    Britannia!

These are the soul of thy renown,
The gems immortal in thy crown,
The suns that never shall go down,
    Britannia!

O, still have faith in truth divine!
Aye sacred be thy seal and sign,
And power and glory shall be thine,
    Britannia!

The Englishman

By Eliza Cook

There's a land that bears a world-known
    name,
  Tho it is but a little spot;
I say 'tis first on the scroll of Fame,
  And who shall say it is not?
Of the deathless ones who shine and live
  In Arms, in Art, or Song;
The brightest the whole wide world can give
  To that little land belong.
'Tis the star of earth, deny it who can;
  The island home of an Englishman.

There's a flag that waves over every sea,
  No matter when or where;
And to treat that flag as aught but the free
  Is more than the strongest dare.
For the lion spirits that tread the deck
  Have carried the palm of the brave;
And that flag may sink with a shot-torn
    wreck,
  But never float over a slave.
Its honor is stainless, deny it who can;
  And this is the flag of an Englishman.

There's a heart that leaps with burning glow,
  The wrong'd and the weak to defend;
And strikes as soon for a trampled foe;
  As it does for a soul-bound friend.
It nurtures a deep and honest love;
  It glows with faith and pride;
And yearns with the fondness of a dove,
  To the light of its own fireside.
'Tis a rich, rough gem, deny it who can:
  And this is the heart of an Englishman.

The Briton may traverse the pole or the
    zone
  And boldly claim his right;
For he calls such a vast domain his own,
  That the sun never sets on his might.
Let the haughty stranger seek to know
  The place of his home and birth;
And a flush will pour from cheek to brow;
  While he tells his native earth.
For a glorious charter, deny it who can;
  Is breathed in the words " I'm an English-
    man."

Sonnet

By William Wordsworth

It is not to be thought of that the flood
  Of British freedom, which, to the open
    sea
Of the world's praise, from dark antiquity
Hath flowed, " with pomp of waters, unwith-
    stood,"

Roused tho it be full often to a mood
  Which spurns the check of salutary bands,
  That this most famous stream in bogs and
    sands
Should perish; and to evil and to good
Be lost forever. In our halls is hung
  Armory of the invincible knights of old:
We must be free or die, who speak the
    tongue
  That Shakespeare spake; the faith and
    morals hold
Which Milton held.—In everything we are
    sprung
Of earth's first blood, have titles manifold.

England and Her Colonies

By William Watson

She stands, a thousand-wintered tree,
  By countless morns impearled;
Her broad roots coil beneath the sea,
  Her branches sweep the world;
Her seeds, by careless winds conveyed,
  Clothe the remotest strand
With forests from her scatterings made,
New nations fostered in her shade,
  And linking land with land.

O ye by wandering tempest sown
  'Neath every alien star,
Forget not whence the breath was blown
  That wafted you afar!
For ye are still her ancient seed
  On younger soil let fall—
Children of Britain's island-breed,
  To whom the Mother in her need
  Perchance may one day call.

National Song

By Alfred Tennyson

There is no land like England
  Where'er the light of day be;
There are no hearts like English hearts,
  Such hearts of oak as they be.
There is no land like England
  Where'er the light of day be;
There are no men like Englishmen,
  So tall and bold as they be.

Chorus

For the French the Pope may shrive 'em,
For the devil a whit we heed 'em:
As for the French, God speed 'em
  Unto their heart's desire,
And the merry devil drive 'em
  Through the water and the fire.

Full Chorus

Our glory is our freedom,
  We lord it o'er the sea;
We are the sons of freedom,
  We are free.

There is no land like England,
  Where'er the light of day be;
There are no wives like English wives,
  So fair and chaste as they be.

There is no land like England,
  Where'er the light of day be;
There are no maids like English maids,
  So beautiful as they be.

CHORUS.—For the French, etc.

Recessional

BY RUDYARD KIPLING

God of our fathers, known of old—
Lord of our far-flung battle line—
Beneath whose awful Hand we hold
  Dominion over palm and pine—
Lord God of Hosts, be with us yet,
Lest we forget—lest we forget!

The tumult and the shouting dies—
  The captains and the kings depart;
Still stands thine ancient sacrifice,
  A humble and a contrite heart,—
Lord God of Hosts, be with us yet,
Lest we forget—lest we forget!

Far-called our navies melt away—
  On dune and headland sinks the fire—
Lo, all our pomp of yesterday
  Is one with Nineveh and Tyre!
Judge of the nations, spare us yet,
Lest we forget—lest we forget!

If, drunk with sight of power, we loose
  Wild tongues that have not Thee in awe;
Such boasting as the Gentiles use,
  Or lesser breeds without the Law—
Lord God of Hosts, be with us yet,
Lest we forget—lest we forget!

For heathen heart that puts her trust
  In reeking tube and iron shard—
All valiant dust that builds on dust,
  And, guarding, calls not Thee to guard—
For frantic boast and foolish word,
Thy mercy on Thy people, Lord!

                                    Amen.

America to Great Britain

BY WASHINGTON ALLSTON

All hail! thou noble land,
  Our Fathers' native soil!
O, stretch thy mighty hand,
  Gigantic grown by toil,
O'er the vast Atlantic wave to our shore!
For thou with magic might
Canst reach to where the light
Of Phoebus travels bright
    The world o'er!

The Genius of our clime,
  From his pine-embattled steep,
Shall hail the guest sublime;
  While the Tritons of the deep
With their conchs the kindred league shall
    proclaim.
Then let the world combine,—
O'er the main our naval line
Like the milky-way shall shine
    Bright in fame!

Tho ages long have past
  Since our Fathers left their home,
Their pilot in the blast,
  O'er untraveled seas to roam,
Yet lives the blood of England in our veins!
And shall we not proclaim
That blood of honest fame
Which no tyranny can tame
    By its chains?

While the language free and bold
  Which the Bard of Avon sung,
In which our Milton told
  How the vault of heaven rung
When Satan, blasted, fell with his host;—
While this, with reverence meet,
Ten thousand echoes greet,
From rock to rock repeat
    Round our coast;—

While the manners, while the arts,
  That mold a nation's soul,
Still cling around our hearts,—
  Between let Ocean roll,
Our joint communion breaking with the Sun:
Yet still from either beach
The voice of blood shall reach,
More audible than speech,
    "We are One."

England

BY ELIZABETH BARRETT BROWNING

Whoever lives true life, will love true love.
I learn'd to love that England. Very oft,
Before the day was born, or otherwise
Through secret windings of the afternoons,
I threw my hunters off and plunged myself
Among the deep hills, as a hunted stag
Will take the waters, shivering with the fear
And passion of the course. And when, at
    last
Escap'd—so many a green slope built on
    slope
Betwixt me and the enemy's house behind,
I dar'd to rest, or wander,—like a rest
Made sweeter for the step upon the grass,—
And view the ground's most gentle dimple-
    ment,
(As if God's finger touch'd but did not
    press
In making England!) such an up and down
Of verdure,—nothing too much up or down,
A ripple of land; such little hills, the sky
Can stoop to tenderly, and the wheatfields
    climb;
Such nooks of valleys, lin'd with orchises,
Fed full of noises by invisible streams;
And open pastures, where you scarcely tell
White daisies from white dew,—at intervals
The mythic oaks and elm-trees standing out
Self-pois'd upon their prodigy of shade,—
I thought my father's land was worthy too
Of being my Shakespeare's . . . .
. . . . Breaking into voluble ecstasy.
I flatter'd all the beauteous country round,
As poets use . . . the skies, the clouds,
    the fields,
The happy violets, hiding from the roads

The primroses run down to, carrying gold,—
The tangled hedgerows, where the cows push out
Impatient horns and tolerant churning mouths
'Twixt dripping ash-boughs,—hedgerows all alive
With birds and gnats and large white butterflies
Which look as if the May-flower had sought life
And palpitated forth upon the wind,—
Hills, vales, woods, netted in a silver mist.
Farms, granges, doubled up among the hills,
And cattle grazing in the water'd vales,
And cottage-chimneys smoking from the woods,
And cottage-gardens smelling everywhere,
Confus'd with smell of orchards. "See," I said,
" And see! is God not with us on the earth?
And shall we put Him down by aught we do?
Who says there's nothing for the poor and vile
Save poverty and wickedness? behold!"
And ankle-deep in English grass I leap'd,
And clapp'd my hands, and call'd all very fair.

England

By John Henry Newman

Tyre of the West, and glorying in the name
  More than in Faith's pure fame!
O trust not crafty fort nor rock renown'd,
  Earn'd upon hostile ground;
Wielding Trade's master-keys, at thy proud will
To lock or loose its waters, England! trust not still.

Dread thine own power! Since haughty Babel's prime,
  High towers have been man's crime.
Since her hoar age, when the huge moat lay bare,
  Strongholds have been man's snare.
Thy nest is in the crags; ah, refuge frail!
Mad counsel in its hour, or traitors, will prevail.

He who scann'd Sodom for His righteous men
  Still spares thee for thy ten;
But, should vain tongues the Bride of Heaven defy,
  He will not pass thee by;
For, as earth's kings welcome their spotless guest,
So gives He them by turn, to suffer or be blest.

Ye Mariners of England

By Thomas Campbell

Ye Mariners of England!
That guard our native seas;
Whose flag has braved, a thousand years,
The battle and the breeze!

Your glorious standard launch again,
To match another foe!
And sweep through the deep,
While the stormy winds do blow;
While the battle rages loud and long,
And the stormy winds do blow.

The spirits of your fathers
Shall start from every wave!
For the deck it was their field of fame,
And Ocean was their grave:
Where Blake and mighty Nelson fell,
Your manly hearts shall glow,
As ye sweep through the deep,
While the stormy winds do blow;
While the battle rages loud and long,
And the stormy winds do blow.

Britannia needs no bulwarks,
No towers along the steep;
Her march is on the mountain-waves,
Her home is on the deep.
With thunders from her native oak,
She quells the floods below—
As they roar on the shore,
When the stormy winds do blow;
When the battle rages loud and long,
And the stormy winds do blow.

The Meteor of England
Shall yet terrific burn,
Till danger's troubled night depart,
And the star of peace return.
Then, then, ye ocean-warriors!
Our song and feast shall flow
To the fame of your name,
When the storm has ceased to blow;
When the fiery fight is heard no more,
And the storm has ceased to blow.

Men of England

By Thomas Campbell

Men of England! who inherit
  Rights that cost your sires their blood!
Men whose undegenerate spirit
  Has been proved on land and flood:—

By the foes ye've fought uncounted,
  By the glorious deeds ye've done,
Trophies captured—breaches mounted,
  Navies conquer'd—kingdoms won!

Yet, remember, England gathers
  Hence but fruitless wreaths of fame,
If the patriotism of your fathers
  Glow not in your hearts the same.

What are monuments of bravery,
  Where no public virtues bloom?
What avail in lands of slavery,
  Trophied temples, arch and tomb?

Pageants!—Let the world revere us
  For our people's rights and laws,
And the breasts of civic heroes
  Bared in Freedom's holy cause.

Yours are Hampden's, Russell's glory,
  Sydney's matchless shade is yours,—
Martyrs in heroic story,
  Worth a hundred Agincourts!

We're the sons of sires that baffled
Crown'd and miter'd tyranny :—
They defied the field and scaffold
For their birthrights—so will we!

Rule, Britannia

By James Thomson

When Britain first at Heaven's command,
Arose from out the azure main,
This was the charter, the charter of the land,
And guardian angels sung the strain :
Rule, Britannia,
Britannia rule the waves,
Britons never shall be slaves.

The nations, not so blest as thee,
Must in their turn to tyrants fall,
While thou shalt flourish, great and free,
The dread and envy of them all.
Rule, Britannia,
Britannia rule the waves,
Britons never shall be slaves.

Still more majestic shalt thou rise,
More dreadful from each foreign stroke;
As the loud blast that rends the skies
Serves but to root thy native oak.
Rule, Britannia,
Britannia rule the waves,
Britons never shall be slaves.

Thee, haughty tyrants ne'er shall tame;
All their attempts to bend thee down
Will but arouse thy generous flame,—
But work their woe and thy renown.
Rule, Britannia,
Britannia rule the waves,
Britons never shall be slaves.

To thee belongs the rural reign,
Thy cities shall with commerce shine;
All thine shall be the subject main,
And every shore encircles thine.
Rule, Britannia,
Britannia rule the waves,
Britons never shall be slaves.

The Muses, still with freedom found,
Shall to thy happy coasts repair,
Blessed Isle! With matchless beauty
crowned,
And manly hearts to guard the fair.
Rule, Britannia,
Britannia rule the waves,
Britons never shall be slaves.

Buonaparte

By Alfred Tennyson

He thought to quell the stubborn hearts of
oak,
Madman!—to chain with chains, and bind
with bands
That island queen that sways the floods and
lands
From Ind to Ind, but in fair daylight woke,
When from her wooden walls, lit by sure
hands,
With thunders, and with lightnings, and with
smoke,
Peal after peal, the British battle broke,
Lulling the brine against the Coptic sands.
We taught him lowlier moods, when Elsinore
Heard the war moan along the distant sea,
Rocking with shattered spars, with sudden
fires
Flamed over: at Trafalgar yet once more
We taught him : late he learned humility
Perforce, like those whom Gideon schooled
with briers.

MEMORIAL DAY*

(May 30)

TRADITION has it that about the time the Civil War broke out, a soldier of the German army came to this country, and, enlisting in our army, served through the war. About the time the war closed he casually remarked one day that it was the custom in Germany for the people to scatter flowers on the graves of soldiers once a year. Nothing more was said at the time, but it is supposed that this was the origin of " Memorial Day."

Be this as it may, early in May, 1868, Adjutant-General N. P. Chipman conferred with National Commander John A. Logan, of the Grand Army of the Republic (an organization then in its infancy) concerning the matter of having that organization inaugurate the custom of spreading flowers on the graves of the Union soldiers all over the Union at some uniform time or day.

The idea seemed to strike General Logan as being a most proper thing to do, and he immediately issued an order in which he named the 30th day of May, 1868, " for the purpose of strewing with flowers, or otherwise decorating the graves of comrades who died in defense of their country during the late rebellion, and whose bodies now lie in almost every city, village, or hamlet churchyard in the land."

After speaking to the Grand Army comrades of their duties he closed with these words, " It is the purpose of the commander-in-chief to inaugurate this observance with the hope that it will be kept up from year to year while a survivor of the war remains to honor the memory of the departed."

As time went on the name of " Decoration " was changed to " Memorial," the former word failing to express the feelings of the comrades, inasmuch as it has too much shallowness for such a grand service as has been inaugurated.

It is well that this day should be kept a high and holy festival. Think of the character of the men who responded thirty-seven years ago to the call of the country! The army was drawn from the average American citizen, and it was constituted from the very best stock in the land. Then think of the high and sacred cause in which they were enlisted.

The men whose graves shall be decorated on Memorial Day were men who ventured their lives, and in multitudes of instances lost them for the sake of great ideas and principles, and for these they counted it honor to deny themselves and endure all things, even death itself.

We cannot do a wiser thing than to honor the memories of the departed defenders of the flag, and in so doing show, not only that we are grateful for what they did, but that we love the Nation whose banner they followed and wish to do something that will prove that we are worthy of the name of Americans.

But the patriot dead are not only those who wore the blue and marched under the flag; not alone their graves do we honor. There were patriots who at home upheld the soldier's heart and inspired him to duty. There were the women, who gave their loved ones, who breathed up prayers for their safety and return, whose needles stitched for them, whose hands wrought for them, whose

* For date of observance of Memorial Day in the South, see table of holidays on p. 465.

letters cheered them, whose love forever embodied itself in something that should comfort and relieve them.

The memory of those patriot women we too would honor, and did we know where their bodies sleep, their graves we would decorate.—N. T. A. (1898.)

ADDRESSES

THIRTY YEARS AFTER *

By Rev. Clark Wright

Mr. President, Gentlemen of the 3d Regimental Association of Georgia:

A private soldier who carried a gun, who was the least of all the men who surround you to-night—is to tell you what you already have learned in your intercourse with the members of the Hawkins Zouave Association of New York, that we are glad to see you, and take great pleasure in bidding you a most cordial welcome to this, the thirtieth anniversary of the organization of the 9th N. Y. Vols. (Hawkins Zouaves).

We most kindly appreciate the hospitality shown our representatives who visited you at one time—who returned declaring that Georgia grapes and watermelons were not only large, but delicious, and were given by the men of the old 3d Georgia with lavish hand, at Fort Valley, thus manifesting your cordiality and regard to the boys (now old men) of the Hawkins Zouaves, for which we are sincerely thankful.

It is very pleasant to have the opportunity to grasp the friendly hand of those who thought so diametrically opposite, thirty years ago. It proves time not only heals, but also cools the blood, gives more mature judgment, enabling each to overlook the past, and while we do not claim to forget those dark hours in our life, nor withdraw an iota. nor impugn the motives or sincerity of an opponent, we can each forgive, and while we let the dead past bury its dead, rejoice in the sunshine of the present, that brings comfort and happiness to all parts of our native land, as we remember above and over all else, we are American citizens. As such this remnant of Hawkins Zouaves sit down and break bread with—and most gladly greet —the survivors of the gallant 3d Regiment of Georgia.

And while the professional politician may rave about the rights of the South, or the rights of the North, we calmly step aside from these noisy windmills of both sections to clasp the hand of these brave heroic men of the South, and bid them a joyful welcome to the metropolis of the Empire State of New York. . . .

We are particularly pleased to see you gentlemen because there are several remarkable parallels, incident in the history of the two regiments whose representatives gather around this board.

1. Both were organized in April, 1861, within seven days of each other; ours on the 19th, yours on the 26th.

2. Both were composed largely of young men, many of whom had not attained their majority.

3. Both were composed of men who, impressed with the righteousness of the cause they represented, and feeling assured they were right, dared that cause maintain.

4. The fortunes of war brought these regiments repeatedly face to face, time after time in most deadly strife, and while each did their best, as soon as the battle ceased, humanity took the place of conflict and the wounded and distressed were cared for without regard to the color of their clothes, whether it was blue or gray, or gray or blue.

5. Altho the records prove few regiments of the last war lost a larger per cent. of those engaged, giving evidence of the terrific fire they experienced, yet neither of them lost a stand of colors, nor were the colors touched by hostile hand, and altho the flags of both have been shot into tatters there is still enough left of each, for the survivors of these regiments annually to gather around, and show our regard for one another, and our love for those who fell fighting beneath their folds.

To-night the stars of Heaven look down upon Georgia and New York clasping hands of friendship and fraternity, while we glory in your record of intrepidity and fortitude, in the manhood you displayed on so many battlefields, in the prosperity of your State and the entire South, in the happiness attending your advancing years, in the glorious fact that Georgia stands side by side with New York in her devotion to the starry flag of Washington, knowing well were a foe to arise from any quarter of the globe and attempt to strike down that emblem of our liberties, the 3d Georgia and 9th New York would stand side by side in defense of our country, our flag, and our homes.

We rejoice the hour has come when we can converse about our early intercourse. Ours was not a hasty acquaintance; most of us grew to manhood before we got within gunshot of each other, and even after we spent a season of varied interest at that breezy watering place on the coast of North Carolina called Hatteras, it was some time

* Delivered when the speaker's old regiment, 9th N. Y. Volunteers, entertained the 3d Georgia under Col (Judge) Sneed.

before we learned that the gentlemen from Georgia were in the vicinity of Hatteras Light House. Learning this we started one day up the coast to seek an introduction to you. Altho some of us have since become gray-haired, we still remember that walk by the side of the poetical, dark blue sea.

We had read Clark Russell's description of the fascinations of the dark blue sea but I think we never realized before how blue it really was; yes, the sea was blue, and before we had walked ten miles in the sand up to our ankles we were blue too, but we trudged on, tired, weary, determined to make your acquaintance. No lover in pursuit of his coy lady could have been more determined than we on our march to Chicamicomico; from this you may judge how we loved you.

But alas we were to prove the truth of the Scottish Bard that

" The best laid plans o' mice and men gang aft aglee,"

for on our arrival we found you had changed your mind, and concluded to defer the matter and let us wait before you would consent to an introduction to the 9th New York. Like the foolish virgins, we learned we were too late for the festivities you had enjoyed that day with an Indiana Regiment, and after a pleasant time had quietly returned from whence you came—not, however, until, like a thoughtful friend, you had compassionately relieved the aforesaid regiment of most of their camp equipage, and eased them of the burden of carrying their heavy overcoats to Hatteras. And so back we went, like a jilted young man, over the same route by the side of the aforesaid deep blue sea, sad and lonely, to wait a more propitious opportunity for an introduction. How often we thought of you!

We knew you were well-dressed gentlemen, for clothing had been sent you from Indiana, and we fancied you went sailing each pleasant afternoon on Albemarle Sound, else you would not have needed the steamboat " Fannie " which a kind Providence and the foresight of Indiana friends placed at your disposal.

I can't tell all we thought and said about you while we enjoyed our savory mullets and sweet potatoe pies served at our hotel by the cooks of Hatteras. Until at last becoming disconsolate we ourselves took steamer and sailed up the sound as far as Roanoke Island, where, possibly fortunately for us, you still concluded to defer the first interview.

We, however, saw your work and finally occupied the " French Flats " (Barracks) you had built; they were the best quarters we had during our term of service and when we took possession of those suburban residences and learned that they were built by the 3d Georgia for our especial use, we knew you loved us, and that you would leave nothing undone to make the 9th happy. Certainly as we recall this evidence of forethought as your part (even at this late day)

we desire to return our most sincere thanks. There in those barracks we tarried until one day, before the historic day of the historic month of April, we bade our island home good-by, to meet on the morrow, April 19th, 1862, as the sequel proved, you the determined men of the 3d Regiment of Georgia.

Concerning that interview held at what you are pleased to call Sawyer's Lane, which we designated Camden, it is unnecessary for me to dwell at great length. We met, exchanged the compliments of the season and parted each with increased respect for the other, thoroughly convinced of the stubborn tenacity and grit characterizing both the men who defended their battery and those who charged for a half mile in front of it.

My recollection is you left us in possession of the field, but if memory serves right that field was like holding a hot poker, while you were in the neighborhood.

So, noiselessly under cover of the darkness, we gently folded up our haversacks (not having much else to fold) and, like the classic Arab, silently took our weary march back to the place from whence we came.

I assure you not many songs were sung that night—not many stories were told, for we were not quite sure you were satisfied, and it was barely possible you might request another interview, and as we had been on the march all the preceding day and a part of the night, we were in no condition to enter into the full enjoyment of an all hands around, even with the gentlemen who had given us such a warm reception, so we went back to the enjoyment of our Island home at Roanoke, to meditate over the interview we had with you on the battle-field of Camden.

. . . And since then the years have passed, and a new generation has come into existence until now. . . .

With mingled feelings of respect and regard we look in your faces to-night. I say respect because one brave man always respects another who stood manfully for what he believed the right. We hold you in kind regard because we recollect the scenes·you passed through, for you are the men who while battling a foe in front, were assailed by starvation in the rear. The battle-fields where opposing hosts contended for victory witnessed no nobler instances of courage and self abnegation than did the homes where ill-clothed Confederates had left wives and children to raise a little corn and tend the flock whereby they might exist.

Our forces experimentally knew nothing of the agony endured by the men in your ranks. We met, fought, buried our dead, cared for our wounded, and gloried in whatever triumph might come. But you not only fought, but you fought amid want.

Of tea, of coffee we had the best in the world; but a pound of tea from Nassau cost you $500. Our army was well shod; if a pair of shoes were worn out after a long march, the Quartermaster would issue another pair. But you were often obliged to go barefooted, while a prominent general of the South has informed us a pair of boots cost $600, and in 1864, it was officially announced that a large number of the Stonewall Brigade were entirely without shoes. Of hard bread we generally had plenty. It is said a Southern captain found one of his soldiers up a persimmon tree eating green persimmons, and when, on asking the reason for such strange action, was told he was eating green persimmons in order to fit his mouth to the size of the rations.

We of the Union Army think of the triumph of our arms and to us they were grand, but it were well for us to ponder over the fact, that while our armies were fighting the Confederates in front, General Starvation was assaulting them on the flank and rear. In January, 1863, the Virginia newspapers quoted flour at $25 per barrel; in January, 1864, $95 per barrel; in January, 1865, $1,000 per barrel. For you heroes of Georgia there was death at the cannon's mouth in front and starvation in the rear. In September, 1861, $1.10 of Confederate money was equal to $1 in United States gold. But in January, 1865, it took $60 Confederate money to buy $1 in gold. It seemed while the money market was going down lower and lower, your courage and pluck mounted higher and higher. A Southern paper gave a list of the dead and wounded, and alongside were directions for the use of boneset as a substitute for quinine. You made pencils to mark roll call from molten bullets, poured into the cavity of small reeds from the cane brakes. The juice of the pokeberry compounded with vinegar furnished ink, while the goose quill (it was all the Yankees left of the goose) took the place of the steel pen to write to the girl you left behind you. Raspberry and sassafras took the place of Hyson, parched rye and dried sweet potatoes took the place of Mocha. Scupanong wine did not continue plentiful after the 9th left North Carolina. Pine tags and potatoes went into the still, to come out pure mountain dew, while the persimmon tree furnished the beer which was called "Possum toddy." Carding combs, the spindle, the loom, was the music coming from the chimney side. Flax joined King Cotton in clothing the people in homespun, while headgear was furnished by robbing the coon or rabbit of his overcoat. According to one authority, buttons, pins, buckles, hooks and eyes, gradually disappeared. While the ladies used devices known to themselves, the men skewered their trousers with wooden pins or locust thorns. We defy the world to show greater pluck and more indomitable courage than was manifested by the South in those four years of terrible war.

But I have thought it was during the holiday seasons of the year the disappointment was keenest, when the little homespun stocking hung on the chimney place at Christmas, when your ingenuity was put to the test to devise so the deprivations you were enduring should not be felt by the little ones around the fireside. Aye, you might have

told them that Hawkins Zouaves had waylaid Santa Claus as he was coming through the lines—you might have told them the Noah's Ark, with its menagerie, the jumping jacks, wagons, and dolls, were all captured by the Yankees. And it might have been true, but it could not soften the feeling of regret in your heart, that at the holiest season of the year, Christmas time, you could not give your little ones the best the world afforded.

But brave souls that you were, this burden also, you took upon your heart as you went forward in the performance of what you conscientiously considered your duty and so those years passed—years of self-sacrifice, years of devotion to what you felt was principle, years of sorrow, of pain, of death, of graves; but they were also years of valor, of courage, of consecration to a given work such as the world never witnessed before, and I doubt if it ever will again.

Each one of you whom we so gladly welcome as our guests were part of that struggle—from Camden to Fredericksburg, wherever we met, amid the lowlands of North Carolina, or the fields of South Mountain, Antietam, or elsewhere, the 9th New York felt in the 3d Regiment of Georgia it had met a foeman worthy its steel.

Your bull dog tenacity, your determined resistance, your courageous valor won from your enemies the highest encomiums of praise, whenever we met you on the field of battle. But now the smoke and rancor of the strife is over and we are enabled carefully to study your history in the light of contemporaneous events (remembering your homes desolate by fire and sword, your bodies illy clad, exposed to the elements, your haversacks empty, while hungry and desolate you sank upon the bare ground to forget for a few moments in sleep the struggle through which you were passing). I say when we recollect these things and then remember the courage exhibited to our eyes, as we met you on the field of battle, we declare we are proud to call you this day brothers, countrymen, Americans.

Well may Georgia honor you with the noblest and best she possesses; well may her orators who meet you at your annual reunions, and were their voices as silvery and sweet as angels, were their powers of description as vivid as the lightning's flash, they would yet be unable to tell the whole story of your faithfulness to that grand Empire State of the South, as we of Hawkins Zouaves who took your fire and saw your determination and valor, as you contended even to the blood and death of the flower of your State, for each and every inch of land you were placed to defend.

The historian and poet is yet to be born who will justly tell the world the whole story of the bravery and heroism of the men of iron nerve, from Georgia. Of the number of men you had engaged, and the loss you suffered at the battle of Antietam I have not the record; but from your determined stand and the withering fire you poured into our regiment at that battle, Hawkins Zouaves lost sixty-three per cent. of those who met you in that one engagement. At the famous charge of the Light Brigade at Balaklava, immortalized by Tennyson, Lord Cardigan took 673 men into action, and lost in killed and wounded 247 men; or, thirty-six and a fraction per cent. of those engaged, of this much praised Light Brigade. But in one engagement with you, Hawkins Zouaves lost sixty-three per cent. or nearly double that of the famous Light Brigade. Your bravery at Antietam exceeded the world-renowned charge of the Light Brigade.

Does the State whose name you bear, or whose flag you defended need more terrible evidence of your fidelity to the trust they reposed in you? If they would have it, let them visit the battlefields of the South, and standing by the hallowed graves of your sacred dead as they mark the different places of conflict where they fell—let these witnesses testify by the very eloquence of their silence, of the integrity, intrepidity, fortitude, and courage of the 3d Regiment of Georgia Volunteers.

Your State abounds in great wealth. It may tell the world of its mines, of its miles upon miles of railroads, of its fertile lands yielding rich harvests to the husbandman; of its factories with its thousands of humming wheels of manufacture; these are good, and well may it glory, and we rejoice you have them; but, its greatest glory, its most priceless gem, its choicest treasure, are the men who, in the face of fire and smoke, starvation and desolation, wounds and death, a hasty burial (aye, so hasty even comrades would forget, and others come and mark the head-board unknown)—yes, these men who literally forsook all and went forth at the behest of the State, these gray-haired, halt, maimed, enfeebled, and the greater number who lie buried amid the Savannahs of the South; these are the choicest treasures, the crown jewels, the sparkling gems in the glittering, scintillating crown of our Sister Empire State of the South.

I know you will pardon me when I say the best men we had in each of these two regiments, are not visibly present with us now; the best and truest of our number lie buried on the battlefields of the South; some were clad in gray, some in blue; no towering monument marks their resting place, nor massive monolith stands sentinel.

But beneath a cedar or a pine,
In solitude austere,
Unknown, unarmed, but not forgotten,
Rests a faithful volunteer.

Buried where they fell, baptizing the soil with their blood, forever consecrating the ground, making it holy, while their life and death tell the world the story of how an American will fight, and if necessary die for what he believes to be the right. And, while I have talked I have thought that these unseen, but not unwelcome guests, are here in our midst to-night; visionary it may be on my part, but I know you will forgive me as I think of these heroes of the 3d Georgia and 9th New York who have long since mingled together in fraternity and love, as we mingle here this hour. They pass before us like a long procession coming from their camping grounds amid the cemeteries, the battlefields, the graveyards of the South. To us they are no longer dead, they live—we can almost hear their well-known voices as with flashing eye, active limb, courageous lion hearts, once more they are with us, side by side, the Blue, the Gray, the private, the officer; on they pass, those who died at Roanoke, at Camden, at South Mountain, at Antietam, at Fredericksburg, and the battlefields of the South. Hayes and McComas, Kimbal, Sturges, Gadsden, Hamilton, Barnett, Wright, Reno, Jackson and Burnside, Grant and Lee.

Oh, ye comrades of '61, friend or foe of those days, we gladly welcome you all, as friends, to this fraternal board. As memory calls your names and recounts your heroic achievements while with us, unseen, you gather here a reunited band of a reunited country beneath the bright folding of our own starry flag.

You who went forth with a mother's benediction; you who bade farewell to the children who received your last embrace at the place of embarkation; you who faced the enemy so boldly in the charge; you who died amid the carnage of battle alone, alone, while the very stars of God seemed to look in pity upon you.

O yes, you, you my countrymen, whether from Georgia or New York, to-night these —the remnant of more than 2,000 men— these your comrades gathered here, salute you as we bring to mind your faithfulness as soldiers, and rejoice with you that our country has passed from the hurricane to the calm; from out of all that crash, of which we were part, to liberty, union, brotherly love, and peace.

But our mind recalls others not present who sitting in their quiet homes here in New York or Georgia, think of this reunion with mingled feelings of joy and sorrow. I seem to look into the mind of dear old gray-haired mother, sitting in yonder home, thinking of the boy on whose head she showered her blessing, around whose neck her arm was clasped, and on whose lips she printed her farewell kiss, as in 1861 he bade her his last good-by. God bless her, to-night, is the prayer of every one around this board, whether she be of Georgia or New York.

And in those other homes, where dwell the widow and her children, made fatherless so early in life. Yes, yes, my friends, they are thinking of these two regiments as they remember the vacant places in our ranks, and the vacant place at their own fireside.

It singeth low in every heart,
We hear it, each and all,
A song of those who answer not
However we may call.

They throng the silence of the heart,
We see them as of yore—
The kind, the true, the brave, the sweet,
Who walk with us no more.

Could we speak to each of these homes,
to-night, we would tell them of the fidelity
and courage of their loved one in the days
of the past, and assure them of our undying
regard for their memory. We would tell
them as we tell you—we shall meet again.
Our comrades are not gone forever, for

When the dreams of life are fled,
When its wasted lamps are dead,
When in cold oblivion's shade
Beauty, power, and fame are laid,
Where immortal spirits reign
There shall we all meet again.

And now, my friends of the 3d Georgia, I
from the left of the line, a private soldier of
the 9th New York who has tried to speak
fitting words on this historic occasion, who,
before I again step back and take my place
in the ranks, do here salute you, and in the
name and in behalf of the 9th Regiment,
N. Y. Volunteers, "Hawkins Zouaves," extend to you, individually and collectively, a
cordial greeting and a most hearty, royal welcome.

Welcome to the old Empire State. Welcome to the ranks of the 9th New York.
Welcome to this our thirtieth anniversary
(1891). Welcome, thrice welcome, 3d Georgia Regimental Association to our city, our
homes, and to our hearts.—P. T.

THE MONUMENT'S MESSAGE *

By Rev. Charles Elmer Allison

The polished granite in front of old Manor
Hall combines strength and grace. " The
quarry has blossomed into the air." Stone
and bronze stand out under the stars, defying the storms and the seasons. Stable and
beautiful they will stand, saluting the far
future, when ours is a buried generation,
sleeping " the iron sleep." A great English
poet, whose pen is a gilded scepter, says
there are sermons in stones. The granite
lips of yonder Color-Bearer are mute, yet
they speak to the spirit's finer ear. All of
those memorial stones, from pedestal to
carved capital and surmounting standard,
have a voice. We bring you the Monument's
Message.

The costly column is reared on American
soil, and America is the garden of the Lord
—great in extent and resources, great in history, great in destiny. Imperial Rome " po-
liced the world." Her empire extended 3,-
000 miles in one direction, and 2,000 in another. As to extent of territory, this Nation
is a modern Rome.

" What shall we say of a Republic of
eighteen states, each as large as Spain, or
one of thirty states, each as large as
Italy, or one of sixty states, each as large
as England and Wales? Take five of the
six first-class Powers of Europe, Great
Britain, and Ireland, France, Germany, Austria and Italy; then add Spain, Portugal,
Switzerland, Denmark and Greece. Let
some greater than Napoleon weld them into
one mighty empire, and you could lay it all
down west of the Hudson River, once and
again, and again—three times."

Of the states and territories west of the
Mississippi, only three are as small as all
New England. Idaho, if laid down in the
East, would touch Toronto, Canada, on the
north, Raleigh, N. C., on the south, while
its southern boundary line is long enough to
stretch from Washington City to Columbus,
Ohio. The greatest measurement of Texas
is nearly equal to the distance from New Orleans to Chicago, or from Chicago to Boston.

Of the resources of the country the half
has not been told. We have hundreds of
thousands more square miles of arable land
than China, and China supports a population of 360,000,000. Transfer all of the
people in the United States to the one State
of Texas, and the population thus concentrated would not be much denser, if any,
than the population of Germany to-day.
Who shall estimate aright the value of
American fields and forests, mines and
mountains, lakes and rivers—nature's highways—orchards and gardens, flocks and
herds, and her broad prairie with their miles
and miles of waving harvests undulating
like ocean billows?

Providence hid this fair land from the old
world for many centuries. It was to be " the
cradle of an illustrious history." True, the
mound builders were here, but they left
mounds, not molding influences. The Indians were here; they left only arrow-heads
and musical names for our lakes, rivers, and
mountains. The Northmen came about the
year 1,000; they left only a foot-print. The
tide of European emigration was not permitted to follow the Northmen. Well it was
for humanity that the Divine Hand kept
that tide back, for then was the midnight of
the dark ages. " Sometimes the bells in the
church steeples were not heard, for the
sound of trumpets and drums." Columbus
embarked in 1492, but his ships carried Spanish influences. The great navigator followed the birds of the air in their flight.
The God of Nations made those birds pilots
to guide Spanish ships away from these
shores. Spain gave form to Mexico and
South America.

* In front of Manor Hall, Yonkers, N. Y., in which city the " Message " was delivered, stands the Sol
diers' Monument.

God works with two hands. While He was hiding this rich land, He was shaping the men who should shape its institutions. Before He gave America to the world, He gave the translated Bible and the printing press to Europe; English, Scotch, Scotch-Irish, Dutch, French, and other illustrious emigrants of like type were the "Creators of Moral America." They were seventeenth century men. Into that superb century were providentially poured the influences of previous centuries. For hundreds of years Europe was at school, learning statecraft and religion. By the translation of the Bible, "the lowly English roof was lifted to take in heights beyond the stars." It was from underneath that roof the Pilgrim fathers came to Plymouth Rock. The Indian's salutation was, not "Welcome, Spaniard," but "Welcome, Englishmen," which, being interpreted, signified, altho the dusky savage did not understand it, "Welcome the open Bible and love of equal rights." Yes, the Monument is reared on American soil, and America, vast in extent, rich in resources and possibilities, was providentially reserved for freemen and freedom's temple.

Firm upon its granite pedestal stands yonder shapely shaft. For us it shall symbolize, by its graceful strength, the American Republic, stable and healthful among the nations of the earth. That group of warriors in bronze represent no holiday soldiers. They stand for heroes in flesh and blood—for stern veterans whose fortitude and valor protected the Commonwealth. They recall those years when a shot fired at the old flag aroused the anger of a great people. Who can describe those historic years?

The heavens were suddenly black. Fierce eagles of war flew across the lurid clouds. The awful storm rolled thunders along the sky. Reverberating, they shook the Atlantic coast and the banks of the Mississippi. They crashed over Antietam, Vicksburg, and Gettysburg. Forked lightnings played among the clouds around Lookout Mountain. Fire ran along upon the ground in Tennessee, and in Virginia, swamps and rivers were turned to blood. It was the Nation's midnight. The death angel was abroad with unsheathed sword. There was a great cry in the land, for there was not a house among half a million where there was not one dead. Four years the storm raged. The iron hail rattled incessantly, prostrating armed men, and crushing woman's heart. It was a deluge of blood. Then muttering thunders ceased; the clouds broke away, and out of the blue sky a dove came, and lo! in her mouth was an olive leaf. More than a quarter of a century has passed. Peace still abides. "Over the cannon's mouth the spider weaves his web." But while mighty people are busied with great enterprises, they do not forget—cannot forget—the brave men who purchased peace by their valor and blood.

We recall with gratitude profound and peculiarly tender, the private soldier and sailor. Men praise the brave commanders, and they do well; but what could generals have accomplished without the heroes in the ranks? With swift zeal the rank and file —a great host—sprang to arms. They gathered from near and far. "The earth trembled under their tread like a floor beaten with flails." "All the avenues of our great cities ran with rivers of burnished steel." We can hear again their measured tramp, tramp, tramp, and their lusty song, "We are coming, Father Abraham, three hundred thousand more." Hark! Veterans, hear ye not again your comrades singing around the flickering fires which lighted up their noble faces, "We are tenting to-night on the old camp ground." Listen! Hear again the battle hymn of the Republic, how it echoes down the corridors of the years, and will echo until time is no more:

He has sounded forth the trumpet that shall never call retreat;
He is sifting out the hearts of men before His judgment seat.
Oh! be swift, my soul, to answer Him! be jubilant, my feet:
Our God is marching on.

In the beauty of the lilies Christ was born across the sea,
With a glory in His bosom that transfigures you and me;
As He died to make men holy, let us die to make men free,
While God is marching on.

When the war began thousands of young men, the flower of American youth, were looking out of college halls upon a future bright with professional honors. They flung books aside and seized rifles. They became "History's Graduates." Hundreds of thousands of young Americans were anticipating a future replete with the profits and emoluments which reward business genius and integrity. Straightway they abandoned cherished life plans in order to defend free institutions.

Did the officer love his home? With an equal tenderness the private soldier loved his. He knew, should a bullet prostrate him, it would shatter the strong staff upon which the aged father had hoped to lean in his declining years. It gave him a heart-break to see his mother's pale face and quivering lip as he kissed her good-by, holding in one arm his rifle and with the other tenderly embracing her trembling form. There were "tears in his voice" when he said farewell, perhaps a final farewell, to the fair friend with whom he had hoped to stand at the marriage altar. Thousands of husbands and fathers realized that their enlistment might leave wives widowed, and little children fatherless. When the private soldier rushed into the battle's fire and smoke, he knew that, after victories were won, the names of officers would be heralded over the land; but should he fall, the type would print after his name only one word—"missing," or "wounded," or "dead." And when that

one dread word should be read in the distant northern home, loved faces would " grow white instantly, as if sprinkled with the dust of ashes by an unseen hand."
Yet for the old banner the soldier made the sacrifice. As a lonely vidette he kept faithful watch in the darkness, while death lurked near, "with foot of velvet and hand of steel." He helped drag heavy cannon through deep mud; he trudged weary miles on forced marches, and endeavored to sleep, when hungry and cold, on the wet ground. Or he tossed on a hospital cot with a "band of pain around his brow." And now, we twine a laurel wreath for that brow. Thousands of those brave men fell, not knowing what would be the result of the conflict. Other thousands were permitted to return and enjoy for a period the blessings they purchased for their countrymen. Then they, too, fell by the wayside, weary with the march of life. They fought for freedom, not for fame, yet honor claims them as her own:

On Fame's eternal camping ground
Their silent tents are spread,
And glory guards with solemn round
The bivouac of the dead.

Who can estimate the value of their splendid services? The Union Army demonstrated the stability of representative government. In the estimation of Europe the American Republic was an experiment. Would it go to pieces by the earthquake shock of civil war? Jealous kings said " Yes," but when the red lips of Grant's cannon thundered " No ! " thrones trembled. Should a government of and for and by the people perish from the earth?
The army demonstrated the solidity of the Nation's credit. At one period the war expenses aggregated $2,000,000 a day, but victories inspired confidence, and many of the soldiers poured their own silver and gold into the coffers of the Nation to sustain the government.
Soldiers of the Union, what shall a grateful people render you in return for your priceless services? Surely the Government should care for the aged and the crippled veteran. A wealthy nation should not permit a soldier's deserving widow or orphan to suffer want. But we are confident that your sentiments are voiced by this declaration. The return for their services which veterans desire is a determination on the part of their fellow-citizens to protect faithfully the free institutions the Grand Army fought to preserve.
Underneath yonder polished pillar is a granite die inscribed with patriotic sentences. For us that lettered die shall symbolize popular education, which sustains the Republic. Books are better than bayonets. Giant truths are mightier than giant powder. The strongest fortresses are school-houses. The mightiest standing army in the world is the great host of American school-children. The seal of the Board of Education in this city is a pictured pen lying across a broken sword. The pen is mightier than the sword. The pens of Adams, Jefferson, Franklin, and Hamilton broke the sword of tyranny in 1776. The pens of Webster, Sumner, Phillips, Garrison, Beecher, Seward and Lincoln broke the swords of secession and slavery. The men in bronze find firm footing on yonder lettered block of granite. They carry thinking weapons. No man " scoops out the brains " of the American civilian or soldier. He has the Bible, and thinks for himself. He has the ballot and governs himself. The only scepter to which he bows is the scepter of truth.
This is a nation of readers—a nation of sovereigns. " We live under a government of men and morning newspapers. The talk of the sidewalk to-day is the law of the land to-morrow." Who shapes public thought is the uncrowned king. His pen is his scepter. Public schools and newspapers are the people's university. When Louis Napoleon was in this country he expressed surprise because he saw a farmer reading a newspaper. Germany has about 5,500 newspapers, Great Britain about 5,000, France about 2,000, Italy about 1,400, Asia—exclusive of Japan— about 850, Russia about 800, and the United States more than 15,000. The enemy of the American public school system is the enemy of the Commonwealth. If you would realize how unstable governments are without public schools, read the history of Mexico and of South America. Taught by costly experience, they have now introduced public education.
Thousands of the youth in our public schools come from homes where they learn little or nothing about the history and the spirit of American institutions. Let the public schools teach them that history, and inspire them with that spirit. Teach the public school youth that it is a high honor to be able to say, " I am an American citizen." Let them hear the shot which the embattled farmers fired at Lexington—" the shot that was heard around the world." Let them catch the peals of the old Liberty bell and the spirit of Independence Day. Let them hear the night-watchman in Philadelphia calling out: " Ten o'clock and Cornwallis taken." Let them hear Washington's soldiers singing on the banks of the Hudson: " No King but God." Let them hear again and again the shining story of the valor and the victories of the men who, uniformed in Heaven's livery, fought with Hooker, Hancock, Mead, Thomas, Foote, Farragut, Kilpatrick, with the chivalrous Kitching, and Fremont, the free-hearted. Teach them that when they arrive at manhood's estate, they should never absent themselves from the polls, preferring private gain to the welfare of city, state, or nation. Let them always vote—and vote for principle.
Underneath yonder carved die are four massive granite blocks, a solid base, on which the stable structure rests, as the American Republic rests secure upon the solid foundations of a true Christianity. Palsied be the vandal hands which would attempt to re-

move those tons of granite, and substitute as a base rotten timber. Palsied be the hands which would attempt to remove the Bible, the Sabbath, the Church and the Christian home, and substitute, as a foundation for our Republic, infidelity, anarchy, and the rotten saloon!

Gladstone, the illustrious Englishman, said to an eminent American: "Talk about questions of the day, there is but one question, and that is the Gospel. It can and will correct everything needing correction. All men at the head of great movements are Christian men. During the many years I was in the Cabinet I was brought into association with sixty master minds, and all but five of them were Christians. My only hope for the world is the bringing the human mind into contact with Divine revelation." This emphasizes the teachings of American patriots. Above all the clamor of Castle Garden statesmen we hear the calm voices of the fathers and preservers of the Republic. One of these patriotic fathers, who was a member of the convention assembled to draft the Constitution of the United States, when moving that the proceedings be opened with prayer, addressed the President in these memorable words: "I have lived, sir, a long time, and the longer I live the more convincing proofs I see of the truth that God governs in the affairs of men; and if a sparrow cannot fall to the ground without His notice, is it probable that an empire can rise without His aid?"

To a trusted friend who visited him during the dark days of the Civil War, President Lincoln said, with emotion: "I do not doubt, I never doubted for a moment, that our country would finally come through safe and undivided. But do not misunderstand me. I do not know how it can be. I do not rely on the patriotism of our people, tho no people have rallied around their king as ours have rallied around me. I do not trust in the bravery and devotion of the boys in blue. God bless them! God never gave a prince or a conqueror such an army as He has given me. Nor yet do I rely on the loyalty and skill of our generals tho I believe we have the best generals in the world at the head of our armies. But the God of our fathers, who raised up this country to be a refuge and the asylum of the oppressed and down-trodden of all nations, will not let it perish now. I may not live to see it"—and he added, after a pause—"I do not expect to see it, but God will bring us through safe."

What a noble company of our youthful citizens is assembled here on this broad platform. That in coming years, as they pass and repass the Monument, they may be reminded of the truths here spoken, permit me to address them a few words. Young Americans, when you have reached mature years, and our lips are dust, the children of the future will look at yonder graceful granite, and will ask, "What mean these stones?" You will tell them how you saw with your own eyes the soldiers of the Union represented by those stern bronze warriors. You will speak of successive Memorial Days, when you saw veteran soldiers embroider with fragrant flowers the mounds made sacred by the dust of their comrades. You will not forget to strew flowers upon their graves. You will interpret for the future generation the message of those voiceful stones.

That you may the more distinctly remember their message, we would have you see on the gray granite four shining gold letters. On the solid base, which symbolizes the foundation of our Republic, a true Christianity, we would have you see the letter F, standing for Faith in God. On the lettered die, which symbolizes a solid education, we would have you see the letter L, standing for Learning. As the polished shaft, by its massive strength and grace, symbolizes the Republic, stable and beautiful among the nations, we would have you see affixed to it the letter A, standing for America. And as our flag is always associated with renown, we would have you see on that granite standard the gold letter G, reflecting the rays of the morning, and standing for Glory. Remember to tell the children of the future that those memorial stones symbolize Faith, Learning, America and Glory. It will not be difficult for you to remember this message and to bear it to the future, because those initial gold letters spell the word FLAG.

Soldiers of the Union, I have now discharged the duty you assigned me. We bring you gratitude, and congratulations—gratitude for arduous and illustrious services; congratulations that a kind Providence mercifully spared your lives for some good purpose. A thousand fell at your side, and ten thousand at your right hand, but He covered you with His feathers. Through the iron hailstones He brought you safe to greet your loved ones, to receive the plaudits of your fellow-citizens, and to enjoy the prosperity of the Commonwealth. Each of you wears the honored title, "A Soldier of the Union." Soon you will be gathered to your fathers. Yonder memorial will perpetuate your honor.

Surely we voice your sentiments when we proclaim that the granite Standard-Bearer represents no citizen who defends organized wrong. He represents neither infidel nor Anarchist. Nor does he stand for the citizen who fails to distinguish between a license to do wrong, and liberty to do right—the only true liberty. He does not represent the citizen who with one hand holds up the flag, and with the other hand tears its pure folds to tatters by defending a traffic which shatters the hearth-stone, smites the smile from the happy face of a sweet child, and murders the soul for which the Son of God shed His blood. But yonder Standard-Bearer does represent, in his massive strength, the loyal American who stands firm for the Bible, the Sabbath, the Church, the Home; for Solid Learning, for Union and Freedom, for the Maintenance of Private and Public Credit, and for Peace on Earth. His sword symbolizes the freeman's weapons—the pen, the pure ballot, and the keen Damascus blade.

So long as the bed-rock principles of the fathers are maintained, the Republic itself will continue to stand, a monument to freedom, stable and beautiful, and seen by the whole world. Because he realizes this, the American citizen, while holding his Nation's ensign in defense of it, and of the granite principles of which it is the glorious symbol, lays his good right hand upon the hilt of his sword.

This, sir, as we interpret it, is the Monument's message.—P. M.

DECORATION DAY ADDRESS *

By James A. Garfield

[Extract from an oration delivered at Arlington, Va., May 30, 1868.]

I am oppressed with a sense of the impropriety of uttering words on this occasion. If silence is ever golden, it must be here beside the graves of fifteen thousand men, whose lives were more significant than speech, and whose death was a poem, the music of which can never be sung. With words we make promises, plight faith, praise virtue. Promises may not be kept; plighted faith may be broken; and vaunted virtue be only the cunning mask of vice. We do not know one promise these men made, one pledge they gave, one word they spoke; but we do know they summed up and perfected, by one supreme act, the highest virtues of men and citizens. For love of country they accepted death, and thus resolved all doubts, and made immortal their patriotism and their virtue. For the noblest man that lives, there still remains a conflict. He must still withstand the assaults of time and fortune, must still be assailed with temptations, before which lofty natures have fallen; but with these the conflict ended, the victory was won, when death stamped on them the great seal of heroic character, and closed a record which years can never blot.

I know of nothing more appropriate on this occasion than to inquire what brought these men here; what high motive led them to condense life into an hour, and to crown that hour by joyfully welcoming death? Let us consider.

Eight years ago this was the most unwarlike nation of the earth. For nearly fifty years no spot in any of these states had been the scene of battle. Thirty millions of people had an army of less than ten thousand men. The faith of our people in the stability and permanence of their institutions was like their faith in the eternal course of nature. Peace, liberty, and personal security were blessings as common and universal as sunshine and showers and fruitful seasons; and all sprang from a single source, the old American principle that all owe due submission and obedience to the lawfully expressed will of the majority. This is not one of the doctrines of our political system—it is the system itself. It is our political firmament, in which all other truths are set, as stars in Heaven. It is the encasing air, the breath of the Nation's life. Against this principle the whole weight of the rebellion was thrown. Its overthrow would have brought such ruin as might follow in the physical universe if the power of gravitation were destroyed, and

" Nature's concord broke,
Among the constellations war were sprung,
Two planets, rushing from aspect malign
Of fiercest opposition, in mid-sky
Should combat, and their jarring spheres confound."

The Nation was summoned to arms by every high motive which can inspire men. Two centuries of freedom had made its people unfit for despotism. They must save their Government or miserably perish. As a flash of lightning in a midnight tempest reveals the abysmal horrors of the sea, so did the flash of the first gun disclose the awful abyss into which rebellion was ready to plunge us. In a moment the fire was lighted in twenty million hearts. In a moment we were the most warlike Nation on the earth. In a moment we were not merely a people with an army—we were a people in arms. The Nation was in column—not all at the front, but all in the array.

I love to believe that no heroic sacrifice is ever lost; that the characters of men are molded and inspired by what their fathers have done; that treasured up in American souls are all the unconscious influences of the great deeds of the Anglo-Saxon race, from Agincourt to Bunker Hill. It was such an influence that led a young Greek, two thousand years ago, when musing on the battle of Marathon, to exclaim, " The trophies of Miltiades will not let me sleep!" Could these men be silent in 1861; these, whose ancestors had felt the inspiration of battle on every field where civilization had fought in the last thousand years? Read their answer in this green turf. Each for himself gathered up the cherished purposes of life—its aims and ambitions, its dearest affections—and flung all, with life itself, into the scale of battle.

And now consider this silent assembly of the dead. What does it represent? Nay, rather, what does it not represent? It is an epitome of the war. Here are sheaves

*From The Works of James A. Garfield.

reaped, in the harvest of death, from every battle-field of Virginia. If each grave had a voice to tell us what its silent tenant last saw and heard on earth, we might stand, with uncovered heads, and hear the whole story of the war. We should hear that one perished when the first great drops of the crimson shower began to fall, when the darkness of that first disaster at Manassas fell like an eclipse on the Nation; that another died of disease while wearily waiting for winter to end; that this one fell on the field, in sight of the spires of Richmond, little dreaming that the flag must be carried through three more years of blood before it should be planted in that citadel of treason; and that one fell when the tide of war had swept us back till the roar of rebel guns shook the dome of yonder Capitol, and re-echoed in the chambers of the Executive Mansion. We should hear mingled voices from the Rappahannock, the Rapidan, the Chickahominy and the James; solemn voices from the Wilderness, and triumphant shouts from the Shenandoah, from Petersburg, and the Five Forks, mingled with the wild acclaim of victory and the sweet chorus of returning peace. The voices of these dead will forever fill the land like holy benedictions.

What other spot so fitting for their last resting place as this, under the shadow of the Capitol saved by their valor? Here, where the grim edge of battle joined; here where all the hope and fear and agony of their country centered; here let them rest, asleep on the Nation's heart, entombed in the Nation's love!

SUGGESTIVE THOUGHTS

ARMY-BLUE, The Faded Overcoat of.—Decoration Day is duly observed over the land. What seemed a faded overcoat of army-blue, carried upon a soldier's arm, is the most striking object in our procession. It will not be long before garments, flags, weapons, and all that belonged to the War of the Rebellion will only be found here and there as rare relics. And perhaps it is better so. The old gun-locks are already turning in our busy wheels, and the worn shreds of clothing are making soft our floors, just as the issues for which battle was joined have knit themselves into our better peace and prosperity. And may a kind Providence withhold from us all wars henceforth!—Ch. St.

DEAD, Honor Our Patriot.—Memorial Day is consecrated to the soldiers; it is dedicated to patriotism; around this sacred day cluster precious memories of our fallen brave. Over the silent chambers of our sleeping comrades we wreathe garlands of flowers—symbols of our love and gratitude. These graves are the Nation's shrine, the Mecca to which patriots journey to renew their devotion to the cause for which these patriots died. The fruits of their victories are a united country. This is a sacred heritage purchased by their valor and sealed by their blood. History is their encomium. Battle-fields attest their courage.

" Sleep, heroes sleep;
  Your deeds shall never die."
                            C. G.

DEAD, Our Honored.—Oh, tell me not that they are dead—that generous host, that airy army of invisible heroes! They hover as a cloud of witnesses above this Nation. Are they dead that yet speak louder than we can speak, and a more universal language? Are they dead that yet act? Are they dead that yet move upon society, and inspire the people with nobler motives and more heroic patriotism? . . .

Every mountain and hill shall have its treasured name, every river shall keep some solemn title, every valley and every lake shall cherish its honored register; and till the mountains are worn out, and the rivers forget to flow—till the clouds are weary of replenishing springs, and the springs forget to gush, and the rills to sing, shall their names be kept fresh with reverent honors which are inscribed upon the book of National Remembrance!—HENRY WARD BEECHER.

DEFENDERS, Our Country's.—Blessed is that country whose soldiers fight for it and are willing to give the best they have, the best that any man has, their own lives, to preserve it because they love it. Such an army the United States has always commanded in every crisis of her history. From the War of the Revolution to the late Civil War, the men followed that flag in battle because they loved that flag and believed in what it represented.

That was the stuff of which the volunteer army of '61 was made. Every one of them not only fought but thought. And many of them did their own thinking and did not always agree with their commander. A young soldier in the late war was on the battle line ahead with the color-guard, bearing the stars and stripes way in front of the line, but the enemy still in front of him. The general called out to the color-bearer, " Bring those colors back to the line," and quicker than any bullet that young soldier answered back, " Bring the line up to the colors." It was the voice of command; there was a man behind it, and there was patriotism in his heart.

So nigh is grandeur to our dust;
  So near to God is man,
When duty whispers low, " Thou must,"
  The youth replies, " I can."

And so, more than two million brave men thus responded and made up an army grander than any army that ever shook the earth with its tread, and engaged in a holier cause than ever engaged soldiers before.

What defenders, my countrymen, have we now? We have the remnant of this old, magnificent, matchless army, of which I have been speaking, and then, as allies in any future war, we have the brave men who fought against us on Southern battle fields. The army of Grant and the army of Lee are together. They are one now in faith, in hope, in fraternity, in purpose, and in an invincible patriotism. And, therefore, the country is in no danger. In justice strong, in peace secure, and in devotion to the flag all one.—WILLIAM McKINLEY.

HEROES, The Graves of.—And every village graveyard will have its green mounds, that shall need no storied monument to clothe them with a peculiar consecration—graves that hold the dust of heroes—graves that all men approach with reverent steps—graves out of whose solemn silence shall whisper inspiring voices, telling the young from generation to generation how great is their country's worth and cost, and how noble and beautiful it was to die for it.—PUTNAM.

LIBERTIES, Cost of Our.—This is a busy world we live in; this is a busy age; and this, our land, is the busiest country of the age. In the intensity of the struggle for future achievement we are prone to lose sight of the past. We do not think often enough of the cost of our liberties.—*Selected.*

MARTYRS, An Army of.—Through all history, from the beginning, a noble army of martyrs have fought fiercely and fallen bravely for that unseen mistress, their country. So, through all history, to the end, as long as men believe in God, that army must still march and fall, recruited only from the flower of mankind, cheered only by their own hope of humanity, strong only in the confidence of their cause.—GEORGE WILLIAM CURTIS.

MEMORIAL DAY.—Memorial Day, with its sad and sacred memories, has again come. And as each new one makes its advent, we recall anew the great and tragic events that made the occasion for the day. Time in his rapid flight has borne us on till we are thirty-one years from the close of the great Civil War, in which thousands of lives were sacrificed and billions of treasure expended to save our country from dismemberment. The asperities and alienations engendered by the great struggle between freedom and slavery have largely passed away; and those who participated as soldiers on both sides, who are still living, fraternize with each other as brothers and fellow-citizens of one common country, on whose glorious banner is inscribed forever, *E pluribus unum*. It is meet that those who sacrificed and died in the struggle, or who sacrificed and have since died, should be remembered and honored for the invaluable service they have rendered their country and humanity. Let the graves of the dead soldiers be decorated with flowers and wreaths of laurel, and the memory of their noble deeds revived anew in oratory and song.—*Selected.*

MEMORIAL DAY REMINDERS.—Let no vandalism of avarice or neglect, no ravages of time, testify to the present or to the coming generations, that we have forgotten, as a people, the cost of a free and undivided Republic.—GENERAL JOHN A. LOGAN.

We honor our heroic and patriotic dead by being true men, as true men by faithfully fighting the battles of our day as they fought the battles of their day.—DAVID GREGG, D.D.

I love to believe that no heroic sacrifice is ever lost, that the characters of men are molded and inspired by what their fathers have done; that treasured up in American souls are all the unconscious influences of the great deeds of the Anglo-Saxon race, from Agincourt to Bunker Hill.—JAMES A. GARFIELD.

The supporters of religion gave their lives for a principle. These martyrs of patriotism gave their lives for an idea.—SCHUYLER COLFAX.

MESSAGES, Patriotic, for Memorial Day.—The broad, deep Americanism which pulses through the great heart of the Republic to-day will grow broader and deeper with the passing years. I am thankful that I have lived to see this noble result of the war springing into vast and virile life. The passions of the titanic struggle will finally enter upon the sleep of oblivion, and only its splendid accomplishments for the cause of human freedom and a united nation, stronger and richer in patriotism because of the great strife, will be remembered.—GENERAL JAMES LONGSTREET, *a Lieutenant-General in the Confederate Army during the Civil War.*

Liberty can never die. The generations of men appear and pass away, but the aspirations of their natures are immortal.—HON. GEORGE S. BOUTWELL, *Secretary of the Treasury in the Cabinet of President Grant.*

As a basis for permanently satisfactory results of the war, we should recognize the claims of justice and equal rights to all classes and sections, a fair apportionment of public burdens and benefits, with special privileges and exemptions to none. Careful and practical teachings along this line will be a patriotic work.—JUDGE JAMES W. LAPSLEY.

Memorial Day, in my opinion, is one of the most significant and beautiful occasions of the year. It shows the sentiment of the people toward those who gave their lives for a good cause, and it teaches a lesson in patriotism which is without a parallel. Memorial Day cannot be too tenderly revered by old and young, by those who participated in one of the Nation's great struggles, or by those who simply know of it as history. Our common country each year is paying a greater tribute of respect to the soldiers, living and dead, and it is my hope that this rule may be expanded still more in the years to come.—G. R.

PRESENT? Are Dead Heroes.—Why may not the men themselves, who died beneath their country's flag, be now among their homes to which their last living thoughts were turned, and here with us to-day? We do not know, but can we not in hope believe, with a solid, substantial, reasonable belief and hope, that our heroes now stand about us, unseen and unheard, as we join to do honor to their memories? The naked human eye is not made to disclose the presence of the myriad forms that exist about us, and the human ear is not attuned to note the solemn symphonies of the music of the spheres.—*Selected.*

UNKNOWN, Tribute to the.—We pay the tribute of respect and reverence to the gallant men who sacrificed their lives to the perpetuation of the Union, and who now lie in common graves marked "unknown." It was fitting at this season of vernal bloom, when nature is joyful with life, that our thoughts should turn to those who gave their lives, as dear to them as ours to us, and that their memory should be honored and reverenced.—SENIOR VICE-COMMANDER BURRAGE.

POETRY

The Bivouac of the Dead

BY THEODORE O'HARA

[Written on the occasion of removing to their native land the remains of Kentuckians who fell in the battle of Buena Vista.]

The muffled drum's sad roll has beat
The soldier's last tattoo;
No more on life's parade shall meet
That brave and fallen few.
On Fame's eternal camping-ground
Their silent tents are spread,
And glory guards, with solemn round,
The bivouac of the dead.

No rumor of the foe's advance
Now swells upon the wind;
No troubled thought at midnight haunts
Of loved ones left behind;
No vision of the morrow's strife
The warrior's dream alarms;
No braying horn or screaming fife
At dawn shall call to arms.

Their shivered swords are red with rust;
Their pluméd heads are bowed;
Their haughty banner, trailed in dust,
Is now their martial shroud;
And plenteous funeral-tears have washed
The red stains from each brow;
And the proud forms, by battle gashed,
Are free from anguish now.

The neighing troop, the flashing blade,
The bugle's stirring blast,
The charge, the dreadful cannonade,
The din and shout, are past.
Not war's wild note, nor glory's peal,
Shall thrill with fierce delight
Those breasts that never more may feel
The rapture of the fight.

Like the fierce northern hurricane
That sweeps his great plateau,
Flushed with the triumph yet to gain,
Comes down the serried foe.

Who heard the thunder of the fray
Break o'er the field beneath,
Knew well the watchword of that day
Was "Victory or death!"

Full many a norther's breath has swept
O'er Angostura's plain,
And long the pitying sky has wept
Above its moldered slain.
The raven's scream, or eagle's flight,
Or shepherd's pensive lay,
Alone now wakes each solemn height
That frowned o'er that dread fray.

Sons of the Dark and Bloody Ground,
Ye must not slumber there,
Where stranger-steps and tongues resound
Along the heedless air!
Your own proud land's heroic soil
Shall be your fitter grave:
She claims from War its richest spoil—
The ashes of her brave.

Thus, 'neath their parent turf they rest,
Far from the gory field,
Borne to a Spartan mother's breast
On many a bloody shield.
The sunshine of their native sky
Smiles sadly on them here,
And kindred eyes and hearts watch by
The heroes' sepulcher.

Rest on, embalmed and sainted dead!
Dear as the blood ye gave,
No impious footstep here shall tread
The herbage of your grave;
Nor shall your glory be forgot
While Fame her record keeps,
Or Honor points the hallowed spot
Where valor proudly sleeps.

Yon marble minstrel's voiceless stone
In deathless song shall tell,
When many a vanished year hath flown,
The story how ye fell.
Nor wreck nor change, nor winter's blight,
Nor Time's remorseless doom,
Can dim one ray of holy light
That gilds your glorious tomb.

The Blue and the Gray

By F. M. Finch

[The following poem was suggested by reading that the women of Columbus, Miss., strewed flowers alike on the graves of the Confederate and of the Union soldiers:]

By the flow of the inland river,
  Whence the fleets of iron have fled,
Where the blades of the grave-grass quiver,
  Asleep are the ranks of the dead;
    Under the sod and the dew,
      Waiting the judgment-day—
    Under the one the Blue,
      Under the other the Gray.

These in the robings of glory,
  Those in the gloom of defeat,
All with the battle-blood gory,
  In the dusk of eternity meet;
    Under the sod and the dew,
      Waiting the judgment-day—
    Under the laurel the Blue,
      Under the willow the Gray.

From the silence of sorrowful hours
  The desolate mourners go,
Lovingly laden with flowers
  Alike for the friend and the foe;
    Under the sod and the dew,
      Waiting the judgment-day—
    Under the roses the Blue,
      Under the lilies the Gray.

So with an equal splendor
  The morning sun-rays fall,
With a touch impartially tender,
  On the blossoms blooming for all;
    Under the sod and the dew,
      Waiting the judgment-day—
    Broidered with gold the Blue,
      Mellowed with gold the Gray.

So when the summer calleth,
  On forest and field of grain
With an equal murmur falleth
  The cooling drip of the rain;
    Under the sod and the dew,
      Waiting the judgment-day—
    Wet with the rain the Blue,
      Wet with the rain the Gray.

Sadly, but not with upbraiding,
  The generous deed was done;
In the storm of the years that are fading,
  No braver battle was won;
    Under the sod and the dew,
      Waiting the judgment-day—
    Under the blossoms the Blue,
      Under the garlands the Gray.

No more shall the war-cry sever,
  Or the widening rivers be red;
Our anger is banished forever
  When are laureled the graves of our dead!
    Under the sod and the dew,
      Waiting the judgment-day—
    Love and tears for the Blue,
      Tears and love for the Gray.

A Ballad of Heroes

By Austin Dobson

" Now all your victories are in vain."

Because you passed, and now are not—
  Because in some remoter day
Your sacred dust in doubtful spot
  Was blown of ancient airs away—
Because you perished—must men say
  Your deeds were naught, and so profane
Your lives with that cold burden? Nay,
  The deeds you wrought are not in vain.

Tho it may be, above the plot
  That hid your once imperial clay,
No greener than o'er men forgot
  The unregarding grasses sway;
Tho there no sweeter is the lay
  Of careless bird; tho you remain
Without distinction of decay,
  The deeds you wrought are not in vain.

No, for while yet in tower or cot
  Your story stirs the pulse's play,
And men forget the sordid lot—
  The sordid cares—of cities gray;
While yet they grow for homelier fray
  More strong from you, as reading plain
That Life may go, if Honor stay,
  The deeds you wrought are not in vain.

ENVOY.

Heroes of old! I humbly lay
  The laurel on your graves again;
Whatever men have done, men may—
  The deeds you wrought are not in vain.

Decoration Day

By S. F. Smith

Strew the fair garlands where slumber the
    dead,
  Ring out the strains like the swell of the
    sea;
Heart-felt the tribute we lay on each bed:
  Sound o'er the brave the refrain of the
    free,
Sound the refrain of the loyal and free,
  Visit each sleeper and hallow each bed:
Waves the starred banner from sea-coast to
    sea;
  Grateful the living and honored the dead.

Dear to each heart are the names of the
    brave;
  Resting in glory how sweetly they sleep!
Dew-drops at evening fall soft on each
    grave,
  Kindred and strangers bend fondly to
    weep;
Kindred bend fondly, and drooping eyes
    weep
  Tears of affection o'er every green grave;
Fresh are their laurels and peaceful their
    sleep:
  Love still shall cherish the noble and
    brave.

Peace o'er this land, o'er these homes of the free,
Brood evermore with her sheltering wing;
God of the nation, our trust is in Thee—
God, our Protector, our Guide, and our King;
God, our Protector, our Guide, and our King,
Thou art our refuge, our hope is in Thee;
Strong in Thy blessing and safe 'neath Thy wing,
Peace shall encircle these homes of the free.

Sleep of the Brave

By William Collins

How sleep the brave, who sink to rest,
By all their country's wishes blessed!
When Spring, with dewy fingers cold,
Returns to deck their hallowed mold,
She there shall dress a sweeter sod
Than Fancy's feet have ever trod.

By fairy hands their knell is wrung;
By forms unseen their dirge is sung;
There Honor comes, a pilgrim gray,
To bless the turf that wraps their clay;
And Freedom shall awhile repair,
To dwell a weeping hermit there!

Three Cheers for the Olden Time

By Fanny Crosby

Three cheers, three cheers for the olden time,
And the brave that knew no fear;
They stood erect as the giant oak,
And laughed when the storm was near.

Like them we'll boast of the land we love,
And her proud flag streaming high;
We'll sing aloud for the bright green hills,
While the ocean waves reply.

They dared to look in the flashing eye
Of the storm-king when he passed;
A shout went up, and a peal of joy
Rang out on the wintry blast.

The grass is green where they calmly rest,
Those veterans true and brave;
Their memory shines like a radiant star
O'er the land they died to save.

Cover Them Over

By Will Carleton

Cover them over with beautiful flowers;
Deck them with garlands, those brothers of ours;
Lying so silent, by night and by day,
Sleeping the years of their manhood away:
Years they had marked for the joys of the brave,
Years they must wave in the sloth of the grave.
All the bright laurels that promised to bloom
Fell to the earth when they went to the tomb.

Give them the meed they have won in the past,
Give them their honors their merits forecast;
Give them the chaplets they won in the strife,
Give them the laurels they lost with their life.
Cover them over—yes, cover them over—
Parent, and husband, and brother, and lover:
Crown in your heart these dear heroes of ours,
And cover them over with beautiful flowers!

Cover the faces that motionless lie,
Shut from the blue of the glorious sky;
Faces once lighted with smiles of the gay—
Faces now marred with the frown of decay.
Eyes that beamed friendship and love to your own;
Lips that sweet thoughts of affection made known;
Brows you have soothed in the day of distress;
Cheeks you have flushed by the tender caress.
Faces that brightened at War's stirring cry;
Faces that streamed when they bade you good-by.
Faces that glowed in the battle's red flame,
Paling for naught, till the Death Angel came.
Cover them over—yes, cover them over—
Parent, and husband, and brother, and lover:
Kiss in your hearts these dead heroes of ours,
And cover them over with beautiful flowers!

Cover the hands that are resting, half-tried,
Crossed on the bosom, or low by the side;
Hands to you, mother, in infancy thrown;
Hands that you, father, close hid in your own;
Hands where you, sister, when tried and dismayed,
Hung for protection and counsel and aid;
Hands that you, brother, for faithfulness knew;
Hands that you, wife, wrung with bitter adieu.
Bravely the cross of their country they bore;
Words of devotion they wrote with their gore;
Grandly they grasped for a garland of light,
Catching the mantle of death-darkened night.
Cover them over—yes, cover them over—
Parent, and husband, and brother, and lover:
Clasp in your hearts these dear heroes of ours,
And cover them over with beautiful flowers!

Cover the feet that, all weary and torn,
Hither by comrades were tenderly borne:
Feet that have trodden, through love-lighted ways,
Near to your own, in the old happy days;
Feet that have pressed, in Life's opening morn,
Roses of pleasure, and Death's poisoned thorn.
Swiftly they rushed to the help of the right,
Firmly they stood in the shock of the fight.
Ne'er shall the enemy's hurrying tramp

Summon them forth from the death-guarded
camp;
Ne'er till Eternity's bugle shall sound,
Will they come out from their couch in the
ground.
Cover them over—yes, cover them over—
Parent, and husband, and brother, and lover:
Rough were the paths of those heroes of
ours—
Now cover them over with beautiful flowers!

Cover the hearts that have beaten so high,
Beaten with hopes that were born but to
die;
Hearts that have burned in the heat of the
fray,
Hearts that have yearned for the homes far
away;
Hearts that beat high in the charge's loud
tramp,
Hearts that low fell in the prison's foul
damp.
Once they were swelling with courage and
will,
Now they are lying all pulseless and still;
Once they were glowing with friendship and
love,
Now the great souls have gone soaring
above.
Bravely their blood to the nation they gave,
Then in their bosom they found them a
grave.
Cover them over—yes, cover them over—
Parent, and husband, and brother, and lover:
Press to your hearts these dead heroes of
ours,
And cover them over with beautiful flowers!

One there is, sleeping in yonder low tomb,
Worthy the brightest of flow'rets that bloom.
Weakness of womanhood's life was her part;
Tenderly strong was her generous heart.
Bravely she stood by the sufferer's side,
Checking the pain of the life-bearing tide;
Fighting the swift-sweeping phantom of
Death,
Easing the dying man's fluttering breath;
Then, when the strife that had nerved her
was o'er,
Calmly she went to where wars are no more.
Voices have blessed her now silent and
dumb;
Voices will bless her in long years to come.
Cover her over—yes, cover her over—
Blessings, like angels, around her shall
hover;
Cherish the name of that sister of ours,
And cover her over with beautiful flowers!

Cover the thousands who sleep far away—
Sleep where their friends can not find them
to-day;
They who in mountain, and hillside and dell
Rest where they wearied, and lie where they
fell.
Softly the grass-blade creeps round their
repose;
Sweetly above them the wild flow'ret blows;
Zephyrs of freedom fly gently o'erhead,
Whispering names for the patriot dead.

So in our minds we will name them once
more,
So in our hearts we will cover them o'er;
Roses and lilies and violets blue,
Bloom in our souls for the brave and the
true.
Cover them over—yes, cover them over—
Parent, and husband, and brother, and lover:
Think of those far-away heroes of ours,
And cover them over with beautiful flowers!

When the long years have crept slowly away,
E'en to the dawn of Earth's funeral day;
When, at the Archangel's trumpet and tread,
Rise up the faces and forms of the dead;
When the great world its last judgment
awaits;
When the blue sky shall swing open its
gates,
And our long columns march silently
through,
Past the great Captain, for final review;
Then for the blood that has flown for the
right,
Crowns shall be given, untarnished and
bright;
Then the glad ear of each war-martyred
son
Proudly shall hear the good judgment,
"Well done."
Blessings for garlands will cover them
over—
Parent, and husband, and brother, and lover:
God will reward those dead heroes of ours,
And cover them over with beautiful flowers!

W. C. M.

The Nation's Dead

ANONYMOUS

Four hundred thousand men
The brave—the good—the true,
In tangled wood, in mountain glen,
On battle plain, in prison pen,
Lie dead for me and you!
Four hundred thousand of the brave
Have made our ransomed soul their grave,
For me and you!
Good friend, for me and you!

In many a fevered swamp,
By many a black bayou,
In many a cold and frozen camp,
The weary sentinel ceased his tramp,
And died for me and you!
From western plain to ocean tide
Are stretched the graves of those who died
For me and you!
Good friend, for me and you!

On many a bloody plain
Their ready swords they drew,
And poured their life-blood, like the rain
A home—a heritage to gain,
To gain for me and you!
Our brothers mustered by our side;
They marched, they fought, and bravely died
For me and you!
Good friend, for me and you!

Up many a fortress wall
　They charged—those boys in blue—
'Mid surging smoke, the volley'd ball;
The bravest were the first to fall!
　To fall for me and you!
These noble men—the Nation's pride—
Four hundred thousand men have died
　　　For me and you!
　Good friend, for me and you!

In treason's prison-hold
　Their martyr spirits grew
To stature like the saints of old,
While amid agonies untold;
　They starved for me and you!
The good, the patient, and the tried,
Four hundred thousand men have died
　　　For me and you!
　Good friend, for me and you!

A debt we ne'er can pay
　To them is justly due,
And to the Nation's latest day
Our children's children still shall say,
　"They died for me and you!"
Four hundred thousand of the brave
Made this, our ransomed soil, their grave,
　　　For me and you!
　Good friend, for me and you!

　　　　　　　　　　G. F.

Decoration Day

BY ELBRIDGE BROOKS

Do you know what it means, you boys and
　　girls
　Who hail from the North and South?
Do you know what it means—
This twining of greens
　Round the silent cannon's mouth;
This strewing with flowers the grass-grown
　　grave;
This decking with garlands the statues brave;
　　This flaunting of flags,
　　All in tatters and rags;
　　This marching and singing·
　　Those bells all a-ringing;
Those faces grave and these faces gay;
This talk of the Blue and this talk of the Gray,
In the North and the South, Decoration Day?

Not simply a show-time, boys and girls,
　Is this day of falling flowers;
　　Not a pageant, a play,
　　Nor a holiday
Of flags and floral bowers;
It is something more than the day that starts
War memories a-throb in veteran hearts:
　For across the years,
　To the hopes and the fears,
　　To the days of battle,
　　Of roar and of rattle—
To the Past that now seems so far away,
Do the sons of the Blue and the sons of the
　　Gray
Gaze—hand clasping hand—Decoration Day.

For the wreck and the wrong of it, boys and
　　girls,
　For the terror and loss, as well,
　　Our hearts must hold
　　A regret untold
As we think of those who fell;

But their blood, on whichever side they
　　fought,
Remade the Nation, and Progress bought!
　We forget the wo;
　For we live, and know
　　That the fighting and sighing,
　　The falling and dying,
Were but the steps toward the Future—the
　　martyrs' way!
Adown which the sons of the Blue and Gray
Look with love and with pride, Decoration
　　Day.

Decoration Day

BY THOMAS DUNN ENGLISH

No more for these the cannon's thunder
　　pealing,
　No more for these the pride of martial
　　　tramp;
No lurking spy around their rest is stealing;
　No sentry walks to guard the silent camp.

No more the soldiers toil in weary marches,
　No more the hosts engage in deadly fray;
And now, beneath the gloomy yews and
　　larches
　They wait the trumpet of the Judgment
　　　Day.

Strew ye their graves with pansies, rose,
　　and lily;
　Pansies for memory, roses for their fame,
Lilies for love which never may grow chilly
　But fan the patriot's fervor into flame.

No sound is heard to-day of warlike clangor,
　Of sharp command, or bugles' warning
　　　blast;
But here arise, without a thought of anger,
　The stirring memories of the long time
　　past.

From cloudless skies there came a peal of
　　thunder,
　And all men stood awestruck and sore
　　amazed
To see disunion strive to rend asunder
　The stately fabric which our fathers raised.

The Dragon's teeth were sown; and quick
　　upspringing
　From field and workshop, came men's
　　heavy tread;
And bold defiance to all foemen flinging,
　War drew the sword and Peace in terror
　　fled.

Brandished the Northern Thor his mighty
　　hammer,
　Wielded the Southern Mars his falchion
　　keen;
And then arose throughout the land the
　　clamor
　Of such a fight as ne'er before was seen.

From home and fireside in the olden manor,
　Leaving behind their children, wives and
　　kin,
They rallied underneath our glorious banner,
　And gave their lives the sacred fight to
　　win.

They brought with them self-sacrifice, devotion,
Ready to fight and die, if die they must,
Ere that old flag, supreme o'er earth and ocean,
Should fall and trail, dishonored in the dust.

They fought no dwarfs; each grappled with a giant;
Each champion's heart was filled with martial fire;
Each on his inborn courage was reliant;
None brought to shame the surname of his sire.

These saved the Union—union which had perished
But for the courage which their deeds revealed;
No stripes were taken from the flag they cherished,
No star was blotted from its azure field.

The old survivors of that fight victorious,
Some still remain, yet leave us one by one;
They die, but never die their actions glorious—
They die, but lives the work so nobly done.

They pass away as pass the summer roses,
Each withering slowly on the stalk of life;
Each soon shall join some comrade who reposes,
Forever freed from human care and strife.

They fought no cowards in those days of terror,
Each hero wrestled with a hero foe.
'Twas four long years ere truth prevailed o'er error,
Ere patriot union laid disunion low.

Peace reigns supreme, and War is here no longer,
The dark-faced Hate slinks scowling to his den,
The broken chain of union welded stronger;
And warring states once foes, are friends again.

Then speak not harshly of the foes who fought us,
Who bravely for their cause threw life away;
Honor the Blue for all the good they wrought us,
But drop a tear of kindness for the Gray.

I.

Ode for Decoration Day

BY HENRY PETERSON

Bring flowers, to strew again
With fragrant purple rain
Of lilacs, and of roses white and red,
The dwellings of our dead—our glorious dead!
Let the bells ring a solemn funeral chime,
And wild war-music bring anew the time
When they who sleep beneath
Were full of vigorous breath,

And in their lusty manhood sallied forth,
Holding in strong right hand
The fortunes of the land,
The pride and power and safety of the North!
It seems but yesterday
The long and proud array—
But yesterday when e'en the solid rock
Shook as with earthquake shock—
As North and South, like two huge icebergs, ground
Against each other with convulsive bound,
And the whole world stood still
To view the mighty war,
And hear the thunderous roar,
While sheeted lightnings wrapped each plain and hill.

Alas! how few came back
From battle and from wrack!
Alas! how many lie
Beneath a Southern sky,
Who never heard the fearful fight was done,
And all they fought for won!
Sweeter, I think, their sleep,
More peaceful and more deep,
Could they but know their wounds were not in vain,
Could they but hear the grand triumphal strain,
And see their homes unmarred by hostile tread.
Ah! let us trust it is so with our dead—
That they the thrilling joy of triumph feel,
And in that joy disdain the foeman's steel.

We mourn for all, but each doth think of one
More precious to the heart than aught beside—
Some father, brother, husband, or some son,
Who came not back, or, coming, sank and died:
In him the whole sad list is glorified!
" He fell 'fore Richmond, in the seven long days
When battle raged from morn till blood-dewed eve,
And lies there," one pale widowed mourner says,
And knows not most to triumph or to grieve.
" My boy fell at Fair Oaks," another sighs;
" And mine at Gettysburg," his neighbor cries,
And that great name each sad-eyed listener thrills.
I think of one who vanished when the press
Of battle surged along the Wilderness.
And mourned the North upon her thousand hills.

O gallant brothers of the generous South!
Foes for a day, and brothers for all time,
I charge you by the memories of our youth,
By Yorktown's field and Montezuma's clime.
Hold our dead sacred; let them quietly rest
In your unnumbered vales, where God thought best!

Your vines and flowers learned long since
    to forgive,
And o'er their graves a broidered mantle
    weave;
Be you as kind as they are, and the word
Shall reach the Northland with each sum-
    mer bird,
And thoughts as sweet as summer shall
    awake
Responsive to your kindness, and shall make
Our peace the peace of brothers once again,
And banish utterly the days of pain.

And ye, O Northmen! be ye not outdone
    In generous thought and deed.
We all do need forgiveness, every one;
    And they that give shall find it in their
        need.
Spare of your flowers to deck the stranger's
    grave,
    Who died for a lost cause:
A soul more daring, resolute, and brave
Ne'er won a world's applause!
(A brave man's hatred pauses at the tomb.)
For him some Southern home was robed in
    gloom,
Some wife or mother looked with longing
    eyes
Through the sad days and nights with tears
    and sighs—
Hope slowly hardening into gaunt Despair.
Then let your foeman's grave remembrance
    share:
Pity a higher charm to Valor lends,
And in the realms of Sorrow all are friends.

Yes, bring fresh flowers and strew the
    soldier's grave,
    Whether he proudly lies
    Beneath our Northern skies
Or where the Southern palms their branches
    wave!
Let the bells toll, and wild war-music swell,
    And for one day the thought of all the
        past—
Full of those memories vast—
Come back and haunt us with its mighty
    spell!
Bring flowers, then, once again,
And strew with fragrant rain
Of lilacs, and of roses white and red,
The dwellings of our dead.

Dirge for a Soldier

By G. H. Boker

Close his eyes; his work is done!
    What to him is friend or foeman,
Rise of moon or set of sun,
    Hand of man or kiss of woman?
Lay him low, lay him low,
In the clover or the snow!
What cares he? he cannot know
Lay him low!

As man may, he fought his fight,
    Proved his truth by his endeavor;
Let him sleep in solemn night,
    Sleep forever and forever.

Lay him low, lay him low,
In the clover or the snow!
What cares he? he cannot know.
Lay him low!

Fold him in his country's stars,
    Roll the drum and fire the volley!
What to him are all our wars?—
    What but death-bemocking folly?
Lay him low, lay him low,
In the clover or the snow!
What cares he? he cannot know.
Lay him low!

Leave 'him to God's watching eye;
    Trust him to the hand that made him.
Mortal love weeps idly by;
    God alone has power to aid him.
Lay him low, lay him low,
In the clover or the snow!
What cares he? he cannot know.
Lay him low!

Killed at the Ford

By Henry Wadsworth Longfellow

He is dead! the beautiful youth,
The heart of honor, the tongue of truth;
He, the life and light of us all,
Whose voice was blithe as a bugle-call,
Whom all eyes followed with one consent,
The cheer of whose laugh, and whose pleas-
    ant word
Hushed all murmurs of discontent.

Only last night, as we rode along
Down the dark of the mountain-gap
To visit the picket-guard at the ford,
Little dreaming of any mishap,
He was humming the words of some old
    song:
"Two red roses he had in his cap,
And another he bore at the point of his
    sword."

Sudden and swift a whistling ball
Came out of the wood, and the voice was
    still;
Something I heard in darkness fall,
And for a moment my blood grew chill;
I spoke in a whisper, as he who speaks
In a room where some one is lying dead;
But he made no answer to what I said.

We lifted him up to his saddle again,
And through the mire and the mist and the
    rain
Carried him back to the silent camp,
And laid him as if asleep on his bed:
And I saw by the light of the surgeon's
    lamp
Two white roses upon his cheeks,
And one, just over his heart, blood-red!

And I saw in a vision how far and fleet
That fatal bullet went speeding forth
Till it reached a town in the distant North,
Till it reached a house in a sunny street,
Till it reached a heart that ceased to beat
Without a murmur, without a cry;

And a bell was tolled in that far-off town
For one who had passed from cross to crown,
And the neighbors wondered that she should
die.

Forget and Forgive

By Major Jonathan W. Gordon

What, comrades, shall I sing to-day,
  To you who know the story well,
Of that sublime, transcendent fray
  In which these silent heroes fell?
You shared their toils, you saw them die,
  And know that self defiled them never
They died to keep yon flag on high,
  And make the Nation one forever.

If there was fault, be it forgot;
  While Union, Freedom, Peace abide
We'll share the good their blood has brought
  And cease to hate, malign, and chide.
No matter how the strife befell,
  To yon dear flag the day was given;
And all again with rapture swell
  To see it float supreme in Heaven.

'Tis quite enough for grief and shame,
  That such a strife e'er smote the land;
And quite enough for praise and fame,
  That Union, Law, and Freedom stand.
Forgive the strife, wash out the shame
  In Lethe's unrevealing river;
But build a monument to fame,
  And glorify these dead forever.

What's Hallowed Ground?

By Thomas Campbell

What's hallowed ground? Has earth a clod
Its Maker meant not should be trod
By man, the image of his God,
    Erect and free,
Unscourged by Superstition's rod
    To bow the knee?

What hallows ground where heroes sleep?
'Tis not the sculptured piles you heap:
In dews that heavens far distant weep,
    Their turf may bloom:
Or Genii twine beneath the deep
    Their coral tomb.

But strew his ashes to the wind,
Whose sword or voice has saved mankind,—
And is he dead, whose glorious mind
    Lifts thine on high?
To live in hearts we leave behind,
    Is not to die!

Is't death to fall for Freedom's right?—
He's dead alone that lacks her light!
And murder sullies, in heaven's sight,
    The sword he draws:—
What can alone ennoble fight?—
    A noble cause!

Give that; and welcome War to brace
Her drums, and rend heaven's welkin space!
The colors planted face to face,
    The charging cheer,
Tho Death's pale horse lead on the chase,
    Shall still be dear!

And place our trophies where men kneel
To Heaven!—but Heaven rebukes my zeal,
The cause of truth and human weal,—
    O God above!—
Transfer it from the sword's appeal
    To peace and love!

Peace, love,—the cherubim that join
Their spread wings o'er devotion's shrine,—
Prayers sound in vain, and temples shine,
    Where they are not;
The heart alone can make divine
    Religion's spot!

What's hallowed ground? 'Tis what gives
    birth
To sacred thoughts in souls of worth!
Peace! Independence! Truth! go forth
    Earth's compass round;
And your high priesthood shall make earth
    All hallowed ground!

Memorial Day

By Richard Watson Gilder

She saw the bayonets flashing in the sun,
  The flags that proudly waved; she heard
    the bugles calling;
She saw the tattered banners falling
About the broken staffs, as one by one
The remnant of the mighty army passed;
And at the last
Flowers for the graves of those whose fight
    was done.

She heard the trampling of ten thousand
    feet
As the long line swept round the crowded
    square;
She heard the incessant hum
That filled the warm and blossom-scented
    air—
The shrilling fife, the roll and throb of drum,
The happy laugh, the cheer. Oh, glorious
    and meet
To honor thus the dead,
Who chose the better part,
And for their country bled!
—The dead! Great God! she stood there in
    the street,
Living, yet dead in soul, and mind, and
    heart—
While far away
His grave was decked with flowers by
    strangers' hands to-day.

Eve of Memorial Day

The Rev. S. F. Smith, author of " My
country, 'tis of thee," was once at the house
of a friend, on the afternoon before Memorial
Day, where were gathered about thirty children and young ladies. The young people
were gathering many cut flowers into bouquets, and while they worked they sang from
time to time the national hymn, " My country, 'tis of thee."
This led Dr. Smith to write the following
beautiful lines:

" Sweet in the innocence of youth,
　　Born of the brave and free,
They wove fair garlands while they sung
　　' My country, 'tis of thee.'
How every bosom swelled with joy,
　　And thrilled with grateful pride,
As fond and whispering cadence breathes
　　' Land where my fathers died.'

" Fair flowers in sweet bouquets they tied,
　　Breaths from the vale and hills,
While childish voices poured the strain,
　　' I love thy rocks and rills;'
Each face grew radiant with the thought,
　　' Land of the noble free,'
Each voice seemed reverent as it trilled,
　　' Sweet land of liberty.'

" And bud, and bloom, and leaf they bound,
　　And bade the living keep
Unharmed and pure the cherished graves
　　Where brave men calmly sleep;
And thus while infant lips begin
　　To lisp ' Sweet freedom's song,'
Manhood's deep tones, from age to age,
　　Shall still ' the sound prolong.'

" I hailed the promise of the scene,
　　Gladness was in the strain;
The glorious land is safe while love
　　Still swells the fond refrain;
And what shall be our sure defense?
　　Who guards our liberty?
Not man—not arms alone—we look,
　　' Our fathers' God, to thee.' "
　　　　　　　　　　　Selected.

New England's Dead

BY ISAAC M'LELLAN

New England's dead! New England's dead!
　　On every hill they lie;
On every field of strife made red
　　By bloody victory.
Each valley, where the battle poured
　　Its red and awful tide,
Beheld the brave New England sword
　　With slaughter deeply dyed.
Their bones are on the Northern hill,
　　And on the Southern plain,
By brook and river, lake and rill,
　　And by the roaring main.

The land is holy where they fought,
　　And holy where they fell;
For by their blood that land was bought—
　　That land they loved so well.
Then glory to that valiant band,
　　The honored saviors of the land!
Oh, few and weak their numbers were—
　　A handful of brave men—
But to their God they gave their prayer,
　　And rushed to battle then.
The God of battles heard their cry,
　　And sent to them the victory.

They left the plowshare in the mold,
　　Their flocks and herds without a fold,
The sickle in the unshorn grain,
　　The corn half garnered on the plain,

And mustered, in their simple dress,
　　For wrongs to seek a stern redress—
To right those wrongs, come weal, come wo,
　　To perish, or o'ercome their foe.

And where are ye, O fearless men?
　　Oh, where are ye to-day?
I call: the hills reply again
　　That ye have passed away;
That on old Bunker's lonely height,
　　In Trenton, and in Monmouth ground
The grass grows green, the harvest bright,
　　Above each soldier's mound.

The bugle's wild and warlike blast
　　Shall muster them no more;
An army now might thunder past,
　　And they not heed its roar.
The starry flag, 'neath which they fought
　　In many a bloody day,
From their old graves shall rouse them not,
　　For they have passed away.
　　　　　　　　　　　Selected.

The Young Patriot

BY PAUL PASTNOR

" Drum as you never drummed before! "
　　What a thrill in the Colonel's tone,
As he turned to the drummer-boy of the
　　　corps!
" Drum as if upon you alone
　　The battle hung! Forward—guide right!"
And the long line breasted the smoke-clad
　　height.

'Twas an errand of death on which they
　　went—
Up the hill to the cannons' throats;
　　A thousand men to the shambles sent
With as little heart as a herd of goats!
　　Yet some one knew that the move was wise;
Some one ordered the sacrifice.

The little drummer-boy marched at the fore,
　　Capless, stained with the smoke and dust,—
Soldier and hero to the core,
　　Worthy his brave commander's trust;
While sharp and clear as alarum's clang
The beat of his drum down the column rang.

The bullets shrieked through the blinding
　　smoke,
And men went down by three and by four;
　　But, oft as the column shook and broke,
The ring of the drum midst the cannon's
　　roar
Heartened the ranks, and they formed anew
A solid front of the blood-stained Blue!

Almost up to the rampart grim!
　　One more charge—but the drum was still!
Bleeding, faint, with a shattered limb,
　　Lay the drummer-boy on the hill.
Heart of the regiment ceased to beat;
Nothing could hinder the wild retreat!

Then the drummer-boy, roused with dread,
　　Groped for his trusty drum once more,
Thought of the words that the Colonel said—
　　" Drum as you never drummed before!

And sitting there, while his blood ebbed fast,
He cheered and played, as the soldiers
    passed.

They won it, the frowning fortress wall—
    They, the few who were left to fight;
Won by the beat of the drumsticks small,
    And the face of the drummer-boy brave
        and bright!
Honor the hero who proved in truth,
The patriot-zeal of the heart of youth!

I.

A Christopher of the Shenandoah

Island Ford, Snicker's Gap, July 18th, 1864

[TOLD BY THE ORDERLY]

By EDITH M. THOMAS

Mute he sat in the saddle—mute midst our
    full acclaim,
As three times over we gave to the mountain
    echo his name.
Then, " But I couldn't do less!" in a mur-
    mur remonstrant came.

This was the deed his spirit set and his hand
    would not shun,
When the vale of the Shenandoah had lost
    the glow of the sun,
And the evening cloud and the battle smoke
    were blending in one.

Retreating and ever retreating, the bank of
    the river we gained,
Hope of the field was none, and choice but
    of flight remained,
When there at the brink of the ford his horse
    he suddenly reined.

For his vigilant eye had marked where,
    close by the oozy marge,
Half-parted its moorings, there lay a bat-
    tered and oarless barge.
" Quick! gather the wounded in!" and the
    flying stayed at his charge.

They gathered the wounded in, whence they
    fell by the river-bank,
Lapped on the gleaming sand, or aswoon
    'mid the rushes dank;
And they crowded the barge till its sides low
    down in the water sank.

The river was wide, was deep, and heady
    the current flowed,
A burdened and oarless craft!—straight into
    the stream he rode,
By the side of the barge, and drew it along
    with its moaning load.

A moaning and ghastly load—the wounded—
    the dying—the dead!
For ever upon their traces followed the
    whistling lead,
Our bravest the mark, yet unscathed and
    undaunted, he pushed ahead.

Alone?—save for one that from love of his
    leader or soldierly pride
(Hearing his call for aid, and seeing that
    none replied),
Plunged and swum by the crazy craft on the
    other side.

But Heaven! what weary toil!—for the river
    is wide, is deep;
Plunged and swum by the crazy craft on the
    further side is steep.
'Tis reached at last, and a hundred of ours
    to the rescue leap.

Oh, they cheered as he rose from the stream
    and the water-drops flowed away!
" But I couldn't do less!" in the silence
    that followed we heard him say;
Then the wounded cheered, and the swoon-
    ing awoke in the barge where they lay.

And I?—Ah, well, I swam by the barge on
    the other side;
But an orderly goes wherever his leader
    chooses to ride.
Come life or come death I couldn't do less
    than follow his guide.

I.

Home They Brought Her Warrior

By ALFRED TENNYSON

Home they brought her warrior dead:
    She nor swooned, nor uttered cry;
All her maidens, watching, said,
    " She must weep or she will die."

Then they praised him, soft and low,
    Called him worthy to be loved,
Truest friend and noblest foe:
    Yet she neither spoke nor moved.

Stole a maiden from her place,
    Lightly to the warrior stept,
Took the face-cloth from the face:
    Yet she neither moved nor wept.

Rose a nurse of ninety years,
    Set his child upon her knee:
Like summer tempest came her tears—
    " Sweet, my child, I live for thee."
        —From " *The Princess.*"

FLAG-RAISING DAY

(June 14)

FLAG-RAISING DAY is one of the youngest of our national anniversaries, but is fast finding a large place in the hearts of the American people, especially in the schools. The day was first recognized June 14, 1894, when the Governor of New York ordered that the Stars and Stripes be raised on all public buildings in the State on June 14, 1897, the one hundred and seventeenth anniversary of the adoption by Congress of our present national flag. This action the Governor took at the request of the " Sons of the Revolution." Flag-raising Day was also fittingly observed in Philadelphia on the same date by request of the " Colonial Dames of America."

The Revolutionary Statesmen in session in the old City Hall at Philadelphia in 1777 appointed a committee to consider and report on the subject of a general standard for the troops of all the colonies. On June 14th of that year Congress passed the famous resolution that the flag of the United States be thirteen stripes alternately white and red, and that the union be thirteen white stars in a blue field, representing a new constellation.

Tradition says that General George Washington, who was a member of the Committee, with Robert Morris and Colonel Ross, took a rough sketch of the proposed design to a Mrs. John Ross, an upholsterer, who was noted for her neatness as a seamstress. She lived on Arch Street, and her home still stands, a shrine frequently visited by patriotic pilgrims. The story runs that the stars in the design had six points; but Mrs. Ross much preferred stars with five points. So with a few clips of her scissors she deftly cut out a five-pointed star for her illustrious callers, who, satisfied of its greater beauty, accepted the change.

Mrs. Ross made a flag which was approved by Congress. It was raised at once in Philadelphia, and the design copied everywhere by the patriots.

When Kentucky and Vermont were admitted into the Union in 1794, the Stars and Stripes were each increased to fifteen; but, in 1818, Congress voted to restore the original thirteen stripes and to add a new star on the 4th of July following the admission of each new state.

The observance of Flag-raising Day in our public schools is very general, and is at once a delightful and efficient means of inspiring the rising generation with the noble sentiment of patriotism.

HISTORICAL

THE HISTORY OF THE FLAG

By ZITELLA COCKE

Our splendid national emblem is a very familiar sight to the young people of this great country, but it is probable that very many who hail it with enthusiastic cheers are quite ignorant of the circumstances which gave rise to its adoption. There is a striking resemblance between the design of our flag and the arms of General Washington, which consisted of three stars in the upper portion and three bars running across the escutcheon, and it is believed by many that the American flag was derived from this heraldic design. A careful investigation of facts reveals the truth that several flags were used by the people of the States before the present one was adopted.

In the month of March, 1775, a red flag was hoisted in New York, bearing on one side the inscription, " George Rex and the liberties of America," and on **Flags** the other side, " No Popery." **Previous** In July, 1775, on Prospect Hill, **to 1777** General Israel Putnam raised a flag, upon which was inscribed the motto of the Commonwealth of Massachusetts, " *Qui transtulit sustinet,*" and on the reverse were written the words, " An Appeal to Heaven." In October, 1775, the floating batteries of Boston carried a flag with the motto, " An Appeal to Heaven," the design being a pine tree on a white field. Virginia carried a flag in 1775—design, a rattlesnake coiled as if about to strike, and the motto, " Don't tread on me." Her State motto in the present time resembles this, " *Sic semper tyrannis,*" but it was not until January 18, 1776, that the grand union flag, bearing stars and stripes, was raised on the heights near Boston. It has been said that when the regulars—British troops—saw it, they supposed it was an evidence of submission to the King, who had just issued his proclamation.

An extract from the *British Register* of 1776 reads thus; " The rebels burnt the King's speech, and changed their colors from a plain red ground to a flag with thirteen stripes, as a symbol of the number and union of the colonies." A letter written from Boston to the Pennsylvania *Gazette* in 1776 says: " The union flag was raised on the second, a compliment to the united colonies." So we see that a series and number of flags appeared—the rattlesnake **The Stars** the pine tree, and the stripes, **and** the various designs of the dif- **Stripes** ferent colonies—until July, 1777, when the blue union of the stars was added to the stripes, and the law adopt-

ed this flag as the great national emblem. After the adoption of this flag, a stripe was added with every new state; but as it became manifest that in time the beauty of the emblem would be marred by the enormous proportions acquired with additional states, Congress reduced the stripes to the original thirteen, and the stars were made to correspond with the number of states.

Perhaps no flag on sea or land shows its grace and beauty of design so well as the emblem of the United States, as its proportions are perfect when it is accurately and properly made—one-half as broad as it is long—the first stripe at the top red, the next white, and these alternating colors make the last stripe red, the blue field for the stars being the width and square of the first seven stripes.

The Continental Congress appointed a committee to supervise the union of the different parts of the national flag, and the following description of their design and significance was prepared:

" The stars of the new flag represent the new constellation of states rising in the West. The idea was taken from the great constellation of Lyra, which in **Symbolism** the hand of Orpheus signifies harmony. The blue in the field was taken from the edges of the Covenanter's banner in Scotland, significant of the league covenant of the United States against oppression, incidentally involving the virtues of vigilance, perseverance, and justice.

The stars were disposed in a circle, symbolizing the perpetuity of the union; the ring, like the serpent of the Egyptians, signifying eternity. The thirteen stripes showed with the stars the number of the united colonies, and denoted the subordination of the states to the Union, as well as equality among themselves. The whole was the blending of the various flags of the army. and the white ones of the floating batteries. The red color, which in Roman days was the signal of defiance, denoted daring; and the white, purity."— H. Y. P.

THE STARS AND STRIPES

By A. Y. Leech

Probably all Americans believe that they know their national flag when they see it, yet many are certainly unable to distinguish between the standard Stars and Stripes and its spurious imitations. It is desirable for all to remember that the flag is not a haphazard arrangement of alternate stripes of red and white, with stars on a blue field, but an emblem fashioned in a manner prescribed by law and official regulations.

The first national legislation on the subject bears date June 14, 1777, when Congress, in session at Philadelphia, adopted the following:

" Resolved, That the flag of the thirteen United States be thirteen stripes, alternate red and white; that the union be thirteen stars, white in a blue field, representing a new constellation."

This was about one year subsequent to the Declaration of Independence. Prior to that time colonial flags, and those improvised by the parties using them, were publicly displayed as occasion demanded, but these were in no sense the " national standard."

The thirteen stripes had been introduced, in alternate white and blue, on the upper left-hand corner of a standard presented to the

Philadelphia Light Horse Company by its captain in the early part of 1775. Moreover, the flag of the thirteen united colonies raised at Washington's headquarters at Cambridge, January 2, 1776, had the thirteen stripes just as they are this day; but it also had the cross of St. George and St. Andrew on a blue ground in the corner.

There is no satisfactory evidence, however, that *any* flag bearing the union of the stars had been in public use before the resolution of June, 1777.

Some writers assert that the first and original United States flag, instead of thirteen stars, each representing a revolted colony or state, contained only twelve stars, because Georgia was not entitled to a vote. Such a flag is said to have been made by the ladies of Philadelphia from the design of the escutcheon of the Washington family, and it is said that Washington himself cut out the five-pointed stars.

It is alleged that this flag was presented to John Paul Jones; that he sailed with it up and down the Schuylkill, to show the people the appearance of the flag of their country; that it was adopted by Congress; that Jones carried it with him on his ship *Bon Homme Richard,* that in his great fight the flag was shot away from its staff and fell in the sea, and that Lieutenant Stafford leaped overboard after it, brought it safely to the ship and nailed it to the masthead.

The tale may be true, but the flag was not the national flag. The act of Congress of June 14, 1777, shows that *no* standard was recognized by the Nation until that date.

It has been impossible to decide with certainty who designed the American flag as first adopted by Congress, but the best recorded evidence gives part of the credit of designing it and all the credit of making it to Mrs. John Ross, an upholsterer, who resided on Arch Street, Philadelphia. Her descendants assert that a committee of Congress, accompanied by General Washington, who was in Philadelphia in June, 1776, called upon Mrs. Ross and engaged her to make the flag from a rough drawing. This drawing was, at her suggestion, redrawn by General Washington with pencil, in her back parlor, and the flag thus designed was adopted by Congress.

Altho the resolution establishing the flag was not officially promulgated by the Secretary of Congress until September 3, 1777, it seems well authenticated that the regulation Stars and Stripes was carried at the battle of the Brandywine, September 11, 1777, and thenceforward during the battles of the Revolution.

Soon after its adoption the new flag was hoisted on the naval vessels of the United States. The ship *Ranger,* bearing the Stars and Stripes and commanded by Captain Paul Jones, arrived at a French port about December 1, 1777. Her flag received on February 14, 1778, the first salute ever paid to the American flag by foreign naval vessels.

No further action relative to the flag was taken by Congress until after Vermont and Kentucky were admitted to the Union. Then, on January 13, 1794, Congress enacted:

"That from and after the first day of May, 1795, the flag of the United States be fifteen stripes, alternate red and white: that the union be fifteen stars, white in a blue field."

This flag was the national banner from 1795 to 1818, during which period occurred the war of 1812 with Great Britain. But soon five additional states—Tennessee, Ohio, Louisiana, Indiana, and Mississippi—were admitted to the Union and required representation on the flag. So Congress, on April 4, 1818, enacted:

First. "That from and after the fourth day of July next, the flag of the United States be thirteen horizontal stripes, alternate red and white; that the Union have twenty stars, white in a blue field."

Second. "That on the admission of every new state into the Union one star be added to the union of the flag, and that such addition shall take effect on the Fourth of July next succeeding such admission."

The debate in Congress shows that the return to the thirteen stripes of the 1777 flag was due, in a measure, to a reverence for the standard of the Revolution; but it was also due to the fact that a further increase of the number of stripes would make the width of the flag out of proportion to its length, unless the stripes were narrowed, and this would have made it hard to see them at a distance.

A newspaper of the time, still kept in the government archives, said, "By this regulation the thirteen stripes will represent the number of states whose valor and resources originally effected American independence, and additional stars will mark the increase of the states since the present Constitution."

No act has since been passed by Congress, altering this feature of the flag, and the standard is the same as originally adopted, except as to the number of stars in its union.

In the war with Mexico the national flag bore twenty-nine stars in its union; during the late Civil War it had thirty-five, and since July 4, 1891, it has borne forty-five stars.

In none of the acts of Congress relating to the flag has the manner of arranging the stars been prescribed, and in consequence there has been a striking lack of uniformity in this matter. Designs of the flag in the keeping of the government show that the early custom was to insert the stars in parallel rows across the blue field. This custom has, it is believed, been observed in the navy, at least since 1818, at which time the President ordered the stars to be arranged in this manner on the national flag used in the navy.

In the army, too, it is believed, the stars have always been arranged in horizontal rows across the blue field, but not always in vertical rows; the effect, however, being about the same as the naval flag. Hereafter there will be no difference in the arrangement of stars between the army and navy, as an agreement has been arrived at between the War and Navy Departments.

American bunting only is now used in the manufacture of the Stars and Stripes, and these flags are woven for the government on American looms.

While the sizes of the government flags are not prescribed by statute law, they are fixed by regulations of the Departments of the War and Navy, which have been based upon convenience, utility and beauty, and the exigencies of the service.

The storm and recruiting flags measure each eight feet in length by four feet two inches in width. The post flag measures twenty feet in length by ten feet in width.

The garrison flag, hoisted only on great occasions and national holidays, measures thirty-six feet in length by twenty feet in width. The union is always one-third of the length of the flag, and extends to the lower edge of the fourth red stripe from the top.

The national colors carried by regiments of infantry and artillery and the battalion of engineers, on parade or in battle, are made of silk. They are six feet six inches long and six feet wide, and are mounted on staffs. The field of the colors is thirty-one inches in length, and extends to the lower edge of the fourth red stripe from the top.—Y. C.

BETSY ROSS AND THE FLAG

By Harry Pringle Ford

On the 14th day of June, 1777, the Continental Congress passed the following resolution:

"Resolved, That the flag of the thirteen United States be thirteen stripes, alternate red and white; and that the union be thirteen stars, white in a blue field, representing a new constellation."

This resolution, the first recorded legislative action, so far as known, relating to the adoption of a national flag in this country, was taken on the recommendation of Robert Morris, the famous financier and treasurer of the Revolution, and George Ross, a Pennsylvania signer of the Declaration of Independence, who, at some time during the previous year, had been appointed a committee to consider the subject of adopting a general standard for all the colonies—various banners and devices having been in use, not only by the colonies, but also by the different regiments, up to this time.

The committee, accompanied by General Washington, called at the house of Betsy Ross, 239 Arch Street, on a day between the 23d of May and the 4th of June, 1776, and left with her an order to make a flag from designs which they submitted. This she did so successfully as to lead to the adoption of the above resolution the following year.

Mrs. Ross, whose maiden name was Elizabeth Griscom, was born January 1st, 1752, of Quaker parentage. She was noted for her exquisite skill in needlework; and that she was engaged in the flag-making business previous to the adoption of the national standard in June, 1777, is evident from the fact that in the preceding May, Congress made an order on the Treasury "to pay Betsy Ross £14. 12s. 2d. for flags for the fleet in the Delaware River." In the latter part of 1773 she married John Ross, the son of the Rev. Æneas Ross, an Episcopal clergyman, of Newcastle, Delaware, a brother to the Hon. George Ross mentioned above.

The young married couple carried on the upholstery business at 239 Arch Street, Philadelphia. Their happiness, however, was destined to be short lived. The spirit of liberty was awakening, and hundreds of patriots were sacrificing the pleasures of home on the altar of their country. Among the foremost of these was young John Ross. One night, whilst guarding, with several other young men, some military stores on one of the city wharves along the Delaware River, he received so serious an injury that he died from the effects of it, after long and anxious nursing on the part of his faithful and devoted young wife. He was buried in the Christ Church burying ground, Fifth and Arch Streets, January 20, 1776. The Ross pew, marked with a national flag, is still preserved in the historic old church.

Left a widow at the early age of twenty-four, Mrs. Ross heroically determined to maintain her independence, if possible, by continuing the upholstering business; and it was not long after the death of her husband that she was called on by the Committee of Congress in reference to making a sample flag for the Nation.

Mr. George Canby, a grandson of Mrs. Ross, who is still living in Philadelphia, and who well remembers his grandmother, gives the following interesting incident of this historic visit:

"The committee asked her if she thought she could make a flag from a design, a rough drawing of which General Washington exhibited. She replied with diffidence and becoming modesty that 'she did not know, but would try.' She noticed, however, that the stars, as drawn, had six points, and informed the committee that the correct star should have but five points. They answered that they understood this, but that a great number of stars would be required, and the more regular form with six points could be more easily made than one with five. She responded in a practical way, by deftly folding a scrap of paper, and then with a single clip of her scissors, she displayed a true, symmetrical, five-pointed star.

"This at once decided that point in her favor. After the design was partially re-drawn on the table in her little back parlor, she was left to make her sample flag according to her own ideas of the arrangement of the stars, the proportions of the stripes and the general form of the whole. Some time after its completion, it was presented to Congress, and the committee soon thereafter had the pleasure of reporting to her that her flag was accepted as the national standard, and she was authorized to proceed at once to the manufacture of a large number for disposal by the Continental Congress."

Mr. Canby has in his possession the old family Bible of his grandmother. It contains many interesting entries. No authentic likeness of Mrs. Ross exists. She was married three times. Her second husband was Captain Joseph Ashburn, to whom she was united in the Old Swedes Church, Philadelphia, June 15th, 1777. He died a prisoner of war, March 3d, 1782, in the old Mill Prison, Plymouth, England. His friend, John Clay-poole, who was a prisoner with him, was finally released, and became the third husband of our fair heroine, May 8th, 1783. Mr. Claypoole died August 3d, 1817. His wife died January 30th, 1836, at the advanced age of eighty-four years, having lived to see our government firmly established and our Nation taking its rightful place among the foremost powers of the world.

The quaint little brick birthplace of the flag at 239 Arch Street, is still standing, altho more than a century and a half old. The front ground floor is now used as a cigar store; the room just back of it, about twelve by eighteen feet in size, is the one in which the flag is said to have been made. It remains quite as it was in the old days, and gives every evidence of belonging to a time not our own. We trust that the old house may long be preserved to keep alive in patriotic hearts the memories that are inseparably associated with the origin of our beautiful banner, the glorious Stars and Stripes.—F.

ABOUT FLAGS

By Eliza E. Clarke

Our flag has been called by various names, in song and story, as "Star-Spangled Banner," "Flag of the Free," "Banner of Liberty," "The Starry Flag," "Stripes and Stars," "Old Glory," etc. But by whatever name it may be called, the true American feels an enthusiastic sentiment of patriotism stirring in his heart, whenever its stripes and stars are unfolded to his sight.

Previous to the adoption of the stripes and stars as our national emblem, while each colony had its own flag, several attempts were made to arrange one which might serve the purpose of all. One of these consisted of thirteen alternate stripes of red and white, with a rattlesnake uncoiled diagonally upon it, the warning "Don't tread on me," being suggestive of the ruling sentiment of the times.

There are various flags in common use of interest to all. Among them, the flag of truce bears an important part. It is a white flag, which is displayed to an enemy to show a desire for consultation, and which protects the bearer from injury from the enemy's fire when approaching their lines. After a battle, when both armies wish to send parties to the field to bury their dead and carry off the wounded, they go with safety under the flag of truce, as it is never fired upon in honorable warfare.

A black flag is a piratical emblem, and means "no quarter;" or, in other words, death to all who are captured by the ship over which it floats. We can well imagine the dismay it must have carried to the hearts of those whose misfortune it was to see its dismal folds displayed at the masthead of an approaching vessel.

A yellow flag floating over a building, or from the mast of a ship shows that some contagious disease is prevailing there.

The expression, "dipping a flag," means lowering it slightly and raising it again as a salute to a vessel or fort.

If the President of the United States makes a sea voyage the flag is carried at the bow of his barge, or at the masthead of the ship he is on, which is then called a flagship. The same is true of the ship commanded by a commodore of the United States Navy.

"The flag of Fort McHenry," whose "broad stripes and bright stars" inspired Francis Key to write our national song. "The Star-Spangled Banner," still exists in a tolerable state of preservation, and is in the possession of Mr. Eben Appleton, of Yonkers, N. Y., a grandson of Col. Armistead, the gallant defender of Fort McHenry. The stripes are two feet wide, and the stars are two feet from point to point. The flag is thirty feet wide and was originally forty feet long, without doubt; but in its present curtailed dimensions is only thirty-two feet long.—E. G.

THE SCHOOL FLAG

The boys are moving in the matter of raising the flag of the United States over the school-houses on national and festive days. The girls are helping them with sympathy and subscriptions. Now and then a rich man puts his hand into his pocket and gives a fine large flag outright, tho it is better to raise the money by moderate subscriptions. We are too much in the habit of looking to rich men to do what we ought to do ourselves.

A flag of the best American bunting, large enough for most school-houses, costs from five to fifteen dollars. Then there are the staff, the halyards, the putting up of the staff, and a nice box to keep the flag in when it is not flying. All this can be done for a sum that is easily raised in almost any town of the United States.

For a small country school-house, the scholars of which know how to use their heads a little, nothing need be bought but the flag itself and some cord. The boys can cut and erect the pole. On last Thanksgiving Day (1899) many flags were raised over school-houses in New England, the money for which was raised in a few hours.

Various questions arise in connection with these flag-raisings.

Who is to have charge of the flag? Who is to raise it on the approved days, lower it, and put it away? Some teachers suggest a Flag Committee composed of the head boy of each class in the school. This plan would give a committee of five, at the most. To avoid confusion and disagreement, the boy at the head of the advanced class should be chairman, with power to direct proceedings. The announcement of the Flag Committee by the principal of the school, at the close of the monthly examination, would be an interesting event.

On what days should the flag be raised? We should say *not* on days that have a party or sectarian character. For example not on days set apart for the celebration of a Republican or Democratic victory at the polls. On the other hand, the inauguration of a president, a governor, a mayor, is not a party event, altho it results from a party victory. The flag might properly be raised on such days.

There are certain birthdays which will suggest themselves to every one: those of Washington, Franklin, Lafayette, Lincoln and others. Here, locality might assert its claims. In New England, the birthdays of Whittier and Longfellow might be honored, while New York might prefer Irving and Cooper.

Such events as the Landing of the Pilgrims could not be overlooked in New England; New York would remember the completion of the first telegraph or the laying of the Atlantic cable; Philadelphia the coming of William Penn; and all schools the admission of their State into the Union, or the acceptance of the Constitution.

In selecting the great days of the late war, the Flag Committees will naturally be careful not to wound sectional pride, nor excite unprofitable controversy. All can join in commemorating that day of days on which President Lincoln issued his proclamation of freedom to the slaves, and that other grand day when General Grant gave back to General Lee and his exhausted troops their side-arms and their horses, and told them to go in peace and raise a crop.

With good sense on the part of the pupils and sympathetic tact on the part of teachers, the school flag may furnish pleasant and salutary incidents in the routine of the school year. The raising of the flag just before school in the morning, and the lowering of it just after school in the afternoon, will be a lesson in history to the neighborhood.

We suggest also that a little, not too much, ceremony in the raising and lowering of the flag will add to the impressiveness of the occasion. The boys are probably aware that it is a part of the etiquette of flag-raising and lowering on the naval vessels that the flag shall never be allowed to touch the deck.

To be sure the flag is only a bit of bunting, and the country does not suffer a loss of dignity if the flag be permitted to touch the dust; but it is also an emblem. For the moment it represents the honor and glory of our native land, and it is not sentimentality but true sentiment that forbids that the stars and stripes be suffered to be soiled by contact with the earth.—Y. C.

FLAG PRESENTATION

During our Civil War the colonel of a fine Union regiment came to his general, in a high state of excitement.

"General," said he, "I was waited on by two lovely ladies, this morning, who wish to present a flag to my regiment, on the coming Fourth of July."

As the brigade was at that time quartered in a very hostile Southern city, this produced considerable surprise on the part of the general; but he finally said:

"Well, it will be worth seeing. Turn out your regiment and let the ceremonies go on."

When the famous day arrived, every soldier was clad in his best, and the colonel looked fairly resplendent in his finest uniform. There was quite a large number of spectators present. The young ladies appeared, escorted by some of their male friends, and were given a post of honor.

One of them made a speech, in which she mentioned liberty as among the choicest blessings in the world, and extolled the conduct of our brave Revolutionary forefathers. It was a very eloquent address, and was heard by all with approval and delight.

At its close, she uncovered and unrolled the flag, and with a smile upon her face, said, sweetly,

"I now have the pleasure of presenting, sir, to you and your regiment, the grandest and most characteristic symbol of the liberty for which our forefathers fought, that has ever seen the light of day."

She unrolled the flag, which, to the unlimited surprise of most of those present, proved to be a Confederate one!

For a moment, there was an intense silence. The Southerners present did not dare to cheer, however much they felt like it; the soldiers were sternly restrained by their officers as well as by their natural chivalry toward the sex.

The colonel's eyes flashed fire; but he was a man of the world, and had been an accomplished politician before entering the war; and, with a gentle and engaging smile, he advanced, and received the flag from the hand of his fair (and unfair) guest. Then, in a clear resonant Fourth-of-July tone, he responded:

"Madame, you are my guest, and a lady. I am the colonel of this regiment, which is composed entirely of gentlemen as well as soldiers, and, I trust, I am deserving the same appellations.

"We have listened with interest to your views as to which is the symbol most typical of freedom of any in the world. We (looking at the colors of the regiment) hold a different opinion, or we should not be here. We are glad to know, too, that our views are gradually gaining ground. We have already received in surrender several flags similar to the one you have just handed me, and shall keep this as a token, that at last even the fair daughters of the Confederacy have decided that their cause is a hopeless one, and have commenced capitulating their colors —eulogizing them, very naturally, as they so do."

The turning of the tables had been accomplished so neatly, that the crowd cheered, in spite of themselves; the young lady, who had perhaps harbored an idea that she would be arrested, and made a sort of martyr, rushed away in confusion; and the colonel marched his regiment back to quarters with flying colors. He afterwards received a merry note from his acquaintance of a day, apologizing for the trick she had attempted to play upon him, thanking him for the gentlemanly manner in which he had treated her, and acknowledging that he had had the best of the incident.

During a late visit to the Nashville Exposition, he enjoyed the pleasure of meeting her —now a handsome "Colonial Dame"—and of laughing with her over the incident.—E.

SUGGESTIVE THOUGHTS

FLAG, Loved the.—The author of PERSONAL RECOLLECTIONS OF THE REBELLION tells a good flag story. At an auction sale in Charleston, just before the breaking out of the war, the auctioneer, after knocking down odd lots of dry goods and remnants, picked up an American flag and cast it down with the contemptuous remark that he would not ask a bid for that useless rag.

This was too much for one of the bystanders, a rough-looking man, and he called out: "I bid ten dollars!"

At the word he elbowed his way through the crowd, took the flag and bore it off.— Y. C.

FLAG, Our.—A great many years ago our people fought for a free land. They wanted a flag all their very own—a flag to wave over their homes and lead their soldiers in battle. They asked George Washington and a friend to have just the right kind of a flag made. It was not to be like any other flag.

Washington drew a picture of a flag with stars and stripes, and took it to a lady to be made. He told her just how to make it.

The stripes were to be red and white, and the stars white upon a blue sky. This was our first flag. And now shall I tell you what our flag means? When you see it waving in the air, it says to you: "This is a free land." The colors tell us something, too. The red says, "Be brave;" the white says, "Be pure;" the blue says, "Be true."— ELSIE M. WHITING.

FLAG, Our.—One dreary morning late in the autumn of 1864, a number of Union prisoners were piloted up the Savannah River, past the historic Fort Pulaski, past the blockade of sunken vessels, and up within the Confederate lines.

Then down the river came a Confederate steamer, and as it turned a curve and came in sight of the Union vessels, there was heard, as if from somewhere within the steamer's depths, a muffled shout, "Hurrah! hurrah! hurrah!"

This meeting at Savannah was for an exchange of prisoners between the Union and Confederate forces. Two steamers were lashed together, gang-planks thrown across, and the exchange begun. Man for man, a steady double line, one line of Union prisoners and the other of Confederates, walked across the gang-planks for days.

"What was that hurrahing for, as the steamer turned the bend?" one of the prisoners was asked, as he came to the United States vessel.

He smiled grimly and said, " Why, you see, some of us happened to be where we could see down the river, and we caught sight of the old flag, the Stars and Stripes. We told the rest of them, and then they gave the three cheers you heard. They weren't much for strength, but they were the best we could give.

" You, who haven't been where you couldn't see the flag if you wanted to," the prisoner went on, " haven't any idea what it meant to us. In the first place it meant freedom—and freedom's a big word to us who've been penned up so long. Then it meant home—and I guess our boys like that word, too! Ask that boy sitting on the stairs; it meant life to him, and a good many more like him."

The boy on the stairway seemed quite willing to speak, but it was necessary to bend down and listen closely in order to hear his words.

" I was one of them that couldn't see the flag," he whispered, " but I could see them that could see it, and I cheered with the rest. I couldn't make much noise, but I did some loud shouting inside just the same!"— Y. C.

FLAG, The.—This very interesting little incident occurred in China a few years ago. At a Fourth of July dinner in Shanghai, the English consul in toasting the British flag, said:

" Here is to the Union Jack—the flag of flags—the flag that has floated on every continent and on every sea for a thousand years —the flag on which the sun never sets."

It was such a strong sentiment that the Americans were a little overawed, until the American humorist, Eli Perkins, was called to toast the Stars and Stripes. Looking directly in the faces of the Englishmen, he said:

" Here is to the Stars and Stripes of the New Republic; when the setting sun lights up her stars in Alaska, the rising sun salutes her on the rock-bound coast of Maine. It is the flag of Liberty, never lowered to any foe, and the only flag that whipped the flag on which the sun never sets."

In these days the American flag is very much in evidence.—*Selected.*

FLAG, The, and the Hymn.—The sights and sounds which most impressed Richard Harding Davis, the war correspondent, were those not of battle but of the interludes of peace. Within sight of the walls of the jail which confined Hobson, he writes, lay our trenches in the shape of a vast horseshoe, the five miles of which were planted with American flags. When they fluttered in the wind at full length and the sun kissed their colors, they made one of the most inspiring pictures of the war. The men would crouch for hours in the pits with these flags rustling over them, feeling well repaid for their service; while evening by evening they crept

closer to the prisoner, signaling silent messages of hope and encouragement.

Then at sunset the band played the Star-Spangled Banner and the national anthem, proclaiming something of a call to arms and something of a call to prayer. The discomforts of the day ceased to exist. The murmurs of the rifle pit, which were like the hum of a great bazaar, were suddenly silent, and the men before the fire rose stiffly from their knees, and those in the trenches stood upright. On every hill as far as one could see, motionless figures stood with heads uncovered and with eyes fixed on the flags where their hands had planted them.

When the music had ceased the men pulled on their hats again and once more began to fry a piece of hardtack in a layer of fat, but for a moment they had seen the meaning of it all, and had been carried back to the country for which they were encountering weariness and hardships and disease and death, and were inspired with fresh courage and fresh resolve.

" It is merely a matter of sentiment," one of Napoleon's generals once said to him.

" Sentiment? " came the quick reply; " then it concerns what most enriches life." And Napoleon was right. The aim of life and life's self-denial, as proved by the men in the trenches, are inspired rather than retarded by beautiful sights and melodious sounds. The flag and the hymn are intensely practical.—Y. C. (S. M.)

FLAG, The Largest.—The largest flag in the world was made in San Francisco for Hawaii, and is eighty feet long. It consumed seven hundred yards of bunting, and will fly from a pole one hundred and fifty feet long.—Y. C.

GLORY, Old.—There are some lessons suggested to us by the colors of the flag. The white is the symbol of purity. It stands for the ideal virtue which should be exercised under certain circumstances and conditions. In a statesman it would stand for a pure and incorrupt citizenship; in a judge it would stand for integrity; in a business man it would stand for honesty; in view of sickness it would stand for humility, and in relation to the poor it stands for charity. In fact, it stands for everything that is godly.

The red stands for love. This color receives its symbolism from the blood, and reminds us that every true patriot should be willing to die for the love of country; to shed his blood, if necessary in the hour of the Nation's peril. But more particularly does the red symbolize that divine love which should dwell in every breast and be the ruling passion in every soul.

The stars upon the azure are symbols of light and heavenly protection. They teach us that every state should be a symbol of light, of righteousness, of truth. They remind us, also, that Heaven is above us, underneath, and around us, and that in the darkest hour of the Nation's peril God's eye is upon us.

All hail, Old Glory, flag of the brave and the free! All hail, thou glorious banner, God bless thee and help thee!—A. S. GUMBART, D.D.

REPUBLIC, The Hope of the.—Law, learning, charity are insufficient to save our Nation from vice, ignorance, and infidelity. All have been tried and found wanting. But add to them the practical morality of Christianity, and a pure and honorable citizenship is assured beyond all fear. It is hard to convince the people of this tremendous fact, sustained by all history, ancient and modern, Jewish and pagan. I believe in churches, colleges, and houses of mercy, and support them all; but my hope is in a citizenship born of Christian faith and practise. Give us these and the Republic will live forever. We are in danger of forgetting the sad fact in history that the fate of republics is empire.

Can we reverse the verdicts of history? I believe we can, by the application of the principles of Christianity to American citizenship.—BISHOP NEWMAN.

"UNCLE SAM" WAS CHRISTENED, How.—The term "Uncle Sam" came into use during the War of 1812 and originated at Troy, N. Y. The government inspector there was Samuel Wilson, universally known as "Uncle Sam." Whenever he inspected supplies furnished the government he would brand them "U. S.," meaning United States, but the abbreviation being then new and not generally recognized, the workmen supposed it to mean "Uncle Sam," the inspector. Afterward the story was repeated and got into print, and from that time the name has been facetiously applied to the United States.—N. Y. T.

POETRY

The Color Guard

By CHARLES W. HARWOOD

There were waving hands and banners, as the crowded car rolled by,
There were shouts from merry children ringing to the summer sky;
Then a strain of music rose and swelled and pealed along the street,
As their gay, tumultuous clamor melted in a chorus sweet:
> O say, can you see, by the dawn's early light,
> What so proudly we hailed at the twilight's last gleaming?—
> Whose broad stripes and bright stars, through the perilous fight,
> O'er the ramparts we watched were so gallantly streaming!

Ah, the starry flag is glorious, and the children love it, too;
And the land is safe and happy where the children's hearts are true.
How their youthful ardor thrilled me, as the revelation came
That the Guard is ever changing, but the flag remains the same.

We were born too late for glory, but we still in memory keep
Stirring echoes from the battlefields where warrior fathers sleep,
We have held the flag as ours, but, lo! the years are passing by,
And a newer generation waves the Stars and Stripes on high.

Better thus! for now the rancors of the strife no more appal;
And the children know no faction, and the flag belongs to all.

Be it so! we yield the prestige, for the New Guard comes apace,
With the strength of youthful millions, loyal purpose in its face.

Flag of peace or flag of battle! Children, it is *yours* to love!
Will you honor and defend it, as the gift of God above?
Ah! the children's hearts are loyal! From a myriad array
North and South there comes the answer, as it came that summer day:
> Then conquer we must, when our cause it is just,
> And this be our motto, "In God is our trust;"
> And the star-spangled banner in triumph shall wave
> O'er the land of the free and the home of the brave.

Y. C.

Our Colors

By LAURA E. RICHARDS

Red! 'tis the hue of battle,
The pledge of victory;
In sunset light, in northern night,
It flashes brave and free.
"Then paint with red thy banner,"
Quoth Freedom to the Land,
"And when thy sons go forth to war,
This sign be in their hand!"

White! 'tis the sign of purity,
Of everlasting truth;
The snowy robe of childhood,
The stainless mail of youth.
Then paint with blue thy banner,
And pure as northern snow
May these thy stately children
In truth and honor go.

Blue! 'tis the tint of heaven,
The morning's gold-shot arch,
The burning deeps of noontide,
The stars' unending march.
Then paint with blue thy banner,
And bid thy children raise
At daybreak, noon, and eventide
Their hymn of love and praise.

Valor and truth and righteousness,
In threefold strength to-day
Raise high the flag triumphant,
The banner glad and gay.
"And keep thou well thy colors,"
Quoth Freedom to the Land,
"And 'gainst a world of evil
Thy sons and thou shall stand."
                                    Y. C.

Cross and Flag

By FREDERICK L. HOSMER

From age to age they gather, all the brave
    of heart and strong,
In the strife of truth with error, of the
    right against the wrong;
I can see their gleaming banner, I can hear
    their triumph song;
        The Truth is marching on!

"In this sign we conquer;" 'tis the symbol
    of our faith,
Made holy by the might of love, triumph-
    ant over death;
He finds his life who loseth it, forever
    more it saith:
        The Right is marching on!

The earth is circling onward, out of shadow
    into light;
The stars keep watch above our way, how-
    ever dark the night;
For every martyr's stripe there glows a
    bar of morning bright;
        For Love is marching on!

Lead on, O cross of martyr faith, with thee
    is victory!
Shine forth, O stars and reddening dawn,
    the full day yet shall be!
On earth His kingdom cometh, and with
    joy our eyes shall see:
        Our God is marching on!
                                    C. G.

E Pluribus Unum

By G. W. CUTTER

Tho many and bright are the stars that ap-
    pear
In that flag by our country unfurled;
And the stripes that are swelling in majesty
    there,
Like a rainbow adorning the world,
Their lights are unsullied as those in the
    sky,
By a deed that our fathers have done;
And they're leagued in as true and as holy a
    tie,
In their motto of " Many in one."

From the hour when those patriots fearlessly
    flung
That banner of starlight abroad,
Ever true to themselves, to that motto they
    clung,
As they clung to the promise of God:
By the bayonet traced at the midnight of
    war,
On the fields where our glory was won;
Oh! perish the heart or the hand that would
    mar
Our motto of " Many in one."

'Mid the smoke of the contest—the cannon's
    deep roar—
How oft hath it gathered renown!
While those stars were reflected in rivers of
    gore,
When the cross and the lion went down;
Tho few were their lights in the gloom of
    that hour,
Yet the hearts that were striking below
Had God· for their bulwark, and truth for
    their power,
And they stopped not to number their foe.

From where our green mountain-tops blend
    with the sky,
And the giant St. Lawrence is rolled,
To the waves where the balmy Hesperides
    lie,
Like the dream of some prophet of old;
They conquered—and dying, bequeathed to
    our care—
Not this boundless dominion alone—
But that banner, whose loveliness hallows
    the air,
And their motto of " Many in one."

We are many in one, while there glitters a
    star
In the blue of the heavens above;
And tyrants shall quail 'mid their dungeons
    afar,
When they gaze on that motto of love.
It shall gleam o'er the sea, 'mid the bolts of
    the storm,
Over tempest and battle and wreck,
And flame where our guns with their thun-
    der grow warm
'Neath the blood on the slippery deck.

The oppressed of the earth to that standard
    shall fly,
Wherever its folds shall be spread;
And the exile shall feel 'tis his own native
    sky
Where its stars shall float over his head.
And those stars shall increase, till the fulness
    of time
Its millions of cycles has run—
Till the world shall have welcomed its mis-
    sion sublime,
And the nations of earth shall be one.

Tho the old Alleghany may tower to heaven,
    And the Father of waters divide,
The links of our destiny cannot be riven,
    While the truth of these words shall abide.

Oh, then let them glow on each helmet and
    brand,
Tho our blood like our rivers shall run:
Divide as we may in our own native land,
    To the rest of the world we are one.

Then, up with our flag—let it stream on the
    air,
Tho our fathers are cold in their graves;
They had hands that could strike, had souls
    that could dare,
And their sons were not born to be slaves.
Up, up with that banner, where'er it may
    call,
Our millions shall rally around;
A nation of freemen that moment shall fall
When its stars shall be trailed on the
    ground.

Flags

Forthwith from the glittering staff unfurled
The imperial ensign; which, full high ad-
    vanced,
Shone like a meteor streaming to the wind,
With gems and golden luster rich em-
    blazed,
Seraphic arms and trophies.
              MILTON—*Paradise Lost.*
                    Bk. I. Line 535.

Ten thousand thousand ensigns high ad-
    vanced,
Standards and gonfalons.
              MILTON—*Paradise Lost.*
                    Book V. Line 588.

The ensigns of their power.
              MILTON—*Paradise Regained.*
                    Bk. IV. Line 65.

The sooty flag of Acheron,
Harpies and Hydras.
              MILTON—*Comus.* Line 604.

Under spread ensigns marching.
              MILTON—*Paradise Lost.*
                    Bk. II. Line 886.

Under spread ensigns moving nigh, in slow
But firm battalion.
              MILTON—*Paradise Lost.*
                    Bk. VI. Line 533.

Bastard Freedom waves
Her fustian flag in mockery over slaves.
    MOORE—*To the Lord Viscount Forbes.*

The flag of our Union forever!
    GEORGE P. MORRIS—*The Flag of Our*
                          Union.

              A garish flag,
To be the aim of every dangerous shot.
          Richard III. Act IV. Sc. 4.

This token serveth for a flag of truce
Betwixt ourselves and all our followers.
       Henry VI. Pt. I. Act III. Sc. 1.

Flag and Cross

BY ALFRED J. HOUGH

The bands were playing in the street,
    The bells were clanging loud,
And all around were restles feet
    And voices of a crowd.

A starry flag shot through the air,
    Its folds the breezes stirred,
And as it swayed and floated there
    Cheer after cheer was heard.

A young man rose and traced with skill
    His country's past renowned;
A nation born at Bunker Hill,
    At Appomattox crowned.

And when he cried: " With Time's last years
    That flag its goal shall reach!"
The people hailed him with their cheers,
    And glorified his speech.

An old man took the speakers' stand,
    His head was crowned with gray;
He raised aloft a trembling hand,
    The tumult died away.

" I see," he said, " unfurled above
    The stars and stripes so fair,
Another flag, the flag of love,
    And God has set it there.

" The stars and stripes will fail alone,
    And fall, forever furled,
With other flags, to-day unknown,
    That once rose o'er the world.

" In fadeless light the stars will shine,
    The stripes untarnished flow,
Illumined by the cross divine,
    And guided where they go."

No answer ringing loud and long,
    In cheers the message brought,
But silence still was on the throng,
    The silence of deep thought.—C. G.

The Flag of Our Union Forever

BY GEORGE P. MORRIS

A song for our banner, the watchword **recall,**
    Which gave the Republic her station,
" United we stand, divided we fall,"
    It made and preserved us a Nation.

CHORUS:

The union of lakes, the union of lands,
    The union of states none can sever,
The union of hearts, the union of hands,
    And the flag of our Union forever.

What God in His infinite wisdom designed,
    And armed with the weapons of thunder,
Not all the earth's despots or factions com-
    bined,
Have the power to conquer or sunder
The union of lakes, the union of lands,
    The union of states none can sever,
The union of hearts, the **union** of hands
    And the flag of our Union forever.

Oh, keep that flag flying! The pride of the van!
To all other nations display it!
The ladies for union are to a—man!
And not to the man who'd betray it.
Then to the union of lakes, the union of lands,
The union of states none can sever!
The union of hearts, the union of hands,
And the flag of the Union forever.

Our Country's Starry Flag

By Margaret E. Sangster

It's streaming from the house-tops, it's flying from the ships,
Ten thousand times ten thousand, we cheer with hearts and lips,
And the guns in muffled thunder salute its folds unfurled,
The starry flag of Freedom, the bravest in the world.

Oh, sweet and shrill the bugles their silver music play,
And loud and stormy beat the drums along the crowded way;
The soldiers in procession are marching down the street,
And the children and the mothers their tattered banners greet.

Not every flag they carry is smooth and bright and new;
Some flags have felt the baptism of battle's fiery dew;
Till the red hath grown full redder in the blood of heroes slain,
And rent and stained the white and blue have tossed in battle's rain.

Somehow our throats are aching, there's a clutching at the breast;
For whoever may be living, our dead are of the best;
Our dead who sleep in lowly graves, afar from war's alarms,
God's peace forever keeping them, where they have grounded arms.

Fling that flag from every steeple, garland every home and school,
Roof and spire and cot and mansion happy 'neath its blessed rule;
Sing that flag where children gather; love that flag by Freedom crowned;
Loyal legions proudly hail it, shout on lips, and hands all round!

Dear old flag of stars triumphant over sea and over land;
Dear old flag of fame unsullied, of a story clean and grand;
On our day of days we pledge thee, all our hearts, and all our toil,
God and country still our watch-word as we stand on Freedom's soil!

E. W.

Salute the Flag

By H. C. Bunner

Off with your hat as the flag goes by!
And let the heart have its say;
You're man enough for a tear in your eye
That you will not wipe away.

You're man enough for a thrill that goes
To your very finger-tips—
Ay! the lump just then in your throat that arose
Spoke more than your parted lips.

Lift up your boy on your shoulder high,
And show him the faded shred—
Those stripes would be red as the sunset sky
If death could have dyed them red.

The old tune thunders through all the air,
And strikes right into the heart;
If ever it calls for you, boy, be there!
Be there, and ready to start.

Off with your hat as the flag goes by!
Uncover the youngster's head!
Teach him to hold it holy and high,
For the sake of its sacred dead.

C. G.

Flag Song

(Air, " Yankee Doodle.")

By Harriet Prescott Spofford

Out upon the four winds blow,
Tell the world your story;
Thrice in hearts' blood dipped before
They called your name Old Glory!
Stream, Old Glory, bear your stars
High among the seven;
Stream a watchfire on the dark,
And make a sign in Heaven!

Mighty harvests gild your plains,
Mighty rivers bear them,
Everywhere you fly you bid
All the hungry share them:
Blooms the wilderness for you,
Plenty follows after,
Underneath your shadow go
Peace and love and laughter.

When from sky to sky you float,
Far in wide savannas,
Vast horizons lost in light
Answer with hosannas.
Symbol of unmeasured power,
Blessed promise sealing,
All your hills are hills of God,
And all your founts are healing!

Still to those the wronged of earth
Sanctuary render;
For hope and home and Heaven they see
Within your sacred splendor!
Stream, Old Glory, bear your stars
High among the seven;
Stream a watchfire on the dark,
And make a sign in Heaven!

I.

The Flag Goes By

By H. H. Bennett

Hats off!
Along the street there comes
A blare of bugles, a ruffle of drums,
A flash of color beneath the sky:
Hats off!
The flag is passing by!

Blue and crimson and white it shines,
Over the steel-tipped, ordered lines.
Hats off!
The colors before us fly;
But more than the flag is passing by.

Sea-fights and land-fights, grim and great,
Fought to make and to save the State;
Weary marches, and sinking ships;
Cheers of victory on dying lips;

Days of plenty and years of peace;
March of a strong land's swift increase;
Equal justice, right and law,
Stately honor and reverent awe;

Sign of a Nation, great and strong
To ward her people from foreign wrong:
Pride and glory and honor, all
Live in the colors to stand or fall.

Hats off!
Along the street there comes
A blare of bugles, a ruffle of drums;
And loyal hearts are beating high:
Hats off!
The flag is passing by!

Y. C.

The Flag of Stars

By Grace Ellery Channing

Oh not alone the eager South—
Alone the steadfast North—
Saw with wet eyes beneath spring skies,
Our flag of stars go forth!
Oh not alone the elder East,
Nor the young-hearted West,
Smiled high with pride where side by side
The Nation's children pressed!

But North and South and East and West,
The mountain and the plain,
The prairie and the desert,
Yielded their flower again.
East and West and South and North,
The flower of the land,
Hearing the mother's call went forth
To stand at her right hand.

We be many hands in labor,
But one arm for the right;
One blood to shed, one heart till dead,
One good sword for the fight:
We be many-tongued and minded,
But one mind and one tongue
When once wide-sent through a continent
The Nation's word has rung!

Then Northern tongues sing Dixie
Beneath the ancient flag;
And the Southerner dies to rebaptize
His own the " Yankee rag! "

Brothers!—to keep for Freedom's sake
The flag of stars unfurled
Beneath the stars of Heaven—to make
The starlight of the world!

Y. C.

The Flag

By Bishop H. C. Potter

O, banner blazoned in the sky,
Fling out your royal red;
Each deeper hue of crimson dye
Won by our sainted dead.

Ye bands of snowy whiteness clean
That bar the waning day,
Stand as the prophecy of things unseen
Toward which we hew our way.

Fair field of blue, a symbol true
Of Right, of Faith, of God,
O'erarch us as we seek anew
The path our fathers trod.

Ye clustered stars that gleam above,
Our darkness turn to light;
Reveal to men Heaven's law of love—
Then ends the world's long night.

The American Flag

By Joseph Rodman Drake

[An almost pathetic interest attaches to the story of this stirring poem of our early national history. Probably nine out of ten of the native-born male inhabitants of the United States have recited it, or heard it recited, in clarion schoolboy tones; but the author of it died at the age of twenty-five, without knowing that he had made himself famous. When he was on his death-bed, a friend asked what he would like to have done with his poems.

" Oh, burn them! " he said. " They are quite valueless."

" The American Flag " was written between May 20 and May 25, 1819, and was the last of the once famous " Croaker Pieces " written for a New York paper, the *Evening Post.* Drake wrote the first four poems alone, but after that he collaborated with Fitz-Greene Halleck, and the pieces were signed, " Croaker & Co." The poem originally concluded with the following lines:

As fixed as yonder orb divine,
That saw the bannered blaze unfurled,
Shall thy proud stars resplendent shine,
The guard and glory of the world.

The author was not satisfied, and said to Halleck, " Fitz, can't you suggest a better stanza?" Whereupon Halleck sat down and wrote four lines, which Drake adopted, and which appear in the poem now.—Y. C.]

When Freedom from her mountain height
Unfurled her standard to the air,
She tore the azure robe of night,
And set the stars of glory there.
She mingled with its gorgeous dyes

The milky baldric of the skies,
And striped its pure, celestial white
With streakings of the morning light;
Then from his mansion in the sun
She called her eagle-bearer down,
And gave into his mighty hand
The symbol of her chosen land.

Majestic monarch of the cloud,
  Who rear'st aloft thy regal form,
To hear the tempest trumpings loud
And see the lightning lances driven,
  When strive the warriors of the storm,
And rolls the thunder-drum of Heaven,
Child of the sun! to thee 'tis given
  To guard the banner of the free,
To hover in the sulphur smoke,
To ward away the battle-stroke,
And bid its blendings shine afar,
Like rainbows on the cloud of war,
  The harbingers of victory!

Flag of the brave! thy folds shall fly,
The sign of hope and triumph high,
When speaks the signal trumpet tone,
And the long line comes gleaming on,
Ere yet the life-blood, warm and wet,
Has dimm'd the glistening bayonet,
Each soldier eye shall brightly turn
To where thy sky-born glories burn;
And as his springing steps advance,
Catch war and vengeance from the glance.
And when the cannon-mouthings loud
Heave in wild wreaths the battle-shroud,
And gory sabers rise and fall
Like shoots of flame on midnight's pall;
  Then shall thy meteor glances glow,
And cowering foes shall shrink beneath
  Each gallant arm that strikes below
That lovely messenger of death.

Flag of the seas! on ocean wave
Thy stars shall glitter o'er the brave;
When death, careering on the gale,
Sweeps darkly round the bellied sail,
And frighted waves rush wildly back
Before the broadside's reeling rack,
Each dying wanderer of the sea
Shall look at once to Heaven and thee,
And smile to see thy splendors fly
In triumph o'er his closing eye.

Flag of the free heart's hope and home!
  By angel hands to valor given,
The stars have lit the welkin dome,
  And all thy hues were born in Heaven.
Forever float that standard sheet!
  Where breathes the foe but falls before us,
With Freedom's soil beneath our feet,
  And Freedom's banner streaming o'er us?

The Tattered Flag

By James Buckham

What a line of them, brave and bright, flags
    that toss in the summer breeze,
Bars of crimson and bars of white—cluster'd
    stars like the Pleiades!
Not a rent in the shining silk, not a stain
    that the eye can see;
Hands that fashioned them white as milk—
    very fair should the emblem be!

Ah! but yonder what tattered thing, shreds
    and ribbons of shabby rags?
Sure, a mockery—fit to swing just as a foil
    to the brighter flags!
Dark the gash in the azure field—stars thrust
    out—and the wide-mouthed wounds
Left to gape with their lips unsealed! Sport
    for all, as it goes its rounds!

What! a cheer and a three times three
    swelling up for the tattered flag?
Staff held high for the crowd to see, all hats
    doffed to the dingy rag?
Brothers' blood for the stains, you say?
    Foeman's lead for the rents uncouth?
Gleam of those lost stars led the way storm-
    ing straight to the cannon's mouth?

Well, then, thus do I make amend—fling my
    cap as the flag goes by,
Count no cost of the breath I spend—who
    cheers lustier, you or I?
Brave old flag with its flaunting shreds!
    dear old flag with its spattered blue!
Cheer it on, with uncovered heads—think in
    what hail of death it flew!

Every shred in the rippling wind tells its tale
    of the bitter fight;
Soldiers stricken and dropped behind, col-
    umns shattered to left and right;
Shriek of the wounded, and, overhead, shriek
    of the awful wraith-like shell;
Hard-clasped hands of the ghastly dead;
    blaze of the guns like the glare of hell.

Who that lived through it came away whole
    in body or whole in mind,
Spirit tuned to the light and gay, fit to trifle
    with human-kind?
All were torn like the flags they bore, all
    came back with the wound and stain;
Haunted by battles, they fight them o'er still
    in the smoke of the purpled plain!

Hail to the flag with its broken staff! hail to
    the heroes who bore it through!
Bitter the cup which they dared to quaff—
    equal the praise and the honor due.
Lift up the flag to the smiling sun, lift it up
    to dear Freedom's sky;
Let it tell of the battles won—tell of the
    graves where the victors lie!
                                        Y. C.

The Stars and Stripes

By Kate Sumner Burr

Let us sing of the Banner of Freedom
  Which floats o'er Columbia's domain;
In the city, the village, the country,
  We'll join in the cheerful refrain.
Oh! how dear every stripe of that ensign;
  And above them the stars shine so true;
'Tis of Freedom and Peace the fair token:
  Three cheers for the Red, White, and
      Blue!

Should one say, in the years yet before us,
  "Declare why so fond thine esteem
For the flag which is now floating o'er us
  Whose stripes and whose stars brightly
      gleam?"

From the dawn of our life as a nation
" Old Glory's " bright record we view;
As we point to the pages historic,
    Three cheers for the Red, White, and
    Blue!

In the folds of our flag we discover
    A beauty exalted, sublime!
We may search seas and continents over,
    There floats none so fair in any clime!
'Tis endeared by our Fathers' devotion,
    To their Land and their God they were
    true;
Now it waves o'er a free, happy people;
    Three cheers for the Red, White, and
    Blue!

Let this pole-star of hope light the races
    Till Tyranny's blight fall no more;
Let oppressors be hurled from high places
    Till right reign supreme on each shore;
Then shall maids, wives, and dear little chil-
    dren,
Fathers, husbands, all lovers so true,
Ever praising the Author of Freedom,
    Rejoice 'neath the Red, White, and Blue.
                        Selected.

The Star Spangled Banner

By Francis Scott Key

[Key's immortal ballad is said to have been
first sung, when fresh from the press, in a
small one-story frame house occupied as a
tavern next to the Holiday Street Theater in
Baltimore. The tavern had been kept by
the Widow Berling and later by a Captain
MacCauley. It was " a house where players
most did congregate " to prepare for the
daily military drill in Jay Street, every able
man being at that time—1814—a soldier.
    Captain Eades, the printer who struck off
the copies of the song for Key, dropped in at
the tavern one day in the latter part of September, not long after Key had been liberated. Eades had a fresh copy of the new
song, and read it aloud to the assembled
volunteers, who cheered every verse. The
old air of " Anacreon in Heaven " had been
adapted to it by its author, and Ferdinand
Durang, mounting a rush-bottom chair, sang
the lines for the first time, unless Key had
sung them to himself.
    When the theater opened, the new song
was sung every night after the play. There
has been much discussion as to what became
of the flag referred to in the song. It has
been located " positively " in various places.
    The version of the song printed below is
taken from the volume, POEMS OF THE LATE
FRANCIS S. KEY, ESQ., published in New
York, in 1857, with an introductory letter by
Mr. Key's brother-in-law, Chief Justice
Taney.—Y. C.]

O say, can you see, by the dawn's early light,
    What so proudly we hailed, at the twi-
    light's last gleaming?
Whose broad stripes and bright stars through
    the perilous fight,

O'er the ramparts we watched, were so
    gallantly streaming;
And the rockets' red glare, the bombs burst-
    ing in air,
Gave proof through the night that our flag
    was still there:
O say, does that Star Spangled Banner yet
    wave
O'er the land of the free and the home of the
    brave?

On that shore, dimly seen through the mists
    of the deep,
    Where the foe's haughty host in dread
    silence reposes,
What is that which the breeze, o'er the tow-
    ering steep,
    As it fitfully blows, now conceals, now dis-
    closes?
Now it catches the gleam of the morning's
    first beam,
In full glory reflected now shines in the
    stream:
'Tis the Star Spangled Banner; O long may
    it wave
O'er the land of the free and the home of the
    brave!

And where are the foes who so vauntingly
    swore
    That the havoc of war, and the battle's
    confusion,
A home and a country should leave us no
    more:
    Their blood has washed out their foul
    footsteps' pollution;
No refuge could save the hireling and slave
From the terror of flight, or the gloom of the
    grave;
And the Star Spangled Banner in triumph
    doth wave
O'er the land of the free and the home of the
    brave!

O thus be it ever, when freemen shall stand
    Between their loved homes and the war's
    desolation;
Blest with victory and peace, may the heav'n-
    rescued land
    Praise the Power that hath made and pre-
    served us a nation!
Then conquer we must, when our cause it is
    just,
And this be our motto, " In God is our
    trust;"
And the Star Spangled Banner in triumph
    shall wave
O'er the land of the free and the home of the
    brave!

Union and Liberty

By Oliver Wendell Holmes

Flag of the heroes who left us their glory,
    Borne through their battle-fields' thunder
    and flame,
Blazoned in song and illumined in story,
    Wave o'er us all who inherit their fame.
    Up with our banner bright,
    Sprinkled with starry light,

Spread its fair emblems from mountain to
 shore,
 While through the sounding sky
 Loud rings the Nation's cry—
UNION AND LIBERTY! ONE EVERMORE!

Light of our firmament, guide of our Nation,
 Pride of her children, and honored afar,
Let the wide beams of thy full constellation
 Scatter each cloud that would darken a
 star!

Empire unsceptered! what foe shall assail
 thee
 Bearing the standard of Liberty's van?
Think not the God of thy fathers shall fail
 thee,
 Striving with men for the birthright of
 man!

Yet if, by madness and treachery blighted,
 Dawns the dark hour when the sword thou
 must draw
Then with the arms to thy million united,
 Smite the bold traitors to Freedom and
 Law!

Lord of the universe! shield us and guide us,
 Trusting Thee always, through shadow and
 sun!
Thou hast united us, who shall divide us?
 Keep us, O keep us the MANY IN ONE!
 Up with our banner bright,
 Sprinkled with starry light,
Spread its fair emblems from mountain to
 shore,
 While through the sounding sky
 Loud rings the Nation's cry—
UNION AND LIBERTY! ONE EVERMORE!

DOMINION DAY

(July 1)

DOMINION DAY, the first of July, is one of the few legal holidays celebrated in Canada, and is only second in importance to Empire Day, a national British holiday celebrated throughout the whole British Empire.

The significance of Dominion Day is purely Canadian, and it celebrates an event of unparalleled importance in the political history of Canada, namely, the passing of the North America Act of 1867, which united all the Canadian colonies under one great confederation, henceforth to be known to the world as the Dominion of Canada, a nation, not independent of, nor in any way disloyal to the mother country, but nevertheless, a free and self-governing people.

The progress of the people of Canada toward freedom and self-government has been slow and secured only through struggle and self-sacrifice. The first Parliament met in 1792, with sixteen representatives, appointed by the people, and eight councilors, appointed by the Crown for life. Until this time Canada had been governed by the laws of England and Orders-in-Council; but the Constitutional Act of 1791, with the consequent meeting of Parliament, gave an impulse to the spirit of self-government which grew stronger and stronger until it was consummated in the British North America Act of 1867.

Dominion Day, therefore, arouses a national enthusiasm, which is a most important factor in the development of any nation. Large importance is attached to the day in educational circles. School exercises are conducted in connection with which a Canadian sentiment is inculcated. The apprehension that the development of this spirit would lead directly to the separation of Canada from the mother country so far has proved unfounded. The alliance between the two nations is to-day maintained and promises so to be continued, while the national enthusiasm and Canadian spirit which Dominion Day fosters, has served to make the people of British North America not only loyal to their own beloved Canada, but also, to an even greater degree, loyal to the British Empire.

HISTORICAL

HISTORICAL SUMMARY*

1497. Canada discovered by Cabot; 1535, Jacques Cartier takes possession for France; Port Royal (now Annapolis, Nova Scotia) founded in 1605—the first permanent settlement in Acadia.

1608. Champlain founds Quebec, beginning settlement of what French called Canada; in 1609 Champlain helps Hurons and Algonquins to defeat Iroquois and wins the undying hatred of Iroquois for French. Company of One Hundred Associates takes over government of Canada, 1628, promising to settle the country in exchange for monopoly of fur trade. In same year Kirke with English fleet captures French fleet on its way to Quebec; 1629, Champlain surrenders Quebec to Kirke. England restores Canada and Acadia to France. 1632, Champlain first governor of Canada. Death of Champlain, 1635. In 1649 Iroquois attack and destroy Huron missions, putting to death with terrible torture, Jesuit missionaries Brebœuf and Lalemant. Hurons almost annihilated.

*CANADA. By E. R. Peacock, M.A., pp. 5-8. Toronto: Warwick Bro's & Ritter.

In 1663, charter of Hundred Associates revoked and royal government begins in Canada under a governor, intendant and bishop. Frontenac appointed governor, 1672—the only man who always kept the Iroquois under proper control. Terrible massacre of French at Lachine, near Montreal, by Iroquois in 1689. Frontenac, who had been recalled to France returns to Canada to save it from annihilation by the Iroquois. His vigorous measures soon check Indians.

1698. Death of Frontenac. For many years thereafter there were frequent outbreaks of border warfare between the English settlers to the south with their allies the Iroquois and the French settlers with their Indian allies.

In 1713, by Treaty of Utrecht, England finally obtains possession of Acadia (Nova Scotia and New Brunswick).

In 1735 a Frenchman builds Fort Rouge, near spot where Winnipeg now stands, and shortly afterwards discovers the Rocky Mountains.

1745. Louisburg, strong French fortress on Cape Breton Island, captured by English colonials under Pepperell but restored three years later by treaty of Aix-la-Chapelle. City of Halifax founded by English 1749. Much fighting on borders between English and French settlers—many atrocities by Indian allies.

1755. General Braddock, with 1,200 men, defeated and killed by French near Fort du Quesne, where Pittsburg now stands. English carry off the French settlers from Acadia. Montcalm takes command of French in Canada, 1756, and France declares war against England—the Seven Years War.

1757. Loudon fails to take Louisburg from French; Montcalm besieges British in Fort William Henry and garrison surrenders, but his Indians massacre many of English prisoners.

1758. Montcalm defeats Abercrombie at Ticonderoga with great loss; Amherst, Boscawen and Wolfe take the great fortress of Louisburg; Abercrombie superseded by Amherst.

In 1759, Wolfe and his army scale heights above Quebec, defeat French in battle of Plains of Abraham. Both Wolfe and Montcalm killed, but Quebec capitulates to English.

1760. French from Montreal besiege British in Quebec all winter, but in spring are driven off by the fleet; British troops concentrate around Montreal but French capitulate and hand over all Canada. Military rule till 1763, when Peace of Paris confirms Britain's right to Canada. In same year famous Indian Chief Pontiac forms a conspiracy to take all British border forts, but is foiled. Quebec Act, 1774, establishes government by governor and council appointed by Crown.

1775. Revolutionary Americans invade Canada, but fail to take Quebec.

In 1784, 25,000 British Loyalists leave United States and settle in Canada and Acadia. They were afterwards known as United Empire Loyalists.

1791. Constitutional Act grants slight measure of representative government and divides Canada into two provinces—Upper Canada and Lower Canada, English criminal law to prevail everywhere; but in Lower Canada French law to prevail in civil cases. This is still the case. First parliaments meet at Newark (Niagara) in Upper Canada, and in Lower Canada at Quebec. Population of Upper Canada, 20,000, of Lower Canada, 130,000.

1807. Parliament of Upper Canada makes provision for beginning of school system.

1812. United States declares war against England and invades Canada at three points, but driven back; Canadians capture Detroit. General Brock, Canadian Commander-in-Chief, killed at Queenston Heights.

In 1813, Americans capture British fleet on Lake Erie, take York and retake Detroit, hold western part of Upper Canada. French-Canadians beat back a greatly superior force of Americans at Chateauguay, and an American force is also beaten at Chrysler's Farm. Americans abandon Western Canada.

In 1814 Americans invade Upper Canada near Niagara, defeat Canadians at Chippewa but are defeated at bloody battle of Lundy's Lane and driven back. Peace signed between Britain and United States.

1817. Bank of Montreal founded.

Between 1820 and 1832 the Lachine, the Welland and the Rideau canals constructed.

1837. Rebellions in Upper and Lower Canada on behalf of responsible government.

1841. Upper and Lower Canada united and granted responsible government; Nova Scotia and New Brunswick given similar privilege in 1847.

1843. First settlement in British Columbia on Vancouver Island. A governor appointed for this new settlement 1850.

1867. Canada, Nova Scotia and New Brunswick unite to form Dominion of Canada with Ottawa as capital. Canada divided into two provinces, Ontario and Quebec. John A. Macdonald, the first Prime Minister of the Dominion. British North America Act, the Dominion Constitution.

1869. Red River rebellion of half-breeds at Fort Garry. Col. Wolsley (now Lord Wolsley) leads 1,300 men through the wilderness to suppress the rebellion but rebels retire quietly before he arrives. Rupert's Land and North-west Territory bought from Hudson's Bay Company. Part of it formed into Province of Manitoba which enters confederation in 1870. Fort Garry becomes Winnipeg the capital.

1871. British Columbia enters the Dominion on condition that a railway be built to connect British Columbia with the east.

1873. Prince Edward Island enters confederation.

1881. Contract let for Canadian Pacific Railway which was completed in 1886.

1882. Four districts—Alberta, Assiniboia, Athabasca and Saskatchewan—formed in North-west Territories, and given local government with capital at Regina.

1885. A rebellion of half-breeds and Indians in North-west Territories put down after considerable loss of life.

1887. The Canadian Pacific Railway opens its line of steamships between Vancouver and Hong Kong.

1891. Death of 'Sir John A. Macdonald, first Premier of the Dominion of Canada.

1894. Great conference held at Ottawa of delegates from all parts of British Empire to discuss means of furthering trade between British Colonies.

CANADA AS A NATION: MATERIAL AND INTELLECTUAL DEVELOPMENT—POLITICAL RIGHTS *

By James G. Bourinot

The population of the whole Dominion—still chiefly confined to the St. Lawrence valley and the Atlantic provinces—does not yet exceed 5,000,000 souls, tho it has **Population** increased nearly five times since 1837.† Of this population, 1,300,-000 are French Canadians; the majority are English, Scotch, and Irish. At least 2,000,-000 profess the Roman Catholic religion. The immigration of late years has been very insignificant, and has been practically nullified by the constant movement of Canadians into the United States—a movement which has been somewhat decreasing since the opening up of the Northwest and the greater facilities offered by the Dominion to energy and enterprise. Under these conditions the natural-born population amounts to about 85 per cent. of the whole.

The people of Canada have already won for themselves a large amount of wealth from the riches of the land, forest, and seas, and an aggregate of the imports **Resources** and exports now reaches $255,-000,000 a year, or an increase of $145,000,000 within half a century. The Northwest already raises upward of 36,000,-000 bushels of wheat, or an increase of 18,-000,000 in five years. Nearly $360,000,000 are invested in manufactures, chiefly of cotton and woolen goods. Some fourteen lines of ocean steamers call at the port of Montreal, which has now a population of over 250,000 souls. Toronto comes next in population, about 190,000, whilst the other cities, like Quebec, Halifax, St. John, Ottawa, Hamilton, and London, range from 70,000 to 30,000. The total revenue of the Dominion, apart from the local and provincial revenues, is about $36,000,000 a year—against only $300,000 in 1837—raised mainly from customs and excise duties, which are high, owing to the "national" or protective policy, altho lower than those on similar goods in

the United States. The expenditures of Canada, very heavy of late years for a small population, have been mainly caused by the development of the Dominion, and by the necessity of providing rapid means of intercommunication for trade and population in a country extending between two oceans,‡ Canals, lighthouses, the acquisition and opening of the Northwest railways, government buildings, have absorbed at least $240,000,-000 since 1867, and it is not remarkable, under these circumstances, that **Improve-** a gross debt has been accumu-**ments** lated within half a century of about $315,000,000, against which must be set valuable assets in the shape of buildings and public works necessary to the progress of a new country. The public buildings, churches, and universities display within a quarter of a century a great improvement in architectural beauty, whilst the homes of the people show, both in the interior and exterior, decided evidences of comfort, convenience, and culture. Instead of the fourteen miles of railway which existed in 1837, there are about 15,000 miles in actual operation, affording facilities for trade and commerce not exceeded by any country in the world.

The mental outfit of the Dominion compares favorably even with that of older countries. The Universities of Canada,—McGill in Montreal, Laval in Quebec, **Univer-** Queen's in Kingston, Dalhousie **sities** in Halifax, and Trinity and Toronto Universities in Toronto —stand deservedly high in the opinion of men of learning in the Old World and the United States, whilst the grammar and common school system, especially of Ontario, is creditable to the keen sagacity and public spirit of the people. We have already seen the low condition of education of fifty years ago, only one in fifteen at school; but now

---

* From The Story of Canada. New York: G. P. Putnam's Sons, 1896.

† Population of the Dominion at last census in 1891, 4,833,239; estimated population, 1900, about 5,300,000. Over 86 per cent. of inhabitants natives of British North America; foreign born, 647,362 — 475,456 from Great Britain; 80,915 born in United States. English speaking, 3,428,265; French, 1,404,974."—From Canada, by E. R. Peacock, M.A.

‡ The figures (of trade and commerce) for the year ending June 30, 1900, showed a phenomenal increase in trade. The total exports amounted to $175,656,947, an increase over 1896 of $46,440,165. The goods entered for consumption were valued at $183,209,273, compared with $154,051,593 for the previous year. In the fiscal year 1899 the total trade was $308,388,068; in 1900 it was $358,866,220.

Mr. W. S. Fielding, as Finance Minister, presented his budget to Parliament on March 23 (1900). He declared that the past fiscal year had been the most prosperous in Canadian history; that the revenue had been $46,741,249, the expenditure $41,905,500, and the surplus $4,837,749.—Condensed from Appleton's Annual Encyclopedia, 1900,

there are 1,000,000 pupils in the educational institutions of the country,* or one in five, at a cost to the people of upwards of $12,000,-000, contributed for the most part by the taxpayers of the different municipalities in connection with which the educational system is worked out. **Education** In Ontario the class of school-houses is exceptionally good, and the apparatus excellent tho there is an injurious tendency to burden pupils with too many subjects, and in that way encourage superficiality. In French Canada there is an essentially literary activity. The intellectual work of the English-speaking people has been chiefly in the direction of scientific, constitutional, and historical literature, in which departments they have shown an amount of knowledge and research which has won for many of them laurels outside of their own country.

The working out of a system of government adapted to the necessities of countries with distinct interests and nationalities, has **Statesmen** developed in Canada a class of statesmen and writers with broad national views and a large breadth of knowledge. On all occasions when men have risen beyond the passion and narrowness of party, the debates of the legislature have been distinguished by a keenness of argument and by a grace of oratory —especially in the case of some French Canadians—which would be creditable to the Senate of the United States in its palmy days. Anyone who reviews the twelve volumes already published by the Royal Society of Canada, founded by the Marquis of Lorne, when Governor-General, will see how much scholarship and ability the writers of Canada bring to the study of scientific, antiquarian, and historical subjects. The names of Todd, Kingsford, Scadding, Read, Pope, Stewart, Patterson, and Withrow will be recognized by Canadians as those of conscientious workers in history and constitutional learning. In **Science and Poetry** science the names of Sir William Dawson, Dr. George M. Dawson, and of other native Canadians on the list of the English and Canadian Royal Societies are well known in the parent State and wherever science has its votaries and followers. The poets, William Kirby, Archbishop O'Brien, John Reade, Charles Roberts, Bliss Carman, Frederick L. Scott, Pauline Johnson, Ethelwyn Wetherald, Archibald Lampman, Duncan Campbell Scott, James David Edgar, and Wilfred Campbell have won recognition even in a country like Canada, where still is wanting the inspiration of a wide field of culture, and of that generous encouragement which can hardly be expected in a country of prosaic needs. Miss Pauline Johnson is the child of an English mother and a head-chief of the Mohawks at Brantford. **Literary Workers** The historical novels of Major Richardson, William Kirby and Gilbert Parker, show the rich materials our past annals offer for romance.

Mr. Gilbert Parker's enthusiasm for his theme is sustained by his bright, attractive style. Sam Slick's SAYINGS AND DOINGS is still the only noteworthy evidence we have of the existence of humor among a practical people, and his "wise saws" and "sayings" were uttered more than half a century ago. Yet, on the whole, if great works are wanting nowadays, the intellectual movement is in the right direction, and according as the intellectual soil of Canada becomes enriched with the progress of culture, we may eventually look for a more generous fruition.

Canadian art has hitherto been imitative, rather than creative, tho of late years, as the Chicago Exposition proved, Canadian artists **Art** have produced several pictures which show an individuality of expression, color, feeling and a knowledge of technique which illustrate the influence of study and experience in the best European schools, especially of Paris. The names of L. R. O'Brien, George Reid, Bell-Smith, Robert Harris, J. W. L. Forster, W. Brymner, and Miss Bell are among the most notable names of English Canadian artists. The Marquis of Lorne and the Princess Louise, during their residence in Canada, did much to stimulate a wider taste for art by the establishment of a Canadian academy, and the holding of annual exhibitions.

Self-government exists in the full sense of the term. At the base of the political structure lie those municipal institutions **Government** which, for completeness, are not excelled in any other country. It is in the enterprising province of Ontario that the system has attained its greatest development. The machinery of these municipalities is used in Ontario to raise the taxes necessary for the support of public schools. Free libraries can be provided in every municipality whenever the majority of the taxpayers choose. Then we go up higher to the provincial organizations governed by a lieutenant-governor, nominated and removable by the government of the Dominion, and advised by a council responsible to the people's representatives, with a legislature composed, in only two of the provinces, of two houses—a council appointed by the Crown, and an elective assembly; in all the other provinces, there is simply an assembly chosen by the people on a very liberal franchise. manhood suffrage in the majority of cases. The fundamental law, or the British North America Act of 1867, gives jurisdiction to the provincial governments over administration of justice (except in criminal matters), municipal and all purely local affairs. In the territories, not yet constituted into provinces, there is a small elective body or house who select a financial committee to assist the lieutenant-governor. These territories are also represented in the two houses of the Dominion Parliament. The central or general government of the Dominion is administered by a governor-general, with the assistance of a ministry responsible to a Parliament, composed of a

---

* In 1900 there were 1,100,000.

Senate appointed by the Crown, and a House of Commons elected under an electoral franchise, practically on the very threshold of universal suffrage. This government has jurisdiction over trade and commerce, post-office, militia and defense, navigation and shipping, fisheries, railways, and public works of a Dominion character, and all other matters of a general or national import. Education is under the control of the provincial governments, but the rights and privileges of a religious minority with respect to separate or denominational schools are protected by the Constitution. The common law of England prevails in all the provinces except in French Canada, where the civil law still exists. The criminal law of England obtains throughout the Dominion. The central government appoints all the judges, who are irremovable, except for cause. Altho the Constitution places in the central government the residue of all powers, not expressly given to the provincial authorities; conflicts of jurisdiction are constantly arising between the general and local governments. Such questions, however, are being gradually settled by the decisions of the courts—the chief security of a written constitution—altho at times the rivalry of parties and the antagonisms of distinct nationalities and creeds tend to give special importance to certain educational and other matters which arise in the operation of the Constitution. All these are perils inseparable from a federal constitution governing two distinct races.

The appointment of the governor-general by the Crown, the power of disallowing bills which may interfere with imperial obligations, and the right which Canadians still enjoy of appealing to the judicial committee of the monarch's Privy Council from the subordinate courts of the provinces, including the Supreme Court of Canada; the obligation which rests upon England to assist the colony in the time of danger by all the power of her army and fleet, together with the fact that all treaties with foreign powers must be necessarily negotiated through the imperial authorities, will be considered as the most patent evidences of Canada being still a dependency of the Empire. Even the restraint imposed upon Canada with respect to any matters involving negotiations with foreign powers has been modified to a great degree, by the fact that England has acknowledged for over thirty years that Canada should be not only consulted in every particular, but actually represented in all negotiations that

A Dependency of the Empire

may be carried on with foreign powers affecting her commercial or territorial interests. A notable example of this new imperial policy was the Washington Convention of 1871, which settled the Alabama Claims and other questions of difference between the United States and Canada. England recognized the direct interest of the Dominion in the subjects under discussion, by the selection of the able Premier of the Liberal-Conservative government, Sir John Macdonald, as one of the commissioners. The most satisfactory result of this conference was the appointment of a commission which, after full deliberation, gave Canada and Newfoundland a compensation of five millions and a half of dollars for certain concessions that were made to the United States on the valuable fishing grounds of British North America. In the diplomatic discussions between England and the United States as a sequence of the seizure of Canadian vessels engaged in catching seals in the open waters of Bering Sea, the English Government was largely influenced by the opinions of the Canadian ministry in relation to a matter affecting Dominion interests.

One of the members of the court of arbitration, which assembled at Paris in 1892, and decided the question at issue in accordance with the principles of international law, fought for by the British and Canadian governments, was Sir John Thompson, an able lawyer of Nova Scotia, who became Premier of the Dominion soon after the death of Sir John Macdonald, and was himself struck down only a few months after the settlement of the Bering Sea question, when summoned to Windsor Castle to take before the Queen the oath of a privy councillor of England—a dramatic close to a short tho exceptionally successful career.

Sir John Macdonald

It was an imperial man of war that brought the remains of Sir John Thompson to the city of Halifax, where representatives of all parts of Canada buried him with honors which few statesmen have ever received. This tribute of respect was due to a Canadian statesman whose appointment on the Paris arbitration commission was a direct acknowledgment of the importance of Canada in imperial councils. With the national development of Canada the conditions of the relations between England and Canada are such as to insure unity of policy so long as each government considers the interests of England and of the dependency as identical, and keeps ever in view the obligations, welfare, and unity of the Empire at large.

ADDRESSES

CONFEDERATION *

By Hon. George Brown

[In the Canadian Parliament, on the Confederation of the Provinces of British North America.]

One hundred years have passed away since the conquest of Quebec, but here we sit, the children of the victor and the vanquished, all avowing hearty attachment to the British Crown, all earnestly deliberating how we shall best extend the blessings of British institutions; how a great people may be established on this continent, in close and hearty connection with Great Britain. Where, sir, in the page of history, shall we find a parallel to this? Will it not stand as an imperishable monument to the generosity of British rule? And it is not in Canada alone that this scene has been witnessed. Four other colonies are at this moment occupied as we are—declaring their hearty love for the parent State, and deliberating with us how they may best discharge the great duty entrusted to their hands, and give their aid in developing the teeming resources of these vast possessions.

And well, Mr. Speaker, may the work we have unitedly proposed rouse the ambition and energy of every true man in British America. Look, sir, at the map of the continent of America. Newfoundland, commanding the mouth of the noble river that almost cuts our continent in twain, is equal in extent to the Kingdom of Portugal. Cross the straits to the mainland, and you touch the hospitable shores of Nova Scotia, a country as large as the Kingdom of Greece. Then mark the sister Province of New Brunswick—equal in extent to Denmark and Switzerland combined. Pass up the St. Lawrence to Lower Canada—a country as large as France. Pass on to Upper Canada —twenty thousand square miles larger than Great Britain and Ireland put together. Cross over the continent to the shores of the Pacific, and you are in British Columbia, the land of golden promise—equal in extent to the Austrian Empire. I speak not now of the vast Indian territories that lie between, greater in extent than the whole soil of Russia—and that will, ere long, I trust, be opened up to civilization, under the auspices of the British American Confederation. Well, sir, the bold scheme in your hands is nothing less than to gather all these countries into one; to organize them under one government, with the protection of the British flag, and in heartiest sympathy and affection with our fellow-subjects in the land that gave us birth. Our scheme is to establish a government that will seek to turn the tide of immigration into this northern half of the American continent; that will strive to develop its great national resources, and that will endeavor to maintain liberty, and justice, and Christianity throughout the land.

What we propose now is but to lay the foundations of the structure, to set in motion the governmental machinery that will, one day, we trust, extend from the Atlantic to the Pacific. And we take especial credit to ourselves, that the system we have devised, while admirably adapted to our present situation, is capable of gradual and efficient expansion in future years to meet all the purposes contemplated by our scheme. But, if honorable gentlemen will recall to mind, that when the United States seceded from the Mother Country, and for many years afterwards, their population was not nearly equal to ours at the present moment, that their internal improvements did not then approach to what we have already attained; and that their trade and commerce was not a third of what ours has already reached, I think they will see that the fulfilment of our hopes may not be so very remote, as at first sight might be imagined. And they will be strengthened in that conviction, if they remember that what we propose to do is to be done with cordial sympathy and assistance of that great Power, of which it is our happiness to form a part.

And, said I not rightly, Mr. Speaker, that such a scheme is well fitted to fire the ambition and rouse the energy of every member of this House? Does it not lift us above the petty politics of the past, and present to us high purposes and great interests, that may well call forth all the intellectual ability, and all the energy and enterprise to be found amongst us? I readily admit all the gravity of the question; and that it ought to be considered cautiously and thoroughly before adoption. Far be it from me to deprecate the closest criticisms, or to doubt for a moment the sincerity or patriotism of those who feel it their duty to oppose the measure. But in considering a question on which hangs the future destiny of half a continent, ought not the spirit of mere fault-finding to be hushed? Ought not the spirit of mere partisanship to be banished from our debates? Ought we not to sit down and discuss the arguments presented, in the earnest and candid spirit of men, bound by the same interest, seeking a common end, and loving the same country?

Some honorable gentlemen seem to imagine that the members of the Government have

* PATRIOTIC RECITATIONS, p. 141, by George W. Ross, LL.D. Toronto: Warwick Bro's & Rutter.

a deeper interest in this scheme than others; but what possible interest can any of us have, except that which we share with every citizen of the land? What risk does any one run from this measure, in which all of us do not fully participate? What possible inducement could we have to urge this scheme, except our earnest and heartfelt conviction that it will conduce to the solid and lasting advantages of our country? There is one consideration, Mr. Speaker, which cannot be banished from this discussion, and that ought, I think, to be remembered in every word we utter; it is that the constitutional system of Canada cannot remain as it is now. Something must be done. We cannot stand still. We cannot go back to chronic sectional hostility and discord—to a state of perpetual ministerial crisis. The events of the last eight months cannot be obliterated; the solemn admissions of men of all parties can never be erased. The claims of upper Canada must be met and met now. I say, then, that every one who raises his voice in hostility to this measure is bound to keep before him, when he speaks, all the perilous consequences of its rejection. I say, then, that no man who has a true regard for the well-being of Canada can give a vote against this scheme, unless he is prepared to offer, in amendment, some better remedy for the evils and injustice that have so long threatened the peace of our country.

Sir, the future destiny of these great Provinces may be affected, by the decision we are about to give, to an extent, which at this moment we may be unable to estimate. But, assuredly the welfare, for many years, of four millions of people hangs on our decision. Shall we then rise equal to the occasion? Shall we approach this discussion without partisanship, and free from every personal feeling, but the earnest resolution to discharge, conscientiously, the duty which an overruling Providence has placed upon us? Sir, It may be that some among us may live to see the day when, as the result of this measure, a great and powerful people shall have grown up in these lands: when the boundless forest all around us shall have given way to smiling fields and thriving towns, and when one united government, under the British flag, shall extend from shore to shore; but who could desire to see that day, if he could not recall with satisfaction the part he took in this discussion? Mr. Speaker, I have done. I leave the subject to the conscientious judgment of the House, in the confident expectation and belief that the decision it will render will be worthy of the Parliament of Canada.

CANADA AND THE UNITED STATES

By Joseph Howe

We are here to determine how best we can draw together, in the bonds of peace, friendship, and commercial prosperity, the three great branches of the British family. In the presence of this great theme all petty interests should stand rebuked. We are not dealing with the concerns of a city, a province or a state, but with the future of our race in all time to come.

Why should not these three great branches of the family flourish, under different systems of government, it may be, but forming one grand whole, proud of a common origin and of their advanced civilization? The clover lifts its trefoil leaves to the evening dew, yet they draw their nourishment from a single stem. Thus distinct, and yet united, let us live and flourish. Why should we not? For nearly two thousand years we were one family. Our fathers fought side by side at Hastings, and heard the curfew toll. They fought in the same ranks for the sepulcher of our Savior. In the earlier and later civil wars, we can wear our white and red roses without a blush, and glory in the principles those conflicts established. Our common ancestors won the great Charter and the Bill of Rights—established free parliaments, the habeas corpus, and trial by jury. Our jurisprudence comes down from Coke and Mansfield to Marshall and Story, rich in knowledge and experience which no man can divide. From Chaucer to Shakespeare our literature is a common inheritance. Tennyson and Longfellow write in one language, which is enriched by the genius developed on either side of the Atlantic. In the great navigators from Cortereal to Hudson, and in all their "moving accidents by flood and field" we have a common interest.

.   .   .   .   .   .

But it may be said we have been divided by two wars. What then? The noble St. Lawrence is split in two places—by Goat Island and Anticosti—but it comes down to us from the same springs in the same mountain sides; its waters sweep together past the pictured rocks of Lake Superior, and encircle in their loving embrace the shores of Huron and Michigan. They are divided at Niagara Falls as we were at the Revolutionary War, but they come together again on the peaceful bosom of Ontario. Again they are divided on their passage to the sea; but who thinks of divisions when they lift the keels of commerce, or when, drawn up to Heaven, they form the rainbow or the cloud? It is true that in eighty-five years we have had two wars—but what then? Since the last we have had fifty years of peace, and there have been more people killed in a single campaign in the late civil war than there were in the two national wars between this country and Great Britain. The people of the United States hope to draw together the two conflicting elements and make them one people. In that task I wish them God-speed! And in the same way I feel that we ought to rule out everything disagreeable in the recollection of our old wars, and unite together as one people for all time to come. I see around the door the flags of the two countries. United as they are there, I would have them draped together, fold within fold, and let

" Their varying tints unite,
And form in Heaven's light,
One arch of peace."

SUGGESTIVE THOUGHTS

ADVANTAGES, Natural.—A single glance at an ordinary school geography shows Canada to be one of the most favored portions of the globe; and as if Providence had kept in reserve its best gifts for this latest born of nations, we have, wafted into our spacious western harbors and along our picturesque Pacific coast, the balmy winds of the Western Ocean, and with them that ocean stream which makes flowers bloom and trees bud near the Arctic circle, as early as on the Mississippi or the St. Lawrence, just as the great stream poured out by the Mexican Gulf foils the Ice King's blockade of the magnificent harbors of our Eastern coasts, and nourishes those deep-sea pastures of which Canada possesses the richest in the world. As a means of access to the interior of this favored land, Nature has cleft our rugged Eastern coast with mighty rivers and great lakes which bear the home hunter to the verge of our great Cereal Table-land, where, through future wheat fields, turn and wind the rivers of the great plain, the Red, Assiniboine, Souris, Qu'Appelle, and Saskatchewan.

This great country bounded by three oceans has the greatest extent of coast line; the greatest number of miles of river and lake navigation; the greatest extent of coniferous forest; the greatest coal measures; the most varied distribution of precious and economic minerals; the most extensive salt and fresh water fisheries; and the greatest extent of arable and pastoral land of any country in the world.—JOHN SCHULTZ.

ADVANTAGES, Racial.—This great northern heritage so vast in area and resources and which we call our own country, is possessed by a northern race and ruled by a northern monarch. Its national characteristics are northern, it is the Norland of this continent; to the northern races of the old world whence we sprang we look for our national characteristics.

We have in this Dominion more Celts than had Brian when he placed his heel on the neck of Odin, more Saxons than had Alfred when he founded his kingdom, more Normans than had William when he drew from them the armed host with which he invaded England, more of Norse blood than there were Norsemen when their kings ruled Britain and their galleys swept the sea. We are the descendants of all the northern kingdom-founders of Western Europe. We have the laws of Edward, the Magna Charta and the Roman Code; we have copied the Constitution which English statesmen, legislators, patriots, and martyrs lived or died to secure and save. We have resources by sea and land, civil and religious liberty; we are heirs equally with those who live in the British Isles, to the glory and traditions of the British Empire. Canadians have fought side by side with the Englishman, Irishman, and Scot on the burning sands of India and Africa, and on the bleak battlefields of the Crimean Peninsula, and they have died as bravely, too, as any of them.—JOHN SCHULTZ.

CANADA, Future of.—What can we say as to our future? What of our destiny? Our destiny under a kind Providence will be just what we will make it. It rests in our own hands. We may in the face of all our advantages, mar it if we will. As it is with individual destiny, so is it with national destiny; we are largely the architects of our own fortunes. We have laid, as I have shown, deep and safe and broad the foundations for a bright future. What country can show legislation more advanced or leading up to better results than ours? In what land do we find a people enjoying more fully than we do the rights of self-government, or where is there a people more fitted to be entrusted with that precious right? Our laws have been well administered. Our courts of justice have won the unlimited confidence of the people. Imbued with the healthy sentiment which has prevailed in ' the mother land for centuries, attached to her forms of government, cherishing her precedents and traditions, we have passed from childhood to youth. We are approaching manhood, and its strength and vigor must depend upon ourselves. What is needed, then? We must appease inter-provincial jealousies; we must modify mere local patriotism; we must cultivate an increased national feeling and show in every way we can that we have crossed the line of youth and pupilage.—RICHARD HARCOURT.

CANADA, Loyalty to.—Let us remember that Canada is our home; that while we think with gratitude of the land of our birth, while our hearts are filled with the warmest patriotism when its history and its heroes are recalled to mind, we should not forget that we have great duties and responsibilities, not of a sectional, but of a national, character to discharge and that we ought to devote ourselves faithfully and honestly to the task of creating and upholding a Canadian spirit, Canadian sentiment, and Canadian enthusiasm; in a word, a spirit of nationality always British, but still Canadian. The patriotism of the British people and government will ever be with us, and we in turn hope always to reside under the shadow of the grand old flag of Britain, at once the symbol of power and civilization. These sentiments I believe to be an expression of the aspirations which animate the great body—may I not say the whole of the Canadian people.—ALEXANDER MACKENZIE.

CANADA, Progress of.—While with just pride we remember the deeds of our ancestors for the past thousand years, and know that when necessary the blood of the sea-kings, the sturdy Saxon, the gallant Norman, and the fiery Celt, which is in our veins, will assert itself again, yet thanks be to Almighty God, our national life began and has continued in peace; and as we chose for our national emblems the Canadian beaver and the maple leaf, so have we sought to build up, harmonize, and beautify our splendid heritage by the arts of peace and not by the arts of war. During the short period, less than a quarter of a century, of our national life, we have girded the continent with bands of steel, piercing mountains, spanning torrents; and crossing the snow-capped giants of the Rocky and Selkirk chains we have linked our young Canadian empire to Japan and China, the oldest empires of the Orient. We have justified our traditions on the sea, in making Canada third in rank of the maritime nations of the world; and at this moment the sails of Canadian ships whiten every sea, commanded by Canadian descendants of Drake and Hawkins, Frobisher and Richard Grenville, Nelson and Collingwood, Cartier and D'Iberville. Better still than even this material progress is the fact that our nationality is founded upon the mutual respect and confidence of the people, surrounded by the sanctity of religion, and crowned with its only appropriate capital, Lawful Constitutional Authority.—JOHN SCHULTZ.

CANADA'S DIFFICULTIES.—We have to contend with political difficulties consequent upon our singular semi-dependent position as a small state between two very great ones, with both of which we have very close relations; with geographical difficulties caused by the great stretches of barren wilderness interposed between the three great divisions of our territory—which have often caused me to wish we lived rather in three islands, with the sea as a means of connection and communication; with national or race difficulties, arising from the circumstances of our early settlement, and lastly with economical difficulties, partly natural and partly of our own making, but none the less real, notwithstanding. What we need, and we need it very badly, is more public spirit—a larger share of the true instinct of patriotism—and to become thoroughly im-

pregnated with the feelings which inspired that well-known passage of Sir Walter Scott:

" Breathes there a man with soul so dead
Who never to himself hath said,
This is my own—my native land?
If such there be, go mark him well,
For him no minstrel numbers swell;
High tho his title, proud his name,
Boundless his wealth as wish can claim,
The wretch concentered all in self,
Living shall forfeit all renown,
And doubly dying shall go down
To the vile dust from which he sprung—
Unwept, unhonored, and unsung."
SIR RICHARD CARTWRIGHT.

CANADIAN POWER, Sources of.—The country you call Canada, and which your sons and your children's children will be proud to know by that name, is a land which will be a land of power among the nations. Mistress of a zone of territory favorable for the maintenance of a numerous and homogeneous white population, Canada must, to judge from the increase in her strength during the past, and from the many and vast opportunities for the growth of that strength in her new provinces in the future, be great and worthy her position on the earth. Affording the best and safest highway between Asia and Europe, she will see traffic from both directed to her coasts. With a hand upon either ocean, he will gather from each for the benefit of her hardy millions a large share of the commerce of the world. To the east and to the west she will pour forth of her abundance, her treasures of food and the riches of her mines and of her forests, demanded of her by the less fortunate of mankind. In no other land have the last seventeen years, the space of time which has elapsed since your Federation, witnessed such progress. Other countries have seen their territories enlarged and their destinies determined by trouble and war, but no blood has stained the bonds which have knit together your free and order-loving populations, and yet in this brief period, so brief in the life of a nation, you have attained to a union whose characteristics from sea to sea are the same. A judicature above suspicion, a strong central government to direct all national interests, the toleration of all faiths with favor to none, a franchise recognizing the rights of labor by the exclusion only of the idler, a government ever susceptible to the change of public opinion and ever open, through a responsible ministry, to the scrutiny of the people—these are the features of your rising power.—LORD LORNE.

CIVILIZATIONS, Canada's Two.—To the political and historical student, probably the chief interest of Canada lies in the existence, side by side, of two civilizations of different types,—French speaking Quebec with its racial peculiarities, its people devotedly attached to their own language, laws, and literature, and their own religious traditions and forms, wedged in between the English speaking maritime provinces on the one side and Ontario and the great west on the other.

Will gradual fusion take place between those widely sundered elements and a nation be formed combining the best qualities of both, as Norman, Saxon, and Cymri fused in England, Teuton, Norseman and Celt in Scotland, and equally composite elements in Ireland? Oracles gloomily predict political strife, ending some day in open conflict, and possibly with not a few of these, the wish is father to the thought; but careful students of our actual development during the last fifty years—the period in which both races have worked together harmoniously in provincial and federal affairs, since their emancipation from the Colonial office—take a very different view. They entertain no doubts concerning our future. The interaction of the two elements gives distinctive color to our national life. To despair of a peaceful solution of the problem, on a continent where English speech and constitutional forms are so overwhelmingly predominant, argues astonishing lack of faith in our own ideals and moral forces and in the far reaching results of free institutions.—Principal G. M. Grant, LL.D.

COMMERCIAL RELATIONS, Anglo-Canadian.—In discussing the commercial relations of Canada and Great Britain, Mr. George W. Ross, the Ontario Premier, said: " If the Canadian seller in the British market had a preference of ten per cent. or even five per cent. over the United States seller, the effect upon Canadian trade would be simply incalculable. Apply it to the millions of bushels of wheat which England buys with which to feed her subjects, and let the Canadian agriculturist on the prairie feel that he has the advantage over the United States agriculturist, then you would speedily see your prairies filled with a teeming population, and the wheat trade of America change its course. The same would apply to the products of our forests and our mines. I hope such a preference may some day be given to us, altho British statesmen as yet have not shown any disposition to consider it seriously. I know of nothing Britain could do that would be more helpful to us in building up Canada, and strengthening the relations between us and the Mother Country."—C. Y. B. (1900).

EPOCHS, Heroic.—Canada has had heroic epochs of different kinds in the course of her development. Parkman describes those of the old or French régime, from the time of Champlain to the day when Wolfe and Montcalm fell on one battlefield behind the old city founded by Champlain. Stories crowd his glowing pages concerning adventurous explorers, Indian ambuscades, and horrors, infantile faith, and splendid martyrdoms of Jesuit and Recollet fathers, and wars waged against the British, and British colonists on sea, lake, land, and river.—Principal G. M. Grant, LL.D.

EPOCHS, Historic.—The real history of Canada begins with the Peace of Paris, when France withdrew from the long conflict waged for " a few arpents of snow," in 1763,

when practically the whole of the North American continent was handed over to Great Britain, to be developed under a freer air than Latin civilization breathed at home or permitted abroad. In the very next decade came the schism of the British race, with the vain struggle of the revolutionists to win or to conquer Canada, a struggle repeated with overwhelming numbers through successive campaigns in 1812-15 and then defeated still more decisively. But that which makes the true life of a nation is to be found not only in the stirring events of war but in the piping times of peace. In our case, it should be looked for in the unrecorded privations endured by the United Empire Loyalists, while they hewed out, from the forest primeval, farms for their children, and in similar work done by hearts of oak from the highlands of Scotland, by Irish peasants and English gentlemen and laborers, by hardy fisher folk on the lower St. Lawrence and the Atlantic coast, by lumbermen in the backwoods and by recent pioneers to the prairies of the great Northwest and the mountain ranges of British Columbia. In the lives of those emigrants amid strange surroundings; in their struggles with isolation, poverty, and a winter sterner than they had ever known before; in the experiences of their children who as sons of the soil readily adapted themselves to its conditions; in the formation by them of infant settlements which have developed into prosperous communities; in the growth of municipal life and the struggles for constitutional freedom, until, in 1867, Canada rose to be a confederation of Provinces which soon after extended from ocean to ocean, and in its subsequent expansion into its present assured position of junior partnership in the Empire,—our true history is to be found.—Principal G. M. Grant, LL.D.

GOVERNMENT, Canada's.—You possess the best form of government with which any historical nation has ever been blessed. The excellency of the British Constitution, with the self-expanding energies it embodies, is an ancient story which I need not insist upon, but as there are always external forces which disturb the working of the most perfect mechanism, so in an old country like England, many influences exist to trouble the harmonious operations of the political machine; but here our Constitution has been set agoing entirely disencumbered of those entanglements which traditional prejudices and social complications have given birth to at home. My advice to you, then, would be to guard and cherish the characteristics of your Constitution with a sleepless vigilance. —Lord Dufferin.

GOVERNMENT, Canada's.—It is common for us to hear of that great experiment in government in which the vast republic near us is engaged. But in the Provinces of British North America we have an experiment going on, of no light interest to our glorious mother country, or to mankind. We occupy a particular and somewhat critical position on this continent, and more than we can foresee may probably depend upon the manner in which our descendants may be able to sustain themselves in it. It will be their part, as it is now ours, to demonstrate that all such freedom of action as is consistent with rational liberty, with public peace, and with individual security, can be enjoyed under a constitutional monarchy as fully as under the purest democracy on earth; to prove that, in proportion as intelligence increases, what is meant by liberty is better understood, and what is soundest and most stable in government is better appreciated and more firmly supported. The glorious career of Britain among the nations of the world, demands of us this tribute to the tried excellence of her admirable Constitution; it should be our pride to show that, far removed as we are from the splendors of Royalty and the influences of the Court, monarchy is not blindly preferred among us from a senseless attachment to antiquated prejudices, nor reluctantly tolerated from a sense of duty or a dread of change; but that, on the contrary, it is cherished in the affections, and supported by the free and firm will of an intelligent people, whose love of order has been strengthened as their knowledge has increased—a people who regard with loyal pleasure the obligations of duty which bind them to the Crown, and who value their kingly form of government not only because they believe it to be the most favorable to stability and peace, but especially for the security it affords to life and property, the steady support which it gives to the laws, and the certainty with which it ensures the actual enjoyment of all that deserves to be dignified with the name " Freedom."— Sir John Beverly Robinson.

IMMIGRATION.—The reason why we have not hitherto attracted and retained more people in Canada from the other side of the Atlantic, is because we have not made our country attractive to them; because we are not known as a nation abroad; because these isolated Provinces have not impressed the imagination of the emigrating classes. Who in the byways of Germany, or even of Britain, knew anything of Canada, until the other day? In those hives of human labor, they knew only one country—America —and only one seaport—New York. But once give our united Provinces the aspect of empire, make them a power and a name, and the reputation and credit of the Dominion will be our best emigration agent abroad. . . . I cannot, for one, agree that the best way to make ourselves respected abroad, and to secure impunity from attack, is to depreciate the sources of our strength; but rather to make the most of what Lord Bacon, in his True Greatness of Britain, considers the main element of a nation's strength, its " breed of men." By the breed of men, that brings a nation safely through its destinies, Lord Bacon meant—not only the muscle of men, their bodily hardihood, but also their *morale*—their courage, docility, and capacity

for combination—the wisdom of the few to command, and the wisdom of the many to cooperate. I do not disparage the power of numbers; I do not underrate the power of wealth; but above both I place the safety of any state, great or small, in the spirit and unity of its inhabitants.

The policy of self-abasement I cannot see in the light of policy at all. View it how we may; turn it round and round; hang it in any light you like, it will not wear the lineaments of prudence, or fortitude or patriotism. While we should, on the one hand, avoid all bravado as unbecoming our position, we should, on the other hand, endeavor to elevate and not depress the public spirit of the country. We should strengthen the faith of our people in their own future, the faith of every Canadian in Canada, and of every Province in its sister Province. This faith wrongs no one; burdens no one; menaces no one; dishonors no one; and, as it was said of old, faith moves mountains, so I venture reverently to express my own belief, that if the difficulties of our future as a Dominion were as high as the peaks of the Alps or Andes, yet that the pure patriotic faith of a united people would be all sufficient to overcome and ultimately, to triumph over all such difficulties.—Hon. D'Arcy McGee.

IMPERIALISM, The Future of.—Canadians can do a great service to the Empire and to humanity by throwing all their influence on the side of restraint; holding themselves ready to take their fair share in the defense of the Empire, but doing all that they honorably can to preserve peace; allying themselves with the sober patriotism of the United Kingdom, not suffering themselves to dance to any tune that the London music halls may play, and being exceedingly careful that the growth of power is not accompanied by the growth of a domineering spirit. Great are the sacrifices that have been made on the battlefields of South Africa; yet there is probably no more valuable service that has been rendered to the Empire than the maintenance of good relations with the United States, without loss of national self-respect, and the maintenance of good relations between French Canadians and people of British descent in Canada. If we were continually quarreling with our neighbors we should be a burden and a source of anxiety instead of a source of comfort to the Empire. So it would be if we were continually quarreling with our French-Canadian fellow-citizens, and continually appealing to England to settle our disputes. On the whole, and making allowance for some little outbreaks of irritation, we have avoided these mistakes. We have achieved such a settlement of the race question that it is looked upon as the ideal of all who are working for the reconciliation of Dutch and English in South Africa. When once that reconciliation is accomplished it will be regarded as a triumph of statesmanship, and any man who would wantonly imperil it would be branded not only as a reckless demagog, but as a traitor to his country. In the desire for new achievements in Imperialism, it will be wise not to lose sight of what has already been done in the building up of a free and united Canada.—JOHN LEWIS. (Can. M.)

INDIES, Canada the Northwest Passage to the.—The supposed existence of a northwest passage to the Indies was the dream that allured hardy navigators who believed in the earth's rotundity but had not the data for determining its size. In our day it has been found that that great northwest passage is not by sea or river but by land. We have discovered that the shortest way from the old world to the world of Japan and China. is across Canada, and therefore Canada feels herself now to be the link between old Europe and the older East and also the link between the three great self-governing parts of the British Empire.—PRINCIPAL GRANT.

LOYALTY TO THE OLD COUNTRY.—Quebec has a Valhalla of departed heroes distinctly its own; yet still it does not turn its back upon the older France, but lives in the past, inspired by its spirit to work out the problem of a new nationality in its own way. There is no more patriotic Canadian than the Frenchman, and he is also the proudest of his origin and race. There is nothing, then, to forbid the English-speaking Canadian from revering the country of his fathers, be it England, Scotland, or Ireland; on the contrary, it may be laid down as a national maxim, that the unpatriotic Englishman, Scot, or Irishman. will be sure to prove a very inferior specimen of the Canadian.—W. J. RATTRAY.

LUNDY'S LANE, The Battle of.—The Battle of Lundy's Lane marks an epoch in Canadian history, and an epoch of which all Canadians are proud. The battle occurred on the evening of the 25th of July, 1814, and resulted in a decisive victory for the Canadian and British forces. The contest raged for four hours; at one time the Americans gained a slight advantage and captured (for a brief period only) a few of our guns. Before midnight the guns were recaptured, the enemy were in full retreat, and the Canadian forces held possession of the field. The anniversary of the Battle of Lundy's Lane is celebrated each year with becoming ceremony, and in fact the celebration is attracting more attention as time goes on.—C. Y. B. (1900).

PIONEERS, The.—He must have a dull and sluggish soul, who can look without emotion on the quiet graves of the early settlers of this country. who can tread upon their moldering bones without a thought of their privations and their toils, who can, from their tombs, look out upon the rural loveliness—the fruitfulness and peace by which he is surrounded, nor drop a tear to the memories of the dead, who won, by the stoutness of their hearts, and the sweat of their brows, the blessings their children have only to cherish and enjoy. They plunged into the forest, not as we do now, for a summer day's ramble, or an hour of tranquil musing, but to win a home from the ruggedness of uncultivated nature, and in despite of the dusky savage thirsting for their blood. Oh! for the muse of Gray to pour out a befitting tribute to the dead.—JOSEPH HOWE.

POLITICAL DEVELOPMENT OF CANADA.—Our political evolution has had the same lesson for us. It has taught us to borrow ideas with equal impartiality from sources apparently opposite. We have borrowed the federal idea from the United States, and our parliamentary and judicial systems from Britain, and so we have formed a Constitution better than that which either the mother country or the older daughter enjoys. At any rate, we made it ourselves and it fits us; and we have thus been taught that ideas belong to no one people, that they are the common property of mankind, and that we should borrow new thoughts from every country that has found by experiment that they will work well.—PRINCIPAL GRANT.

QUEEN, Canadian Attachment to the.—Our attachment to the Queen, our own Victoria, is mingled with a tenderness not inconsistent with the sterner sentiment which it softens and embellishes without enervating. Let her legitimate authority as a constitutional monarch; let her reputation as a woman be assailed, and notwithstanding the lamentation of Burke, that the age of chivalry was past, thousands of swords would leap from their scabbards to avenge her. Ay, and they would be drawn as freely, and wielded as vigorously and bravely in Canada—in Nova Scotia—as in England. Loyalty! love of British institutions! They are engrafted in our very nature; they are part and parcel of ourselves; and I can no more tear them from my heart even if I would, and lacerate all its fibers, than I would sever a limb from my body. And what are those institutions? A distinguished American statesman recently answered this question. He said: "The proudest government that exists upon the face of the earth is that of Great Britain, and the great Pitt her proudest statesman, when he would tell of Britain's crowning glory—did not speak as he might have done, of her widespread Dominion, upon which the sun never sets. He did not speak of martial achievements, of glorious battlefields, and of splendid naval conflicts; but he said, with swelling breast, and kindling eye, that the poorest man of Great Britain in his cottage might bid defiance to all the forces of the Crown. It might be frail, its roof might shake, the wind might blow through it, the storm might enter, the rain might enter; but the King of England could not enter it. In all his power he dare not cross the threshold of that ruined tenement."—SIR WILLIAM YOUNG.

RELIGIOUS DEVELOPMENT.—Our religious evolution has taught us the same thing. We have been enabled to accomplish a measure of religious unification greater than either the mother land or the United States has found possible. Eighteen years ago, for instance, all the Presbyterian denominations united into one Church, wide as the Dominion of Canada. Immediately thereafter the Methodist Churches took the same step, and this very month the Anglicans are doing likewise. Still farther, these great Protestant Churches have appointed committees to see whether it is not possible to have a wider union, and the young life of Canada says " Amen" to the proposal.—PRINCIPAL GRANT.

SLAVERY.—Slavery was gradually extinguished in Upper Canada by an act of the Legislature passed July 9, 1793, but slavery still existed in York on March 1, 1811.—C. Y. B. (1900).

TRADE, Increase of.—In 1868 the total exports amounted to $57,567,888, the total imports to $73,459,644, the grand total being $131,027, 532. In 1899 the exports amounted to $158,896,905, the total imports to $162,764,308, the grand total being $321,661,213.—C. Y. B. (1900).

UNITY, Canadian.—We are here a nation, composed of the most heterogeneous elements—Protestants and Catholics, English, French, German, Irish, Scotch, every one, let it be remembered, with his traditions, with his prejudices. In each of these conflicting antagonistic elements, however, there is a common spot of patriotism, and the only true policy is that which reaches that common patriotism and makes it vibrate in all toward common ends and common aspirations.—WILFRID LAURIER.

POETRY

Annapolis Royal

BY EDWARD BLACKADDER

I loiter here within this ancient town—
Long time agone the rising hope of France,
The seed of future empire—as in trance,
'Mid storied scenes, I wander up and down.

Here are the grass-grown walls which bore the frown
Of death-disgorging cannon long ago,
And wide the gleaming basin gleams below,
Where thunder-bearing ships no more are known.

Yea, death hath reaped its harvest in this place;
Along these shores have hundreds bled and died
To save this jewel for the Gallic crown.
Stern fate ordained it for another race:
The sturdy Saxon tills yon meadows wide;
Peace rules o'er all; war's trumpet sleeps unblown.

Our Beautiful Land

BY HELEN M. JOHNSON

What land more beautiful than ours?
What other land more blest?
The South with all its wealth of flowers?
The prairies of the West?

O no! there's not a fairer land
Beneath Heaven's azure dome—
Where Peace holds Plenty by the hand,
And Freedom finds a home.

The slave who but her name hath heard,
Repeats it day and night;—
And envies every little bird
That takes its northward flight!

As to the Polar star they turn
Who brave a pathless sea,—
So the oppressed in secret yearn,
Dear native land for thee!

How many loving memories throng
Round Britain's stormy coast!
Renowned in story and in song,
Her glory is our boast!

With loyal hearts we still abide
Beneath her sheltering wing;—
While with true patriot love and pride
To Canada we cling!

We wear no haughty tyrant's chain,—
We bend no servile knee,
When to the mistress of the main
We pledge our fealty.

She binds us with the cords of love,—
All others we disown;
The rights we owe to God above
We yield to Him alone.

May He our future course direct
By His unerring hand;
Our laws and liberties protect,
And bless our native land!

Canada

BY CHARLES G. D. ROBERTS

O Child of Nations, giant-limbed,
Who stand'st among the nations now
Unheeded, unadorned, unhymned,
With unanointed brow,

How long the ignoble sloth, how long
The trust in greatness not thy own?
Surely the lion's brood is strong
To front the world alone!

How long the indolence ere thou dare
Achieve thy destiny, seize thy fame,
Ere our proud eyes behold thee bear
A nation's franchise, nation's name?

To Canada

By Charles G. D. Roberts

Awake, my country, the hour of dreams is
 done
Doubt not, nor dread the greatness of thy
 fate,
Tho faint souls fear the keen, confronting sun
And fain would bid the morn in splendor wait!
Tho dreamers wrapped in starry visions cry:
" Lo, yon thy future, yon thy faith, thy
 fame!"
And stretch vain hands to stars. Thy fame
 is nigh,
Here in Canadian hearth, and home and
 name;
This name which yet shall grow till all the
 nations know
Us for a patriot people, heart and hand,
Loyal to our native hearth, our native land.

Canadians, Awake

By A. M. Taylor

Ye sons of Canada, awake!
The star of morn has left the sky;
Your fathers' flag of victory,—
That glorious banner floats on high,
Earth is beneath and God above;
And human life is heavenly love;
Arise, young legions, onward move!

Ye sons of Canada, awake!
Protect the rights your sires have won!
The heritage of sire to son,
The Crown of Peace,—Hope's rising sun.
'Tis valor to adore the light;
'Tis honor to make free with might;
'Tis glory to establish right.

Ye sons of Canada, awake!
Stretch forth the mighty arm of toil;
Embattle, beautify the soil
Your fathers won by brave turmoil;
And, while your glory swells, behold
Your virgin empire still unfold
Her halcyon hope, her wealth untold.

Ye sons of Canada, awake!
Let Christian mercy shrine your heart;
Let vice and vanity depart;
The poor may fight their country's part;—
Extend the hand of brotherhood
To honest hearts and loyal blood,—
The truly brave are truly good.

Ye sons of Canada, awake!
While in your loyal bosoms, burns
The patriot's fire, the heart that warns,
That victory loves, that thraldom spurns,—
Bid those, who would oppress you, know
You dread not death, you fear no foe;—
Your swords are sharp, your bosoms true.

Ye sons of Canada, awake!
Behold the grass on which ye tread,
Behold the white stars overhead,
All labor for a common need.
'Tis sacred dust beneath your feet;
Your fathers' graves in memory sweet,
Their patriot spirits ever beat.

Arouse Ye, Brave Canadians

By J. D. Edgar

*Lines suggested by General Brock's stirring
appeal to the people of Upper Canada at
the opening of the war of 1812.*

Canadian arms are stout and strong,
 Canadian hearts are true;
Your homes were in the forest made,
 Where pine and maple grew.
A haughty foe is marching
 Your country to enthrall;
Arouse ye, brave Canadians,
 And answer to my call!

Let every man who swings an ax,
 Or follows at the plow,
Abandon farm and homestead,
 And grasp a rifle now!
We'll trust the God of Battles,
 Altho our force be small;
Arouse ye, brave Canadians,
 And answer to my call!

Let mothers, tho with breaking hearts,
 Give up their gallant sons;
Let maidens bid their lovers go,
 And wives their dearer ones!
Then rally to the frontier,
 And form a living wall;
Arouse ye, brave Canadians,
 And answer to my call!

Our Canadian Dominion

By Pamelia S. Vining

Fair land of peace! to Britain's rule and
 throne
Adherent still, yet happier than alone,
And free as happy, and as brave as free.
Proud are thy children,—justly proud, of
 thee;—
Thou hast no streams renowned in classic
 lore,
No vales where fable heroes moved of yore,
No hills where Poesy enraptured stood,
No mythic fountains, no enchanted wood;
But unadorned, rough, cold, and often stern,
The careless eye to other lands might turn,
And seek, where nature's bloom is more in-
 tense,
Softer delights to charm the eye of sense.

We cannot boast those skies of milder ray,
'Neath which the orange mellows day by
 day;
Where the Magnolia spreads her snowy flow-
 ers,
And Nature revels in perennial bowers;—
Here, Winter holds his long and solemn
 reign,
And madly sweeps the desolated plain;—
But Health and Vigor hail the wintry strife,
With all the buoyant glow of happy life;
And by the blazing chimney's cheerful
 hearth,
Smile at the blast 'mid songs and household
 mirth.

But we who know thee proudly point the hand
Where thy broad rivers roll serenely grand—
Where, in still beauty 'neath our northern sky,
Thy lordly lakes in solemn grandeur lie—
Where old Niagara's awful voice has given
The floods' deep anthem to the ear of Heaven—
Through the long ages of the vanished past;
Through summer's bloom and winter's angry blast,—
Nature's proud utterance of unwearied song,
Now, as at first, majestic, solemn, strong,
And ne'er to fail, till the archangel's cry
Shall still the million tones of earth and sky,
And send the shout to ocean's farthest shore:—
" Be hushed ye voices!—time shall be no more! "

Here, Freedom looks o'er all these broad domains,
And hears no heavy clank of servile chains;
Here man, no matter what his color be,
Can stand erect, and proudly say, " I'M FREE ! "—
No crouching slaves cower in our busy marts,
With straining eyes and anguish-riven hearts.

The beam that gilds alike the palace walls
And lowly hut, with genial radiance falls
On peer and peasant,—and the humblest here
Walks in the sunshine, free as is the peer.
Proudly he stands with muscle strong and free,
The serf—the slave of no man doomed to be.
His own, the arm the heavy ax that wields;
His own, the hands that till the summer fields;
His own, the babes that prattle in the door;
His own, the wife that treads the cottage floor;
All the sweet ties of life to him are sure;
All the proud rights of MANHOOD are secure.

Blest land of peace!—O may'st thou ever be
Even as now the land of LIBERTY!
Treading serenely thy bright upward road,
Honored of nations, and approved of God!
On thy fair front emblazoned clear and bright—
FREEDOM, FRATERNITY, AND EQUAL RIGHT!

Dominion Day

BY AGNES MAULE MACHAR

With loud huzzas and merry bells, and cannon's thundering peal,
And pennons fluttering on the breeze, and serried rows of steel,
We greet, again, the birthday morn of our young giant's land,
From the Atlantic stretching wide to far Pacific strand;
With flashing rivers, ocean lakes, and prairies wide and free,
And waterfalls and forests dim, and mountains by the sea;
A country on whose birth-hour smiled the genius of romance,

Above whose cradle brave hands waved the lily-cross of France;
Whose infancy was grimly nursed in peril, pain, and wo;
Whose gallant hearts found early graves beneath Canadian snow;
When savage raid and ambuscade and famine's sore distress,
Combined their strength, in vain, to crush the dauntless French noblesse;
When her dim, trackless forest lured, again and yet again,
From silken court of sunny France, her flower, the brave Champlain.
And now, her proud traditions boast four blazoned rolls of fame,—
Crecy's and Flodden's deadly foes our ancestors we claim;
Past feud and battle buried far behind the peaceful years,
While Gaul and Celt and Briton turn to pruning-hooks their spears;
Four nations welded into one,—with long historic past,
Have found in these our western wilds, one common life, at last;
Through the young giant's mighty limbs, that stretch from sea to sea,
There runs a throb of conscious life—of waking energy.
From Nova Scotia's misty coast to far Columbia's shore,
She wakes,—a band of scattered homes and colonies no more,
But a young nation, with her life full beating in her breast,
A noble future in her eyes—the Britain of the West.
Hers be the noble task to fill the yet untrodden plains
With fruitful, many-sided life that courses through her veins;
The English honor, nerve, and pluck,—the Scotsman's love of right,—
The grace and courtesy of France,—the Irish fancy bright,—
The Saxon's faithful love of home, and home's affection blest;
And, chief of all, our holy faith,—of all our treasures best.
A people poor in pomp and state, but rich in noble deeds,
Holding that righteousness exalts the people that it leads;
As yet the waxen mold is soft, the opening page is fair;
It rests with those who rule us now, to leave their impress there,—
The stamp of true nobility, high honor, stainless truth;
The earnest quest of noble ends; the generous heart of youth;
The love of country, soaring far above dull party strife;
The love of learning, art, and song,—the crowning grace of life;
The love of science, soaring far through Nature's hidden ways;
The love and fear of Nature's God,—a nation's highest praise.

So, in the long hereafter, this Canada shall
   be
The worthy heir of British power and British
   liberty;
Spreading the blessings of her sway to her
   remotest bounds,
While, with the fame of her fair name, a
   continent resounds.
True to her high traditions, to Britain's ancient glory
Of patient saint and martyr, alive in deathless story;
Strong in their liberty and truth, to shed
   from shore to shore
A light among the nations, till nations are
   no more.

Hurrah For the New Dominion

By A. McLachlan

Let others raise the song, in praise
   Of lands renown'd in story;
The land for me, of the maple tree,
   And the pine, in all his glory!

Hurrah! for the grand old forest land,
   Where Freedom spreads her pinion;
Hurrah! with me, for the maple tree,
   Hurrah! for the New Dominion!

Be hers the light, and hers the might,
   Which Liberty engenders;
Sons of the free, come join with me—
   Hurrah! for her defenders.

And be their fame in loud acclaim—
   In grateful songs ascending;
The fame of those, who met her foes,
   And died, her soil defending.

Hurrah! for the grand old forest land
   Where freedom spreads her pinion;
Hurrah! with me, for the maple tree,
   Hurrah! for the New Dominion!

Freedom's Journey

By Thomas D'Arcy McGee

Freedom! a nursling of the North,
   Rocked in the arms of stormy pines,
On fond adventure wander'd forth
   Where south the sun superbly shines;
The prospect shone so bright and fair,
She dreamt her home was there, was
   there.

She lodged 'neath many a gilded roof,
   They gave her praise in many a hall,
Their kindness checked the free reproof,
   Her heart dictated to let fall;
She heard the negro's helpless prayer,
And felt her home could not be there.

She sought through rich Savannah's green,
   And in the broad palmetto grove,
But where her altar should have been
   She found nor liberty nor love;
A cloud came o'er her forehead fair,
She found no shrine to Freedom there.

Back to her native scenes she turn'd,
   Back to the hardy, kindly North,
Where bright aloft the pole-star burned,
   Where stood her shrine by every hearth;
" Back to the North I will repair,"
   The Goddess cried, " my home is there."

Here's To the Land

By William Wye Smith

Here's to the land of the rock and the pine;
   Here's to the land of the raft and the
   river!
Here's to the land where the sunbeams shine,
   And the night that is bright with the
   north-light's quiver!

Here's to the land of the ax and the hoe!
   Here's to the stalwarts that give them
   their glory;—
With stroke upon stroke, and with blow upon
   blow,
   The might of the forest has passed into
   story!

Here's to the land with its blanket of
   snow;—
   To the hero and hunter the welcomest
   pillow!
Here's to the land where the stormy winds
   blow
   Three days, ere the mountains can talk to
   the billow!

Here's to the buckwheats that smoke on her
   board!
   Here's to the maple that sweetens their
   story;
Here's to the scythe that we swing like a
   sword,
   And here's to the fields where we gather
   our glory!

Here's to her hills of the moose and the
   deer;
   Here's to her forests, her fields, and her
   flowers!
Here's to her homes of unchangeable cheer,
   And the maid 'neath the shade of her own
   native bowers!

The Battle of La Prairie (1691)

By William D. Schuyler-Lighthall

That was a brave old epoch
   Our age of chivalry
When the Briton met the Frenchman
   At the fight of La Prairie;
And the manhood of New England,
   And the Netherlanders true
And Mohawks sworn, gave battle
   To the Bourbon's lilied blue.

That was a brave old governor
   Who gathered his array,
And stood to meet, he knew not what,
   On that alarming day.
Eight hundred, amid rumors vast
   That filled the wild wood's gloom,
With all New England's flower of youth,
   Fierce for New France's doom.

And the brave old half five hundred!
  Theirs should in truth be fame;
Borne down the savage Richelieu,
  On what emprise they came!
Your hearts are great enough, O few:
  Only your numbers fail,
New France asks more for conquerors
  All glorious tho your tale.

It was a brave old battle
  That surged around the fort,
When D'Hosta fell in charging,
  And 'twas deadly strife and short,
When in the very quarters
  They contested face and hand,
And many a goodly fellow
  Crimsoned yon La Prairie sand.

And those were brave old orders
  The colonel gave to meet
That forest force with trees entrenched
  Opposing the retreat:
" De Calliere's strength's behind us,
  And in front your Richelieu;
We must go straightforth at them;
  There is nothing else to do."

And then the brave old story comes,
  Of Schuyler and Valrennes,
When " Fight " the British colonel called,
  Encouraging his men,
" For the Protestant Religion
  And the honor of our King!"—
" Sir, I am here to answer you!"
  Valrennes cried, forthstepping.

Were those our brave old races?
  Well, here they still abide;
And yours is one or other,
  And the second's at your side;
So when you hear your brother say,
  " Some loyal deed I'll do,"
Like old Valrennes, be ready with
  " I'm here to answer you! "

Ottawa

By Duncan Campbell Scott

City about whose brow the north winds
    blow,
Girdled with woods and shod with river
    foam,
Called by a name as old as Troy or Rome,
Be great as they, but pure as thine own
    snow;
Rather flash up amid the auroral glow,
The Lamia city of the northern star,
Than be so hard with craft or wild with
    war,
Peopled with deeds remembered for their
    wo.
Thou art too bright for guile, too young
    for tears,
And thou wilt live to be too strong for
    Time;
For he may mock thee with his furrowed
    frowns,
But thou wilt grow in calm throughout the
    years,
Cinctured with peace and crowned with
    power sublime,
The maiden queen of all the towered towns.

The Story of a People

By Louis Honore Fréchette

O history of my country, set with pearls un-
    known,
With love I kiss thy pages venerated. . . .

Hail first to thee, O Cartier, brave and hardy
    sailor,
Whose footsteps sounded on the unexplored
    shores
Of our immense St. Lawrence. Hail, Cham-
    plain,
Maisonneuve, illustrious founders of two
    cities,
Who show above our waves their rival
    beauties.
There was at first only a group of Bretons
Brandishing the sword-blade and the wood-
    man's ax,
Sea-wolves bronzed by sea-winds at the port
    of St. Malo;
Cradled since their childhood beneath the sky
    and water,
Men of iron and high of heart and stature,
They, under eye of God, set sail for what
    might come—
Seeking, in the mazes of the foggy ocean,
Not the famous El Dorados, but a soil where
    they might plant,
As symbols of their saving, beside the cross
    of Christ,
The flag of France.

Snowshoeing Song

By Arthur Weir

Hilloo, hilloo, hilloo, hilloo!
Gather, gather, ye men in white;
The winds blow keenly, the moon is bright,
The sparkling snow lies firm and white;
Tie on the shoes, no time to lose,
We must be over the hill to-night.

Hilloo, hilloo, hilloo, hilloo!
Swiftly in single file we go,
The city is soon left far below,
Its countless lights like diamonds glow;
And as we climb we hear the chime
Of church bells stealing o'er the snow.

Hilloo, hilloo, hilloo, hilloo!
Like winding-sheet about the dead,
O'er hill and dale the snow is spread,
And silences our hurried tread;
The pines bend low, and to and fro
The magpies toss their boughs o'erhead.

Hilloo, hilloo, hilloo, hilloo!
We laugh to scorn the angry blast,
The mountain top is gained and past.
Descent begins, 'tis ever fast—
One short quick run, and toil is done,
We reach the welcome inn at last.

Shake off, shake off the clinging snow;
Unloose the shoe, the sash untie,
Fling tuque and mittens lightly by;
The chimney fire is blazing high,
And, richly stored, the festive board
Awaits the merry company.

Remove the fragments of the feast!
The steaming coffee, waiter, bring.
Now tell the tale, the chorus sing,
And let the laughter loudly ring;
Here's to our host, drink down the toast,
Then up! for time is on the wing.

Hilloo, hilloo, hilloo, hilloo!
The moon is sinking out of sight,
Across the sky dark clouds take flight,
And dimly looms the mountain height;
Tie on the shoes, no time to lose,
We must be home again to-night.

A Canadian Folk-Song

By William Wilfred Campbell

The doors are shut, the windows fast,
Outside the gust is driving past,
Outside the shivering ivy clings,
While on the hob the kettle sings.
  Margery, Margery, make the tea,
  Singeth the kettle merrily.

The streams are hushed up where they flowed,
The ponds are frozen along the road,
The cattle are housed in shed and byre,
While singeth the kettle on the fire.
  Margery, Margery, make the tea,
  Singeth the kettle merrily.

The fisherman on the bay in his boat
Shivers and buttons up his coat;
The traveler stops at the tavern door,
And the kettle answers the chimney's roar.
  Margery, Margery, make the tea,
  Singeth the kettle merrily.

The firelight dances upon the wall,
Footsteps are heard in the outer hall,
And a kiss and a welcome that fill the room,
And the kettle sings in the glimmer and gloom.
  Margery, Margery, make the tea,
  Singeth the kettle merrily.

The Heroes of Fish Creek and Batoche

Not in the quiet churchyard, near those who
    loved them best;
But by the wild Saskatchewan, they laid
    them to their rest.
A simple soldier's funeral in that lonely spot
    was theirs,
Made consecrate and holy by a nation's tears
    and prayers,
Their requiem—the music of the river's surg-
    ing tide;
Their funeral wreaths, the wild flowers that
    grow on every side;
Their monument—undying praise from each
    Canadian heart,
That hears how, for their country's sake,
    they nobly bore their part.
                                    Selected.

INDEPENDENCE DAY

(July 4)

TO every loyal American one day stands out preeminently in all the list of holidays. Independence Day—the Fourth of July—is observed in each and every state of the Union, and in the District of Columbia, as our one great distinctive national holiday. And this is assuredly as it should be, for the event which it celebrates is beyond question the most important in the history of the United States.

Independence Day celebrates the signing, on the Fourth of July, 1776, of the Declaration of Independence by the members of the Continental Congress, then assembled in the State House at Philadelphia. Until this time the colonists had protested that they were not rebels, but " petitioners in arms," only desiring their rights as loyal subjects of the King of England. But wrongs unredressed, complaints unheeded, and petitions unanswered had exhausted the patience of the American people. The Declaration of Independence resulted and was the culminating act in the long train of events which led up to the final severance of the American colonies from the Mother Country and the making of them a free and independent Nation.

It came with no sudden explosion nor violent eruption. War had already been declared and the American people were already in arms, prepared, however, at any intimation of concession on England's part, to suspend hostilities; but patience and hope were at length exhausted, and when Congress met in May, 1776, its members would no longer consent to petition England, and a strong sentiment for separation from the Mother Country began to be felt. On June 7th, Richard Henry Lee, of the Virginia delegation, instructed, he said, by the unanimous vote of the Council of Virginia, presented the following resolution:

" That these United Colonies are and of right ought to be, free and independent States: that they are absolved from all allegiance to the British Crown; that all political connection between them and Great Britain is, and ought to be, totally absolved."

John Adams, who had long favored the idea of independence, even wnen it was popularly believed to be a most unwise and extreme measure, was quickly upon his feet to second the motion. Then followed a debate of four days' duration. John Adams, Samuel Adams, Roger Sherman, Oliver Wolcott, R. H. Lee and George Wythe were probably the great speakers in favor of separation, while John Dickinson, followed by able men, such as John Jay, James Wilson, and Robert R. Wilson, led the opposition. We have, however, no actual, authenticated record of the debates and those who participated, for the extreme danger to the men involved caused the omission of all such reports from the Congressional Journal. New York, New Jersey, Pennsylvania, Maryland, Delaware, and South Carolina opposed the measure. Massachusetts, Rhode Island, New Hampshire, Connecticut, Virginia, North Carolina, and Georgia favored it. Unanimity was, however, regarded as so desirable that a final vote was postponed until July 1st. Meantime a committee was appointed by ballot, consisting of Thomas Jefferson,

Benjamin Franklin, John Adams, Roger Sherman, and R. R. Livingstone, to prepare a declaration stating to the world the grievances which drove the Colonies to separate from Great Britain.

That this document was the work of Thomas Jefferson there can be no reasonable doubt, altho in after years much severe criticism was directed against him for its lack of originality and use of current expression. That such criticism is unjust is equally true, for in no sense did the document claim for itself any virtue on account of originality. The gist of it was in the thoughts of every man who thought at all. The current phrases and the popular wording of the great principles which it defended, together with the long list of grievances it recited were upon the lips of every one. The skill which Jefferson showed was in his power of selection and in his formal statement, in clear and forcible style, of the grievances and the conditions which were familiar to all.

On June 28th this document was laid before Congress. Meantime most earnest work had been done throughout the colonies, as well as with the congressional delegates who opposed the measure. On the night of July 1, New York, Pennsylvania, Delaware, and South Carolina still held back, but on July 2 all delegates but those from New York solemnly voted in favor of the motion which "absolved" the colonies "from all allegiance to the British Crown" and made them "free and independent States." Thus "Independence" was really declared on July 2, but Jefferson's document was not acted upon until July 4, when, after a long debate, and one or two corrections, it was finally accepted and signed by the President of Congress, John Hancock, and the Secretary, Charles Thompson. Within a week the Provincial Congress of New York had finally expressed its approval. August 2nd an engrossed copy of The Declaration of Independence was laid before Congress and received the signatures of the delegates from every one of the thirteen colonies.

Thus was completed the foundation act in the history of the United States of America. It is a privilege and a duty of the American people to celebrate the anniversary of an event so vitally important to them. At the time of the passing of the act, John Adams wrote to his wife a letter which has become historic. " I am apt to believe," he wrote, " that it (the day) will be celebrated by succeeding generations as the great anniversary festival. It ought to be commemorated as the day of deliverance, by solemn acts of devotion to God Almighty. It ought to be solemnized with pomp and parade, with shows, games, sports, guns, bells, bonfires, and illuminations, from one end of this continent to the other, from this time forward for evermore." These words have proved prophetic. That as a people, Americans have emphasized the lighter part of the prophecy in the spirit of their celebration is greatly to be deplored. The day at times appears rather to be an orgy than a solemn festival; a time of noise and self-indulgence rather than of patriotic joy and thankfulness. But underneath these mistaken methods of celebration there is a deeper feeling in the hearts of American citizens. There is a growing sentiment in favor of the abolition of the less worthy attempts to mark the day, and the encouragement of all and every means to make Independence Day what it should be, the proud and glad observance of the Nation's birthday, a time when every loyal citizen should in public functions and in private life rejoice in the welfare of his country, and, with solemn thanksgiving to his God, pledge himself anew to the service of America.

PATRIOTISM IN THE SCHOOLS

The development of the virtue of love of country, which is symbolized by the raising of so many new and beautiful flags over school-houses, should not end, by any means, with the hanging out of these banners. Unless there is, in the teaching of the schools, a distinct and intelligent care to ground the pupils in the true love of country which comes with intelligent knowledge of it, and to inspire the young with something of the air, the light, the life and beauty of the land, the flags may as well be left to flutter into shreds.

Genuine love of our country cannot be founded upon words alone, nor upon the mere recitation of deeds of heroism and past public services. To be the true spirit which has always animated great peoples, our American patriotism must have a special tie to the soil—a feeling which allies itself to the trees, the flowers, the birds, the prairies, their soil, and story, and their manifold productions and colorings, the hills, the wild creatures of the woods, and fields, and everything that is distinctively American.

Acquaintance with the episodes of our history and a knowledge of our Constitution and laws are a highly important part of the education of an American citizen. But his equipment should not end with them. They represent the intellectual part of one's patriotism; the *heart* of it is nourished from its romance, its natural features, its soil and its products, the animals, the atmosphere, the skies—all things which make the earliest and most lasting impression upon the individual, and through which every sentiment is typified to him.

If we take the writings of a great patriotic poet, like Whittier, we find that these natural things are well known to him, and their shaping influence upon character appreciated.

In Whittier's poems there is a constant reference of sentiments and ideas to the soil and the aspects of nature. He makes no mistake about the flowers and trees which he weaves into his songs, nor about the birds which warble through them. There is abundance of native light and color.

But the ignorance of these things among many Americans is striking. Not long since there went the rounds of a portion of the press of this country an extract which told " what birds sing earliest in the morning." It was stated that the skylark sang at about such an hour, the chaffinch at another hour, the tomtit at another, and so on through a somewhat long list.

Now every bird in this list was an European bird, and not one of them could be heard in this country save in a cage or an aviary. Yet this extract, which came from an English periodical, was given in good faith by many American journals as a statement of the order in which American birds begin their singing in the morning.

Many Americans, in their natural love for trees, plant, sometimes in ignorance of their foreign origin, trees which will not thrive or reach their full beauty in our soil, passing by native trees and shrubs of superior beauty, vigor, and significance. For there is significance in natural things as well as in facts and figures, and more healthy sentiment in the natural sciences than some people suppose.

The enormous immigration which is pouring into our country, and which consists in much larger proportion than ever before of peoples very unlike our own population in character, habits, and traditions, makes it desirable and even necessary to instil into the rising generation of these people as much of the knowledge and feeling of American life and nature as possible.

It is not practicable, in our elementary schools, to give thorough instruction in geology, botany, and ornithology; but it is practicable to impart to the pupils a certain amount of accurate foundation knowledge of the natural things about them. It is especially practicable to convey this knowledge in informal talks and in the half-unconscious side instruction which often takes the deepest lodgment in a boy's or girl's brain.

This fact should not be lost sight of by our teachers in the school year, nor in the normal instruction which is given to teachers themselves.—Y. C.

HISTORICAL

THE DECLARATION OF INDEPENDENCE

It may seem strange to some young people that the memories of the fifty-six signers of that wonderful paper should be so honored in this country. Said a bright boy recently, " Why was it any very great thing to sign a paper of that kind? I think the man who wrote it was great, but don't see why the others were."

The reason they were great was that they

were both patriotic and brave. They believed that it was not right for this country to be subject to and taxed by Great Britain while having no voice in the government. A committee, consisting of Thomas Jefferson, of Virginia; John Adams, of Massachusetts; Benjamin Franklin, of Pennsylvania; Roger Sherman, of

The Signers of the Declaration

Connecticut, and Robert R. Livingstone, of New York, was appointed to write out a declaration to this effect. Thomas Jefferson, tho at this time but thirty-three years of age, was one of the best classically educated men in public life, and composed the Declaration, which, without his other public services, would have made his name famous.

The American colonies were represented by fifty-six members in the assemblage which met on July 4, 1776, and decided to adopt the Declaration of Independence. As a matter of fact, only the president of the assembly, John Hancock, signed the paper on that day. On August 2d, it was signed by all but one of the fifty-six—Matthew Thornton, of New Hampshire—who signed in November.

As to the reason why it was brave: The thirteen colonies were subject to England. In declaring that they would be "absolved from all allegiance to the British **The** crown," they placed themselves **Danger** in rebellion, and if they failed in **of Signing** the struggle that must follow, the signers of that paper would be regarded as traitors and treated accordingly. John Hancock, as the paper was being signed, said, "We must all hang together." "Ay," answered Benjamin Franklin, "We must all hang together, else we shall all hang separately."

Someone suggested to Charles Carroll that as there were a great many men of that name, if the cause should fail, the English would not know which one to arrest. "Yes, they will," he said, and immediately wrote "of Carrollton" after his name.

They all understood fully the danger, but were proud to meet it, and deserve the greatest honor from each succeeding generation.

They were, as a whole, comparatively young men, for the average age of all was only forty-three years and ten months. Edward Rutledge, of South Carolina, was the youngest, being but twenty-**The Pro-** seven, and Benjamin Franklin, **fessions** the oldest, was seventy. Five **of the** were physicians, thirty lawyers, **Signers** seven farmers, eight merchants, and two mechanics; John Witherspoon, of New Jersey, was a clergyman, Abraham Clark, of New Jersey, a surveyor, Roger Sherman, of Connecticut, a shoemaker, and Franklin, a printer.

Richard Henry Lee, of Virginia, deserves special mention, as he started the movement by presenting to the assembly on June 7, 1776, this resolution:

"*Resolved:* That these united colonies are, and of right ought to be, free and independent states; that they are absolved from all allegiance to the British crown; and that all political connection between them and the State of Great Britain is, and ought to be dissolved."

As the mover of this resolution, when a committee was appointed he would naturally have been made chairman, but was called away by illness in his family, and Mr. Jefferson was chosen. He served later in several congresses and was the first senator from Virginia.

A rather remarkable coincidence is that Thomas Jefferson, the author of the Declaration of Independence, and John Adams, one of the signers and its great supporter, both afterward President of the United States, died on the same day, and that Independence Day, 1826. On June 30th of that year someone asked John Adams, who was then very ill, for a toast to be given in his name on the Fourth of July. He replied, "*Independence forever!*" When the day came, hearing the noise of bells and cannon, he asked the cause, and, on being told, he murmured, "Independence forever!" and before evening was dead.
—C. A.

THE EARLIEST CELEBRATIONS OF INDEPENDENCE

By Paul Leicester Ford

John Adams' prediction as to the celebration of the Declaration of Independence was verified within six days, for it was first celebrated on July 8th, 1776, on a "warm, sunshine morning." Marshall states, in the yard of the State House, "where, in the presence of a great concourse of people, the Declaration of Independence was read by John Nixon. The company declared their approbation by three repeated huzzas. The King's Arms were taken down in the Court Room, State House [at the] same time, ... after which, went [to] the Commons, where the same was proclaimed at each of the five Battalions. . . . Fine starlight, pleasant evening. There were bonfires, ringing bells, with other great demonstrations of joy upon the unanimity and agreement of the Declaration."

One day later, on July 9th, the Declaration was celebrated at New York, in a manner directed by Washington, who in **In 1776** the General Orders for that day announced:

"The Honr: Continental Congress, impelled by the dictates of duty, policy, and necessity, having been pleased to dissolve the Connection which subsisted between this Country and Great Britain, and to declare the United Colonies of America free and independent States, The Several brigades are to be drawn up this evening on their respective Parades at six o'clock, when the declaration of Congress, showing the grounds & reasons of this Measure, is to be read with an audible voice. The General hopes this important Event will serve as a fresh incentive to every officer and soldier, to act with Fidelity and Courage, as knowing that now the peace and safety of his Country, depends (under God) solely on the success of our Arms: And that he is now in the service of a State, possessed of sufficient power to reward his merit, and advance him to the highest Honors of a free Country."

And Washington notified the Congress that "Agreeably to the request of Congress I caused the Declaration to be proclaimed before all the army under my immediate command; and have the pleasure to inform them, that the measure seemed to have their most hearty assent; the expressions and behavior, both of officers and men, testifying their warmest approbation of it."

Not content with thus celebrating freedom, Webb relates that

"Last night the statue of George III. was tumbled down and beheaded, the troops having long had an inclination to do so, thought the time of publishing a declaration of independence a favorable opportunity, for which they received a check in this day's orders."

After this, each recurring Fourth of July was observed by the army. In 1777, at Morristown, it was celebrated by a **In 1777 and 1778** *feu de joie* and every soldier was ordered an extra gill of rum. In 1778 the General Orders announced that

"To-morrow, the anniversary of the Declaration of Independence, will be celebrated by firing thirteen pieces of cannon and a *feu de joie* of the whole line. The army will be formed on the Brunswick side of the Raritan, at five o'clock in the afternoon, on the ground pointed out by the Quartermaster-General."

In 1779 the day brought joy to the wrongdoer, for the orderly book directed that **In 1779** "This day being the anniversary of our glorious independence, will be commemorated by the firing of thirteen cannon from West Point at 1 o'clock P. M. The Commander-in-Chief thinks proper to grant a general pardon to all prisoners in this army, under sentence of death. They are to be released from confinement accordingly."

The last celebration of the army, in 1782, was described as follows: **In 1782** "On the 4th, the anniversary of the Declaration of our Independence was celebrated in camp. The whole army was formed on the banks of the Hudson, on each side of the river. The signal of thirteen cannon being given at West Point, the troops displayed and formed line, when a general *feu de joie* took place throughout the whole army."

Of the first celebration by Congress, we have a good description in a letter from John Adams to his daughter, which is **First Celebration by Congress** doubly interesting as showing how impromptu the affair was: "Yesterday, being the anniversary of American Independence, was celebrated here with a festivity and ceremony becoming the occasion. I am too

old to delight in pretty descriptions, if I had a talent for them, otherwise a picture might be drawn which would please the fancy of a Whig, at least. The thought of taking any notice of this day was not conceived until the second of this month, and it was not mentioned until the third. It was too late to have a sermon, as every one wished, so this must be deferred another year. Congress determined to adjourn over that day, and to dine together. The general officers and others in town were invited, after the President and Council and Board of War of this State. In the morning the *Delaware* frigate, several large galleys, and other continental armed vessels, the *Pennsylvania* ship and row-galleys, and guard-boats, were all hauled off in the river, and several of them beautifully dressed in the colors of all nations displayed about the masts, yards and rigging. At one o'clock the ships were all manned; that is, the men were all ordered aloft and arranged upon the topyards and shrouds, making a striking appearance of companies of men drawn up in order in the air.

"Then I went on board the *Delaware* with the President and several gentlemen of the Marine Committee; soon after which we were saluted with a discharge of thirteen guns, which was followed by thirteen others from each other armed vessel in the river, then the galleys followed the fire and after them the gunboats. Then the President and company returned in the barge to the shore, and were saluted by three cheers from every ship, galley and boat in the river. The wharves and shores were lined with a vast concourse of people all shouting and huzzaing in a manner which gave great joy to every friend of this country, and the utmost terror and dismay to every lurking Tory. At three we went to dinner, and were very agreeably entertained with excellent company, good cheer, fine music from the band of Hessians taken at Trenton, and continual volleys between every toast from a company of soldiers drawn up in Second Street before the city tavern, where we dined. The toasts were in honor of our country and the heroes who had fallen in their pious efforts to defend her. After this, two troops of light horse, raised in Maryland, accidentally here on their way to camp, were paraded through Second Street; after them a train of artillery, and then about a thousand infantry, now in this city on their march to camp, from North Carolina. All these marched into the common, where they went through their firings and maneuvers; but I did not follow them. In the evening I was walking about the streets for a little fresh air and exercise, and was surprised to find the whole city lighting up their candles at the windows. I walked most of the evening, and I think it was the most splendid illumination I ever saw—a few surly houses were dark, but the lights were very universal. Considering the lateness of the design and the suddenness of the execution, I was amazed at the universal joy and alacrity that was discovered, and at the brilliancy and splendor of every part of this joyful exhibition. I had forgot the ringing of bells all day and evening, and the bonfires in the streets, and the fireworks played off. Had General Howe been here in disguise, or his master, this show would have given them the heartache."

The celebration of 1778, was quite different and was described by Richard Henry Lee in the following words:

In 1778 "We had a magnificent celebration of the anniversary of independence yesterday. when handsome fireworks were displayed. The Whigs of the city dressed up a woman of the town with the monstrous head-dress of the Tory ladies, and escorted her through [the streets] with a great concourse of people. Her head was elegantly and expensively dressed, I suppose about three feet high and proportionate

width, with a profusion of curls, etc., etc., etc. The figure was droll and occasioned much mirth. It has lessened some heads already, and will probably bring the rest within the bounds of reason, for they are monstrous, indeed. The Tory wife of Dr. Smith has christened this figure Continella, or the Duchess of Independence, and prayed for a pin from her head by way of relic. The Tory women are very much mortified, notwithstanding this."

It is interesting to know that throughout the whole country the celebration of independence sprang into custom in these very early years and accounts of them could be multiplied almost indefinitely; but the foregoing are sufficient to show how the men who had made independence thought fit to celebrate it.—I.

A RENAISSANCE OF PATRIOTISM

By George J. Manson

Within the past few years there has been what ex-President Harrison once happily termed "a *renaissance* of patriotism." It started with the centennial anniversaries of 1776, which had the effect of carrying the memories of the people back to the period of the Nation's birth, and subsequently resulted in the formation of several societies which will be the means of fostering the patriotic spirit, love of country, and recall remembrances of our Revolutionary struggle. The organizers of these societies found that there was a growing lack of what may be called national patriotism—the patriotism that grows out of a lively recollection of the early making of the country through battle, toil, and hardship of the fathers. This lukewarm spirit was not charged to the flood of immigration, or to the lapse of time, but was principally due to neglect on the part of the descendants of Revolutionary heroes to perform their duty of keeping before the public mind the memory of the services of their ancestors. the times in which they lived and the principles for which they contended.

One of the first of these societies to be started was the "Sons of the Revolution." This was organized February 22, 1876, reorganized December 4, 1883, and **The Sons** incorporated May 3, 1884. The **of the** aim of this society is to perpet**Revolution** uate the memory of the men who, in military, naval or civil service, by their acts or counsel, achieved American independence. The members promote and assist in the proper celebration of the anniversaries of Washington's Birthday, the battles of Lexington and Bunker Hill, the 4th of July, the capitulation of Saratoga and Yorktown, and the formal evacuation of New York by the British army, December 3, 1783, as a relinquishment of territorial sov-

ereignty, and other prominent events relating to or connected with the War of the Revolution.

The roll-book of the members is something more than a mere list of names. Before each name is the year, showing when the member was admitted into the society, and there is also given in a paragraph his genealogical history so far as it relates to his ancestors who were in any way connected with the Revolutionary struggle. There is a general, or national society, divided into state societies which regulate their own affairs. Under the rules of the New York State society, ten or more members can organize within any county outside of the county of New York. such a body being called a local chapter. The total membership is now about six thousand. When membership is asked on the ground of an ancestor having been a "sailor" or "marine," it must be shown that such service was other than shore duty and regularly performed in the Continental navy, or the navy of one of the original thirteen states, or on an armed vessel other than a merchant ship. When the ancestor has been an "official" his service must have been sufficiently important in character to have rendered him specially liable to arrest and imprisonment, if captured by the enemy, as well as liable to conviction of treason against the Government of Great Britain.

A few years ago the society stimulated interest in its work by offering two prizes to the cadets of the United States Naval Academy, at Annapolis, Md.—a gold medal and a silver medal—for the best original essays upon the subject, "The Navy in the Revolution." A singular and patriotic feature of these essays was that they were not to contain less than 1776 words. A gold medal is likewise annually awarded by the New York society to a student in the College of the City of New York, for the best essay on a patriotic subject, and gold, silver, and bronze medals to the scholars of the high schools throughout the State for like essays. Similar prizes are awarded by the societies in other states.

Congress has also been urged, by the Sons of the Revolution as a body, to pass a bill which has already been introduced in that body, making an appropriation of a sum of money to erect a monument to John Paul Jones. It has also memorialized Congress to enact such a law as will secure the publication of all the archives of the United States Government relating to the War of the Revolution, in a manner similar to the publication of the records of the War of the Rebellion.

The seal of the society is an interesting study, suggesting as it does, in small compass, the spirit of patriotism the society desires to cultivate. The seal consists of the figure of a minuteman, in Continental uniform, standing on a ladder leading to a belfry. In his right hand he holds a musket and an olive branch, while his left hand grasps a bell-rope. Above is seen the cracked Liberty bell, from which issues a ribbon bearing the motto of the society: *Exegi monumentum aere perennius*. Many members of this society did gallant service in the war with Spain.

The second important patriotic society is the "Sons of the American Revolution," a name very similar to that of the organization **Sons of the** just mentioned. The first branch **American** of this society was formed in **Revolution** California in 1876 by a body of descendants of officers, soldiers, and seamen of the Revolution gathered in San Francisco for the purpose of celebrating the one hundredth anniversary of the Declaration of Independence. Similar societies were therefore organized in other states, and, on April 30, 1889, these societies with two or three exceptions, celebrated the centennial inauguration of Washington as first President of the United States. This meeting was held in Fraunce's Tavern, in New York City, in the identical long room (now marked with a commemorative tablet) in which Washington bade farewell to his officers, December 3, 1783. The national organization was formed on the occasion of this meeting.

This society exists in about thirty states, and numbers about five thousand members. A singular and interesting feature in connection with this and kindred organizations is that their existence has led to and greatly stimulated genealogical research, a species of investigation to which Americans, as a rule, have given but little attention. Persons who have become interested in these societies, it has been found, have rescued unrecorded facts from the aged members of their families who were destined soon to pass away, information which could have been obtained in no other way and which would have been lost forever in a few years.

The "Sons of the American Revolution" prides itself on being a practical and not merely a sentimental and ornamental organization. It has been particularly active in saving throughout the country valuable historical landmarks, such as the headquarters of Jonathan Trumbull, in Connecticut, which has been obtained and is now used for a museum. It is marking historical spots and, directly and indirectly, securing the erection of memorials of the Revolutionary heroes, such as the Bennington Monument, near that famous battle-field, the statue of Gen. John Stark, in New Hampshire, and a monument to be erected in Baltimore to Maryland's heroes of the Revolution. It has obtained from Congress a law providing for the collection and indexing of the records of service of the Revolution. It has stimulated the general observance of national patriotic holidays, and was influential in setting apart June 14th as "flag day," in commemoration of the adoption of the Stars and Stripes as the national standard.

"The Society of Colonial Wars," originated in New York, and was instituted August 18, 1892, and incorporated October 18, 1892.

In May, 1893, the New York so-**The** ciety with the societies in the **Society of** states of Pennsylvania, Mary-**Colonial** land, Massachusetts, Connecti-**Wars** cut, and the District of Columbia organized the General Society, these states having been previously chartered by the society in the State of New York. The objects of the organization are similar to the previously named societies, from which they differ only in minor details. The present membership is approximately 3,000. On June 14th of this year (1898) this society joined with the Sons of the Revolution in appropriate ceremonies attending the unveiling of commemorative tablets at Fort Ticonderoga, intended to perpetuate the memories of the capture of the fort by Colonel Ethan Allen and his gallant band, the Colonial battles fought in the vicinity of Fort Ticonderoga, etc.

"The Military Order of Foreign Wars" is, as its name implies, a military organization with patriotic objects, having for its scope **The** the period of American history **Military** since national independence. The **Order of** principal feature of the Order is **Foreign** the perpetuating of the names, **Wars** as well as the services, of commissioned officers who served in either the War of the Revolution, the War with Tripoli, the War of 1812, the Mexican War, or the War with Spain. Veteran companionship is conferred upon such officers, and Hereditary Companionship upon their direct lineal descendants in the male line. The present membership is 1,400, which is rapidly growing. Other societies that merit more extended notice but which can here only be named are the "Order of Cincinnati," the "Society of the War of 1812," the "Aztec Club," the "Loyal Legion," the "Grand Army of the Republic," the "Flag Association," "Colonial Order of the Acorn," "Order of Washington," the "Pilgrim Society," and some others.

It is quite natural that women, whose

patriotic services during the late Civil War have often been the subject of grateful eulogy, should become interested in this new movement. There are several patriotic societies, composed exclusively of women, the objects of which are practically the same as the organizations which have just been mentioned. The society known as the "Daughters of the Revolution" was organized by Mrs. Flora Adams Darling, September 9, 1891. In October, 1890, was organized the more important society known as the "Daughters of the American Revolution," which now has a membership of about 3,500. This society has state chapters existing in most of the states. To become a member of this society a woman must be not less than eighteen years of age, and be the descendant of an ancestor who loyally rendered material aid as a soldier, sailor or civil officer to the cause of independence. The Daughters of the American Revolution have presented to the City of Paris an equestrian statue of Washington, designed and executed by Daniel C. French. It was intended to be a return of the compliment to the American people conveyed by the French Government when it presented to the United States the statue of Washington which is now at the National Capital. The unveiling took place with imposing ceremonies on July 3d.

The Colonial Dames of America The "Colonial Dames of America," an organization incorporated in 1893, requires of a member that she shall be descended in her own right from some ancestor of worthy life who came to reside in the American colony prior to

The Daughters of the Revolution

1750. This ancestor, or some one of his descendants, shall be a lineal ascendant of the applicant, and shall have rendered efficient service to his country during the colonial period, either in the founding of the commonwealth, or of an institution which has survived and developed into importance, or who shall have held an important position in the Colonial Government and by distinguished services shall have contributed to the founding of the Nation. Services rendered after 1783 are not recognized.

Still another woman's patriotic organization is known as the "United States Daughters, 1776-1812." This society was founded by Mrs. Flora Adams Darling, and incorporated in 1892. Ladies to be eligible must be lineal descendants of an ancestor who assisted in the wars of 1776-1812, either as a military or naval officer, soldier, sailor, or in any way gave aid to the cause, tho the society reserves to itself the privilege of rejecting any nomination that may not be acceptable to it.

United States Daughters, 1776-1812

Another patriotic woman's organization, tho not of recent date, which has for years rendered important service, is the "Mount Vernon Ladies' Association," of Washington, D. C. This association has under its care and direction the Washington estate at Mount Vernon, Va. In 1895 a volume entitled ANCESTRY was published by Bailey, Banks & Biddle (Philadelphia) in connection with their Department of Heraldry that contained a complete list of the various patriotic societies, then forty-seven in number. Since the publication of this volume many new societies have sprung up.—I.

ADDRESSES

FREEDOM OR SLAVERY

BY PATRICK HENRY

[Delivered in Richmond, Va., March, 1775.]

Mr. President, it is natural to man to indulge in the illusions of hope. We are apt to shut our eyes against a painful truth, and listen to the song of that siren, till she transforms us to beasts. Is this the part of wise men, engaged in a great and arduous struggle for liberty? Are we disposed to be of the number of those who, having eyes, see not, and having ears, hear not, the things which so nearly concern our temporal salvation? For my part, whatever anguish of spirit it may cost, I am willing to know the whole truth; to know the worst, and to provide for it.

I have but one lamp by which my feet are guided; and that is the lamp of experience. I know of no way of judging of the future but by the past. And judging by the past, I wish to know what there has been in the conduct of the British Ministry for the last ten years to justify those hopes with which gentlemen have been pleased to solace themselves and the House? Is it that insidious smile with which our petition has been lately received? Trust it not, sir: it will prove a snare to your feet. Suffer not yourselves to be "betrayed with a kiss!" Ask yourselves, How this gracious reception of our petition comports with those warlike preparations which cover our waters and darken our land? Are fleets and armies necessary to a work of love and reconciliation? Have we shown ourselves so unwilling to be reconciled, that force must be called in to win back our love? Let us not deceive ourselves, sir. These are the implements of war and subjugation, the last "arguments" to which kings resort.

I ask gentlemen, sir, what means this martial array, if its purpose be not to force us to submission? Can gentlemen assign any other possible motive for it? Has Great Britain any enemy in this quarter of the world, to call for all this accumulation of navies and armies? No, sir, she has none. They are meant for us; they can be meant for no other. They are sent over to bind and to rivet upon us those chains which the British Ministry have been so long forging. And what have we to oppose to them? Shall we try argument? Sir, we have been trying that for the last ten years. Have we anything new to offer upon the subject? Nothing. We have held the subject up in every light of which it is capable; but it has been all in vain. Shall we resort to entreaty and humble supplication? What terms shall we find which have not been already exhausted? Let us not, I beseech you, sir, deceive ourselves longer. Sir, we have done everything that could be done, to avert the storm which is now coming on. We have petitioned, we have remonstrated, we have supplicated, we have prostrated ourselves before the throne, and have implored its interposition to arrest the tyrannical hands of the Ministry and Parliament. Our petitions have been slighted; our remonstrances have produced additional violence and insult; our supplications have been disregarded, and we have been spurned with contempt from the foot of the throne. In vain, after these things, may we indulge the fond hope of peace and reconciliation. There is no longer any room for hope. If we wish to be free, if we mean to preserve inviolate those inestimable privileges for which we have been so long contending; if we mean not basely to abandon the noble struggle in which we have been so long engaged, and which we have pledged ourselves never to abandon until the glorious object of our contest shall be obtained. we must fight; I repeat it, sir, we must fight! An appeal to arms, and to the God of Hosts, is all that is left us!

They tell us, sir, that we are weak—"unable to cope with so formidable an adversary!" But when shall we be stronger? Will it be the next week, or the next year? Will it be when we are totally disarmed, and when a British guard shall be stationed in every house? Shall we gather strength by irresolution and inaction? Shall we acquire the means of effectual resistance, by lying supinely on our backs, and hugging the delusive phantom of hope, until our enemies have bound us hand and foot? Sir, we are not weak, if we make a proper use of those means which the God of Nature hath placed in our power. Three millions of people, armed in the holy cause of Liberty, and in such a country as that which we possess, are invincible by any force which our enemy can send against us.

Besides, sir, we shall not fight our battles alone. There is a just Power who presides over the destinies of nations, and who will raise up friends to fight our battles for us. The battle, sir, is not to the strong alone; it is to the vigilant, the active, the brave. Besides, sir, we have no election. If we were base enough to desire it, it is now too late to retire from the contest. There is no retreat, but in submission and slavery. Our chains are forged. Their clanking may be heard on the plains of Boston. The war is inevitable; and let it come! I repeat it, sir, let it come! It is in vain, sir, to extenuate the matter. Gentlemen may cry "Peace, peace!" but there is no peace! The war is actually begun! The next gale that sweeps from the north will bring to our ears the clash of resounding arms! Our brethren are already in the field! Why stand we here idle? What is it that gentlemen wish? What would they have? Is life so dear, or peace so sweet, as to be purchased at the price of chains and slavery? Forbid it, Almighty Powers! —I know not what course others may take; but as for me, give me liberty or give me death!

THE MORAL FORCES WHICH MAKE AMERICAN PROGRESS *

By Edward Everett

Sir, in our views of the glorious future that awaits the Union, we are apt to regard geographical extension as the measure and the index of our country's progress. I do not deny the general correctness of that impression. It is necessary for the formation of the highest type of national character that it should be formed and exhibited upon a grand and extensive scale. It cannot be developed within the bounds of a petty state. Nor do I admit that this idea of geographical extension necessarily carries with it—tho

it does perhaps by natural association—that of collision with other powers. But, sir, I think there is no fear, so far as geographical extension is necessary, but that we shall, in the natural progress of things, have as much of it, and as rapidly as the best interests of the country admit or require.

In the meantime, if we wish a real, solid, substantial growth—a growth which will not bring us in collision with foreign powers —we shall have it in twenty-five years to our heart's content; not by the geographical

* Peroration of the Speech of March 21, 1853, on the Clayton-Bulwer Treaty.

accession of dead acres, not by the purchase of Cuba or by the partition of Mexico, but by the simple, peaceful increase of our population.

Sir, have you well considered that that mysterious law which was promulgated on the sixth day of the Creation: "Be fruitful and multiply and replenish the earth," will, in twenty-five years of peace and union, —for it is all wrapped up in that,—aided by the foreign immigration, give us another America of living men as large as that which we now possess? Yes, sir, as far as living men are concerned, besides replacing the millions which will have passed off the stage, it will give us all that the arm of Omnipotence could give us, if it should call up from the depths of the Pacific and join to the Union another America as populous as ours.

If, by any stroke of power or policy, you could to-morrow extend your jurisdiction from Hudson's Bay to Cape Horn, and take in every state and every government, and all their population, it would not give to you a greater amount of population, including your own, than you will have at the end of twenty-five years by the simple law of increase, aided by immigration from abroad.

I shall not live to see it. My children probably will. The Senator from Illinois, in all human probability, will live to see it, and there is, perhaps, no one more likely than he to impress his views of public policy upon the mind of those growing millions, and to receive from them in return all the honors and trusts which a grateful people can bestow upon those they respect and love.

Let me adjure him, then, to follow the generous impulses of his nature, and after giving, like a true patriot, his first affections to his own country, to be willing to comprehend all the other friendly countries of the earth within the scope of a liberal consideration, and, above all, to cultivate the spirit and arts of peace.

Sir, it is the opposite spirit of military aggrandizement, the spirit of conquest that has forged those chains in Europe, which the Senator so eloquently deplores. It was this that brought down Asia to the dust in the morning of the world, and has kept her seated in sackcloth and ashes ever since. This blasted Greece; this destroyed Rome. It was not a foreign enemy that laid the ax to the root of Rome's freedom; it was her own proconsuls coming home from the successful wars of Asia, gorged with the gold of conquered provinces

The spirit of military aggrandizement and conquest has done the same thing for Europe. Will they not do it here, if we indulge them? Do not let the Senator think that I suspect he wishes to indulge them; but will they not do it? Will they not give us vast standing ar-mies, overshadowing navies, colossal military establishments, frightful expenditures, contracts, jobs, corruption which it sickens the heart to contemplate? And how can our simple republican institutions, our elective magistracies, our annual or biennial choice of those who are to rule over us, unsupported by hereditary claims or pretorian guards, be carried on under such influences?

Do not mistake, however, sir. I counsel no pusillanimous doctrine of nonresistance. Heaven forbid! Providence has placed us between the two great world oceans, and we shall always be a maritime power of the first order. Our commerce already visits every sea, and wherever it floats, it must be protected. Our immense inland frontier will always require a considerable army, and it should be kept in the highest state of discipline.

The schools at Annapolis and West Point ought to be the foster children of our Republic. Our arsenals and our armories ought to be kept filled with every weapon and munition of war, and every vulnerable point on the coast ought to be fortified. But while we act on the maxim, "In peace prepare for war" let us also remember that the best preparation for war is peace. This swells your numbers; this augments your means; this knits the sinews of your strength; this covers you all over with a panoply of might; and then, if war must come in a just cause, no power on earth—no, sir, not all combined—can send forth an adversary from whose encounter you need shrink.

But give us these twenty-five years of peace. I do believe that the coming quarter of a century is to be the most important in our whole history, and I do beseech you, let us have the twenty-five years, at least, of peace.*

Let our fertile wastes be filled up with swarming millions; let the tide of immigration continue to flow in from Europe; let the steamer, let the canal, let the railway, especially the Great Pacific Railway, subdue these mighty distances, and bring this vast extension into a span; let us pay back the ingots of California gold with bars of Atlantic iron; let agriculture clothe our vast wastes with waving plenty; let the industrial and mechanic arts erect their peaceful fortresses at the waterfalls of our rivers; and then, in the train of this growing population, let the printing office, the lecture room, the school room, and the village church be scattered over the country; and, sir, in these twenty-five years, we shall exhibit a spectacle of national prosperity, such as the world has never seen on so large a scale, and yet within the reach of a sober, practical contemplation. —W. B. O.

* Edward Everett's prayer for peace was not answered. The Civil War of 1860-1865, with all its horrors came. But the growth of the population of the United States between 1853 and 1878, notwithstanding the War, confirmed the truth of Edward Everett's position. The population in 1853 was about 24,000,000 ; in 1860, about 32,000,000 ; and in 1878, about 46,000,000.

A RHAPSODY

By Cassius Marcellus Clay

I may be an enthusiast; but I cannot but give utterance to the conceptions of my own mind. When I look upon the special developments of European civilization; when I contemplate the growing freedom of the cities, and the middle class which has sprung up between the pretenders to divine rule on the one hand, and the abject serf on the other; when I consider the Reformation, and the invention of the press, and see, on the southern shore of the continent, an humble individual, amidst untold difficulties and repeated defeats, pursuing the mysterious suggestions which the mighty deep poured unceasingly upon his troubled spirit, till at last, with great and irrepressible energy of soul, he discovered that there lay in the far western ocean a continent open for the infusion of those elementary principles of liberty which were dwarfed in European soil,—I conceive that the hand of destiny was there!

When I see the immigration of the Pilgrims from the chalky shores of England,—in the night fleeing from their native home,—so dramatically and ably pictured by Mr. Webster in his celebrated oration,—when father, mother, brother, wife, sister, lover, were all lost by those melancholy wanderers—" stifling," in the language of one who is immortal in the conception, "the mighty hunger of the heart," and landing, amidst cold and poverty and death, upon the rude rocks of Plymouth,—I venture to think the will of Deity was there!

When I have remembered the Revolution of '76,—the Seven Years' War—three millions of men in arms against the most powerful nation in history, and vindicating their independence,—I have thought that their suf-

ferings and death were not in vain! When I have seen the forsaken heartstone,—looked upon the battlefield, upon the dying and the dead,—heard the agonizing cry, " Water, for the sake of God! water; " seeing the dissolution of being,—pale lips pressing in death the yet loved images of wife, sister, lover,—I have not deemed—I will not deem all these things in vain! I cannot regard this great continent, reaching from the Atlantic to the far Pacific, and from the St. John's to the Rio del Norte, as the destined home of a barbarian people of third-rate civilization.

Like the Roman who looked back upon the glory of his ancestors, in wo exclaiming,

" Great Scipio's ghost complains that we are slow,
And Pompey's shade walks unavenged among us,"

the great dead hover around me:—Lawrence, " Don't give up the ship."—Henry, " Give me liberty or give me death! "—Adams, " Survive or perish, I am for the Declaration "—Allen, " In the name of the living God, I come! "

Come then, Thou Eternal, who dwellest not in temples made with hands, but who, in the city's crowd or by the far forest stream, revealest Thyself to the earnest seeker after the true and right, inspire my heart; give me undying courage to pursue the promptings of my spirit; and, whether I shall be called in the shades of life to look upon as sweet and kind and lovely faces as now, or shut in by sorrow and might, horrid visions shall gloom upon me in my dying hour—O, my country, mayest thou yet be free!—W. B. O.

SERMONS

THE HAND OF GOD IN AMERICAN HISTORY

By Rev. Morgan Dix, D.D.

Glory be to God! and here, throughout the land, far and near, through all our homes, be peace, good will, and love. As one family, one people, one nation, we keep the birthday of our rights, our liberty, our power, and strength. Let us do this with eyes and hearts raised to the Fountain of life, the Beginning of glory and might; with words of praise and thanks to God who rules on high; for He is the living God and stedfast forever, and His Kingdom that which shall not be destroyed, and His dominion shall be even unto the end. Wherefore as He is our strength and hope, let all begin and all go on, first and ever, with glory to God Most High.

There are great things to think about to-

day; the growth of the people, unparalleled in history: the vastness of their empire, a wonder of the latter days; the bands by which the mighty frame is held together—so slight to the eye, so hard to break; the many races wedded into one; the marvelous land, with its oceans, its lakes themselves like lesser oceans, its icebergs and glaciers, its torrid deserts, its mountain ranges and rich, fat valley land, its climates of every kind, its rivers, its wealth in all that rock, and earth, and water can supply; and then the people—active, able, full of enterprise and force, acting with the power of a myriad of giants, speaking one language, living under one flag, bound by common interests, and, as to-day, kindled by one common feeling of devotion, pride, joy, hope: sure there is enough to fill the soul and make the head giddy. But let these things be spoken of elsewhere; let others dwell upon them.

We have a definite share in the national celebration; our part is to lift to God a great voice which He shall hear amid all the other voices of the hour. Why do we gather here? Is it to recount the praises of men and their mighty achievements? Is it to make display of our national greatness, to tell over our victories and conquests, to celebrate the names and acts of chieftains, statesmen, and rulers of the land, of brave and patient people who gave fortune, life, and sacred honor to the State, of any of those who deserve remembrance to-day? Let this be done elsewhere, as is right and fitting; let men stand up when it is convenient, and in set oration and address do honor to the dead and the living, point the moral of our history, hold up the ideals of patriotism, virtue, and unselfish love of home and native land. But we must be about our Father's business; we have other words to speak, deeper, further reaching; our work here is to offer praise and glory to God; to bless Him in His relations to the Nation as its Lord and King, as Ruler and Governor, as Providence, Law-giver, and Judge. Without God nothing of what we properly value to-day could have been. Without God there could have been neither Nation, nor Nation's birthday. It is He that hath made and kept us one. The office of the Church is to bless and sanctify the Nation's feast day. She cannot be indifferent nor unmoved. We are citizens of the earthly house as well as of the heavenly. We act in that double capacity in praising God Almighty, while with our brethren we keep the feast.

And oh! what ground for thankfulness to-day. Think of the mighty hand that hath led us and upheld us through these years—what it has done for us—what that right hand of the Most High hath wrought! Look back to the humble beginnings—to the poor little colonists with their scant store, their modest ambitions; think of their long-suffering patience, and also of their honorable resolve not to submit to injustice and oppression; remember the band of men who met together, more than one hundred years ago, to sign the Declaration, how they did it—not, as popular legends tell us, with transports of enthusiasm and amid bell-ringing and general jubilation, but in secret session of Congress, with an awful sense of what it meant, with a vision of the gibbet and the ax before their eyes, and well aware of the toil, and blood, and grief that it must cost to maintain their attitude before the world. Think with what dread and sinking of heart, with what tears and partings, with what conflicts of spirit, and what doubts as to the duty of the hour, the foundations were laid; and let us have a tender heart toward the old fathers of the State, the men who took their lives in their hands, and so brought the new Nation to the birth. And then think amid what untold trials and sufferings they carried on their war! Think of the great hearts ready to break, of the starved and ragged armies with that mighty spirit under their hunger-worn ribs, more frequently retreating than advancing, wasted by sickly summer heat, and often in winter standing barefoot in snow; that squalid, sorrowful, anxious force working their sure way through cloud, and storm, and darkness to the victory, perfect and finished, at the end.

It is touching to read the memorials of those days, and to think of all that has come since then; how we are entered into their labors, and are at peace because they went through all that; they sowed in tears and we reap in joy. So then let there be thanks to God for the past, out of which He has evoked the present grandeur of our State, and let us remember what we owe to those who went before, for a part of that debt is obvious; to imitate the virtues and return to the simple mind, the pure intention, the unselfish devotion to the public weal which marked the founders of the Republic. It is a far cry to those days, but there still shine the stars which guided them on their way, the light of Heaven illuminating the earth, the bright beacons of honesty, truth, simplicity, sincerity, self-sacrifice, under which, as under an astrological sign, the little one was born. Pray Heaven those holy lights of morality and public virtue may not forever fade away. Surely it is a marvelous thing to see how nations rise and grow; how they gather strength; how they climb to the meridian of their noonday light and glory; how they blaze awhile, invested with their fullest splendors at that point, and thence, declining, rush downward into the evening, and the night, and the darkness of a long, dead sleep, whence none can awake any more.

This history is not made without God. His hand is in it all. His decrees on Nation and State are just, in perfect justice, as on each one of its men. And must it all be told over again in our case? Is there no averting the common doom? Must each people but repeat the monotonous history of those who went before? God only knows how long the course will be till all shall be accomplished.

But certainly we, the citizens, may do something; we may live pure, honest, sober lives, for the love of country also, as well as for the love of Christ. We may, by taking good heed to ourselves, help to purify the whole Nation, and so obtain a lengthening of our tranquillity. We want much more of this temper; we need to feel that each man helps, in his own way, to save or to destroy his country. Every good man is a reason in God's eyes why He should spare the Nation and prolong its life; every bad man, in his vicious, selfish, evil life, is a reason why God should break up the whole system to which that worthless, miserable being belongs.

If we love our country with a true, real love we shall show it by contributing in ourselves to the sum of collective righteousness what it may be in our power, aided by

God's grace, to give. They are not true men who have no thanks to bring to the Lord this day. They are not true men who simply shout and cry, and make noisy demonstration, and speak great swelling words, without reason, or reflection, or any earnest thought to duty, to God, and the State. From neither class can any good come; not from the senselessly uproarious, not from the livid and gloomy children of discontent. They were thoughtful, patriotic, self-sacrificing men who built this great temple of civil and religious liberty. By such men only can it be kept in repair and made to stand for ages and ages. No kingdom of this world can last forever, yet many endure to a great age. The old mother country, England, in her present constitutional form, is more than eight hundred years old—a good age, a grand age, with, we trust and pray, many bright centuries to come hereafter, as good, as fair. Let us remember that for us, as for all people, length of days and long life and peace depend on the use we make of our gifts, on the fidelity with which we discharge our mission. And that is the reason why every one of us has, in part, his country's life in his own hands. But I detain you from the duty of the hour. We meet to praise not man, but God; to praise Him with a reasonable and devout purpose; to bless Him for this day which He permits us to see, for our homes, our liberties, our peace, our place among the powers of the earth. It is all from Him, whatever good we have, and to Him let us ascribe the honor and the glory. And let us say, with them of old time:

"Blessed art thou, O Lord God of our fathers; and to be praised and exalted above all forever.

"Yea, let us bless the Most High, and praise and honor him that liveth forever, whose dominion is an everlasting dominion, and his kingdom is from generation to generation. And all the inhabitants of the earth are reputed as nothing; and he doeth according to his will in the army of heaven and among the inhabitants of the earth."—P. T.

SUGGESTIVE THOUGHTS

"**AMERICA.**"—The origin of the words of the patriotic hymn, "America," has been somewhat recently celebrated by an anniversary. The air, as is well known, is that of the national anthem of England, "God Save the King." As such it has been in use, in one form or another, since the middle of the last century.

In 1832, Dr. S. F. Smith came upon it in a "book of German music," and on the spur of the moment, as it appears, wrote for it the hymn "America." This was in Andover, Mass., in February, 1832. The hymn was first sung publicly at a children's celebration at the Park Street Church, Boston, on July 4th of that year.

"If I had anticipated the future of it, doubtless I should have taken more pains with it," wrote Doctor Smith, in 1872. "Such as it is, I am glad to have contributed this mite to the cause of American freedom." —*Selected.*

AMERICA FIRST.—This is the season when Young America celebrates the glorious deeds of the forefathers, when they cut the leading-strings that bound them to the Old World, and stepped forth with the independence of manhood.

It took Rome five hundred years, five centuries of war, intrigue, and arrogance, to overspread Southern Europe. In a little more than one century America has grown to a magnitude, in area and perhaps in population also, equal to that of Rome in its most magnificent days.

"Civis Romanus sum!" was the proudest boast that could fall from the lips of man at the beginning of the Christian era. Is there to-day an American who rates his citizenship in the Great Republic at a lower value than Roman freedom nineteen hundred years ago?

The day for "spread-eagle" brag is long past, but there is no reason why we should hesitate to say what not we alone but all the people of the world believe, that it is the destiny of this country to become the greatest, the strongest, the wealthiest, the most self-supporting, of all the nations of the earth. It is already the greatest self-governing community the world has ever seen.

How can we make it greater? By standing together as Americans. We shall not magnify, but shall belittle ourselves, if we swagger before our neighbors—using bravado for the strong, and insolence in our treatment of the weak. But we should take American views instead of party views, when questions arise between this government and others.

The motto "America against the world" would be a contemptible motto. Yet is it not better to adopt even such a motto than to take the side of the world against America, or to be indifferent when the interests of one's own country are assailed?

The Fourth of July is a good time for us all to resolve that we will be Americans at heart. Not that we will build up our own country on the ruins of others, but that when there is a clashing of interests those of our native land shall have our hearty support. —Y. C.

COUNTRY, Love of.—If love were the offspring of merit, then patriotism would find no difficulty in showing why a country is worth loving. But the Russian loves a land that has no freedom; the Spaniard, like the Irishman, loves a country that has no prosperity; the Chinaman loves a land that has no inspiration; the Eskimo loves a land that has for others no natural beauty. Men of each of these nationalities love their home land apparently for no other reason than because it is their own.

So long as being born in a country makes its patriots, there will be no better reason to give. If patriots would make their country, —if the people would all help to make their country better worth loving,—the word patriotism would not sometimes mean so little. It is poorly worth the name if it implies no more than the habit of association that attaches the savage to his hunting-ground or brings back the exiled cat to its wonted garret. True patriotism is something more than blind instinct.

Neither is it a partisanship or a worship. It has been said there is no such thing as a Turkish patriot. The Turk is first and last a Mohammedan.

Nor is patriotism a mere sentiment. It is a principle of duty; and it becomes more beneficent as it grows more enlightened. That will be when patriots cease to cry, "Our country, right or wrong!" and insist that its public life and its politics shall have nothing in them of which they need feel ashamed.—Y. C.

DECLARATION, How the, Was Adopted.—It was desirable that a fact of such supreme importance as the birth of thirteen new nations should not remain merely a matter of logical inference. It must be embodied in a declaration incapable of misinterpretation, not open to be explained away by ingenious constructions or canceled by technical arguments. Independence could not be left to be gathered among the recitals of a preamble. . . . On June 7 Richard Henry Lee, of Virginia, moved "certain resolutions respecting independency." John Adams seconded the motion. Its consideration was referred to the next morning at ten o'clock, when members were "enjoined to attend punctually." A debate of three days ensued. It appeared that four New England colonies and three Southern colonies were prepared to vote at once in the affirmative; but unanimity was desirable, and could probably be obtained by a little delay. So a postponement was voted until July 1. . . . Three committees were appointed; one was charged with drafting the document itself, so that it should be ready for adoption on July 1. The members of this committee, in order of precedence, were Thomas Jefferson, John Adams, Benjamin Franklin, Roger Sherman, and Robert R. Livingston. On July 1 debate was resumed in committee of the whole on the original resolution of Mr. Lee, which was reported to Congress and carried by that body on the next day. The Declaration was then at once reported and discussed until late on July 4. The question of independence was really settled July 2, but posterity has selected July 4, the anniversary of the adoption of Jefferson's Declaration.—JOHN T. MORSE, JR., in LIFE OF JOHN ADAMS.

ENGLAND AND AMERICA.—This is a memorable day to Englishmen as well as to Americans. It is to us a day both of regret and of rejoicing: of regret at the severance of the political connection which bound the two branches of our race together, and of regret even more for the unhappy errors which brought that severance about, and the unhappy strife by which the memory of it was embittered. But it is also a day of rejoicing, for it is the birthday of the eldest daughter of England—the day when a new nation, sprung from our own, first took its independent place in the world. And now with the progress of time rejoicing has prevailed over regret, and we in England can at length join heartily with you in celebrating the beginning of your national life. All sense of bitterness has passed away, and been replaced by sympathy with all which this anniversary means to an American heart.

England and America now understand one another far better than they ever did before. In 1776 there was on one side a monarch and a small ruling caste, on the other side a people. Now our government can no longer misrepresent the nation, and across the ocean a people speaks to a people. We have both come, and that most notably within recent months, to perceive that all over the world the interests of America and of England are substantially the same.

The sense of our underlying unity over against the other races and forms of civilization has been a potent force in drawing us together. It is said that the Fourth of July is a day of happy augury for mankind. This is true because on that day America entered on a course and proclaimed principles of government which have been of profound significance for mankind. Many nations have had a career of conquest and of civilizing dominion: but to make an immense people prosperous, happy, and free is a nobler and grander achievement than the most brilliant conquests and the widest dominion.—JAMES BRYCE.

ENGLAND AND THE FOURTH OF JULY.—I wish with all my heart that we could adopt the Fourth of July as the Festival Day of the whole English-speaking race. If this suggestion should seem strange to Americans, it is not unfamiliar to many Englishmen. We consider that the triumph of the American revolt against George III. was a vindication of the essentially English idea of democratic self-government, and we believe that we have benefited by it almost as much as the Americans. It taught us a lesson which made the British Colonial Empire a possibility, and if we are now involved in a suicidal war in South Africa, it is largely because our Government has forgotten the principles of George Washington, and has gone back to the principles of George III.

For some years past I have presided at a distinctly British celebration of the Fourth of July at my brother's settlement in Southeast London, at Browning Hall, and I have always repudiated the idea that Americans should be allowed to monopolize the Fourth of July. It is one of the great days of the English-speaking race in the celebration of which all members of the English-speaking

nations should participate.—W. T. Stead.
(I.)

FAMILY, A Patriotic.—The father of a small family, at the outbreak of the Rebellion, felt that he could not stay at home while his neighbors went to the war. The boys agreed to take care of the place, and help mother, while the father fought for the flag. Each did his part well. The boys' farming elicited the commendation of a passing gentleman, to whom one of them said, "Father's fighting, I'm digging, and mother's praying."—"Fighting, digging, and praying!" cried the gentleman. "That's the patriotism that will bring the country out of her distress."—F. II.

HEROISM, Example of.—The plague was making a desert of the city of Marseilles. Death was everywhere. The physicians could do nothing. In one of their counsels, it was decided that a corpse must be dissected; but it would be death to the operator. A celebrated physician of the number arose and said, "I devote myself for the safety of my country. Before this numerous assembly I swear in the name of humanity and religion, that to-morrow, at the break of day, I will dissect a corpse, and write down, as I proceed, what I observe." He immediately left the room, made his will, and spent the night in religious exercises. During the day, a man had died in his house of the plague; and at daybreak on the following morning, the physician, whose name was Guyon, entered the room, and critically made the necessary examinations, writing down all his surgical observations. He then left the room, threw the papers into a vase of vinegar, that they might not convey the disease to another, and retired to a convenient place, where he died in twelve hours.—F. I.

INDEPENDENCE DAY.—The second day of July, 1776, will be the most memorable epoch in the history of America. I am apt to believe that it will be celebrated by succeeding generations as the great anniversary festival. It ought to be commemorated as the day of deliverance by solemn acts of devotion to God Almighty. It ought to be solemnized with pomp and parade, with shows, games, sports, bells, bonfires, and illuminations, from one end of this continent to the other, from this time forward forevermore. You will think me transported with enthusiasm, but I am not. I am well aware of the toil and blood and treasure that it will cost us to maintain this Declaration, and support and defend these States. Yet through all the gloom I can see the rays of ravishing light and glory. I can see that the end is more than worth all the means; and that posterity will triumph in that day's transaction, even tho we should rue it, which I trust in God we shall not.—John Adams. From a letter to his wife.

LIBERTY AND LAW.—All freedom has its birthright and its protection in law. Are you free? Law has given the priceless gift to you.

Law once volleyed, and thundered, and raged with lips of fire and face of blood, to bespeak for four million slaves the mercy of freedom. Law gives freedom, and true freedom abides in the lowly hut of obedience.

"Ye shall know the truth, and the truth shall make you free." There is, then, no liberty for humanity, but the liberty which flames out from God's law of truth. The most independent and happy moment of life is when a soul can say: "I'm a slave of Jesus." It is the soul's true declaration of independence.—*Selected.*

NATIONAL SAFETY.—A selfish nation may make money, but it will be unmade by its money.

Nations, like men, are never safe when their chief thought is their own safety.

Unless God founded the nation, it is not worth saving; if God founded it, He will aid it in its salvation.

No nation is safe until its citizens care more about its safety than their own.

The salvation of a nation comes by way of its few best men, "the remnant."

"Blessed is the nation whose God is the Lord," and who see in this their blessedness.—*Selected.*

NATIONS, Crises of.—There are brief crises in which the drift of individual and national history is determined, sometimes unexpectedly; critical moments on which great decisions hang; days which, like a mountain in a plain, lift themselves above the dead level of common days into everlasting eminence. Our Day of Independence was such a day; so was the day of Marathon, and the day of Waterloo. Napoleon admitted that the Austrians fought grandly on the field of Rivoli, and said, "They failed because they do not understand the value of minutes." Humboldt refers the discovery of America to "a wonderful concatenation of trivial circumstances," including a flight of parrots.—Dr. Foss.

PATRIOTISM.—Patriotism is love of country, and loyalty to its life and weal.

Take patriotism away, and the nation's soul has fled.

Next to God is country, and next to religion is patriotism.

America is the country of human dignity, and human liberty.

The duty of patriotism is the duty of justice and gratitude.

The safety of the Republic lies in the vigilant and active patriotism of the American people. This patriotism, America, thou shalt have. I speak for veterans. I speak for their brother citizens.—Archbishop Ireland.

PATRIOTISM.—A true patriot is known by his interest in education.—James Ellis.

The factious man is apt to mistake himself for a patriot.—Marquis d'Argensen.

No nation can expect to prosper and become great without ardent and devoted patriotism; it is irresistible, unconquerable, universal.—J. E. E. D. Acton.

Patriotism is usually truer and more intense in small than in large countries, and in countries rough and barren than in those smoother and more fertile.—H. WINSLOW.

When virtue and genuine patriotism predominate, offices will seek good and competent men, who should answer the call as a matter of duty, not of pleasure or profit.—L. C. JUDSON.

We join ourselves to no party that does not carry the flag and keep step to the music of the Union.—RUFUS CHOATE. Letter to the Whig Convention.

This Nation, under God, shall have a new birth of freedom, and that government of the people, by the people, for the people, shall not perish from the earth.—LINCOLN. Speech at Gettysburg, Nov. 19, 1863.

Liberty and Union, now and forever, one and inseparable.—DANIEL WEBSTER. Second Speech on Foot's Resolution.

Cum tempus necessitasque postulat, decertandum manu est, et mors servituti turpidinique anteponenda.

When time and need require, we should resist with all our might, and prefer death to slavery and disgrace.—CICERO.

Nihil ex omnibus rebus humanis est præclarius aut præstantium quam de republicâ bene mereri.

Of all human things nothing is more honorable or more excellent than to deserve well of one's country.—CICERO.

O fortunata mors quæ, naturæ debita, pro patriâ potissimum redita!

O happy death, which tho due to nature is most nobly given for our country.—CICERO.

Patria est communis omnium parens.

Our country is the common parent of all.—CICERO.

Nullum est imperium tutum nisi benevolentiâ munitum.

No government is safe unless protected by the good-will of the people.—NEPOS.

Amor patriæ ratione valentior.

The love of country is more powerful than reason itself.—OVID.

Nescio quâ natale solum dulcedine captos Ducit, et immemores non sinit esse sui.

Our native land charms us with inexpressible sweetness, and never allows us to forget that we belong to it.—OVID.

Patria est ubicumque vir fortis sedem elegerit.

A brave man's country is wherever he chooses his abode.—QUINTUS CURTIUS RUFUS.

Non exercitus, neque thesauri, præsidia regni sunt, verum amici.

The safety of a kingdom is not its armies, nor its treasures, but its friends.—SALLUST.

Præferre patriam liberis regem decet.

A king should prefer his country to his children.—SENECA.

Servare cives, major est virtus patriæ patri.

To preserve the life of citizens, is the greatest virtue in the father of his country.—SENECA.

Patriotism is love of one's country; the passion which aims to serve one's country, either in defending it from invasion, or protecting its rights, and maintaining its laws and institutions in vigor and purity; it is the characteristic of a good citizen, the noblest passion that animates a man in the character of a citizen.—N. WEBSTER. (C. G.)

PATRIOTISM, Pleasure of.—Neither Montaigne in writing his essays, nor Descartes in building new worlds, nor Burnet in framing an antediluvian earth, no, nor Newton in discovering and establishing the true laws of nature on experiment and a sublime geometry, felt more intellectual joys than he feels who is a real patriot, who bends all the force of his understanding, and directs all his thoughts and actions, to the good of his country.—BOLINGBROKE.

PATRIOTISM, Pure.—Do you know how much money Washington received for his services as commander-in-chief of the army in the time of the American Revolution? Not one farthing. His successors in the army have received their $17,000 or $19,000 salary a year. But for Valley Forge, and Monmouth, and the Delaware crossing, and all the other horrors of the Revolution, Washington received not a farthing.

What but pure love of country inspired Governor Nelson, of Virginia, during the Revolutionary War, when, at the siege of Yorktown, Lafayette asked him to what point the cannon had better be directed, and Governor Nelson answered, " Point to that house; it is mine, and the best house in town; and Lord Cornwallis will surely be occupying that as his headquarters? " What but patriotism led Bismarck, when at one time he was threatened with death because of his effort to get Germany away from the Austrian clutches, to cry out, " What care I if they hang me provided the rope by which I am hanged binds this new Germany firmly to the Prussian throne? "—TALMAGE.

PATRIOTISM, True Spartan.—Lycurgus taught his citizens to think nothing more disagreeable than to live for themselves. Like bees, they acted with one impulse for the public good, and always assembled about their prince. They were possessed with a thirst for honor and enthusiasm bordering upon insanity, and had not a wish but for their country.

These sentiments are confirmed by some of their aphorisms. When Pædaretus lost his election for one of the three hundred, he went away rejoicing that there were three hundred better men than himself found in the city. Pisistratides going with some others, ambassador to the King of Persia's lieutenants, was asked whether they came with a public commission or on their own account, to which he answered, " If successful, for the public; if unsuccessful, for ourselves."—PLUTARCH.

PATRIOT, The True.—He loves his country, but he loves still more the Kingdom of God.

He cares too much for his country to uphold her in any wrong.

He does not reserve his patriotism until he has a chance to die for his country; he lives for her.

He does not urge the selection of the best men for candidates, and then refuse to serve when called upon, tho at the cost of time and money and inclination.

He does not vote for bad men, and then plead that he did not know they were bad. He takes time to investigate the characters of candidates.—*Selected*.

RELIGIOUS PURPOSE OF THE FOUNDERS.—To tell the story of the Hebrews and leave out religion is impossible: equally impossible is such omission in telling the story of our country. Columbus, in his journal, speaks of "the means to be taken for the conversion" of the natives to Christianity. Parkman shows the spirit higher than advantage or the pursuit of wealth which actuated the French discoverers. Sir Humphrey Gilbert, saying, "We are as near to Heaven by sea as by land," reveals the spirit of not a few of the early English discoverers. "Every enterprise of the Pilgrims," says Bancroft, "began with God." Lord Baltimore had a religious purpose in the founding of Maryland. Christian philanthropy was the controlling thought of Oglethorpe in Georgia. William Penn founded Pennsylvania as a religious movement; and he is blind who does not see the same purpose in the beginning of our national councils and the wonderful career of the Father of his Country.—Rev. John Lee.

UNION, The Perpetuity of the.—When my eyes shall be turned to behold, for the last time, the sun in Heaven, may I not see him shining on the broken and dishonored fragments of a once glorious Union; on States dissevered, discordant, belligerent; on a land rent with civil feuds, or drenched, it may be, in fraternal blood! Let their last feeble and lingering glance, rather, behold the gorgeous ensign of the Republic, now known and honored throughout the earth, still full high advanced, its arms and trophies streaming in their original luster, not a stripe erased or polluted, not a single star obscured, bearing for its motto no such miserable interrogatory as What is all this worth? nor those other words of delusion and folly, Liberty first, and Union afterward, but everywhere, spread all over in characters of living light, blazing on all its ample folds, as they float over the sea and over the land, and in every wind under the whole heavens, that other sentiment, dear to every true American heart, Liberty and Union now and forever, one and inseparable.—Daniel Webster.

POETRY

The Heroic Age

By Richard Watson Gilder

He speaks not well who doth his time deplore,
Naming it new and little and obscure,
Ignoble and unfit for lofty deeds.
All times were modern in the time of them,
And this no more than others. Do thy part
Here in the living day, as did the great
Who made old days immortal! So shall men,
Gazing back to this far-looming hour,
Say: "Then the time when men were truly men,
Tho wars grew less, their spirits met the test
Of new conditions; conquering civic wrong;
Saving the State anew by virtuous lives;
Guarding the country's honor as their own,
And their own as their country's and their sons';
Defying leagued fraud with single truth;
Not fearing loss; and daring to be pure.
When error through the land raged like a pest,
They calmed the madness caught from mind to mind
By wisdom drawn from eld, and counsel sane.
And as the martyrs of the ancient world
Gave Death for man, so nobly gave they Life;
Those the great days, and that the heroic age."

America

By Samuel Francis Smith

My country, 'tis of thee,
Sweet land of liberty,
Of thee I sing;
Land where my fathers died,
Land of the pilgrims' pride,
From every mountain-side,
Let freedom ring.

My native country, thee,
Land of the noble, free,
Thy name I love;
I love thy rocks and rills,
Thy woods and templed hills,—
My heart with rapture thrills,
Like that above.

Let music swell the breeze,
And ring from all the trees
Sweet freedom's song;
Let mortal tongues awake,
Let all that breathe partake,
Let rocks their silence break,
The sound prolong.

Our fathers' God, to Thee,
Author of liberty,
To Thee we sing;
Long may our land be bright
With freedom's holy light,—
Protect us by Thy might,
Great God, our King.

The Battle Cry of Freedom

By Geo. F. Root

Yes, we'll rally round the flag, boys, we'll
  rally once again,
Shouting the battle cry of Freedom,
We'll rally from the hillside, we'll gather
  from the plain,
Shouting the battle cry of Freedom!

Chorus:

The Union forever, hurrah! boys, hurrah!
Down with the traitor, up with the star,
While we rally round the flag, boys, rally
  once again,
Shouting the battle cry of Freedom!

We are springing to the call of our brothers
  gone before,
Shouting the battle cry of Freedom;
And we'll fill the vacant ranks with a million
  freemen more,
Shouting the battle cry of Freedom!—Cho.

We will welcome to our number the loyal,
  true and brave,
Shouting the battle cry of Freedom;
And altho they may be poor, not a man shall
  be a slave,
Shouting the battle cry of Freedom!—Cho.

So we're springing to the call from the East
  and from the West,
Shouting the battle cry of Freedom;
And we'll hurl the rebel crew from the land
  we love the best,
Shouting the battle cry of Freedom!—Cho.

Battle Hymn of the Republic

By Julia Ward Howe

Mine eyes have seen the glory of the coming
  of the Lord;
He is tramping out the vintage where the
  grapes of wrath are stored;
He has loosed the fearful lightning of His
  terrible swift sword.
  His truth is marching on.

I have seen Him in the watch-fire of a hundred circling camps;
They have builded Him an altar in the evening dews and damps;
I can read His righteous sentence by the dim
  and flaring lamps.
  His day is marching on.

I have read a fiery gospel writ in burnished
  rows of steel;
"As ye deal with My contemners, so with
  you My grace shall deal;
Let the Hero, born of woman, crush the
  serpent with his heel,
  Since God is marching on."

He has sounded forth the trumpet that shall
  never call retreat!
He is sifting out the hearts of men before
  His judgment seat;
Oh, be swift, my soul, to answer Him! Be
  jubilant, my feet!
  Our God is marching on.

In the beauty of the lilies Christ was born
  across the sea,
With a glory in His bosom that transfigures
  you and me.
As He died to make men holy, let us die to
  make men free,
  While God is marching on.

Columbia, the Land of the Brave

By David T. Shaw

O Columbia, the gem of the ocean,
  The home of the brave and the free,
The shrine of each patriot's devotion,
  A world offers homage to thee.
Thy mandates make heroes assemble,
  When Liberty's form stands in view,
Thy banners make tyranny tremble,
  When borne by the Red, White, and Blue.

Chorus:

When borne by the Red, White, and Blue,
When borne by the Red, White, and Blue,
Thy banners make tyranny tremble,
  When borne by the Red, White, and Blue.

When war winged its wide desolation,
  And threatened the land to deform,
The ark then of Freedom's foundation,
  Columbia, rode safe through the storm,
With the garlands of victory around her,
  When so proudly she bore her brave crew,
With her flag proudly floating before her,
  The boast of the Red, White, and Blue.
  Chorus.

The wine-cup, the wine-cup bring hither,
  And fill you it true to the brim.
May the wreaths they have won never wither,
  Nor the stars of their glory grow dim.
May the service united ne'er sever,
  But they to their colors prove true!
The Army and Navy forever!
  Three cheers for the Red, White, and Blue!
  Chorus.

Our Country Saved

[*Extract from "Ode Recited at the Harvard
  Commemoration, July 21, 1865.*]

By James Russell Lowell

Boom, cannon, boom to all the winds and
  waves!
  Clash out, glad bells, from every rocking
  steeple!
Banners, advance with triumph, bend your
  staves!
  And from every mountain-peak
Let beacon-fire to answering beacon speak,
Katahdin tell Monadnock, Whiteface he,
And so leap on in light from sea to sea,
  Till the glad news be sent
Across a kindling continent,
Making earth feel more firm and air breathe
  braver:
Be proud! for she is saved, and all have
  helped to save her!

She that lifts up the manhood of the poor,
She of the open soul and open door,
With room about her hearth for all mankind!
The fire is dreadful in her eyes no more;
From her bold front the helm she doth unbind,
Sends all her handmaid armies back to spin,
And bids her navies, that so lately hurled
Their crashing battle, to hold their thunders in,
Swimming like birds of calm along the unharmful shore.
No challenge sends she to the older world,
That looked askance and hatred; a light scorn
Plays o'er her mouth, as round her mighty knees
She calls her children back, and waits the morn
Of nobler day, enthroned between her subject seas.

Bow down, dear land, for thou hast found release!
Thy God, in these distempered days,
Hath taught thee the sure wisdom of His ways,
And through thine enemies hath wrought thee peace!
Bow down in prayer and praise!
No poorest in thy borders but may now
Lift to the juster skies a man's enfranchised brow.
O Beautiful! my Country! ours once more!
Smoothing thy gold of war-disheveled hair
O'er such sweet brows as never other wore,
And letting thy set lips
Freed from wrath's pale eclipse,
The rosy edges of their smile lay bare,
What words divine of lover or of poet
Could tell our love and make thee know it,
Among the nations bright beyond compare?
What were our lives without thee?
What all our lives to save thee?
We reck not what we gave thee;
We will not dare to doubt thee,
But ask whatever else, and we will **dare**!

Dixie

BY DANIEL DECATUR EMMETT

I wish I was in de land ob cotton,
Old times dar am not forgotten,
Look away! Look away! Look **away**!
In Dixie Land where I was born in,
Early on a frosty mornin',
Look away! Look away! Look **away**!

CHORUS:

Den I wish I was in Dixie,
Hooray! Hooray!
In Dixie Land, I'll take my stand,
To lib and die in Dixie,
Away! Away!
Away down south in Dixie.

Old Missus marry " Will-de-weaber,"
William was a gay deceaber;
Look away! Look away! Look away!

But when he put his arm around 'er,
He smiled as fierce as a forty pounder,
Look away! Look away! Look away!
CHORUS.

His face was as sharp as a butcher's cleaber,
But dat did not seem to greab 'er;
Look away! Look away! Look away!
Old Missus acted de foolish part,
And died for a man dat broke her heart.
Look away! Look away! Look away!
CHORUS.

Now here's a health to de next old Missus,
And all de gals dat want to kiss us;
Look away! Look away! Look away!
But if you want to drive 'way sorrow,
Come and hear dis song to-morrow,
Look away! Look away! Look away!
CHORUS.

Dar's buckwheat cakes an' Injen batter,
Makes you fat or a little fatter;
Look away! Look away! Look away!
Den hoe it down and scratch your grabble,
To Dixie's Land I'm bound to trabble,
Look away! Look away! Look away!
CHORUS.

Origin of Fireworks

BY H. M. GREENLEAF

Away, far off in China,
In the days of Nanke-chin,
Lived a funny little fellow,
Who was priest and mandarin,
And ever through his shaven head,
A strain of music rang,
Which seemed to him like " Fizz
And crackle, fizz and crackle,—BANG."

One day this little fellow,
As he trolled his merry song,
Chanced to meet the royal viceroy,
As he rode in state along,
Who stopping, listened with delight,
To what he gaily sang,
And begged at once the music rare,
Of " Fizz and crackle,—BANG,"

But naught had he of music,
Nor a note had ever read,
For this strain so shrill and stirring,
Was but running in his head;
Nor could the gongs nor kettle-drums,
With all their noisy clang,
Express a bit of what he meant
By " Fizz and crackle,—BANG."

Then said this little fellow,
" I will try what I can do,"
And he straightawav set to molding
Rockets, Roman candles too;
But what he sought and most desired,
Was something with a twang,
That could express in all its force,
His " Fizz and crackle,—BANG."

But e'en while he was planning,
Burst his rockets with such noise,
Frightened came the whole town running
To behold the dreadful toys;

Then madly danced the mandarin,
And cried, " O, I will hang,
If I've not found the very thing,
To make my ' Crackle,—BANG.' "

* * * * *

Now sound the rattling crackers,
As in days of Nanke-chin,
(For the Fourth, to be well honored,
Must have clangor, clash, and din,)
The banners all are waving,
And the drums and trumpets clang,
Awaking echoes far and near,
Of " Fizz and crackle,—BANG."

And when the day departing,
Does the evening opén out,
Sparkling, fiery little demons
Leap from wheels and dance about,
And hissing rockets upward fly,
Amidst prolonged huzza,
While crowds astonished, gaping,
Cry out, "*Sst!* Boom! *A-A-A-A-H!*"
Y. C.

Freedom

Hereditary bondsmen! Know ye not
Who would be free themselves must strike
the blow?
BYRON—*Childe Harold.* Canto II.
St. 67.

Freedom has a thousand charms to show,
That slaves howe'er contented, never know.
COWPER—*Table Talk.*—Line 260.

He is the freeman, whom the truth makes
free,
And all are slaves besides.
COWPER—*The Task.* Bk. V. Line 733.

When Freedom from her mountain height
Unfurled her standard to the air,
She tore the azure robe of night,
And set the stars of glory there.
DRAKE—*The American Flag.*

My angel,—his name is Freedom,—
Choose him to be your king;
He shall cut pathways east and west,
And fend you with his wing.
EMERSON—*Boston Hymn.*

Yes, to this thought I hold with firm persist-
ence;
The last result of wisdom stamps it true;
He only earns his freedom and existence
Who daily conquers them anew.
GOETHE—*Faust.*

Know ye why the Cypress tree as Freedom's
tree is known?
Know ye why the Lily fair as Freedom's
flower is shown?
Hundred arms the Cypress has, yet never
plunder seeks;
With ten well-developed tongues the Lily
never speaks!
OMAR KHAYYAM—Frederich Bodenstedt,
Translator.

What is freedom? Rightly understood,
A universal license to be good.
HARTLEY COLERIDGE.

Marching Through Georgia

By HENRY CLAY WORK

Bring the good old bugle boys, we'll sing
another song,
Sing it with a spirit that will start the world
along,
Sing it as we used to sing it fifty thousand
strong,
While we were marching through Georgia.

CHORUS:

Hurrah! Hurrah! We bring the jubilee!
Hurrah! Hurrah! The flag that makes
you free!
So we sang the chorus from Atlanta to the
sea,
While we were marching through Georgia.

How the darkies shouted when they heard
the joyful sound!
How the turkeys gobbled which our com-
missary found!
How the sweet potatoes even started from
the ground,
While we were marching through Georgia.
CHORUS.

Yes, and there were Union men who wept
with joyful tears,
When they saw the honored flag they had
not seen for years,
Hardly could they be restrained from break-
ing forth in cheers.
While we were marching through Georgia.
CHORUS.

" Sherman's dashing Yankee boys will never
reach the coast! "
So the saucy rebels said, and 'twas a hand-
some boast,
Had they not forgot, alas! to reckon with
the host,
While we were marching through Georgia.
CHORUS.

So we made a thoroughfare for Freedom
and her train,
Sixty miles in latitude; three hundred to
the main;
Treason fled before us, for resistance was in
vain,
While we were marching through Georgia.
CHORUS.

The Glory of the State

By SIR WILLIAM JONES

What constitutes a state?
Not high-raised battlements or labored
mound,
Thick wall or moated gate;
Not cities proud with spire and turret
crowned;
Not bays and broad-armed ports,
Where, laughing at the storm, rich navies
ride;
Not starred and spangled courts,
Where low-browed baseness wafts perfume
to pride;

No; *men*, high-minded *men*,
　　With powers as far above dull brutes en-
　　　dued
In forest, brake, or den,
　　As beasts excel cold rocks and brambles
　　　rude;
Men who their duties know,
　　But know their rights, and knowing dare
　　　maintain.

Hail Columbia

BY JOSEPH HOPKINSON.

Hail, Columbia, happy land!
Hail, ye heroes, heaven-born band!
Who fought and bled in Freedom's cause,
Who fought and bled in Freedom's cause,
And when the storm of war was gone,
Enjoyed the peace your valor won.
Let independence be our boast,
Ever mindful what it cost,
Ever grateful for the prize,
Let its altar reach the skies.
　　Firm—united—let us be.
　　Rallying round our liberty;
　　As a band of brothers joined,
　　Peace and safety we shall find.

Immortal patriots! rise once more;
Defend your rights, defend your shore;
Let no rude foe, with impious hand,
Let no rude foe, with impious hand,
Invade the shrine where sacred lies
Of toil and blood the well-earned prize,
While offering peace sincere and just,
In Heaven we place a manly trust,
That truth and justice will prevail,
And every scheme of bondage fail.

Sound, sound the trump of fame!
Let Washington's great name,
Ring through the world with loud applause,
Ring through the world with loud applause:
Let every clime to Freedom dear
Listen with a joyful ear.
With equal skill and godlike power,
He governs in the fearful hour
Of horrid war; or guides with ease
The happier times of honest peace.

Behold the Chief who now commands,
Once more to serve his country stands—
The rock on which the storm will beat,
The rock on which the storm will beat:
But armed in virtue firm and true,
His hopes are fixed on Heav'n and you.
When Hope was sinking in dismay,
When glooms obscured Columbia's day,
His steady mind, from changes free.
Resolved on death or liberty.

Liberty

The people never give up their liberties but
under some delusion.
　　BURKE—*Speech at a County Meeting*
　　　　　　of Bucks, 1784.

Liberty's in every blow!
Let us do or die.
　　BURNS—*Bannockburn.*

What is liberty without wisdom and without virtue? It is the greatest of all possible
evils; for it is folly, vice, and madness, without tuition or restraint.
　　BURKE—*Reflections on the Revolution*
　　　　　　in France.

For freedom's battle once begun,
Bequeath'd by bleeding sire to son,
Tho baffled oft is ever won.
　　BYRON—*The Giaour.* Line 123.

The poorest man may in his cottage bid
defiance to all the force of the crown.
　　EARL OF CHATHAM—*Speech on the*
　　　　　　Excise Bill.

'Tis liberty alone that gives the flower
Of fleeting life its luster and perfume;
And we are weeds without it.
　　COWPER—*The Task.* Bk. V. Line 446.

The love of liberty with life is given,
And life itself the inferior gift of Heaven.
　　DRYDEN—*Palemon and Arcite*
　　　　　　Bk. II. Line 291.

This is true liberty when freeborn men,
Having to advise the public, may speak free:
Which he who can and will deserves high
　　praise:
Who neither can nor will may hold his peace.
What can be juster in a state than this?
　　MILTON—Trans. *Horace.* Ep. I.
　　　　　　16, 40.

Give me again my hollow tree
A crust of bread, and liberty!
　　POPE—*Imitations of Horace.* Bk. II.
　　　　　　Satire VI. Line 220.

O Liberty! Liberty! how many crimes are
committed in thy name!
　　MADAME ROLAND—*Macaulay. Mirabeau.*

Patriotism

Who would not be that youth? what pity
　　is it
That we can die but once to save our
　　country.
　　ADDISON—*Cato.* Act IV. Sc. 4.

Our ships were British oak,
And hearts of oak our men.
　　S. J. ARNOLD—*Death of Nelson.*

True patriots all; for be it understood
We left our country for our country's good.
　　GEORGE BARRINGTON. *New South Wales.*
　　Prologue for the Opening of the Play-
　　House at New South Wales, Jan. 16,
　　1796.

Washington's a watchword such as ne'er
Shall sink while there's an echo left to air.
　　BYRON—*Age of Bronze.* St. 5.

The patriot's boast, where'er we roam,
His first, best country, ever is at home.
　　GOLDSMITH—*The Traveller.* Line 73.

Strike—for your altars and your fires;
Strike—for the green graves of your sires;
　　God, and your native land.
　　FITZ-GREENE HALLECK—*Marco Bozzaris.*

Thou too, sail on, O ship of State!
Sail on, O Union, strong and great!
Humanity with all its fears,
With all the hopes of future years,
Is hanging breathless on thy fate!
LONGFELLOW—*The Building of the Ship.*

A song for our banner? The watchword re-
call
Which gave the Republic her station;
" United we stand—divided we fall! "
It made and preserves us a nation!
GEORGE P. MORRIS—*The Flag of our
Union.*

The bullet comes—and either
A desolate hearth may see;
And God alone to-night knows where
The vacant place may be!
The dread that stirs the peasant
Thrills nobles' hearts with fear;
Yet above selfish sorrow
Both hold their country dear.
ADELAIDE A. PROCTOR—*Lesson of
the War.*

Be just, and fear not:
Let all the ends thou aim'st at, be thy coun-
try's,
Thy God's, and truth's; then if thou fall'st,
O Cromwell,
Thou fallest a blessed martyr.
Henry VIII. Act III. Sc. 2.

Had I a dozen sons,—each in my love
alike, . . . I had rather have eleven die
nobly for their country, than one voluptu-
ously surfeit out of action.
Coriolanus. Act I. Sc. 3.

I do love
My country's good, with a respect more ten-
der,
More holy, and profound, than mine own life.
Coriolanus. Act III. Sc. 3.

Dulce et decorum est pro patriâ mori.
It is sweet and glorious to die for one's
country. HORACE.

Non ille pro charis amicis
Aut patriâ timidus perire.
He dares for his country or his friends to
die. HORACE.

Patriotism

BY SIR WALTER SCOTT

Breathes there the man with soul so dead
Who never to himself hath said,
This is my own, my native land!
Whose heart hath ne'er within him burned,
As home his footsteps he hath turned
From wandering on a foreign strand!
If such there breathe, go, mark him well;
For him no minstrel raptures swell;
High tho his titles, proud his name,
Boundless his wealth as wish can claim,
Despite those titles, power, and pelf,
The wretch, concentered all in self,
Living shall forfeit fair renown,
And, doubly dying, shall go down
To the vile dust from whence he sprung,
Unwept, unhonored, and unsung.

Love Patriotism

BY SUSAN COOLIDGE

He serves his country best
Who lives pure life, and doeth righteous
deed,
And walks straight paths, however others
stray,
And leaves his sons as uttermost bequest,
A stainless record which all men may read;
This is the better way.

No drop but serves the slowly lifting tide;
No dew but has an errand to some flower;
No smallest star but sheds some helpful ray,
And man by man, *each helping all the rest,*
Make the firm bulwark of the country's
power;
There is no better way.

The Ship of State

[*From " The Building of the Ship."*]

BY HENRY WADSWORTH LONGFELLOW

Thou too sail on, O Ship of State!
Sail on, O Union, strong and great.

We know what master laid thy keel,
What workman laid thy ribs of steel,
Who made each mast and sail and rope,
In what a forge, with what a heat
Were shaped the anchors of thy hope.
Fear not each sudden sound and shock,
'Tis of the wave and not the rock,
'Tis but the flapping of the sail,
And not the rent made by the gale.
In spite of rocks and tempest roar,
In spite of false lights on the shore,
Sail on, nor fear to breast the sea!
Our hearts, our hopes are all with thee;
Our hearts, our hopes, our prayers, our tears,
Our faith triumphant o'er our fears,
Are all with thee; are all with thee!

Unguarded Gates

BY THOMAS BAILEY ALDRICH

Wide open and unguarded stand our gates,
Named of the four winds—North, South,
East, and West;
Portals that lead to an enchanted land
Of cities, forests, fields of living gold,
Vast prairies, lordly summits touched with
snow,
Majestic rivers sweeping proudly past
The Arab's date palm and the Norseman's
pine—
A realm wherein are fruits of every zone,
Airs of all climes, for lo! throughout the
year
The red rose blossoms somewhere—a rich
land,
A later Eden planted in the wilds,
With not an inch of earth within its bound
But if a slave's foot press it sets him free!
Here it is written, Toil shall have its wage,
And Honor honor, and the humblest man
Stands level with the highest in the law.

Of such a land have men in dungeons
dreamed,
And with the vision brightening in their
eyes
Gone smiling to the fagot and the sword.

Wide open and unguarded stand our gates,
And through them press a wild, a motley
throng—
Men from the Volga and the Tartar steppes,
Featureless figures of the Hoang-Ho,
Malayan, Scythian, Teuton, Kelt, and Slav,
Flying the Old World's poverty and scorn;
These bringing with them unknown gods
and rites.
Those tiger passions, here to stretch their
claws.
In street and alley what strange tongues are
these,
Accents of menace alien to our air,
Voices that once the Tower of Babel knew!
O Liberty, White Goddess! is it well
To leave the gate unguarded? On thy breast
Fold Sorrow's children, soothe the hurts of
fate,
Lift the down-trodden, but with the hand of
steel
Stay those who to thy sacred portals come
To waste the gifts of freedom. Have a care
Lest from thy brow the clustered stars be
torn
And trampled in the dust. For so of old
The throning Goth and Vandal trampled
Rome,
And where the temples of the Cæsars stood
The lean wolf unmolested made her lair.

At. M.

Yankee Doodle

Father and I went down to camp
  Along with Cap'n Goodin',
And there we saw the men and boys
  As thick as hasty-puddin'.

CHORUS:

  Yankee Doodle, keep it up,
    Yankee Doodle, dandy,
  Mind the music and the step,
    And with the girls be handy.

And there we see a thousand men,
  As rich as Squire David;
And what they wasted every day
  I wish it would be savéd.
          CHORUS.

The 'lasses they eat every day
  Would keep a house a winter;
They have so much that I'll be bound
  They eat it when they've mind ter.
          CHORUS.

And there I see a swamping gun,
  Large as a log of maple,
Upon a ducéd little cart,
  A load for father's cattle.
          CHORUS.

And every time they shoot it off,
  It takes a horn of powder,
And makes a noise like father's gun,
  Only a nation louder.
          CHORUS.

I went as nigh to one myself
  As 'Liah's underpinning;
And father went as nigh again,—
  I thought the deuce was in him.
          CHORUS.

Cousin Simon grew so bold,
  I thought he would have cocked it;
It scared me so, I shrinked it off
  And hung by father's pocket.
          CHORUS.

And Cap'n Davis had a gun,
  He kind of clap't his hand on't,
And stuck a crooked stabbing iron
  Upon the little end on't.
          CHORUS.

And there I see a pumpkin shell
  As big as mother's basin;
And every time they touched it off,
  They scampered like the nation.
          CHORUS.

I see a little barrel, too,
  The heads were made of leather;
They knocked upon 't with little clubs,
  And called the folks together.
          CHORUS.

And there was Cap'n Washington,
  And gentle folks about him;
They say he's grown so 'tarnal proud,
  He will not ride without 'em.
          CHORUS.

He got him on his meeting clothes,
  Upon a strapping stallion.
He set the world along in rows,
  In hundreds and in millions.
          CHORUS.

The flaming ribbons in his hat,
  They looked so taring fine, ah!
I wanted dreadfully to get
  To give to my Jemima.
          CHORUS.

I see another snarl of men,
  A digging graves they told me,
So 'tarnal long, so 'tarnal deep,
  They 'tended they should hold me.
          CHORUS.

It scared me so I hooked it off,
  Nor stopped, as I remember,
Nor turned about till I got home,
  Locked up in mother's chamber.
          CHORUS.

LABOR DAY

(September)

IN Congress (1894) a bill became a law making the first Monday in September a legal public holiday, or "national holiday," in the same sense that Christmas Day, New Year's Day, Washington's Birthday and the Fourth of July are already national holidays.

In the act creating the new holiday, the first Monday in September is formally defined as "the day celebrated and known as Labor's Holiday." The day is more commonly known as "Labor Day."

This law is a recognition by the national government of the importance and significance of the new holiday, which had already been made a legal holiday in twenty-seven states and one territory.

It must not be supposed, however, that the new law makes Labor Day a holiday, or *dies non,* to all intents and purposes in those states which have not decreed it to be such by the enactment of their own legislatures. So far as ordinary business is concerned—the signing and falling due of notes, the lawfulness of customary transactions, the fulfillment of contracts to labor, and so forth—Congress has no power to create a holiday in the states.

Though the first of January is a truly national holiday, it is not a legal holiday in the States of Massachusetts, New Hampshire, and Rhode Island. All ordinary transactions are legal in those States on that day, and contracts made on them may be enforced.

The same is true as to the 22d of February in Arkansas, Iowa, and Mississippi, and as to the 30th of May in several states.

The Congressional enactment makes Labor Day a legal public holiday in the District of Columbia, and places the closing of all Federal offices throughout the Union under the same regulations on this day as on Christmas, New Year's, Memorial Day, and Independence Day.

Congress and the Executive have simply done what is in their power to give to the day chosen by organized labor as its special anniversary equal honor with the birthday of the Nation, the birthday of Washington and the other general holidays.—Y. C.

HISTORICAL

A FACTORY BASED ON THE GOLDEN RULE

A great factory system organized upon principles of brotherhood, openly professing the Golden Rule as its doctrine, advocating the care and training of men's minds and spirits, while employing their hands, is so unique, so altogether captivating, that it would require not above half an hour's inspection most effectually to silence for the time being the loudest grumbler at modern industrial conditions. Quite the most unique thing about it all, too, is the naive confession by the company (The National Cash Register Company) that they find business profit in what they are doing for their people. Enter the women's dining hall on the upper floor of the Administration Building, or the "rest-room," or the bathrooms, or bicycle sheds, or the working-rooms, kept as clean as your mother's kitchen, painted in Colonial yellow to be easy for the eye—everywhere the same frank placard greets you—" It Pays."

The company pays good wages and gives unusual attention to matters of sanitation, cleanliness, light, ventilation, heating, and ornamentation. The health of the employees is made a first consideration. Several years ago the president found a young woman heating coffee in a tomato can on a heater for the noon lunch. He promptly furnished a stove for heating lunches, and from this has grown the generous noon lunch provided to the young women, at a cost of one cent. The dining-room contains flowers, rugs, pictures, a piano and a " rest-room " adjoining, with couches and medicines. The lunch is estimated to cost three cents, but the company figures that the increased efficiency of this department amounts to five cents per person. The young women are required to wear white aprons and cuffs, which are furnished and laundered at the company's expense. They go to work an hour later than the men in the morning, and leave ten minutes earlier in the evening. There is a ten-minute recess each morning and afternoon for calisthenics or rest. They also have regular holidays. They receive ten hours' pay for eight hours' work. The chairs have high backs and foot-rests. The young women in the binderies and at the machines look as neat as high-school girls. The object lesson in cleanliness is too plain to be mistaken. The men work nine hours and a half, with ten hours' pay. Weekly baths are granted to all on the company's time.

The lawns and grounds were carefully planned by a landscape gardener. One of the streets near the factory has been pronounced in summer time the most beautiful in the world. The section of the city in which the factory is located was formerly " Slidertown," disreputable and unsightly. Now it is " South Park," and is rightly named. The employees themselves have formed the " South Park Improvement Association." For many squares about the factory the effect of the factory's attention to beauty is seen in the homes, in a window-box of flowers, a vine-clad porch, a well-trimmed lawn, or a well-kept back yard. There are no strikes here and no lockouts.

Why, indeed, should there be? A prominent German Socialist, visiting the factory, said: " This is all I mean by Socialism." Another said: " You make money and happiness at the same time." All this costs the company a large sum, but, besides getting its own profits, the lives of thousands of men and women are broadened and made more happy. When capital becomes generous to labor, labor becomes generous to capital. The employer realizes that it is to his interest to make the employee as much of a man as possible, physically, intellectually, morally. This represents a distinct advance in factory life. The workman is not merely a " hand; " he is a " soul." Put more into his soul, give him more to think about, give him a better dwelling and better surroundings, open new vistas of life, and he will, out of his strengthened manhood, give you a better service.

The House of Usefulness is the social settlement. Here resides the deaconess, and here center all the social organizations—boys' and girls' clubs, musical organizations, kindergarten, mothers' meetings, relief associations. The leverage obtained here upon the lives of boys and girls seems incalculable.

The Sunday-school has seven hundred members, and meets on the third floor of one of the factory buildings. A printed program is used, with a Scripture lesson. First there is a drill of the Boys' Brigade; then a choir processional; then singing and responsive reading, and quotation of selected verses, Scriptural and otherwise; then a twenty-minute address, and remarks by the deaconess. The subjects of study are practical life lessons, such as " Work," " Charity," " Child Life," " Liberty." The basis of the study is the Scriptures, but illustrative material from every source is welcome. Often the stereopticon is used in the school to show scenes of travel, the beauties of nature, best methods of homemaking or landscape gardening.

There is nothing traditional, nothing hoary-headed about this factory system, not even in the Sunday-school. Walking amidst these new industrial conditions, one feels as if he had already pushed through the door of the new century.—I.

HOUSING THE CITY POOR

It is coming to be recognized more and more that the housing of the poor vitally affects the health and safety of the rest of the people in every community. We partake of one another's sufferings, whether we will or no. This consideration, if no higher one, gives interest to figures presented to show how the lowly in New York and other large cities are compelled to live.

Mr. Jacob A. Riis, well known as an expert on the condition of New York's poor, tells us, in an article in *The Atlantic Monthly,*

that more than half of New York's millions live in tenements, not counting those who live in the better class of flats. The tenth ward, which holds the unenviable eminence of being the most crowded in the world, contained 643 persons to the acre in 1895, and was still growing rapidly. One block was crowded to the rate of 1,526 to the acre, and one in the eleventh ward to 1,774. Frequent murders and suicides by those who live in the crowded districts bear witness to the fact that their miserable condition leads them to place a cheap value on human life.

It would cost only ten per cent. more to build the tenements fireproof, and the extra outlay would come back in decreased insurance rates and repair expense, yet this fact finds no echo in legislation, or in the practise of builders. The law permits a tenement to cover only sixty-five per cent. of its lot, yet some of them go far over this limit, one house covering ninety-three per cent., leaving but seven per cent. for the light and air to struggle through for from 100 to 150 people. Many of the worst are built in the back yards of other tenement-houses, shut out from light and air themselves, and cutting off the light and air from the tenements near.

It was in such barracks as these that the infant death-rate rose one year to 325 per 1,000—one in three had to die. In a list of sixty-six old houses it was found that one-quarter of the 5,460 tenants died in five years. The results of the sins of the landlords are visited upon the tenants. Yet the worst feature of the tenement "blight," as Mr. Riis calls it, is the fact that it makes real homes impossible. Self-respect and morality cannot be preserved where the separateness and sacredness of the home are interfered with as they are in the crowded tenement-houses.

The cure for the blight is being attempted, with encouraging success, by a company of wealthy men, who, with a capital stock of $2,000,000, are putting up model tenement-houses in which the evils mentioned above are provided against. Over 350 families have already been housed in these, and more tenements are in process of building. The same company has built a hundred cottages in the suburbs of Brooklyn, and has sold most of them to families who would otherwise be in tenement-houses.—H. R.

OUR WORKING-WOMEN

Among the saddest chapters in industrial history are those which record the treatment to which women and children have been subjected. The changes in their favor have been great, such as are due to the factory acts in England and to legislation in their behalf in other countries. Even where workmen are thought capable of managing their own affairs it is admitted that the condition of women and children in the industries is such as to require legal enactments for their welfare. Investigations in the most advanced countries have shown that the legal protection received is not sufficient, that abuses are still frequent, and that for their deliverance from existing evils something besides legislative action is needed.

Compared with England and other European countries, the position of American working-women is favorable. The proportion of those obliged to work in factories is certainly not as large in the United States as in continental industrial nations. The average wage of women in the English industries is reported at a little more than three dollars a week. Many for hard work and long days receive only a few shillings a week, say from four to six or seven, and the standard of living is necessarily low. With all the improvements due to the factory laws, to inspectors, and to other causes, recent official investigations in England have revealed conditions among the women workers which are shocking. Some are obliged to work over one hundred hours a week; sanitary arrangements are often defective; what should be conveniences are frequently filthy and outrageously indecent; and the moral character is endangered. The reports of the existing horrors are extensively discussed, and English reformers are eagerly searching for the means to remove them.

American optimism is so sure that things are moving along smoothly, that each can best take care of his own interests, and that evils will right themselves, that the condition of our working-women has not received the attention it deserves. Perhaps our traditional chivalry makes it self-evident that their treatment is admirable. Fortunately, we have definite information before us in the Fourth Annual Report of the United States Commissioner of Labor. The report is based on statistics gathered from twenty-five cities, north, south, east, and west, and may be taken as truly representative of the country at large. "The study comprehends three hundred and forty-three distinct industries of the large number now open to women. . . . By working-women is meant that class of women who earn their living in the occupations calling for manual labor. . . . Those women who work in great city manufactories upon light manual or mechanical labor, and in stores, are the ones that we recognize under the popular term 'working-women.'" Those engaged in families as servants are therefore excluded. The investigation included the affairs of 17,427 working-women, from six to seven per cent. of the whole number of women engaged in the industrial pursuits investigated. Of those whose family relations were examined 15,387 were single; 745 married; 1,038 widows; 12,020 are in comfortable home conditions; of 4,693 the home was poor, and "poor in this investigation means poor indeed." The average earnings of the working-women in the industries of our great cities is $5.24, a large amount compared with the earnings of working-women in other lands.

Saddest of all is the condition when the earnings of the father must be supplemented by the toil of the wife and children in factories, and when a widowed mother is obliged to support her children by work away from home. The percentage of such is probably smaller than in other lands, yet it is too large. How can there be a proper home-life, with the wife and mother at work all day in a factory? Of those who are single, many are thrown on their own resources and obliged to give part of their earnings for the support of the family, while others are not driven by the same necessity, but want to add to their income from the family and to become more independent. Very many, of course, earn much less than the average given above. When away from home, as a large proportion are, it becomes a difficult problem how to make the meager income meet the expense of lodging, board, and dress, to say nothing of recreation. Many a worker is obliged to live in a gloomy, badly furnished room, in a crowded and unhealthy part of the city. Company must be received in this one room or not at all. Fuel may be too dear, and a comfortable public place may present irresistible attractions. The dangers of such a situation are apparent. For those who are at home, or have some family connection, the circumstances are, of course, far more favorable.

Peculiar difficulties are connected with statistics as to morals and religion; we cannot get at the heart but must estimate them according to their outward manifestations. The church attendance of over 16,000 of the working-women was ascertained. The number attending Protestant churches was 5,854; 7,769 attended Roman Catholic services, and 369 the Jewish synagog; but the large number of 2,309 attended no church.

The view, prevalent in some quarters, that the girls and women engaged in the industries furnish an undue proportion of the professional prostitutes is not confirmed by the investigation; the private morals were of course not a subject of inquiry. With pleasure we record the following result: "From all that can be learned one need not hesitate in asserting that the working-women of the country are as honest and as virtuous as any class of our citizens." This is significant, and deserves emphasis. The report well says: "The virtuous character of our working-women is all the more attractive when the cost of their virtue is recognized. With their poor pay, if they continue virtuous they are the more entitled to our applause, and certainly one must recognize the heroic struggle they make to sustain life, to appear fairly well, and to remove what every honorable-minded man and woman seeks to remove, the appearance of poverty."

The investigation was conducted by women and included inquiries into the former occupations of prostitutes. Of 3,866 prostitutes in different cities it was found that 1,155, or 29.88 per cent. had been engaged in housework, hotel-work, table-work, and cooking. Most surprising, and most instructive, is the fact that 1,236 or 31.97 per cent., nearly one-third of the whole, entered prostitution directly from their homes! One of the many

lessons that the home, the family, must be improved if society is to be regenerated and public morality advanced.

Of the particular conditions in certain cities we can refer to a few only; and they are mentioned in the hope that the ministers and churches in these cities will investigate the facts and undertake the removal of the wrong.

It is into the poorer quarters that our working-women are driven, often the slums, and they are obliged to share all the evils of the surroundings. The report thus describes parts of Brooklyn inhabited by them: "Whole streets and districts of tenement-houses are given over to poverty, filth, and vice, the sanitary and moral unwholesomeness of which is manifest."

We are sure that few in the wealthier sections and elegant suburbs of Cincinnati are aware of the abominations to which many of their workers are subjected. These workers live where "the streets are dirty and closely built up with ill-constructed houses, holding from two to six families. Many poorer parts of Cincinnati are as wretched as the worst European cities, and the population looks as degraded."

This seems incredible; yet this official report is not the only testimony respecting this degraded condition. We turn to New York, with respect to which we are prepared to believe almost anything. Yet of that city we read: "The crowded condition of the poor and struggling is beyond belief unless actually witnessed. This brings with it disease, death, immorality, etc. Tall rear tenements block up the small air-spaces that are insufficient even for the front, and often a third house stands behind the second. Sewerage is lacking or defective, and stenches of all kinds prevail in the poorer quarters. . . . As respects ventilation, a properly regulated workshop is the exception. The average room is either stuffy and close, or hot and close, and even where windows abound they are seldom opened. Toilet facilities are generally scant and inadequate, a hundred workers being dependent sometimes on a single closet or sink, and that too often out of order."

It is common to regard laborers as mere machines, not as personalities. This we know, and yet we are shocked when the brutal reality is stated as plainly as in the following quotation from the report: "Whenever the employer was personally acquainted with his people the standard of conduct was apt to be excellent. In many an instance, however, the employer openly declared that so long as his work was done he did not inquire or care how bad the girls might be." Were we prepared for this, even in New York? After we have duly pondered this, and relieved our American conscience by the reflection that this disgraceful condition must be due to the foreign element, let us close our meditation with this statement: "Foreigners are often found to be more considerate of their help than native-born men."

Philadelphia, the city of homes and of

brotherly love, presents much more favorable conditions than New York. Yet even of the Quaker City we learn with respect to the mills that " the sanitary condition of most is open to criticism. . . . The worsted-yarn mills employ very young girls, sometimes violating the law against child-labor." Little Rhode Island ought to be able to overlook its small territory and present a model condition to the larger states. Yet we read of Providence: " The older mills are defective in light, ventilation, and space, are often without dressing rooms, and frequently the ordinary sanitary arrangements are disregarded."

Various Christian associations, Protestant and Catholic, are doing noble work in behalf of the working-women; yet it is a very insignificant part of what might and ought to be done. Many of the girls need home and companionship, sympathy and help. Cannot their cause be laid on the hearts of our churches. To our Christian women an appeal comes from the condition of their toiling sisters for consecration and sacrifice in their behalf; and the work to be done in this re-spect is as noble and as urgently needed as that in any foreign mission field.

Gladly we make room for one more quotation. Yet the query arises, Why is it called for in a governmental report? Perhaps the saddest fact in this official document is the fact that things which ought to be self-evident to a Christian conscience must be urged on the attention of Christians. We trust that this quotation will serve to emphasize Christian duty:

" The honest working-woman is entitled to the respect of all honest-minded people. She should be welcomed in the churches of the cities, and should be drawn into the best associations, where social and moral surroundings would aid her in cultivating her own self-respect, and in which mutual assistance could be rendered. At least, it should not be possible to class her as the ' forgotten woman,' for her struggle is too heroic, her hardships too painful, her lot too dreary, for Christian people thoughtlessly to pass her by."—H. R.

REPRESENTATIVE WORKINGMEN

By H. D. Jenkins, D.D.

When at one time application was made to Judge Hallet, of Denver, for the interposition of the Federal Government to restore order in the state, he replied that if a state chose to select for executive positions " socialists and imbeciles " it must suffer the consequences; and it was not the province of the General Government to save a commonwealth from its own folly. Several of our western states have had a severe lesson, and it may be hoped that they will profit by it. Demagogs find it for their profit to pose as the " friends of the workingmen," ignoring the simple fact that the real workingman's best friend is himself.

Our own Iowa was once the dumping ground of " industrial armies," from the further West, shoved across the Missouri by officials, like one mayor of Omaha, who would not permit them to set foot on Nebraska soil. but who, immediately that the horde of irresponsible wanderers was safely in another state, began vociferous protests against the " inhumanity " which refused free rides as well as free meals to men who would not work and could scarce be forced to walk.

It seemed to me at this time worth all it would cost to ascertain by personal investigation the condition of the working classes, the manual laborers, in our own cities. I heard of " naked thousands," of " starvation wages," until I really began to think that labor was, perhaps, more oppressed in this country than in the Old World from which so many of our discontented came. Accordingly I visited workshops of all the prominent trades, and investigated the men found at labor as to their sources and amounts of income, their personal habits, the condition of their families, and their relation to the higher interests of society. I was especially interested to know whether our churches were " driving the poor men out by excessive costs," a question of especial interest to me as a pastor of a church where. during my whole pastorate, there never had been a pew rented. It seemed to me that the only way to know the facts concerning the workingman was to go to him at his work, and not to take the word of some fellow who might apply at the back door of the parsonage for cold victuals. And I give below the unvarnished statements of our Iowa workingmen from their own lips.

The first man I interviewed was the smith who shoes my horse. He is a young Scotchman who has been in this country seven years. When he landed he had just $15 in his pocket. He lost the first three years of his residence in this country largely through the attempt to become a farmer in Dakota. When he recognized that the conditions of success in that must first be learned before they could be put into practice, he fell back upon his trade. He has now been at work four years; he owns his shop; has accumulated $6,000 worth of property, part of which is drawing interest; his income last year was $2,000 or upward, and he has sent $1,500 lately home to make life more cheerful for the " old folks " in the land beyond the sea. He is not married, and attends no church, but contributes $12 a year to one. Beer costs him about $1 a month, mostly for treating customers. He thinks this a pretty good country for a workingman, and does not care to have Congress donate to tramps what it cost him industry to acquire.

The next man I sought at his home. He is a carpenter, and during the dull time has been "pretty close." When at work he gets $2.50 to $3 a day; is married and has two children. Up to last year he has been steadily employed; has saved nothing, and contributed nothing to church or benevolence; does not go to church, altho his parents did. He never drinks, but likes a good cigar and does not deny himself this "when he feels like it." He takes in all the ball games when not at work. His wife contributes to the support of the family by taking in boarders. Sundays he "brushes up," reads the papers, and enjoys his smoke. He owns nothing, but owes nothing, and trusts to have "better luck this year." This man is American born, has not a single vicious habit, is a kind husband and father; but, despite the fact that his annual income for some years has never before fallen below $700 to $900 a year, he is to-day largely dependent upon the assistance of his wife for the well-being of the family.

The next man was a butcher's helper. He gets $60 a month. He is married and has one child. When married his whole worldly possessions consisted of a horse and buggy and a cottage organ. To-day he has his home, worth $2,000, nearly paid for, and upon this he makes regular monthly payments, by which it will presently be cleared. He is a church member, and contributes $18 a year to the maintenance of that, but spends nothing for liquors or tobacco. He keeps up a $2,000 insurance upon his life.

Walking into the composing room of one of our dailies I addressed the first printer I met, a perfect stranger. He gets $3 a day, and has $150 a year besides as an official in the Typographical Union, making up an income of $1,050 a year. He is not married, seldom goes to church, and contributes nothing regularly to church or Y. M. C. A. He pays $150 a year for life insurance, and this is all he saves. He does not drink; but his pipe costs him about $12 a year. He pays $312 a year for board, $150 a year for his clothes and $10 to his union. He does not know what becomes of the rest of the income, but "it goes."

The bookbinder in the next room gets $925 a year; is married and has three children. Rent and food cost about half of this. He pays $21 a year in an assessment company for $2,000 insurance. He is not a church member and contributes nothing in religious societies, but spends $50 a year for cigars. He does not own his home or help in the support of any indigent relatives. He is satisfied with his condition, and thinks he could save a little something, but it would cut pretty close. Would cut off his cigar most likely.

Down the street I found my next representative in a wholesale fruit house as a porter. He earns $10 a week, $520 a year. He is married and has one child. He has paid for his home through a building association. He has besides his home a cow, a lot of poultry, and a garden. His life insurance costs him $20 a year. He is not a church member; but his wife is, and gives $12 a year.

His neighbor, a tinner, earns $750 a year. This man is married, and has one child. He owns his own home, bought through a building association, and worth $1,500. He saves in the bank about $180 yearly, altho he spends $50 a year for tobacco. He is not a church member, and contributes nothing to religious causes; but his lodge costs him $7 a year.

My colored friend, the janitor, told me that he earns about $540 a year. Out of this he is paying for some lots in an "addition," upon which he has laid down several hundred dollars, and will soon own them in fee simple. He owns a place of three acres, upon which his wife's father supports himself now. He has a small pension, $72 a year; but he gives this to his mother. He is a member of the African Church, and contributes $18 a year to that. The lodge costs him $30 a year; but he spends nothing for liquors or tobacco.

The next man I stopped upon the street was also colored—a jovial, happy-go-lucky man-of-all-work. He was born a slave; is not married; does all sorts of odd jobs, and picks up about $365 a year. He taught himself to read, and owns about $200 worth of standard books, and takes the leading magazines and reviews, or reads such as he does not take at the public library, He has invested about $140 in some lots, but does not think he made a very good bargain, and does not know whether to complete payment; could do so if he thought best. He is also a member of the church, and contributes $18 a year to that; but he smokes $50 worth of cigars a year. "Does not like a pipe."

To make up the number to ten I buttonholed a railroad employee, who tends the lamps that hang upon the switches at one of our stations. He said he was not married, was a member of the church, and contributed $18 a year to that. He is temperate, and does not use liquor or tobacco. It cost him for board about $200 a year; but for this he has a good table and an exceptionally clean and wholesome room. He put about $640 of his savings into some real estate, which he later sold for $800, and this he has at interest. He likes his work, and has nothing to complain of in this country, of which he is a native-born citizen.

Here are ten men, representing as many different kinds of manual labor. Instead of it being impossible for a man to support a family in such employments, I found that the married men were almost the only ones "getting ahead" in the world. Instead of finding that the church was "an intolerable burden," the highest any workingman was paying to the church was $18 or $20 a year, while three of the ten spent $50 a year for tobacco. That so little was spent for liquor was simply due to the fact that in hard times the drinking men "must go," and they have been long since "fired" from shop and forge, and are now presumably tramping over the country and demanding "relief," presenting "petitions in boots," it may be.

The question of prosperity, I soon found, resolved itself not into one of wages so much as into one of character. Nothing impressed me more favorably than the self-respect of these men, who were almost wholly strangers to me. The church members, as a rule, were by far the most prosperous instead of the most burdened. There was no hostility to religion manifest, but at the most indifference. Between such as these and the church there exists no impassable gulf. The study was of incalculable value to me as a pastor, and I present its methods and results to any who may be interested to know the facts in an issue which seems to be joined largely upon false statements of the real condition of the social problem.—I

LABOR'S GRIEVANCES

By Rev. C. H. Parkhurst, D.D.

A reliable statistician says that between '60 and '81 wages increased thirty-one per cent., while prices of staple commodities increased forty-one per cent.—the laborer received more wages, but not so much more as food, clothes, and rent cost him more. But alongside of that put the fact that during that time the national wealth nearly trebled; and the wage-worker knows perfectly well that it was in considerable measure by his own perspiration that that national wealth was trebled; whether justly or unjustly, he is convinced that he is not receiving nearly his share of the profit that his own brawn is helping to produce.

And then, just at the time when he is barely making the ends meet, he reads in the papers that in one year ten Wall Street men made an aggregate profit of eighty million dollars. We do not say that that newspaper statement is true; we do not say that, even if it were, the poor wage-worker ought not to go on serenely picking his bone and sweetly munching his crust. We are simply trying at love's behest, to feel our way into the circumstances of these people, so as to survey facts from their standpoint and be able to judge whether it is only at the impulse of unreasoning malignity that these people confer and organize and confront combinations of capital with combinations of labor.

Add to this the fact, so commonly true, that labor is treated as pure commodity, as impersonal a matter as cotton or wheat. The dealer in grain, coffee, tobacco, wool, buys in the cheapest market. Purchase and sales are regulated by the law of supply and demand. The employer, so it is urged, nine cases out of ten, proceeds on the same impersonal principle; contracts with the employee with no reference to the human element that differentiates him from an ox, an ass, or a barrel of potatoes; is bound to the wage-worker by only a "cash-nexus;" does not remunerate him with any reference to his actual worth to him; will make 300 per cent. off his labor, if possible, without such a profit seeming even to suggest that market rates of labor ought not to be altogether trusted as criterion of compensation; and so from first to last holds himself to his hireling in the same relation in which the merchant stands to his wares and the teamster to his cattle. Labor reduces to chattel, and the wage-worker to a marketable animal.

And not only that. Not only does capital use labor as a tool, but in this, as in all instances, the tool is a good deal more likely to depreciate than appreciate with the usage. The severe competition of modern mercantile and productive interests has brought about one peculiar condition that fifty years ago was utterly unknown. I mean division of labor. In order that the mechanic may best promote the interests of his employer, he is taught to do only one thing. If he is a piano-maker, he is confined to only one minutely specialized part of the instrument. If he is a needle manufacturer, he is limited to one only of the many processes necessary to its production; and as competition grows sharper, labor is more and more minutely divided. Now the important principle in the case is that a man is always narrowed to the scope of his employment. What can you expect of a man in a bank who does nothing from morning till night but draw checks? of a man on the elevated railway whose only employment it is to punch tickets? of a factory employee who ten hours a day for twenty years has been doing nothing but point pins? Such is the stress and trend of things that the employer not only is using his employee, but is using him up, is coining hireling intelligence into dividends, and so is grinding soul as well as body into grist to satisfy rapacity or meet the exigencies of competition.

Now, however the wage-worker may be given to exaggeration, there is an element of truth in all these complaints, and the first thing that Christianity has to do is frankly to acknowledge it. So long as there remains one track of unbaptized self-seeking in the human heart, the man that is on the top will always tend to make a slave and a chattel of the man that is under. And when we have frankly acknowledged that to a degree labor has been wronged, then the next step is to right the wrong. When we deal justly with the just elements in the indictment, the unjust elements will fall to pieces of themselves. The strength of all error is the truth that is mixed with it. My confidence in the average man is so complete that I believe labor will show itself reasonable when reasonably approached, and will show itself manly to the degree in which capital deals with it in the capacity of manhood, and not at the grade of a chattel or serf.

SUGGESTIVE THOUGHTS

CARLYLE'S VIEW OF THE LABOR QUESTION.—Carlyle taught that work is a social function, and property a social trust. Again, he discerned and proclaimed that the great economic problem of the age is the proper division of the fruits of labor; and that we can no longer leave that division "to be scrambled for by the Law of the Strongest, Law of Supply and Demand, Law of *Laissez-faire,* and other idle laws and unlaws." "A fair day's wage for a fair day's work, is as just a demand as governed men ever made of governors. It is the everlasting right of man."—W. S. LILLY.

CRIME AND THE PRICE OF BREAD. —Crime increases when the price of bread goes up. is the conclusion reached by Professor Brentano, the well-known Berlin specialist on sociology. He has just published statistical comparisons between the price of grain used for bread and the number of thefts per 100,000 of population in Bavaria, and the result shown is, that on the average since 1835, for every penny of increase in the price of grain there has been a corresponding increase of one in the number of thefts. When the price of bread goes down, the thefts are diminished in proportion. Here are the figures from 1882 to 1891:

Year	Thefts per 100,000 of pop.	Grain, Pennies per kilo.
1882	535	152.3
1883	518	144.7
1884	509	143.3
1885	486	140.6
1886	480	130.6
1887	470	120.9
1888	459	134.5
1889	434	153.5
1890	494	170.0
1891	511	211.2

H. R.

LABOR.—Labor at first inflicted as a curse, seems to be the gentlest of all punishments, and is fruitful of a thousand blessings: the same Providence which permits diseases, produces remedies; when it sends sorrows, it often sends friends and supporters; if it gives a scanty income, it gives good sense, and knowledge, and contentment, which love to dwell under homely roofs; with sickness come humility, and repentance, and piety; and affliction and grace walk hand in hand.—JORTIN.

LABOR.—Labor is one of the great elements of society—the great substantial interest on which we all stand. Not feudal service, or predial toil, or the irksome drudgery by one race of mankind subjected to another, but labor, intelligent, manly, independent, thinking and acting for itself, earning its own wages, accumulating those wages into capital, educating childhood, maintaining worship, claiming the right of elective franchise, and helping to uphold the great fabric of the state. That is American labor, and all my sympathies are with it, and my voice, till I am dumb, will be for it.—DANIEL WEBSTER.

LABOR AGITATIONS? What is Likely to Be the End of the.—What seems likely here and to-day seems unlikely in another place and next week. A banker recently asked a similar question; and, when pressed to give his own view, he admitted that he saw no way out except by means of legislation; but he neither knew what legislation was required, nor did he believe that any legislation would afford a remedy unless better executed than economic legislation is at present. The question itself is becoming more frequent. It is asked now by many until recently indifferent to the social problem. The time is past when laborers alone are supposed to be interested in the question. This growth of interest in the problem is itself a hopeful sign. Our hope of a peaceable solution rests on the belief that all classes will consider the problem and cooperate in its solution. This hope is bright in exact proportion as the Gospel of Christ is applied to the burning industrial questions. —H. R.

LABOR, Eminence and.—When we read the lives of distinguished men in any department, we find them almost always celebrated for the amount of labor they could perform. Demosthenes, Julius Cæsar, Henry of France, Lord Bacon, Sir Isaac Newton, Franklin, Washington, Napoleon, different as they were in their intellectual and moral qualities, were all renowned as hard workers. We read how many days they could support the fatigues of a march; how early they rose; how late they watched; how many hours they spent in the field, in the cabinet, in the court; how many secretaries they kept employed; in short, how hard they worked.— EDWARD EVERETT.

LABORERS, Hiring.—Morier, in the record of his second journey through Persia, mentions having noted in the market-place at Hamadan, a custom like that alluded to in the parable of the laborers. "Here we observed every morning before the sun rose, that a numerous band of peasants were collected with spades in their hands, waiting to be hired for the day, to work in the surrounding fields. This custom struck me as a most happy illustration of our Savior's parable, particularly when, passing by the same place late in the day, we found others standing idle, and remembered His words, ' Why stand ye here all the day idle? ' as most applicable to their situation, for on putting the very same question to them, they answered us, ' Because no man hath hired us.' " Josephus says that Ananus paid the workmen who were employed in the rebuilding or beautifying of the temple, a whole day's pay, even tho they should have labored but a single hour.—F. II.

LABORERS, Parable of the.—Lightfoot quotes from the Talmud concerning a celebrated rabbi, who died at a very early age, as follows: " To what was R. Bon Bar Chaiza like? To a king who hired many laborers, among whom there was one hired who performed his task extraordinarily well. What did the king? He took him aside, and walked with him to and fro. When even was come, those laborers came that they might receive their hire, and he gave him a complete hire with the rest. And the laborers murmured, saying, ' We have labored hard all the day, and this man only two hours, yet he hath received as much wages as we.' The king said to them, ' He hath labored more in those two hours than you in the whole day.' So R. Bon plied the law more in eight and twenty years than another in a hundred years."—F. II.

LABOR, Faithful in.— Bonaventura, the Seraphic Doctor, was general of the Franciscan order, one of whose rules required a rotation of work among the members. Gregory X. sent him a cardinal's hat by two nuncios, who found him in the kitchen washing the plates after dinner. The nuncios were amazed. The Seraphic Doctor, without a blush, excused himself from attending to their business till he had finished his dishes. So the cardinal's hat was hung on a dog-wood tree near the kitchen door, till the dishes were finished and the new cardinal's hands were dried.—F. II.

LABOR, Healthfulness of.—There is a story in the Arabian Nights' Tales of a king who had long languished under an ill habit of body, and had taken abundance of remedies to no purpose. At length, a physician cured him by the following method: He took a hollow ball of wood, and filled it with several drugs; after which he closed it up so artfully that nothing appeared. He likewise took a mall, and after having hollowed the handle, and that part which strikes the ball, he closed in them several drugs after the same manner as in the ball itself. He then ordered the Sultan, who was his patient, to exercise himself early in the morning with these rightly prepared instruments till such time as he should sweat; when, as the story goes, the virtue of the medicaments

perspiring through the wood had so good an influence on the Sultan's constitution, that they cured him of an indisposition which all the compositions he had taken inwardly had not been able to remove. This Eastern allegory is finely contrived to show us how beneficial bodily labor is to health, and that exercise is the most effectual physic.—ADDISON.

LABOR, Honors to.—Statues in every public place should record its wonders; oratorios should be composed in its honor; its insignia—the plow, the spade, and the loom —should decorate state carriages, and ornament churches and public halls; while its successful votaries should wear the honored decoration of " The Order of Industry."—J. JOHNSON.

LABOR, Incessancy of.—The more we accomplish, the more we have to accomplish. All things are full of labor; and, therefore, the more we acquire, the more care and the more toil to secure our acquisitions. Good men can never retire from their works of benevolence; their fortune is never made. I never heard of an apostle, prophet, or public benefactor, retiring from their respective fields of labor. Moses, and Paul, and Peter, died with their harness on. So did Luther, and Calvin, and Wesley, and a thousand others as deserving, tho not so well known to fame. We are inured to labor. It was first a duty; it is now a pleasure. Still there is such a thing as overworking man and beast, mind and body. The mainspring of a watch needs repose, and is the better for it. The muscles of an elephant, and the wings of a swift bird, are at length fatigued. Heaven gives rest to the earth because it needs it; and winter is more pregnant with blessings to the soil than summer with its flowers and fruits. But in the war for truth and against error, there is no discharge.—A. CAMPBELL.

LABOR, Law of.—There is nothing truly valuable which can be purchased without pains and labor. The gods have set a price upon every real and noble pleasure. If you would gain the favor of the Deity, you must be at the pains of worshiping Him; if the friendship of good men, you must study to oblige them; if you would be honored by your country, you must take care to serve it. In short, if you would be eminent in war or peace, you must become master of all the qualifications that can make you so.—ADDISON.

LABOR, Life-character of.—Labor is life: from the inmost heart of the worker rises his God-given Force—the sacred celestial life-essence breathed into him by the Almighty God!—CARLYLE.

LABOR, Need of.—King Antigonus, when he had not for a long time seen Cleanthes, the philosopher, said to him, " Dost thou yet, O, Cleanthes, continue to grind? " " Yes, sir," replied Cleanthes, " I still grind, and that I do to gain my living, and not to depart from philosophy." How great and generous was the courage of this man, who, coming from the mill and the kneading-trough, did with the same hand which had been employed in turning the stone and molding the dough, write of the nature of the gods, moon, stars, and sun.—PLUTARCH.

LABOR, No Rest from.—Miserable is he who slumbers on in idleness, miserable the workman who sleeps before the hour of his rest, or who sits down in the shadow while his brethren work in the sun. There is no rest from labor on earth. There are always duties to perform and functions to exercise, functions which are ever enlarging and extending in proportion to the growth of our moral and mental station. Man is born to work, and he must work while it is day. "Have I not," said a great worker, "an eternity to rest in?"—TUNMAN.

LABOR, Place for.—See the spider casting out her film to the gale, she feels persuaded that somewhere or other it will adhere and form the commencement of her web. She commits the slender filament to the breeze, believing that there is a place provided for it to fix itself. In this fashion, should we believingly cast forth our endeavors in this life, confident that God will find a place for us. He who bids us play and work will aid all our efforts and guide us in His Providence in a right way. Sit not still in despair, O son of toil, but again cast out the floating thread of hopeful endeavor and the wind of love will bear it to its resting place.—SPURGEON.

LABOR, Power for.—Karamsin, the Russian traveler, having observed Lavater's diligence in study, visiting the sick, and relieving the poor, greatly surprised at his activity, said to him, "Whence have you so much strength of mind and power of endurance?" "My friend," replied he, "man rarely wants the power to work, when he possesses the will; the more I labor in the discharge of my duties, so much the more ability and inclination to labor do I constantly find within myself."—F. II.

LABOR, Prayer and.—Labor is of noble birth; but prayer is the daughter of Heaven. Labor has a place near the throne, but prayer touches the golden scepter. Labor, Martha-like, is busy with much serving; but prayer sits with Mary at the feet of Jesus. Labor climbs the mountain-side with Moses; but prayer soars upward, with Elijah, in a chariot of fire. Labor has the raven's wing, yet sometimes goes forth in vain; but prayer has the pinions of the dove, and never returns but with the olive-leaf of blessing!—W. H. GROSER.

LABOR, Prayer with.—Anthony the hermit, was sitting in his cell in the wilderness, grievously tempted with importunate thoughts, and fell into sadness and darkness. Then he prayed, "Lord, I desire to be saved, but my thoughts are a hindrance to me. What shall I do in my present affliction?

How shall I be saved?" Soon after he went outside of his cell and saw a man sitting and working, then leaving his work to pray, afterwards sitting down to his work twisting a palm rope, and after a time engaging again in prayer. He concluded this to be an angel sent from God to instruct him in duty. Then the angel addressed him and said, "Do so, and thou shalt be saved." Thereafter the great hermit and all his followers were diligent in labor and in prayer.—F. II.

LABOR, Value of.—God is constantly teaching us that nothing valuable is ever obtained without labor; and that no labor can be honestly expended without our getting its value in return. He is not careful to make everything easy to man. The Bible itself is no light book; human duty no holiday engagement. The grammar of deep personal religion, and the grammar of real practical virtue, are not to be learned by any facile Hamiltonian methods.—BINNEY.

POVERTY AND BIRTHRATE.—The fact that the birthrate is higher in the poor districts than in the rich is often remarked upon, but it is seldom made the subject of official inquiry and report. M. Jacques Bertillon, in a bulletin of the International Institute of Statistics, makes an interesting treatment of the variations in the birthrate in the different strata of society in Paris, Berlin, Vienna and London. He finds that the birth-rate is invariably low among the rich and high among the poor. The following table, for Paris, for the period of 1889-93, shows the number of births per thousand women between the ages of 15 and 50:

In 5 very poor districts	108	per 1,000
In 3 poor "	95	" "
In 5 comfortable "	72	" "
In 2 very comf'ble "	65	" "
In 4 rich "	53	" "
In 1 very rich district	34	" "

In Berlin for the period 1886-94 the births per thousand adult women were as follows:

In 2 very poor districts	157	per 1,000
In 3 poor "	129	" "
In 4 comfortable "	114	" "
In 3 very comf'ble "	96	" "
In 3 rich "	68	" "
In 1 very rich district	47	" "

London revealed a similar condition:

In 5 very poor districts	147	per 1,000
In 5 poor "	140	" "
In 3 comfortable "	107	" "
In 6 very comf'ble "	107	" "
In 7 rich "	87	" "
In 2 very rich "	63	" "

Vienna, too, showed a result of the same character, namely:

In 4 very poor districts	200	per 1,000
In 4 poor "	164	" "
In 3 comfortable "	155	" "
In 2 very comf'ble "	153	" "
In 5 rich "	107	" "
In 1 very rich district	71	" "

These tables, representing peoples of different nationality, language, and customs, are so similar that it cannot be far wrong to take the proportions shown here as true for the cities of all civilized countries.—H. R.

SOCIOLOGICAL STUDY, A.—The interests of the laboring classes lie close to if not well within the religious field. But unfortunately writers take their data too often from the inner consciousness of the reporter or the campaign orator than from the researches of patient investigators. The Statistical Society of Great Britain is an honorable body of economic experts, and one of their most valuable reports was that read before a meeting held in London (1900). If the poor be steadily growing poorer this association, whose duty it is to know the facts, has failed to discover it. A statistical study of the working classes of Great Britain covering the past thirty or forty years was presented showing conclusively from official and trades-union data that the laboring classes of England have within one generation increased their money wages 105 per cent., and their per capita consumption of staple foods and their use of textile fabrics 45 per cent. This showing is not made by examining the condition of some single family or isolated hamlet, but is the result of a careful investigation of reports made both by government inspectors and by the laborers' associations. The scale of living has notably advanced so that the rise of money wages has not been wholly offset by any rise in prices, for the laboring classes are better housed and better clothed and better fed than they were in 1860, the year from which the computations start. A very interesting chart was presented, drawn on a logarithmic scale, in which one could trace by the eye the rise in wages, the increase in purchase of home-comforts and a corresponding increase in the number of marriages. Contrary to the theories of certain economists, there was shown with the increase in wages an increase in the number employed. This latter number, by the way, is nothing like what those who write of "the struggle for bread" would have us believe. In 1860 the unemployed amounted to but 2.71 in a hundred; and now, despite the introduction of so much machinery, it is but 3.25 per hundred. It was also shown by means of this chart that when money wages rose, consumption, employment, and marriages rose, while in-door pauperism fell. With a drop in wages everything else dependent dropped, but in-door pauperism rose. That shows us how perilously close to the line of dependence the majority of workmen still live. Periods of depression in trade which used to occur about once in ten years now come round once in seven, as it takes but a shorter time to-day to overstock the market. Whatever may be the faults and defects of our present systems it is indisputably true that the condition of the laborer is steadily improving in every Christian land. —In.

STRIKES.—While the United States in five years had 7,229 strikes, there were 4,526 in Great Britain and Ireland during the same period, 1,866 in France, 1,075 in Italy in fifteen years, and 205 in two years in Austria-Hungary.—*Selected.*

TOIL, The Dignity of.—In the world's life, just as in the life of a man, there are certain periods of eager and all-absorbing action, and these are followed by periods of memory and reflection. We then look back upon our past and become for the first time conscious of what we are, and of what we have done. We then see the dignity of toil, and the grand results of it; the beauty and the strength of faith, and the fervent power of patriotism.—WILLIAM HURRELL MALLOCK.

WORK.—Oh, it is great, and there is no other greatness. To make some nook of God's Creation a little fruitfuler, better, more worthy of God; to make some human hearts a little wiser, manfuler, happier,—more blessed, less accursed! It is work for a God. . . .

Noble fruitful Labor, growing ever nobler, will come forth,—the grand sole miracle of Man; whereby man has risen from the low places of this earth, very literally, into divine Heavens.—THOMAS CARLYLE.

POETRY

American Aristocracy

BY JOHN G. SAXE

Of all the notable things on earth,
The queerest one is pride of birth
Among our "fierce democracy!"
A bridge across a hundred years,
Without a prop to save it from sneers,
Not even a couple of rotten *peers,*—
A thing for laughter, fleers, and jeers,
Is American aristocracy!

English, and Irish, French and Spanish,
Germans, Italians, Dutch and Danish,

Crossing their veins until they vanish
In one conglomeration!
So subtle a tangle of blood, indeed,
No Heraldry Harvey will ever succeed
In finding the circulation.

Depend upon it, my snobbish friend,
Your family thread you can't ascend,
Without good reason to apprehend
You may find it *waxed,* at the farther end,
By some plebeian vocation:
Or, worse than that, your boasted line
May end in a loop of stronger twine,
That plagued some worthy relation!

Clear the Way

By Charles Mackay

Men of thought, be up and stirring night and
    day:
Sow the seed—withdraw the curtain—clear
    the way!
Men of action, aid and cheer them, as ye may!
    There's a fount about to stream,
    There's a light about to beam,
    There's a warmth about to glow,
    There's a flower about to blow;
There's a midnight blackness changing into
    gray.
Men of thought and men of action, clear
    the way!

Once the welcome light has broken, who
    shall say
What the unimagined glories of the day?
What the evil that shall perish in its ray?
    Aid the dawning, tongue and pen;
    Aid it, hopes of honest men,
    Aid it, paper; aid it, type;
    Aid it, for the hour is ripe,
And our earnest must not slacken into play.
Men of thought and men of action, clear
    the way!

Lo! a cloud's about to vanish from the day;
And a brazen wrong to crumble into clay.
Lo! the right's about to conquer; clear
    the way!
    With the right shall many more
    Enter smiling at the door:
    With the giant wrong shall fall
    Many others, great and small,
That for ages long have held us for their
    prey,
Men of thought and men of action, clear
    the way!

Cleon and I

By Charles Mackay

Cleon hath a million acres—ne'er a one have
    I;
Cleon dwelleth in a palace—in a cottage, I;
Cleon hath a dozen fortunes—not a penny, I;
But the poorer of the twain is Cleon, and
    not I.

Cleon, true, possesseth acres—but the land-
    scape, I;
Half the charms to *me* it yieldeth, money
    cannot buy;
Cleon harbors sloth and dullness—freshening
    vigor, I;
He in velvet, I in fustian; richer man am I.

Cleon is a slave to grandeur—free as thought
    am I;
Cleon fees a score of doctors—need of none
    have I.
Wealth-surrounded, care-environed, Cleon
    fears to die;
Death may come—he'll find me ready—hap-
    pier man am I.

Cleon sees no charm in nature—in a daisy, I;
Cleon hears no anthem ringing in the sea and
    sky.

Nature sings to me forever—earnest listener,
    I;
State for state, with all attendants, who would
    change? Not I.

The Song of the Forge

Anonymous

Clang, clang! the massive anvils ring;
Clang, clang! a hundred hammers swing;
Like the thunder-rattle of a tropic sky,
The mighty blows still multiply,—
Clang, clang!
Say, brothers of the dusky brow,
What are your strong arms forging now?

Clang, clang!—we forge the coulter now,—
The coulter of the kindly plow.
Sweet Mary Mother, bless our toil!
May its broad furrow still unbind
To genial rains, to sun and wind,
The most benignant soil!

Clang, clang!—our coulter's course shall be
On many a sweet and sheltered lea,
By many a streamlet's silver tide;
Amidst the song of morning birds,
Amidst the low of sauntering herds,
Amidst soft breezes, which do stray
Through woodbine hedges and sweet May,
Along the green hill's side.

When regal Autumn's bounteous hand
With wide-spread glory clothes the land,—
When to the valleys, from the brow
Of each resplendent slope, is rolled
A ruddy sea of living gold,—
We bless, we bless the plow.

Clang, clang!—again, my mates, what grows
Beneath the hammer's potent blows?
Clink, clank!—we forge the giant chain,
Which bears the gallant vessel's strain
Midst stormy winds and adverse tides;
Secured by this, the good ship braves
The rocky roadstead, and the waves
Which thunder on her sides.

Anxious no more, the merchant sees
The mist drive dark before the breeze,
The storm-cloud on the hill;
Calmly he rests.—tho far away,
In boisterous climes, his vessel lay,—
Reliant on our skill.

Say on what sands these links shall sleep,
Fathoms beneath the solemn deep?
By Afric's pestilential shore;
By many an iceberg, lone and hoar;
By many a balmy western isle,
Basking in Spring's perpetual smile;
By stormy Labrador.

Say, shall they feel the vessel reel,
When to the battery's deadly peal
The crashing broadside makes reply;
Or else, as at the glorious Nile,
Hold grappling ships, that strive the while
For death or victory?

Hurrah!—cling, clang!—once more, what
glows,
Dark brothers of the forge, beneath
The iron tempest of your blows,
The furnace's red breath?

Clang, clang!—a burning torrent, clear
And brilliant of bright sparks, is poured
Around, and up in the dusky air,
As our hammers forge the sword.

The sword!—a name of dread! yet when
Upon the freeman's thigh 'tis bound,—
While for his altar and his hearth,
While for the land that gave him birth,
The war-drums roll, the trumpets sound,—
How sacred is it then!
Whenever for the truth and right
It flashes in the van of fight,—
Whether in some wild mountain pass,
As that where fell Leonidas;
Or on some sterile plain and stern,
A Marston or a Bannockburn;
Or amidst crags and bursting rills,
The Switzer's Alps, gray Tyrol's hills;
Or as, when sunk the Armada's pride,
It gleams above the stormy tide,—
Still, still, whene'er the battle word
Is liberty, when men do stand
For justice and their native land,—
Then Heaven bless the sword!

The Man with the Hoe

By Edwin Markham

Bowed by the weight of centuries he leans
Upon his hoe and gazes on the ground,
The emptiness of ages in his face,
And on his back the burden of the world.
Who made him dead to rapture and despair,
A thing that grieves not and that never
hopes,
Stolid and stunned, a brother to the ox?
Who loosened and let down this brutal jaw?
Whose was the hand that slanted back this
brow?
Whose breath blew out the light within this
brain?

Is this the Thing the Lord God made and
gave
To have dominion over sea and land;
To trace the stars and search the Heavens
for power;
To feel the passion of Eternity?
Is this the Dream He dreamed who shaped
the suns
And pillared the blue firmament with light?
Down all the stretch of Hell to its last gulf
There is no shape more terrible than this—
More tongued with censure of the world's
blind greed—
More filled with signs and portents for the
soul—
More fraught with menace to the universe.

What gulfs between him and the seraphim!
Slave of the wheel of labor, what to him
Are Plato and the swing of Pleiades?
What the long reaches of the peaks of song,

The rift of dawn, the reddening of the rose?
Through this dread shape the suffering ages
look;
Time's tragedy is in that aching stoop;
Through this dread shape humanity betrayed,
Plundered, profaned, and disinherited,
Cries protest to the Judges of the World,
A protest that is also prophecy.

O masters, lords, and rulers in all lands,
Is this the handiwork you give to God,
This monstrous thing distorted and soul-
quenched?
How will you ever straighten up this shape;
Give back the upward looking and the light;
Rebuild in it the music and the dream;
Touch it again with immortality;
Make right the immemorial infamies,
Perfidious wrongs, immedicable woes?

O masters, lords, and rulers in all lands,
How will the Future reckon with this Man?
How answer his brute question in that hour
When whirlwinds of rebellion shake the
world?
How will it be with kingdoms and with
kings—
With those who shaped him to the thing he
is—
When this dumb Terror shall reply to God
After the silence of the centuries?

Labor

Toil is the lot of all, and bitter wo
The fate of many.
Bryant's *Homer's Iliad*. Bk. XXI.
Line 646.

Such hath it been—shall be—beneath the sun
The many still must labor for the one.
Byron—*The Corsair*. Canto I. St. 8.

Labor, wide as the Earth, has its summit
in Heaven.—Carlyle—*Essays*. *Work*.

Without Labor there were no Ease, no
Rest, so much as conceivable.—Carlyle—
Essays. Characteristics.

Labor is discovered to be the grand conqueror, enriching and building up nations
more surely than the proudest battles.—
Channing—*War*.

Work, feed thyself, to thine own powers
appeal,
Nor whine out woes, thine own right-hand
can heal.
Crabbe—*Parish Register*. Pt. III.

Honest labor bears a lovely face.
Thos. Dekker—*Patient Grissell*.
Act I. Sc. 1.

Men must work and women must weep.
Charles Kingsley—*The Three Fishers*.

From labor there shall come forth rest.
Longfellow—*To a child. Line* 162.

Taste the joy
That springs from labor.
Longfellow—*Masque of Pandora.*
Pt. VI. *In the Garden.*

The heights by great men reached and kept
  Were not attained by sudden flight,
But they, while their companions slept,
  Were toiling upward in the night.
      Longfellow—*The Ladder of St.
                      Augustine.*

No man is born into the world, whose work
Is not born with him; there is always work,
And tools to work withal, for those who will;
And blessed are the horny hands of toil!
                          Lowell.

      Let no one till his death
Be called unhappy. Measure not the work
Until the day's out and the labor done.
              E. B. Browning.

And many strokes, tho with a little ax,
Hew down and fell the hardest-timber'd oak.
   Henry VI. Pt. III. Act. II. Sc. I.

  Now the hungry lion roars,
    And the wolf behowls the moon;
  Whilst the heavy plowman snores,
    All with weary task fore-done.
  Midsummer Night's Dream. Act V.
                    Sc. 2.

The labor we delight in, physics pain.
    Macbeth. Act II. Sc. 3.

Why such impress of shipwrights whose sore
  task
Does not divide the Sunday from the week.
      Hamlet. Act I. Sc. I.

I worked with patience which is almost
  power.—E. B. Browning.

  Light is the task when many share the toil.
                 Bryant.

Labor is Worship

By Frances S. Osgood

Pause not to dream of the future before us;
Pause not to weep the wild cares that come
  o'er us;
Hark, how Creation's deep, musical chorus,
  Unintermitting, goes up into Heaven!
Never the ocean wave falters in flowing;
Never the little seed stops in its growing;
More and more richly the rose-heart keeps
  glowing,
  Till from its nourishing stem it is riven.

" Labor is worship! "—the robin is singing;
" Labor is worship! "—the wild bee is singing;
Listen! that eloquent whisper upspringing
  Speaks to thy soul from out Nature's great
  heart.
From the dark cloud flows the life-giving
  shower;
From the rough sod blows the soft-breathing
  flower;
From the small insect, the rich coral bower;
  Only *man,* in the plan, ever shrinks from
  his part.

Labor is life! 'Tis the still water faileth;
Idleness ever despaireth, bewaileth;
Keep the watch wound, for the dark rust as-
  saileth;
  Flowers **droop and die in** the stillness of
  noon.

Labor is glory!—the flying cloud lightens;
Only the waving wing changes and brightens;
Idle hearts only the dark future frightens;
  Play the sweet keys, wouldst thou keep
  them in tune.

Labor is rest from the sorrows that greet us,
Rest from all petty vexations that meet us,
Rest from sin-promptings that ever entreat
  us,
  Rest from world-sirens that lure us to ill.
Work—and pure slumbers shall wait on thy
  pillow;
Work—thou shalt ride over Care's coming
  billow;
Lie not down wearied 'neath Wo's weeping-
  willow;
  Work with a stout heart and resolute will!

Labor is health. Lo, the husbandman reaping
How through his veins goes the life current
  leaping!
How his strong arm, in its stalwart pride
  sweeping,
  True as a sunbeam the swift sickle guides.
Labor is wealth! In the sea the pearl grow-
  eth;
Rich the queen's robe from the frail cocoon
  floweth;
From the fine acorn the strong forest blow-
  eth;
  Temple and statue the marble block hides.

Droop not, tho shame, sin, and anguish are
  round thee;
Bravely fling off the cold chain that hath
  bound thee;
Look to yon pure Heaven smiling beyond
  thee;
  Rest not content in thy darkness—a clod.
Work for some good, be it ever so slowly;
Cherish some flower, be it ever so lowly;
Labor! all labor is noble and holy;
  Let thy great deeds be thy prayer to thy
  God.

Burden of Labor

By Henry Wadsworth Longfellow

Labor with what zeal we will,
  Something still remains undone,
Something uncompleted still
  Waits the rising of the sun.

By the bedside, on the stair,
  At the threshold, near the gates,
With its menace or its prayer,
  Like a mendicant it waits;

Waits. and will not go away;
  Waits, and will not be gainsaid;
By the cares of yesterday
  Each to-day is heavier made;

Till at length the burden seems
  Greater than our strength can **bear,**
Heavy as the weight of dreams,
  Pressing on us everywhere.

And we stand from day to day,
  Like the dwarfs of times gone **by,**
Who, as northern legends say,
  On their shoulders held the sky.

The Village Blacksmith

By Henry Wadsworth Longfellow

Under a spreading chestnut-tree
    The village smithy stands;
The smith, a mighty man is he,
    With large and sinewy hands;
And the muscles of his brawny arms
    Are strong as iron bands.

.   .   .   .

Week in, week out, from morn till night,
    You can hear his bellows blow;
You can hear him swing his heavy sledge,
    With measured beat and slow,
Like sexton ringing the village bell,
    When the evening sun is low.

.   .   .   .

Toiling, rejoicing, sorrowing,
    Onward through life he goes;
Each morning sees some task begin,
    Each evening sees it close;
Something attempted, something done,
    Has earned a night's repose.

Thanks, thanks to thee, my worthy friend,
    For the lesson thou hast taught!
Thus at the flaming forge of life
    Our fortunes must be wrought;
Thus on its sounding anvil shaped
    Each burning deed and thought!

Objects of Labor

By William Drummond

A good that never satisfies the mind,
A beauty fading like the April flowers,
A sweet with floods of gall that runs com-
    bined,
A pleasure passing ere in thought made ours,
An honor that more fickle is than wind,
A glory at opinion's frown that lowers,
A treasury which bankrupt time devours,
A knowledge than grave ignorance more
    blind,
A vain delight our equals to command,
A style of greatness, in effect a dream,
A swelling thought of holding sea and land,
A servile lot, decked with a pompous name,
Are the strange ends we toil for here below,
Till wisest death make us our errors know.

Original Labor

By John Milton

Now came still evening on, and twilight
    gray
Had in her sober livery all things clad;
Silence accompanied; for beast and bird,
They to their grassy couch, these to their
    nests,
Were slunk, all but the wakeful nightingale;
She all night long her amorous descant sung.
Silence was pleased; now glowed the firma-
    ment
With living sapphires; Hesperus, that led
The starry host, rode brightest, till the moon,
Rising in clouded majesty, at length
Apparent queen, unveiled her peerless light,
And o'er the dark her silver mantle threw.
    When Adam thus to Eve: "Fair consort,
    the hour
Of night, and all things now retired to rest,
Mind us of like repose, since God hath set
Labor and rest, as day and night, to men
Successive; and the timely dew of sleep,
Now falling with soft slumberous weight, in-
    clines
Our eyelids. Other creatures all day long
Rove idle, unemployed, and less need rest;
Man hath his daily work of body or mind
Appointed, which declares his dignity,
And the regard of Heaven on all his ways;
While other animals unactive range,
And of their doings God takes no account.
To-morrow, ere fresh morning streak the east
With first approach of light, we must be risen,
And at our pleasant labor, to reform
Yon flowery arbors, yonder alleys green,
Our walk at noon, with branches overgrown,
That mock our scant manuring, and require
More hands than ours to lop their wanton
    growth.
Those blossoms also, and those dropping
    gums
That lie bestrewn, unsightly and unsmooth,
Ask riddance, if we mean to tread with ease;
Meanwhile, as Nature wills, night bids us
    rest."—*Paradise Lost.*

Mrs. Lofty and I

Anonymous

Mrs. Lofty keeps a carriage,
                    So do I;
She has dapple grays to draw it,
                    None have I;
She's no prouder with her coachman
                    Than am I
With my blue-eyed laughing baby
                    Trundling by;
I hide his face, lest she should see
The cherub boy, and envy me.

Her fine husband has white fingers,
                    Mine has not;
He could give his bride a palace,
                    Mine a cot;
Her's comes beneath the star-light,
                    Ne'er cares she;
Mine comes in the purple twilight,
                    Kisses me.
And prays that He who turns life's sands,
Will hold his lov'd ones in His hands.

Mrs. Lofty has her jewels,
                    So have I;
She wears hers upon her bosom,
                    Inside I;
She will leave hers at death's portals,
                    By and by:
I shall bear the treasure with me,
                    When I die;
For I have love, and she has gold;
She counts her wealth, mine can't be told.

She has those that love her station,
                    None have I;
But I've one true heart beside me,
                    Glad am I;

I'd not change it for a kingdom,
           No, not I;
God will weigh it in his balance,
           By and by;
And then the diff'rence 'twill define
'Twixt Mrs. Lofty's wealth and mine.

The Night Cometh

By S. Dyer

Work, for the night is coming;
  Work, through the morning hours;
Work, while the dew is sparkling;
  Work, 'mid springing flowers;
Work, when the day grows brighter,
  Work, in the glowing sun;
Work, for the night is coming,
  When man's work is done.

Work, for the night is coming,
  Work through the sunny noon;
Fill brightest hours with labor,
  Rest comes sure and soon.
Give every flying minute
  Something to keep in store:
Work, for the night is coming,
  When man works no more.

Work, for the night is coming,
  Under the sunset skies;
While their bright tints are glowing,
  Work,' for daylight flies.
Work till the last beam fadeth,
  Fadeth to shine no more;
Work while the night is darkening,
  When man's work is o'er.

The Song of the Shirt

By Thomas Hood

With fingers weary and worn,
  With eyelids heavy and red,
A woman sat, in unwomanly rags,
  Plying her needle and thread—
Stitch! stitch! stitch!
  In poverty, hunger, and dirt,
And still, with a voice of dolorous pitch,
  She sang the " Song of the Shirt!"

" Work! work! work!
  While the cock is crowing aloof:
And work—work—work!
  Till the stars shine through the roof!
It's oh! to be a slave
  Along with the barbarous Turk,
Where woman has never a soul to save,
  If this is Christian work!

" Work—work—work!
  Till the brain begins to swim!
Work—work—work!
  Till the eyes are heavy and dim!
Seam, and gusset, and band,
  Band, and gusset, and seam,
Till over the buttons I fall asleep,
  And sew them on in my dream!

" Oh! men with sisters dear!
  Oh! men with mothers and wives!

It is not linen you're wearing out,
  But human creatures' lives!
Stitch—stitch—stitch!
  In poverty, hunger, and dirt,
Sewing at once, with a double thread,
  A shroud as well as a shirt!

" But why do I talk of death,
  That phantom of grisly bone?
I hardly fear his terrible shape,
  It seems so like my own—
It seems so like my own,
  Because of the fast I keep:
O God! that bread should be so dear,
  And flesh and blood so cheap!

" Work—work—work!
  My labor never flags;
And what are its wages? A bed of straw,
  A crust of bread—and rags:
A shatter'd roof—and this naked floor—
  A table—a broken chair—
And a wall so blank, my shadow I thank
  For sometimes falling there!

" Work—work—work!
  From weary chime to chime:
Work—work—work!
  As prisoners work for crime!
Band, and gusset, and seam,
  Seam, and gusset, and band,
Till the heart is sick, and the brain be-
    numb'd,
  As well as the weary hand!

" Work—work—work!
  In the dull December light;
And work—work—work!
  When the weather is warm and bright:
While underneath the eaves
  The brooding swallows cling,
As if to show me their sunny backs,
  And twit me with the spring.

" Oh! but to breathe the breath
  Of the cowslip and primrose sweet;
With the sky above my head,
  And the grass beneath my feet:
For only one short hour
  To feel as I used to feel,
Before I knew the woes of want,
  And the walk that costs a meal!

" Oh! but for one short hour!
  A respite, however brief!
No blessed leisure for love or hope,
  But only time for grief!
A little weeping would ease my heart—
  But in their briny bed
My tears must stop, for every drop
  Hinders the needle and thread!"

With fingers weary and worn,
  With eyelids heavy and red,
A woman sat, in unwomanly rags,
  Plying her needle and thread:
Stitch—stitch—stitch!
  In poverty, hunger, and dirt;
And still with a voice of dolorous pitch—
Would that its tone could reach the rich!—
  She sung this " Song of the Shirt!"

DISCOVERY DAY
PRESIDENT'S PROCLAMATION
1892

By the President of the United States of America. A Proclamation.

WHEREAS, By joint resolution, approved June 29, 1892, it was resolved by the Senate and House of Representatives of the United States of America, in Congress assembled, " That the President of the United States be authorized and directed to issue a proclamation recommending to the people the observance in all their localities of the four-hundredth anniversary of the discovery of America, on the twenty-first day of October, 1892, by public demonstrations and by suitable exercises in their schools and other places of assembly."

Now, therefore, I, Benjamin Harrison, President of the United States of America, in pursuance of the aforesaid joint resolution, do hereby appoint Friday, October 21, 1892, the four-hundredth anniversary of the discovery of America by Columbus, as a general holiday for the people of the United States. On that day let the people, so far as possible, cease from toil and devote themselves to such exercises as may best express honor to the discoverer, and their appreciation of the great achievements of the four completed centuries of American life.

Columbus stood in his age as the pioneer of progress and achievement. The system of universal education is in our age the most prominent and salutary feature of the spirit of enlightenment, and it is peculiarly appropriate that the schools be made by the people the center of the day's demonstration. Let the national flag float over every school-house in the country, and the exercises be such as shall impress upon our youth the patriotic duties of American citizenship.

In the churches and in other places of assembly of the people let there be expressions of gratitude to Divine Providence for the devout faith of the discoverer, and for the Divine care and guidance which has directed our history, and so abundantly blessed our people.

In testimony whereof, I have hereunto set my hand and caused the seal of the United States to be affixed.

Done at the City of Washington this twenty-first day of July, in the year of our Lord, one thousand eight hundred and ninety-two, and of the Independence of the United States the one hundred and seventeenth.

BENJAMIN HARRISON.

By the President.

JOHN W. FOSTER, *Secretary of State.*

ADDRESSES

FOUR CENTURIES COMPLETED

By Francis Bellamy

[Address prepared under the auspices of the " Youth's Companion " for the National School
Exercises, October 26, 1892.]

The spectacle America presents this day is unique, without precedent in history. From ocean to ocean, in city, village, and country-side, children of the states are marshaled and marching under the banner of the Nation; citizens are gathering around the school-house. The attention of the world is focused on the American schoolmaster and his pupils.

Men are recognizing to-day the most impressive anniversary since Rome celebrated her thousandth year,—the four-hundredth anniversary of the stepping of a hemisphere into the world's life; four completed centuries of a new social order; the celebration of liberty and enlightenment organized into a civilization. And while, during these hours, the Federal Government of these United States strikes in one chosen spot the key-note of this great American day, we, the people, assemble around the common American institution, which not only unites us all, but also embodies the American principle of universal enlightenment and equality and is itself the most characteristic product of the four centuries of American life,—the Free School,—and take up the solemn and ex-ultant music.

Four hundred years ago this morning the *Pinta's* gun broke the silence and announced the discovery of this hemisphere.

It was a virgin world. Human life hitherto upon it had been without significance. European eyes that possibly had beheld it were holden that they should not see and report its opportunities. In the Old World for thousands of years civilized men had been trying experiments in social order, and they had been found wanting. But here an untouched soil lay ready for a new experiment in civilization. From the dawn of time nature had been preparing this place for the civilization of enlightenment.

In the fulness of time Columbus came. All things were ready. A new method was present for a new civilization. New forces had come to light of late,—the mariner's compass, gunpowder, printing, the spur of intellectual awakening; these were new things for Europe, and full of overturning power in the Old World. But in the New World they were to work together in a mighty harmony.

It was for Columbus, when the right hour struck, forced and propelled by this fresh life, to reveal the land where these new principles were to be brought, and where the awaited trial of the new civilization was to be made.

To-day we reach our most memorable milestone. We look backward and we look forward.

Backward, we see the first mustering of modern ideas; their long conflict with Old World theories also transported hither. We see stalwart men and brave women, one moment on the shore, then disappearing in dim forests. We hear the ax; we see the flames of burning cabins, and hear the cry of the savage. We see the never-ceasing wagon-trains always toiling westward. We behold log cabins becoming villages, then cities. We watch the growth of institutions out of little beginnings,—schools becoming an educational system; meeting-houses leading into organic Christianity; town-meetings growing to political movements; county discussions developing federal governments. We see these hardy men, with intense convictions, grappling, struggling, often amid battle-smoke, and some idea characteristic of the New World always triumphing. We see settlements knitting together into a nation with singleness of purpose. We note the birth of the modern system of industry and commerce, and its striking forth into undreamed-of wealth, making the millions members one of another as sentiment could never bind. And under it all, and through it all, we fasten on certain principles ever operating and regnant, —the leadership of manhood; equal rights for every soul; universal enlightenment as the source of progress. These are the principles that have shaped America; these principles are the true Americanism.

We look forward. We are conscious we are in a period of transition. Ideas in education, in political economy, in social science, are undergoing revision. There is a large uncertainty about the outcome. But faith in the underlying principles of Americanism and in God's destiny for the Republic makes a firm ground of bright hope. Whatever else may come, it may at least be held as certain that the coming century will be more than ever the age of the people; that it will develop a greater care for the rights of the weak; that it will disclose an increased purpose that every one shall start in life without handicaps; that it will make a more solid provision for the rounded development of each individual in the education that meets his need.

Had our fathers of a century ago celebrated the three-hundredth anniversary of America, could any prophet of them have pictured what the new century was to do? No lesson drawn from America's three earlier centuries could have even hinted the bewildering rush of her fourth century.

No man can this day reach out and grasp the hundred years that are now beginning. On the victorious results of the completed centuries the persisting principles of Americanism will build our fifth century. Its material progress will be too amazing for man to try to imagine. But, holding our hand on the currents that are passing, we may be sure that in the social relations of men with men the most important gains are to be expected. America's fourth century has been glorious. America's fifth century must be made happy.

One institution more than any other has wrought out the achievements of the past, and is to-day most trusted for the future. Our fathers in their wisdom knew that the foundations of liberty, equality, and fraternity must be universal education. The free school, therefore, was conceived the cornerstone of the Republic. Washington and Jefferson recognized that the education of citizens is not the prerogative of Church or of other private interest; that while religious training belongs to the Church, and while technical and higher culture may be given to private institutions, the training of citizens in the common knowledge and the common duties of citizenship belongs irrevocably to the state.

We, therefore, on this anniversary of America, present the Public School as the proudest and noblest expression of the principle of enlightenment which Columbus grasped by faith. We uplift the system of free and universal education as the master-force which, under God, has been informing each of our generations with the peculiar truths of Americanism. America, therefore, gathers her sons around the schoolhouse to-day as the institution closest to the people, most characteristic of the people, and fullest of hope for the people.

To-day America's fifth century begins. The world's twentieth century will soon be here. To the thirteen millions now in the American schools the command of the coming years belongs. We, the youth of America, who to-day unite to march as one army under the sacred flag, understand our duty. We pledge ourselves that the flag shall not be stained, and that America shall mean equal opportunity and justice for every citizen, and brotherhood for the world.

MEMORIAL DESERTS OF COLUMBUS

Well might the mail-clad monarchs of the earth refuse their countenance to Columbus and reward his matchless exploit with beggary and chains. He projected and he accomplished that which, in its ultimate and inevitable consequences, was to wrest from their hands the implements of their ferocious sport, to "break their bow and snap their spear in sunder,' and all but to extinguish the sources of their proudest and most absolute prerogative.

"No kingly conqueror, since time began
The long career of ages, had to man
A scope so ample given for trade's bold range,
Or caused of earth's wide stage such rapid, mighty change."

From the discovery of the New World, the mercantile spirit has been rapidly gaining upon its old antagonist; and the establishment upon these shores of our Republic, whose union was the immediate result of commercial necessities, whose independence found its original impulse in commercial oppression, and of whose Constitution the regulation of commerce was the first leading idea, may be regarded as the epoch at which the martial spirit finally lost its supremacy, which, it is believed and trusted, it can never again acquire.—ROBERT C. WINTHROP.

Necessity is the mother of invention, and there was little or no necessity of that sort at Syracuse. But everything for which a demand existed Archimedes was able to supply, and actually did supply it. It was not reserved for him to find a place for doing more. It was not his destiny to discover the fulcrum, by poising his mighty lever upon which the world, as he knew it, could be moved. But sixteen hundred years afterwards, at the head of the very gulf on which Sicily stands, the man was born to whom that lofty destiny was vouchsafed. Columbus, a native of Genoa, discovered the New World, and the Old World has been moving ever since.— ROBERT C. WINTHROP.

I drove along this incomparable road (the Cornice Road, near the Mediterranean) during three days of delicious weather, and on the fourth day entered that superb city, which a grander admiral than Farragut might well have been proud to claim as his birthplace, Christopher Columbus, a native of Genoa.

A noble monument to Columbus, recently finished, surmounted by a striking likeness of him, and adorned by a series of bas-reliefs illustrating the strange, eventful history of his life, from which I need hardly say the discovery of America was not wholly omitted, greeted us at the gates with the simple inscription, in Italian, " To Christopher Columbus, from his Country." And as I gazed upon it with admiration, I could not help feeling that it was not there alone that a monument and a statue were due to his memory; but that upon the shores of our own hemisphere, too, there ought to be some worthy memorial of the discoverer of the New World, an exact reproduction of this admirable monument at Genoa, so that hemisphere should seem to respond to hemisphere in a common tribute to the heroic and matchless old navigator. It would be some sort of atonement, I thought, on the part of America.—tardy and inadequate, indeed, but better than nothing.—for having allowed another, however meritorious, to usurp the place to which his name was so preeminently entitled in the geographical nomenclature of the globe. —ROBERT C. WINTHROP.

From the hour when Columbus and his compeers discovered our continent, its ultimate political destiny was fixed. At the very gateway of the Pantheon of American liberty and American independence might well be seen a triple monument, like that to the old inventors of the art of printing at Frankfort, including Columbus, Americus Vespucius, and Cabot.

They were the pioneers in the march to independence. They were the precursors in the only progress of freedom which was to have no backward steps. Liberty had struggled long and bravely in other ages and in other lands. It had made glorious manifestations of its power in Athens and in Rome; in the medieval republics of Italy; on the plains of Germany; along the dikes of Holland; among the icy fastnesses of Switzerland, and, more securely and hopefully still, in the sea-girt isle of Old England. But it was the glory of these old navigators to reveal a standing-place for it, at last, where its lever could find a secure fulcrum and rest safely until it had moved the world.—ROBERT C. WINTHROP. (Col. S.)

THE COLUMBIAN ORATION

BY CHAUNCEY M. DEPEW

[Delivered at the Dedication Ceremonies of the World's Fair at Chicago, October 21st, 1892.]

This day belongs not to America, but to the world. The results of the event it commemorates are the heritage of the peoples of every race and clime. We celebrate the emancipation of man. The preparation was the work of almost countless centuries; the realization was the revelation of one. The cross on Calvary was hope; the cross raised on San Salvador was opportunity. But for the first, Columbus would never have sailed; but for the second, there would have been no place for the planting, the nurture, and the expansion of civil and religious liberty. Ancient history is a dreary record of unstable civilizations. Each reached its zenith of material splendor, and perished. The Assyrian, Persian, Egyptian, Grecian, and Roman empires were proofs of the possibilities and limitations of man for conquest and intellectual development. Their destruction involved a sum of misery and relapse which made their creation rather a curse than a blessing. Force was the factor in the government of the world when Christ was born, and force was the source and exercise of authority both by Church and State when Columbus sailed from Palos. The Wise Men traveled from the East toward the West under the guidance of the Star of Bethlehem. The spirit of the equality of all men before God and the law moved westward from Calvary with its revolutionary influence upon old institutions, to the Atlantic Ocean. Columbus carried it westward across the seas. The emigrants from England, Ireland, Scotland, and Wales, from Germany and Holland, from Sweden and Denmark, from France and Italy, from Spain and Portugal, under its guidance and inspiration, moved west. and again west, building states and founding cities until the Pacific limited their march. The exhibition of arts and sciences, of industries and inventions, of education and civilization, which the Republic of the United States will here present, and to which, through its chief Magistrate, it invites all nations, condenses and displays the flower and fruitage of this transcendent miracle.

The anarchy and chaos which followed the breaking up of the Roman Empire necessarily produced the feudal system. The people, preferring slavery to annihilation by robber chiefs, became the vassals of territorial lords. The reign of physical force is one of perpetual struggle for the mastery. Power which rests upon the sword neither shares nor limits its authority. The king destroyed the lords, and the monarchy succeeded feudalism. Neither of these institutions considered or consulted the people. They had no part but to suffer or die in this mighty strife of masters for the mastery. But the throne, by its broader view and greater resources, made possible the construction of the highways of freedom. Under its banner, races could unite and petty principalities be merged, law substituted for brute force and right for might. It founded and endowed universities, and encouraged commerce. It conceded no political privileges, but unconsciously prepared its subjects to demand them.

.   .   .   .   .   .

Fifty years before Columbus sailed from Palos, Gutenberg and Faust had forged the hammer which was to break the bonds of superstition and open the prison doors of the mind. They had invented the printing press and movable types. The prior adoption of a cheap process for the manufacture of paper at once utilized the press. Its first service, like all its succeeding efforts, was for the people. The universities and the schoolmen, the privileged and the learned few of that age, were longing for the revelation and preservation of the classic treasures of antiquity, hidden, and yet insecure in monastic cells and libraries. But the firstborn of the marvelous creation of these primitive printers of Mayence was the printed Bible. The priceless contributions of Greece and Rome to the intellectual training and development of the modern world came afterwards, through the same wondrous machine. The force, however, which made possible America and its reflex influence upon Europe was the open Bible by the family fireside. And yet neither the enlightenment of the new learning, nor the dynamic power of the spiritual awakening, could break through the crust of caste which had been forming for centuries. Church and State had so firmly and dexterously interwoven the bars of privilege and authority that liberty was impossible from within. Its piercing light and fervent heat must penetrate from without.

Civil and religious freedom are founded upon the individual and his independence, his worth, his rights, and his equal status and opportunity. For his planting and development a new land must be found where, with limitless areas for expansion, the avenues of progress would have no bars of custom or heredity, of social orders or privileged classes. The time had come for the emancipation of the mind and soul of humanity. The factors wanting for its fulfilment were the new world and its discoverer.

. . . .

Neither realism nor romance furnishes a more striking and picturesque figure than that of Christopher Columbus. The mystery about his origin heightens the charm of his story. That he came from among the toilers of his time is in harmony with the struggles of our period. Forty-four authentic portraits of him have descended to us, and no two of them are the counterfeits of the same person. Each represents a character as distinct as its canvas. Strength and weakness, intellectuality and stupidity, high moral purpose and brutal ferocity, purity and licentiousness, the dreamer and the miser, the pirate and the Puritan, are the types from which we may select our hero. We dismiss the painter, and piercing with the clarified vision of the dawn of the twentieth century the veil of four hundred years, we construct our Columbus.

The perils of the sea in his youth on the rich argosies of Genoa, or in the service of the licensed rovers who made them their prey, had developed a skilful navigator and intrepid mariner. They had given him a glimpse of the possibilities of the unknown beyond the highways of travel, which roused an unquenchable thirst for adventure and research. The study of the narratives of previous explorers and diligent questionings of the daring spirits who had ventured far towards the fabled West gradually evolved a theory which became in his mind so fixed a fact that he could inspire others with his own passionate beliefs. The words, " That is a lie," written by him on the margin of nearly every page of a volume of the travels of Marco Polo, which is still to be found in a Genoese library, illustrate the skepticism of his beginning, and the first vision of the New World, the fulfilment of his faith.

To secure the means to test the truth of his speculations, this poor and unknown dreamer must win the support of kings and overcome the hostility of the Church. He never doubted his ability to do both, tho he knew of no man living who was so great in power, or lineage, or learning, that he could accomplish either. Unaided and alone, he succeeded in arousing the jealousies of sovereigns, and dividing the councils of the ecclesiastics. " I will command your fleet and discover for you new realms, but only on condition that you confer on me hereditary nobility, the Admiralty of the Ocean and the Vice-Royalty and one-tenth the revenues of the New World," were his haughty terms to King John of Portugal. After ten years of disappointment and poverty, subsisting most of the time upon the charity of the enlightened monk of the Convent of Rabida, who was his unfaltering friend, he stood before the throne of Ferdinand and Isabella, and, rising to imperial dignity in his rags, embodied the same royal conditions in his petition.

. . . .

It was a happy omen of the position which woman was to hold in America that the only person who comprehended the majestic scope of his plans and the invincible quality of his genius was the able and gracious Queen of Castile. Isabella alone of all the dignitaries of that age shares with Columbus the honors of his great achievement. She arrayed her kingdom and her private fortune behind the enthusiasm of this mystic mariner, and posterity pays homage to her wisdom and faith.

The overthrow of the Mohammedan power in Spain would have been a forgotten scene in one of the innumerable acts in the grand drama of history had not Isabella conferred immortality upon herself, her husband, and their dual crown, by her recognition of Columbus. The devout spirit of the Queen and the high purpose of the explorer inspired the voyage, subdued the mutinous crew, and prevailed over the raging storms. They covered with the divine radiance of religion and humanity the degrading search for gold and the horrors of its quest, which filled the first century of conquest with every form of lust and greed.

The mighty soul of the great admiral was undaunted by the ingratitude of princes and the hostility of the people by imprisonment and neglect. He died as he was securing the means and preparing a campaign for the rescue of the Holy Sepulcher at Jerusalem from the infidel. He did not know what time has revealed, that while the mission of the crusades of Godfrey of Bouillon and Richard of the Lion Heart was a bloody and fruitless romance, the discovery of America was the salvation of the world. The one was the symbol, the other the spirit; the one death, the other life. The tomb of the Savior was a narrow and empty vault, precious only for its memories of the supreme tragedy of the centuries, but the new continent was to be the home and temple of living God.

The rulers of the Old World began with partitioning the New. To them the discovery was expansion of empire and grandeur to the throne. Vast territories, whose properties and possibilities were little understood, and whose extent was greater than the kingdoms of the sovereigns, were the gifts to court favorites and the prizes of royal approval. But individual intelligence and independent conscience found here haven and refuge. They were the passengers upon the caravel of Columbus, and he was unconsciously making for the port of civil and religious liberty. Thinkers who believed men capable of higher destinies and larger responsibilities, and pious people who preferred the Bible to that union of Church and State where each serves the other for the temporal benefit of both, fled to those distant and hospitable lands from intolerable and hopeless oppression at home. It required three hundred years for the people thus happily situated to understand their own powers and resources and to break bonds which were still reverenced or loved, no matter how deeply they wounded or how hard they galled.

The nations of Europe were so completely absorbed in dynastic difficulties and devastating wars, with diplomacy and ambitions, that, if they heard of, they did not heed the growing democratic spirit and intelligence in their American colonies. To them these provinces were sources of revenue, and they never dreamed that they were also schools of liberty. That it exhausted three centuries under the most favorable conditions for the evolution of freedom on this continent demonstrates the tremendous strength of custom and heredity when sanctioned and sanctified by religion. The very chains which fettered became inextricably interwoven with the habits of life, the associations of childhood, the tenderest ties of the family, and the sacred offices of the Church from the cradle to the grave. It clearly proves that if the people of the Old World and their descendants had not possessed the opportunities afforded by the New for their emancipation, and mankind had never experienced and learned the American example, instead of living in the light and glory of nineteenth-century conditions they would still be struggling with medieval problems.

The northern continent was divided among England, France, and Spain, and the southern between Spain and Portugal. France, wanting the capacity for colonization, which still characterizes her, gave up her western possessions and left the English, who have the genius of universal empire, masters of North America. The development of the experiment in the English domain makes this day memorable. It is due to the wisdom and courage, the faith and virtue, of the inhabitants of this territory, that government of the people, for the people, and by the people was inaugurated and has become a triumphant success. The Puritan settled in New England and the Cavalier in the South. They represented the opposites of spiritual and temporal life and opinions. The processes of liberty liberalized the one and elevated the other. Washington and Adams were the new types. Their union in a common cause gave the world a Republic both

stable and free. It possessed conservatism without bigotry, and liberty without license. It founded institutions strong enough to resist revolution, and elastic enough for indefinite expansion to meet the requirements in government of ever-enlarging areas of population and the needs of progress and growth. It was nurtured by the toleration and patriotism which bound together in a common cause the Puritans of New England and the Catholics of Maryland, the Dutch Reformers of New York and the Huguenots of South Carolina, the Quakers and Lutherans of Pennsylvania and the Episcopalians, Methodists, Presbyterians, Baptists, and religionists of all and of opposite opinions in the other colonies.

The *Mayflower*, with the Pilgrims, and a Dutch ship laden with African slaves were on the ocean at the same time, the one sailing for Massachusetts, and the other for Virginia. This company of saints and first cargo of slaves represented the forces which were to peril and rescue free government. The slaver was the product of the commercial spirit of Great Britain, and the greed of the times to stimulate production in the colonies. The men who wrote in the cabin of the *Mayflower* the first charter of freedom, a government of just and equal laws, were a little band of Protestants against every form of injustice and tyranny. The leaven of their principles made possible the Declaration of Independence, liberated the slaves, and founded the free commonwealths which form the Republic of the United States.

Platforms of principles, by petition or protest or statement, have been as frequent as revolts against established authority. They are a part of the political literature of all nations. The Declaration of Independence proclaimed at Philadelphia, July 4, 1776, is the only one of them which arrested the attention of the world when it was published and has held its undivided interest ever since. The vocabulary of the equality of man had been in familiar use by philosophers and statesmen for ages. It expressed noble sentiments, but their application was limited to classes or conditions. The masses cared little for them, nor remembered them long. Jefferson's superb crystallization of the popular opinion that "all men are created equal, that they are endowed by their Creator with certain inalienable rights, that among these are life, liberty, and the pursuit of happiness," had its force and effect in being the deliberate utterance of the people. It swept away in a single sentence kings and nobles, peers and prelates. It was Magna Charta and the Petition of Rights planted in the virgin soil of the American wilderness, and bearing richer and riper fruit. Under its vitalizing influence upon the individual, the farmer left his plow in the furrow, the lawyer his books and briefs, the merchant his shop, and the workman his bench, to enlist in the patriot army. They were fighting for themselves and their children. They embodied the idea in their Constitution in the immortal words with which that great instrument of liberty and order began:—

"We, the people of the United States, do ordain."

The scope and limitations of this idea of freedom have neither been misinterpreted nor misunderstood. The laws of nature in their application to the rise and recognition of men according to their mental, moral, spiritual, and physical endowments are left undisturbed. But the accident of birth gives no rank and confers no privilege. Equal rights and common opportunity for all have been the spurs of ambition and the motors of progress. They have established the common schools and built the public libraries. A sovereign people have learned and enforced the lesson of free education. The practise of government is itself a liberal education. People who make their own laws need no lawgivers. After a century of successful trial, the system has passed the period of experiment, and its demonstrated permanency and power are revolutionizing the governments of the world. It has raised the largest armies of modern times for self-preservation, and at the successful termination of the war returned the soldiers to the pursuits of peace. It has so adjusted itself to the pride and patriotism of the defeated that they vie with the victors in their support of and enthusiasm for the old flag and our common country. Imported anarchists have preached their baleful doctrines, but have made no converts. They have tried to inaugurate a reign of terror under the banner of the violent seizure and distribution of property only to be defeated, imprisoned, and executed by the law made by the people and enforced by juries selected from the people, and judges and prosecuting officers elected by the people. Socialism finds disciples only among those who were its votaries before they were forced to fly from their native land, but it does not take root upon American soil. The State neither supports nor permits taxation to maintain the Church. The citizen can worship God according to his belief and conscience, or he may neither reverence nor recognize the Almighty. And yet religion has flourished, churches abound, the ministry is sustained, and millions of dollars are contributed annually for the evangelization of the world. The United States is a Christian country, and a living and practical Christianity is the characteristic of its people.

Benjamin Franklin, philosopher and patriot, amused the jaded courtiers of Louis XVI. by his talks about liberty, and entertained the scientists of France by bringing lightning from the clouds. In the reckoning of time, the period from Franklin to Morse, and from Morse to Edison is but a span, and yet it marks a material development as marvelous as it has been beneficent. The world has been brought into contact and sympathy. The electric current thrills and unifies the people of the globe. Power and production, highways and transports have been so multiplied and improved by inventive genius, that within the century of our independence sixty-four millions of people have happy homes and improved conditions within our borders. We have accumulated wealth far beyond the visions of the Cathay of Columbus or the El Dorado of De Soto. But the farmers and freeholders, the savings banks and shops illustrate its universal distribution. The majority are its possessors and administrators. In housing and living, in the elements which make the toiler a self-respecting and respected citizen, in avenues of hope and ambition for children, in all that gives broader scope and keener pleasure to existence, the people of this Republic enjoy advantages far beyond those of other lands. The unequaled and phenomenal progress of the country has opened wonderful opportunities for making fortunes, and stimulated to madness the desire and rush for the accumulation of money. Material prosperity has not debased literature nor debauched the press; it has neither paralyzed nor repressed intellectual activity. American science and letters have received rank and recognition in the older centers of learning. The demand for higher education has so taxed the resources of the ancient universities as to compel the foundation and liberal endowment of colleges all over the Union. Journals, remarkable for their ability, independence, and power, find their strength, not in the patronage of government, or the subsidies of wealth, but in the support of a Nation of newspaper readers. The humblest and poorest person has, in periodicals whose price is counted in pennies, a library larger, fuller, and more varied than was within the reach of the rich in the time of Columbus.

The sum of human happiness has been infinitely increased by the millions from the Old World who have improved their conditions in the New, and the returning tide of lesson and experience has incalculably enriched the Fatherlands. The divine right of kings has taken its place with the instruments of medieval torture among the curiosities of the antiquary. Only the shadow of kingly authority stands between the government of themselves, and the people of Norway and Sweden. The union in one empire of the States of Germany is the symbol of Teutonic power and the hope of German liberalism. The petty despotisms of Italy have been merged into a nationality which has centralized its authority in its ancient capitol on the hills of Rome. France was rudely roused from the sullen submission of centuries to intolerable tyranny by her soldiers returning from service in the American Revolution. The wild orgies of the Reign of Terror were the revenges and excesses of a people who had discovered their power, but were not prepared for its beneficent use. She fled from herself into the arms of Napoleon. He, too, was a product of the American experiment. He played with kings as with toys and educated France for liberty. In the processes of her evolution from darkness to light, she tried Bourbon and Orleanist and the third Napoleon, and cast them aside. Now in the fulness of time, and through the training in the school of hardest experience, the French people have reared and enjoy a permanent republic. England of the *Mayflower* and of James II., England of George

III. and of Lord North, has enlarged suffrage and is to-day animated and governed by the democratic spirit. She has (1892) her throne admirably occupied by one of the wisest of sovereigns and best of women, but it would not survive one dissolute and unworthy successor. She has her hereditary peers, but the House of Lords will be brushed aside the moment it resists the will of the people.

The time has arrived for both a closer union and greater distance between the Old World and the New. The former indiscriminate welcome to our prairies and the present invitation to these palaces of art and industry mark the passing period. Unwatched and unhealthy immigration can no longer be permitted to our shores. We must have a national quarantine against disease, pauperism, and crime. We do not want candidates for our hospitals, our poorhouses or our jails. We cannot admit those who come to undermine our institutions and subvert our laws. But we will gladly throw wide our gates for, and receive with open arms, those who by intelligence and virtue, by thrift and loyalty, are worthy of receiving the equal advantages of the priceless gift of American citizenship. The spirit and object of this exhibition are peace and kinship.

Three millions of Germans, who are among the best citizens of the Republic, send greeting to the Fatherland, expressing their pride in its glorious history, its ripe literature, its traditions and associations. Irish, equal in number to those who still remain upon the Emerald Isle, who have illustrated their devotion to their adopted country on many a battlefield, fighting for the Union and its perpetuity, have rather intensified than diminished their love for the land of the shamrock and their sympathy with the aspirations of their brethren at home. The Italian, the Spaniard, and the Frenchman, the Norwegian, the Swede, and the Dane, the English, the Scotch, and the Welsh, are none the less loyal and devoted Americans because in this congress of their kin the tendrils of affection draw them closer to the hills and valleys, the legends and the loves associated with their youth.

Edmund Burke, speaking in the British Parliament with prophetic voice, said: "A great revolution has happened—a revolution made, not by chopping and changing of power in any of the existing states, but by the appearance of a new state, of a new species, in a new part of the globe. It has made as great a change in all the relations and balances and gravitations of power as the appearance of a new planet would in the system of the solar world." Thus was the humiliation of our successful revolt tempered to the motherland by pride in the state created by her children. If we claim heritage in Bacon, Shakespeare, and Milton, we also acknowledge that it was for liberties guaranteed Englishmen by sacred charters our fathers triumphantly fought. While wisely rejecting throne and caste and privilege and an Established Church in their newborn state, they adopted the substance of English liberty and the body of English law. Closer relations with England than with other lands, and a common language rendering easy interchanges of criticisms and epithet, sometimes irritate and offend, but the heart of republican America beats with responsive pulsations to the hopes and aspirations of the people of Great Britain.

The grandeur and beauty of this spectacle are the eloquent witnesses of peace and progress. The Parthenon and the cathedral exhausted the genius of the ancient, and the skill of the medieval architects, in housing the statue or spirit of Deity. In their ruins or their antiquity they are mute protests against the merciless enmity of nations, which forced art to flee to the altar for protection. The United States welcome the sister republics of the Southern and Northern continents, and the nations and peoples of Europe and Asia, of Africa and Australia, with the products of their lands, of their skill and of their industry, to this city of yesterday, yet clothed with royal splendor as the queen of the Great Lakes. The artists and architects of the country have been bidden to design and erect the buildings which shall fitly illustrate the height of our civilization and the breadth of our hospitality. The peace of the world permits and protects their efforts in utilizing their powers for man's temporal welfare. The result is this park of palaces. The originality and the boldness of their conceptions, and the magnitude and harmony of their creations, are the contributions of America to the oldest of the arts and the cordial bidding of America to the peoples of the earth to come and bring the fruitage of their age to the boundless opportunities of this unparalleled exhibition.

If interest in the affairs of this world is vouchsafed to those who have gone before, the spirit of Columbus hovers over us to-day. Only by celestial intelligence can it grasp the full significance of this spectacle and ceremonial.

From the first century to the fifteenth counts for little in the history of progress, but in the period between the fifteenth and twentieth is crowded the romance and reality of human development. Life has been prolonged, and its enjoyment intensified. The powers of the air and the water, the resistless forces of the elements, which in the time of the Discoverer were the visible terrors of the wrath of God, have been subdued to the service of man. Art and luxuries which could be possessed and enjoyed only by the rich and noble, the works of genius which were read and understood only by the learned few, domestic comforts and surroundings beyond the reach of lord or bishop, now adorn and illumine the homes of our citizens. Serfs are sovereigns and the people are kings. The trophies and splendors of their reign are commonwealths, rich in every attribute of great States, and united in a Republic whose power and prosperity and liberty and enlightenment are the wonder and admiration of the world.

All hail, Columbus, discoverer, dreamer, hero, and apostle! We here, of every race and country, recognize the horizon which bounded his vision and the infinite scope of his genius. The voice of gratitude and praise for all the blessings which have been showered upon mankind by his adventure is limited to no language, but is uttered in every tongue. Neither marble or brass can fitly form his statue. Continents are his monument, and unnumbered millions present and to come, who enjoy in their liberties and their happiness the fruits of his faith, will reverently guard and preserve, from century to century, his name and fame.—W. B. O.

SERMONS

CHRISTOPHER COLUMBUS: A MODERN ABRAHAM

By Rev. Robert S. McArthur, D.D.

And he went out not knowing whither he went.—Hebrews xi: 8

I need scarcely remind you that these words were originally spoken of Abraham, the father of the faithful. You know that he was ignorant of the country to which he was to be led. Doubtless he had some intimation of its nature, and also of the general direction in which it lay; but it must be remembered that his knowledge of geography was very imperfect, that the country, judged by the mode of travel of that day, was very distant, that it lay beyond a trackless desert, and that probably no traveler had ever made the journey and returned to report. Abraham's position, therefore, was trying in the extreme. Strong faith was needed on his part; strong faith was possessed by him, and a grand result in glory to God and in blessing to the race was secured as the result of that faith.

Had these words been written by the pen of inspiration of Columbus they could not more fittingly state the facts in his case. He, too, went out not knowing whither he went, and he never fully knew; he died under an utter misapprehension of the nature of the country he had visited and of the character of the discoveries he had made. He, too, realized the necessity of great faith, and of divine guidance. God went before Abraham, and before even Columbus, altho he was a very imperfect man, as truly as when by the pillar of cloud by day and the pillar of fire by night He went before the children of Israel on their weary march.

This journey on the part of Columbus was begun during a time of great interest in the history of Spain, and in the history of the world. It was the time of the revival of learning; the time of the birth of the great Protestant Reformation, and with it came a vast increase of intelligence. The days of monkish ignorance were happily passing away, and the dawn of light and liberty was at hand. About this time came the invention of the printing-press, and the discovery of the mariner's compass, and soon the discovery of America itself. Then came many navigators such as Vespucci, Cabot, Verrazani and others; and later those who laid the foundations of this republic, planting the seeds which have blossomed and bloomed into the flower and fruit of the liberty we enjoy today. It may be well, however, for us to glance for a moment or two at some of the previous voyages which we have reason to believe were made to our shores. Our esteemed friend, Mr. Frederick Saunders, the librarian of the Astor Library, in his recent book entitled THE STORY OF THE DISCOVERY OF THE NEW WORLD, reminds us that in the fifth century of our era the Chinese sent Hoei-Shin, a Buddhist monk, who, it is believed, reached this continent and visited what is now called Mexico. Then came the Northmen. They were the sea-rovers of the world; they were the terror of Europe from the North Sea to the Mediterranean Sea. In 860 of our era they discovered Iceland; having been driven by a fierce storm they landed upon what was to them an unknown shore, a shore, which became a permanent settlement of their countrymen. A similar accident drove them to the coasts of what is now Greenland. Two of their number, named Leif and Bjarni, voyaged along the coast and discovered what is now Newfoundland. A little later, pressing their way onward, they reached Nova Scotia, which they called Markland because they found it well wooded. After two days more of sailing they made land on the coast of New England, perhaps at Plymouth County, Massachusetts. There is evidence leading us to suppose that on the shores of the Charles River near Cambridge, there are traces of houses erected by these Northmen. The more this subject is investigated the more conclusive the evidence of this seems to be. It is stated that the first child born of European parents on this continent—the first certainly so far as known—was Snorri, son of Karlsfre, born in what was called Vineland—in the year 1007 of our era; and what is very interesting, it is affirmed—I think on reasonably solid grounds—that Thorwaldsen, the great Danish sculptor, was a descendant of this first child of European parents born on American soil. The manuscripts that are now preserved in the Royal Library of Copenhagen, manuscripts that were found in a monastery on the Island of Flato, on the west coast of Iceland, are authority for these statements. These manuscripts lay forgotten for centuries, but they have recently been discovered, and they confirm the opinion that many had vaguely cherished previous to their discovery.

There are stories also of a Welsh colony, stories which seem to have an historical basis. It is said that this colony with Prince Madoc in command reached this country in the year 1170. They made discoveries which are proving valuable in the development of American history. It is believed that some tribes of Indians as a result of this intermingling of races are partially of Welsh origin. Among these were the Mandans, whose color, whose hair ' and whose eyes were different from those of most Indian tribes. Their religious rites, their domestic habits, their mode of building their tents after the form of druidical abodes, such as we see in Great Britain, all point to an element of British life in this Indian race. I have been interested also in the discovery that the so-called Pawnee tribe are believed to have in them an intermingling of Welsh blood. The name of this tribe was originally spelled " Panis," but pronounced " Pawnee," and so we have come to have the spelling that is common in our own day.

It would be quite unfair in any historical summary to pass over the work done by Prince Henry of Portugal. He was one of the great navigators of the Portuguese race. He stimulated many travelers and made many interesting discoveries in the Mediterranean and in other seas. He gave up the pleasures of the court and lived on the promontory of Sagres, in which secluded and inhospitable place he devoted himself to the study of nautical science, building observatories, collecting charts, and with princely liberality securing the aid of the most skilled and the bravest navigators.

The times in which Columbus lived, and especially those which marked the beginning of his voyages, were times of profoundest interest to all students of history. The great wars in Spain, leading to the expulsion of the Moors, were still in progress during the earlier part of his residence in that country, but were nearing their completion. Isabella and Ferdinand were united in hand and heart under a patriotic and religious movement for the conquest of the Moors and for driving them from Spanish soil. It was a time of great excitement throughout the entire land of Spain. Columbus himself was present at the battle and conquest of Granada. When this last stronghold of the Moors was taken Isabella and Ferdinand entered into Granada in triumph, while 300,000 Moors marched out, bedewing the soil of their beloved city with their patriotic tears and with their heart's blood. Columbus was present. He, perhaps, saw Cardinal Mendoza ascend the Torre de la Vela and first raise the Christian flag, while he shouted, " Granada is taken! Granada is taken! " It was also the time of the Inquisition. This is a page of Spanish history which many eulogists of Spain and encomiasts of Columbus will not mention today. It is a page of history not very welcome to us, standing beneath this American

flag and standing upon this American soil; but he would be a faithless historian and an unjust narrator who should not make allusion to this vile blot on the history of Spain, on the name of Christianity and on the human race itself. Isabella never gave willingly her consent to the introduction of the Inquisition. It was, as Prescott has reminded us, wrung from her under the influence of her priestly confessors; and it was, as Prescott further says, the only stain in the pure white marble of Isabella's life. But it should be borne in mind that Prescott is unduly eulogistic of this Queen; more candid writers are now showing her in her true character as a woman of at least the average cruelty of her time and Church. She was induced to give her consent to the Inquisition because of the greater glory which she was led to believe it would bring to the Roman Church; but Ferdinand endorsed it because of the gold it would bring into the Spanish coffers. Wherever there was a rich Jew he became the subject of the Inquisition; wherever there was a Protestant, rich or poor, he must be tortured by the Inquisition. God had a great purpose in the discovery of America just at that hour. Europe was overcrowded; liberty was strangled; hope was dying. The Jews were driven from Spain, the Moors soon crossed the strait to their native soil, and God flung wide open the doors of this New World that there might be a place where Liberty could breathe, and where a republic could be born.

Time permits me only to touch the history of Columbus very briefly, and I do not regard it as very necessary that I should dwell in detail upon the hsitory. His name is itself interesting. Columbus is its Latin form, Colombo the Italian form, and Colon is its Spanish form. Christoval Colon is his Spanish name. The feminine form of Columbus means a dove, and Christopher means "Christbearer." He was born in Genoa, probably in the year 1436, tho some say 1446. His origin was very obscure; and the details of his life are extremely meager. His father was Dominico Colombo, and was a woolcarder or comber by trade. In a will dated 1494 he speaks of himself as " formerly a weaver." Some suppose that Columbus was of illustrious descent; but his son Fernando, the son of the Cordovan woman, but not the Cordovan wife, used wise words when he said, " I am of the opinion that I should derive less dignity from any nobility of ancestry than from being the son of such a father." The mother of Columbus was named Susanna Fontanrossa, and there were in the family three sons and one daughter. The brothers were named Bartholomew, Giacomo, and Diego. Bartholomew was sent to England to interview Henry VII.; the King gave him encouragement, and but for the action of Isabella, England would have had the glory of the great discovery. The sister married a man in very humble life, a man whose name was Giacomo Baravello, but a man of no importance. In his boyhood Columbus was sent to the University of Pavia, where his studies were history, cosmography, philosophy and other sciences, and especially drawing.

But at the age of fifteen he became a sailor, a fact which contributed much to his later taste for navigation. A relative of Columbus, who was named Columbus also, was commander of a cruiser in the service of René, Count of Provence, and Columbus made journeys with him to the Isle of Thule, now supposed to be Iceland. Doubtless many of these excursions were piratical, and he doubtless was a youthful pirate; but that was in an age when piracy was considered legitimate activity for the brave and dashing spirits of the youthful Genoese. During a sea-fight, when the opposing vessels were chained together, a fire broke out that was likely to destroy both vessels, and Columbus, it is said, leaped into the sea with an oar in his hand and swam six miles, reaching the coast of Portugal, and then walked to Lisbon, which was at that time the headquarters of a number of navigators. This was probably about the year 1470, altho all these dates are doubtful. His son Ferdinand, of whom I have spoken, has written an account of his father's personal appearance at this time. Altho young, the son tells us that his hair was perfectly white, that he was tall and was commanding in appearance and in manner. He was married to Felipa Monis de Palestrello, daughter of an Italian cavalier, who was an able navigator, and had been governor of Porto Santo, but who became poor and died leaving little except charts and instruments. Columbus helped in the support of his father's family and also his wife's by making maps and charts. At this time fables of unknown lands were constantly repeated—fables of the Island of the Seven Cities and of the Island of St. Brandan, on which the Scottish priest landed in the sixth century. There came from Greece the story of Atlantis, which Plato was said to have learned from the Egyptians. The idea of a western nation was conceived when there came floating pieces of wood, strangely carved, great reeds, and especially when the discovery was made of two bodies of a race widely different from the European. The idea of a western ocean-way to India filled the mind of Columbus, and soon he entered into correspondence with Toscanelli, who greatly strengthened his theories.

With this conviction Columbus applied to Genoa, but Genoa refused the application; then to Venice, but Venice refused. Then to John II. of Portugal, who long kept him waiting with half promises, finally dismissed him, and then sent out an expedition of his own, trying to secure the honor of discovery and to rob Columbus of his due. His wife died about this time, and he left Portugal in disgust at the treatment of the court and in deep domestic grief, and went first to Spain in 1484. He proposed to the Duke of Medina Sidonia and afterward to the Duke of Medina Celi that they organize an excursion for discovery, but they declined. We find him next at Cordova, where the court was held for a time, and where preparations were making for the final onset which resulted in the fall of Granada and the expulsion of the Moors. A few weeks ago I went one Thursday morning through the streets of Cordova. Cordova is to-day only an echo, only a ghost of what it was then. It is now a decaying city; but the tramp of horsemen and splendor of the chivalry of the days of Ferdinand and Isabella were recalled to my mind. I sat for an hour and a half in the Grove of Oranges waiting for my train to arrive, and I could picture the silent streets with the flower and chivalry of Spain marching under the banner of Castile and Leon, and I could picture Columbus following the court to Cordova to press his suit. From Cordova he went to Salamanca, where he pleaded his cause before the learned professors and philosophers, who laughed him to scorn. The mariner stood alone before that brilliant company of officials, civil and ecclesiastic, and heard them sneer at his proposals, and was himself almost overwhelmed by their opposition.

We follow him as he turned his steps toward the Convent La Rabida, with his little boy, Diego, the son born at Porto Santo, the son of his dead wife, asking for bread and water, father and boy hungry, thirsty, friendless, and unknown. But in his soul great thoughts were burning; while every ear was deaf and every heart was cold, his ear was open to the divine voice, which he was constantly hearing, and his heart was aglow with great plans. The prior became deeply interested, and gave him letters to Fernando de Talevera, confessor to Isabella. With these letters he hastened once more to the court; but the exchequer is empty and he leaves with little hope. I follow him for a moment as he comes down past Santa Fé and reaches the Bridge of Pines on his way to France. He turns his back on Spain; he is going to France, and France or England shall have the glory of the discovery. Bartholomew, his brother, has gone to England. Will these countries help? It is a critical moment; imperishable history is now making. There comes to Isabella a message from Luis de Santangel, begging her to listen to Columbus. He secures her consent, a messenger is despatched and reaches Columbus at the Bridge of Pines, and he turns and comes back into the presence of the Queen. This was a turning-point in the history of Columbus—in the history of Spain. Isabella consented to an expedition, but Ferdinand complained that the war with the Moors had exhausted his exchequer. But she declared that she would undertake it for her own crown of Castile, and that she would sell her jewels for the money if necessary. All honor to Isabella! All honor to woman! Woman made the discovery of Columbus possible, and on her head to-day I put the crown of glory. Ferdinand finally acquiesced and the contract was signed by the sovereigns at Santa Fé, April 17, 1492.

August the 3d, 1492, before daylight Columbus is watching the direction of the winds from the little monastery of La Rabida. The voice of prayer is in his ear. It is eight o'clock. The winds fill the sails, and from Palos, with one hundred and twenty men on the *Nina,* the *Pinta,* and the *Santa Maria,* he starts upon his immortal journey.

It is not necessary, as my aim is not to give what can readily be found in books of reference, that I trace this journey or his subsequent discoveries; neither is it necessary that I should call your attention to the fact that through the influence of Bobadilla he was finally sent back in chains to Spain; nor that I should remind you that on May 20, 1506, alone and friendless, moneyless and helpless, he died at Valladolid. Isabella was dead. Ferdinand was ungrateful; he never had the heart of a man. He finally gave Columbus a pompous funeral and a magnificent monument. It would have been better if he had given him bread when he was starving and friendship when he was friendless!

Will you allow me now in the few further minutes that I may claim to sum up the characteristics of this great man?

Columbus was very far from being a perfect man; he does not even come up to the best ideas of his own age and religion. More than that, perhaps, we ought not to expect; less than that we cannot permit without reasonable criticism. Attention has been called to the fact that during all these Columbian festivities (1892) not one descendant of the race discovered by Columbus will be present. The Carib race was utterly destroyed in a few years. All writers agree that the " Indians," so-called by Columbus, were healthy and robust. It is also certain from many allusions that their numbers were great; but during the last twenty years the most careful research reveals no trace of the race. There is nothing more certain than that these early discoverers were thirsty for blood and greedy for gold. They enslaved these kind-hearted people, and drove them from the face of the earth. Las Casas tells us that 40,000 perished on one group of islands " in a short time by the sword of the soldier and the lash of the driver." The name of Columbus, it must be admitted, is stained by the blood of these innocent thousands, whose hospitality he readily received and whom he wickedly destroyed. In a large measure, his glory is purely imaginary. He has had the credit of discovering America, and now America is discovering him. He died without any accurate knowledge of the country which he had discovered, and we have lived until lately without any accurate knowledge of him. We have idealized and so idolized him too long. School books have utterly misled the youth of our land. But the critical historic method of recent days shows Columbus in his true character.

It shows us that he was a consummate deceiver; that he made deception a fine art; and that he cannot be called a chivalrous knight until theft, murder, and slave-making are chivalrous acts. All who had dealings with him, from the sovereign to the sailor, as Dunlop has shown, treated him with distrust and aversion. In early life his voyage from the kingdom of Naples was marked by deception, and he dwells upon his crimes with special pride. Deception characterized his entries on the log-book of his western journey. It is very doubtful if he saw the light which he claims to have seen on the night of Oct. 11th, but it is quite certain that he made a claim for the thirty crowns a year which " their highnesses " promised to him who should first see land, and that he cheated Benejo, the sailor to whom the honor and money belonged. His selfishness and arrogance are shown in his demands for liberal terms before he would enter upon his voyage of discovery, and yet he and those who would canonize him call this greedy, deceptive, and cruel man the " Christ-bearer."

He was as perfidious as he was pious, and it is not at all improbable that from Alonzo Sanchez, who died in his house, leaving charts and maps, he derived the knowledge which made his discoveries possible. It is well known that the Arabs enlightened Spain and all the world for centuries on all cosmographical questions. Bishop Boyle, who was appointed by the Pope as apostolic vicar in these western lands, was so disgusted with the avarice, licentiousness, and brutality of those under Columbus that he desired to return to Spain. Finally, acting with the authority of his position, he excommunicated Columbus. Columbus took revenge by refusing to furnish the Pope's vicar with necessary provisions, and as a result he was obliged to leave the New World. After Columbus had sent 500 Indians to Spain as slaves he attacked these innocent savages in the New World, who had so confidently welcomed him as their guest, with twenty bloodhounds, and with horsemen more savage than the dogs, he butchered them with spear and lance, and the bloodhounds tore them in a manner too horrible to describe. Even Washington Irving has to admit the throwing of Moxica from the walls of the fortress into the fosse below, tho this biographer softens the act by euphemistic phrase. He affirmed that gold was the greatest of blessings, as it not only secures happiness here, but he declared in so many words that it procured eternal salvation hereafter. Some of the innocent " heathen," seeing his love for gold, would hold a bit of it up and say, " Behold the Christian's god! " If his besetting sin was not impurity it was cupidity. As the originator of American slavery he never can receive the unqualified praise of those who, by blood and treasure destroyed American slavery.

Isabella, who has been altogether overpraised by Prescott and others, pretended to be much shocked at the slavery which he introduced, but in 1503 she signed an order obliging these innocent Americans to toil as slaves. Against them it is likely that the charge of cannibalism made by Columbus was false, and was made to justify his cruelty toward them. It is almost certain that he wilfully misrepresented the facts concerning his discoveries in such matters as finding a race of men with tails, and equally foolish statements. He constantly contradicts himself concerning the events of his own life. His son Fernando affirms that his father knew better than to suppose that he was on the border of Cathay, and states that he gave out this impression, and named the people Indians, because all Europeans knew the immense wealth of the Indies. Koselly de Lorgues and other would-be canonizers claim for Columbus all the virtues of a saint. Bancroft only incidentally mentions him, but correctly sets forth his many infirmities. Prescott, as is well known, tends constantly to adulation; but even he, when discussing the vagaries of Columbus, suspects "a temporary alienation of mind." Aaron Goodrich shows a constant tendency to depreciation and even to denunciation. Dr. Shea, the Romanist, recognizes the fact that Columbus could never attach to himself either those above or below him so that there were but few "who adhered loyally to his cause." Washington Irving has written of Columbus as if he had accepted a retainer to magnify all his merits and to deny, or at least minimize, all his demerits. His statements must often be taken with many grains of salt. Justin Winsor has written with equal intelligence and fairness. He has presented what seems to be the true picture of Columbus; this volume will be the standard for years to come. He has given both praise and blame, and sums up his character with historical accuracy and judicial candor. The volume by Mr. Frederick Saunders, of the Astor Library, will serve an admirable purpose as a popular presentation of the man and his times.

We shall all give him praise for his great perseverance. He overcame almost all the disadvantages of his youth; he overcame disappointments which might have dampened the ardor of almost any discoverer or inventor. Amerigo Vespucci received the honor of giving his name to the New World, but I ought to say that Vespucci was not responsible for this honor. We are indebted for the name of America to a German professor. Part of the writings of Vespucci were published in German, and this German professor gave to the new country the name of America. Humboldt, I think, has shown very clearly that Vespucci was not at all to blame, that he had no idea of robbing Columbus of honor; indeed, Columbus has had too much honor in connection with the discovery of this Western continent. Humiliating, indeed, it was to Columbus that he should have been sent back to Spain in irons, but he never lost hope. never lost courage; he preserved those irons to the very last; he had them hung up where his friends could see them, and he regarded them as a mark of honor. His perseverance never failed; when rejected at Genoa, rejected at Venice, rejected in Portugal, delayed in England and delayed in Spain, he still persevered, amid all the trials of his immortal voyage until on the morning of the 12th of October, 1492, he saw the sand glistening on the shores of the New World, and in a little while heard one of the men on the *Pinta* call out, "Land! land!" and a new world was discovered.

But most of all we emphasize the piety of Columbus, altho it was often of a very questionable kind. The success of his enterprise was due to two errors—the supposed extent of Asia to the east, and the supposed smallness of the earth. Columbus never knew the land he discovered; he thought all the while he was going to 'India, and he stumbled on America. That is why he called the islands " West Indies," and why the inhabitants were called " Indians." He thought he was going to Asia; he thought Cuba was Japan. He was under the influence of Marco Polo, and constantly interpreted all he saw by the prejudices existing already in his mind, and he died without knowing the lands he had discovered, unless we can adopt the explanation which his son has given. He died utterly in error as to their nature or as to the continent itself. God overruled these errors. Columbus was wrong in the main question, and his opponents at Salamanca were right when they affirmed that he could not find Asia by going in that direction, but he clung to his purpose. He heard voices in dreams; he believed that he was prophesied of in many parts of the Word of God; that he was the subject of the prophecy in the nineteenth Psalm and the fourth verse, and the thought gave him hope and cheer: " Their line is gone out through all the earth and their words to the end of the world." That was his thought. He wrote the sacred name of Christ on his banner and gave Him all honor. He landed on the shores of this New World dressed in the resplendent robes of an admiral, with a sword in one hand and the banner of Christ in the other. The company fell upon their knees and praised God for His wonderful goodness. This New World was consecrated to God from the very moment of its first discovery. This country is a Christian land; the highest authority has recently pronounced it to be a Christian land, and it ought to be recognized as a Christian land, and the holy Sabbath be observed when the great Columbian Exposition shall be held. Wo to us as a people if we lower our flag, if we dishonor our history, if we forsake our God!

When he had returned to Barcelona and had told his story before the King and Queen, all fell upon their knees and joined in singing the *Te Deum*. Columbus was not a great man; in many important respects he was weak and wicked. But he was great in his perseverance; he was great in a certain conception which he had of religious truth; but he blundered constantly. He was in utter error as to the course he pursued and the countries he discovered. He was an utter failure as a planter of colonies and a ruler of men. No greater failure in the effort to plant colonies in any land can be discovered than the failure of Columbus in that regard. I want to hold the balances justly. I want to give praise where praise is due, and I want to withhold it from him where praise is not due. No sooner had he left the colonists than everything went to destruction. I have emphasized his failures and rightly, and I have striven to give him the due meed of praise; but there are chapters in the life of Columbus which are a reproach to a noble manhood, which are opposed to the laws of man and which are rebuked by the laws of God. Historians have immortalized him, poets have idealized him, and priests now would canonize him, altho once some of them were ready to cannonade him. In the Biblioteca Colombina is his tract, placed there by his son Fernando, written when he was afraid of the tortures of the Inquisition, because the priests believed that his discovery was against the Church and against their traditional interpretations of the Bible.

He was buried at Valladolid, where he died; but soon his remains were taken to the Carthusian monastery of Las Cuevas, in Seville; the remains of Diego, the second admiral, were also buried there. But in 1536 the bodies of father and son were taken over the sea to Hispaniola, or San Domingo, and interred in the cathedral. In 1795 or 1796, on the occasion of the cession of that island to the French, the relics were transferred to the cathedral of Havana, where they now repose; if, indeed, the remains re-exhumed and reburied were those of Columbus, a matter which must remain doubtful.*

My beloved friends, life is a strange voyage. Beyond it is an unknown country. You and I are voyagers. There is only one bark in which we can safely sail—the bark of faith. There is only one banner under which we may make the journey—the banner of Christ. Columbus was an Abraham, for he went out not knowing whither he went. Columbus was a Moses, for he endured as seeing Him who is invisible. Only the man of faith is the man of power. Only he who can see the invisible can do the impossible. God grant that to-day in that bark we may be wafted by God's blessing, and may land at last on the shores of Heaven, where we shall sing a sweeter *Te Deum* than that which awoke the echoes on the soil of virgin America, or those amid the splendors of the court at Barcelona.—P. T.

SUGGESTIVE THOUGHTS

AMERICA, Discovering.—The statement is sometimes made that Queen Isabella of Spain pawned her jewels in order to provide funds for fitting out the expedition for the discovery of America. This is a very old story, first told not long after the death of Columbus, and, tho it is not true, its origin is not difficult to discover. As every fact about the great voyage is of interest to Americans, we will briefly give the facts about the raising of the money.

Columbus went to the Spanish court to lay his ambitious project before the King and Queen just as the last great stronghold of the Moors, Granada, had surrendered to the forces of Ferdinand and Isabella.

In some respects it was an inopportune time. The country was exhausted by the war which had just closed with this splendid success, and the joint monarchs were not inclined to embark upon any new and uncertain adventure; and what was more important, the treasuries of both Aragon and Castile were nearly empty. Queen Isabella, in fact, had been obliged to pledge her jewels to get money for the prosecution of the war against the Moors.

The Genoese navigator pleaded his cause in vain. Both King and Queen listened coldly to his enthusiastic plans, in which the recovery of the Holy Sepulcher from the Turks was strangely mingled. They refused to assist his enterprise, and Columbus in despair left Granada, intending to make a final effort for assistance at the French court.

At his audience with the Spanish monarchs, however, there were two persons who were convinced of the truth of his daring theories, or at least of the wisdom of attempting to prove them to be true. They were, singularly, the finance ministers of the two crowns, St. Angel for Aragon and Quintanilla for Castile.

St. Angel obtained an audience as soon as possible with the Queen, and so warm was his advocacy of the theories of the Genoese stranger, so convincing his arguments for assisting him, that Isabella, fired by his enthusiasm, exclaimed, " I undertake the enterprise for my own crown of Castile, and will pledge my private jewels to raise the necessary funds."

The minister assured her that this generous measure would be unnecessary, and hastened from the royal presence to send a messenger after Columbus, who speedily returned to Granada. The arrangements for the expedition were speedily made. St. Angel supplied about seventeen thousand florins from the treasury of Aragon.

The three Pinzon brothers, ship-builders at Palos de Moguer, loaned Columbus one-eighth of the necessary money, he having assumed this share of the expense in consideration of his receiving one-eighth of the profits. They also furnished additional money and two of the vessels, and all three of the brothers went on the expedition, two as captains of the caravels *La Niña* and *La Pinta*, the other as a pilot. The third vessel, *Santa Maria* was impressed, to the great terror of the owner and the crew.

It may be well to add that Columbus repaid the loan made by St. Angel with the

---

* The remains of Columbus were transferred on December 12, 1898, from the Cathedral in Havana to the gunboat *Conde de Venadigo* which, escorted by the *Alfonso XII*. and the *Infanta Isabel*, were sent to take the ashes of the discoverer to Spain.—Col. An.

gold which he brought back from the New World on his first voyage. A portion of this gold was employed in gilding the vaults and ceilings of the royal saloon of King Ferdinand's grand palace at Zaragoza, or Saragossa, the Aljaferia, where possibly it may still be visible to the American pilgrim.—Y. C.

AMERICA, Future of.—Agassiz says the American continent was the first created; it will be the last in the fulfilment of the designs of the Creator. A cosmopolitan land—cosmopolitan in the intentions of its founders, in the bloody struggle of its defenders—God has in store for you who people it the accomplishment of admirable results. Northward are the Esquimaux; southward is Africa. You summon from walled China the unmoving people to dwell amid the moving Nation, the stationary to mingle with the progressive; all impelled by the breath of you, the great humanitarian people. The foundation of your people is the Bible, the book that speaks of God, the living word of Jesus Christ. In an admirable manifesto from your President there shines through his words the Christian faith. A belief in Jesus is at the root of this Nation; and when I return I shall tell Europe that I have found here liberty associated with Christianity, and have been among a people who do not think that to be free they must be parted from God.—HYACINTHE.

AMERICA, Imperial.—There is danger in the current shouting for "Imperial America," if it be for the glory of the American people rather than for the glory of God. Lust for territory, eagerness for the expansion of the national limits, may be the outcome of mere pride and vainglory, and may easily result in dangerous or even disastrous complications. There is all the greater necessity, therefore, that the man in the pulpit—who can so greatly help to mold and direct public opinion—should keep his head level and his heart right with God. He should remember that at the outset it was settled once for all that the war with Spain was not entered upon for conquest and imperial expansion, but in the interest of freedom and humanity. The course of preacher and Nation alike should be decided in full recognition of that fact. Nevertheless the war bids fair to change not only the map, but also the history, of the world, and the new and altogether unlooked for conditions must be recognized and reckoned with.

The advent of the United States as a Sixth Power in the world has made obsolete all the traditions and diplomacy that have known only the Five Great Powers of Europe. Six months have made the United States one of the greatest factors in the history of the future by making this Nation the disinterested champion of freedom in the world. The die is cast. There can be no retreat, no drawing back. It is demanded of our Government and people, that they shall take their place in the councils of the nations, and inaugurate and carry out, in the spirit of disinterestedness, a Christian policy and diplomacy, in accomplishing the extraordinary task providentially assigned to them.

In taking its new and larger place, this Nation, if it remembers its solemn promises to God and man, will see to it that no foot of land over which its flag has been raised—from Porto Rico to the farthest of the Philippines—shall be remanded again to Spanish oppression and butchery or to monkish tyranny and robbery. The duty of assuring freedom and good government—self-government, if possible, which is the nearest to that, next in order—rests upon the Nation and cannot safely be shirked. The unexpected commercial and political development doubtless demands the stations requisite for our new lines of intercourse and commerce, but that may be reconciled with our promises and duty to the races involved and interested. The task may be great, but it is a God-appointed one, and so carries with it, if the Nation honestly essays it, the promise of Divine help and assured success in the interests of the Kingdom of God.—GREGORY. (H. R.)

AMERICA, Land of.—Before Columbus and the one hundred and twenty men embarked on board the *Santa Maria*, the *Pinta*, and the *Nina*, on their eventful voyage, what did they do? Took the Sacrament of our Lord Jesus Christ. Coming in sight of land, what song goes up from all three decks? "*Gloria in Excelsis.*" What did they first do stepping from shipboard to solid ground? All knelt in prayer, consecrating the New World to God. What did the Huguenots do, landing in the Carolinas; and the Hollanders, landing in New York; and the Puritans, landing in New England? With bent knees, uplifted faces and heaven-beseeching prayer, they took possession of this Continent for God. How did they open the first American Congress? With prayer in the name of Christ. Beside that, see what God has done for us. Open the map of our North American Continent, and see how the land was shaped for immeasurable prosperities. Behold the navigable rivers, greater and more numerous than those of any other land, running down to the sea in all directions—prophecy of large manufactures and easy commerce. Look at the great ranges of mountains, timbered with wealth on the tops and sides, and metaled with wealth underneath; 180,000 square miles of coal; 180,000 square miles of iron. The land so contoured that extreme weather seldom lasts more than three days. For the most of the year the climate is bracing, and favorable for brawn and brain. All fruits, all minerals, all harvests. Scenery which displays an autumnal pageantry which no other land pretends to rival. No South American earthquakes. No Scotch mists. No English fogs. No Egyptian plagues. No Germanic divisions. The happiest people on the earth are the people of the United States. The poor man has more chance, the industrious man more opportunity. How good God was to our fathers! How good God is to us and our children! To Him, blessed be His mighty name, to Him of the Cross and the triumph, to Him who still remembers the prayers of the Pilgrim Fathers and Huguenots and Holland refugees, to Him this land shall be consecrated.—TALMAGE.

"AMERICA," Why?—How did it happen that the Continent discovered by Christopher Columbus received its name from Americus Vespucius? Thanks to the zeal with which investigation has been recently pushed into all these matters, this most natural query can be answered now much more intelligently than it could a few years ago. The first printed map on which the name America appears was published at Lyons in 1516, ten years after the death of Columbus. But it was in 1507 that there issued from the obscure college press of the town of St. Dié in Lorraine a little book or pamphlet, called COSMOGRAPHIÆ INTRODUCTIO, by Martin Waldseemüller, in which such use of the name was first proposed. It came about in this way:

Vespucius, a Florentine of high repute as a navigator, a friend of Columbus, stirred by his discoveries, went with Ojeda in 1499 to explore the northern coast of South America, and again in 1501-1503 he made voyages which opened up to knowledge the coast of Brazil.

He wrote, soon after, an account of his travels so racy and graphic that it instantly became popular and passed through many editions in the various tongues of Europe. One of these booklets fell into the hands of the little band of scholars at St. Dié, and gave rise to their suggestion that a good name for the New World which Vespucius had done so much to bring to the notice of the Old World, and which lay directly over against *Africa*, would be *America*.

There was no thought whatever at this time of appending the name to anything but the continental mass, of unknown shape and size, which lay behind the Brazilian shore, and which was looked upon as a totally distinct region from the islands which had been discovered by Columbus, while as to any continent north of the islands there was as yet very little knowledge.

With this Brazilian land, first seen through an accident by Cabral in 1500, no other name was now so prominently and legitimately connected as that of Americus Vespucius.

No protest was raised against the proposed name by the heirs or friends of Columbus. It was not regarded as in any way invading or invalidating the claims and rights of the discoverer of the regions farther north. The name, therefore, as applied to the southern continent easily came into general acceptance. It soon became widely adopted, especially in the German and French maps and globes, and in fact throughout central and northern Europe.

Vespucius died in 1512. There is no evidence connecting him with the naming, or with any false pretension in regard to the discovery.

Not till 1541, by which time it began to be certain that the northern lands were not, as had been previously supposed, a part of Asia, did any map appear giving the name America to the whole of the Western Continent, and not till a few years previons to this did it seem to occur to any that injustice was being done, or might be done, by this name, to the superior claims of Columbus.

Las Casas and other friends spoke up now for "Columba;" but it was too late—the mischief had been wrought. And all had been done, as is quite evident, with entire innocence and naturalness.

Had the prominent thing in connection with Columbus' discoveries been the Continent instead of the islands, and had not his fame been under so great an eclipse at the time of his death and for quite a period afterward, and had Spain pursued a less selfish, exclusive, secretive policy in regard to all its information about the New World, it would not have been left to other lands to name this Continent and to take from Spain's great admiral this deserved recognition.—Y. C.

COLUMBUS BOOK OF PRIVILEGES,* The.—The origin of this remarkable volume is explained by Mr. Harrisse in the Introduction which he, better than any other man, was qualified to write for it.

When Columbus was on the eve of his last voyage in 1502 he was full of misgivings lest his rights should not descend to his son Diego. The Crown lawyers advised that the capitulations embodying his rights were void; and with the view of placing the proof of his rights beyond the reach of his enemies, Columbus, before he sailed, had four copies made and lodged in safe places. Two were to be sent to Genoa, one to the monastery of Las Cuevas, where his body reposed for a time previous to its transmission to San Domingo. These three were made with extreme care on parchment. A fourth copy, made on paper, was sent to this country, and lost, being probably consumed by worms and ants in San Domingo. There is some reason to believe that the copy sent to Las Cuevas came into the possession of Edward Everett and, tho now lost, may be recovered.

The other two copies were carried to Genoa by Nicolo Oderigo, special envoy of the Republic, to Ferdinand and Isabella, and apparently a friend of the admiral. One of these copies was sent inclosed in a bag of Cordovan leather with a silver clasp, which is now shown at Genoa and is reproduced in the volume we are considering. The other was among the plunder carried off by Napoleon to Paris and not included in the general return made after the Restoration by the allies.

* CHRISTOPHER COLUMBUS. HIS OWN BOOK OF PRIVILEGES, 1502. Photographic Facsimile of the Manuscript in the Archives of the Foreign Office in Paris, for the First Time Published, with Expanded Text Translation into English, and an Historical Introduction. The Translation and Transliteration by George F. Barwick, of the British Museum; the Introduction by Henry Harrisse; the Whole Compiled and Edited, with Preface, by Benjamin Franklin Stevens. London: 4 Trafalgar Square, Charing Cross: B. F Stevens. Limited Edition. Foolscap folio, thick, handmade paper, half pigskin, with plankwood sides and clasps, pp. lxv, 284. $30.00.

It was supposed to be lost until, in 1880, when M. de Freycinet became Minister of Foreign Affairs, the archives of the department were thrown open to the public, and here in the collection in the Palace of the Quai d'Orsay, May 31, 1880, Mr. Harrisse, to his surprise and delight, laid his hand upon a volume bound in green morocco and stamped with the initials of the French Republic, which proved to be the lost copy of the privileges, patents and concessions granted to Columbus, and originally taken by Oderigo to Genoa.

These are the documents which are reproduced in the COLUMBUS BOOK OF PRIVILEGES. Apart from the history which is full, clear and sufficient on all points, the documents are attested by comparison with the original series owned by the present Duke of Veragua.

These documents, forty-four in number and bound under the general title, CODEX DIPLOMATICUS OF CHRISTOPHER COLUMBUS, are reproduced by Mr. Stevens in the BOOK OF PRIVILEGES (1502) with unsurpassed fidelity and intelligence. First we have in his own Preface a full account of his general method of reproduction and of the plan on which the work was to be done. The volume itself matches in size and style the others in the series of elegant and useful Stevens' FACSIMILES OF MANUSCRIPTS IN EUROPEAN ARCHIVES relating to America. Every manuscript page is reproduced in facsimile, and inset in the volume so as to have on the pages opposite an exact transliteration of the Spanish text and a correct translation into English.

The substantial facts of his discovery were made known by Mr. Harrisse in 1884, in his LIFE OF COLUMBUS, published that year. They are presented again with careful elaboration in the Introduction to this volume. The case as to the lost manuscript of Las Cuevas does not seem to be quite so hopeless as Mr. Harrisse appears to think. Tho it has disappeared it is not impossible that it may be found, and meantime we know rather more about it than Mr. Harrisse supposed through a brief description in the *North American Review* (October, 1825) by Caleb Cushing.

The editor has added at the end reproductions and illustrations, in the same style, of three Columbus letters, introduced into the collection, we suppose, for their allusions, to the Admiral's interest in the evidence he was collecting in this way to substantiate his rights.

The volume has a novel and extremely appropriate binding in pigskin back, with beechwood boards oddly clasped to complete the covers. The paper is heavy linen-laid parchment with uncut edges in foolscap folio size. —I.

COLUMBUS, The Wife of.—The traditional high standing of Christopher Columbus seems likely to suffer not a little at the hands and by the standards of our modern historians. Says *The Voice*: He has been presented to us during the generations past as a man of heroic mold, of stern morality, deep piety, and of such unyielding confidence in his own conclusions, that the opposition of the whole world and the lapse of many years could not daunt him. And now comes a historian from Boston (Justin Winsor), in a work highly commended for accuracy, and gives us this picture of Columbus:

"Hardly a name in profane history is more august than his. Hardly another character in the world's record has made so little of its opportunities. His discovery was a blunder; his blunder was a new world, the new world is his monument! Its discoverer might have been its father; he proved to be its despoiler. He might have given its young days such a benignity as the world likes to associate with a maker; he left it a legacy of devastation and crime. He might have been an unselfish promoter of geographical science; he proved a rabid seeker for gold and a viceroyalty. He might have won converts to the fold of Christ by the kindness of his spirit; he gained the execrations of the good angels. He might, like Las Casas, have rebuked the fiendishness of perverted belief. The triumph of Barcelona led down to the ignominy of Valladolid, with every step in the degradation palpable and resultant."

This is relentless. So is the same writer's characterization of Queen Isabella as "an unlovely woman at the best, and an obstructor of Christian charity." For one, we will not accept the portraits as true ones, until they are endorsed by a reasonably unanimous vote of the historians. But what a wrecking of the honored reputations of heroes of the past this generation has had to submit to! One is almost tempted to protest that even the demands of historical truth should leave sacred the memories the world has learned to revere. But John Locke's words come to mind on second thought: "To love truth for truth's sake is the principal part of human perfection in this world, and the seed-plot of all other virtues."

It may be that the halo which has crowned the head of the husband hitherto, is now to circle about Mrs. Columbus. It is suggested that to the wife of Columbus is due a large portion of the credit for his discoveries, and the meager record of her life goes far to substantiate this idea. It is known that her father was himself a navigator of considerable distinction; that his daughter frequently accompanied him on his geographical investigations and entered with enthusiasm into all his projects. To Columbus she brought not only the invaluable charts and records which her father had compiled during his lifetime, but better than all. she brought her own ripe experience and mature judgment. Altho history is silent on this point, it is very probable that to his ambition for exploration more than to his skill as a suitor, Columbus owed the fact that he won this woman for his wife. Neither is it unlikely that to her encouragement more than to the jewels of Queen Isabella the world owes the result of his life work.—E.

COUNTRY, Some Facts About Our.—It is the largest political subdivision in the

Western Hemisphere, having a total land and water area of 3,594,880 square miles.

Its largest state, Texas, has an area of 265,780 square miles; its smallest, Rhode Island, 1,085 square miles.

Its largest territory is Alaska, with an area of 570 000 square miles, whose principal river, the Yukon, is now claimed to be larger than the Mississippi.

Its most populous states are: New York, Pennsylvania, Illinois, and Ohio. The two former have more than 5,000,000, and the two latter more than 3,000,000 inhabitants respectively.

It contains three of the eleven cities in the world numbering respectively more than 1,000,000 population. London, Paris, Tokio, Berlin, Vienna, St. Petersburg, Canton and Peking are the other cities that enjoy this distinction.

"Union" is the word most used in naming the various localities, there being 356 bearing this appellation. "Liberty" is also a a favorite name. Next in order come the names of presidents and other prominent public men, that of the "Father of His Country" leading with more than 300 places named in his honor.
—W. Hinton. (Y. C.)

POETRY

America

(The Morning of the Discovery, October 21, 1492.)

By Hezekiah Butterworth

Immortal morn, all hail,
That saw Columbus sail
　　By Faith alone.
The skies before him bowed,
Back rolled the ocean proud,
And every lifting cloud
　　With glory shone.

Fair Science then was born
On that celestial morn,
　　Faith dared the sea;
Triumphant o'er her foes,
Then Truth immortal rose,
New heavens to disclose
　　And earth to free.

Strong Freedom then came forth
To liberate the earth
　　And crown the right:
So walked the pilot bold
Upon the sea of gold,
And darkness backward rolled
　　And there was light.

Sweep, sweep across the seas,
Ye rolling jubilees,
　　Grand chorals raise;
The world adoring stands,
And with uplifted hands
Offers from all the lands,
　　To God its praise.

Ye hosts of Faith, sing on;
The victories ye have won
　　Shall time increase,
And, like the choral strain
That fell on Bethlehem's plain,
Inspire the perfect reign
　　Of Love and Peace.
　　　　　　　　　Col. S.

An Ode to America

The great exhibition in Paris was naturally marked by an interchange of courtesies among the representatives of all the nations. There were speeches of friendship at dozens of ceremonies. These addresses, however, were in prose, with but one exception. On the occasion of the inauguration of the American pavilion M. Edouard Lance read at the American Club an original composition in verse. Of this "Ode à l'Amérique" a copy has reached us, and we transcribe it, in appreciative mood, as follows:

À L'AMÉRIQUE

Avec les souvenirs de leurs gloires passées,
L'Amérique et la France, en ce jour enlacées,
　　Ne forment qu'une nation.
Le Commerce et les Arts scellent leur alliance,
Et leurs brillants travaux célèbrent la puissance
　　De la civilisation.

De même qu'autrefois ce siècle à son aurore
A vu flotter les plis du drapeau tricolore,
　　Au tien uni dans le devoir,
Il voit, à son déclin, claquer les bandes franches
Où rouge et blanc et bleu, semés d'étoiles blanches,
　　Font un firmament plein d'espoir!

Que n'êtes-vous vivants, Rochambeau, Lafayette,
Vous qui vintes, après la sublime conquête,
　　Faire entendre vos mâles voix,
Afin de contempler votre œuvre, si féconde:
La Liberté, de loin éclairant le vieux Monde,
　　Et frappant de stupeur les rois!

Car elle a triomphé, superbe, épanouie,
Couronnant les efforts de la lutte inouïe
　　Des Franklins et des Washingtons.
Et vous, Américains, fils de sa chère fille
Gardez comme un trésor la clef de la Bastille,
　　Fétiche pour vos rejetons.

Sous le fier bouclier de chaque République,
Unissons les drapeaux de France et d'Amérique,
　　Marchons en nous serrant les mains.
Liberté! Liberté! Bientôt la Providence
Nous fera triompher dans la sainte défense
　　De tous les grands progrès humains!
　　　　　　　　　N. Y. T.

The American Eagle

BY CHARLES WEST THOMSON

Bird of Columbia, well art thou
An emblem of our native land;
With unblanched front and noble brow,
Among the nations doomed to stand;
Proud like her mighty mountain woods;
Like her own rivers wandering free;
And sending forth from hills and floods
The joyous shout of liberty.
Like thee, majestic bird, like thee,
She stands in unbought majesty,
With spreading wing, untired and strong
That dares a soaring far and long,
That mounts aloft, nor looks below,
And will not quail tho tempests blow.

The admiration of the earth,
In grand simplicitv she stands;
Like thee, the storms beheld her birth,
And she was nursed by rugged hands;
But, past the fierce and furious war,
Her rising fame new glory brings,
For kings and nobles come from far
To seek the shelter of her wings.
And like thee, rider of the cloud,
She mounts the heavens, serene and proud,
Great in a pure and noble fame,
Great in her spotless champion's name,
And destined in her day to be
Mighty as Rome,—more nobly free.

My native land, my native land,
To her my thoughts will fondly turn;
For her the warmest hopes expand,
For her the heart with fears will yearn.
Oh, may she keep her eye, like thee,
Proud eagle of the rocky wild,
Fixed on the sun of Liberty,
By rank. by faction, unbeguiled;
Remembering still the rugged road
Our venerable fathers trod,
When they through toil and danger pressed
To gain their glorious bequest,
And from each lip the caution fell
To those who followed, " Guard it well."

Col. S.

Christophorus, the " Christ-Bearer "

BY HENRY B. CARRINGTON

(Historical Columbian Ode for School Exercise.)

The myth which gives the origin of the name Christopher, from the Greek Χριστός, " Christ," and the verb φέρω, " I carry," is fragrant with sweetness.

The four centuries which succeeded the discovery of America are traced by the foot-steps of Christian progress, however re-tarded or misdirected at times by human avarice, ambition, and passion.

Each of the sixteen quarter-centuries de-veloped some type of discovery, invention, or struggle, which found a fit place in the maturity which had its world-wide recogni-tion October 21, 1892.

The free constitutions of Aragon and Cas-tile, which guaranteed the liberties of the people through the Cortes, or representative governments of those kingdoms before rep-resentation was granted the commons of any other European country, are suggestive of the broader and grander sway of the people, then so faintly foreshadowed and now realized.

The Columbian Ode, with its historic gen-eral trend, has for its purpose to emphasize other by-gone centuries in their relations to Christianity as the fundamental and ultimate basis of all genuine liberty.

The story of Columbus is full of sug-gestive facts, and through tablets, declama-tion, and essays there may be found fresh stimulus for historical research and study by accepting the syllabus as a guide. It may be placed upon a blackboard, or on the margin of a tablet-sheet, and thus elicit in-terest and willing work on the part of youth.

SYLLABUS OF COLUMBIAN ODE

I.—The Royal Marriage. The Queen's Choice.
II.—The Conquest of Granada.
III.—Peace and its New Plans Unfold.
IV.—Foreign Adventure and Conquest As-sert Their Claims.
V.—The Brave but Humble Volunteer, Christopher.
VI.—The Royal Outfit and its Departure.
VII.—Visions of Glory Dimmed by Envy.
VIII.—The Queen's Benediction. The Hero's Faith.
IX.—The Perilous Voyage and its Inci-dents.
X.—The Vision Realized. The New World Found.
XI.—Rival Ventures and Cunning Schemes Fail.
XII.—Passion and Plunder in the Ascend-ant.
XIII.—Slavery Bars the Sway of Christoph-orus.
XIV.—The Rights of Man Assert Their Sway. Freedom Advances.
XV.—Columbia Delivered. Church and School Assert Their Higher Law.
XVI.—Henceforth Man's Best Aim to be " The Christ-bearer."

The Golden Age of Andalusian pride
Matured when Aragon and bright Castile
Their wedded sovereigns seated side by side
Upon a double throne, all feuds to heal;
And the bride, so fair, held chiefly precious
To be, in faith and deed, CHRISTOPHORUS.

Granada's great Alhambra felt the tread
Of Spanish lords, their knightly spurs to win,
And Moorish chiefs sought rest at night, in dread
Of morning's dawn, fresh conflict to begin;
While heathen hate, so stern and treach-erous,
Shrank back appalled before CHRISTOPHORUS.

Then Peace her mantle cast about the throne,
  To shield the trophies by high valor won;
The Standard-Bearer by himself, alone
  Bemoaned the end of strife and battles done;
Yet still the Queen, intent and serious,
Sought other fields to prove CHRISTOPHORUS.

New worlds to compass, new realms to conquer,
  New pathways trace to India's golden strands;
New gems to find, and never-failing treasure,
  New converts seek in waiting heathen lands;
While, as the State waxed strong and prosperous,
No knight arose to be CHRISTOPHORUS.

One seaman bold, with richly-cultured brain,
  Who deftly handled either helm or spar,
Repelled at other Courts, paid court to Spain
  For grant to search the regions distant far,
O'er Ocean's wildest Seas, tempestuous,
And prove himself to be CHRISTOPHORUS.

The anxious Queen this royal grant procured,
  Her ready purse supplied the ample means:
Three fragile barks and needed crews secured,
  Her pledge, once made, this gift in full redeems.
So sails the fleet with wishes generous,
And, to execute her will, CHRISTOPHORUS.

No venture e'er before like object sought,
  Nor shared so many hopes with doubting fears;
No other Age so well the spirit caught,
  Which grasps at once the fate of coming years;
While yet the proud, benighted, envious,
Had naught but scorn for this CHRISTOPHORUS.

The Queen's own banner waved the fleet "Adieu,"
  And trumpet echoes cheered the hero bold,
Imparting courage to the humble crew,
  His plans and hopes to help unfold;
And he, with nerve high-strung, but courteous,
With prayer joined faith to be CHRISTOPHORUS.

No lashing seas, nor tempests fierce and wild,
  No angry threats his earnest life to take,
No chafing of his temper, firm and mild,
  Could make him from his solemn purpose break;
But as such strokes grew madly furious,
The more he dared to be CHRISTOPHORUS.

The seas once crossed, the New World surely found,
  He gave it hallowed name, "Salvator Blest,"
And planted royal banner in the ground,
  With honors duly borne from East to West.
By faith discerning nations numerous,
The future subjects of CHRISTOPHORUS.

From other Eastern lands and British Isles
  As years rolled on, the swift-winged transports flew
On rival ventures, and by cunning wiles
  Sought each to bind the Old World to the New,
Yet lost, through methods harsh and tyrannous,
The spirit of a true CHRISTOPHORUS.

Then, maddened year by year through treasure found,
  And Passion's greed for titles, lands, and pelf,
The natives of the soil, in bondage ground
  Were used alone to meet behests of Self
And Christ-like graces, pure and plenteous
Were lost to view without CHRISTOPHORUS.

And thus it came, while kings and mighty thrones
  Made merchandise of men for selfish ends
Despising man, as man, his wail and groan
  And each with other only plunder blends
The New-Found World, so fair and beauteous,
Must longer wait for true CHRISTOPHORUS.

The years rolled on, and many score were told,
  Till centuries twain, and more sad record made,
When, as the rights of man their claims unfold,
  Just rights for all, whate'er their race or grade,
There sprang to view, with Freedom glorious,
The sway and charm of known CHRISTOPHORUS.

And thus Columbia's soil, set free at last
  From rule by brutish force and selfish aims,
Through INDEPENDENCE gained and dangers passed,
  A higher law, the Law of Right, maintains;
While Church and School, with savor gracious,
Proclaim the conquests of CHRISTOPHORUS.

Henceforth, the aim of nations to be great
  Win lasting wealth, and compass true renown,
While each the other's merit seeks to mate
  And only honor's course with glory crown
Shall be to prove most wise and virtuous,
And man become indeed CHRISTOPHORUS.
                                    Col. S.

Columbus

By Richard E. Burton

I see a galleon of Spanish make
That westward like a wingéd creature flies
Above a sea dawn-bright, and arched with
skies
Expectant of the sun and morning-break.
The sailors from the deck their land-thirst
slake
With peering o'er the waves, until their eyes
Discern a coast that faint and dream-like lies,
The while they pray, weep, laugh,—or madly
take
Their shipmates in their arms and speak no
word.
And then I see a figure, tall, removed
A little from the others, as behooved,
That since the dawn has neither spoke nor
stirred;
A noble form the looming mast beside,
Columbus, calm, his prescience verified.

Selecetd.

The Vision of Columbus *

By Joel Barlow

(Soliloquy of Columbus in prison. Written
in 1807)

Land of delights, ah, dear, delusive coast,
To these fond, aged eyes forever lost,
No more thy flowery vales I travel o'er,
For me thy mountains rear the head no
more,
For me thy sparkling rocks no gems unfold,
Nor streams luxuriant wear their paths in
gold:
From realms of promised peace forever
borne,
I hail mute anguish, and in secret mourn.
But dangers past, a world explored in
vain,
And foes triumphant, show but half my
pain.
Dissembling friends, each early joy who
gave,
And fired my youth the storms of fate to
brave,
Swarmed in the sunshine of my happier
days,
Pursued the fortune and forsook the praise,
Now pass my cell with smiles of sour
disdain,
Insult my woes, and triumph in my pain.
One gentle guardian once could shield the
brave;
But now that guardian slumbers in the grave.
Hear from above, thou dear departed shade,
As once my hopes, my present sorrows aid;
Burst, my full heart,—afford that last
relief,—
Breathe back my sighs, and reinspire my
grief.
Still in my sight thy royal form appears,
Reproves my silence, and demands my tears.
Even on that hour no more I joy to dwell,
When thy protection bade the canvas swell,
When kings and churchmen found their
factions vain,

Blind Superstition shrunk beneath her chain,
The sun's glad beam led on the circling way,
And isles rose beauteous in Atlantic day;
For on those silver shores, that new domain,
What crowds of tyrants fix their murderous
reign!
Her infant realm, indignant Freedom flies,
Truth leaves the world, and Isabella dies.

(Hesper, visiting Spirit, addresses Columbus, and bears him upward where the outspread earth gladdens his eyes and the future
of the New World is unfolded to his mental
vision.)

Rise, trembling chief, to scenes of rapture
rise,
This voice awaits thee from the western
skies:
Indulge no longer that desponding strain,
Nor count thy toils nor deem thy labor vain.
Thou seest in me the guardian power who
keeps
The new-found world that skirts Atlantic
deeps,
Hesper my name,—my seat the brightest
throne
In Night's whole Heaven,—my sire the living
sun.
This hand which formed and in the tides of
time
Laves and improves the 'meliorating clime,
Which taught thy prow to cleave the track-
less way,
And hailed thee first in occidental day,
To all thy worth shall vindicate thy claim,
And raise up nations to revere thy name.
In this dark age the blinded faction sways,
And wealth and conquest gain the palm of
praise;
Awed into slaves, while groveling millions
groan,
And blood-stained steps lead upward to a
throne.
Far other wreaths thy virtuous temples
twine,
Far nobler triumphs crown a life like thine.
Thine be the joys that minds immortal grace.
As thine the deeds that bless a kindred race.
Now raise thy sorrowed soul to views more
bright,
The visioned ages rushing on thy sight.
Worlds beyond worlds shall bring to light
their stores;
Time, Nature, Science, blend their utmost
powers,
To show, concentered in one blaze of fame.
The ungathered glories that await thy name.

Long gazed the mariner, when thus the
guide:
"Here spreads the world thy daring sail
descried,
'Hesperia' called, from my anterior claim,
But now Columbia, from thy patriarch name.
Ages unborn shall bless the happier day
That saw thy streamer shape the guideless
way,
Their bravest heroes trace the path you
lead,

* From THE COLUMBIAD.

And sires of nations through the regions
spread.
A-north from that broad gulf where ver-
dant rise
Those gentler mounds that skirt the temper-
ate skies,
A happier hemisphere invites thy view.
'Tis there the Old World shall embrace the
New,
Where Europe's better sons their seat shall
trace,
And change of government improve the race.
Through all the mid-sky zones, to yon blue
pole,
Their green hills lengthen, their bright rivers
roll,
And sloping westward, how their cham-
paigns run,
How slope their uplands to the morning sun.
There lies the path thy future sons shall
trace,—
Plant here their arts and rear their vigorous
race,—
A race predestined in these choice abodes
To teach mankind to tame their fluvial
floods;
Retain from ocean, as their work requires,
Those great auxiliars raised by solar fires;
Force them to form ten thousand roads, and
girth
With liquid belts each verdant mound of
earth;
To aid the colon's as the carrier's toil;
To drive the coulter and to fat the soil;
Learn all mechanic arts, and oft regain
Their native hills, in vapor and in rain.
But now no more the patriotic mind
To narrow views and local laws confined,
Makes patriot views and moral views the
same,
Works with enlightened zeal, to see com-
bined
The strength and happiness of humankind.
At this blest period, when the total race
Shall speak one language and all truths
embrace.
Instruction clear a speedier course shall find,
And open earlier on the infant mind,
Nor dark authorities, nor names unknown,
Fill the learned head with ignorance not its
own,
But Wisdom's eye with beams unclouded
shine,
And simplest rules her native charms define;
Triumphant Virtue, in the garb of Truth,
Win a pure passage to the heart of youth,
Pervade all climes where suns or oceans roll,
And warm the world with one great moral
soul.—
To see, facilitate, attain the scope
Of all their labor and of all their hope."

Thus heard Columbus, eager to behold
The famed Apocalypse its years unfold,
The soul still speaking through his gazing
eyes,
And thus his voice:

      " Oh, let the vision rise!
Command, celestial guide, from each far
pole,

John's visioned morn to open on my soul,
And raise the scene by his reflected light,
Living and glorious, to my longing sight.
Let Heaven, unfolding, show the eternal
throne,
And all the conclave flame in one clear sun;
On clouds of fire, with angels at his side,
The Prince of Peace, the King of Salem
ride,
With smiles of love to greet the bridal earth,
Call slumbering ages to a second birth,
With all His white-robed millions fill the
train,
And here commence His interminable reign."
" Such views," the saint replies, " for
sense too bright,
Would seal thy vision in eternal night;
Man cannot face nor seraph power display
The mystic beams of such an awful day.
Enough for thee that thy delighted mind
Should trace the temporal actions of thy
kind."
   .   .   .   .   .

" Here, then," said Hesper with a blissful
smile,
" Behold the fruits of thy long years of toil.
To yon bright borders of Atlantic day.
Thy swelling pinions led the trackless way,
And taught mankind such useful deeds to
dare,
To trace new seas and happy nations rear,
Till by fraternal hands their sails unfurled
Have waved at last in union o'er the world.
Then let thy steadfast soul no more com-
plain
Of dangers braved and griefs endured in
vain,
Of courts invidious, Envy's poisoned stings,
The loss of empire, and the frown of kings,
While these broad views thy better thoughts
compose,
To spurn the malice of insulting foes,
And all the joys descending ages gain
Repay thy labors and remove thy pain."
                         Col. S.

The Discovery

By Mary Isabella Forsyth

Beneath a summer sky,
One sailed of old, in eager, earnest quest,
Who heard an unborn nation's voiceless cry
     Afar, from out the West.

His heart expectant swelled.
The Christ, whose name he bore, his hope
inspired.
A force Divine his onward course impelled,
     His inner vision fired.

He cleft far wider seas
Than met his gaze.—He never heard the
roar
Of waves of wondrous human destinies
     Upon that farther shore.

The sweep of centuries
Shows sails unnumbered following his wake.
Far more to men than pleasure, comfort,
ease,
     To hear those billows break!

Forever must they roll,
Till all humanity has understood
That highest liberty means self-control,
And law means brotherhood.

Y. C.

The Prophet Bird—1492

By HEZEKIAH BUTTERWORTH

The sails hung listless on the pictured sea
Where green Sargasso meadows pulsed and
    dreamed
In liquid atmosphere; the sea birds free,
On silken pinions, sank and rose and
    gleamed—
A sea of glass and mingling gold it seemed.
The great sun rose, an open gate of Heaven,
And landless seas filled the horizon broad.
Columbus gazed; when, from some far shore
    driven
By venturous wings, a happy land bird came
And sang upon the spars.   The Prophet
    Pilot heard
That wingéd messenger, on seas aflame,
That the dead air with mystic warblings
    stirred,
And, as a lone discoverer, hailed the bird
Sent out to lead the New World's ark of
    God.

So, when the soul draws near its final haven,
The advent anthem palpitates the light,
The sea grows calm, tho in the morn and
    even
No hills of palms rise radiant on the sight,
Nor silver shores, nor crowns of temples
    white.
Monitions come, impalpable to sense,
The sea winds feel the distant highland's
    breath,
And venturous birds the songs of Providence
Waft through the air above the tides of
    death.
We know celestial airs around us glow,
We know celestial tides course through the
    sea,
Of spheres unseen we feel the influence,

The eye of faith looks forward and believes,
And lo! the white-winged dove brings olive
    leaves.

Y. C.

Our Country for the World

By DENIS WORTMAN, D.D.

Our country for the World! we sing,
    But in no worldly way:
Our Country to the Lord we bring
    And fervent for her pray:
God make her true; God make her pure;
    God make her wise and good;
And through her may the Christ make sure
Man's world-wide Brotherhood!
        America! America!
'Gainst wrong thy might be hurled;
For thee we lift our loud Huzza!
    Our Country for the World!

Oh, broader than her wide domains
    Be her designs divine;
And richer than her golden veins
    Her charities divine;
Firmer than stalwart mountain-tower
    Her fixéd faith in Thee,
Her triumphs nobler through Thy power
    Than gain on land or sea!
        America! America!
'Gainst wrong thy might be hurled;
For thee we lift our loud Huzza!
    Our Country for the World!

Great God! our Country for the World,
    And all the world for Thee!
Christ's banners o'er all lands unfurled
    In high exultancy!
O Day of God, speed on, speed on!
    Speed truth and peace and love!
Till all below for Him be won—
    Who reigns o'er realms above!
        America! America!
'Gainst wrong thy might be hurled;
For thee we lift our loud Huzza!
    Our Country for the World!

C. G.

ELECTION DAY

(November)

THE BALLOT-BOX

I AM aware that the ballot-box is not everywhere a consistent symbol; but to a large degree it is so. I know what miserable associations cluster around this instrument of popular power. I know that the arena in which it stands is trodden into mire by the feet of reckless ambition and selfish greed. The wire-pulling and the bribing, the pitiful truckling and the grotesque compromises, the exaggeration and the detraction, the melodramatic issues and the sham patriotism, the party watchwords and the party nicknames, the schemes of the few paraded as the will of the many, the elevation of men whose only worth is in the votes they command,—vile men, whose hands you would not grasp in friendship, whose presence you would not tolerate by your fireside—incompetent men, whose fitness is not in their capacity as functionaries, or legislators, but as organ pipes;—the snatching at the slices and offal of office, the intemperance and the violence, the finesse and the falsehood, the gin and the glory; these are indeed but too closely identified with that political agitation which circles around the ballot-box.

But, after all, they are not essential to it. They are only the masks of a genuine grandeur and importance. For it is a grand thing,—something which involves profound doctrines of right,—something which has cost ages of effort and sacrifice,—it is a grand thing that here, at last, each voter has just the weight of one man; no more, no less; and the weakest, by virtue of his recognized manhood, is as strong as the mightiest. And consider, for a moment, what it is to cast a vote. It is the token of inestimable privileges, and involves the responsibilities of an hereditary trust. It has passed into your hands as a right, reaped from fields of suffering and blood. The grandeur of history is represented in your act. Men have wrought with pen and tongue, and pined in dungeons, and died on scaffolds, that you might obtain this symbol of freedom, and enjoy this consciousness of a sacred individuality. To the ballot have been transmitted, as it were, the dignity of the scepter and the potency of the sword.

And that which is so potent as a right, is also pregnant as a duty; a duty for the present and for the future. If you will, that folded leaf becomes a tongue of justice, a voice of order, a force of imperial law; securing rights, abolishing abuses, erecting new institutions of truth and love. And, however you will, it is the expression of a solemn responsibility, the exercise of an immeasurable power for good or for evil, now and hereafter. It is the medium through which you act upon your country,—the organic nerve which incorporates you with its life and welfare. There is no agent with which the possibilities of the Republic are more intimately involved, none upon which we can fall-back with more confidence than the ballot-box.—EDWIN H. CHAPIN, D.D.   (G. F.)

HISTORICAL

POLITICAL AND PERSONAL LIBERTY

By Judge David J. Brewer

[U. S. Supreme Court]

Liberty has been the dream of humanity through all the ages; and this side the waters there have been two great steps forward in the way of realizing its high ideals. The first was in that proclamation whose anniversary we celebrate—the proclamation of political liberty, the great Declaration which ushered into the world a government of and by and for the people, which dethroned a single monarch and made all men rulers, and which gave to the world a Nation whose career has been and is the hope and inspiration of humanity. Only in a new world where the traditions of monarchy had faded away, where the divine right of the king had become an obsolete thought, where men felt the touch and inspiration of the free air which blows over our mountains and prairies, and looked to themselves as the immediate messengers of the divine purpose to lift each man up into a personal and inalienable inheritance, was such a declaration and such a nation then possible.

A century and more has passed, and as the foundations of this Government are more firmly settled, as the great structure reared by the fathers now spans the continent from ocean to ocean, and has victoriously established its right to be, political liberty has ceased to be the mere dream of the enthusiast, and has become the everyday fact of the men of thought and action in the world.

This was the first step; and we are here to glory in it, and to boast of those ancestors who suffered and toiled and fought to accomplish it.

The second came in our day. Political liberty did not mean personal liberty. On the southern horizon was a dark cloud, ever threatening the peace and life of the Nation— the cloud of slavery. A multitude of human beings, as vast as the whole population of the colonies in 1776, were held as chattels. Wealth and political power perpetuated the injustice, and it seemed so fully intrenched within constitutional protection as to be beyond the danger of disturbance. But "whom the gods would destroy, they first make mad." Untimely greed precipitated the irrepressible conflict. That lone, strange man, John the Baptist of the New Dispensation, struck with his single lance the grim monster. John Brown died upon the scaffold. In that rare heroic hour of death, as the eye grew dim to the visions of sense, did the Good Master bless him with a glimpse, by faith, of the glory whose door he was thus unlocking for Humanity. He "lost, but losing, won." The dormant conscience of the Nation was aroused, lethargic patriotism was wondrously startled, and from Maine to California the glad refrain of the responsive song. "We are coming, Father Abraham, three hundred thousand more," was the *Jubilate Deo* of the new era. It was the crisis of the Nation's life. We saw the awful horror of civil war; the wrong and suffering of the slave were balanced in the equipoise of eternal justice, by the blood and tears of the race that enslaved him; the trailing garments of universal sorrow still linger and shadow every home, and Decoration Day is the great *In Memoriam* of the Nation's sacrifice. But out of that struggle came personal liberty, and for the first time there was written into the Constitution of the United States, in the thirteenth amendment, the terrible word *slavery;* and written in it only to contain the Nation's declaration that it should nevermore exist within its borders. Personal liberty became the universal affirmation of the law, and the second great step forward along the lines of human freedom was taken.—I.

THE CONTROL OF CITIES

The problem of the control of cities has at last become a pressing one. We have had many other important questions to settle in the United States and have given but little attention hitherto to the science of municipal government. Now that the evils of our lack of system have become so widespread, so evident, and so intolerable, men have set themselves to work in earnest to see what can be done, and the first thing that we find, to our surprise, is that we are far behind the rest of the world in this important matter. In the exuberance of our zeal for republican institutions, and of our pride in what we have accomplished, we like to speak occasionally of the "effete" institutions of old Europe and to flatter ourselves that there is nothing in the form of effective government of the people which we do not understand and which we have not illustrated in our own country.

But we have had our eyes opened, and it now seems strange to us that we should have been blind so long to our shortcomings in the matter of the government of our cities. We have had large and important cities for many years; but in the last quarter of a century our urban population has increased so rapidly, and so many large and flourishing cities have sprung up, that the problem of the control of our cities becomes palpably a more important one every year, and we begin to understand how necessary it is to our prosperity as a people, that our cities should be honestly and efficiently governed.

The business interests represented by the administration of a large city are much larger than those of the state in which it is situated. Take New York City, for example. Its finances are (1894) five or six times as great as those of the State to which it belongs. In 1893 the receipts of the city treasury were nearly $92,000,000, and the payments almost a million larger, while those of the State, for the same period, were about $18,000,000. The State, fortunately, has no debt, but the present indebtedness of the city is over $103,000,000. These enormous figures show how important are the finances which the rulers of this great city must manage. For so great a financial trust, business men would at once admit that officers of the highest character and of the widest experience should be chosen. And yet, as some point out, these are the very men who most generally neglect their duty as voters, and allow the politicians and the rabble to control the nominations and city elections. Such large business interests are represented in the government of a great city, and there are so many salaried positions and so many contracts to be awarded, that the politicians find in municipalities the largest scope for their shrewdness and the largest rewards for their activity.

It is to our discredit as an independent and progressive people that we have not seemed to be aware of the extent and character of the evils of our municipal government, and that we have made but little study of methods and systems. The city campaigns fit in nicely with the plans of the politicians, and we have blindly allowed the national parties to control, through their machinery, the affairs of our cities. When we come to turn the question over in our minds we see at once that there is absolutely no reason why Republicans and Democrats, as such, should nominate our municipal tickets, and make themselves responsible for our municipal government. There are great national questions with which as partisans they are properly concerned. But what has the management of the finances, the care of the streets, the parks, the health, peace, order and safety of our cities to do with the tariff, or with the silver question, or with the admission of new states, or with our foreign policy, or indeed with any of the great interests which are national in their scope and character? Municipal policies are widely different from national policies, and ought to be separated in our politics.

Many writers agree that:

(1) Municipal elections should be entirely separate from state and national elections. The reasons for this they give at length, and few can read them without agreeing that they are conclusive. The problems of the city differ from those of the state, and there is no sufficient reason why the elections should be combined.

(2) The interests of the city are chiefly business interests, and honest and efficient men, men of experience, should be selected to control them.

(3) The decent and intelligent element should take a larger and more constant interest in municipal elections. Many who have large business affairs which they look after very carefully, pay no attention whatever to their duties as citizens. They allow the saloon-keeper and the practical politician to have things their own way, and are only roused to their duty when the evils of bad government become unendurable. We cannot have good local government unless the best citizens do their part in securing and maintaining it.

(4) The cities should have home rule. They should not be subject to the constant interference of state legislatures. The frequent changes made in city charters are not often in the interest of better government. They are more likely to give larger scope to the machinations of those who manage municipal politics for the income they get.—I.

THE QUESTION OF PATRIOTISM

A distinguished minister, speaking generally and not for print, made a query which has occurred to many minds: Why should a man's patriotism be doubted because he is in honest and conscientious opposition to a foreign policy of his government? Is not this an attempt to terrorize the exercise of a right upon which the safety and even the existence of free government depend? A free government must have, in order to its good administration, an opposition, a party watchful and ever eager to detect and expose flaws. Where a policy reaches over into the field of morals, as nearly all policies do, is there not even a higher necessity for a moral " opposition? "

Is it not therefore both unreasonable and tyrannical to question a man's patriotism because he is in opposition?

But opposition has its limitations; and the history of our own country has furnished the data for surveying it with approximate accuracy—the line which the consensus of patriotic public opinion has, at every new exigency, drawn through the same points. The people were divided at the time immediately preceding the Revolution, in their loyalty to the then existing government, the British crown. It was held then, and since, by the verdict of history, that both parties were equally entitled to rank as patriots up to the battle of Bunker Hill. That battle made an armed struggle between the colonies and the crown inevitable. The verdict of history is that it was, after that battle, unpatriotic for a colonist to stand by the crown against his fellow countrymen.

The war of 1812 was strenuously opposed by the Federal party. This did not discount the patriotism of the Federalists up to the time when Congress declared war. Because the opposition was continued after the declaration of war, the Federalist party became so odious to the people that it ceased to exist.

The Mexican war gave another equally impressive example. That was a war of unprovoked aggression and conquest in the interest of the extension of slavery. The opposition to it was therefore intense. The Whig party was in opposition and maintained it, during the war. In 1848 it righted itself politically by nominating General Taylor and won, temporarily, but that was its last campaign. In 1852 it tried the same tactics, nominating General Scott, but was beaten to death, and disappeared.

The Democratic party was in opposition during the Civil War. With great advantages on its side, it seated but one man in the presidential chair between the years 1856 and 1900, or forty-four years.

The verdict of the American people affirmed, and three times reaffirmed, appears to be this, that opposition must cease in the presence of an armed enemy. This was mistranslated into a thoroughly false principle, a false patriotism—"Our country right or wrong." An honest man cannot say that. Patriotism is a virtue, but honest manhood is a higher virtue. A true man will not turn his conscience over to the keeping of an administration. That which is inherently wrong cannot be made conventionally right. What then is the significance of a now well-established line between legitimate and illegitimate opposition? We must not say that it is an arbitrary and an immoral line. The consensus for a century and a quarter, of the opinion of the most enlightened of nations would not crystallize an immoral principle into a law, a law that is none the less provided with sanctions because it is unwritten.

The British opposition is now giving the answer. They say that they will bow to the will of the majority, because that is a condition precedent to the existence of free government; that they will support the armies and do nothing to discourage them, because that is the shortest way out of a bad situation, and because they are morally bound to back the men who are putting their lives between the flag and the enemy. Thus they say that new moral factors come into the question when war is declared against their country, and that these moral considerations for the time preponderate and must control. But they also say, that having discharged their patriotic duty during an exigency for which they were not responsible, and to the precipitation of which they were actively opposed, they purpose, when it is past, to take hold of the government with clean, irreproachable and strong patriotic hands, and fling it out of power, and proceed to right any wrongs that the government may have committed.—In.

FUNDS FOR POLITICAL PURPOSES

By Thomas L. James

[Ex-Postmaster-General of the United States.]

The approach of a presidential canvass always provokes more or less discussion on the subject of the use of money in elections. I am requested by *The Independent* to give my views on this subject.

Of course, money must be had to carry on any enterprise, good or bad; because all human undertakings require a certain amount of work, and that work has to be paid for in money. The first question of moral importance is, How is the money for a presidential campaign raised? In political campaigns, so far as my knowledge goes, money is raised by contributions. The prominent, especially the wealthy men of the party, are approached by managers of the organization, or their agents, who attend to the details of party management, and are requested to donate as large a sum as they can afford toward the expenses of the campaign. A considerable sum is raised before the meeting of the nominating convention. I have been informed that some men pay or contribute a certain sum for the privilege of being delegates to the national convention. This is the first time that I have heard of such a thing being done, and tho there may be such cases, I think they must be very rare, because the honor of attending such a national gathering is all-sufficient for hundreds of prominent and competent men who are able to represent the interests of the party on such an occasion. Then, again, if a man is more or less actively interested in politics, the fact that he has been a member of a national convention is of value to him in the eyes of the party; it is a sort of political asset and, when combined with ability, character, and influence, helps him later on to obtain some position of honor or emolument within the gift of higher officials. Delegates to a national convention pay all their own expenses, the occasion is not one where a free excursion and "a good time" can be had at the expense of the party.

Where does the money that is raised for political purposes go to? It goes to build and furnish the big convention hall, to pay for music, flags, transparencies, and, when the campaign opens, speakers, singers and their traveling expenses, the printing of political documents, posters, handbills, advertising, and a hundred incidental expenses, which, in the aggregate, amount to a considerable sum. These are all legitimate expenses. It may be asked, Who pays for the time and the expenses of the carloads of shouters who leave the large cities in the interests of their favorite candidate, and whose business it is to "work up" enthusiasm for him in the convention city? A large proportion of them, like the delegates, pay their own expenses; and, just as the delegates esteem it an honor and, in a certain sense, a political advantage to be able to attend such a gathering, so the more prominent "shouters" are more thoroughly identified with the party by their attendance; and, in case of its success, have a better chance of securing recognition from an official from whom they may desire to obtain a political appointment. The expenses of many are paid by political clubs or organizations in the cities, who raise money for party purposes on their own account, and who naturally desire to do all that they can to win success for the national ticket.

Altho I believe the contributions are generally used for proper purposes, there is no doubt that a certain class of politicians believe in using money for the purchase of delegates and voters. There is a story told by a prominent politician of New York, which peculiarly illustrates the business-like methods of such proceedings. Some few years ago, the members of the colored delegation from one of the Southern states to a national convention were considered rather "uncertain" in regard to their allegiance to the favorite candidate. They intimated that they were open to the power of persuasion, if it came to them in a financial form. Mr. B., who had charge of the funds, saw their leader, and agreed to defray the expenses of the delegates, they having been elected for a certain candidate whom they were to vote for in the convention. He paid $3,000. The convention was held, and the colored members voted for another candidate. Immediately after the convention they had the ef-

frontery to demand $1,000 more, claiming that their expenses amounted to $4,000 and saying that if he did not pay them promptly they would sue him for it.

As a matter of policy alone, aside from the violation of good morals, the improper use of money in political campaigns is really a source of weakness instead of strength. Its use does a party more harm than good. The people who are in politics simply for pay and for what they can "get out of it" are really of no benefit to an organization. Among our public speakers, the most distinguished ones, and those who render the greatest service to the party—men, for instance, like Chauncey M. Depew, Warner Miller, Charles Emory Smith, Joseph H. Choate, and many others who might be named in both of the great parties—such men do not receive pay for their speeches.

Any man who will take pay for his vote, either in a nominating convention or at the polls, should be disfranchised and sent to prison for the offense. Such a crime strikes at the very foundation of our Government. Our country would soon cease to be representative among the nations of the earth, without a free and honest ballot and an equally honest expression of the public voice in the choice of presidential nominees at the great national conventions. But, because election campaigns cost so much money at the present time, we must not become pessimistic and say that it is altogether the result of corruption. The campaign in this State, in 1856, I do not believe, cost more than $20,000, and that was fought very bitterly, from start to finish; but, in considering the large sums spent now, we must remember the changed conditions of modern life. The population is much larger. We are more luxurious in our ideas. We spend more money in every direction. The methods of carrying on a political campaign, owing to the increase in population, must necessarily be more complex and diversified than they were forty years ago, when the style of living, as well as the manner of conducting all public affairs, was simpler than it is at the present time. In other words, large expenditure of campaign funds is not, necessarily, a sign of political corruption.—I.

THE USE OF MONEY IN POLITICAL CAMPAIGNS

By Silas W. Burt

The large use of money, both before and after election, in the political campaigns of the present day, is a phase of modern public life that represents one of the great changes in our political methods since our forefathers established and practised the principles laid down in the Constitution. The Constitution, as we know, was based on the pure democratic idea of government, in which all power and imitation should proceed from the

people themselves. Gradually we have substituted for this, which we might call the spontaneous expression of the people, a mechanism by which, instead of the people's instructing their delegates, the presumption is that the delegates are going to instruct the people. In other words, we have absolutely inverted the original idea that lay at the basis of our political fabric.

Concurrently with this has been introduced

into the political or partisan practises the mercenary idea which appears to taint every part of the political fabric to-day. This is demonstrated in many ways: by the purchase of places in the Senate of the United States; by the large contributions that are levied upon the men who want to be nominated or appointed to office; by the immense sum for campaign funds that is raised and disbursed without any audit. . It has been sought to remedy some of these evils by legislation, in which there should be a publication of these contributions and a limitation of the uses to which they might be applied. This legislation, however, has been deplorably defective in the fact, so far, that it does not require an accounting from political committees, but only from individual candidates.

It is difficult to estimate the cost of a great presidential campaign. There is no doubt but what it might be measured by millions of dollars, apart from the loss involved in the general destruction of business. It has been said that frequent elections have their value in keeping alive public interest in public affairs, and in educating the people upon the great questions that are to be solved. But when we recollect that a great part of the expenses of the campaign are spent in badges, torchlight processions, and other appeals to the imagination and sensation rather than to reason, it seems probable that a very large part of this expenditure is practically valueless, so far as the education of the people is concerned, and is really spent to pervert their intelligence.

We have long had the "political boss," who has taken advantage of his power to levy contributions upon corporations and others interested in legislation and also in procuring the spoils of office for his "heelers;" but a new figure is now projected upon the political stage, and that is "the president maker."

It is difficult to devise a prompt remedy for these evils that have become gradually embedded in our political methods. The reform of the civil service is wresting from the bosses the offices so long used as bribes or rewards. This will weaken the machinery by which they control and sell legislation, tho this outrageous abuse can be effectively cured only by such an awakening of the public conscience as shall make such practices as odious as treason, of which indeed they are a phase. There remains the potent remedy of partisan independence at the ballot boxes, that has achieved much of good in recent years, and is a constantly increasing force that terrifies the " political workers."

Parties are an essential part of representative governments, and can be effective only by organization; but when organization degenerates into a brutal machinery that stifles intelligence and true patriotism, the republic is moribund. As the perfunctory and bigoted exercise of the suffrage has gradually extinguished much of the manhood of American citizenship, so the restoration of intelligence, conscience, and individual independence in this prime duty will be the sole effective means of curing many existing evils and preventing others that might be equally dangerous.—I.

HOW BAD MEN ARE CHOSEN TO RULE

By Fulton McMahon

One of the greatest living theologians has published an essay in which he brings home to Christian citizens the duty of making their influence felt in politics. It does not, perhaps, detract from the absolute value of the exhortation to know that the celebrated author has, during a long life in a ring-ridden city, never cast a ballot; but it incites reflection. This excellent man clearly belongs to the better—indeed what ought to be the best "element." His neighbors are of the same general class. When he and they discuss problems of sociology and local administration, much is said about foreign illiterates, the great undercurrent of official immorality, the deterioration of civic virtue, and the exploitation by bad men of politics as a business. Yet in that neighborhood, which contains no ignorant immigrants and no professional politicians, there are, within one block, twenty-five homes that did not send a single voter to the polls.

Who is to blame if our cities are badly governed? Let us look at New York. Some men of intelligence and reputed character are publicly declaring that the city is not only well, but excellently governed. This, however, need not deter us from affirming that the metropolis presents nearly every phase of bad municipal administration. Great effort is constantly making to correct these evils by improving the form of the government. Since the city is a quasi-corporation, a creature of the State, it has been easy to experiment with theories by tinkering with the charter. It may safely be said that these alterations, so far as they were conscious efforts to improve matters, were nearly all induced by the bad character of the men who were in power when the changes were demanded. Good men did not realize that in adopting, and relying upon, such means to remedy evils they were abandoning the one ground on which they could stand in ultimate victory. They have gone on perfecting a system which only serves the evil purposes of bad men a little better than did the old systems. This should be kept in mind, also, by the people who are expecting great reforms through the action of the last Constitutional Convention (1894). It is a fact beyond dispute that our existing form of local government is adequate to all our needs.

If the right kind of men were in control, a few minor modifications, conservatively made, would afford us as good an administration of public affairs as we may reasonably desire.

The trouble is not in our institutions, imperfect as they doubtless are. The crying necessity for reform springs from the fact that while our institutions are representative theoretically, our public officials are not so, actually. The normal operation of social and political laws would only rarely and sporadically elevate to positions of trust and power such men as now give the character to our municipal public service. The question thus raised concerns the explanation of this unnatural condition of things. What prevents the best men from being chosen to office? This question need, perhaps, not to be answered; for we know there are numerous considerations, not here relevant, that commonly preclude the selection of the very best men on the ground of non-availability. But what is the hindrance to the choice of good men and fit?

Do good citizens knowingly elect bad officials? Yes, in many instances. Sometimes they are deceived, but too often they are morally responsible for great public wrongs. Blind partisanship in national politics conduces to the sacrifice of principle in local matters as a means hallowed by an end. " Our ticket, tho Satan head it," is the motto of thousands who dare not utter it. This same spirit has to be contended with in every effort looking to an extension of civil service reform. Indeed, the city problem is nothing else than that. Men who take this or that view of the tariff and who have come to blame the very weather or the opposition party cannot readily be brought to forego any even imaginary partisan advantage by the discontinuance of the patronage system. The local machine is so built that its cogs form an integral part of the national complex. Patronage is the oil that makes it go. That which the Nation and State afford is not enough, especially when the party is in opposition; so the local spoils must be used. Campaign funds are raised and treated in a like manner. Such mutuality of tickling leads to a hopeless entanglement of national and local interests. Moreover, the city men who really go into politics on principle generally confine their appreciative participation to national affairs and naturally regard the local organizations merely as means to national success. But meantime the vital local matters of taxation, justice, order, health, and comfort have been made to sink or swim with the wholly irrelevant contest over high and low tariff. Yes, let it again be replied, good citizens do knowingly elect bad men to local offices, and for no better reason than that a party boss has said the local sacrifice conditions national victory. When this question is seriously considered in all its aspects, Christian men must see that morality as well as expediency enters into it. Shall attachment to political theories usurp the place of conscience?

Many citizens who see the unreasonableness of choosing city officials on a national platform continue to support this system, on the ground that no' other is practicable. Such is the refuge of all men who have no real faith in the moral principles they profess. Very few thinkers any longer pretend that there is a true analogy between municipal and state or federal government. An assumed analogy of this kind has been the cause of great confusion in the modern treatment of the subject. It would, further, explain in large measure why Mr. James Bryce is able to state so positively that our institutions break down in cities. It has also brought about the present condition of the uninformed public mind, which honestly imagines that these or those opinions regarding national policy are proper qualifications for a local court clerk or tax officer. With the further spread of right ideas about civil service such false conceptions will cease to confuse intelligent minds. But the men who reject non-partisan city government solely on the ostensible ground of impracticability, expose themselves either to the charge of moral insincerity or to the imputation of self-interested action.

Granting that there is rightfully no politics in local affairs such as police justice and street-cleaning, men of character and intelligence are bound in the performance of their simplest public duty to combine their efforts to eliminate this irrelevant and disturbing element. Shall the Christian merchant be driven to commercial cheating because, forsooth, the failure to adopt such an expedient may give his business competitor an advantage? Where, in that event, is his Christianity? Shall the Christian citizen of one national party continue his support of an unnatural and immoral intermingling of unrelated interests—shall he refuse to lend his aid to obtaining a purely business administration of local affairs—because, forsooth, such action may threaten to strengthen the other national party? Where, in that event, is his Christianity? Observe that this is not illegitimately identifying a popular reform movement with our religion. We are assuming that the men so appealed to honestly entertain the conviction, as great numbers avowedly do, that the now prevalent balancing and trading of national and local interests are wrong and unnecessary save as they may seem to be demanded by expediency. And since when has mere difficulty of realization become a sufficient excuse for the abandonment of ideals? If we know, or are convinced, that a thing is right, we are bound to make it practicable. The attainment of a personal Christian character is not a result, but a process. and an unending striving after the unattainable. So also there is no practicable perfection in human society or government, but a Christian citizenship has no right to follow the line of least resistance.

There are some religionists of correct lives who refuse to employ the services in any capacity of persons holding a different faith from their own. We do not regard this as a high type of religion. No more can we accept as a high standard of Christian citizenship the man who does not believe a neighbor of another political faith worthy to be intrusted with local administrative functions. A little observation will disclose how amazingly common this attitude is among men whose first law of mind and action should be charity. Universal mugwumpery would be a sad state for a free people, and fortunately impossible; but it need not impair a man's party loyalty one iota to declare and prove himself absolutely and unqualifiedly an Independent in municipal elections. Until intelligent Christian men take this broad view, and also flee the reproach of indifference to civic obligations, there is little ground for hope that our cities will speedily be freed from ring rule.—I.

THE SOURCE OF PARTY WISDOM

By James A. Garfield

I have seen the sea lashed into fury and tossed into spray, and its grandeur moves the soul of the dullest man; but I remember that it is not the billows, but the calm level of the sea, from which all heights and depths are measured. When the storm has passed and the hour of calm settles on the ocean, when the sunlight bathes its smooth surface, then the astronomer and surveyor, take the level from which to measure all terrestrial heights and depths. Gentlemen of the convention, your present temper may not mark the healthful pulse of our people when our enthusiasm has passed. When the emotions of this hour have subsided, we shall find that calm level of public opinion below the storm, from which the thoughts of a mighty people are to be measured, and by which their final action will be determined. Not here in this brilliant circle, where fifteen thousand men are assembled, is the destiny of the Republican party to be declared. Not here, where I see the faces of seven hundred and fifty-six delegates waiting to cast their votes in the urn and determine the choice of the Republic, but by four million Republican firesides, where the thoughtful voters, with wives and children about them, with the calm thoughts inspired by the love of home and country, with the history of the past, the hopes of the future, and a knowledge of the great men who have adorned and blessed our Nation in days gone by—there God prepares the verdict that shall determine the wisdom of our work to-night. Not in Chicago, in the heats of June, but in the sober quiet that comes to them between now and November; in the silence of deliberate judgment will the great question be settled.—*Selected.*

SERMONS

THE RELATION OF THE CHURCH TO POLITICAL MORALITY

By Rev. Bernard Paine

This question, which demands a practical solution in the states and in the Nation, suggests a larger one, viz.: the relation of Christianity to the moral condition and the moral improvement of society. In this discussion, therefore, we consider the Church as synonymous with Christianity. When the Christian Church is true to its mission, and just so far as it is true to the teachings and to the example of Christ, it is the salt of the earth. It saves it from utter corruption and purifies it with a new life and a new morality. The truth is, if we examine closely into Christ's work, we learn that immediately, constantly, and by indirect methods as well. He was correcting the relations of people in society. His words let the light in, and smote the sources of wrong moral conduct. One thing which He was ever enforcing was the proper estimate of man apart from his condition.

Every man is a child of God. This is His great revelation as to man. Christ has given to every man on earth the charter of his liberty, the right to a filial and equal relation in God's family, and to the moral and inalienable right to be, as a man, on a fundamental equality with every other man. Boundaries of Nations cannot fence off and cast out any men regardless of their rights as men. The color of the skin cannot obliterate the man, or make him anything else than a man. Education, culture, refinements of society, occupation —especially the luxurious living of the wealthy —may make a striking difference in the external appearance of those who are so favored from those of the large majority whose hands are bony and calloused with daily toil, and whose dress is plain and worn. The innocent and amiable will carry a sweet face, while the ugly and vicious will betray their vices to the world in the countenances that they wear.

But notwithstanding these wide diversities, there is the human soul under all beating with common impulses, feelings, and desires; and Christ opened the door of hope and life to each and to all.

In close connection with this, Jesus taught the duty and Christian privilege of self-sacrifice in place of selfishness. In this He showed the only practicable way of exercising love for our neighbor. If a Christian loves his neighbor as himself, there will be no end of opportunities to assist him out of trouble and help to better things; and in doing these things, he will be denying himself and making personal sacrifices in order to attain his end, and bringing to his brother man everywhere the help that he needs. And it is in relation to this wide opportunity afforded in this free land of ours—a Nation so open to all kinds of effort and influence for the uplifting of great masses of human brothers—it is at this point of view that we should cultivate our Christian patriotism, and learn to honor and love our native land. We need not condone her faults; but with all the faults and imperfections of our country, for this liberty in Christ's work we love her still.

The relation of the Church to the moral condition of society in our land and to its improvement is one of responsibility as well as privilege. Take one instance—the family. Upon its sacredness and peace, its unity and virtue, the whole structure of society rests. Whatever touches its integrity or weakens its life tends to destroy the home and spread the virus of unfaithfulness and libertinism through the land. Now, Christianity has lifted marriage to the level of a sacrament. It elevates the relation between husband and wife to a holy unity, symbolizing the relation between Christ and His Church. It holds up before us the relative duties and affections of parents and children as an affecting mirror in which we behold the face of our Heavenly Father, and the filial piety that is due to Him from all His earthly children. Every Christian family is a pivot on which the Church moves the lever of personal life to herald forth and carry Christ to the people. The families of a Church are like planetary stars, of varying brightness, sending light into the intervening spaces from Christ, the central luminary. This light is their good works, which men see and for which they bless God, because they come from God. This testimony is not weak, but purifying and aggressive. The Church never will rest or be silent so long as the laws of the state make it easy for the marriage covenant to be annulled. It cannot cease to cry aloud until the laws of the state are made parallel to the law of Christ. We see in this one instance how closely the Church is related to the moral condition of society, and how it constantly and powerfully works for the improvement of that condition. We also may see how this aggressive power for good may be increased through the enactment of laws which favor the virtue and sanctity of the family. Every Christian man is a citizen of a free, self-governed nation. He need not go out of the

kingdom of Heaven to become a citizen, but remains in it, a Christian man. The Church has a mighty, aggressive power to exert through her citizen membership.

And now we approach another phase of our subject. We speak of the suffrages of the people, and of the ballot in the hands of a freeman. Let us not be ashamed to ask, What is a ballot? A ballot is a vote upon some question, or measure, or law, as a constitutional law, brought before the citizen voters to decide. More commonly, it is a vote by which each citizen makes his choice of the men that he prefers should hold certain offices of trust, especially for men, whether in the state or nation, who are to enact and to execute laws. The ballot is a piece of paper. It means nothing except in the hands of a citizen who is privileged to show by his use of it what kind of a man he is. By a figure of speech, the term "ballot" is used to cover the power, use, and privilege of the voting citizen in the making of laws, and in the governing of the Nation. When we speak of the purification of the ballot, we mean the purification of the men and their acts in the use or misuse of the ballot. We have been taught from the early days of the Republic that a free nation depends for its stability and prosperity upon the virtue and intelligence of her citizens. It is a maxim of freedom's defenders. The ballot is the true measure of the virtue and intelligence of a citizen. Upon the sacredness of the ballot rests the future of the Nation. Whatever corrupts it strikes a blow at the life of the Republic. Is such corruption at all prevalent in our State and Nation?

Professor McCook, of Trinity College, Hartford, has made a careful inquiry. Having been chosen chairman of a committee to examine into the expenditures for alms and charity in the city of Hartford, his report of the facts was given to the world, and made the basis of a reformation in that city. He then extended his investigations to the State, more especially to learn the facts concerning the amount of venality at the polls. These facts have been given out through various periodicals. He discusses the subject in *The Homiletic Review* for June, 1893. Speaking of the manner in which the practical politician gets into office, he says: "It has come to pass that 20,000 votes of Connecticut's 166,-000 votes are liable to be cast for money or some other valuable consideration. The gauge has been thrust into the barrel at haphazard in three places—two country towns and one city ward—bringing up 11.3 per cent. of venal. Again, it has gone down into 17 towns and one large city and brought up 15.9 per cent. As a result, the mean number of voters for sale in the open market is 22,576, and the sums paid have been found to range from $1.50 to $50.

This information comes from the practical politician "unembarrassed," as the writer says, "by the consciousness of moral guilt or civic delinquency." Professor McCook further testifies that "The practical politician effects bribery of this kind through money, flour, cows; through shooting parties, with free conveyance and free refreshment, both solid and liquid, attached, and like gross rewards." Let us smother our moral feelings and coolly look these facts in the face. More than one-eighth of the citizen voters of this State, this famed " land of steady habits " can be purchased for such various mercenary rewards. Moreover they are being purchased. What does this mean? It means, for one thing, that this venal vote rules the election in every doubtful state, and probably in every doubtful town and city. What, now, becomes of the ballot, the power and glory of the Republic? Where are the virtuous and intelligent American citizens, who, whether in one party or the other, may be outvoted by a band of lawless tramps and drunkards, who are bought by money, cows, or beer? What kind of men will get into office while such voting prevails? Will not the practical politician get to the State Capitol? " One has only to follow the proceedings of a state legislature day by day," says Professor McCook, " to find the evidence of bribery no less real, tho perhaps less gross." Then, besides, there is the venal influence and work of the third house. Only a few years since, the lobby of the Massachusetts Legislature underwent an investigation. It was found that hundreds of thousands of dollars were in the hands of this lobby, and operated with the connivance of prominent politicians.

An article in the March *Forum* (1894) shows how municipal corruption is reduced to a science. The writer says: " Municipal government is corrupt simply because corrupt and corruptible men are elected to office. Corrupt men are elected to office because office 'pays,' and corruptible men yield because they make money by yielding. If municipal governments had no profitable contracts to award, if school boards had no text-books to select, we should have no 'municipal problem.' " In this way the writer opens up a vast but well-defined system of bribery on the part of business firms, operating upon city councils, the selectmen of towns, and the school boards of town and city to introduce water-works, school-books, heating apparatus, etc. These things are being practised widely all over the country. But the spirit of righteous reform is not dead. It was such righteous reform that abolished the Tweed ring in New York City. It was such a national spirit of protest and revolt that withered the reputation of every man whose name was in any way connected with the " Credit Mobilier " scandal in Congress. This righteous spirit of reform has its source in the Christian Church.

One of the most iniquitous forms of taking from an American citizen his right to a free ballot is through intimidation. This is not bribery; it is oppression. It is oppression in a free land. It is practised by **both** parties, sometimes through corporations and capitalists, and sometimes by threats of violence at the polls. The evidence is spread before the Nation that it is practised at elections in various states at the South for the suppression of the colored voters. I do not know what

legislation is wise in such a crisis; but one thing the Church knows, and that is that the Ethiopian as well as the Caucasian is a man in Christ's view, and as an American citizen he has the right to a free ballot; and whenever force or intimidation drives him from the polls, the Nation has the duty and the power to protect him. Is anything being done to correct these evils that surround the elections? Yes; and the current of reform is in this case started from across the water. Fortunately, we have a very encouraging example in the very thorough legislation upon the corrupt practises at elections which was effected in the Parliament of Great Britain in 1883. This was one of the great achievements of Mr. Gladstone's cabinet, and the man who had special charge of the work was Sir Henry James, the attorney-general at that time. The author of the act gives a very interesting account of it in the April (1894) number of the *Forum*. The evil had become gigantic, spreading and taking deeper root for many generations. It seemed to defy reform. Many attempts had been made and laws passed, but they had little effect. Says Sir Henry: " A most unsatisfactory aspect of the matter was that in many localities bribery and treating were resorted to by men in responsible positions, who seemed to be blind to any moral evil in the corrupt practises they had almost openly resorted to. From the reports it was found that justices of the peace, members of the governing local bodies, and professional men were conspicuous offenders." But as these corrupt practises were investigated and exposed, the public demanded reform and the press of the whole realm did valiant service. A striking feature of this law is its thoroughness. The courts and mode of conviction were clearly marked and the penalties severe. For example, " If upon the trial of an election petition, the Election Court reports that the offenses of bribery and personation have been committed by or with the knowledge and consent of a candidate, or that the offenses of treating or undue influence have been committed by a candidate, such candidate shall not be capable of being elected to a sitting in the House of Commons for the county or borough to which the report refers, and if elected, his election is void." The same result follows if a candidate is guilty " by his agents." The act has been in existence ten years. The author says: " Corrupt practises have in most localities ceased to exist. No member since the passing of the act has been unseated for bribery."

The act passed by the Massachusetts Legislature in 1892 for a similar purpose is also set forth in the same number of the *Forum* by its author, Hon. Josiah Quincy. He says: " While it defines and forbids certain acts as constituting 'corrupt practices,' its main provisions are directed merely to securing a full and public account of all political expenditures; but no limitation is imposed upon their amount, and they are not confined to certain specified objects, as they are in the English act." These expenditures must be made through a political committee. Each such committee must have a treasurer, and this treasurer is obliged to keep a record of all moneys received and paid out, with names of each person contributing, and the amount given. He is not allowed to solicit or make any assessment upon any candidate. Within thirty days after election this treasurer must make a sworn statement of all the receipts and disbursements. Mr. Quincy says: "The Massachusetts act has worked so well at its first trial as to afford decided encouragement for the introduction of similar legislation elsewhere." Mr. Bishop, of New York, criticizes the Massachusetts law, as well as those in New York and Michigan, in not making sufficiently definite the courts before which the offenses are to be tried and the manner of bringing them to trial. The proposed Connecticut act, which goes to the next General Assembly (1894) seems to me to remedy this defect. This proposed act "to suppress corrupt practices at elections" is published, together with an improved ballot law, with the acts of the last Assembly, a copy of which ought to be in the hands of every citizen of the State and read. This law ought to be enacted. It should be so well understood by the public as to call forth a strong public sentiment in its support, so that it shall not be weakened by the amendments of practical politicians, but, if necessary, made stronger by the corrections and additions of the framers and friends of the bill. This reform has come; it is a pressing need, and it hastens to its goal What is the sphere of the Church in such a reform? A brief outline must suffice in my closing words:

1. It must recognize and hold up before men the moral character of this corruption of the ballot. Bribery is a sin. It is condemned in the laws of Moses: "And thou shalt take no gift; for a gift blindeth the wise, and perverteth the words of the righteous." These words are as true to-day as when they were written. The warning is repeated in Deuteronomy and other parts of the Bible: "Thou shalt not wrest judgment; thou shalt not respect persons; neither take a gift; for a gift doth blind the eyes of the wise, and pervert the words of the righteous." If it will blind the eyes of the wise, what effect must it have upon the common people—upon the foolish? Will it not destroy the moral sense? When Simon the Sorcerer tried to bribe Peter with money, he said to him: "Thy money perish with thee, because thou hast thought that the gift of God may be purchased with money." Even our Lord was made subject to the temptation of bribery by the arch-deceiver. He showed him all the kingdoms of this world, their riches, and the glory of them, and said, "All these will I give thee, if thou wilt fall down and worship me." But this was most abhorrent to the holy nature of Christ. His reply was quick, with disgust and sharp rebuke: "Get thee behind me, Satan." Bribery under all circumstances is wicked; but in the political life of a people, it is most degrading. Corruption is the proper word.

2. The Church furnishes a standard for political morality. Outside of Christianity, there is no one standard of morality for all people and times. Governments are of various forms. Circumstances and customs call forth diverse ideals and tests of what is justifiable and right. But God does not change. Jesus Christ "is the same, yesterday, to-day, and forever." In setting up His kingdom, there is to be—there is only one standard; it is the will of God. How repugnant to bribery is the thought of God! God's love does not trifle with the rights and privileges of the weak. It does not permit a stumbling-block to rest before the feet of our brother.

3. Once more, for the elevation of political morality the Church is to furnish motives. The motives furnished by the State in its regulation of conduct are limited in their range. They appeal to fears, chiefly in the restraints put upon personal liberty and the disgrace of convict life. The State does well to call in the Church and her ministers to help reform the character of the convicts. But what can the State do toward changing the moral character of the people in the community at large? How rid them of a wrong bias? How straighten the crooked places in man's fallen nature? How restore the lost balance? She knows nothing of these things. Dr. Parker says concerning Christ's work of adjusting human relations: "A very subtle thing is the equipoise. An extra handful of dust on the side of a plant might endanger the universe." There is something in human nature that the State cannot reach. A writer in *Lux Mundi* says: "If states and societies are as the individuals who compose them, then any theory of society must rest upon the theory of man; and the theory of man is imperfect unless it recognizes the fact of sin. This fact of sin, of course, is broader and deeper than any acts, whether moral or immoral. The State, therefore, needs the Church to furnish the motives for the elevation of political morality. Her resources for this are quite inadequate, and need to be supplemented by those of Christianity. The State fails to give principles and motives which apply to all moral conduct." And again we quote these conclusive words: "The State can only secure a minimum of morality, shifting with the general morality of the community. It is in its appeal to the higher motives that the State is weak; it is in its appeal to the higher motives that the Church is strong."

Brethren, we believe in the coming of a better future to the world. We have not lost the vision of the seers. We are now living in the bright to-morrow of ancient days; and every to-morrow will be brighter than the one before it. But how is this hope of the ages to be realized? The prophets, with one voice, say, by the increase of righteousness. "Righteousness exalteth a nation," and nothing else can. "He that soweth to the flesh shall of the flesh reap corruption." Sodom found it so; Nineveh had experience of the truth; so did Babylon, Rome; and the nations of heathenism in every age affirm the truth. The kingdom of God is not to be a kingdom of saloons. It is said the brewers of New York city rule the entire municipality. How? By mortgaging 6,000 saloons, and holding the keepers in political subjection. Does not the city need Dr. Parkhurst and the churches behind him to smite the vampire of debauchery and corruption? "And a highway shall be there, and the unclean shall not walk therein." The better to-morrow will see a great diminution of almhouses and miseries of poverty. Professor McCook says more than 56 per cent. of the expense of almhouses and charity in Hartford is due to intemperance. In 1890 intemperance cost the city the sum of $68,432 in alms and charity. The kingdom of God that we are praying for is not a far-away kingdom, somewhere in the outside universe. It is coming on the earth. The inhabitants shall not want. Poverty and sickness will be swept away. The strife of tongues shall cease. Peace shall reign on earth as in Heaven. The New Jerusalem comes down to earth. It is "four-square." It hath foundations. The measuring line in its erection is the plummet of righteousness. Its cornerstone is Christ. Through His reign righteousness and peace are promised throughout the world.

In every movement that Christianity makes to eradicate the corrupt practises of men in political and in social life Christ is setting up His kingdom on the earth.—H. R.

THE USE AND ABUSE OF PARTY POLITICS

By Rev. Hugh Price Hughes

Let your forbearance be known unto all men.—Phil. iv: 5

In the Authorized Version, as every one knows, it is translated "moderation." It is a very good thing, probably, to get rid of that word, because so many people imagine that it has some special or exclusive reference to the use of strong drink. Of course the apostle is not thinking of anything of the sort. "Let your *forbearance* be known unto all men." In the margin, as an alternative suggestion, the word *gentleness* is used—"Let your *gentleness* be known unto all men." Many will remember that Matthew Arnold translated the word, with much of his usual verbal felicity, *sweet reasonableness*—"Let your *sweet reasonableness* be known unto all men." The word, in fact, is, in itself, a very high tribute to the delicate and lofty morality which the best Greek minds have reached, and it expresses the state of mind in which we make due allowance for the conduct of others, and especially of our opponents, and in which we are alive to our own mental defects.

Now I need scarcely remind you or prove to you that there is no sphere of life in which this moderation or forbearance or gentleness or sweet reasonableness is more urgently demanded than in the region which men call politics; and I have to speak this afternoon of "The Use and Abuse of Party Politics." But before I say a word about party politics, I must try to bring home to everybody's mind, altho there seems to be some extraordinary difficulty in the process, that there is an immense difference between politics and party politics, altho the great majority of those who either speak or think or write upon the subject seem to be incapable of grasping the idea that there is anything which may be called politics except that with which we are almost too familiar, and which is more properly called party politics.

But what is politics, in the legitimate sense of that word? Why, it is the science of Social Conduct! And every act of your life outside the domestic circle is a political act. There are a great many acts of your life, also, inside the domestic circle, which are strictly political. So that the man who says, as a great many unthinking or ill-informed men say, that he is not a politician is like that remarkable man, in the well-known French play, who expressed his astonishment at the discovery that he had been talking grammar all his life without knowing it. Why, everybody is a politician! You cannot help being a politician. You cannot live for an hour without being a politician. But what a man generally means when he says that he is not a politician I am afraid is this— that he has been all his life enjoying his political privileges and grossly neglecting his political duties; and in that sense the observation is scarcely to his credit. As a matter of fact, politics, properly understood, is simply Science of Life—the doctrine of the way in which I am to do my duty to my neighbor, which is an essential part of true religion. It is nothing in the world, except Religion applied to human society; in fact, it is the practical recognition of the Second Table of the Law of God.

But if this is so, how is it that so many persons who sincerely desire to please God, and to do the will of God, speak so suspiciously and so disparagingly of politics? How is it that politics have been so much misunderstood and disparaged? It is because politics, as I have already said, have been confounded with party politics; have often been contemptible and wicked beyond description; and, indeed, when not carried so far as that, there are a great many persons who positively cannot discuss politics without losing their temper. And this is so well known that the subject is tabooed to a very great extent in polite society, so-called, so that if you go to a dinner party the one thing of which you must not speak is politics, and the place that might reasonably be occupied by noble and instructive conversation about the science and art of life, and human progress, is occupied by inane, and worse than inane, gossip.

Then, again, it is very much too common on the part of those who either talk or write about politics to impute the vilest motives to their political opponents, and to carry on their observations in a perfect shower of personalities. And I am bound to add further that, in consequence of these pollutions, and of this unhappy temper of mind, the arguments in which a great many persons who discuss politics indulge are of the most puerile and even asinine character. I am bound, with some reluctance and shame, to add that I know not a few Christians, sincere Christians, who have been so eaten up with party politics that they have even sacrificed their church to the supposed interests of their political party, have put loyalty to their party chiefs before loyalty to Jesus Christ; and you cannot imagine anything more disgraceful than that on the part of a Christian.

Moreover, party political prejudice and passion have been carried so far in this country that a public speaker, like myself, never dares to mention in a mixed assembly the name of any great statesman, because the moment you do that, not only will his friends and supporters cheer him, which is an innocent and inoffensive amusement on their part, but a number of geese in the audience begin at once to hiss. Now, I say that a country in which that takes place is not yet civilized; that if a man cannot restrain his feelings so far as to abstain from insulting those with whom he does not happen to agree, the man is a savage; because, one of the fundamental distinctions between a savage and a civilized man is, that a civilized man is able to restrain himself. But every one who listens to me is aware that this miserable party spirit has been carried so far in this country that public speakers like myself are never able to quote prominent politicians even on issues that have nothing whatever to do with party politics, because we hear these offensive sounds. The truth is, political discussions have been carried on in this country hitherto so completely outside the pale of religion, and even of ordinary social restraints, that when men discuss politics they seem to give a free rein to their temper, and to take leave of their reason.

Now, this being to a very great extent the case, what ought we and I to do? Some one might say: "Take no part in politics at all." I have heard a great many persons say that. The great majority of my co-religionists said it when I was a boy; I do not think they say it now. But there are a great many people who do say it. Some excellent Christians said so to me last week, and I found they were strongly urging me to take no part in politics because they imagined that I did not agree with their political opinions, which is not a sufficient reason, in all cases, for abstention. I very much astonished them by saying that I had never taken part in party politics, that I had never voted, except for my university, and that I had never appeared upon a party political platform. But the difficulty of such excellent persons is, that they have never yet distinguished between politics and party politics. I, for my part, hold very strongly that, as a rule, Christian ministers would do well to abstain from taking an active part in party politics; but I am bound to say that, if politicians choose to discuss questions that have moral issues, I am not going to be gagged and muzzled. For I have a prior claim to be heard on everything that affects righteousness and character and morality.

But not referring to persons who, like myself, are Christian ministers, and who therefore occupy a somewhat exceptional position, and who are bound to remember that in their congregations they have every variety of political opinion—what is the course under these painful circumstances which ordinary Christians ought to take? The hasty and superficial reply of many, as I have already said, is this: As people cannot discuss politics without losing their tempers, as so much mud is flung about, as it is so disturbing to the serene spirit of the devout man—take no part in politics whatever. There are several objections to that; but, perhaps, one that I may name will suffice—*it is advice that it is impossible to take,* for, as I have already explained, everybody must be a politician if he happens to live in a country like this. If he takes himself off with his wife and children to a solitary island, perhaps he may live without being, in the strict sense of the word, a politician; but the moment he employs a servant politics enters, for his relation to the person whom he employs has to be determined. It is very difficult, therefore, even in a very thinly populated island, to avoid being a politician; but it is absolutely impossible in England, and it is all nonsense to talk about it. It only indicates a man's ignorance, that he should suppose it is possible for him to abstain from being a politician. I quite admit, as I have already said, that he may abstain in the sense of neglecting his political duty, and allowing the country to go to the devil as far as he is concerned, but that is not the sort of example a Christian minister can commend, or that would have any commendation whatever in the Bible. So far as men abstain from discharging their political duties, because that discharge involves annoyance, or perhaps loss in business, or introduces some painful element into life, they are cowards. They are treacherous to Jesus Christ, they are deserting the post of duty; and, so far as they are concerned, they are handing over all the resources of civilization to the devil, to which I, personally, strongly object. I have fully admitted that political activity is liable to abuse, but all good things are liable to abuse, and the better they are the more liable are they to abuse; but the fact that this peril exists should not reduce us to political impotence, but should set us on our guard, and teach us to set our neighbors a better example. Free and just political institutions are absolutely essential to the progress and development both of the individual and of the race.

I know there are some persons—they must be very ill-informed, and they must be absolutely ignorant of history—who cherish the delusion that personal happiness and the interests of religion are not dependent in any sense upon political institutions. This is the exact opposite of the truth. I appeal to the whole course of human history from its dawn. The great outburst of ancient thought and art in Greece took place among the free citizens of Athens, and not among the military slaves of Sparta. It was just the same in the Middle Ages. It is just the same in Modern Europe to-day. It is a lesson drawn from the history of all ages, that Literature, Art, Science, as well as Religion, always follow the fortunes, and flourish under the flag, of political freedom. It is, therefore, a part of our high duty to God and man to use all our influence in every direction to establish and to extend political freedom, and just political institutions. It is a matter of life and death to everybody who loves God and his neighbor to do his duty in this direction. Yes, you say, that may be all right, it is quite evident to any one who takes an intelligent and scriptural sense of the scope of human duty that it is impossible for us to neglect our political duty without neglecting both our duty to God and man, but what of party politics? That is no duty.

It is an old saying among thinkers that every man who is born into this world is naturally either a follower of Plato or a follower of Aristotle; and we might say with respect to life that everybody is naturally a Conservative or a Liberal, and that there must always therefore be, in some form or other, and with some name or other, these two great tendencies of the human mind expressing themselves in two great organizations. The Conservative is predominantly anxious to conserve existing good, and he is very sensitively alive to the perils of change. On the other hand the Liberal is predominantly anxious to realize further improvement, and he is so conscious of that that he gladly runs the risk of any peril that improvement may involve. But whatever view we may take of political opinion, when we think over the matter calmly we must admit that there is no justification whatever for the violent language which politicians are too apt to use with respect to their opponents. Probably the best excuse for it is that really they do not believe it themselves, and use it simply in a Pickwickian sense. When politicians address great gatherings of their own adherents, they seem to think it is necessary to put all that pepper, mustard, and vinegar into their speech so as to keep the meeting lively, and if it is quite understood that it means nothing I do not know that it does very much harm. But at any rate this is certain—looking at this important phase of human life, especially on the eve of the General Election—that every Christian is bound, if he is a real Christian, to keep his temper when he discusses politics, and that any Chris-

tian who loses his temper ought to be excommunicated until he publicly repents. I say that he is not only not a Christian but he is not a civilized man, and has no pretense whatever to elementary civilization. We have been far too tolerant of the naughty tempers of people when they discuss politics, and we must insist upon the introduction of politeness and courtesy into public life. The Speaker of the House of Commons insists upon it there, where no doubt his influence is very much needed in that direction. I think that the chairman of a public meeting ought to have a similar power of restraining the impetuosity of ardent advocates. Unless there is some very exceptional occasion we ought to admit that those who differ from us are, as a rule, quite as honest as we are, that their ideal is a lofty one, even if we prefer our own; and that, as a matter of fact, there is no political party which has the absolute monopoly of Right and Truth, and that it would not really be to the permanent advantage of the British Empire that either of the two great political parties should disappear.

I think, further, that we are fully agreed that every intelligent Christian ought to take a keen and active interest in politics, and if any one doubts that, I need simply utter the words ",United States." Let any one go to the United States of America, as I did last year; let him consider the awful state of New York; let him consult intelligent men in any part of the States with respect to the condition of public affairs, and he will find a general consensus of opinion among the upright citizens of America that politics there have become so unscrupulous and so mercenary and so dirty that good men cannot afford to touch them. To that, of course, my answer was: " Your good men are the cause; for if you had been touching them they would never have been found in the position in which they are to-day."

What is it that has saved this old country, with all its corruption and with all its tendency to these abuses, from sinking so low? One has said, " Monarchy." I do not wish to discuss that question now, but I am afraid that the mere existence of monarchy in itself is not sufficient without the co-operation of all good citizens to secure the objects which are desired. I should like to remind my friend, without in the least degree disputing the immense importance of monarchy in this country—which I never have done—that there are some monarchical countries in this world that are even more degraded than the United States; and that, as a matter of fact, the most degraded countries in the world at this moment are monarchical. I might also say that in some respects the Monarchy in this country is not so powerful as the Presidency is in America, so long as it lasts. But this is rather taking us off the logical line of thought. By all means, at the right time, let us advocate the immense importance of monarchy; but I am sure of this, that whether you happen to call the Constitution of your country Monarchical or Republican—and the difference is very often more verbal than real—whatever be its title, it is impossible to maintain the purity of public life, and to prevent bribery and corruption and the utmost degradation of the State unless every individual citizen discharges his duty as constantly and honestly as I am proud to think Queen Victoria has during her public life. For my own part, I confess that I am very anxious in all possible ways to secure the co-operation of good women as well as of good men in the public service of my country.

It is very astonishing that so many people talk so much about politics without having ever studied them and without knowing anything about them. I am afraid the majority of the free and independent electors of this country really do not know much about politics. I think if you pursue your inquiries in the cities, as well as in the villages, you will find that there are a great many persons who vote who really know nothing at all about politics. It is a very serious thing when we consider that the great interests of the British Empire, and through the British Empire of the human race, are very largely dependent upon the votes of persons who have never taken the least trouble to understand either the history of their country or the meaning of political terms.

Politics is the only serious subject that men think themselves qualified to act upon without any previous education or instruction whatever. If it happened to be astronomy, or botany, or medicine, or law, he would never be allowed to work in any of these arts, or to take a decisive part in the history of any one of these sciences without having, at least, acquired the A B C of it; but the awful fact of politics is that we do not take the trouble seriously to understand the political situation. I am afraid most men who even try to acquire some information from the newspapers —a very ambiguous source of information— constantly read those with which they agree instead of those with which they differ. I confess it gives me no pleasure to read those with which I agree; I spend all my time in reading the papers with which I do not agree. It is not always very pleasant reading, but I am sure it is more profitable than merely hearing my own views echoed.

Now, I do implore those who are listening to me to realize the gravity of all these questions. There is nothing that you do in all your life for which you are more accountable to God, or which is more serious, than the vote which many of you are going to give at the approaching General Election (1892). I dare say you have already made up your mind which party you are going to vote for, but I confess I have some suspicion that, even in an unusually intelligent audience like this, if I brought some of you up to this platform and elicited from you for whom you were going to vote, and then were permitted to cross-examine you as to why you were going to give that vote, the answers which you would give would not satisfy yourselves or the audience. It is a very serious matter. You may have time, even now, before the General Election, to acquire a more intelligent knowledge of the questions which will be submitted to the people of this country when that grave event takes place.

Let me say, in conclusion, that I hope we shall all learn two lessons—deeply religious lessons, from one of the greatest political thinkers of our race—Edmund Burke. One is this, that party politics are inevitable, that we must tolerate the existence of two great parties in the State, which from time to time will hold office under the Crown; and, therefore, our business is to try and narrow the area of controversy and to cultivate to the utmost extent mutual confidence and mutual good will.

And, secondly, let those of us who feel most keenly and most deeply on these questions—as the best Christians and those who have most of the mind of Christ must feel—remember the great saying of Edmund Burke: " Compromise is the soul of politics." As the human race is inevitably divided into two great parties, as we cannot help looking at different sides of the shield, as the very constitution of our minds compel us to take somewhat divergent standpoints—it is perfectly ridiculous for any man to expect that he is going to have all his own way, or that the party to which he belongs must triumph all along the line, and must carry out its policy absolutely. The real progress of this country, and the absence hitherto of the bitter strife which has desolated families and churches, has been due to a sort of saving common sense which has characterized the British people, and especially the English people, which has led those who are most opposed to certain changes to accept them and to have done with them when they have become inevitable; and which has led the reformers to realize that they must consult the convictions of others as well as their own, and that the honorable solution of all controversy is some reasonable compromise.

I have already referred to the splendid and imperishable services which the Queen has rendered to this country from time to time, but of all her great services I think that none was greater, more courageous, or more sagacious than the course which she took on a certain occasion, when there seemed to be a possibility of a deadlock between the two Houses of Parliament, and some bitter and disastrous strife, in relation to the last extension of the franchise, when she used her immense influence to compel all political parties to come together, and by an honorable compromise to accept that Extension of the Franchise and Redistribution of Seats under which we now live. The Queen herself used her great influence on that occasion to bring the controversy to an end and to secure a peaceful solution. And I cannot but think, with respect to other bitter controversies, about which opinion is inevitably divided, that the Queen herself could occupy no nobler or more patriotic position than that of a peacemaker, and of one who will compel politicians of all parties to avoid the falsehood of extremes.—H. R.

WHAT CAN THE MINISTRY DO TO PURIFY OUR POLITICS?

BY HOWARD CROSBY, D.D.

There is an idea common to the worldly mind, as shown in the newspaper press, that the Church is a sort of police arrangement to busy itself with poverty and crime, and provide for every form of distress. Some Christians who are readily led by the newspapers, are foolish enough to foster this idea. It is this notion put into operation that made the Church of the early centuries grow into a political power of gigantic magnitude, by which transmutation it became fearfully corrupt and cruelly tyrannical. The Church, as Christ made it, is a spiritual body designed to preserve and nourish its own spirituality, and to convert unbelievers to the Savior. Its high province is to hold and hold forth the truth of God in Christ. As true believers in Christ are generally despised and oppressed by the world, the Church is to look after *its* own poor and needy ones, and to make due provision for their wants. This is all the relation that the Church, as an organization, bears to the poor.

But the doctrines of Christ are doctrines of love and helpfulness toward all men, and hence the individual Christian is to seek every man's good. To this end, he can and ought to unite with others in benevolent enterprises, and show practical kindness to every form of need. But the Church organization has nothing to do with this. If, as an organization, it takes hold of public affairs outside of its own limits, it inevitably loses its spirituality in secular work, and as invariably becomes a political party, either to be crushed or to become a tyrant. Pastors, elders, deacons, church councils, presbyteries, synods, and all other church governments, must confine themselves to their own spiritual fields, if they would remain pure and true to Christ. It looks very pious for a Church to run itself out into committees and meetings for the poor. And the public will applaud, but a church which spends its strength in that way will have very little spiritual life. It will reduce the Gospel standard of piety, which demands a holy life, to the care of the poor, which the Church can attend to at the same time that it upholds theaters and fashionable follies. Why are we to have the world tell us what piety is? A true piety is in the communion of the soul with God, and the religion that flows from such piety will necessarily visit the widow and the fatherless. But if visiting the widow and the fatherless (or rather having them visited by paid agents) is made the core of piety, then communion with God will be neglected, and the man will not keep himself unspotted from the world.

There is an enormous amount of error afloat on this subject, simply because Christians go to the world to know how they ought to live, when they should go only to God's word, where they will find that the soul's relation to God is the first and main thing, and that the Church is the spiritual household of faith, the fruits of which faith, in doing good to every one as we have opportunity, are to be seen in the Christian individual life. But the doing of good to certain classes is not to be considered the main thing, nor is it to be a substitute for vital union with God, nor is it a *Church* duty in any way, but a *Christian* duty, in which Christians are free to act with any one in or out of the Church. I have given these thoughts as preliminary to answering the question at the head of this article, "What Can the Ministry Do to Purify our Politics?" In accordance with these thoughts, I reply:

1. *The ministry as such have nothing to do with politics.* They are ministers of the Church of Christ, not of the nation, nor of the world. The nation and the world have no more claim on them as ministers than they have on the presidents of banks or the head-masters of schools. Their function is to minister to God's people—if pastors, then to the special flock that each is called to tend. Before the nation and the world, the minister is simply a *man,* a Christian man, bound to use his influence as any other Christian (no less and no more) for the good of all. Putting the clergy (as they are falsely called) into the secular government as clergy, as the Papacy did wholly when it had a temporal kingdom, and as England does partially to-day with its lord-bishops in Parliament, is an enormity calculated to do evil, and only evil, both to Church and State. It is putting two things together that have totally different aims and totally different functions, and hence, friction, collision, and destruction are necessary consequences. The Church has as its aim the conversion of men to God and the upbuilding of God's people in their spiritual lives, and its function is to use the divine means to this end. The State has as its aim, the preservation of the persons and property of men in this world, and its function is to pass laws and enforce them that will achieve this object. The spheres of operation are dissimilar. There is a point of contact between them, it is true, but that point of contact is made by the *individual.* It is the individual Christian who can promote the preservation of persons and property by good laws. The Church has nothing to do with this. The individual Christian can do this, as a *man,* but the Church is not a man, but an aggregate of men in a spiritual capacity, having no earthly functions. Hence our proposition that the ministry as such have nothing to do with politics.

2. *The ministry can instruct their people*

in their duty to promote righteousness as individuals. A faithful setting forth of Christian duty at the polls, not to vote for this or that man, but to vote conscientiously as before God, and to make the use of the franchise a solemn duty to be prayerfully performed, is a part of the minister's function, when he is teaching his people how to live on earth as representatives of God's truth. If a minister goes beyond this, and, as a minister, advocates a special political course on which good men differ, or a special candidate, when there are several, he is using his spiritual position carnally and degrading the ministry. He may, as a man and citizen, when great causes are at stake, exercise his liberty and advocate the righteous cause and what he believes to be the righteous man, but he must keep this matter clear from his Church duties. He is not to drag the Church into his private views, however important and intense they may be. His pulpit is not for politics of any kind, nor is his pastoral work to propagate his political views. And because many will not discriminate between the man and the minister, he is to be careful in regard to his liberty as a man to advocate causes and men. He ought to do something in this way—it is his duty as a citizen, which he has no right to lay aside—but he must do it prudently, and ever with an eye to the preservation of the spiritual character of his office as a minister. It is a bad thing for a minister to be counted a politician. He makes a poor minister and a poor politician. A minister may be patriotic and public-spirited, and yet not compromise his holy office. He will never be a partisan while he urges his people to use their influence for purifying the politics of the State. He is in the world, and is to instruct his people as to their conduct in the world, and their relation to the State cannot rightfully escape his attention.

3. *The ministry can place clearly before their people any gross injustice or glaring wickedness in law or its administration, which calls for Christian action.* They can concentrate and systematize thought about it, so as to suggest a plan of activity, which merely a vague notion could not bring about. People generally are so immersed in their secular vocations that they only descry an evil and groan over it, but do not take time to examine its character and causes, and discern its cure. The minister accustomed to deal with such matters, and not having secular affairs to absorb him, can more readily digest the subject for his people and guide them to the activity of reform.

In this, again, the minister is to be careful lest he take up a doubtful cause. The case must be a clear one. It may be cruelty to children, or cruelty to animals, or the protection of evil houses, or the shielding of lawbreakers, or any matter regarding the right and wrong in which there cannot be a question. If the laws or the law officers plainly are guilty of these outrages, then it is also plainly the duty of the minister to speak plainly to his people about it that they may act plainly in the matter. A minister's common sense should tell him where the boundary line is here, beyond which he would be only a partisan and not a Christian minister. And if a minister has not common sense to discern this, the sooner he leaves the ministry the better.

I end, as I began, with an earnest protest against political preaching and political preachers. They mingle the Church and the world to the sad detriment of the Church, and without the slightest good to the world. Instead of leading the soul upward to the holy contemplation of Christ, they lead their hearers into the dust and turmoil of political factions, where the soul becomes smirched and loses its power to rise to heavenly contemplations. And I also protest against the flimsy newspaper doctrine which reduces religion to economics and makes the Church merely a benevolent society. Bringing the Church thus down to their level the glib writers presume to instruct it and to give it their approbation or condemnation, as the case may be.

Ministers and churches that listen to such nonsense and are moved by it disgrace themselves. What is the Church of Christ that it should go to the world for guidance? Has Christ, its Guide and Savior, abandoned it? Has the Holy Spirit, promised by Him, failed? Has the truth left the Church and taken up its residence in the editors of the journals that publish prize-fights and licentious advertisements? Away with this foul blot upon God's Church! As our Savior drove out from the holy precincts of the Temple the changers of money and those that bought and sold, so let us, in His holy name, drive out from the Church this carnalism that would secularize all holy things and would guide divine matters by the groveling expediencies of the selfish and greedy world. Let the ministry hold high and fast the standard of Christ's cross, which means pardon and renewal to every sinner that repents and trusts in His atoning sacrifice. Let this be the first and main work of the Christian ministry, and from this, as a source, let the life of both minister and people be fitted to discharge the personal duties which belong to them both as men and citizens. So will the ministry best work to purify our politics and to serve the State.—H. R.

SUGGESTIVE THOUGHTS

BALLOT-BOX, The Christian and the. —State and municipal elections call for the most strenuous efforts on the part of all true citizens to secure the success of those who truly represent the supreme interests of the people. Occasionally one among the many is able to make his political power felt most forcibly in some other function than that of a voter. So Dr. Parkhurst, as President of the Society for the Prevention of Crime; so, too, John W. Goff, in his conduct of the examination into the scandals of the metropolitan police force, before the Lexow Committee. But the average citizen impresses his individuality upon the state more strongly at the ballot-box than anywhere else.

" His individuality," we say. For the ballot-box is expressive not simply of choice, but of the character behind the choice. Ever over against it stands a balance in which is weighed the man who casts the ballot. To vote for a candidate known to be unworthy is to declare one's self unworthy to exercise the prerogative of the voter. To exalt the party and its interest above the city or state and its good, is to forfeit, morally, the right of franchise. Patriotism is a grace second only to godliness; but partisanship may be a disgrace second only to devilishness. Especially true is this, if a given party supports in its platform a plank that gives encouragement to immorality, or countenances in its policy any form of public evil. The dictum of a well-known ex-United States Senator that the Decalog and the Golden Rule have no place in politics was answered a few years ago with his retirement. His constituents doubtless felt that such an assertion was too much of the nature of a self-arraignment. The men needed for all our offices are men to whom righteousness, temperance, and judgment are obligations which they feel called upon to fulfil—not men who, like Felix, tremble, self-convicted, when these are urged upon them. A candidate for office should be as white in principle and in practise as his title indicates or suggests that he is.—H. R.

ELECTION DAY.—The Men for Office. " Look even out the best and meetest of your master's sons, and set him on his father's throne, and fight for your master's house.—2 Kings x: 3.

Wanted, a Man. " I defy the armies of Israel this day: give me a man, that we may fight together."—I Sam. xvii: 10.

Bossism *vs.* Conscientiousness. " No man can serve two masters: for either he will hate the one and love the other; or else he will hold to the one and despise the other."—Matt. vi: 24.—H. R.

OFFICE, Disappointed Seeker of.—Pædaretus, when he was not chosen among the three hundred (which was the highest office and honor in the city), went away cheerfully and smiling, saying he was glad if the city had three hundred better citizens than himself.—PLUTARCH.

OFFICE, Love of.—Profligacy in taking office is so extreme, that we have no doubt public men may be found. who for half a century would postpone all remedies for a pestilence, if the preservation of their places depended upon the propagation of the virus. —S. SMITH.

OFFICE-SEEKERS, Hungry.—A fox, while crossing a river, was driven by the stream into a narrow gorge, and lay there for a long time, unable to get out, covered with myriads of horse-flies that had fastened themselves upon him. A hedgehog, who was wandering in that direction, saw him; and, taking compassion on him, asked him if he should drive away the flies that were so tormenting him. But the fox begged him to do nothing of the sort. " Why not? " asked the hedgehog. " Because," replied the fox, " these flies that are upon me now, are already full, and draw but little blood, but should you remove them, a swarm of fresh and hungry ones will come, who will not leave a drop of blood in my body."—F. II.

POLITICAL AGITATION.—All hail, Public Opinion! To be sure, it is a dangerous thing under which to live. It rules to-day in the desire to obey all kinds of laws, and takes your life. It rules again in the love of liberty, and rescues Shadrach from Boston Court House. It rules to-morrow in the manhood of him who loads the musket to shoot down—God be praised!—the man-hunter Gorsuch. It rules in Syracuse, and the slave escapes to Canada. It is our interest to educate this people in humanity, and in deep reverence for the rights of the lowest and humblest individual that makes up our numbers. Each man here, in fact, holds his property and his life dependent on the constant presence of an agitation like this of anti-slavery. Eternal vigilance is the price of liberty: power is ever stealing from the many to the few. The manna of popular liberty must be gathered each day, or it is rotten. The living sap of to-day outgrows the dead rind of yesterday. The hand intrusted with power, becomes either from human depravity or *esprit de corps*, the necessary enemy of the people. Only by continual oversight can the democrat in office be prevented from hardening into a despot; only by unintermitted agitation can a people be kept sufficiently awake to principle not to let liberty be smothered in material prosperity.

All clouds, it is said, have sunshine behind them, and all evils have some good result; so slavery, by the necessity of its abolition, has saved the freedom of the white race from being melted in the luxury or buried beneath the gold of its own success. Never look, therefore, for an age when the people can be quiet and safe. At such times Despotism, like a shrouding mist, steals over the mirror of Freedom. The Dutch, a thousand years ago, built against the ocean their bulwarks of willow and mud. Do they trust to that? No. Each year the patient, industrious peasant gives so much time from the cultivation of his soil and the care of his children to stop the breaks and replace the willow which insects have eaten, that he may keep the land his fathers rescued from the water, and bid defiance to the waves that roar above his head, as if demanding back the broad fields man has stolen from their realm.—WENDELL PHILLIPS.

POLITICAL IDEAS.—Political parties are based upon ideas. They are the organized expression of public thought.

The size of the idea determines the size of the party. Local interests may be inflated into a national importance, but a reaction is sure to follow. A part can never be made to equal the whole.

When the idea and its representative separate, then loyalty to a party becomes loyalty to a name. The living tenant has moved out and nothing remains but an empty house. Bigotry is adverse to motion. It seldom leads and never follows. The result is the political bigot sits on the door step and doesn't know the house is empty.

There is no real reform that does not touch and transform the internal idea. Every mob has its mission. It may be chaotic and lost sight of, but a central dominant idea exists somewhere. The mob may be dispersed, but until the idea is met and satisfied the difficulty still remains. The execution of John Brown was one thing, but to halt the march of his soul quite another. The politics of Heaven are ideal. They are not dependent upon men or methods. Men die and methods change, but Right is a perpetual nominee. Defeated and beaten, it arises out of its grave and claims recognition. The campaigns of God are not ended at sunset. They go on and on and on, into the most distant generations. The issues that were raised under Abraham, Saul, Herod, Charles or George appear in the reign of Victoria. Right is the heir to every crown, and until its claims are recognized the throne is vacant.

Under God's government the judges stood for justice, but the people clamored for might, so the Lord gave them a king. From that day until this the king has been a political necessity. But his hereditary right was disputed from the first. The sons of Saul became subjects. Revolutions are the birth throes of republics and to that end has ever been the trend of history. Few nations have reached that degree of moral fitness by which this is possible. And here comes in the recognition of that eternal something we call Right. Our Revolutionary fathers, with all their worth, failed to realize its importance. They fought for the equality of man, and at the same time made color the test of manhood. It was an injustice to the black man and still more so to the white. That wrong has been the whip with which God has scourged the back of this Republic. War decides nothing beyond the relative strength of the contestants. It gained the black man his liberty and then forced upon him privileges for which he had no preparation. No one can vote for another; that question must be decided by the voter himself. The black man must be lifted up to the ballot box, else the country has still an account to settle with God.—*Selected.*

POETRY

The Ballot

By William G. Haeselbarth

As noiseless fall those printed slips
As fall the silent dews of night,
Yet never words from human lips
Had greater majesty and might.
They are the fiat and the will
Of patriots who love their land,
Who aim their duty to fulfil,
And on that firmly take their stand.

Millions on millions through the land
Fall noiseless as the rain and snow,
A puff of wind may from the hand
Release and whirl it to and fro.
Administrations rise and fall,
And parties rise or cease to be,
Obedient to the ballot's call,
The weapon of a people free.

Over the noisy, wordy war
And jangle of opposing views,
The ballot falls—a word and law
That none may question or refuse.
More powerful far than shot or shell,
Because no wounds are left to heal,
Each one can feel that all is well,
And safe and well the Commonweal.

Long may a ballot pure proclaim
The Nation's righteous, sovereign will,
Their highest thought and loftiest aim
Their own high mission to fulfil.
Thus shall the ballot prove a guide
To point the way that should be trod,
And prove to them no less, beside,
The people's voice the voice of God.
C. W.

An Eclectic

By James Russell Lowell

I'm an eclectic; ez to choosin'
T'wixt this an' thet, I'm plaguy lawth;
I leave a side thet looks like losin',
But (wile there's doubt) I stick to both;
I stan' upon the Constitution,
Ez preudunt statesmen say, who've planned
A way to git the most profusion
O' chances ez to ware they'll stand.

God Will Weigh the Votes

By Joel Swartz

Men may count but God will weigh
Votes cast on election day;
'Mid the voters He will stand,
With a winnow in His hand,

And will purge the threshing floor
Of the Land from shore to shore,
And will garner every grain
Which the voters' chests contain;
But the chaff, in righteous ire,
Will consume with flaming fire.

U. S.

What Mr. Robinson Thinks

BY JAMES RUSSELL LOWELL

Guvener B. is a sensible man;
  He stays to his home and looks arter his
  folks;
He draws his furrer ez straight ez he can,
  An' into nobody's tater patch pokes;
    But John P.
    Robinson he
Sez he wunt vote for Guvener B.

My! ain't it terrible! Wut shall we du?
  We can't never choose him o' course—
  thet's flat;
Guess we shall hev to come round, (don't
  you?)
  An' go in fer thunder an' guns, an' all
  that;
    Fer John P.
    Robinson he
Sez he wunt vote for Guvener B.

Gineral C. is a dreffle smart man;
  He's ben on all sides thet give places or
  pelf;
But consistency still was a part of his plan;
  He's ben true to one party,—an' thet is
  himself;—
    So John P.
    Robinson he
Sez he shall vote fer Gineral C.

Gineral C. he goes in fer the war;
  He don't vally principle more'n an old cud;
Wut did God make us raytional creetur's fer,
  But glory an' gunpowder, plunder an'
  blood?
    So John P.
    Robinson he
Sez he shall vote fer Gineral C.

We were gittin' on nicely up here to our village,
  With good old idees o' wut's right an' wut
  ain't,

We kind o' thought Christ went agin war an'
  pillage
  An' thet eppyletts wornt the best mark of a
  saint;
    But John P.
    Robinson he
Sez this kind o' thing's an exploded idee.

The side of our country must ollers be took
  An' President Polk, you know, he is our
  country.
An' the angel thet writes all our sins in a
  book,
  Puts the debit to him, an' to us the per con-
  try;
    An' John P.
    Robinson he
Sez this is his view o' the thing to a T.

Parson Wilbur he calls all these argiments
  lies;
  Sez they're nothin' on airth but jest fee, faw,
  fum:
An' thet all this big talk of our destinies
  Is half on it ign'ance, an' t'other half rum;
    But John P.
    Robinson he
Sez it ain't no sech thing; an' of course, so
  must we.

Parson Wilbur sez *he* never heerd in his life
  Thet th' apostles rigged out in their swal-
  ler-tail coats,
An' marched round in front of a drum an' a
  fife,
  To git some on 'em office, an' some on 'em
  votes;
    But John P.
    Robinson he
Sez they didn't know everythin' down in
  Judee.

Wal, it's a marcy we've got folks to tell us
  The rights an' the wrongs o' these matters,
  I vow,—
God sends country lawyers, an' other wise
  fellers
  To start the world's team wen it gits in a
  slough;
    Fer John P.
    Robinson he
Sez, the world'll go right, ef he hollers out,
  Gee!

FOREFATHERS' DAY

(December 21)

AMONG the sentiments which appeal most profoundly to men and which operate most powerfully upon their characters, we find the impulse to revere and honor their forefathers. With it we find coupled the love of posterity, and the two together exercise a potent influence on nations as well as individuals. That chieftain of the ancient Britons who endeavored to rally his followers for one more struggle against the Roman invader struck a responsive chord in the hearts of those barbarians when he cried aloud to them, " Think of your forefathers and of your posterity! "

Affectionate reverence for ancestors appeals in greater or less measure to all nations, but to the American people the veneration of our forefathers must appeal with peculiar power. The nations of Europe in attempting to trace their ancestry must follow the line back into a maze of tradition and myths. The oriental nations, while perhaps their history extends farther back into antiquity, must still, with the exception of the Jewish nation, lose their beginnings in vague legends and stories. The American nation, on the other hand, had a distinct and authenticated beginning, and the American who honors his forefathers looks back to men who in reality, not in myths, stood for those qualities and principles which have made the American people; and, therefore, there is every reason why the celebration of Forefathers' Day should meet a response in the heart of every loyal citizen of our country.

The day itself, December 21, celebrates particularly the landing of the Puritan Pilgrims at Plymouth, Mass., December 21, 1620, and was at first brought into prominence in New England and in the Congregational churches throughout the country. While it is in no state a legal holiday, Forefathers' Day is, nevertheless, loved and revered in many states of the Union, and the event which it commemorates is lauded and memorialized in schools, in public meetings, and at banquets and other functions both private and public.

But Forefathers' Day has a broader and deeper significance than simply the commemoration of the landing of the Pilgrims at Plymouth. It calls upon the American people to honor these men, truly, but with them all those first settlers of our land who were actuated by the same noble motives, and in whose hearts thrilled the same love of freedom and hatred of oppression. Forefathers' Day in its broadest acceptance glorifies the memory of the Puritans from England, the Beggars from Holland, the Huguenots from France, the Covenanters from Scotland, the Scotch-Irish from Ireland, and any other people from any other nations, who, from noble and exalted motives, abandoned their native lands and devoted their lives to the founding and continuance of America upon those principles which should enable her to become the home of political and religious liberty, a Nation whose God is the Lord, and whose people rejoice in that chiefest among national and individual blessings, a God-given freedom.

HISTORICAL

THE PILGRIMS

By John G. Whittier

A worthy New England deacon once described a brother in the church as a very good man Godward, but rather hard manward. It cannot be denied that some very satisfactory steps have been taken in the latter direction, at least, since the days of the Pilgrims. Our age is tolerant of creed and dogma, broader in its sympathies, more keenly sensitive to temporal need, and practically recognizing the brotherhood of the race; wherever a cry of suffering is heard its response is quick and generous. It has abolished slavery, and is lifting woman from world-old degradation to equality with man before the law. Our criminal codes no longer embody the maxim of barbarism, "An eye for an eye, and a tooth for a tooth," but have regard not only for the safety of the community, but to the reform and well-being of the criminal. All the more, however, for this amiable tenderness do we need the counterpoise of a strong sense of justice. With our sympathy for the wrong-doer we need the old Puritan and Quaker hatred of wrongdoing; with our just tolerance of men and opinions a righteous abhorrence of sin. All the more for the sweet humanities and Christian liberalism which, in drawing men nearer to each other, are increasing the sum of social influences for good or evil, we need the bracing atmosphere, healthful, if austere, of the old moralities. Individual and social duties are quite as imperative now as when they were minutely specified in statute-books and enforced by penalties no longer admissible. It is well that stocks, whipping-post, and ducking-stool are now only matters of tradition; but the honest reprobation of vice and crime which they symbolized should by no means perish with them. The true life of a nation is in its personal morality, and no excellence of constitution and laws can avail much if the people lack purity and integrity. Culture, art, refinement, care for our own comfort and that of others, are all well; but

truth, honor, reverence, and fidelity to duty are indispensable.

The Pilgrims were right in affirming the paramount authority of the law of God. If they erred in seeking that authoritative law, and passed over the Sermon on the Mount for the stern Hebraisms of Moses; if they hesitated in view of the largeness of Christian liberty; if they seemed unwilling to accept the sweetness and light of the good tidings,—let us not forget that it was the mistake of men who feared more than they dared to hope, whose estimate of the exceeding awfulness of sin caused them to dwell upon God's vengeance rather than His compassion; and whose dread of evil was so great that, in shutting their hearts against it, they sometimes shut out the good. It is well for us if we have learned to listen to the sweet persuasion of the Beatitudes; but there are crises in all lives which require also the emphatic "Thou shalt not" of the Decalog which the founders wrote on the gate-posts of their commonwealth.

Let us, then, be thankful for the assurances which the last few years have afforded us that

"The Pilgrim spirit is not dead,
But walks in noon's broad light."

We have seen it in the faith and trust which no circumstances could shake, in heroic self-sacrifice, in entire consecration to duty. The fathers have lived in their sons. Have we not all known the Winthrops and Brewsters, the Saltonstalls and Sewalls, of old times, in gubernatorial chairs, in legislative halls, around winter camp-fires, in the slow martyrdoms of prison and hospital? The great struggle through which we have passed has taught us how much we owe to the men and women of the Plymouth Colony,—the noblest ancestry that ever a people looked back to with love and reverence. Honor, then, to the Pilgrims! Let their memory be green forever!—*Selected.*

SALEM'S BONFIRES

By Rev. James L. Hill, D.D.

Come to Salem, all of you who lament the absence of great gatherings with noise and music and banners on Independence Day, and who believe that pure, clean patriotism is no longer powerful enough to give us the ardent celebrations which were once the joy and glory of our Nation's natal morning. Just as the clock is striking twelve, thus add-

ing another year to the era of American Independence, your eyes will be drawn irresistibly to a towering monument of hogsheads and barrels and casks that raises its huge form one hundred and thirty-five feet high, and bulks against the midnight sky. This topgallant monticle is stacked as symmetrically as a church steeple.

At the impressive moment, by means of a wire tackle, a bundle of cotton waste saturated with oil is raised to the turret, ignited, and thus a crown of flame is laid upon the beetling pile. The high pyramid usually burns evenly all round, and stands persistently up until it is at least two-thirds gone. Hear the great wave of indistinct "Oh's" and "Ah's" which seem to issue unbidden from the surging sea of faces, that, lighted up by the fountain of fire, suggest the imposing audiences in the vast amphitheater of ancient Rome. Salem sits in the bottom of the saucer, nearly environed by communities that come in throngs, bringing whole stores of noise-producers which are not seen until they are heard. Horses cannot seem to understand the Fourth of July. Steam-cars and trolley-cars assemble the people to the number of twenty thousand.

Two rival demonstrations excite their wonder and admiration. The Gallows Hill Bonfire Association lights its exalted beacon on an historic eminence where nineteen victims of the witchcraft delusion were hung. The Broad Street Social Club stacks its twenty-four tiers of oily barrels on Lookout, which is nearer the city. The small boys have their miniature pillars of flame, which by common consent, as boys are impatient, are earliest ignited, and in the light of whose glittering splendor the mastodons whose doom is imminent stand forth in their amazing proportions.

These incinerations, one of them having been lighted by the same hand for a quarter of a century, have so taken hold of the public mind that the youngsters about Collins Cave, near Fort Avenue, love to build a raft, pile it high with barrels, and let the gorgeous spectacle float out into the open water. These blazing summits, engaging in responsive service and announcing widely that the night has turned into the morning of a new year of liberty, are vivid reminders of those beacon-fires once lighted on Olivet to announce to the scattered Jews the exact moment of the rising of the paschal moon, which were instantly answered by lights on mountains more remote, these flames being thus projected, a line of fiery telegraphs, until they were mirrored in the waters of the Euphrates, where the children of the Hebrews wept as they remembered Zion. Hawthorne was born in Salem on the Fourth of July. That victory over the Spanish fleet announced to the American people on our Independence Day (1898) caused every star in our banner to flash anew with liberty. The vestal

fires of truest patriotism burn with perennial purity upon our American altars. Two days before our anniversary was inaugurated, July 2, 1776, John Adams in writing to his wife about an appropriate celebration suggested "bells, bonfires, and illuminations." Salem rises to his suggestion. The substratum of sound is of cow-bells, any bells, while the general din is punctuated by pistol-shots, cannon, and those huge crackers loaded with dynamite that give an ear-splitting detonation. Brass bands are employed to entertain the multitude until time for the pageant, and as much of the music as can be heard is excellent.

John Adams in his next specification must have held Salem in prophecy. Eight thousand barrels burning in one shaft, and throwing a flame higher than Bunker Hill Monument, illuminating the heavens for miles around, would have gratified the heart of the old man eloquent. Nothing surpasses or equals Salem's bonfires in New England, and probably not in the world. Preparations begin weeks in advance. Guards are stationed to keep away fun-loving boys who might be playing with matches on the day before the Fourth. Four thousand barrels have been bought in one lot for the great event, besides thirty-eight greasy hogsheads to stand at the base and hold combustible material.

The cylinder at the top is painted in the national colors. Previous to the fire Old Glory waves from the summit. Thus decorated, the colossus looms up at night like a ship in a fog. The stars that may have hid their faces at certain scenes enacted upon these promontories designed by nature for these peaceful displays, look kindly down upon young America, full of the fresh feeling of life when one must run up steep places. Time and money—one hundred dollars is appropriated by the city—are better spent in celebrating the birth of freedom than in the synagogs of Satan.

Like a magnificent building after an earthquake, nothing but a pile of débris is soon left to tell the story of the labors of many hours during summer evenings and holidays. In about an hour the crowd usually feels itself in the wrong place, and then comes an *exeunt omnes*. None need to be rocked to sleep when they have sought their beds.

Patriotism grows by its expression. Like religion it must have utterance. It is not enough to feel patriotic; for, if the sentiment never manifests itself, even its existence is held upon a very uncertain tenure. —C. E. W.

IN PILGRIM PLYMOUTH

By Priscilla Leonard

Practically, one goes to Plymouth by train from Boston, and lands in the side streets of the modern town. But historically one must land at Plymouth Rock. It may be that

Mary Chilton did not step first upon it, but it is the beginning of New England history none the less. It may also be that the Pilgrim Fathers themselves did not first land there, but anchored the *Mayflower* for a month instead in the harbor of what is now

Plymouth Rock Provincetown. Cape Cod, while they explored the coast for a suitable place to settle. These are shocks to the lover of tradition, but they do not hinder the fact that Forefathers' Rock is a foundation stone of American liberty. It is also something of a shock to find that Plymouth Rock is very small and retiring in appearance. It is the only bit of stone, apparently, for miles round. Far out on the outer face of Manomet, south of the entrance to the harbor, the " breaking waves " may occasionally " dash high " against the rocks, but everywhere else the beach is a low, long, level stretch of yellow-gray sand, and the wide, shallow bay is as pretty and peaceful as possible. Still, tho the coast was not rock-bound, it must have been freezingly cold and bleak when the " band of exiles " moored their bark " there ; and, indeed, we are told that the first exploring party was nearly frozen on Clark's Island ; so that the faith and courage of the Pilgrims was quite enough tried.

Plymouth Rock, by the way, would be exceedingly difficult to land upon nowadays, because it is quite a distance from the water. It is the real historic rock, however, and the sea must have lapped its sides in those long-ago days, because Elder Thomas Faunce, of Duxbury, in 1741 (being then a man of ninety-five), was brought thither in an arm-chair, and sitting upon the Rock,

Its History made public declaration that when a boy he had been frequently told by the Pilgrims themselves, and by his father, who came over in 1623, that a landing was made upon this identical stone. " The aged elder then took his last look at the spot so endeared to his memory, and bedewing it with tears, bade it farewell." That must have been one of the most dramatic scenes the Rock has witnessed. However, part of it has had rather an adventurous career ; for in 1774 the top was split off and drawn to the Town Hall by twenty yoke of oxen, to be used as the pedestal of a liberty pole, whose flag bore the patriotic motto, " Liberty or Death." Here the Pilgrim relic remained until 1834, when, on the Fourth of July, it was removed, accompanied by a formal procession, to the front of Pilgrim Hall. Meanwhile the rest of the Rock was preserved on the original site, surrounded by a stone pavement. In 1859 the present canopy over it was built. It took eight years to complete this, which is one of the homeliest structures ever designed by mortal man. In 1880 the vagrant top was restored to its place and firmly cemented there, to roam no more. Anyone can now go into the little kiosk, and sit on the sacred stone, or step on it, as preferred. Most people sit on it, for sight-seeing is weary work. But if one wants to see all Plymouth, the rest here must be only a momentary one, for there is no time to spare.

The proper place to begin in Plymouth, historically, is, as has been said, the Rock.

The best spot, geographically, is the hill from which the National Monument to the Forefathers overlooks town and harbor. From a broad, open space the great granite pile rises, surmounted by the massive statue of Faith, one hand holding a Bible, the other pointing upward to Heaven. On the four corners of the pedestal are emblematic figures of Morality, Law, Education, and Freedom. From its foot, looking down over the tree-shaded, rambling, irregular streets below, one soon gets the bearings of Plymouth, and can trace the old town lying within its four streets, with Burial Hill as its fortress site. Below, nearer the Rock on the shore, is Cole's Hill, where the dead were buried in that terrible " first sickness " and where corn was planted next season to hide the graves from the Indians, so that they might not know how reduced the little colony had become. The " labors, sacrifices, and sufferings " of the Pilgrim band, commemorated in the inscription on the monument, seem very real as we look down at the spot where they struggled so bravely for God and liberty against many foes in an inhospitable land.

Going down from the monument hill one can ramble round the older part of Plymouth at leisure, finding something of interest at every step. Here is the " town brooke," into which the " many delicate springs " still run—a favorite spot for artists. Here is Leyden Street, the

Leyden Street first one laid out by the Pilgrims who built here their " common house " where all could rendezvous while the work was going on, and then proceeded to " measure out " the grounds ; and " first wee tooke notise how many families there were, willing all single men that hadde no wives to join with some family as they thought fitte, soe that wee might build fewer houses ; which was done, and wee reduced them to nineteen families. To greater families wee allotted larger plots ; to every person half a pole in breadth and three in length, and soe lots were cast where every man should lie ; which was done and staked out," and thus Leyden Street was built, running up from the water's edge to the fort and watchtower on Burial Hill. Where Main Street now crosses it stood Governor Bradford's house, with four guns mounted, " so as to flank along the streets."

But the governor's house has long ago vanished, and so have fort and watchhouse. The wide outlook from the watchhouse over town and sea made it valuable to the tiny garrison. Its brick foundation is still there, about a foot below the surface, and the very hearthstone on which the Pilgrims built their watch-fires lies on the southern side, where they placed it more than two centuries and a half ago. To-day, when all America is the home of religion and civilization, it is hard to realize the splendid courage necessary to this group of pioneers, who met the unknown forces of a continent without fear, trusting in God with a deep and victorious faith, willing to die in the wilderness rather than surrender a pure worship of Him. The sea was behind them, the trackless woods in front; they stood alone against a mighty and mysterious land of savagery, and yet they were not dismayed. Here, on Burial Hill, in their rude fort, they held their worship, and took courage from it to strive and toil and conquer; and the most careless heart feels a thrill in this hallowed and historic spot.

The feeling is intensified as one visits Pilgrim Hall. There has been so much joking about the furniture brought over in the *Mayflower,* that one thinks of it as handsome and valuable. It is in reality very different. Plain, rudely-carved chairs, solid **Pilgrim** tables and stools, chipped with **Hall** long use, iron cooking pots, pewter platters, everything was of the simplest and strongest kind, for those colonists were in marching and fighting trim and needed no luxuries. They were cultured—many of them had coats of arms, indeed; but they were of true Spartan breed; and met their new conditions with resolute adaptability. One book they had and read—their Bible. Alden's Bible is here, and Winslow's, and Brewster's Commentaries on The Proverbs. The Proverbs were just such meat as these righteous, sturdy men and women of Plymouth needed and enjoyed. One can imagine that little Wrestling Brewster (whose christening blanket is preserved here, and is about as thick as a piece of unbleached muslin—poor child!) and Peregrine White, the first white child born in New England, and Lora Standish, must have learned The Proverbs by heart in early childhood. They did not learn the three R's very well, however—at least, Peregrine White's will is signed only by his mark, a queer, trembly " P. W.," which has to be interpreted liberally to be anything at all.

John Alden and Priscilla Molines (not Mullins) are very much in evidence at Pilgrim Hall. It is a pretty romance, and one hesitates to find Longfellow in the wrong in any way; but it is only fair to the facts to mention that Priscilla did not ride on a milkwhite steer through the woods to her new home, as the poet pictures her, **Longfel-** for two reasons: first there were **low's John** no domestic animals larger than **and** goats in Plymouth when John **Priscilla** and Priscilla were married; and, secondly, there was no settlement on the other side of the bay at that

period. Only the two rows of houses on Leyden Street were standing, and there were therefore no woods to go through to reach Alden's home on the slope of Burial Hill. Still, in 1627, not so many years afterwards, the young couple did remove to Duxbury, and John Alden built first a small house, and then a larger and more substantial one, which is standing to this day, and round which memories of the Pilgrim pair cling in abundance, much to the satisfaction of the John of the seventh generation, who inhabits the old homestead, and to the satisfaction, too, of five thousand other Alden descendants, scattered over the United States. Governor Bradford is the only Pilgrim whose descendants outnumber those of John and Priscilla, it is said.

Indeed, of the forty-one who signed the compact in the cabin of the *Mayflower,* as she lay off Provincetown that cold November day (their names, by the way, are duly inscribed on the forty-one festoons of the remarkable railing round the tablet which commemorates the compact) **The Forty-** nearly all have many descendants. **One** The curator at Pilgrim Hall, **Signers** himself descended from eight of the signers, receives daily letters from East and West asking for information about the Pilgrim ancestors of the writers. Far and wide the descendants of the *Mayflower* band have gone, carrying everywhere the faith, the energy, and the high ideals of their forefathers. The great West and the awakening South have felt the influence of the same sturdy endurance, enterprise, and resolute faith that drove the famous little company to brave the unknown dangers of a bleak and hostile country. Plymouth, historic and filled with interest as it is, does not, and cannot, hold the full story of the Pilgrims. That story is written in letters of light over the whole continent; all over the country, wherever they have gone, they have carried with them a respect for law, a reverence for God, education and freedom of worship, and a courage to uphold them, that has made this our great Nation the " land of the free and the home of the brave." May America, with her churches, her schools, her civil and religious liberty, her great past and her glorious future be truly and forever the " land of the Pilgrims' pride."—C. E. W.

PERSONAL RESPONSIBILITY

By WILLIAM T. ELLIS

" My country, 'tis of thee." Yes, she is *my* country, and not the country of the professional politician and office-holder, appearances to the contrary notwithstanding. The country is the heritage of the individual citizen. To him she looks for protection; upon him she leans for support. When he ceases to love her with an ardent love, and when he

becomes indifferent to her welfare, then the saddest day in her history will have dawned.

There is a great difference between a home and a hotel, and the home is the more precious of the two, tho it may be but a humble cottage, while the hotel may be a palace. It is the sense of possession that makes the difference. The home is ours. It does not belong to the public; it is sacred to us alone. Therefore we prize it and guard it. The same spirit of personal relation is needed toward our country. We have a proprietary interest in her; she belongs to us. There is no person alive who has a better right than every one of us who live beneath the flag to say, " This is my country."

" I am the State! " cried a famous king. In no such arrogant and selfish sense, but even more truly, the least American may say. " I am the State." The government is not a thing distinct from the governed. The people are the Nation. All its responsibilities are our responsibilities. Its burdens are our burdens. Its problems are problems that are to be settled, not by the government in the abstract, but by the individual citizen in the aggregate.

A patriot cannot turn his troubles over to the policemen, or to any other officeholder. Citizenship has its burdens, and we must bear them. That is the price we pay for a republican form of government. The instant we withdraw our shoulders from under our share of the national load, trouble begins for our country. By that act we imperil, to a degree, the national stability. For the Nation is only sure and strong when her people are awake to their duties to the State.

Private indifference to public affairs is the greatest menace that confronts America. Good men relegate the direction of the Nation to politicians, who are too often greedy and unpatriotic. Then they wonder why their prayers for her purity and peace are not always answered. This is a case wherein God will hear only the prayers of our hands and our feet. He will not perform our duties for us. If we are not enough interested to assume to the last ounce our obligations of citizenship, we cannot expect him miraculously to intervene to save the country from her enemies within.

It should be a personal offense to every citizen when an officeholder goes wrong. Any man who deals dishonorably by the government deserves, and should receive, the manifest condemnation of every patriot. A more vigorous treatment of political evil doers, on the part of citizens, is urgently demanded in these times. We should be readier to measure out punishment—and ostracism— to offenders against the State than to offenders against our personal rights—and such, indeed, are the former, and in larger degree. A quickened public spirit needs to be awakened in this respect, that Americans may understand that he who betrays an official trust insults and injures every individual in the community.

Indifference is unpatriotic. The best friend of the Nation's foes is the man who does not concern himself about public affairs. The political evil doers ask only that the sense of personal responsibility be dulled in the minds of the people; for this means success to their worst schemes. If the community will only concern itself altogether with business and pleasure seeking, and pay no attention to matters of government or politics, the politicians and spoilsmen will waste no gray matter in anxiety. Their safety and success— and the Nation's danger and failure—lie in the indifference of the people.

Here is a serious need of our Nation: The arousal of her citizens to an appreciation of their personal responsibility. Give us a people who are awake to all the questions of the hour, and who view with jealous eye the conduct of public servants, and America will arise to a might and a purity undreamed of by our fathers. Her destiny will be glorious because her inhabitants are true.

" God give us men; a time like this demands
  Great hearts, strong minds, true faith, and
    willing hands,
Men whom the lust of office does not kill;
  Men whom the spoils of office cannot buy;
  Men who possess opinions and a will;
  Men who have honor; men who will not
    lie."

C. E. W.

ADDRESSES

ORATION AT PLYMOUTH *

By John Quincy Adams

Among the sentiments of most powerful operation upon the human heart, and most highly honorable to the human character, are those of veneration for our forefathers, and of love for our posterity. They form the connecting links between the selfish and the social passions. By the fundamental principle of Christianity, the happiness of the individual is interwoven, by innumerable and imperceptible ties, with that of his contemporaries. By the power of filial reverence and parental affection, individual existence is extended beyond the limits of individual life, and the happiness of every age is chained in mutual dependence upon that of every other. Respect for his ancestors excites, in the breast of man, interest in their history, attachment to their characters, concern for their errors, involuntary pride in their virtues. Love for his posterity spurs him to exertion for their support, stimulates him to virtue for their example, and fills him with the tenderest solicitude for their welfare. Man, therefore, was not made for himself

* Delivered at Plymouth on the twenty-second day of December, 1802, in Commemoration of the Landing of the Pilgrims.

alone. No, he was made for his country, by the obligations of the social compact; he was made for his species, by the Christian duties of universal charity; he was made for all ages past, by the sentiment of reverence for his forefathers; and he was made for all future times, by the impulse of affection for his progeny. Under the influence of these principles, "Existence sees him spurn her bounded reign."

They redeem his nature from the subjection of time and space; he is no longer a "puny insect shivering at a breeze;" he is the glory of creation, formed to occupy all time and all extent; bounded, during his residence upon earth, only to the boundaries of the world, and destined to life and immortality in brighter regions, when the fabric of nature itself shall dissolve and perish.

The voice of history has not, in all its compass, a note but answers in unison with these sentiments. The barbarian chieftain, who defended his country against the Roman invasion, driven to the remotest extremity of Britain, and stimulating his followers to battle by all that has power of persuasion upon the human heart, concluded his persuasion by an appeal to these irresistible feelings. "Think of your forefathers and of your posterity." The Romans themselves, at the pinnacle of civilization, were actuated by the same impressions, and celebrated, in anniversary festivals, every great event which has signalized the annals of their forefathers. To multiply instances where it were impossible to adduce an exception would be to waste your time and abuse your patience; but in the Sacred Volume, which contains the substance of our firmest faith and of our most precious hopes, these passions not only maintain their highest efficacy, but are sanctioned by the express injunctions of the Divine Legislator to His chosen people.

The revolutions of time furnish no previous example of a nation shooting up to maturity and expanding into greatness with the rapidity which has characterized the growth of the American people. In the luxuriance of youth, and in the vigor of manhood, it is pleasing and instructive to look backwards upon the helpless days of infancy; but in the continual and essential changes of a growing subject, the transactions of that early period would soon be obliterated from the memory but for some periodical call of attention to aid the silent records of the historian. Such celebrations arouse and gratify the kindliest emotions of the bosom. They are faithful pledges of the respect we bear to the memory of our ancestors and of the tenderness with which we cherish the rising generation. They introduce the sages and heroes of ages past to the notice and emulation of succeeding times; they are at once testimonials of our gratitude, and schools of virtue to our children.

These sentiments are wise; they are honorable; they are virtuous; their cultivation is not merely innocent pleasure; it is incumbent duty. Obedient to their dictates, you, my fellow-citizens, have instituted and paid frequent observance to this annual solemnity. And what event of weightier intrinsic importance, or of more extensive consequences was ever selected for this honorary distinction?

In reverting to the period of our origin, other nations have generally been compelled to plunge into the chaos of impenetrable antiquity, or to trace a lawless ancestry into the caverns of ravishers and robbers. It is your peculiar privilege to commemorate, in this birthday of your Nation, an event of which the principal actors are known to you familiarly, as if belonging to your own age; an event of a magnitude before which imagination shrinks at the imperfection of her powers. It is your further happiness to behold, in those eminent characters, who were most conspicuous in accomplishing the settlement of your country, men upon whose virtue you can dwell with honest exultation. The founders of your race are not handed down to you, like the father of the Roman people, as the sucklings of a wolf. You are not descended from a nauseous compound of fanaticism and sensuality, whose only argument was the sword, and whose only paradise was a brothel. No Gothic scourge of God, no Vandal pest of nations, no fabled fugitive from the flames of Troy, no bastard Norman tyrant, appears among the list of worthies who first landed on the Rock, which your veneration has preserved as a lasting monument of their achievement. The great actors of the day we now solemnize were illustrious by their intrepid valor no less than by their Christian graces, but the clarion of conquest has not blazoned forth their names to all the winds of Heaven. Their glory has not been wafted over oceans of blood to the remotest regions of the earth. They have not erected to themselves colossal statues upon pedestals of human bones, to provoke and insult the tardy hand of heavenly retribution. But theirs was "the better fortitude of patience and heroic martyrdom." Theirs was the gentle temper of Christian kindness, the rigorous observance of reciprocal justice, the unconquerable soul of conscious integrity. Worldly fame has been parsimonious of her favor to the memory of those generous companions. Their numbers were small; their stations in life obscure; the object of their enterprise unostentatious; the theater of their exploits remote; how could they possibly be favorites of worldly Fame—that common crier, whose existence is only known by the assemblage of multitudes; that pander of wealth and greatness, so eager to haunt the palaces of fortune, and so fastidious to the houseless dignity of virtue; that parasite of pride, ever scornful to meekness, and ever obsequious to insolent power; that heedless trumpeter whose ears are deaf to modest merit, and whose eyes are blind to bloodless, distant excellence?

When the persecuted companions of Robinson, exiles from their native land, anxiously sued for the privilege of removing a thousand leagues more distant to an untried soil, a rigorous climate, and a savage wilderness, for the sake of reconciling their sense of religious duty with their affections for their country, few, perhaps none of them, formed a conception of what would be, within two centuries, the result of their undertaking. When the jealous and niggardly policy of their British sovereign denied them even that humblest of requests, and instead of liberty would barely consent to promise connivance, neither he nor they might be aware that they were laying the foundations of a power, and that he was sowing the seeds of a spirit, which, in less than two hundred years, would stagger the throne of his descendants, and shake his united kingdoms to the center. So far is it from the ordinary habits of mankind to calculate the importance of events in their elementary principles, that had the first colonists of our country ever intimated as a part of their designs the project of founding a great and mighty nation, the finger of scorn would have pointed them to the cells of bedlam as an abode more suitable for hatching vain empires than the solitude of a transatlantic desert.

These consequences, then so little foreseen, have unfolded themselves, in all their grandeur, to the eyes of the present age. It is a common amusement of speculative minds to contrast the magnitude of the most important events with the minuteness of their primeval causes, and the records of mankind are full of examples for such contemplations. It is, however, a more profitable employment to trace the constituent principles of future greatness in their kernel; to detect in the acorn at our feet the germ of that majestic oak, whose roots shoot down to the center, and whose branches aspire to the skies. Let it be, then, our present occupation to inquire and endeavor to ascertain the causes first put in operation at the period of our commemoration, and already productive of such magnificent effects; to examine with reiterated care and minute attention the characters of those men who gave the first impulse to a new series of events in the history of the world; to applaud and emulate those qualities of their minds which we shall find deserving of our admiration; to recognize with candor those features which forbid approbation or even require censure, and, finally, to lay alike their frailties and their perfections to our own hearts, either as warning or as example.

Of the various European settlements upon this continent, which have finally merged in one independent Nation, the first establishments were made at various times, by several nations, and under the influence of different motives. In many instances, the conviction of religious obligation formed one and a powerful inducement of the adventures; but in none, excepting the settlement at Plymouth, did they constitute the sole and exclusive actuating cause. Worldly interest and commercial speculation entered largely into the views of other settlers, but the commands of conscience were the only stimulus to the emigrants from Leyden. Previous to their expeditions hither, they had endured a long banishment from their native country. Under every species of discouragement, they undertook the voyage; they performed it in spite of numerous and almost insuperable obstacles; they arrived upon a wilderness bound with frost and hoary with snow, without the boundaries of their charter, outcasts from all human society, and coasted five weeks together, in the dead of winter, on this tempestuous shore, exposed at once to the fury of the elements, to the arrows of the native savage, and to the impending horrors of famine.

Courage and perseverance have a magical talisman, before which difficulties disappear and obstacles vanish into air. These qualities have ever been displayed in their mightiest perfection, as attendants in the retinue of strong passions. From the first discovery of the Western Hemisphere by Columbus until the settlement of Virginia which immediately preceded that of Plymouth, the various adventurers from the ancient world had exhibited upon innumerable occasions that ardor of enterprise and that stubbornness of pursuit which set all danger at defiance, and chained the violence of nature at their feet. But they were all instigated by personal interests. Avarice and ambition had tuned their souls to that pitch of exaltation. Selfish passions were the parents of their heroism. It was reserved for the first settlers of New England to perform achievements equally arduous, to trample down obstructions equally formidable, to dispel dangers equally terrific, under the single inspiration of conscience.

To them even liberty herself was but a subordinate and secondary consideration. They claimed exemption from the mandates of human authority, as militating with their subjection to a superior power. Before the voice of Heaven they silenced even the calls of their country.

Yet, while so deeply impressed with the sense of religious obligation, they felt, in all its energy, the force of that tender tie which binds the heart of every virtuous man to his native land. It was to renew that connection with their country which had been severed by their compulsory expatriation, that they resolved to face all the hazards of a perilous navigation and all the labors of a toilsome distant settlement. Under the mild protection of the Batavian government, they enjoyed already that freedom of religious worship, for which they had resigned so many comforts and enjoyments at home; but their hearts panted for a restoration to the bosom of their country. Invited and urged by the openhearted and truly benevolent people who had given them an asylum for the persecution of their own kindred to form their settlement within the territories then under their jurisdiction, the love of their country predominated over every influence save that of conscience alone, and they preferred the precarious chance of relaxation from the bigoted rigor of the English government to the certain liberality and alluring offers of the Hollanders. Observe, my countrymen, the generous patriotism, the cordial union of soul, the conscious yet unaffected vigor which beam in their application to the British monarch:

"They were well weaned from the delicate milk of their mother country, and inured to the difficulties of a strange land. They were knit together in a strict and sacred bond, to take care of the good of each other and of the whole. It was not with them as with other men, whom small things could discourage, or small discontents cause to wish themselves again at home."

Children of these exalted Pilgrims! Is there one among you who can hear the simple and pathetic energy of these expressions without tenderness and admiration? Venerated shades of our forefathers! No, ye were indeed, not ordinary men! That country which had ejected you so cruelly from her bosom you still delighted to contemplate in the character of an affectionate and beloved mother. The sacred bond which knit you together was indissoluble while you lived; and oh, may it be to your descendants the example and the pledge of harmony to the latest period of time! The difficulties and dangers, which so often had defeated attempts of similar establishments, were unable to subdue souls tempered like yours. You heard the rigid interdictions; you saw the menacing forms of toil and danger, forbidding your access to this land of promise; but you heard without dismay; you saw and disdained retreat. Firm and undaunted in the confidence of that sacred bond; conscious of purity, and convinced of the importance of your motives, you put your trust in the protecting shield of Providence, and smiled defiance at the combining terrors of human malice and elemental strife. These, in the accomplishment of your undertaking, you were summoned to encounter in their most hideous forms; these you met with that fortitude, and combated with that perseverance, which you had promised in their anticipation; these you completely vanquished in establishing the foundations of New England, and the day which we now commemorate is the perpetual memorial of your triumph.

It were an occupation peculiarly pleasing to cull from our early historians, and exhibit before you every detail of this transaction; to carry you in imagination on board their bark at the first moment of her arrival in the bay; to accompany Carver, Winslow, Bradford, and Standish, in all their excursions upon the desolate coast; to follow them into every rivulet and creek where they endeavored to find a firm footing, and to fix, with a pause of delight and exultation, the instant when the first of these heroic adventurers alighted on the spot where you, their descendants, now enjoy the glorious and happy reward of their labors. But in this grateful task, your former orators, on this anniversary, have anticipated all that the most ardent industry could collect, and gratified all that the most inquisitive curiosity could desire. To you, my friends, every occurrence of that momentous period is already familiar. A transient allusion to a few characteristic instances, which mark the peculiar

history of the Plymouth settlers, may properly supply the place of a narrative, which to this auditory, must be superfluous.

One of these remarkable incidents is the execution of that instrument of government by which they formed themselves into a body politic, the day after their arrival upon the coast, and previous to their landing. This is perhaps, the only instance in human history of that positive, original social compact, which speculative philosophers have imagined as the only legitimate source of government. Here was a unanimous and personal assent, by all of the individuals of the community, to the association by which they became a nation. It was the result of circumstances and discussions which had occurred during their passage from Europe, and is a full demonstration that the nature of civil government, abstracted from the political institutions of their native country, had been an object of their serious meditation. The settlers of all the former European colonies had contented themselves with the powers conferred upon them by their respective charters, without looking beyond the seal of the royal parchment for the measure of their rights and the rule of their duties. The founders of Plymouth had been impelled by the peculiarities of their situation to examine the subject with deeper and more comprehensive research. After twelve years of banishment from the land of their first allegiance, during which they had been under an adoptive and temporary subjection to another sovereign, they must naturally have been led to reflect upon the relative rights and duties of allegiance and subjection. They had resided in a city, the seat of a university, where the polemical and political controversies of the times were pursued with uncommon fervor. In this period they had witnessed the deadly struggle between the two parties, into which the people of the United Provinces after their separation from the crown of Spain, had divided themselves. The contest embraced within its compass not only theological doctrines, but political principles, and Maurice and Barnevelt were the temporary leaders of the same rival factions, of which Episcopius and Polyander were the ecclesiastical champions.

That the investigation of the fundamental principles of government was deeply implicated in these dissensions is evident from the immortal work of Grotius, upon the rights of war and peace, which undoubtedly originated from them. Grotius himself had been a most distinguished actor and sufferer in those important scenes of internal convulsion, and his work was first published very shortly after the departure of our forefathers from Leyden. It is well known that in the course of the contest Mr. Robinson more than once appeared, with credit to himself, as a public disputant against Episcopius; and from the manner in which the fact is related by Governor Bradford, it is apparent that the whole English Church at Leyden took a zealous interest in the religious part of the controversy. As strangers in the land, it is presumable that they wisely and honorably avoided entangling themselves in the political contentions involved with it. Yet the theoretic principles, as they were drawn into discussion, could not fail to arrest their attention, and must have assisted them to form accurate ideas concerning the origin and extent of authority among men, independent of positive institutions. The importance of these circumstances will not be duly weighed without taking into consideration the state of opinion then prevalent in England. The general principles of government were there little understood and less examined. The whole substance of human authority was centered in the simple doctrine of royal prerogative, the origin of which was always traced in theory to divine institution. Twenty years later, the subject was more industriously sifted, and for half a century became one of the principal topics of controversy between the ablest and most enlightened men in the Nation. The instrument of voluntary association executed on board the *Mayflower* testifies that the parties to it had anticipated the improvement of their Nation.

Another incident, from which we may derive occasion for important reflections, was the attempt of these original settlers to establish among them that community of goods and of labor, which fanciful politicians, from the days of Plato to those of Rousseau, have recommended as the fundamental law of a perfect republic. This theory results, it must be acknowledged, from principles of reasoning most flattering to the human character. If industry, frugality, and disinterested integrity were alike the virtues of all, there would, apparently, be more of the social spirit, in making all property a common stock, and giving to each individual a proportional title to the wealth of the whole. Such is the basis upon which Plato forbids, in his Republic, the division of property. Such is the system upon which Rousseau pronounces the first man who enclosed a field with a fence, and, said, "This is mine," a traitor to the human species. A wiser and more useful philosophy, however, directs us to consider man according to the nature in which he was formed; subject to infirmities, which no wisdom can remedy; to weaknesses, which no institution can strengthen; to vices, which no legislation can correct. Hence, it becomes obvious that separate property is the natural and indisputable right of separate exertion; that community of goods without community of toil is oppressive and unjust; that it counteracts the laws of nature, which prescribe that he only who sows the seed shall reap the harvest; that it discourages all energy, by destroying its rewards; and makes the most virtuous and active members of society the slaves and drudges of the worst. Such was the issue of this experiment among our forefathers, and the same event demonstrated the error of the system in the elder settlement of Virginia. Let us cherish that spirit of harmony which prompted our forefathers to make the attempt, under circumstances more favorable to its success than, perhaps, ever occurred upon earth. Let us no less admire the candor with which they relinquished it, upon discovering its irremediable inefficacy. To found principles of government upon too advantageous an estimate of the human character is an error of inexperience, the source of which is so amiable that it is impossible to censure it with severity. We have seen the same mistake, committed in our own age, and upon a larger theater. Happily for our ancestors, their situation allowed them to repair it before its effects had proved destructive. They had no pride of vain philosophy to support, no perfidious rage of faction to glut, by persevering in their mistakes until they should be extinguished in torrents of blood.

As the attempt to establish among themselves the community of goods was a seal of that sacred bond which knit them so closely together, so the conduct they observed towards the natives of the country displays the steadfast inherence to the rules of justice and their faithful attachment to those of benevolence and charity.

No European settlement ever formed upon this continent has been more distinguished for undeviating kindness and equity towards the savages. There are, indeed, moralists who have questioned the right of the Europeans to intrude upon the possessions of the aboriginals in any case, and under any limitations whatsoever. But have they maturely considered the whole subject? The Indian right of possession itself stands, with regard to the greatest part of the country, upon a questionable foundation. Their cultivated fields; their constructed habitations; a space of ample sufficiency for their subsistence, and whatever they had annexed to themselves by personal labor, was undoubtedly, by the laws of nature, theirs. But what is the right of the huntsman to the forest of a thousand miles over which he has accidentally ranged in quest of prey? Shall the liberal bounties of Providence to the race of man be monopolized by one of ten thousand for whom they were created? Shall the exuberant bosom of the common mother, amply adequate to the nourishment of millions, be claimed exclusively by a few hundreds of her offspring? Shall the lordly savage not only disdain the virtues and enjoyments of civilization himself, but shall he control the civilization of the world? Shall he forbid the wilderness to blossom like a rose? Shall he forbid the oaks of the forest to fall before the ax of industry, and to rise again, transformed into the habitations of ease and elegance? Shall he doom an immense region of the globe to perpetual desolation, and to hear the howlings of the tiger and the wolf silence forever the voice of human gladness? Shall the fields and valleys, which a beneficent God has formed to teem with the life of innumerable multitudes, be condemned to everlasting barrenness? Shall the mighty rivers, poured out by the hand of nature, as channels of communication between numerous nations, roll their waters in sullen silence and eternal solitude to the deep? Have hundreds of commodious harbors, a thousand leagues of coast, and a boundless ocean, been spread in the front of this land, and shall every purpose of utility to which they could apply be prohibited by the tenants of the woods? No, generous philanthropists! Heaven has not been thus inconsistent in the works of its hands. Heaven has not thus placed at irreconcilable strife its moral laws with its physical creation. The Pilgrims of Plymouth obtained their right of possession to the territory on which they settled, by titles as fair and unequivocal as any human property can be held. By their voluntary association they recognized their allegiance to the government of Britain, and in process of time received whatever powers and authorities could be conferred upon them by a charter from their sovereign. The spot on which they fixed had belonged to an Indian tribe, totally extirpated by that devouring pestilence which had swept the country shortly before their arrival. The territory, thus free from all exclusive possession, they might have taken by the natural right of occupancy. Desirous, however, of giving ample satisfaction to every pretense of pride or right, by formal and solemn conventions with the chiefs of the neighboring tribes, they acquired the further security of the purchase. At their hands the children of the desert had no cause for complaint. On the great day of retribution, what thousands, what millions of the American race will appear at the bar of judgment to arraign their European invading conquerors! Let us humbly hope that the fathers of the Plymouth Colony will then appear in the whiteness of innocence. Let us indulge in the belief that they will not only be free from all accusation of injustice to these unfortunate sons of nature, but that the testimonials of their acts of kindness and benevolence towards them will plead the cause of their virtues, as they are now authenticated by the record of history upon earth.

Religious discord has lost her sting; the cumbrous weapons of theological warfare are antiquated; the field of politics supplies the alchemists of our times with materials of more fatal explosion, and the butchers of mankind no longer travel to another world for instruments of cruelty and destruction. Our age is too enlightened to contend upon topics which concern only the interests of eternity; the men who hold in proper contempt all controversies about trifles, except such as inflame their own passions, have made it a commonplace censure against your ancestors, that their zeal was enkindled by subjects of trivial importance; and that however aggrieved by the intolerance of others, they were alike intolerant themselves. Against these objections, your candid judgment will not require an unqualified justification; but your respect and gratitude for the founders of the State may boldly claim an ample apology. The original grounds of their separation from the Church of England were not objects of a magnitude to dissolve the bonds of communion, much less those of charity, between Christian brethren of the same essential principles. Some of them,

however, were not inconsiderable, and numerous inducements concurred to give them an extraordinary interest in their eyes. When that portentous system of abuses, the Papal dominion, was overturned, a great variety of religious sects arose in its stead in the several countries, which for many centuries before had been screwed beneath its subjection.

The fabric of the Reformation, first undertaken in England upon a contracted basis, by a capricious and sanguinary tyrant, had been successively overthrown and restored, renewed and altered, according to the varying humors and principles of four successive monarchs. To ascertain the precise point of division between the genuine institutions of Christianity and the corruptions accumulated upon them in the progress of fifteen centuries, was found a task of extreme difficulty throughout the Christian world. Men of the profoundest learning, of the sublimest genius, and of the purest integrity, after devoting their lives to the research, finally differed in their ideas upon many great points, both of doctrine and discipline. The main question, it was admitted upon all hands, most intimately concerned the highest interests of man, both temporal and eternal. Can we wonder that men who felt their happiness here and their hopes of hereafter, their worldly welfare and the kingdom of Heaven at stake, should sometimes attach an importance beyond their intrinsic weight to collateral points of controversy, connected with the all-involving object of the Reformation? The changes in the forms and principles of religious worship were introduced and regulated in England by the hand of public authority.

But that hand had not been uniform or steady in its operations. During the persecutions inflicted in the interval of Popish restoration under the reign of Mary, upon all who favored the Reformation, many of the most zealous reformers had been compelled to fly their country. While residing on the continent of Europe, they had adopted the principles of the most complete and rigorous reformation, as taught and established by Calvin. On returning afterwards to their native country, they were dissatisfied with the partial reformation, at which as they conceived, the English establishment had rested; and claiming the privilege of private conscience, upon which alone any departure from the Church of Rome could be justified, they insisted upon the right of adhering to the system of their own preference, and, of course, upon that of nonconformity to the establishment prescribed by the royal authority. The only means used to convince them of error and reclaim them from dissent was force, and force served but to confirm the opposition it was meant to suppress. By driving the founders of the Plymouth Colony into exile, it constrained them to absolute separation from the Church of England; and by the refusal afterward to allow them a positive toleration, even in this American wilderness, the council of James I. rendered that separation irreconcilable. Viewing their religious liberties here, as held only by sufferance, yet bound to them by all the ties of conviction, and by all their sufferings for them, could they forbear to look upon every dissenter among themselves with a jealous eye? Within two years after their landing, they beheld a rival settlement attempted in their immediate neighborhood; and not long after, the laws of self-preservation compelled them to break up a nest of revelers, who boasted of protection from the mother country, and who had recurred to the easy but pernicious resource of feeding their wanton idleness, by furnishing the savages with the means, the skill, and the instruments of European destruction. Toleration, in that instance, would have been self-murder, and many other examples might be alleged, in which their necessary measures of self-defense have been exaggerated into cruelty, and their most indispensable precautions distorted into persecution. Yet shall we not pretend that they were exempt from the common laws of mortality, or entirely free from all the errors of their age. Their zeal might sometimes be too ardent, but it was always sincere. At this day, religious indulgence is one of our clearest duties, because it is one of our undisputed rights. While we rejoice that the principles of genuine Christianity have so far triumphed over the prejudices of a former generation, let us fervently hope for the day when it will prove equally victorious over the malignant passions of our own.

In thus calling your attention to some of the peculiar features in the principles, the character, and the history of our forefathers, it is as wide from my design, as I know it would be from your approbation, to adorn their memory with a chaplet plucked from the domain of others. The occasion and the day are most peculiarly devoted to them, and let it never be dishonored with a contracted and exclusive spirit. Our affections as citizens embrace the whole extent of the Union, and the names of Raleigh, Smith, Winthrop, Calvert, Penn, and Oglethorpe, excite in our minds recollections equally' pleasing and gratitude equally fervent with those of Carver and Bradford. Two centuries have not elapsed since the first European foot touched the soil which now constitutes the American Union. Two centuries more and our numbers must exceed those of Europe itself. The destinies of this empire, as they appear in prospect before us, disdain the powers of human calculation. Yet, as the original founder of the Roman state is said once to have lifted upon his shoulders the fame and fortunes of all his posterity, so let us never forget that the glory and greatness of all our descendants is in our hands. Preserve in all their purity; refine, if possible, from all their alloy, those virtues which we this day commemorate as the ornament of our forefathers. Adhere to them with inflexible resolution, as to the horns of the altar; instil them with unwearied perseverance into the minds of your children; bind your souls and theirs to ,the national Union as the chords of life are centered in the heart, and you shall soar with rapid and steady wing to the summit of human glory. Nearly a century ago, one of those rare minds to whom it is given to discern future greatness in its seminal principles, upon contemplating the situation of this continent, pronounced, in a vein of poetic inspiration, " Westward the star of empire takes its way." Let us unite in ardent supplication to the Founder of nations and the Builder of worlds, that what then was prophecy may continue unfolding into history,—that the dearest hopes of the human race may not be extinguished in disappointment, and that the last may prove the noblest empire of time.—W. B. O.

THE HEROISM OF THE EARLY COLONISTS

By Rufus Choate

If one were called on to select the most glittering of the instances of military heroism to which the admiration of the world has been constantly attracted, he would make choice, I imagine, of the instance of that desperate valor, in obedience to the laws, Leonidas and his three hundred Spartans cast themselves headlong, at the passes of Greece, on the myriads of their Persian invaders. From the simple page of Herodotus, longer than from the Amphictyonic monument, or the games of the commemoration, that act speaks still to the tears and praise of all the world.

Judge, if that night, as they watched the dawn of the last morning their eyes could ever see; as they heard with every passing hour the stilly hum of the invading host, its dusky lines stretched out without end, and now almost encircling them round; as they remembered their unprofaned home, city of heroes and the mother of heroes,—judge if, watching there, in the gateway of Greece, this sentiment did not grow to the nature of madness, if it did not run in torrents of literal fire to and from the laboring heart; and when morning came and passed, and they had dressed their long locks for battle, and when, at a little after noon, the countless invading throng was seen at last to move, was it not with a rapture, as if all the joy, all the sensation of life, was in that one moment, that they cast themselves, with the fierce gladness of mountain torrents, headlong in that brief revelry of glory?

I acknowledge the splendor of that transaction in all its aspects. I admit its morality too, and its useful influence on every Grecian heart, in that greatest crisis of Greece.

And yet, do you not think that whoso could, by adequate description, bring before you that winter of the Pilgrims,—its brief sunshine; the nights of storm, siow waning; the damp and icy breath, felt to the pillow of the dying; its destitutions, its contrasts with all their former experience in life, its utter insulation and loneliness, its deathbeds and burials, its memories, its apprehensions, its hopes; the consultations cf the prudent; the prayers of the pious; tne occasional cheerful hymn, in which the strong heart threw off its burden, and, asserting its unvanquished nature, went up, like a bird of dawn, to the skies;—do ye not think that whoso could describe them calmly waiting in that defile, lonelier and darker than Thermopylæ, for the morning that might never dawn or might show them, when it did, a mightier arm than the Persian raised as in act to strike, would he not sketch a scene of more difficult and rarer heroism? A scene, as Wordsworth has said, "melancholy, yea, dismal, yet consolatory and full of joy;" a scene even better fitted to succor, to exalt, to lead the forlorn hopes of all great causes, till time shall be no more! I have said that I deemed it a great thing for a nation, in all the periods of its fortunes, to be able to look back to a race of founders, and a principle of institution, in which it might rationally admire the realized idea of true heroism. That felicity, that pride, that help, is ours. Our past, with its great eras, that of settlement, that of independence, should announce, should compel, should spontaneously evolve as from a germ, a wise, moral, and glowing future. Those heroic men and women should not look down on a dwindled posterity. That broad foundation, sunk below frost or earthquake, should bear up something more permanent than an encampment of tents, pitched at random, and struck when the trumpet of march sounds at next daybreak. It should bear up, as by a natural growth, a structure in which generations may come, one after another, to the great gift of the social life.— W. B. O.

THE DUTY OF ENTHUSIASM

By M. W. Stryker, D.D., LL.D.

Mr. President, Sisters and Brothers: I have always prayed that I might be delivered from my traducers and from my introducers. I have suffered many things of many presidents. I stand before you to-day as the victim of circumstances. I have been delighted, as you all have been, to hear the honorable member from the Worcester District sauce Massachusetts. There is no one outside the bounds of Massachusetts who can speak his mind so freely about Harvard College. I should begin the words I have to say this day by an apology for ever having graduated from a college! I should make a further apology for having anything to do with the faculty of a college. But I do not impugn the logic of my friend, because I remember that there are colleges and colleges, that as "they didn't know everything down in Judee," so they do not know everything even in the great colleges of New England, tho they know a little of everything. There are colleges and colleges. There are Congressmen and Congressmen. I suppose our friend who preceded me (Representative Walker of Massachusetts), does not want free sugar in his, but there are some Congressmen who do. I desire to put myself outside the range of his syllogisms, and to say, that, however humble may be my relation to college work, I will not stand in the shoes of any cold-blooded expounder of what has been so well called The Dismal Science, because it first leaves out God, and second, it leaves out man.

. . . .

This is not the first time that I have had a chance to detain the eyes and ears of New Englanders, and if I can help it, it shall not be the last time that I shall do so. There is a certain independence in speaking to people who are like the farmer to whom Whittier loaned his copy of "Plato," who came back and said: "I like that fellow; he has some of my idees." The New Englander takes his ideas always mixed with brains. The multitude of those who are gathered here to-day are not to be measured by arithmetic, but by ethics, rather. New Englanders are not to be counted, but are to be weighed. You do not take yours by the dozen, but by the pound. This is a representative audience.

I feel as if I were speaking into a telephone that had universal connections. I hope that I shall be heard at the other end of the line with as much emphasis as was illustrated by what happened at one of the telephones when a farmer went into the office and was having the thing explained to him. and was asked to put his ear to it. Just then there was a clap of thunder, and he called up his wife and exclaimed: "That's Maria!" He recognized the voice. One of our speakers said something about the boycotts that were such a trouble, or blessing not unmixed, and a friend of mine who sat near me, and who always sits very near to me, suggested that the girl-cotts had something to do with it, too. I am thankful for both the boycotts and the girl-cotts of that sort. I think the women, who make the majority of this and perhaps every other crowd in New England —and out of it, too—where brains are at all in demand, may well take comfort to themselves from a toast which was given at a New England dinner in New York, in which a man said that he would like to propose a toast to the Pilgrim Mothers; that they endured all that the Pilgrim Fathers had endured; and they had endured the Pilgrim Fathers besides.

I am glad we started off to-day with "Yankee Doodle." It is a good tune. It is classic, with something better than the classicism of art. Every New Englander ought to know that story of how when the first regiment went down from these great hills that hold down the memories of an honorable race, and they were gathered into the Astor House in New York, the first New England regiment to go to the front, Broadway from curb to curb was thronged, and as the first glitter and flash of the front file issued from the doorway of that historic inn, about ten o'clock in the morning, the band struck up "Yankee Doodle," of all tunes in the world, and the people set up such a mighty roar and tempest of sympathy and determination that it seemed to rock the very granite walls. There was no uncertainty after New England had set that tune of how the city of New York would go.

This concourse to-day (July 4, 1894) is a witness that patriotism is not a lost art, and the day that gathers us is not simply a bright legend. We stand here on classic, on sacred ground. We are in the heart of venerable New England—a name that is written on no map, but a name that shines wherever law, truth, faith, are held in reverence. We stand within the bounds of no mean commonwealth (Connecticut), rather of one whose historic honor is so bright that when one reads her annals, it is to wonder what is left to record for the fame of the other stars of our constellation. It is a record legible and luminous all the way from Buckingham to Morris. Under what better motto could we gather than Connecticut's "*Qui transtulit sustinet*"! But to-day, men and women of a score of states, perhaps of every state, where that dear banner answers the heavens with its stellar and auroral beauty—to-day we are each and all Americans! Thanks to the host (Henry C. Bowen), who calls us here.* Joy to the hearts that answer him! Peace, plenty, above all piety, unsullied, unbounded, unfaltering, to the land we love and call our own! But we are all here not only to remember; we are also here to resolve, highly, humbly, fervently and with unanimous consecration. No one can attempt to voice your wills with a deeper sense of inadequacy than mine is as I think how many notable and noble souls have brought their best to this illustrious rendezvous. How poor shall be the largess that the best can bring to this great love feast of our loyalty!

Dear America! "Beautiful my country!" "Nation and company of nations!" I hail my privilege to lay my offering among the laurels of this day of days. Massachusetts, the mother of Adams; New York, proud foster mother of Alexander Hamilton; Illinois, dear to us forever for those two sons of Anak who smote home for the cause of mankind's emancipation and enfranchisement —I have loved all these with a filial love; but were any or all of them to lift recreant and insane hands against the District of Columbia, I am for my whole country! Thank

God, undistinguishable, indisseverable, all those stars blend in one ever crescent light. How shall Texas say "This is mine," or Ohio say "This is mine?" All are ours, and we are for them all!

But we are here for a mission. That were but tawdry declamation that should deal in glittering vagueness. A duty summons us —a divine, a holy trust is in our hands at such an hour, in such a land, when still portent and promise are so strangely blended. It is ours in the name of the fathers who "having served their generation by the will of God have fallen asleep," to recognize the demands upon our total powers and to pledge ourselves that the hastening future of our fatherland shall be epical and not tragic.

I am asked to speak to you to-day of The Duty of Enthusiasm. I wanted a big text, and it is a big one. Enthusiasm is a great word. A true master of our English utterance who gave language new form by his idiomatic use of it—Isaac Taylor—wrote a book once upon the NATURAL HISTORY OF ENTHUSIASM. But his whole treatment of his theme dealt with the lower and oblique associations of that word and gave warning against perverse, unreasoned, and mistaken zeal. He noted the quixotic and fanatical elements of the mere rhapsodist—the dogmatism and violence of the self-opinionate—the passion that lacks wisdom and the ecstasy that is sanguine without sense. It is of the better and truer significance of enthusiasm that I would speak. The word means full of the god. It shall stand with us for inspiration, for consecration, for that joyful and dauntless purpose which never rests in the superficiality of averages and which hastens the kingdom of that truth which it is persuaded of and hails from afar. True enthusiasm means daring and uncompromising devotion. It is not a sentiment and an intoxicant, but an ardent and quenchless hope that what should be shall be! This is dedication—the sublime surrender of the whole being to the guidance of the ever ongoing God. And this is duty. Because it is a duty it is a possibility. It is our privilege and our right. I summon your souls to see that nothing less than such a surrender to our Maker can answer the voices of the times and fulfill the obligations of high manhood and womanhood.

It is the conquest of the soul by great and profound ideals that makes great. This is the stuff whereof pioneers and prophets are made. Said Swedenborg: "Such as the love is, such is the wisdom." Men see with their hearts, and the heart that counts no sacrifice costly if ultimate truth may reign is the heart that is full of the god. The three great elements of power are these—judgment, imagination, hope. He who has these is complete and furnished to every good work. One may have either without the others—then he is gibbous instead of spherical. The true leader and the true follower —each is one who will take great risks for great reasons.

"He either fears his fate too much,
 Or his deserts are small,
Who will not put it to the touch,
 And win or lose it all."

But this non-prudential eagerness does not forget the critical, it rather consummates its conclusions in executive decisions. There is to-day a cant of moderation. It is one of the affectations of conventional propriety to suppress impulse and to cry down intensity of conviction. This *blasé* theory of behavior, this *ennui* of life avoids elemental seriousness. It never breathes deep enough to breathe hard. It skims the mere rim of reality. It dwells in petty fads, and gushes over them with abundant adjectives. It is superlative because it is not positive, and takes the whole English language in vain to ornament a whim. It lives in the subjunctive instead of the indicative mood. It wishes, but it never wills. The simulation of enthusiasm is its death. Shallow intent destroys the very capacity of high thoughts and deep life. Dawdling selfishness is the damnation of dudes and impotents.

"For life is not as idle ore,
 But iron dug from central gloom,
And heated hot with burning fears,
And dipped in baths of hissing tears,
 And battered with the stroke of doom,
To shape and use."

We need to read and get by heart Paul's characterization of Epaphroditus, who "for the work of God was nigh unto death, gambling away his life."

A wise Frenchman wrote a book upon the proposition that "Eloquence is a Virtue." It is a faithful saying. When the real man arrives he speaks with tones that smite his time of stupidity as the thunders break the oppression of the heavy summer day. John the Baptist, Martin Luther, Cromwell, Mirabeau, Samuel Adams, O'Connell, John Bright, Garrison, Phillips, Lincoln—these are the men whose enthusiasm interrupts and crushes the stolidity of custom and irresolution of policy. The great orator is the implacable *man*. With molten speech, with the naked power of a conviction that scorns half-truths, a terror to the bad and to the timid, impeaching that absolute infidelity to the hour and the opportunity which often intrenches itself in the most consummate orthodoxy *in thesi*— not sinister and never merely dextrous, but two-handed and whole-hearted the Voice leaps alive into the midst of a stagnant and querulous time, challenging its practical atheisms with all the sublimity and mastery of the truth itself. Such men God sends as the couriers of repentance, and they are the herald angels of the Evangel. They disdain the paltry evasions and subterfuges of expediency, and trembling themselves in the reality of that kindling ideal which both consumes and compels them—taking fire like meteors by the rapidity and friction of their passage- they are the avatars of the message they announce!

But to us all God is ever saying: "Whom shall I send, and who will go for us?" A deep voice sounding out the lonely truth is like a midnight bell; it rings into innumerable ears, which wake, and listen, and thank God for another day. God guide and guard that prophet, who, in the face of vast reproach, is rousing the hypnotized conscience of Manhattan Island. The Tammany Goliath may vaunt, and the Republican Eliab may sneer, but this latest David, not in the Saul's armor of the place holder and pelf distributor, but with the smooth stone slung true shall slay his tens of thousands. The one great mission of the Hebrew Prophets was to preach righteousness to their times—they were in politics for all they were worth! It is an antediluvian heresy that denies the right or neglects the duty of such an enthusiasm as knows how to perceive the power of contemporary iniquity and to arraign it with the voice of a Micah or a Joel.

Enthusiasm is the characteristic alike of the scientist, the historian, the poet, the true statesman, the apostle, the saint. Inspiration is the note and accent of every life that touches its age with the dateless law of duty. They who "prefer bondage with ease to strenuous liberty" are those who have said of the idols of material success—"these be thy gods." Shall it be Aaron, with the cultus of the calf—the worship of the visible—or Moses, with "Thou shalt have no other gods before me!" There is no slavery so base and blind as the prostitution of enthusiasm at the altars of Mammon—where to-day "the great man boweth down, and the mean man humbleth himself." The last question is, who shall reign? The sovereignty of God is the final truth. Deep and ominous, if we heed it not, the long roll is already beating, and from gate to gate the whisper will swell to a voice like the storm "who is on the Lord's side."

Americans are, of all people on earth, most avid of congratulation and averse to censure. But a merely provincial patriotism that worships either knowledge or skill or strength or plenty will no more preserve our semi-Christian civilization from becoming godless than these saved Babylon! Americans do not love their Jeremiahs; but they well may heed them. We are not in such danger to-day from foreigners as we are from ourselves. I for one, because I am a patriot, will remember that the best part of the word "fatherland" is the first part; and, repudiating that toast of Stephen Decatur's "Our Country Right or Wrong," I will pray "Our Father which art in Heaven," and "Our Country Right and Never Otherwise." "*Vox Dei, vox populi*" must be the new patriotism. It is only the discipline of obedience to the high God that can apply the power of enthusiasm to public life, eagerness of conscience must be trained by common consent to effective programs. We need to-day a new oath of allegiance to that God whom upon our coinage we say we trust. We need to publish a new Declaration of *Dependence*. Public opinion is not infallible. Majorities are not final. Righteous minorities are the real rulers—not screaming themselves hoarse with that terrestrial apotheosis of man in the "*Aux armes les braves*" of the "Marseillaise," but chorusing the deeper purpose and the sublimer enthusiasm of "*Ein feste Burg ist unser Gott!*"

Liberty's statue yonder in New York Harbor is but a hollow idol unless it upholds the lamp that God alone can kindle and keep! Providential America, daughter of privilege and opportunity, understand thyself by that philosophy of history which thine open Bible gives thee, by that enthusiasm, that fulness of God, whose prayers become prophecies! For here is truest taught and easiest learned what makes a nation happy and keeps it so, what ruins kingdoms and lays cities flat. Upon the Saxon race lies the triple mission of Greek, Roman, and Hebrew. It stands triply for culture, for law, for reverence. Not alone in these tongues, but in our own dear English let it be written—in the tongue of Wiclif and Milton, and Tennyson, and Whittier, and Lanier, "This is the King!"

The Saxon never wore the yoke easily or long. With the power of conscience and the enthusiasm of truth, he has conquered his' conquerors. He may perish, but he can only perish by his own moral suicide. The Saxon is invited to the headship of the nations. He rules as Cæsar never dreamed of ruling. He holds the commanding influence in four continents, and is sole master of the fifth. He girdles the round earth with nations. His righteous will may be law for the planet. He must not swerve from God. Christ has raised up this solid front of a hundred million men. What pencil dipped in the dawn can write its possible glories, or dipped in the smoke of Hell can limn its obloquy! The switch points are set close for either line.

"*To-day* we fashion destiny, the web of fate we spin,
To-day for all hereafter choose we holiness or sin;
E'en now from starry Gerizim or Ebal's cloudy crown
We call the dews of blessing or the bolts of cursing down."

There is an optimism which boasts in its own strength and there is a pessimism which cravenly invites the woes it dreads. There is a *tertium quid*, the cross of Christ; above us Heaven, beneath us the pit, about us God! Not optimism, not pessimism, but enthusiasm. There are dangers dire and dark, demagogs and monopolists, poltroons and panderers, with sophisms that slander manhood and doubts that slander God! But by the arm of God we can beat them down!

Back in 1871, when men in Chicago were hanging themselves to lamp-posts and drowning themselves in the lake, a man put an advertisement in one of the papers, reading: "Men of Chicago. Take hope. Our fathers raised her from the bog, and we can raise her from the ashes." It is that spirit that has raised that Phenix City by the shore of Lake Michigan. It is that Chicago spirit translated and transfigured by the Gospel of Christ that we need to-day, every one of us, to put whole souls into all our affairs. God will give us light if we ask Him for it. Hope is creative, doubt is abortive. Let us hope, let us act. The men who are willing to deny themselves any possible gain, who forget that a vote is a vow, who forget that a candidate is a man clad-in-white, who forget the patriotism of paying taxes, who forget that law is like a bicycle and that the way to keep it standing is to keep it going, whose very bones are flabby with civil neglect, whose minds are mere kennels for vagrant theories, and who recant the old-fashioned law of duty and "the faith that comes by self-control," and by self-sacrifice, too—these moral spendthrifts and soul paupers, these are the *incubi* of the times. Such a man is not a man, but a manikin. But upon the souls who are full of the enthusiasm of duty rests the unconquerable State. To these "the Christ that is to be" flings wide His effectual doors. Ruled by such a ken, life can never seem shabby nor hope irrational. To him who truly lives and does, the veil of the visible becomes more and more diaphanous. Such an one shall be able to say, with brave Walter Scott, what he so simply uttered as he drew near the end of his life of honor: "I think that next week I shall be in the secret." There are such men. We do not always listen to hear the deep breathing of the people ready to respond to the prophet of conscience; we bite into one blasted ear, and forget the green sabers of the corn that array a thousand prairies. We find one brackish pool, and forget the trickling of a myriad translucent springs; we see one whirling, copper cloud, and doubt the sun. But God reigns! God reigns! God reigns!

On some level shores the tides rise, invisibly percolating all the sands. One instant it is shore, and the next up comes the ocean and it is sea; the ebb is no more, the flood tide is on. Such is the apparent spontaneity and instantaneousness of many a great movement under the Sovereign Spirit.

Thou who didst steer the little *Mayflower* to her desired haven, bring America to port! Grant that upon this gathering of the people our dear flag may shine with the light of an Evangel, pure as the sweet influences of the Pleiades and firm as the bands of Orion. Thou who dost guide Arcturus, grant that those stars may glow in the coronet of Christ. In the enthusiasm of loyalty to God and serried against the evils and forebodings of the time we will march in the footsteps of a believing ancestry. Let every flagstaff and belfry, every throbbing dome and thundering cannon, every eloquent orator and voice of multitudes, every prayer of gratitude and every tear of joy, carry the name that is above every name and swear it with a mighty oath: "This God is our God, as he was our father's God, and he shall be ours forever and forever." And we can say with all high confidence after the great poet now asleep:

"Are there thunders moaning in the distance?
Are there specters moving in the darkness?
Trust the hand of light will guide His people

Till the thunders pass, the specters vanish,
And the light is victor, and the darkness
Dawns into the jubilee of the ages."

GOD SAVE AMERICA! I.

SUGGESTIVE THOUGHTS

FOREFATHERS' DAY, The True.—It is conceded that Captain Jones of the *Mayflower* sighted Cape Cod November 9, 1620, O. S., but a landing on Plymouth Rock is mentioned December 22, 1620, N. S. Old style was the calendar of Julius Cæsar, dating from the third century, which made the days too long, and provided too many leap years. In 1582 Pope Gregory found there had been ten superfluous leap years and took ten days out of the calendar, and reduced the future number of leap years. In 1752 the English adopted the system, allowing eleven days for error, as it had been constantly increasing. This is a very simple matter, but it has puzzled old heads.

The *Mayflower* remained in Provincetown harbor thirty-four days, during which Peregrine White, the first child, was born, and Dorothy May Bradford, the wife of the future Governor and historian, died. Three expeditions were sent out, the third of which, consisting of sixteen men, four of whom were seamen of the *Mayflower,* reached Plymouth December 11, 1620, O. S., and immediately returned to the *Mayflower* at Provincetown. The date was clearly December 21, N. S., and that, and not December 22, is the true Forefathers' Day.—CHARLES W. FELT. (N. Y. S.)

MARRIAGE IN PURITAN DAYS.—The brides of old-time Puritan days were solemnly adjured to wear:

Something old and something new;
Something borrowed, something blue.

They were seldom married in church; often in the new house that was destined to be their home, and you may believe it was generally bleak enough to give an almost funereal aspect to the affair. It was bad luck to look in the mirror after the toilet was completed—even the maidens of that day were superstitious.

The wedding gown was first displayed in public at meetings. Indeed, there was no other place where the bride could surely count upon finding all her friends together.

The bride and groom and bridal party began the display by proudly walking in a little procession through the narrow streets to the meeting house on the Sabbath following the marriage.

In Larned's HISTORY OF WINDHAM COUNTY, CONN., may be found a description of such an amusing scene in Brooklyn, Conn.

Further public notice was drawn to the bride by allowing her to choose the text for the sermon preached on the first Sunday of the coming out of the newly married couple. Much ingenuity was exercised in finding appropriate and sometimes startling Bible texts for these wedding sermons.

The instances are well known of the marriage of Parson Smith's two daughters, one of whom selected the text. "Mary hath chosen that good part," while the daughter Abbie, who married John Adams, decided upon the text, "John came neither eating nor drinking, and they say he hath a devil." —*Selected.*

MAYFLOWER AND OCEANIC.—Those persons who are on the lookout for coincidences may find one in the sailing of the *Mayflower* with the Pilgrim fathers and the departure of the *Oceanic* on her first voyage.

The *Mayflower* sailed from Plymouth for the land of the West on Wednesday, September 6, 1620. The new *Oceanic* sailed from Liverpool for New York on Wednesday, September 6, 1899.

It will be of interest also to compare the size of the *Mayflower* with that of the *Oceanic.* The *Mayflower* was said to be 180 tons burden. The *Oceanic* is 17,274 tons, gross measurement. The former carried 100 passengers. The latter will carry 1,575 passengers and 450 crew.

A male child born on board the *Mayflower* was christened Oceanus. A resident in Belfast who was presented with a daughter on January 14, 1899, the day of the launching of the *Oceanic,* christened the child with the name of the new ship.—*Selected.*

MAYFLOWER, The.—That little ship, the *Mayflower,* was destined for a memorable place in history. Within its cabin this Republic had its origin in the compact that was signed by brave and religious men, declaring their faith in God and the right of men to worship Him according to the dictates of conscience, a compact sealed with tears of faith and made holy by prayer.

The last Sabbath of that voyage was spent upon the vessel in holy worship. Earnest, fervent prayers were offered. Hymns of praise were sung and covenants with God were renewed.

"Amidst the storm they sang,
And the stars heard and the sea,
And the sounding aisles of the dim woods rang
To the anthems of the free."

The Pilgrims are dead. The *Mayflower's* little company all sleep along the shores of their New World home. But the songs which awakened the echo upon that wintry

Sabbath morning are still floating through the forests and over the hills and plains of our land in unison with the song of peace and good-will to men. They being dead yet speak. The music of that grand chorus rings in our ears to-day! And down in the future, when the singers are forgotten, it will still have its influence as an educating power among the masses.—Rev. John W. Sayers (C. G.)

POETRY

That Gray, Cold Christmas Day

By Hezekiah Butterworth

They sailed away from Provincetown Bay
In the fireless light of the sun,
And they came at night to a havened height,
And the journey at last was done.
With rain and sleet were the tall masts iced,
And frosty and dark was the air,
But they looked from the crystal sails to Christ
As they moored in the harbor fair.
The sky was cold and gray,
And there were no ancient bells to ring,
No priests to chant, no choirs to sing,
No chapel of baron, lord or king,
That gray, cold winter day.

The snow came down on the vacant seas
And deep on the lone rocks lay;
But their axes rung 'mid the evergreen trees,
And followed the Sabbath day.
The Christmas came, in a crimson haze,
And the workmen said at dawn:
" Shall our axes swing on this day of days
When the Lord of Light was born?"
The sky was cold and gray,
And there were no ancient bells to ring,
No priests to chant, no choirs to sing,
No chapel of baron, lord or king,
That gray, cold Christmas day.

" The old town's bells we seem to hear:
They are ringing sweet on the Dee;
They are ringing sweet on the Haarlem Meer,
And sweet on the Zuyder Zee.
The pines are frosted with snow and sleet.
Shall we our axes wield,
When the bells of Lincoln are ringing sweet
And the bells of Austerfield?"
The sky was cold and gray,
And there were no ancient bells to ring,
No priests to chant, no choirs to sing,
No chapel of baron, lord or king,
That gray, cold Christmas day.

Then the master said: " Your axes wield;
Remember ye Malabarre Bay,
And the covenant there with the Lord ye sealed;
Let your axes ring to-day.
You may talk of the old town's bells to-night,
When your work for the Lord is done;
And your boats return, and the shallops light
Shall follow the light of the sun.
The sky is cold and gray,
And here are no ancient bells to ring,
No priests to chant, no choirs to sing,
No chapel of baron, lord or king,
This gray, cold Christmas day.

" If the Lord was born on Christmas Day,
And the day of Him is blest,
Then low at His feet the evergreens lay,
And cradle His Church in the West.
Immanuel waits at the temple gates
Of the nation to-day ye found,
And the Lord delights in no empty rites—
To-day let your axes sound!"
The sky was cold and gray,
And there were no ancient bells to ring,
No priests to chant, no choirs to sing,
No chapel of baron, lord or king,
That gray, cold Christmas day.

Their axes rang through the evergreen trees,
Like the bells on the Thames and Tay,
And they, cheering, sang by the windy seas,
And they thought of Malabarre Bay.
On the lonely heights of Burial Hill
The old Precisioners sleep,
But did ever men with a nobler will
A goodlier Christmas keep—
When sky was cold and gray,
And there were no ancient bells to ring,
No priests to chant, no choirs to sing,
No chapel of baron, lord or king,
That gray, cold Christmas day?
F.

The Storming of Bunker Hill

By Francis Zuri Stone

Twice on the low redoubt, ere noon, the Regulars advanced,
And from their burnished bayonets the sun of morning glanced;
Twice all the bristling fire-locks flashed behind that sullen mound,
And with a coronet of flame the thundering rampart crowned.
And twice the English columns red, like Fundy's mighty tide,
Rolled back and left their stranded wreck heaped up on ev'ry side:
Down, down the flame-whipped, shot-scourged slope, the panting soldiers fled,
While through the smoke clouds, glowed like coals, strewn on the ground, their dead!

Now reinforced by Clinton's troops, over their comrades slain,
With faces grim the grenadiers move to assault again;
But ere to storm that stubborn height they form in close array,
As swimmers strip to buffet tides, their knapsacks cast away.
No empty volleys herald them:—this time the King shall deal
His mercy to the " Rebel " horde on gleaming rows of steel!

The anchored ships their broadsides cease,
and silence settles down,
Save that the church-bells, cannon-jarred,
still clang in Boston town.

"Once more stand firm, ye heroes, stand!
Once more repel the foe!
God for our Cause! Stand fast, ye Brave,
and meet the final blow!
Stand! for your wives and children watch
from every belfry high,
And when such prayers attend his soul, what
patriot fears to die?
See, where in seething billows red the flames
o'er Charlestown roll!
Hark! thundering from its steeple burned,
hear ye the church-bell toll!
It summoned ye to worship once—now with
expiring breath
It summons ye to victory, or to a glorious
death!"

"Halt!" And a hedge of bayonets fronts
each determined line,
Like icicles in winter's sun the musket barrels shine.
"Charge!" and as the myriad autumn leaves
before a gale are whirled,
Lord Howe against that wall of earth his
mad battalions hurled.
Now 'neath the tattered pine-tree flag a line
of fire runs
Along the curtain of the fort, and empty are
the guns,
And wave on wave of grenadiers against the
breastwork surge,
To fall as breakers from a rock the Equi-
noxes scourge!

Yet as successive waves, flung back, return
with heavier stroke,
So o'er the parapet at last the spray of bayo-
nets broke,
And as when Ocean conquers dikes she hides
the barrier crossed,
Beneath that crest of British steel the wall
to sight was lost!
So from the long-contested ground our
smoke-grimed troops retreat,
And carry with them victory from such a
dear defeat
And tho forced back 'cross Charlestown
Neck they doggedly withdrew,
The battle-storm had only ceased, to burst
the sky anew!

But like a master-mariner who will not leave
his post
Tho sinks his ship beneath his feet, so
lingered 'gainst the host
The champion of Young Liberty, and gal-
lant Warren fell,
Not unremembered in the land for which he
fought so well;
For where, on land or sea, shall float our
proud flag from its staff,
There towers in her Stars and Stripes the
Patriot's cenotaph!

Y. C.

The Lexington Minute-Man

By Laura E. Richards

'Twas the gray of the morning, Revere at the
gate
With whipstock and fist he did din it, man!
"The British are marching, the hour is late!
Make ready, each Lexington minute-man!"

A hand to the musket—a word to the wife—
The cockade, who but she then should pin
it, man?
And there in the doorway she leaned for her
life,
Gazing after her Lexington minute-man.

And hurry and scurry we ran to the green;
Not a lad but was bound he'd be in it, man!
There Hadley and Muzzy and Parker were
seen,
All proud of the name of the minute-man.

And Raymond and Harrington ran with
Munroe,
And Winship and Wyman did spin it, man!
And Comee and Farmer and Estabrook too
Sprang quick to the call for the minute-
man.

Now shoulder to shoulder, and eyes to the
front!
The shooting, leave them to begin it, man!
The Nation's behind us, but we bear the
brunt;
Stand fast, every Lexington minute-man!

If they will have a war, let its first shot be
here!
They begin, but we'll end it and win it,
man!
So steady, in valor and constancy clear,
Stand fast, every Lexington minute-man!

Ah! well, 'tis long over! our land is long
free;
My hair, Time's beginning to thin it, man!
But still at my work or my rest tho I be,
My heart beats the tune of the minute-man!

And tho my old limbs should be paralyzed
clean;
Ay! e'en tho the grave I were in it, man,
Yet it's odds but you'd find me on Lexington
green,
If the drum beat the call for the minute-
man.

Y. C.

The Pilgrim's Vision

By Oliver Wendell Holmes

I saw in the naked forest our scattered
remnant cast,
A screen of shivering branches between them
and the blast;
The snow was falling round them, the dying
fell so fast;
I looked to see them perish, when, lo! the
vision passed.

Again mine eyes were opened: the feeble had
    waxed strong,
The babes had grown to sturdy men, the
    remnant was a throng;
By shadowed lake and winding stream, and
    all the shores along,
The howling demons quaked, to hear the
    Christians' godly song.

They slept, the village fathers, by rivers,
    lake, and shore,
When far adown the steep of Time the vision
    rose once more;
I saw along the winter snow a spectral col-
    umn pour,
And high above their broken ranks a tattered
    flag they bore.

Their leader rode before them, of bearing
    calm and high,
The light of Heaven's own kindling throned
    in his awful eye;
These were the Nation's champions, her dread
    appeal to try!
" God for the right! " I faltered, and, lo! the
    train passed by.

Once more: the strife was ended, the solemn
    issue tried:
The Lord of Hosts, His mighty arm, had
    helped our Israel's side;
Gray stone and grassy hillock told where her
    martyrs died,
And peace was in the borders of victory's
    chosen bride.

A crash, as when some swollen cloud cracks
    o'er the tangled trees!
With side to side, and spar to spar, whose
    smoking decks are these?
I know St. George's blood-red cross, thou
    mistress of the seas;
But what is she, whose streaming bars roll
    out before the breeze?

Ah! well her iron ribs are knit, whose thun-
    ders strive to quell
The bellowing throats, the blazing lips, that
    pealed the Armada's knell!
The mist was cleared; a wreath of stars rose
    o'er the crimsoned swell,
And wavering from its haughty peak, the
    cross of England fell!

O trembling Faith! tho dark the morn, a
    heavenly torch is thine!
While feebler races melt away, and paler
    orbs decline,
Still shall the fiery pillar's ray along thy
    pathway shine,
To light the chosen tribe that sought this
    Western Palestine!

I see the living tribe roll on; it crowns with
    flaming towers
The icy capes of Labrador, the Spaniard's
    " land of flowers; "
It streams beyond the splintered ridge that
    parts the northern showers,—
From eastern rock to sunset wave the conti-
    nent is ours.

Landing of the Pilgrim Fathers

By Felicia Dorothea Hemans

The breaking waves dashed high
    On a stern and rock-bound coast,
And the woods against a stormy sky
    Their giant branches tossed.

And the heavy night hung dark
    The hills and waters o'er,
When a band of exiles moored their bark
    On the wild New England shore.

Not as the conqueror comes,
    They, the true-hearted, came;
Not with the roll of the stirring drums,
    And the trumpet that sings of fame.

Not as the flying come,
    In silence and in fear;
They shook the depths of the desert gloom
    With their hymns of lofty cheer.

Amidst the storm they sang,
    And the stars heard, and the sea;
And the sounding aisles of the dim woods
    rang
To the anthem of the free.

The ocean eagle soared
    From his nest by the white wave's foam;
And the rocking pines of the forest roared—
    This was their welcome home!

There were men with hoary hair
    Amidst that pilgrim band;—
Why had they come to wither there,
    Away from their childhood's land?

There was woman's fearless eye,
    Lit by her deep love's truth;
There was manhood's brow serenely high,
    And the fiery heart of youth.

What sought they thus afar?
    Bright jewels of the mine?
The wealth of seas, the spoils of war?
    They sought a faith's pure shrine!

Ay, call it holy ground,
    The soil where first they trod;
They left unstained what there they found—
    Freedom to worship God.

Appendix

BIBLIOGRAPHY

General

[Holy Days and Holidays in General.]

AMERICAN LIBRARY ASSOCIATION.—Index to General Literature. (Houghton, Mifflin & Co., Boston.)

ANGLICAN AND AMERICAN PULPIT LIBRARY.— [5 vols.] (E. S. Gorham, New York.)

AUGUSTI, JOHANN C. W.—Handbuch der Christlichen Archäologie. [3 vols.] (Leipzig. 1817-31.)

BENHAM, W.—Sermons for the Church Year. [2 vols.] (E. P. Dutton & Co., New York.)

BENNETT, C. W.—Christian Archaeology. (Phillips & Hunt, New York.)

BINGHAM, JOSEPH.—Origines Ecclesiasticae, or The Antiquities of the Christian Church. [2 vols.] (London, England.)

CHAMBERS, R.—The Book of Days. [2 vols.] (J. B. Lippincott Co., Philadelphia.)

COLEMAN, LYMAN.—Ancient Christianity Exemplified. (J. B. Lippincott Co., Philadelphia.)

FOSTER, ELON.—New Cyclopedia of Poetical Illustrations. [First and Second Series.] (Funk & Wagnalls Co., New York.)

FOSTER, ELON.—New Cyclopedia of Prose Illustrations. [First and Second Series.] (Funk & Wagnalls Co., New York.)

GERHARDT, PAUL.—Spiritual Songs. [Tr. by John Kelly.] (Alexander Strahan, London, England.)

GRANT, ALEXANDER H.—Church Seasons. (Thomas Whittaker, New York.)

HOMILETIC REVIEW.—[Vols. i-xlii.] (Funk & Wagnalls Co., New York.)

HONE, WILLIAM.—Every Day Book. (Ward, Lock & Co., London, England.)

HONE, WILLIAM.—Year Book. (Ward, Lock & Co., London, England.)

HOSPINIAN, RUDOLPH.—De Origine Festorum Christianorum. (Original Ed., Zurich, 1612.)

KEBLE, JOHN.—The Christian Year. (Thomas Nelson & Sons, New York.)

KEN, BISHOP THOMAS.—Hymns for all the Festivals in the Year. (B. M. Pickering. London, England.)

LOCKYER, J. N.—Origin of the Year. [*Nature,* vol. xlv, p. 487; xlvi, p. 104; xlvii, pp. 32, 228.] (New York.)

LYRA GERMANICA.—Tr. by Catherine Winkworth. (Longmans, Green & Co., London and New York.)

MACARTHUR, ROBERT S.—The Christian Year. [Current Questions for Thinking People, p. 325.] American Baptist Publication Society, Philadelphia.)

MATSON, HENRY.—References for Literary Workers. (A. C. McClurg & Co., Chicago.)

NEALE, JOHN MASON.—Church Festivals and Their Household Words. (J. T. Hayes, London, England.)

NEALE, JOHN MASON.—Hymns of the Eastern Church. (J. T. Hayes, London, England.)

NEALE, JOHN MASON.—Mediaeval Hymns and Sequences. (Joseph Masters, London, England.)

NEWMAN, JOHN H.—Use of Saints' Days. [Sermons, vol. ii, p. 393.] (Rivingtons, London, England. 1884.)

NOBLE, FRANKLIN.—Thoughts for the Occasion, Anniversary and Religious. (E. B. Treat & Co., New York.)

POOLE, WILLIAM F.—Index to Periodical Literature. (Houghton, Mifflin & Co., Boston.)

RIDDLE, JOSEPH E.—Manual of Christian Antiquities. (John W. Parker, London, England.)

SACRED LYRICS FROM THE GERMAN.—(Presbyterian Board of Publication, Philadelphia.)

SANDERSON, JOSEPH.—Thoughts for the Occasion, Patriotic and Secular. (E. B. Treat & Co., New York.)

SCHAFF AND GILMAN.—Library of Religious Poetry. (Funk & Wagnalls Co., New York.)

TREASURY OF RELIGIOUS THOUGHT. [Vols. i-xix.] (E. B. Treat & Co., New York.)

VENNER, G. U.—The Church Year. [*Lutheran Quarterly,* vol. xxiv, p. 455.] (Gettysburg, Pa.)

Holy Days

NEW YEAR'S DAY

BANKS, LOUIS A.—Motto for the Year. [Paul and His Friends. p. 1.] (Funk & Wagnalls Co., New York. 1898.)

BOSWELL, JAMES.—New Year Day Observed. [Life of Samuel Johnson, p. 134.] (Henry Washbourne, London, England.)

GRANT, A. H.—Circumcision of Christ.

[Church Seasons, p. 73.] (Thomas Whittaker, New York. 1893.)

GRAY, J. COMPER.—New Year's Day. [Biblical Museum. r. e. Gen. to ii, Kings, pp. 270, 439.] (E. R. Herrick & Co., New York. 1898.)

HEPWORTH, GEORGE H.—A Happy New Year.

[Herald Sermons, p. 46.] (E. P. Dutton & Co., New York. 1894.)

McLaren, Alexander.—The New Year. [Secret of Power, p. 187.] (The Macmillan Co., London and New York.)

Neander, August.—New Year's Festival. [History of the Christian Religion and Church, vol. ii, pp. 350-351.] (Houghton, Mifflin & Co., Boston. 1871.)

Parkhurst, C. H.—Looking Forward to the New Year. [Treasury of Religious Thought, vol. xvii, p. 686.] (E. B. Treat & Co., New York.)

Spurgeon, C. H.—A New Year's Benediction. [Sermons, vol. vii, p. 11.] (Funk & Wagnalls Co., New York.)

Talmage, T. D.—Forward. [The Brooklyn Tabernacle Sermons, p. 389.] (Funk & Wagnalls Co., New York.)

EPIPHANY

Brooks, Phillips.—The Heroism of Foreign Missions. [Sermons, vol. v, p. 1.] (E. P. Dutton & Co., New York.)

Century of Christian Progress, A.—(Fleming H. Revell Co., New York.)

Christlieb, Theodor.—Protestant Foreign Missions. (Congregational House, Boston.)

Dennis, James S.—Christian Missions and Social Progress. [3 vols.] (Fleming H. Revell Co., New York.)

Encyclopedia of Missions.—[2 vols.] (Funk & Wagnalls Co., New York.)

Evangelization of the World. (Fleming H. Revell Co., New York.)

Leonard, D. L.—A Hundred Years of Missions. (Funk & Wagnalls Co., New York.)

Pierson, Arthur T.—Crisis of Missions. (Baker & Taylor Co., New York.)

Pierson, Arthur T.—The Miracles of Missions. [First, Second, and Third Series.] (Funk & Wagnalls Co., New York.)

Storrs, Richard S.—Addresses on Foreign Missions. (Congregational House, Boston.)

Upham, Prof. F. W.—The Star of Our Lord. (Nelson & Phillips, New York.)

Upham, Prof. F. W.—The Wise Men: Who They Were. (Nelson & Phillips, New York.)

LENT

Brooks, Phillips.—Sermons. [Vol. ii, p. 200.] (E. P. Dutton & Co., New York. 1881.)

Bruce, Alexander B.—Fasting. [The Training of the Twelve, p. 69.] (T. & T. Clark, Edinburgh. 1877.)

Collier, Price.—A Lenten Sermon. [Sermons, p. 161.] (E. P. Dutton & Co., New York. 1892.)

Farrar, Dean F. W.—A Study of Temptation. [The Homiletic Review, vol. xxx, p. 126.] (Funk & Wagnalls Co., New York.)

Hodge, Charles.—Mortify the Deeds of the Body.—[Conference Papers, 1879, p. 150.] (Charles Scribner's Sons, New York.)

Hodge, Charles.—Fasting. [Conference Papers 1879, p. 262.] (Charles Scribner's Sons, New York.)

Parkhurst, Charles H.—A Man of Sorrows. [Homiletic Review, vol. xxv, p. 230.] (Funk & Wagnalls Co., New York.)

Peck, J. O.—Revival Methods. [Homiletic Review, vol. ix, p. 351.] (Funk & Wagnalls Co., New York.)

Potter, Henry C.—Revival Agencies. [Homiletic Review, vol. xxi, p. 331.] (Funk & Wagnalls Co., New York.)

Robertson, Frederick W.—Worldliness. [Sermons, p. 330.] (Harper & Brothers, New York. 1870.)

PALM SUNDAY

Beecher, Henry Ward.—Palm Sunday Sermon. [Christian World Pulpit, vol. viii, p. 100.] (London.)

Hoare, Charles James.—The Exaltation of Christ. [Sermons for the Church's Year, edited by W. Benham, p. 296.] (E. P. Dutton & Co., New York.)

Lives of Christ [in loco.]

McCulloch, D.D.—The Man on the Throne. [The Evangelical Church, ed. by Henry Tullidge, p. 700.] (Thomas Whittaker, New York. 1879.)

Palm Sunday.—[Christian World Pulpit, vol. xix, p. 140.] (London.)

Robinson, Edward.—Researches. [3 vols., vol. i, p. 473.] (Crocker & Brewster, Boston. 1887.)

Spurgeon, Charles H.—Sermons. [Vol. xii, p. 96; xiv, p. 90.] (Funk & Wagnalls Co., New York.)

Stanley, Arthur P.—Sinai and Palestine. [pp. 188-191.] (Charles Scribner's Sons, New York, 1868.)

Talmage, T. D.—Christ Over All. [Pulpit Power and Eloquence, 723.] (F. M. Barton, Cleveland.)

Thomson, William M.—The Land and the Book. [3 vols., vol. i, pp. 408-414.] (Harper & Brothers, New York. 1880.)

COMMUNION SUNDAY

Beecher, C.—Emblems in the Lord's Supper. [New England Magazine, vol. xli, p. 516.] (Warren F. Kellogg, Boston.)

Brandt, John L.—The Lord's Supper. (The Standard Publishing Co., Cincinnati.)

Bruce, Alexander Balmain.—The Training

of the Twelve. [p. 359.] (A. C. Armstrong & Son, New York. 1900.)

EARLE, A. M.—Church Communion Tokens. [*Atlantic Monthly*, vol. lxxiv, p. 210.] (Houghton, Mifflin & Co., Boston.)

KOHLER, K.—Jewish View of the Lord's Supper. [*Public Opinion*, vol. xiii, p. 238.] (New York.)

MAURICE, FREDERICK D.—The Eucharist Considered as a Declaration of Christ's Death to Mankind. [Lincoln's Inn Sermons, 6 vols., vol. iv, p. 97.] (The Macmillan Co., New York.)

MURRAY, ANDREW.—The Lord's Table. (Fleming H. Revell Co., New York.)

NEW ENGLAND MAGAZINE.—The Lord's Supper a Eucharistic Service. [Vol. xlv, p. 868.] (Warren F. Kellogg, Boston.)

ROBERTSON, FREDERICK W.—The Sacrifice of Christ. [Sermons, 1870, p. 495.] (Harper & Brothers, New York.)

SIGMUND, W. S.—Lutheran Doctrine of Lord's Supper. [*Lutheran Quarterly Review*, vol. xxvi, p. 248.] (Gettysburg, Pa.)

GOOD FRIDAY

ATONEMENT, THE, IN MODERN RELIGIOUS THOUGHT. A THEOLOGICAL SYMPOSIUM. (Thomas Whittaker, New York. 1901.)

COOK, JOSEPH.—The Conquering Cross of Christ. [*Our Day*, vol. xiii, p. 541.] (Our Day Publishing Co., Boston.)

CORWIN, C. E.—Development of the Doctrine of the Atonement, from the Time of Christ until 730 A. D. [*Reformed Quarterly*, vol. xliii, p. 375; 730-1710, p. 497]. (Reformed Church Publication Society, Philadelphia, Pa.)

HEISLER, C. W.—The Day of the Crucifixion of Jesus Christ. [*Lutheran Quarterly Review*, vol. xxv, p. 209.] (Gettysburg, Pa.)

HOLCK, L. G.—Real Meaning of the Crucifixion. [*New Church Review*, 1883, vol. iii, p. 504.] (Fairbanks & Palmer, Chicago.)

KING, E.—The Seven Words from the Cross. [The Sermon Year Book, for 1891, p. 136.] (Funk & Wagnalls Co., New York.)

LANE, C. R.—The Suffering of Jesus Christ: Was It in His Divine Nature? [*Reformed Quarterly*, vol. xxxix, p. 173.] (Reformed Church Publication Society, Philadelphia.)

ROBERTSON, FREDERICK W.—The Loneliness of Christ. [Sermons, p. 168.] (Harper & Brothers, New York. 1870.)

SMYTH, J. K.—Gladstone on the Atonement. [*New Church Review*, vol. ii, p. 112.] (Fairbanks & Palmer, Chicago.)

VOIGHT, A. G.—New Testament Idea of the Atonement. [*Lutheran Quarterly*, vol. xxv, p. 310.] (Gettysburg Pa.)

EASTER

BENT, J. T.—Easter in Greece. [*Living Age*, vol. clii, p. 402.] (Living Age Co., Boston.)

CHAMPION, T. E.—Easter Observances. [*Canadian Magazine*, vol. ii, p. 458.] (Ontario Publishing Co., Toronto.)

EASTER.—[T. M. Clark, A. G. Haygood, and others. *Magazine of Christian Literature*, vol. vi, p. 142.] (Christian Literature Publishing Co., New York.)

EASTER, DATE OF.—[*Leisure Hour*, vol. xxv, pp. 256, 494.] (London, England.)

EASTER IN ROME.—[*Catholic World*, vol. xli, p. 120.] (Catholic World Magazine, New York.)

GOTWALD, L. A.—Resurrection of Jesus

Christ. [*Lutheran Quarterly*, vol. xxiv, p. 546.] (Gettysburg, Pa.)

MILLIGAN, WILLIAM.—The Resurrection of Our Lord. (The Macmillan Co., London and New York.)

RICE, W. N.—The Credibility of the Resurrection of Christ. [*Methodist Review*, vol. lv, p. 177.] (Methodist Quarterly Review, New York.)

WESTCOTT, BROOKE F.—The Gospel of the Resurrection. (The Macmillan Co., London and New York.)

WESTCOTT, B. F.—The Revelation of the Risen Lord. (The Macmillan Co., London and New York.)

SUNDAY

CRAFTS, WILBUR F.—The Sabbath for Man. (Funk & Wagnalls Co., New York.)

CRAFTS, WILBUR F.—Sabbath Reform Practicable. [*Our Day*, vol. xiii, p. 520.] (Boston.)

ELLIS, A. B.—Origin of Sabbaths and Weeks. [*Popular Science Monthly*, vol. xlvi, p. 329.] (McClure, Phillips & Co., New York.)

GARDINER, G. W.—Sabbath, Shall We Have One and How? [*Baptist Review*, vol. ii, p. 584.] (Baptist Publication Society, Philadelphia.)

GILFILLAN, JAMES.—The Sabbath. (American Tract Society, New York.)

LORD'S DAY, EIGHT STUDIES OF THE.— (Houghton, Mifflin & Co., Boston.)

OSWALD, F. L.—Sabbatarianism an Expensive Delusion. [*North American Review*, vol. clxii, p. 125.] (Harper & Brothers, New York.)

ROBINSON, S.—Sunday Laws in the U. S. [*Catholic Presbyterian*, vol. ii, p. 87.] (A. D. F. Randolph, New York.)

SABBATH, THE ENGLISH AND AMERICAN.— [*The Nation*, vol. lvi, p. 122.] (Evening Post Publishing Co., New York.)

WARD, J. H.—Future of Sunday Journalism. [*Forum*, vol. i, p. 389.] (Forum Publishing Co., New York.)

ASCENSION DAY

BANKS, LOUIS ALBERT.—Christ and His Friends. [The Divine Magnet, p. 324.] (Funk & Wagnalls Co., New York. 1895)

BRUBAKER, J.—Ascension of Jesus Christ. [*Lutheran Quarterly Review*, vol. xxiv, p. 155.] (Gettysburg, Pa.)

EXPOSITORS' BIBLE.—Commentary on Acts i: 9-11. [p. 43.] (Funk & Wagnalls Co., New York. 1900.)

KINGSLEY, CHARLES.—Ascension Day. [All Saints' Day and Other Sermons, p. 116.] (Charles Scribner's Sons, New York. 1878.)

MILLIGAN, WILLIAM.—The Ascension and Heavenly Priesthood of Our Lord. (The Macmillan Co., London and New York.)

PEARSON, JOHN.—Pearson on the Creed. [Article VI.] (Henry G. Bohn, London, England.)

SPURGEON, CHARLES H.—Lessons of the Ascension. [Sermons, vol. xvii, p. 381.] (Funk & Wagnalls Co., New York.)

WESTCOTT, BROOKE F.—The Revelation of the Risen Lord. [Chapters x, xi.] (The Macmillan Co., London and New York.)

WHITSUNDAY

CHURCH AT ITS DAWN, THE.—[*New Church Review*, vol. i, p. 196.] (Fairbanks & Palmer, Chicago.)

CONGREGATIONALIST, THE.—Theories of the Church. [Vol. vii, p 174.] (Boston.)

CROSBIE, W.—The Lesson of Pentecost. [*The Congregationalist*, vol. vii, p. 577.] (Boston.)

LANE, C. R.—The Holy Spirit. [*Reformed Quarterly*, vol. xxxiii, p. 439.] (The Reformed Church Publication Society, Philadelphia.)

LONDON QUARTERLY REVIEW.—The Holy Spirit Between the Resurrection and Pentecost. [Vol. lx, p. 165.] (London, England.)

MAURICE, FREDERICK DENISON.—The Mean-

ing of the Gift of Tongues. [Sermons, 6 vols, p. 14.] (The Macmillan Co., London and New York. 1892.)

PEPPER, G. D. B.—The Holy Spirit the Need of the Church.—[*Baptist Review*, vol. vi, p. 13.] (Baptist Publication Society, Philadelphia.)

RENNELL, T.—Christians the Temple of the Spirit. [Sermons for the Church Year. Edited by W. Benham, vol. i, p. 382.] (E. P. Dutton & Co., New York.)

ROBERTSON, FREDERICK W.—The Dispensation of the Spirit. [Sermons, p. 455.] (Harper & Brothers, New York. 1870.)

WATERHOUSE, C. W.—Day of Pentecost. [*Baptist Review*, vol. vii, p. 229.] (Baptist Publication Society, Philadelphia.)

CHILDREN'S DAY

CHESEBROUGH, AMOS S.—Children Trained for Disciple-ship. (Hartford, Conn.)

CRAFTS, WILBUR F.—Talks to Boys and Girls About Jesus. (Funk & Wagnalls Co., New York. 1881.)

FOSTER'S CYCLOPEDIA OF PROSE AND POETICAL ILLUSTRATIONS—4 vols. [See under "Child", "Boy", "S. S.", etc.] (Funk & Wagnalls Co., New York.)

HOWATT, J. REID—The Children's Pew. (Thomas Whittaker, New York.)

HOWATT, J. REID—The Children's Preacher. (Thomas Whittaker, New York.)

NOBLE, FRANKLIN.—Thoughts for the Occa-

sion, Anniversary and Religious. [Index under Children's Day.] (E. B. Treat & Co., New York.)

STALL, SYLVANUS.—Five-Minute Object Sermons to Children. (Funk & Wagnalls Co., New York.)

STORIES OF THE FESTIVALS, FASTS, AND SAINTS' DAYS OF THE CHURCH. (Thomas Whittaker, New York.)

SUNDAY SCHOOL WAYS OF WORKING.—(J. D. Wattles & Co., Philadelphia.)

TRUMBULL, HENRY CLAY.—Hints on Child Training. (J. D. Wattles & Co., Philadelphia.)

TRINITY SUNDAY

APPLE, T. G.—God in Christ. [*Reformed Quarterly Review*, vol. xxix, p. 131.] (Reformed Church Publication Society, Philadelphia.)

MAURICE, FREDERICK D.—The Uniting Name. [Sermons, 6 vols., vol. iv, p. 29.] (The Macmillan Co., London and New York.)

SHERWOOD, E.—Mystery of the Trinity. [*Methodist Quarterly Review*, vol. liv, p. 584.]. (New York.)

SPURGEON, C. H.—Personality of the Holy Ghost. [Sermons, vol. i, p. 55.] (Funk & Wagnalls Co., New York.)

STRONG, A. H.—The Two Natures of Christ. [Philosophy and Religion, p. 201.] (A. C. Armstrong & Son, New York.)

TRINITY REALLY UNITY.—[*New Church Review*, vol. iii, p. 258.] (Fairbanks & Palmer, Chicago.)

VAN PELT, D.—*Reformed Quarterly Review*. [Vol. xxix, p. 232.] (Reformed Church Publication Society, Philadelphia.)

VAUGHAN, J. S.—Trinity as Seen in Material Creation. [*Dublin Review*, vol. cxii, p. 16.] (Dublin, Ireland.)

WALLACE, H.—Human Nature a Witness to the Trinity. [*British and Foreign Evangelical Review*, vol. xxxii, p. 35.] (London, England.)

WALWORTH, C. A.—The Trinity in Simple English. [*Catholic World*, vol. xlii, p. 289.] (New York.)

ALL SAINTS' DAY

DEEMS, CHARLES F.—In Memoriam. [Sermons, p. 172.] (Funk & Wagnalls Co., New York.)

HAVEN, GILBERT.—Two Greek Books on the Life Beyond. [Pulpit Power and Eloquence, p. 325.] (F. M. Barton, Cleveland, 1901.)

KINGSLEY, CHARLES.—All Saints' Day. [All Saints' Day and Other Sermons, p. 1.] (Charles Scribner's Sons, New York.)

LITTLE, W. J. KNOX.—The Resurrection of the Body. [The Perfect Life, p. 189.] (Longmans, Green & Co., London and New York.)

PLUMPTRE, E. H.—Our Life in Heaven. [Sermons for the Church's Year. Edited by W. Benham, 2 vols., vol. ii, p. 322.] (E. P. Dutton & Co., New York.)

ROBINSON, FREDERICK W.—God's Revelation of Heaven. [Sermons, p. 23.] (Harper & Brothers, New York. 1870.)

SPURGEON, CHARLES H.—Remains of the Dust of the Saints. [Sermons, vol. iv, p. 164.] (Funk & Wagnalls Co., New York.)

SPURGEON, CHARLES H.—Saints Are in Christ's Companionship. [Sermons, vol. xvii, p. 82.] (Funk & Wagnalls Co., New York.)

STALKER, JAMES.—Heaven. [Pulpit Power and Eloquence, p. 699.] (F. M. Barton, Cleveland.)

TALMAGE, T. DEWITT.—Shall We Know Each Other There? [The Brooklyn Tabernacle Sermons, p. 49.] (Funk & Wagnalls Co., New York.)

THANKSGIVING DAY

DA COSTA, B. F.—Origin of Thanksgiving Day. [Magazine of American History, vol. xiv, p. 556.] (New York.)

GIBSON, J. MONRO.—The Chain of Blessing. [Thanksgiving Sermons and Outlines, p. 64.] (Wilbur B. Ketcham, New York.)

GRACEY, L. L.—Beginnings of Thanksgiving Day in the U. S. [Chautauquan Magazine, vol. xvi, p. 174.] (Cleveland.)

HARDY, E. J.—Thankfulness. [Good Words, vol. xxiv, p. 241.] (London, England.)

MACMILLAN, HUGH.—The Table Prepared in Presence of Foes. [Thanksgiving Sermons and Outlines, p. 11.] (Wilbur B. Ketcham, New York.)

NORTON, C. L.—Thanksgiving Day Past and Present. [Magazine of American History, vol. xiv, p. 556.] (New York.)

SPURGEON, CHARLES H.—Thanksgiving. [Morning by Morning, p. 321.] (Passmore & Alabaster, London, England.)

STANLEY, ARTHUR P.—The National Thanksgiving. [Sermons on Special Occasions, p. 15, Harper's Franklin Square Library.] (Harper & Brothers, New York.)

THANKSGIVING TIME FANCIES.—[Scribner's Magazine, vol. xviii, p. 557.] (Charles Scribner's Sons, New York.)

WHITFORD, J. B.—The Hand of God in History. [Pulpit Treasury, vol. xii, p. 441.] (E. B. Treat & Co., New York.)

ADVENT

BEECHER, HENRY WARD.—The Second Advent. [Christian World Pulpit, vol. xiv, p. 88.] (The Christian World, London, England.)

BUTLER, H. M.—The Three Comings of Christ. [Sermon Bible, vol. xii, p. 102.] (Funk & Wagnalls Co., New York.)

GUINNESS, H. H.—Watch. [Pulpit Power and Eloquence, p. 270.] (F. M. Barton, Cleveland.)

HALL, JOHN.—What Shall the End Be? [Questions of the Day, p. 225.] (Dodd, Mead & Co., New York.)

JEBB, BISHOP.—Children of the Night and of the Day. [Sermons for the Church's Year, W. Benham, p. 1.] (E. P. Dutton & Co., New York.)

KINGSLEY, CHARLES.—All Saints' Day and Other Sermons. [p. 41.] (Charles Scribner's Sons, New York.)

MAN'S INCREASED RESPONSIBILITY THROUGH THE ADVENT OF CHRIST. [Spence and Exell, in Homiletical Library, vol. i, p. 1.] (A. D. F. Randolph & Co., New York.)

MOZLEY, J. B.—The Reversal of Human Judgment. [Pulpit Power and Eloquence, p. 543.] (F. M. Barton, Cleveland.)

PREPARATION FOR THE COMING DAY.—[Spence and Exell, in Homiletical Library, vol. i, p. 10.] (A. D. F. Randolph & Co., New York.)

SPURGEON, CHARLES H.—Paul the Ready. [Pulpit Power and Eloquence, p. 695.] (F. M. Barton, Cleveland.)

CHRISTMAS DAY

BANKS, LOUIS ALBERT.—God's Love and Its Gift. [Christ and His Friends, p. 139.] (Funk & Wagnalls Co., New York. 1895.)

BROOKS, PHILLIPS.—Christmas Sermon. [Century Magazine, vol. xxv, p. 179.] (The Century Company, New York.)

BUCHANAN, CLAUDIUS.—The Star in the East. [Pulpit Power and Eloquence, p. 46.] (F. M. Barton, Cleveland. 1901.)

CHAMBERS' JOURNAL.—Christmas in Other Countries. [Vol. lxii, p. 801.] London, England.)

CRAFTS, WILBUR F.—The Birth of Jesus.

[Talks to Boys and Girls About Jesus, p. 68.] (Funk & Wagnalls Co., New York. 1881.)

DEEMS, CHARLES F.—No Room for Jesus. [Sermons, p. 66.] (Funk & Wagnalls Co., New York. 1885.)

HEPWORTH, GEORGE H.—Christ's Glorious Coming. [Treasury of Religious Thought, vol. i, p. 462.] (E. B. Treat & Co., New York.)

RUSKIN, JOHN.—The Birth of Jesus. [Talks to Boys and Girls About Jesus, p. 75.] (Funk & Wagnalls Co., New York. 1881.)

STOCKTON, THOMAS H.—Glory to God. [Pulpit Power and Eloquence, p. 707.] (F. M. Barton, Cleveland. 1901.)

WARNER, CHARLES DUDLEY.—Christmas in Former Times. [Harper's Magazine, vol. lxxx, p. 1.] (Harper & Brothers, New York.)

OLD YEAR DAY

BAILEY, PHILIP JAMES.—Life. [Library of Choice Literature, Compiled by A. R. Spofford, vol. vi, p. 25.] (Gebbie Publishing Co., Philadelphia. 1895.)

BANCROFT, THOMAS.—Man's Life. [Library of Choice Literature, Compiled by A. R. Spofford, vol. ii, p. 329.] (Gebbie Publishing Co., Philadelphia. 1895.)

BANKS, LOUIS ALBERT.—Burning the Bridges in the Rear. [Paul and His Friends, p. 110.] (Funk & Wagnalls Co., New York. 1898.)

BISHOP, SAMUEL.—Man's Life. [Library of Choice Literature, Compiled by A. R. Spofford, vol. ii, p. 328.] (Gebbie Publishing Co., Philadelphia. 1895.)

CAMPBELL, THOMAS.—The Last Man. Poem. [Poems, p. 261.] (E. Moxon, Son, & Co., London, England.)

CUYLER, THEODORE L.—The Last Words of the Dying Year. [Homiletic Review, vol. ii, p. 139.] (Funk & Wagnalls Co., New York.)

DEEMS, CHARLES F.—How Old Art Thou? [Sermons, p. 198.] (Funk & Wagnalls Co., New York. 1885.)

HEPWORTH, GEORGE H.—A Wasted Life. [Herald Sermons, p. 68.] (E. P. Dutton & Co., New York. 1894.]

ROBERTSON, FREDERICK W.—Christian Progress by Oblivion of the Past. [Sermons, p. 57.] (Harper & Brothers, New York. 1870.)

TAYLOR, WILLIAM M.—Providence. [Limitations of Life, p. 249.] (A. C. Armstrong & Son, New York. 1879.)

Holidays

LINCOLN'S BIRTHDAY

ARNOLD, I. N.—Life of Abraham Lincoln. (A. C. McClurg & Co., Chicago.)

ATLANTIC MONTHLY.—[Vols. xxxvii, 21; xli, 366, 454; lviii, 556; lxvii, 721.] (Houghton, Mifflin & Co., Boston.)

BEECHER, HENRY WARD.—Abraham Lincoln. [p. 701.] (Fords, Howard & Hulbert, New York. 1889.)

HAPGOOD, NORMAN.—Abraham Lincoln, the Man of the People. (The Macmillan Co., London and New York.)

HERNDON AND WEIK.—Abraham Lincoln. [3 vols.] (D. Appleton & Co., New York. 1889.)

HOLLAND, JOHN G.—Abraham Lincoln. (C. A. Nichols, Springfield, Mass.)

INDEPENDENT, THE.—Symposium on Abraham Lincoln. [The Independent, Apr. 4, 1895.] (New York.)

LAMON, W. H.—Recollections of Lincoln. (A. C. McClurg & Co., Chicago.)

NICOLAY AND HAY.—Complete Works of Lincoln. (The Century Co., New York.)

NICOLAY AND HAY.—Abraham Lincoln. [10 vol. ed. and 2 vol. ed. (The Century Co., New York. 1890.)

TARBELL, IDA M.—Life of Abraham Lincoln. [2 vols.] (McClure, Phillips & Co., New York.)

WASHINGTON'S BIRTHDAY

ALLIBONE, SAMUEL AUSTIN.—Dictionary of Authors. [Gives Opinions of Eminent Authors, vol. iii, p. 2596.] (J. B. Lippincott Co., Philadelphia.)

BANCROFT, GEORGE.—History of the U. S. (D. Appleton & Co., New York. 1884.)

EVERETT, EDWARD.—Orations and Speeches. [4 vols.; vol. i, 564; iv, 3.] (Little, Brown & Co., Boston.)

FORD, W. C.—Complete Works of George Washington. [14 vols.] (G. P. Putnam's Sons, New York.)

HALE, EDWARD EVERETT.—Life of Washington. (G. P. Putnam's Sons, New York.)

HEADLEY, J. T.—Washington and His Generals. (Charles Scribner's Sons, New York.)

INDEPENDENT, THE.—Washington Number. [April 25, 1889, pp. 1-18, 22-24.] (New York.)

IRVING, WASHINGTON.—Life of George Washington. [5 vols.] (G. P. Putnam's Sons, New York.)

LODGE, HENRY CABOT.—Life of George Washington. [American Statesmen Series, 2 vols.] (Houghton, Mifflin & Co., Boston.)

WEBSTER, DANIEL.—Washington. [Webster's Works, 6 vols.; vol. i, p. 219.] (Little, Brown & Co., Boston.)
WHIPPLE, EDWARD P.—Character and Char-

acteristic Men. [p. 293.] (Houghton, Mifflin & Co., Boston.)
WILSON, WOODROW.—George Washington. (Harper & Brothers, New York. 1900.)

ARBOR DAY

ARBOR DAY ANNUAL.—[Write to State Superintendent of Public Schools in the capital cities of Nebraska, Kansas, Wisconsin, Illinios, New York, and other States.]
BALDWIN, JAMES.—Harper's School Speaker: Arbor Day and Memorial Day. (Harper & Brothers, New York.)
FULLER, ANDREW S.—Practical Forestry. [A Treatise on the Proper Planting and Cultivation, with a Description, and the Botanical and Popular Names of all the Indigenous Trees of the U. S., both Evergreen and Deciduous, together with Notes on a large number of the most valuable Exotic Species. Illustrated.] (Orange Judd Co., New York.)
FURNAS, ROBERT W.—Arbor Day. [1888.] (State Journal Co., Printers, Lincoln, Neb.)
MUELLER, FERDINAND VON.—Select Extra-Tropical Plants Readily Eligible for Industrial Culture or Naturalization, with Indications of their Native Countries and

Some of Their Uses. (George S. Davis, Detroit, Mich.)
PINCHOT, GIFFORD.—A Primer of Forestry. [Part I: The Forest. Part II: Practical Forestry. Washington, Bulletin 24, U. S. Department of Agriculture, Division of Forestry, 2d ed. Authorized by Congress, April 18, 1900.]
SUDWORTH, GEORGE B.—Check List of the Forest Trees of the U. S., Their Names and Ranges, Pamphlet. 1898. [Prepared under the direction of B. E. Fernow, Chief of the Division of Forestry, Washington, U. S. Department of Agriculture.] (Bulletin No. 17.)
TOUMEY, J. W.—Practical Tree Planting in Operation. [Pamphlet. Washington. U. S. Department of Agriculture, Division of Forestry. 1900.]
WESTERN SCHOOL JOURNAL. [March Number of each Year.] (Topeka, Kansas.)
WILLIS, ANNIE I.—Exercises for Arbor Day. (New England Publishing Co., 3 Somerset St., Boston, Mass.)

EMPIRE DAY

BEDE, VENERABLE.—Description of Britain. [Library of Choice Literature, A. R. Spofford, vol. vii, p. 353.] (The Gebbie Publishing Co., Philadelphia.)
DICKENS, CHARLES.—Child's History of England. (Chapman & Hall, London.)
FROUDE, JAMES ANTHONY.—History of England. [12 vols.] (Charles Scribner's Sons, New York.)
GREEN, JOHN RICHARD.—History of the English People. [1 vol. ed., 4 vol. ed.] (Harper & Brothers, New York.)
KNIGHT, CHARLES.—History of England. [2 vols.] (Funk & Wagnalls Co., New York.)
LITTELL'S LIVING AGE.—Reign of Victoria.

[Vol. cviii, p. 450.] (Living Age Co., Boston.)
MACAULAY, THOMAS B.—History of England. [5 vols.] Harper & Brothers, New York.)
McCARTHY, JUSTIN.—Political Influence of Queen Victoria. [Outlook, vol. 67, p. 297. February, 1901.] (New York.)
MITCHELL, DONALD G.—English Lands, Letters and Kings. (Charles Scribner's Sons, New York.)
STEAD, W. T.—King Edward VII., A Character Study. [Review of Reviews, vol. xxiii, No. 134, Mar. 1901, p. 294.] (New York.)

MEMORIAL DAY

BECK, J. M.—War, the Distress of Nations. [American Magazine of Civics, vol. vii, p. 1.] (A. J. Palm & Co., New York.)
BURTON, R.—Memorial Day. (Copeland & Day, Boston.)
COPELAND, H.—Memorial Day at the Corners. [New England Magazine, vol. xiv, p. 472.] (Warren F. Kellogg, Boston.)
DOANE, WILLIAM C.—Follies and Horrors of War. [North American Review, vol. clxii, p. 190.] (Harper & Brothers, New York.)
FISKE, A. W.—Decadence of the Grand Army. [The Nation, vol. lx, p. 342.] (Evening Post Publishing Co., New York.)

HOW TO AVOID WAR.—[North American Review, vol. clxii, p. 119.] (Harper & Brothers, New York.)
HUBBARD, G. H.—Cost of War. [New Englander, vol. lvi, p. 222.] (New Haven, Conn.)
JEWETT, S. O.—Decoration Day: A Story. [Harper's Magazine, vol. lxxxviii, p. 84.] (Harper & Brothers, New York.)
MENDES, H. P.—The Solution of War. [North American Review, vol. clxi, p. 161.] (Harper & Brothers, New York.)
TAYLOR, H. C.—Study of War. [North American Review, vol. clxii, p. 181.] (Harper & Brothers, New York.)

FLAG-RAISING DAY

CHAMPION, MRS. S. E.—Our Flag. (Tuttle, Morehouse & Taylor, New Haven, Conn.)

GRIFFIS, W. E.—First Salute to the U. S. Flag. [*New England Magazine*, vol. viii, p. 576.] (Warren F. Kellogg, Boston.)

HOLDEN, E. B.—Our Country's Flag and Flags of Foreign Countries. (D. Appleton & Co., New York.)

HULME, F. E.—Flags of the World. [Illustrated.] (Frederick Warne & Co., New York.)

KELLOGG, E. L.—1898—Flag Day in the School Room. (E. L. Kellogg & Co., New York.)

MORRIS, R. A.—Washington, Lincoln, and the American Flag. [Patriotic Birthday Exercises.] (Helman, Taylor Co., Cleveland, Ohio.)

RANDOLPH, JOHN C.—Patriotic Songs for School and Home. (Oliver Ditson & Co., Boston.)

STREET, G. G.—Our Flag. (Courier Co., Buffalo.)

TITHERINGTON, R. H.—Story of the Flag. [*Munsey's Magazine*, vol. xiii, p. 401.] (Frank A. Munsey, New York.)

DOMINION DAY

BOURINOT, J. G.—Canada. (G. P. Putnam's Sons, New York.)

BOURINOT, J. G.—Canada Under British Rule. [1796-1900.] (The Macmillan Co., London and New York.)

DUFFERIN, LADY.—My Canadian Journal. (D. Appleton & Co., New York.)

PARKMAN, FRANCIS.—The Old Régime in Canada. (Little, Brown & Co., Boston.)

PEACOCK, E. R.—Canada. (Warwick Brothers & Rutter, Toronto.)

PEPPER, MARY S.—Maids and Matrons of New France. (Little, Brown & Co., Boston.)

RALPH, JULIAN.—On Canada's Frontier. (Harper & Brothers, New York.)

RAND, THEODORE H.—Treasury of Canadian Verse. (William Briggs, Toronto.)

ROSS, G. W.—Patriotic Recitations. (Warwick Brothers & Rutter, Toronto.)

WARNER, CHARLES DUDLEY.— Baddeck. (Houghton, Mifflin & Co., Boston.)

INDEPENDENCE DAY

BAUSLIN, D. H.—Civil Liberty and the Reformation. [*Lutheran Quarterly*, vol. xxii, p. 547.] (Gettysburg, Pa.)

CABOT, E. T.—E. Atkinson—Personal Liberty. [*Popular Science Monthly*, vol. xl, p. 433.] (McClure, Phillips & Co., New York.)

DESHLER, C. D.—How the Declaration was Received in the Old Thirteen. [*Harper's Magazine*, vol. lxxxv, p. 165.] (Harper & Brothers, New York.)

HOWE, J. W.—How the Fourth of July Should Be Celebrated. [*The Forum*, vol. xv, p. 567.] (Forum Publishing Co., New York.)

SMITH, J. M.—Limits of Individual Liberty and State Authority. [*American Magazine* of Civics, vol. ix, p. 288.] (A. J. Palm & Co., New York.)

SPRAGUE, H. B.—The Mayflower Compact and the Jeffersonian Heresy. [*Our Day*, vol. xiv, p. 145.] (Our Day Publishing Co., Boston.)

STORY OF THE DECLARATION OF INDEPENDENCE. —[*Open Court*, vol. v, p. 2859.] (Open Court Publishing Co., Chicago.)

STRONG, JOSIAH.—Our Country. (Baker & Taylor Co., New York.)

WERNER, E. S.—Readings and Recitations. (E. S. Werner Publishing Co., New York.)

WILLIAMS, ELIZABETH M.—Anecdotes of the First Fourth of July. [*Magazine of American History*, vol. xxx, p. 91.] (New York.)

LABOR DAY

BARNES, WILLIAM E.—The Labor Problem. (Harper & Brothers, New York.)

BEHRENDS, A. J. F.—Socialism and Christianity. (Baker & Taylor Co., New York.)

BLISS, WILLIAM D. P. [ED.]—The Encyclopedia of Social Reforms. (Funk & Wagnalls Co., New York.)

FRANKE, K.—Socialistic Situation in Germany. [*The Nation*, vol. lxi, p. 132.] (The Evening Post Publishing Co., New York.)

GILMAN, NICHOLAS P.—Socialism and the American Spirit. (Houghton, Mifflin & Co., Boston.)

INDEPENDENT, THE.—Strife between Labor and Capital. A Symposium. [Feb. 7, 1895.] (New York.)

INDEPENDENT, THE.—Labor Unions. A Symposium. [May 2, 1895. 1900, vol. 52.] (New York.)

LAUGEL, A.—Socialism and Militarism in France. [*The Nation*, vol. lviii, p. 8. 1894.] (The Evening Post Publishing Co., New York.)

SUMNER, WILLIAM GRAHAM.—What Social Classes Owe to Each Other. (Harper & Brothers, New York.)

TREVOR, J.—Religion of the Labor Movement. [*Forum*, vol. xviii, p. 597.] (The Forum Publishing Co., New York.)

DISCOVERY DAY

ANDERSON, R. B.—Stephens on the Discovery of America by Madoc. [*The Dial*, vol. xvi, p. 138.] (Chicago.)

CASTELAR, E.—Christopher Columbus. [*Century Magazine*, vol. xxii, pp. 123-921.] (The Century Co., New York.)

HUBBARD, G. G.—Discoveries of America. [*National Geographic Magazine*, vol. iv, p. 1.] (Washington.)

INDEPENDENT, THE.—Symposium on Columbus. [June 2, 1892.] (New York.)

KIEFFER, JOHN B.—Causes Which Led to the Discovery of America. [*Reformed Quarterly Review*, vol. xl, p. 122.] (Reformed Church Publication Society, Philadelphia.)

LITTELL'S LIVING AGE.—Discovery of America. [Vol. cxciv, p. 771.] (Boston.)

LONG, R. S.—Discovery of America by the Chinese. [*Eclectic Magazine*, vol. cxx, p. 201.] (Living Age Co., Boston.)

NEWBERRY, J. S.—Ancient Civilization of America. [*Popular Science Monthly*, vol. xli, p. 187.] (McClure, Phillips & Co., New York.)

RUGE, S.—Christopher Columbus. [*Harper's Magazine*, vol. lxxxv, p. 681.] (Harper & Brothers, New York.)

WINSOR, J.—The Discovery and Naming of America. [*The Nation*, vol. lxiii, p. 143.] (The Evening Post Pub. Co., New York.)

ELECTION DAY

BISHOP, J. B.—Secret Voting. [*The Nation*, vol. v, p. 368.] (The Evening Post Pub. Co., New York.)

BISHOP, J. B.—Power of the Independent Vote in the U. S. [*The Nation*, vol. liv, p. 164.] (The Evening Post Pub. Co., New York.)

DEMBITZ, L. N.—Advent of the Australian Ballot. [*The Nation*, vol. liv, pp. 32, 87.] (The Evening Post Pub. Co., New York.)

LUSK, H. H.—The American Ballot. [*The Forum*, vol. xxii, p. 225.] (The Forum Publishing Co., New York.)

MACE, J.—Universal Suffrage in France. [*North American Review*, vol. clvi, p. 27.] (Harper & Brothers, New York.)

McCOOK, J. J.—Alarming Proportion of Venal Voting. [*The Forum*, vol. xiv, p. 1.] (The Forum Publishing Co., New York.)

McCOOK, J. J.—Venal Voting Methods and Remedies. [*The Forum*, vol. xiv, p. 159.] (The Forum Publishing Co., New York.)

NORDHOFF, CHARLES.—Politics for Young Americans. (Harper & Brothers, New York.)

SATTERTHWAITE, L.—Independence in Politics. [*New Englander*, vol. lvi, p. 180.] (Wm. L. Kingsley, New Haven.)

ST. JOHN, W. P.—A National Platform for the American Independents of 1896. [*The Arena*, vol. xvi, p. 67.] (The Arena Publishing Co., New York.)

TUFTS, W. W.—Defects of Patent Ballot Boxes. [*The Nation*, vol. lvii, p. 155.] (The Evening Post Pub. Co., New York.)

FOREFATHERS' DAY

BRAINERD, CEPHAS.—The New-England Society Orations, 1820-1885. (The Century Co., New York.)

CAMPBELL, DOUGLAS.—The Puritans in Holland, England and America. (Harper & Brothers, New York.)

DOW, J. G.—Puritans and Jews. [*Jewish Quarterly*, vol. iii, p. 52.] (D. Nutt, London.)

DUTCH, INFLUENCE IN AMERICA.—[*Atlantic Monthly*, vol. lxx, p. 698.] (Houghton, Mifflin & Co., Boston.)

EARLE, A. M.—Puritanism, Influence on National Character. [*Nineteenth Century*, vol. xxxviii, p. 312.] (Leonard Scott Publishing Co., New York.)

FISKE, JOHN.—The Dutch and Quaker Colonies in America. (Houghton, Mifflin & Co., Boston.)

FISKE, JOHN.—The Beginnings of New England. (Houghton, Mifflin & Co., Boston.)

GRAVES, H.—The Huguenots in New England. [*New England Magazine*, n. s., vol. xi, p. 497.] (Warren F. Kellogg, Boston.)

HIGGINSON, THOMAS W.—The Puritans in New England. [Atlantic Essays, p. 189.] (Houghton, Mifflin & Co., Boston.)

WENDELL, B.—Characteristics of the Puritans. [*Harvard Monthly*, vol. xiv, p. 45.] (Cambridge, Mass.)

TOPICAL INDEX

ᕼoly Days

NEW YEAR'S DAY

NEW YEAR'S DAY — Continued

COMMUNION SUNDAY

GOOD FRIDAY

EASTER — Continued

SUNDAY

ASCENSION DAY

ASCENSION DAY — Continued

WHITSUNDAY

WHITSUNDAY — Continued

CHILDREN'S DAY

TRINITY SUNDAY

TRINITY SUNDAY — Continued

ALL SAINTS' DAY

THANKSGIVING DAY

THANKSGIVING DAY — Continued

ADVENT

CHRISTMAS DAY

OLD YEAR DAY

OLD YEAR DAY — Continued

Holidays

LINCOLN'S BIRTHDAY

LINCOLN'S BIRTHDAY — Continued

WASHINGTON'S BIRTHDAY

ARBOR DAY

ARBOR DAY — Continued

EMPIRE DAY

MEMORIAL DAY

MEMORIAL DAY — Continued

FLAG-RAISING DAY

DOMINION DAY

DOMINION DAY — Continued

INDEPENDENCE DAY

LABOR DAY

DISCOVERY DAY

ELECTION DAY

ELECTION DAY — Continued

FOREFATHERS' DAY

INDEX TO AUTHORS

INDEX TO TEXTS